Cambridge Tracts in Theoretical Computer Science 58

Temporal Logics in Computer Science

This comprehensive text provides a modern and technically precise exposition of the fundamental theory and applications of temporal logics in computer science. Part I presents the basics of discrete transition systems, including constructions and behavioural equivalences. Part II examines the most important temporal logics for transition systems and Part III looks at their expressiveness and complexity. Finally, Part IV describes the main computational methods and decision procedures for model checking and model building – based on tableaux, automata and games – and discusses their relationships.

The book contains a wealth of examples and exercises, as well as an extensive annotated bibliography. Thus, the book is not only a solid professional reference for researchers in the field but also a comprehensive graduate textbook that can be used for self-study as well as for teaching courses.

STÉPHANE DEMRI is a CNRS directeur de recherche at Laboratoire Spécification et Vérification (LSV), ENS de Cachan, and he is currently the head of LSV. His current research interests include verification of infinite-state systems, temporal logics and analysis of systems with data. He has participated in numerous international and national projects and has been co-responsible for bilateral projects with Poland, South Africa and Australia. He is regularly involved in teaching, in program committees, in steering committees and in editorial boards. He has co-authored more than 125 publications in the field of formal/logical methods for analysing computer systems, including a monograph, 4 edited proceedings, 6 book chapters and 50 articles in international journals.

VALENTIN GORANKO is currently a professor of logic and theoretical philosophy at Stockholm University. He has more than 30 years of university teaching and research experience in mathematics, computer science and philosophy in universities in Bulgaria, South Africa, Denmark and Sweden. His main expertise and research interests are in theory and applications of modal and temporal logics to computer science, artificial intelligence, multiagent systems and philosophy. He has authored and co-authored more than 100 publications, including two recent textbooks on logic and discrete mathematics. He is a member of several editorial boards and steering bodies of professional organisations and is currently the vice-president of the Association for Logic, Language and Information (FoLLI).

MARTIN LANGE is currently a professor in theoretical computer science at the University of Kassel, Germany. His research interests include model checking and general decision procedures for logics in computer science with a focus on temporal logics. He has published more than 80 papers in international journals and conference proceedings. He received an ERC Starting Grant in 2010 and a Heisenberg professorship from the German Research Council in 2013.

CAMBRIDGE TRACTS IN THEORETICAL COMPUTER SCIENCE 58

Titles in the series
A complete list of books in the series can be found at
www.cambridge.org/computerscience.
Recent titles include the following:

Temporal Logics in Computer Science

Finite-State Systems

STÉPHANE DEMRI
Centre National de la Recherche Scientifique (CNRS), France

VALENTIN GORANKO
Stockholms Universitet

MARTIN LANGE
Universität Kassel, Germany

CAMBRIDGE
UNIVERSITY PRESS

CAMBRIDGE
UNIVERSITY PRESS

University Printing House, Cambridge CB2 8BS, United Kingdom

Cambridge University Press is part of the University of Cambridge.

It furthers the University's mission by disseminating knowledge in the pursuit of
education, learning and research at the highest international levels of excellence.

www.cambridge.org
Information on this title: www.cambridge.org/9781107028364

First published 2016

Printed in the United Kingdom by Clays, St Ives plc

A catalogue record for this publication is available from the British Library

ISBN 978-1-107-02836-4 Hardback

Contents

Contents

1

Introduction

Temporal logics provide a generic logical framework for modelling and reasoning about time and temporal aspects of the world. While stemming from philosophical considerations and discussions, temporal logics have become over the past 50 years very useful and important in computer science, and particularly for formal specification, verification and synthesis of computerised systems of various nature: sequential, concurrent, reactive, discrete, real time, stochastic, etc. This book provides a comprehensive exposition of the most popular discrete-time temporal logics, used for reasoning about transition systems and computations in them.

1.1 Temporal Logics and Computer Science: A Brief Overview

We begin with a brief historical overview of temporal reasoning and logics and their role in computer science.

1.1.1 Historical Origins of Temporal Reasoning and Logics

The study of time and temporal reasoning goes back to the antiquity. For instance, some of Zeno's famous paradoxical arguments refer to the nature of time and the question of infinite divisibility of time intervals. Perhaps the earliest scientific reference on temporal reasoning, however, is Aristotle's *'Sea Battle Tomorrow'* argument in the *Organon II – On*

Interpretation, Chapter 9, claiming that *future contingents*, i.e. statements about possible future events which may or may not occur, such as 'There will be a sea-battle tomorrow', should not be ascribed definite truth values at the present time. A few decades later the philosopher Diodorus Cronus from the Megarian school illustrated the problem of future contingents in his famous *Master Argument* where he, inter alia, defined 'possible' as '*what is or will ever be*' and 'necessary' as '*what is and will always be*'.

Philosophical discussions on temporality, truth, free will and determinism, and their relationships continued during the Middle ages. In particular, William of Ockham held that propositions about the contingent future cannot be known by humans as true or false because only God knows their truth value now. However, he argued that humans can still freely choose amongst different possible futures, thus suggesting the idea of a future-branching model of time with many possible time-lines (histories), truth of propositions being relativised to a possible actual history. This model of time is now often called *Ockhamist* or *actualist*. Later, several philosophers and logicians raised and analysed problems relating temporality with nondeterminism, historical necessity, free will, God's will and knowledge, etc., proposing various different solutions. Still, little tangible progress in the formal study of temporal reasoning occurred until some new ideas emerged in the late 19th to early 20th century, including the developments of Minkowski's four-dimensional space time model and its application to Einstein's relativity theory, of Reichenbach's theory of temporality and tenses in natural language, as well as some informal philosophical studies of temporal reasoning by C. Peirce, McTaggart, B. Russell, W. Quine, J. Findley, J. Łukasiewicz and others. However, temporal logic as a formal logical system only emerged in the early 1950s when the philosopher Arthur Prior set out to analyse and formalise such arguments, leading him, inter alia, to the invention of (as Prior called it) Tense Logic, of which he developed and discussed several formal systems. Prior's seminal work initiated the modern era of temporal logical reasoning, leading to numerous important applications not only to philosophy, but also to computer science, artificial intelligence and linguistics.

Prior introduced the following basic temporal modalities:

P   'It *has at some time in the past been* the case that ...'
F   'It *will at some time in the future be* the case that ...'
H   'It *has always been* the case that ...'
G   'It *will always be* the case that ...'

Put together in a formal logical language they allow complex temporal patterns to be expressed, for instance:

There is a solstice ∧ *there is a lunar eclipse* → GP '*There is a solstice and a lunar eclipse*'

means that if there is a solstice and there is a lunar eclipse now then it will always be the case that there has been a solstice and a lunar eclipse at the same moment of time.

Subsequently, other temporal modalities were introduced, notably *Nexttime* and the binary operators *Since* and *Until* in Kamp's (1968) very influential doctoral thesis. The simplest and most common models of time are linear-ordered time flows and Prior's temporal operators, as well as Since and Until, have natural interpretation in them. The resulting temporal logics for linear time are quite expressive. A classical expressiveness result, due to Kamp (1968) states that the temporal logic with Since and Until is as expressive as first-order logic. The temporal logic with operators for Next-time and Until interpreted on the time flow of natural numbers, known as the *linear-time temporal logic* LTL, became since the late 1970s the most popular temporal logic used in computer science.

Coming back to Prior's philosophical studies of temporal reasoning: in his analysis of Diodorus's Master Argument Prior argued that its fallacy lay in Diodorus's assumption that whatever is, or is not, or will be, or will never be, has in the past been necessarily so – thus, in effect assuming that the future is deterministic. Prior supported Aristotle's view that 'while it is now beyond the power of men or gods to affect the past, there are alternative futures between which choice is possible'. In order to resolve the problems pointed out by Aristotle and Diodorus, Prior wanted, inter alia, to capture the *logic of historical necessity*. His philosophical analysis and the quest for formalisation of the arguments for 'the incompatibility of foreknowledge (and fore-truth) and indeterminism' lead him to consider two formalisations of temporal logic of branching time, reflecting the 'Peircean' and the 'Ockhamist' (or, 'actualist') views, underlying respectively the ideas behind the *branching-time temporal logics* CTL and CTL* presented here. For further reading on the history of temporal reasoning and logics, see Øhrstrøm and Hasle (1995). In particular, for details on Prior's views and motivating analyses, see Prior (1967, Chapter VII) and Øhrstrøm and Hasle (1995, Chapters 2.6 and 3.2). A broad but concise overview of temporal logics is Goranko and Galton (2015).

1.1.2 The Role of Temporal Logics in Computer Science

Temporal aspects and phenomena are pervasive in computer and information systems. These include: scheduling of the execution of programs by an operating system; concurrent and reactive systems and, in particular, synchronisation of concurrent processes; real-time processes and systems; hardware verification; temporal databases, etc. Many of these are related to specification and verification of properties of *transition systems* and *computations* in them. Formally, transition systems are directed graphs consisting of states and transitions between them. They are used to model sequential and concurrent processes. There can be different types of transitions (e.g. affected by different types of actions) which we indicate by assigning different labels to them. Thus, more generally, we talk about *labelled transition systems*. A state in a transition system may satisfy various properties: it can be *initial, terminal, deadlock, safe or unsafe*, etc. One can describe state properties by formulae of a suitable state-description language; on propositional level these are simply atomic propositions. The set of such propositions that are true at a given state is encoded in the *label* of that state, and a transition system where every state is assigned such label will be called an *interpreted transition system*. In terms of the semantics of modal logics, transition systems are simply Kripke frames, and the labelling of states corresponds to a valuation of the atomic propositions in such frames, so interpreted transition systems are just Kripke models. A *computation* in a transition system is, intuitively, the observable trace of a run – a sequence of states produced by following the transition relations in the system, viz. the sequence of the labels of these states. It can be regarded as a record of all observable successive intermediate results of the computing process.

Early work implicitly suggesting applications of temporal reasoning to modelling and analysis of deterministic and stochastic transition systems is the theory of processes and events in Rescher and Urquhart (1971, Chapter XIV). The use of temporal logic for specification and verification of important properties of reactive and concurrent systems, such as *safety*, *liveness* and *fairness*, was first explicitly proposed in Amir Pnueli's (1977) seminal paper (see also Abrahamson 1979; Lamport 1980; Ben-Ari et al. 1981, 1983; Clarke and Emerson 1981). In particular, Pnueli proposed and developed, together with Zohar Manna, versions of the temporal linear-time logic LTL, in Manna and Pnueli (1979, 1981) as logical framework for deductive verification of such systems. Other influential early works on temporal logics of programs and processes include Abrahamson (1979, 1980) and Kröger (1987).

Since the late 1970s temporal logics have found numerous other applications in computer science. The key for their success and popularity is that temporal logics are syntactically simple and elegant, have natural semantics in interpreted transition systems, are well expressive for properties of computations and – very importantly – have good computational behaviour. Thus, they provide a very appropriate logical framework for formal specification and verification of programs and properties of transition systems. Depending on the type of systems and properties to specify and verify, two major families of temporal logics have emerged: *linear-time and branching-time logics*. Manna and Pnueli (1992) is a comprehensive reference on the early use of (linear time) temporal logics for specification of concurrent and reactive systems, and Manna and Pnueli (1995) is its continuation showing how that can be used to guarantee safety of such systems.

Two major developments, both starting in the 1980s, contributed strongly to the popularity and success of temporal logics in computer science. The first one is the advancement of *model checking* as a method for formal verification by Clarke and Emerson (1981), followed by Clarke et al. (1983, 1986), and independently by Queille and Sifakis (1982a). Introductions to model checking can be found in Huth and Ryan (2000) and Clarke and Schlingloff (2001), and for more comprehensive expositions, see Clarke et al. (2000) and Baier and Katoen (2008). The second major development is the emergence of *automata-based methods* for verification, initially advocated in a series of papers by Streett (1982), Sistla, Vardi and Wolper (1987), Vardi and Wolper (1986a,b) and Emerson and Sistla (1984), and further developed in Sistla et al. (1987), Emerson and Jutla (1988), Muller et al. (1988), Streett and Emerson (1989), Thomas (1990), Emerson and Jutla (1991), Vardi (1991), Vardi and Wolper (1994), Vardi (1996, 1997), Wolper (2000), Kupferman et al. (2000), Löding and Thomas (2000), etc. See also Vardi and Wilke (2007), Vardi (2007) and Grädel et al. (2002) for broader overviews and further references.

1.1.3 The Influence of Computer Science on the Development of Temporal Logics

The applications of temporal logics for specification and verification of computer systems have in turn strongly stimulated the study of their expressiveness and computational complexities and the development of efficient algorithmic methods for solving their basic logical decision problems.

The first proof systems developed for temporal logics were Hilbert-style axiomatic systems (see e.g. Rescher and Urquhart 1971; Goldblatt 1992; Reynolds 2001), as well as tableaux-style calculi and some Gentzen-type systems (see e.g. Fitting 1983; Wolper 1985; Goré 1991; Schwendimann 1998b; Goré 1999). In particular, efficient and intuitively appealing tableau-based methods for satisfiability testing of temporal formulae were developed in the early 1980s, by Wolper (1983, 1985) for the linear-time logic LTL, Ben-Ari, Manna and Pnueli (1981) for the branching-time logic UB and Emerson and Halpern (1982, 1985) for the branching-time logic CTL. The increasing demand coming from the field of formal verification for efficient algorithmic methods solving verification problems has led to the subsequent development of new methods, based on automata (see earlier references) and games (Stirling 1995, 1996; Stevens and Stirling 1998; Lange and Stirling 2000, 2001, 2002; Grädel 2002; Lange 2002a; see also Grädel et al. 2002 for a comprehensive coverage and further references). Other methods, such as temporal resolution, have also been developed recently (see e.g. Fisher 2011).

Whereas traditional systems of logical deduction and tableaux-style calculi can be qualified as direct methods, since they handle temporal formulae directly, the automata-based and the game-theoretic approaches work by reducing the decision problems for temporal logics to decision problems about automata and games, respectively. For instance, the automata-based approach is based on reducing logical to automata-based decision problems in order to take advantage of known results from automata theory (D'Souza and Shankar 2012). The most standard target problems on automata used in this approach are the *language nonemptiness problem* (checking whether an automaton admits at least one accepting computation) and the *language inclusion problem* (checking whether the language accepted by an automaton $\mathcal{A}$ is included in the language accepted by another automaton $\mathcal{B}$). In a pioneering work, Richard Büchi (1962) introduced a class of automata on infinite words and showed that these automata are equivalent in a precise sense to formulae in the monadic second-order theory (MSO) of the structure $(\mathbb{N}, <)$, which eventually resulted in Büchi's proof of the decidability of that theory. Later this idea and the result were extended by Rabin (1969) in his seminal paper to automata on trees and the decidability of the MSO theory of the infinite binary tree (equivalently, the MSO theory of two successor functions). These results provide the theoretical foundation of the automata-based decision methods in temporal logics.

Likewise, in the game-theoretic approach, the question of whether a temporal formula is satisfiable corresponds to the question of whether some designated player has a winning strategy in an associated satisfiability game. More generally, the existence of winning strategies of a given player in model-checking games and satisfiability-checking games provide uniform characterisations of the model checking and the satisfiability-testing problems for many temporal logics. These game-theoretic characterisations are of particular interest in the context of program verification.

As we demonstrate in this book, the methods for solving decision problems of temporal logics, based on automata, tableaux and games are closely related, both conceptually and technically, while each of them has pros and cons compared to the other. Because of the conceptual elegance and technical power and convenience, the automata-based methods have generally been favoured by the researchers in the area of verification and most of the tools that have been implemented are based on automata. On the other hand, tableau-based methods for model checking and satisfiability checking of temporal logics have so far been less developed for practical purposes and less tested for industrial applications, but are arguably more natural and intuitive from logical perspective, easier for execution by humans and potentially more flexible and practically efficient, if suitably optimised.

1.2 Structure and Summary of the Book Content

With this book we aim to offer a comprehensive, uniform, technically precise and conceptually in-depth exposition of the field, focusing on the intrinsically logical aspects of it and including both classical and recent results and methods of fundamental importance. The book has been written with the specific intention to be suitable both as a comprehensive graduate textbook and as a professional reference on the current state of the art in the field. For that purpose, it presents an essentially self-contained and rigorous treatment of the content, with precise definitions, statements and many detailed proofs, as well as numerous examples and exercises. Many easy or routine proofs are omitted in the main text but are explicitly left as exercises.

Except for the introductory chapter, we do not make references and credits to specific results in the main text, but provide such references in the bibliographic notes at the end of every chapter, where we also mention related topics not treated in the book and provide a number of additional references.

The book consists of 15 chapters structured in four parts. Here we will give a concise summary of their contents and will mention a few highlights in each chapter. More detailed summaries can be found at the beginning of each chapter.

Part I, 'Models', presents the basic theory of the abstract models for the temporal logics studied further, viz. transition systems and computations in them.

Chapter 2, 'Preliminaries and Background I', provides some preliminary material that will be needed further, including basics of sets, binary relations and orders, fixpoint theory, computational complexity and 2-player games on graphs. We do not intend to teach this material here but rather to recall the most basic definitions, terminology and notation, mainly for readers' convenience, as a quick reference.

Chapter 3, 'Transition Systems', introduces the basic concepts and facts related to transition systems, computations and important types of their properties. In particular, we provide simple algorithms solving the basic reachability problems in transition systems. Besides, we discuss transition systems as abstract models of the behaviour of real systems with respect to transitions between states. A real transition system can be modelled by different abstract transition systems and at different levels of detail. The chapter addresses the important question of when two transition systems should be considered behaviourally equivalent, that is, modelling essentially equivalent real transition systems. That question leads to the fundamental notion of bisimulation, the main versions of which are introduced and studied in the chapter. In particular, we introduce bisimulation games and relate the existence of winning strategies for one of the players in such games to the existence of bisimulation between the transitions systems on which the game is played. This is the first place in the book where games are considered and they will be one of its main themes.

Part II, 'Logics', is the core part of the book, presenting and studying the most important temporal logics used for specification and verification of discrete transition systems and many variations of them. In a relatively uniform manner we introduce the syntax and semantics of each of these logical systems, discuss and illustrate their use for formal specification of properties of transition systems and computations, study their expressiveness and the basic logical decision problems (model checking, satisfiability and validity testing) for them, relate them to standard verification tasks and present algorithms for solving some of these decision problems. The expositions are written from the primary perspective of computer science rather than from the perspective of pure modal and temporal logics. Thus, we have emphasised the more relevant topics associated with transition systems, such as expressiveness, bisimulation invariance, model checking, small model property and deciding satisfiability, while other fundamental logical topics, such as deductive systems and proof theory (except for short sections on axiomatic systems and derivations in them), model theory, correspondence theory, algebraic semantics, duality theory, etc. are almost left untouched here, but references are given in the bibliographic notes to other books where they are treated in depth.

Following is a brief summary of the chapters in this part.

Chapter 4, 'Preliminaries and Background II', provides some common background, terminology and notation related to logical decision problems and deductive systems. It assumes some knowledge of propositional logic, upon which all temporal logics studied here are built.

Chapter 5, 'Basic Modal Logics', is a concise introduction to the multimodal logic BML, regarded here as the basic temporal logic for reasoning about interpreted transition systems. Highlights on that chapter include: invariance of BML formulae under bisimulations and characterising the existence of bounded bisimulations between interpreted transition systems with BML formulae; study of the logical decision problems of model checking and satisfiability testing for BML, model-checking games and an axiomatic system for BML. Inter alia, we provide a simple optimal algorithm for testing satisfiability in BML that runs in polynomial space. These are further adapted to the extension BTL of BML with past-time operators. This chapter can also be viewed as a stepping stone towards the more expressive and interesting branching-time temporal logics CTL, CTL* and the modal μ-calculus, presented further.

Chapter 6, 'Linear-Time Temporal Logics', is devoted to temporal logics for linear-time models, representing single computations (i.e. infinite sequences of states generated by the transition relations), rather than entire transition systems. Here we present and study in detail the linear-time temporal logic LTL. We focus again on the logical and computational properties of this logic, viz. its semantics, expressiveness, model checking and testing of satisfiability and validity. We provide conceptually simple decision procedures for satisfiability testing and model-checking problems for LTL based on the so-called ultimately periodic model property and discuss how these can be refined and transformed into optimal decision procedures. (Alternative decision methods, essentially using the same property but based on tableaux and automata, are developed further, respectively in Chapters 13 and 14.) We also present and discuss here some of the most interesting extensions of LTL over linear models: with past-time operators, automata-based operators, propositional quantification, etc. At the end, we provide a complete axiomatic system for LTL and illustrate it with some derivations.

Chapter 7, 'Branching-Time Temporal Logics', introduces and studies a variety of the most important and expressive branching-time temporal logics extending BML with global temporal operators capturing different reachability properties and with quantifiers over paths/computations. These include, inter alia, the temporal logic of reachability TLR, the more expressive computation tree logic CTL, and the full computation tree logic CTL* combining CTL with LTL, plus several fragments, variations and extensions of it. We establish the tree-model property for CTL*, extend the bisimulation invariance result to it and discuss the expressiveness of the family of branching-time logics. In particular, we show that formulae of TLR suffice to characterise every finite interpreted transition system up to bisimulation equivalence. We then study the logical decision problems for CTL and CTL*. We present the linear-time labelling algorithm for model checking CTL formulae and show how model checking in CTL* can be reduced to repeated model checking of LTL formulae. Lastly, we briefly present complete axiomatic systems for TLR and CTL and illustrate them with some derivations.

Chapter 8, 'The Modal Mu-Calculus', presents the most expressive of all temporal logics studied in this book. The modal μ-calculus $\mathcal{L}_\mu$ extends BML with the fundamental syntactic construct of a least fixpoint operator and its dual, the greatest fixpoint operator. Using these, all previously studied temporal operators in the linear and branching-time logics can be defined simply and elegantly. The chapter provides a detailed and technically involved exposition of the key syntactic and semantic concepts of the modal μ-calculus, including the technical machinery needed to understand and evaluate its formulae, viz. approximants, signatures and games. We present the embedding of all previously studied (single-action) temporal logics, including CTL^*, into the μ-calculus, as well as related topics such as modal equation systems, model-checking games and results about structural complexity of formulae. The chapter also offers a comparison with other logical formalisms, such as monadic second-order logic and linear-time μ-calculus.

Chapter 9, 'Alternating-Time Temporal Logics', introduces concurrent game structures as multiagent generalisation of the transition systems considered so far and the respective multiagent extensions of the branching-time logics, known as alternating-time temporal logics, which enable strategic reasoning in open and multiagent transition systems and have recently been gaining increasing popularity. Formulae in the alternating-time temporal logics can quantify over strategies of agents and over all computations consistent with a given collective strategy of a coalition of agents, which is a refinement of the path quantification in CTL^*, thus enabling the expression of properties of the type *'the group of agents C has a collective strategy to achieve a given (LTL-definable) temporal objective on all computations consistent with that strategy'*. Following the general structure of the previous chapters, we present the syntax and semantics of the multiagent analogues ATL and ATL^* of the branching-time logics CTL and CTL^*, discuss their expressiveness and study their logical decision problems. In particular, we show that the linear-time labelling algorithm for model checking CTL extends smoothly to ATL. We also generalise the notion of bisimulation to alternating bisimulation and extend the bisimulation invariance property to ATL. This chapter is relatively independent from the rest of the book, as we do not study alternating-time temporal logics further, but it provides sufficient material for their further study.

Part III, 'Properties', is dedicated to two fundamental generic questions about temporal logics: their expressiveness and the computational complexity of their main logical decision problems. We provide a uniform treatment by proposing a synthetic and unified approach to both questions. These topics are also discussed in the rest of the book, but in a less systematic way. A summary of Part III follows.

Chapter 10, 'Expressiveness', provides an in-depth study of the relationships and comparisons between the different temporal logics introduced in Part II with respect to the temporal properties of interpreted transition systems that can, or cannot, be expressed by formulae in a given particular logic. A way to address such questions is to look at the entire spectrum of all temporal logics. We can naturally compare the expressiveness of two logics by asking whether every property that is formalisable in one of them can also be formalised in the other. This yields a preorder on all temporal logics of the same kind, i.e. with semantics based on the same class of models. A temporal formula can be identified with the class of (rooted) interpreted transition systems in which that formula is valid. Thus, a formula of one logic being expressible by a formula in another logic simply amounts to the two formulae being equivalent in the usual logical sense, i.e. being valid in the same class of models.

The structure of this chapter reflects the two main kinds of results that are presented there. The first two sections contain positive results of expressive inclusions, by means of translations from one logic to another, where the two different families of logics – for linear time and for branching time – are treated in separate sections. For instance, we show that all the different major extensions of LTL introduced earlier – with automata-based operators (ETL), with propositional quantification (QLTL), the linear μ-calculus LT_μ and the industrial standard Property Specification Language (PSL) – have the same expressiveness. With regards to branching-time logics, we present, for instance, the embedding of CTL* into $\mathcal{L}_\mu$. The last part of Chapter 10 presents negative expressiveness results of the kind that some properties in one logic are not expressible in another. For instance, we show that LTL is expressively weaker than its extensions mentioned earlier, pinpoint the expressive power of CTL by separating it from the other branching-time logics and prove that higher degree of fixpoint alternation in $\mathcal{L}_\mu$ yields greater expressiveness.

Chapter 11, 'Computational Complexity', is devoted to analysing the computational complexity of the main decision problems for temporal logics, which is of great importance for the assessment of their practical suitability as tools for formal verification. The chapter proposes a unifying picture of the computational complexity of most of the temporal logics studied here, by characterising the complexities of their satisfiability and model-checking problems. Complexity upper bounds for these problems are obtained by providing respective decision procedures in the other chapters, by using either concretely described algorithms presented there or by developing general decision methods such as semantic tableaux, automata or games. These upper bounds are revisited in that chapter and matching complexity lower bounds are established there, thus establishing the optimal complexities of the respective decision problems. In particular, the chapter presents a hierarchy class of problems, namely tiling problems and their variants involving games, thus providing a uniform and powerful framework for obtaining lower bound complexity results.

In the last part, **Part IV, 'Methods',** we present three fundamental methods for solving decision problems for temporal logics, namely: the tableaux-based, the games-based and the automata-based methods, by devoting a chapter to each of these. These technical frameworks are closely related and we discuss briefly their relationships and compare their pros and cons in the brief opening **Chapter 12, 'Frameworks for Decision Procedures',** provided to help the understanding of the bridges between these methods. Here is a brief summary of the other chapters in this part.

Chapter 13, 'Tableaux-Based Decision Methods', provides a systematic and uniform exposition of (a suitable adaptation) of the method of semantic tableaux, for constructive satisfiability testing and model building for formulae of the logics BML, LTL, TLR and CTL, by organising a systematic search for a satisfying model of the input set of formulae.

We begin the chapter by sketching a generic tableaux construction for testing satisfiability, illustrated with the basic modal logic BML. This construction builds on, and optimises further, a blend of ideas going back to the incremental tableaux method introduced for the propositional dynamic logic PDL in Pratt (1979, 1980) and further developed for LTL by Wolper (1983, 1985) and for CTL by Emerson and Halpern (1985). That version of the tableaux method differs essentially from the more traditional approach to tableaux-based calculi presented in Fitting (1983) and Goré (1999), because of the need for special treatment of the fixpoint definable temporal operators. Following the generic construction we develop and illustrate with running examples the tableau constructions for the logics LTL and CTL and present in detail proofs of their termination, soundness and completeness. The most distinctive features of the tableaux building methodology presented in Chapter 13 are uniformity, conceptual simplicity and flexibility. That methodology, however, does not extend readily to the more expressive logics CTL* and the $\mathcal{L}_\mu$, for which alternative decision methods, using automata and games, have been developed. Such alternative methods are developed, also for LTL and CTL, respectively in the two subsequent chapters.

In Chapter 14, 'The Automata-Based Approach', we present in detail that approach for a variety of temporal logics and classes of automata and compare the advantages and the drawbacks of the different constructions. The automata-based approach consists in reducing logical decision problems to decision problems about automata and their languages and takes advantage of known results and decision procedures from automata theory. Here temporal logical formulae are represented by automata and their models are considered to be of uniform nature, viz. infinite words (representing infinite computations, for linear-time logics) or trees (representing tree-unfoldings of transition systems, for the branching-time logics). Thus, the question of truth of a temporal formula in a model is equivalently replaced by the question of acceptance of that model by the automaton representing the formula. Respectively, the satisfiability problem for the formula is reduced to the language nonemptiness problem of its representing automaton. Based on this generic transformation, in this chapter we develop the automata-based approach for solving logical decision problems for several logics, mainly LTL and its variants (ETL, PSL) as well as the branching-time temporal logic CTL (and its fragment BML) for which we present several reductions from formulae to automata. To do so, we make use of notions from previous chapters but also we provide some original reductions, e.g. using alternating automata, thus also illustrating the diversity of automata-based methods. Moreover, we present several methods for LTL-like logics, as well as analogous methods for CTL, as a generalisation of some of the methods for LTL. The chapter does not deal with CTL* and with modal μ-calculus. Instead, we provide decision methods based on verification games for those two logics in the next Chapter 15.

Chapter 15, 'The Game-Theoretic Framework', develops the approach to the main decision problems for temporal logics based on special logical games. We present model-checking games and satisfiability-checking games and use them to characterise the respective decision problems for temporal logics. These games are defined by means of an arena

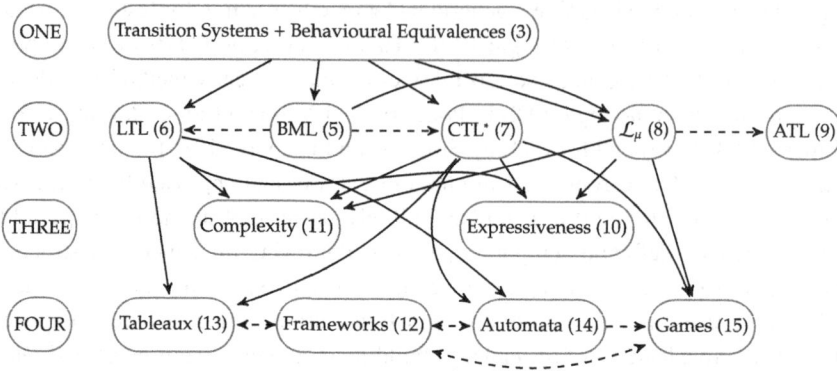

Figure 1.1 Dependencies between the different parts and chapters.

on which two players perform plays. Then we relate the model-checking problem – i.e. the question of whether a given state of an interpreted transition system satisfies a temporal formula – to the existence of a winning strategy for the proponent player in the respective model-checking game. Likewise, the satisfiability problem corresponds to the question of whether the proponent player has a winning strategy in the respective satisfiability game. The chapter is divided into four sections. The first one builds the general game-theoretic framework and concludes with the Main Reduction Theorem which shows how to obtain reductions to parity games. In the next section we provide the necessary automata-theoretic constructions for such reductions. The last two sections contain the actual definitions of games for temporal logics.

1.3 Using the Book for Teaching or Self-Study

The book can be used for a variety of introductory and advanced courses. An introductory course could cover most of Parts I and II (perhaps, excluding the chapter on the modal μ-calculus and more advanced topics from the previous chapters). More advanced courses could add quite independently parts from the chapters in Parts III and IV, see the dependencies between the chapters in the book illustrated in Figure 1.1. The leftmost column indicates the parts, and each chapter is identified by a keyword and by its number. Arrows specify dependencies between the parts/chapters where a normal arrow indicates that the chapter at the arrow's source should be read before the chapter at the arrow's target. A dashed arrow means that it is helpful to read it first. The preliminary chapters 2 and 4 are not represented in the figure; their content may be needed in the entire book.

Acknowledgements

First of all, we are indebted to many researchers who have contributed over the years to the development of the area of temporal logics in computer science and have thus produced much of the content of the book. We have provided detailed references at the end of each chapter, but for such a huge and dynamic field of research omissions are inevitable, so we also apologise here en bloc for all – certainly unintended, but nevertheless unfortunate – omissions to give due credit.

We are grateful to many colleagues who have contributed in one way or another to our work on the book, from proofreading preliminary parts to discussing its content or related topics over the years. In particular, we thank Florian Bruse, Paul Gastin, Markus Latte, Omer Mermelstein, Philippe Schnoebelen and Steen Vester. We also thank Ivan Danov for the help with the design of the book's website.

Valentin Goranko and Martin Lange have both been supported by visiting professorships from the École Normale Supérieure de Cachan in France. Much of the work that has gone into this book was done during these visits.

Special thanks are due to the representatives of Cambridge University Press: David Tranah and Clare Dennison for their infinite patience and understanding during the multiple delays and extensions of the target dates for the completion of this book, as well as their continual help and support.

Last but not least, we wish to thank our families for the understanding and moral support during the many years of work on the book. In addition, Valentin is particularly grateful to his partner Nina for the valuable technical support with the preparation of many figures.

Part I
Models

Part I

2

Preliminaries and Background I

This chapter presents preliminaries on set-theoretical notions, binary relations, linear orderings, fixpoint theory and computational complexity classes. Mainly, we provide notations for standard notions rather than giving a thorough introduction to these notions. More definitions are provided in the book, and we invite the reader to consult textbooks on these subjects for further information. For instance, in Moschovakis (2006) any reader can find material about set-theoretical notions, ordinals or fixpoints far beyond what is sketched in this chapter. Still, we implicitly assume that the reader has basic set-theoretic background. As stated already in Chapter 1, we do not intend to teach this material here but rather to recall the most basic notions, terminology and notation. The current chapter is included for the convenience of the reader as a quick reference.

Structure of the chapter. The chapter is divided into two sections. The first section contains standard material on sets and relations. Section 2.1.1 presents standard set-theoretical notions that are used throughout the book. Binary relations are ubiquitous structures in this volume, and Section 2.1.2 is dedicated to standard definitions about them. In Section 2.1.3, we provide basic definitions about partial and linear orders.

The second section contains material that is more specialised and needed for the development of a theory of and algorithms for temporal logics. Section 2.2.1 presents the basics of fixpoint theory; Chapter 8, which deals with the modal μ-calculus with fixpoint operators, uses some of the results stated herein. In Section 2.2.2, we recall standard complexity classes defined via deterministic and nondeterministic time- and space-bounded Turing machines. Other classes, in particular involving alternating Turing machines, are discussed in Chapter 11. Section 2.2.3 provides an introduction to 2-player zero-sum games of perfect information that are useful, for instance, in defining the game-theoretic approach to temporal logics.

2.1 Sets and Relations

2.1.1 Operations on Sets

Throughout this book we use the standard notations for set-theoretical notions: membership ($\in$), inclusion ($\subseteq$), strict (or proper) inclusion ($\subset$), union of sets ($\cup$), intersection of sets ($\cap$), difference of sets ($\setminus$) and product of sets ($\times$). The empty set is denoted by $\emptyset$.

By X^n we denote the product $X \times \cdots \times X$ with n factors. A disjoint union $\uplus$ of the sets X and Y is the set $X \uplus Y = (X \times \{1\}) \cup (Y \times \{2\})$. The union and the intersection of an indexed family $(X_i)_{i \in I}$ of sets are denoted by $\bigcup_{i \in I} X_i$ and $\bigcap_{i \in I} X_i$, respectively.

$\mathbb{N}$, $\mathbb{Z}$, $\mathbb{R}$ and $\mathbb{Q}$ denote the sets of all natural numbers, integers, real numbers and rational numbers, respectively. By $\mathcal{P}(X)$ we denote the powerset of the set X, which is the family of all subsets of X. By $\text{card}(X)$ we denote the cardinality of the set X.

A family $(X_i)_{i \in I}$ of subsets of Y is

- a **cover** of Y iff $\bigcup_{i \in I} X_i = Y$ and
- a **partition** of Y iff it is a cover of Y such that for all $i, j \in I$, we have that $i \neq j$ implies $X_i \cap X_j = \emptyset$.

2.1.2 Binary Relations

A **binary relation between sets X and Y** is any subset of $X \times Y$. In particular, a **binary relation in a set X** is any subset of $X^2 = X \times X$.

Let $R \subseteq X \times Y$. Some notation: if $(x, y) \in R$, we will also write xRy or $R(x, y)$ and say that x **is R-related to** y.

Given sets X and Y and $R \subseteq X \times Y$ we define the **domain of R**,

$$\text{dom}(R) := \{x \in X \mid \text{ there is } y \in Y \text{ such that } (xRy)\},$$

and the **range of R**

$$\text{ran}(R) := \{y \in Y \mid \text{ there is } x \in X \text{ such that } (xRy)\}.$$

We recall some special relations on a set X:

- the **empty relation** $\emptyset$,
- the **equality relation** (also known as the **identity** relation or the **diagonal** relation): $E_X := \{(x, x) \mid x \in X\}$ and
- the **universal relation** X^2.

Since binary relations are sets themselves, all Boolean operations $\cup, \cap$ and $\setminus$ apply to them, too. Also, the **complement** of a relation $R \subseteq X \times Y$ is defined as $\overline{R} := (X \times Y) \setminus R$.

Note that we can always assume that two relations are defined between the same sets, because if $R_1 \subseteq X_1 \times Y_1$ and $R_2 \subseteq X_2 \times Y_2$, we can assume that $R_1 \subseteq (X_1 \cup X_2) \times (Y_1 \cup Y_2)$ and $R_2 \subseteq (X_1 \cup X_2) \times (Y_1 \cup Y_2)$.

Inverse and Composition

Let $R \subseteq X \times Y$. The **inverse of** R is the relation $R^{-1} \subseteq Y \times X$ defined as

$$R^{-1} := \{(y, x) \mid (y, x) \in R\}.$$

Thus, we have xRy iff $yR^{-1}x$.

Let $R \subseteq X \times Y$ and $S \subseteq Y \times Z$. The **composition of** R **and** S is the binary relation $R \circ S \subseteq X \times Z$ defined by

$$R \circ S := \{(x, z) \mid \text{ there is } y \in Y \text{ such that } (xRy \text{ and } ySz)\}.$$

In particular, when $R \subseteq X^2$, then $R \circ R$ is defined, and it is denoted by R^2.

The composition of binary relations is associative, i.e. $(R \circ S) \circ T = R \circ (S \circ T)$. However, the composition of binary relations is generally *not* commutative.

For any binary relations R, S, we have $(R \circ S)^{-1} = S^{-1} \circ R^{-1}$.

Some Special Binary Relations

A binary relation $R \subseteq X^2$ is called

- **reflexive** if, for all $x \in X$, we have $(x, x) \in R$;
- **irreflexive** if, for all $x \in X$, we have $(x, x) \notin R$;
- **serial**, or **total**, if, for all $x \in X$, there is $y \in X$ such that $(x, y) \in R$;
- **functional** or **deterministic** if, for all $x \in X$, there is a unique $y \in X$ such that $(x, y) \in R$;
- **symmetric** if, for all $x, y \in X$, we have $(x, y) \in R$ iff $(y, x) \in R$;
- **antisymmetric** if, for all $x, y \in X$, we have that if $(x, y) \in R$ and $(y, x) \in R$, then $x = y$;
- **connected** if, for all $x, y \in X$, either $(x, y) \in R$ or $(y, x) \in R$;
- **transitive** if, for all $x, y, z \in X$, if $(x, y) \in R$ and $(y, z) \in R$, then $(x, z) \in R$;
- **equivalence relation** if it is reflexive, symmetric and transitive;
- **pre-order** (or **quasi-order**) if it is reflexive and transitive;
- **partial order** if it is reflexive, transitive and antisymmetric, i.e. an antisymmetric preorder;
- **strict partial order**, if it is irreflexive and transitive;
- **linear order** (or **total order**) if it is a connected partial order;
- **strict linear** (or **total**) **order**, if it is a connected strict partial order.

Example 2.1.1.

1. The divisibility relation in $\mathbb{Z} \setminus \{0\}$ and the relation 'not longer than' in the set of English words are pre-orders, but not partial orders.
2. The divisibility relation in $\mathbb{N} \setminus \{0\}$ and the relation $\subseteq$ in any power set $\mathcal{P}(X)$ are partial orders, but not linear orders, unless X has at most one element.
3. The relation $\leq$ in any of $\mathbb{N}, \mathbb{Z}, \mathbb{Q}, \mathbb{R}$ is a linear order.
4. The relation $<$ in any of $\mathbb{N}, \mathbb{Z}, \mathbb{Q}, \mathbb{R}$ is a strict linear order.

Many of the special binary relations listed can be characterised in a purely relational language, without referring to the elements of their domains and ranges. For any set X and binary relation $R \subseteq X^2$, the following hold:

1. R is reflexive iff $E_X \subseteq R$.
2. R is symmetric iff $R^{-1} \subseteq R$ iff $R^{-1} = R$.
3. R is antisymmetric iff $R^{-1} \cap R \subseteq E_X$.
4. R is connected iff $R \cup R^{-1} = X^2$.
5. R is transitive iff $R^2 \subseteq R$.

The **graph** of a function (mapping) $\mathfrak{f} : X \to Y$ is the binary relation $G_\mathfrak{f} \subseteq X \times Y$ defined by $G_\mathfrak{f} := \{(x, \mathfrak{f}(x)) \mid x \in X\}$.

A relation $R \subseteq X \times Y$ is functional iff it is the graph of a function from X to Y.

Closure Operations

Recall that R^2 denotes the binary relation obtained from the composition $R \circ R$. More generally, let us define R^i for all $i \in \mathbb{N}$, where R is a binary relation in $X \times X$, as follows:

- $R^0 := E_X$, i.e. R^0 is the diagonal relation on X and
- $R^{i+1} := (R^i \circ R)$ for all $i \in \mathbb{N}$.

We define the **transitive closure** of the binary relation R as follows:

$$R^+ := \bigcup_{i=1}^{\infty} R^i.$$

We also define the **reflexive and transitive closure** R^* of R as

$$R^* := \bigcup_{i=0}^{\infty} R^i = R^0 \cup R^+.$$

It is easy to show that, indeed, R^+ is transitive, while R^* is reflexive and transitive. Section 3.2 contains generalisations of this definition by considering families of binary relations, as well as other parameters.

Equivalence Relations

Recall that an equivalence relation in a set X is a reflexive, symmetric and transitive relation in X. For instance, the relations of equality ($=$) and congruence modulo n ($\equiv_n$) in $\mathbb{Z}$ are equivalence relations. (Recall: $m \equiv_n m'$ for $m, m' \in \mathbb{Z}$ iff n divides $m - m'$.)

Let $R \subseteq X^2$ be an equivalence relation and $x \in X$. The subset of X: $[x]_R := \{y \in X \mid xRy\}$ is called the **equivalence class** or the **cluster** of x generated by R.

For every equivalence relation R in a set X and $x, y \in X$ the following hold:

1. $x \in [x]_R$.
2. $x \in [y]_R$ implies $[x]_R = [y]_R$.
3. $x \notin [y]_R$ implies $[x]_R \cap [y]_R = \emptyset$.

Let $R \subseteq X^2$ be an equivalence relation. The set $X/R := \{[x]_R \mid x \in X\}$ is called the **quotient-set of** X **generated by** R.

The element $[x]_R$, also denoted by x/R, is called the **quotient-element of** x **generated by** R. The mapping $\eta_R : X \to X_R$ defined by $\eta_R(x) := x/R$ is called the **canonical mapping** of X onto X/R.

Note that the canonical mapping η_R is surjective, i.e. for every $y \in X_R$, there is some $x \in X$ such that $\eta_R(x) = y$.

Let $\mathfrak{f} : X \to Y$. Then the following three statements hold:

1. The binary relation $\tilde{\mathfrak{f}}$ in X defined by

$$x\tilde{\mathfrak{f}}y \quad \text{iff} \quad \mathfrak{f}(x) = \mathfrak{f}(y)$$

 is an equivalence relation in X, called the **kernel equivalence** of $\mathfrak{f}$.
2. The mapping $\mathfrak{g} : X/\tilde{\mathfrak{f}} \longrightarrow Y$ defined by

$$\mathfrak{g}(x/\tilde{\mathfrak{f}}) := \mathfrak{f}(x)$$

 is a well-defined injection, such that $\mathfrak{f} = \mathfrak{g}\eta_{\tilde{\mathfrak{f}}}$.
 To see this, let $x/\tilde{\mathfrak{f}} = y/\tilde{\mathfrak{f}}$. Then $x\tilde{\mathfrak{f}}y$, hence $\mathfrak{f}(x) = \mathfrak{f}(y)$, i.e. $\mathfrak{g}(x/\tilde{\mathfrak{f}}) = \mathfrak{g}(y/\tilde{\mathfrak{f}})$, so $\mathfrak{g}$ is well defined. Conversely, if $\mathfrak{g}(x/\tilde{\mathfrak{f}}) = \mathfrak{g}(y/\tilde{\mathfrak{f}})$, then $\mathfrak{f}(x) = \mathfrak{f}(y)$, i.e. $x\tilde{\mathfrak{f}}y$, hence $x/\tilde{\mathfrak{f}} = y/\tilde{\mathfrak{f}}$, so $\mathfrak{g}$ is an injection. Finally, $(\mathfrak{g}\eta_{\tilde{\mathfrak{f}}})(x) = \mathfrak{g}(\eta_{\tilde{\mathfrak{f}}}(x)) = \mathfrak{g}(x/\tilde{\mathfrak{f}}) = \mathfrak{f}(x)$.
3. Moreover, if $\mathfrak{f}$ is surjective, then $\mathfrak{g}$ is bijective. This follows immediately from the previous point.

These statements show, inter alia, that every mapping can be represented as a composition of a surjective mapping followed by an injective mapping.

Partitions

A **partition** of a set X is any family $\mathcal{P}$ of nonempty and pairwise disjoint subsets of X, the union of which is X.

For every equivalence relation $R \subseteq X^2$, the quotient-set $\{[x]_R \mid x \in X\}$ is a partition of X.

If $\mathcal{P}$ is a partition of a set X, then the relation $\sim_{\mathcal{P}} \subseteq X^2$ defined by

$$x \sim_{\mathcal{P}} y \quad \text{iff} \quad x \text{ and } y \text{ belong to the same member of } \mathcal{P}$$

is an equivalence relation in X. Thus, equivalence relations in X and partitions of X are two faces of the same coin.

2.1.3 Partial and Linear Orders

Pre-Orders and Partial Orders

Recall that a pre-order is a reflexive and transitive relation, while a partial order is an antisymmetric pre-order. We consider a typical application of the quotient construction. Let R be a pre-order in X. Then the following hold:

1. The relation $\sim$ in X defined by

$$x \sim y \quad \text{iff} \quad xRy \text{ and } yRx$$

   is an equivalence relation in X.
2. The relation $\tilde{R}$ in $X/_\sim$, defined by

$$x/_\sim \tilde{R} \, y/_\sim \quad \text{iff} \quad xRy,$$

   is a well-defined partial order in X (called **the partial order induced by** R).

Let $\leq$ be a (fixed) partial order in the set X. Then X is called a **partially ordered set**, abbreviated as **poset**. We will use standard notation, in particular $x \geq y$ for $y \leq x$; $x < y$ for $x \leq y$ and $x \neq y$; and $x > y$ for $y < x$.

Note that every subset Y of a poset X is a poset with respect to the restriction of the partial order in X to Y.

Extremal Elements

Let X be a poset and $Y \subseteq X$. A **lower** (resp. **upper**) **bound for** Y **in** X is any $x \in X$ such that $x \leq y$ (resp. $x \geq y$) for every $y \in Y$. The least of all upper bounds of Y, if it exists, is also called the **supremum** of Y; the greatest of all lower bounds of Y, if it exists, is called the **infimum** of Y.

If a lower (resp. upper) bound of Y belongs to Y, it is called a **least** (resp. **greatest**) element of Y.

Note the following:

- Neither infimum nor supremum of Y need to exist, but if one exists, it must be unique.
- If a least (greatest) element of Y exists, it is the infimum (supremum) of Y and therefore is unique.
- However, the infimum (supremum) of Y need not belong to Y and therefore need not be a least (resp. greatest) element of it.

An element $x \in Y$ is called **minimal** in Y if there is no element of Y strictly less than x, i.e. for every $y \in Y$, if $y \leq x$, then $x = y$. It is called **maximal** in Y if there is no element of Y strictly greater than x, i.e. for every $y \in Y$, if $y \geq x$, then $x = y$.

Note that the least (resp. greatest) element of Y, if it exists, is minimal (resp. maximal).

Example 2.1.2. The poset $\mathbb{N}$ with respect to divisibility has a least element, viz. 1, but no maximal (hence no greatest) elements.

However, the poset $\{2, 3, 4, \ldots\}$ has no least element with respect to divisibility, while it has infinitely many minimal elements, viz. all primes.

Trees

A **tree** is defined as a pair $\text{Tr} = (X, R)$, where X is a nonempty set of **nodes** and R is a binary relation on X such that there is a designated element r of X (the **root**) such that

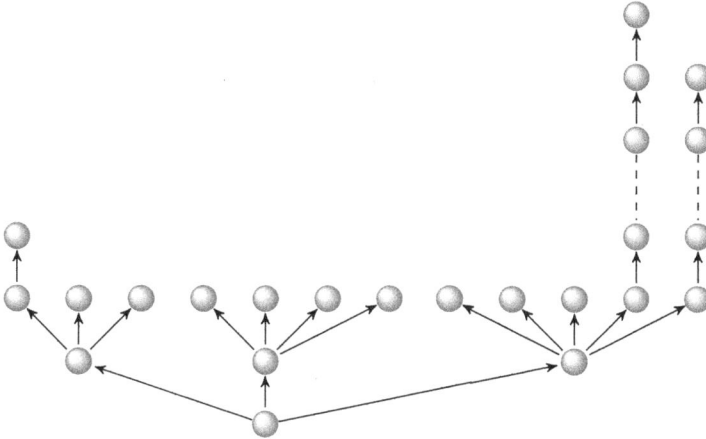

Figure 2.1 A tree with 12 branches.

$R^{-1}(r) = \emptyset$, $R^*(r) = X$ (i.e. every element of X is reachable by an R-path from r) and for every $x \in X \setminus \{r\}$, $R^{-1}(x)$ is a singleton set.

If $(x, x') \in R$, then we say that x is the **parent** of x' and x' is a **child** of x. If $(x, x') \in R^+$, then we say that x is an **ancestor** of x'. The elements of X are called the **nodes** of the tree $\text{Tr} = (X, R)$.

A **branch** Br is a subset of X such that the restriction of (X, R) to Br, i.e. (Br, $R \cap \text{Br} \times \text{Br}$), is a total order and that for any proper extension Br $\subset Y$, $(Y, R \cap Y \times Y)$ is not a total order. Depending on the 'order type' of (Br, $R \cap \text{Br} \times \text{Br}$), a branch can be represented by a maximal sequence $x_0, x_1, \ldots$ such that $x_0 = r$, and for every $i \geq 1$, $(x_i, x_{i+1}) \in R$. Figure 2.1 contains a tree with 12 branches.

The **level** of $x \in X$, denoted by $|x|$, is the distance from the root, i.e. the number of R-transitions from the root to x. In particular, $|r| = 0$. Equivalently, $|x| = n$ iff there is a branch Br $= x_0, x_1, \ldots, x_n, \ldots$ such that $x = x_n$. The nodes x of X such that $R(x) = \emptyset$ are called the **leaves**.

A tree $\text{Tr} = (X, R)$ over $\mathbb{N}$ is a tree such that X is a subset of $\mathbb{N}^*$ (set of finite sequences of natural numbers), and if $x \cdot i \in X$, where $x \in \mathbb{N}^*$ and $i \in \mathbb{N}$, then $(x, x \cdot i) \in R$ and $x \cdot (i - 1) \in X$ if $i > 1$.

Let Σ be a (finite) alphabet. A Σ-**labelled tree** is a pair $(\text{Tr}, \mathfrak{f})$ such that $\text{Tr} = (X, R)$ is a tree and $\mathfrak{f} : X \to \Sigma$ is a map. We often refer to $\mathfrak{f}$ as a labelled tree, leaving its domain implicit.

Well-Ordered Sets

An **ascending** (resp. **strictly ascending**) **chain** in a poset $(X, \leq)$ is any, finite or infinite, sequence $x_1 \leq x_2 \leq \ldots$ (resp. $x_1 < x_2 < \ldots$) of elements of X. A **descending** (resp. **strictly descending**) chain is defined analogously.

A poset is called **well founded** if it contains no infinite strictly descending chains.

Every finite poset is well founded. Similarly, the linearly ordered set $(\mathbb{N}, <)$ is well founded. The poset $(\mathcal{P}(X), \subseteq)$, where X is any infinite set, is not well founded.

A well-founded linear order is called **well-order** (or **complete order**).

Example 2.1.3. $(\mathbb{N}, \leq)$ is a well-order, while $(\mathbb{Z}, \leq)$, $(\mathbb{Q}, \leq)$ and $(\mathbb{R}, \leq)$ are not. The **lexicographic order** in $\mathbb{N}^2$ defined by $(x_1, y_1) \leq (x_2, y_2)$ iff $x_1 < x_2$ or $(x_1 = x_2$ and $y_1 \leq y_2)$ is a well-order in $\mathbb{N}^2$.

A poset $(X, <)$ is well founded iff every nonempty subset of X has a minimal element. In particular, $(X, <)$ is a well-order iff every nonempty subset of X has a least element.

Theorem 2.1.4. Let $(X, \leq)$ be a well-founded set and $Y \subseteq X$ be such that for every $x \in X$, if all elements of X less than x belong to Y, then x itself belongs to Y. Then $Y = X$. ∎

Proof. Assume the contrary, i.e. $X \setminus Y \neq \emptyset$. Then $X \setminus Y$ has a minimal element x. Then all elements of X less than x belong to Y, hence x must belong to Y which is a contradiction. □

Order Types and Ordinal Numbers

Two ordered sets $(X, \leq)$ and $(Y, \leq')$ have the same **order type** when the sets are **order isomorphic**. This means that there is a bijection $\mathfrak{f} : X \to Y$ such that

- for all $x, y \in X$, $x \leq y$ implies $\mathfrak{f}(x) \leq' \mathfrak{f}(y)$ and
- for all $x', y' \subset Y$, $x' \leq' y'$ implies $\mathfrak{f}^{-1}(x') \leq \mathfrak{f}^{-1}(y')$.

Ordinals are defined as equivalence classes of isomorphic well-ordered sets; so, when $(X, \leq)$ is a well-ordered set, its order type can be understood as the unique ordinal isomorphic to $(X, \leq)$; see the following basics on ordinals (see also Rosenstein 1982; Moschovakis 2006). Ordinals can be defined alternatively by considering a well-ordered set for each ordinal that canonically represents the equivalence class of well-ordered sets corresponding to the ordinal. So, the ordinals can be more conveniently defined inductively by the following:

- The empty set (in that context, usually written 0) is an ordinal.
- If α is an ordinal, then $\alpha \cup \{\alpha\}$ (in that context, usually written $\alpha + 1$) is an ordinal.
- If X is a set of ordinals, then $\bigcup_{\alpha \in X} \alpha$ is an ordinal.

The ordering is defined by $\beta < \alpha$ iff $\beta \in \alpha$. An ordinal α is a **successor** ordinal iff there exists an ordinal β such that $\alpha = \beta + 1$. An ordinal which is not 0 or a successor ordinal is a **limit** ordinal. The first limit ordinal is written ω.

Addition, multiplication and exponentiation of ordinals can be defined inductively. Here is the definition for addition:

- $\alpha + 0 = \alpha$,
- $\alpha + (\beta + 1) = (\alpha + \beta) + 1$ and
- $\alpha + \beta = sup\{\alpha + \gamma : \gamma < \beta\}$, where β is a limit ordinal. Note that here, *sup* corresponds to set union. Limit ordinals are sometimes denoted by κ.

Multiplication and exponentiation are defined similarly. The principle behind the definition of addition is **transfinite induction**, which is an extension of induction to well-ordered sets. In a nutshell, let $p(\alpha)$ be a property defined for all ordinals α. Suppose that if $p(\beta)$ for all the ordinals $\beta < \alpha$, then $p(\alpha)$ holds true. Transfinite induction guarantees that the property $p(\alpha)$ is true for all the ordinals α. Such a principle can also be used to define operations on ordinals, as done for addition, for example. Indeed, the class of ordinals is known to be well ordered, and therefore Theorem 2.1.4 applies to it. In particular, any nonempty set of ordinals has a least element. Usually, proving $p(\alpha)$ for all α can be divided into three cases: (1) prove that $p(0)$ holds; (2) prove that for all ordinals α, if $p(\alpha)$ holds, then $p(\alpha + 1)$ holds; (3) prove that for limit ordinal κ, if, for all $\alpha < \kappa$, we have $p(\alpha)$ holds, then $p(\kappa)$ holds. Similar cases appear for defining objects/sets/operations indexed by ordinals.

An ordinal that cannot be put in one-to-one correspondence with any smaller ordinal is called a **cardinal**. Furthermore, assuming the Axiom of Choice, every set X can be put in a one-to-one correspondence with an ordinal. The least ordinal for which there is a one-to-one correspondence with X is a cardinal, called the **cardinality of X** and denoted card(X).

2.2 Some Fundamental Preliminaries

2.2.1 Fixpoints in Powerset Lattices

Given a set X, a mapping $F : \mathcal{P}(X) \to \mathcal{P}(X)$ is called an **operator on** X. An operator F on X can be iterated **upwards** α times, denoted F^α, for any ordinal α. The upwards iteration F^α is defined by transfinite induction on α as follows ($Y \subseteq X$):

- $F^0(Y) := Y$,
- $F^{\alpha+1}(Y) := F(F^\alpha(Y))$ and
- $F^\alpha(Y) = \bigcup_{\beta < \alpha} F^\beta(Y)$ for limit ordinals α.

Likewise, F can be iterated **downwards** α times, denoted F_α, for any ordinal α, and the iteration F_α is defined by transfinite induction on α as follows:

- $F_0(Y) := Y$,
- $F_{\alpha+1}(Y) := F(F_\alpha(Y))$ and
- $F_\alpha(Y) = \bigcap_{\beta < \alpha} F_\beta(Y)$ for limit ordinals α.

Definition 2.2.1. An operator $F : \mathcal{P}(X) \to \mathcal{P}(X)$ is **monotone** if, for all $Y_1, Y_2 \subseteq X$, if $Y_1 \subseteq Y_2$ then $F(Y_1) \subseteq F(Y_2)$. $\qquad\qquad \nabla$

Definition 2.2.2. Given an operator $F : \mathcal{P}(X) \to \mathcal{P}(X)$, a set $Y \subseteq X$ is

- a **fixpoint** of F if $F(Y) = Y$,
- a **pre-fixpoint** of F if $F(Y) \subseteq Y$,
- a **post-fixpoint** of F if $F(Y) \supseteq Y$,
- a **least fixpoint** if Y is a fixpoint and $Y \subseteq Z$ for every fixpoint Z,
- a **least pre-fixpoint** if Y is a pre-fixpoint and $Y \subseteq Z$ for every pre-fixpoint Z,

- a **greatest fixpoint** if Y is a fixpoint and $Y \supseteq Z$ for every fixpoint Z,
- a **greatest post-fixpoint** if Y is a post-fixpoint and $Y \supseteq Z$ for every post-fixpoint Z.   ▽

Clearly, if F has a least fixpoint or a least pre-fixpoint, it is unique. Likewise for greatest fixpoints and greatest post-fixpoints. If F has a least fixpoint, it is denoted by μF. Likewise, the greatest fixpoint of F, if it exists, is denoted by νF.

Theorem 2.2.3 (Knaster–Tarski). Let $F : \mathcal{P}(X) \to \mathcal{P}(X)$ be a monotone operator. Then

(I) F has a least fixpoint μF, which is also the least pre-fixpoint of F, and has a greatest fixpoint νF, which is also the greatest post-fixpoint of F;

(II) $\mu F = \bigcap \{ Y \subseteq X \mid F(Y) = Y \} = \bigcap \{ Y \subseteq X \mid F(Y) \subseteq Y \}$; and

(III) $\nu F = \bigcup \{ Y \subseteq X \mid F(Y) = Y \} = \bigcup \{ Y \subseteq X \mid F(Y) \supseteq Y \}$.   ■

Theorem 2.2.3 is due to B. Knaster and A. Tarski, and its proof can be found e.g. in (Kozen 2006, Lecture A). The preceding statement is actually a restricted form of Knaster–Tarski's Theorem. In full generality, one can assume that F is an order-preserving function operating on a complete lattice. The proofs of the claims in Theorem 2.2.3 are nice elementary exercises.

The last part of Knaster–Tarski's Theorem actually says more than what meets the eye: owing to the monotonicity of F, it is easy to see that $F^{\alpha}(Y) \subseteq F^{\beta}(Y)$ and $F_{\alpha}(Y) \supseteq F_{\beta}(Y)$ whenever $\alpha < \beta$, i.e. both sequences are monotone, hence they are bound to reach their fixpoints by the κth iteration where κ is the successor cardinal of $\mathrm{card}(X)$, i.e. the least cardinal greater than $\mathrm{card}(X)$.

The least (resp. greatest) fixpoint can be obtained by simply applying the successive iterations of F, beginning with $\emptyset$ for μ, or with X for ν, until a fixpoint is reached. Often it is practically easier to compute, or at least analyse, these iterations (also known as **unfoldings**) of F than the intersection (resp. union) of all pre-fixpoints (resp. post-fixpoints).

2.2.2 Complexity Classes

In the following, we recall a few basic concepts about complexity theory; for further information and definitions, we invite the reader to consult e.g. Arora and Barak (2009).

Complexity theory provides a means of assigning a measure to algorithms/problems described in a given computation model. This measure is supposed to express how difficult a problem is, for instance by comparing its measure with the measure of other problems. A **decision problem**, or simply **problem**, is a subset of Σ^* for some finite alphabet Σ. This is of course an abstract way to define a problem, and in the sequel, we shall use the following presentation to introduce a given problem $\mathrm{L} \subseteq \Sigma^*$.

Input: $u \in \Sigma^*$

Question: Is $u \in \mathrm{L}$?

Most of the time, the alphabet Σ is implicit when dealing with inputs that are not directly finite words, such as logical formulae, finite transition systems or game arenas. A reasonably succinct encoding for inputs is always assumed, unless it is explicitly provided.

The two most common measures of complexity are time (number of elementary steps of a computation) and space (size of the memory used during a computation). These two measures are understood as asymptotic functions in the length of the inputs, and in this book we deal with worst-case complexity.

In order to determine the complexity of a problem $\mathcal{P}$, we first have to choose a model of computation, that is to define a class of (abstract) machines that will be used for solving $\mathcal{P}$. In this book, if needed, we use Turing machines (TMs). However, we do not work directly with Turing machines but with a more intuitive model of computation for which our complexity results transfer easily to TMs. We follow a standard practice and discuss algorithms in an almost model-independent manner. Our informal demonstrations should be taken as an indication of how this could be done formally.

For every map $\mathfrak{f} : \mathbb{N} \to \mathbb{R}$, we write $\mathcal{O}(\mathfrak{f}(n))$ to denote the class of maps $\mathfrak{g} : \mathbb{N} \to \mathbb{N}$ such that there exist an n_0 and a value $c \in \mathbb{N}$ such that for all $n > n_0$, $\mathfrak{g}(n) < c \cdot \mathfrak{f}(n)$. $\mathcal{O}(\mathfrak{f}(n))$ is the class of functions whose asymptotic growth is bounded by $c \cdot \mathfrak{f}(n)$ for some constant c. Let $\mathfrak{F}$ be a class of maps $\mathbb{N} \to \mathbb{R}$. NTIME($\mathfrak{F}$) is the class of problems accepted by non-deterministic Turing machines which accept within time $\mathfrak{f}(n)$ for some $\mathfrak{f} \in \mathfrak{F}$. Similarly, DTIME($\mathfrak{F}$) (resp. DSPACE($\mathfrak{F}$)) is the class of problems accepted by deterministic Turing machines which accept within time (resp. space) $\mathfrak{f}(n)$ for some $\mathfrak{f} \in \mathfrak{F}$. We write *Poly* to denote the class of polynomial functions with domain $\mathbb{N}$. The complexity classes of particular interest in this book are the following (some more can be found in Chapter 11):

$$
\begin{aligned}
\text{PTIME} \quad &:= \text{DTIME}({\textstyle\bigcup}_{\mathfrak{f}(n)\in Poly}\,\mathcal{O}(\mathfrak{f}(n))), \\
\text{NP} \quad &:= \text{NTIME}({\textstyle\bigcup}_{\mathfrak{f}(n)\in Poly}\,\mathcal{O}(\mathfrak{f}(n))), \\
\text{PSPACE} \quad &:= \text{DSPACE}({\textstyle\bigcup}_{\mathfrak{f}(n)\in Poly}\,\mathcal{O}(\mathfrak{f}(n))), \\
\text{EXPTIME} \quad &:= \text{DTIME}({\textstyle\bigcup}_{\mathfrak{f}(n)\in Poly}\,\mathcal{O}(2^{\mathfrak{f}(n)})), \\
\text{2EXPTIME} \quad &:= \text{DTIME}({\textstyle\bigcup}_{\mathfrak{f}(n)\in Poly}\,\mathcal{O}(2^{2^{\mathfrak{f}(n)}})).
\end{aligned}
$$

It is known that PTIME $\subseteq$ NP $\subseteq$ PSPACE $\subseteq$ EXPTIME $\subset$ 2EXPTIME, and that PTIME $\neq$ EXPTIME. Moreover, by Savitch's Theorem, PSPACE = NPSPACE (Savitch 1970), where NPSPACE (resp. NEXPSPACE) denotes the class of problems that can be solved in polynomial space (resp. exponential space) with a nondeterministic Turing machine.

Let $\mathcal{P} \subseteq \Sigma^*$ and let $\mathcal{P}' \subseteq \Sigma'^*$. $\mathcal{P}$ is polynomial-time-reducible (resp. logarithmic-space-reducible) to $\mathcal{P}'$ if there is $\mathfrak{f} : \Sigma^* \to \Sigma'^*$ such that $\mathfrak{f}$ can be computed in polynomial time (resp. logarithmic space) and for every $x \in \Sigma^*$, $x \in \mathcal{P}$ iff $\mathfrak{f}(x) \in \mathcal{P}'$. This notion happens to be very useful to characterise problems that are as complex as a whole class of problems; the definitions are provided in the following.

Let $\mathcal{C}$ be a class of problems and let $\mathcal{P}$ be a problem.

$\mathcal{C}$-hardness. $\mathcal{P}$ is said to be $\mathcal{C}$-**hard** (with respect to logarithmic-space reductions) if, for every problem $\mathcal{P} \in \mathcal{C}$, there is $\mathfrak{f} : \Sigma^* \to \Sigma'^*$ such that $\mathfrak{f}$ can be computed in logarithmic

space and, for every $x \in \Sigma^*$, $x \in \mathcal{P}$ iff $\mathfrak{f}(x) \in \mathcal{P}'$. So $\mathcal{P}$ is at least as difficult as any problem in the class $\mathcal{C}$. In a sense, $\mathcal{P}$ captures the difficulty of a whole complexity class.

C-completeness. $\mathcal{P}$ is said to be $\mathcal{C}$-**complete** with respect to $\mathcal{C}'$ if $\mathcal{P}$ is $\mathcal{C}$-hard and $\mathcal{P} \in \mathcal{C}$.

So $\mathcal{P}$ is $\mathcal{C}$-complete when it captures the class $\mathcal{C}$ in terms of computational complexity; in the book we provide numerous decision problems (using logics, automata, games, etc.) that are shown to be $\mathcal{C}$-complete for some $\mathcal{C}$ in NP, PSPACE, EXPTIME, 2EXPTIME, etc.

2.2.3 Two-Player Games

Arenas and Winning Conditions

In the game-theoretic approach to temporal logics, the logical decision problems get reduced to the problem of solving a game, i.e. to determine which one of two players has a winning strategy for this game. We will only be concerned with very restricted classes of games from a game-theoretic point of view: 2-player zero-sum games of perfect information. For algorithmic purposes we are also particularly interested in finite games. Typically, these games are infinite-duration games, too (see the following definitions).

Such a game is defined by its **arena** and its **winning conditions**. Formally, the arena is a directed, 2-partitioned graph in which each node represents a certain state that the game can be in and the edges represent the transitions that the game can evolve along. Playing the game can be seen as pushing a token along the edges of the graph. The particular graph structure is owed to the particular restricted class of games that we want to consider:

- **Finiteness** of the games means that there are only finitely many different game positions.
- The partitioning of the node set into two sets realises a **2-player** game: each node belongs to exactly one of two players whose responsibility is to make the game proceed by chosing a successor node once a play has reached one of their nodes.
- Being a **perfect information** game means that both players always have full information about the state of the game. A simple model like directed graphs does not conceal any information. For games of imperfect information, like most card games, one would have to consider extensions of such a model.
- An **infinite-duration** game is one in which the underlying arena is sink-less, i.e. each node has at least one successor. Thus, maximal paths in this graph are of infinite length, and these maximal paths represent the plays of the game. A game model that is most used for temporal logics allows both infinite and finite plays, i.e. also ones represented by maximal paths in the arena that end in a dead-end node. It is not difficult to imagine that finite plays can be seen as special cases of infinite ones, for example by moving from a dead-end node to a designated new node which only has an edge to itself.
- Finally, the games are **zero-sum**, which means that one player's win is the other player's loss, and vice versa. The winning condition of the game partitions the set of all plays into those won by one player and those won by the other player.

We begin with the formal definition of a game arena.

Definition 2.2.4. The **arena** of a **2-player, zero-sum game of perfect information and infinite duration**, henceforth simply called a **game arena**, is a triple (V, Own, E) where (V, E) is a directed graph with finite node set V and edge relation $E \subseteq V \times V$ such that for every $v \in V$, there is some $w \in V$ with $(v, w) \in E$. Furthermore, $Own : V \to \{0, 1\}$ assigns to each node the player who owns the node. In this abstract setting, we refer to the two players as player 0 and player 1. In order to better distinguish between them, we will use female pronouns for player 0 and male ones for player 1. We will also simply write V_i for $\{v \in V \mid Own(v) = i\}$ when $i \in \{0, 1\}$. Note that V_0 and V_1 – even just one of them – uniquely determines the owner function Own. $\triangledown$

Example 2.2.5. We use the following convention to graphically represent game arenas. Nodes that are being owned by player 0 are drawn as circles, whereas nodes that are being owned by player 1 are drawn as boxes. The starting node is marked with an incoming edge that originates nowhere. For instance, the following represents a game arena:

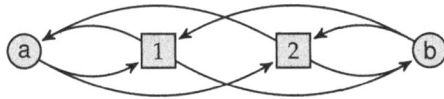

This arena represents a 2-player game in which both players always have the choice between two options. Player 0 can choose to move to 1 or 2, whereas player 1 responds from either of these positions with a choice to go to a or b.

Formally, the game arena is $(\{a, b, 1, 2\}, Own, E, a)$, with the owner function implicitly given by $V_0 = \{a, b\}$ and $V_1 = \{1, 2\}$. The edge relation E can easily be read off the preceding graph.

Any game played in this particular arena is **turn-based** – the two players always move in turn. This is a coincidence; the games we consider in this book will in general not be turn-based.

Note that the previous example does not specify when a player has won. This is the task of the winning condition. Adding a winning condition to an arena makes it a game. In order to talk about winning, we need the notion of a play.

Definition 2.2.6. Let (V, Own, E) be a game arena. A **play** is an infinite sequence $\lambda = v_0, v_1, \ldots$ such that $(v_i, v_{i+1}) \in E$ for every $i \in \mathbb{N}$. We will say that this play starts in v_0.

Let $v \in V$. We write $\Pi(v)$ for the set of all possible plays in this arena that start in v. Note that $\Pi(v) \subseteq V^\omega$.

A **game** is a tuple $\mathcal{G} = (V, Own, E, v_I, Win)$ where (V, Own, E) forms a game arena, v_I is a designated starting node and $Win : \Pi(v_I) \to \{0, 1\}$ is the **winning condition** that assigns a winner to every play that starts in v_I.

Since we will often consider winning conditions that depend on the infinite occurrences of nodes in a play, we define $\inf(v_0, v_1, \ldots) := \{v \mid$ there are infinitely many $i \in \mathbb{N}$ with $v = v_i\}$. Note that on finite graphs, we have $\inf(\lambda) \neq \emptyset$ for any play λ. $\triangledown$

Remark 2.2.7. For technical convenience, we will also sometimes consider games in which not all arena nodes have a successor. A play can then also be a maximal finite sequence $v_0, \ldots, v_n$ of nodes in the arena. We introduce the convention that the winner of such a play is always $1 - Own(v_n)$, i.e. the player who cannot move any further in the last node of that play loses it. It should be clear that this really is just a technical convenience. It is always possible to turn such a game into one with total arenas by adding two more nodes w_i, $i = 0, 1$, with additional edges

$$\{(v, w_i) \mid E(v) = \emptyset \text{ and } Own(v) = 1 - i\} \cup \{(w_0, w_0), (w_1, w_1)\}$$

and letting player i win any play that eventually (only) visits the node w_i.

Clearly every play is an infinite sequence of nodes, but not every infinite sequence of nodes is a play unless the edge relation of the underlying game arena is the full relation $E = V \times V$. Intuitively, the two players move in the arena by pushing a token along the edges, and the result after infinitely many steps is a play. The winning condition then names the winner. Different choices could have led to a different play with a different winner.

Example 2.2.8. Consider the game $\mathcal{G}_1 = (V, Own, E, \text{a}, Win_{\text{fair}})$ with the arena of Example 2.2.5 and the winning condition defined by

$$Win_{\text{fair}}(\lambda) = \begin{cases} 0, & \text{if a} \in \inf(\lambda) \text{ implies } 1 \in \inf(\lambda), \\ 1, & \text{otherwise.} \end{cases}$$

For example, player 0 would win the play that cycles on a, 1, b, 2, but player 1 would win the play a, 1, b, 2, a, 2, a, 2, …

As a second example, consider the game $\mathcal{G}_2$ which is obtained from $\mathcal{G}_1$ by replacing the winning condition with the following one:

$$Win_{\text{count}}(\lambda) = \begin{cases} 0, & \text{if } \max(\inf(\lambda) \cap \{1, 2\}) = \text{card}(\inf(\lambda) \cap \{\text{a}, \text{b}\}), \\ 1, & \text{otherwise.} \end{cases}$$

In other words, player 0 wins a play in which player 1 chose both a and b infinitely often only if she chose 2 infinitely often. If player 1 chose only one of them infinitely often, then player 0 must have chosen 2 only finitely often.

Strategies

It is pretty obvious how player 0 can enforce a win in the game $\mathcal{G}_1$: she simply always chooses 1. Since the game is turn-based and from every position in V_0 she can move to 1, every resulting play will visit 1 infinitely often which makes player 0 the winner of that play.

It is less obvious to see whether she can equally enforce a win in $\mathcal{G}_2$. Intuitively, this is difficult because of two facts. First, regardless of what she chooses in a single move, this does not make it occur infinitely often or not. Second, it looks like she would have to know in advance all the choices that player 1 makes among a and b in order to be able to decide between playing 1 or 2 infinitely often. We will see that, nevertheless, she can also enforce a win in this game. However, we need to formally define what this enforcement is meant to be. We need to introduce strategies.

Definition 2.2.9. Let $\mathcal{G} = (V, Own, E, v_I, Win)$ be a game. A **history** is a finite sequence $\eta = v_0, \ldots v_n$ for some $n \in \mathbb{N}$ such that $v_0 = v_I$ and $(v_i, v_{i+1}) \in E$ for every $i = 0, \ldots, n - 1$. The owner of a history $v_0, \ldots, v_n$ is $Own(v_n)$. A **strategy** for player **P** is a (partial) function $\mathfrak{str} : V^*V_{\mathbf{P}} \to V$ which assigns to every history $v_0, \ldots, v_n$ owned by player **P** a node $w \in V$ with $(v, w) \in E$.

A play $\lambda = v_0, v_1, \ldots$ **conforms** to a strategy $\mathfrak{str}$ for player **P** if for every $i \in \mathbb{N}$ with $v_i \in V_{\mathbf{P}}$ we have $v_{i+1} = \mathfrak{str}(v_0, \ldots, v_i)$.

A **winning strategy** for player **P** is a strategy for him or her such that every play that conforms to this strategy is also winning for him or her. $\qquad \triangledown$

Thus, in a play that conforms to strategy $\mathfrak{str}$ for player **P**, his/her choices have always been guided by the strategy in the sense that in each of his/her positions she always chose the successor which the strategy has assigned to the current history.

Example 2.2.10. Reconsider the game $\mathcal{G}_1$ from Example 2.2.8. The winning condition requires player 0 to choose 1 infinitely often whenever a is chosen infinitely often. As mentioned earlier, player 0 has a trivial winning strategy for $\mathcal{G}_1$ given as $\mathfrak{str}_0(\eta) = 1$ for every history η that is owned by her. She also wins with the following nonconstant strategy $\mathfrak{str}_1$ defined as

$$\mathfrak{str}_1(v_0, \ldots, v_n) \;=\; \begin{cases} 1, & \text{if } v_n = \mathsf{a}, \\ 2, & \text{otherwise.} \end{cases}$$

Thus, any play that conforms to $\mathfrak{str}_1$ and contains a infinitely often will also contain 1 infinitely often. Moreover, any such play that contains a only finitely often would also do so for the node 1.

On the other hand, suppose that the edge $(\mathsf{a}, 1)$ is removed from the game arena. Then player 1 has a winning strategy $\mathfrak{str}_2$ given by $\mathfrak{str}_2(\eta) = \mathsf{a}$.

Example 2.2.11. Now consider the game $\mathcal{G}_2$ from Example 2.2.8 in which player 0 has to choose that number among 1 and 2 infinitely often that equals the number of letters from $\{\mathsf{a}, \mathsf{b}\}$ which player 1 chooses infinitely often. There is a relatively simple strategy for player 0 to win this game. All she needs to know is to remember player 1's last two choices. Note that they are given in the history of a moment in a play. Whenever player 1's last two choices have differed, she chooses 2, otherwise she chooses 1. Formally,

$$\mathfrak{str}_3(v_0, \ldots, v_{n-2}, v_{n-1}, v_n) \;=\; \begin{cases} 2, & \text{if } n \geq 2 \text{ and } v_{n-2} \neq v_n, \\ 1, & \text{otherwise.} \end{cases}$$

To see that this is indeed a winning strategy consider an arbitrary play $\lambda = v_0, v_1, \ldots$ which conforms to $\mathfrak{str}_3$. Let $m = \mathrm{card}(\inf(\lambda) \cap \{a, b\})$. There are two cases.

If $m = 1$ then from some moment on player 1 will only have chosen, say, a. The case with b is entirely identical. Thus, there is some even i such that $v_{i+2j} = a$ for all $j \geq 0$. Since λ conforms to $\mathfrak{str}_3$, we have $v_{i+2j+1} = 1$ for all $j \geq 0$ and therefore $\max(\inf(\lambda) \cap \{1, 2\}) = 1$.

On the other hand, if $m = 2$ then player 1 has chosen both a and b infinitely often in λ. Then there must be infinitely many even i such that $v_i = a$ and $v_{i+2} = b$ or vice versa. Note that for each such i we have $v_{i+3} = 2$ because λ conforms to $\mathfrak{str}_3$. Thus, we have $\max(\inf(\lambda) \cap \{1, 2\}) = 2$ in that case.

These examples accentuate two important aspects of winning strategies in such games. The first one is determinacy.

Definition 2.2.12. A class of games $\mathfrak{G}$ is called **determined** if for every game $\mathcal{G} \in \mathfrak{G}$ either player 0 or player 1 has a winning strategy. ∇

It should be clear that there is no game for which both players have a winning strategy. A formal proof is left as Exercise 15.1. The far more interesting part of determinacy is the other one: why should one player have a winning strategy just because the other one does not? Nevertheless, the games that we consider here will all enjoy determinacy, and we will be able to use determinacy to prove important game-theoretic characterisations of decision problems for temporal logics.

The second important aspect that is exemplified earlier is the dependency on memory of a winning strategy.

Definition 2.2.13. A strategy $\mathfrak{str}$ for player **P** in a game with node set V is called **memoryless**, or **positional**, if, for all histories η, η' and all $v \in V_{\mathbf{P}}$, we have $\mathfrak{str}(\eta, v) = \mathfrak{str}(\eta', v)$. ∇

In other words, the choices made by a memoryless strategy do not depend on the entire history of the current moment but only on the position in the game. We will also define memoryless strategies for player **P** as functions of type $V_{\mathbf{P}} \to V$.

Note that the strategies $\mathfrak{str}_0$, $\mathfrak{str}_1$ and $\mathfrak{str}_2$ defined in Example 2.2.8 are in fact memoryless, whereas strategy $\mathfrak{str}_3$ from Example 2.2.10 is not. It is not too hard to see that player 0 has in fact no memoryless winning strategy for that game. A formal proof of this is left as Exercise 15.2.

Combining these two aspects yields the following definition.

Definition 2.2.14. A class of games $\mathfrak{G}$ is said to have **memoryless determinacy** if for every game $\mathcal{G} \in \mathfrak{G}$ either player 0 or player 1 has a memoryless winning strategy. ∇

A generalisation of the concept of a memoryless strategy is that of a finite-memory strategy. Here, the choice made by a strategy does not depend on the entire history of a play either but on a part of it that can be represented using bounded memory.

Definition 2.2.15. A strategy $\mathfrak{str}$ for player **P** in a game with node set V is called k-bounded if there is an equivalence relation $\sim\,\subseteq V^* \times V^*$ such that

- $\sim$ has at most k many equivalence classes, and
- for all $w, w' \in V^*$ and all $v \in V_\mathbf{P}$: if $w \sim w'$ then $\mathfrak{str}(w, v) = \mathfrak{str}(w', v)$.

We say that $\mathfrak{str}$ is **finite-memory** if it is k-bounded for some $k \geq 1$. $\qquad\qquad \nabla$

Regular Games

A class of games that is of particular importance for algorithmic purposes is the class of 'regular games'. The name is derived from the property that the set of winning plays for either player, when seen as a formal language of infinite words, satisfies a regularity property. An ω-regular language is one that can be recognised by a nondeterministic Büchi automaton (see Chapter 14) or a deterministic parity automaton (see Chapter 15), respectively or that can be described by an ω-regular expression (see Chapter 10). Those who are (yet) unfamiliar with such concepts can simply regard this as a natural extension from finite-state recognisability on finite words to infinite words.

Note that *Win* – originally defined as a function of type $\Pi(v_I) \rightarrow \{0, 1\}$ – can in fact be seen as a formal language over the alphabet V which is finite for finite games.

Definition 2.2.16. Let $\mathcal{G} = (V, \textit{Own}, E, v_I, \textit{Win})$ be a game with Π being the set of all plays in $\mathcal{G}$. Then $\mathcal{G}$ belongs to $\mathfrak{G}_{\mathsf{reg}}$ iff $\{\lambda \in \Pi \mid \textit{Win}(\lambda) = 0\}$ is an ω-regular language. $\quad \nabla$

The choice of player 0 in this definition as the one whose set of winning plays determines whether the game is regular, is an arbitrary one. Note that $\{\lambda \in \Pi(v_I) \mid \textit{Win}(\lambda) = 0\}$ is a regular language iff $\{\lambda \in \Pi(v_I) \mid \textit{Win}(\lambda) = 1\}$ is a regular language.

The concept of a regular game can also be extended to infinite games, for example by mapping game nodes to a finite alphabet and then considering the language of the image of all winning plays under this map. This will not play a major role for our purposes, though.

Finally, we lay the foundations for an algorithmic treatment of games by introducing the most obvious decision problem for such games.

Definition 2.2.17. The decision problem of **solving** for a class $\mathfrak{G}$ of games is: given some $\mathcal{G} \in \mathfrak{G}$, determine whether player 0 has a winning strategy for $\mathcal{G}$.

The computation problem of solving additionally asks for a winning strategy to be returned. $\qquad\qquad \nabla$

Note how memoryless determinacy of a class of games $\mathfrak{G}$ makes the game solving problem(s) meaningful: if $\mathfrak{G}$ enjoys determinacy then determining whether player 0 has a winning strategy is as good as doing so for player 1. For classes of games without determinacy, one may have to introduce two decision problems of solving for each player separately. Moreover, note that memoryless winning strategies are finite objects, namely subsets of the edge relation of a finite graph, whereas winning strategies in general may be infinite objects.

In that case, only winning strategies for which there is some finite representation could be computed and returned.

Reconsider the winning strategy str_3 from Example 2.2.10 that is not memoryless. Since player 0's choices with this strategy only ever depend on the last three nodes of the history, it is in fact possible to represent it finitely as a function of type $V_0^2 \to V_1$: player 0 needs to remember the last two choices made by player 1, i.e. the last two visits to V_0 in order to determine where to move next. We leave it as an exercise to form a reduction of this game to one with memoryless winning strategies by simply increasing the node space to all triples of consecutive nodes in this game.

3

Transition Systems

Transition systems are widely used to model computer programs and systems. They consist of states, representing possible configurations, and transitions, representing possible state changes. Such changes may be governed by an action induced by the system itself or by an external event. This is a fundamental model to define the semantics of computer systems or abstract computational devices such as finite state machines, pushdown systems, Turing machines, counter machines, timed automata, etc. Besides, many other models of sequential, parallel, reactive and interactive processes and computations, such as Petri nets, process calculi such as CCS and CSP, etc., can naturally be recast as transition systems.

Transition systems are mathematically quite simple, as they can be viewed as (possibly infinite) directed graphs with labels on vertices or on edges. Yet, theoretical tools developed for them have allowed striking breakthroughs to be made for software verification, in particular due to the approach of verification by model checking.

In the context of this book, transition systems appear in two capacities: as object of primary interest and study, in Part I of the book, and as models for the temporal logics which we will study further. A real system can be modelled by different abstract transition systems and in different levels of detail. It is therefore important to have precise criteria whether a given abstract model faithfully captures the formally specified *behaviour* of the given real transition system. For that it is necessary to have a precise notion of behaviour of a transition system, so later in this chapter we also address the question:

When should two transition systems be considered to be behaviourally equivalent?

This question does not have a unique answer, as the notion of equivalence depends on the behavioural features of transition systems that are considered of importance for the real systems they model. Such features may involve local behaviour (pre- and postconditions), generated paths and computations, as well as reachability, safety, liveness, fairness, etc., types of system properties. Accordingly, a variety of natural notions of behavioural equivalence arise. We will concentrate on two of them – *bisimilarity* and *trace equivalence* – because they are inherently linked to the notion of logical equivalence. A natural question that arises in the study of logics over any kind of structures like transition systems is:

What is the most general relation between two transition systems that preserves the truth of all temporal formulae in them?

As we will demonstrate in Chapter 5 and further, these two questions turn out to be closely related and, under some quite natural conditions, their answers turn out to be essentially equivalent.

Structure of the chapter. Section 3.1 presents the basic concepts related to transition systems and provides a series of examples. In Section 3.1.5, we present a basic classification and discussion of the main types of important properties on transition systems and the main verification problems associated with them. Section 3.2 forms the basis for procedures that verify properties of transition systems: it takes a systematic look at various reachability properties and problems, and it provides algorithmic solutions for them.

Section 3.3 presents and illustrates the notion of bisimulation between interpreted transition systems, including bounded, finite and unbounded bisimulation. In Section 3.4 we consider the concept of bisimilarity as being the largest bisimulation and present algorithms for computing it. We also consider a game-theoretic interpretation of bisimilarity which can be used not only to compute it, but most of all to build an intuition of which transition systems are bisimilar. Finally, in Section 3.5 we consider the weaker notion of trace equivalence, relate it to bisimilarity and give an algorithm for deciding trace equivalence between two transition systems.

3.1 Basic Concepts

Transition systems consist of states and transitions between them. They are used to model sequential and concurrent processes, which can be autonomous, reactive or interactive. The states in a transition system can be thought of as program states, control states, configuration states, memory registers, etc. The transitions are caused by actions, that can represent program instructions, procedures or whole programs, autonomous processes, agents' actions, etc. In this book we adopt an abstract view on transition systems and do not discuss the nature of the transitions much, except for Chapter 9, where this plays an essential role.

3.1.1 Interpreted Transition Systems

We begin with the general notion of transition system, where transitions can be affected by different actions or processes, and to distinguish different types of transitions, we assign different labels to them.

Definition 3.1.1. A **rooted, interpreted transition system** is a structure

$$\mathcal{T} = (S, \{\xrightarrow{a}\}_{a \in Act}, L, s)$$

consisting of

- a nonempty set S of **states**, called the **state space** of $\mathcal{T}$;
- a nonempty set Act of **action names** (or, **action labels**); each of these acts – possibly nondeterministically – on states and produces **successor states**;
- a binary **transition relation** $\xrightarrow{a} \subseteq S \times S$ associated with every action name $a \in Act$;
- a (possibly empty) set PROP of **atomic propositions**; each of these holds in a particular set of states;
- a **labelling function** $L : S \to \mathcal{P}(\text{PROP})$ which assigns to every state s the set $L(s)$ of atomic propositions true at s, called the **description**, or just the **label**, of that state;
- a designated **initial state** s called the **root** of $\mathcal{T}$.

We also call the pair (Act, PROP), determining the possible actions and atomic propositions in a transition system, its **signature** or **type**. ∇

Such structures are **rooted transition systems** because of the designated initial state which acts as a root from which the temporal behaviour modelled by such a transition system evolves.

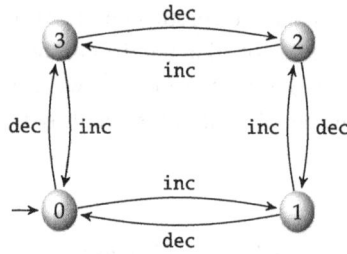

Figure 3.1 A transition system for counting modulo 4.

A state may have various properties: it can be initial, terminal, accepting, deadlock, safe or unsafe, etc., depending on the scenario that is modelled with such a transition system. Such properties of states are described by formulae of a suitable state description language. On propositional level these are indicated by the **atomic propositions**. It is the labelling function assigning such atomic properties to states which make these structures **interpreted transition systems**.

Such rooted interpreted transition systems are the models for temporal logics. Henceforth, we will shortly speak of **transition systems** (TS) or **interpreted transition systems** (ITS) only.

When referring to transition systems where states have a specific structure – such as states of pushdown automata, Turing machines, counter automata, Petri nets, etc. – we will often use the term '**configuration**' as a synonym of 'state'. Also, depending on the context, sometimes we will talk about '**control states**' or '**locations**' instead of 'states', and about **actions**, or **processes**, instead of 'transitions'.

We write $s \xrightarrow{a} r$ to indicate that the action a can transform the state s into the state r and say that s is an a-**predecessor** of r, while r is an a-**successor** of s.

Example 3.1.2. In Figure 3.1 we present a simple transition system with four states that models the evolution of an integer variable modulo four. The transition system has two actions: `inc` for increment and `dec` for decrement and no atomic propositions. We use a short incoming arrow to depict the transition systems initial states, i.e. 0 in this case.

To emphasise the distinction between the transitions with different action labels, such transition systems are sometimes called **labelled**. When a transition system involves only one action label, we sometimes call it a **mono-transition system**. Then we omit the action label and typically denote it as (S, R, L, s) where R is a binary relation on S. Every transition system $\mathcal{T} = (S, \{\xrightarrow{a}\}_{a \in Act}, L, s)$ induces a mono-transition system by simply 'forgetting' the action names. It is also called **union transition system**, and it uses as transition relation the following one instead.

$$R_{\mathcal{T}} := \bigcup_{a \in Act} \xrightarrow{a}.$$

Figure 3.2 Mono-transition system ($\mathbb{N}$, succ).

Thus, for any states $s, r \in S$, the relation $sR_T r$ holds iff there is at least one transition that relates s to r.

Sometimes we are interested in a transition system as a global structure where the particular initial state is irrelevant. In that case we simply omit it and denote a transition system as (S, R, L) for instance. If the set of atomic propositions is empty, then the labelling function is constant and can therefore be omitted as well. For example, Figure 3.2 shows the mono-transition system ($\mathbb{N}$, succ) where succ is the successor function on $\mathbb{N}$.

In logical terminology, a description of a state is usually called a **truth assignment** at the given state. Sometimes one uses **valuations** instead; these are functions $V : \text{PROP} \to \mathcal{P}(S)$ assigning to each atomic proposition from PROP the set of states where it is true. Clearly, the two formalisms are inter-definable and we will make use of both, for different purposes. For instance, we will use valuations in the context of global model checking, where with every formula of the logic we associate (and compute) its **extended valuation**, or just **extension**, being the set of states in the given interpreted transition system where that formula is true.

Transition systems can be finite or infinite, and much of our treatment here will apply to either. However, for some specific topics, e.g. model checking, we will assume them to be finite; this requirement can be weakened to being finitely presentable. Still, even finite transition systems display infinite behaviour, which is in the focus of this book.

Given an interpreted transition system $T = (S, R, L)$ over a set of atomic propositions PROP, we denote

$$\text{PROP}(T) := \bigcup \{L(s) \mid s \in S\}.$$

Definition 3.1.3. An interpreted transition system $T = (S, R, L)$ is **finite** if both S and $\text{PROP}(T)$ are finite. ∇

Note that when PROP is finite, the second constraint is automatically satisfied.

3.1.2 Paths and Computations

The infinite behaviour of transition systems can be expressed in terms of *paths* and *computations* in them.

Definition 3.1.4. A **path** π in a transition system T is a finite or an infinite sequence of states and (names of) actions which transform every state into its successor:

$$s_0 \xrightarrow{a_0} s_1 \xrightarrow{a_1} s_2 \ldots$$

The path is said to be rooted at s_0. A path π consisting of n transitions is said to have **length** n, denoted $|\pi| = n$.

A path in a transition system is **maximal** if it is either infinite, or is finite and ends in a **deadlock**, i.e. a state with no successors.   ▽

The following is a path in the transition system of Figure 3.1:

$$2 \xrightarrow{\text{inc}} 3 \xrightarrow{\text{inc}} 4 \xrightarrow{\text{dec}} 3 \xrightarrow{\text{inc}} 4 \xrightarrow{\text{dec}} 3 \xrightarrow{\text{dec}} 2 \xrightarrow{\text{inc}} 3 \xrightarrow{\text{dec}} \ldots$$

We will sometimes use the terms '**run**' or '**execution**' as synonyms of 'path', for instance when referring to some special cases of transition systems, such as automata, Petri nets, etc.

We will usually consider the case when the (union) transition relation R is **serial**, i.e. every state has at least one R-successor. In that case we also call the underlying transition system **total**.

In a mono-transition system, a path is simply a sequence of states $s_0, s_1, \ldots$, every one of which is related to the next by the transition relation. Formally, a path in such a transition system can be defined as a mapping $\pi : \mathbb{N} \to S$, for infinite paths, respectively $\pi : [0, n] \to S$ for finite paths, where $[0, n] = \{0, 1, \ldots, n\}$. So, we will often denote the successive states of a path π by $\pi(0), \pi(1), \pi(2), \ldots$.

Definition 3.1.5. A finite path in a transition system is a **cycle** if its first and its last state coincide. In particular, a **loop** is a cycle of length 1, i.e. $s \xrightarrow{a} s$.   ▽

Definition 3.1.6. A transition system is

- **acyclic** if it does not contain cycles;
- **forest-like** if it is acyclic and every state has at most one predecessor state;
- **tree-like** if it is forest-like, in which at most one state has no predecessor states. If such a state exists, it is called the **root** and the transition system is called a **tree**. ▽

The trace of a path in a transition system, that is 'visible' to the user, is the corresponding sequence of labels of states along the path, which we call a *computation*.

Definition 3.1.7. A **computation**, or **trace**, in a transition system $(S, \{\xrightarrow{a}\}_{a \in Act}, L)$ is a (finite or infinite) sequence of state descriptions and respective actions along a path: $L(s_0) \xrightarrow{a_0} L(s_1) \xrightarrow{a_1} L(s_2) \ldots$.   ▽

Thus, intuitively, a computation is the observable effect (the 'trace') of a path in a transition system. It can be regarded as a record of all successive intermediate results of the computing process. The idea is that the information encoded by the state descriptions includes all that is essential in the computation, including the values of all important variables.

If a path or a computation is finite, it is also called **terminating**. As mentioned earlier, we will mainly be discussing nonterminating computations, so, for technical convenience we can always append to any finite path a transition to an **idle state** (or, **terminating state**) that loops to itself and has no other outgoing transitions. Thus every path and computation in a transition system can be considered infinite.

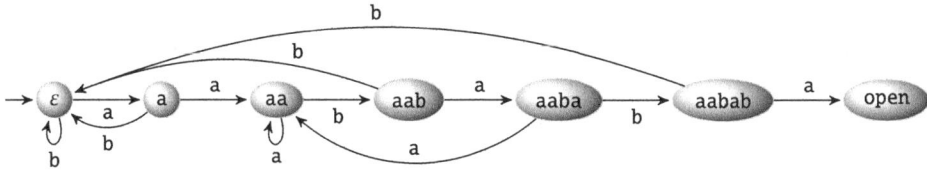

(a) With key 'aababa'.

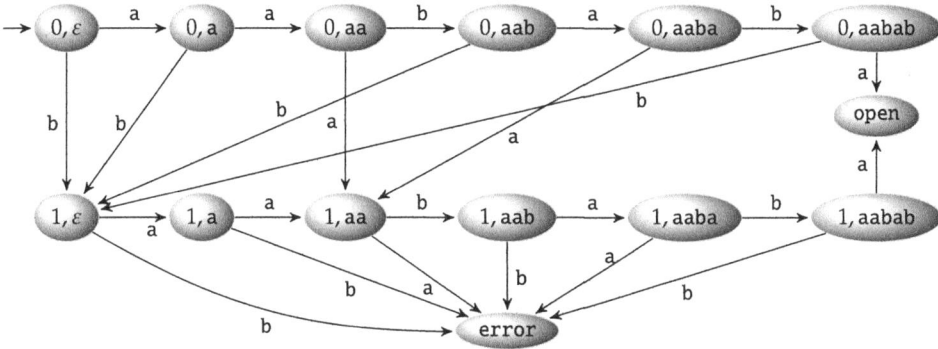

(b) With key 'aababa' and at most one error.

Figure 3.3 Transition systems modelling digicode systems.

When the actions are not important, we will omit them from the description of paths and computations and will represent them simply as $s_0, s_1, s_2, \ldots$ and respectively $L(s_0), L(s_1), L(s_2), \ldots$.

Sometimes, when we are not interested in the specific path generating a given computation (or, when the transition system has only one path, as in $(\mathbb{N}, \mathtt{succ})$) we can bypass the notion of a path altogether and introduce the notion of **abstract computation** being simply a mapping $\sigma : \mathbb{N} \to \mathcal{P}(\mathrm{PROP})$. Accordingly, we will denote the successive labels in a computation σ by $\sigma(0), \sigma(1), \sigma(2), \ldots$.

3.1.3 Transition Systems as Models of Computation

As discussed earlier, transition systems are ubiquitous in computer science; they serve not just as models for temporal logics but as structures defining the semantics of operational devices such as finite-state machines, pushdown automata, Turing machines, Petri nets, counter machines, rewriting systems, timed automata. Moreover, real-life examples, such as clocks, vending machines, payphones, semaphores, lifts, etc., can be modelled by such structures. Here we will provide a selection of representative examples.

Digicode. Figure 3.3(a) presents a simple digicode system with two keys 'a' and 'b', where the door opens when 'aababa' is pressed. It is designed in such a way that errors are possible and each error does not necessarily bring you back to the 'initial' state ε. For instance, there is an infinite path from the state ε such that the key 'b' is pressed infinitely, which entails that the transition system described in Figure 3.3 is not terminating. Other options are possible and some would be even more faithful to a physical digicode system. For instance, in Figure 3.3(b) we present another transition system related to the digicode where at most one error is allowed. Assuming that at most n errors are allowed, the appropriate way to model the digicode would be to first design an operational model (a counter machine for instance) that can count the errors with a counter and then to interpret this model as a transition system by using the usual semantics for counter machines. The transition system presented in Figure 3.3(b) would be the outcome of the interpretation when $n = 1$. Unlike the transition system in Figure 3.3(a), the one in Figure 3.3(b) is terminating from any state, i.e. no infinite path can be defined from it.

A machine with two counters. Counter machines are well-known formalisms that can be viewed as finite-state automata enriched with variables ranging over natural numbers (counters). Simple actions on counters include increment, decrement or zero-test (as in **Minsky machines**) but more complex actions are possible and this can be combined with guards (i.e. linear constraints on counter values) in order to be allowed to trigger a transition. Imagine a simple **counter machine** with two counters and only two possible actions: both counters are incremented simultaneously or both counters are decremented simultaneously. Such a counter machine has an obvious operational semantics, leading to the transition system presented in Figure 3.4 where the set of states is precisely $\mathbb{N}^2$ (the set of possible values for the pair of counters).

Dijkstra's mutual exclusion problem. An important type of transition systems are those modelling, or prescribing, the behaviour of concurrent or reactive systems. A well-known example is associated with Dijkstra's *mutual exclusion problem*, stated as follows: two concurrent processes use a common resource. Only one of them can access the resource at a time, and then that process is said to be in its *critical section*, so only one process can be in a critical section at any time instant. At the start each process is in noncritical section and whenever a process is in a noncritical section it can keep trying to enter a critical section arbitrarily often. The problem is to design a reasonable 'mutual exclusion' protocol prescribing the possible runs of the system. What is reasonable is not precisely specified, but can involve various requirements, such as:

- **Safety:** Both processes may not be in a critical section at the same time.
- **Nonblocking:** If a process is not in a critical section, it can try to enter it at a next state.
- **Liveness:** If a process ever tries to enter a critical section, then it will eventually enter it.
- **Fairness:** If a process keeps trying to enter a critical section, then it will eventually enter it.
- **No strict alternation:** The processes need not enter their critical sections in strict alternation.

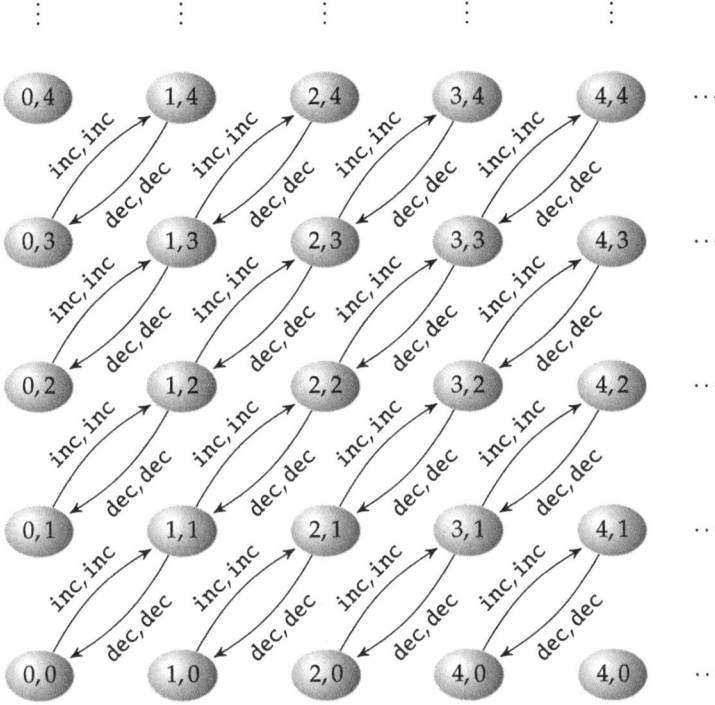

Figure 3.4 Transition system induced by a simple counter machine.

Some of these requirements are obligatory, others desirable. Eventually, the protocol should ensure correct and efficient behaviour of the system.

In order to use transition systems to model a protocol solving this problem, we must first formalise the requirements. This we will do later, in Chapter 7, where we will introduce logical languages that are sufficiently expressive for that purpose. Here we will only introduce suitable atomic propositions and will propose a possible protocol. We choose to use the following special atomic propositions, for $i = 1, 2$:

- N_i: process i is in a noncritical section.
- T_i: process i is trying (requesting) to enter a critical section.
- C_i: process i is in a critical section.

The interpreted transition system in Figure 3.5 is a model of a possible protocol for the mutual exclusion problem, by specifying the possible states and transitions of the system. The transitions where process 1 changes status are given with dashed lines, and those where process 2 changes status are given with solid lines.

We will revisit this example in Chapter 7. Meanwhile, the reader may wish to contemplate which of the requirements specified previously are satisfied by this model.

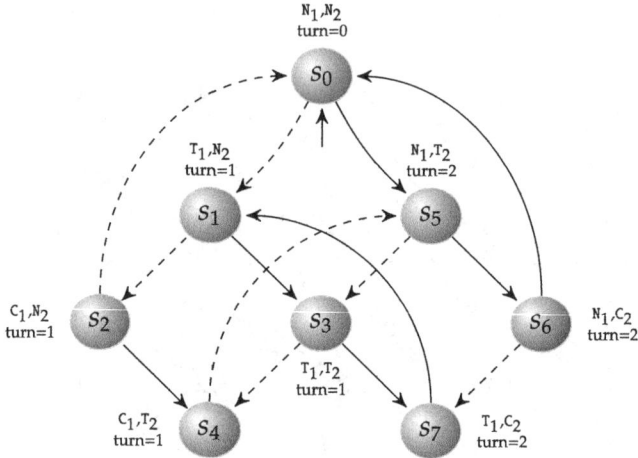

Figure 3.5 A TS modelling of a mutual exclusion protocol. Legend: $\mathtt{N}$ = noncritical, $\mathtt{T}$ = trying, $\mathtt{C}$ = critical.

3.1.4 Immediate Predecessors and Successors

Let $\mathcal{T} = (S, \{\xrightarrow{a}\}_{a \in Act})$ be a transition system, $B \subseteq Act$ and $X \subseteq S$. We define the set

$$\text{post}(B, X) := \{r \mid \text{there exist } s \in X \text{ and } a \in B \text{ such that } s \xrightarrow{a} r\}.$$

It contains the **immediate successors** of X with transitions labelled by actions from B. When $\mathcal{T}$ is a mono-transition system (S, R), we write $\text{post}(X)$ to denote the set $\{r \mid \text{there exist } s \in X \text{ such that } sRr\}$. Similarly, when X is a singleton set $X = \{t\}$, we may write $\text{post}(B, t)$ or $\text{post}(t)$ instead of $\text{post}(B, \{t\})$ or $\text{post}(\{t\})$, respectively. A similar convention applies for other sets. More generally, we write $\text{post}(X)$ instead of $\text{post}(B, X)$ when $B = Act$.

Similarly, we define

$$\text{pre}(B, X) := \{r \mid \text{there exist } s \in X \text{ and } a \in B \text{ such that } r \xrightarrow{a} s\}.$$

The set $\text{pre}(B, X)$ contains the **immediate predecessors** of X with transitions labelled by actions from B. When $\mathcal{T} = (S, R)$, we write $\text{pre}(X)$ to denote the set $\{r \mid \text{there exist } s \in X \text{ such that } rRs\}$. Again, we write $\text{pre}(X)$ instead of $\text{pre}(B, X)$ when $B = Act$. We will also write $\text{pre}(a, X)$ instead of $\text{pre}(\{a\}, X)$ for any $a \in Act$. Note that, even though the sets $\text{post}(B, X)$ and $\text{pre}(B, X)$ depend on the transition system $\mathcal{T}$, we omit the subscript $\mathcal{T}$ since the transition system will usually be fixed by the context.

For example, one can compute the following sets:

- in the transition system defined in Figure 3.3:
  $\text{post}(aab) = \{\varepsilon, aaba\}$ and $\text{pre}(aab) = \{aa\}$, while $\text{pre}(aa) = \{a, aa, aaba\}$.
- in the transition system in Figure 3.4:
  $\text{pre}((0, 0)) = \{(1, 1)\}$ and $\text{pre}((1, 2)) = \text{post}((1, 2)) = \{(0, 1), (2, 3)\}$.

Now we extend the operators `post` and `pre` to capture the sets of all successors, resp. predecessors, reachable within a given number of steps. First, for the sets of successors we define:

- $\text{post}^{\leq 0}(B, X) := X$ and,
- for every $i \geq 0$, $\text{post}^{\leq i+1}(B, X) := \text{post}^{\leq i}(B, X) \cup \text{post}(B, \text{post}^{\leq i}(B, X))$.

The sets of predecessors from which the set X is reachable within i steps are defined likewise:

- $\text{pre}^{\leq 0}(B, X) := X$ and,
- for every $i \geq 0$, $\text{pre}^{\leq i+1}(B, X) := \text{pre}^{\leq i}(B, X) \cup \text{pre}(B, \text{pre}^{\leq i}(B, X))$.

We leave it to the reader to show (see Exercise 3.5) by induction on i, that $\text{post}^{\leq i}(B, X)$ contains the set of states that can be reached from some states in X with a finite path of length at most i, while $\text{pre}^{\leq i}(B, X)$ consists of those states from which states in X can be reached with a finite path of length at most i.

For example, in the transition system $(\mathbb{N}, \text{succ})$ defined in Figure 3.2, for every $i, j \in \mathbb{N}$, the set $\text{post}^{\leq j}(i)$ contains exactly $j + 1$ elements, namely $\text{post}^{\leq j}(i) = \{i, \ldots, i + j\}$.

It is worth noting that

$$\text{pre}^{\leq 0}(X) \subseteq \text{pre}^{\leq 1}(X) \subseteq \text{pre}^{\leq 2}(X) \subseteq \ldots$$

and

$$\text{post}^{\leq 0}(X) \subseteq \text{post}^{\leq 1}(X) \subseteq \text{post}^{\leq 2}(X) \subseteq \ldots$$

With small modifications of the preceding inductive definitions, one can also define the sets of successors or predecessors that contain the states that can be reached in *exactly i* steps. We leave these as Exercise 3.6.

3.1.5 Temporal Properties

There are several types of practically important properties of transition systems which we will briefly discuss here.

Local Properties

Local properties of transition systems refer to immediate successors or predecessors of the current state s and therefore involve the sets $\text{post}(s)$ and $\text{pre}(s)$. A typical example of a local property is the requirement that some immediate successor or predecessor of the current state satisfies a given constraint (which can itself be an atomic property or a more complex one). Important examples of local properties are the **preconditions** and **postconditions** associated with program instructions.

Here are examples of more abstract local properties:

- 'The system may enable the process `pr` at the next state'.
- 'The process `pr` will be enabled at the next state, no matter how the system evolves'.

- 'If the process `pr` is currently enabled, the scheduler must have disabled the process `pr` at the previous state'.

   Here are some more concrete examples:

- 'If the elevator is on the top floor, it will start moving down'.
- 'If the light was red at the previous state and is orange now, it must turn green at the next state'.
- 'If the train is entering the tunnel now, the semaphore at the other end must have been red at the previous moment'.

More generally, a local property may refer to a bounded time neighbourhood of a state s and therefore can be expressed by making use of the sets $\mathrm{post}^{\leq d}(s)$ and $\mathrm{pre}^{\leq d}(s)$ for a fixed finite distance $d \in \mathbb{N}$. However, local properties cannot refer to states which are reachable by *any* finite path, i.e. they cannot express *unbounded reachability* properties. For instance, 'The system will reach termination within 100 steps' is an (iterated) local property, while 'The system will eventually reach termination' is not. All temporal logics presented in Chapter 5 can express local properties and when the property refers to states reachable in less than d transitions, at the level of logical formulae this corresponds to considering formulae of **modal depth** $\leq d$.

Invariance and Safety

Invariance properties describe what must *always hold* throughout the computation, while **safety properties** describe what must *never happen* during the computation. Thus, both invariance and safety properties are *universal* properties and sometimes the distinction between these is only contextual. Here are some examples of safety properties:

- 'No more than one process can be in its critical section at any moment'.
- 'A resource will never be used by two or more processes simultaneously'.
- 'No deadlock will ever occur'.

   Here are some more concrete examples:

- 'The traffic lights will never show green in both directions'.
- 'A train will never pass a red semaphore'.
- 'The reactor will not overheat'.

   A very important type of property of sequential programs that can be phrased as an invariance property is **partial correctness**: 'If a precondition $\mathcal{P}$ holds at the input of the program, then whenever it terminates (if it does at all) a postcondition $\mathcal{P}'$ will hold at the output'.

   Safety properties admit a more formal definition which is omitted here, but it is important to note that its violation can be witnessed by a finite path. For instance, for disproving the property that all the reachable states are in the set X, it is sufficient to find a finite path leading to a state outside of X.

Eventualities and Liveness

Eventuality and **liveness properties** describe *what must eventually happen* during the computation. So, these are **existential** properties. Here are some examples:

- 'The execution of the process will eventually terminate'.
- 'If a message is sent, it will eventually be delivered'.
- 'Once a printing job is activated, it will eventually be completed'.
- 'If the train has entered the tunnel, it will eventually leave it'.

A typical example of a (bad) eventuality property is **deadlock**: when the system reaches a state from which it can make no further transition.

Another, very important type of property of sequential programs that can be phrased as an eventuality property is *total correctness*: 'If a precondition $\mathcal{P}$ holds at the input of the program, then it will terminate and a postcondition $\mathcal{P}'$ will hold at the output'.

Fairness

Fairness properties reflect the idea that *all processes must be treated 'fairly' by the operating system (scheduler, etc.)*. There is a whole variety of fairness properties and a lot of literature devoted to them. They express important requirements in **concurrent systems**, i.e. systems whereby several processes sharing resources are run concurrently by an operating system which is to schedule their execution in a 'fair' way. A typical situation arises in Dijkstra's mutual exclusion problem: a process is ready for the next step of its execution and sends a request for scheduling. It may or may not be immediately scheduled for execution, because it is competing with the other processes for resources, but a *fair scheduling* would mean that if the process is persistent for long enough then eventually its request will be granted.

Here are some types of fairness properties with examples.

Weak fairness 'Every continuous request will be eventually granted'.
Strong fairness 'If a request is repeated infinitely often then it is eventually granted'.
Impartiality 'Every process will be scheduled infinitely often'.

Precedence Properties

Often a specification of a system involves requirements regarding the precedence of events, such as: 'The event e will occur before the event e' (which may or may not occur at all)'. Here are some examples:

- 'If the train has entered the tunnel, it must leave it before any other train has entered'.
- 'Before the traffic light turns green in a given direction, it must have turned red in the intersecting road'.

State, Path and Tree Properties

There are different types of properties in transition systems, not only in terms of what they express, but also in terms of the sort of objects they refer to: states, single paths, or trees consisting of all paths starting from a given state in the transition system. The latter can still be regarded as a state property, but of a higher order. For instance, being a 'safe state' is a state property, staying always in a 'safe region' can be a property of a single computation or of some or all computations starting from a given state, and 'always terminating' is a property of all computations starting from a given state in a transition system. The following is a more involved property that combines state, path and tree properties: 'there exists a path starting from the current state and reaching a state satisfying the property A such that every path starting from it eventually reaches a state satisfying the property B'.

Later we will introduce various temporal logics, suitable for specifying different types of properties. For instance, the basic modal logic for transition systems, BML, introduced in Chapter 5 is suitable for specifying and reasoning about local state properties, while the linear-time temporal logic LTL (Chapter 6) is mainly suited for reasoning about path properties of single computations in transition system and the branching-time temporal logic CTL* (Chapter 7) is intended to reason about state, path and tree properties alike.

Lastly, we note that the right choice of a logical language depends on their expressiveness and conciseness (see Chapter 10), but also on their computational price in terms of the computational complexity of reasoning tasks and decision problems in them (see Chapter 11).

Verification Problems

Several algorithmic problems for verification tasks naturally arise in transition systems. We will classify the most important ones here.

First, the following are the main algorithmic verification problems associated with a given state property φ:

- **Local model checking:** given a transition system $\mathcal{T}$ and a state s, determine whether s _satisfies_ φ.
- **Model satisfiability checking:** given a transition system $\mathcal{T}$, determine whether _there is a state s in $\mathcal{T}$ satisfying φ._
- **Satisfiability testing**: determine whether _there is an interpreted transition system $\mathcal{T}$ and a state s in $\mathcal{T}$ satisfying φ._

Global model checking is a search problem and the other three are decision problems. Often, we are interested in _constructive_ satisfiability testing, i.e. not only obtaining a Yes/No answer, but actually finding a satisfying rooted interpreted transition system when there is one.

Likewise, the main algorithmic verification problems associated with a given path property φ are:

- **Path model checking:** given a computation σ in a transition system, determine whether σ _satisfies_ φ.
- **Universal path model checking:** given a transition system $\mathcal{T}$ and a state s in it, determine whether _every computation σ in $\mathcal{T}$ starting from s satisfies φ._

- **Existential path model checking:** given a transition system $\mathcal{T}$ and a state s in it, determine whether *there is a computation σ in $\mathcal{T}$ starting from s and satisfying φ.*
- **Path satisfiability testing**: determine whether *there is any computation σ satisfying φ.*

Most of the preceding problems listed above can be reduced to solving one or several *reachability problems* in transition systems, which we discuss in the next section.

3.2 Reachability

Many important properties of transition systems can be expressed in terms of *reachability* or *nonreachability* of states with specific properties, by means of finite paths in the transition system. For instance, eventuality is just reachability of a 'good state', while safety is nonreachability of 'bad states'; many fairness properties can be stated in terms of repeated (recurrent) reachability, etc. Here we will look more systematically at the various types of abstract reachability properties, starting with some technical preparation.

3.2.1 Reachability Sets

The set of states reachable forwards or backwards from the set $X \subseteq S$ (relative to a set B of actions used in transitions) are denoted respectively by $\mathrm{post}^\star(X)$ and $\mathrm{pre}^\star(X)$, and are defined as follows.

$$\mathrm{post}^\star(B, X) := \bigcup_{i \geq 0} \mathrm{post}^{\leq i}(B, X); \quad \mathrm{pre}^\star(B, X) := \bigcup_{i \geq 0} \mathrm{pre}^{\leq i}(B, X).$$

In particular, we provide the following definitions:

$$\mathrm{post}^\star(X) := \bigcup_{i \geq 0} \mathrm{post}^{\leq i}(X); \quad \mathrm{pre}^\star(X) := \bigcup_{i \geq 0} \mathrm{pre}^{\leq i}(X).$$

When $\mathcal{T}$ is a mono-transition system (S, R), we have $r \in \mathrm{post}^\star(s)$ iff $(s, r) \in R^*$, where $R^* := \bigcup_{n=0}^{\infty} R^n$ is the **reflexive and transitive closure** of R. For example, in the transition system in Figure 3.4, we have

$$\mathrm{post}^\star(\{(0, i) : i \in \mathbb{N}\}) = \{(k, l) \in \mathbb{N}^2 : l - i = k\}.$$

Also, for all $(k, l) \in \mathbb{N}^2$, we have $\mathrm{post}^\star(\{\mathsf{inc}\}, (k, l)) = \mathrm{pre}^\star(\{\mathsf{dec}\}, (k, l))$.

Sometimes we need to consider the states that can be reached in at least one step, defined accordingly:

$$\mathrm{post}^+(B, X) := \bigcup_{i \geq 1} \mathrm{post}^{=i}(B, X); \quad \mathrm{pre}^+(B, X) := \bigcup_{i \geq 1} \mathrm{pre}^{=i}(B, X)$$

and in particular,

$$\mathrm{post}^+(X) := \bigcup_{i \geq 1} \mathrm{post}^{=i}(X); \quad \mathrm{pre}^+(X) := \bigcup_{i \geq 1} \mathrm{pre}^{=i}(X).$$

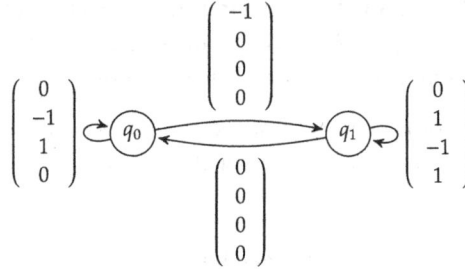

Figure 3.6 A simple VASS with two control states.

The set $\mathrm{post}^{=i}(B, X)$ (resp. $\mathrm{pre}^{=i}(B, X)$) denotes the set of successors (resp. predecessors) that can be reached in exactly i steps from X via transitions labelled by the actions in B. The sets $\mathrm{post}^{=i}(X)$ and $\mathrm{pre}^{=i}(X)$ are defined similarly.

The reachability sets $\mathrm{post}^{\star}(X)$, $\mathrm{pre}^{\star}(X)$, $\mathrm{post}^{+}(X)$ and $\mathrm{pre}^{+}(X)$ admit simple characterisations in terms of fixpoints of monotone functions, as follows. Given a transition system $\mathcal{T} = (S, \{\xrightarrow{a}\}_{a \in Act})$ and $X \subseteq S$, consider the function $\mathfrak{f} : \mathcal{P}(S) \to \mathcal{P}(S)$ such that $\mathfrak{f}(Y) := X \cup \mathrm{post}(Y)$. Since $(\mathcal{P}(S), \subseteq)$ is a **complete lattice** and the map $\mathfrak{f}$ is a monotone operator, by the Knaster–Tarski Theorem (Theorem 2.2.3), the map $\mathfrak{f}$ has a unique least fixpoint. We leave to the reader (see Exercise 3.8) to show that the least fixpoint of $\mathfrak{f}$ is precisely $\mathrm{post}^{\star}(X)$. Likewise, $\mathrm{pre}^{\star}(X)$ is the least fixpoint of the map $\mathfrak{g} : \mathcal{P}(S) \to \mathcal{P}(S)$ where

$$\mathfrak{g}(Y) := X \cup \mathrm{pre}(Y).$$

Example 3.2.1. A **vector addition system with states** (VASS for short) is a finite-state automaton with transitions labelled by tuples of integers viewed as update functions. Formally, a **VASS** is a structure $\mathcal{V} = (Q, n, \delta)$ where Q is a nonempty finite set of **control states**, $n \geq 1$ is the **dimension** and δ is the **transition relation** defined as a finite set of triples in $Q \times \mathbb{Z}^n \times Q$. Elements $t = (q, \vec{b}, q') \in \delta$ are called **transitions** and are often represented by $q \xrightarrow{\vec{b}} q'$. Figure 3.6 presents a VASS of dimension 4 with two control states.

A **configuration** of $\mathcal{V}$ is defined as a pair $(q, \vec{x}) \in Q \times \mathbb{N}^n$. Given two configurations $(q, \vec{x})$, $(q', \vec{x'})$ and a transition $t = q \xrightarrow{\vec{b}} q'$, we write $(q, \vec{x}) \xrightarrow{t} (q', \vec{x'})$ whenever $\vec{x'} = \vec{x} + \vec{b}$. The operational semantics of VASS updates configurations. Runs in such systems are essentially paths in the transition system $(Q \times \mathbb{N}^n, \{\xrightarrow{t}\}_{t \in \delta})$. For the VASS in Figure 3.6, one can show that

$$\left\{ \begin{pmatrix} a \\ b \\ d \end{pmatrix} \in \mathbb{N}^3 \mid \exists \begin{pmatrix} a' \\ b' \\ c' \end{pmatrix} \in \mathbb{N}^3, \; (q_0, \begin{pmatrix} a' \\ b' \\ c' \\ d \end{pmatrix}) \in \mathrm{post}^{\star}\left((q_0, \begin{pmatrix} a \\ b \\ 0 \\ 0 \end{pmatrix}) \right) \right\}$$

$$= \left\{ \begin{pmatrix} a \\ b \\ d \end{pmatrix} \in \mathbb{N}^3 : d \leq a \times b \right\}.$$

This equality applies in the induced TS $(\{q_0, q_1\} \times \mathbb{N}^4, \{\xrightarrow{t}\}_{t \in \delta})$.

3.2.2 Reachability Problems

There is a rich variety of reachability problems in transition systems. Generally, we talk about reachability of a state or a set of states along some or all paths starting from a given state (or, set of states); this is *forward reachability*. Likewise we may be interested in the states from which a state (or a set of states) is reachable; this is *backward reachability*.

Here is a sample of the more important reachability problems:

- **State-to-state reachability:** Given a transition system $\mathcal{T}$ and states s and r, is there a path in $\mathcal{T}$ from s to r? In other words, we ask whether $r \in \texttt{post}^\star(s)$, or equivalently, whether $s \in \texttt{pre}^\star(r)$.
- **State-to-set reachability** (existential version)**:** Given a transition system $\mathcal{T}$, a state s and a set of states X, is there a path in $\mathcal{T}$ from s to some state in X? Otherwise said, we ask whether $s \in \texttt{pre}^\star(X)$. This generalises the state-to-state reachability problem.
- **State-to-set reachability** (universal version)**:** Given a transition system $\mathcal{T}$, a state s and a set of states X, is every state in X reachable from s in $\mathcal{T}$?
- **Set-to-set reachability:** Given a transition system $\mathcal{T}$ and sets of states X and Y, is every state in Y reachable from some state in X?

Reachability problems may have more involved structure, referring to *repeated*, or *recurrent* reachability, for example:

- **Recurrent state-to-set reachability:** Given a transition system $\mathcal{T}$, a state s and a set of states X, is X reachable *infinitely often* from r in $\mathcal{T}$? That is, is there a path starting from s and passing through states in X infinitely often?
- **Generalised recurrent state-to-set reachability:** Given a transition system $\mathcal{T}$, a state s and sets of states $X_1, \ldots, X_k$, is there are an infinite path in $\mathcal{T}$ starting from s and reaching infinitely often each of the sets X_i for every $i \in [1, k]$?

Lastly, some important reachability problems impose additional constraints on the paths realising the reachability, e.g. reachability of a desired state while staying in a *safe region* of the transition system. For example:

- **State-to-set constrained reachability:** Given a transition system $\mathcal{T}$, a state s and sets of states X and Z, is X reachable from s by a path within Z? That is, is there a path from s to a state in X, every state of which is in Z?

When we consider interpreted transition systems, reachability problems can be stated *symbolically*, in terms of the state labels, rather than on explicit sets of states.

Thus, a fundamental type of question is whether a given transition system with distinguished states or sets of states satisfies a given reachability property. Abstractly, such generic questions can be answered by directly applying the definitions related to paths, reachability, etc. However, if we are interested in providing *algorithmic* answers to such questions we need to specify how the transition systems and sets of states are finitely encoded. In that case, the questions are turned into **decision problems** for reachability.

Obviously, when all involved sets of objects (i.e. states, actions, atomic propositions) are finite, or finitely representable (for instance, by dealing with regular sets, with the appropriate notion for regularity), we can effectively design decision problems for reachability.

Instead of formulating and solving every reachability problem ad hoc, a better approach would be to design a formal language to express generically reachability questions and to ask whether *any question* that can be formally expressed in that language can be answered on a given transition system. Such formal languages for expressing reachability problems on transition systems will be provided by the more expressive temporal logics introduced in the forthcoming chapters, and these problems will be solved uniformly with algorithms for model checking for these logics.

3.2.3 Deciding Reachability

In this section, we consider several decision problems that are reachability problems on (finite) transition systems and we analyse their computational complexity. Our purpose is to present algorithmic solutions of concrete instantiations of reachability questions mentioned in the previous sections and also to provide a simple complexity analysis that will be helpful in the forthcoming chapters. A thorough complexity analysis will be provided in Chapter 11 where the complexities of decision problems for temporal logics are more systematically investigated.

The simplest reachability problem REACH on transition systems can be stated as follows:

Input: A finite rooted transition system $(\mathcal{T}, s)$ and a state $r \in S$.

Question: Is $r \in \text{post}^\star(s)$?

We present in what follows an algorithmic solution of the problem REACH.

First, we need to define the size of the input in terms of which we measure the complexity of the algorithms. The size $|\mathcal{T}|$ of a transition system $\mathcal{T} = (S, \{\xrightarrow{a}\}_{a \in Act}, s)$ is defined as the sum

$$\text{card}(S) + \sum_{a \in Act} \text{card}(\xrightarrow{a}) + \text{card}(Act).$$

The problem REACH is indeed tractable as it can be solved by an algorithm that runs in polynomial time.

Theorem 3.2.2. REACH can be solved with a nondeterministic algorithm in logarithmic space.   ∎

Proof. Whenever $r \in \text{post}^\star(s)$, there is a path from r to s of length at most $\text{card}(S)$ (there is no need to visit twice the same state). We introduce a counter that counts up to $\text{card}(S)$ (and therefore uses only space in $\mathcal{O}(\log(\text{card}(S))$ with a binary representation of the natural numbers) and we need to store the current state of the path. Whenever we guess a new state, we need to check that it is a direct successor of the previous state. We stop if either the counter has reached a value greater than $\text{card}(S)$ or if the target state r is reached. At any step, we need to store the counter value and two states that can also be encoded with space in $\mathcal{O}(\log(\text{card}(S)))$.

Here is a more formal presentation of that nondeterministic algorithm:

1: $i \leftarrow 0; x \leftarrow s$;
2: **while** $x \neq r$ and $i < \text{card}(S)$ **do**
3:      guess x' such that $x \xrightarrow{a} x'$ for some $a \in Act$;
4:      $i \leftarrow i + 1; x \leftarrow x'$
5: **end while**
6: **if** $x = r$ **then accept**
7: **abort**

To repeat, the algorithm requires only $\mathcal{O}(\log(\text{card}(S)))$ bits to encode the states x, x', r and the counter i. In the algorithm preceding, 'guess x such that x satisfies property P holds' is equivalent to 'guess x; if x does not satisfy property P then abort'. This works, because the algorithm is nondeterministic, so one accepting execution suffices. $\qquad\qquad\square$

3.2.4 Deciding Repeated Reachability

An important variant of the reachability problem asks whether a state from a given set of states can be reached from a given initial state and can be reached again from itself, in at least one step. This type of reachability is used to define the acceptance condition for Büchi automata (see Chapter 14). It leads to the following **repeated reachability problem** RREACH:

Input: A finite rooted transition system $(\mathcal{T}, s)$ and a subset $F \subseteq S$.

Question: Is there any $r \in F$ such that $r \in \text{post}^{\star}(s)$ and $r \in \text{post}^{+}(r)$?

With respect to worst-case complexity, the repeated reachability problem is not more difficult than the reachability problem.

Theorem 3.2.3. RREACH can be solved in logarithmic space with a nondeterministic algorithm. $\qquad\qquad\blacksquare$

The idea is similar to the one for solving the simple reachability problem but this time two paths are guessed on the fly, namely one for $r \in \text{post}^{\star}(s)$ and another one for $r \in \text{post}^{+}(r)$. We formally present a nondeterministic algorithm that uses only logarithmic space in $\mathcal{O}(|(\mathcal{T}, s)| + \text{card}(F))$, so it is in $\mathcal{O}(|\mathcal{T}|)$.

1: guess $x_f \in F$;
2: $i \leftarrow 0; x \leftarrow s$;
3: **while** $x \neq x_f$ and $i < \text{card}(S)$ **do**
4:      guess x' such that $x \xrightarrow{a} x'$ for some $a \in Act$
5:      $i \leftarrow i + 1; x \leftarrow x'$.
6: **end while**
7: **if** $x \neq x_f$ **then abort**

8: $i \leftarrow 0$;
9: **while** $i < \text{card}(S)$ **do**
10:     guess x' such that $x \xrightarrow{a} x'$ for some $a \in Act$;
11:     $i \leftarrow i + 1; x \leftarrow x'$
12: **end while**
13: **if** $x = x_f$ **then accept**
14: **abort**

The repeated reachability problem RREACH is a special case of the **generalised repeated reachability problem** GREACH, used for checking nonemptiness of so-called **generalised Büchi automata**, see Chapter 14:

Input: A finite rooted transition system $(\mathcal{T}, s)$ and a finite list $F_1, \dots, F_k \subseteq S$.

Question: Are there $r_1, \dots, r_k \in F_1, \dots, F_k$ such that:

1. $r_1 \in \text{post}^\star(s)$,
2. $r_{i+1} \in \text{post}^+(r_i)$ for every $i \in [1, k-1]$,
3. and $r_1 \in \text{post}^+(r_k)$?

Again, with respect to worst-case complexity, the generalised repeated reachability problem is not more difficult than the reachability problem.

Theorem 3.2.4. GREACH can be solved in logarithmic space with a nondeterministic algorithm.   ∎

The NLOGSPACE algorithm for the problem GREACH is similar to the one solving the problem RREACH and its design is left as Exercise 3.12.

Computing Transitive Closure and Strongly Connected Components

Here we present two standard results about simple algorithms in directed graphs, that will be used in the labelling algorithm for model checking of the computation tree logic CTL in Chapter 7, and specifically in the proof of Theorem 7.3.6. References on these can be found in the bibliographical notes.

The first result that we will need is related to the cost for computing the transitive closure R^+ (i.e. the smallest transitive relation containing R) of the edge relation R in a given directed graph.

Lemma 3.2.5. Let $G = (S, R)$ be a directed graph encoded by lists of neighbours and $X \subseteq S$. Computing the set $\bigcup \{R^+(s) \mid s \in X\}$ can be done in time $\mathcal{O}(\text{card}(S) + \text{card}(R))$.   ∎

The other result that we will need is about the cost of computing strongly connected components in a directed graph. A **strongly connected component** (SCC) C for (S, R) is a subset of S such that for all $s \neq s' \in C$, there is an R-path from s to s' and an R-path from s' to s. It is called **nontrivial** if either $\text{card}(C) > 1$, or $C = \{s\}$ and $(s, s) \in R$. An SCC is **maximal** whenever it is maximal with respect to set inclusion.

Lemma 3.2.6. Let $G = (S, R)$ be a directed graph represented by lists of neighbours. Computing the partition of G into maximal strongly connected components can be done in time $\mathcal{O}(\mathrm{card}(S) + \mathrm{card}(R))$. ∎

The **topological order** of SCCs in a directed graph is a partial order $\preceq$ such that $C \preceq C'$ iff every node in C' is reachable from every node in C. Note that this is indeed a partial order, mainly because it does not contain cycles.

3.3 Bisimulation Relations

Perhaps the most important behavioural equivalence between two models of computation is the one that guarantees that any computational step performed in one model can be 'simulated' in the other, and vice versa. This idea is at the heart of the notion of **bisimulation**. We assume that the type of the transition systems, i.e. set of actions and propositions, considered hereafter is arbitrary but fixed.

3.3.1 Definitions and Examples

Definition 3.3.1. Let $\mathcal{T}_1 = (S_1, \{\xrightarrow{a}_1\}_{a \in Act}, L_1)$ and $\mathcal{T}_2 = (S_2, \{\xrightarrow{a}_2\}_{a \in Act}, L_2)$ be two transition systems of the same type. A relation $\beta \subseteq S_1 \times S_2$ is a **bisimulation between** $\mathcal{T}_1$ **and** $\mathcal{T}_2$, denoted $\mathcal{T}_1 \overset{\beta}{\leftrightarrows} \mathcal{T}_2$, if it satisfies the following conditions for every pair of states (s_1, s_2) such that $s_1 \beta s_2$ and $a \in Act$ is any transition label:

Forth: If $s_1 \xrightarrow{a}_1 r_1$ for some $r_1 \in S_1$, then there is an $r_2 \in S_2$ such that $r_1 \beta r_2$ and $s_2 \xrightarrow{a}_2 r_2$. It is displayed in Figure 3.7(a). A continuous arrow stands for a universally quantified transition, a dashed one for an existentially quantified one. Hence, it demands that for every a-transition on the left there must be one on the right with the corresponding properties on states. The dotted arrows depict the bisimulation relation.

Back: Conversely, if $s_2 \xrightarrow{a}_2 r_2$ for some $r_2 \in S_2$, then there is $r_1 \in S_1$ such that $r_1 \beta r_2$ and $s_1 \xrightarrow{a}_1 r_1$. It is displayed in Figure 3.7(b).

Atom equivalence: For every $p \in \mathrm{PROP}$: $p \in L_1(s_1)$ iff $p \in L_2(s_2)$. That is, β-related states must satisfy the same atomic propositions. We will write $s_1 \simeq s_2$ in that case. ▽

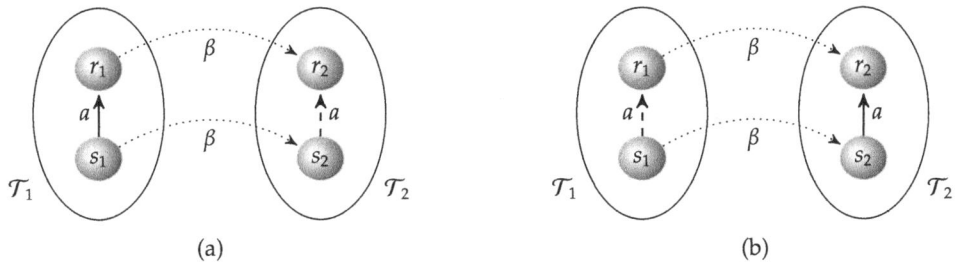

Figure 3.7 The (a) Forth and (b) Back conditions on a bisimulation.

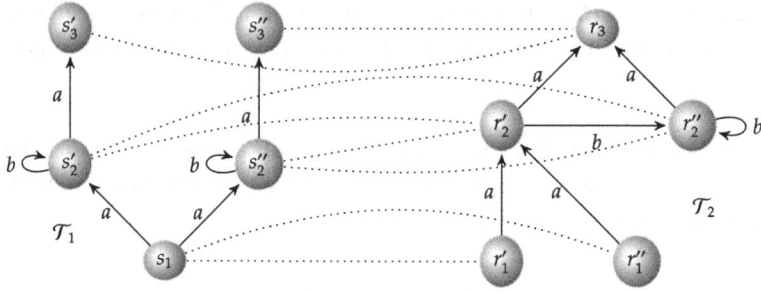

Figure 3.8 Globally bisimilar transition systems.

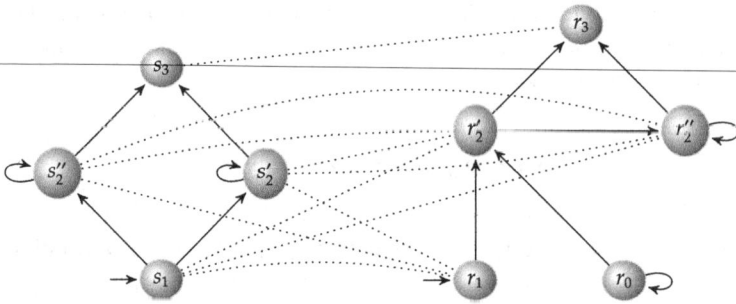

Figure 3.9 Locally bisimilar rooted transition systems.

We say that two states $s \in T_1$ and $r \in T_2$ are **bisimulation equivalent** or **bisimilar**, if there is a bisimulation β between T_1 and T_2 such that $(s, r) \in \beta$. $\triangledown$

Note that, by the preceding definition, the empty relation is always a bisimulation. Hence, nontrivial properties can only be achieved with special bisimulations.

If a bisimulation exists between T_1 and T_2 that links every state in T_1 to some state of T_2 and vice versa, we also say that T_1 and T_2 are **(globally) bisimulation equivalent**, or just **(globally) bisimilar**, denoted $T_1 \rightleftarrows T_2$.

If the two transition systems under consideration are rooted, i.e. have explicitly given initial states, then we call them **locally bisimilar** if the two initial states are bisimilar.

Example 3.3.2. We leave it as Exercise 3.18 to show that the symmetric relation given by the dotted lines in Figure 3.8 is a global bisimulation between the two transition systems T_1 and T_2. They do not use atomic propositions, hence, the condition on satisfying the same set of propositions is trivially satisfied for every pair of states. The same holds for the two rooted transition systems in Figure 3.9 which are locally but not globally bisimilar.

Figure 3.10 shows a (global) bisimulation between two interpreted transition systems over the set of propositions PROP $= \{p, q\}$.

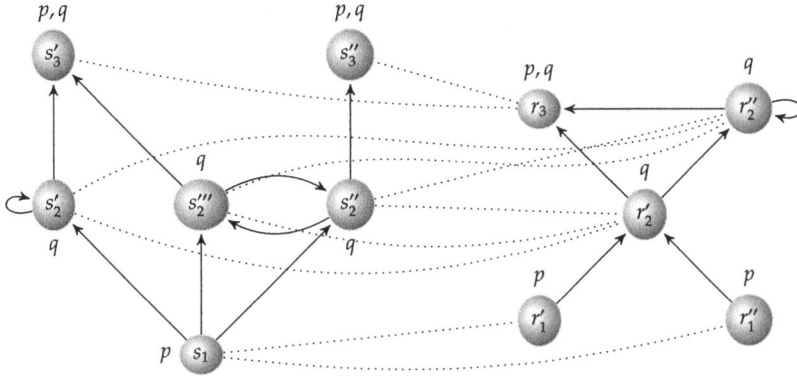

Figure 3.10 Globally bisimilar interpreted transition systems.

Lemma 3.3.3.

(I)   The identity relation in any transition system $\mathcal{T}$ is a bisimulation between $\mathcal{T}$ and itself.

(II) The inverse relation of a bisimulation between transition systems is a bisimulation. More precisely, if $\mathcal{T}_1 \overset{\beta}{\rightleftarrows} \mathcal{T}_2$ then $\mathcal{T}_2 \overset{\beta^{-1}}{\rightleftarrows} \mathcal{T}_1$.

(III) The composition of two bisimulations between transition systems is a bisimulation. More precisely, if $\mathcal{T}_1 \overset{\beta'}{\rightleftarrows} \mathcal{T}_2$ and $\mathcal{T}_2 \overset{\beta''}{\rightleftarrows} \mathcal{T}_3$ then $\mathcal{T}_1 \overset{\beta' \circ \beta''}{\rightleftarrows} \mathcal{T}_3$. ∎

The proofs are routine and are left to the reader, see Exercise 3.16.

Corollary 3.3.4. Bisimulation equivalence between transition systems is an equivalence relation. ∎

This corollary allows us to formally use the notion of a (global or local) **bisimulation type** of a given transition system as the class of all systems that are globally, resp. locally bisimulation equivalent to it.

Proposition 3.3.5. The union of any family of bisimulations between transition systems is a bisimulation between these transition systems. ∎

The various notions of bisimulations and bisimulation types introduced here will be characterised in logical terms in Chapter 5.

So far we have formally considered bisimulation relations between two transition systems. An important particular case arises when the two are the same. When $\mathcal{T} \overset{\beta}{\rightleftarrows} \mathcal{T}$ holds we say that β is a **bisimulation in** $\mathcal{T}$. Hence, it relates states within $\mathcal{T}$ that exhibit the same behaviour in $\mathcal{T}$. This is of course no essentially different case: bisimulation between two different transition systems is also covered by bisimulation within one transition system, namely the one that arises as the disjoint union of the two. We will shift between one and the other perspective as it is convenient for us.

We consider a particular consequence of Lemma 3.3.3. Every (global) bisimulation $\overset{\beta}{\rightleftharpoons}$ between transition systems $\mathcal{T}$ and $\mathcal{T}'$ generates a (global) bisimulation $\beta \circ \beta^{-1}$ within $\mathcal{T}$. Another such useful consequence is the following.

Lemma 3.3.6. For every interpreted transition system $\mathcal{T}$ and a bisimulation β in $\mathcal{T}$, the reflexive, symmetric and transitive closure β^* of β is an equivalence relation and a bisimulation in $\mathcal{T}$, too.   ∎

The fact that β^* is an equivalence relation in $\mathcal{T}$ is by definition. The proof that it is a bisimulation in $\mathcal{T}$ is left as Exercise 3.17. The bisimulation β^* will be called the **equivalence closure of β in $\mathcal{T}$**.

Next, note that the relation between the states in a transition system $\mathcal{T}$, given by realising the same bisimulation type, i.e. being related by some bisimulation in $\mathcal{T}$, is an equivalence relation. Moreover, the following holds.

Corollary 3.3.7. The relation $\beta_{\mathcal{T}}$ that relates exactly those pairs of states in an interpreted transition system $\mathcal{T}$ that realise the same bisimulation type is a bisimulation in $\mathcal{T}$.   ∎

Proof. Follows from Proposition 3.3.5 because $\beta_{\mathcal{T}}$ is a union of bisimulations in $\mathcal{T}$.   □

We can now define the **bisimulation type** of a state s in a given interpreted transition system $\mathcal{T}$ as the respective equivalence class of s with respect to $\beta_{\mathcal{T}}$.

3.3.2 Bounded and Finite Bisimulations

Sometimes, we are only interested in behavioural equivalence of two rooted transition systems up to a given number of transition steps, i.e. up to a given distance from the roots. This leads to the weaker notion of **bounded bisimulation**.

Definition 3.3.8. Let $\mathcal{T}_1 = (S_1, \{\overset{a}{\longrightarrow}_1\}_{a \in Act}, L_1)$ and $\mathcal{T}_2 = (S_2, \{\overset{a}{\longrightarrow}_2\}_{a \in Act}, L_2)$ be two transition systems of the same type.

The property of some relation $\beta \subseteq S_1 \times S_2$ being a k-**bounded-bisimulation** (or just k-**bisimulation**) between the rooted transitions systems $(\mathcal{T}_1, s_1)$ and $(\mathcal{T}_2, s_2)$, denoted $(\mathcal{T}_1, s_1) \overset{\beta}{\rightleftharpoons}_k (\mathcal{T}_2, s_2)$ is inductively defined over $k \in \mathbb{N}$ as follows.

(B$_0$) $(\mathcal{T}_1, s_1) \overset{\beta}{\rightleftharpoons}_0 (\mathcal{T}_2, s_2)$ iff $L_1(s_1) = L_2(s_2)$.

(B$_{k+1}$) $(\mathcal{T}_1, s_1) \overset{\beta}{\rightleftharpoons}_{k+1} (\mathcal{T}_2, s_2)$ iff $L_1(s_1) = L_2(s_2)$ and for every $a \in Act$:

   Forth: If $s_1 \overset{a}{\longrightarrow}_1 r_1$ for some $r_1 \in S_1$, then there is $r_2 \in S_2$ such that $s_2 \overset{a}{\longrightarrow}_2 r_2$ and $(\mathcal{T}_1, r_1) \overset{\beta}{\rightleftharpoons}_k (\mathcal{T}_2, r_2)$;

   Back: Conversely, if $s_2 \overset{a}{\longrightarrow}_2 r_2$ for some $r_2 \in S_2$ then there is $r_1 \in S_1$ such that $s_1 \overset{a}{\longrightarrow}_1 r_1$ and $(\mathcal{T}_1, r_1) \overset{\beta}{\rightleftharpoons}_k (\mathcal{T}_2, r_2)$.

A relation β is a **finite bisimulation** between the rooted transition systems $(\mathcal{T}_1, s_1)$ and $(\mathcal{T}_2, s_2)$, denoted $(\mathcal{T}_1, s_1) \overset{\beta}{\rightleftharpoons}_{\text{fin}} (\mathcal{T}_2, s_2)$, if $(\mathcal{T}_1, s_1) \overset{\beta}{\rightleftharpoons}_k (\mathcal{T}_2, s_2)$ for every $k \in \mathbb{N}$.   ▽

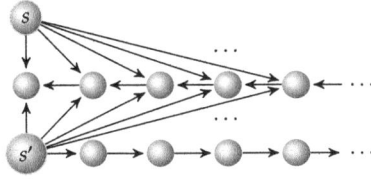

Figure 3.11 Nonbisimilar but finitely bisimilar states.

Clearly, every k-bisimulation between rooted transition systems is an m-bisimulation between them, for every $m \leq k$.

If there is a k-bisimulation between the rooted transition systems $(\mathcal{T}_1, s_1)$ and $(\mathcal{T}_2, s_2)$, i.e. they are k-bisimilar, then we denote that by $(\mathcal{T}_1, s_1) \rightleftharpoons_k (\mathcal{T}_2, s_2)$; likewise for finite bisimilarity.

Clearly, every bisimulation between the rooted (interpreted or not) transition systems is a finite bisimulation between them. The converse, however, is not always true, as shown by the transition system $\mathcal{T}$ in Figure 3.11 and the two states s and s'. We claim that $(\mathcal{T}, s) \not\rightleftharpoons (\mathcal{T}', s')$ while $(\mathcal{T}, s) \rightleftharpoons_k (\mathcal{T}', s')$ for every $k \in \mathbb{N}$. We will prove these claims later, in Theorem 3.4.4.

Still, the equivalence between bisimulations and finite bisimulations holds for the natural class of finitely branching transition systems.

Definition 3.3.9. An interpreted transition system is **finitely branching** if every state in that transition system has only finitely many immediate successors. ∇

Later we will show that $\rightleftharpoons_{\mathsf{fin}}$ coincides with $\rightleftharpoons$ on the class of finitely branching systems. This is known as the Hennessy–Milner Theorem (cf. Theorem 3.4.5). We will use techniques developed later in Section 3.4.1 for proving it.

3.3.3 Unfolding

We examine an important construction on transition system: unfolding it into a tree. This is done here in the context of bisimulation because the most important result about unfolding is that a bisimulation can always be found between a transition system and its unfolding. This has major consequences for the model theory of temporal logics, to be studied in later chapters.

Definition 3.3.10. The **unfolding** of the transition system $\mathcal{T} = (S, \{\overset{a}{\rightarrow}\}_{a \in Act}, L, s)$ is again a transition system $\widehat{\mathcal{T}} = (\widehat{S}, \{\overset{a}{\Longrightarrow}\}_{a \in Act}, \widehat{L}, \widehat{s})$ where:

- $\widehat{S}$ consists of all *finite paths* in $\mathcal{T}$, including all single states s, regarded as paths $\widehat{s}$ of length 0. The last state of a finite path π will be denoted by $\mathtt{last}(\pi)$.
- $\pi \overset{a}{\Longrightarrow} \pi'$ holds if π' is a one-step extension of π along the transition a, i.e.
  - $\pi = \pi(0) \overset{a_0}{\longrightarrow} \pi(1) \overset{a_1}{\longrightarrow} \cdots \overset{a_{n-1}}{\longrightarrow} \pi(n)$ and,
  - $\pi' = \pi(0) \overset{a_0}{\longrightarrow} \pi(1) \overset{a_1}{\longrightarrow} \cdots \overset{a_{n-1}}{\longrightarrow} \pi(n) \overset{a}{\longrightarrow} \pi(n+1)$.

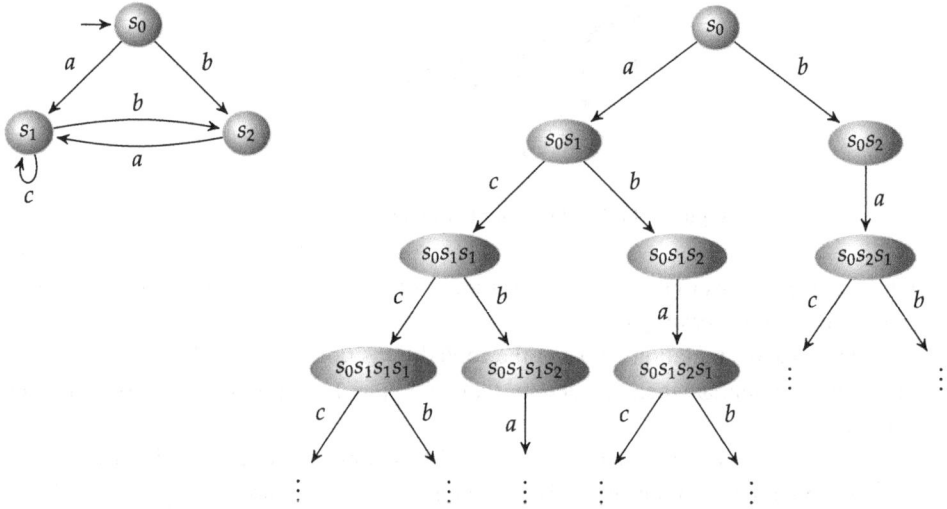

Figure 3.12 Rooted ITS at the left, and its unfolding from the root on the right.

- Such finite paths inherit their labels from their last state: $\widehat{L}(\pi) := L(\mathtt{last}(\pi))$ for every $\pi \in \widehat{\mathcal{T}}$. ∇

A rooted transition system and its unfolding from the state s_0 are shown in Figure 3.12.

Note that every unfolding of a transition system from a particular state is a tree, and the unfoldings of a transition system from various states form a forest. Also, note that $\pi_0 \xrightarrow{a_0} \pi_1 \xrightarrow{a_1} \pi_2 \cdots$ is a path in $\widehat{\mathcal{T}}$ iff

$$\mathtt{last}(\pi_0) \xrightarrow{a_0} \mathtt{last}(\pi_1) \xrightarrow{a_1} \mathtt{last}(\pi_2) \cdots$$

is a path in $\mathcal{T}$. Consequently,

$$\widehat{L}(\pi_0) \xrightarrow{a_0} \widehat{L}(\pi_1) \xrightarrow{a_1} \widehat{L}(\pi_2) \cdots$$

is a computation in $\widehat{\mathcal{T}}$ iff

$$L(\mathtt{last}(\pi_0)) \xrightarrow{a_0} L(\mathtt{last}(\pi_1)) \xrightarrow{a_1} L(\mathtt{last}(\pi_2)) \cdots$$

is (the same) computation in $\mathcal{T}$.

Thus, paths and computations in $\mathcal{T}$ and in $\widehat{\mathcal{T}}$ are in one-to-one correspondence: the last states of a path in $\widehat{\mathcal{T}}$ form the corresponding path in $\mathcal{T}$. This correspondence naturally maps $\widehat{\mathcal{T}}$ onto $\mathcal{T}$ and it is possible to show that this correspondence is a bisimulation.

Since the paths and computations in a rooted interpreted transition system $(\mathcal{T}, s)$ are explicitly represented by the branches of the trees in the unfolding $(\widehat{\mathcal{T}}, \widehat{s})$, the latter is also called the **computation tree** of $(\mathcal{T}, s)$.

Given a rooted interpreted transition system $(\mathcal{T}, s)$ and $n \in \mathbb{N}$, the subtree of $(\widehat{\mathcal{T}}, \widehat{s})$ rooted at $\widehat{s}$ and consisting only of those states that are labelled with finite paths in $\mathcal{T}$ starting

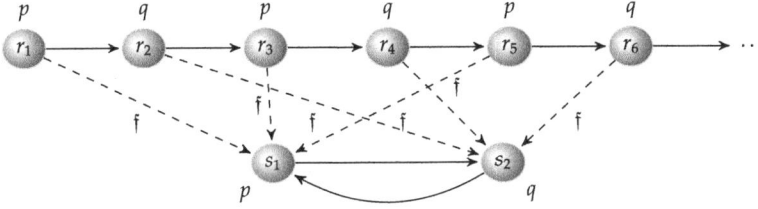

Figure 3.13 Bounded morphism for Example 3.3.12.

at s and of length at most n, with the transition relation between them inherited from $(\widehat{T}, \widehat{s})$, is called the **computation tree of depth** n of (T, s).

In order to show the aforementioned result about the existence of a bisimulation between a transition system and its unfolding, we introduce a closely related concept of **bounded morphism** which formalises a special case of a bisimulation.

Definition 3.3.11. Let T_1 and T_2 be two interpreted transition systems of the same type with domains S_1 and S_2, respectively. A mapping $\mathfrak{f}: S_1 \to S_2$ is a **bounded morphism** from T_1 to T_2, denoted $\mathfrak{f}: T_1 \xrightarrow{\rightleftarrows} T_2$, if its graph is a bisimulation between T_1 and T_2.

If $\mathfrak{f}$ is surjective, then T_2 is called a **bounded morphic image of** T_1. $\qquad \triangledown$

Thus, a bounded morphism $\mathfrak{f}$ associates with each $s \in S_1$ a unique bisimilar state $\mathfrak{f}(s) \in S_2$. This simplifies the bisimulation conditions for a bounded morphism between two transition systems. We invite the reader to formulate it in detail.

Example 3.3.12. In Figure 3.13 the mapping $\mathfrak{f}$ from the ITS on top to the one below it, satisfying $\mathfrak{f}(r_{2k-1}) = s_1$, $\mathfrak{f}(r_{2k}) = s_2$ for all $k > 0$, is a bounded morphism.

Lemma 3.3.13. Let $T = (S, \{\xrightarrow{a}\}_{a \in Act}, L)$ be an interpreted transition system. Then the mapping $\texttt{last} : \widehat{S} \to S$ associating to every path π its last state $\texttt{last}(\pi)$ is a bounded morphism from $\widehat{T}$ onto T. $\qquad \blacksquare$

The proof is left as Exercise 3.22.

Corollary 3.3.14. Every rooted interpreted transition system is bisimilar to a tree-like interpreted transition system. $\qquad \blacksquare$

We conclude this section by presenting two notions related to generated subsystems. Given a transition system $T = (S, (\xrightarrow{a})_{a \in Act}, L)$ and a state $s \in S$, we write $T[s] := (S', (\xrightarrow{a}_g)_{a \in Act}, L')$ to denote the **generated subsystem** defined as follows:

- $S' := \{s' \in S \mid s (\bigcup_{a \in Act} \xrightarrow{a})^* s'\}$ (in particular $s \in S'$),
- L' is the restriction of L to the states in S',
- for all $a \in Act$, the transition relation $\xrightarrow{a}_g$ is the restriction of $\xrightarrow{a}$ to S'.

Similarly, given $T = (S, (\xrightarrow{a})_{a \in Act}, L)$ a state $s \in S$, and $n \in \mathbb{N}$, we write $T^n[s] := (S', (\xrightarrow{a}_g)_{a \in Act}, L')$ to denote the generated subsystem up to depth n defined as follows:

- $S' := \{s' \in S \mid s \bigcup_{i \in [0,n]} (\bigcup_{a \in Act} \overset{a}{\rightarrow})^i s'\}$,
- L' is the restriction of L to the states in S',
- for all $a \in Act$, the transition relation $\overset{a}{\rightarrow}_g$ is the restriction of $\overset{a}{\rightarrow}$ to S'.

3.4 Bisimilarity

Checking behavioural equivalence can, in particular, be used in order to compare a 'real' transition system with an ideal transition system built as a model from given specifications. In this section we first analyse the concept of bisimilarity, i.e. existence of a bisimulation relation, in a game-theoretic way, then examine its algebraic properties and present a method for deciding this existence.

3.4.1 Bisimulation Games

Bisimulation equivalences between transition systems can be characterised in a more intuitive and animated way as existence of winning strategies for one player in corresponding *model comparison games*, in the case of modal logics also called *bisimulation games*. We illustrate the concept in the case of bisimulation games for interpreted mono-transition systems; the generalisation to labelled transition systems is straightforward.

Let T_1 and T_2 be interpreted transition systems of the same type. The **bisimulation game** $\mathcal{G}(T_1, T_2)$ over T_1 and T_2 is played by two players **I** and **II** with two pebbles, one placed at the root state s_1 in T_1 and the other at the root state s_2 in T_2, to mark the 'current' states in each structure. Sometime, when T_1 and T_2 differ only by their root states, we may write $\mathcal{G}(T_1, T_1)$ but specify explicitly what the initial configuration is. A **configuration** in the game $\mathcal{G}(T_1, T_2)$ is a pair of states (r_1, r_2) where $r_1 \in T_1$ and $r_2 \in T_2$ mark the current positions of the two pebbles.

The game starts from the initial configuration given by the two states to be checked for bisimilarity. It is turn-based, and each round is played as follows. Player **I**, also known as **Challenger**, **Falsifier** or **Spoiler**, selects one of the two pebbles and moves it forwards along a transition in the respective structure, to a successor state. Player **II**, known as **Defender**, **Verifier** or **Duplicator**, has to respond by similarly moving the pebble forwards along a transition (with the same label) in the other structure. After each move of any of the players, the current configuration changes accordingly.

Intuitively, the objective of Player **I** in the game is to detect and demonstrate a behavioural difference between the two rooted interpreted transition systems in the initial configuration by choosing a sequence of transitions that eventually cannot be properly simulated by the other player. On the other hand, the objective of Player **II** is to defend the claim that the two rooted interpreted transition systems in the initial configuration are behaviourally equivalent, so she tries to reply with transitions maintaining that equivalence for the duration of the game.

During the game, Player **II** loses if she cannot respond correctly to the move of Player **I**, or if the two pebble positions in the resulting new configuration are *not in* *atom-correspondent states*, i.e. these states are distinguished by an atomic proposition. On the other hand, Player **I** loses during the game if he cannot make a move in the current round because both pebbles are in states without successors.

The bisimulation game can be played for a predetermined number of rounds, or indefinitely. The *n*-**round bounded bisimulation game** between T_1 and T_2, denoted $\mathcal{G}^n(T_1, T_2)$, terminates after n rounds, or earlier, if either player loses during one of these rounds. In such case, the other player wins. If the *n*th round is completed without violating the atom equivalence in any configuration, Player **II** wins the game. Respectively, the **(unbounded) bisimulation game** is played until some of the players lose, otherwise forever. An infinite path of the game (which continues through an infinite sequence of rounds), played correctly according to the preceding rules, is won by Player **II**.

In the terminology of abstract 2-player games on graphs, as introduced in Section 2.2.3, the bisimulation game on T_1 and T_2 is of the following form. Let $T_i = (S_i, \rightarrow, s_0^i, L_i)$ for $i = 1, 2$ be two rooted interpreted transition systems. Then $\mathcal{G}(T_1, T_2) = (V, Own, E, v_I, Win)$ with

- node set $V = S_1 \times S_2 \times \{\mathbf{I}, \mathbf{II}\}$,
- owner function defined by $Own(s, t, \mathbf{I}) = 1$ and $Own(s, t, \mathbf{II}) = 0$,
- initial vertex $v_I = (s_0^1, s_0^2, \mathbf{I})$,
- edges in the arena given by

$$E = \{((s, t, \mathbf{I}), (s', t, \mathbf{II})) \mid s \rightarrow s'\} \cup \{((s, t, \mathbf{II}), (s, t', \mathbf{I})) \mid t \rightarrow t'\},$$

- a winning condition *Win* that makes Player **I** the winner of all infinite plays. Moreover, finite plays may exist in these plays, too (cf. Remark 2.2.7). As usual, they are won by the opponent of the player who gets stuck in the last configuration of that play.

Proposition 3.4.1. Every bisimulation game is determined, i.e. one of the players has a winning strategy. Moreover, if a player has a winning strategy in a given (bounded or unbounded) bisimulation game, then that player has a positional winning strategy in that game. ∎

Determinacy follows from that result for a much larger class of games, known as the Gale–Stewart Theorem. We do not give a detailed proof of this result for bisimulation games here. Instead we remark that bisimulation games are special cases of parity games, to be defined in Chapter 15, for which this result is stated as Theorem 15.1.21 and proved in detail there.

Example 3.4.2. In the transition system T in Figure 3.14, Player **II** has a winning strategy in the 2-round bisimulation game $\mathcal{G}^2(T, T)$ with initial configuration (s_1, r_1), while Player **I** has a winning strategy in the 3-round bisimulation game $\mathcal{G}^3(T, T)$ with the same initial configuration.

Now suppose there was a loop in state r_4 instead of r_3. Then Player **II** has a winning strategy even for the unbounded bisimulation game with initial configuration (s_1, r_1), by

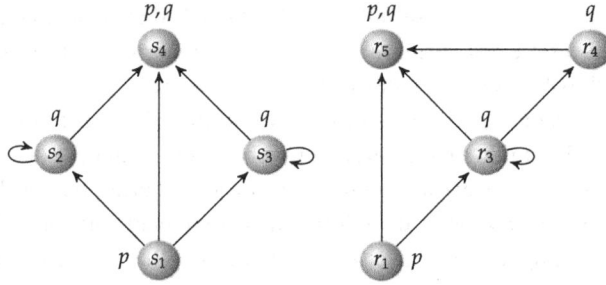

Figure 3.14 Two transition systems for some bisimulation games.

always responding to any move of Player **I** by playing the respective pebble in a state which is atom-equivalent to the state where Player **I** has moved.

The intuition of player **I** challenging the claim of bisimilarity in the current configuration, while player **II** defending that claim, is formalised as follows.

Theorem 3.4.3.

(I) Player **II** has a winning strategy in the n-round game $\mathcal{G}^n(\mathcal{T}_1, \mathcal{T}_2)$ with initial configuration (s_1, r_1) if and only if $(\mathcal{T}_1, s_1) \rightleftharpoons_n (\mathcal{T}_2, r_1)$.

(II) Player **II** has a winning strategy in the unbounded bisimulation game $\mathcal{G}(\mathcal{T}_1, \mathcal{T}_2)$ with initial configuration (s_1, r_1) if and only if $(\mathcal{T}_1, s_1) \rightleftharpoons (\mathcal{T}_2, r_1)$.   ∎

Proof. We will sketch the unbounded case, as it subsumes the bounded one. Indeed, any bisimulation $(\mathcal{T}_1, s_1) \overset{\beta}{\rightleftharpoons} (\mathcal{T}_2, r_1)$ provides a nondeterministic winning strategy for Player **II**: she merely needs to select her responses so that the currently pebbled states remain linked by β. The atom equivalence condition on β guarantees that atom equivalence between pebbled states is maintained; the *forth* condition guarantees a matching response to all challenges played by Player **I** in $\mathcal{T}_1$; the *back* condition similarly guarantees a matching response to challenges played by Player **I** in $\mathcal{T}_2$.

Conversely, we claim that the set of all configurations – regarded as pairs of states (t, t') – from which Player **II** has a winning strategy is a bisimulation between the respective transition systems. The proof of this claim is left as an exercise.   □

Using the preceding theorem, we can now prove the earlier claim that the two rooted transition systems shown in Figure 3.11 – in fact, they are shown as one transition system with two different states therein – are finitely bisimilar but not bisimilar.

Theorem 3.4.4. There are rooted transition systems that are finitely bisimilar but not bisimilar.   ∎

Proof. Take $(\mathcal{T}, s)$ and $(\mathcal{T}, s')$ from Figure 3.11. Let Player **I** move in $\mathcal{T}$ from t up the infinite branch; then Player **II** must move to one of the successors on the finite branches in $\mathcal{T}$. Let then Player **I** lead the play in $\mathcal{T}$ along the infinite branch. Player **II** gets stuck and loses at some finite round, when the end of the branch in $\mathcal{T}$ has been reached. On the other hand, $(\mathcal{T}, s) \rightleftarrows_n (\mathcal{T}, s')$ for every $n \in \mathbb{N}$, since any two paths of lengths greater than or equal to n look exactly the same in an n-round game. □

Now we can also prove the following result, mentioned already before.

Theorem 3.4.5 (Hennessy–Milner Theorem). Let $\mathcal{T}$ and $\mathcal{T}'$ both be finitely branching interpreted transition system. Then $(\mathcal{T}, s) \rightleftarrows_{\text{fin}} (\mathcal{T}', s')$ implies $(\mathcal{T}, s) \rightleftarrows (\mathcal{T}', s')$. ∎

Proof. The argument is best given via bisimulation games. We claim that Player **II** can maintain $(\mathcal{T}, r) \rightleftarrows_{\text{fin}} (\mathcal{T}', r')$ indefinitely – i.e. in all configurations throughout the game – which gives her a winning strategy for the infinite game. For instance, let Player **I** play in $\mathcal{T}$ and move the pebble from s to r. Suppose that for all responses r' available to Player **II** in $\mathcal{T}'$, $(\mathcal{T}, r) \not\rightleftarrows_{\text{fin}} (\mathcal{T}', r')$. As there are only finitely many choices for r' due to finite branching, we can find a sufficiently large $n \in \mathbb{N}$ such that $(\mathcal{T}, r) \not\rightleftarrows_n (\mathcal{T}', r')$ for all r' with $(s', r') \in R'$. But this would imply $(\mathcal{T}, s) \not\rightleftarrows_{n+1} (\mathcal{T}', s')$, contradicting the assumption that $(\mathcal{T}, s) \rightleftarrows_{\text{fin}} (\mathcal{T}', s')$. □

3.4.2 Largest Bisimulations

It follows from Proposition 3.3.5 that the union of all bisimulation relations between two given transition systems is again a bisimulation between them, hence it is the **largest bisimulation** with respect to set inclusion between these transition systems.

Actually, we have already seen the largest bisimulation between two interpreted transition systems. Recall that $(\mathcal{T}_1, s_1)$ and $(\mathcal{T}_2, s_2)$ are locally bisimilar, that is, $(\mathcal{T}_1, s_1) \rightleftarrows (\mathcal{T}_2, s_2)$, if there is a bisimulation β between $\mathcal{T}_1$ and $\mathcal{T}_2$ such that $s_1 \beta s_2$. If that is the case, then s_1 and s_2 are related by the largest bisimulation $\tilde{\beta}$ between $\mathcal{T}_1$ and $\mathcal{T}_2$, and vice versa, $s_1 \tilde{\beta} s_2$ implies $(\mathcal{T}_1, s_1) \rightleftarrows (\mathcal{T}_2, s_2)$.

In the particular case when $\mathcal{T}_1 = \mathcal{T}_2 = \mathcal{T}$ we talk about the largest bisimulation in $\mathcal{T}$.

Lemma 3.4.6. For every interpreted transition system $\mathcal{T}$, its largest bisimulation is an equivalence relation in $\mathcal{T}$. ∎

This is an immediate corollary of Lemma 3.3.6.

Again, we have already seen earlier the largest bisimulation in $\mathcal{T}$ as the union $\beta_{\mathcal{T}}$ of all bisimulations in $\mathcal{T}$. We can relate the largest bisimulations in both cases as follows.

Proposition 3.4.7. Given two interpreted transition systems of the same type, $\mathcal{T}_1$ with state space S_1 and $\mathcal{T}_2$ with state space S_2, let $\mathcal{T} := \mathcal{T}_1 \uplus \mathcal{T}_2$ be their disjoint union.

(I) The largest bisimulation $\beta_{\mathcal{T}}$ in $\mathcal{T}$, restricted to $S_1 \times S_2$, determines the largest bisimulation $\beta_{\mathcal{T}_1, \mathcal{T}_2}$ between $\mathcal{T}_1$ and $\mathcal{T}_2$.

(II) Conversely, the largest bisimulation $\beta_{\mathcal{T}_1, \mathcal{T}_2}$ between $\mathcal{T}_1$ and $\mathcal{T}_2$ determines the largest bisimulation $\beta_{\mathcal{T}}$ in $\mathcal{T}$ as the reflexive, symmetric and transitive closure of $\beta_{\mathcal{T}_1, \mathcal{T}_2}$ in $\mathcal{T}$. ∎

The proof is by a routine verification and is left as Exercise 3.34.

Note that, in case (II), the reflexive and transitive closure of β_{T_1,T_2} does not add more relations between the states in S_1 and the states in S_2, for β_{T_1,T_2} is the largest bisimulation between T_1 and T_2. All that is added in β_T are the equivalence relations within S_1 and within S_2 generated from the bisimulation $\beta_{T_1,T_2} \circ (\beta_{T_1,T_2})^{-1}$ in T_1 and respectively $(\beta_{T_1,T_2})^{-1} \circ \beta_{T_1,T_2}$ in T_2. Note that these are also the largest bisimulations respectively in T_1 and in T_2.

3.4.3 Bisimulation Quotients

Hereafter we denote the largest bisimulation in T by $\sim_T$. It is also called the **coarsest stable (bisimulation) partition of** T. Being an equivalence relation, $\sim_T$ defines a partition in T and generates a quotient structure of T, called the **bisimulation quotient of** T, that identifies the $\sim_T$-bisimilar states, i.e. the states with the same bisimulation type in T. We give a precise definition of bisimulation quotient for the case of mono-transition systems; the generalisation to labelled transition systems is straightforward.

Definition 3.4.8. Let $T = (S, R, L)$ be an interpreted transition system. The **bisimulation quotient** of T is the interpreted transition system

$$T/\!\sim_T \; := (S_{\sim_T}, R_{\sim_T}, L_{\sim_T})$$

where:

- $S_{\sim_T} := \{[s]_{\sim_T} \mid s \in S\}$, where $[s]_{\sim_T}$ for the equivalence class of s in S;
- $R_{\sim_T} := \{([s]_{\sim_T}, [r]_{\sim_T}) \in S_{\sim_T} \times S_{\sim_T} \mid (s', r') \in R \text{ for some } s' \in [s]_{\sim_T}, r' \in [r]_{\sim_T}\}$.
- $L_{\sim_T}([s]_{\sim_T}) := L(s)$. ∇

We leave it as Exercise 3.27 to verify that the preceding definition is correct in the usual sense: the definitions of $R_{\sim_T}$ and $L_{\sim_T}$ do not depend on the choice of representatives of their arguments.

Example 3.4.9. Consider the two transition systems shown in Figure 3.10. Both their bisimulation quotients are the following one.

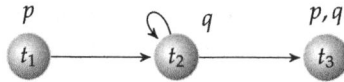

The bisimulation quotient of the ITS on top of each of Figure 3.13 is the ITS below it. Each of the two ITS in Figure 3.14 coincides with its bisimulation quotient.

The following is immediate from the definitions and left as Exercise 3.34; it is also a particular case of Proposition 3.4.11, coming up soon.

Proposition 3.4.10. The canonical projection $\mathfrak{f}: S \to S_{\sim_T}$ from T onto its bisimulation quotient $T/\!\sim_T$ is a (surjective) bounded morphism.   ■

Consequently, every interpreted transition system is globally bisimilar to its bisimulation quotient. Intuitively, the bisimulation quotient of the interpreted transition system $\mathcal{T}$ provides a canonical minimal representation up to bisimulation equivalence of that interpreted transition system. It is minimal, in a sense that every bisimulation type of a state in $\mathcal{T}$ is realised at one, and only one, state of $\mathcal{T}_\sim$. Since every interpreted transition system which is globally bisimilar to $\mathcal{T}$ must contain *at least one* representative of each bisimulation type of states in $\mathcal{T}$, it follows that $\mathcal{T}_\sim$ is *minimal* among all interpreted transition systems which are globally bisimilar to $\mathcal{T}$. Furthermore, any global bisimulation between two bisimulation quotients is uniquely determined by the bisimulation types of the states in $\mathcal{T}$, and is therefore an isomorphism. The following proposition gives a more precise sense to these claims.

Proposition 3.4.11. Let $\mathcal{T}' \overset{\beta}{\rightleftharpoons} \mathcal{T}$ be a global bisimulation.

(I) The mapping $\mathfrak{f}_\beta : \mathcal{T}' \to \mathcal{T}/\!\sim_\mathcal{T}$ defined by $\mathfrak{f}_\beta(s) := [r]_{\sim_\mathcal{T}}$ iff $s\beta r$, is a well-defined surjective bounded morphism from $\mathcal{T}'$ to $\mathcal{T}/\!\sim_\mathcal{T}$.
(II) The mapping $\tilde{\mathfrak{f}}_\beta : \mathcal{T}'/\!\sim_{\mathcal{T}'} \to \mathcal{T}/\!\sim_\mathcal{T}$ defined by $\tilde{\mathfrak{f}}_\beta([s]_{\sim_{\mathcal{T}'}}) := \mathfrak{f}_\beta(s)$ is well defined and is an isomorphism between $\mathcal{T}'/\!\sim_{\mathcal{T}'}$ and $\mathcal{T}/\!\sim_\mathcal{T}$. ∎

The proof is left as Exercise 3.34.

The analogue of bisimulation quotient for a rooted interpreted transition system $(\mathcal{T}, s)$ is based on the quotient $\mathcal{T}[s]/\!\sim_\mathcal{T}$ taken after restriction to the generated subsystem rooted at s. It provides a *canonical representative* of the bisimulation type of s, in the sense of being uniquely determined up to isomorphism, for locally bisimilar rooted interpreted transition system. The following summarises the findings on bisimulation quotients.

Corollary 3.4.12. Let $\mathcal{T}$ and $\mathcal{T}'$ be transition systems and $\mathcal{T}' \overset{\beta}{\rightleftharpoons} \mathcal{T}$ be a global bisimulation.

(I) $\mathcal{T}$ and $\mathcal{T}'$ are globally bisimilar if and only if their bisimulation quotients are isomorphic.
(II) The rooted transition systems $(\mathcal{T}, s)$ and $(\mathcal{T}', s')$ are locally bisimilar iff the following bisimulation quotients are isomorphic:

$$(\mathcal{T}[s]/\!\sim_{\mathcal{T}[s]}, [s]_{\sim_{\mathcal{T}[s]}}) \qquad (\mathcal{T}'[s']/\!\sim_{\mathcal{T}'[s']}, [s']_{\sim_{\mathcal{T}'[s']}}).$$

∎

3.4.4 Largest Bisimulations as Greatest Fixpoints

The largest bisimulations can also be defined and computed as the greatest fixpoint of suitable monotone operators. We sketch this construction for largest bisimulations between two mono-transition systems with a single transition relation R. Let $\mathcal{T}_1$ with state space S_1 and $\mathcal{T}_2$ with state space S_2 be two transition systems of the same type, let $X \subseteq S_1 \times S_2$ and let $s_1 \in S_1$ and $s_2 \in S_2$ be atom equivalent states (i.e. $s_1 \simeq s_2$). We say that the pair (s_1, s_2) has the **back-and-forth property with respect to X** iff Player **II** has a single round strategy to lead the bisimulation game from the configuration (s_1, s_2) to a configuration $(r_1, r_2) \in X$, that is the Back and Forth conditions are satisfied with respect to the pair (s_1, s_2) and the relation X. Note that the *back*-and-*forth* conditions for a bisimulation relation β say that each of its pairs has the *back*-and-*forth* property with respect to β itself.

Consider the following operator $F = F_{(\mathcal{T}_1, \mathcal{T}_2)}$ on subsets $X \subseteq S_1 \times S_2$:

$$F(X) := \big\{ (s_1, s_2) \in X \mid (s_1, s_2) \text{ has the } back\text{-and-}forth \text{ property w.r.t. } X \big\}.$$

It is easy to show that the operator F is monotone in the sense that $X \subseteq Y$ implies that $F(X) \subseteq F(Y)$, which is left as Exercise 3.26.

Therefore, by the Knaster–Tarski Theorem (Theorem 2.2.3), F has a (unique) greatest fixpoint in restriction to any subset of $S_1 \times S_2$. We are interested in the greatest fixpoint of F that respects atom equivalence, and therefore consider the restriction F_0 of F to $X_0 := \{ (s_1, s_2) \in S_1 \times S_2 \mid s_1 \simeq s_2 \}$. Let $\nu F_0 \subseteq X_0$ be this greatest fixpoint. Being a fixpoint of F within X_0, νF_0 respects atom equivalence and has the *back*-and-*forth* property. So, νF_0 is a bisimulation. As any bisimulation between $\mathcal{T}_1$ and $\mathcal{T}_2$ must also be a fixpoint of F_0, νF_0 is the largest one.

Thus, the evaluation of νF_0 on finite interpreted transition systems $\mathcal{T}_1$ and $\mathcal{T}_2$ goes through a finite sequence of stages, producing a monotonically decreasing sequence of subsets $X_n \subseteq S_1 \times S_2$ defined as follows

$$
\begin{aligned}
X_0 &:= \{ (s_1, s_2) \in S_1 \times S_2 \mid s_1 \simeq s_2 \} \\
X_{n+1} &:= F_0(X_n)
\end{aligned}
$$

which eventually stabilises with value νF_0.

How many iteration steps are needed to reach that fixpoint? An immediate answer is: not more than $\mathrm{card}(S_1) \cdot \mathrm{card}(S_2)$, because every iteration either removes at least one pair of states or reaches the fixpoint. However, a more careful analysis implies a better bound on the number of iterations. The key observation is the following lemma.

Lemma 3.4.13. Let $\mathcal{T}$ be an interpreted transition system with a state space S and F be an operator on subsets X of $S \times S$. Then for every equivalence relation X in S its image $F(X)$ is an equivalence relation, too. ∎

The proof is by routine verification and it is left as Exercise 3.34.

Theorem 3.4.14. Over finite interpreted transition systems $\mathcal{T}_1$ and $\mathcal{T}_2$ (with respective sets of states S_1 and S_2) the limit νF_0 is reached within a number of iterations bounded above by $\mathrm{card}(S_1) + \mathrm{card}(S_2)$. Furthermore, one iteration of the evaluation of F_0 can be computed in quadratic time. Consequently, the largest bisimulation is computable in time polynomial in $\mathrm{card}(S_1) + \mathrm{card}(S_2)$. ∎

Proof. Suppose, without any loss of generality, that the interpreted transition systems $\mathcal{T}_1$ and $\mathcal{T}_2$ have disjoint state spaces S_1 and S_2 and let $S = S_1 \cup S_2$. Then note that the starting set $X_0 \subseteq S \times S$, defined earlier, is an equivalence relation in S. Now, consider the operator F, defined earlier, as applied in the (disjoint) union $\mathcal{T}_1 \cup \mathcal{T}_2$. By Lemma 3.4.13, every iteration $F^n(X_0)$ is an equivalence relation in S. Since every equivalence relation in S can be identified with the partition in S that it generates, it follows that every iteration step of the computation of νF_0 corresponds to a refinement of the previous partition of S. Since every chain of refinements of partitions that is strict w.r.t. inclusion must be bounded in length by the number of elements of the underlying set which is S, we conclude that the number of the iterations of the computation of νF_0, until stabilisation, is bounded above by $\text{card}(S_1) + \text{card}(S_2)$. Since every iteration is computable in time polynomial in $\text{card}(S_1) + \text{card}(S_2)$, so is the largest bisimulation.

In order to show that each iteration requires quadratic time, we assume that $X \subseteq S \times S$ is an equivalence relation. The computation of $F(X)$ can be done in time $\mathcal{O}(d^2)$ where d is the maximal out-degree in $\mathcal{T}_1 \cup \mathcal{T}_2$, using the following algorithm.

> **for all** $(s,t) \in X$ **do**
>> let $U = E(t)$ in
>> **for all** $s' \in E(s)$ **do**
>>> check that there is $t' \in U$ with $(s',t') \in X$
>> **end for**
>> let $U = E(s)$ in
>> **for all** $t' \in E(t)$ **do**
>>> check that there is $s' \in U$ with $(s',t') \in X$
>> **end for**
> **end for**

We assume that the sets can be built and lookups performed in constant time. $\Box$

So, νF_0 can be computed in time $\mathcal{O}((\text{card}(S_1) + \text{card}(S_2))d^2)$ where d is the maximal out-degree in $\mathcal{T}_1 \cup \mathcal{T}_2$.

Corollary 3.4.15. Computing the largest bisimulation, and hence the bisimulation quotient, in any finite interpreted transition system $\mathcal{T}$ can be done within a number of iterations of the operator F that is bounded above by its number of states.   ∎

Now we can look at the iteration procedure computing the largest bisimulation between $\mathcal{T}_1$ and $\mathcal{T}_2$ from the perspective of bounded bisimulations.

Proposition 3.4.16. For every $n \in \mathbb{N}$:

$$X_n = \big\{ (s_1, s_2) \in S_1 \times S_2 \mid (\mathcal{T}_1, s_1) \rightleftarrows_n (\mathcal{T}_2, s_2) \big\}.$$ ∎

The proof is by induction on $n \in \mathbb{N}$, using the definition of the operator F. This is left as Exercise 3.34.

Closure within $m = \text{card}(S_1) + \text{card}(S_2)$ steps for finite interpreted transition systems implies that, in restriction to $\mathcal{T}_1$ and $\mathcal{T}_2$, m-bisimulation equivalence $\rightleftarrows_m$ coincides with full bisimulation equivalence $\rightleftarrows$. Therefore, we can rephrase the preceding claim in terms of bisimulation games.

Corollary 3.4.17. Let $\mathcal{T}_1$ and $\mathcal{T}_2$ be finite interpreted transition systems such that $m = \text{card}(S_1) + \text{card}(S_2)$, and let $s_1 \in \mathcal{T}_1$, $s_2 \in \mathcal{T}_2$.

(I) If Player **II** has a winning strategy in the m-round bisimulation game between $(\mathcal{T}_1, s_1)$ and $(\mathcal{T}_2, s_2)$ then Player **II** has a winning strategy in the unbounded bisimulation game between $(\mathcal{T}_1, s_1)$ and $(\mathcal{T}_2, s_2)$.

(II) If Player **I** has a winning strategy in the unbounded bisimulation game between $(\mathcal{T}_1, s_1)$ and $(\mathcal{T}_2, s_2)$ then Player **I** has a winning strategy in the m-round bisimulation game between $(\mathcal{T}_1, s_1)$ and $(\mathcal{T}_2, s_2)$.   ■

Now, for readers familiar with basics of **ordinals** we discuss the general case of possibly infinite transition systems. Then the stages of the evaluation of νF_0 produce a monotonically decreasing ordinal-indexed sequence of subsets $X_\alpha \subseteq S_1 \times S_2$ according to

$$X_0 := \{(s_1, s_2) \in S_1 \times S_2 \mid s_1 \simeq s_2\}$$
$$X_{\alpha+1} := F_0(X_\alpha) \qquad \text{(successor stage)}$$
$$X_\kappa := \bigcap_{\alpha < \kappa} X_\alpha \qquad \text{(limit stage)}$$

which eventually stabilises with value νF_0.

Proposition 3.4.16 can now be extended with

$$X_\omega = \{(s_1, s_2) \in S_1 \times S_2 \mid (\mathcal{T}_1, s_1) \rightleftarrows_{\mathsf{fin}} (\mathcal{T}_2, s_2)\}.$$

The least ordinal α such that $X_{\alpha+1} = X_\alpha$ is called the **closure ordinal** of this greatest fixpoint evaluation.

Lemma 3.4.18. The closure ordinal of the greatest fixpoint evaluation over the interpreted transition systems $\mathcal{T}_1$ and $\mathcal{T}_2$ is bounded by the cardinal number of bisimulation types realised in $\mathcal{T}_1$ and $\mathcal{T}_2$.   ■

Proof. This is done by extending the argument in Lemma 3.4.6 to infinite cardinalities.   □

3.4.5 Computing Bisimulation Quotients

Using bisimulation quotients is often desirable for complexity reasons, for instance for model checking of bisimulation invariant properties, typically all those definable in temporal logics. As shown in Theorem 3.4.14, the bisimulation quotient of any finite interpreted transition system can be computed efficiently, but exactly *how efficiently?* Here we will present the simplest and most popular algorithm, known as the **Kanellakis–Smolka algorithm**, which implements the iterative procedure underlying the proof of Theorem 3.4.14 and Corollary 3.4.15. It is not the practically most efficient algorithm, and several improved algorithms have been proposed, see the bibliographic notes.

The algorithm of Kanellakis and Smolka takes as an input a finite interpreted transition system $\mathcal{T}$ and produces as an output its bisimulation quotient. It is a simple iterative procedure using the following notion.

Definition 3.4.19. Given an ITS $\mathcal{T} = (S, \{\xrightarrow{a}\}_{a\in Act}, L)$, let $\mathfrak{P}$ be a partition of S into blocks (clusters) $\{B_1, \ldots, B_k\}$. A block B_j is a **splitter** for a block B_i with respect to an action $a \in Act$ if the set

$$B_i \cap \mathtt{pre}(\{a\}, B_j) = \{s \in B_i \mid s \xrightarrow{a} t \text{ for some } t \in B_j\}$$

is a proper and nonempty subset of B_i.

If no such pair of blocks exists for a given action $a \in Act$, the partition $\mathfrak{P}$ is called **stable with respect to** a. The partition $\mathfrak{P}$ is **stable** if it is stable with respect to every action $a \in Act$. $\qquad\qquad \nabla$

The existence of a splitter B_j for a block B_i in the partition $\mathfrak{P}$ indicates that $\mathfrak{P}$ is not yet a bisimulation partition because the elements of $B_i \cap \mathtt{pre}(\{a\}, B_j)$ are not behaviourally equivalent to those in $B_i \setminus \mathtt{pre}(\{a\}, B_j)$ with respect to a-transitions and the target set B_j. Therefore, a natural refinement of the current partition $\mathfrak{P}$ that resolves this 'defect' is to replace the block B_i by two new blocks, $B_i \cap \mathtt{pre}(\{a\}, B_j)$ and $B_i \setminus \mathtt{pre}(\{a\}, B_j)$. Note that they are disjoint and their union is B_i, hence the resulting family of sets is again a partition of S, where B_j is not a splitter with respect to the transition a of either of the newly added blocks.

The algorithm starts with the coarsest partition of S, viz. $\mathfrak{P}_0 = \{S\}$ and iterates until reaching stabilisation over the same step: identify blocks B_j and B_i in the current partition such that B_j is a splitter for B_i with respect to a transition a, if there is such a pair of blocks, and replace B_i with two new blocks, $B_i \cap \mathtt{pre}(\{a\}, B_j)$ and $B_i \setminus \mathtt{pre}(\{a\}, B_j)$.

This procedure is guaranteed to terminate, in at most $card(S)$ iteration steps, because every iteration step refines the current partition and the finest partition is certainly stable. It is easy to see that the current partition upon termination is the coarsest stable bisimulation partition of $\mathcal{T}$, that is, its largest bisimulation $\sim_{\mathcal{T}}$.

We leave it to the reader to complete the details, write the algorithm in pseudo-code and prove its correctness.

3.5 Trace Equivalence

Intuitively, a bisimulation relates states of two (possibly equal) transition systems if every transition from one of these states to some successor state can be matched by a transition from the other state ending in a successor which is related by the bisimulation relation to the first successor, and vice versa. This guarantees local behavioural equivalence from every pair of related states. In particular, it takes the branching at every state into account.

In this section we examine another weaker notion of behavioural equivalence which only takes the global branching into account, namely is defined by considering the entire set of traces, resp. computations of rooted transitions systems.

These two different views onto behavioural equivalence will later re-occur in the form of two different kinds of temporal logics: branching-time and linear-time logics. The former can make assertions about the branching in particular states; hence they have close

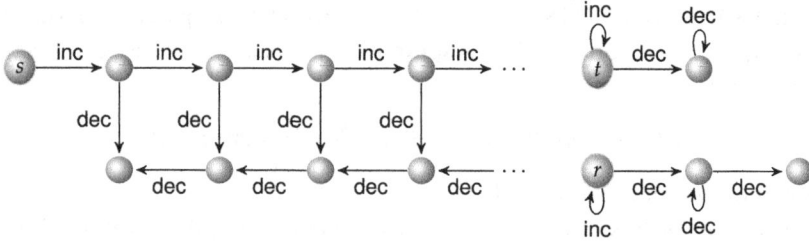

Figure 3.15 Trace (non-)inclusion between rooted transition systems.

connections to bisimilarity. The latter are interpreted over computation paths; thus they are oblivious to what is possible in a particular state. Consequently, such logics exhibit connections to trace equivalence.

3.5.1 A Weaker Equivalence Than Bisimilarity

We write $\text{traces}_T(s)$ for the set of all *maximal* traces in the transition system T that emerge from the state s. Remember that a trace is an alternating sequence between state labels, i.e. sets of atomic propositions and action names. Hence, a trace – as opposed to a path – can exist in several transition systems. Maximality means that the trace is either infinite or ends in a terminal state. If the underlying transition system T can be derived from the context then we may also simply write $\text{traces}(s)$ instead of $\text{traces}_T(s)$.

Definition 3.5.1. Let (T_1, s_1) and (T_2, s_2) be two rooted transition systems of the same type. We define a relation **trace inclusion**, written $\rightsquigarrow$, on such rooted transition systems by

$$(T_1, s_1) \rightsquigarrow (T_2, s_2) \quad \text{iff} \quad \text{traces}_{T_1}(s_1) \subseteq \text{traces}_{T_2}(s_2).$$

We say that (T_1, s_1) and (T_2, s_2) a **trace equivalent**, written $(T_1, s_1) \leftrightsquigarrow (T_2, s_2)$, if $(T_1, s_1) \rightsquigarrow (T_2, s_2)$ and $(T_2, s_2) \rightsquigarrow (T_1, s_1)$ both hold. ∇

It should be clear that trace equivalence is indeed an equivalence relation because it is defined via equality on the set of traces in a state. Equally, trace inclusion – sometimes also called containment – is a pre-order. We also may speak of **computational equivalence** instead of trace equivalence.

Example 3.5.2. Consider the transition system T with states s, t and r in Figure 3.15. Since there are no atomic propositions, we can describe maximal traces as finite and infinite sequences of actions. We have

$$\text{traces}_T(s) = \{\text{inc}^\omega\} \cup \{\text{inc}^n \, \text{dec}^n \mid n \geq 1\}$$
$$\text{traces}_T(t) = \{\text{inc}^\omega\} \cup \{\text{inc}^n \, \text{dec}^\omega \mid n \geq 0\}$$
$$\text{traces}_T(r) = \{\text{inc}^\omega\} \cup \{\text{inc}^n \, \text{dec}^m \mid n \geq 0, m \geq 2\} \cup \{\text{inc}^n \, \text{dec}^\omega \mid n \geq 0\}.$$

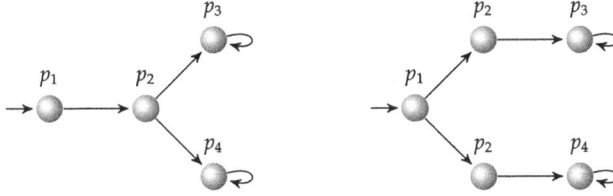

Figure 3.16 Computationally equivalent rooted ITS that are not locally bisimilar.

So the only case in which trace inclusion holds between these three states is $t \rightsquigarrow r$. In particular, s and t are incomparable with respect to $\rightsquigarrow$.

We are particularly interested in the relationship between trace equivalence and bisimilarity, since both are natural notions of behavioural equivalence.

Theorem 3.5.3. Let $\mathcal{T}_1 = (S, \{\xrightarrow{a}\}_{a \in Act}, L, s_1)$ and $\mathcal{T}_2 = (S', \{\xrightarrow{a}\}_{a \in Act}, L', t_1)$ be two rooted transition systems. If $\mathcal{T}_1 \rightleftarrows \mathcal{T}_2$ then $\mathcal{T}_1 \leftrightsquigarrow \mathcal{T}_2$. ∎

Proof. Suppose that $\mathcal{T}_1 \rightleftarrows \mathcal{T}_2$. Since bisimilarity is an equivalence relation it is symmetric. So it suffices to show that $\mathcal{T}_1 \rightsquigarrow \mathcal{T}_2$ holds.

So assume that there is a trace $\sigma = L_1 \xrightarrow{a_1} L_2 \xrightarrow{a_2} \ldots \in \texttt{traces}_{\mathcal{T}_1}(s_1)$. Then we obviously have $L_1 = L(s_1)$. Since $\mathcal{T}_1 \rightleftarrows \mathcal{T}_2$ there is a bisimulation β such that $\mathcal{T}_1 \overset{\beta}{\rightleftarrows} \mathcal{T}_2$. In particular, we have $(s_1, t_1) \in \beta$. But then we get that $L(s_1) = L'(t_1)$. Moreover, there must be a state $s_2 \in S$ with $s_1 \xrightarrow{a_1} s_2$ such that $L_2 = L(s_2)$. Again, by the definition of a bisimulation, there must be a state $t_2 \in S'$ with $t_1 \xrightarrow{a_1} t_2$ such that $(s_2, t_2) \in \beta$. This can be iterated through σ, constructing a path $t_1 \xrightarrow{a_1} t_2 \xrightarrow{a_2} \ldots$ through $\mathcal{T}_2$ which has the same trace as σ. Hence, $\sigma \in \texttt{traces}_{\mathcal{T}_2}(t_1)$, too, and therefore $\mathcal{T}_1 \rightsquigarrow \mathcal{T}_2$. □

On the other hand, trace equivalence is weaker than bisimulation equivalence. For instance, the two rooted interpreted transition systems in Figure 3.16 are computationally equivalent but there is no local bisimulation between them.

In the next subsection we want to give an algorithm for deciding trace inclusion between two transition systems. This is not too difficult, but it benefits from the restriction to the case of TS with total transition relations. We therefore briefly discuss how to reduce inclusion of maximal traces in arbitrary TS to that in total TS (where maximal traces are all infinite).

Lemma 3.5.4. Let $\mathcal{T}$ be a transition system over some set of actions Act. Take a new action # and let $\mathcal{T}'$ be the transition system over $Act \cup \{\#\}$ which results from $\mathcal{T}$ by adding a new state s_{end} and transitions $s \xrightarrow{\#} s_{\text{end}}$ for every deadlock state s, as well as a transition $s_{\text{end}} \xrightarrow{\#} s_{\text{end}}$. Then there is a one-to-one correspondence $\mathfrak{f}$ between maximal traces in $\mathcal{T}$ and those in $\mathcal{T}'$ given as

$$\mathfrak{f}(\sigma) := \begin{cases} \sigma, & \text{if } \sigma \text{ is infinite,} \\ \sigma \, (\# \emptyset)^\omega, & \text{otherwise.} \end{cases}$$

Proof. Clearly, $\mathfrak{f}$ maps every maximal trace of $\mathcal{T}$ onto an infinite and therefore maximal trace in $\mathcal{T}'$. Moreover, every infinite trace σ' in $\mathcal{T}'$ either only visits states that also exist in $\mathcal{T}$. Hence, it is also a maximal trace in $\mathcal{T}$. Or it eventually visits state s_{end} and loops in it with action #. Then its unique prefix given by the states other than s_{end} defines a maximal trace in $\mathcal{T}$. The claim is finished by observing that this mapping of infinite traces in $\mathcal{T}'$ to maximal ones in $\mathcal{T}$ is exactly what $\mathfrak{f}^{-1}$ does.   □

As a consequence of this simple reduction, we can simply assume – whenever this is convenient – that maximal traces are always infinite.

3.5.2 Computing Trace Inclusion

We finish this section on trace equivalence by giving an algorithm for deciding whether two rooted transition systems are behaviourally equivalent with respect to this notion. It will be particularly convenient to use nondeterminism for this. Note that it suffices to give a procedure for trace inclusion – calling it twice, the second time with inverted arguments, can be used to decide trace equivalence. Even more so, we will give a nondeterministic algorithm that decides trace noninclusion between two transition systems $\mathcal{T}_1$ and $\mathcal{T}_2$. Intuitively it guesses a trace in $\mathcal{T}_1$ step by step and follows all paths in $\mathcal{T}_2$ that have the same trace. This is very similar to a technique known as powerset construction in finite automata theory. Using the observation after Lemma 3.5.4, we assume transition systems to be total.

For the sake of simplicity we assume that the procedure is being given a single total interpreted transition system with two designated states s and t.

```
 1: procedure TRACENONINCL(S, {─a→ | a ∈ Act}, L, s, t)              ▷ n = card(S)
 2:     if L(s) ≠ L(t) then return true
 3:         count ← 0
 4:         x ← s
 5:         X ← {t}
 6:     while count < n · 2^n do
 7:         if X = ∅ then return true
 8:         guess y ∈ S and a ∈ Act such that x ─a→ y
 9:         x ← y
10:         X ← post(a, X) ∩ {r | L(r) = L(x)}
11:         count ← count + 1
12:     end while
13:     return false
14: end procedure
```

Theorem 3.5.5. Procedure TRACENONINCL decides trace noninclusion in nondeterministic polynomial space.   ■

Proof. It is clear that TRACENONINCL is nondeterministic. It is also not hard to see that it uses polynomial space only: it stores a state x which requires space $\lceil \log n \rceil$, a set of states X requiring space n and a counter of maximal value $n \cdot 2^n$ which requires space $\lceil \log(n \cdot 2^n) \rceil$ which is $\mathcal{O}(n)$.

It remains to be seen that it is sound and complete. We start with completeness. Suppose therefore that we have $s \not\rightarrow t$, i.e. there is a trace $\sigma \in \text{traces}(s)$ such that $\sigma \notin \text{traces}(t)$. By successively guessing the path underlying σ, the value of X will eventually become $\emptyset$ for the following reason. Let $\sigma = L_1 \xrightarrow{a_1} L_2 \xrightarrow{a_2} \ldots$. Since $\sigma \notin \text{traces}(t)$, there must be a smallest k such that for every path $t_1 \xrightarrow{a_1} t_2 \xrightarrow{a_2} \ldots$ with $t_1 = t$ we have that $L(t_k) \neq L_k$ but $L(t_i) = L_i$ for all $i < k$. Hence, if *count* ever reaches the value k then we get $X = \emptyset$ and therefore a positive return.

It remains to be seen that we must have $k < n \cdot 2^n$. Suppose this was not the case. Let $x_0, x_1, x_2, \ldots, x_k$ and $X_0, X_1, X_2, \ldots, X_k$ denote the values of the variables x and X in the first $k + 1$ iterations of the while loop. Hence, by assumption we have $k \geq n \cdot 2^n$ and $X_k = \emptyset$. But there are only n many different values for the x_i and only 2^n many different ones for the X_i. Hence, there must be $i < j < n \cdot 2^n$ such that $x_i = x_j$ and $X_i = X_j$. Since TRACENON-INCL's behaviour in each iteration of the while-loop only depends on the values of these two variables, there would have been another trace and therefore better guesses such that the condition $X = \emptyset$ would have been met earlier. This argument can be iterated to show that a maximal trace σ' could have been found in $\text{traces}(s)$ which is not in $\text{traces}(t)$ such that all prefixes of σ' starting in t contain at most $n \cdot 2^n - 1$ many transitions.

Finally, we need to show that TRACENONINCL is correct. Clearly, if it returns true in the first line then we have trace noninclusion between s and t. Otherwise assume that it returns true during the while-loop. It is not hard to see that the successive values of x can be used to construct a trace $\sigma \in \text{traces}(s)$. Moreover, the values of X track the set of all states that would be reached by the prefixes of this trace when started in t. Since X becomes $\emptyset$, it must be impossible to extend σ to a maximal trace in $\text{traces}(t)$. $\qquad\qquad\square$

3.6 Exercises

Exercises on designing transition systems

Exercise 3.1. Design a transition system modelling a digicode system with two keys 'a' and 'b' such that the door opens when 'baabba' is pressed. An unbounded number of errors is possible.

Exercise 3.2. Design a labelled transition system modelling a coffee vending machine working with coins of 10, 20 and 50 cents, and dispensing single expresso for 40c, or double espresso for 70c, by choice of the customer made at the beginning, not accepting more coins after a credit of 40c (if single expresso is selected), resp. 70c (if double expresso is selected), is reached and returning change, when due. (Hint: label transitions with 'single', 'double', '10', '20', '50', etc., and use suitable atomic propositions to indicate the currently accumulated credit.)

Exercise 3.3. Design a labelled transition system modelling a buffer that can store in a queue an up to 2-letters word over a 3-letter alphabet $\{a, b, c\}$, with the following possible actions/transitions:

- *push(x)*: push a letter x in the input of the buffer, if it is not full;
- *pop*: pop the last letter from the buffer, if it is not empty.

Exercise 3.4. Consider the transition system in Figure 3.1. Show that the set of infinite paths starting at the state '0' is uncountable.

Exercises on reachability sets

Exercise 3.5. Show by induction on i that $\mathtt{post}^{\le i}(B, X)$ contains the set of states that can be reached from some states in X with a finite path of length at most i, while $\mathtt{pre}^{\le i}(B, X)$ consists of those states from which states in X can be reached with a finite path of length at most i.

Exercise 3.6. Modify the inductive definitions of $\mathtt{post}^{\le i}(B, X)$ and $\mathtt{pre}^{\le i}(B, X)$ to define the sets of successors or predecessors that contain the states that can be reached in *exactly* i steps.

Exercise 3.7. Consider the transition system $(Q \times \mathbb{N}^n, \{\overset{t}{\to}\}_{t \in \delta})$ defined from the vector addition system with states in Figure 3.6. Is there a state $(q_0, \vec{x}) \in Q \times \mathbb{N}^n$ such that $\mathtt{post}^\star\big((q_0, \vec{x})\big)$ is infinite?

Exercise 3.8. Let $\mathcal{T} = (S, \{\overset{a}{\to}\}_{a \in Act})$ be a transition system and $X \subseteq S$. Let $\mathfrak{f} : \mathcal{P}(S) \to \mathcal{P}(S)$ be such that $\mathfrak{f}(Y) := X \cup \mathtt{post}(Y)$. Show that $\mathtt{post}^\star(X)$ is the least fixpoint of the operator $\mathfrak{f}$.

Likewise, show that $\mathtt{pre}^\star(X)$ is the least fixpoint of the map $\mathfrak{g} : \mathcal{P}(S) \to \mathcal{P}(S)$ where $\mathfrak{g}(Y) := X \cup \mathtt{pre}(Y)$.

Exercise 3.9. Let $\mathcal{T} = (S, \{\overset{a}{\to}\}_{a \in Act})$ be a transition system and $X \subseteq S$.

(a) Define operators on $\mathcal{P}(S)$ whose least fixpoints are respectively $\mathtt{post}^+(X)$ and $\mathtt{pre}^+(X)$. Prove your claims.
(b) Define an operator on $\mathcal{P}(S)$ whose least fixpoint is the set of states reachable in an even number of steps from X. Prove your claim.

Exercise 3.10. Which of the properties listed in Section 3.1.3 are satisfied by the mutual exclusion protocol modelled by the transition system in Figure 3.5?

Exercise 3.11. Redesign the transition system in Figure 3.5 to enforce strict alternation of the two processes entering their critical sections when they both have requested to enter a critical section. Then determine which of the properties listed in Section 3.1.3 are satisfied by the resulting transition system.

Exercises on algorithms

Exercise 3.12. Design a nondeterministic algorithm to solve the problem GREACH in logarithmic space.

Exercise 3.13. Consider the following reachability problem:

Input: A finite rooted transition system $(\mathcal{T}, s)$ and $\{F_1, \ldots, F_k\} \subseteq \mathcal{P}(S)$.

Question: Is there some $i \in [1, k]$ such that $r \in \text{post}^\star(s)$ for some $r \in F_i$ and there is a nonempty path from r to r for which exactly the states in F_i are visited.

The existence of such paths is closely related to the acceptance condition in Muller automata recognising ω-words. Show that this problem can be solved in nondeterministic logarithmic space in $|\mathcal{T}| + \sum_i \text{card}(F_i)$.

Exercises on behavioural equivalences

Exercise 3.14. Construct the unfoldings of the following labelled transition system $\mathcal{T}$ from each of its states.

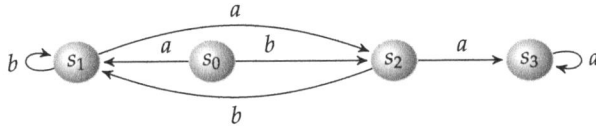

Exercise 3.15. Consider the following interpreted transition systems:

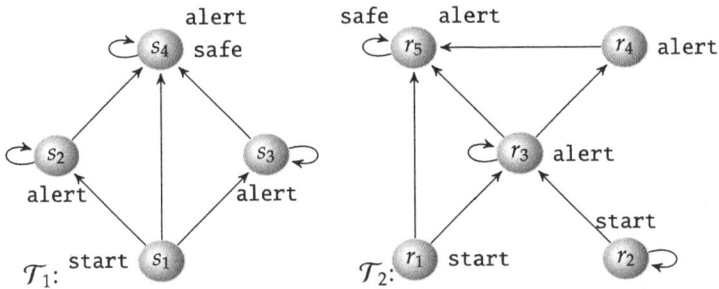

(a) Determine whether $\mathcal{T}_1$ and $\mathcal{T}_2$ are globally bisimilar. If so, define a global bisimulation between them; otherwise give an argument.
(b) Determine whether $(\mathcal{T}_1, s_1)$ and $(\mathcal{T}_2, r_1)$ are locally bisimilar. If so, define a local bisimulation between them; otherwise give an argument.

Exercise 3.16. Prove Lemma 3.3.3 and Proposition 3.3.5.

Exercise 3.17. Complete the proof of Lemma 3.3.6.

Exercise 3.18. In Example 3.3.2, show that the symmetric relation given by the dotted lines in Figure 3.8 is a global bisimulation between $\mathcal{T}_1$ and $\mathcal{T}_2$.

Exercise 3.19. Prove that if $\mathcal{T}$ and $\mathcal{T}'$ are ITS and $\mathcal{T} \overset{\beta}{\rightleftarrows} \mathcal{T}'$ then the relation $\sim_\beta$ in $\mathcal{T}$ defined by $s \sim_\beta r$ iff there is $t \in \mathcal{T}'$ such that $s\beta t$ and $r\beta t$ is a bisimulation in $\mathcal{T}$ which is symmetric and transitive. Furthermore, if β is a global bisimulation, then $\sim_\beta$ is an equivalence relation in $\mathcal{T}$.

Exercise 3.20. Verify that the mapping defined in Example 3.3.12 is a bounded morphism.

Exercise 3.21. Show that in the following figure there is a bounded morphism from the left transition system to the right one.

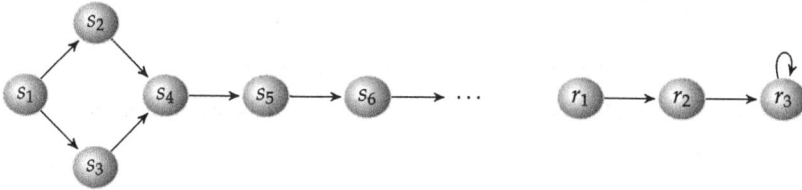

Exercise 3.22. Prove Lemma 3.3.13.

Exercise 3.23. Prove the existence of the winning strategies claimed in Example 3.4.2.

Exercise 3.24. Prove the claim at the end of the proof of Theorem 3.4.3, that the set of pairs (t, t') in all configurations $(\mathcal{T}_1, s_1; \mathcal{T}_2, r_1)$ from which Player **II** has a winning strategy, if nonempty, is a bisimulation.

Exercise 3.25. Given two interpreted transition systems $\mathcal{T}_1$ and $\mathcal{T}_2$, let $\beta_{\mathcal{T}_1, \mathcal{T}_2}$ be the largest bisimulation between $\mathcal{T}_1$ and $\mathcal{T}_2$. Then show that $\beta_{\mathcal{T}_1, \mathcal{T}_2} \circ (\beta_{\mathcal{T}_1, \mathcal{T}_2})^{-1}$ in $\mathcal{T}_1$ and $(\beta_{\mathcal{T}_1, \mathcal{T}_2})^{-1} \circ \beta_{\mathcal{T}_1, \mathcal{T}_2}$ in $\mathcal{T}_2$ are the largest bisimulations respectively in $\mathcal{T}_1$ and in $\mathcal{T}_2$.

Exercise 3.26. Show that the operator F defined in Section 3.4 is monotone with respect to set inclusion.

Exercise 3.27. Verify that the definition of a bisimulation quotient (Definition 3.4.8) is correct in sense that $R_{\sim_{\mathcal{T}}}$ and $L_{\sim_{\mathcal{T}}}$ do not depend on the choice of representatives of their arguments.

Exercise 3.28. Verify the claims about the bisimulation quotients in Example 3.4.9. (See also Exercise 3.32.)

Exercise 3.29. Prove Lemma 3.4.6.

Exercise 3.30. Show that the kernel equivalence $\sim_\mathfrak{f}$ of every bounded morphism $\mathfrak{f}\colon \mathcal{T}_1 \to \mathcal{T}_2$, defined in $\mathcal{T}_1$ as $s \sim_\mathfrak{f} r$ iff $\mathfrak{f}(s) = \mathfrak{f}(r)$, is a bisimulation in $\mathcal{T}_1$.

Exercise 3.31. Write the Kanellakis–Smolka algorithm for computing bisimulation quotients in pseudo-code and prove its correctness.

Exercise 3.32. Apply the Kanellakis–Smolka algorithm for computing the bisimulation quotients of the two ITS given in Figure 3.10, and show that they have the same bisimulation quotient, namely the ITS given in Example 3.4.9.

Exercise 3.33. Show that Algorithm TRACENONINCL is not correct for nontotal transition systems.

Exercise 3.34. Prove Corollary 3.3.7, Proposition 3.4.7. Proposition 3.4.10, Proposition 3.4.11, Lemma 3.4.13 and Proposition 3.4.16.

3.7 Bibliographical Notes

Transition systems are a fundamental formalism for capturing the operational semantics of dynamic systems, in particular programs (Plotkin, 1981). Early notable references on transition systems include Keller (1976), Sifakis (1980) and Queille and Sifakis (1982b). The first more systematic studies of transition systems go back to the works of Arnold and Nivat (see e.g. Arnold and Nivat 1982 (in French); Arnold 1994; Hoare 1985). See also Bergstra and Klop (1985) for a more algebraic approach. The book by Arnold (1994) contains a detailed exposition of finite transition systems, the use of temporal logics for specifying their most fundamental properties and behavioural equivalences between transition systems. Transition systems are also dealt with in Stirling (1992), Clarke et al. (2000), Schneider (2004) and Baier and Katoen (2008).

Transition systems with structured actions. In the framework of temporal logics presented here the structure of actions and transitions is usually hidden and this is one of the abstractions of this approach to formalisation of the notion of computation. In this framework, an action is just a black box, and all that matters is how it transforms states, i.e. the transition relation it generates. An alternative approach can consider the computations from the viewpoint of the *internal structure* of the actions or programs: these can be built from 'atomic' actions or programs using some action/program constructs, such as *composition, conditional branching, iteration*, etc. Transition systems with appropriately structured sets of actions provide a convenient formalism for specifying operational semantics of programming languages and are typically used in modelling sequential programs in logical languages such as the propositional dynamic logic PDL (Fischer and Ladner 1979; Pratt 1980; Kozen and Tiuryn 1990; Harel et al. 2000) and of various logics of processes (Plotkin 1981; Kozen and Tiuryn 1990; Stirling 1992, 2001; German and Sistla 1992).

Kripke structures. From a technical viewpoint, transition systems can be regarded as **Kripke frames**, and interpreted transition systems as **Kripke models**, used to provide relational semantics for modal logics since the late 1950s, originating in Kanger (1957), Hintikka (1962) and Kripke (1963); see also Copeland (2002). Jónsson and Tarski (1951) can be viewed as an algebraic counterpart to possible worlds semantics. For a more recent comprehensive treatment of Kripke frames and models and the possible worlds semantics of modal logics, see Blackburn et al. (2001, 2007). The two views on transition systems, as Kripke models and processes, are related in van Benthem et al. (1993).

Examples and properties of transition systems In Lamport (1977), two important classes of properties have been introduced: safety properties (something bad never happens) and liveness properties (something good eventually happens). For a brief survey on safety and liveness properties, see Kindler (1994). Emerson (1990) identifies fairness as the link between concurrency and nondeterminism: '*concurrency = nondeterminism + fairness*'. For more on fairness, see Gabbay et al. (1980), Lamport (1980), Lehmann et al. (1981) and Francez (1986). More on properties of transition systems can be found in Manna and Pnueli (1979, 1981, 1990, 1992, 1995), Kröger and Merz (2008) and Baier and Katoen (2008). The latter also studies in detail more general regular and ω-regular properties of transition systems, i.e. properties definable by finite automata on finite and on infinite words. Every ω-regular property can be defined as the intersection of a safety ω-regular property and a liveness ω-regular property (Alpern and Schneider 1987; Baier and Katoen 2008).

Reachability problems. The reachability problems presented in this chapter are variants of well-known problems in graph theory, such as the Graph Accessibility Problem (GAP). Many decision problems considered in this book (satisfiability of a logical formula, nonemptiness of a language accepted by an automaton or the existence of a winning strategy in a game) can be reduced to several instances of reachability problems as presented in this chapter. The proofs of Lemma 3.2.5 and 3.2.6 can be found in Aho et al. (1974, 1983). One of the most popular algorithms for computing SCCs, as used in Lemma 3.2.6, is Tarjan's (1972).

Operations on transition systems. In this chapter we have not considered operations for constructing transition systems from others, apart from unfolding since it is fundamental for the study of bisimulation-invariance. Often, transition systems are used to model concrete systems made up of several components that are interacting. This can be modelled using products of transition systems, for instance synchronised products (Arnold and Nivat 1982; Arnold 1994; see also Bérard et al. 2001; Baier and Katoen 2008). For interleaving (asynchronous products) of transition systems, see Baier and Katoen (2008).

Bisimulation. The notion of bisimulation was introduced in the theory of processes by Park (1981), extending Milner's notion of simulation in Milner (1980) and Hennessy and Milner's (1980) iterative version based on stratified simulation relations. Park's work was following numerous studies of simulation between programs and processes, as well as weak homomorphisms between automata and transition systems in the 1970s (see Sangiorgi 2009). Independently, bisimulation was introduced in modal and temporal logics by van Benthem (1976) in his PhD dissertation under the name '*p-relation*', later renamed in van Benthem (1984) to '*zig-zag relation*' as a relational extension of the functional notion of *pseudo-morphism* introduced by Segerberg (1971) in his dissertation. It was used as one of the basic constructions on Kripke models preserving truth of modal formulae. For further details on the origins of that notion, see Sangiorgi (2009) as well as Sangiorgi and Rutten (2012) for further advanced topics on bisimulations and their coinductive interpretation.

There is some analogy between bisimulation quotients and filtrations, discussed in Chapter 5. Filtrations are quotient structures, too, but with respect to equivalences generated by sets of formulae, rather than with respect to largest bisimulations.

Bisimilarity checking. An algorithm for computing bisimulation minimisation was first explicitly proposed by Kanellakis and Smolka (1983), later improved by Paige and Tarjan (1987) and Fernandez (1990) (see also Baier and Katoen 2008; Aceto et al. 2012a). It decides bisimilarity in time $\mathcal{O}(m \cdot \log(n))$ over state spaces with n nodes and m edges.

Bisimulation games. The game-theoretic characterisation of bisimilarity can be found in Stirling (1999). The exposition on bisimulation games presented here partly follows Goranko and Otto (2007). See Stirling (2001) for further discussion and examples on bisimulation games, and also for a proof of their positional determinacy, i.e. that for every bisimulation game one of the players has a positional winning strategy. Here we referred to the Gale–Stewart Theorem which can be found in Gale and Stewart (1953).

Other behavioural equivalences and pre-orders. Simulation is a behavioural pre-order that can be used to explain that one program's behaviour supersedes another one's. It was introduced in Milner (1980) and Hennessy and Milner (1980). Trace equivalences, simulations and bisimulations between labelled transition systems were studied from a logical perspective in van Benthem et al. (1993) and van Benthem and Bergstra (1995). Also, some other variations of bisimulations, e.g. for transition systems with silent transitions were studied in van Benthem et al. (1993). There is a rich theory of behavioural equivalences between bisimilarity and trace equivalence known as the *linear-time branching-time spectrum* (Glabbeek 2001).

Part II

Logics

4

Preliminaries and Background II

In this chapter we outline some common terminology, notation and facts about syntactic and semantic logical concepts that are used, *mutatis mutandis*, in all chapters in the part.

We assume that the reader has basic background on propositional and first-order classical logic. Some general references are listed in the bibliographic notes.

4.1 Preliminaries on Modal Logic

Modal Logical Languages and Connectives

Throughout the book we assume that the generic notion of **modal logic** subsumes the one of **temporal logic**. That applies, in particular, to modal languages, operators, formulae, etc. For instance, whenever we say 'modal formulae', that also refers, in particular, to temporal formulae, unless otherwise specified.

Modal languages. Hereafter we assume an arbitrarily fixed multimodal language L with an alphabet containing a possibly infinite set of atomic propositions PROP, a sufficient set of propositional connectives from which all others are definable – typically something like conjunction and negation – plus an abstract family of (usually, unary or binary) modal operators $\mathcal{O}$. We call the pair $(\mathcal{O}, \text{PROP})$ the **signature** of the language. For instance, given the set of actions *Act*, we will use the set of modal operators $\mathcal{O} = \{\text{EX}_a, \text{AX}_a \mid a \in Act\}$. The modal μ-calculus introduced in Chapter 8 follows a slightly different syntax for modal operators, see Section 8.1.1.

Logical connectives. Throughout this book we will use standard notation for the propositional logical connectives, as follows.

- ⊤ for **truth**;
- ⊥ for **falsum**;
- ¬ for **negation**;
- ∧ for **conjunction**;
- ∨ for **disjunction**;
- → for **implication** (a.k.a., **conditional**);
- ↔ for **bi-implication** (a.k.a., **bi-conditional**). Often this is also called 'equivalence'. We will reserve the use of this word for *relations of equivalence*, e.g. between formulae.

Here we will denote an abstract modal operator by O.

Metavariables. We will use the following typical **metavariables** for the most commonly used logical objects:

- atomic propositions: p, q, r;
- modal formulae: φ, ψ, χ;
- sets of modal formulae: $\Gamma, \Delta, \Psi, \Theta$.

An n-ary **operator** O applied to an n-tuple of formulae $\varphi_1, \ldots, \varphi_n$ produces the formula $O(\varphi_1, \ldots, \varphi_n)$. In the case of unary O we simply write $O\varphi_1$, whereas for binary operators O we will typically write $\varphi_1 O \varphi_2$.

By way of example, the set of formulae built from the the atomic propositions in $\{p_1, p_2, \ldots\}$, the truth constants $\bot, \top$, the Boolean connectives ¬ and ∧, the unary modal operator X and the binary modal operator U, is represented/defined by the following grammar

$$\varphi, \psi ::= \bot \mid \top \mid p_i \mid \neg\varphi \mid (\varphi \wedge \psi) \mid X\varphi \mid (\varphi U \psi).$$

Note that, for the sake of unique readability, parentheses are imposed in the preceding grammar with the application of every binary connective. However, for the sake of simplicity, these parentheses will often be omitted, when a danger of ambiguity of confusion does not arise. This convention will apply to the syntax of all logics introduced in the book.

A **constant formula** is a formula containing no atomic propositions, for instance $\neg(\bot U \neg \top)$.

Basic Syntactic Concepts and Notations

Throughout this book we see formulae as represented by directed acyclic graphs (DAG). This allows nodes to be shared which is not possible in a syntax tree representation. For instance, the formula $(p U \neg Xp) \vee \neg(\neg p U \neg Xp)$ of the syntax can be represented by the following DAG.

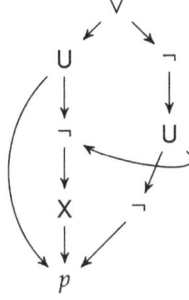

All the syntactical notions can be derived from this.

In order to analyse the computational complexity of logical decision problems or reductions we need to define the notion of formula size. The **size** of a formula φ shall be denoted by $|\varphi|$ and it equals the number of nodes in its syntax DAG. It is well known that the size can be exponentially smaller than the length of a string representation for the formula. So complexity upper bounds measured in the size are *a priori* more difficult to obtain than with respect to length. Consider, as an example, the family of formulae $(\varphi_i)_{i \in \mathbb{N}}$ such that $\varphi_0 = p$ and $\varphi_{i+1} = \varphi_i \wedge \mathsf{X} \neg \varphi_i$ for all $i \geq 0$. Then we have $|\varphi_n| = \mathcal{O}(n)$ whereas its length is in $\Omega(2^n)$.

The set of all **subformulae** of a formula φ will be denoted by $sub(\varphi)$. It is defined recursively on structure of the formula φ.

$$sub(\bot) := \{\bot\}$$
$$sub(\top) := \{\top\}$$
$$sub(p) := \{p\}$$
$$sub(\mathsf{O}(\varphi_1, \ldots, \varphi_n)) := \bigcup_{i=1}^{n} sub(\varphi_i) \cup \{\mathsf{O}(\varphi_1, \ldots, \varphi_n)\}$$

where O is an n-ary connective. Likewise, the set of all subformulae of a set of formulae Γ will be denoted by $sub(\Gamma)$, and it is $sub(\Gamma) := \bigcup \{sub(\varphi) \mid \varphi \in \Gamma\}$. Note that $|\varphi| = \text{card}(sub(\varphi))$.

The **main connective** of φ will be denoted by $maincon(\varphi)$. It is the connective at the root of the formula's syntax DAG. The **main subformulae** of φ will be denoted by $mainsub(\varphi)$. They are the formulae occurring immediately under the root.

$$mainsub(\bot) = mainsub(\top) = mainsub(p) := \text{undefined}$$
$$mainsub(\mathsf{O}(\varphi_1, \ldots, \varphi_n)) := \{\varphi_1, \ldots, \varphi_n\}$$
$$maincon(\bot) := \text{undefined}$$
$$maincon(\top) := \text{undefined}$$
$$maincon(p) := \text{undefined}$$
$$maincon(\mathsf{O}(\varphi_1, \ldots, \varphi_n)) := \mathsf{O}.$$

Note that the definition for subformulae with modal operators simply generalises the definition that is used for propositional connectives.

The **modal degree/depth** $mdeg(\varphi)$ of a formula φ is the greatest number of nested occurrences of modal operators in it, i.e. on the longest path from the root of the syntax DAG to a leaf.

$$mdeg(\bot) := 0$$

$$mdeg(p) := 0$$

$$mdeg(\neg\varphi) := mdeg(\varphi)$$

$$mdeg(\varphi_1 O \varphi_2) := \max(mdeg(\varphi_1), mdeg(\varphi_2)) \qquad \text{(Boolean connective O)}$$

$$mdeg(O(\varphi_1, \ldots, \varphi_n)) := \max(mdeg(\varphi_1), \ldots, mdeg(\varphi_n)) + 1 \qquad \text{(modal operator O)}.$$

For instance, $mdeg(\neg O_2(\neg O_1 O_1 \neg p \to q, p \wedge O_1 q)) = 3$. For any modal language L, the **fragment** L^n of L comprises all formulae of L with modal depth $\leq n$.

Let φ, ψ, χ be formulae. We denote by $\varphi[\psi/\chi]$ the result of the **uniform simultaneous substitution** of all occurrences (if any) of χ as a subformula of φ by ψ. Note that the syntax of formulae in all logical languages that we will use is such that any two different occurrences of χ as a subformula of φ are disjoint, so there is no danger of ambiguity here.

We introduce the following notation: for any formula φ we denote by $\sim\varphi$ the negation of φ, after dropping a double negation in front, if applicable. Formally:

$$\sim\varphi := \begin{cases} \psi, & \text{if } \varphi = \neg\psi \\ \neg\varphi, & \text{otherwise.} \end{cases}$$

Assuming that $\neg$ is interpreted by the classical negation (as in propositional logic), for all the temporal logics consider in the book, $\sim\varphi$ and $\neg\varphi$ shall denote formulae with equivalent meaning. A set Γ is closed under $\sim$ whenever it is closed under classical negation $\neg$ and newly introduced double negations are eliminated.

Definition 4.1.1. The set of **main components** of a formula φ is defined as follows:

$$maincomp(\bot) := \text{undefined}$$

$$maincomp(p) := \text{undefined}$$

$$maincomp(\neg p) := \text{undefined}$$

$$maincomp(O(\varphi_1, \ldots, \varphi_n)) := \{\varphi_1, \ldots, \varphi_n\}$$

$$maincomp(\neg O(\varphi_1, \ldots, \varphi_n)) := \{\sim\varphi_1, \ldots, \sim\varphi_n\}. \qquad \triangledown$$

In particular, $maincomp(\neg\neg\varphi) := \{\sim\neg\varphi\} = \{\varphi\}$. Thus, the main components of a formula φ are like its main subformulae, but with preserving their polarity in φ. Thus, *not* every main component of a formula is its subformula. For instance, if EX is a unary modal operator then $maincomp(\neg EX p) = \{\neg p\}$ and $\neg p$ is not a subformula of $\neg EX p$.

The **closure** of a formula φ is understood as a set of formulae that are used to determine the satisfiability or validity status of φ. Such a set is usually finite and only formulae from the closure set can occur in the decision procedure (if any) to determine satisfiability or validity. The exact definition depends very much on the proof method but – as a rule of thumb – the closure of a formula φ, usually denoted by $cl(\varphi)$, is at least closed under taking main components, but it may also be closed under the pseudo-negation $\sim$ or under subformulae. Moreover, one may go a bit beyond subformulae or their negations by considering superformulae obtained by unfolding fixpoints. For instance, assuming that U is a binary modal operator, X is a unary modal operator (as defined for LTL in Chapter 6) and $\psi_1 \mathsf{U} \psi_2$ is logically equivalent to $\psi_2 \vee (\psi_1 \wedge \mathsf{X}(\psi_1 \mathsf{U} \psi_2))$, we could consider the following properties. If Γ is a closed set and $\psi_1 \mathsf{U} \psi_2 \in \Gamma$, then the following formulae would also belong to Γ:

$$\psi_1, \psi_2, \psi_2 \vee (\psi_1 \wedge \mathsf{X}(\psi_1 \mathsf{U} \psi_2)), (\psi_1 \wedge \mathsf{X}(\psi_1 \mathsf{U} \psi_2)), \mathsf{X}(\psi_1 \mathsf{U} \psi_2).$$

In what follows, we provide a definition for closure sets that is used by default (variants will be considered too along the chapters).

Definition 4.1.2. The **closure of a formula** φ is the least set of formulae $cl(\varphi)$ containing φ, closed under taking subformulae and closed under $\sim$. The closure of a set of formulae Γ, denoted $cl(\Gamma)$, is defined as the union of the closures of the formulae in Γ, that is, $cl(\Gamma) := \bigcup \{ cl(\varphi) \mid \varphi \in \Gamma \}$. A set of formulae Γ is **closed** if and only if $cl(\Gamma) = \Gamma$. ▽

The term 'closure' is actually quite appropriate since $cl(\cdot)$ from Definition 4.1.2 satisfies the three fundamental properties of closure operator:

1. $\varphi \in cl(\varphi)$,
2. $\Gamma \subseteq \Gamma'$ implies $cl(\Gamma) \subseteq cl(\Gamma')$,
3. $cl(cl(\Gamma)) = cl(\Gamma)$.

The following claims are straightforward and are left as exercises.

Lemma 4.1.3. For every modal formula φ:

(I) The closure $cl(\varphi)$ is finite and $card(cl(\varphi)) \leq 2 \times card(sub(\varphi))$.
(II) For every $\psi \in sub(\varphi)$, both ψ and $\sim\psi$ are in $cl(\varphi)$.
(III) Every main subformula of φ has a size smaller than the size of φ.
(IV) If $\neg\psi \in cl(\varphi)$, then $\psi \in sub(\varphi)$. ■

Obviously, properties of Lemma 4.1.3 depend very much on Definition 4.1.2 but more generally, for alternative definitions of $cl(\varphi)$, we shall at least expect that the cardinality of $cl(\varphi)$ is polynomial in the size of φ and for every subformula ψ of φ, either there is a formula in the closure equivalent to ψ (typically ψ itself) or there is a formula in the closure equivalent to $\neg\psi$ (typically $\neg\psi$ or $\sim\psi$).

Definition 4.1.4. A set of formulae Γ is **patently inconsistent** if Γ contains $\bot$, $\neg\top$, or a contradictory pair of formulae of the form either ψ and $\neg\psi$, or ψ and $\sim\psi$.

A set of formulae Γ is **propositionally expanded**, or simply **expanded**, if:

1. Γ is not patently inconsistent,
2. $\neg\neg\psi \in \Gamma$ implies $\psi \in \Gamma$,
3. $\psi_1 \wedge \psi_2 \in \Gamma$ implies $\psi_1, \psi_2 \in \Gamma$,
4. $\psi_1 \vee \psi_2 \in \Gamma$ implies $\psi_1 \in \Gamma$ or $\psi_2 \in \Gamma$,
5. $\neg(\psi_1 \wedge \psi_2) \in \Gamma$ implies $\sim\psi_1 \in \Gamma$ or $\sim\psi_2 \in \Gamma$,
6. $\neg(\psi_1 \vee \psi_2) \in \Gamma$ implies $\sim\psi_1 \in \Gamma$ and $\sim\psi_2 \in \Gamma$. ∇

In Definition 4.1.4, neither is it assumed that Γ is closed nor is it supposed that the implications can be turned into equivalences. The next definition provides more restricted conditions, in particular by assuming an underlying closed set and by requiring that the implication can be turned into equivalences.

Let X be a closed set of formulae (in the sense of Definition 4.1.2). A set of formulae Γ is **maximally consistent** with respect to X, or simply maximally consistent, if:

1. Γ is not patently inconsistent.
2. For every $\psi \in X$, either $\psi \in \Gamma$ or $\sim\psi \in \Gamma$ (but not both).
3. For every $\neg\neg\psi \in X$, $\psi \in \Gamma$ iff $\neg\neg\psi \in \Gamma$.
4. For every $\psi_1 \wedge \psi_2 \in X$, $\psi_1 \wedge \psi_2 \in \Gamma$ iff $\{\psi_1, \psi_2\} \subseteq \Gamma$.
5. For every $\psi_1 \vee \psi_2 \in X$, $\psi_1 \vee \psi_2 \in \Gamma$ iff either $\psi_1 \in \Gamma$ or $\psi_2 \in \Gamma$.

When Γ is maximally consistent, we can conclude also that for every $\neg(\psi_1 \wedge \psi_2) \in X$, $\neg(\psi_1 \wedge \psi_2) \in \Gamma$ iff either $\psi_1 \notin \Gamma$ or $\psi_2 \notin \Gamma$. Similarly, for every $\neg(\psi_1 \vee \psi_2) \in X$, $\neg(\psi_1 \vee \psi_2) \in \Gamma$ iff $\psi_1 \notin \Gamma$ and $\psi_2 \notin \Gamma$. It is worth mentioning that the number of maximally consistent sets with respect to $cl(\varphi)$ is bounded by $2^{\mathrm{card}(sub(\varphi))}$.

Basic Semantic Concepts and Notations

The semantics of a logic explains the meaning of its formulae as statements about the class of structures that it is interpreted over. In this book we consider temporal logics that are interpreted in transition systems in a particular way. For instance, formulae of the simple branching-time temporal logic CTL to be introduced in Section 7.1.3 are interpreted in a *state* of a transition system; formulae of the linear-time temporal logic LTL (see Chapter 6) on the other hand are interpreted in paths. We will even see situations in which formulae need to be interpreted in a state on a particular path of a transition system. In any case, the semantics is given by a relation $\models$ between objects like states or paths on one side and formulae on the other. This relation determines the **truth** of a formula φ at that object of the transition system. For instance, $\mathcal{T}, s \models \varphi$ is to be read as 'the formula φ holds in state s of the transition system $\mathcal{T}$'.

Definition 4.1.5. The **extension** of a formula φ – interpreted in states – in a model $\mathcal{T}$ is the set of states in $\mathcal{T}$ satisfying φ, i.e. $[\![\varphi]\!]^{\mathcal{T}} := \{s \mid \mathcal{T}, s \models \varphi\}$. ∇

Truth and extension are interchangeable. In Chapter 8 for instance, it is more convenient to give the semantics by defining the extension directly. In such a case, truth can be derived from it: a formula is satisfied in a state if that state belongs to the formula's extension in the underlying transition system.

The notion of truth will be defined separately for each of the specific logics that we study here, typically by induction on the structure of the formula. A **logic** shall then be understood as an abstract modal language L equipped with a class $\mathcal{C}$ of structures in which its formulae can be interpreted and equipped with a notion of truth. Given that notion, we introduce the following generic terminology for logics that are interpreted in states:

Given an L-model $\mathcal{T}$, a state s in $\mathcal{T}$ and a formula φ of L, we say that φ is

- **satisfied at** s **in** $\mathcal{T}$ or that $(\mathcal{T}, s)$ is a **model** of φ, if $\mathcal{T}, s \models \varphi$;
- **satisfiable in** $\mathcal{T}$ if $\mathcal{T}, r \models \varphi$ for some state $r \in \mathcal{T}$;
- **satisfiable**, if it is satisfied in some model $\mathcal{T}$;
- **valid in** $\mathcal{T}$, denoted $\mathcal{T} \models \varphi$, if $\mathcal{T}, r \models \varphi$ for every state $r \in \mathcal{T}$; we then also say that $\mathcal{T}$ **is a model of** φ;
- **valid in a class of models** $\mathcal{C}$, denoted $\mathcal{C} \models \varphi$, if $\mathcal{T} \models \varphi$ for every $\mathcal{T} \in \mathcal{C}$;
- **valid**, denoted $\models \varphi$, if it is valid in every L-model.

For logics interpreted differently, for instance in paths rather than states, these notions are defined likewise.

A set of L-formulae Γ is **satisfiable** if there is an L-model $\mathcal{T}$ and a state $s \in \mathcal{T}$ such that $\mathcal{T}, s \models \varphi$ for every $\varphi \in \Gamma$. Note that satisfiability of a finite set Γ is equivalent to satisfiability of the single formula $\bigwedge \Gamma$ where $\bigwedge \Gamma := \varphi_1 \wedge \cdots \wedge \varphi_n$ with $\Gamma = \{\varphi_1, \ldots, \varphi_n\}$ (assuming that binary conjunction belongs to L).

An L-formula φ is a **logical consequence** of a set of L-formulae Γ, denoted $\Gamma \models \varphi$, if $\mathcal{T}, s \models \varphi$ for every model $\mathcal{T}$ and a state s such that $\mathcal{T}, s \models \psi$ for every formula $\psi \in \Gamma$. We then also say that φ **follows logically** from Γ and that Γ **logically implies** φ.

Two L-formulae, φ and ψ, are **(logically) equivalent**, denoted $\varphi \equiv \psi$, if $\models \varphi \leftrightarrow \psi$, that is, if $\mathcal{T}, s \models \varphi$ iff $\mathcal{T}, s \models \psi$ for every model $\mathcal{T}$ and state s in it.

The notions of validity, satisfiability and logical consequence are related in a generic way that applies to all logics that we study here. The proof is left as an exercise.

Lemma 4.1.6. For every L-formula φ and for every set of L-formulae Γ the following are equivalent:

(I) $\Gamma \models \varphi$.
(II) $\Gamma \cup \{\neg\varphi\}$ is not satisfiable.
(III) $\models (\bigwedge \Gamma) \to \varphi$, when Γ is finite. ∎

4.2 Logical Decision Problems

Satisfiability and validity. A logic $\mathfrak{L}$ comes with

- its language, i.e. set of all formulae, L,
- a class of L-models $\mathcal{C}$ and,
- notions for truth.

In the following, an $\mathcal{L}$-formula is understood as a formula built from L whereas an $\mathcal{L}$-model is understood as an L-model from $\mathcal{C}$, typically a transition system.

The notion of truth, given by a relation $\models$ between $\mathcal{L}$-models and $\mathcal{L}$-formulae, induces decision problems that are fundamental to the modelling and verification of, and reasoning about, program behaviour. The **satisfiability-testing problem**, also called in here **satisfiability-checking problem**, for a logic $\mathcal{L}$ interpreted in states of a transition system, denoted by SAT($\mathcal{L}$), is defined as follows.

Input: an $\mathcal{L}$-formula φ.

Question: Is there an interpreted transition system $\mathcal{T}$ of $\mathcal{L}$ and a state s in $\mathcal{T}$ such that $\mathcal{T}, s \models \varphi$?

The dual **validity problem** VAL($\mathcal{L}$), is defined similarly.

Input: an $\mathcal{L}$-formula φ.

Question: Is it the case that $\models \varphi$?

For logics interpreted over paths for instance, satisfiability then asks for the existence of a path instead of a state.

In any case, the satisfiability problem is therefore to decide, for a given formula φ, whether there is a model for it, regardless of what the exact nature of this model is, depending on the logic $\mathcal{L}$. Validity quantifies universally over models instead.

Satisfiability and validity are duals of each other: a formula φ is valid iff $\neg\varphi$ is not satisfiable; respectively, φ is satisfiable iff $\neg\varphi$ is not valid. Indeed, all the logics considered in this book admit classical negation that allows to perform the preceding reasoning.

Note that the problem SAT($\mathcal{L}$) only asks for *existence* of a model, not for the *construction* of one. However, we will show (see e.g. Chapter 13) that it can actually be solved constructively for each of the temporal logics studied here, by producing a *finite* model of a bounded size for any satisfiable formula of $\mathcal{L}$.

Model checking. Another fundamental generic logical question is whether a given formula of a given logic $\mathcal{L}$ is true (locally at a given state, or globally) in a given model for $\mathcal{L}$. Hence the problem of **model checking** is to decide the relation $\models$, given an $\mathcal{L}$-model and an $\mathcal{L}$-formula. The exact nature of this problem differs with the underlying logic, depending on whether formulae are interpreted in states, paths, etc. For the simplest case of interpretation in states, we consider two variants.

The **local model-checking problem** for $\mathcal{L}$, denoted by MC($\mathcal{L}$), is defined as follows:

Input: an $\mathcal{L}$-formula φ, a finite $\mathcal{L}$-model $\mathcal{T}$ and a state s in $\mathcal{T}$.

Question: Is it the case that $\mathcal{T}, s \models \varphi$?

The **global model-checking problem** for $\mathcal{L}$, denoted by GMC($\mathcal{L}$), is defined as follows:

Input: an $\mathcal{L}$-formula φ and a finite $\mathcal{L}$-model $\mathcal{T}$.

Output: the set $[\![\varphi]\!]^{\mathcal{T}}$.

For logics interpreted in paths, the situation is a bit more complex. We can consider the problem in which we are given a finite (interpreted) transition system and a path in it together with a formula, and we have to decide whether truth holds between the path and the formula. Now note that paths in finite (interpreted) transition system can be infinite objects. Hence, we need to require the path to be finitely represented at least. Another approach is discussed in detail in Chapter 6 where we externally enforce some mechanism that turns truth in a path to truth in a state, and then the two preceding model-checking problems are defined as well.

4.3 Expressive Power

Temporal formulae in the context of this book represent statements about the behaviour of programs modelled as transition systems. An important question that arises with the study of logics is the one concerning **expressive power**. It can be used to compare different logics and relate them with respect to the question of whether anything that can be said in one logic can also be said in the other.

A natural framework for comparing the expressive powers of two logics first requires that they are interpreted over the same classes of semantical structures (models) and that their semantics refer to the same objects in the models. We introduce a simple and standard methodology for comparing the expressive powers of two logics and will set a few conventions for that. We have branching-time temporal logics specifically in mind (see Chapter 7) but the following definitions may be used in a much more general settings, too.

Let $\mathfrak{L}_1$ and $\mathfrak{L}_2$ be two logics with formulae whose semantics is defined on rooted interpreted transition systems from the class $\mathcal{C}$. We say that the logic $\mathfrak{L}_1$ is **not more expressive than** $\mathfrak{L}_2$, written $\mathfrak{L}_1 \sqsubseteq \mathfrak{L}_2$, if for every formula φ in $\mathfrak{L}_1$ there is a formula φ' in $\mathfrak{L}_2$ such that $\varphi \equiv \varphi'$ (relatively to $\mathcal{C}$). We say that $\mathfrak{L}_1$ is **strictly less expressive than** $\mathfrak{L}_2$, written $\mathfrak{L}_1 \sqsubset \mathfrak{L}_2$, if $\mathfrak{L}_1 \sqsubseteq \mathfrak{L}_2$ and not $\mathfrak{L}_2 \sqsubseteq \mathfrak{L}_1$. Similarly, we say that $\mathfrak{L}_1$ and $\mathfrak{L}_2$ are **equi-expressive**, written $\mathfrak{L}_1 \equiv \mathfrak{L}_2$, whenever $\mathfrak{L}_1 \sqsubseteq \mathfrak{L}_2$ and $\mathfrak{L}_2 \sqsubseteq \mathfrak{L}_1$.

Note that the symbol '$\equiv$' is already overloaded with different uses, but this should not cause any confusion in the sequel since one use involves (logically equivalent) formulae whereas the other use refers to (equally expressive) temporal logics. Previously, we have assumed that the logics $\mathfrak{L}_1$ and $\mathfrak{L}_2$ have the same class $\mathcal{C}$ of models but this is not necessary for comparison. The definition of $\sqsubseteq$ can be generalised as follows: let $\mathcal{C}'$ be a class of models that are both $\mathfrak{L}_1$-models and $\mathfrak{L}_2$-models. We say that the logic $\mathfrak{L}_1$ is **not more expressive than** $\mathfrak{L}_2$ relatively to $\mathcal{C}'$, written $\mathfrak{L}_1 \sqsubseteq_{\mathcal{C}'} \mathfrak{L}_2$, if for every formula φ in $\mathfrak{L}_1$ there is a formula φ' in $\mathfrak{L}_2$ such that $\varphi \equiv \varphi'$ relatively to $\mathcal{C}'$.

Note that $\sqsubseteq$ and $\sqsubset$ are transitive relations whereas $\equiv$ is an equivalence relation between logics. Also, note that whenever $\mathfrak{L}_1$ is a syntactic fragment of $\mathfrak{L}_2$, we have $\mathfrak{L}_1 \sqsubseteq \mathfrak{L}_2$.

4.4 Deductive Systems

The fundamental concept in logic is logical consequence, which is the basis of logically correct reasoning. It extends the concept of logical validity but is also generally reducible to it, so one can focus on the study of the latter. Verifying logical validity in classical propositional logic is conceptually simple and technically easy (though, possibly computationally expensive), but this is not so anymore for the full first-order logic, nor for the various nonclassical logics, including the temporal logics studied here. In fact, verifying logical validity, in propositional modal and temporal logics, is in principle an *infinite task*, as it requires checking infinitely many possible models, rather than a finite number of simple truth assignments. In logics with a 'small model property' this task becomes finite, but the enumeration and checking of all models within the limit size is usually practically unfeasible.

Thus, a different approach for proving logical validity, not based on the semantic definition, becomes practically necessary. Such a different approach is provided by the notion of **deductive system**: a formal, mechanical – or, at least mechanisable – procedure for *derivation (inference, deduction)* of formulae, or lists ('sequents') of formulae, by applying precise *inference rules* and possibly using some formulae that are postulated as derived, called *axioms*. The underlying idea of deductive systems, which goes back to Aristotle, is to *simulate* and *substitute* the semantic notions of logical consequence and validity with the formal, syntactic notions of *deductive consequence and theoremhood* which are based only on the syntactic shape of the formulae but not on their meaning. Thus, at least theoretically, any person with no knowledge and understanding of the meaning of logical formulae and logical consequence, or even a suitably programmed computer, should be able to do successful derivations in a given deductive system.

When the logic under consideration is decidable, deductive systems for it are in principle replaceable by *logical decision procedures*. These may be practically more efficient but are conceptually inferior as they usually reduce the logical reasoning task to combinatorial manipulations and replace the search for a logical argument by algorithmic search for a satisfying model. Therefore, while this book is primarily focused on algorithmic treatment of temporal logics, we will discuss the deductive approach, too.

The most popular types of logical deductive systems are *axiomatic systems*, *sequent calculi*, *natural deduction*, *semantic tableaux* and *resolution*. Of these, in Part II we will only treat, briefly, axiomatic systems, as sections in each of the chapters in this part. Semantic tableaux will be treated in detail in Chapter 13. In the case of temporal logics treated here, the method of semantic tableaux can be regarded both as a deductive system and a decision procedure.

Basic Concepts of Deductive Systems

There are different types of deductive systems, but they all share several common aspects and principles. A deductive system works within a *formal logical language* with a precise syntax of the set of formulae. The main component of a deductive system is the notion of **derivation (inference, deduction) from a given set of assumptions**, based on a set of precisely specified **rules of inference**. The derivations are performed on formulae or lists of formulae. The idea, again, is that by applying these rules systematically, one can **derive** (**infer, deduce**) formulae from other formulae that are either already derived, or are *assumed* as given, and called **assumptions** (**premises**). In addition, axiomatic systems also allow for an initial set of formulae, called **axioms**, to be accepted as derived without applying any rules of inference. Thus, the axioms can always be used as premises in derivations.

Here are some basic notions related to derivations in the deductive system $\mathcal{D}$.

- A formula φ is **derivable** (or, follows deductively) in $\mathcal{D}$ from a set of formulae Γ, denoted $\Gamma \vdash_{\mathcal{D}} \varphi$, if φ can be derived from all axioms of $\mathcal{D}$ and the formulae from Γ by applying the rules of inference of $\mathcal{D}$. If $\Gamma \vdash_{\mathcal{D}} \varphi$, we also say that Γ **deductively implies** φ in $\mathcal{D}$.
- In particular, if $\Gamma = \emptyset$, we write $\vdash_{\mathcal{D}} \varphi$ and say that φ is a **theorem** of $\mathcal{D}$. If $\Gamma \vdash_{\mathcal{D}} \varphi$ is not the case, we write $\Gamma \nvdash_{\mathcal{D}} \varphi$.
- A set of formulae Γ is **consistent in** $\mathcal{D}$ (or, $\mathcal{D}$-**consistent**) if $\Gamma \nvdash_{\mathcal{D}} \bot$; otherwise Γ is **inconsistent in** $\mathcal{D}$ (or, $\mathcal{D}$-**inconsistent**).

In every deductive system $\mathcal{D}$ for the logics we consider here, $\{\varphi\} \vdash_{\mathcal{D}} \bot$ is equivalent to $\vdash_{\mathcal{D}} \neg\varphi$. Thus, a formula φ is consistent in $\mathcal{D}$ iff $\nvdash_{\mathcal{D}} \neg\varphi$. More generally, the relationship between consistency and derivability can be extended as follows:

$$\Gamma \cup \{\varphi\} \text{ is } \mathcal{D}\text{-consistent} \quad \text{iff} \quad \Gamma \nvdash_{\mathcal{D}} \neg\varphi;$$

and, respectively, $\Gamma \vdash_{\mathcal{D}} \varphi$ iff $\Gamma \cup \{\neg\varphi\}$ is $\mathcal{D}$-inconsistent.

Soundness, Completeness and Adequacy of Deductive Systems

A very important aspect of deductive systems is that derivations in them are completely mechanisable procedures that, in principle, do not require any intelligence or understanding of the meaning of the formulae or rules involved; in fact, such meaning need not be specified at all. Thus, derivations in a given deductive system can be performed by a mechanical device, such as a computer, without any human intervention, as long as the axioms and rules of inference of the deductive system have been programmed into it.

While deductive systems are not explicitly concerned with the meaning (semantics) of the formulae they derive, they are designed with the purpose to derive only valid logical consequences from the assumptions. A deductive system with this property is called sound. In particular, every theorem of such a deductive system must be a valid formula.

Formally, a deductive system $\mathcal{D}$ is **sound** (or, **correct**) for a given logical semantics (that is, well-defined notions of logical validity and consequence) if $\mathcal{D}$ can *only* derive logically valid consequences, i.e.:

$$\varphi_1, \ldots, \varphi_n \vdash_{\mathcal{D}} \psi \quad \text{implies} \quad \varphi_1, \ldots, \varphi_n \models \psi.$$

In particular, $\vdash_{\mathcal{D}} \psi$ implies $\models \psi$.

A deductive system $\mathcal{D}$ is **complete** for a given logical semantics if $\mathcal{D}$ can derive *every* valid logical consequence (as defined in that semantics), i.e.:

$$\varphi_1, \ldots, \varphi_n \models \psi \quad \text{implies} \quad \varphi_1, \ldots, \varphi_n \vdash_{\mathcal{D}} \psi.$$

In particular, $\models \psi$ implies $\vdash_\mathcal{D} \psi$, that is, a complete deductive system can derive *every* logically valid formula.

We say that a deductive system $\mathcal{D}$ is **adequate** for a given semantics if it is both sound and complete for it, i.e.:

$$\varphi_1, \ldots, \varphi_n \models \psi \text{ if and only if } \varphi_1, \ldots, \varphi_n \vdash_\mathcal{D} \psi.$$

In particular, we have then $\models \psi$ if and only if $\vdash_\mathcal{D} \psi$.

The soundness of a deductive system can be guaranteed, and proved easily in principle, as long as the following two conditions hold:

(i) *All axioms (if any) must be valid.*
(ii) *All rules of inference must be sound*, i.e. they must always produce true conclusions when applied to true assumptions. Such rules, in particular, preserve validity. Thus, validity propagates from the axioms to all theorems.

Axiomatic System for the Classical Propositional Logic

Axiomatic systems are not well suited for practical deduction because they employ very few and simple rules of inference that do not allow for well-structured derivations. However, axiomatic systems are usually easier to construct and to prove their soundness, completeness and other meta-properties than other types of deductive systems. Besides their universality, the main importance of a sound and complete axiomatic system is that it captures precisely the semantics and provides some understanding of the logically valid principles of the given logic.

Here we present a standard version of a sound and complete axiomatic system for the classical propositional logic PL. We assume the language of PL to contain the logical connectives $\top, \neg, \wedge, \vee, \rightarrow$, for the sake of presenting characterising axioms for each of these, while $\bot$ and $\leftrightarrow$ will be assumed definable as usual: $\bot := \neg\top$, $\varphi \leftrightarrow \psi := (\varphi \rightarrow \psi) \wedge (\psi \rightarrow \varphi)$.

Before presenting the axiomatic system we need to define the notion of **formula scheme**. This is the set of all **substitution instances** obtained from a given formula by applying uniform substitutions, as follows. Let $\varphi = \varphi(p_1, \ldots, p_n)$ be a formula built over the atomic propositions $p_1, \ldots, p_n$ and let $\psi_1, \ldots, \psi_n$ be formulae. Then $\varphi' = \varphi[\psi_1/p_1, \ldots, \psi_n/p_n]$ is the formula obtained from φ by simultaneously replacing every occurrence of p_i by ψ_i, for each $i = 1, \ldots, n$. We say that φ' is a **substitution instance** (or, just an **instance**) of φ.

For example, $((p \wedge q) \wedge \neg\neg p) \rightarrow (\neg(p \wedge q) \vee \neg p)$ is the instance of $(p \wedge \neg q) \rightarrow (\neg p \vee q)$ in which p is substituted by $(p \wedge q)$ and q is substituted by $\neg p$.

The scheme of all substitution instances of the formula $\varphi(p_1, \ldots, p_n)$ can be written simply as $\varphi[\psi_1/p_1, \ldots, \psi_n/p_n]$, where $\psi_1, \ldots, \psi_n$ are regarded not as specific formulae, but as *metavariables* for formulae. Then the formulae of the scheme are the instances obtained by substituting formulae for these metavariables. Thus, the scheme generated from the formula $(p \wedge \neg q) \rightarrow (\neg p \vee q)$ can be written as $(\varphi \wedge \neg\psi) \rightarrow (\neg\varphi \vee \psi)$.

Now, the axiomatic system, denoted by AxSys_{PL}, will consist of several **axiom schemes**, which are formula schemes the instances of which are taken as **axioms**, and one simple **rule of inference**.

The axiom schemes of AxSys_{PL} are the following, where φ, ψ, χ are metavariables that stand for any formulae of PL.

$$(\top) \quad \top$$
$$(\to 1) \quad \varphi \to (\psi \to \varphi)$$
$$(\to 2) \quad (\varphi \to (\psi \to \chi)) \to ((\varphi \to \psi) \to (\varphi \to \chi))$$
$$(\to 3) \quad (\neg\psi \to \neg\varphi) \to ((\neg\psi \to \varphi) \to \psi)$$
$$(\wedge 1) \quad (\varphi \wedge \psi) \to \varphi$$
$$(\wedge 2) \quad (\varphi \wedge \psi) \to \psi$$
$$(\wedge 3) \quad (\varphi \to \psi) \to ((\varphi \to \chi) \to (\varphi \to \psi \wedge \chi))$$
$$(\vee 1) \quad \varphi \to \varphi \vee \psi$$
$$(\vee 2) \quad \psi \to \varphi \vee \psi$$
$$(\vee 3) \quad (\varphi \to \chi) \to ((\psi \to \chi) \to (\varphi \vee \psi \to \chi)).$$

The only rule of inference is **Modus Ponens**:

$$\text{MP} \quad \frac{\vdash \varphi, \ \vdash \varphi \to \psi}{\vdash \psi}.$$

A **derivation** in AxSys_{PL} from a set of assumptions Γ is a finite sequence $\varphi_1, \ldots, \varphi_n$ such that for every $i \in \{1, \ldots, n\}$, either $\varphi_i \in \Gamma$, or φ_i is an axiom of AxSys_{PL}, or there are $j, k < i$ such that φ_k is equal to $\varphi_j \to \varphi_i$. Then, we write $\Gamma \vdash_{\text{AxSys}_{\text{PL}}} \varphi_n$. A formula φ is said to be **derivable** in AxSys_{PL}, or a **theorem** of AxSys_{PL}, denoted as $\vdash_{\text{AxSys}_{\text{PL}}} \varphi$, if $\emptyset \vdash_{\text{AxSys}_{\text{PL}}} \varphi$.

The notion of derivation from a set of assumptions is the deductive analogue of logical consequence in PL. Thus, in order to derive the claim that '$\varphi_1, \ldots, \varphi_n$ logically imply ψ' we add the assumptions $\varphi_1, \ldots, \varphi_n$ to the set of axioms and try to derive ψ.

Example 4.4.1. We show that $\vdash_{\text{AxSys}_{\text{PL}}} (p \wedge (p \to q)) \to q$ holds.

1. $\vdash_{\text{AxSys}_{\text{PL}}} (p \wedge (p \to q)) \to p$,   by $(\wedge 1)$;
2. $\vdash_{\text{AxSys}_{\text{PL}}} (p \wedge (p \to q)) \to (p \to q)$,   by $(\wedge 2)$;
3. $\vdash_{\text{AxSys}_{\text{PL}}} ((p \wedge (p \to q)) \to (p \to q)) \to (((p \wedge (p \to q)) \to p) \to ((p \wedge (p \to q)) \to q))$,   by $(\to 2)$;
4. $\vdash_{\text{AxSys}_{\text{PL}}} (p \wedge (p \to q)) \to p) \to ((p \wedge (p \to q)) \to q)$,   by MP from 2,3;
5. $\vdash_{\text{AxSys}_{\text{PL}}} (p \wedge (p \to q)) \to q$,   by MP from 1,4.

This example looks overly complicated for the simple tautology that it derives, but it is illustrative of how complex derivations in axiomatic systems can be. Still, it can be proved that AxSys_{PL} can derive every valid logical consequence and, therefore, every valid tautology.

In general, the derivations in AxSys_{PL} can be simplified significantly by using the following important result which allows introduction and elimination of auxiliary assumptions in the derivations. See e.g. Sundholm (2001) or van Dalen (2004)) for a proof.

Theorem 4.4.2 (Deduction Theorem for PL). For any formulae φ, ψ and a set of formulae Γ we have $\Gamma \cup \{\varphi\} \vdash_{\text{AxSys}_{\text{PL}}} \psi$ iff $\Gamma \vdash_{\text{AxSys}_{\text{PL}}} \varphi \rightarrow \psi$. ∎

Proof. The direction from right to left is an immediate application of Modus Ponens. The proof of the other direction requires a more involved argument, by induction on the derivations. We leave that as an exercise. □

Using the Deduction Theorem, derivations such as $\vdash_{\text{AxSys}_{\text{PL}}} p \rightarrow p$ become straightforward. The derivation in Example 4.4.1 can be substantially simplified. DT stands for an application of the Deduction Theorem.

1. $p \wedge (p \rightarrow q) \vdash_{\text{AxSys}_{\text{PL}}} p$,   by ($\wedge$1) and DT;
2. $p \wedge (p \rightarrow q) \vdash_{\text{AxSys}_{\text{PL}}} p \rightarrow q$,   by ($\wedge$2) and DT;
3. $p \wedge (p \rightarrow q) \vdash_{\text{AxSys}_{\text{PL}}} q$,   by 1,2 and MP;
4. $\vdash_{\text{AxSys}_{\text{PL}}} (p \wedge (p \rightarrow q)) \rightarrow q$,   by 3 and DT.

Remark 4.4.3. If any of $\wedge$, $\vee$ and $\rightarrow$ is considered definable in terms of the others, the corresponding axioms become redundant, as they can be shown to be derivable from the others. However, the presence of the implication $\rightarrow$ is vital for making good sense of the derivations in axiomatic systems, so throughout this section we will assume it always present in the language.

Recall the notion of deductive consistency. In particular, we say that a set of PL formulae Γ is AxSys_{PL}-inconsistent if $\Gamma \vdash_{\text{AxSys}_{\text{PL}}} \bot$; otherwise Γ is AxSys_{PL}-consistent.

The following proposition gives some useful generic characterisations of consistency that apply in particular to AxSys_{PL}. The proofs are left as exercises. They can be found easily in the logic literature, too.

Proposition 4.4.4. The following are equivalent for any set of PL formulae Γ.

(I) Γ is AxSys_{PL}-inconsistent.
(II) $\Gamma \vdash_{\text{AxSys}_{\text{PL}}} \varphi$ for every PL formula φ.
(III) There is a formula φ such that $\Gamma \vdash_{\text{AxSys}_{\text{PL}}} \varphi$ and $\Gamma \vdash_{\text{AxSys}_{\text{PL}}} \neg\varphi$.
(IV) There are formulae $\varphi_1, \dots, \varphi_n \in \Gamma$ such that $\vdash_{\text{AxSys}_{\text{PL}}} \neg(\varphi_1 \wedge \cdots \wedge \varphi_n)$. ∎

Even though not very suitable for practical derivations, the axiomatic system AxSys_{PL} adequately captures the concept of logical consequence, and in particular, validity, in PL.

Theorem 4.4.5. The axiomatic system AxSys_{PL} is sound and complete, i.e.:

$$\varphi_1, \dots, \varphi_n \vdash_{\text{AxSys}_{\text{PL}}} \psi \text{ if and only if } \varphi_1, \dots, \varphi_n \models \psi.$$

In particular, $\vdash_{\text{AxSys}_{\text{PL}}} \psi$ if and only if ψ is a tautology. ∎

This theorem can be equivalently reformulated in terms of satisfiability and consistency:

Theorem 4.4.6. Any set of formulae Γ of PL is satisfiable if and only if it is AxSys_{PL}-consistent. ∎

We leave the proof that the two formulations of the soundness and completeness theorem are equivalent, i.e. each implies the other, as an exercise.

To prove the soundness of AxSys_{PL} it suffices to check that all axioms of AxSys_{PL} are tautologies. Therefore, since the rule Modus Ponens preserves validity, AxSys_{PL} can only derive tautologies when using axioms as premises. By the same argument, AxSys_{PL} can only derive valid logical consequences.

The proof of completeness is more involved and uses the method, going back to Henkin, of building a satisfying model out of a maximal consistent set containing the given consistent set of formulae Γ. All axiomatic systems for temporal logics presented further will extend AxSys_{PL} with additional axioms and rules of inference. The proof of completeness for AxSys_{PL} will be subsumed by the proof of completeness for the axiomatic system for BML, outlined in Chapter 5.

5

Basic Modal Logics

This chapter is a brief introduction to the basic multimodal logic BML, interpreted as the simplest natural temporal logic for reasoning about transition systems. Indeed, transition systems are nothing but Kripke frames and interpreted transition systems are simply Kripke models, so a standard Kripke semantics is provided for a multimodal language with modal operators $\Box_a$ and $\Diamond_a$, associated with each transition relation R_a. These bear natural meaning in interpreted transition systems, stating what *must* be true in all /respectively, what *may* be true at some/ R_a-successors of the current state. In order to emphasise these readings of the modal operators, we will use a notation that is unusual for modal logic, but is more suitable in the context of temporal logics: AX_a (read as *for all paths starting from the current state, at the next state*) and EX_a (*for some path starting from the current state, at the next state*). Thus, BML is the minimal natural logical language to specify *local properties* of transition systems.

Since the chapter is written from the primary perspective of transition systems, rather than from modal logic perspective, we have put an emphasis on certain topics such as expressiveness, bisimulation, model checking, the finite model property and deciding satisfiability, while other fundamental topics in modal logic – such as deductive systems and proof theory, model theory, correspondence theory, algebraic semantics and duality theory – are almost left untouched here. Of all deductive systems developed for modal logics we only mention the axiomatic system for BML here and present a version of the tableau-based method for it in Chapter 13; for the rest we only provide basic references in the bibliographic notes.

This chapter can also be viewed as a stepping stone towards the more expressive and interesting temporal logics that are presented further.

Structure of this chapter. Section 5.1 presents the syntax and semantics for BML. The relational translation from BML into first-order logic (FO) is also presented emphasising the fact that BML can be viewed as a fragment of classical first-order predicate logic. Section 5.2 presents some techniques for renaming and transformation of BML formulae to equisatisfiable ones in certain normal form of modal depth two. Section 5.3 relates modal and bisimulation equivalence of transition systems and bisimulation invariance of BML formulae (van Benthem's Characterisation Theorem) and introduces characteristic formulae for finite interpreted transition system under a fixed depth. Section 5.4.3 is dedicated to a game-based approach to solve the model-checking problem for BML. Section 5.5.1 briefly presents the standard filtration method for modal logic, consisting of building small finite models by collapsing states satisfying the same formulae from a given finite set of formulae. In particular, we establish the finite model property for BML. Section 5.5.2 presents an algorithmic solution to solve the satisfiability problem for BML. Section 5.6 introduces the basic tense logic BTL extending BML by adding past-time operators. We explain how the basic theory of BML can easily be extended to BTL. Section 5.7 introduces an axiomatic system for BML, illustrates it with some derivations, outlines a proof of the completeness theorem for it and extends it to an axiomatic system for BTL. These last two sections are more sketchy and most of the proofs are left to the reader.

5.1 The Basic Modal Logic BML

5.1.1 Syntax and Semantics

With every type $\tau = (Act, \text{PROP})$ of interpreted transition systems we associate a multimodal language BML_τ with a set of atomic propositions PROP and a family of modal operators $(\text{EX}_a)_{a \in Act}$, one for each transition label $a \in Act$. So the language BML_τ has the **signature** $(\mathcal{O}_\tau, \text{PROP})$ with $\mathcal{O}_\tau = \{\text{EX}_a \mid a \in Act\}$ (see Section 4.1).

The inductive definition of formulae of BML_τ is:

$$\varphi := p \mid \bot \mid \neg\varphi \mid (\varphi \wedge \varphi) \mid \text{EX}_a\varphi$$

where $p \in \text{PROP}$ and $a \in Act$. The other logical connectives: $\top, \rightarrow, \vee, \leftrightarrow$ are defined as usual; besides, the *dual* of each modal operator EX_a is AX_a, defined as $\text{AX}_a\varphi := \neg\text{EX}_a\neg\varphi$. Parentheses will often be omitted, when a danger of ambiguity does not arise.

The fragment of the logic BML_τ consisting only of constant formulae is known as **Hennessy–Milner logic** here denoted as HML_τ. When the type τ is assumed fixed or arbitrary, we will write just BML instead of BML_τ.

The modal depth of a formula φ, written $mdeg(\varphi)$, follows developments from Chapter 4. Moreover, **BML^n** comprises all formulae of BML with modal depth at most n.

The semantics of BML_τ is the standard possible-worlds semantics in interpreted transition systems. The basic semantical notion of **truth of a formula at a state s of an interpreted transition system** $\mathcal{T} = (S, \{\xrightarrow{a}\}_{a \in Act}, L)$ is defined inductively as follows.

$$\mathcal{T}, s \not\models \bot$$
$$\mathcal{T}, s \models p \qquad \text{iff} \quad p \in L(s)$$
$$\mathcal{T}, s \models \neg\varphi \qquad \text{iff} \quad \mathcal{T}, s \not\models \varphi$$
$$\mathcal{T}, s \models \varphi \wedge \psi \qquad \text{iff} \quad \mathcal{T}, s \models \varphi \text{ and } \mathcal{T}, s \models \psi$$
$$\mathcal{T}, s \models \text{EX}_a\varphi \qquad \text{iff} \quad \mathcal{T}, s' \models \varphi \text{ for some } s' \in S \text{ such that } s \xrightarrow{a} s'.$$

The derived truth definition of AX_a becomes the following.

$$\mathcal{T}, s \models \text{AX}_a\varphi \quad \text{iff} \quad \mathcal{T}, s' \models \varphi \text{ for every } s' \in S \text{ such that } s \xrightarrow{a} s'.$$

Example 5.1.1. Consider the transition system $\mathcal{T}$ in Figure 5.1. The following hold.

- $\mathcal{T}, s_0 \models p \wedge \neg q \wedge \text{EX}_a(\neg p \wedge \neg r) \wedge \text{EX}_a(p \wedge r) \wedge \text{AX}_a\neg q \wedge \text{AX}_b\bot$.
- $\mathcal{T}, s_1 \models \neg p \wedge \neg q \wedge \neg r \wedge \text{AX}_b(q \wedge \text{EX}_a(p \wedge r \wedge \text{EX}_b\top))$.
- $\mathcal{T}, s_3 \models \text{AX}_a\bot \wedge \text{AX}_b p \wedge \neg\text{EX}_b p$.
- $\mathcal{T}, s_4 \models \neg(p \wedge q) \wedge \text{EX}_b(r \wedge \text{AX}_a\bot \wedge \text{EX}_c\text{EX}_a\neg\text{AX}_b\text{EX}_b\neg(q \wedge \neg q))$.

We leave to the reader to find the unique state in which the formula $\psi = (\neg\text{AX}_a p \vee \neg\text{AX}_b q) \wedge \neg\text{AX}_b\neg\text{AX}_c\neg\text{AX}_b\text{EX}_a\top$ is true.

The semantic definitions of satisfiability, validity in a model, logical validity, logical implication and any related notions are naturally taken from Section 4.2 but instantiated to the logic BML, since we have defined the notions of BML formulae, the BML models (transition systems) and the satisfaction relation ($\models$).

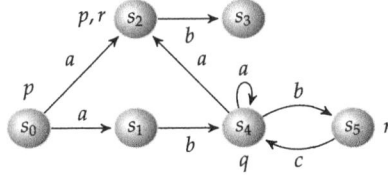

Figure 5.1 A transition system.

For instance, we have $\{EX_a(p \wedge q), AX_a(\neg p \vee r)\} \models EX_a(r \wedge q)$, while $\neg EX_a(p \vee q) \equiv AX_a \neg p \wedge AX_a \neg q$. Satisfiability, validity and logical consequence in BML are related as in Lemma 4.1.6.

The extension of a formula in a transition system, written $[\![\varphi]\!]^T$ (see Chapter 4), can be viewed as the extensional meaning of the formula in the transition system. The next result states that, thanks to the inductive definition of the satisfaction relation $\models$, the extension of a formula can be computed inductively from the extensions of its subformulae, if any. Conversely, the semantics for BML can be defined in terms of extensions instead of using the satisfaction relation.

Lemma 5.1.2. The **extension** of a formula $[\![\varphi]\!]^T$ can be computed inductively on the construction of φ:

- $[\![\bot]\!]^T = \emptyset$,
- $[\![p]\!]^T = \{s \mid p \in L(s)\}$,
- $[\![\neg\psi]\!]^T = S \setminus [\![\psi]\!]^T$,
- $[\![\psi_1 \wedge \psi_2]\!]^T = [\![\psi_1]\!]^T \cap [\![\psi_2]\!]^T$,
- $[\![EX_a\psi]\!]^T = \text{pre}(a, [\![\psi]\!]^T) = \{s \in S \mid \{s' \in S : s \xrightarrow{a} s'\} \cap [\![\psi]\!]^T \neq \emptyset\}$. ∎

The proof of Lemma 5.1.2 is left as Exercise 5.7.

The logical decision problems for BML such as satisfiability, validity, local model checking and global model checking are defined along the lines of Section 4.2. We recall that when a transition system T is finite, its size is defined as

$$|T| := \text{card}(S) + \sum_{a \in Act} \text{card}(\xrightarrow{a}) + \sum_{s \in S} \text{card}(L(s)).$$

Example 5.1.3. Consider the transition system T in Figure 5.2.

- $T, s_1 \models AX(\neg\texttt{ready} \rightarrow \texttt{safe})$, because the only successor states of s_1 in which 'ready' is not true are s_2 and s_4, and they both satisfy 'safe'. Therefore, the formula $AX(\neg\texttt{ready} \rightarrow \texttt{safe})$ is obviously satisfiable in T.
- $[\![EX\texttt{crash}]\!]^T = \{s_3, s_5\}$ because these are all states which have a successor satisfying 'crash'.
- $[\![EXEX\texttt{crash}]\!]^T = \{s_2, s_3, s_4, s_5\}$ because these are all states which have a successor in $[\![EX\texttt{crash}]\!]^T$. (Note the recursive argument here.)

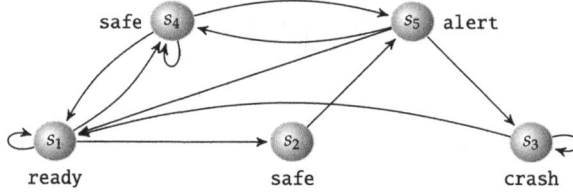

Figure 5.2 Another transition system.

- $\llbracket \neg \mathsf{ready} \leftrightarrow \mathsf{EXEX}\mathsf{crash} \rrbracket^{\mathcal{T}} = \{s_1, s_2, s_3, s_4, s_5\}$, because $\{s_2, s_3, s_4, s_5\}$ are precisely the states in which 'ready' is not true.
- Hence, $\mathcal{T} \models \neg\mathsf{ready} \leftrightarrow \mathsf{EXEX}\mathsf{crash}$.
  Therefore, the formula $\neg\mathsf{ready} \wedge \mathsf{AXAX}\neg\mathsf{crash}$ is not satisfiable in $\mathcal{T}$.
- On the other hand, $\mathcal{T}, s_3 \not\models \mathsf{AX}(\neg\mathsf{alert} \to \neg\mathsf{EX}\,\mathsf{crash})$, i.e.
  $\mathcal{T} \not\models \mathsf{AX}(\neg\mathsf{alert} \to \neg\mathsf{EX}\,\mathsf{crash})$. Hence, $\mathsf{EX}(\neg\mathsf{alert} \wedge \mathsf{EX}\,\mathsf{crash})$ is satisfiable in $\mathcal{T}$.

5.1.2 The Standard Translation into Classical Logic

With every type $\tau = (Act, \mathrm{PROP})$ of interpreted transition systems, where $\mathrm{PROP} = \{p_0, p_1, \ldots\}$, we associate a relational first-order language FO_τ having a family of unary predicates $\{P_i\}_{p_i \in \mathrm{PROP}}$, a family of binary predicates $\{R_a\}_{a \in Act}$ and a set of first-order variables $\mathrm{VAR} = \{x_0, x_1, \ldots\}$. We regard the models of FO_τ as interpreted transition systems in a natural sense: the interpretations of the binary predicates are the transition relations, and the interpretations of the unary predicates define a valuation: $V(p_i) := P_i$, and therefore, a state description function $L(s) := \{ p_i \mid s \in P_i \}$. Note that we use the same notation for the transition relations in interpreted transition systems and for the binary predicates in the associated first-order structure; this should cause no confusion.

Thus, we now have two notions of truth and validity in an interpreted transition system: the modal and the first-order one. Wherever necessary, we will highlight the distinction by writing $\models_{\mathrm{FO}}$ to explicitly refer to first-order semantics.

In fact, truth and validity of a BML-formula in an interpreted transition system *are first-order notions*, in the following sense. The formulae of BML_τ are translated into FO_τ by means of the following **standard translation**, parameterised with the variables from VAR. The idea behind the translation is to express the existential quantification EX_a in the target first-order language, by faithfully mimicking the semantics for BML.

$$\mathrm{ST}(p_i, x_j) := P_i(x_j) \text{ for every } p_i \in \mathrm{PROP}$$
$$\mathrm{ST}(\bot, x_j) := \bot$$
$$\mathrm{ST}(\neg\varphi, x_j) := \neg\mathrm{ST}(\varphi, x_j)$$
$$\mathrm{ST}(\varphi_1 \wedge \varphi_2, x_j) := \mathrm{ST}(\varphi_1, x_j) \wedge \mathrm{ST}(\varphi_2, x_j)$$
$$\mathrm{ST}(\mathsf{EX}_a\varphi, x_j) := \exists y(R_a(x_j, y) \wedge \mathrm{ST}(\varphi, y)),$$

where y is the first variable not occurring in $\mathrm{ST}(\varphi, x_j)$. The respective clause for AX_a can now be derived as

$$\mathrm{ST}(\mathsf{AX}_a\varphi, x_j) \ := \ \forall y(R_a(x_j, y) \rightarrow \mathrm{ST}(\varphi, y)),$$

where y is chosen as earlier. Note that x_j is the only free variable in $\mathrm{ST}(\varphi, x_j)$. Furthermore, it suffices to use in the standard translation only *two variables*, x_0 and x_1, as free or bound, quantified over in an alternating fashion, by amending the choice of y in the clause for $\mathrm{ST}(\mathsf{EX}_a\varphi, x_j)$ as follows: $y := x_{1-j}$. This yields a translation of BML_τ into the *two-variable fragment* FO2 of the respective first-order language. We have, for instance:

$$\mathrm{ST}(\mathsf{EX}_a\mathsf{EX}_b p_1, x_0) = \exists x_1 (R_a(x_0, x_1) \wedge \exists x_0(R_b(x_1, x_0) \wedge P_1(x_0))).$$

We also note that the standard translation of any modal formula falls into the **guarded fragment** of first-order logic. This standard translation is semantically faithful in the following sense.

Lemma 5.1.4. For every rooted interpreted transition system $(\mathcal{T}, s)$ and $\varphi \in \mathrm{BML}$: $\mathcal{T}, s \models \varphi$ iff $\mathcal{T} \models_{\mathrm{FO}} \mathrm{ST}(\varphi, x_0)[x_0 := s]$. ∎

Proof. We will provide the proof for the version of the standard translation ST that appropriately recycles the variables x_0 and x_1. We show that for all $i \in \{0, 1\}$, for all formulae ψ and for every interpreted transition system $\mathcal{T} = (S, \{\xrightarrow{a}\}_{a \in Act}, L)$, also viewed as the first-order structure $\mathcal{T} = (S, (R_a)_{a \in Act}, (P_i)_{p_i \in \mathrm{PROP}})$, and for every $s \in S$, we have

$$\mathcal{T}, s \models \psi \text{ iff } \mathcal{T} \models_{\mathrm{FO}} \mathrm{ST}(\psi, x_i)[x_i := s].$$

The proof is by structural induction. The base case for $\bot$ and the cases in the induction steps for the Boolean connectives are straightforward.

Case $\psi = p_j$. We have $\mathcal{T}, s \models p_j$ iff $p_j \in L(s)$ iff $s \in P_j$ iff $\mathcal{T} \models_{\mathrm{FO}} P_j(x_i)[x_i := s]$ iff $\mathcal{T} \models_{\mathrm{FO}} \mathrm{ST}(\psi, x_i)[x_i := s]$.

Case $\psi = \mathsf{EX}_a\psi'$. The following are equivalent:

- $\mathcal{T}, s \models \psi$,
- $\mathcal{T}, s' \models \psi'$ for some $s' \in S$ such that $s \xrightarrow{a} s'$ (by definition of $\models$),
- $\mathcal{T}, s' \models \psi'$ for some $s' \in S$ such that $R_a(s, s')$ (by definition of R_a),
- $\mathcal{T} \models_{\mathrm{FO}} \mathrm{ST}(\psi', x_{1-i})[x_{1-i} := s']$ for some $s' \in S$ such that $R_a(s, s')$ (by the induction hypothesis),
- $\mathcal{T} \models_{\mathrm{FO}} \exists x_{1-i}(R_a(x_i, x_{1-i}) \wedge \mathrm{ST}(\psi', x_{1-i}))[x_i := s]$ (by definition of $\models_{\mathrm{FO}}$),
- $\mathcal{T} \models_{\mathrm{FO}} \mathrm{ST}(\psi, x_i)[x_i := s]$ (by definition of ST). □

Thus, with a slight abuse of terminology, we can say that every formula φ of BML is logically equivalent to its standard translation $\mathrm{ST}(\varphi, x)$. Then, a natural question arises: *which formulae $\gamma(x)$ of FO_τ are logically equivalent, in the same sense, to modal formulae from BML?* We will address that question in Section 5.3.

We note that the translation ST can easily be adapted to variants of BML for which transition relations satisfy first-order properties such as reflexivity, totality, symmetry, or transitivity. In order to mechanise the reasoning for modal logics, the translation is helpful because a unique theorem-prover for first-order logic suffices and the principle is flexible enough to be adapted to numerous basic modal logics. However, there is also an obvious drawback: validity and logical consequence in first-order logic is undecidable. This problem can be eluded by noting that the translation of modal formulae falls into decidable fragments of FO such as the guarded fragment or the two-variable fragment. Still, using the standard translation is not always possible, for instance when the required properties on transition relations are not first-order definable, e.g. well-foundedness, or when transitive closure relations are required.

5.1.3 Specifying Local Properties

Local properties – that refer to some or all successors of the current state – are naturally expressed in BML, for instance:

- 'The system may enable the process pr at the next state' is expressed by

$$\text{EX enabled}(pr).$$

- 'The process pr will be enabled at the next state, no matter how the system evolves' is expressed by

$$\text{AX enabled}(pr).$$

- In order to directly express the property 'If the process pr_1 is currently enabled, the scheduler must have disabled the process pr_2 at the previous state' one needs past modal operators, referring to the predecessors of the current state. Still, one can specify this property in BML, too, by first realising that it is supposed to hold at *every* state, and then changing the temporal perspective and rephrasing it to '(At any state) if the process pr_2 is currently not disabled, the scheduler may not enable the process pr_1 at the next state':

$$\neg\text{disabled}(pr_2) \rightarrow \text{AX}\neg\text{enabled}(pr_1).$$

- Likewise, 'If the light was red at the previous state and is orange now, it must turn green at the next state' can be rephrased and formally specified in BML as follows:

$$\text{red} \rightarrow \text{AX}(\text{orange} \rightarrow \text{AXgreen}).$$

Note that these formal specifications circumvent the restricted expressiveness of the language, by suitably repositioning the state of reference. When more expressive modal operators are added further on this will no longer be necessary and usually the important properties can be stated already at the initial state of the interpreted transition system.

5.2 Renaming and Normal Forms

We provide basic definitions related to the renaming of subformulae in a given formula. Usually, occurrences of a subformula are substituted by occurrences of a (new) atomic proposition. The satisfiability status of the formula can be preserved if the renaming is accompanied with the satisfaction of an additional subformula that logically relates the new atomic proposition and the substituted subformula. Renaming of subformulae is quite useful to transform formulae, for instance to obtain a simplified form in order to solve logical decision problems such as satisfiability or validity more easily. To formally justify the relevance of renamings that are translations at the syntactic level, renamings at the semantical level (i.e. updates of the labelling map in transition systems) are also presented below. A few propositions shall relate these two types of renaming (see for example Lemma 5.2.4).

5.2.1 The Renaming Technique

We start with the notion of **renaming** at the semantical level. To do so, first, we formally define what it means for two transition systems to differ by the interpretation of at most one atomic proposition.

Definition 5.2.1. Let p be an atomic proposition and, $\mathcal{T}_1 = (S_1, R_1, L_1)$ and $\mathcal{T}_2 = (S_2, R_2, L_2)$ be two transition systems. $\mathcal{T}_1$ and $\mathcal{T}_2$ are p-**variants** iff they only differ by the interpretation of the atomic proposition p, i.e. $(S_1, R_1) = (S_2, R_2)$ and for all $s \in S_1$, we have $L_1(s) \setminus \{p\} = L_2(s) \setminus \{p\}$. $\qquad\qquad\nabla$

A similar notion is introduced in Section 6.7.2 (for linear transition systems) for a notion of invariants that strictly involve more than one atomic proposition. Let us provide some more notation.

Definition 5.2.2. Given a transition system $\mathcal{T} = (S, R, L)$, an atomic proposition p and a formula ψ, we write $\mathcal{T}[p \leftarrow \psi]$ to denote the unique p-variant of $\mathcal{T}$ (with the labelling map L') such that for all $s \in S$, we have

$$L'(s) := (L(s) \setminus \{p\}) \cup \begin{cases} \emptyset, & \text{if } \mathcal{T}, s \not\models \psi \\ \{p\}, & \text{otherwise.} \end{cases}$$

So the interpretation of the atomic proposition p in the transition system $\mathcal{T}[p \leftarrow \psi]$ is uniquely determined by the satisfaction of ψ in $\mathcal{T}$. $\qquad\qquad\nabla$

Let φ, ψ, χ be BML formulae. Recall that $\varphi[\psi/\chi]$ is the result of uniform simultaneous substitution of all occurrences (if any) of χ as a subformula of φ by ψ.

Now we introduce a few more definitions about formulae. Given a formula φ and $n \in \mathbb{N}$, we define the formula $\mathsf{AX}^{(n)}\varphi$ that states that φ holds at all states reachable from the current state with a path of length at most n. In order to define $\mathsf{AX}^{(n)}\varphi$, it is sufficient to take the conjunction of the cases when φ holds at the current state and at all states at distance $1, \ldots, n$:

$$\mathsf{AX}^{(n)}\varphi := \varphi \wedge \mathsf{AX}\varphi \wedge \cdots \wedge \mathsf{AX}^n\varphi.$$

The formula $\mathsf{AX}^{(n)}\varphi$ contains several occurrences of the formula φ. However, since the size of formulae is measured by the number of subformulae, the size of $\mathsf{AX}^{(n)}\varphi$ is in $\mathcal{O}(|\varphi| + n)$. Finally, the formula $\varphi[\psi/\chi]^{(n)}$ defined further performs a uniform substitution with the addition of a conjunct that states that two subformulae are equivalent for all states reachable from the current state with a path of length at most n:

$$\varphi[\psi/\chi]^{(n)} := \mathsf{AX}^{(n)}(\psi \leftrightarrow \chi) \wedge \varphi[\psi/\chi].$$

Lemma 5.2.3 relates the syntactic operation of substituting an atomic proposition p by a formula ψ and the semantical operation of interpreting p by the extension of ψ.

Lemma 5.2.3. Let χ, ψ be BML formulae and p be an atomic proposition. Then for every transition system $\mathcal{T}$ we have $[\![\chi[\psi/p]]\!]^{\mathcal{T}} = [\![\chi]\!]^{\mathcal{T}[p \leftarrow \psi]}$. ∎

The proof is by easy structural induction on χ and it is left as Exercise 5.7. Similarly, Lemma 5.2.4 states that a subformula in a formula φ can be substituted by an atomic proposition p without changing its extension (i.e. its interpretation), as soon as in the interpreted transition system the newly introduced atomic proposition is itself interpreted as the extension of the substituted subformula.

Lemma 5.2.4. Let φ, ψ be BML formulae and p be an atomic proposition not occurring in φ. Then for every ITS $\mathcal{T}$ we have $[\![\varphi]\!]^{\mathcal{T}} = [\![\varphi[p/\psi]]\!]^{\mathcal{T}[p \leftarrow \psi]}$. ∎

Lemma 5.2.4 immediately follows from Lemma 5.2.3 by taking $\chi = \varphi[p/\psi]$ and noting that $(\varphi[p/\psi])[\psi/p] = \varphi$.

Finally, Lemma 5.2.5 states that a subformula ψ can be substituted by another formula χ in a given formula φ without changing its satisfaction status at a state s, as soon as ψ and χ agree on all states reachable from s in at most n steps, where n is the modal depth of φ. Indeed, a formula of BML with modal depth n, holding at a state s, cannot impose constraints on the states that are not reachable from s in at most n steps, see Section 5.3.1.

Lemma 5.2.5. Let φ, ψ, χ be BML formulae, $n \in \mathbb{N}$ such that $mdeg(\varphi) \leq n$ and p be an atomic proposition. Then

$$\models \mathsf{AX}^{(n)}(\psi \leftrightarrow \chi) \rightarrow (\varphi[\psi/p] \leftrightarrow \varphi[\chi/p]).$$

Proof. The proof is by induction on n, using in the inductive step the soundness of the Necessitation rule, $\models \varphi_1$ implies $\models \mathsf{AX}\varphi_1$, and the validity of the scheme $\mathsf{AX}(\varphi_1 \rightarrow \varphi_2) \rightarrow (\mathsf{AX}\varphi_1 \rightarrow \mathsf{AX}\varphi_2)$. We leave the details as Exercise 5.7. □

Lemma 5.2.6. Let φ, ψ be BML formulae and p be an atomic proposition not occurring in φ and ψ. Then for any $n \geq mdeg(\varphi)$, an interpreted transition system $\mathcal{T}$, and a state $s \in \mathcal{T}$:

$$\mathcal{T}, s \models \varphi \quad \text{iff} \quad \mathcal{T}', s \models \varphi[p/\psi]^{(n)}$$

for some p-variant $\mathcal{T}'$ of $\mathcal{T}$. ∎

Proof. If $\mathcal{T}, s \models \varphi$ then $\mathcal{T}[p \leftarrow \psi], s \models \varphi[\psi/p]$, by Lemma 5.2.4. Moreover, $\mathcal{T}[p \leftarrow \psi] \models p \leftrightarrow \psi$ (because p does not occur in ψ), hence $\mathcal{T}[p \leftarrow \psi], s \models AX^{(m)}(p \leftrightarrow \psi)$ for every m. Therefore $\mathcal{T}[p \leftarrow \psi], s \models \varphi[\psi/p]^{(n)}$.

Conversely, let $\mathcal{T}', s \models \varphi[p/\psi]^{(n)}$ for some p-variant $\mathcal{T}'$ of $\mathcal{T}$.

Then $\mathcal{T}', s \models AX^{(n)}(p \leftrightarrow \psi)$. Note that $mdeg(\varphi[p/\psi]) \leq mdeg(\varphi) \leq n$. Then, by Lemma 5.2.5, $\mathcal{T}', s \models (\varphi[p/\psi])[\psi/p] \leftrightarrow (\varphi[p/\psi])[p/p]$, that is, $\mathcal{T}', s \models \varphi \leftrightarrow \varphi[p/\psi]$. Therefore, $\mathcal{T}', s \models \varphi$, hence $\mathcal{T}, s \models \varphi$ because p does not occur in φ. $\qquad\square$

5.2.2 Flat Normal Form

Using repeated renaming, all subformulae of a given BML formula can subsequently be 'extracted' and replaced by new atomic propositions, thus transforming the formula into an equivalent one in a special, 'flat' normal form. It can be viewed as an analogue of the Scott normal form in classical predicate logic.

We call BML formulae containing exactly one logical connective **simple**. Note that every BML formula which is not an atomic proposition or a logical constant among $\top$ or $\perp$ contains at least one simple subformula. The first occurrence (from left to right) of a simple subformula in a formula φ will be called **the first simple subformula of φ**.

With every BML formula φ and a simple BML formula χ we associate an atomic proposition $p_{\varphi,\chi}$ which does not occur in φ.

Let us define the map $fiat(\cdot)$ that transforms a formula into a flat one by using substitutions and equivalences. The definition is by structural induction and for every atomic proposition p, we have $fiat(p) := p$. Now let φ be a BML formula of modal depth $n \geq 0$ and let χ be the first simple subformula of φ. We then recursively define

$$fiat(\varphi) := AX^{(n)}(p_{\varphi,\chi} \leftrightarrow \chi) \wedge fiat(\varphi[p_{\varphi,\chi}/\chi]).$$

Note that $\varphi[p_{\varphi,\chi}/\chi]$ has one occurrence of a logical connective less than φ and this guarantees well-foundedness of the recursive definition.

Example 5.2.7. Let $\varphi = \neg AX(EXAX\,p_0 \vee \neg AX\,p_0)$. For simplicity of the notation, let us assume that $PROP = \{p_0, p_1, \ldots\}$.

$$
\begin{aligned}
fiat(\varphi) &= AX^{(3)}(p_1 \leftrightarrow AX\,p_0) \wedge fiat(\neg AX(EX\,p_1 \vee \neg p_1)) \\
&= AX^{(3)}(p_1 \leftrightarrow AX\,p_0) \wedge AX^{(2)}(p_2 \leftrightarrow EX\,p_1) \wedge fiat(\neg AX(p_2 \vee \neg p_1)) \\
&= AX^{(3)}(p_1 \leftrightarrow AX\,p_0) \wedge AX^{(2)}(p_2 \leftrightarrow EX\,p_1) \wedge AX^{(1)}(p_3 \leftrightarrow \neg p_1) \wedge \\
&\quad fiat(\neg AX(p_2 \vee p_3)) \\
&= AX^{(3)}(p_1 \leftrightarrow AX\,p_0) \wedge AX^{(2)}(p_2 \leftrightarrow EX\,p_1) \wedge AX^{(1)}(p_3 \leftrightarrow \neg p_1) \wedge \\
&\quad AX^{(1)}(p_4 \leftrightarrow (p_2 \vee p_3)) \wedge fiat(\neg AX\,p_4) \\
&= AX^{(3)}(p_1 \leftrightarrow AX\,p_0) \wedge AX^{(2)}(p_2 \leftrightarrow EX\,p_1) \wedge AX^{(1)}(p_3 \leftrightarrow \neg p_1) \wedge \\
&\quad AX^{(1)}(p_4 \leftrightarrow (p_2 \vee p_3)) \wedge AX^{(0)}(p_5 \leftrightarrow AX\,p_4) \wedge fiat(\neg p_5) \\
&= AX^{(3)}(p_1 \leftrightarrow AX\,p_0) \wedge AX^{(2)}(p_2 \leftrightarrow EX\,p_1) \wedge AX^{(1)}(p_3 \leftrightarrow \neg p_1) \wedge \\
&\quad AX^{(1)}(p_4 \leftrightarrow (p_2 \vee p_3)) \wedge AX^{(0)}(p_5 \leftrightarrow AX\,p_4) \wedge \\
&\quad AX^{(0)}(p_6 \leftrightarrow \neg p_5) \wedge fiat(p_6) \\
&= AX^{(3)}(p_1 \leftrightarrow AX\,p_0) \wedge AX^{(2)}(p_2 \leftrightarrow EX\,p_1) \wedge AX^{(1)}(p_3 \leftrightarrow \neg p_1) \wedge \\
&\quad AX^{(1)}(p_4 \leftrightarrow (p_2 \vee p_3)) \wedge (p_5 \leftrightarrow AX\,p_4) \wedge (p_6 \leftrightarrow \neg p_5) \wedge p_6.
\end{aligned}
$$

Lemma 5.2.8. Let φ be any BML formula. Then for any interpreted transition system $\mathcal{T} = (S, R, L)$ and a state $s \in S$:

$$\mathcal{T}, s \models \varphi \quad \text{iff} \quad \mathcal{T}', s \models \text{fiat}(\varphi)$$

for some ITS $\mathcal{T}'$, such that $\mathcal{T}$ and $\mathcal{T}'$ coincide on all atomic propositions occurring in φ and $\mathcal{T}'$ is also based on the transition system (S, R).   ■

The ITS $\mathcal{T}'$ is defined and the claim is proved by simultaneous induction on the number of logical connectives in φ, using Lemma 5.2.6. The proof is left as Exercise 5.7.

The flat normal forms can be used, for instance, when constructing automata associated with BML formulae in a well-structured way, see Chapter 14. For logics such as TLR, CTL or CTL* defined in Chapter 7, propagating equivalences between subformulae can be done in a more simple way, thanks to the presence of the temporal operator of reachability EF that can specify constraints on any state reachable by any finite path.

5.3 Modal and Bisimulation Equivalence

In this section we present the fundamental relationship between bisimulation equivalence and modal equivalence of interpreted transition systems and we show that BML formulae can be used to characterise interpreted transition systems up to bisimulation equivalence, while invariance under bisimulation equivalence is characteristic for those properties of interpreted transition systems which are definable by formulae of BML.

All results in this section about bisimulation invariance of BML-formulae in interpreted transition systems apply likewise to bisimulation invariance of formulae of Hennessy–Milner logic HML_τ in plain (noninterpreted) transition systems.

5.3.1 Modal Equivalence

The following definition introduces the notion of BML-equivalence between two rooted ITS.

Definition 5.3.1. Two rooted interpreted transition systems $(\mathcal{T}_1, s_1)$ and $(\mathcal{T}_2, s_2)$ are **BML-equivalent** denoted $(\mathcal{T}_1, s_1) \equiv_{\text{BML}} (\mathcal{T}_2, s_2)$, if they satisfy the same BML-formulae. Moreover, $(\mathcal{T}_1, s_1)$ and $(\mathcal{T}_2, s_2)$ are **BML^n-equivalent**, denoted $(\mathcal{T}_1, s_1) \equiv_{\text{BML}}^n (\mathcal{T}_2, s_2)$, if they satisfy the same BML-formulae of modal depth up to n.   ▽

The following theorem says that two rooted interpreted transition systems that are n-bisimilar satisfy exactly the same modal formulae of modal depth at most n.

Theorem 5.3.2 (Bounded bisimulation invariance). If $(\mathcal{T}_1, s_1)$ and $(\mathcal{T}_2, s_2)$ are rooted interpreted transition systems and $n \in \mathbb{N}$ is such that $(\mathcal{T}_1, s_1) \leftrightarroweq_n (\mathcal{T}_2, s_2)$, then $(\mathcal{T}_1, s_1) \equiv_{\text{BML}}^n (\mathcal{T}_2, s_2)$.   ■

Proof. We will use the characterisation in Theorem 3.4.3 of n-bisimulations by means of n-round bisimulation games to prove the contraposition of the claim: if $\mathcal{T}_1, s_1 \models \varphi$ and $\mathcal{T}_2, s_2 \models \neg \varphi$ for some $\varphi \in \mathrm{BML}^n$, then Player **I** has a winning strategy in the n-round game on $(\mathcal{T}_1, s_1; \mathcal{T}_2, s_2)$, and therefore $(\mathcal{T}_1, s_1) \not\rightleftarrows_n (\mathcal{T}_2, s_2)$. This is shown by induction on the modal depth of the formula φ. If $mdeg(\varphi) = 0$, a distinction in BML^0 means violated atomic correspondence – a configuration in which Player **II** has lost.

For the induction step, assume that $(\mathcal{T}_1, s_1)$ is distinguished from $(\mathcal{T}_2, s_2)$ by a formula $\varphi \in \mathrm{BML}^{n+1}$. Propositional connectives in φ can be preprocessed, so that without loss of generality φ can be assumed of the form $\mathsf{EX}\psi$ for some $\psi \in \mathrm{BML}^n$. Suppose then that for instance $\mathcal{T}_2, s_2 \models \neg\varphi$, while $\mathcal{T}_1, s_1 \models \varphi$. Suppose in that case Player **I** moves the pebble in $\mathcal{T}_1$ from s_1 to some r_1, where $\mathcal{T}_1, s_1 \models \psi$. As $\mathcal{T}_2, s_2 \models \neg\mathsf{EX}\psi$, any available response for Player **II** can only lead to a configuration $(\mathcal{T}_1, r_1; \mathcal{T}_2, r_2)$ in which $(\mathcal{T}_1, r_1)$ and $(\mathcal{T}_2, r_2)$ are distinguished by $\psi \in \mathrm{BML}^n$. Therefore, by the inductive hypothesis, Player **I** has a winning strategy for the remaining n rounds of the game. $\qquad\square$

Corollary 5.3.3 (Bisimulation invariance). The formulae of BML are invariant under bisimulations: if $(\mathcal{T}_1, s_1)$ and $(\mathcal{T}_2, s_2)$ are rooted interpreted transition systems, such that $(\mathcal{T}_1, s_1) \rightleftarrows (\mathcal{T}_2, s_2)$, then $(\mathcal{T}_1, s_1) \equiv_{\mathrm{BML}} (\mathcal{T}_2, s_2)$. $\qquad\blacksquare$

In particular, if $(\mathcal{T}_2, s_2)$ is a bounded morphic image of $(\mathcal{T}_1, s_1)$ (see Definition 3.3.11) then $(\mathcal{T}_1, s_1) \equiv_{\mathrm{BML}} (\mathcal{T}_2, s_2)$.

Corollary 5.3.4. For every (uninterpreted) rooted transition systems $(\mathcal{T}_1, s_1)$ and $(\mathcal{T}_2, s_2)$: if $(\mathcal{T}_1, s_1) \rightleftarrows (\mathcal{T}_2, s_2)$, then $(\mathcal{T}_1, s_1) \equiv_{\mathrm{HML}} (\mathcal{T}_2, s_2)$. $\qquad\blacksquare$

Generated subsystems have been introduced in Section 3.3.3. In what follows, we provide properties about the satisfaction of formulae on them. We recall that we write $\mathcal{T}[s]$ to denote the generated subsystem from s.

Corollary 5.3.5. Given a transition system $\mathcal{T} = (S, (\xrightarrow{a})_{a \in Act}, L)$, a state $s \in S$ and a formula φ in BML:

(I) For every state r in $\mathcal{T}[s]$, we have $\mathcal{T}, r \models \varphi$ iff $\mathcal{T}[s], r \models \varphi$.
(II) $\mathcal{T} \models \varphi$ implies $\mathcal{T}[s] \models \varphi$.

Similarly, we write $\mathcal{T}^n[s]$ to denote the generated subsystem from s until depth n. The next corollary says that a BML formula of modal depth n cannot see beyond the (depth-n) generated subsystem rooted at the current state.

Corollary 5.3.6. For every transition system $\mathcal{T}$, state $s \in \mathcal{T}$ and formula φ of BML:

(I) $\mathcal{T}, s \models \varphi$ iff $\mathcal{T}[s], s \models \varphi$.
(II) If $mdeg(\varphi) = n$ then $\mathcal{T}, s \models \varphi$ iff $\mathcal{T}^n[s], s \models \varphi$.

Thus, to check the truth of a formula of modal depth n at a given state s of an interpreted transition system $\mathcal{T}$ it suffices to consider the depth n generated substructure of $\mathcal{T}$ rooted at s.

Corollary 5.3.7. Every satisfiable formula of BML of modal depth n is satisfiable at the root of a tree-like interpreted transition system of height n.   ■

Later on, we will show that the satisfying tree can always be chosen to be finitely branching, and therefore finite (see Section 5.5.1 and Section 5.5.2).

5.3.2 Bisimulation-Invariant First-Order Properties

When restricted to state properties definable in first-order logic, it turns out that bisimulation invariance is not only necessary, but also a sufficient condition for definability in BML, as the following classical result shows.

Definition 5.3.8. A formula $\varphi(x) \in \text{FO}_\tau$ of one free variable x is **bisimulation invariant** if, for all interpreted transition systems $(\mathcal{T}, s)$ and $(\mathcal{T}', s')$, such that $(\mathcal{T}, s) \rightleftarrows (\mathcal{T}', s')$, we have that

$$\mathcal{T} \models_{\text{FO}} \varphi[x := s] \text{ iff } \mathcal{T}' \models_{\text{FO}} \varphi[x := s']. \qquad \nabla$$

In Lemma 5.1.4, we have seen that a modal formula ψ and its translation $\text{ST}(\psi, x)$ in FO are equivalent. We say that $\varphi(x) \in \text{FO}_\tau$ of one free variable x is logically equivalent to a modal formula ψ if the formula $\forall x(\varphi(x) \leftrightarrow \text{ST}(\psi, x))$ is valid in FO.

Proposition 5.3.9 (van Benthem's Characterisation Theorem). Let $\varphi(x) \in \text{FO}_\tau$. Then, the following arc equivalent:

(I) φ is bisimulation invariant.
(II) $\varphi(x)$ is logically equivalent to a modal formula $\widetilde{\varphi} \in \text{BML}$.   ■

For a proof of van Benthem's Characterisation Theorem, see the bibliographical references. As a consequence, we also obtain that any first-order formula $\varphi(x)$ that is bisimulation invariant is equivalent to a formula $\varphi'(x)$ in FO2.

5.3.3 Characteristic Formulae

Hereafter we assume that the set PROP is finite and, for technical simplicity, we consider the case of one transition relation. The generalisation to arbitrary signatures is routine. In the particular case of PROP $= \emptyset$ we obtain respective results about Hennessy–Milner logic HML and plain (noninterpreted) transition systems.

Here we introduce special BML formulae associated with rooted interpreted transition systems which characterise them up to n-bisimulations. More precisely, for a given rooted interpreted transition system $(\mathcal{T}, s)$, its characteristic formula of depth n, for any $n \geq 0$, is satisfied by those rooted interpreted transition systems that are n-bisimilar (hence, BML_n-equivalent) to $(\mathcal{T}, s)$.

First, note that, since PROP is assumed to be finite, say PROP $= \{p_1, \ldots, p_k\}$, there are finitely many essentially distinct (i.e. nonequivalent) formulae in BML^n. More precisely, given $n \geq 0$, one can compute a *finite* subset X^n of BML^n such that any formula $\varphi \in \mathrm{BML}^n$ is equivalent to some $\psi \in X^n$ (ψ can be viewed as the canonical representative for φ) and two distinct formulae ψ_1, ψ_2 in X^n are not logically equivalent, i.e. $\psi_1 \leftrightarrow \psi_2$ is not a valid formula.

Using the set X^n, for any (possibly infinite) subset Y of BML^n we can form infinite conjunctions or disjunctions over Y, such as

$$\bigvee_{\psi \in Y} \psi \quad \text{or} \quad \bigwedge_{\psi \in Y} \mathrm{EX}\,\psi$$

by equivalently reducing them to finite ones, where every formula in Y is replaced by its equivalent representative from X^n and then using propositional equivalences, such as $(\varphi \vee \psi \vee \psi) \equiv (\varphi \vee \psi)$ and $(\varphi \wedge \psi \wedge \psi) \equiv (\varphi \wedge \psi)$.

Definition 5.3.10. With every rooted interpreted transition system $(\mathcal{T}, s)$, where $\mathcal{T} = (S, R, L)$ and $n \in \mathbb{N}$ we associate a **characteristic formula** $\chi_{[\mathcal{T},s]}^n$ of depth n, inductively defined as follows.

$$\chi_{[\mathcal{T},s]}^0 := \left(\bigwedge_{p \in \mathrm{PROP} \cap L(s)} p \right) \wedge \left(\bigwedge_{p \in \mathrm{PROP} \setminus L(s)} \neg p \right).$$

The formula $\chi_{[\mathcal{T},s]}^{n+1}$ is defined as follows, assuming that characteristic formulae of depth n are already defined:

$$\chi_{[\mathcal{T},s]}^{n+1} := \chi_{[\mathcal{T},s]}^0 \wedge \left(\bigwedge_{(s,r) \in R} \mathrm{EX}\, \chi_{[\mathcal{T},r]}^n \right) \wedge \left(\mathrm{AX} \bigvee_{(s,r) \in R} \chi_{[\mathcal{T},r]}^n \right). \qquad \nabla$$

In the preceding definition, a disjunction [resp. conjunction] over an empty set is defined, as usual, as $\bot$ [resp. $\top$].

Note that $\chi_{[\mathcal{T},s]}^n$ is of modal depth at most n, and therefore it belongs to BML^n. Intuitively, $\chi_{[\mathcal{T},s]}^n$ combines the atomic description of s and the characteristic formulae of depth $n-1$ for all successors of s and only of them. In the long run, it describes the part of $\mathcal{T}$ seen from s within n steps – but, as we will show, only up to n-bisimulation equivalence.

Since BML^n has only a finite number of nonequivalent formulae, it follows that there are only finitely many nonequivalent characteristic formulae of depth n, even though a state s may have infinitely many successors. Thus, every formula $\chi_{[\mathcal{T},s]}^n$ is well defined. More precisely, the set X^0 of all characteristic formulae of depth 0 has cardinality 2^{2^k} (the number of Boolean functions built over the set of atomic propositions $\{p_1, \ldots, p_k\}$) and, inductively, for every $n \geq 0$, the set X^{n+1} of all characteristic formulae of depth $n+1$ has cardinality in $2^{2^{O(\mathrm{card}(X^n))}}$.

Example 5.3.11. The characteristic formula $\chi_{[\mathcal{T},s_4]}^2$ for the state s_4 in the interpreted transition system with type $(\{a, b, c\}, \{p, q, r\})$, presented in Figure 5.1, is:

$$\chi_{[\mathcal{T},s_4]}^2 = \chi_{[\mathcal{T},s_4]}^0 \wedge \mathrm{EX}_a\, \chi_{[\mathcal{T},s_2]}^1 \wedge \mathrm{EX}_a\, \chi_{[\mathcal{T},s_4]}^1 \wedge \mathrm{AX}_a\, (\chi_{[\mathcal{T},s_2]}^1 \vee \chi_{[\mathcal{T},s_4]}^1) \wedge$$
$$\mathrm{EX}_b\, \chi_{[\mathcal{T},s_5]}^1 \wedge \mathrm{AX}_b\, \chi_{[\mathcal{T},s_5]}^1 \wedge \mathrm{AX}_c \bot$$

where

$$\chi^0_{[\mathcal{T},s_2]} = p \wedge q \wedge \neg r$$
$$\chi^0_{[\mathcal{T},s_3]} = \neg p \wedge \neg q \wedge \neg r$$
$$\chi^0_{[\mathcal{T},s_4]} = \neg p \wedge \neg q \wedge r$$
$$\chi^0_{[\mathcal{T},s_5]} = \neg p \wedge q \wedge \neg r$$
$$\chi^1_{[\mathcal{T},s_2]} = \chi^0_{[\mathcal{T},s_2]} \wedge \mathsf{AX}_a \bot \wedge \mathsf{EX}_b \, \chi^0_{[\mathcal{T},s_3]} \wedge \mathsf{AX}_b \, \chi^0_{[\mathcal{T},s_3]} \wedge \mathsf{AX}_c \bot$$
$$\chi^1_{[\mathcal{T},s_4]} = \chi^0_{[\mathcal{T},s_4]} \wedge \mathsf{EX}_a \, \chi^0_{[\mathcal{T},s_2]} \wedge \mathsf{EX}_a \, \chi^0_{[\mathcal{T},s_4]} \wedge \mathsf{AX}_a \, (\chi^0_{[\mathcal{T},s_2]} \vee \chi^0_{[\mathcal{T},s_4]}) \wedge$$
$$\qquad \mathsf{EX}_b \, \chi^0_{[\mathcal{T},s_5]} \wedge \mathsf{AX}_b \, \chi^0_{[\mathcal{T},s_5]} \wedge \mathsf{AX}_c \bot$$
$$\chi^1_{[\mathcal{T},s_5]} = \chi^0_{[\mathcal{T},s_5]} \wedge \mathsf{AX}_a \bot \wedge \mathsf{AX}_b \bot \wedge \mathsf{EX}_c \, \chi^0_{[\mathcal{T},s_4]} \wedge \mathsf{AX}_c \, \chi^0_{[\mathcal{T},s_4]}.$$

The proof of the following lemma can be done by induction on n and is left as Exercise 5.7.

Lemma 5.3.12. For every rooted interpreted transition system $(\mathcal{T}, s)$ and $n \in \mathbb{N}$, we have $\mathcal{T}, s \models \chi^n_{[\mathcal{T},s]}$. ∎

The formula $\chi^n_{[\mathcal{T},s]}$ describes $(\mathcal{T}, s)$ up to n-bisimulation, which can be stated more precisely as follows.

Theorem 5.3.13. For every rooted ITS $(\mathcal{T}, s)$ and $(\mathcal{T}', s')$ the following are equivalent:

(I) $\mathcal{T}', s' \models \chi^n_{[\mathcal{T},s]}$.
(II) Player **II** has a winning strategy in the n-round bisimulation game on $(\mathcal{T}, s; \mathcal{T}', s')$.
(III) $(\mathcal{T}, s) \leftrightarrows_n (\mathcal{T}', s')$. ∎

Proof. (I) $\Rightarrow$ (II): We show that if $\mathcal{T}', s' \models \chi^n_{[\mathcal{T},s]}$ then Player **II** has a winning strategy in the n-round bisimulation game on $(\mathcal{T}, s; \mathcal{T}', s')$ by induction on n. For $n = 0$ the claim follows by definition. Assuming it holds for n, let us look again at $\chi^{n+1}_{[\mathcal{T},s]}$ from the perspective of the game:

$$\chi^0_{[\mathcal{T},s]} \wedge (\underbrace{\bigwedge_{(s,r) \in R} \mathsf{EX} \, \chi^n_{[\mathcal{T},r]}}_{\text{forth}}) \wedge (\mathsf{AX} \underbrace{\bigvee_{(s,r) \in R} \chi^n_{[\mathcal{T},r]}}_{\text{back}}).$$

The conjunct $\chi^0_{[\mathcal{T},s]}$ guarantees that the game is not lost already.

The *back*-and-*forth* conjuncts tell Player **II** how to provide suitable responses in the first round to challenges from Player **I** played respectively in $\mathcal{T}$ (*forth*) or in $\mathcal{T}'$ (*back*). The *forth* part says that for all moves from s to some r in $\mathcal{T}$, it holds that $\mathcal{T}', s' \models \mathsf{EX}\chi^n_{[\mathcal{T},r]}$, and any R'-successor r' of s' such that $\mathcal{T}', r' \models \chi^n_{[\mathcal{T},r]}$ provides a response for Player **II** that will allow her to succeed through another n rounds.

Similarly the *back* part says that for all moves from s' to some r' in $\mathcal{T}'$ there is a R-successor r of s in $\mathcal{T}$ such that $\mathcal{T}', r' \models \chi^n_{[\mathcal{T},r]}$. Such r is a response for Player **II** that is good for another n rounds.

(II) $\Rightarrow$ (III) is done by Theorem 3.4.3.

(III) $\Rightarrow$ (I) follows from Lemma 5.3.12 and Theorem 5.3.2, because $\chi^n_{[T,s]} \in$ BML^n. $\qquad\qquad\qquad\qquad\qquad\qquad\qquad\qquad\qquad\qquad\qquad\quad$ $\square$

5.3.4 Characterisations of Modal Equivalence

Now we can put together bisimulations, bisimulation games, logical equivalence and characteristic formulae, as an immediate consequence from Theorem 5.3.2 and Theorem 5.3.13:

Theorem 5.3.14. For every rooted interpreted transition system (T, s) and (T', s') the following are equivalent:

(I) $T', s' \models \chi^n_{[T,s]}$.
(II) $(T, s) \equiv^n_{\mathrm{BML}} (T', s')$.
(III) $(T, s) \leftrightarrows_n (T', s')$.
(IV) Player **II** has a winning strategy in the n-round bisimulation game on $(T, s; T', s')$. ∎

As corollaries we obtain a corresponding characterisation of full modal equivalence, and a normal form for BML formulae.

Corollary 5.3.15. For every rooted interpreted transition system (T, s) and (T', s') of finite type $\tau = (Act, \mathrm{PROP})$ (Act and PROP are finite) the following are equivalent:

(I) For every $n \in \mathbb{N}$, $T', s' \models \chi^n_{[T,s]}$.
(II) $(T, s) \equiv_{\mathrm{BML}} (T', s')$.
(III) $(T, s) \leftrightarrows_{\mathrm{fin}} (T', s')$ (see Section 3.3.2).
(IV) For every $n \in \mathbb{N}$ Player **II** has winning strategies in the n-round bisimulation games on $(T, s; T', s')$. ∎

Corollary 5.3.16. Over interpreted transition systems of any finite type, finite bisimulation equivalence coincides with modal equivalence. ∎

As a consequence from the Hennessy–Milner Theorem 3.4.5, we also obtain the following.

Corollary 5.3.17. Over finitely branching interpreted transition system, modal equivalence coincides with bisimulation equivalence. ∎

Another useful consequence from the preceding results is that every formula of BML is equivalent to a disjunction of characteristic formulae.

Corollary 5.3.18. Any formula $\varphi \in$ BML^n is logically equivalent to the disjunction

$$\bigvee_{T,s\models\varphi} \chi^n_{[T,s]}.$$ ∎

Note that, even though the number of rooted interpreted transition systems satisfying φ may be infinite, the preceding disjunction is finite up to equivalence, as there are only finitely many, up to logical equivalence, such χ^n in the type of φ.

A class $\mathcal{C}$ of rooted interpreted transition systems is **closed under bisimulation** if, whenever $(\mathcal{T}, s) \in \mathcal{C}$ and $(\mathcal{T}, s) \rightleftarrows (\mathcal{T}', s')$ then $(\mathcal{T}', s') \in \mathcal{C}$. Classes closed under n-bisimulations and finite bisimulations are defined likewise.

Corollary 5.3.19. Any class $\mathcal{C}$ of rooted interpreted transition systems of a finite type that is closed under n-bisimulation is definable in BML^n by the disjunction

$$\bigvee \left\{ \chi^n_{[\mathcal{T},s]} \mid (\mathcal{T}, s) \in \mathcal{C} \right\}.$$

The proof is left as Exercise 5.7. The following proposition follows from Corollary 3.4.17.

Corollary 5.3.20. Let $(\mathcal{T}_1, s_1)$ and $(\mathcal{T}_2, s_2)$ be finite rooted interpreted transition systems with respectively n_1 and n_2 states, such that $(\mathcal{T}_1, s_1) \rightleftarrows_{(n_1+n_2)} (\mathcal{T}_2, s_2)$. Then $(\mathcal{T}_1, s_1) \rightleftarrows (\mathcal{T}_2, s_2)$. ∎

Corollary 5.3.21. Let $(\mathcal{T}, s)$ and $(\mathcal{T}', s')$ be finite rooted interpreted transition systems with respectively n_1 and n_2 states, for which any of the equivalent conditions in Theorem 5.3.14 holds for some $n \geq (n_1 + n_2)$. Then $(\mathcal{T}, s) \rightleftarrows (\mathcal{T}', s')$. ∎

Thus, in a finite interpreted transition system $\mathcal{T}$ every state s can be characterised up to bisimulation equivalence by the characteristic formula $\chi^n_{[\mathcal{T},s]}$ for any large enough n. We will denote by $\chi_{[\mathcal{T},s]}$ the formula for the least suitable n. Thus, we have the following.

Corollary 5.3.22. For every finite rooted interpreted transition system $(\mathcal{T}, s)$ and for all states s, r in $\mathcal{T}$, the following are equivalent:

(I) $\mathcal{T}, r \models \chi_{[\mathcal{T},s]}$.
(II) $(\mathcal{T}, s) \rightleftarrows (\mathcal{T}, r)$.

Lastly, we recall that finite bisimulation generally does not imply full bisimulation (Chapter 3), but this is the case for finitely branching transition system, as stated in the Hennessy–Milner Theorem (Theorem 3.4.5). ∎

5.4 Model Checking

5.4.1 From Model Checking to Validity

The logical problems of model checking and validity testing are quite different, and not always reducible to each other at low computational cost. However, we will show that MC(BML) can be reduced to validity testing, by using characteristic formulae to describe the given interpreted transition system up to bisimulation bounded by the modal depth of the given formula. Even though the reduction itself is not computationally expensive (it requires only logarithmic space), it cannot serve as a serious alternative to the design of dedicated algorithms for model checking since MC(BML) and VAL(BML) will be shown to be of quite different computational complexity. However, the reduction we present here is helpful to understand the concepts introduced so far.

Let $\mathcal{T} = (S, \{\xrightarrow{a}\}_{a \in Act}, L)$ be an interpreted transition system and $s \in S$. Let φ be a formula of modal depth n. We would like to build a formula φ^* such that $\mathcal{T}, s \models \varphi$ iff φ^* is valid in BML.

Let $\chi^n_{[\mathcal{T},s]}$ be the characteristic formula built in Section 5.3.3. By Theorem 5.3.14, for every rooted interpreted transition system $(\mathcal{T}', s')$, we have $\mathcal{T}', s' \models \chi^n_{[\mathcal{T},s]}$ iff $(\mathcal{T}, s) \equiv^n_{\mathrm{BML}}$ $(\mathcal{T}', s')$. We will show that the formula $\chi^n_{[\mathcal{T},s]} \to \varphi$ is the right candidate for φ^*. Indeed, if $\mathcal{T}, s \models \varphi$, then $\chi^n_{[\mathcal{T},s]} \to \varphi$ is valid. Conversely, if $\chi^n_{[\mathcal{T},s]} \to \varphi$ is valid, we get $\mathcal{T}, s \models \varphi$, since $\mathcal{T}, s \models \chi^n_{[\mathcal{T},s]}$ (see Lemma 5.3.12). Therefore, we have the following result for reducing the model-checking problem to the validity problem.

Theorem 5.4.1. Let $\mathcal{T}$ be a transition system, s be a state in $\mathcal{T}$ and φ be a formula in BML. Then we have $\mathcal{T}, s \models \varphi$ iff $\chi^n_{[\mathcal{T},s]} \to \varphi$ is valid. ∎

5.4.2 The Labelling Algorithm

Here we provide a simple algorithm to solve the local model-checking problem for MC(BML) in polynomial time. This is a standard labelling algorithm that can easily be extended, for instance to basic tense logic BTL or to the branching-time logic CTL, which we introduce further.

Algorithm 1 Checking whether $\mathcal{T}, s \models \varphi$.

```
 1: procedure MC_BML(T, s, φ)
 2:     case φ of
 3:     p:  return p ∈ L(s)
 4:     ¬φ':  return (not MC_BML(T, s, φ'))
 5:     φ₁ ∧ φ₂:  return (MC_BML(T, s, φ₁) and MC_BML(T, s, φ₂))
 6:     EXφ':
 7:         if ∃s' ∈ R(s) with MC_BML(T, s', φ') = true then
 8:             return true
 9:         end if
10:         return false
11:     end case
12: end procedure
```

Algorithm 1 is a straightforward implementation of the definition of the satisfaction relation $\models$. It can be viewed as a procedure for the recursive top-down labelling of the states by subformulae with truth values.

Lemma 5.4.2. Given a BML formula φ, a finite interpreted transition system $\mathcal{T}$, and a state s in $\mathcal{T}$, $\mathrm{MC}_{\mathrm{BML}}(\mathcal{T}, s, \varphi)$ returns true iff $\mathcal{T}, s \models \varphi$. ∎

The proof is by structural induction on φ. It essentially relies on properties stated in Lemma 5.1.2.

We can now provide a complexity upper bound for MC(BML).

Corollary 5.4.3. MC(BML) is in PTIME.   ∎

Proof. We update the computation of $\mathrm{MC}_{\mathrm{BML}}(\mathcal{T}, s, \varphi)$ slightly so that it can be computed in time polynomial in $|\mathcal{T}| + |\varphi|$. We use a standard trick from dynamic programming by introducing an array T of dimension two such that $\mathrm{T}[s, \psi]$ can take one of the following values:

- false if $\mathrm{MC}_{\mathrm{BML}}(\mathcal{T}, s, \psi)$ has been already computed and it returns false,
- true if $\mathrm{MC}_{\mathrm{BML}}(\mathcal{T}, s, \psi)$ has been already computed and it returns true,
- unkown otherwise.

Algorithm 1 is modified in such a way that it first checks whether $\mathrm{T}[s, \psi]$ is different from unkown. If it is the case, it directly returns the value $\mathrm{T}[s, \psi]$. (Initially, the array is initialised to unkown everywhere before the outermost call to $\mathrm{MC}_{\mathrm{BML}}$.) Otherwise, the current code is executed except that before returning the final Boolean value, it is stored in the array T by providing a new value to $\mathrm{T}[s, \psi]$.   □

As for global model checking, it can, of course, be reduced to local model checking at each state in the system. However, this is generally not optimal. We will defer the presentation of an optimal algorithm for global model checking to Chapter 7 when we will present it for the more expressive branching-time logic CTL (see also Section 9.3.2).

5.4.3 A Game-Theoretic Approach

We will introduce another conceptual formalism for doing model checking. It can easily be used to obtain a decision procedure for model checking BML, however, this is not our primary focus. Model-checking games are of great value for understanding the properties that are expressed by given temporal formulae. The games provide an interactive semantics for temporal (and modal) logics. While BML is surely a rather harmless logic when it comes to formulae that are difficult to understand, we already start the introduction of the concept of model-checking games here where the formulae pose no additional difficulty. Later, when we discuss more complex logics like the modal μ-calculus in Chapter 8 for instance, we can assume the basic concepts of how the evaluation of a formula in an interpreted transition system can be seen as a game to be known.

The game is played between two players on an underlying ITS $\mathcal{T}$ and a BML formula φ. The two players decompose the formula and trace states in the ITS in order to figure out whether it holds. For literals this can be seen immediately, so if the game has reached a position with a literal then it ends and the winner is determined. If the formula at hand is nonatomic then one of the players will make a choice that should, intuitively, take them closer to seeing whether the formula is satisfied in the current state.

A vital prerequisite for what follows is the presentation of φ in negation normal form where formulae are built from literals, i.e. atomic propositions and their negations, using the operators $\vee$, $\wedge$, EX and AX only. Here we only consider the mono-modal version of BML with modalities EX and AX rather than EX_a and AX_a for actions a. The extension of this framework to multimodal BML is easy and left as Exercise 5.10. Assuming negation normal form is not restrictive as the following result shows. Its proof is left as Exercise 5.14.

Lemma 5.4.4. For every BML formula φ there is an equivalent ψ in negation normal form such that $|\psi| \leq 2 \cdot |\varphi|$. ∎

The operators of BML can be divided into two groups: 'existential' operators are those for which it is easier to prove than to refute, and 'universal' ones, for which it is easier to refute than to prove that the formula holds. The existential operators in BML are disjunction and existential modalities; note that a disjunction holds in a state if *one* of the two disjuncts holds there. Thus, it can 'easily' be proved in the sense that its satisfaction is witnessed by *some* disjunct. A conjunction on the other hand is a universal construct; its satisfaction is *refuted* by *some* conjunct whereas it is witnessed only by *all* conjuncts just like the satisfaction of a disjunction is refuted by all disjuncts.

Similar considerations can be made for the modal operators. The fact that some state s satisfies a formula of the form $\text{EX}\,\psi$ is witnessed by *some* successor of s that satisfies ψ whereas it would only be refuted by *all* successors not satisfying ψ.

This dichotomy is reflected in the characterisation of the model-checking problem as a game between two players: one's role is to make choices whenever something can easily be witnessed, the other one makes choices whenever something can easily be refuted. In other words, the one player's goal is to show that the given formula is satisfied by the given ITS, whereas the other player attempts to show the converse. Hence, we will refer to the players as **Verifier** and **Refuter**, abbreviated as **V** and **R**.

Definition 5.4.5. Given a rooted ITS $(\mathcal{T}, s_0)$ with $\mathcal{T} = (S, \rightarrow, L)$ and a BML formula φ in negation normal form, the **model-checking game** $\mathcal{G}^{\mathcal{T}}(s_0, \varphi)$ is a 2-player game with arena (V, Own, E) such that

- $V = S \times sub(\varphi)$,
- $Own(s, \psi) = 0$ iff ψ is of the form $\psi_1 \vee \psi_2$ or $\text{EX}\,\psi$.

Thus, game nodes are pairs of states in the underlying ITS and subformulae. We will often speak of such nodes as **configurations** because they represent a moment in which the satisfaction relation between a state and a formula is being examined. In order to stress this point we will also write such a configuration as $s \vdash \psi$ rather than (s, ψ) because of its notational similarity to $s \models \psi$. ∇

The definition of the edge relation and the winning conditions in these games require a little bit of preparatory discussion.

$$(\vee) \ \frac{s \vdash \psi_1 \vee \psi_2}{s \vdash \psi_i} \ \mathbf{V} \qquad\qquad (\wedge) \ \frac{s \vdash \psi_1 \wedge \psi_2}{s \vdash \psi_i} \ \mathbf{R}$$

$$(\mathrm{EX}) \ \frac{s \vdash \mathsf{EX}\psi}{t \vdash \psi} \ \mathbf{V}, s \rightarrow t \qquad\qquad (\mathrm{AX}) \ \frac{s \vdash \mathsf{AX}\psi}{t \vdash \psi} \ \mathbf{R}, s \rightarrow t$$

Figure 5.3 The BML model-checking game rules.

We present the edge relation in this game arena, i.e. the possible moves that the players can make in it, in a rule-based style. Such rules are to be read from top to bottom: there is an edge from the configuration on the top to any configuration at the bottom. We may use meta-variables in order to represent several possibilities for successor configurations. In order to refer to particular rules, they can be given a name stated to the left. We state the player who makes a choice in the top configuration to the right of the rule. This is of course redundant in this particular case since we have explained the ownership in the BML model-checking games already in the preceding definition. However, the rule-based denotation is more convenient and we will adopt that for the future instead of the more technical exposition of an ownership function. It should be clear that the two ways are equivalent for as long as no more than one rule applies to each configuration. It is easily checked that this is the case for the BML model-checking games.

The **rules** of the BML model-checking games are presented in Figure 5.3. Thus, in configurations with disjunctions **V** chooses one of the disjuncts. Likewise, whenever a play reaches a conjunction then player **R** chooses one of the conjuncts. Whenever it reaches a configuration in which the formula starts with a modal operator, the players – depending on whether it is the existential or the universal modal operator – must choose a successor state to the one in the current configuration, and the play continues with the examination of this successor state and the formula following the modal operator.

Definition 5.4.6 (Winning conditions in BML model-checking games). Let $\lambda = C_0$, ..., C_n be a play in the model-checking game $\mathcal{G}^{\mathcal{T}}(s_0, \varphi)$. Then C_n cannot have any successor configurations in this game, and it is easily seen from the game rules that C_n must be of one of four possible forms. In each case we assign a winner to the play as follows. Player **V** wins λ if

- there is a state t and an atomic proposition q such that $C_n = t \vdash q$ and $q \in L(t)$, or $C_n = t \vdash \neg q$ and $q \notin L(t)$;
- there is a state t and a formula ψ such that $C_n = t \vdash \mathsf{AX}\psi$, and t has no successor in $\mathcal{T}$.

Likewise, player **R** wins λ if

- there is a state t and an atomic proposition q such that $C_n = t \vdash q$ and $q \notin L(t)$, or $C_n = t \vdash \neg q$ and $q \in L(t)$;
- there is a state t and a formula ψ such that $C_n = t \vdash \mathsf{EX}\psi$, and t has no successor in $\mathcal{T}$. $\qquad\qquad \nabla$

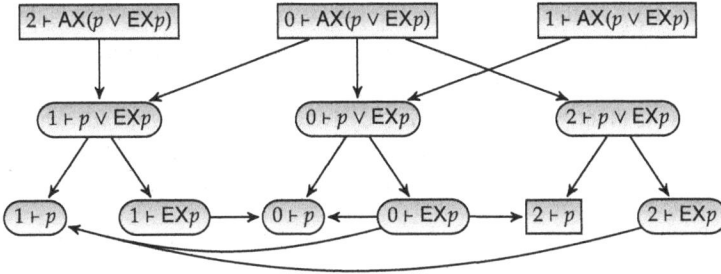

Figure 5.4 A BML model-checking game.

When analysing a rooted ITS with root s_0 with respect to a BML property φ then we are of course interested in the question of whether the state s_0 satisfies φ which amounts to considering all plays starting in the configuration $s_0 \vdash \varphi$. Hence, the game-based approach is particularly prone to capturing local model checking.

Example 5.4.7. Consider the following ITS $\mathcal{T}$

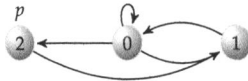

and the BML formula $\varphi = \mathsf{AX}(p \vee \mathsf{EX}p)$. The arena of the model-checking game $\mathcal{G}^{\mathcal{T}}(0, \varphi)$ is shown in Figure 5.4. In fact, it is also the arena of the games $\mathcal{G}^{\mathcal{T}}(1, \varphi)$ and $\mathcal{G}^{\mathcal{T}}(2, \varphi)$. The only difference between these games is the question for which state 0, 1, 2 we want to know whether they satisfy φ.

We introduce the general convention that nodes owned by player **V** are shown rounded, i.e. with half-circles at the sides, while player **R**'s nodes are shown as rectangles. We will use the same geometric shapes for nodes that are technically not owned by either of the players because any play through them ends there. We will use round shapes for those nodes that make player **R** win the corresponding play and rectangular ones for those that make **V** win. This may seem strange at first sight, but at second it makes perfect sense. This way, a dead-end node marked with a circle looks like a choice for player **V**, and if taken as a choice by her then it also looks like **R** should win there because **V** cannot come up with a choice of a successor configuration.

It is not too hard to see that **R** has a winning strategy starting from the configuration $0 \vdash \mathsf{AX}(p \vee \mathsf{EX}p)$. It consists of first moving to $1 \vdash p \vee \mathsf{EX}p$. Then, regardless of where player **V** moves in the next step or two steps, we either reach $0 \vdash p$ or $1 \vdash p$. According to the winning conditions, **R** wins in both.

We want to show that the model-checking games characterise the model-checking problem in the sense that winning for player **V** corresponds to satisfaction of the underlying formula in the underlying state of the underlying ITS. To this end, we analyse player

R's winning strategy in the preceding example more closely. Note that indeed we have $\mathcal{T}, 0 \not\models AX(p \vee EX p)$ because we also have $1 \not\models p \vee EX p$. This holds because we neither have $1 \models p$ nor $0 \models EX p$ since we have $0 \not\models p$. Now compare this reasoning to player **R**'s winning strategy: evidently, his strategy is only following the reasons for why the pair in a configuration does not belong to the satisfaction relation $\models$. This can be generalised to the whole of BML (and later on to more complex temporal formulae).

Lemma 5.4.8. Let $\mathcal{G}^{\mathcal{T}}(s_0, \varphi)$ be a model-checking game for some ITS $\mathcal{T}$ with root s_0 and some BML formula φ. If $\mathcal{T}, s_0 \models \varphi$ then player **V** has a winning strategy for the game starting in configuration $s_0 \vdash \varphi$.   ∎

Proof. Let us call a configuration $t \vdash \psi$ **true**, if $t \models \psi$ holds. By assumption, the game starts in a true configuration. We now observe three simple facts:

- Every play of $\mathcal{G}^{\mathcal{T}}(s_0, \varphi)$ is finite. This is simply because every game rule strictly reduces the formula component in a configuration.
- Whenever player **V** has to make a choice in a true configuration then she can do so by preserving truth, i.e. she can choose a true successor configuration. This holds because she makes choices in disjunctions with rule ($\vee$) for which some disjunct must be satisfied, and for existential modalities with rule (EX) for which their argument must be satisfied on some successor state.
- Whenever player **R** has to make a choice in a true configuration then he must preserve truth, i.e. all successor configurations are also true. This can be seen by inspection of the rules ($\wedge$) and (AX).
- When a play ends in a configuration then it is true iff player **V** wins the play at this point.

This yields a winning strategy for player **V**: she simply preserves truth in her choices.

Now let us check whether this is indeed a winning strategy, i.e. take any play $C_0, \ldots, C_n$ in which player **V** has always moved according to her strategy. Because of the first fact, we can indeed assume it to be finite. By assumption, C_0 is true. We can iteratively use facts (2) and (3) to show that C_1 and all other subsequent configurations including C_n must be true, too. Then fact (4) tells us that **V** is indeed the winner of this play.   □

The converse direction holds, too. Its proof follows from Lemma 5.4.9. It works by considering a suitable notion for the other player, namely falsity of a configuration.

Lemma 5.4.9. Let $\mathcal{G}^{\mathcal{T}}(s_0, \varphi)$ be a model-checking game for some ITS $\mathcal{T}$ with root s_0 and some BML formula φ. If $\mathcal{T}, s_0 \not\models \varphi$ then player **R** has a winning strategy for the game starting in configuration $s_0 \vdash \varphi$.   ∎

Altogether, we obtain a game-based characterisation of the BML model-checking problem.

Theorem 5.4.10. Let $\mathcal{G}^{\mathcal{T}}(s_0, \varphi)$ be a model-checking game for some ITS $\mathcal{T}$ with root s_0 and some BML formula φ. Then $\mathcal{T}, s_0 \models \varphi$ iff player **V** has a winning strategy for the game starting in configuration $s_0 \vdash \varphi$.   ∎

Proof. The 'only if' was shown in Lemma 5.4.8. For the 'if'-direction assume that player **V** has a winning strategy for this game starting in this particular configuration. It should be clear that player **R** cannot have a winning strategy at the same time. According to Lemma 5.4.9 we cannot have $\mathcal{T}, s_0 \not\models \varphi$ either, i.e. we have $\mathcal{T}, s_0 \models \varphi$ which completes the proof. $\qquad\square$

5.5 Satisfiability and the Tree Model Property

5.5.1 Filtration

Recall that finite model property of a logic $\mathcal{L}$ means that every satisfiable formula of $\mathcal{L}$ is satisfiable in a finite model. The finite model property is a characteristic feature of modal and temporal logics, accounting for most of the decidability results for them. Clearly, logics with the finite model property and with a decidable model-checking problem have recursively enumerable sets of satisfiable formulae. So, combined with a recursive axiomatisation (and hence, recursive enumeration of the validities), the finite model property provides a standard, though practically inefficient, method for proving decidability by running two semidecision procedures in parallel – one trying to derive a formula, and the other systematically searching for a finite model of its negation.

A traditional and most widely used method for establishing the finite model property for modal logics is the **filtration method**, which we will outline here and will illustrate on BML. In fact, as we will show further, BML has an even stronger property. For simplicity, we consider transition systems with only one transition relation; the generalisation is straightforward.

Given a formula φ of BML and a model $\mathcal{T}$, we want to produce a *finite* interpreted transition system $\widetilde{\mathcal{T}}$ satisfying φ. The method of filtration provides a transformation from $\mathcal{T}$ to a finite interpreted transition system $\widetilde{\mathcal{T}}$ in a uniform manner with respect to φ and $\mathcal{T}$. Before sketching the construction, note that the satisfiability of a BML formula φ in an interpreted transition system only depends on the truth of the (finitely many) subformulae of φ in various states of that structure. Therefore, two states in an interpreted transition system that satisfy the same subformulae of φ are *indistinguishable* from the viewpoint of φ. Sometimes it is necessary to extend the set of subformulae of φ to a wider but still finite set of formulae, called the *closure of* φ and denoted by $cl(\varphi)$ (see also Definition 4.1.2). Thus, $cl(\varphi)$ partitions the model into *finitely many equivalence classes* of states, all states in each class satisfying the same subset of $cl(\varphi)$. The underlying idea of the filtration method is to collapse the (infinite) model to its finite quotient with respect to the equivalence relation generated by that partition, in a way that preserves the truth of all formulae in $cl(\varphi)$, and hence of φ itself.

The equivalence relation itself can be thought of as a coarse-grained approximation to bisimulation equivalence that is specific to the given formula φ. It is meant to preserve φ but needs to do so at a coarser level than bisimulation in order to be of finite index. Note that n-bisimulation $\underleftrightarrow{}_n$ can also serve as a finite-index approximation but, because of its graded nature, does not lend itself to taking quotients in the desired global manner. This is because $(\mathcal{T}, s) \rightleftharpoons_n (\mathcal{T}, s')$ (i.e. that s and s' are of the same n-bisimulation type) does not imply that the same n-bisimulation types are accessible from s and from s'.

Take any interpreted transition system $\mathcal{T} = (S, R, L)$ and a set of formulae Γ, which is assumed to be closed under subformulae and single negations (i.e. if $\varphi \in \Gamma$ is not a negation itself, then $\neg \varphi \in \Gamma$). So, Γ is closed in the sense of Definition 4.1.2. Define an equivalence relation $\sim_\Gamma$ on $\mathcal{T}$ as follows:

$$s \sim_\Gamma r \quad \overset{\text{def}}{\Leftrightarrow} \quad \text{for every } \varphi \in \Gamma : \mathcal{T}, s \models \varphi \text{ iff } \mathcal{T}, r \models \varphi.$$

Let $[r]_\Gamma$ be the equivalence class of r with respect to $\sim_\Gamma$ and $S_\Gamma := \{[r]_\Gamma \mid r \in S\}$. Note that if Γ is finite then S_Γ is finite, too. Furthermore, the state description L is collapsed to a state description L_Γ in a canonical way: $L_\Gamma([r]) \cap X = L(r) \cap X$ where X is the set of atomic propositions occurring in Γ. Therefore, we can adopt the definition $L_\Gamma([r]) := L(r) \cap X$.

Now we say that an interpreted transition system $\widetilde{\mathcal{T}} = (S_\Gamma, \widetilde{R}, L_\Gamma)$ is a **filtration of** $\mathcal{T}$ **with respect to** Γ if for every $\varphi \in \Gamma$ and $r \in S$: $\mathcal{T}, r \models \varphi$ iff $\widetilde{\mathcal{T}}, [r]_\Gamma \models \varphi$. With a slight abuse of terminology, we also say that $\widetilde{R}$ is a filtration of R with respect to Γ.

There are two simple conditions on the relation $\widetilde{R}$ which guarantee that it is a filtration of R with respect to Γ. They give lower and upper bounds for that relation, respectively:

(MIN) For all $s, r \in S$, if sRr, then $[s]_\Gamma \widetilde{R}[r]_\Gamma$.
(MAX) For all $[s]_\Gamma, [r]_\Gamma \in S_\Gamma$, if $[s]_\Gamma \widetilde{R}[r]_\Gamma$, then for every $\mathsf{AX}\varphi \in \Gamma$:
      if $\mathcal{T}, s \models \mathsf{AX}\varphi$, then $\mathcal{T}, r \models \varphi$.

Note that none of these conditions depends on the choice of representatives s and r, as $\varphi, \mathsf{AX}\varphi \in \Gamma$.

By induction on φ one can prove that for every $\widetilde{R}$ satisfying these conditions, the structure $\widetilde{\mathcal{T}} = (S_\Gamma, \widetilde{R}, L_\Gamma)$ is indeed a filtration of $\mathcal{T}$ with respect to Γ. This claim is known as the *filtration lemma*. Often, the conditions (MIN) and (MAX) are adopted as the definition of a filtration of R, and the filtration lemma then claims that they imply that $\mathcal{T}_\Gamma$ has the desired property.

Does every interpreted transition system have a filtration with respect to any set of formulae Γ? Yes: converting the implication to equivalence in either of the conditions (MIN) and (MAX) defines a relation that satisfies the other condition, too, and hence renders a filtration. Thus, at least two filtrations always exist:

- the **minimal filtration** $\mathcal{T}_\Gamma^{\min} := (S_\Gamma, R_\Gamma^{\min}, L_\Gamma)$ where $R_\Gamma^{\min} := \{([s]_\Gamma, [r]_\Gamma) \mid (s, r) \in R\}$.
- the **maximal filtration** $\mathcal{T}_\Gamma^{\max} := (S_\Gamma, R_\Gamma^{\max}, L_\Gamma)$ where,

$$R_\Gamma^{\max} := \{([s]_\Gamma, [r]_\Gamma) \mid \text{ for every } \mathsf{AX}\varphi \in \Gamma, \ \mathcal{T}, s \models \mathsf{AX}\varphi \text{ implies } \mathcal{T}, r \models \varphi\}.$$

Clearly, every relation $\widetilde{R}$ such that $R_\Gamma^{\min} \subseteq \widetilde{R} \subseteq R_\Gamma^{\max}$ is a filtration, too.

Figure 5.5 presents an interpreted transition system and its minimal filtration with $\Gamma = \{p, \neg p, \mathsf{EX}p, \neg\mathsf{EX}p\}$. Observe that $\sim_\Gamma$ has three equivalence classes and that the filtration does not coincide with the bisimulation quotient.

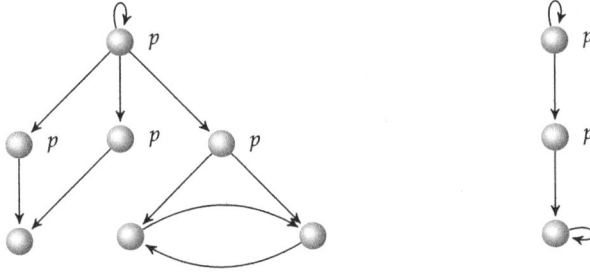

Figure 5.5 An interpreted transition system and its minimal filtration.

Now, given a formula $\varphi \in$ BML and a rooted interpreted transition system $(\mathcal{T}, s)$ such that $\mathcal{T}, s \models \varphi$, applying the filtration construction to $\Gamma = cl(\varphi)$ produces a finite rooted interpreted transition system $(\widetilde{\mathcal{T}}, [s]_\Gamma)$ that satisfies φ. Therefore, BML has the finite model property and, since it has a recursive axiomatisation, we obtain a decidability result.

Theorem 5.5.1. The satisfiability problem SAT(BML) is decidable. ∎

This can also be shown as a direct consequence of the filtration method by using the fact that MC(BML) is decidable too, as we have seen a bit earlier, by noting that the size of the filtered model is bounded above by an exponent of the length of the input formula; see e.g. Section 4.2 for a generic definition for the local model-checking problem MC($\mathcal{L}$) given a logic $\mathcal{L}$. Indeed, given a formula φ, if there is a rooted interpreted transition system $(\mathcal{T}, s)$ such that $\mathcal{T}, s \models \varphi$, then $\mathcal{T}_\Gamma^{\min}, [s]_\Gamma \models \varphi$ where Γ is the closure of φ and $\mathcal{T}_\Gamma^{\min}$ is the minimal filtration of $\mathcal{T}$. Since $\mathcal{T}_\Gamma^{\min}$ has at most $2^{|\varphi|}$ states (maximal number of equivalence classes for the equivalence relation $\sim_\Gamma$), φ is then satisfiable in a model whose number of states is bounded by $2^{|\varphi|}$. This yields a simple decision procedure for checking satisfiability: enumerate the (nonisomorphic) finite rooted interpreted transition systems with at most $2^{|\varphi|}$ states and restricted to the atomic propositions occurring in φ, check for satisfiability in those rooted interpreted transition systems, which can be effectively done since MC(BML) is decidable.

This leads to an exponential-space upper bound in the length of the input formula. Alternatively, one can guess a rooted interpreted transition system of size exponentially bounded in the length of the input formula and then check in time exponentially bounded in the length of the formula whether it satisfies it, whence a nondeterministic exponential-time upper bound. In Section 5.5.2, the satisfiability problem will be solved much more efficiently (in polynomial space, instead of exponential space with the preceding algorithm) even though we cannot avoid that some satisfiable formulae have models of exponential size.

The filtration method can be refined to establish the finite model property for various axiomatic extensions of BML, by adjusting the definition of $\widetilde{R}$ so as to preserve desired properties of the original structure $\mathcal{T}$, such as transitivity, linearity etc., or to impose such properties on the resulting structure $\widetilde{\mathcal{T}}$.

The filtration method can also be adapted or used in a very specific way to establish the finite model property for most of the expressive extensions of BML studied in the forthcoming chapters; for detailed filtration constructions for these logics see bibliographical references in Section 5.9. Instead, we will obtain the finite model properties for these logics using other methods, e.g. tableaux constructions in Chapter 13.

Next we will establish a stronger finite model property for BML, viz. the **finite tree model property**.

Lemma 5.5.2. For every $n \in \mathbb{N}$, every rooted interpreted transition system is n-bisimilar to a finite tree-like interpreted transition system. ∎

Proof. Consider the rooted interpreted transition system $(\mathcal{T}, s)$. According to Corollary 3.3.14 (see also Definition 3.3.10), its unfolding $\widehat{\mathcal{T}}, s$ provides a bisimilar tree-like interpreted transition system. As we only need n-bisimulation equivalence, we may cut off $\widehat{\mathcal{T}}$ at depth n from its root s, to obtain a rooted tree-like transition system $\widehat{\mathcal{T}}^n[s]$ such that $(\widehat{\mathcal{T}}^n[s], s) \rightleftarrows_n (\mathcal{T}, s)$ whose depth is bounded by n. This tree-like interpreted transition system may still be infinite, due to infinite branching. In that case, however, we may prune successors at every node to retain at most one representative of each $\rightleftarrows_n$ equivalence class. As $\rightleftarrows_n$ has finite index, the resulting tree is finite. □

Consequently, any satisfiable formula of BML is satisfied at the root of a finite tree-like interpreted transition system. A careful look at the preceding argument enables us to make the claim of Lemma 5.5.2 more precise.

Corollary 5.5.3 (Finite tree model property). Every satisfiable formula φ of BML is satisfiable in a finite tree of height at most $mdeg(\varphi)$ and branching factor bounded by the number of occurrences of modal operators in φ. ∎

Note that we cannot extend the preceding claim for any rooted interpreted transition system $(\mathcal{T}, s)$ in which a directed cycle is reachable from s to full bisimilarity with a finite tree. Locally, however, this can be achieved in partial unfoldings. See also Section 5.5.2 for an alternative proof for Corollary 5.5.3 based on the correctness proof for the algorithm checking BML satisfiability.

Lemma 5.5.4. Let $n \in \mathbb{N}$. Every finite rooted interpreted transition system $(\mathcal{T}, s)$ is bisimilar to a finite rooted interpreted transition system $(\widehat{\mathcal{T}}, \widehat{s})$ whose restriction to depth n from the distinguished node $\widehat{s}$ is a tree. ∎

The proof is left as Exercise 5.14. The finite tree model property is unique to BML. No further extensions that we will consider have that property. However, as noted earlier, they all have the finite model property. Besides, we will show that they all have the (infinite) tree model property.

5.5.2 Satisfiability Testing

Here we present a nondeterministic algorithm for testing satisfiability of BML formulae. For the sake of simplicity, we now assume that the modal operator EX is the only primitive

modal operator. First, we slightly refine the notion of a closure of a formula by introducing
a new parameter n: the distance from the root node to the current node where the formula
is evaluated.

As explained in Chapter 4, the closure set of a formula φ is understood as a finite set of
formulae built from φ that is sufficient to reason about the satisfiability status of φ. Next,
we follow Lemma 4.1.3 and we write $cl(\varphi)$ to denote the **closure** of φ according to that
definition. Consequently, $cl(\varphi)$ is the smallest set that contains φ and that is closed under
taking subformulae and under applications of $\sim$, that is a slight variant of negation.

Each set $ecl(n, \varphi)$ defined subsequently is therefore a subset of $cl(\varphi)$, viewed as subformulae occurring in modal depth at least n. Formally, for each $n \in \mathbb{N}$, $ecl(n, \varphi)$ is the
smallest set such that:

- $ecl(0, \varphi) = cl(\varphi)$,
- for all $n \in \mathbb{N}$, if $\mathsf{EX}\psi$ occurs in some formula of $ecl(n, \varphi)$, then $\psi \in ecl(n + 1, \varphi)$,
- for all $n \in \mathbb{N}$, if $\neg\mathsf{EX}\psi$ occurs in some formula of $ecl(n, \varphi)$, then $\sim\psi \in ecl(n + 1, \varphi)$,
- for every $n \in \mathbb{N}$, $ecl(n, \varphi)$ is closed, in the sense of Definition 4.1.2.

Consider the formula $\varphi = \mathsf{EX}(\neg\mathsf{EX}p \vee \neg\mathsf{EX}q)$. We obtain the following sets:

- $ecl(0, \varphi)$ is equal to $cl(\varphi)$ and therefore it is equal to the set:

$$\{\varphi, \neg\varphi, (\neg\mathsf{EX}p \vee \neg\mathsf{EX}q), \neg(\neg\mathsf{EX}p \vee \neg\mathsf{EX}q), \neg\mathsf{EX}p, \mathsf{EX}p, \neg\mathsf{EX}q, \mathsf{EX}q, p, q, \neg p, \neg q\}$$

- $ecl(1, \varphi)$ is equal to the set:

$$\{(\neg\mathsf{EX}p \vee \neg\mathsf{EX}q), \neg(\neg\mathsf{EX}p \vee \neg\mathsf{EX}q), \neg\mathsf{EX}p, \mathsf{EX}p, \neg\mathsf{EX}q, \mathsf{EX}q, p, q, \neg p, \neg q\}$$

- $ecl(2, \varphi) = \{p, q, \neg p, \neg q\}$ and $ecl(3, \varphi) = \emptyset$.

A set $\Gamma \subseteq cl(\varphi)$ is n-**maximally consistent** iff $\Gamma \subseteq ecl(n, \varphi)$ and Γ is maximally consistent
with respect to $ecl(n, \varphi)$. Maximality of consistency is sufficient for our future needs; propo-
sitional consistency (in the sense of propositionally expanded sets from Definition 4.1.4)
would be also possible, but assuming maximality provides a more explicit approach.

Lemma 5.5.5. *Let φ be a BML formula and $n \in \mathbb{N}$.*

(I) *Every n-maximally consistent set has cardinality at most $|\varphi|$ and can be encoded with
a number of bits linear in $|\varphi|$.*

(II) $ecl(|\varphi|, \varphi) = \emptyset$.

(III) *Given a set $\Gamma \subseteq cl(\varphi)$ of cardinality at most $|\varphi|$ and $n \in \mathbb{N}$, it can be decided in linear
time in $|\varphi|$ whether Γ is n-maximally consistent.* ∎

The proof of Lemma 5.5.5 is an easy verification. Indeed, $\max\{mdeg(\psi) \mid \psi \in
ecl(0, \varphi)\}$ is equal to $mdeg(\varphi)$ and whenever $\max\{mdeg(\psi) \mid \psi \in ecl(n, \varphi)\} = N \geq 1$, we
have $\max\{mdeg(\psi) \mid \psi \in ecl(n + 1, \varphi)\} < N$.

Algorithm 2 A nondeterministic algorithm for satisfiability checking.

1: **procedure** $\text{SAT}_{\text{BML}}(\Gamma, d)$
2:     **if** Γ is not d-maximally consistent **then** abort
3:     **end if**
4:     **if** Γ contains only propositional formulae **then** return $\texttt{true}$
5:     **end if**
6:     **for** $\text{EX}\,\psi \in \Gamma$ **do**
7:         Guess $\Delta \subseteq ecl(d+1, \varphi)$ such that $\psi \in \Delta$ and $\{\sim\psi' : \neg\text{EX}\psi' \in \Gamma\} \subseteq \Delta$
8:         **if** not $\text{SAT}_{\text{BML}}(\Delta, d+1)$ **then** abort
9:         **end if**
10:     **end for**
11: **end procedure**

We present Algorithm 2 computing the function SAT_{BML}, such that the BML formula φ is satisfiable iff there is $\Gamma \subseteq ecl(0, \varphi)$ such that $\varphi \in \Gamma$ and $\text{SAT}_{\text{BML}}(\Gamma, 0)$ has a computation that returns $\texttt{true}$. Thus, the function $\text{SAT}_{\text{BML}}(\Gamma, d)$ is parameterised by the formula φ and this parameter should be understood as a global variable. The first argument Γ is intended to be a subset of $ecl(d, \varphi)$. The algorithm computing SAT_{BML} is nondeterministic but it can be defined as a deterministic one by enumerating possibilities instead of guessing, in the standard way. A call $\text{SAT}_{\text{BML}}(\Gamma, d)$ performs the following actions. First it checks whether Γ is d-maximally consistent and if the modal depth is zero, then it returns $\texttt{true}$ in case of d-maximal consistency. In order to check that Γ is satisfiable, children of the node are guessed. If $\text{EX}\,\psi \in \Gamma$, then we apply recursively $\text{SAT}_{\text{BML}}(\Delta, d+1)$ with $\psi \in \Delta$ to ensure not only that Δ is $(d+1)$-maximally consistent but also that Δ is satisfiable. Hence, if we guess a set Δ that contains some unsatisfiable formula, then $\text{SAT}_{\text{BML}}(\Delta, d+1)$ has no accepting computation which also induces a nonaccepting computation for $\text{SAT}_{\text{BML}}(\Gamma, d)$. Termination is guaranteed by the fact that the modal depth of formulae occurring in a set is decreasing.

Algorithm 2 has the following features:

- it does not rely on any machinery such as automata or tableaux/sequent proof systems for checking satisfiability, but accepting computations are closely related to open tableaux,
- the graph of recursive calls (here, for SAT_{BML}) induces a tree model for the argument formula (see the proof of Lemma 5.5.6).

First we prove that Algorithm 2 is correct.

Lemma 5.5.6.

(I) If for some $\Gamma \subseteq ecl(0, \varphi)$, $\text{SAT}_{\text{BML}}(\Gamma, 0)$ has a computation that returns $\texttt{true}$ and $\varphi \in \Gamma$, then φ is satisfiable.

(II) If φ is satisfiable in some model then for some $\Gamma \subseteq ecl(0, \varphi)$ such that $\varphi \in \Gamma$, $\text{SAT}_{\text{BML}}(\Gamma, 0)$ has an accepting computation. ∎

Proof. (I) Assume that $\mathrm{SAT_{BML}}(\Gamma, 0)$ has an accepting computation with $\varphi \in \Gamma$. Let us build an interpreted transition system $\mathcal{T} = (S, R, L)$ for which there is $s \in S$ such that for every $\psi \in \Gamma$, we have $\psi \in \Gamma$ implies $\mathcal{M}, s \models \psi$.

From an accepting computation of $\mathrm{SAT_{BML}}(\Gamma, 0)$, we consider the following finite tree (S, R, l) that corresponds to the tree of calls.

- (S, R, l) is a finite tree,
- for each $s \in S$, $l(s) = (\Delta, d)$ for some d-maximally consistent set Δ,
- the root node s_0 is labelled by $(\Gamma, 0)$,
- for each node s with $R(s) = \{s_1, \ldots, s_u\}$, the call related to $l(s)$ recursively calls $\mathrm{SAT_{BML}}$ with the respective arguments $l(s_1)$, ..., $l(s_u)$.

The map l takes an abstract state s and returns the arguments (Δ, d) of some accepting computation from $\mathrm{SAT_{BML}}(\Delta, d)$. The model $\mathcal{T}$ we are looking for is precisely $\mathcal{T} = (S, R, L)$ for which $L(s) = \Delta \cap \mathrm{PROP}(\varphi)$ where $l(s) = (\Delta, d)$ for each s.

By structural induction on ψ we show that for all $s \in S$ with $l(s) = (\Delta, d)$, for all $\psi \in ecl(d, \varphi)$, $\psi \in \Delta$ iff $\mathcal{T}, s \models \psi$. If we were dealing with propositionally consistent sets (in the sense of propositionally expanded sets from Definition 4.1.4) instead of maximal consistent sets, we would just need to establish that, if $\psi \in \Delta$, then $\mathcal{T}, s \models \psi$. Consequently, we get $\mathcal{M}, s_0 \models \varphi$. The case when ψ is an atomic proposition is by definition of L.

Induction hypothesis: for all $\psi \in cl(\varphi)$ such that $|\psi| \leq n$, for all $s \in S$ with $l(s) = (\Delta, d)$, if $\psi \in ecl(d, \varphi)$ and $\psi \in \Delta$, then $\mathcal{T}, s \models \psi$.

Let ψ be a formula in $ecl(\varphi)$ such that $|\psi| = n + 1$. The cases when the outermost connective of ψ is Boolean is a consequence of the d-maximal consistency and the induction hypothesis. By way of example, let us consider the case $\psi = \mathsf{EX}\, \psi'$. Let $s \in S$ be such that $L(s) = (\Delta, d)$ and $\psi \in ecl(d, \varphi)$. By definition of S, $\mathrm{SAT_{BML}}(\Delta, d)$ has an accepting computation. If $\psi \in \Delta$, then there is a call $\mathrm{SAT_{BML}}(\Delta', d + 1)$ with $\psi' \in \Delta'$ that has an accepting computation. By induction hypothesis, there is a state s' such that $l(s') = (\Delta, d + 1)$ and $\mathcal{T}, s' \models \psi'$ with sRs'. So, $\mathcal{T}, s \models \psi$.

The case when $\psi = \neg\mathsf{EX}\, \psi'$ is left as an exercise.

(II) Assume that φ is BML satisfiable in some transition system $\mathcal{T} = (S, R, L)$. So there is $s \in S$ such that $\mathcal{T}, s \models \varphi$. We show that for all interpreted transition systems $\mathcal{T}'$ and $s' \in S'$, if $\Gamma = \{\psi \in ecl(d, \varphi) : \mathcal{M}', s' \models \psi\}$ for some $d \in \{0, \ldots, |\varphi|\}$, then $\mathrm{SAT_{BML}}(\Gamma, d)$ has an accepting computation. We recall that Γ is d-maximally consistent. Consequently, we get that $\mathrm{SAT_{BML}}(\{\psi \in ecl(0, \varphi) : \mathcal{T}, s \models \psi\}, 0)$ has an accepting computation.

The proof is by induction on $d_{max} - d$ where d_{max} is the maximal value such that $ecl(d_{max}, \varphi) \neq \emptyset$.

Base case: $d = d_{max}$. Any satisfiable set of propositional formulae included in $ecl(d_{max}, \varphi)$ is d_{max}-maximally consistent and leads to an accepting computation.

Induction hypothesis: for all $|\varphi| \geq d' \geq n \geq 1$ and $\Gamma \subseteq ecl(d', \varphi)$ such that there exist a transition system $\mathcal{T}'$ and a state s' verifying $\Gamma = \{\psi \in ecl(d', \varphi) : \mathcal{T}', s' \models \psi\}$ we have that $\mathrm{SAT_{BML}}(\Gamma, d')$ has an accepting computation.

$$\text{SAT}_{\text{BML}}(\{\varphi, (\neg \text{EX}p \vee \neg \text{EX}q), \text{EX}q, \neg \text{EX}p, p, q\}, 0)$$

$$\text{SAT}_{\text{BML}}(\{\neg(\neg \text{EX}p \vee \neg \text{EX}q), \text{EX}p, \text{EX}q, q, \neg p\}, 1)$$

$$\text{SAT}_{\text{BML}}(\{p, q\}, 2) \qquad\qquad\qquad \text{SAT}_{\text{BML}}(\{q, \neg p\}, 2)$$

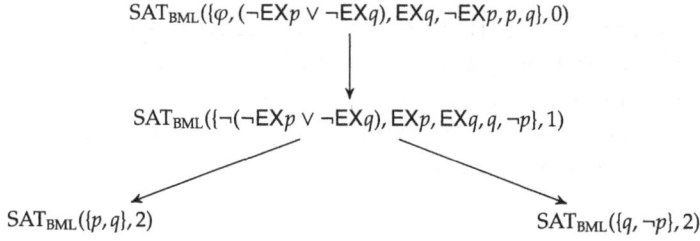

Figure 5.6 A tree of SAT_{BML} calls witnessing the satisfiability status of φ.

Let $d' = n - 1$ and Γ be a subset of $ecl(d', \varphi)$ for which there exist an interpreted transition system $\mathcal{T}'$ and a state s' verifying $\Gamma = \{\psi \in ecl(d', \varphi) : \mathcal{T}', s' \models \psi\}$. The set Γ is therefore d'-maximally consistent and satisfiable, i.e. $\bigwedge_{\psi \in \Gamma} \psi$ is satisfiable. This is sufficient to establish that $\text{SAT}_{\text{BML}}(\Gamma, d')$ has an accepting computation. Indeed, the step (2.) is successful because Γ is d'-maximal consistent.

Let $\text{EX}\psi_1, \ldots, \text{EX}\psi_u$ be the EX-formulae in Γ. So, there are states $s_1, \ldots, s_u \in R(s')$ such that for every $i \in [1, u]$, we have $\mathcal{T}', s_i \models \psi_i$. By the induction hypothesis, for every $i \in [1, u]$, $\text{SAT}_{\text{BML}}(\Delta_i, d' + 1)$ returns $\texttt{true}$ with $\Delta_i = \{\psi \in ecl(d' + 1, \varphi) : \mathcal{T}', s_i \models \psi\}$. Consequently, $\text{SAT}_{\text{BML}}(\Gamma, d')$ has an accepting computation. □

In Figure 5.6, we provide a simple tree of calls that leads to an accepting computation witnessing that the BML formula $\varphi = \neg \text{EX}(\neg \text{EX}p \vee \neg \text{EX}q)$ is satisfiable. Note that this is not the smallest tree that leads to an accepting computation and the computation checks more constraints than what is strictly necessary.

Next we analyse the space needed to run Algorithm 2.

Lemma 5.5.7. For every 0-maximally consistent in $cl(\varphi)$ set Γ, and computation of $\text{SAT}_{\text{BML}}(\Gamma, 0)$:

- the recursive depth is linear in $|\varphi|$,
- each call requires linear space in $|\varphi|$. ■

Proof. By Lemma 5.5.5, the size of the stack of recursive calls to SAT_{BML} is at most $|\varphi|$ since $ecl(|\varphi|, \varphi) = \emptyset$. In the function SAT_{BML}, the steps (2.) and (4.) can obviously be checked in polynomial time in φ (and therefore in polynomial space), see e.g. Lemma 5.5.5(III). In the steps (7.-8.), one needs a counter to count to at most $|\varphi|$, to remember which EX-formulae have not been yet considered. All the nonrecursive instructions in (8.) can be done in polynomial time in $|\varphi|$. □

Corollary 5.5.8. For every 0-maximally consistent in $ecl(\varphi)$ set Γ, existence of an accepting computation from $\text{SAT}_{\text{BML}}(\Gamma, 0)$ requires at most polynomial space in $|\varphi|$. ■

So we have established that a BML formula φ is satisfiable iff for some $\Gamma \subseteq ecl(0, \varphi)$ such that $\varphi \in \Gamma$, $\text{SAT}_{\text{BML}}(\Gamma, 0)$ has a computation that returns $\texttt{true}$, whence the NPSPACE upper bound. By Savitch's Theorem, nondeterminism can be eliminated at low cost, leading to the PSPACE upper bound.

Theorem 5.5.9. SAT(BML) is in PSPACE. ∎

Note that we are able to prove again that every satisfiable formula φ is satisfiable in a finite tree of bounded height and branching factor, as stated in Corollary 5.5.3. Indeed, we have seen that when φ is satisfiable, then there is $\Gamma \subseteq ecl(0, \varphi)$ such that $\varphi \in \Gamma$, $\text{SAT}_{\text{BML}}(\Gamma, 0)$ has a computation that returns true. By the proof of (I) for Lemma 5.5.6, we can then build a finite tree model satisfying φ that is of height $mdeg(\varphi)$ and branching factor bounded by the number of occurrences of modal operators in φ. A related tableau construction can be also found in Section 13.1.

Corollary 5.5.10. Every satisfiable BML formula φ has a finite tree-like model with height and branching factor bounded by $mdeg(\varphi)$. ∎

5.6 The Basic Tense Logic BTL

5.6.1 Adding Past-Time Operators

The **basic tense logic** BTL is the extension of BML in which new modal operators EY_a and AY_a are introduced so that their interpretations are related to the converse of transition relations. This increases the expressive power of BML by allowing the specification of postconditions for instance. $\text{EY}_a p$ can be read as a statement about the existence of a predecessor via the transition relation $\xrightarrow{a}$ that satisfies p.

As for BML, with every type $\tau = (Act, \text{PROP})$, we associate a **multitense language** $\text{BTL} = \text{BTL}_\tau$ with a set of atomic propositions PROP and two families of modal operators $(\text{EX}_a)_{a \in Act}$ and $(\text{EY}_a)_{a \in Act}$. Formulae of BTL are defined according to the following grammar:

$$\varphi := p \mid \bot \mid \neg\varphi \mid (\varphi \wedge \varphi) \mid \text{EX}_a\varphi \mid \text{EY}_a\varphi.$$

We write AY_a to denote the dual operator of EY_a so that $\text{AY}_a\varphi := \neg\text{EY}_a\neg\varphi$. The modal depth of a formula φ is defined as the modal depth for BML formulae, with the added clause $mdeg(\text{EY}_a\varphi) := mdeg(\varphi) + 1$. The semantics of BTL_τ is the standard Kripke semantics in interpreted transition systems where we extend the satisfaction relation $\models$ (for BML) to the past operators as follows:

$$\mathcal{T}, s \models \text{EY}_a\varphi \quad \text{iff} \quad \mathcal{T}, s' \models \varphi \text{ for some state } s' \in S \text{ such that } s' \xrightarrow{a} s.$$

The derived truth definition of AY_a becomes:

$$\mathcal{T}, s \models \text{AY}_a\varphi \quad \text{iff} \quad \mathcal{T}, s' \models \varphi \text{ for all states } s' \in S \text{ such that } s' \xrightarrow{a} s.$$

All notions related to truth, extension of a formula, validity, satisfiability, logical consequence and basic tense theory are defined for BTL exactly as for BML in Section 5.1. The relationship between past and future operators is reflected by the following two important additional validities of BTL.

$$\models p \rightarrow \mathsf{AY}_a\mathsf{EX}_a\, p \quad \text{and} \quad \models p \rightarrow \mathsf{AX}_a\mathsf{EY}_a\, p.$$

Moreover, it is easy to show that if φ in BTL is valid then $\mathsf{AY}_a\varphi$ is valid, too.

Lastly, we note that the extension $[\![\varphi]\!]^T$ of a BTL formula φ in an interpreted transition system T can be computed inductively just like in BML, with the additional clause:

$$[\![\mathsf{EY}_a\psi]\!]^T = \mathrm{post}(a, [\![\psi]\!]^T) = \{s \mid \{s' \in S \mid s' \xrightarrow{a} s\} \cap [\![\psi]\!]^T \neq \emptyset\}.$$

Extending the standard translation into FO2 to BTL is quite straightforward since moving forwards or backwards along a binary relation in first-order logic does not make any essential difference. The translation of subformulae of the form $\mathsf{EY}_a\psi$ goes through the clause:

$$\mathrm{ST}(\mathsf{EY}_a\psi, x_j) := \exists y\, (R_a(y, x_j) \wedge \mathrm{ST}(\psi, y)),$$

where y is the first variable in VAR not occurring in $\mathrm{ST}(\varphi, x_j)$. Like for BML, one can show that for every rooted interpreted transition system (T, s) and BTL formula φ, we have $T, s \models \varphi$ iff $T \models_{\mathrm{FO}} \mathrm{ST}(\varphi, x)[x := s]$ (the proof of Lemma 5.1.4 can easily be adapted).

5.6.2 Satisfiability and Model Checking

Recycling of variables is also possible for BTL and therefore the translation can fall into the two-variable fragment of FO. Since FO2 has a decidable satisfiability problem, we can conclude that the satisfiability and validity problems for BTL are decidable. However, this translation does not directly provide an optimal computational complexity. Here we provide a nondeterministic polynomial-space algorithm for testing satisfiability of BTL formulae, by extending the algorithm for BML from Section 5.5.2. For the sake of simplicity, we now assume that EX and EY are the only modal operators. As in Section 5.5.2, we further refine the notion of extended closure by introducing a new parameter $u \in \{\rightarrow, \leftarrow\}^*$: the sequence of forwards or backwards moves. Each set $ecl(u, \varphi)$ is therefore a subset of $cl(\varphi)$, viewed as subformulae occurring after moving according to the sequence of moves u. Formally, for every $u \in \{\rightarrow, \leftarrow\}^*$, $ecl(u, \varphi)$ is the smallest set of formulae such that:

- $ecl(\varepsilon, \varphi) = cl(\varphi)$,
- for all $u \in \{\rightarrow, \leftarrow\}^*$,
  - if $\mathsf{EX}\psi$ occurs in some formula of $ecl(u, \varphi)$, then $\psi \in ecl(u \cdot \rightarrow, \varphi)$,
  - if $\neg\mathsf{EX}\psi$ occurs in some formula of $ecl(u, \varphi)$, then $\sim\!\psi \in ecl(u \cdot \rightarrow, \varphi)$,
  - if $\mathsf{EY}\psi$ occurs in some formula of $ecl(u, \varphi)$, then $\psi \in ecl(u \cdot \leftarrow, \varphi)$,
  - if $\neg\mathsf{EY}\psi$ occurs in some formula of $ecl(u, \varphi)$, then $\sim\!\psi \in ecl(u \cdot \leftarrow, \varphi)$,
  - $ecl(u, \varphi)$ is closed in the sense of Definition 4.1.2.

For example, consider the formula $\varphi = \text{EX}(\neg\text{EX}p \vee \neg\text{EY}q)$. We obtain the following sets:

- $ecl(\varepsilon, \varphi)$ is equal to $cl(\varphi)$ and therefore it is equal to

$$\{\varphi, \neg\varphi, (\neg\text{EX}p \vee \neg\text{EY}q), \neg(\neg\text{EX}p \vee \neg\text{EY}q), \neg\text{EX}p, \text{EX}p, \neg\text{EY}q, \text{EY}q, p, q, \neg p, \neg q\}.$$

- $ecl(\rightarrow, \varphi)$ is equal to

$$\{(\neg\text{EX}p \vee \neg\text{EY}q), \neg(\neg\text{EX}p \vee \neg\text{EY}q), \neg\text{EX}p, \text{EX}p, \neg\text{EY}q, \text{EY}q,$$

$$p, q, \neg p, \neg q\text{EX}p, \text{EY}q, p, q\}.$$

- $ecl(\rightarrow \cdot \rightarrow, \varphi) = \{p, \neg p\}$ and $ecl(\rightarrow \cdot \rightarrow \cdot \rightarrow, \varphi) = \emptyset$.
- $ecl(\rightarrow \cdot \leftarrow, \varphi) = \{q, \neg q\}$ and $ecl(\rightarrow \cdot \leftarrow \cdot \rightarrow, \varphi) = \emptyset$.

A set $\Gamma \subseteq cl(\varphi)$ is u-**maximally consistent** iff $\Gamma \subseteq ecl(u, \varphi)$ and Γ is maximally consistent with respect to $ecl(u, \varphi)$.

It is worth observing that this definition for $ecl(\cdot)$ actually extends the one for BML. Indeed, let φ be a formula in BML and u be the word $\rightarrow^n$ ('$\rightarrow$' repeated n times). One can show that $ecl(n, \varphi)$ in BML is equal to $ecl(u, \varphi)$ in BTL. There was no need to consider words for defining $ecl(\cdot)$ in BML since the modal operators can only move forwards and only their length matters.

Lemma 5.6.1. Let φ be a BTL formula and $u \in \{\rightarrow, \leftarrow\}^*$.

(I) Every u-maximally consistent set has cardinality at most $|\varphi|$ and can be encoded with a number of bits linear in $|\varphi|$.

(II) $ecl(u, \varphi) = \emptyset$ if $|u| \geq |\varphi|$ (length of u is greater than the size of φ).

(III) Given a set $\Gamma \subseteq cl(\varphi)$ of cardinality at most $|\varphi|$ and $u \in \{\rightarrow, \leftarrow\}^*$, it can be decided in linear time in $|\varphi|$ whether Γ is u-maximally consistent. ∎

The proof of Lemma 5.6.1 is an easy exercise again. Indeed, $\max\{mdeg(\psi) \mid \psi \in ecl(\varepsilon, \varphi)\}$ is equal to $mdeg(\varphi)$ and whenever $\max\{mdeg(\psi) \mid \psi \in ecl(u, \varphi)\} = N \geq 1$, we have $\max\{mdeg(\psi) \mid \psi \in ecl(u \cdot \rightarrow, \varphi) \cup ecl(u \cdot \leftarrow, \varphi)\} < N$.

We present Algorithm 3 for computing the function SAT_{BTL}, such that φ is BTL satisfiable iff there is $\Gamma \subseteq ecl(\varepsilon, \varphi)$ such that $\varphi \in \Gamma$, Γ is ε-maximally consistent and $\text{SAT}_{\text{BTL}}(\Gamma, \varepsilon)$ has a computation that returns true. The function $\text{SAT}_{\text{BTL}}(\Gamma, u)$ is parameterised by the formula φ and this parameter should again be understood as a global variable. The first argument Γ is intended to be a subset of $ecl(u, \varphi)$. A call $\text{SAT}_{\text{BTL}}(\Gamma, u)$ performs the following actions. First, it checks whether Γ is u-maximally consistent and if the modal degree is zero, then it returns true in case of d-maximal consistency. In order to check that Γ is satisfiable, children of the node are guessed. We recursively apply $\text{SAT}_{\text{BTL}}(\Delta, u \cdot \rightarrow)$ or $\text{SAT}_{\text{BTL}}(\Delta, u \cdot \leftarrow)$ to ensure that not only Δ is $(u \cdot \rightarrow)$-maximally consistent or $(u \cdot \leftarrow)$-maximally consistent but also that Δ is satisfiable. Hence, if we guess a set Δ that contains some unsatisfiable formula, then $\text{SAT}_{\text{BTL}}(\Delta, u \cdot \rightarrow)$ or $\text{SAT}_{\text{BTL}}(\Delta, u \cdot \leftarrow)$ has no accepting computation which also induces a nonaccepting computation for $\text{SAT}_{\text{BTL}}(\Gamma, u)$.

Let us first state the correctness of Algorithm 3.

Algorithm 3 A nondeterministic algorithm for BTL satisfiability.

1: **procedure** $\mathrm{SAT_{BTL}}(\Gamma, u)$

2:     **if** Γ is not u-maximally consistent **then** abort

3:     **end if**

4:     **if** Γ contains only propositional formulae **then return** true

5:     **end if**

6:     **for** $\mathrm{EX}\psi \in \Gamma$ **do**

7:        Guess $\Delta \subseteq ecl(u\cdot \rightarrow, \varphi)$ such that

             $\psi \in \Delta, \{\sim\psi' \mid \neg\mathrm{EX}\psi' \in \Gamma\} \subseteq \Delta$ and $\{\sim\psi' \mid \neg\mathrm{EY}\psi' \in \Delta\} \subseteq \Gamma$

8:        **if** not $\mathrm{SAT_{BTL}}(\Delta, u\cdot \rightarrow)$ **then** abort

9:        **end if**

10:     **end for**

11:     **for** $\mathrm{EY}\psi \in \Gamma$ **do**

12:        Guess $\Delta \subseteq ecl(u\cdot \leftarrow, \varphi)$ such that

             $\psi \in \Delta, \{\sim\psi' \mid \neg\mathrm{EY}\psi' \in \Gamma\} \subseteq \Delta$ and $\{\sim\psi' \mid \neg\mathrm{EX}\psi' \in \Delta\} \subseteq \Gamma$

13:        **if** not $\mathrm{SAT_{BTL}}(\Delta, u\cdot \leftarrow)$ **then** abort

14:        **end if**

15:     **end for**

16: **end procedure**

Lemma 5.6.2.

(I) If for some $\Gamma \subseteq ecl(\varepsilon, \varphi)$, $\mathrm{SAT_{BTL}}(\Gamma, \varepsilon)$ has a computation that returns true and $\varphi \in \Gamma$, then the BTL formula φ is satisfiable.

(II) If the BTL formula φ is satisfiable then for some $\Gamma \subseteq ecl(\varphi, \varepsilon)$ such that $\varphi \in \Gamma$, $\mathrm{SAT_{BTL}}(\Gamma, \varepsilon)$ has an accepting computation. ∎

The proof of Lemma 5.6.2 is similar to the proof of Lemma 5.5.6 and it is left as Exercise 5.18. Next we analyse the space needed to run Algorithm 3.

Lemma 5.6.3. For every fully ε-expanded in $cl(\varphi)$ set Γ, and computation of $\mathrm{SAT_{BTL}}(\Gamma, \varepsilon)$:

• the recursive depth is linear in $|\varphi|$,
• each call requires linear space in $|\varphi|$. ∎

Again, the proof is similar to the proof of Lemma 5.5.7.

Corollary 5.6.4. For every ε-maximally consistent set Γ, $\mathrm{SAT_{BTL}}(\Gamma, \varepsilon)$ runs in polynomial space in $|\varphi|$. ∎

So we have established that a BTL formula φ is satisfiable iff for some $\Gamma \subseteq ecl(\varepsilon, \varphi)$ such that $\varphi \in \Gamma$, $\mathrm{SAT_{BTL}}(\Gamma, \varepsilon)$ has a computation that returns true, whence the NPSPACE upper bound (and consequently, the PSPACE upper bound by Savitch's Theorem, see e.g. Section 2.2.2).

Theorem 5.6.5. SAT(BTL) is in PSPACE. ∎

Like for BML, we can conclude that every satisfiable formula φ in BTL is satisfiable in a finite tree of height $mdeg(\varphi)$ and branching factor bounded by the number of occurrences of modal operators in φ.

The model-checking algorithm for BML can easily be adapted for BTL, too, and it runs in the same complexity. Likewise, the model-checking algorithm and the model-checking game for BML can easily be adapted for BTL, too, and an analogue of Theorem 5.4.10 holds. We leave the details as Exercise 5.17.

5.7 Axiomatic Systems

We present a standard axiomatic system AXSYS$_{BML}$ in the mono-modal case (the multimodal extension is straightforward) for the set of valid formulae of BML, extending AXSYS$_{PL}$ with just one axiom scheme plus a simple auxiliary axiom and one extra rule of inference. We assume for technical convenience that the associated language BML contains as primitive connectives $\top, \neg, \wedge, \vee, \rightarrow$ and AX whereas $\bot, \leftrightarrow$ and EX can be assumed definable as usual, by $\mathsf{EX}\varphi := \neg\mathsf{AX}\neg\varphi$.

5.7.1 An Axiomatic System for BML

Recall that an axiom scheme is the set of all instances obtained from a given formula by applying uniform substitutions of formulae for the formula metavariables in the scheme. In our case, the scheme and the formulae to be substituted are BML-formulae. For example, $(\mathsf{AX}(\mathsf{AX}p \rightarrow \mathsf{EX}r) \wedge \mathsf{EXAX}p) \rightarrow \mathsf{AXEX}r$ is the instance of $(\mathsf{AX}(\varphi \rightarrow \psi) \wedge \mathsf{EX}\varphi) \rightarrow \mathsf{AX}\psi$ where φ is substituted by $\mathsf{AX}p$ and ψ is substituted by $\mathsf{EX}r$.

The axioms of AXSYS$_{BML}$ are all instances of the following schemes.

(PL) All axiom schemes of AXSYS$_{PL}$.
(K) $\mathsf{AX}\varphi \wedge \mathsf{AX}(\varphi \rightarrow \psi) \rightarrow \mathsf{AX}\psi$.

The rules of inference are **Modus ponens** (MP) and the rule of **Necessitation**:

$$\mathbf{Nec}: \quad \frac{\vdash \varphi}{\vdash \mathsf{AX}\varphi}.$$

The axiom scheme (K) is the standard K-axiom for basic modal logic. If the seriality condition for the transition relation associated with EX is required, then the following axiom must be added:

(SER) $\mathsf{EX}\top$.

It does not play any essential role for any of the properties of AXSYS$_{BML}$ mentioned further, but is needed when satisfying models are constructed. All basic notions related to derivations and derivability, defined in Chapter 4 for AXSYS$_{PL}$, apply, *mutatis mutandis*, to

$\text{AxSys}_{\text{BML}}$. In particular, deductive consequence from a set of assumptions in $\text{AxSys}_{\text{BML}}$ is defined likewise. The only difference is that the rule **Nec** can be applied in derivations in $\text{AxSys}_{\text{BML}}$ to any theorem (in particular, any axiom) of $\text{AxSys}_{\text{BML}}$, but *not* to the other assumptions.

We will denote derivability in $\text{AxSys}_{\text{BML}}$ by $\vdash_{\text{AxSys}_{\text{BML}}}$ but within this section we sometimes will omit the subscript. We list some useful claims about $\text{AxSys}_{\text{BML}}$, the proof of which we leave to the reader, see, e.g. Exercise 5.30.

Proposition 5.7.1. The Deduction Theorem holds for $\text{AxSys}_{\text{BML}}$: for any BML-formulae φ, ψ and a set of formulae Γ:

$$\Gamma \cup \{\varphi\} \vdash_{\text{AxSys}_{\text{BML}}} \psi \quad \text{iff} \quad \Gamma \vdash_{\text{AxSys}_{\text{BML}}} \varphi \to \psi. \qquad \blacksquare$$

Proposition 5.7.2. The following hold for $\text{AxSys}_{\text{BML}}$:

(I) For any BML-formulae φ, ψ and a set of formulae Γ:
   if $\Gamma \vdash \psi$ then $\Gamma \cup \{\varphi\} \vdash \psi$.
(II) If $\vdash \varphi \to \psi$ then $\vdash \mathsf{AX}\varphi \to \mathsf{AX}\psi$.
(III) $\vdash (\mathsf{AX}\varphi_1 \wedge \cdots \wedge \mathsf{AX}\varphi_n) \to \mathsf{AX}(\varphi_1 \wedge \cdots \wedge \varphi_n)$.
(IV) $\vdash \mathsf{AX}(\varphi_1 \wedge \cdots \wedge \varphi_n) \to (\mathsf{AX}\varphi_1 \wedge \cdots \wedge \mathsf{AX}\varphi_n)$. $\qquad \blacksquare$

Given the soundness of AxSys_{PL}, in order to prove the soundness of $\text{AxSys}_{\text{BML}}$ it suffices to show that the new axiom scheme consists of valid formulae and that the necessitation rule **Nec** preserves validity, which we leave as Exercise 5.23.

Example 5.7.3. $\vdash_{\text{AxSys}_{\text{BML}}} \mathsf{AX}(p \to q) \to (\mathsf{EX}p \to \mathsf{EX}q)$
   (Recall that $\mathsf{EX}\varphi = \neg\mathsf{AX}\neg\varphi$.)

1. $\vdash (p \to q) \to (\neg q \to \neg p)$ \hfill instance of a theorem of AxSys_{PL}
2. $\vdash \mathsf{AX}((p \to q) \to (\neg q \to \neg p))$ \hfill by 1 and **Nec**
3. $\vdash \mathsf{AX}((p \to q) \to (\neg q \to \neg p)) \to (\mathsf{AX}(p \to q) \to \mathsf{AX}(\neg q \to \neg p))$
   \hfill instance of axiom scheme (**K**)
4. $\vdash \mathsf{AX}(p \to q) \to \mathsf{AX}(\neg q \to \neg p)$ \hfill by 2,3 and **MP**
5. $\mathsf{AX}(p \to q) \vdash \mathsf{AX}(\neg q \to \neg p))$ \hfill by 4 and the Deduction Theorem
6. $\vdash \mathsf{AX}(\neg q \to \neg p) \to (\mathsf{AX}\neg q \to \mathsf{AX}\neg p)$ \hfill instance of axiom scheme (**K**)
7. $\mathsf{AX}(p \to q) \vdash \mathsf{AX}(\neg q \to \neg p) \to (\mathsf{AX}\neg q \to \mathsf{AX}\neg p)$ \hfill by 6
8. $\mathsf{AX}(p \to q) \vdash \mathsf{AX}\neg q \to \mathsf{AX}\neg p$ \hfill by 5, 7
9. $\vdash (\mathsf{AX}\neg q \to \mathsf{AX}\neg p) \to (\neg\mathsf{AX}\neg p \to \neg\mathsf{AX}\neg q)$
   \hfill instance of a theorem of AxSys_{PL}
10. $\mathsf{AX}(p \to q) \vdash (\mathsf{AX}\neg q \to \mathsf{AX}\neg p) \to (\neg\mathsf{AX}\neg p \to \neg\mathsf{AX}\neg q)$ \hfill by 9
11. $\mathsf{AX}(p \to q) \vdash \neg\mathsf{AX}\neg p \to \neg\mathsf{AX}\neg q$ \hfill by 8, 10 and **MP**
12. $\mathsf{AX}(p \to q) \vdash \mathsf{EX}p \to \mathsf{EX}q$ \hfill by 11 and the definition of EX
13. $\vdash \mathsf{AX}(p \to q) \to (\mathsf{EX}p \to \mathsf{EX}q)$ \hfill by 12 and the Deduction Theorem

By substituting any formulae φ for p and ψ for q we also obtain a derivation of $\vdash_{\text{AxSys}_{\text{BML}}} \text{AX}(\varphi \to \psi) \to (\text{EX}\varphi \to \text{EX}\psi)$.

Example 5.7.4. $\text{AX}(\text{EX}p \to q), \text{EX}(\text{AX}p \wedge \text{EX}r) \vdash_{\text{AxSys}_{\text{BML}}} \text{EX}q$

1. $\vdash p \to (r \to p)$	instance of an axiom of AxSys$_{\text{PL}}$
2. $\vdash \text{AX}(p \to (r \to p))$	by 1 and **Nec**
3. $\vdash \text{AX}(p \to (r \to p)) \to (\text{AX}p \to \text{AX}(r \to p))$	instance of axiom scheme (**K**)
4. $\vdash \text{AX}p \to \text{AX}(r \to p)$	by 2, 3 and **MP**
5. $\text{AX}p \wedge \text{EX}r \vdash \text{AX}p \to \text{AX}(r \to p)$	by 4
6. $\vdash (\text{AX}p \wedge \text{EX}r) \to \text{AX}p$	instance of an axiom of AxSys$_{\text{PL}}$
7. $\text{AX}p \wedge \text{EX}r \vdash \text{AX}p$	by 6 and the Deduction Theorem
8. $\text{AX}p \wedge \text{EX}r \vdash \text{AX}(r \to p)$	by 5, 7 and **MP**
9. $\vdash \text{AX}(r \to p) \to (\text{EX}r \to \text{EX}p)$	by Example 5.7.3
10. $\text{AX}p \vdash \text{AX}(r \to p) \to (\text{EX}r \to \text{EX}p)$	by 9
11. $\text{AX}p \vdash \text{EX}r \to \text{EX}p$	by 8, 10 and **MP**
12. $\vdash \text{AX}p \to (\text{EX}r \to \text{EX}p)$	by 11 and the Deduction Theorem
13. $\text{AX}p \wedge \text{EX}r \vdash \text{AX}p \to (\text{EX}r \to \text{EX}p)$	by 12
14. $\text{AX}p \wedge \text{EX}r \vdash \text{EX}r \to \text{EX}p$	by 7, 13 and **MP**
15. $\vdash (\text{AX}p \wedge \text{EX}r) \to \text{EX}r$	instance of an axiom of AxSys$_{\text{PL}}$
16. $\text{AX}p \wedge \text{EX}r \vdash \text{EX}r$	by 15 and the Deduction Theorem
17. $\text{AX}p \wedge \text{EX}r \vdash \text{EX}p$	by 14, 16 and **MP**
18. $\vdash (\text{AX}p \wedge \text{EX}r) \to \text{EX}p$	by 17 and the Deduction Theorem
19. $\vdash \text{AX}((\text{AX}p \wedge \text{EX}r) \to \text{EX}p)$	by 18 and **Nec**
20. $\vdash \text{AX}((\text{AX}p \wedge \text{EX}r) \to \text{EX}p) \to (\text{EX}(\text{AX}p \wedge \text{EX}r) \to \text{EXEX}p)$	by Ex. 5.7.3
21. $\vdash \text{EX}(\text{AX}p \wedge \text{EX}r) \to \text{EXEX}p$	by 19, 20 and **MP**
22. $\text{EX}(\text{AX}p \wedge \text{EX}r) \vdash \text{EXEX}p$	by 21 and the Deduction Theorem
23. $\text{AX}(\text{EX}p \to q), \text{EX}(\text{AX}p \wedge \text{EX}r) \vdash \text{EXEX}p$	by 22
24. $\vdash \text{AX}(\text{EX}p \to q) \to (\text{EXEX}p \to \text{EX}q)$	by Example 5.7.3
25. $\text{AX}(\text{EX}p \to q) \vdash \text{EXEX}p \to \text{EX}q$	by 24 and the Deduction Theorem
26. $\text{AX}(\text{EX}p \to q), \text{EX}(\text{AX}p \wedge \text{EX}r) \vdash \text{EXEX}p \to \text{EX}q$	by 25
27. $\text{AX}(\text{EX}p \to q), \text{EX}(\text{AX}p \wedge \text{EX}r) \vdash \text{EX}q$	by 23, 26 and **MP**

Recall the notion of deductive consistency from Chapter 4. In particular, a set of BML formulae Γ is **AxSys$_{\text{BML}}$-inconsistent** if $\Gamma \vdash_{\text{AxSys}_{\text{BML}}} \bot$; otherwise Γ is **AxSys$_{\text{BML}}$-consistent**.

The following lemma, analogous to Proposition 4.4.4, provides some useful generic characterisations of consistency in AxSys$_{\text{BML}}$, used further in the proof of the completeness theorem for AxSys$_{\text{BML}}$.

Lemma 5.7.5. The following are equivalent for any set of BML formulae Γ:

(I) Γ is AxSys$_{\text{BML}}$-inconsistent.
(II) $\Gamma \vdash_{\text{AxSys}_{\text{BML}}} \varphi$ for every BML formula φ.

(III) There is a formula φ such that $\Gamma \vdash_{\text{AxSys}_{\text{BML}}} \varphi$ and $\Gamma \vdash_{\text{AxSys}_{\text{BML}}} \neg\varphi$.

(IV) There are formulae $\varphi_1, \ldots, \varphi_n \in \Gamma$ such that $\vdash_{\text{AxSys}_{\text{BML}}} \neg(\varphi_1 \wedge \cdots \wedge \varphi_n)$. ∎

The proof is essentially the same as that of Proposition 4.4.4 and it is left as Exercise 5.32.

5.7.2 Canonical Models

As with AxSys_{PL}, the soundness and completeness for $\text{AxSys}_{\text{BML}}$ can be stated in two different, yet equivalent forms.

Theorem 5.7.6 (Soundness and Completeness). The axiomatic system $\text{AxSys}_{\text{BML}}$ is sound and complete, i.e. for every set of Γ of BML formulae and any ψ we have:

(I) $\Gamma \vdash_{\text{AxSys}_{\text{BML}}} \psi$ if and only if $\Gamma \models \psi$,

(II) Γ is satisfiable if and only if it is consistent in $\text{AxSys}_{\text{BML}}$.

In particular, $\vdash_{\text{AxSys}_{\text{BML}}} \psi$ if and only if ψ is a tautology. ∎

The proof of soundness of $\text{AxSys}_{\text{BML}}$ is left as Exercise 5.23. We also leave it as Exercise 5.29 to show that the two versions of the soundness and completeness theorem for $\text{AxSys}_{\text{BML}}$ are equivalent. In particular, the soundness direction of the first version is equivalent to the claim that every satisfiable set of BML formulae is consistent in $\text{AxSys}_{\text{BML}}$.

We will sketch the proof of the completeness part of the second characterisation. It states that every set of BML-formulae that is consistent in $\text{AxSys}_{\text{BML}}$ is satisfiable. Given a consistent set Γ we want to construct a model of Γ, i.e. a rooted ITS in which Γ is satisfiable. Actually, we will do more: we will construct **one** ITS that satisfies **all** sets of formulae that are consistent in $\text{AxSys}_{\text{BML}}$. That will be the so called **canonical ITS for $\text{AxSys}_{\text{BML}}$**. To construct it we build on the idea of the completeness proof for PL. The states of that ITS will be the **maximal consistent sets of formulae** of BML, i.e. the $\text{AxSys}_{\text{BML}}$-consistent sets which cannot be extended consistently.

First, we need to establish some fundamental properties of maximal consistent sets (MCS).

Lemma 5.7.7. The following are equivalent for any consistent set of BML formulae Γ:

- Γ is a MCS.
- For every BML-formula φ, either $\varphi \in \Gamma$ or $\neg\varphi \in \Gamma$.
- For every BML-formula φ, $\Gamma \cup \{\varphi\}$ is consistent iff $\varphi \in \Gamma$. ∎

The proof of this lemma is left as Exercise 5.32.

Lemma 5.7.8. If Γ is a MCS then:

- $\neg\varphi \in \Gamma$ iff $\varphi \notin \Gamma$.
- $\varphi \wedge \psi \in \Gamma$ iff $\varphi \in \Gamma$ and $\psi \in \Gamma$.

- $\varphi \vee \psi \in \Gamma$ iff $\varphi \in \Gamma$ or $\psi \in \Gamma$.
- $\varphi \rightarrow \psi \in \Gamma$ iff $\varphi \notin \Gamma$ or $\psi \in \Gamma$. ∎

The proof of this lemma is left as Exercise 5.32. The intuition behind maximal consistent sets is simple but fundamental. Take any state in an ITS. The set of formulae true at that state is a MCS. Thus, maximal consistent sets serve as complete descriptions of (what is true at) states of an ITS. This being the case, one can *identify* a state in an ITS with all that is true at that state, i.e. with the MCS of formulae true there. We now take up this idea and construct the canonical ITS to consist of the set S_{BML} of *all maximal* AxSys$_{BML}$-*consistent sets of BML-formulae*. Next, we need the following fundamental generic fact.

Lemma 5.7.9 (Lindenbaum's Lemma). Every AxSys$_{\mathrm{BML}}$-consistent set of formulae can be extended to a maximal AxSys$_{\mathrm{BML}}$-consistent set. ∎

To prove this lemma we simply arrange all (countably many) formulae of the language in an infinite sequence, pick them one by one and add them to the set if and only if that will preserve consistency. The eventual result will be a MCS. Indeed, derivations, and therefore inconsistency, in BML are *finitary notions*: if the resulting set is inconsistent, that inconsistency should occur at some step of the construction, which is prevented. The details of the proof of Lindenbaum's Lemma are left as Exercise 5.31.

Now, we are ready to construct the **canonical ITS** for AxSys$_{\mathrm{BML}}$ as the interpreted transition system $\mathcal{T}_{\mathrm{BML}} = (S_{\mathrm{BML}}, R_{\mathrm{BML}}, L_{\mathrm{BML}})$ where:

- S_{BML} is the set of maximally consistent sets of AxSys$_{\mathrm{BML}}$.
- For all $\Gamma, \Gamma' \in S_{\mathrm{BML}}$ we have $(\Gamma, \Gamma') \in R_{\mathrm{BML}}$ if and only if, for all φ, $\mathsf{AX}\varphi \in \Gamma$ implies $\varphi \in \Gamma'$.
- For all $\Gamma \in S_{\mathrm{BML}}$ we have $L_{\mathrm{BML}}(\Gamma) := \{p \in \mathrm{PROP} \mid p \in \Gamma\}$.

Note that the axiom (SER) ensures that the relation R_{BML} is serial, i.e. every state has a successor. Omitting the axiom (SER) would not affect the proof of completeness except that the seriality of R_{BML} would not be imposed.

The crucial property of this construction is the following generic claim.

Lemma 5.7.10 (Truth lemma). For every BML-formula φ and a state $\Gamma \in S_{\mathrm{BML}}$, the following holds: $\mathcal{T}_{\mathrm{BML}}, \Gamma \models \varphi$ if and only if $\varphi \in \Gamma$. ∎

That equivalence is proved by structural induction on φ. The case when $\varphi \in \mathrm{PROP}$ is ensured by the definition of L_{BML}. Due to the properties of MCSs mentioned in Proposition 5.7.2 this equivalence propagates through all Boolean connectives. For the final step, for $\varphi = \mathsf{AX}\psi$ for some ψ the claim boils down to the following. Let $\Gamma \in S_{\mathrm{BML}}$ be such that $\mathsf{AX}\psi \notin \Gamma$. Then we have to show that there is some $\Gamma' \in S_{\mathrm{BML}}$ such that $(\Gamma, \Gamma') \in R_{\mathrm{BML}}$ and $\neg\psi \in \Gamma'$. Indeed, it suffices to show that the set $\{\vartheta \mid \mathsf{AX}\vartheta \in \Gamma\} \cup \{\neg\psi\}$ is AxSys$_{\mathrm{BML}}$-consistent, which we leave as Exercise 5.24. Then we apply Lindenbaum's Lemma. We leave the completion of the details of this proof as Exercise 5.31.

Now that we have the Truth Lemma at hand, we are ready to complete the proof of completeness: take a consistent set Δ and extend it to an MCS Γ. It is a state of the canonical ITS $\mathcal{T}_{BML}$. Then, by the Truth Lemma, $\mathcal{T}_{BML}, \Gamma \vDash \varphi$ for every $\varphi \in \Delta$, hence Δ is satisfiable.

Remark 5.7.11. The construction of the canonical ITS and the proof of completeness based on it are generic and universal. They can be applied in principle to prove a general completeness result for any extension of BML. In fact, in order to construct a canonical ITS satisfying a given consistent formula φ, we only need to consider the maximal consistent subsets of its closure $cl(\varphi)$, as defined in Chapter 4, so a suitable modification of the canonical model construction can often be used to prove a finite model property. The canonical model method, however, directly works only when the canonical transition system belongs to the class of transition systems on which the standard semantics of the logic is defined. Logics for which this is the case are called *canonical*. Unfortunately, the logics that we will consider further in the book are *not canonical* and for them additional steps in the completeness proofs will be required.

5.7.3 An Axiomatic System for BTL

The axiomatic system for BTL extends $\textsc{AxSys}_{BML}$ with the analogues of **K** and **Nec** for the past operators, plus additional axioms that reflect the relationships between the future and past operators. The axioms of $\textsc{AxSys}_{BTL}$ are all instances of the following schemes, where φ, ψ stand for any formulae of BTL.

(BML) All axiom schemes of $\textsc{AxSys}_{BML}$.
(K^{-1}) $\mathsf{AY}(\varphi \to \psi) \to (\mathsf{AY}\varphi \to \mathsf{AY}\psi)$.
(XY) $\varphi \to \mathsf{AYEX}\varphi$.
(YX) $\varphi \to \mathsf{AXEY}\varphi$.

The rules of inference are *Modus ponens* and the pair of rules of necessitation:

$$\textbf{Nec} \quad \frac{\vdash \varphi}{\vdash \mathsf{AX}\varphi} \qquad \textbf{Nec}^{-1} \quad \frac{\vdash \varphi}{\vdash \mathsf{AY}\varphi}.$$

The new axioms (XY) and (YX) are needed to ensure that the transition relations associated with AX and AY are inverses to each other.

The Deduction Theorem holds likewise for $\textsc{AxSys}_{BTL}$, the proof of which we leave as Exercise 5.30.

Theorem 5.7.12 (Soundness and Completeness). The axiomatic system $\textsc{AxSys}_{BTL}$ is sound and complete, i.e. for every set of BTL formulae $\{\varphi_1, \ldots, \varphi_n, \varphi\}$:

$$\varphi_1, \ldots, \varphi_n \vdash_{\textsc{AxSys}_{BTL}} \psi \quad \text{if and only if} \quad \varphi_1, \ldots, \varphi_n \vDash \psi.$$

In particular, $\vdash_{\textsc{AxSys}_{BTL}} \psi$ if and only if ψ is a tautology. $\blacksquare$

Given the soundness of AxSys$_{\text{BML}}$, to prove the soundness of AxSys$_{\text{BTL}}$ it suffices to show that all axioms of AxSys$_{\text{BTL}}$ are valid and that the rule **Nec**$^{-1}$ preserves validity. We leave these as Exercise 5.27.

The proof of completeness is quite analogous to the proof for AxSys$_{\text{BML}}$ with the following additional step. The canonical ITS $\mathcal{T}_{\text{BTL}}$ is defined just like $\mathcal{T}_{\text{BML}}$, but built on the set of maximally consistent sets of AxSys$_{\text{BTL}}$. Now, to prove the Truth Lemma for $\mathcal{T}_{\text{BTL}}$, the following property has to be established, stating that the relations corresponding to AX and to AY are each other's inverses:

Lemma 5.7.13. For all $\Gamma, \Gamma' \in S_{\text{BTL}}$ the following are equivalent:

(I) For every BTL formula φ, AX$\varphi \in \Gamma$ implies $\varphi \in \Gamma'$.
(II) For every BTL formula φ, AY$\varphi \in \Gamma'$ implies $\varphi \in \Gamma$. ■

The proof of this lemma uses the additional axioms (XY$_a$) and (YX$_a$) and is left as Exercise 5.32. Once the lemma is proved, the Truth Lemma and the completeness proof for AxSys$_{\text{BTL}}$ follow just like those for AxSys$_{\text{BML}}$.

5.8 Exercises

Exercises on the semantics of BML

Exercise 5.1. Consider the transition system $\mathcal{T} = (S, R, L)$, where:

- $S = \{s, t, u, v, w\}$.
- $R = \{(s, w), (s, t), (s, v), (w, w), (t, u), (t, v)(u, u), (u, v), (v, u), (v, t), (v, s)\}$.
- $L(s) = \{q\}$, $L(t) = \{q\}$, $L(u) = \emptyset$, $L(v) = \{p, q\}$ and $L(w) = \{p\}$.

Draw the graph of $\mathcal{T}$ and determine if each of the following holds.

(a) $\mathcal{T}, s \models \text{AX}(p \to \text{EX}p)$.
(b) $\mathcal{T}, s \models \text{EXAX}(\neg q \land \text{AX}p)$.
(c) $\mathcal{T}, v \models \text{AXEX}(\text{AX}\neg p \to q)$.
(d) $\mathcal{T}, v \models q \to \text{AXEX}q$.

(e) $\mathcal{T}, v \models \text{AX}(q \land \text{EXAX}(\neg q \land \text{AX}p))$.
(f) $\mathcal{T}, s \models \text{EX}(\neg p \lor q)$.
(g) $\mathcal{T}, s \models \text{EX}(\neg q \lor \text{EX}q)$.
(h) $\mathcal{T}, v \models \text{EX}(\text{AX}p \to \text{AXAX}p)$.

Exercise 5.2. Consider the following interpreted transition system.

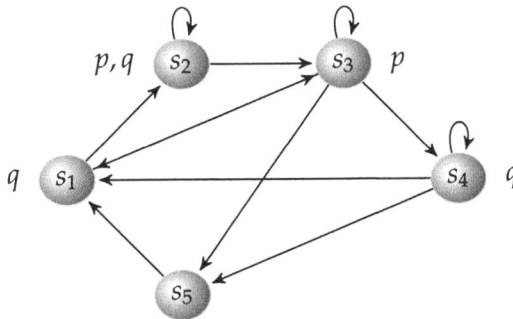

(a) Determine whether $T, s_1 \models \mathsf{AX}(q \rightarrow \mathsf{EX}\neg p)$ holds.

(b) Compute the set $[\![\mathsf{AX}(q \rightarrow \mathsf{EX}\neg p)]\!]^T$.

(c) Determine whether $T \models \mathsf{EXEX}\neg(p \vee q)$ holds.

Exercise 5.3. Consider the interpreted transition system in Figure 5.2.

(a) Determine whether $T, s_1 \models \mathsf{AX}(\mathsf{safe} \rightarrow \neg\mathsf{EX}\,\mathsf{crash})$ holds.

(b) Compute the set $[\![\mathsf{AX}(\mathsf{safe} \rightarrow \neg\mathsf{EX}\,\mathsf{crash})]\!]^T$.

(c) Determine whether $T \models \mathsf{EX}(\mathsf{safe} \wedge \mathsf{EX}\,\mathsf{crash})$ holds.

Exercise 5.4. For each state of T in Exercise 5.3 write a modal formula that describes what is true (but not necessarily what is false) at the state and at its successors. For instance:
$T, s_1 \models \mathsf{ready} \wedge \mathsf{EX}\,\mathsf{ready} \wedge \mathsf{EX}\,\mathsf{safe} \wedge \mathsf{AX}\,(\mathsf{ready} \vee \mathsf{safe})$.

Exercise 5.5. Determine which formulae are valid in BML.

(a) $\mathsf{EX}_a\mathsf{EX}_b p \leftrightarrow \mathsf{EX}_b\mathsf{EX}_a p$.

(b) $\mathsf{EX}_a\mathsf{AX}_a p \leftrightarrow \mathsf{AX}_a\mathsf{EX}_a p$.

(c) $\mathsf{AX}_a\mathsf{AX}_b p \leftrightarrow \mathsf{AX}_b\mathsf{AX}_a p$.

(d) $\mathsf{AX}_a(p \vee q) \leftrightarrow \mathsf{AX}_a p \vee \mathsf{AX}_a q$.

(e) $\mathsf{AX}_a(p \wedge q) \leftrightarrow \mathsf{AX}_a p \wedge \mathsf{AX}_a q$.

(f) $\mathsf{EX}_a(p \wedge q) \leftrightarrow \mathsf{EX}_a p \wedge \mathsf{EX}_a q$.

Exercise 5.6. Translate the following BML formulae into first-order logic using the standard translation from Section 5.1.2.

(a) $\mathsf{AX}\,p \rightarrow \mathsf{AXAX}\,p$.

(b) $\mathsf{AXEX}\,p \rightarrow \mathsf{EXAX}\neg p$.

(c) $\neg\mathsf{EX}\,p \wedge \mathsf{AX}(\neg q \vee \mathsf{AXEX}\,p)$.

Exercise 5.7. Prove Lemma 5.1.2, Lemma 5.1.4, Lemma 5.2.3, Lemma 5.2.8, Lemma 5.3.12 and Corollary 5.3.19. Complete the proof of Lemma 5.2.5.

Exercises on model and satisfiability checking

Exercise 5.8. Run Algorithm 1 on the interpreted transition system in Figure 5.1 with the formula $\varphi = \mathsf{EX}_a\mathsf{EX}_b\neg p$.

Exercise 5.9. Recall the model-checking game in Figure 5.4 and check which player has a winning strategy for the game starting in either of the nodes $1 \vdash \mathsf{AX}(p \vee \mathsf{EX}\,p)$ and $2 \vdash \mathsf{AX}(p \vee \mathsf{EX}\,p)$.

Exercise 5.10. Define model-checking games for a multimodal BML and check whether their correctness proofs need to be extended in order for them to capture the satisfaction relation for this logic.

Exercise 5.11. Let τ be a finite type and $n \geq 0$ be a fixed natural number. Show that the satisfiability problem for formulae in BML_τ^n can be solved in polynomial time. (Recall that BML_τ^n is the fragment of BML restricted to formulae of modal depth at most n.)

Exercise 5.12. Let $\mathcal{C}_\mathbb{N}$ be the set of transition systems of the form $(\mathbb{N}, \mathrm{succ}, L)$ with $\mathrm{succ} = \{(n, n+1) \mid n \in \mathbb{N}\}$. We consider the language of BML with a single modal operator. Show that the satisfiability problem for BML interpreted over $\mathcal{C}_\mathbb{N}$ is in NP.

Exercise 5.13. Consider the class $\mathcal{C}_{S5}$ of transition systems (S, R, L) such that R is an equivalence relation on S, as well as the language of BML with a single modal operator AX. We are interested in the computational complexity of the following satisfiability problem SAT(S5):

Input: a formula φ built over the logical connectives $\neg$, $\wedge$ and AX,

Question: is there an ITS $\mathcal{T} = (S, R, L) \in \mathcal{C}_{S5}$ and $s \in S$ such that $\mathcal{T}, s \models \varphi$?

(a) Explain why SAT(S5) is NP-hard.
(b) Let us denote by $\mathcal{C}'_{S5}$ the subset of $\mathcal{C}_{S5}$ that consists of the ITS (S, R, L) such that $R = S \times S$. Show that the satisfiability problem with $\mathcal{C}_{S5}$ is equivalent to the satisfiability problem with $\mathcal{C}'_{S5}$.
(c) Given a formula φ, $\mathcal{T} = (S, R, L) \in \mathcal{C}'_{S5}$ and $s \in S$ such that $\mathcal{T}, s \models \varphi$, let Γ be the set of subformulae of φ of the form AXψ such that $\mathcal{T}, s \not\models$ AXψ. So, for every AX$\psi \in \Gamma$, there is a state $s_{\neg\psi}$ such that $\mathcal{T}, s_{\neg\psi} \not\models \psi$. Let $\mathcal{T}' = (S', R', L')$ be the interpreted transition system such that
   - $S' := \{s\} \cup \{s_{\neg\psi} : \mathrm{AX}\psi \in \Gamma\}$,
   - $R' := R \cap (S' \times S')$,
   - L' is the restriction of L to the states in S'.
   Show that for every $s' \in S'$, for every subformula ψ of φ, we have $\mathcal{T}, s' \models \psi$ iff $\mathcal{T}', s' \models \psi$.
(d) Given a transition system $\mathcal{T} = (S, R, L)$ and a formula φ, show that checking whether $\mathcal{T} \in \mathcal{C}'_{S5}$ and whether there is $s \in S$ such that $\mathcal{T}, s \models \varphi$ can be done in polynomial time in the size of $\mathcal{T}$ and φ.
(e) Conclude that the satisfiability problem SAT(S5) is in NP.

Exercise 5.14. Prove Lemma 5.4.4, Lemma 5.4.9 and Lemma 5.5.4. Complete the details of the proof of Lemma 5.5.2 and the case (I) in the proof of Lemma 5.5.6.

Exercises on BTL

Exercise 5.15. Let $\mathfrak{swap}$ be a map from BTL formulae to BTL formulae that is homomorphic for Boolean connectives and such that $\mathfrak{swap}(\mathrm{EX}_a\psi) := \mathrm{EY}_a\mathfrak{swap}(\psi)$ and $\mathfrak{swap}(\mathrm{EY}_a\psi) := \mathrm{EX}_a\mathfrak{swap}(\psi)$. Show that φ is satisfiable iff $\mathfrak{swap}(\varphi)$ is satisfiable.

Exercise 5.16. Are the following formulae valid for any φ?

(a) $\varphi \rightarrow \mathrm{AX}_a\mathrm{AY}_a\varphi$.
(b) $\varphi \rightarrow \mathrm{EX}_a\mathrm{EY}_a\varphi$.
(c) $\varphi \rightarrow \mathrm{EX}_a\mathrm{AY}_a\varphi$.
(d) $\varphi \rightarrow \mathrm{EY}_a\mathrm{AX}_a\varphi$.

Give a countermodel in each case of invalidity.

Exercise 5.17.

(a) Adapt the model-checking algorithm for BML to BTL and show that MC(BTL) is in PTIME.
(b) Adapt the model-checking games for BML to BTL and prove the analogue of Theorem 5.4.10.

Exercise 5.18. Prove Lemma 5.5.5, Lemma 5.6.1, Lemma 5.6.2 and Lemma 5.6.3.

Exercises on axiomatic systems

Exercise 5.19. Show that the following are theorems of AxSys$_{BML}$.

(a) $(AX\varphi \wedge AX\psi) \rightarrow AX(\varphi \wedge \psi)$.
(b) $(AX\varphi_1 \wedge \cdots \wedge AX\varphi_n) \rightarrow AX(\varphi_1 \wedge \cdots \wedge \varphi_n)$, for any $n > 1$.
(c) $AX(\varphi \wedge \psi) \rightarrow AX\varphi$.
(d) $(EXq \wedge AXEXp) \rightarrow EXEXp$.
(e) $EX(EXq \wedge AXp) \rightarrow EXEX(p \wedge q)$.
(f) $(EXp \rightarrow AXAX\neg q) \rightarrow \neg EX(p \wedge EXq)$.

Exercise 5.20. Derive the following in AxSys$_{BML}$.

(a) If $\vdash \varphi \rightarrow \psi$ then $\vdash AX\varphi \rightarrow AX\psi$.
(b) $AX\neg p \rightarrow EXq, AX\neg q \vdash EXp$.
(c) $EX\neg p \rightarrow AXq, EX\neg q \vdash AXp$.
(d) $EX\neg p \rightarrow AXq, AX\neg q \vdash AXp$.

(c) $EXp, AX(p \rightarrow AXq) \vdash EXAXq$
(f) $EXAXp, AXEXq \vdash EXEX(p \wedge q)$.
(g) $AX(p \vee EXq), EXAX\neg q \vdash EX\neg p$.

Exercise 5.21. Use derivations in AxSys$_{BML}$ to establish the following logical consequences.

(a) $AXp, EX(\neg p \vee q), AX(q \rightarrow EXq) \models EXEXq$.
(b) $EXp, AX(\neg p \vee AXq), AX(EXq \rightarrow p) \models EXAX\neg q$.
(c) $AXp, AX(\neg q \rightarrow AX\neg p), EXEXp \models EX(p \wedge q)$.

Exercise 5.22. Use derivations in AxSys$_{BML}$ to establish the following logical equivalences.

(a) $EX(p \vee q) \equiv (EXp \vee EXq)$.
(b) $\neg EX(p \vee AXq) \equiv AX(p \rightarrow EX\neg q)$.
(c) $\neg AX(EXp \rightarrow EXq) \equiv EX(EXp \wedge AX\neg q)$.

Exercise 5.23. Show that the additional axiom schemata for AxSys$_{BML}$ over AxSys$_{PL}$ consists of valid formulae and that the Necessitation rule **Nec** preserves validity.

Exercise 5.24. Let Γ be a maximal $\text{AxSys}_{\text{BML}}$-consistent set of BML-formulae such that $\text{AX}\varphi \notin \Gamma$. Then show that the set $\{\psi \mid \text{AX}\psi \in \Gamma\} \cup \{\neg\varphi\}$ is $\text{AxSys}_{\text{BML}}$-consistent. (Hint: suppose the contrary and use Proposition 5.7.2.)

Exercise 5.25. Consider the language of BML with a single modal operator AX and the axiomatic system AxSys_{S4} extending $\text{AxSys}_{\text{BML}}$ with the following additional axiom schemes:

(T) $\text{AX}\varphi \to \varphi$.
(4) $\text{AX}\varphi \to \text{AXAX}\varphi$.

Consider also the class $\mathcal{C}_{\text{S4}}$ of transition systems (S, R, L) such that R is a reflexive and transitive relation. We say that a formula φ is S4-**satisfiable** if it is satisfiable in some ITS $\mathcal{T}$ in $\mathcal{C}_{\text{S4}}$. Similarly, φ is S4-**valid** if $\mathcal{T} \models \varphi$ for all interpreted transition systems $\mathcal{T}$ in $\mathcal{C}_{\text{S4}}$.
    With AX^i we denote the sequence of $i \geq 0$ successive occurrences of AX.

(a) Show that the additional axioms (T) and (4) are S4-valid.
(b) Show that for every $i \geq 0$, the formula $\text{AX}p \to \text{AX}^i p$ is S4-valid.
(c) State and prove a completeness theorem for AxSys_{S4} with respect to the class $\mathcal{C}_{\text{S4}}$. (Hint: show that the canonically defined relation in the canonical ITS for AxSys_{S4} is reflexive and transitive.)

Exercise 5.26. Derive the following in $\text{AxSys}_{\text{BTL}}$.

(a) $\vdash \text{EXAY}p \to p$.
(b) $\vdash \text{EYAX}p \to p$.

Exercise 5.27. Prove the soundness of $\text{AxSys}_{\text{BTL}}$ by showing that all additional axioms of $\text{AxSys}_{\text{BTL}}$ are valid and that the rules **Nec** and **Nec**$^{-1}$ preserve validity.

Exercise 5.28. Consider the extension $\text{AxSys}_{\text{TS4}}$ extending $\text{AxSys}_{\text{BTL}}$ with the following additional axiom schemes:

(T) $\text{AX}\varphi \to \varphi$.
(4) $\text{AX}\varphi \to \text{AXAX}\varphi$.

    Recall from Exercise 5.25 the class of interpreted transition systems $\mathcal{C}_{\text{S4}}$.

(a) Show that the following formulae are S4-valid and derive them as theorems of $\text{AxSys}_{\text{TS4}}$:
    (a) $\text{AY}\varphi \to \varphi$.
    (b) $\text{AY}\varphi \to \text{AYAY}\varphi$.
(b) State and prove a completeness theorem for $\text{AxSys}_{\text{TS4}}$ with respect to the class $\mathcal{C}_{\text{S4}}$.

Exercise 5.29. Show that the two versions of the soundness and completeness theorem for $\text{AxSys}_{\text{BML}}$ are equivalent.

Exercise 5.30. Establish the Deduction Theorem 5.7.1 for $\textsc{AxSys}_{\text{BML}}$ and for $\textsc{AxSys}_{\text{BTL}}$.

Exercise 5.31. Complete the details of the proofs of Lindenbaum's Lemma 5.7.9 and the Truth Lemma 5.7.10.

Exercise 5.32. Prove Lemma 5.7.5, Lemma 5.7.7, Lemma 5.7.8 and Lemma 5.7.13.

5.9 Bibliographical Notes

The logic BML presented in this chapter is a syntactic variant of the modal logic **K** (i.e. the modal logic K equipped with a family of modal operators). Interpreted transition systems are just Kripke models (see e.g. Kanger 1957; Hintikka 1962; Kripke 1963; Copeland 2002), used to provide the possible-worlds semantics for modal logics. We refer the reader to Bull and Segerberg (1984) for fairly complete historical notes on the early development of modal logic whereas the history of mathematical modal logic and possible-world semantics in the 20th century is well presented in Goldblatt (2005).

Classical textbooks introducing modal logics are Lemmon et al. (1977), Chellas (1980), Hughes and Cresswell (1984), van Benthem (1985), Goldblatt (1992), Popkorn (1992) and Hughes and Cresswell (1996). More recent books on modal logics, focusing on technical aspects and results, include Chagrov and Zakharyaschev (1997) and Kracht (1995), whereas Blackburn et al. (2001) is a detailed graduate level textbook on the topic.

Modal logic is actually a generic name for all logics involving modal operators and having Kripke-style semantics. Thus, a lot of useful additional material can be found in books about temporal logics (see e.g. Goldblatt 1992; Huth and Ryan 2000; Fisher 2011), dynamic logics (see e.g. Harel et al. 2000), epistemic logics (see e.g. Fagin et al. 1995), description logics (see e.g. Baader et al. 2003) or multi-dimensional modal logics (see e.g. Marx and Venema 1997; Gabbay et al. 2003). A general and very comprehensive state of the art reference on modal logics is the handbook by Blackburn et al. (2007).

Bisimulations and modal equivalence. Bisimulations were first introduced in the model theory of modal logic and related to modal equivalence in the early 1970s in the works of Segerberg (1971), Lemmon et al. (1977), Fine (1975) and van Benthem (1976); see also Bull and Segerberg (1984) and van Benthem (1985). Van Benthem (1976) proved Proposition 5.3.9. Parallels between transition systems and modal logic, and in particular on the role of bisimulations to characterise modal equivalence, go back to Park, Milner and Hennessy (see Hennessy and Milner 1985), where the Hennessy–Milner logic HML_τ was introduced. For more recent follow-up work on relations between simulations and bisimulations of transition systems and their logical characterisations see van Benthem and Bergstra (1995) and van Benthem et al. (1993), where extended notions of bisimulations, corresponding to several languages for temporal and dynamic logics are also defined and studied.

Much of the material from Section 5.3 is based on Goranko and Otto (2007), where an alternative proof of Proposition 5.3.9 can also be found.

The renaming technique and flat normal form. Renaming technique is a standard means to transform formulae from first-order logic in order to get some helpful normal forms (see e.g. Scott 1962; Boy de la Tour 1992). It has been also intensively used for modal logics; see e.g. an early work in Mints (1988), but nowadays this is a very standard technique (see e.g. Demri and Goré 1999; Fisher et al. 2001; Fisher 2011).

Filtration. Filtration is the most widely used method for proving the finite model property in modal logics, particularly those determined by classes of frames with specific properties of the accessibility relation. This method is originally due to McKinsey who first applied an algebraic version of it in modal logic. Filtration was introduced in its present form by Lemmon and Scott (1977) and further developed and applied by Segerberg (1971). Gabbay (1972) introduced a different version, called *selective filtration*. Later, Fischer and Ladner (1979) proved the finite model property of propositional dynamic logic PDL using filtration. Examples of filtrations for a number of important modal and temporal logics can be found in Lemmon et al. (1977), Goldblatt (1992) and Hughes and Cresswell (1996). The filtration method can also be adapted to establish the finite model property for some expressive extensions of BML studied in the forthcoming chapters; for detailed filtration constructions for these logics, see Goldblatt (1992). In Chagrov and Zakharyaschev (1997, Chapter 5), material about canonical models and filtrations can be found. We note that not every modal logic with the finite model property is decidable, as it may not be recursively axiomatisable. For instance, this is the case for $K \times K \times K$ (see Gabbay et al. 2003).

Translations from modal logics to first-order logic. The **standard translation** of modal logic into first-order logic goes back to the early 1970s and was perhaps first explicitly presented in Fine (1975) and van Benthem (1976), where the foundations of the **Correspondence Theory** between modal logic and first-order logic were laid. One of the early works on translation of modal logics into first-order logic, with the explicit goal to mechanise such logics, was Morgan (1976). Morgan distinguishes two types of translations: the **semantical translation**, which is nowadays known as the **relational translation** (see e.g. Fine 1975; van Benthem 1976, 1985; Moore 1977), and the **syntactic translation**, which consists of reifying modal formulae (i.e. transforming them into first-order terms) and translating the axioms and inference rules from a Hilbert-style proof system into classical logic using an additional provability predicate symbol. So, provability in the proof system is reduced to validity in classical logic. With such a syntactic translation, every propositional normal modal logic with a finite axiomatisation can be translated into classical predicate logic by reducing theoremhood to validity. However, using this general translation, decidability of modal logics is lost in general. Modal formulae in BML produce formulae in first-order logic that are at the intersection of the two-variable fragment (Grädel et al. 1997) and the guarded fragment (Andréka et al. 1998). A general schema to translate modal logics into the guarded fragment restricted to two individual variables can be found in Demri and de Nivelle (2005). A survey on translation methods for modal logics can be found in Ohlbach et al. (2001), where more references are provided, for instance about the **functional translation**

(see e.g. Auffray and Enjalbert 1989; Ohlbach 1993; Gasquet and Herzig 1994; Nonnengart 1996; see also Orłowska 1988; D'Agostino et al. 1995 for other types of translations).

The guarded fragment. It is easy to show that $ST(\varphi, x)$ (defined in Section 5.1) belongs to the guarded fragment of first-order predicate logic that has been introduced in Andréka et al. (1998). By using recycling of variables, we can even define $ST(\varphi, x)$ so that $ST(\varphi, x)$ belongs to the fragment of GF with two variables (called herein GF2) (Gabbay 1981; Grädel et al. 1997).

Both the guarded fragment, introduced in Andréka et al. (1998) (see also de Nivelle 1998; Ganzinger and de Nivelle 1999; Nivelle et al. 2000; de Nivelle and de Rijke 2003) and FO2, the fragment of classical logic with two variables (Scott 1962; Mortimer 1975; Lewis 1980; Gabbay 1981; Grädel et al. 1997; de Nivelle and Pratt-Hartmann 2001), have been used as target logics for the translations of modal formulae. Andréka et al. (1998) explicitly mention the goal of identifying 'the modal fragment of first-order logic' as a motivation for introducing the guarded fragment. Apart from having nice logical properties, the guarded fragment GF (Andréka et al. 1998) has an EXPTIME-complete satisfiability problem when the maximal arity of the predicate symbols is fixed (Grädel 1999). More precisely, the satisfiability problem for GF restricted to predicate symbols of arity at most $k \geq 2$ is EXPTIME-complete (Grädel 1999). Hence, its worst-case complexity is identical to that for some simple extensions of modal logic K, as for example K augmented with universal modality (Spaan 1993a).

Ladner-like algorithms. The algorithm presented in Section 5.5.2 is a variant of the one originally presented in Ladner (1977). PSPACE-completeness for BML satisfiability problem (and therefore the PSPACE upper bound) is due to Ladner (1977). The extension to the basic tense logic BTL presented in Section 5.6 is due to Spaan (1993b). Such algorithms that do not rely on special machineries, such as automata or tableaux, have been considered for richer classes of modal and temporal logics (see e.g. Demri 2003; Demri and Lugiez 2010). A tableaux-based calculus for BML is presented in Chapter 13 and an automata-based decision procedure is given in Chapter 14. These calculi can be viewed as a variant implementation of Ladner's original algorithm in which nondeterminism is resolved in a specific way.

Model checking. Model checking is a well-known approach to verifying behavioural properties of computing systems which has been very successful in the verification of finite-state systems (see e.g. Clarke and Emerson 1981; Queille and Sifakis 1982a; McMillan 1993; Clarke et al. 2000; Bérard et al. 2001). Model-checking for first-order logic has been considered even earlier (see e.g. model-checking games in Grädel 2002).

Tense logic with past operators. The basic tense logic BTL, as the first formal logical treatment of time, was introduced by Arthur Prior (1957, 1967, 1968, 1977). Other early comprehensive treatments of temporal logics include Rescher and Urquhart (1971) and

Gabbay (1976). For more general references on temporal logics with past operators, from both philosophical and technical perspective, see also Burgess (1984), van Benthem (1993, 1995) and Gabbay et al. (1994).

Axiomatic systems. Axiomatic systems are the historically oldest type of logical deductive systems. Their idea goes back to the pioneering works of the founder of formal logic, Aristotle, on the system of Syllogistic and of Euclid on the foundations of geometry and arithmetic. The probably first prototype of an axiomatic system can be found in Euclid's *Elements*. Still, the concept of formal logical deduction was only systematically developed in the late 19th to early 20th centuries by Frege, Pierce, Peano and Russell and particularly promoted by Hilbert, in whose honour axiomatic systems are also commonly called 'Hilbert style systems'. More on classical deductive systems and specifically on axiomatic systems can be found in Smullyan (1968) and Sundholm (2001) or in the first chapters of Huth and Ryan (2000).

Axiomatic systems for modal logics were studied in the first half of the 20th century and these were purely syntactic studies until possible-worlds semantics was introduced in the late 1950s by Hintikka, Kanger, Kripke and others. The first completeness results for axiomatic systems in modal logic were published by Kripke (1963), and a great number of such results were established during the 1960s to 1980s by van Benthem, Bull, Fine, Gabbay, Goldblatt, Lemmon and Scott, Sahlqvist, Segerberg, Thomason and many others (see Segerberg 1971; Lemmon et al. 1977; Fine 1975; van Benthem 1976; Bull and Segerberg 1984; van Benthem 1985; Goldblatt 2005; see also Blackburn et al. 2001, 2007 for general references).

Games. Bibliographical references about games for temporal logics can be found in Section 15.6.

6

Linear-Time Temporal Logics

Linear-time temporal logics formalise reasoning about *single computations* in transition systems, represented by *linear models* over natural numbers, that is, infinite sequences of states of length ω. With linear-time formulae one can specify a rich variety of important properties of infinite computations; not only local ones, like BML, but also related to their *limit behaviour*, such as safety, liveness or fairness. In fact, a classical result by Hans Kamp implies that the most popular linear-time logic LTL, which will be introduced and studied in this chapter, is as expressive as first-order logic on single computations Kamp (1968).

A linear-time formula is normally used in order to specify a property for *all* computations in a given interpreted transition system, reflecting the view of a program as the collection of all its possible executions. This means that LTL cannot express basic branching-time properties, so the expressiveness of LTL on nonlinear transition systems is incomparable to the one of BML (see Chapter 10).

In this chapter we present and study the linear-time logic LTL and some of its most interesting extensions: with past-time operators, automata-based operators, propositional quantification, etc. We will focus on the logical and computational properties of these logics, viz. their semantics, expressiveness, model checking and testing of satisfiability and validity. We will establish the fundamental *ultimately periodic model property* of LTL: every satisfiable formula of that logic is satisfiable in an ultimately periodic linear model, that is, in a computation that, after a certain initial segment, starts repeating forever. Moreover, effective upper bounds, in the worst-case exponential in the length of the formula, can be computed for the length of both the initial segment and the period. Thus, the ultimately periodic model property implies decidability of the satisfiablity (and, hence, of validity, too) in LTL and provides a decision method for that problem. Eventually, that method can be refined and transformed into an optimal decision procedure which will be presented here. Alternative decision procedures, essentially using the same property but based respectively on tableaux and automata, will be developed in Chapters 13 and 14.

Another important property of LTL is that the model checking and satisfiability-testing problems for that logic are inter-reducible, in a complexity-preserving way. Thus, both problems for LTL turn out to be of equal worst-case computational complexity, viz. PSPACE. This, together with the good expressiveness, makes the logic LTL a very suitable and well-balanced logical language for specification and verification of properties of computations. LTL and some of its extensions are some of the most widely used logical formalisms to specify the behaviour of computer systems that require formal verification. It is the basis for numerous specification languages and tools.

Structure of the chapter. Section 6.1.1 provides a smooth introduction to temporal operators involved in LTL, whereas Section 6.1 contains the most basic definitions about the syntax and semantics for LTL. Section 6.2 presents the standard decision problems related to LTL, namely, validity/satisfiability problems and model-checking problems. Section 6.3 establishes that LTL has the ultimately periodic model property, which allows us to design decision procedures for satisfiability and model-checking problems in Section 6.4. Extensions of LTL are introduced in Sections 6.5, 6.7.1, 6.7.2 and 6.7.3, respectively for LTL with past-time operators, extended temporal logic ETL, quantified LTL and PSL. Section 6.6 focuses on the expressive power of LTL.

6.1 Syntax and Semantics on Linear Models

6.1.1 LTL Intuitively

The language of the linear-time temporal logic LTL extends the classical propositional logic with temporal modalities referring to future states of the current computation. More precisely, it involves the temporal operators **Next Time** (or, '**Tomorrow**') X; **Sometime** (in the future) F; **Always** (in the future) G; and **Until** U, in addition to the classical propositional connectives. Now and then we may also use logical constants $\top$ and $\bot$. Before we give the formal semantics we begin with the intuitive meaning of the temporal operators.

Next time. When φ states a property of the current state, $X\varphi$ states that the next state satisfies φ:

Thus, the formula `alert` $\to$ X `halt` says that if the system is currently in a state of alert, then the next state will be a 'halt' state. When using X repeatedly, we denote:

$$X^n\varphi := \underbrace{X \ldots X}_{n \text{ times}} \varphi.$$

Thus, the formula $\varphi \wedge X\varphi \wedge X^2\varphi \ldots \wedge X^n\varphi$ states that φ is currently true and will remain true for the next n states.

Sometime and always. The formula $F\varphi$ states that some future (or possibly, the current) state satisfies φ without specifying explicitly which one that is. Thus, it says that φ will be true **sometime** in the future, or possibly at the current state. Respectively, $G\varphi$ states that *all* future states (including the current one) satisfy φ, i.e. that from now on φ will always be true.

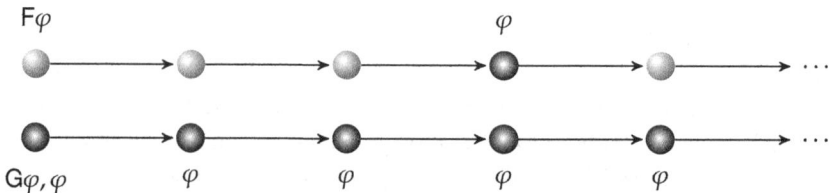

For example, the formula `alert` → `F halt` means that if the system currently is in a state of alert, then it will be in a halt state at some point from then on. Likewise, G(alert → FX halt) means that whenever in the future the system is in a state of alert, it will be in a halt state at some point after that.

The modality G is the *dual* of F: whatever the formula φ may say, if φ is always satisfied, then it is not true that $\neg\varphi$ will ever be satisfied, and conversely. Hence $G\varphi$ and $\neg F\neg\varphi$ are equivalent in their meaning, and therefore will be defined to be logically equivalent.

Until. The binary operator **Until**, denoted by U, is richer and more involved than the operator F. The formula $\varphi U\psi$ states that φ is true until ψ is true – more precisely – that ψ will be true at some future state (or, possibly now) and φ will hold from now on in the meantime.

The example G(alert → F halt) can be refined with the statement that 'starting from a state of alert, the alarm remains activated until the halt state is eventually reached':

$$G(\text{alert} \rightarrow (\text{alarm } U \text{ halt})).$$

Weak until. This is a variation of Until, denoted W. Intuitively, $\varphi W\psi$ still expresses the statement 'φ until ψ', but without the inevitable occurrence of ψ; if ψ never occurs, then φ must remain true forever. Thus, we can regard $\varphi W\psi$ as an abbreviation for $G\varphi \lor (\varphi U\psi)$.

Release. The operator **Release** R is defined as the dual of the until operator U, i.e. $\varphi R\psi :=$ $\neg(\neg\varphi U\neg\psi)$. The formula $\varphi R\psi$ intuitively states that the truth of φ releases the requirement for the truth of ψ; it can be defined as $G\psi \lor \psi U(\psi \land \varphi)$. This means that ψ must remain true until sometime in the future, if ever, when φ becomes true and thus 'releases' ψ from that obligation. Thus, we can regard $G\psi$ as an abbreviation for $\bot R\psi$.

6.1.2 LTL Formally

LTL formulae are defined by the following abstract grammar:

$$\varphi, \psi ::= \overbrace{\bot \mid p \mid \neg\varphi \mid (\varphi \land \psi)}^{\text{propositional calculus}} \mid \overbrace{X\varphi \mid F\varphi \mid G\varphi \mid (\psi U\varphi)}^{\text{temporal extension}},$$

where p ranges over a countably infinite set PROP of atomic propositions. Elements of PROP are obtained by abstracting properties of transition systems, e.g. p may mean 'the current value of the first register is 0'.

As per earlier convention, all other propositional connectives: $\vee$ (disjunction), $\rightarrow$ (material implication), and $\leftrightarrow$ (bi-conditional) will be regarded as definable, unless otherwise specified. Parentheses will be omitted whenever safe to do so, obeying the following precedence rules: unary operators bind stronger than binary ones, and the strength of binding among the binary operators increases in the sequence $\leftrightarrow$, $\rightarrow$, $\vee$, $\wedge$, U.

Given a set of temporal operators $\mathcal{O} \subseteq \{\mathsf{X}, \mathsf{F}, \mathsf{G}, \mathsf{U}\}$, we write $\mathrm{LTL}(\mathcal{O})$ to denote the restriction of LTL to formulae with temporal connectives from $\mathcal{O}$. Given a temporal operator O, an O-formula is an LTL formula whose outermost connective is O; in particular, it cannot be a propositional formula.

Fragments. Just like for BML we introduce a ranking function measuring the depth of nestings of temporal operators in LTL formulae.

Definition 6.1.1. The **modal depth** $mdeg(\varphi)$ of an LTL formula φ is defined as the maximal nesting of temporal operators on a path in its syntax DAG. ∇

For instance, we have $mdeg(\mathsf{G}p \vee (\mathsf{F}p\mathsf{U}\neg\mathsf{X}q)) = 2$.

Now, we write $\mathrm{LTL}_n^k(\mathsf{O}_1, \mathsf{O}_2, \ldots)$ to denote the **fragment** of LTL restricted to formulae such that

- the temporal operators are among $\mathsf{O}_1, \mathsf{O}_2, \ldots$,
- the modal depth is bounded by k,
- at most n distinct atomic propositions occur.

When n (respectively, k) takes the value ω, we mean that there is no restriction on the number of atomic propositions (resp. on the modal depth). In that case, we usually omit ω. So, $\mathrm{LTL}_\omega^2(\mathsf{F})$ denotes the set of LTL formulae of modal depth at most 2 built over the temporal operator F (no restriction on the number of atomic propositions).

Linear models. The intended models for LTL are infinite computations, viewed as ω-sequences of labels being sets of atomic propositions. Formally, a **(linear) model** for LTL is an infinite sequence

$$\sigma : \mathbb{N} \to \mathcal{P}(\mathrm{PROP}),$$

i.e. an ω-word of $(\mathcal{P}(\mathrm{PROP}))^\omega$. For example, the following depicts a prefix of such an LTL model:

Definition 6.1.2. Given a linear model σ, a position $i \in \mathbb{N}$ and a formula φ, we define the **satisfaction relation** $\models$ inductively as follows:

$$\sigma, i \not\models \bot$$

$\sigma, i \models p$	iff	$p \in \sigma(i)$
$\sigma, i \models \neg\varphi$	iff	$\sigma, i \not\models \varphi$
$\sigma, i \models \varphi \wedge \psi$	iff	$\sigma, i \models \varphi$ and $\sigma, i \models \psi$
$\sigma, i \models \mathsf{X}\varphi$	iff	$\sigma, i+1 \models \varphi$
$\sigma, i \models \mathsf{F}\varphi$	iff	there is $j \geq i$ such that $\sigma, j \models \varphi$
$\sigma, i \models \mathsf{G}\varphi$	iff	for all $j \geq i$ we have $\sigma, j \models \varphi$
$\sigma, i \models \psi\mathsf{U}\varphi$	iff	there is $j \geq i$ such that $\sigma, j \models \varphi$ and $\sigma, k \models \psi$ for all k with $i \leq k < j$.

We now define **truth** of an LTL formula φ in a linear LTL model σ as $\sigma \models \varphi \overset{\text{def}}{\Leftrightarrow} \sigma, 0 \models \varphi$.

∇

Given an LTL model σ and $i \geq 0$, we write $\sigma[i, +\infty)$ to denote the LTL model obtained from σ by truncating the i first positions, i.e. for every $j \geq 0$, we have $\sigma[i, +\infty)(j) := \sigma(i + j)$. Respectively, by $\sigma[i, j]$ we denote the segment $\sigma(i), \ldots, \sigma(j)$ of σ.

Lemma 6.1.3. For every LTL formula φ, linear model σ and a position i, we have $\sigma, i \models \varphi$ iff $\sigma[i, +\infty) \models \varphi$. ∎

The proof of Lemma 6.1.3 is left as Exercise 6.21.

Abbreviations. Besides the propositional connectives $\top, \vee, \rightarrow, \leftrightarrow$, we define:

- $\mathsf{F}^{\infty}\varphi := \mathsf{GF}\varphi$ ('φ holds infinitely often').
- $\mathsf{G}^{\infty}\varphi := \mathsf{FG}\varphi$ ('φ holds eventually always').
- $\varphi\mathsf{R}\psi := \neg(\neg\varphi\mathsf{U}\neg\psi)$.
- $\varphi\mathsf{W}\psi := \mathsf{G}\psi \vee (\varphi\mathsf{U}\psi)$.

Note that the operator F can be regarded as a special case of U: the two formulae $\mathsf{F}\varphi$ and $\top\mathsf{U}\varphi$ are logically equivalent.

Example 6.1.4. Consider the following linear model σ, defined as follows: for every $k \geq 0$,

- $p \in \sigma(k)$ iff k is even,
- $q \in \sigma(k)$ iff either $k \in [2, 4]$ or $100 \leq k$,
- $r \in \sigma(k)$ iff $k \equiv_3 1$.

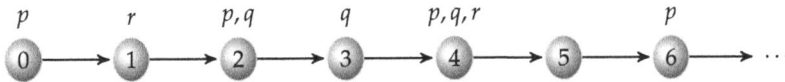

One can show that the following holds in σ:

- $\sigma, 0 \models q \vee \mathsf{XX}\neg r$. Indeed, $\sigma, 2 \not\models r$, hence $\sigma, 2 \models \neg r$, hence $\sigma, 1 \models \mathsf{X}\neg r$, hence $\sigma, 0 \models \mathsf{XX}\neg r$.

- $\sigma, 1 \models \mathsf{F}(q \wedge \mathsf{XX}\neg p)$. Indeed, $\sigma, 3 \models q \wedge \mathsf{XX}\neg p$.
- $\sigma, 1 \models \mathsf{X}(q \mathsf{U} \neg (p \vee q \vee r))$. Indeed, $\sigma, 5 \models \neg(p \vee q \vee r)$ and $\sigma, i \models q$ for $i = 2, 3, 4$, hence $\sigma, 2 \models q \mathsf{U} \neg (p \vee q \vee r)$.
- $\sigma \models \mathsf{F}^{\infty}(\neg p \wedge q \wedge \mathsf{X}r)$. Indeed, $\sigma, i \models \neg p \wedge q \wedge \mathsf{X}r$ for every $i = 6k + 3$ for $k \geq 17$.

Examples

Using LTL formulae one can express various properties of computations, for instance:

- safety: $\mathsf{G}(\texttt{ok})$, $\neg\mathsf{F}(\texttt{deadlock})$,
- liveness: $\mathsf{G}(\texttt{messageSent} \rightarrow \mathsf{F}\,\texttt{messageReceived})$,
- total correctness: $(\texttt{init} \wedge \texttt{precondition}) \rightarrow \mathsf{F}(\texttt{end} \wedge \texttt{postcondition})$ and
- strong fairness: $\mathsf{GF}\,\texttt{processEnabled} \rightarrow \mathsf{GF}\,\texttt{processExecuted}$.

Here are some examples of expressing properties of computations with LTL formulae:

- 'Every occurrence of p will be followed immediately by an occurrence of q which will hold true until p ceases to be true'.

$$\mathsf{G}(p \rightarrow \mathsf{X}(q \wedge q\mathsf{U}\neg p)).$$

- 'Every time when a message is sent, it will not be marked as "sent" before an acknowledgment of receipt is returned'.

$$\mathsf{G}(\texttt{sent} \rightarrow (\neg\texttt{markedSent U ackRet})).$$

- 'Every time when a message is sent, it will be marked as "sent" but only immediately after an acknowledgment of receipt is returned.'

$$\mathsf{G}(\texttt{sent} \rightarrow (\neg\texttt{markedSent U (ackRet} \wedge \neg\texttt{markedSent} \wedge \mathsf{X}\,\texttt{markedSent})).$$

- 'Between every two green signals there will be a red signal'.
  Note that while this specification may sound at first quite OK, it is actually ambiguous. We will not discuss here the issue of validating and disambiguating specifications, but we leave it to the reader to ponder on which of the following LTL formulae, if any, should be the right reading and formalisation of the preceding requirement:

$$\mathsf{G}(\texttt{green} \rightarrow \mathsf{X}(\neg\texttt{green U red}))$$

or

$$\mathsf{G}(\texttt{green} \rightarrow \mathsf{X}(\neg\texttt{green W red}))$$

or

$$\mathsf{G}(\texttt{green} \wedge \mathsf{XFgreen} \rightarrow \mathsf{X}(\neg\texttt{green U red})).$$

Languages of Infinite Words

The set of linear models over a given set of atomic propositions $\Pi \subseteq \mathrm{PROP}$ for a given LTL formula φ such that $\mathrm{PROP}(\varphi) \subseteq \Pi$ can be viewed as a language over the alphabet $\mathcal{P}(\Pi)$:

$$\mathrm{Mod}_{\Pi}(\varphi) \ := \ \{\sigma \in (\mathcal{P}(\Pi))^{\omega} \mid \sigma \models \varphi\}.$$

Often, but not always, we can assume that $\Pi = \mathrm{PROP}(\varphi)$, unless otherwise specified. In that case we will denote $\mathrm{Mod}_{\mathrm{PROP}(\varphi)}(\varphi)$ simply by $\mathrm{Mod}(\varphi)$.

Remark 6.1.5. When dealing with specific temporal formulae, only a finite number of atomic propositions are present. The assumption for finiteness of the set of atomic propositions is sometimes essential, e.g. in automata-based model checking, so in the sequel we will sometimes make the assumption that PROP is finite. However, usually we assume an unlimited supply of atomic propositions, and this assumption can be essential, for instance in order to define (many-one) reductions and to establish fine-tuned complexity results. So, unless otherwise explicitly specified in the context, we will assume that PROP is countably infinite (or, at least finite but unbounded and possibly expandable when necessary).

6.1.3 Truth and Validity in Transition Systems

While the intended models for LTL are linear interpreted transition systems, LTL formulae can naturally be interpreted in any rooted transition system. Recall that, given a rooted transition system $(\mathcal{T}, s)$, we denote by $\mathtt{traces}_{\mathcal{T}}(s)$ the set of computations in $\mathcal{T}$ with initial state s. Also, we denote by $\mathtt{traces}_{\mathcal{T}}$ the set of all computations in $\mathcal{T}$ (see Section 3.5.1). Thus, $\mathtt{traces}_{\mathcal{T}}(s)$ and $\mathtt{traces}_{\mathcal{T}}$ are (possibly infinite) sets of ω-words in $\mathcal{P}(\mathrm{PROP})^{\omega}$.

Definition 6.1.6. An LTL formula φ is **universally true** in a rooted interpreted transition system $(\mathcal{T}, s)$, denoted $\mathcal{T}, s \models_{\forall} \varphi$, if $\sigma \models \varphi$ *for all computations* $\sigma \in \mathtt{traces}_{\mathcal{T}}(s)$.

Likewise, φ is **existentially true** in a rooted ITS $(\mathcal{T}, s)$, denoted $\mathcal{T}, s \models_{\exists} \varphi$, if $\sigma \models \varphi$ *for some computation* $\sigma \in \mathtt{traces}_{\mathcal{T}}(s)$.

When $\mathcal{T}, s \models_{\forall} \varphi$ we simply say that φ is **true** in $(\mathcal{T}, s)$, and usually we write $\mathcal{T}, s \models \varphi$. Then we will also say that $(\mathcal{T}, s)$ *satisfies* φ. $\qquad\qquad \nabla$

Lemma 6.1.7. Given an LTL formula φ and a rooted transition system $(\mathcal{T}, s)$ such that $\mathrm{PROP}(\varphi) \subseteq \mathrm{PROP}(\mathcal{T})$, the following are equivalent:

(I) $\mathcal{T}, s \models_{\forall} \varphi$.
(II) $\mathcal{T}, s \not\models_{\exists} \neg\varphi$.
(III) $\mathtt{traces}_{\mathcal{T}}(s) \subseteq \mathrm{Mod}_{\mathrm{PROP}(\mathcal{T})}(\varphi)$.
(IV) $\mathtt{traces}_{\mathcal{T}}(s) \cap \mathrm{Mod}_{\mathrm{PROP}(\mathcal{T})}(\neg\varphi) = \emptyset$. $\qquad\qquad \blacksquare$

The proof is left as Exercise 6.13.

Example 6.1.8. Consider the following simple transition system, in which on and off are the only atomic propositions. Since they hold in separate and unique states, we also use these propositions as the states' names.

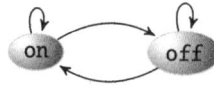

We can show the following, by using direct semantic arguments.

- $\mathcal{T}, \text{on} \models_\exists \neg F^\infty \text{off}$. Indeed, any computation which eventually loops in state on satisfies $G^\infty \neg \text{off}$, which is equivalent to $\neg F^\infty \text{off}$.
- The previous statement can equivalently be rephrased as $\mathcal{T}, \text{on} \not\models_\forall F^\infty \text{off}$. Likewise, $\mathcal{T}, \text{on} \not\models_\forall F^\infty \text{on}$. On the other hand,

$$\mathcal{T}, \text{off} \models_\forall F^\infty \text{on} \vee F^\infty \text{off}$$

  because at least one state must be visited infinitely often.
- $\mathcal{T}, \text{on} \models_\forall G \text{ on} \vee (\text{on U off})$. Indeed, every computation starting from on either stays there forever, or stays at on until it first visits off.

Lemma 6.1.9. For every LTL formula φ the following are equivalent:

(I) $\vdash \varphi$.
(II) $\mathcal{T} \models \varphi$ for every interpreted transition system $\mathcal{T}$.
(III) $\text{Mod}(\neg\varphi) = \emptyset$. ∎

The proof of Lemma 6.1.9 is left as Exercise 6.13.

The notions of validity, satisfiability and logical consequence in LTL are the usual ones, see Section 4.1. Note that an LTL formula φ is **satisfiable** iff $\text{Mod}(\varphi)$ is non-empty. Equivalently, it is **valid** if $\text{Mod}(\varphi)$ is the universal language $\mathcal{P}(\text{PROP}(\varphi))^\omega$ of infinite words in the alphabet $\text{PROP}(\varphi)$.

Example 6.1.10. We leave it to the reader to check that the following LTL formulae are valid.

- $G^\infty \varphi \to F^\infty \varphi$.
- $G\varphi \wedge F\psi \to \varphi U \psi$.
- $\varphi \wedge G(\varphi \to X\varphi) \to G\varphi$.
- $\varphi \wedge G(\varphi \to XF\varphi) \to F^\infty \varphi$.

Validity, satisfiability, etc., are also related in the usual way. In particular, the validities in Example 6.1.10 can be rephrased as logical consequences:

- $G^\infty \varphi \models F^\infty \varphi$.
- $G\varphi, F\psi \models \varphi U \psi$.

- $\varphi, \mathsf{G}(\varphi \to \mathsf{X}\varphi) \models \mathsf{G}\varphi$.
- $\varphi, \mathsf{G}(\varphi \to \mathsf{XF}\varphi) \models \mathsf{F}^{\infty}\varphi$.

We list some important equivalences which will be used further.

Proposition 6.1.11. The following are valid equivalences in LTL.

$$\neg\mathsf{X}\varphi \;\equiv\; \mathsf{X}\neg\varphi.$$
$$\mathsf{F}\varphi \;\equiv\; \top\mathsf{U}\varphi.$$
$$\mathsf{F}\varphi \;\equiv\; \varphi \vee \mathsf{XF}\varphi.$$
$$\neg\mathsf{F}\varphi \;\equiv\; \neg\varphi \wedge \mathsf{X}\neg\mathsf{F}\varphi.$$
$$\mathsf{G}\varphi \;\equiv\; \varphi \wedge \mathsf{XG}\varphi.$$
$$\neg\mathsf{G}\varphi \;\equiv\; \neg\varphi \vee \mathsf{X}\neg\mathsf{G}\varphi.$$
$$\varphi\mathsf{U}\psi \;\equiv\; \psi \vee (\varphi \wedge \mathsf{X}(\varphi\mathsf{U}\psi)).$$
$$\neg(\varphi\mathsf{U}\psi) \;\equiv\; \neg\psi \wedge (\neg\varphi \vee \mathsf{X}\neg(\varphi\mathsf{U}\psi)).$$

∎

The proof of Proposition 6.1.11 is left as Exercise 6.15.

6.2 Logical Decision Problems

6.2.1 Satisfiability and Validity

Satisfiability and validity are fundamental logical notions. They are associated with respective decision problems which are in the focus of this book.

Definition 6.2.1. The **satisfiability problem** for LTL, denoted by SAT(LTL), is defined as follows:

Input: an LTL formula φ.

Question: Is there any model σ such that $\sigma \models \varphi$?
(Equivalently, is it the case that $\mathrm{Mod}(\varphi) \neq \emptyset$?)

The **validity problem** VAL(LTL) is defined similarly:

Input: an LTL formula φ.

Question: Is the case that $\models \varphi$?
(Equivalently, is it the case that $\mathrm{Mod}(\neg\varphi) = \emptyset$?) $\qquad\qquad \nabla$

These two problems are simply reducible to each other's complement: a formula φ is valid iff $\neg\varphi$ is not satisfiable; respectively, φ is satisfiable iff $\neg\varphi$ is not valid. Further we will develop several algorithmic procedures solving the satisfiability problem: first, by an inherently nondeterministic algorithm in Section 6.4, and later, using more constructive methods, such as tableaux, developed in Chapter 13, or automata-based methods, developed in Chapter 14.

6.2.2 Model Checking

A basic question for any given logic $\mathcal{L}$ is whether a given formula of $\mathcal{L}$ is true, or valid, in a given model for $\mathcal{L}$. This is a fundamental *logical* question and, abstractly, such a question is answered generically by applying the semantic definition for truth/validity in $\mathcal{L}$. However, if we are interested in a constructive, *algorithmic* answer to such a question, this becomes the *decision problem* of *model checking*. Such a problem can only be stated, and possibly solved, algorithmically if it is applied to finite, or at least *finitely presentable* models, which can be effectively fed as input to a computer program. Here we will define the necessary notions and state the respective decision problems for the case of LTL, but will present algorithms solving them later, in Section 6.4 (see also Section 4.2).

It is worth observing that even when $(\mathcal{T}, s)$ is finite, the set of computations starting at s may be uncountably infinite. In fact, two states suffice for this, as evident from Example 6.1.8: the set of computations in that transition system, is the set of all words over the two-letter alphabet $\{\text{on}, \text{off}\}$, which is in one-to-one correspondence with the set of all infinite $[0, 1]$ strings, which is in one-to-one correspondence with the set of real numbers in the interval $[0, 1]$.

Path Model Checking in Ultimately Periodic Linear Models

The path model checking in LTL as a logical problem is the question whether a given LTL formula φ is true in a given linear LTL model (computation). Again, abstractly it is solved by applying the semantic truth definition for LTL formulae. In order to treat it as an algorithmic problem, we need to make it finitary, but linear models are by definition infinite. However, an important class of such models, namely those generated by finite ITS that have the shape of a lasso, are finitely presentable. Here is the formal definition.

Definition 6.2.2. A linear model $\sigma : \mathbb{N} \to \mathcal{P}(\text{PROP})$ is **ultimately periodic** if there exist natural numbers i and $l > 0$ such that $\sigma(k) = \sigma(k + l)$ for every $k \geq i$. The (possibly empty) finite sequence $\sigma(0), \ldots, \sigma(i - 1)$ is the **prefix** and $\sigma(i), \ldots, \sigma(i + l)$ is the **loop** of σ. We then say that σ has **prefix length** i and **loop length** l. An ultimately periodic linear model $\sigma : \mathbb{N} \to \mathcal{P}(\text{PROP})$ is **finitary** iff $\bigcup_{i \geq 0} \sigma(i)$ is finite; that is, if it is obtained by unfolding of a lasso-like finite transition system.

The **size** of a finitary ultimately periodic model $\sigma : \mathbb{N} \to \mathcal{P}(\text{PROP})$ with a prefix length i and loop length l is defined as $(i + l) \cdot \text{card}(\bigcup_{i \geq 0} \sigma(i))$. $\qquad\qquad \nabla$

Thus, an ultimately periodic model can be represented by a finite sequence $\Gamma_0, \ldots, \Gamma_{i+l}$ and two integers i and l. The model σ is then defined as

$$\sigma(j) = \begin{cases} \Gamma_j, & \text{if } j < i + l \\ \Gamma_k, \text{ where } k \text{ is least such that } k \geq i \text{ and } k \equiv_l (j - i), & \text{otherwise.} \end{cases}$$

Figure 6.1 presents a simple ultimately periodic model.

We can now formulate the **path model-checking problem for LTL** as a decision problem:

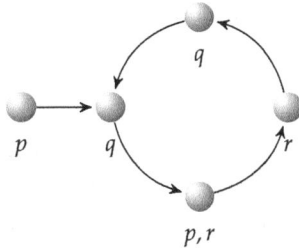

Figure 6.1 Ultimately periodic model with $i = 1$ and $l = 4$.

Input: A finitary ultimately periodic model σ and an LTL formula φ.

Question: Is it true that $\sigma \models \varphi$?

We will present an algorithm solving this problem efficiently in Section 6.4.

The Full Model-Checking Problems for LTL

The full model-checking problem for LTL asks, given a transition system $T = (S, R, L)$, a state s in T and an LTL formula φ, whether some, or all, computations in $\text{traces}_T(s)$ satisfy the formula φ.

In order to state it as an algorithmic decision problem, we need to restrict it to finitely representable transition systems only. In this chapter we will only consider the case of truly finite transition systems.

First we make the necessary notions precise. Given a transition system $T = (S, R, L)$ recall that $\text{PROP}(T)$ is the set of atomic propositions occurring in the image of L. If Π is any set of atomic propositions such that $\text{PROP}(T) \subseteq \Pi$ then we say that T is an interpreted transition system over Π.

Now we can formally state the model-checking problems as decision problems:

1. The **universal model-checking problem for LTL**, denoted by $\text{MC}^\forall(\text{LTL})$, is defined as follows:
   Input: an LTL formula φ, a finite interpreted transition system T and a state $s \in S$.

   Question: Is it the case that $T, s \models_\forall \varphi$?
2. The **existential model-checking problem**, denoted by $\text{MC}^\exists(\text{LTL})$, is defined likewise:
   Input: an LTL formula φ, a finite interpreted transition system T and a state $s \in S$.

   Question: Is there a linear model σ in $\text{traces}_T(s)$ such that $\sigma, 0 \models \varphi$?

Without any loss of generality, in the preceding formulation, we can assume that the codomain of L is restricted to $\mathcal{P}(\text{PROP}(\varphi))$.

Lemma 6.1.7 shows that the problems $\text{MC}^\forall(\text{LTL})$ and $\text{MC}^\exists(\text{LTL})$ are simply inter-reducible, and that they can be reduced to emptiness, respectively nonemptiness, of formal languages of infinite words.

We will present an algorithmic procedure for the existential model-checking problem in Section 6.4.

The logical problems of model checking and validity testing are quite different, and generally not reducible to each other at a low computational cost, but here we provide simple reductions between them for the case of LTL. Later we will use these for reductions of the respective decision problems to each other. Further, in Chapter 14, we will see that these two problems can be solved uniformly, indeed, by applying the automata-based approach.

6.2.3 From Validity to Model Checking and Back

In order to reduce validity testing to model checking in LTL it is sufficient to consider for every set of atomic propositions Π a 'complete' interpreted transition system, the set of traces in which is precisely the set of all LTL models over Π.

Definition 6.2.3. Let Π be a nonempty subset of PROP. We define the **complete interpreted transition system over** Π as $\mathcal{T}_\Pi^c = (S, R, L)$ as follows: $S = \mathcal{P}(\Pi)$, $R = S \times S$ and L is the identity mapping.

In the case when Π is finite and has n elements, we will denote $\mathcal{T}_\Pi^c$ simply by $\mathcal{T}_n^c$ because for what follows, only the size of the set Π will matter. $\triangledown$

Lemma 6.2.4. Let Π be a fixed nonempty subset of PROP. Then for any formula φ built over atomic propositions in Π the following are equivalent:

(I) $\models \varphi$,

(II) $\mathcal{T}_\Pi^c \models \varphi$,

(III) $\mathcal{T}_\Pi^c, \emptyset \models_\forall \mathsf{X}\varphi$.   ■

It suffices to note that every linear model σ over Π belongs to $\mathtt{traces}_{\mathcal{T}_\Pi^c}(\sigma(0))$ and vice versa. We leave the details as Exercise 6.24.

Corollary 6.2.5. VAL(LTL) is constructively reducible to $\mathrm{MC}^\forall$(LTL).   ■

Observe that the reduction is not in logarithmic space since the size of $\mathcal{T}_n^c$ is exponential in n. However, logarithmic-space reductions exist, too, because both VAL(LTL) and $\mathrm{MC}^\forall$(LTL) are known to be PSPACE-complete problems, see e.g. Chapter 11.

For the other direction we assume PROP to be countably infinite, or at least unbounded. Let $\Pi = \{p_1, \ldots, p_n\}$ be again a fixed subset of PROP and $\mathcal{T} = (S, R, L)$ be any finite transition system over Π. First, with each state s in S we associate a special atomic proposition $p_s \notin \Pi$. Let $\mathrm{PROP}(S) := \{p_s \mid s \in S\}$. Then we encode the labelling $L(s)$ by the following formula:

$$AP_s^{\mathcal{T}} := p_s \wedge \bigwedge\{p_i \mid 1 \leq i \leq n, p_i \in L(s)\} \wedge \bigwedge\{\neg p_i \mid 1 \leq i \leq n, p_i \notin L(s)\}.$$

For each state s, we encode the (nonempty) set $R(s)$ of immediate successors of s by the formula:

$$Next_s^{\mathcal{T}} := \mathsf{X}\bigvee\{p_r : r \in R(s)\}.$$

Now, with every state s in $\mathcal{T}$ we associate the formula

$$\chi_s^{\mathcal{T}} := AP_s^{\mathcal{T}} \wedge Next_s^{\mathcal{T}}.$$

Finally, we define the formula

$$\chi^{\mathcal{T}} := \mathsf{G}\left(\bigvee_{s \in S} \chi_s^{\mathcal{T}} \wedge \bigwedge_{s,r \in S, s \neq r} \neg(p_s \wedge p_r)\right).$$

Note that $\chi^{\mathcal{T}}$ belongs to the fragment LTL(X, G).

$\mathcal{T}$ can be expanded to an interpreted transition system $\mathcal{T}^+$ over $\Pi \cup \mathrm{PROP}(S)$ in an obvious way, by adding p_s to the label of s for every $s \in S$. For every computation σ^+ in $\mathtt{traces}_{\mathcal{T}^+}$, there is a trace $\sigma \in \mathtt{traces}_{\mathcal{T}}$ obtained from σ^+ by removing those new atomic propositions in $\mathrm{PROP}(S)$.

The formula $\chi^{\mathcal{T}}$ encodes the set of computations in $\mathcal{T}$ in a way made explicit by the following proposition.

Lemma 6.2.6. Let $\Pi = \{p_1, \dots, p_n\}$ be a fixed subset of PROP and $\mathcal{T} = (S, R, L)$ be any finite transition system over Π. Then the following hold:

(I) $\sigma^+ \models \chi^{\mathcal{T}} \wedge p_{s_0}$ for every infinite path $s_0 \to s_1 \to s_2 \cdots$ in $\mathcal{T}$ where $\sigma^+ = L(s_0) \cup \{p_{s_0}\}, L(s_1) \cup \{p_{s_1}\}, L(s_2) \cup \{p_{s_2}\}, \dots$.
(II) $\mathcal{T}^+ \models_\forall \chi^{\mathcal{T}}$.
(III) For every linear model σ', if $\sigma' \models \chi^{\mathcal{T}}$ then there is a path $s_0 \to s_1 \to s_2 \cdots$ in $\mathcal{T}$ such that $\sigma' = L(s_0) \cup \{p_{s_0}\}, L(s_1) \cup \{p_{s_1}\}, L(s_2) \cup \{p_{s_2}\}, \dots$ and $\sigma' \in \mathtt{traces}_{\mathcal{T}^+}$.
(IV) For every $s \in \mathcal{T}$ and a rooted transition system $(\mathcal{T}', s')$: $\mathcal{T}', s' \models_\forall \chi^{\mathcal{T}} \wedge p_s$ iff $\mathtt{traces}_{\mathcal{T}'}(s') \subseteq \mathtt{traces}_{\mathcal{T}^+}(s)$.
(V) For every LTL formula φ over Π:

$$\mathcal{T}, s \models_\forall \varphi \quad \text{iff} \quad \models (\chi^{\mathcal{T}} \wedge p_s) \to \varphi.$$

Proof. We leave the proof of the first four claims as Exercise 6.24. Now, for the last one, the implication from left to right follows from Claim (III), because $\mathcal{T}, s \models_\forall \varphi$ is equivalent to $\mathcal{T}^+, s \models_\forall \varphi$. Conversely, the implication from right to left follows from Claim (II). □

When MC$^\forall$(LTL) and VAL(LTL) are regarded as decision problems, we can estimate the complexity of the reduction:

Corollary 6.2.7. There is a logarithmic-space reduction from MC$^\forall$(LTL) to VAL(LTL). ∎

Proof. Property 6.2.6 in Lemma 6.2.6 entails that there is a reduction from MC$^\forall$(LTL) to VAL(LTL). It remains to check that $(\chi^{\mathcal{T}} \wedge p_s) \to \varphi$ can be constructed in logarithmic space in the size of φ. This amounts to checking that $\chi^{\mathcal{T}}$ can be built in logarithmic space. Since the construction of χ^T involves conjunctions and disjunctions with a number of arguments in $\mathcal{O}(\text{card}(S))$, we only need counters using space $\mathcal{O}(log(\text{card}(S)))$ to compute these conjunctions and disjunctions since the arguments themselves require also at most space in $\mathcal{O}(log(\text{card}(S)))$ to be constructed.   □

6.3 The Small Model Property

In this section we present a fundamental result about LTL that is the core of most algorithms solving decision problems in LTL and many of its extensions, viz. the **ultimately periodic model property** (Theorem 6.3.3): if an LTL formula has any (linear) model then it has an ultimately periodic (UP) model. Moreover, we will show that both the prefix length and the loop length of such model can be effectively (though, exponentially) bounded in the length of the formula. Then we will introduce the important notion of 'satisfiability witness' for an LTL formula, which can be thought as an ultimately periodic model satisfying the formula, together with a constructive 'evidence' that it is indeed a model of the formula.

6.3.1 The Ultimately Periodic Model Property

First, we need to recall some notations. Given an LTL formula φ, we define its **closure** $cl_{\text{LTL}}(\varphi)$ as done in Section 4.1, Definition 4.1.2. The set $cl_{\text{LTL}}(\varphi)$ contains subformulae that are relevant for checking the satisfiability of φ; it is the smallest set containing φ, closed under subformulae and closed under $\sim$. Indeed, in order to determine the truth of a formula φ one has to consider a number of 'simpler' formulae which appear in the process of the truth evaluation of φ. Herein, these are precisely the formulae in $cl_{\text{LTL}}(\varphi)$.

We recall that $\text{card}(cl_{\text{LTL}}(\varphi)) \leq 2 \times |\varphi|$ where $|\varphi|$ denotes the size of φ. Finally, the number of maximally consistent sets with respect to $cl_{\text{LTL}}(\varphi)$ is bounded by $2^{|\varphi|}$. Furthermore, every main component of a formula φ has a length shorter than the length of φ; therefore it induces a natural well-founded ordering on $cl_{\text{LTL}}(\varphi)$, which will be used in the forthcoming proofs by induction (see Section 4.1).

Given a computation σ and a formula φ, we write $cl_{\text{LTL}}(\varphi, \sigma, i)$ to denote the set of formulae from $cl_{\text{LTL}}(\varphi)$ that hold true at position i, i.e. $cl_{\text{LTL}}(\varphi, \sigma, i) := \{\psi \in cl_{\text{LTL}}(\varphi) \mid \sigma, i \models \psi\}$.

Given a computation σ and an interval $[i, j]$ with $0 \leq i \leq j$, we write $\sigma \backslash [i, j]$ to denote the computation obtained from σ by removing the subsequence $\sigma(i), \ldots, \sigma(j)$. More formally, $\sigma' = \sigma \backslash [i, j]$ is defined as follows:

- $\sigma'(k) := \sigma(k)$ for all $k \in [0, i - 1]$.
- $\sigma'(k) := \sigma(k + 1 + (j - i))$ for all $k \geq i$.

The following lemma states that removing a subsequence between two positions in a computation satisfying the same formulae in $cl_{\text{LTL}}(\varphi)$ does not change the satisfaction of the formulae in $cl_{\text{LTL}}(\varphi)$ in the remaining computation.

Lemma 6.3.1. Let σ be a computation, φ be an LTL formula and i, j be positions such that $i < j$ and $cl_{\mathrm{LTL}}(\varphi, \sigma, i) = cl_{\mathrm{LTL}}(\varphi, \sigma, j)$. Let σ' be $\sigma \backslash [i, j-1]$. Then the following hold:

(I) $cl_{\mathrm{LTL}}(\varphi, \sigma', k) = cl_{\mathrm{LTL}}(\varphi, \sigma, k)$, for every $k \in [0, i-1]$.
(II) $cl_{\mathrm{LTL}}(\varphi, \sigma', k) = cl_{\mathrm{LTL}}(\varphi, \sigma, k + (j-i))$, for every $i \leq k$. ∎

The proof is done by induction on the main components and it is left as Exercise 6.32. Before stating the second lemma, we introduce the notion of **fulfilment**. Let ψ be an U-formula of the form $\psi = \psi_1 U \psi_2$ such that $\sigma, i \models \psi$. We say that ψ is **fulfilled before position** j if $j \geq i$ and there is $i \leq k \leq j$ verifying $\sigma, k \models \psi_2$.

Lemma 6.3.2. Let σ be a computation, φ be an LTL formula and i and $l > 0$ be natural numbers such that $cl_{\mathrm{LTL}}(\varphi, \sigma, i) = cl_{\mathrm{LTL}}(\varphi, \sigma, i+l)$ and every U-formula in $cl_{\mathrm{LTL}}(\varphi, \sigma, i)$ is fulfilled before $i+l$. Let σ' be the (unique) ultimately periodic model with prefix length i and loop length l such that for every $0 \leq k < i+l$, $\sigma'(k) := \sigma(k)$. For every formula $\psi \in cl_{\mathrm{LTL}}(\varphi)$, the following conditions hold true:

(I) $\sigma, k \models \psi$ iff $\sigma', k \models \psi$ for every $k < i+l$,
(II) $\sigma', k \models \psi$ iff $\sigma', k+l \models \psi$ for every $k \geq i$. ∎

Proof. The proof of (II) is obvious since $\sigma' \backslash [0, k-1]$ is equal to $\sigma' \backslash [0, k+l-1]$ and temporal operators in LTL state constraints on the future only ($k \geq i$). The proof of (I) is by induction on the main components. The base case of atomic propositions, as well as the induction steps for the Boolean connectives are straightforward. The remaining cases are as follows.

Case 1: $\psi = X\psi_1$. For every $k < i+l-1$, we have $\sigma, k \models \psi$ iff $\sigma, k+1 \models \psi_1$ iff $\sigma', k+1 \models \psi_1$ (by the induction hypothesis) iff $\sigma', k \models \psi$. Moreover, $\sigma, i+l-1 \models \psi$ iff $\sigma, i+l \models \psi_1$ iff $\sigma, i \models \psi_1$ (by the assumption on positions i and $i+l$) iff $\sigma', i \models \psi_1$ (by the induction hypothesis) iff $\sigma', i+l \models \psi_1$ (by satisfaction of (II)) iff $\sigma', i+l-1 \models \psi$.

Case 2: $\psi = \neg X\psi_1$. Follows from Case 1.

Case 3: $\psi = \psi_1 U \psi_2$. Assume that $\sigma, k \models \psi$ for some $k < i+l$. If $k \leq i$, then by the assumptions of the lemma, there is $\alpha \leq i+l$ such that $\sigma, \alpha \models \psi_2$ and for every $k' \in [k, \alpha]$, we have $\sigma, k' \models \psi_1$. By the induction hypothesis, we get that $\sigma', \alpha \models \psi_2$ and for every $k' \in [k, \alpha]$, we have $\sigma', k' \models \psi_1$. Hence, $\sigma', k \models \psi$. Now suppose that $i < k < i+l$. If ψ is fulfilled before the position $i+l$, then we are done as earlier. Otherwise, for every $k' \in [k, i+l]$, we have $\sigma, k' \not\models \psi_2$ and $\sigma, k' \models \psi_1$. Consequently, $\sigma, i+l \models \psi$ and by assumption on positions i and $i+l$, we get $\sigma, i \models \psi$. Hence, there is $i \leq \alpha < k$ such that $\sigma, \alpha \models \psi_2$ and for every $i \leq k' < \alpha$, we have $\sigma, k' \models \psi_1$. By the induction hypothesis and satisfaction of (II), $\sigma', k \models \psi$ and ψ is fulfilled before the position $(i+l-k) + (\alpha - i) + 1$. The proof for the other direction is analogous.

Case 4: $\psi = \neg(\psi_1 U \psi_2)$. Follows from Case 3. □

We are now ready to state and prove the ultimately periodic model property of LTL.

Theorem 6.3.3 (Ultimately Periodic Model Property). For every satisfiable LTL formula φ, there is an ultimately periodic model σ such that $\sigma \models \varphi$, its loop length is bounded by $|\varphi| \cdot 2^{|\varphi|}$ and its prefix length is bounded by $2^{|\varphi|}$. ∎

Proof. Let φ be an LTL formula and σ be a model such that $\sigma \models \varphi$. Since $cl_{LTL}(\varphi)$ is finite, there are two positions I and $I + L$ with $L > 0$ such that $cl_{LTL}(\varphi, \sigma, I) = cl_{LTL}(\varphi, \sigma, I + L)$ and every U-formula in $cl_{LTL}(\varphi, \sigma, I)$ is fulfilled before the position $I + L$.

Without any further consideration, the values I and L can be arbitrarily large. However, whenever there are $k < k' < I$ such that $cl_{LTL}(\varphi, \sigma, k) = cl_{LTL}(\varphi, \sigma, k')$, by Lemma 6.3.1, we know that $\sigma \backslash [k, k' - 1] \models \varphi$. By applying Lemma 6.3.1 at most I times, we can obtain a model σ' such that there are two positions $i \leq 2^{\text{card}(cl_{LTL}(\varphi))}$ and $i + L$ with $L > 0$ such that $cl_{LTL}(\varphi, \sigma', i) = cl_{LTL}(\varphi, \sigma', i + L)$ and every U-formula in $cl_{LTL}(\varphi, \sigma', i)$ is fulfilled before position $i + L$. Similarly, whenever there are $i < k < k' < i + L$ such that $cl_{LTL}(\varphi, \sigma', k) = cl_{LTL}(\varphi, \sigma', k')$ and no positions in $[k, k' - 1]$ are crucial to fulfil an U-formula from $cl_{LTL}(\varphi, \sigma', i)$, by Lemma 6.3.1, we know that $\sigma' \backslash [k, k' - 1] \models \varphi$. Because there are at most $\text{card}(cl_{LTL}(\varphi))$ many U-formulae to fulfil, and the interval between every two positions fulfilling such formulae can be reduced to $2^{\text{card}(cl_{LTL}(\varphi))}$, after applying Lemma 6.3.1 repeatedly (at most L times) we obtain a model σ'' such that there are two positions, $i \leq 2^{\text{card}(cl_{LTL}(\varphi))}$ and $i + l$ with $0 < l \leq \text{card}(cl_{LTL}(\varphi)) \cdot 2^{\text{card}(cl_{LTL}(\varphi))}$, such that $cl_{LTL}(\varphi, \sigma'', i) = cl_{LTL}(\varphi, \sigma'', i + l)$ and every U-formula in $cl_{LTL}(\varphi, \sigma'', i)$ is fulfilled before position $i + l$. Since each set of the form $cl_{LTL}(\varphi, \sigma, i)$ is maximally consistent with respect to $cl_{LTL}(\varphi)$ (see Lemma 6.3.4) and there are at most $2^{|\varphi|}$ such sets by Lemma 6.3.2, we conclude that there is an ultimately periodic model σ such that $\sigma \models \varphi$, its loop length is bounded by $|\varphi| \cdot 2^{|\varphi|}$ and its prefix length is bounded by $2^{|\varphi|}$. □

6.3.2 Small Satisfiability Witnesses

Existence of ultimately periodic models for satisfiable LTL formulae is a major step towards designing decision procedures for LTL decision problems. However, in order to use their existence in such decision procedures, such models must be effectively verified as models satisfying the given input formulae. In order to provide a given ultimately periodic model with the necessary evidence that it satisfies the given formula φ, it must be expanded with a 'log record' of the path model checking of the formula on it, which is done by enriching every state with the (finite) set of relevant subformulae of φ which are true at that state. Thus, eventually, a satisfying ultimately periodic model for a given formula can be encoded as a sequence of sets of subformulae satisfying respective local conditions and eventuality conditions. Such a sequence is a syntactic object which will be called a 'satisfiability witness' for the formula, and we will be particularly interested in *small* 'satisfiability witnesses', encoding ultimately periodic models of suitably bounded prefix and loop lengths.

In what follows, we use the notion of expanded set of LTL formulae from Definition 4.1.4.

Lemma 6.3.4. Let σ be a computation, φ be an LTL formula and $i \geq 0$. Then, $cl_{\text{LTL}}(\varphi, \sigma, i)$ is maximally consistent. ∎

The proof is left as Exercise 6.32.

Definition 6.3.5. The pair of maximally consistent sets (Γ_1, Γ_2) is **one-step consistent** iff:

1. $\mathsf{X}\psi \in \Gamma_1$ implies $\psi \in \Gamma_2$.
2. $\neg\mathsf{X}\psi \in \Gamma_1$ implies $\sim\psi \in \Gamma_2$.
3. $\psi_1\mathsf{U}\psi_2 \in \Gamma_1$ implies $\psi_2 \in \Gamma_1$ or ($\psi_1 \in \Gamma_1$ and $\psi_1\mathsf{U}\psi_2 \in \Gamma_2$).
4. $\neg(\psi_1\mathsf{U}\psi_2) \in \Gamma_1$ implies $\sim\psi_2 \in \Gamma_1$ and ($\sim\psi_1 \in \Gamma_1$ or $\neg(\psi_1\mathsf{U}\psi_2) \in \Gamma_2$). ▽

In Definition 6.3.5, the consistency condition between two successive maximally consistent sets is very similar to the one in Hintikka traces presented in Definition 13.2.5.

Lemma 6.3.6. Let σ be a computation, φ be an LTL formula and $i \geq 0$. Then the pair of sets $(cl_{\text{LTL}}(\varphi, \sigma, i), cl_{\text{LTL}}(\varphi, \sigma, i+1))$ is one-step consistent. ∎

The proof is left as Exercise 6.32.

Definition 6.3.7. A **small satisfiability witness** for an LTL formula φ is a finite sequence $\Gamma_0, \ldots, \Gamma_i, \ldots, \Gamma_{i+l}$ of subsets of $cl_{\text{LTL}}(\varphi)$, with a distinguished position i, such that

(SSW1) $i \in [0, 2^{|\varphi|}]$ and $l \in [1, |\varphi| \cdot 2^{|\varphi|}]$.
(SSW2) Each Γ_j is maximally consistent, $\varphi \in \Gamma_0$ and $\Gamma_i = \Gamma_{i+l}$.
(SSW3) For every $j \in [0, i+l]$, the pair (Γ_j, Γ_{j+1}) is one-step consistent,
(SSW4) If an U-formula $\psi_1\mathsf{U}\psi_2$ belongs to $\bigcup_{i \leq j < i+l} \Gamma_j$ then ψ_2 belongs to $\bigcup_{i \leq j < i+l} \Gamma_j$.

A **satisfiability witness** is defined as a sequence $\Gamma_0, \ldots, \Gamma_i, \ldots, \Gamma_{i+l}$ satisfying (SSW2)–(SSW4), i.e. without constraints on its length. ▽

In the preceding definition, Condition (SSW1) guarantees that the sequence is not too large whereas Conditions (SSW2) and (SSW3) ensure local consistency as well as initial and final conditions. Combining them with Condition (SSW4) provides an eventuality condition.

Theorem 6.3.3 implies that if an LTL formula is satisfiable then it has a small satisfiability witness. Theorem 6.3.8 implies that the converse is true, too. Thus, we obtain equivalence between the existence of an infinite structure (a model for φ) and the existence of a finite structure (a small satisfiability witness) for any given LTL formula φ.

Theorem 6.3.8. An LTL formula is satisfiable iff it has a small satisfiability witness. ∎

Proof. '⇒'. First assume that the formula φ is satisfiable, i.e. there is a model σ such that $\sigma, 0 \models \varphi$. By Theorem 6.3.3, there is an ultimately periodic model σ' with prefix length $i \leq 2^{|\varphi|}$ and loop length $l \leq |\varphi| \cdot 2^{|\varphi|}$ such that $\sigma', 0 \models \varphi$. It is then easy to check that the sequence

$$cl_{\text{LTL}}(\varphi, \sigma', 0), \ldots, cl_{\text{LTL}}(\varphi, \sigma', i+l)$$

is a small satisfiability witness for φ. We leave this as Exercise 6.28.

'⇐'. For the proof of the other direction, we show that if the formula φ has a small satisfiability witness $\Gamma_0, \ldots, \Gamma_i, \ldots, \Gamma_{i+l}$, then it is satisfiable. Indeed, consider the linear model σ defined as follows:

- For every $j \in [0, i+l]$, $\sigma(j) := \Gamma_j \cap \mathrm{PROP}(\varphi)$.
- For every $j \geq i$, $\sigma(j+l) := \sigma(j)$.

Note that σ is an ultimately periodic model with prefix length i and loop length l. We claim that $\sigma, 0 \models \varphi$. Moreover, we will prove that:

(I) $\Gamma_j \subseteq cl_{\mathrm{LTL}}(\varphi, \sigma, j)$ for all $j \in [0, i+l]$.
(II) $cl_{\mathrm{LTL}}(\varphi, \sigma, j+l) = cl_{\mathrm{LTL}}(\varphi, \sigma, j)$ for all $j \geq i$.

Claim (II) is an immediate consequence of the fact that σ is ultimately periodic and LTL contains only future-time temporal operators.

We will prove Claim (I) by structural induction on the main components of the formulae in $cl_{\mathrm{LTL}}(\varphi)$. The base case for atomic propositions and the induction steps for subformulae with Boolean outermost connectives are straightforward. The remaining cases are the following.

Case 1: $\psi = \mathsf{X}\psi_1 \in \Gamma_j$. In the case $j < i+l$, $\psi \in \Gamma_j$ implies $\psi_1 \in \Gamma_{j+1}$ (by one-step consistency), which implies $\sigma, j+1 \models \psi_1$ (by the induction hypothesis). Consequently, $\sigma, j \models \psi$. Otherwise ($j = i+l$), we have $\psi \in \Gamma_j$ implies $\psi \in \Gamma_i$, which implies $\sigma, i \models \psi$ (by the previous case). Since σ is ultimately periodic, we get $\sigma, i+l \models \psi$.

Case 2: $\psi = \neg\mathsf{X}\psi_1 \in \Gamma_j$. Similar to Case 1 by replacing ψ_1 by $\sim\psi_1$.

Case 3: $\psi = \psi_1\mathsf{U}\psi_2$. The proof is by *reductio ad absurdum*. Let j be the maximal element in $[0, i+l]$ such that $\psi \in \Gamma_j$ and $\sigma, j \not\models \psi$. First suppose that $j < i+l$. By one-step consistency we have

1. $\psi_2 \in \Gamma_j$, or
2. $\psi_1 \in \Gamma_j$ and $\psi \in \Gamma_{j+1}$.

If (1) holds then, by the induction hypothesis, $\sigma, j \models \psi_2$ and therefore $\sigma, j \models \psi$, which leads to a contradiction. If (2) holds then, by maximality of j, we have $\sigma, j + 1 \models \psi_1\mathsf{U}\psi_2$. By the induction hypothesis, $\sigma, j \models \psi_1$ and therefore $\sigma, j \models \psi_1\mathsf{U}\psi_2$, which leads to a contradiction.

Now suppose that $j = i+l$. Since $\Gamma_i = \Gamma_{i+l}$, by Condition (SSW4), there is a minimal $j' \in [i, i+l]$ such that $\psi_2 \in \Gamma_{j'}$. Moreover, by Definition 6.3.5(3), for all $j'' \in [i, j'-1]$, we have that $\psi_1 \in \Gamma_{j''}$. So by induction hypothesis, for $j'' \in [i, j'-1]$, $\sigma, j'' \models \psi_1$ and $\sigma, j' \models \psi_2$. Consequently, $\sigma, i \models \psi$ and by Claim (II), we get $\sigma, i+l \models \psi$ too, which leads to a contradiction.

Case 4: $\psi = \neg(\psi_1\mathsf{U}\psi_2) \in \Gamma_j$. We consider whether j is smaller than i.

Suppose $j < i$. Then, by one-step consistency, one of the following two conditions must hold.

1. for every $j' \in [j, i+l]$, $\sim\psi_2 \in \Gamma_{j'}$, or
2. there is $j' \in [j, i+l]$ such that $\sim\psi_1 \in \Gamma_{j'}$ and for $j'' \in [j, j']$, we have $\sim\psi_2 \in \Gamma_{j''}$.

If (1.) holds then, by induction hypothesis, for every $j' \in [j, i+l]$, $\sigma, j' \models \sim\psi_2$ and therefore $\sigma, j \models \psi$ by using Claim (II).

If (2.) holds then, by induction hypothesis, there is $j' \in [j, i+l]$ such that $\sigma, j' \models \sim\psi_1$ and for $j'' \in [j, j']$, we have $\sigma, j'' \models \sim\psi_2$. Hence, $\sigma, j \models \psi$.

Now suppose that $j \geq i$. Again, by one-step consistency, we have one of the following cases.

- For every $j' \in [i, i+l]$, $\sim\psi_2 \in \Gamma_{j'}$. As for (1.), we can conclude that $\sigma, j \models \psi$.
- There is $j' \in [j, i+l]$ such that $\sim\psi_1 \in \Gamma_{j'}$ and for $j'' \in [j, j']$, we have $\sim\psi_2 \in \Gamma_{j''}$. As for (2.), we can conclude that $\sigma, j \models \psi$.
- There is $j' \in [i, j-1]$ such that $\sim\psi_1 \in \Gamma_{j'}$ and for $j'' \in [i, j'] \cup [j, i+l]$, we have $\sim\psi_2 \in \Gamma_{j''}$. By using the induction hypothesis, the fact that $\Gamma_i = \Gamma_{i+l}$ and Claim (II), we can also establish that $\sigma, j \models \psi$. $\qquad\square$

A satisfiable LTL formula may have more than one small satisfiability witness. The different proof methods for checking satisfiability of LTL formulae can be distinguished by the strategies and heuristics they employ to generate satisfiability witnesses, when they exist. It is worth noting that we can always assume that the prefix length i is at least 1, by shifting the loop. For instance, the goal of the tableau-based approach presented in Chapter 13 consists of generating a tableau that encodes sufficiently many satisfiability witnesses for a given formula by decomposing subformulae on demand and then checking the eventuality conditions. Similarly, in the automata-based approach, presented in Chapter 14, to each formula we associate a **Büchi automaton** that accepts exactly the models of the formula, and checking the nonemptiness of this automaton amounts to finding a small satisfiability witness for the formula.

6.4 Decision Procedures

6.4.1 Satisfiability Checking

As discussed earlier, most methods for checking satisfiability of LTL formulae attempt to find a small satisfiability witness or a variant thereof. A brute force algorithm for that would generate all sequences of subsets of $cl_{\text{LTL}}(\varphi)$ of length at most $2^{|\varphi|} + |\varphi| \cdot 2^{|\varphi|}$ and check whether one of them is a small satisfiability witness. Such an algorithm provides a double exponential-time decision procedure for LTL satisfiability. Alternatively, one can guess a sequence of length at most $2^{|\varphi|} + |\varphi| \cdot 2^{|\varphi|}$ and check that it is a small satisfiability witness. Naively, this would lead to a nondeterministic exponential space procedure. Instead, one can do the guessing step by step and do the check on the fly. We will show here that this can be done in nondeterministic polynomial space. Savitch's Theorem then provides a polynomial-space upper bound.

Algorithm 4 is a nondeterministic procedure which is based on the preceding results. It checks whether a given LTL formula has a small satisfiability witness. The idea is similar to the one for solving the the reachability problem for transition systems, see Section 3.2.2, since a fixed number of maximally consistent sets needs to be stored at any step.

Consider, for example, the formula $\varphi = \mathsf{GF}p \wedge \mathsf{GF}q$ and $\Gamma := \{\varphi, \mathsf{GF}p, \mathsf{GF}q, \mathsf{F}p, \mathsf{F}q\}$. One can check that the following sequence is a small satisfiability witness with $i = 2$ and $l = 4$:

$$\Gamma \cup \{\neg p, \neg q\}, \Gamma \cup \{\neg p, \neg q\}, \Gamma \cup \{p, \neg q\}, \Gamma \cup \{\neg p, \neg q\}, \Gamma \cup \{\neg p, q\},$$
$$\Gamma \cup \{p, q\}, \Gamma \cup \{p, \neg q\}.$$

We invite the reader to run Algorithm 4 when the preceding sequence is guessed and to check that an accepting state is reached.

Theorem 6.4.1. Algorithm 4 for satisfiability checking of LTL formulae is correct and works in space that is polynomial in the size of the input formula. ∎

Proof. Correctness follows from Theorem 6.3.8. In order to check that the nondeterministic algorithm can run in polynomial space, it is sufficient to observe that

---

Algorithm 4 Guessing a small satisfiability witness.

1: guess $i \in [0, 2^{|\varphi|}]$ and $l \in [1, |\varphi|2^{|\varphi|}]$
2: guess $\Gamma \subseteq cl_{\text{LTL}}(\varphi)$ such that $\varphi \in \Gamma$ and Γ is maximally consistent
3: $j \leftarrow 0$
4: **while** $j < i$ **do**
5:     guess maximally consistent Γ' such that (Γ, Γ') is one-step consistent;
6:     $j \leftarrow j + 1$
7:     $\Gamma \leftarrow \Gamma'$
8: **end while**
9: $\Gamma_f \leftarrow \Gamma$
10: $j \leftarrow 0$
11: $\Delta_U \leftarrow \emptyset$
12: $\Delta_U' \leftarrow \emptyset$
13: **while** $j < l$ **do**
14:     $\Delta_U \leftarrow \Delta_U \cup \{\psi_1 U \psi_2 \in cl_{\text{LTL}}(\varphi) : \psi_1 U \psi_2 \in \Gamma\}$
15:     $\Delta_U' := \Delta_U' \cup \{\psi_1 U \psi_2 \in cl_{\text{LTL}}(\varphi) : \psi_2 \in \Gamma\}$
16:     guess maximally consistent Γ' such that (Γ, Γ') is one-step consistent
17:     $j \leftarrow j + 1$
18:     $\Gamma \leftarrow \Gamma'$
19: **end while**
20: **if** $\Gamma = \Gamma_f$ and $\Delta_U \subseteq \Delta_U'$ **then**
21:     accept
22: **else**
23:     abort
24: **end if**

- the values of i and l are at most exponential in the size of the input formula and thus only require a polynomial number of bits to be represented, and
- each subset of $cl_{LTL}(\varphi)$ can be encoded by a polynomial number of bits, and we need to store only five such sets, viz. (Γ, Γ', Γ_f, Δ_U, and Δ_U') and
- the following tests can be performed in polynomial space:
  1. testing whether Γ is maximally consistent,
  2. testing whether (Γ, Γ') is one-step consistent,
  3. checking the equality $\Gamma = \Gamma_f$ and the inclusion $X_U \subseteq X_U'$. □

Recall that, according to Savitch's Theorem, nondeterministic polynomial space is included in deterministic polynomial space. Applying this to LTL satisfiability checking yields the following complexity upper bound.

Corollary 6.4.2. The decision problem of testing satisfiability for LTL formulae is in PSPACE. ■

6.4.2 Existential Model Checking

Now, we will explain why the (existential) model-checking problem for LTL can be solved in polynomial space using arguments similar to those in Section 6.4.1. Even though the principle of the algorithm is similar to the one for checking satisfiability, we provide detailed explanations here because it is important to understand how to handle the restriction of the satisfiability problem in which only traces from a given state in a transition system are allowed.

Let $\mathcal{T} = (S, R, L)$ be a finite transition system, $s \in S$ be a state and φ be an LTL formula. We wish to check whether there is $\sigma \in \text{traces}_{\mathcal{T}}(s)$ such that $\sigma, 0 \models \varphi$. Observe that given a computation σ in $\text{traces}_{\mathcal{T}}(s)$ obtained from the path $s_0 R s_1 R s_2 \cdots$, and an interval $[i, j]$ with $0 \le i \le j$, the trace $\sigma \backslash [i, j]$ is not necessarily in $\text{traces}_{\mathcal{T}}(s)$. However, if $s_i = s_j$, then $\sigma \backslash [i, j] \in \text{traces}_{\mathcal{T}}(s)$. This sufficient condition is all what we need in order to apply Lemma 6.3.1 and Lemma 6.3.2 in the proof of Theorem 6.4.3. It is possible to adapt Theorem 6.3.3 as follows: existence of a trace in $\text{traces}_{\mathcal{T}}(s)$ satisfying φ is equivalent to the existence of an ultimately periodic trace satisfying φ.

Theorem 6.4.3 (Ultimately Periodic Model Property). If there is a trace σ in $\text{traces}_{\mathcal{T}}(s)$ such that $\sigma, 0 \models \varphi$, then there is an ultimately periodic trace σ in $\text{traces}_{\mathcal{T}}(s)$ such that $\sigma \models \varphi$, its loop length is bounded by $\text{card}(S) \cdot |\varphi| \cdot 2^{|\varphi|}$ and its prefix length is bounded by $\text{card}(S) \cdot 2^{|\varphi|}$. ■

Proof. Suppose that there is a trace σ in $\text{traces}_{\mathcal{T}}(s)$ obtained from the path $s_0 R s_1 R s_2 \cdots$, such that $\sigma, 0 \models \varphi$. Since $cl_{LTL}(\varphi)$ is finite, there are two positions I and $I + L$ with $L > 0$ such that

1. $cl_{LTL}(\varphi, \sigma, I) = cl_{LTL}(\varphi, \sigma, I + L)$,
2. every U-formula in $cl_{LTL}(\varphi, \sigma, I)$ is fulfilled before the position $I + L$,
3. $s_I = s_{I+L}$.

Without any further consideration, the values I and L can be arbitrarily large. However, whenever there are $k < k' < I$ such that $s_k = s_{k'}$ and $cl_{\text{LTL}}(\varphi, \sigma, k) = cl_{\text{LTL}}(\varphi, \sigma, k')$, by Lemma 6.3.1, we know that $\sigma \backslash [k, k' - 1] \models \varphi$; furthermore $\sigma \backslash [k, k' - 1]$ belongs to $\text{traces}_{\mathcal{T}}(s)$. By applying Lemma 6.3.1 at most I times, we can obtain a model σ' such that there are two positions $i \leq \text{card}(S) \cdot 2^{\text{card}(cl_{\text{LTL}}(\varphi))}$ and $i + L$ with $L > 0$ such that $cl_{\text{LTL}}(\varphi, \sigma', i) = cl_{\text{LTL}}(\varphi, \sigma', i + L)$ and every U-formula in $cl_{\text{LTL}}(\varphi, \sigma', i)$ is fulfilled before position $i + L$.

Similarly, whenever there are $i < k < k' < i + L$ such that $s_k = s_{k'}$ and $cl_{\text{LTL}}(\varphi, \sigma', k) = cl_{\text{LTL}}(\varphi, \sigma', k')$ and no positions in $[k, k' - 1]$ are crucial to fulfil an U-formula from $cl_{\text{LTL}}(\varphi, \sigma', i)$, by Lemma 6.3.1, we know that $\sigma' \backslash [k, k' - 1] \models \varphi$; furthermore $\sigma \backslash [k, k' - 1]$ belongs to $\text{traces}_{\mathcal{T}}(s)$. Note that there are at most $\text{card}(cl_{\text{LTL}}(\varphi))$ many U-formulae to fulfil, and the interval between every two positions fulfilling such formulae can be reduced to within $\text{card}(S) \cdot 2^{\text{card}(cl_{\text{LTL}}(\varphi))}$. Therefore, after applying Lemma 6.3.1 repeatedly (at most L times) we obtain a model σ'' such that there are two positions, $i \leq \text{card}(S) \cdot 2^{\text{card}(cl_{\text{LTL}}(\varphi))}$ and $i + l$ with $0 < l \leq \text{card}(S) \cdot \text{card}(cl_{\text{LTL}}(\varphi)) \cdot 2^{\text{card}(cl_{\text{LTL}}(\varphi))}$, such that $cl_{\text{LTL}}(\varphi, \sigma'', i) = cl_{\text{LTL}}(\varphi, \sigma'', i + l)$ and every U-formula in $cl_{\text{LTL}}(\varphi, \sigma'', i)$ is fulfilled before position $i + l$ and $s_i = s_{i+l}$. Since $\text{card}(cl_{\text{LTL}}(\varphi)) \leq |\varphi|$ and, by Lemma 6.3.2, we conclude that there is an ultimately periodic model σ in $\text{traces}_{\mathcal{T}}(s)$ such that $\sigma \models \varphi$, its loop length is bounded by $\text{card}(S) \cdot |\varphi| \cdot 2^{|\varphi|}$ and its prefix length is bounded by $\text{card}(S) \cdot 2^{|\varphi|}$. ☐

In order to deal with the existential model-checking problem, we introduce the notion of 'small model-checking witness'. Such a structure is defined as a small satisfiability witness but augmented by a state of the transition system at each position. The one-step consistency condition further requires that two states in successive positions belong to the accessibility relation of the transition system. Another serious difference is that the maximal values for the prefix length and the loop length have an additional factor: the number of states of the transition system (due to Theorem 6.4.3).

Definition 6.4.4. A **small model-checking witness** for $(\mathcal{T}, s, \varphi)$ is a finite sequence $(\Gamma_0, s_0), \ldots, (\Gamma_i, s_i), \ldots, (\Gamma_{i+l}, s_{i+l})$ of pairs for which the first components are subsets of $cl_{\text{LTL}}(\varphi)$ and the second components are states of $\mathcal{T}$, with a distinguished position i, such that

(SSW'1) $i \in [1, \text{card}(S) \cdot 2^{|\varphi|}]$ and $l \in [1, \text{card}(S) \cdot |\varphi| \cdot 2^{|\varphi|}]$.
(SSW'2) Each Γ_j is maximally consistent, $\varphi \in \Gamma_0$ and $\Gamma_i = \Gamma_{i+l}$.
(SSW'3) For every $j \in [0, i + l]$, the pair (Γ_j, Γ_{j+1}) is one-step consistent.
(SSW'4) If an U-formula $\psi_1 \text{U} \psi_2$ belongs to $\bigcup_{i \leq j < i+l} \Gamma_j$ then ψ_2 belongs to $\bigcup_{i \leq j < i+l} \Gamma_j$.
(SSW'5) $s_0 = s$, $s_i = s_{i+l}$ and for every $j \in [0, i + l - 1]$, $s_j \mathrel{R} s_{j+1}$.
(SSW'6) For all $j \in [0, i + l]$ and $p \in sub(\varphi)$, $p \in L(s_j)$ iff $p \in \Gamma_j$. ▽

A model-checking witness is built by synchronising a satisfiability witness and a path in the transition system; synchronisation is performed using propositional valuations.

Theorem 6.4.5. There is a $\sigma \in \text{traces}_{\mathcal{T}}(s)$ such that $\sigma, 0 \models \varphi$ iff $(\mathcal{T}, s, \varphi)$ has a small model-checking witness. ■

The proof is left as Exercise 6.32. It is similar to the proof of Theorem 6.4.5.

Now consider Algorithm 5 that nondeterministically guesses a small model-checking witness.

Algorithm 5 Guessing a small model-checking witness.

1: guess $i \in [1, \mathrm{card}(S) \cdot 2^{|\varphi|}]$ and $l \in [1, \mathrm{card}(S) \cdot |\varphi| 2^{|\varphi|}]$
2: guess $\Gamma \subseteq cl_{\mathrm{LTL}}(\varphi)$ such that $\varphi \in \Gamma$ and Γ is maximally consistent
3: $j \leftarrow 0$
4: $s_{cur} \leftarrow s$
5: **if** (there is $p \in cl_{\mathrm{LTL}}(\varphi)$ s.t. ($p \notin L(s_{cur})$ and $p \in \Gamma$)) or (there is $\neg p \in cl_{\mathrm{LTL}}(\varphi)$ s.t ($p \in L(s_{cur})$ and $\neg p \in \Gamma$)) **then** abort
6: **end if**
7: **while** $j < i$ **do**
8:      guess maximally consistent Γ' such that (Γ, Γ') is one-step consistent;
9:      guess s' such that $s_{cur} R s'$
10:     $j \leftarrow j + 1$
11:     $\Gamma \leftarrow \Gamma'; s_{cur} \leftarrow s'$
12: **end while**
13: $\Gamma_f \leftarrow \Gamma; s_f \leftarrow s_{cur}$
14: $j \leftarrow 0$
15: $X_{\mathsf{U}} \leftarrow \emptyset; X'_{\mathsf{U}} \leftarrow \emptyset$
16: **while** $j < l$ **do**
17:     **if** (there is $p \in cl_{\mathrm{LTL}}(\varphi)$ s.t. ($p \notin L(s_{cur})$ and $p \in \Gamma$)) or (there is $\neg p \in cl_{\mathrm{LTL}}(\varphi)$ s.t ($p \in L(s_{cur})$ and $\neg p \in \Gamma$)) **then** abort
18:         **end if**
19:     $X_{\mathsf{U}} \leftarrow X_{\mathsf{U}} \cup \{\psi_1 \mathsf{U} \psi_2 \in cl_{\mathrm{LTL}}(\varphi) : \psi_1 \mathsf{U} \psi_2 \in \Gamma\}$
20:     $X'_{\mathsf{U}} := X'_{\mathsf{U}} \cup \{\psi_1 \mathsf{U} \psi_2 \in cl_{\mathrm{LTL}}(\varphi) : \psi_2 \in \Gamma\}$
21:     guess maximally consistent Γ' such that (Γ, Γ') is one-step consistent
22:     guess s' such that $s_{cur} R s'$
23:     $j \leftarrow j + 1$
24:     $\Gamma \leftarrow \Gamma'; s_{cur} \leftarrow s'$
25: **end while**
26: **if** $\Gamma = \Gamma_f$ and $s_{cur} = s_f$ and $X_{\mathsf{U}} \subseteq X'_{\mathsf{U}}$ **then**
27:     accept
28: **else**
29:     abort
30: **end if**

Theorem 6.4.6. Algorithm 5 for solving $\mathrm{MC}^3(\mathrm{LTL})$ is correct and works in polynomial space in the size of the input formula. ∎

Proof. By Theorem 6.4.5, there is $\sigma \in \mathtt{traces}_{\mathcal{T}}(s)$ such that $\sigma, 0 \models \varphi$ iff $(\mathcal{T}, s, \varphi)$ has a small model-checking witness. Algorithm 5 nondeterministically guesses a small model-checking witness for $(\mathcal{T}, s, \varphi)$ in polynomial space. By Savitch's Theorem, we get the PSPACE upper bound. $\qquad\square$

Observe that for all traces $\sigma \in \texttt{traces}_{\mathcal{T}}(s)$, we have $\sigma, 0 \models \varphi$ iff not (there is a trace $\sigma \in \texttt{traces}_{\mathcal{T}}(s)$ such that $\sigma, 0 \models \neg\varphi$). Thus, there is a logarithmic-space reduction from $\text{MC}^{\forall}(\text{LTL})$ to the complement problem of $\text{MC}^{\exists}(\text{LTL})$. Since $\text{MC}^{\exists}(\text{LTL})$ is in PSPACE, $\text{MC}^{\forall}(\text{LTL})$ is therefore in co-PSPACE, whence in PSPACE since PSPACE is a complexity class involving deterministic machines (co-PSPACE = PSPACE).

Corollary 6.4.7. The decision problem $\text{MC}^{\forall}(\text{LTL})$ is in PSPACE. $\qquad\blacksquare$

6.4.3 Path Model Checking

The path model-checking problem in ultimately periodic linear models is an important particular case of the full (existential or universal) model-checking problem in finite transition systems, because an ultimately periodic linear model can be regarded as the unfolding of a lasso-shaped finite transition system. Here we will show that the problem of path model checking of LTL formulae in ultimately periodic models is computationally tractable, unlike the full model-checking problem for LTL.

Let σ be a finitary ultimately periodic model of prefix length i and loop length l encoded by the sequence $\Gamma_0, \ldots, \Gamma_{i+l}$ in which each $\Gamma_j \subseteq \text{PROP}$ for some LTL formulae φ. We will present a labelling algorithm that successively marks the positions of the ultimately periodic input model by subformulae of the input formula, of increasing size. It is a simplified version of the labelling algorithm for CTL model checking, see Section 7.3.2.

Let $\psi_1, \ldots, \psi_k$ be the subformulae of φ preordered by increasing size. In particular:

- $\psi_k = \varphi$,
- ψ_1 is an atomic proposition or constant,
- if ψ_a is a strict subformula of ψ_b, then $a < b$,
- $k \leq |\varphi|$.

For every $j \in [0, i + l]$, we build the set of formulae

$$l[j] := \{\psi \in \{\psi_1, \ldots, \psi_k, \neg\psi_1, \ldots, \neg\psi_k\} \mid \sigma, j \models \psi\}.$$

Algorithm 6 presents a labelling technique for checking whether $\sigma, 0 \models \varphi$.

Theorem 6.4.8. Algorithm 6 for path model checking of LTL formulae in ultimately models is correct and works in time polynomial in the sizes of the input formula and ultimately periodic model. $\qquad\blacksquare$

Note that in Algorithm 6, the computation for every $a \in [1, k]$ requires $\mathcal{O}((i + l)^2)$ steps. Thus, $\sigma \models \varphi$ can be checked in time $\mathcal{O}((i + l)^2 \cdot |\varphi|)$. Besides, one can organise

---

Algorithm 6 Checking $\sigma, 0 \models \varphi$.

1: Linearly order the subformulae of φ by increasing size; we obtain $\psi_1, \ldots, \psi_k$

2: **for** $j \in [0, i + l]$ **do** $l[j] \leftarrow \emptyset$ **end for**;

3: **for** $a \in [1, k]$ **do**

4:     **if** ψ_a is an atomic proposition **then**

5:         **for** $j \in [0, i + l]$ **do**

6:             **if** $\psi_a \in \Gamma_j$ **then** $l[j] \leftarrow l[j] \cup \{\psi_a\}$

7:             **else** $l[j] \leftarrow l[j] \cup \{\neg\psi_a\}$

8:             **end if**

9:         **end for**

10:     **else if** $\psi_a = \neg\psi_{a_1}$ **then**

11:         **for** $j \in [0, i + l]$ **do if** $\psi_a \notin l[j]$ **then** $l[j] \leftarrow l[j] \cup \{\neg\psi_a\}$ **end if**

12:         **end for**

13:     **else if** $\psi_a = \psi_{a_1} \wedge \psi_{a_2}$ **then**

14:         **for** $j \in [0, i + l]$ **do**

15:             **if** $\{\psi_{a_1}, \psi_{a_2}\} \subseteq l[j]$ **then** $l[j] \leftarrow l[j] \cup \{\psi_a\}$

16:             **else** $l[j] \leftarrow l[j] \cup \{\neg\psi_a\}$

17:             **end if**

18:         **end for**

19:     **else if** $\psi_a = \mathsf{X}\psi_{a_1}$ **then**

20:         **for** $j \in [0, i + l]$ **do**

21:             **if** $(j < i + l$ and $\psi_{a_1} \in l[j + 1])$ or $(j = i + l$ and $\psi_{a_1} \in l[i + 1])$

22:               **then** $l[j] \leftarrow l[j] \cup \{\psi_a\}$

23:             **else** $l[j] \leftarrow l[j] \cup \{\neg\psi_a\}$

24:             **end if**

25:         **end for**

26:     **else if** $\psi_a = \psi_{a_1} \mathsf{U} \psi_{a_2}$ **then**

27:         **for** $j \in [0, i + l]$ **do**

28:             **if** $\exists \, j' \in [j, i + l]$ s.t. $(\psi_{a_2} \in l[j'] \, \& \, \forall \, j'' \in [j, j' - 1], \psi_{a_1} \in l[j''])$

29:               **then** $l[j] \leftarrow l[j] \cup \{\psi_a\}$

30:             **else**

31:                 **if** $i \leq j \, \& \, \exists \, j' \in [i, j - 1]$ s.t. $(\psi_{a_2} \in l[j'] \, \&$

32:                     $\forall \, j'' \in [j, i + l] \cup [i, j' - 1], \psi_{a_1} \in l[j''])$ **then**

33:                     $l[j] \leftarrow l[j] \cup \{\psi_a\}$

34:                 **else**

35:                     $l[j] \leftarrow l[j] \cup \{\neg\psi_a\}$

36:                 **end if**

37:             **end if**

38:         **end for**

39:     **end if**

40: **end for**

41: **return** '$\varphi \in l[0]$'

---

the model-checking procedure described earlier in a dynamic programming style, by building a Boolean array T of dimension $(i + l + 1) \cdot \text{card}(\text{sub}(\varphi))$ such that $T[j, \psi] = \top$ iff $\sigma, j \models \psi$. The details are left as Exercise 6.22.

Let $\varphi = \mathsf{FG}(q \vee r)$ and σ the finite ultimately periodic model depicted in Figure 6.1. Clearly $\text{sub}(\varphi) = \{\varphi, \mathsf{G}(q \vee r), (q \vee r), q, r\}$. Running Algorithm 6 on φ and σ, the following values for $l[0], l[1], l[2], l[3], l[4]$ are eventually obtained (assuming that the states in the loop are 2, 3 and 4).

1. $l[0] = \{\neg q, \neg r, \neg(q \vee r), \neg \mathsf{G}(q \vee r), \varphi\}$.
2. $l[1] = \{q, \neg r, (q \vee r), \mathsf{G}(q \vee r), \varphi\}$.
3. $l[2] = \{\neg q, r, (q \vee r), \mathsf{G}(q \vee r), \varphi\}$.
4. $l[3] = \{\neg q, r, (q \vee r), \mathsf{G}(q \vee r), \varphi\}$.
5. $l[4] = \{q, \neg r, (q \vee r), \mathsf{G}(q \vee r), \varphi\}$.

We invite the reader to run Algorithm 6 step by step to verify this.

6.5 Adding Past-Time Operators

In this section we will present and study an extension of the logic LTL with temporal operators referring to the past in linear temporal models.

6.5.1 LTL with Past

The temporal operators in LTL refer to the future only. Here we will introduce their past-time counterparts:

- The past-time analogue of the 'Next' operator X is the **Previous** (also known as '**Yesterday**') operator. If φ states a property of the current state, $\mathsf{Y}\varphi$ states that the previous state satisfies φ. If there is no previous state, $\mathsf{Y}\varphi$ is false.

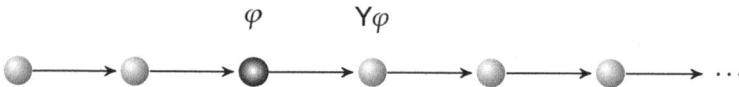

- The operator **Since**, denoted S, is defined as the past-time analogue of U as follows: $\varphi \mathsf{S} \psi$ states that ψ holds true at some past position (or, possibly, the current one) and meanwhile, since then, φ holds true:

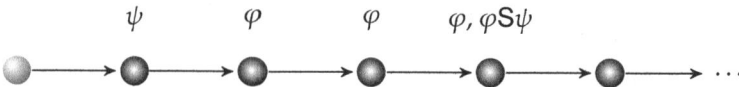

- One can also naturally define the operator F^{-1}, also denoted by P in the literature on philosophical logic, referring to 'sometime in the past'. Thus, $\mathsf{F}^{-1}\varphi$ is true at a current state iff φ is true at that state or at some previous state.

$$\varphi \qquad\qquad\qquad\qquad\qquad\qquad\qquad\qquad \mathsf{F}^{-1}\varphi$$

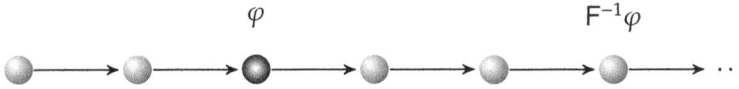

Note that F^{-1} can be defined in terms of Since: $\mathsf{F}^{-1}\varphi := \top\mathsf{S}\varphi$.

- Likewise, we can consider G^{-1}, also denoted by H in the literature on philosophical logic, referring to 'always in the past'. Thus, $\mathsf{G}^{-1}\varphi$ is true at a current state iff φ is true at that state and at every previous state:

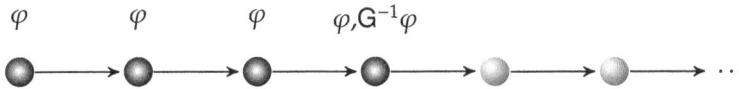

$$\varphi \qquad\qquad \varphi \qquad\qquad \varphi \qquad\quad \varphi,\mathsf{G}^{-1}\varphi$$

The operator G^{-1} can also be defined as $\neg\mathsf{F}^{-1}\neg$.

The **linear-time temporal logic with past**, denoted LTL+Past, is defined as an extension of LTL with the operators Y and S. The formulae of LTL+Past are defined by the following abstract grammar:

$$\varphi, \psi ::= \bot \mid p \mid \neg\varphi \mid (\varphi \wedge \psi) \mid \mathsf{X}\varphi \mid \mathsf{Y}\varphi \mid (\psi\mathsf{U}\varphi) \mid (\psi\mathsf{S}\varphi).$$

We use $\mathsf{F}^{-1}\varphi$ as an abbreviation for $\top\mathsf{S}\varphi$ and $\mathsf{G}^{-1}\varphi$ as an abbreviation for $\neg\mathsf{F}^{-1}\neg\varphi$. LTL+Past and LTL have the same models, and the definition of the satisfaction relation $\models$ is extended with the following clauses:

- $\sigma, i \models \mathsf{Y}\varphi$ iff $\sigma, i-1 \models \varphi$ and $i > 0$,
- $\sigma, i \models \psi\mathsf{S}\varphi$ iff there is $0 \leq j \leq i$ such that $\sigma, j \models \varphi$ and $\sigma, k \models \psi$ for all $j < k \leq i$.

Adding past-time operators to temporal logics may lead to more natural specifications. For instance, one may not only want to specify that every request is eventually granted but also that every grant is preceded by a request, which can be naturally expressed in LTL+Past in more than one (nonequivalent) ways, e.g.:

- $\mathsf{G}(\mathtt{grant} \rightarrow \mathsf{F}^{-1}\mathtt{request})$.
- $\mathsf{G}(\mathtt{grant} \rightarrow \mathsf{Y}(\neg\mathtt{grant}\,\mathsf{S}\,\mathtt{request}))$.

Similarly, one may specify the requirement that an alarm may not go off since it was reset unless a problem has occurred, e.g. by:

$$\mathsf{G}((\mathtt{alarm} \rightarrow \mathsf{F}^{-1}(\mathtt{problem} \wedge \mathsf{F}^{-1}\mathtt{reset}))\,\mathsf{S}\,\mathtt{reset}).$$

For some statements about LTL+Past it is, as with other logics as well, useful not to have negation operators at arbitrary positions in the formula. We therefore introduce negation normal form for LTL+Past.

Definition 6.5.1. An LTL+Past formula is in **negation normal form** if it is built from $\mathsf{Y}\top$, $\neg\mathsf{Y}\top$ and literals (i.e. atomic propositions and their negations), using $\wedge$, $\vee$, and the temporal operators X, U, G, Y, S and G^{-1}. ∇

Lemma 6.5.2. For every LTL+Past formula φ there is a LTL+Past formula φ' that is in negation normal form and equivalent to φ, such that $|\varphi'| = \mathcal{O}(|\varphi|)$. ∎

Proof. The required φ' can be obtained from φ by successively pushing negation operators inwards, using the well-known de Morgan laws, elimination of double negation ($\neg\neg\psi \equiv \psi$), as well as the following equivalences.

$$\neg\mathsf{X}\psi \equiv \mathsf{X}\neg\psi$$
$$\neg\mathsf{Y}\psi \equiv \neg\mathsf{Y}\top \vee \mathsf{Y}\neg\psi$$
$$\neg(\psi_1\mathsf{U}\psi_2) \equiv \big(\neg\psi_2\mathsf{U}(\neg\psi_1 \wedge \neg\psi_2)\big) \vee \mathsf{G}\neg\psi_2$$
$$\neg(\psi_1\mathsf{S}\psi_2) \equiv \big(\neg\psi_2\mathsf{S}(\neg\psi_1 \wedge \neg\psi_2)\big) \vee \mathsf{G}^{-1}\neg\psi_2.$$

It should be clear that the size of the resulting formula is linear in the size of φ (formulae are encoded as DAGs by default). Note that $\neg\mathsf{Y}\psi$ is not logically equivalent to $\mathsf{Y}\neg\psi$, except if the formulae are interpreted over $\mathbb{Z}$. □

Now we will introduce a variant of the notion of equivalence of formulae, which is not of independent importance for LTL, but is of relevance here.

Definition 6.5.3. Two formulae, φ and ψ, of LTL+Past are **initially equivalent**, denoted $\varphi \equiv_0 \psi$, whenever for all models σ, we have $\sigma, 0 \models \varphi$ if and only if $\sigma, 0 \models \psi$. ▽

The following explains why initial equivalence is not an important concept for LTL, yet it is one for LTL+Past.

Lemma 6.5.4.

(I) For every LTL formulae φ and ψ, it holds that $\varphi \equiv_0 \psi$ iff $\varphi \equiv \psi$.
(II) There are LTL+Past formulae φ and ψ such that $\varphi \equiv_0 \psi$ but not $\varphi \equiv \psi$. ∎

The proof is left as Exercise 6.40.

6.5.2 Bi-infinite Models

When past-time operators are involved, models based on $\mathbb{Z}$ can be considered instead of $\mathbb{N}$. For formal verification, it is unclear whether this is reasonable mainly because any system has initial configurations. However, this makes good sense from a logical perspective.

A $\mathbb{Z}$-**model** is a map $\sigma : \mathbb{Z} \to \mathcal{P}(\text{PROP})$ and $\text{LTL}^{\mathbb{Z}}$+Past is defined as LTL+Past except that $\mathbb{Z}$-models are considered and the satisfaction relation with past-time operators is updated as follows ($i \in \mathbb{Z}$):

- $\sigma, i \models \mathsf{Y}\varphi$ iff $\sigma, i-1 \models \varphi$,
- $\sigma, i \models \varphi_1\mathsf{S}\varphi_2$ iff there is $j \leq i$ such that $\sigma, j \models \varphi_2$ and $\sigma, k \models \varphi_1$ for all $j < k \leq i$.

Lemma 6.5.5. There is a logarithmic-space reduction from the $\text{LTL}^{\mathbb{Z}}$+Past satisfiability problem into the LTL+Past satisfiability problem. ∎

Consequently, LTL+Past on $\mathbb{Z}$-models can be simply encoded by LTL+Past on $\mathbb{N}$-models and, therefore, there is no special need to consider specifically this natural variant.

Proof. Let φ be a formula in LTL$^{\mathbb{Z}}$+Past with atomic propositions $p_1, \ldots, p_n$. First, we associate with each p_i a pair of new, distinct atomic propositions, p_i^+, p_i^-. For each linear model $\sigma : \mathbb{Z} \to \mathcal{P}(\{p_1, \ldots, p_n\})$, we associate a linear model $\sigma' : \mathbb{N} \to \mathcal{P}(\{p_1^+, p_1^-, \ldots, p_n^+, p_n^-\})$ that encodes σ. Moreover, we construct a formula φ' such that for every model σ of LTL$^{\mathbb{Z}}$+Past, $\sigma \models \varphi$ iff $\sigma' \models \varphi'$. The models σ and σ' are related by the following property: for $j \in \mathbb{N}$, $p_i \in \sigma(j)$ iff $p_i^+ \in \sigma'(j)$ and $p_i \in \sigma(-j)$ iff $p_i^- \in \sigma'(j)$. This construction shows that φ is satisfiable in LTL$^{\mathbb{Z}}$+Past iff φ' is satisfiable in LTL+Past.

We define the following map $t(\cdot, \cdot)$ recursively from which it is then easy to get φ':

- $t(p_j, sg) := p_j^{sg}$ with $sg \in \{+, -\}$,
- t is a homomorphism with respect to the Boolean connectives,
- $t(\mathsf{X}\psi, +) := \mathsf{X}\, t(\psi, +)$,
- $t(\mathsf{X}\psi, -) := (\mathsf{Y}\top \to \mathsf{Y}\, t(\psi, -)) \wedge (\neg\mathsf{Y}\top \to \mathsf{X}\, t(\psi, +))$,
- $t(\mathsf{Y}\psi, -) := \mathsf{X}\, t(\psi, -)$,
- $t(\mathsf{Y}\psi, +) := (\mathsf{Y}\top \to \mathsf{Y}\, t(\psi, +)) \wedge (\neg\mathsf{Y}\top \to \mathsf{X}\, t(\psi, -))$,
- analogous clauses are defined for the binary temporal operators U and S:
  - $t(\psi_1 \mathsf{U} \psi_2, +) := t(\psi_1, +)\, \mathsf{U}\, t(\psi_2, +)$.
  - $t(\psi_1 \mathsf{U} \psi_2, -)$ is defined as the disjunction:

$$((t(\psi_1, -) \wedge \mathsf{Y}\top)\, \mathsf{S}\, t(\psi_2, -)) \vee ((t(\psi_1, -) \wedge \mathsf{Y}\top)\, \mathsf{S}\, (\neg\mathsf{Y}\top \wedge t(\psi_1, +)\, \mathsf{U}\, t(\psi_2, +)).$$

  - $t(\psi_1 \mathsf{S} \psi_2, -) := t(\psi_1, -)\, \mathsf{U}\, t(\psi_2, -)$.
  - $t(\psi_1 \mathsf{S} \psi_2, +)$ is defined as the disjunction:

$$((t(\psi_1, +) \wedge \mathsf{Y}\top)\, \mathsf{S}\, t(\psi_2, +)) \vee ((t(\psi_1, +) \wedge \mathsf{Y}\top)\, \mathsf{S}\, (\neg\mathsf{Y}\top \wedge t(\psi_1, -)\, \mathsf{U}\, t(\psi_2, -)).$$

The formula φ' is defined as:

$$\varphi' := t(\varphi, +) \wedge \bigwedge_{1 \leq i \leq n} (p_i^- \leftrightarrow p_i^+).$$

The second part of the conjunction is motivated by the fact that satisfiability is defined at position 0 and at that position, the atomic propositions p_i^- and p_i^+ should be equivalently true. We will show that φ is satisfiable iff φ' is satisfiable. The proof is by structural induction on φ, by observing that a $\mathbb{Z}$-model σ restricted to $\{p_1, \ldots, p_n\}$ can be viewed as an $\mathbb{N}$-model σ' restricted to $\{p_1^-, \ldots, p_n^-, p_1^+, \ldots, p_n^+\}$. For all $i \in \mathbb{N}$ and all $j \in [1, n]$,

- $p_j \in \sigma(i)$ iff $p_j^+ \in \sigma'(i)$,
- $p_j \in \sigma(-i)$ iff $p_j^- \in \sigma'(i)$.

It should be noted that φ' can be of polynomial size in the size of φ. Remember that the size of formulae is defined with respect to their DAG-size. $\qquad\square$

6.5.3 The Succinctness of LTL with Past

Here we consider linear models based on $\mathbb{N}$ again. It is easy to see that the translation of an LTL+Past formula into an LTL formula comes at a nontrivial blow-up of size. It may involve iterated transformations into conjunctive or disjunctive normal form, and it certainly duplicates subformulae which may be handled differently subsequently. Thus, one should expect that the blow-up is at least exponential. It turns out that *every* such transformation has to involve an at least exponential blow-up. This phenomenon is known as **succinctness**, intuitively meaning that there are (families of) properties which can be expressed using much shorter formulae in one logic (here: LTL+Past) than the other (here: LTL).

Note that this is only interesting if one considers families of properties, i.e. sequences of growing formulae. This way, we can compare the asymptotic growth of formulae required to express certain properties in one logic or the other and make such considerations independent of the actual size of operators in a logic. We will therefore speak of an **exponential succinctness gap** between two logics $\mathcal{L}_1$ and $\mathcal{L}_2$, if there is a sequence $\{\varphi_n\}_{n\in\mathbb{N}}$ of formulae in $\mathcal{L}_1$ such that for every sequence $\{\psi_n\}_{n\in\mathbb{N}}$, satisfying $\psi_n \equiv \varphi_n$ for all $n \in \mathbb{N}$, we have that the sizes of the ψ_n grow exponentially in the sizes of the φ_n.

In order to prove such an exponential succinctness gap between LTL+Past and LTL we consider languages $Init_n$ and All_n, for $n \geq 1$, of computations over an increasing number of atomic propositions $q_0, \ldots, q_n$, where:

1. $Init_n$ consists of all computations that satisfy the following property: *any state that agrees with state 0 on the truth of the propositions $q_1, \ldots, q_n$ must also agree with it on the truth of q_0.*
2. All_n consists of all computations satisfying the following property: *any two states that agree on the truth of the propositions $q_1, \ldots, q_n$ must also agree on the truth of proposition q_0.*

Formally:

$$Init_n := \{\sigma \in (\mathcal{P}(\{q_0, \ldots, q_n\}))^\omega \mid \forall i \in \mathbb{N} : \text{if } q_k \in \sigma(i) \text{ iff } q_k \in \sigma(0) \,\forall\, k \in [1, n]$$
$$\text{then } q_0 \in \sigma(i) \text{ iff } q_0 \in \sigma(0)\}$$

$$All_n := \{\sigma \in (\mathcal{P}(\{q_0, \ldots, q_n\}))^\omega \mid \forall i, j \in \mathbb{N} : \text{if } q_k \in \sigma(i) \text{ iff } q_k \in \sigma(j) \,\forall\, k \in [1, n]$$
$$\text{then } q_0 \in \sigma(i) \text{ iff } q_0 \in \sigma(j)\}.$$

We will establish three claims:

1. The languages $Init_n$ are expressible in LTL+Past using formulae of size $\mathcal{O}(n)$.
2. If $Init_n$ are expressible in LTL using formulae of some size $g(n)$, then All_n are expressible using formulae of size $g(n) + 1$.
3. If All_n are expressible in LTL using formulae $\{\psi_n\}_{n\in\mathbb{N}}$ then ψ_n must have size $2^{\Omega(n)}$.

For the first claim, consider the following formulae of LTL+Past, where $n \geq 1$:

$$\varphi_n := \mathsf{G}\Big(\big(\bigwedge_{i=1}^{n}(q_i \to \mathsf{F}^{-1}\mathsf{G}^{-1}q_i) \wedge (\neg q_i \to \mathsf{F}^{-1}\mathsf{G}^{-1}\neg q_i)\big) \to$$

$$\big((q_0 \to \mathsf{F}^{-1}\mathsf{G}^{-1}q_0) \wedge (\neg q_0 \to \mathsf{F}^{-1}\mathsf{G}^{-1}\neg q_0)\big)\Big).$$

Lemma 6.5.6. For every $n \geq 1$ we have $\mathrm{Mod}(\varphi_n) = Init_n$. ∎

Proof. Immediately from the definition of $Init_n$, observing that on all linear models based on $\mathbb{N}$, the formula $\mathsf{F}^{-1}\mathsf{G}^{-1}\psi$ says that ψ must hold in state 0. □

The second claim follows from the next lemma.

Lemma 6.5.7. Let ψ_n, $n \geq 1$ be a family of LTL formulae such that $\mathrm{Mod}(\psi_n) = Init_n$ for every $n \geq 1$. Then $\mathrm{Mod}(\mathsf{G}\psi_n) = All_n$ for every $n \geq 1$. ∎

Proof. Immediate from the definition of $Init_n$, All_n and the semantics of the operator G. □

For the last claim, note that there are $N := 2^n$ many different valuations (that is, possible labels of a state) P of the atomic propositions $q_1, \ldots, q_n$. Let v_n be a finite sequence of N states in which each P is the label of exactly one state; for instance, take

$$v_n = \emptyset \cdot \{q_1\} \cdot \{q_2\} \cdot \{q_1, q_2\} \cdot \{q_3\} \cdot \ldots \cdot \{q_1, \ldots, q_n\}.$$

For any set of positions $T \subseteq [1, 2^n]$ – for technical convenience we assume them to start at 1 – let w_n^T be obtained from v_n by adding q_0 to all positions in T and only them, i.e. $w_n^T(i) := v_n(i) \cup \{q_0\}$ if $i \in T$ and $w_n^T(i) := v_n(i)$ otherwise.

Note that there are $2^N = 2^{2^n}$ many different such T. Fix an arbitrary one of them as T_0 and consider the computations $\rho_n^T := (w_n^T)^\omega$ and $\sigma_n^T := w_n^{T_0} \cdot \rho_n^T$ for every $T \subseteq [1, 2^n]$. It should be clear that $\rho_n^T \in All_n$ for every T, and $\sigma_n^T \in All_n$ iff $T = T_0$.

We are now ready to prove the main result.

Lemma 6.5.8. Let ψ_n be a family of LTL formulae such that for all $n \geq 1$ we have $\mathrm{Mod}(\psi_n) = All_n$. Then we have $|\psi_n| = 2^{\Omega(n)}$. ∎

Proof. Let σ_n^T be defined as earlier for every $T \in \mathcal{P}([1, 2^n])$. We consider those formulae of the closure of ψ_n that hold in position 0 and in position 2^n of each such word. Suppose they were equal, i.e. $cl_{\mathrm{LTL}}(\psi_n, \sigma_n^T, 0) = cl_{\mathrm{LTL}}(\psi_n, \sigma_n^T, 2^n)$. According to Lemma 6.3.1 we could remove the part $0, \ldots, 2^n - 1$ from σ_n^T resulting in ρ_n^T, and we would have $\sigma_n^T \models \psi_n$ iff $\rho_n^T \models \psi_n$. But we have $\rho_n^T \in All_n = \mathrm{Mod}(\psi_n)$ for every T and $\sigma_n^T \notin All_n$ for almost every T, namely for $2^{2^n} - 1$ many T. Thus, there must be at least $2^{2^n} - 1$ many different subsets of $cl_{\mathrm{LTL}}(\psi_n)$ which is only possible if $|\psi_n| = 2^{\Omega(n)}$. □

Putting Lemma 6.5.6, 6.5.7 and 6.5.8 together yields an exponential succinctness gap between LTL+Past and LTL.

Theorem 6.5.9. There are LTL+Past formulae φ_n, $n \geq 1$, such that for every family ψ_n of LTL formulae with $\psi_n \equiv \varphi_n$ for all $n \geq 1$ we have: $|\psi_n| = 2^{\Omega(|\varphi_n|)}$. ∎

We remark that this result does not prove an exponential succinctness gap over a *finite* set of propositions. In order to do so, one can encode the valuation of n atomic propositions in a single state using a single atomic proposition along $\lceil \log n \rceil$ many states. However, then it is unknown whether the property used earlier can be defined in LTL+Past using formulae of linear length. Still, it is possible to define it with formulae of size $\mathcal{O}(n \log n)$, resulting in a sub-exponential succinctness gap. The question of whether there is also an exponential succinctness gap over a fixed set of atomic propositions is still open.

6.6 Invariance Properties

In this section, we present a selection of results about the expressiveness of LTL and variants, from the point of view of invariance properties. This is complemented by material presented on Chapter 10 especially dedicated to the expressive power of temporal logics. Expressive power of temporal logics can be measured by several means, one of them being to compare temporal logics with standard logical formalisms, such that first-order logics or monadic second-order logics, as done in Chapter 10. Alternatively, analysing the classes of linear models definable by LTL is another way to get some hints on the expressive power of LTL formulae. For instance, in Section 6.6.2, we explain why LTL(U) defines precisely the classes of models invariant modulo stuttering that can be defined with LTL formulae. In Section 6.6.1, we establish that two rooted transition systems satisfy the same LTL formulae iff their sets of traces are identical. This is clearly another way to approach the expressiveness of LTL. Kamp's Theorem (see the bibliographic notes) is probably even more explicit since it provides an equivalence between LTL formulae and first-order formulae over $\mathbb{N}$.

6.6.1 Trace Equivalence

To begin with, note that whenever two rooted transition systems have the same computations, they satisfy (in existential and in universal sense) the same LTL formulae.

The converse need not always be true if the set of atomic propositions PROP is infinite, see Exercise 6.41. However, we will show that it holds when PROP is finite. Indeed, we will show that every ultimately periodic model σ over a finite set PROP can be characterised precisely by an LTL formula.

First, for any given (finite) subset $\Pi \subseteq$ PROP we denote

$$\bigwedge_{\text{PROP}} \Pi := \bigwedge_{p \in \Pi} p \wedge \bigwedge_{p \notin \Pi} \neg p.$$

Now, let σ have a prefix length i and a loop length l. Then we define

$$\chi_\sigma := \bigwedge_{0 \leq j \leq i+l} \mathsf{X}^j \left(\bigwedge_{\text{PROP}} \sigma(j) \right) \wedge \mathsf{X}^i \left(\bigwedge_{\Gamma \subseteq \text{PROP}} \mathsf{G} \left(\left(\bigwedge_{\text{PROP}} \Gamma \right) \to \mathsf{X}^l \left(\bigwedge_{\text{PROP}} \Gamma \right) \right) \right).$$

Note that the formula χ_σ belongs to the fragment LTL(X, G).

Lemma 6.6.1. Let PROP be a finite set of atomic propositions and σ, σ' be computations over PROP, that is $\sigma, \sigma' \in (\mathcal{P}(\text{PROP}))^\omega$. Then

$$\sigma' \models \chi_\sigma \text{ iff } \sigma' = \sigma.$$ ∎

The proof of Lemma 6.6.1 is left as Exercise 6.42.

We write $\text{traces}_{\mathcal{T}}^{\text{UL}}(s)$ to denote the ultimately periodic computations in $\text{traces}_{\mathcal{T}}(s)$ and put $\Sigma := \mathcal{P}(\text{PROP})$.

Theorem 6.6.2. Let $(\mathcal{T}, s)$ and $(\mathcal{T}', s')$ be two finite rooted transition systems. The following are equivalent:

(I) For every LTL formula φ, we have $\mathcal{T}, s \models_\exists \varphi$ iff $\mathcal{T}', s' \models_\exists \varphi$.
(II) For every LTL formula φ, we have $\mathcal{T}, s \models_\forall \varphi$ iff $\mathcal{T}', s' \models_\forall \varphi$.
(III) $\text{traces}_{\mathcal{T}}(s) = \text{traces}_{\mathcal{T}'}(s')$.
(IV) $\text{traces}_{\mathcal{T}}^{\text{UL}}(s) = \text{traces}_{\mathcal{T}'}^{\text{UL}}(s')$. ∎

Proof. The equivalence of (I) and (II) is straightforward. Likewise are the implications from (III) to (I), (II) and (IV). The implication from (I) to (IV) follows from Lemma 6.6.1.

Lastly, to prove that (IV) implies (III), suppose, for instance, that $\sigma \in \text{traces}_{\mathcal{T}}(s) \setminus \text{traces}_{\mathcal{T}'}(s')$. Then, we claim that there is a finite prefix $\sigma[0, k]$ of σ which is not a prefix of any computation in $\text{traces}_{\mathcal{T}'}(s')$. Indeed, consider the tree Tr where the nodes are all finite paths $t_1, \ldots, t_m$ in $\mathcal{T}'$ that start at $t_1 = s'$ and are such that the sequences of their labels in $\mathcal{T}'$ are prefixes of σ; the successors of a node ρ in Tr are the nodes in Tr that extend ρ by a single state. Clearly, Tr is finitely branching, because any node can have no more than $|\mathcal{T}'|$ successors. Furthermore, Tr has no infinite branches, because any such branch would generate the computation σ in $\mathcal{T}'$. Therefore, by Kőnig's Lemma, Tr is finite. Now, take a longest branch in Tr. It generates a finite prefix $\sigma[0, k-1]$ of σ in $\mathcal{T}'$. Then, the prefix $\sigma[0, k]$ is as required.

Now, $\sigma[0, k]$ can be extended to a computation from $\text{traces}_{\mathcal{T}}^{\text{UL}}(s)$ and, by construction of $\sigma[0, k]$, any such computation is not in $\text{traces}_{\mathcal{T}'}(s')$. Indeed, to construct such computation take any path in $\mathcal{T}$ that generates $\sigma[0, k]$ – which is guaranteed by the totality and finiteness of $\mathcal{T}$ – and extend it until it reaches a self-reachable state; then continue with an infinite repetition of the loop from that state. □

6.6.2 Stuttering Invariance

The next result characterises the expressive power of LTL(U).

Definition 6.6.3. For any computation σ the **stuttering collapse** of σ is the unique computation stcol(σ) obtained by replacing all maximal subsequences of states with identical labels in σ by a single state with the same label, except for the last infinite repetition of a label in σ, if any. ▽

For instance, the stuttering collapse of the computation

$$\{p, q\}^5 \cdot \emptyset^7 \cdot \{p\} \cdot \{q\}^4 \cdot \{p\}^\omega$$

is the computation

$$\{p, q\} \cdot \emptyset \cdot \{p\} \cdot \{q\} \cdot \{p\}^\omega$$

whereas the stuttering collapse of

$$\{p, q\}^5 \cdot (\emptyset^7 \cdot \{p\} \cdot \{p, q\}^4)^\omega$$

is

$$\{p, q\} \cdot (\emptyset \cdot \{p\} \cdot \{p, q\})^\omega.$$

Definition 6.6.4. We say that the computations σ and σ' are **equivalent modulo stuttering**, written $\sigma \approx \sigma'$, if $stcol(\sigma) = stcol(\sigma')$. ∇

For instance, the following sequences are equivalent modulo stuttering:

$$\{p, q\}^5 \cdot \{p\} \cdot \emptyset^7 \cdot \{q\}^2 \cdot \emptyset^\omega \quad \{p, q\}^2 \cdot \{p\}^3 \cdot \emptyset^2 \cdot \{q\} \cdot \emptyset^\omega \quad \{p, q\} \cdot \{p\} \cdot \emptyset \cdot \{q\} \cdot \emptyset^\omega.$$

We say that an LTL formula φ is **invariant modulo stuttering** whenever if $\sigma \in \text{Mod}(\varphi)$ and $\sigma \approx \sigma'$ then $\sigma' \in \text{Mod}(\varphi)$. Clearly, not every LTL formula is invariant modulo stuttering, for instance $X\neg p$, as witnessed by the equivalent sequences. It is easy to show that if $\varphi \in \text{LTL}(U)$, then $\text{Mod}(\varphi)$ is invariant modulo stuttering. Note that the preceding example relies on the presence of the X-operator. Actually, we will show that LTL(U) is exactly the fragment of LTL that defines languages invariant modulo stuttering.

Theorem 6.6.5. Let φ be an LTL formula. The following statements are equivalent.

(I) φ is invariant modulo stuttering.
(II) There is a formula $\psi \in \text{LTL}(U)$ such that $\varphi \equiv \psi$.   ∎

Proof. The fact that (II) implies (I) can easily be proved by induction on the structure of ψ. We leave the details as an exercise.

(I) implies (II): First we construct, by induction on the structure of φ, its LTL(U)-counterpart $tr(\varphi)$. This is straightforward in almost all cases, e.g. $tr(p) := p$, $tr(\psi_1 \vee \psi_2) := tr(\psi_1) \vee tr(\psi_2)$, $tr(\neg\psi) := \neg tr(\psi)$, $tr(\psi_1 U \psi_2) := tr(\psi_1) U tr(\psi_2)$. The only nontrivial case is that of $\varphi = X\psi$ because the X-operator is not available in LTL(U). Recall the assumption of φ being invariant modulo stuttering. Thus, in order to prove that $X\psi \equiv tr(X\psi)$ it suffices to show that for every computation σ:

$$stcol(\sigma) \models X\psi \text{ iff } stcol(\sigma) \models tr(X\psi).$$

Take any computation σ and let $\sigma' = stcol(\sigma)$. Note that there are two possible cases for σ':

1. σ' consists of states with equal labels only. In this case, ψ can be required to hold immediately, rather than after one step because σ' and $\sigma'[1, +\infty)$ are identical.
2. The labels of the first and the second state in σ' differ in at least one atomic proposition, say p. Then p can be used to signal the *next* state in σ', where ψ must hold. For that, one simply needs to require that no other atomic proposition changes truth value in between the current state and the one where p changes value: because σ' is a stuttering collapse, there can be no intermediate such state in σ'.

Now let LIT(φ) be the set of literals over the atomic propositions occurring in φ. Here is the formal definition of $tr(\mathsf{X}\psi)$, encoding both preceding cases:

$$tr(\mathsf{X}\psi) := \left(tr(\psi) \wedge \bigwedge_{\ell \in \mathrm{LIT}(\varphi)} (\ell \to \mathsf{G}\ell)\right) \vee$$

$$\bigvee_{\ell \in \mathrm{LIT}(\varphi)} \left(((\neg\ell)\mathsf{U}(\ell \wedge tr(\psi))) \wedge \bigwedge_{\ell' \in \mathrm{LIT}(\varphi)} ((\ell'\mathsf{U}\ell) \vee ((\neg\ell')\mathsf{U}\ell))\right).$$

We leave it as an exercise to check that for any computation σ we have $\mathrm{stcol}(\sigma) \models \mathsf{X}\psi$ iff $\mathrm{stcol}(\sigma) \models tr(\mathsf{X}\psi)$, by considering the earlier two cases. □

6.7 Extensions of LTL

6.7.1 Automata-Based Temporal Operators

It is not always easy to figure out whether a set of computations can be defined by an LTL formula. For instance, is there any LTL formula φ such that $\mathrm{Mod}(\varphi)$ is precisely the set of computations σ for which the atomic proposition p belongs to $\sigma(i)$ for every even position i (and, possibly to some odd-numbered states, too)? We invite the reader to determine, before reading further, whether any of the following formulae is adequate for that:

$$\varphi_1 = p \wedge \mathsf{X}\neg p \wedge \mathsf{G}(p \leftrightarrow \mathsf{X}\mathsf{X}p)$$
$$\varphi_2 = p \wedge \mathsf{G}(p \to \mathsf{X}\mathsf{X}p)$$
$$\varphi_3 = q \wedge \mathsf{X}\neg q \wedge \mathsf{G}(q \leftrightarrow \mathsf{X}\mathsf{X}q) \wedge \mathsf{G}(q \to p).$$

For instance, formula φ_1 defines a unique model and enforces that p does not belong to $\sigma(i)$ when the position i is odd. How about formula φ_2? As for formula φ_3, note that it does the job, but uses an extra atomic proposition q, which prevents it from characterising the desired language.

We will prove further that this property cannot be expressed in LTL, see Theorem 10.3.3.

Theorem 6.7.1. There is no LTL formula φ built over the unique atomic proposition p such that $\mathrm{Mod}(\varphi)$ is exactly the set of linear models such that p holds on every even position. ∎

As we will show in Chapter 14, LTL formulae can be translated into 'equivalent' automata. In particular, the temporal operators in LTL can be 'simulated' by automata.

Moreover, it is intuitively clear that a simple automaton can be designed to read the LTL model and check the property 'truth at every even state' discussed previously. This suggests considering an extension of LTL by adding *all* temporal operators that can be defined with (finite-state) automata.

We illustrate the idea on a simple example. Consider an LTL model σ such that $\sigma, i \models \varphi\mathsf{U}\psi$ for some position i and U-formula $\varphi\mathsf{U}\psi$. So, there is $j \geq i$ such that $\sigma, j \models \psi$ and for $k \in [i, j-1]$, we have $\sigma, k \models \varphi$. This can be illustrated by the schema.

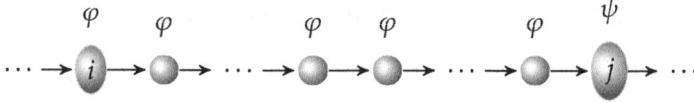

Let $\Sigma = \{\varphi, \psi\}$ and $\mathrm{L} \subseteq \Sigma^*$ be the regular language $\varphi^* \cdot \psi$. It is clear that $\sigma, i \models \varphi\mathsf{U}\psi$ iff there is a word in L, say $\mathsf{a}_0 \cdots \mathsf{a}_N$ with $N \geq 0$, such that for $j \in [0, N]$, $\sigma, i + j \models \mathsf{a}_j$. In particular, $\sigma, i \models \mathsf{F}\psi$ iff there is $\mathsf{a}_0 \cdots \mathsf{a}_N \in \top^* \cdot \psi$ (over the alphabet $\{\top, \psi\}$) such that for $j \in [0, N]$, $\sigma, i + j \models \mathsf{a}_j$. More generally, given a finite alphabet $\Sigma = \{\varphi_1, \ldots, \varphi_k\}$ and a regular language $\mathrm{L} \subseteq \Sigma^*$, we define that $\sigma, i \models \mathrm{L}$ iff there is $\mathsf{a}_0 \cdots \mathsf{a}_N \in \mathrm{L}$ such that for $j \in [0, N]$, $\sigma, i + j \models \mathsf{a}_j$. Such a use of regular languages can obviously capture the until operator, as well as the next-time operator.

The **extended temporal logic** (ETL), defined subsequently, extends LTL with these new temporal connectives, based on regular languages defined with the help of finite-state automata. (An equivalent definition can be given with right-linear grammars or regular expressions.)

ETL formulae are defined by the following abstract grammar:

$$\varphi ::= \bot \mid p \mid \neg\varphi \mid (\varphi \wedge \psi) \mid \mathcal{A}(\varphi_1, \ldots, \varphi_k)$$

where $\mathcal{A}$ is a finite-state automaton built over the alphabet $\Sigma = \{\mathsf{a}_1, \ldots, \mathsf{a}_k\}$ and we assume that the letters in Σ are linearly ordered (the order is implicit in the sequel). We assume an unbounded supply of finite-state automata and each finite-state automaton can be viewed as a temporal operator (see the following semantics). ETL models are precisely LTL models and it remains to define the satisfaction relation for formulae of the form $\mathcal{A}(\varphi_1, \ldots, \varphi_k)$. Intuitively, the relation $\sigma, i \models \mathcal{A}(\varphi_1, \ldots, \varphi_k)$ holds when a finite pattern induced from $\mathrm{L}(\mathcal{A})$ exists from position i. First, there is a correspondence between the sequence of letters $\mathsf{a}_1, \ldots, \mathsf{a}_k$ and the sequence of argument formulae $\varphi_1, \ldots, \varphi_k$. A word $\mathsf{a}_{l_1}\mathsf{a}_{l_2} \ldots \mathsf{a}_{l_N} \in \mathrm{L}(\mathcal{A})$ induces a sequence of argument formulae $\varphi_{l_1}\varphi_{l_2} \ldots \varphi_{l_N}$ with the intention to provide constraints on the N positions. Formally:

$\sigma, i \models \mathcal{A}(\varphi_1, \ldots, \varphi_k)$ iff

- either there is $\mathsf{a}_{l_1}\mathsf{a}_{l_2} \ldots \mathsf{a}_{l_N} \in \mathrm{L}(\mathcal{A})$ such that for every $j \in [0, N-1]$, $\sigma, i + j \models \varphi_{l_{j+1}}$,
- or $\varepsilon \in \mathrm{L}(\mathcal{A})$.

Observe that in this condition, the index of the jth letter (with $j \in [0, N-1]$) determines which argument must hold at the jth next position, namely φ_{l_j}. Here we present a model for the ETL formula $\mathcal{A}(p, q)$ with $L(\mathcal{A}) = \{ab^i a \mid i \geq 0\}$ and a $<$ b.

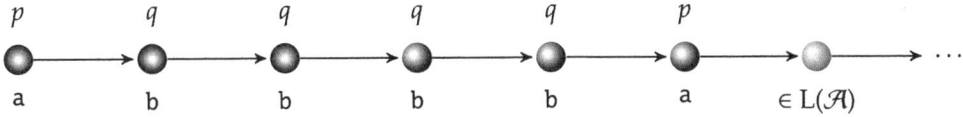

$$
\begin{array}{cccccc}
p & q & q & q & q & p \\
\bullet \!\!\rightarrow & \bullet \!\!\rightarrow & \bullet \!\!\rightarrow & \bullet \!\!\rightarrow & \bullet \!\!\rightarrow & \bullet \!\!\rightarrow \cdots \\
a & b & b & b & b & a \qquad \in L(\mathcal{A})
\end{array}
$$

The formula $\mathcal{A}(p, q)$ can be alternatively encoded by the finite-state automaton (formulae are letters)

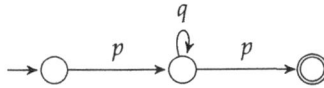

$$
\rightarrow \bigcirc \xrightarrow{\ p\ } \bigcirc \!\!\circlearrowleft^{q} \xrightarrow{\ p\ } \circledcirc
$$

The deficiency of LTL established in Theorem 6.7.1 can be fixed within ETL: the formula $\neg \mathcal{A}(\top, \neg p)$ with $L(\mathcal{A}) = (a^2)^* b$ holds exactly in models such that the atomic proposition p holds on every even position.

6.7.2 Propositional Quantification

We introduce here another natural extension of LTL, that turns out to have the same expressiveness as ETL. In this context we assume that formulae are built over propositional variables instead of atomic propositions, because we will introduce quantification over them. Given a set Π of propositional variables, and LTL models σ and σ', we write $\sigma \approx_{\Pi} \sigma'$ whenever for every $i \geq 0$, we have $(\sigma(i) \setminus \Pi) = (\sigma'(i) \setminus \Pi)$; i.e. σ and σ' are equal, possibly except on the interpretation of the propositional variables in Π.

We introduce the logic **QLTL** which is an extension of LTL with quantification on propositional variables. Formally, we extend the syntax of LTL by also allowing formulae of the form $\exists p \, \psi$ with the following semantics: $\sigma, i \models \exists p \, \psi$ iff there exists σ' such that $\sigma \approx_{\{p\}} \sigma'$ and $\sigma', i \models \psi$.

As for LTL, given an QLTL formula φ with free propositional variables in Π, we write $\text{Mod}(\varphi)$ to denote the set of models of φ over the alphabet $\mathcal{P}(\Pi)$.

The renaming technique. We illustrate the power of QLTL with the renaming technique. A standard method for reducing the complexity of formulae in various logical formalisms is to rename subformulae, at the cost of introducing new predicate symbols or propositional variables, see Section 5.2.1. LTL can also benefit from this technique, thanks to the presence of the temporal operator G. The idea: given an LTL formula φ with subformula ψ and a propositional variable p not occurring in φ, we have that φ is satisfiable iff $G(p \leftrightarrow \psi) \wedge \varphi[p/\psi]$ is satisfiable where $\varphi[p/\psi]$ is obtained from φ by replacing every occurrence of ψ by p.

Lemma 6.7.2. $\mathrm{Mod}(\varphi) = \mathrm{Mod}(\exists p(\mathsf{G}(p \leftrightarrow \psi) \wedge \varphi[p/\psi]))$.   ∎

The proof for Lemma 6.7.2 is left as Exercise 6.51, see also Section 5.2.1.

We show why any ETL formula can be reduced to a QLTL formula while preserving completely the set of models.

Theorem 6.7.3. For every ETL formula φ, there is a QLTL formula φ' such that $\mathrm{Mod}(\varphi) = \mathrm{Mod}(\varphi')$.   ∎

Proof. As a start, consider an ETL formula φ of the form $\mathcal{A}(p_1, \ldots, p_k)$; then we consider the general case. Let $\mathcal{A} = (\Sigma, Q, Q_0, \delta, F)$ be a finite-state automaton with $Q = \{q_1, \ldots, q_\alpha\}$ and $\Sigma = \{\mathsf{a}_1, \ldots, \mathsf{a}_k\}$. We build a QLTL formula φ' such that $\mathrm{Mod}(\varphi) = \mathrm{Mod}(\varphi')$. Without any loss of generality, we can assume that $\mathrm{L}(\mathcal{A}) \neq \emptyset$. Recall that $\sigma, i \models \mathcal{A}(p_1, \ldots, p_k)$ iff there is $\mathsf{a}_{l_1} \mathsf{a}_{l_2} \ldots \mathsf{a}_{l_N} \in \mathrm{L}(\mathcal{A})$ such that for $j \in [0, N-1]$, $\sigma, i+j \models p_{l_{j+1}}$. Then $\mathsf{a}_{l_1} \mathsf{a}_{l_2} \ldots \mathsf{a}_{l_N} \in \mathrm{L}(\mathcal{A})$ iff there is an accepting run of the form $q'_0 \xrightarrow{\mathsf{a}_{l_1}} q'_1 \xrightarrow{\mathsf{a}_{l_2}} q'_2 \ldots \xrightarrow{\mathsf{a}_{l_N}} q'_N$.

When $\sigma, i \models \mathcal{A}(p_1, \ldots, p_k)$, there are $X_1, \ldots, X_\alpha \subseteq \mathbb{N}$ such that:

- $\{X_1, \ldots, X_\alpha\}$ is a partition of $[0, N-1]$,
- for all $j \in [1, \alpha]$, $X_j = \{i \in [0, N-1] : q'_i = q_j\}$,

By definition of accepting runs, these sets satisfy the conditions

1. $0 \in X_j$ for some $q_j \in Q_0$.
2. $(N-1) \in X_j$ for some $q_j \in F$.

In order to build φ', for each state q_i, we introduce an atomic proposition q_i that contains the positions on which the current state is q_i. We also introduce a new atomic proposition in that holds true only on the positions of the finite run. We write φ' to denote the conjunction of the following formulae prefixed by $\exists\, q_1, \ldots, q_\alpha, \mathsf{in}$:

1. The accepting run is finite: $\mathsf{in} \wedge (\mathsf{in} \mathbin{\mathsf{U}} \mathsf{G}\neg\mathsf{in})$.
2. The first state is in Q_0: $\bigvee_{q_j \in Q_0} q_j$.
3. A state in F ends the run: $\bigvee_{q_j \in F} \mathsf{F}(q_j \wedge \mathsf{in} \wedge \mathsf{X}\neg\mathsf{in})$.
4. Each position is labelled by a unique state and by a unique letter (standard formula omitted herein).
5. The labelling of the positions respects the transition relation δ:

$$\mathsf{G} \bigwedge_{q_i} (q_i \wedge \mathsf{in}) \to \left(\bigvee_{q_i \xrightarrow{\mathsf{a}_j} q_{i'} \in \delta} p_j \wedge \mathsf{X}\, q_{i'} \right).$$

One can show that $\mathrm{Mod}(\varphi) = \mathrm{Mod}(\varphi')$.

Consider the translation $\mathfrak{f}$ from ETL formulae to QLTL formulae such that $\mathfrak{f}$ is the identity for atomic propositions, $\mathfrak{f}$ is homomorphic for Boolean connectives and $\mathfrak{f}(\mathcal{A}(\psi_1, \ldots, \psi_k))$ is equal to $\varphi'(\mathfrak{f}(\psi_1), \ldots, \mathfrak{f}(\psi_k))$ where φ' is the translation of $\mathcal{A}(p_1, \ldots, p_k)$ where each

occurrence of p_i is replaced by $\mathfrak{f}(\psi_i)$. When $\varepsilon \in L(\mathcal{A})$, $\mathfrak{f}(\mathcal{A}(\psi_1, \ldots, \psi_k))$ is simply equal
to $\top$. $\square$

The logic QLTL is expressive enough to capture ETL (actually, ETL and QLTL turn
out to have the same expressive power) and it can explicitly internalise renamings by
introducing new propositional variables. In terms of computational complexity, however,
there is a huge difference between QLTL and ETL: indeed, the satisfiability problem for
ETL is PSPACE-complete as for plain LTL whereas it is nonelementary for QLTL, see
Section 11.2.

6.7.3 The Industrial Specification Language (PSL)

In this section we present another extension of LTL which has more expressive power than
LTL itself. The inability to express ω-regular properties like 'at all even positions' makes
LTL too weak for certain specification and verification purposes (see Theorem 6.7.1). Nevertheless, a need for temporal logics as formal specification languages has been established
in system design. Moreover, several major players in this area have joint forces and defined
a specification language which is supposed to lay down the standards, mainly in hardware
design and verification. This **Property Specification Language**, PSL for short, is a rich
logic that features all sorts of operators and various facets for different purposes like linear-
time vs. branching-time scenarios or finite runs versus infinite runs. Here we present an
extension of LTL which contains the most important features of the linear-time part of PSL
interpreted over infinite runs. As it is commonly done in the academic literature, we take
the liberty of calling this logic PSL, too.

Syntax and Semantics

Formulae of PSL are formed in a three-stage process. A **Boolean expression** over PROP
is any expression using atomic propositions in PROP, the constants $\bot$ and $\top$, as well as
the usual Boolean connectives $\land$, $\lor$, $\neg$, etc. Such a Boolean expression b is interpreted
in the labelling of a state in a computation in the usual way. If $\Pi \subseteq$ PROP then we write
$\Pi \models b$ to denote that the Boolean expression b evaluates to *true* under the usual rules for
the connectives when each element of Π is interpreted by *true* and elements of PROP $\setminus \Pi$
are interpreted by *false*.

Definition 6.7.4. Semi-extended regular expressions (SEREs) are built on top of
Boolean expressions using the following grammar.

$$E ::= b \mid E \cup E \mid E \cap E \mid E; E \mid E^*$$

where b is a Boolean expression over PROP. ∇

So, semi-extended regular expressions involve the regular operations plus intersection. Such
SEREs are interpreted over *finite* sequences of sets of atomic propositions, i.e. by finite parts
of a computation $\rho : [n] \to \mathcal{P}(\text{PROP})$ for some $n \in \mathbb{N}$ as follows.

$$\rho \models b \qquad \text{iff} \quad |\rho| = 1 \text{ and } \rho(0) \models b$$
$$\rho \models E \cup F \quad \text{iff} \quad \rho \models E \text{ or } \rho \models F$$
$$\rho \models E \cap \beta \quad \text{iff} \quad \rho \models E \text{ and } \rho \models F$$
$$\rho \models E; F \quad \text{iff} \quad \text{there are } \rho', \rho'' \text{ with } \rho = \rho'\rho'', \ \rho' \models E \text{ and } \rho'' \models F$$
$$\rho \models E^* \quad \text{iff} \quad \text{there are } m \geq 0 \text{ and } \rho_1, \dots, \rho_m \text{ with } \rho = \rho_1 \dots \rho_m \text{ and }$$
$$\rho_i \models E \text{ for all } i = 1, \dots, m.$$

Finally, formulae of PSL are interpreted over infinite sequences $\sigma : \mathbb{N} \to \mathcal{P}(\text{PROP})$. They are obtained by extending the syntax of LTL with two new temporal operators. The **and-then** operator is a binary one that takes a SERE E and a formula φ and expresses that there is a finite prefix which satisfies the SERE E such that the suffix beginning in the last state of that prefix satisfies φ. Formally,

$$\sigma, i \models E \diamondsuit\!\!\to \varphi \quad \text{iff} \quad \text{there is } j \geq i \text{ with } \sigma(i) \dots \sigma(j) \models E \text{ and } \sigma, j \models \varphi.$$

Example 6.7.5. Take for example the formula $(q; \neg q)^* \cap (p^*; \neg p^*) \diamondsuit\!\!\to r$ and the computation σ defined as follows.

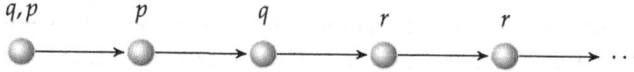

Then we have $\sigma, 0 \models (q; \neg q)^* \cap (p^*; \neg p^*) \diamondsuit\!\!\to r$ because $\rho \models (q; \neg q)^*$ and $\rho \models p^*; \neg p^*$ where $\rho = \sigma(0) \dots \sigma(3)$ and $\sigma, 3 \models r$.

Note that atomic propositions can be used in PSL formulae in two different ways, as in the preceding example. Propositions p and q are used to describe single states through Boolean expressions, while proposition r is actually a formula which is interpreted on an infinite sequence of states.

The dual of the *and-then* operator is also used. It can be read as **triggers**:

$$E \,\square\!\!\to \varphi := \neg(E \diamondsuit\!\!\to \neg\varphi).$$

Thus, it describes all computations which do not have a finite prefix described by E such that the corresponding suffix satisfies $\neg\varphi$. In other words, whenever a prefix satisfies E then the corresponding suffix must satisfy φ, i.e. φ is *triggered* by E on this computation.

The second operator that PSL features in addition to LTL is the **closure** operator. It turns an SERE E – interpreted over finite sequences – into a formula being interpreted over an infinite sequence in the way that $\text{Cl}(E)$ intuitively states that at every moment in a computation it looks like one could see a prefix that models E. Formally, it is defined as follows.

$$\sigma, i \models \text{Cl}(E) \quad \text{iff} \quad \text{for all } j \geq i \text{ there is } \sigma' \text{ with } \sigma(i) \dots \sigma(j)\sigma' \models E \diamondsuit\!\!\to \top.$$

Example 6.7.6. Consider the very simple SERE $E = \neg p^*; p$ describing finite computation parts which satisfy p in their last state. The computation σ defined as

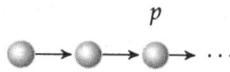

is a model of $Cl(E)$ simply because any of its prefixes $\sigma(0)\ldots\sigma(j)$ can be extended by the corresponding suffix $\sigma(j+1)\ldots$ in order to form a computation which begins with a part that satisfies the SERE E. However, the computation

in which p holds nowhere is also a model of $Cl(E)$ even though E requires p to hold eventually. Remember that the closure operator requires the SERE to hold on a prefix of *some* computation for any prefix of σ. In detail, every prefix $\sigma(0)\ldots\sigma(j)$ can be extended by a suffix which contains a state satisfying p, and then this extension has a prefix which satisfies E.

6.8 An Axiomatic System for LTL

6.8.1 Derivations in the System AxSys$_{LTL}$

Here we provide a sound and complete axiomatic system for LTL, extending AxSys$_{PL}$ with a minimal set of additional axioms for X ensuring seriality and linearity, as well as axioms expressing the fixpoint characterisations of G and U, plus the inference rule of Necessitation for G. For the formulae of LTL we will assume that the primitive temporal operators are X, G, U, even though G is definable in terms of X and U. The other connectives and temporal operators definable as usual.

The axiomatic system AxSys$_{LTL}$.
Axiom schemata:

(PL)	All axiom schemes of AxSys$_{PL}$
(K$_X$)	$X(\varphi \to \psi) \to (X\varphi \to X\psi)$
(SER)	$X\top$
(FUNC)	$X\neg\varphi \leftrightarrow \neg X\varphi$
(PostFP$_G$)	$G\varphi \to (\varphi \wedge XG\varphi)$
(GFP$_G$)	$G(\psi \to (\varphi \wedge X\psi)) \to (\psi \to G\varphi)$
(PreFP$_U$)	$(\psi \vee (\varphi \wedge X(\varphi U\psi))) \to (\varphi U\psi)$
(LFP$_U$)	$G((\psi \vee (\varphi \wedge X\chi)) \to \chi) \to ((\varphi U\psi) \to \chi)$.

The **rules of inference** are **Modus Ponens** (MP) and the rules of **Necessitation**:

$$\text{Nec}_X \; \frac{\vdash \varphi}{\vdash X\varphi} \qquad \text{Nec}_G \; \frac{\vdash \varphi}{\vdash G\varphi}.$$

In technical terms, the axiom PreFP$_G$ says that $G\varphi$ is a post-fixpoint of the operator Γ_G defined by '$\Gamma_G(\psi) = \varphi \wedge X\psi$', whereas GFP$_G$ says that $G\varphi$ is (set-theoretically, in terms of its extension) a *greatest post-fixpoint* of Γ_G. Likewise, the axiom PreFP$_U$ says that $\varphi U\psi$ is a pre-fixpoint of the operator Γ_U defined by '$\Gamma_U(\psi') = \psi \vee (\varphi \wedge X\psi')$', whereas LFP$_U$ says that $\varphi U\psi$ is a least pre-fixpoint of Γ_U. As we show further, in Lemma 6.8.1, items (VII) and (VIII), the axioms imply something stronger, namely that $G\varphi$ and $\varphi U\psi$ are respectively a *greatest fixpoint* and a *least fixpoint* of the respective operators; in fact, they are unique such fixpoints up to equivalents.

Note that GFP_G generalises the following *Induction axiom*

(IND): $G(\varphi \to X\varphi) \to (\varphi \to G\varphi)$.

In fact, the axiom GFP_G can be replaced by the following induction rule, easily derivable in the preceding system:

IND-Rule: If $\vdash \psi \to \varphi \wedge X\psi$ then $\vdash \psi \to G\varphi$.

Likewise, LFP_U can be replaced by an inductive inference rule, see Lemma 6.8.3 further.

All basic notions related to derivations and derivability, defined for AxSys_{BML} in Section 5.7, apply likewise to AxSys_{LTL}. In particular, deductive consequence from a set of assumptions in AxSys_{LTL} is defined likewise, where the rules **Nec** can be applied in derivations in AxSys_{LTL} to any theorem (in particular, any axiom) of AxSys_{LTL}, but *not* to the other assumptions.

Since AxSys_{LTL} is an extension of AxSys_{PL}, all derivable formulae and rules in AxSys_{PL} listed in Section 5.7 are derivable in AxSys_{LTL}, as well. Besides, the Deduction theorem, as stated for AxSys_{BML} in Section 5.7, holds here likewise. Moreover, we list some additional useful facts about AxSys_{LTL} in the following proposition, in the proof of which we will illustrate derivations in AxSys_{LTL}.

Lemma 6.8.1. The following are derivable in AxSys_{LTL}.

(I) $G\varphi \to X\varphi$

(II) G-monotonicity rule G-**Mon**:
  if $\vdash_{\text{AxSys}_{LTL}} \varphi \to \psi$ then $\vdash_{\text{AxSys}_{LTL}} G\varphi \to G\psi$.

(III) $XG\varphi \to GX\varphi$

(IV) $\varphi \wedge GX\varphi \to G\varphi$

(V) $GX\varphi \to XG\varphi$

(VI) K_G: $G(\varphi \to \psi) \to (G\varphi \to G\psi)$

(VII) FP_G: $G\varphi \leftrightarrow (\varphi \wedge XG\varphi)$

(VIII) FP_U: $\varphi U\psi \leftrightarrow (\psi \vee (\varphi \wedge X(\varphi U\psi)))$

(IX) FP_F: $F\varphi \leftrightarrow (\varphi \vee XF\varphi)$

(X) LFP_F: $G((\varphi \vee X\psi) \to \psi) \to (F\varphi \to \psi)$. ∎

Proof. We will sketch some of the derivations in AxSys_{LTL}, skipping some easy steps done in BML. We will omit the subscript AxSys_{LTL}.

(I) $\vdash G\varphi \to X\varphi$:

1.1	$\vdash G\varphi \to (\varphi \wedge XG\varphi)$	by Axiom (PostFP$_G$) and PL
1.2	$\vdash G\varphi \to \varphi$	by 1.1 and PL
1.3	$\vdash G\varphi \to XG\varphi$	by 1.1 and PL
1.4	$\vdash X(G\varphi \to \varphi)$	by 1.2 and **Nec**$_X$
1.5	$\vdash X(G\varphi \to \varphi) \to (XG\varphi \to X\varphi)$	by Axiom (K$_X$)
1.6	$\vdash XG\varphi \to X\varphi$	by 1.4, 1.5 and **MP**
1.7	$G\varphi \vdash XG\varphi$	by 1.3 and the Deduction Theorem

1.8 $\ \mathsf{G}\varphi \vdash \mathsf{X}\varphi$ by 1.6, 1.7 and **MP**

1.9 $\ \vdash \mathsf{G}\varphi \to \mathsf{X}\varphi$ by 1.8 and the Deduction Theorem

(II) Assume $\vdash \varphi \to \psi$.

2.1 $\ \vdash \mathsf{G}\varphi \to \varphi$ by Axiom (PostFP$_\mathsf{G}$) and PL

2.2 $\ \vdash \mathsf{G}\varphi \to \psi$ by 1.1, assumption and PL

2.3 $\ \vdash \mathsf{G}\varphi \to \mathsf{XG}\varphi$ by Axiom (PostFP$_\mathsf{G}$)

2.4 $\ \vdash \mathsf{G}\varphi \to \psi \wedge \mathsf{XG}\varphi$ by 2.2, 2.3 and PL

2.5 $\ \vdash \mathsf{G}(\mathsf{G}\varphi \to \psi \wedge \mathsf{XG}\varphi)$ by 2.4 and **Nec$_\mathsf{G}$**

2.6 $\ \vdash \mathsf{G}(\mathsf{G}\varphi \to \psi \wedge \mathsf{XG}\varphi) \to (\mathsf{G}\varphi \to \mathsf{G}\psi)$ by Axiom (GFP$_\mathsf{G}$)

2.7 $\ \vdash \mathsf{G}\varphi \to \mathsf{G}\psi$ by 2.5, 2.6 and **MP**

(III) $\vdash \mathsf{XG}\varphi \to \mathsf{GX}\varphi$:

3.1 $\ \vdash \mathsf{G}\varphi \to \varphi \wedge \mathsf{XG}\varphi$ by Axiom (PostFP$_\mathsf{G}$)

3.2 $\ \vdash \mathsf{XG}\varphi \to \mathsf{X}(\varphi \wedge \mathsf{XG}\varphi)$ by 3.1, Axiom (FP$_\mathsf{X}$), **Nec$_\mathsf{X}$** and PL
(See also Proposition 5.7.2.)

3.3 $\ \vdash \mathsf{X}(\varphi \wedge \mathsf{XG}\varphi) \to (\mathsf{X}\varphi \wedge \mathsf{XXG}\varphi)$ by Axiom (FP$_\mathsf{X}$) and PL
(See also Proposition 5.7.2.)

3.4 $\ \vdash \mathsf{XG}\varphi \to \mathsf{X}\varphi \wedge \mathsf{XXG}\varphi$ by 3.2, 3.3 and PL

3.5 $\ \vdash \mathsf{G}(\mathsf{XG}\varphi \to \mathsf{X}\varphi \wedge \mathsf{XXG}\varphi)$ by 3.4 and **Nec$_\mathsf{G}$**

3.6 $\ \vdash \mathsf{G}(\mathsf{XG}\varphi \to \mathsf{X}\varphi \wedge \mathsf{XXG}\varphi) \to (\mathsf{XG}\varphi \to \mathsf{GX}\varphi)$
by Axiom (GFP$_\mathsf{G}$)

3.7 $\ \vdash \mathsf{XG}\varphi \to \mathsf{GX}\varphi$ by 3.5, 3.6 and **MP**

(IV) The proof is left as an exercise.

(V)] $\vdash \mathsf{GX}\varphi \to \mathsf{XG}\varphi$:

5.1 $\ \vdash \varphi \wedge \mathsf{GX}\varphi \to \mathsf{G}\varphi$ by 4

5.2 $\ \vdash \mathsf{X}(\varphi \wedge \mathsf{GX}\varphi \to \mathsf{G}\varphi)$ by 5.1 and **Nec$_\mathsf{X}$**

5.3 $\ \vdash \mathsf{X}(\varphi \wedge \mathsf{GX}\varphi) \to \mathsf{XG}\varphi$ by 5.2, Axiom (K$_\mathsf{X}$) and PL

5.4 $\ \vdash (\mathsf{X}\varphi \wedge \mathsf{XGX}\varphi) \to \mathsf{X}(\varphi \wedge \mathsf{GX}\varphi)$ by Axiom (K$_\mathsf{X}$) and PL

5.5 $\ \vdash (\mathsf{X}\varphi \wedge \mathsf{XGX}\varphi) \to \mathsf{XG}\varphi$ by 5.2, 5.3 and PL

5.6 $\ \vdash \mathsf{GX}\varphi \to \mathsf{X}\varphi \wedge \mathsf{XGX}\varphi$ by Axiom (PostFP$_\mathsf{G}$)

5.7 $\ \vdash \mathsf{GX}\varphi \to \mathsf{XG}\varphi$ by 5.5, 5.6 and PL

(VI) K$_\mathsf{G}$: $\mathsf{G}(\varphi \to \psi) \to (\mathsf{G}\varphi \to \mathsf{G}\psi)$

6.1 $\ \vdash \mathsf{G}\varphi \to \varphi \wedge \mathsf{XG}\varphi$ by Axiom (PostFP$_\mathsf{G}$)

6.2 $\ \varphi \to \psi \vdash \mathsf{G}\varphi \to \varphi \wedge \mathsf{XG}\varphi$ by 6.1

6.3 $\ \varphi \to \psi \vdash \mathsf{G}\varphi \to \psi \wedge \mathsf{XG}\varphi$ by 6.2 and PL

6.4 $\ \vdash (\varphi \to \psi) \to (\mathsf{G}\varphi \to \psi \wedge \mathsf{XG}\varphi)$ by 6.3 and Deduction Theorem

6.5 $\ \vdash \mathsf{G}(\varphi \to \psi) \to \mathsf{G}(\mathsf{G}\varphi \to \psi \wedge \mathsf{XG}\varphi)$ by G-**Mon**

6.6 $\ \vdash \mathsf{G}(\mathsf{G}\varphi \to \psi \wedge \mathsf{XG}\varphi) \to (\mathsf{G}\varphi \to \mathsf{G}\psi)$ by Axiom (PostFP$_\mathsf{G}$)

6.7 $\ \vdash \mathsf{G}(\varphi \to \psi) \to (\mathsf{G}\varphi \to \mathsf{G}\psi)$ by 6.5, 6.6 and PL

(VII) To derive $\mathsf{G}\varphi \leftrightarrow (\varphi \wedge \mathsf{XG}\varphi)$ it suffices to derive the implication from right to left since the other implication is Axiom (PostFP$_\mathsf{G}$). Let us denote $\psi := \varphi \wedge \mathsf{XG}\varphi$. The idea is to apply Axiom (GFP$_\mathsf{G}$) for this ψ.

7.1 $\ \vdash \mathsf{G}\varphi \to (\varphi \wedge \mathsf{XG}\varphi)$ by Axiom (PostFP$_\mathsf{G}$)

7.2 $\vdash X(G\varphi \to (\varphi \land XG\varphi))$ by 7.1 and $\mathbf{Nec_X}$
7.3 $\vdash X(G\varphi \to (\varphi \land XG\varphi)) \to XG\varphi \to X(\varphi \land XG\varphi)$ by Axiom (K_X)
7.4 $\vdash XG\varphi \to X(\varphi \land XG\varphi)$ by 7.2, 7.3 and $\mathbf{MP}$
7.5 $\vdash \varphi \land XG\varphi \to X(\varphi \land XG\varphi)$, i.e. $\vdash \psi \to X\psi$ by 7.4 and PL
7.6 $\vdash \psi \to \varphi$ by PL
7.7 $\vdash \psi \to \varphi \land X\psi$ by 7.5, 7.6 and PL
7.8 $\vdash G(\psi \to \varphi \land X\psi)$ by 7.7 and $\mathbf{Nec_G}$
7.9 $\vdash G(\psi \to \varphi \land X\psi) \to (\psi \to G\varphi)$ by Axiom (GFP_G)
7.10 $\vdash \psi \to G\varphi$, i.e. $\vdash \varphi \land XG\varphi \to G\varphi$ by 7.8, 7.9 and $\mathbf{MP}$

We leave the last three derivations as exercises. The derivation of (VIII) is similar to the previous one and will be done, in the existentially quantified version for the logic CTL, in Section 7.5. The remaining two derivations can be easily extracted from the respective axioms for U, using the definition of F in terms of U, or from those for G, by using the duality with F.   □

Here are some additional useful claims about $\textsc{AxSys}_{\text{LTL}}$, the proofs of which we leave as exercises.

Lemma 6.8.2. The following are derivable in $\textsc{AxSys}_{\text{LTL}}$.

   (I) $G\varphi \to GG\varphi$
  (II) $FG\varphi \to GF\varphi$
 (III) $\varphi U\psi \to F\psi$
  (IV) $G\varphi \land F\psi \to \varphi U\psi$
   (V) $\varphi \land G(\varphi \to XF\varphi) \to GF\varphi$
  (VI) $(\varphi \to \chi)U\psi \to (\varphi U\psi \to \chi U\psi)$
 (VII) $G(\psi \to \vartheta) \to (\varphi U\psi \to \varphi U\vartheta)$
(VIII) $\varphi U\psi \to \varphi U(\varphi U\psi)$
  (IX) If the operator G is assumed definable as $Gp := \neg(\top U \neg p)$, then the axioms $PostFP_G$ and GFP_G are derivable from the rest in $\textsc{AxSys}_{\text{LTL}}$.   ■

Lemma 6.8.3. The following rule of inference is derivable in $\textsc{AxSys}_{\text{LTL}}$:
U-Induction Rule: If $\vdash \psi \lor (\varphi \land X\chi) \to \chi$ then $\vdash (\varphi U\psi) \to \chi$. Furthermore, the axiom LFP_U of $\textsc{AxSys}_{\text{LTL}}$ can be derived from the rest of $\textsc{AxSys}_{\text{LTL}}$ using this additional rule of inference.   ■

Thus, the axiom LFP_U can be equivalently replaced in $\textsc{AxSys}_{\text{LTL}}$ by the U-Induction Rule.

6.8.2 *Soundness and Completeness of* $\textsc{AxSys}_{\text{LTL}}$

Like for the previous axiomatic systems, the soundness and completeness for $\textsc{AxSys}_{\text{LTL}}$ can be stated in two different forms.

Theorem 6.8.4. The axiomatic system $\text{AxSys}_{\text{LTL}}$ is sound and (weakly) complete, i.e. for every finite set of LTL formulae $\{\varphi_1, \ldots, \varphi_n, \varphi\}$:

$$\varphi_1, \ldots, \varphi_n \vdash_{\text{AxSys}_{\text{LTL}}} \psi \text{ if and only if } \varphi_1, \ldots, \varphi_n \models \psi.$$

Equivalently, every set of LTL formulae is satisfiable if and only if it is consistent in $\text{AxSys}_{\text{LTL}}$. In particular, $\vdash_{\text{AxSys}_{\text{LTL}}} \psi$ if and only if ψ is a valid LTL formula. ∎

Remark 6.8.5. The completeness part of the theorem is only stated for *finite* sets of LTL formulae. Because of the fixpoint axioms, implying induction properties, the completeness claim does not hold in general for infinite sets of LTL formulae. Indeed, the set of formulae $\{F\neg p, p, Xp, XXp \ldots X^n p, \ldots\}$ is clearly unsatisfiable, but it is $\text{AxSys}_{\text{LTL}}$-consistent, for any derivation of a contradiction, say $\bot$, would only involve finitely many of these formulae. On the other hand, every finite set of the type $\{F\neg p, p, Xp, XXp \ldots X^n p\}$ is clearly satisfiable, and therefore must be $\text{AxSys}_{\text{LTL}}$-consistent. Logics with such property are called *noncompact* and for such logics only *weak completeness*, with respect to finite sets of formulae, hold.

Proof. (Sketch). Given the soundness of $\text{AxSys}_{\text{BML}}$, in order to prove the soundness of $\text{AxSys}_{\text{LTL}}$ it suffices to show that the new axiom schemes consist of valid LTL formulae and that the necessitation rules preserves validity, which we leave as exercises.

Because of the fixpoint axioms, the logic LTL is not canonical so additional constructions and further steps are needed for the completeness proof of $\text{AxSys}_{\text{LTL}}$, as compared to the one for $\text{AxSys}_{\text{BML}}$. We are not going to give a detailed proof of the completeness part but only a sketch of the main steps.

- The proof starts with a construction of a state-generated canonical ITS $\mathcal{T}_\Gamma$ for a given finite input set of LTL formulae Γ which is assumed $\text{AxSys}_{\text{LTL}}$-consistent. Due to the axioms and the derived LTL formulae in Lemma 6.8.1 and 6.8.2, it can be proved that the transition relation in $\mathcal{T}_\Gamma$ is reflexive, transitive and functional, that is, a linear ordering with an initial state and in which every state has a (unique) immediate successor. However, it need *not* be of the order type of the natural numbers, hence it is not a standard linear LTL model, i.e. one consisting of a single infinite computation. Therefore, further steps are needed to produce a satisfying standard model of length ω.
- One method to produce such model is to do *filtration* of $\mathcal{T}_\Gamma$ over the closure of the set Γ.
- The result is a *finite* (so, not yet based on $\mathbb{N}$) ITS satisfying Γ at its initial state. It looks like a balloon, with a finite tail representing an initial segment of $\mathbb{N}$ and ending with a cluster of points related to each other.
- After some technical work one can show that this balloon can be unfolded into a bisimilar infinite computation, i.e. an ITS based on a copy of $\mathbb{N}$, ensuring that a copy of every point from the head of the balloon appears infinitely many times in the unwinding. This will take care of the satisfaction of the eventualities and, combined with the bisimulation, will guarantee satisfaction of Γ. □

References to detailed proofs of completeness for variations of $\text{AxSys}_{\text{LTL}}$ can be found in the bibliographic Section 6.10. An alternative approach for proving Theorem 6.8.4 would be to reduce it to the proof of soundness and completeness of the system of semantic tableaux for LTL developed in Chapter 13, see Theorem 13.2.20. For such a reduction it suffices to show that the tableaux for LTL closes if and only if the input set of formulae is inconsistent in $\text{AxSys}_{\text{LTL}}$. This claim can be proved by modifying the respective proof that the tableaux closes if and only if the input set of LTL formulae is unsatisfiable, by replacing the semantic arguments there with syntactic ones, based on derivations in $\text{AxSys}_{\text{LTL}}$.

6.9 Exercises

Exercises on the semantics of LTL

Exercise 6.1. Is it possible to define the property $\bigwedge_{i=0}^{n} X^i \varphi$ (cf. Section 6.1.1) with an LTL formula that only grows linearly in n?

Exercise 6.2. Define $\varphi R \psi$, respectively $\varphi W \psi$, using the other constructs.

Exercise 6.3. Define in LTL the operator **Before** B with meaning $\varphi B \psi$: 'if ψ ever occurs (becomes true) then φ will occur before ψ occurs'. Then define the operator **Strong Before** SB with meaning of $\varphi SB \psi$: 'ψ will eventually occur (becomes true) and φ will occur before ψ occurs'.

Exercise 6.4. Give semantic definitions of G^∞ and F^∞ by means of explicit truth conditions for $\sigma, i \models G^\infty \varphi$ and $\sigma, i \models F^\infty \varphi$, as in Definition 6.1.2.

Exercise 6.5. Simplify, up to logical equivalence: $GF^\infty p$, $FF^\infty p$, $GG^\infty p$, $FG^\infty p$, $F(pUq)$.

Exercise 6.6. Express the following specifications in LTL.

(a) 'Every green light will be followed by a yellow light, which will be followed by a red light, which will be followed by a green light.'
(b) 'Whenever the event φ occurs in the future, it will not hold at the next moment, but will occur again later in the future.'
(c) 'A train may not enter the tunnel unless the light on the other end of the tunnel is red.'
(d) 'A train may only enter the tunnel after the light on the other end of the tunnel has turned red.'
(e) 'Whenever a train enters the tunnel, the light on the other end of the tunnel must be red and will stay red until the train has left the tunnel.'
(f) 'The event φ will occur infinitely often, unless every occurrence of φ is followed by an occurrence of ψ.'
(g) 'The event φ may occur not more than twice in the future, at least two time units apart.'

Exercise 6.7. Translate the following LTL specifications into English in the most natural way you can.

(a) $G^\infty(q \to Xp)$.

(b) $F(p \wedge XG\neg p)$.

(c) $F(p \wedge (qU\neg p))$.

(d) $F^\infty(pU\neg p)$.

Exercise 6.8. Consider the linear model σ, from Example 6.1.4. Recall that its labelling is defined as follows: for every $k \geq 0$,

- $p \in \sigma(k)$ iff k is even,
- $q \in \sigma(k)$ iff either $k \in [2, 4]$ or $100 \leq k$,
- $r \in \sigma(k)$ iff $k \equiv_3 1$.

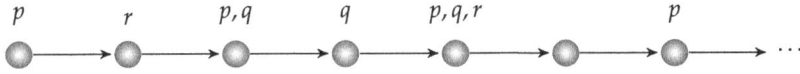

Show that the following hold in σ:

(a) $\sigma, 2 \models G(p \to X\neg p)$.

(b) $\sigma \not\models \neg qU(p \wedge r)$.

(c) $\sigma \models \neg qU(qUr)$.

(d) $\sigma \not\models G^\infty\neg(p \wedge q)$.

(e) $\sigma \models F^\infty\neg(p \wedge q)$.

(f) $\sigma \models FGF(p \wedge q \wedge r)$.

(g) $\sigma \models F^\infty((p \wedge \neg r)Ur)$.

(h) $\sigma \not\models G^\infty(\neg p \vee F\neg q \vee X\neg r)$.

(i) $\sigma \models F^\infty(rUX(\neg p \wedge Xr))$.

(j) $\sigma \not\models (\neg XrU\neg Xq)UGq$.

Exercise 6.9. Consider the following LTL model:

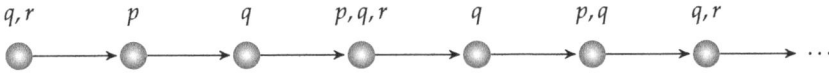

The model σ is defined as follows: for every $k \geq 0$,

- $p \in \sigma(k)$ iff $k \equiv_2 1$,
- $q \in \sigma(k)$ iff either $3 \leq k \leq 100$ or ($102 \leq k$ and $k \equiv_2 0$),
- $r \in \sigma(k)$ iff $k \equiv_3 0$.

Represent that model as an ultimately periodic model. Then determine whether each of the following holds by using the definition of $\models$:

(a) $\sigma, 0 \models F(q \wedge XXp)$.

(b) $\sigma, 1 \models F(q \wedge X(\neg q \wedge \neg p))$.

(c) $\sigma, 2 \models G(r \to X(q \vee \neg p))$.

(d) $\sigma \models \neg qU(qUr)$.

(e) $\sigma \models G(r \to X\neg r \wedge XX\neg r)$.

(f) $\sigma \models G^\infty\neg(q \wedge Xr)$.

(g) $\sigma \models F^\infty(p \wedge Xr)$.

(h) $\sigma \models F^\infty\neg(q \wedge r)$.

(i) $\sigma \models FGF(p \wedge q \wedge r)$.

(j) $\sigma \models F(qU\neg(p \vee q \vee r))$.

(k) $\sigma \models G^\infty F^\infty(rU(\neg p \wedge X\neg r))$.

(l) $\sigma \models F^\infty G^\infty((p \wedge \neg r)U\neg p)$.

Exercise 6.10. Consider the simple transition system from Example 6.1.8, in which on and off are the only atomic propositions:

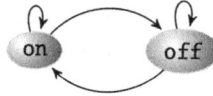

Show the following, by using direct semantic arguments.

(a) $\mathcal{T}, \text{on} \models_\exists F^\infty\text{on} \wedge F^\infty\text{off}$
(b) $\mathcal{T}, \text{on} \models_\exists G(\text{on} \rightarrow XX\,\text{off})$
(c) $\mathcal{T}, \text{on} \models_\forall F\,\text{off} \rightarrow ((\text{on} \wedge F\,\text{off})\,U\,\text{off})$
(d) $\mathcal{T}, \text{on} \not\models_\forall F\,\text{off} \rightarrow (\text{on} \wedge X\,\text{off})\,U\,\text{off}$
(e) $\mathcal{T}, \text{on} \not\models_\exists (\text{on} \wedge X\,\text{on})\,U\,\text{off}$
(f) $\mathcal{T}, \text{on} \models_\exists (\text{on} \wedge XX\,\text{on})\,U\,\text{off}$.

Exercise 6.11. Consider the following transition system.

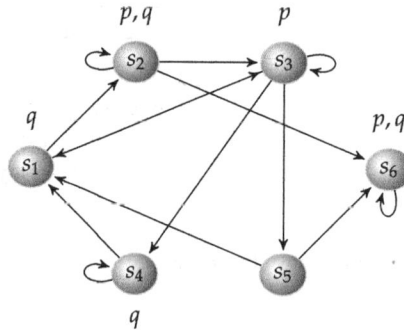

Determine the following by only using the definitions of $\models_\exists$ and $\models_\forall$:

(a) $\mathcal{T}, s_1 \models_\exists Gp$
(b) $\mathcal{T}, s_1 \models_\exists XGp$
(c) $\mathcal{T}, s_1 \models_\exists G(q \rightarrow Xp)$
(d) $\mathcal{T}, s_1 \models_\forall G(q \rightarrow Xp)$
(e) $\mathcal{T}, s_1 \models_\forall F^\infty(p \vee q)$
(f) $\mathcal{T}, s_1 \models_\forall G^\infty(\neg p \rightarrow Xq)$
(g) $\mathcal{T}, s_1 \models_\exists X(pUGq)$
(h) $\mathcal{T}, s_3 \models_\exists \neg qU(pUGq)$
(i) $\mathcal{T} \models_\exists G^\infty(p \vee q)$
(j) $\mathcal{T} \models_\forall F^\infty(p \vee q)$.

Exercise 6.12. Consider the following transition system $\mathcal{T}$, where the labels in the states are the sets of atomic propositions holding true at these states:

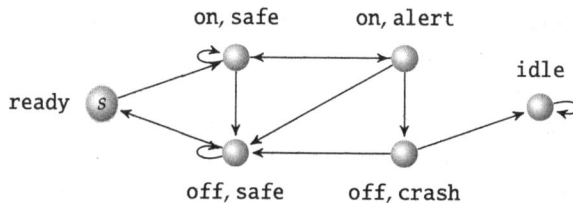

Verify the following by using any method.

(a) $\mathcal{T}, s \models_\exists \neg G(\texttt{alert} \to F \texttt{off})$
(b) $\mathcal{T}, s \models_\forall F^\infty \texttt{crash} \to F^\infty \texttt{ready}$
(c) $\mathcal{T}, s \models_\forall F^\infty(\texttt{off} \to XX \texttt{safe})$
(d) $\mathcal{T}, s \models_\forall G^\infty \texttt{idle} \vee F^\infty(X \texttt{safe} U (\texttt{off} \vee \texttt{alert}))$
(e) $\mathcal{T} \models_\exists (F^\infty \texttt{crash} \wedge F^\infty(\texttt{on} \wedge X \texttt{safe}))$
(f) $\mathcal{T} \models_\forall (F^\infty \texttt{alert} \to F^\infty(\texttt{safe} \vee \texttt{crash}))$
(g) $\mathcal{T} \not\models_\forall (G^\infty \neg \texttt{alert} \to F^\infty \texttt{safe})$.

Exercise 6.13. Prove Lemma 6.1.7 and Lemma 6.1.9.

Exercise 6.14. Prove the validity of each of the LTL formulae listed in Example 6.1.10 by using the semantic definition.

Exercise 6.15. Prove each of the equivalences listed in Proposition 6.1.11 by using the semantic definition.

Exercise 6.16. Prove the following validities and equivalences of LTL formulae by using the semantic definition.

(a) $\varphi U \psi \equiv (\psi \vee \varphi) \wedge (\psi \vee X(\varphi U \psi))$
(b) $\neg(\varphi U \psi) \equiv (\neg\psi \wedge \neg\varphi) \vee (\neg\psi \wedge X\neg(\varphi U \psi))$
(c) $\varphi R \psi \equiv \psi \wedge (\varphi \vee X(\varphi R \psi))$
(d) $\neg(\varphi U \psi) \equiv G\neg\psi \vee (\neg\varphi U(\neg\varphi \wedge \neg\psi))$
(e) $\varphi U(\psi \vee \chi) \equiv (\varphi U \psi) \vee (\varphi U \chi)$
(f) $(\varphi \wedge \psi)U\chi \equiv (\varphi U \chi) \wedge (\psi U \chi)$
(g) $(\varphi \to \chi)U\psi \wedge \varphi U \psi \to \chi U \psi$
(h) $G((\psi \vee (\varphi \wedge X\chi)) \to \chi) \to (\varphi U \psi \to \chi)$.

Exercise 6.17. Check each of the following logical consequences of LTL formulae using the semantic definition. If not valid, give a countermodel.

(a) $F^\infty \varphi \models G^\infty \varphi$
(b) $\varphi, G(\varphi \to F\varphi) \models GF\varphi$.

Exercise 6.18. Check each of the following equivalences of LTL formulae using the semantic definition. If not valid, give a countermodel: a linear LTL model on which one formula is true while the other false.

(a) $(\varphi \vee \psi)U\chi \equiv (\varphi U \chi \vee \psi U \chi)$
(b) $(\varphi \wedge \psi)U\chi \equiv (\varphi U \chi \wedge \psi U \chi)$
(c) $\psi U(\varphi \wedge \chi) \equiv (\psi U \varphi \wedge \psi U \chi)$
(d) $\psi U(\varphi \vee \chi) \equiv (\psi U \varphi \vee \psi U \chi)$.

Exercise 6.19. A unary modality for LTL is a nonempty sequence $M \in \{F, G, X\}^+$. We say that two unary modalities M and M' are equivalent whenever $Mp \leftrightarrow M'p$ is valid. A modality M is minimal iff there is no modality M' such that (1) M is equivalent to M', (2) $|M'| < |M|$ and (3) $M \in \{F, G\}^* \cdot \{X\}^*$.

(a) Characterise the set of minimal unary modalities for LTL.
(b) Show that every unary modality is equivalent to a minimal one.

Exercise 6.20. Define the binary relation $\preceq$ on linear models as follows: $\sigma \preceq \sigma'$ iff for all $i \in \mathbb{N}$, $\sigma(i) \subseteq \sigma'(i)$. We write $\sigma \prec \sigma'$ when $\sigma \preceq \sigma'$ and $\sigma \neq \sigma'$. A linear model σ for an LTL formula φ is minimal whenever $\sigma \models \varphi$ and there is no σ' such that $\sigma' \prec \sigma$ and $\sigma' \models \varphi$.

(a) Design a (simple) satisfiable LTL formula φ that has no minimal model.
(b) Define a logarithmic-space reduction from the problem of checking the existence of minimal models for LTL formulae into the satisfiability problem for QLTL.
(c) Let LTL$_{guarantee}$ be a fragment of LTL defined by

$$\varphi ::= p \mid \neg p \mid \varphi \wedge \varphi \mid \varphi \vee \varphi \mid \varphi U \varphi \mid X\varphi.$$

Show that for every formula φ in the fragment LTL$_{guarantee}$, φ is LTL satisfiable iff φ has a minimal model (see also Exercise 6.36).

Exercise 6.21. Prove Lemma 6.1.3.

Exercises on decision procedures

Exercise 6.22. Reorganise the path model-checking procedure for LTL formulae presented in Theorem 6.4.8 by building a Boolean array T of dimension $(i + l + 1) \times \text{card}(sub(\varphi))$ such that $T[j, \psi] = \top$ iff $\sigma, j \models \psi$, where the values $T[j, \psi_m]$ are computed in increasing order of $m \in [1, k]$.

Exercise 6.23. Give an alternating algorithm that uses logarithmic space only and solves the path model-checking problem for LTL on ultimately periodic linear models.

Exercise 6.24. Prove Lemma 6.2.4 and the first four statements in Lemma 6.2.6.

Exercises on ultimately periodic models

Exercise 6.25. Consider the following ultimately periodic model, with prefix length $i = 3$ and a loop length $l = 4$.

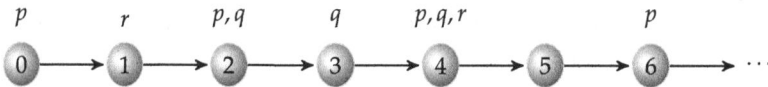

Using the path model-checking algorithm in Section 6.4 determine which statements hold:

- $\sigma \models G(q \rightarrow Xp)$.
- $\sigma \models G(\neg p \rightarrow Xp)$.
- $\sigma \models F^\infty(\neg q \wedge Xq)$.

- $\sigma \models G^\infty \neg (p \wedge q)$.
- $\sigma \models G^\infty ((\neg p \wedge \neg q) \rightarrow X((p \vee q)Ur))$.

Exercise 6.26. Design a family of LTL formulae $(\varphi_n)_{n \geq 1}$ such that the size of φ_n is in $\mathcal{O}(n)$, φ_n is satisfiable and any ultimately periodic model for φ_n has loop length and prefix length in $\mathcal{O}(2^n)$.

Exercise 6.27. Design a family of LTL formulae $(\psi_n)_{n \geq 1}$ such that the size of ψ_n is in $\mathcal{O}(n)$, ψ_n is satisfiable and there is an ultimately periodic model for ψ_n with loop length and prefix length in $\mathcal{O}(n)$. Show that LTL satisfiability restricted to formulae in $(\psi_n)_{n \geq 1}$ is in NP.

Exercise 6.28. In the proof of Theorem 6.3.8 show that the ultimately periodic model σ' generates a small satisfiability witness.

Exercise 6.29. Show Theorem 6.4.8 by establishing the correctness of Algorithm 6.

Exercise 6.30. Let LTL(X, U, W) be the extension of LTL obtained by adding the weak until operator W as a primitive temporal operator. Recall that $pWq \equiv (Gp) \vee (pUq)$. Show that the satisfiability problem for LTL(X, U, W) can be solved in polynomial space.

Exercise 6.31. Design a logarithmic-space reduction from the model-checking problem for LTL(U) to the model-checking problem for LTL(U) restricted to two atomic propositions.

Exercise 6.32. Prove Lemma 6.3.4, Lemma 6.3.6 and Theorem 6.4.5. Complete the proof of Lemma 6.3.1.

Exercises on fragments

Exercise 6.33. The goal of this exercise is to show that satisfiability and existential model-checking problems for LTL(F) can be solved in nondeterministic polynomial time. Given φ in LTL(F), we write $sub_F(\varphi)$ to denote the set $\{\psi : F\psi \in sub(\varphi)\}$. Let σ be a model such that $\sigma, 0 \models \varphi$. From σ, we define the following objects:

- $X_\emptyset = \{\psi \in sub_F(\varphi) : \sigma, 0 \models G\neg\psi\}$,
- $X_{fin} = \{\psi \in sub_F(\varphi) : \sigma, 0 \models F(\psi \wedge XG\neg\psi)\}$,
- $X_{inf} = \{\psi \in sub_F(\varphi) : \sigma, 0 \models GF\psi\}$,
- l_σ is the minimal number such that for every $i \geq l_\sigma$, for every $\psi \in X_{fin}$, we have $\sigma, i \not\models \psi$.

(a) Show that $X_\emptyset$, X_{fin}, X_{inf} is a partition of $sub_F(\varphi)$.

(b) Suppose $X_{fin} = \{\psi_1, \ldots, \psi_\alpha\}$, $X_{inf} = \{\psi_{\alpha+1}, \ldots, \psi_{\alpha+\beta}\}$ and $\beta \geq 1$. For every $s \in [1, \alpha]$, let i_s by the maximal number such that $\sigma, i_s \models \psi_s$. We order $\psi_1, \ldots, \psi_\alpha$ in such a way so that $i_1 \leq i_2 \leq \cdots \leq i_\alpha$. Similarly, let $l_\sigma \leq i_{\alpha+1} \leq i_{\alpha+2} \leq \cdots \leq i_{\alpha+\beta}$ such that for every $s \in [\alpha+1, \alpha+\beta]$, $\sigma, i_s \models \psi_s$. Let σ' be the model

$\sigma(0)\sigma(i_1)\cdots\sigma(i_\alpha)(\sigma(i_{\alpha+1})\cdots\sigma(i_{\alpha+\beta}))^\omega$. Let $\mathfrak{f}:\mathbb{N}\to\mathbb{N}$ be the map such that $\mathfrak{f}(0)=0$, for every $s\in[1,\alpha]$, $\mathfrak{f}(s)=i_s$ and for all $k\geq 0$ and $\gamma\in[1,\beta]$, we have $\mathfrak{f}(\alpha+k\times\beta+\gamma)=i_{\alpha+\gamma}$. Show that for every $\psi\in sub(\varphi)$, for every $t\in\mathbb{N}$, we have $\sigma',t\models\psi$ iff $\sigma,\mathfrak{f}(t)\models\psi$.

(c) When $\beta=0$, i.e. $X_{inf}=\emptyset$, adapt the preceding definition for σ' by building from σ an ultimately periodic model σ'' such that $\sigma'',0\models\varphi$.

(d) Prove that for every satisfiable LTL(F) formula φ, there is an ultimately periodic model σ such that $\sigma\models\varphi$ and its loop length plus its prefix length is bounded by the size of φ.

(e) Show that the satisfiability problem for LTL(F) is in NP.

(f) Show that the existential model-checking problem for LTL(F) is in NP.

(g) Prove that both problems are NP-hard.

Exercise 6.34. The goal of this exercise is to establish that $SAT(LTL^1(X,U))$ and $MC(LTL^1(X,U))$ are in NP. In particular, this means that the model-checking problem restricted to LTL formulae of temporal depth at most one can be solved in polynomial time with a nondeterministic algorithm.

Let $\sigma:\mathbb{N}\to\mathcal{P}(PROP)$ be an LTL model and $u=(n_i)_{i\in\mathbb{N}}$ be an infinite sequence of natural numbers such that there is $k\geq 0$ satisfying $n_0<\cdots<n_k$ and for all $j>k$, we have $n_j\geq n_k$. The LTL model $\sigma':\mathbb{N}\to\mathcal{P}(PROP)$ is **extracted** from σ and u whenever for all $i\in\mathbb{N}$, we have $\sigma'(i)=\sigma(n_i)$.

Let $\sigma:\mathbb{N}\to\mathcal{P}(PROP)$ be an LTL model and φ be a formula in $LTL^1(X,U)$. Define the (finite) set $X_{\sigma,\varphi}$ of **witness positions** as the smallest set satisfying the conditions:

- always $0\in X_{\sigma,\varphi}$,
- if there is $X\psi\in sub(\varphi)$, then $1\in X_{\sigma,\varphi}$,
- for each subformula $\psi_1U\psi_2\in sub(\varphi)$,
  - if $\sigma,0\models\psi_1U\psi_2$, then $i\in X_{\sigma,\varphi}$, where i is the minimal position such that $\sigma,i\models\psi_2$,
  - if $\sigma,0\models\neg(\psi_1U\psi_2)\wedge F\psi_2$, then $i\in X_{\sigma,\varphi}$, where i is the minimal position such that $\sigma,i\not\models\psi_1$.

(If $\sigma,0\not\models F\psi_2$, then no witness is required.)

(a) Let φ be the formula defined as follows:

$$((p\vee\neg r)Uq)\wedge\neg(pUq)\wedge(\neg Xp\vee\neg(pUr))\wedge\neg r$$

and be σ be the LTL model $\{p\}^4\cdot\emptyset\cdot\{p\}\{q\}^2\{p\}\cdots$. Compute the set of witnesses $X_{\sigma,\varphi}$.

(b) Let $\sigma:\mathbb{N}\to\mathcal{P}(PROP)$ be an LTL model and $u=(n_i)_{i\in\mathbb{N}}$ be a sequence of natural numbers satisfying the preceding requirements and such that $X_{\sigma,\varphi}\subseteq\{n_0,\ldots,n_k\}$. Let σ' be the LTL model extracted from σ and u. Show that for all $\psi\in sub(\varphi)$, we have $\sigma,0\models\psi$ iff $\sigma',0\models\psi$.

(c) Let $\varphi\in LTL^1(X,U)$. Show that if φ is satisfiable then there is an LTL model σ such that $\sigma,0\models\varphi$ and for all $i,j\geq|\varphi|$, we have $\sigma(i)=\sigma(j)$. Conclude that $SAT(LTL^1(X,U))$ is in NP.

(d) Let $\mathcal{T} = (S, R, L)$ be a finite transition system, $s \in S$ and $\varphi \in \text{LTL}^1(\text{X}, \text{U})$ such that $\mathcal{T}, s \models_\exists \varphi$. Show that there is a computation σ from s such that $\sigma, 0 \models \varphi$, and σ is ultimately periodic with both the prefix length and the loop length bounded by $\text{card}(S) \times |\varphi|$.

(e) Conclude that $\text{MC}(\text{LTL}^1(\text{X}, \text{U}))$ is in NP.

Exercise 6.35.

(a) Let φ be an LTL formula that contains some subformula ψ. Show that φ is satisfiable iff $\varphi[p/\psi] \wedge \text{G}(p \leftrightarrow \psi)$ is satisfiable where p is a new atomic proposition not occurring in φ.

(b) Conclude that there is a logarithmic-space reduction from SAT(LTL) (resp. SAT(LTL(F))) to SAT(LTL) (resp. SAT(LTL(F))) restricted to formulae of temporal depth at most 2.

Exercises on LTL with past

Exercise 6.36. Let φ be an LTL formula built over the connectives $\neg, \vee, \wedge, \text{X}$ and U and such that $\neg$ occurs only in front of atomic propositions. Show that if $\sigma, 0 \models \varphi$, then there is $N \geq 0$ such that for every LTL model σ' that agrees with σ on the N first positions, $\sigma', 0 \models \varphi$. (That is, φ defines a **guarantee property**, see e.g. Manna and Pnueli (1990).)

Exercise 6.37. Extend the ordered set $(\mathbb{N}, <)$ by $(\mathbb{N} \cup \{\infty\}, <)$ with $i < \infty$ for all $i \in \mathbb{N}$. An extended linear model σ is of the form $\sigma : \mathbb{N} \cup \{\infty\} \to \mathcal{P}(\text{PROP})$. Formulae in $\text{LTL}(\text{X}, \text{F})$ can then be interpreted on $(\mathbb{N} \cup \{\infty\}, <)$ by considering extended linear models. Main clauses for the satisfaction relation $\models$ are the following ($i \in \mathbb{N} \cup \{\infty\}$):

$$\sigma, i \models \text{X}\varphi \quad \text{iff} \quad i \in \mathbb{N} \text{ and } \sigma, i+1 \models \varphi$$
$$\sigma, i \models \text{F}\varphi \quad \text{iff} \quad \text{there is } j \geq i \text{ such that } \sigma, j \models \varphi.$$

As usual, $\text{G}\varphi$ is an abbreviation for $\neg \text{F} \neg \varphi$.

(a) Define a logarithmic-space reduction from the LTL satisfiability problem restricted to $\text{LTL}(\text{X}, \text{F})$ into the satisfiability problem for $\text{LTL}(\text{X}, \text{F})$ with extended linear models.

(b) Show that $(p \wedge \text{G}(p \to \text{X}p)) \to \text{G}p$ is not valid in the class of extended linear models but valid in the class of linear models over $\mathbb{N}$.

(c) Define a reduction from the satisfiability problem for $\text{LTL}(\text{X}, \text{F})$ with extended linear models into the LTL satisfiability problem for $\text{LTL}(\text{X}, \text{F})$.

(d) Let $(\mathbb{N} \times \{1, 2\}, <)$ be another linear ordering such that $(n, a) < (m, b)$ iff either $a < b$ or ($a = b$ and $n < m$). Extended linear models are now of the form $\mathbb{N} \times \{1, 2\} \to \mathcal{P}(\text{PROP})$. Design a reduction from the satisfiability problem for $\text{LTL}(\text{X}, \text{F})$ with this new class of linear models into the satisfiability problem for LTL+Past.

Exercise 6.38. Show the following equivalences in LTL+Past:

(a) $\text{X}(\varphi \text{U} \psi) \equiv (\text{X}\varphi)\text{U}\text{X}\psi$ and $\text{X}(\varphi \text{S} \psi) \equiv (\text{X}\varphi)\text{S}\text{X}\psi$,

(b) $Y(\varphi U \psi) \equiv (Y\top) \wedge (Y\varphi)U(Y\psi)$ and $Y(\varphi S \psi) \equiv (Y\varphi)S(Y\psi)$,

(c) $XG\varphi \equiv GX\varphi$ and $XG^{-1}\varphi \equiv G^{-1}X\varphi$,

(d) $YG\varphi \equiv GY\varphi$ and $YG^{-1}\varphi \equiv G^{-1}Y\varphi$,

(e) $XY\varphi \equiv \varphi$ and $YX\varphi \equiv (Y\top) \wedge \varphi$.

Exercise 6.39. Show the following equivalences in LTL+Past:

(a) $(\varphi_1 \wedge \varphi_2)U\psi \equiv (\varphi_1 U\psi) \wedge (\varphi_2 U\psi)$ and $(\varphi_1 \wedge \varphi_2)S\psi \equiv (\varphi_1 S\psi) \wedge (\varphi_2 S\psi)$,

(b) $\psi U(\varphi_1 \vee \varphi_2) \equiv (\psi U\varphi_1) \vee (\psi U\varphi_2)$ and $\psi S(\varphi_1 \vee \varphi_2) \equiv (\psi S\varphi_1) \vee (\psi S\varphi_2)$,

(c) $G(\varphi_1 \wedge \varphi_2) \equiv G\varphi_1 \wedge G\varphi_2$ and $G^{-1}(\varphi_1 \wedge \varphi_2) \equiv G^{-1}\varphi_1 \wedge G^{-1}\varphi_2$.

Exercise 6.40. Prove Lemma 6.5.4 and complete the proof of Lemma 6.5.5 as well as the details in the proofs of Lemma 6.5.6 and Lemma 6.5.7.

Exercises on invariance properties

Exercise 6.41. Show that if the set of atomic propositions PROP is infinite, two rooted interpreted transition systems may satisfy, e.g. universally, the same LTL formulae yet not have the same computations. (*Hint:* a computation may involve infinitely many atomic propositions.)

Exercise 6.42. Prove Lemma 6.6.1. Complete the proof of Theorem 6.6.2. In the proof of Theorem 6.6.5:

(a) Prove direction (II) $\implies$ (I).

(b) Complete the details in the last step of the proof of direction (I) $\implies$ (II).

Exercises on extensions of LTL

Exercise 6.43. Show that $\neg\mathcal{A}(\top, \neg p)$ with $L(\mathcal{A}) = (a^2)^*b$ holds exactly in models such that the atomic proposition p holds on every even position.

Exercise 6.44.

(a) Is there an LTL formula equivalent to $\mathcal{A}(p, q)$ with $L(\mathcal{A}) = (a \cdot b)^*$?

(b) Is there an LTL formula equivalent to $\mathcal{A}(p, q, r)$ with $L(\mathcal{A}) = (a \cdot b)^*c$?

(c) Is there an LTL formula equivalent to $\mathcal{A}(p, q, r)$ with $L(\mathcal{A}) = a^* \cdot (b \cdot c)$?

Exercise 6.45. Let $\mathcal{A}_1$, $\mathcal{A}_2$ and $\mathcal{A}_3$ be finite-state automata with $L(\mathcal{A}_1) = a \cdot b$, $L(\mathcal{A}_2) = a^* \cdot b$ and $L(\mathcal{A}_3) = a^+ \cdot b$. Show that $\mathcal{A}_3(p, q)$ is equivalent to $\mathcal{A}_1(\top, \mathcal{A}_2(p, q))$.

Exercise 6.46. It is possible to extend the definition of ETL by replacing formulae of the form $\mathcal{A}(\varphi_1, \ldots, \varphi_n)$ by formulae of the form $L(\varphi_1, \ldots, \varphi_n)$ where L is a language of finite words specified within a fixed formalism. The language L is again viewed as a set of patterns, not necessarily regular. For a class $\mathcal{C}$ of languages, we write LTL[$\mathcal{C}$] to denote the extension of LTL with formulae of the form $L(\varphi_1, \ldots, \varphi_n)$ for some $L \in \mathcal{C}$. Obviously,

ETL is precisely equivalent to LTL[REG] where REG is the class of regular languages represented by finite-state automata. Let L be a language of finite words and L' be a finite language. Define a reduction from the existential model-checking problem for LTL[{L}] into the existential model-checking problem for LTL[{L \ L'}].

Exercise 6.47. Let $(\Sigma, Q, Q_0, \delta, F)$ be a deterministic finite-state automaton. We write $min(\mathcal{A})$ to denote the language

$$\{w \in L(\mathcal{A}) \mid \text{ for all } v \in L(\mathcal{A}), \ v \leq w \text{ implies } v = w\},$$

where $\leq$ is the prefix relation.

(a) Build an automaton $\mathcal{A}'$ such that $L(\mathcal{A}') = min(\mathcal{A})$, justify the correctness of the construction and provide an example of automaton $\mathcal{A}$ such that $min(\mathcal{A})$ is infinite.
(b) Suppose that $card(\Sigma) = n \geq 1$. Show that for all formulae $\varphi_1, \ldots, \varphi_n \in$ ETL, $\mathcal{A}(\varphi_1, \ldots, \varphi_n) \leftrightarrow \mathcal{A}'(\varphi_1, \ldots, \varphi_n)$ is a valid formula where $\mathcal{A}' = min(\mathcal{A})$.
(c) Now, suppose that $min(\mathcal{A})$ is finite. Define a translation t from formulae built over the operators $\neg$, $\wedge$ and $\mathcal{A}$ (fragment denoted by PC[L($\mathcal{A}$)]) into LTL(X) such that for every total and finite transition system $\mathcal{M} = (S, R, L)$ and for every $s \in S$, $\mathcal{M}, s \models_\exists \varphi$ iff $\mathcal{M}, s \models_\exists t(\varphi)$.
(d) Evaluate the size of $t(\varphi)$ in terms of the size of φ and the number of subformulae of $t(\varphi)$ in terms of the number of subformulae of φ.
(e) Show that for every deterministic finite-state automaton $\mathcal{A}$ such that $min(\mathcal{A})$ is finite, the model-checking problem for PC[L($\mathcal{A}$)] is in NP.

Exercise 6.48. Let σ_0, σ_1 be two computations. Their **zip** $\sigma_0 \curlywedge \sigma_1$ is obtained by alternatingly taking states from these two computations, forming a new computation.

$$(\sigma_0 \curlywedge \sigma_1)(i) = \begin{cases} \sigma_0(j), & \text{if } i = 2j \\ \sigma_1(j), & \text{if } i = 2j+1. \end{cases}$$

We extend the zip operation to languages in the natural way: $L_0 \curlywedge L_1 := \{\sigma_0 \curlywedge \sigma_1 \mid \sigma_i \in L_i \text{ for } i = 0, 1\}$. Prove or refute:

(a) If L_0 and L_1 are LTL-definable, then so is $L_0 \curlywedge L_1$.
(b) If L_0 and L_1 are ETL-definable, then so is $L_0 \curlywedge L_1$.

Exercise 6.49. We extend ETL by replacing the formulae $\mathcal{A}(\varphi_1, \ldots, \varphi_k)$ by formulae of the form $L(\varphi_1, \ldots, \varphi_k)$ where L is a context-free language of finite words specified within a fixed formalism. The language L is again viewed as a set of patterns, this time not necessarily regular. We write LTL[CF] to denote the extension of LTL with formulae of the form $L(\varphi_1, \ldots, \varphi_k)$ for some context-free language L. Show that the validity problem for LTL[CF] is undecidable by reducing the undecidable universality problem on context-free languages.

Exercise 6.50. Explain what the models of the following formula are.

$$\exists\, q\, (q \wedge \mathsf{G}(q \leftrightarrow \neg\mathsf{X}q) \wedge \mathsf{G}(q \to p)).$$

Exercise 6.51. Prove Lemma 6.7.2.

Exercises on axiomatic systems

Exercise 6.52. Show that **IND-Rule** is derivable in $\textsc{AxSys}_{\text{LTL}}$ and that axiom GFP_G is derivable in $\textsc{AxSys}_{\text{LTL}}$ where it is replaced by the Induction rule **IND-Rule**.

Exercise 6.53. Complete the derivations in Lemma 6.8.1.

Exercise 6.54. Given the soundness of $\textsc{AxSys}_{\text{BML}}$, prove the soundness of $\textsc{AxSys}_{\text{LTL}}$.

Exercise 6.55. Prove Lemma 6.8.2 and Lemma 6.8.3.

6.10 Bibliographical Notes

The linear-time temporal logics are intended to reason about linear models, representing single computations. The most popular linear-time temporal logic LTL was first studied in the form presented here in Gabbay et al. (1980), based on the early works of Kamp (1968) and Pnueli (1977) – the strict Until operator, that can express all temporal operators in LTL, was first proposed in Kamp (1968) while temporal logics were proposed as a framework for formal verification of programs in Pnueli (1977). Notably, the next-time operator was introduced in Manna and Pnueli (1979) in order to define LTL restricted to the operators Next-time and Sometime; see also a similar language in Pnueli (1979).

The temporal operators 'sometimes' F, 'always' G and their past-time versions have been introduced in Prior (1967), which, building on earlier book of Prior (1957), laid the foundations of the modal approach to temporal logic.

Nowadays, LTL is one of the most standard logical formalisms to specify the behaviours of computer systems in view of formal verification. It has also been the basis for several specification languages, such as PSL (Eisner and Fisman 2006) (see Section 6.7.3), and it is used as a logical specification language in various tools such as SPIN (Holzmann 1997) and SMV (McMillan 1993).

Ultimately Periodic Model Property. Theorem 6.3.3 was originally proved by Sistla and Clarke (1985, Theorem 4.7). The proof of the existence of a small satisfiability witness can be generalised to various extensions of LTL such as LTL+Past and ETL as shown in Sistla and Clarke (1985). Corollary 6.4.2 and Corollary 6.4.7 are shown in Sistla and Clarke (1985).

Path model checking. Variants of the path model-checking problem obtained by modifying the encoding of the ultimately periodic model or the specification language have been studied in Markey and Schnoebelen (2003). Recently, it has been shown in Kuhtz and Finkbeiner (2009) that the path model-checking problem for LTL is in the complexity class AC^2 related to circuit complexity. On a slightly related subject, the proof of Lemma 6.2.6 follows the argument presented in (Sistla and Clarke, 1985, page 740).

Stuttering. Theorem 6.6.5 is shown in Peled and Wilke (1997). A general stuttering theorem for LTL(U, X) can be found in Kučera and Strejček (2005).

Extensions. Various extensions of LTL have been proposed and studied. The most notable of them include LTL with past-time operators (Lichtenstein et al. 1985; Laroussinie and Schnoebelen 2000; Laroussinie et al. 2002; Markey 2002), Wolper's extended temporal logic ETL (Wolper 1981, 1983; Vardi and Wolper 1994) and the linear μ-calculus (Vardi 1988) (see also Chapter 8). ETL has been introduced in Wolper (1983) and decision procedures for the corresponding model checking and satisfiability problems have been considered in Sistla and Clarke (1985) and Vardi and Wolper (1994). An automata-based construction for ETL formulae can be found in Wolper (1983), leading to Theorem 11.4.2. The PSPACE upper bound can also be obtained by a small satisfiability witness argument (Sistla and Clarke 1985). A concise variant has been studied in Kupferman et al. (2001) in which one-way finite-state automata are replaced by two-way alternating automata for temporal connectives. The PSPACE upper bound is preserved for such an extension (Kupferman et al. 2001). Furthermore, Henriksen and Thiagarajan (1999) contains another variant for which the until operator is indexed by a regular expression. Even though ETL formulae are seldom used in specification languages, its main theoretical value is in its high expressive power and in the relatively low complexity of satisfiability and model-checking problems. Nevertheless, the lack of ω-regularity for LTL may have practical significance, as argued in Vardi (2009).

LTL versus LTL+Past. Past operators played a central role in early work on temporal logic, in particular since they were needed to establish the equi-expressiveness of the temporal logic LTL to the much better studied (at that time) first-order logic. The need for past operators is discussed in Chapter 10; one of the highlights is Gabbay's Separation Theorem (Theorem 10.1.22) which is stated in Gabbay et al. (1980), but this paper does not contain a proof. Instead, it points at unpublished work of Gabbay's from 1979 under the title 'The Separation Property of Tense Logic' which is supposed to contain a syntactic proof. A proof is included in Gabbay (1989), which was published much later.

Theorem 6.5.9 was proved in Laroussinie et al. (2002).

QLTL. Modal logics with propositional quantifiers have been considered in Bull (1969). The logic BML with such propopositional quantifiers has been shown undecidable in Fine (1970) by reduction from second-order arithmetic. Hence, adding propositional quantifiers to a logic increases considerably its expressive power. In the case of QLTL, considering linear models allows to preserve the decidability of LTL but at the cost of nonelementary complexity, a consequence of Meyer (1973). As far as we know, QLTL has been introduced in Sistla (1983) and further studied in Sistla et al. (1987) and Vardi and Wolper (1994), especially for computational complexity issues. QLTL is as expressive as ETL (Vardi and Wolper, 1994).

PSL. The property specification language PSL (Accellera Organization 2004) was invented in response to LTL's weak expressive power, namely the fact that there are ω-regular properties not expressible in LTL. Some stronger formalisms had been designed by hardware manufactors who needed that extended expressive power: FORSPEC used by Intel (Armoni et al. 2002), SUGAR used by IBM (Beer et al. 2001), 'e' used by Verisity (Iman and Joshi 2004), CBV used by Motorola (Abadir et al. 2003) and SYSTEMVERILOG used by Synopsys (Rich 2003). SUGAR is in fact a branching-time logic whereas the others are linear-time formalisms. The need for a single standardised specification language for correct hardware design was seen by all players and – not surprisingly – each of them thought of their own language as the one that should be used by everyone. The dispute was finally settled by the invention of PSL – largely based on SUGAR – which is mainly a linear-time logic (as presented here) but in its full entirety also includes branching-time features. It was originally developed under the auspicies of the industrial consortium Accellera which maintains the standards of various hardware specification formalisms. PSL has subsequently become the IEEE standard 1850.

PSL shows how practical demands in industrial applications and theoretical results from academia can work together well: for instance, automata based decision procedures provide necessary tool support for system verification using PSL (Bustan et al. 2005). Theoretical properties like complexity and expressiveness of its operators have been examined in Lange (2007), for instance.

7

Branching-Time Temporal Logics

In the previous two chapters we presented temporal logics for reasoning about local properties of interpreted transition systems (BML) and about global properties of linear time models, that is, single computations (LTL). Neither of these, however, is expressive enough to reason about *global properties of all computations* in the transition system. This is where branching-time temporal logics come into play. They combine the full repertoire of temporal operators of LTL, on one hand, with the ability to quantify over paths, and hence over computations, starting at the current state.

The temporal operators X and U of LTL navigate forwards along a particular run and express global properties about it. Thus, LTL is suited for reasoning about *single computations* in a transition system, but does not provide any syntactic means to look at alternative runs in the system. On the other hand, BML provides the means to look at all immediate successors of the current state, but not any further. So, the idea of the branching-time framework is to put temporal operators and path quantifiers together and enable global reasoning about *all possible computations* starting from a given state, and eventually about what happens in the *entire* transition system. In particular, the path quantification can be regarded as a generalisation of both existential and universal model checking in LTL, but it also enables much more, viz. any Boolean combination of both, as well as iterating these by nesting path quantifiers. In the simplest cases of interaction between path quantifiers and temporal operators, these are required to alternate strictly and that restriction generates the simplest natural branching-time logics TLR and CTL which we study here. Gradually extending the admissible patterns of combinations of temporal and Boolean operators over what patterns of path quantification is allowed produces a growing hierarchy of more expressive logics, eventually leading to the fully unrestricted language of the branching-time logic CTL*.

We present in this chapter the most popular species of branching-time logics and discuss and compare their expressiveness. Nevertheless, the proofs about expressiveness results are deferred to Chapter 10 that is exclusively dedicated to those questions.

Why do we need to study different logics to reason about the same class of models? Because there is always a trade-off between expressiveness of a given logic and the computational cost of solving its basic logical decision problems: the more expressive the logic is, the higher the computational complexities of its decision problems one can expect. Thus, one can try to optimise one or the other but not both and, as we will see, the quest for best balance between expressiveness and computational cost often produces a variety of logical systems with different properties. To sum up, expressiveness, complexity of satisfiability and complexity of the model-checking problems will be our main criteria for judging the suitability and desirability of a logic. Part III of this book is dedicated to formally establish such expressiveness results and complexity characterisations.

Structure of the chapter. In Section 7.1 we introduce a hierarchy of the most popular branching-time logics and discuss their expressiveness. We begin the section with an informal discussion of the branching-time framework. Then we introduce the basic reachability logic TLR that extends BML by allowing modal operators for reachability and universal coverability and can naturally express safety and liveness properties. This is then followed by the computation tree logic CTL extending TLR with an operator expressing universal eventualities. We then introduce the full computation tree logic CTL* which subsumes both LTL and CTL and allows, in addition to safety and liveness, all kinds of fairness conditions to be expressed. In Section 7.1.5 we provide important fixpoint characterisations of the temporal operators in CTL, used further in the satisfiability-testing and model-checking algorithms for CTL.

Section 7.2 studies the interplays between bisimulation equivalence and logical equivalence for the richer branching-time logics (compared to the basic modal logic BML). We show that all formulae of CTL* are invariant under bisimulation and that the reachability logic TLR is already expressive enough to describe every finite rooted ITS up to bisimulation equivalence. An important consequence of bisimulation invariance is the tree-model property for CTL*. More precisely, we show that every satisfiable formula of CTL* is satisfiable in a tree of uniform and small branching degree.

Section 7.3 studies the model-checking problems for branching-time logics. We present an optimal algorithm for CTL* by a reduction to LTL model checking, as well as the polynomial-time labelling algorithm for global CTL model checking. As an illustration, we apply these to the specification and verification of models of Dijkstra's mutual exclusion problem. Algorithms for satisfiability checking of branching-time temporal logics are deferred to the later chapters in Part IV because they need some technical developments.

In Section 7.4 we introduce and discuss some important fragments of CTL*, including CTL with fairness, CTL^2, CTL^+, as well as extensions of these with past operators. We also present a general framework for extending CTL with a finite number of additional operators obtained by path-quantification on LTL formulae.

Section 7.5 presents axiomatic systems for TLR, CTL and some of its extensions.

7.1 A Hierarchy of Branching-Time Logics

In this section we introduce the branching-time temporal logics TLR, CTL and CTL*, present their syntax and semantics and discuss and compare their expressiveness.

7.1.1 State and Path Formulae

A key feature of the branching-time temporal logics consists of having in the object level the ability to quantify over runs, by using operators of the form E or A. In this way, satisfaction of a formula does not only involve the existence of a single run or only the nonexistence of a run satisfying a given property. Instead, satisfaction of a formula may involve more than a single run and each run witnesses a specific property participating in the satisfaction of the formula.

We have already seen examples of combinations of temporal operators with path quantifiers and the properties that are expressed through such combinations. For instance, the existence of a run such that the next position satisfies p, which can be written down 'E X p', is precisely the modal operator EX from the basic modal logic BML. Similarly, stating that for all the runs, the next position satisfies p, which can be written 'A X p' is again precisely the modal operator AX. Also, the existence of a run such that a future position satisfies p, which can be written EFp, simply states that there is a reachable state satisfying p. The semantics for a formula of the form E(pUq) could be defined analogously, by first

Figure 7.1 Two ITS with identical sets of computations.

existentially quantifying over a run and then checking the existence of a prefix witnessing the satisfaction of $p\mathsf{U}q$. Dually, stating that for all runs and for all positions p holds true can be written $\mathsf{AG}p$. This is equivalent to stating that all reachable states satisfy p. So, the combination 'AG', syntactically made up of a universal quantifier over paths and a universal quantifier over positions, can also be regarded as a primitive temporal operator in branching-time logics.

Example 7.1.1. Consider the following property in either of the two transition systems in Figure 7.1: there exists a run reaching a state satisfying p for which there is a run such that each future position satisfies p and there is a run such that every future position does not satisfy p. Such a property can be written syntactically as

$$\mathsf{EF}(p \wedge \mathsf{EXG}p \wedge \mathsf{EXG}\neg p).$$

Note that s satisfies this property but t does not, even though both have the same set of computations.

Hence, the ability to quantify over paths in some inductive way allows the branching nature of an ITS to be expressed in temporal logics. Compare this also with the examples showing the difference between bisimilarity and trace equivalence (cf. Figure 3.16).

Informally, we use E as an existential quantifier over paths and F, X and G as temporal operators interpreted over linear structures (i.e. over computations). Boolean connectives have their standard meaning. When inspecting the formula of the preceding example more closely, we notice that the subformulae $\mathsf{EXG}p$ and $\mathsf{EXG}\neg p$ are intended to be interpreted on a state. Such subformulae are called **state formulae**. By contrast, subformulae of the form $\mathsf{XG}p$ or $\mathsf{F}(p \wedge \mathsf{EXG}p \wedge \mathsf{EXG}\neg p)$ are interpreted on a computation, i.e. on a path in the transition system by extracting its labeling, and such formulae are called **path formulae**. This is why we have to make a distinction between two types of formulae in order to design more expressive branching-time temporal logics, since expressive power is gained from the ability to combine path quantification and path formulae. Some logics like TLR and CTL will only feature state formulae; consequently they are less expressive than CTL*. We have also seen an implicit branching-time logic, which features path formulae only, viz. LTL with implicit universal path quantification, as it is done for model checking for instance. It can be considered to be a degenerated branching-time temporal logic in that sense.

The distinction between state and path formulae can be reconciled; every state formula is naturally a path formula because every path has a unique first state in which the formula at hand is interpreted. The other direction is not true; a state only defines a unique path in linear structures but not in general in arbitrary transition systems.

7.1.2 The Reachability Logic TLR

Recall that, given a transition system $\mathcal{T} = (S, \{\xrightarrow{a}\}_{a \in Act})$, we denote by $\xrightarrow{a}^*$ the reflexive and transitive closure of the transition relation $\xrightarrow{a}$, that is: $s \xrightarrow{a}^* t$ iff there exists a finite path $s_0 \xrightarrow{a} s_1 \ldots \xrightarrow{a} s_n$ with $n \geq 0$, $s = s_0$ and $t = s_n$.

Thus, $\xrightarrow{a}^*$ is the **reachability relation** for the transitions of type a, and it is very natural to associate a new modal operator with it, called the **reachability operator** or **reachability modality** which we will denote EF_a, expressing 'forward reachability along some a-computation'.

The temporal logic of reachability, abbreviated TLR and hereafter called **reachability logic**, extends BML introduced in Chapter 5 with additional reachability operators EF_a for each transition relation $\xrightarrow{a}$. The syntax of TLR is defined formally by the following grammar.

$$\varphi = p \mid \bot \mid \neg\varphi \mid (\varphi \wedge \varphi) \mid \mathsf{EX}_a\varphi \mid \mathsf{EF}_a\varphi.$$

As usual, here and further in the chapter, we will use standard abbreviations for logical connectives and will often omit parentheses when ambiguity does not arise. We also define, as in BML, the **dual** of each modal operator EX_a as $\mathsf{AX}_a\varphi := \neg\mathsf{EX}_a\neg\varphi$. Analogously, for each reachability operator EF_a we define its dual AG_a, which is also called the **coverability operator**, as $\mathsf{AG}_a\varphi := \neg\mathsf{EF}_a\neg\varphi$.

The formulae of TLR are interpreted over total rooted transition systems and the satisfaction relation $\models$ naturally extends the one for BML (Section 5.1) with the additional clause:

$$\mathcal{T}, s \models \mathsf{EF}_a\varphi \quad \text{iff} \quad \mathcal{T}, r \models \varphi \text{ for some } r \in S \text{ such that } s \xrightarrow{a}^* r.$$

Thus, $\mathsf{EF}_a\varphi$ is true at the state s if φ is true at *some* state r reachable from s along the transition relation $\xrightarrow{a}$.

The derived clause for the truth of $\mathsf{AG}_a\varphi$ is:

$$\mathcal{T}, s \models \mathsf{AG}_a\varphi \quad \text{iff} \quad \mathcal{T}, r \models \varphi \text{ for all } r \in S \text{ with } s \xrightarrow{a}^* r.$$

Thus, $\mathsf{AG}_a\varphi$ is true at the state s if φ is true at *every* state r reachable from s along the transition relation $\xrightarrow{a}$. The meaning of $\mathsf{AG}\varphi$ is illustrated in Figure 7.2 on the unfolding of a mono-transition system.

The logic TLR naturally allows **eventuality properties** of the type $\mathsf{EF}\varphi$ and **safety properties** of the type $\mathsf{AG}\varphi$ to be expressed. For example, given three processes the following formula expresses a typical safety property stating that by only executing the relation $\xrightarrow{a}$ any two of them will never be in a critical section – marked by the proposition cs_i for $i \in \{1, 2, 3\}$ – at the same time.

$$\mathsf{AG}_a\neg\big((\mathsf{sc}_1 \wedge \mathsf{sc}_2) \vee (\mathsf{sc}_1 \wedge \mathsf{sc}_3) \vee (\mathsf{sc}_2 \wedge \mathsf{sc}_3)\big).$$

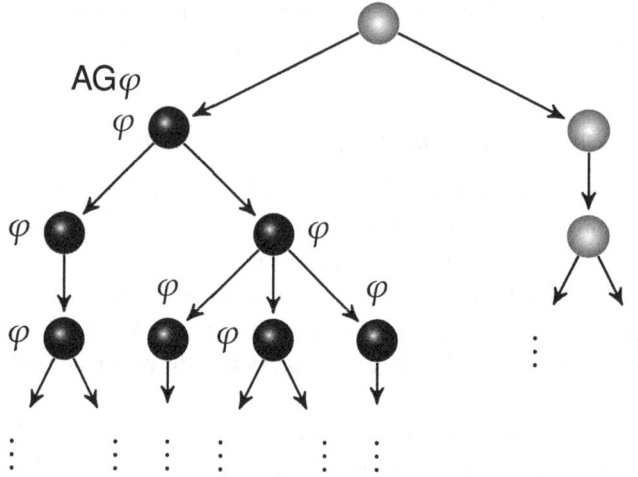

Figure 7.2 AGφ: φ holds true at every reachable state.

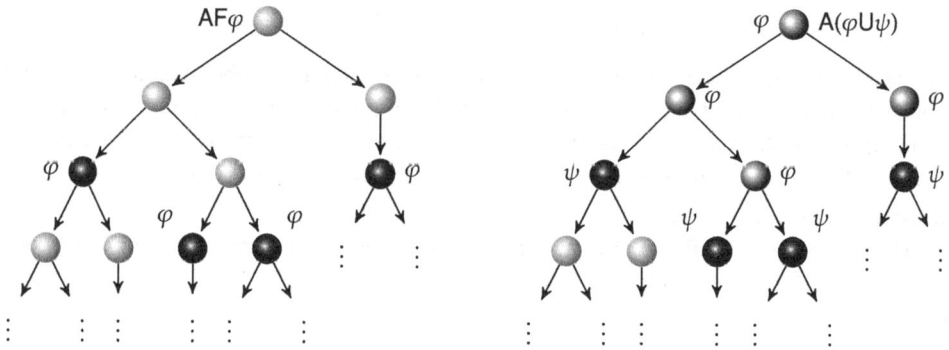

Figure 7.3 Illustration of AFφ and A(φUψ).

The logic TLR shares most of the nice properties of BML; in particular, it has the small model property and satisfiability is decidable. The proofs require more involved arguments, though. Since there is no particular gain in just considering TLR in this context, we refer to the corresponding results for the stronger logic CTL, to be defined next. Decidability of satisfiability and the small model property for CTL are proved in Section 13.3.4.

7.1.3 The Computation Tree Logic CTL

While TLR is considerably more expressive than BML, it still lacks the expressiveness of some important properties, for instance claiming reachability not on some, but *on all* computations starting from the current state. Formally, TLR lacks the expressiveness of the operator 'AF', which is illustrated on the left of Figure 7.3.

In the rest of this chapter we only consider transition systems with a single transition relation. We also assume them to be serial. Consequently, paths are also always infinite from now on. These are, of course, restrictions of the general case. They simplify the technicalities but they also have some logical implications. For instance, on serial systems $A\varphi \to E\varphi$ is valid whereas in general it is not.

The Syntax and Semantics

The language of CTL extends the language of BML with additional modal operators for existential and universal **constrained reachability**, obtained by combining the existential, respectively, universal path quantifier with the Until operator. Formally, the syntax of CTL is defined by the following grammar.

$$\varphi ::= p \mid \perp \mid \neg\varphi \mid (\varphi \wedge \varphi) \mid \mathsf{EX}\varphi \mid \mathsf{E}(\varphi\mathsf{U}\varphi) \mid \mathsf{A}(\varphi\mathsf{U}\varphi).$$

The meaning of the formula $A(\varphi \mathsf{U} \psi)$ is naturally obtained by combining the Until property with universal path quantification: ψ must eventually hold on all paths, and φ holds on each moment before that on all these paths. It is illustrated on the right side of Figure 7.3.

Like in BML and TLR, all other propositional connectives are considered as definable, as well as AX, as dual of EX. The reachability operator of TLR is now definable as $\mathsf{EF}\varphi := \mathsf{E}(\top\mathsf{U}\varphi)$. The universal reachability operator is definable, too: $\mathsf{AF}\varphi := \mathsf{A}(\top\mathsf{U}\varphi)$. It has a dual, denoted EG, which expresses the existence of a computation on which φ is an invariant, i.e. holds at every moment: $\mathsf{EG}\varphi := \neg\mathsf{AF}\neg\varphi$. Illustrating this operator is left as Exercise 7.1.

The semantics of CTL is based on total transition systems, where the definition of truth of a CTL formula at a state extends the truth definition for TLR (Section 7.1.2) with the following clauses for the new operators (recall that 'path' means an infinite path):

$$\mathcal{T}, s \models \mathsf{E}(\varphi_1\mathsf{U}\varphi_2) \quad \text{iff} \quad \text{there is a path } \pi \text{ starting at } s \text{ and an } i \geq 0$$
$$\text{such that } \pi(0) = s, \mathcal{T}, \pi(i) \models \varphi_2 \text{ and}$$
$$\text{for every } j \in [0, i-1], \text{ we have } \mathcal{T}, \pi(j) \models \varphi_1,$$

$$\mathcal{T}, s \models \mathsf{A}(\varphi_1\mathsf{U}\varphi_2) \quad \text{iff} \quad \text{for all paths } \pi \text{ such that } \pi(0) = s, \text{ there is } i \geq 0$$
$$\text{such that } \mathcal{T}, \pi(i) \models \varphi_2 \text{ and for every } j \in [0, i-1],$$
$$\text{we have } \mathcal{T}, \pi(j) \models \varphi_1.$$

Note the natural link between the semantics of CTL and the semantics of LTL: according to the truth definitions, a state s in $\mathcal{T}$ satisfies $E(\varphi_1\mathsf{U}\varphi_2)$ if and only if there is a computation starting at s and satisfying $\varphi_1\mathsf{U}\varphi_2$ in the sense of LTL. Likewise, s satisfies $A(\varphi_1\mathsf{U}\varphi_2)$ if and only if every computation starting at s satisfies $\varphi_1\mathsf{U}\varphi_2$ in the sense of LTL. Of course, this does not reduce the semantics of CTL to that of LTL because the formulae φ_1, φ_2 are generally not LTL formulae as they may contain nested path quantifiers, but the analogy is clear. The same analogy applies, in particular, to all other definable operators EF, AF, EG and AG. We will get back to this idea later, in Section 7.4.2 where we will generalise the pattern of turning linear time into branching time formulae.

Examples

Besides eventualities and safety, already expressible in TLR, with CTL formulae one can also express **progress properties** or **liveness** of the form: whenever a process i sends a request at a given state to enter in a critical section, this request will eventually be granted on any computation evolving from that state:

$$\mathsf{AG}(\mathtt{req}_i \;\rightarrow\; \mathsf{AF}\; \mathtt{cs}_i).$$

CTL can also be used to express various other *global* properties, such as partial and total correctness of terminating executions of a nondeterministic program, represented as finite initial segments of infinite computations, with respect to a given precondition φ and postcondition ψ. Thus, using the atomic proposition $\mathtt{terminal}$ to label the terminal states of the execution we express partial correctness along every possible execution using

$$\varphi \rightarrow \mathsf{AG}(\mathtt{terminal} \rightarrow \psi).$$

For partial correctness along *some* possible execution we simply replace the operator AG by EG. If we are interested in *total* correctness, i.e. additionally also want to require termination then we can do this via

$$\varphi \rightarrow \mathsf{AF}(\mathtt{terminal} \wedge \psi)$$

or using EF, depending on whether it should hold along all computations or just some.

The Problem of Separating Logics with Respect to Expressive Power

CTL extends TLR with additional operators. Hence, every TLR formula is also a CTL formula, so CTL is **at least as expressive** as TLR. An interesting question that arises immediately is whether CTL is **strictly more expressive** than TLR, i.e. whether there is a property that is CTL-definable but not TLR-definable. Such questions are in general highly nontrivial; it is not enough to argue that some formula in CTL cannot be expressed syntactically in TLR (which is of course very easy to show). Consider for instance the operator AU. As it turns out, it can be expressed in terms of EG and EU.

Lemma 7.1.2. The following logical equivalence holds in CTL.

$$\mathsf{A}(p\mathsf{U}q) \equiv \neg(\mathsf{EG}\neg q \vee \mathsf{E}((\neg q)\mathsf{U}(\neg q \wedge \neg p)))$$

The proof is left as Exercise 7.7.

So in order to show inexpressibility of a property one has to argue semantically that there is *no* formula expressing it. For instance, we would have to show that every TLR formula, regardless of how complex it is, does not express $\mathsf{E}(p\mathsf{U}q)$. It should be clear that the standard proof technique for such statements about all formulae of a logic – induction on the formula structure – is not applicable here because (in-)expressibility of a property is generally noncompositional. For instance, neither $\neg\mathsf{EG}\neg q$ nor $\neg\mathsf{E}(\neg q \,\mathsf{U}\, \neg q \wedge \neg p)$ is equivalent to a subformula of $\mathsf{A}(p\mathsf{U}q)$ but their conjunction is equivalent to $\mathsf{A}(p\mathsf{U}q)$, according to Lemma 7.1.2.

Thus, stronger principles are needed in order to show inexpressibility of certain temporal properties and then to separate temporal logics with respect to expressive power. The study of such a principle and results is deferred to Chapter 10, more precisely Section 10.3.

That chapter also contains results about **equi-expressiveness** of branching-time logics (cf. Section 10.2). For instance, with Lemma 7.1.2 we know that the two logics obtained from TLR by extending it syntactically with AU on one hand, and EU as well as EG on the other, have the same expressive power. Such results of equi-expressiveness are not always as easy to get either; it may be the case that there is a syntactic translation of formulae of one logic into those of another which preserves the expressed temporal properties, but this translation may have to take the entire formula into account instead of translating formulae operator-wise. Such results are naturally a bit more complicated and are therefore developed in detail in Chapter 10.

The fact that there are results of equi-expressiveness which are obtained by means of translations between temporal operators along the lines of Lemma 7.1.2 raises questions on how to define the syntax of a logic. The set of primitive temporal operators for CTL chosen here is irreducible, i.e. no operator is definable in terms of the others, but alternative options are possible.

7.1.4 The Full Computation Tree Logic CTL*

In TLR and CTL we have combined certain temporal operators like X or U with path quantifiers in certain ways. This immediately raises the question after a 'most general' branching-time logic in which such operators can be combined freely. This is what the full branching-time logic CTL* is which is introduced in the following.

The Syntax

The logic CTL* unifies the definitions for LTL and CTL in the sense that it includes both 'state formulae' evaluated at states of ITS and 'path formulae' interpreted over computations in ITS. Thus, CTL* strictly extends both LTL and CTL syntactically.

State formulae φ and **path formulae** ϑ of CTL* are defined by mutual recursion with the grammar

$$\varphi ::= \bot \mid p \mid \neg\varphi \mid (\varphi \wedge \varphi) \mid \mathsf{A}\vartheta$$
$$\vartheta ::= \varphi \mid \neg\vartheta \mid (\vartheta \wedge \vartheta) \mid \mathsf{X}\vartheta \mid (\vartheta\mathsf{U}\vartheta)$$

where $p \in \mathrm{PROP}$.

As usual, the other propositional connectives $\top$, $\rightarrow$, $\vee$, $\leftrightarrow$ and the temporal operators F and G are defined as usual and the existential path quantification is defined as a dual of the universal one: $\mathsf{E}\varphi := \neg\mathsf{A}\neg\varphi$. Besides, we will use the abbreviations known from LTL: $\mathsf{G}^\infty\vartheta := \mathsf{FG}\vartheta$ and $\mathsf{F}^\infty\vartheta := \mathsf{GF}\vartheta$.

Note that syntactically every state formula is also a path formula according to this grammar, and this reflects the fact that a path uniquely identifies a state in which a formula is interpreted: its starting state. Path formulae can be turned into state formulae by prefixing them with a path quantifier. Hereafter, unless otherwise specified, by a 'CTL* formula' we generally mean a state formula, and we use φ to refer to any CTL* formula; when we want to refer only to path formulae, we will make it explicit and use the respective notation.

Note also that LTL is precisely the fragment of CTL* consisting of all **pure path formulae**, i.e. those containing no path quantifiers. On the other hand, CTL can be regarded as the **pure state formulae** fragment of CTL*. By immediately prefixing every path operator with a path quantifier, the combination of these two can be regarded as an atomic operator which makes every subformula a state formula.

The Semantics

We first present the semantics for CTL* in a style where the distinction between state formulae and path formulae is explicit. Later on, we provide an equivalent, somewhat simpler version of that semantics, in which the distinction is implicit. Section 7.4.4 provides a third variant, with past-time operators, that differs slightly from the definitions in this section, but is eventually equivalent to them on the fragment of the original CTL* with future operators only.

The semantics for CTL* is based on transition systems with two satisfaction relations $\models_s$ and $\models_p$. The first one relates states to state formulae, the second one paths to path formulae. Later we will omit subscripts for the satisfaction relations assuming no risk of confusion and we will freely use $\models$ instead, for both of them.

Given a transition system $T = (S, \rightarrow, L)$ and an infinite path π in it, as usual we define the path $\pi[k, +\infty)$ as obtained from π by chopping off the first k states, i.e. $\pi[k, +\infty) := \pi(k), \pi(k+1), \pi(k+2), \ldots$.

The two satisfaction relations are defined as follows.

$$T, s \not\models_s \bot$$

$T, s \models_s p$	iff	$p \in L(s)$
$T, s \models_s \neg\varphi$	iff	$T, s \not\models_s \varphi$
$T, s \models_s \varphi \wedge \psi$	iff	$T, s \models_s \varphi$ and $T, s \models_s \psi$
$T, s \models_s \mathsf{E}\vartheta$	iff	there is a path π starting at s such that $T, \pi \models_p \vartheta$
$T, s \models_s \mathsf{A}\vartheta$	iff	for all paths π starting at s, we have $T, \pi \models_p \vartheta$
$T, \pi \models_p \varphi$	iff	$T, \pi(0) \models_s \varphi$ for state formulae φ
$T, \pi \models_p \neg\vartheta$	iff	$T, \pi \not\models_s \vartheta$
$T, \pi \models_p \vartheta \wedge \vartheta'$	iff	$T, \pi \models_p \vartheta$ and $T, \pi \models_p \vartheta'$
$T, \pi \models_p \mathsf{X}\vartheta$	iff	$T, \pi[1, +\infty) \models_p \vartheta$
$T, \pi \models_p \vartheta\mathsf{U}\vartheta'$	iff	there is $i \geq 0$ such that $T, \pi[i, +\infty) \models_p \vartheta'$ and for every $j \in [0, i-1]$, we have $T, \pi[j, +\infty) \models_p \vartheta$.

Remark 7.1.3. The atomic propositions are evaluated *relative to states, not to paths* and then the satisfaction of an atomic proposition p on a path is reduced to the truth valuation of p at the first state $\pi(0)$ of the path. This is the **locality condition** which we adopt hereafter, but versions of CTL* have also been studied where atomic propositions are evaluated relative to paths, see references in the bibliographic notes.

Remark 7.1.4. Despite the apparent complexity of the preceding definition, the relation $\models_p$ behaves like the satisfaction relation for LTL, except that the 'atomic' formulae for it are now state formulae, whereas the relation $\models_s$ behaves like the satisfaction relation for CTL, except that path quantifications are more liberal.

The notions of truth, satisfiability, validity, logical equivalence and consequence for CTL* formulae transfer naturally from LTL and CTL. However, one needs to be careful with the two sorts of formulae. For instance, satisfiability of a state formula asks for the existence of a rooted transition system in which the formula is satisfied; satisfiability of a CTL* path formula would ask for the existence of a transition system and a path in it that satisfies it, etc. However, we define **truth of a path formula** ϑ **at a state** by the following convention, as in LTL:

$$\mathcal{T}, s \models_s \vartheta \overset{\text{def}}{\Leftrightarrow} \mathcal{T}, s \models_s \mathsf{A}\vartheta.$$

Thus, $\mathcal{T}, s \models_s \vartheta$ iff $\mathcal{T}, \pi \models_s \vartheta$ for every path π in $\mathcal{T}$ such that $\pi(0) = s$.

Recall that every state formula is a path formula, too, and therefore by applying the preceding convention to a state formula φ leads to $\mathcal{T}, s \models \varphi$ also meaning that $\mathcal{T}, s \models \mathsf{A}\varphi$. This, however, is unproblematic because, as we will see later, $\mathsf{A}\varphi \equiv \varphi$ for every state formula φ.

Remark 7.1.5. Due to the different sorts of CTL* formulae, validity in CTL* *is not closed under uniform substitutions*, unlike in most traditional logics. Indeed, $p \to \mathsf{A}p$ is valid for any $p \in \mathrm{PROP}$, while $\mathsf{G}p \to \mathsf{AG}p$ is not valid since the state formula $\mathsf{A}(\mathsf{G}p \to \mathsf{AG}p)$ admits countermodels (Exercise 7.8). Still, validity in CTL* is preserved under *uniform substitutions which only replace atomic propositions by state formulae*.

Examples

For invariance and eventuality properties, CTL is essentially as good as CTL*. However, CTL is not suitable for expressing **fairness properties** where G^∞ and F^∞ are essentially used, while these can be naturally expressed in CTL*. For instance, **fairness along some possible computation** is expressed by

$$\mathsf{E}(\mathsf{GFreq} \to \mathsf{Fgrant})$$

while the following formula expresses fairness along *every* possible computation.

$$\mathsf{A}(\mathsf{GFreq} \to \mathsf{Fgrant}).$$

What seems to be the closest translation of the latter in CTL, namely

$$\mathsf{AGAFreq} \to \mathsf{AFgrant},$$

is in fact different, see Exercise 7.16.

We give a few more examples of expressing properties with CTL*. The assertion that 'there is no computation on which some q-state starts a computation on which p is never true' is expressed by

$$\neg EF(q \wedge EG \neg p).$$

'For every future state s on every computation where p is true, every successor state starts a computation on which q is true, until p becomes false'.

$$AG(p \rightarrow AXE(qU\neg p)).$$

'If φ is eventually true on every computation starting from the current state, then there is a future state after which ψ will remain false until φ becomes true'.

$$AG^{\infty}\varphi \rightarrow EFA(\neg \psi U\varphi).$$

The One-Sorted Semantics

Since every state formula of CTL* is also a path formula, it is natural to merge the two sorts and assume that all CTL* formulae are path formulae. We will briefly present the syntax and semantics of this version. For the sake of consistency with the rest of the book, hereafter we will use the notation φ, ψ – previously used for state formulae only – to denote *any* CTL* formulae, unless explicitly stated otherwise. The set of all formulae of CTL* is now defined recursively as follows:

$$\varphi ::= \bot \mid p \mid \neg \varphi \mid (\varphi \wedge \varphi) \mid X\varphi \mid (\varphi U\varphi) \mid A\varphi$$

where $p \in$ PROP. The other logical connectives $\top, \rightarrow, \vee, \leftrightarrow$, the temporal operators F and G and the existential path quantifier E are definable as before.

Now all CTL* formulae are regarded as path formulae and the basic semantical notion is *truth of a formula relative to a path in an interpreted transition system*. Given an ITS $\mathcal{T} = (S, R, L)$ and a path π in $\mathcal{T}$, the inductive definition for $\mathcal{T}, \pi \models \varphi$ is as follows:

$$
\begin{aligned}
&\mathcal{T}, \pi \not\models \bot \\
&\mathcal{T}, \pi \models p && \text{iff} && p \in L(\pi(0)) \text{ for every } p \in \text{PROP} \\
&\mathcal{T}, \pi \models \neg \varphi && \text{iff} && \mathcal{T}, \pi \not\models \varphi \\
&\mathcal{T}, \pi \models \varphi \wedge \psi && \text{iff} && \mathcal{T}, \pi \models \varphi \text{ and } \mathcal{T}, \pi \models \psi \\
&\mathcal{T}, \pi \models X\varphi && \text{iff} && \mathcal{T}, \pi[1, +\infty) \models \varphi \\
&\mathcal{T}, \pi \models \varphi U\psi && \text{iff} && \mathcal{T}, \pi[j, +\infty) \models \psi \text{ for some } j \in \mathbb{N} \text{ and } \mathcal{T}, \pi[i, +\infty) \models \varphi \\
& && && \text{for every } i \text{ such that } i \in [0, j-1] \\
&\mathcal{T}, \pi \models A\varphi && \text{iff} && \mathcal{T}, \pi' \models \varphi \text{ for every path } \pi' \text{ in } \mathcal{T} \\
& && && \text{such that } \pi(0) = \pi'(0).
\end{aligned}
$$

We leave it as Exercise 7.12 to check that the two notions of satisfiability and validity coincide, which can be shown by simply proving the following properties by structural induction.

Proposition 7.1.6. Let $\models$ denote the satisfaction relation of the one-sorted CTL*, and $\models_s$ and $\models_p$ those of the two-sorted CTL*. Let $\mathcal{T}$ be a transition system, and π a path in it. Then the following hold.

a) For any state formula φ we have $\mathcal{T}, \pi \models \varphi$ iff $\mathcal{T}, \pi(0) \models_s \varphi$.
b) For any path formula φ we have $\mathcal{T}, \pi \models \varphi$ iff $\mathcal{T}, \pi \models_p \varphi$. ∎

Remark 7.1.7. The semantics of CTL* can be modified to evaluate every atomic proposition, and hence every formula, on paths. Then, the same atomic proposition p may be true with respect to one path, while false with respect to another, starting at the same state. The resulting logic, however, becomes undecidable and much less intuitive, see references in the bibliographic notes.

A Generalised Semantics

The semantics of CTL* given previously takes all paths in the transition system into account. This is not always necessary, and sometimes it is even *not reasonable* because some paths could be forbidden by liveness or fairness conditions, exogenously imposed on the transition system. On the other hand, in order to give meaningful semantics, there ought to be *sufficiently many* available paths, satisfying some basic conditions.

We are now going to generalise the semantics of CTL* by considering models based on pairs $(\mathcal{T}, \Pi)$ where $\mathcal{T}$ is a labelled transition system and Π is a family of *recognised paths* in $\mathcal{T}$. A minimal reasonable requirement for such a family is that it must be **covering**: every state must belong to some recognised path. This, however, is not sufficient, because the truth definitions of the temporal operators invoke suffixes of a path, which may not be in the family. Recall that a suffix of a path π is every path $\pi[k, +\infty)$ obtained from π by chopping off the first k states. Thus, we impose the additional requirement of **suffix closure**: every suffix of a path from Π must be in Π.

Definition 7.1.8. A pair $(\mathcal{T}, \Pi)$ where $\mathcal{T}$ is a transition system and Π is a covering and suffix closed family of paths in $\mathcal{T}$ will be called a **generalised branching-time structure**. A generalised branching-time structure $(\mathcal{T}, \Pi)$ where Π is the set of all paths in $\mathcal{T}$ will be called a **standard model** or **R-generated model**. ▽

The semantics of CTL* can be generalised over such structures with no complications, by restricting the path quantifications to the paths in the family Π. This generalised semantics is *not equivalent* to the standard one, because not every formula valid in all transition systems is valid in all generalised branching-time structures. One example is $\mathsf{AX}\varphi \to \mathsf{XA}\varphi$. The reason for the possible failure of that formula is that a path falsifying φ may belong to Π while its extension one step backwards is not in Π.

Thus, another natural closure condition emerges: a family of paths Π is **prefix closed** if whenever a path π belongs to Π and $sR\pi(0)$ then the path $s\pi$ obtained by prefixing π with s must belong to Π, too.

Given two paths π and π', such that $\pi(n) = \pi'(m)$, the path $\pi[0, n]\,\pi'[m+1, +\infty)$ obtained by appending $\pi'[m+1, +\infty)$ onto $\pi[0, n]$ is called a **fusion** of π and π'. A family of paths is called **fusion closed** if every fusion of paths from Π belongs to Π.

We leave it as an Exercise 7.17 to show that fusion closure implies prefix closure, while suffix closure and prefix closure together imply fusion closure. Hereafter we will use fusion closure, not prefix closure.

Adding the condition of fusion closure to generalised branching-time structures still produces an essentially more general semantics for CTL*. Indeed, e.g. Burgess's formula AGEF$\varphi \to$ EGFφ is valid in all standard models but fails in some suffix and fusion closed generalised branching time structures (Exercise 7.18). The reason is the failure of another natural and important closure condition satisfied by standard models, viz. **limit closure** of the family of paths Π: if π is a path such that for every $n \in \mathbb{N}$ there is a path ρ^n such that the fusion $\pi[0, n]\,\rho^n[n+1, +\infty)$ belongs to Π, then π – which can be viewed as the limit of the sequence of such fusions paths – must belong to Π, too.

Proposition 7.1.9. A generalised branching time model $(\mathcal{T}, \Pi)$ is R generated iff it is fusion and limit closed.   ∎

The proof of this claim is left as Exercise 7.24 and a reference for it can be found in the bibliographic notes.

7.1.5 Fundamental Equivalences and Validities

The Interaction of Path Quantifiers with Other Operators

Some understanding of the meaning of branching-time formulae can be gained by studying equivalences and validities. We start with the easy observation that universal path quantifiers commute with conjunctions, and existential path quantifiers commute with disjunctions.

$$A(\varphi \wedge \psi) \equiv A\varphi \wedge A\psi, \quad E(\varphi \vee \psi) \equiv E\varphi \vee E\psi. \tag{7.1}$$

Clearly, if all paths satisfy φ and ψ, then all paths must satisfy φ, and all paths must satisfy ψ, and vice versa. The second equivalence can be justified in a similar way, or it can be derived from the first one via the de Morgan laws and $E\varphi \equiv \neg A\neg\varphi$.

It should be clear that universal path quantification does in general not commute with disjunctions. Consider for instance $A(Xp \vee X\neg p)$. This is a validity since any successor of any state must either satisfy p or $\neg p$. However, $AXp \vee AX\neg p$ is not valid; the following is a countermodel.

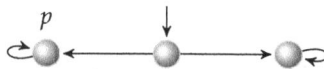

Note that the two disjuncts in this example are genuine path formulae. This is in fact necessary; universal path quantification does commute with disjunctions in the special case of state formula disjuncts. Consider for instance $\mathsf{A}(p \vee \neg p)$. It is valid, and so is $\mathsf{A}p \vee \mathsf{A}\neg p$. This example is of course very simple and we cannot conclude from it that this works for any state formula. So, a formal statement and proof is needed for the general case. It is helpful, though, to consider first how path quantification acts on state formulae.

Lemma 7.1.10. Let φ be a state formula and $\mathcal{Q} \in \{\mathsf{A}, \mathsf{E}\}$. Then we have $\mathcal{Q}\varphi \equiv \varphi$. ∎

Proof. Let s be any state of any ITS. We first show the statement for universal path quantifiers. The case for existential quantifiers is done in the same way.

'$\Rightarrow$' Suppose $s \models \mathsf{A}\varphi$. Then for any path π starting in s we have $\pi \models \varphi$. Since φ is a state formula we have $\pi(0) \models \varphi$ for any of these which is in fact the same as $s \models \varphi$.

'$\Leftarrow$' Suppose $s \models \varphi$. Now take any path π such that $\pi(0) = s$. Since φ is a state formula we get $\pi \models \varphi$ for any path π with $\pi(0) = s$, using the convention of how state formulae are interpreted as path formulae. Thus, we have $s \models \mathsf{A}\varphi$. □

Lemma 7.1.11. Let φ be a state formula and ψ be any CTL* formula. Then we have

a) $\mathsf{A}(\varphi \vee \psi) \equiv \varphi \vee \mathsf{A}\psi$,
b) $\mathsf{E}(\varphi \wedge \psi) \equiv \varphi \wedge \mathsf{E}\psi$. ∎

Proof. We only show part (a) since part (b) can be done in the same way. Alternatively, it follows from part (a) with the de Morgan laws and duality between A and E.

'$\Rightarrow$' Suppose $s \models \mathsf{A}(\varphi \vee \psi)$. Thus, any path π starting in s satisfies φ or ψ. We distinguish two cases. In the first case, *all* such paths satisfy ψ. Then we clearly have $s \models \mathsf{A}\psi$ and therefore $s \models \varphi \vee \mathsf{A}\psi$.

In the second case there is at least one path π such that $\pi \models \varphi$. Now remember that φ is a state formula, hence, $\pi(0) \models \varphi$. Since $\pi(0) = s$ we have $s \models \varphi$ and therefore $s \models \varphi \vee \mathsf{A}\psi$.

'$\Leftarrow$' Suppose $s \models \varphi \vee \mathsf{A}\psi$. Then there are two cases. First, if $s \models \varphi$ then by Lemma 7.1.10 we also have $s \models \mathsf{A}\varphi$ and therefore also $s \models \mathsf{A}(\varphi \vee \psi)$ since, if all paths starting in s satisfy φ then clearly all of these satisfy φ or ψ.

In the second case we have $s \models \mathsf{A}\psi$. With the same argument about the impossibility to falsify formulae by adding more disjunctive choices we also get $s \models \mathsf{A}(\varphi \vee \psi)$. □

Next we consider the interplay between path quantification and temporal operators. We can ask whether we get general commutativity results as well. The answer is negative in general. We leave it as Exercise 7.22 to show that the following pairs of formulae are in general not equivalent, where $\mathcal{Q} \in \{\mathsf{A}, \mathsf{E}\}$.

- $\mathcal{Q}\mathsf{G}\varphi$ and $\mathsf{G}\mathcal{Q}\varphi$,
- $\mathcal{Q}\mathsf{F}\varphi$ and $\mathsf{F}\mathcal{Q}\varphi$,
- $\mathcal{Q}\mathsf{X}\varphi$ and $\mathsf{X}\mathcal{Q}\varphi$.

There is a way, though, in which path quantification can be 'moved across' the modal next-step operator.

Lemma 7.1.12. For any CTL* formula φ and any $\mathcal{Q} \in \{A, E\}$ we have that $\mathcal{Q}X\varphi \equiv \mathcal{Q}X\mathcal{Q}\varphi$. ∎

Proof. First we consider the case of $\mathcal{Q} = E$.

'$\Rightarrow$' Suppose $s \models EX\varphi$, i.e. there is a path π such that $\pi(0) = s$ and $\pi[1, +\infty) \models \varphi$. Then clearly we have $\pi(1) \models E\varphi$ and therefore $s \models EXE\varphi$.

'$\Leftarrow$' Suppose $s \models EXE\varphi$. Then there is a path π with $\pi(0) = s$ and $\pi[1, +\infty) \models E\varphi$. Since $E\varphi$ is a state formula this is equivalent to $\pi(1) \models E\varphi$. Hence, there is a path π' starting in $\pi(1)$ such that $\pi' \models \varphi$. By suffix closure, the path $\pi'' = \pi(0)\pi'$ is also a path starting in s, and it satisfies $X\varphi$. Hence, we get $s \models EX\varphi$.

The case of $\mathcal{Q} = A$ is easily obtained from this. If $EX\varphi \equiv EXE\varphi$ then we also have $\neg EX\varphi \equiv \neg EXE\varphi$ and, by duality of the path quantifiers then also $A\neg X\varphi \equiv A\neg XE\varphi$. Since negation commutes with X we also get $AX\neg\varphi \equiv AX\neg E\varphi \equiv AXA\neg\varphi$. But CTL* is closed under negation, i.e. if this equivalence holds for any φ then it also holds for any $\neg\varphi$ and therefore we also get $AX\varphi \equiv AXA\varphi$ for any φ. □

Next lemma states yet another simple but useful fact, the proof of which we leave as an exercise.

Lemma 7.1.13. For any CTL* formulae φ and ψ, if $\varphi \equiv \psi$ then $E\varphi \equiv E\psi$ and $A\varphi \equiv A\psi$. ∎

Unfolding Principles

The equivalences developed so far can be used to derive an **unfolding principle** for CTL comparable to the one for LTL:

$$\varphi U\psi \equiv \psi \vee (\varphi \wedge X(\varphi U\psi)). \tag{7.2}$$

First of all we note that this must also be valid in CTL*. In fact, there is a simple general correspondence between LTL and CTL* validities.

Theorem 7.1.14. Let φ be a valid LTL formula. Then φ is valid in CTL* as well. ∎

Proof. By contraposition. Suppose φ was not valid as a CTL* formula, i.e. there is an ITS $\mathcal{T}$ with a path π such that $\mathcal{T}, \pi \not\models \varphi$. Then clearly the computation π exists and φ cannot hold in every computation. □

Now consider a CTL formula $E(\varphi U\psi)$. From the equivalence (7.2), using Lemma 7.1.13 we get

$$E(\varphi U\psi) \equiv E(\psi \vee (\varphi \wedge X(\varphi U\psi))).$$

This holds generally for any CTL* formulae φ and ψ. In the special case of CTL formulae φ and ψ we can simplify the right-hand side considerably. Note that in this case the left-hand side is a CTL formula but the right-hand side is not.

Remember that a CTL formula is always a CTL* state formula, so we can apply the principles worked out earlier to obtain the following.

$$E(\varphi U\psi) \equiv E(\psi \vee (\varphi \wedge X(\varphi U\psi)))$$

$$\equiv E\psi \vee E(\varphi \wedge X(\varphi U\psi)) \qquad \text{by Equation 7.1}$$

$$\equiv \psi \vee E(\varphi \wedge X(\varphi U\psi)) \qquad \text{by Lemma 7.1.10}$$

$$\equiv \psi \vee (\varphi \wedge EX(\varphi U\psi)) \qquad \text{by Lemma 7.1.11}$$

$$\equiv \psi \vee (\varphi \wedge EXE(\varphi U\psi)) \qquad \text{by Lemma 7.1.12.}$$

This has simplified the unfolding principle from a general one for CTL* to a special one for CTL considerably. The last formula is syntactically a CTL formula. Moreover, it also realises a genuine unfolding principle for $E(\varphi U\psi)$ in the sense that this formula occurs syntactically on the right-hand side, i.e. in its own unfolding.

Likewise, we obtain unfolding principles for CTL formulae using universal path quantification and/or the Release operator.

Theorem 7.1.15. The following equivalences are valid in CTL.

$$E(\varphi U\psi) \equiv \psi \vee (\varphi \wedge EXE(\varphi U\psi))$$

$$A(\varphi U\psi) \equiv \psi \vee (\varphi \wedge AXA(\varphi U\psi))$$

$$E(\varphi R\psi) \equiv \psi \wedge (\varphi \vee EXE(\varphi R\psi))$$

$$A(\varphi R\psi) \equiv \psi \wedge (\varphi \vee AXA(\varphi R\psi)). \qquad \blacksquare$$

Proof. The first one is derived previously, the others can be derived from the corresponding LTL unfolding principles in the same way, or by duality. $\qquad \square$

It is important to note that these CTL equivalences inherit the fixpoint nature of the underlying LTL equivalences. The next theorem states set-theoretic versions of these equivalences, in terms of the extensions of the respective formulae.

Theorem 7.1.16. Let $\mathcal{T}$ be an ITS and φ, ψ be CTL formulae.

- $[\![E(\varphi U\psi)]\!]^{\mathcal{T}}$ is the **least fixpoint** of the monotone operator

$$\mathbf{EU}_{\varphi,\psi}(X) := [\![\psi]\!]^{\mathcal{T}} \cup ([\![\varphi]\!]^{\mathcal{T}} \cap \mathrm{pre}(X)).$$

- $[\![A(\varphi U\psi)]\!]^{\mathcal{T}}$ is the **least fixpoint** of the monotone operator

$$\mathbf{AU}_{\varphi,\psi}(X) := [\![\psi]\!]^{\mathcal{T}} \cup ([\![\varphi]\!]^{\mathcal{T}} \cap \overline{\mathrm{pre}}(X)).$$

- $[\![E(\varphi R\psi)]\!]^{\mathcal{T}}$ is the **greatest fixpoint** of the monotone operator

$$\mathbf{ER}_{\varphi,\psi}(X) := [\![\psi]\!]^{\mathcal{T}} \cap ([\![\varphi]\!]^{\mathcal{T}} \cup \mathrm{pre}(X)).$$

- $[\![A(\varphi R\psi)]\!]^{\mathcal{T}}$ is the **greatest fixpoint** of the monotone operator

$$\mathbf{AR}_{\varphi,\psi}(X) := [\![\psi]\!]^{\mathcal{T}} \cap ([\![\varphi]\!]^{\mathcal{T}} \cup \overline{\mathrm{pre}}(X)). \qquad \blacksquare$$

By the Knaster–Tarski Theorem 2.2.3, these sets are the least pre-fixpoints, respectively largest post-fixpoints of the corresponding unfoldings operators, whence the following theorem.

Theorem 7.1.17. The following logical consequences hold in CTL.

$$
\begin{aligned}
&\text{(LFP}_{\text{EU}}) && AG((\psi \vee (\varphi \wedge EX\chi)) \to \chi) \models E(\varphi U\psi) \to \chi \\
&\text{(LFP}_{\text{AU}}) && AG((\psi \vee (\varphi \wedge AX\chi)) \to \chi) \models A(\varphi U\psi) \to \chi \\
&\text{(LFP}_{\text{EF}}) && AG((\psi \vee EX\chi) \to \chi) \models EF\psi \to \chi \\
&\text{(LFP}_{\text{AF}}) && AG((\psi \vee AX\chi) \to \chi) \models AF\psi \to \chi \\
&\text{(GFP}_{\text{EG}}) && AG(\psi \to (\varphi \wedge EX\psi)) \models \psi \to EG\varphi \\
&\text{(GFP}_{\text{AG}}) && AG(\psi \to (\varphi \wedge AX\psi)) \models \psi \to AG\varphi.
\end{aligned}
$$

The proof is left as Exercise 7.4.

Other Logical Validities

We conclude the section on equivalences and validities by stating some more, which will be used further or are interesting and may not be obvious.

Proposition 7.1.18. The following schemes of formulae, where φ and ψ are CTL* formulae, are valid:

(I) $A\varphi \to \varphi$
(II) $A\varphi \to AA\varphi$
(III) $A\varphi \to AE\varphi$
(IV) $\varphi \to A\varphi$, for any state formula φ
(V) $AX\varphi \to XA\varphi$
(VI) $AG\varphi \to GA\varphi$
(VII) $A(\varphi \to \psi) \to (A\varphi \to A\psi)$
(VIII) The result of uniform substitution of any state formulae for atomic propositions in φ, for any valid formula φ.

We also list some validities that essentially use the fact that all paths that can be generated in the ITS are present in the model (cf. Exercise 7.18).

Proposition 7.1.19. The following schemes of formulae, where φ, ψ, χ are any CTL* state formulae, are valid:

(I) $AGEF\varphi \to EGF\varphi$
(II) $AG(\varphi \to EX\varphi) \to (\varphi \to EG\varphi)$
(III) $AG(\varphi \to EXF\varphi) \to (\varphi \to EGF\varphi)$
(IV) $AG(E\varphi \to EX((E\psi \, U \, E\chi))) \to (E\varphi \to EG((E\psi \, U \, E\chi)))$.

The first one is known as **Burgess's formula**, the last one as **Reynold's limit closure formula**. Verifying the claims in these preceding two propositions is left as Exercise 7.14.

Observe that none of the formulae in Proposition 7.1.19 (I)–(III) is valid for all path formulae. In particular, for the formulae (II) and (III), this assumes that a universal path quantifier prefixes the formulae.

Indeed, consider the infinite binary tree $\mathcal{T} = (\{0, 1\}^*, R, L)$ with $L(u) = \emptyset$ if u ends by '0', otherwise $L(u) = \{p\}$ and φ be equal to $p \wedge \mathsf{XG}\neg p$.

For every $u \in \{0, 1\}^*$, $\pi, |u| \models \mathsf{F}(p \wedge \mathsf{XG}\neg p)$ where π is the infinite path encoded by $u \cdot 1 \cdot 0^\omega$. Therefore, $\mathcal{T}, \varepsilon \models \mathsf{AGEF}(p \wedge \mathsf{XG}\neg p)$. However, $\mathcal{T}, \varepsilon \not\models \mathsf{EGF}(p \wedge \mathsf{XG}\neg p)$ since $\mathsf{GF}(p \wedge \mathsf{XG}\neg p)$ is an unsatisfiable LTL formula. This invalidates Proposition 7.1.19(I) with an arbitrary formula φ.

The formula $\mathsf{A}(\mathsf{AG}(\varphi \to \mathsf{EX}\varphi) \to (\varphi \to \mathsf{EG}\varphi))$ can be equivalently transformed to $\mathsf{AG}(\varphi \to \mathsf{EX}\varphi) \to \mathsf{A}(\varphi \to \mathsf{EG}\varphi)$ and then one can check that $\mathcal{T}, \varepsilon \models \mathsf{AG}(p \wedge \mathsf{XG}\neg p \to \mathsf{EX}(p \wedge \mathsf{XG}\neg p))$. Indeed, for every $u \in \{0, 1\}^*$, $\pi, |u| \models \mathsf{X}(p \wedge \mathsf{XG}\neg p)$ where π is the infinite path encoded by $u \cdot 1 \cdot 0^\omega$. Let us consider the path π_0 encoded by 0^ω. We have $\pi_0, 0 \models p \wedge \mathsf{XG}\neg p$ but there is no path satisfying $\mathsf{G}(p \wedge \mathsf{XG}\neg p)$ since that formula is not LTL satisfiable. Consequently, not $\mathcal{T}, \varepsilon \models \mathsf{AG}(\varphi \to \mathsf{EX}\varphi) \to \mathsf{A}(\varphi \to \mathsf{EG}\varphi)$ with φ equal to $p \wedge \mathsf{XG}\neg p$. This invalidates Proposition 7.1.19(II) with an arbitrary formula φ.

A similar reasoning leads to the nonvalidity of $\mathsf{A}(\mathsf{AG}(\varphi \to \mathsf{EXF}\varphi) \to (\varphi \to \mathsf{EGF}\varphi))$ with φ being $p \wedge \mathsf{XG}\neg p$, which invalidates Proposition 7.1.19 (III) with an arbitrary formula φ.

A Simple Normal Form

For the sake of technical convenience we sometime consider the version of CTL* with path quantifiers A and E and the linear-time temporal operators Until U and Release R as primitive connectives. Then the formulae of CTL* are defined by the following grammar.

$$\varphi ::= \perp \mid p \mid \neg\varphi \mid (\varphi \wedge \varphi) \mid \mathsf{X}\varphi \mid (\varphi \mathsf{U}\varphi) \mid (\varphi \mathsf{R}\varphi) \mid \mathsf{A}\varphi \mid \mathsf{E}\varphi.$$

A **pure path formula** is understood as a path formula built over the temporal connectives X, U and R (but without any occurrence of A or E).

Lemma 7.1.20. For every CTL* state formula φ, there is an equivalent CTL* state formula φ' in negation normal form (NNF) such that $|\varphi'| \leq 2 \cdot |\varphi|$, i.e. all occurrences of the negation $\neg$ in φ' can only occur in front of atomic propositions. ∎

The proof is by easy verification and it is left as Exercise 7.24.

Lemma 7.1.21. Let φ be a state formula in NNF, ψ be a state subformula of φ that is not a negated atomic proposition and p be an atomic proposition that does not occur in φ.

(I) φ is satisfiable iff the following formula φ' is satisfiable:

$$\varphi' = \mathsf{AG}(p \to \psi) \wedge \varphi[p/\psi].$$

(II) If $\mathcal{T}, s \models \varphi'$, then $\mathcal{T}, s \models \varphi$. ∎

The proof is similar to the proof of Lemma 5.2.6 and it is left as Exercise 7.24.

Before defining the new normal form for CTL* formulae (called simple formulae later on), we need to consider the following equivalences that are valid CTL* formulae when ψ is a pure path formula:

$$\mathsf{AG}(p \to \mathsf{E}\psi) \leftrightarrow \mathsf{AGE}(p \to \psi)$$
$$\mathsf{AG}(p \to \mathsf{A}\psi) \leftrightarrow \mathsf{A}(\mathsf{G}(p \to \psi)).$$

A CTL* formula is **simple** iff it is a conjunction of the form

$$p \wedge \Big(\bigwedge_{i \in I} \mathsf{AGE}(q_i \to \psi_i) \Big) \wedge \Big(\bigwedge_{i \in I'} \mathsf{AG}(r_i \to \chi_i) \Big)$$

where the ψ_i's and χ_i's are pure path formulae.

Theorem 7.1.22. For any CTL* formula, one can build a simple CTL* formula φ' such that

  (I) φ' can be built in linear-time in $|\varphi|$.
  (II) The number of subformulae of the form $\mathsf{E}\psi$ in φ' is bounded by the number of path quantifiers in φ with an existential polarity. (If φ is already in NNF, this amounts to the number of occurrences of existential path quantifier E in φ.)
  (III) For all $k \geq 0$, φ is satisfiable in a k-branching tree iff φ' is satisfiable in a k-branching tree.   ∎

The notion of k-branching tree is presented in Definition 7.2.5.

Theorem 7.1.22 (I) is established by using Lemma 7.1.20, a repeated application of the transformation in Lemma 7.1.21 and the validity of the preceding formulae. Theorem 7.1.22 (II) is obtained by a simple analysis of the translation, whereas Theorem 7.1.22 (III) is a consequence of Lemma 7.1.21 (II).

7.2 Bisimulation Invariance

In this section we study the interplay between bisimulation equivalence and branching-time temporal logics. Remember that LTL cannot distinguish models that are trace equivalent, but there are examples of trace equivalent systems which can be distinguished using BML. Bisimilarity is a finer behavioural equivalence than trace equivalence, and we have already seen a close connection between bounded bisimilarity and modal formulae. Now with operators at hand that allow properties like reachability to be expressed, the question of the relationship between bisimilarity and branching-time temporal logics arises.

7.2.1 Indistinguishability of Bisimilar Models

The next result states that CTL* cannot distinguish bisimilar models. Note that this is a positive property, as it makes CTL* suitable for the specification of program behaviour.

Theorem 7.2.1. If $(\mathcal{T}_1, s_1) \rightleftarrows (\mathcal{T}_2, s_2)$, then $(\mathcal{T}_1, s_1)$ and $(\mathcal{T}_2, s_2)$ satisfy the same state formulae of CTL*.   ∎

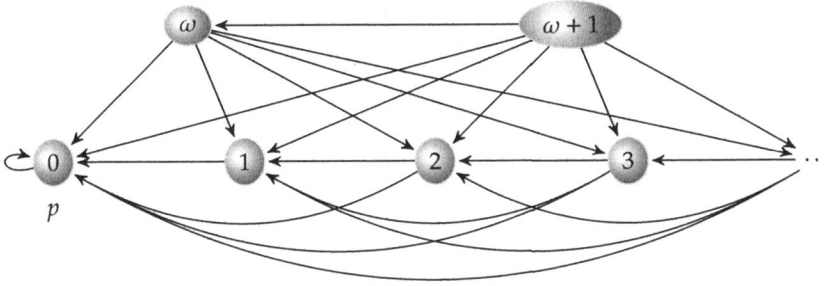

Figure 7.4 ω and $\omega + 1$ cannot be distinguished by CTL* formulae.

Proof. (Sketch) The proof relies on Theorem 3.5.3. More precisely, two bisimilar states, s_1 and s_2, not only generate the same set of computations but also for every infinite path π from s_1, there is an infinite bisimilar path π' from s_2. This means that for any $i \in \mathbb{N}$, the states at position i in π and π' respectively, are pairwise bisimilar. The proof is then by structural induction of (state and path) formulae by using the following two induction hypotheses.

- For all $s \in \text{post}^\star(s_1)$ and $s' \in \text{post}^\star(s_2)$ such that $s \rightleftarrows s'$, for all state formulae φ of size less than N, we have $\mathcal{T}_1, s \models \varphi$ iff $\mathcal{T}_2, s' \models \varphi$.
- For all the paths $\pi = r_0, r_1, \ldots$ starting by a state in $\text{post}^\star(s_1)$, for all the paths $\pi' = r'_0, r'_1, \ldots$ starting by a state in $\text{post}^\star(s_2)$ such that for all $i \in \mathbb{N}$, $r_i \rightleftarrows r'_i$, we have for all $i \in \mathbb{N}$ and for all path formulae φ of size less than N, the equivalence $\pi, i \models \varphi$ iff $\pi', i \models \varphi$ holds.

The rest of the proof is left as Exercise 7.24 and the induction follows the construction rules for CTL* formulae. $\square$

The converse is not true; there are systems $(\mathcal{T}_1, s_1)$ and $(\mathcal{T}_2, s_2)$ that satisfy the same state formulae of CTL* but are not locally bisimilar. However, such counterexamples necessarily need to be infinite since nonbisimilarity of two states in finite systems can already be revealed with a BML formula that is true in one but false in the other state. In Figure 7.4, we present a (total) transition system $\mathcal{T}$ with the set of states $S = \{0, 1, 2, \ldots, \omega, \omega + 1\}$ and for all ordinals $\alpha, \beta \leq \omega + 1$, we have $\beta \to \alpha$ iff ($\alpha < \beta$ or $\alpha = \beta = 0$) and 0 is the only state such that p holds true on it. For the sake of clarity, not all the edges have been drawn in Figure 7.4. It is easy to show that $\mathcal{T}, \omega \not\rightleftarrows \mathcal{T}, \omega + 1$ whereas ω and $\omega + 1$ agree on all CTL* formulae, which is left as Exercise 7.21.

7.2.2 Characteristic Formulae in TLR

While bisimulation-invariance shows that a program logic is expressively *weak* enough not to distinguish systems that model programs with equivalent behaviour, it is also interesting to see whether such logics are *strong* enough to describe such behaviour in detail. This is justified by the existence of characteristic formulae with respect to the desired behavioural equivalence. Such formulae describe a transition system up to bisimilarity, i.e. they show that the logic is strong enough to distinguish (certain) models that are not to be considered behaviourally equivalent. We will show that TLR is expressive enough to describe every finite rooted ITS up to bisimulation equivalence.

First, recall from Section 5.3.3 that with every rooted ITS $(\mathcal{T}, s)$, where $\mathcal{T} = (S, R, L)$ and $n \in \mathbb{N}$ we associate a characteristic formula $\chi_{[\mathcal{T},s]}^{n} \in$ BML of depth n. Furthermore, when $\mathcal{T}$ is finite, with every $s \in \mathcal{T}$ we associate the characteristic formula $\chi_{[\mathcal{T},s]}$ (which is $\chi_{[\mathcal{T},s]}^{n}$ for a large enough n) characterising s up to bisimulation equivalence, *within* $\mathcal{T}$.

Theorem 7.2.2. For every finite rooted ITS $\mathcal{T} = (S, R, L, s)$ there is a TLR formula $\Phi_{[\mathcal{T},s]}$ that characterises $(\mathcal{T}, s)$ up to bisimulation equivalence in the sense that for any ITS $\mathcal{T}'$ with root s' we have $\mathcal{T}', s' \models \Phi_{[\mathcal{T},s]}$ iff $(\mathcal{T}', s') \rightleftarrows (\mathcal{T}, s)$. ∎

Proof. We first define for every $r \in \mathcal{T}$ the formula

$$\Xi_{[\mathcal{T},r]} := \mathsf{AG}\Big(\chi_{[\mathcal{T},r]} \to \bigwedge_{rRt} \mathsf{EX}\chi_{[\mathcal{T},t]} \wedge \mathsf{AX} \bigvee_{rRt} \chi_{[\mathcal{T},t]}\Big).$$

Recall (Corollary 5.3.22) that for every state $r' \in \mathcal{T}$ we have that $\mathcal{T}, r' \models \chi_{[\mathcal{T},r]}$ if and only if $(\mathcal{T}, r) \rightleftarrows (\mathcal{T}, r')$. Consequently, $\mathcal{T}, r \models \Phi_{[\mathcal{T},r]}$ for every $r \in \mathcal{T}$. Then let

$$\Phi_{[\mathcal{T},s]} := \chi_{[\mathcal{T},s]} \wedge \bigwedge_{r \in S} \Xi_{[\mathcal{T},r]}.$$

It remains to be seen that the models of $\Phi_{[\mathcal{T},s]}$ are exactly the states that are bisimilar to s in $\mathcal{T}$.

'$\Leftarrow$' This follows from bisimulation invariance of TLR formulae which is a special case of Theorem 7.2.1, and because $\mathcal{T}, s \models \chi_{[\mathcal{T},s]}$.

'$\Rightarrow$' It suffices to define a winning strategy for Player **II** for the bisimulation game $\mathcal{G}(s', s)$, using the formula $\Phi_{[\mathcal{T},s]}$ as follows: at every round of the game, Player **II** responds to the choice of Player **I** by choosing a state satisfying the same characteristic formula $\chi_{[\mathcal{T},t]}$ as the choice of Player **I**. The existence of this strategy can be proved by induction on the number of rounds: at round 0 this follows from the fact that $\mathcal{T}', s' \models \chi_{[\mathcal{T},s]}$. Now, suppose that $\mathcal{T}', r' \models \chi_{[\mathcal{T},r]}$, i.e. the condition of the winning strategy is satisfied by the current configuration $(\mathcal{T}, r; \mathcal{T}', r')$ of round n. This and the assumption $\mathcal{T}', s' \models \Phi_{[\mathcal{T},s]}$ imply that

1. $\mathcal{T}', r' \models \bigwedge_{rRt} \mathsf{EX}\chi_{[\mathcal{T},t]}$ and
2. $\mathcal{T}', r' \models \mathsf{AX} \bigvee_{rRt} \chi_{[\mathcal{T},t]}$.

Now consider the two cases for the possible moves of Player **I**. If Player **I** chooses a successor t of r in $\mathcal{T}$, then, by (1), $\mathcal{T}', t' \models \chi_{[\mathcal{T},t]}$ for some $t' \in \mathcal{T}'$ and any such t' is a good choice of Player **II**.

If Player **I** chooses a successor t' of r' in $\mathcal{T}'$, then, by (2), $\mathcal{T}', t' \models \chi_{[\mathcal{T},t]}$ for some $t \in \mathcal{T}$ and any such t is a good choice of Player **II**. □

Combining this with bisimulation invariance of TLR yields the following link between logical and behavioural equivalence.

Corollary 7.2.3. Two finite rooted interpreted transition systems are locally bisimilar if and only if they satisfy the same TLR formulae. ∎

7.2.3 Tree Models

Recall the unfolding construction from Section 3.3.3. It implies that any rooted ITS $(\mathcal{T}, s)$ is locally bisimilar to its rooted unfolding $(\widehat{\mathcal{T}}, \widehat{s})$, where $\widehat{s}$ is the 1-state path starting at s. Combining this with Theorem 7.2.1 gives us the tree model property for CTL*.

Corollary 7.2.4. Every satisfiable CTL* state formula has a tree model. ∎

Satisfiability in Uniformly Branching Trees

Thus, we see that the semantics of CTL* (both standard and general) can be restricted to tree-like transition systems. In fact, it turns out that a simple type of uniformly branching trees is sufficient.

Definition 7.2.5. Let $k \in \mathbb{N}$. A k-**branching tree** is a tree in which every node has exactly k successors. A tree that is k-branching for some k is called **uniformly branching**. ▽

It is our goal to show that every satisfiable state formula of CTL* is satisfiable in a uniformly branching tree.

Theorem 7.2.6. Every satisfiable state formula φ in negation normal form of CTL* is satisfiable in a k-branching tree with $k \leq m + 1$, where m is the number of existential path quantifiers occurring in φ. ∎

Proof. Without any loss of generality, we can assume that φ is a simple CTL* formula (see Theorem 7.1.22) with m occurrences of E: $\mathsf{E}\psi_1, \ldots, \mathsf{E}\psi_m$. Let $\mathcal{T} = (S, R, L)$ be a (total) transition system and $s_0 \in S$ be such that $\mathcal{T}, s_0 \models \varphi$. We will build an $(m + 1)$-branching tree transition system $\mathcal{T}' = (S', R', L')$ with $\varepsilon \in S'$ such that $\mathcal{T}', \varepsilon \models \varphi$.

- $S' = [0, m]^*$, i.e. S' is the set of finite sequences built over the finite alphabet $[0, m]$.
- uRv iff there is $i \in [0, m]$ such that $v = u \cdot i$.
- It remains to define the labelling map L' which is done by induction on the length of the states. To do so, we introduce an auxiliary map $\mathfrak{f} : S' \to S$ such that $\mathfrak{f}(\varepsilon) := s_0$ and $L'(\varepsilon) := L(s_0)$. More generally, we require that $L'(u) = L(\mathfrak{f}(u))$ for all $u \in S$.

  Since $\mathcal{T}$ is total, there is an infinite path $\pi = s_0, s_1, s_2, \ldots$ starting at the state s_0. For every $i \geq 1$, we set $\mathfrak{f}((0)^i) := s_i$ and $L'((0)^i) := L(s_i)$.

Now let $u \in S'$ such that $\mathfrak{f}(u)$ is defined (say, equal to r) as well as $L'(u \cdot (0)^i)$ for all $i \geq 0$, but $L'(u \cdot j)$ is undefined ($j \in [1, m]$). If $\mathcal{T}, \mathfrak{f}(u) \not\models \mathsf{E}\psi_j$, then consider an arbitrary infinite path $\pi = r_0, r_1, r_2, \ldots$ starting at the state r. We set $\mathfrak{f}(u \cdot j) = r_1$, $L'(u \cdot j) = L(r_1)$, and for all $i \geq 1$, we set $\mathfrak{f}(u \cdot j \cdot (0)^i) := r_{i+1}$ and $L'(u \cdot j \cdot (0)^i) := L(r_{i+1})$.

If $\mathcal{T}, \mathfrak{f}(u) \models \mathsf{E}\psi_j$ then there is an infinite path $\pi = r_0, r_1, r_2, \ldots$ starting at the state r such that $\mathcal{T}, \pi \models \psi_j$. We set $\mathfrak{f}(u \cdot j) := r_1$, $L'(u \cdot j) := L(r_1)$, and for all $i \geq 1$, $\mathfrak{f}(u \cdot j \cdot (0)^i) := r_{i+1}$ and $L'(u \cdot j \cdot (0)^i) := L(r_{i+1})$.

Now, one can show the following:

- All computations/traces from ε in $\mathcal{T}'$ are also computations in $\mathcal{T}$.
- For all $u \in S'$ and for all $\mathsf{E}\psi_j$, if $\mathcal{T}, \mathfrak{f}(u) \models \mathsf{E}\psi_j$ then $\mathcal{T}', u \models \mathsf{E}\psi_j$.

This allows to conclude that $\mathcal{T}', \varepsilon \models \varphi$ (since φ is a simple CTL* formula). Checking these properties is left as Exercise 7.24. Then, by Theorem 7.1.22 (III), we get that φ is satisfiable in an $(m + 1)$-branching tree.   □

Consequences for Satisfiability Checking

Here we state the complexity results regarding the satisfiability-testing problems for the main branching-time logics.

1. The satisfiability problem for TLR and CTL is in ExpTime and
2. The satisfiability problem for CTL* is in 2ExpTime.

We defer the proofs to later chapters where we use special methods, namely tableaux (Chapter 13), automata (Chapter 14) and games (Chapter 15) to obtain decision procedures for these logics (and others). Here we just remark that the richer structure of branching-time models as opposed to linear-time models makes decision procedures conceptually a bit more difficult, and this is just why we cannot present a procedure comparable to what was done in Chapter 6.

These statements about the complexity of deciding satisfiability are included at the end of this section, on bisimulation invariance, because it is the tree model property and the refined Theorem 7.2.6 which form a starting point for automata-theoretic decision procedures. They allow the satisfiability problem to be reduced to the nonemptiness problem for automata working on infinite trees of fixed branching degree.

We remark that the tableaux for CTL and the games for CTL* we present in those later chapters do not need this result about satisfiability in trees; instead we can derive Theorem 7.2.6 from them. Moreover, we get the finite model property, and even a small model theorem using these methods (including automata). The following hold:

a) Every satisfiable CTL formula has a model of exponential size,
b) Every satisfiable CTL* formula has a model of doubly exponential size.

Here, (double) exponential is to be understood as a function of the size of the underlying formula. For proofs consider, for example, Corollary 13.3.25 and Theorem 15.4.34.

7.3 Model Checking

Unlike satisfiability checking for branching-time logics which needs some technical developments, model checking is in fact very simple. We consider two cases: CTL* and CTL. Clearly, every model-checking procedure for CTL* is also one for CTL. Still it makes sense to consider these two separately: the best known procedures for CTL* require exponential time – the problem is in fact PSPACE-hard (cf. Theorem 11.4.9) – whereas model checking for CTL (and then also for TLR) can be done in polynomial time.

7.3.1 A Reduction from CTL* to LTL

We will show here that, even though CTL* is a branching-time logic, the model-checking problem for it can be reduced to repeated LTL global model checking, by applying a combination of a dynamic programming approach and a simple renaming technique.

Theorem 7.3.1. The model-checking problem for CTL* can be solved in polynomial space. ■

Proof. We sketch a simple, recursive top-down procedure illustrating the method. First, note that the CTL* formulae with no path quantifiers are precisely the LTL formulae. Now, given any CTL* formula φ and a CTL* model $\mathcal{T}$, we identify the maximal state subformulae $\psi_1, \ldots, \psi_n$ of φ starting with a path quantifier and replace them uniformly with new atomic propositions $p_1, \ldots, p_n$.

Here we assume that A is the only primitive path-quantifier in the language of CTL*, whereas E is definable in terms of it. Then each ψ_i is a formula of the type Aχ where χ is a CTL*-formula containing strictly less nested path quantifiers than φ. Substituting $p_1, \ldots, p_n$ for $\psi_1, \ldots, \psi_n$ in φ results in an LTL formula φ'.

Using this procedure recursively, we can globally model check each of $\psi_1, \ldots, \psi_n$ and compute the sets of states $X_1, \ldots, X_n$ in the model $\mathcal{T}$ where each of them is true. Then we modify $\mathcal{T}$ to a model $\mathcal{T}'$ by assigning the atomic propositions $p_1, \ldots, p_n$ to be true respectively in the sets of states $X_1, \ldots, X_n$. Now the global model checking of φ in $\mathcal{T}$ is reduced to the global model checking of the LTL formula φ' in $\mathcal{T}'$.

According to Corollary 6.4.7, global LTL model checking can be done in polynomial space. The space needed for this CTL* model-checking procedure is still polynomial: in addition to the space needed to run the algorithm for LTL, it needs a number of new labels to the states of the underlying transition system that is bounded in the number of path quantifiers of φ. □

Alternatively, the same method can be organised as an inductive bottom-up procedure, by first computing the extensions of the *smallest* state subformulae starting with path

quantifiers and replacing them by fresh atomic propositions, before dealing likewise with
larger formulae. At every such replacement step the number of occurrences of path quantifiers in the formula decreases by 1, which guarantees termination.

Example 7.3.2. Take the formula

$$\varphi = \mathsf{E}\neg\mathsf{F}\mathsf{A}(p\mathsf{U}\mathsf{F}q) \to (\mathsf{E}\mathsf{F}\mathsf{G}\neg q \vee \neg\mathsf{E}\mathsf{G}\mathsf{F}\,\mathsf{A}(p\mathsf{U}\mathsf{F}q))$$

and an arbitrary finite ITS $\mathcal{T}$.

We begin by identifying the smallest state subformulae starting with a path quantifier:
$\varphi_1 = \mathsf{A}(p\mathsf{U}\mathsf{F}q)$ and $\varphi_2 = \mathsf{E}\mathsf{F}\mathsf{G}\neg q$. After replacing these with fresh atomic propositions p_1
and p_2, the resulting formula is $\varphi' = \mathsf{E}\neg\mathsf{F}p_1 \to (p_2 \vee \neg\mathsf{E}\mathsf{G}\mathsf{F}p_1)$. Running the algorithm
for solving $\mathrm{MC}^\exists(\mathrm{LTL})$ on $\mathcal{T}$, φ_2 for every $s \in S$ and running the algorithm for solving
$\mathrm{MC}^\forall(\mathrm{LTL})$ on $\mathcal{T}$, φ_1 for every $s \in S$ produce the valuations of p_1 and p_2 in $\mathcal{T}$. Let $\mathcal{T}'$
be the expansion of $\mathcal{T}$ with these. We now proceed inductively by identifying the small-
est state subformulae starting with a path quantifier in φ': $\varphi_3 = \mathsf{E}\neg\mathsf{F}p_1$ and $\varphi_4 = \mathsf{E}\mathsf{G}\mathsf{F}p_1$.
After replacing these with fresh atomic propositions p_3 and p_4, the resulting formula is
$\varphi'' = p_3 \to (p_2 \vee \neg p_4)$. Running $\mathrm{GMC}^\exists_{\mathrm{LTL}}(\mathcal{T}', \varphi_3)$ and $\mathrm{GMC}^\exists_{\mathrm{LTL}}(\mathcal{T}', \varphi_4)$ produces the valuations of p_3 and p_4 in $\mathcal{T}'$. It remains to model check φ'', which has no more path quantifiers,
in the resulting expansion $\mathcal{T}''$ of $\mathcal{T}'$ with these atomic propositions.

7.3.2 The Labelling Algorithm for CTL

As we mentioned earlier, the logic CTL became a very popular language for specification and verification of transition systems because of its tractable model-checking problem, for which we present a simple algorithm here. Without loss of generality, we can
assume that the only temporal connectives in the language are EX, EU and EG, while AX,
AG and AU are definable (recall Lemma 7.1.2). This does not increase the cost of model
checking beyond polynomial time because the size of a formula is measured in terms of its
number of subformulae and this only grows linearly when rewriting, e.g., an AU using EU
and EG.

The idea of the global model-checking algorithm for CTL is, given an ITS $\mathcal{T}$ and a CTL
formula φ as input, to compute the extension $[\![\varphi]\!]^{\mathcal{T}}$ inductively on the structure of φ by using
the fixpoint characterisations of the temporal operators EU and EG from Theorem 7.1.16.
The pseudocode is given in Algorithm 7.

Lemma 7.3.3. Algorithm MCCTL terminates on every finite transition system and any
CTL formula.   ∎

Proof. There are no recursive descends because the formula argument gets strictly smaller
in each recursive call. Thus, all that is needed for termination of the entire algorithm is
to show that the two repeat-until loops terminate. This is a simple consequence of the
fact that the maps realised in lines 18 and 24 which take a set T and compute a set (that

---

Algorithm 7 An algorithm for global CTL model checking.

1: **procedure** MCCTL($\mathcal{T}, \varphi$)
2:     **case** φ **of**
3:       p: **return** $\{s \in S \mid p \in L(s)\}$ $\triangleright\ p \in$ PROP
4:       $\neg\vartheta$:
5:           $F \leftarrow$ MCCTL($\mathcal{T}, \vartheta$)
6:           **return** $S \setminus F$
7:       $\vartheta_1 \wedge \vartheta_2$:
8:           $F_1 \leftarrow$ MCCTL($\mathcal{T}, \vartheta_1$); $F_2 \leftarrow$ MCCTL($\mathcal{T}, \vartheta_2$)
9:           **return** $F_1 \cap F_2$
10:      EXϑ:
11:          $F \leftarrow$ MCCTL($\mathcal{T}, \vartheta$)
12:          **return** pre(F)
13:      E(ϑ_1Uϑ_2):
14:          $F_1 \leftarrow$ MCCTL($\mathcal{T}, \vartheta_1$); $F_2 \leftarrow$ MCCTL($\mathcal{T}, \vartheta_2$); $T \leftarrow \emptyset$
15:          **repeat**
16:             $T' \leftarrow T$; $T \leftarrow F_2 \cup (F_1 \cap \text{pre}(T))$
17:          **until** $T = T'$
18:          **return** T
19:      EGϑ:
20:          $F \leftarrow$ MCCTL($\mathcal{T}, \vartheta$); $T \leftarrow S$
21:          **repeat**
22:             $T' \leftarrow T$; $T \leftarrow F \cap \text{pre}(T)$
23:          **until** $T = T'$
24:          **return** T
25:     **end case**
26: **end procedure**

---

is then stored in T again) are monotonic with respect to $\subseteq$. The loop in the EU-clause therefore computes an increasing chain of sets of states, while the other one computes a decreasing chain. In a transition systems with n states, the maximal length of such chains is bounded by $n + 1$ before a fixpoint must be reached and the until-condition of the loop applies.   □

Termination is important for the correctness analysis because it means that we can argue by induction. Since the termination argument is closely linked to the structure of the formula to be checked, we can even do induction over the formula.

Lemma 7.3.4. Algorithm MCCTL returns, given a finite transition system $\mathcal{T}$ and a CTL formula φ, the extension $[\![\varphi]\!]^{\mathcal{T}}$.   ■

Proof. Let $\mathcal{T} = (S, R, L)$ be a transition system and φ be a CTL formula. The statement of the lemma can be proved by induction on the structure of φ. All cases are straightforward apart from the two of $\varphi = \mathsf{E}(\vartheta_1 \mathsf{U} \vartheta_2)$ and $\varphi = \mathsf{EG}\vartheta$.

Case $\varphi = \mathsf{E}(\vartheta_1 \mathsf{U} \vartheta_2)$. Let T be the set of states in $\mathcal{T}$ that is returned by MCCTL in the corresponding clause in line 18. We need to show $T = [\![\varphi]\!]^{\mathcal{T}}$ assuming that $F_i = [\![\vartheta_i]\!]^{\mathcal{T}}$ for $i \in \{1, 2\}$.

For the direction '$\supseteq$' assume that $s \in [\![\mathsf{E}(\vartheta_1 \mathsf{U} \vartheta_2)]\!]^{\mathcal{T}}$, i.e. there is a path $s_0, \ldots, s_n$ such that $s = s_0$, $s_n \models \vartheta_2$ and $s_i \models \vartheta_1$ for $i = 0, \ldots, n - 1$. Then we have $s_n \in F_2$ and $s_i \in F_1$ for $i = 0, \ldots, n - 1$. Now note that variable set T contains s_n after the first iteration, s_{n-1} after the second, etc. In general, the ith iteration adds s_{n-i+1} to T. Since the loop only terminates when no more states are being added to T, we get that s is included in the return value of this clause.

For the direction '$\subseteq$' assume that s is included in the return value of this clause. Let T_i be the value of the variable set T *before* the ith iteration of the repeat-until loop, respectively and assume that the nth iteration is the last one to be carried out before the loop terminates. Note the following two facts:

- $T_1 = F_2$,
- for every $i = 2, \ldots, n$ and every $t \in T_i$ we have $t \in F_2$, or $t \in F_1$ and there is a $t' \in T_{i-1}$ such that $t' \in T_{i-1}$.

So if $s \in T_n$ then either $s \models \vartheta_2$ or $s \models \vartheta_1$ and there is an $s' \in T_{n-1}$ with sRs'. This can now be iterated, constructing a path starting in s such that all states either satisfy ϑ_2, or they satisfy ϑ_1 and their successor on this path does the same. The length of this path is bounded by n because any state in T_1 must satisfy ϑ_2. Then this path witnesses that $s \models \mathsf{E}(\vartheta_1 \mathsf{U} \vartheta_2)$.

Case $\varphi = \mathsf{EG}\vartheta$. Again, let T be the set of states returned in line 24, assuming that $F = [\![\vartheta]\!]^{\mathcal{T}}$. We show $T = [\![\varphi]\!]^{\mathcal{T}}$.

Part '$\supseteq$'. Suppose $s \models \mathsf{EG}\vartheta$. Then there is an infinite path $s_0, s_1, \ldots$ of states, all of which satisfy ϑ and are therefore included in F, such that $s_0 = s$. Since $\mathcal{T}$ is assumed to be finite, there are $m' < m$ such that $s_{m'} = s_m$. We now claim that $S^\star := \{s_0, \ldots, s_{m-1}\}$ is included in the value of T after any iteration of the repeat-until loop in this clause of the algorithm. It should be clear that it is included in there *before* the first iteration. Then for every $i = 0, \ldots, m - 1$ we have that s_i has a successor which is in $S^\star$ itself. This is trivial for $s_0, \ldots, s_{m-2}$, and for s_{m-1} it holds because $s_m = s_{m'}$. Note that a new value of T is computed by taking all predecessors of states in T that belong to F. By definition, we have $S^\star \subseteq F$. Hence, if $S^\star$ is included in the value of T before an iteration, then it is so after the iteration. Since $s \in S^\star$, we also get that s is included in the return value in this clause.

Part '$\subseteq$' is proved by contraposition. Suppose that $s \notin [\![\mathsf{EG}\vartheta]\!]^{\mathcal{T}}$, i.e. any path starting in s must eventually hit a state not satisfying ϑ or, equivalently, a state that is not in F. Assuming that $\mathcal{T}$ has n states, it should be clear that such a state must be reached after at most n steps on any path in $\mathcal{T}$. We will show that s is not included in the return value in this case. Define the sets $T'_0, \ldots, T'_n$ as follows: T'_i contains all those states t such that any path starting in t hits a state that does not belong to F after at most i steps. Then we have

- $T'_0 = S \setminus F$,
- for any state t and any $i < n$: if all of t's successors belong to T'_i then t belongs to T'_{i+1}.

The latter means that if some successor of t does not belong to T'_i then t does not belong to T'_{i+1}. Now let $T_i := S \setminus T'_i$. We observe that the T_i are exactly the values of the variable T after the ith iteration of the repeat-until loop: after the first iteration T contains all states that belong to F and have some successor. Since we assume transition systems to be serial, T equals F at this point. In the following iterations, a state t gets eliminated from T if all its successors do not belong to the last value of T.

Now if all paths starting in s hit a state not belonging to F after at most n steps, then we have $s \in T'_n$ by definition and therefore $s \notin T_n$ which means that it cannot belong to the set of states returned by MCCTL in this clause. $\square$

Now we turn to analysis of the time complexity of Algorithm 7. First we note that a naïve implementation of this algorithm, as it is presented here, might have exponential running time. The reason is to be found in the way that the input size is measured. Remember that the size of a formula φ is the number of its distinct subformulae. This corresponds to a DAG representation of formulae in which a subformula can be used in several places but is only stored once. Algorithm 7 would compute the extension of such a subformula twice even though the result is the same in both cases. So what is needed in order to obtain a running time that is linear in the size of the input formula is a mechanism that remembers the results of recursive calls and re-uses them later if necessary. This can be done using **labelling**.

Let φ be given and $\psi_1, \ldots, \psi_k$ be all its subformulae in order of increasing size. W.l.o.g. we can assume ψ_1 to be an atomic proposition. Hence, the states of the underlying $\mathcal{T}$ that satisfy ψ_1 are already labelled with ψ_1. Algorithm MCCTLLABEL successively extends the state labels with $\psi_1, \ldots, \psi_k$. It uses a procedure MCCTL' which is very similar to MCCTL but instead of recursive calls it maintains these labels. It is obtained from MCCTL by applying the following modifications.

- Replace the clause for atomic propositions by a 'skip' step.
- Replace every recursive call MCCTL$(\mathcal{T}, \psi)$ by $\{s \in S \mid \psi \in L(s)\}$.
- Replace every statement of the form '**return** T' by

  for all $s \in T$ **do**
      $L(s) \leftarrow L(s) \cup \{\varphi\}$
  end for

where φ is the formula that the case-statements switch on.

Then the CTL labelling algorithm for global model checking becomes:

1: **procedure** MCCTLLABEL($\mathcal{T}, \varphi$)
2:     let $\psi_1, \ldots, \psi_k$ be φ's subformulae in ascending order of size
3:     **for** $i = 1, \ldots, n$ **do**
4:         MCCTL'($\mathcal{T}, \psi_i$)
5:     **end for**
6: **end procedure**

Lemma 7.3.5. For any ITS $\mathcal{T}$ and any CTL formula φ, Algorithms MCCTL and MCCTLLABEL compute the same result.   ∎

We leave the proof of this lemma as Exercise 7.37.

Theorem 7.3.6. The global model-checking problem for CTL can be solved in time linear both in the size of the input formula and the size of the transition system. More precisely, given a finite ITS $\mathcal{T} = (S, R, L)$ and a CTL formula φ, the extension $[\![\varphi]\!]^{\mathcal{T}}$ can be computed in time $\mathcal{O}(\mathrm{card}(R) \cdot |\varphi|)$.   ∎

Proof. Lemma 7.3.5 transfers the correctness of Algorithm MCCTL to MCCTLLABEL. Thus, all we need to do is to analyse its running time. Clearly, it takes $|\varphi|$ many iterations of the loop through all subformulae. Now all that is needed is to see that a single call to MCCTL' can be made to run in time $\mathcal{O}(\mathrm{card}(R) + \mathrm{card}(S))$, i.e. in time $\mathcal{O}(\mathrm{card}(R))$ since $\mathcal{T}$ is total. This should be clear for the cases of atomic propositions and Boolean formulae. Computing $\mathrm{pre}(F)$ for a given F can be done in time $\mathcal{O}(\mathrm{card}(R))$. Finally, the repeat-until loops in the cases of EU- and EG-formulae can also be made to run in time $\mathcal{O}(\mathrm{card}(R))$ because they can be implemented such that every transition is only considered once by starting with F_2 for instance and then successively visiting predecessors.   □

Corollary 7.3.7. GMC(CTL) is in PTIME.   ∎

Example 7.3.8. Consider the ITS $\mathcal{T}$ in Figure 7.5. Using the algorithm for GMC(CTL) we can compute the following.

$$[\![p \wedge \mathsf{EX}\neg q]\!] = \{s_2, s_3\}$$
$$[\![\mathsf{AX}(p \wedge \mathsf{EX}\neg q)]\!] = \{s_1, s_2\}$$
$$[\![\mathsf{EG}\neg q]\!] = \{s_3\}$$
$$[\![\mathsf{AG}(p \vee \neg q)]\!] = \{s_2, s_6\}$$
$$[\![\mathsf{E}(q\mathsf{U}(p \wedge \mathsf{EX}\neg q))]\!] = \{s_1, s_2, s_3, s_4\}$$
$$[\![\mathsf{A}(q\mathsf{U}(p \wedge \mathsf{EX}\neg q))]\!] = \{s_1, s_2, s_3\}.$$

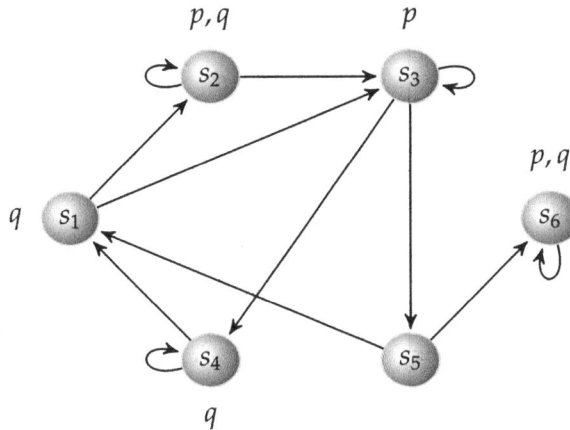

Figure 7.5 The ITS for Example 7.3.8.

7.3.3 A Verification Example

For an easy but useful example of the application of model checking CTL and CTL* to program verification we revisit Dijkstra's mutual exclusion problem (MEP) from Section 3.1.3. It is about two concurrent processes using a common resource. Only one of them can access the resource at a time, and then that process is said to be in its *critical section*. So, only one process can be in a critical section at any time instant. At the start each process is in noncritical section and whenever a process is in a noncritical section it can keep trying to enter a critical section arbitrarily often. The problem is to design a 'mutual exclusion' protocol prescribing the possible runs of the system and satisfying several requirements, such as:

- **Safety:** both processes may not be in a critical section at the same time.
- **Nonblocking:** if a process is not in a critical section, it can try to enter it at a next state.
- **Liveness:** if a process ever tries to enter a critical section, then it will eventually enter it.
- **Fairness:** if a process keeps trying to enter a critical section, then it will eventually enter it.
- **No strict alternation:** the processes need not enter their critical sections in strict alternation.

We are now in a position to formalise these requirements in the branching-time logics introduced here. Recall that we introduced the following special atomic propositions, for $i = 1, 2$:

- N_i: process i is in noncritical section.
- T_i: process i is trying (requesting) to enter a critical section.
- C_i: process i is in critical section.

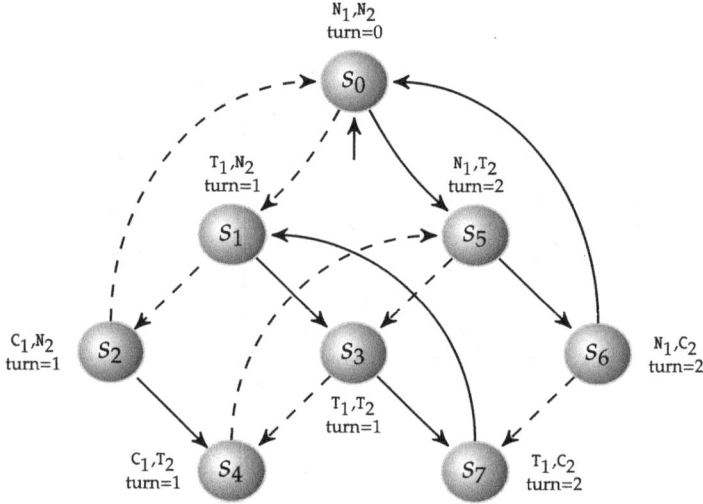

Figure 7.6 The ITS from Section 3.1.3 modelling a mutual exclusion protocol. Legend: N = noncritical, T = trying, C = critical.

Using these, we can formalise some of the earlier requirements as follows:

- **Safety:** $AG\neg(C_1 \wedge C_2)$.
- **Nonblocking:** $AG(N_1 \to EX\, T_1) \wedge AG(N_2 \to EX\, T_2)$.
- **Liveness:** $AG(T_1 \to AF\, C_1) \wedge AG(T_2 \to AF\, C_2)$.

Note that all of these are in CTL. In fact, the formulae **Safety** and **Nonblocking** are even in TLR.

The transition system $\mathcal{T}_{MEP}^1$ in Figure 7.6 was presented in Section 3.1.3 as a model of a possible protocol for the MEP, by specifying the possible states and transitions of the system. The transitions where process 1 changes status are given with dashed lines, and those where process 2 changes status are given with solid lines. We check whether the formally specified requirements are satisfied by this model. Running the labelling algorithm for GMC(CTL) from the previous section, we find that $\mathcal{T}_{MEP}^1$ satisfies **Safety** and **Nonblocking** at the initial state s_0, but does not satisfy any of the two **Liveness** conditions there. The reason, intuitively speaking, is that one of the processes can be held in a state in which it requests to enter the critical section forever, without ever entering in it. Thus, the protocol modelled by the ITS $\mathcal{T}_{MEP}^1$ in Figure 3.5 is not a good solution of the MEP. A revised version $\mathcal{T}_{MEP}^2$ of that protocol is presented in Figure 7.7.

Running the labelling algorithm for GMC(CTL) again, we find that $\mathcal{T}_{MEP}^2$ now satisfies all **Safety** and **Nonblocking** and **Liveness** conditions at the initial state s_0, so it solves the problem we found with $\mathcal{T}_{MEP}^1$. However, we have not specified yet any fairness conditions

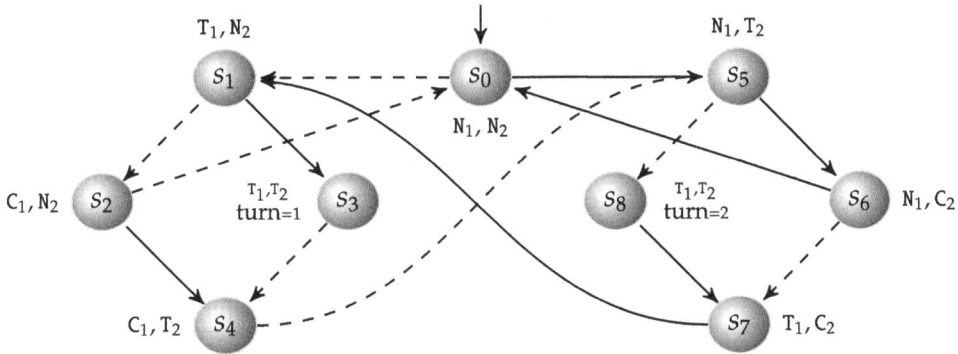

Figure 7.7 The ITS $\mathcal{T}_{MEP}^2$ modelling the revised mutual exclusion protocol. Legend: N = noncritical, T = trying, C = critical.

for the mutual exclusion protocol yet. Various fairness requirements can be specified in CTL* and then verified. Some examples of such fairness requirements are the following.

- **Fair1:** $\mathsf{AG}(T_1 \to F^\infty C_1)$, and likewise $\mathsf{AG}(T_2 \to F^\infty C_2)$.
- **Fair2:** $\mathsf{AG}(F^\infty T_1 \to F^\infty C_1)$, and likewise $\mathsf{AG}(F^\infty T_2 \to F^\infty C_2)$.
- **Fair3:** $\mathsf{AG}(F^\infty T_1 \to EF^\infty C_1)$, and likewise $\mathsf{AG}(F^\infty T_2 \to EF^\infty C_2)$.
- **Fair4:** $\mathsf{AG}(F^\infty T_1 \to AF^\infty C_1)$, and likewise $\mathsf{AG}(F^\infty T_2 \to AF^\infty C_2)$.

We invite the reader to contemplate how these conditions are ordered in terms of their logical strength, i.e. which implies which of them, and also which of these conditions can be assumed reasonable and which of them are too strong to impose.

When running the algorithm for GMC(CTL*) on $\mathcal{T}_{MEP}^2$ we find that it satisfies the conditions **Fair2–Fair4**, but not **Fair1**. We leave it as an exercise to verify these claims.

7.4 Some Fragments and Extensions of CTL*

We present a selection of fragments of CTL* introduced with the motivation to optimise the balance between expressiveness and computational complexity. Some of them, like ECTL and CTL^2 are more expressive than CTL while still having tractable (i.e. solvable in poly-nomial time) model-checking problems. Others, like CTL^+ or CTL_{lp}^* allow some properties to be expressed much more concisely than it is possible using CTL. This section also aims at contributing to a better understanding of how the path quantifiers and the temporal oper-ators interact in CTL*.

It is worth noting that the expressive power of linear time logics such as LTL or ETL can naturally be characterised with respect to other standard formalisms such as first-order logic (Kamp's Theorem) or Büchi automata. For branching-time temporal logics such char-acterisations are more rare. Thus, comparisons are rather made within the world of temporal logics, see Chapter 10 for a more detailed discussion thereof.

7.4.1 Adding Fairness Operators

Let ECTL denote the extension of CTL with the additional temporal operators EF^∞ and AF^∞. Intuitively, $EF^\infty\varphi$ states that there is a computation on which φ holds true infinitely often; AF^∞ demands this for all computations starting in a state at hand.

The semantics of these operators can be inherited from CTL* because of $F^\infty\varphi := GF\varphi$, or it can be defined explicitly as expected:

$$\mathcal{T}, s \models EF^\infty\varphi \quad \text{iff} \quad \text{there is an infinite path } \pi \text{ starting from } s$$
$$\text{such that for every } i \geq 0, \text{ there is } j \geq i \text{ with } \mathcal{T}, \pi(j) \models \varphi$$
$$\mathcal{T}, s \models AF^\infty\varphi \quad \text{iff} \quad \text{for all paths } \pi \text{ starting from } s \text{ and every } i \geq 0$$
$$\text{there is a } j \geq i \text{ such that } \mathcal{T}, \pi(j) \models \varphi.$$

The operators AG^∞ and EG^∞ are defined as duals of these. See Exercise 7.31 for some new validities and nonvalidities in ECTL.

It is natural to ask whether ECTL is more expressive than CTL. Indeed, we cannot a priori exclude the possibility that the operators EF^∞ and AF^∞ could be expressed in CTL by some clever encoding. This, actually, is the case for the second one: if φ is a state formula then we have $AGF\varphi \equiv AGAF\varphi$. Hence, the addition of the operator for fairness along *all* computations to CTL does *not* increase its expressive power. However, fairness along *some* computation is, in fact, not expressible in CTL, and thus, ECTL is really a stronger logic than CTL.

Proposition 7.4.1. There is no CTL formula φ such that $\varphi \equiv EF^\infty p$. ■

Consequently, ECTL $\not\subseteq$ CTL (see also Section 4.3). The proof is deferred to Chapter 10, see Theorem 10.3.7. In that chapter we present a general technique for proving such inexpressibility results. We invite the reader to contemplate why such a technique might be necessary, in particular why a proof could not just consider two transition systems such that $EGFq$ holds in one but not the other. The reason is that they would have to differ essentially in their behaviour in order to realise this. But then this difference could be pointed out using a simple formula of BML already. So there is no chance of showing that any CTL formula does not distinguish between them.

It should be clear that, as a consequence of Proposition 7.4.1, there is also no CTL formula φ that is equivalent to $AFGp$. This shows that there are properties which can be expressed in LTL but not in CTL.

The polynomial-time labelling algorithm for GMC(CTL) can easily be adapted to GMC(ECTL) (Exercise 7.30). Indeed, to handle the case of formulae of the type $EF^\infty\varphi$ it is sufficient to compute the strongly connected components in the ITS in which at least one state satisfies φ, and then compute all the states that can reach such components. Thus, we obtain the following.

Proposition 7.4.2. GMC(ECTL) is in PTIME. ■

7.4.2 From LTL Formulae to Branching-Time Logics

Recall that, while the syntax of CTL* permits path quantifiers applied to path formulae built with arbitrary combinations of linear time operators, in CTL formulae a path quantifier must be immediately followed by a single temporal operator only. A natural relaxation of that restriction is the extension ECTL which also allows the combination GF of two linear-time operators in such positions. Going further down that road, one can allow path quantifiers to be immediately followed by *any* combination of at most two linear-time operators, possibly negated. The resulting fragment is called CTL^2. For instance, $EG(pUp')$ is a formula in CTL^2 but not in CTL. Similarly, $E\neg(pU(p'Up''))$ is also a formula in CTL^2, but not in CTL. However, we will see that the latter formula has an equivalent formula in CTL, while the former one does not. Thus, CTL^2 is strictly more expressive than ECTL (see the forthcoming Corollary 7.4.3). However, we will see later that it still has tractable model checking. Can we strengthen it further while preserving tractability of model checking? The answer is *Yes*. Actually, it turns out that we can add any finite number of patterns with combinations of temporal operators and the resulting fragment of CTL* will still have that desirable property.

Here we present more formally a general scheme of defining such fragments of CTL* and will prove that model checking each of them is possible in polynomial time. The proof of this more general result is postponed to Exercise 7.35 but here we will illustrate the key ideas for the case of CTL^2.

A General Framework

First we rewrite the semantics of the CTL operator EU in a way slightly different from that in Section 7.1.3, viz. in an 'LTL-based style':

$\mathcal{T}, s \models E\varphi_1 U\varphi_2$ iff there is an infinite path π in $\mathcal{T}$ such that $\pi(0) = s$ and $\sigma, 0 \models p_1 U p_2$
    where

(i) p_1 and p_2 are auxiliary new atomic propositions,
(ii) σ is an LTL model built over π for the language extended with p_1 and p_2, such that each p_i, for $i \in \{1, 2\}$, is true precisely at those positions on π at which the state formula φ_i is true in $\mathcal{T}$. Formally, for each $k \geq 0$, $p_i \in \sigma(k)$ iff $\pi(k) \in \llbracket \varphi_i \rrbracket^{\mathcal{T}}$. All other atomic propositions inherit their truth valuations from $\mathcal{T}$.

The semantics of the temporal operator AU can be redefined likewise.

Now we generalise this. Let PROP be a fixed set of atomic propositions and let $p_1, \ldots, p_N \notin$ PROP be auxiliary new atomic propositions. Consider any LTL formula ϑ built over $p_1, \ldots, p_N$. We can turn this formula into two temporal connectives of arity N, $E\vartheta$ and $A\vartheta$, producing state formulae of CTL*. The LTL-style of semantic definition of EU readily extends to the semantics of the operator $A\vartheta$ as follows. For any ITS $\mathcal{T}$ over the set PROP, state $s \in \mathcal{T}$, and state formulae $\varphi_1, \ldots, \varphi_N$ we define:

$\mathcal{T}, s \models E\vartheta(\varphi_1, \ldots, \varphi_N)$ iff there is an infinite path π in $\mathcal{T}$ such that $\pi(0) = s$ and $\sigma, 0 \models$
    $\vartheta(p_1, \ldots, p_N)$, where σ is the LTL model for the language over PROP extended with

$p_1, \ldots, p_N$, built over π so that all atomic propositions in PROP inherit their truth valuations in σ from $\mathcal{T}$ and each p_i, for $i \in \{1, \ldots, N\}$, is true precisely at those positions on π at which the state formula φ_i is true in $\mathcal{T}$. Formally, for each $k \geq 0$, $p_i \in \sigma(k)$ iff $\pi(k) \in [\![\varphi_i]\!]^{\mathcal{T}}$.

The semantics of the connective $A\vartheta$ is defined likewise.

Clearly, $E\vartheta(\varphi_1, \ldots, \varphi_N)$ and $A\vartheta(\varphi_1, \ldots, \varphi_N)$ are CTL* state formulae for any CTL* state formulae $\varphi_1, \ldots, \varphi_N$. Thus, adding $E\vartheta$ and $A\vartheta$ to CTL produces a fragment of CTL*. More generally, any finite set of LTL formulae $\{\vartheta_1, \ldots, \vartheta_M\}$ induces such a fragment of CTL* obtained by inductively extending propositional logic PL with the pair of connectives $E\vartheta$ and $A\vartheta$ for each $\vartheta_1, \ldots, \vartheta_M$, with semantics defined as earlier. We denote that fragment of CTL* by $BT(\vartheta_1, \ldots, \vartheta_M)$. Thus, the formulae of that fragment are defined with the abstract grammar:

$$\varphi ::= \bot \mid p \mid (\varphi \wedge \varphi) \mid \neg\varphi \mid$$
$$E\vartheta_1(\varphi, \ldots, \varphi) \mid \cdots \mid E\vartheta_M(\varphi, \ldots, \varphi) \mid$$
$$A\vartheta_1(\varphi, \ldots, \varphi) \mid \cdots \mid A\vartheta_M(\varphi, \ldots, \varphi).$$

For instance, the logic BML corresponds to $BT(\vartheta_1)$, CTL corresponds to $BT(\vartheta_1, \vartheta_2)$ and its extension ECTL corresponds to $BT(\vartheta_1, \vartheta_2, \vartheta_3)$, where

$$\vartheta_1 := Xp_1, \quad \vartheta_2 := p_1 U p_2, \quad \vartheta_3 := GF p_1.$$

We may also write $BT(X)$ for BML, $BT(X, U)$ for CTL and $BT(X, U, F^\infty)$ for ECTL. By using the duality between the path quantifiers E and A and the fact that formulae are closed under negation, it is easy to show that $BT(\vartheta_1, \ldots, \vartheta_M)$ is expressively equivalent to $BT(\vartheta_1, \ldots, \vartheta_M, \neg\vartheta_1, \ldots, \neg\vartheta_M)$.

The Logic CTL²

As a particular case of the general scheme presented earlier, now we can define the fragment CTL² of CTL*. **CTL²** is defined as the logic $BT(\vartheta_1, \ldots, \vartheta_M)$ so that $\{\vartheta_1, \ldots, \vartheta_M\}$ contains a subset of LTL formulae

- with at most *two* occurences of temporal operators X and U and
- every atomic proposition is in the scope of some temporal operator.

A formal and precise definition will follow. The first condition is the essential one, while the second condition is added to limit the cardinality of the set $\{\vartheta_1, \ldots, \vartheta_M\}$ satisfying the first condition, without restricting the expressiveness. For instance,

$$E(p_1 \wedge X(p_2 U \neg\neg p_3)) \equiv p_1 \wedge EX(p_2 U p_3)$$

and therefore there is no need to consider $\vartheta = p_1 \wedge X(p_2 U \neg\neg p_3)$ since $X(p_2 U p_3)$ suffices. Alternatively, formulae from CTL² can be defined by using the following abstract grammar where φ ranges over the set of (state) formulae for CTL², ϑ_1 ranges over path formulae with exactly one outermost linear operator and ϑ_2 ranges over path formulae with exactly two

$$\mathsf{E}\,\mathsf{X}\mathsf{X}p_1 \equiv \mathsf{E}\mathsf{X}\,\mathsf{E}\mathsf{X}\,p_1$$

$$\mathsf{A}\,\mathsf{X}\mathsf{X}p_1 \equiv \mathsf{A}\mathsf{X}\,\mathsf{A}\mathsf{X}\,p_1$$

$$\mathsf{E}\,\mathsf{X}(p_1\mathsf{U}p_2) \equiv \mathsf{E}\mathsf{X}\,\mathsf{E}(p_1\,\mathsf{U}\,p_2)$$

$$\mathsf{E}\,\mathsf{X}\neg(p_1\mathsf{U}p_2) \equiv \mathsf{E}\mathsf{X}\,\neg\mathsf{A}(p_1\,\mathsf{U}\,p_2)$$

$$\mathsf{A}\,\mathsf{X}(p_1\mathsf{U}p_2) \equiv \mathsf{A}\mathsf{X}\,\mathsf{A}(p_1\,\mathsf{U}\,p_2)$$

$$\mathsf{A}\,\mathsf{X}\neg(p_1\mathsf{U}p_2) \equiv \neg\mathsf{E}\mathsf{X}\,\mathsf{E}(p_1\,\mathsf{U}\,p_2)$$

$$\mathsf{E}\,p_1\mathsf{U}(\mathsf{X}p_2) \equiv \mathsf{E}(p_1\,\mathsf{U}\,\mathsf{E}\mathsf{X}\,p_2)$$

$$\mathsf{A}\,p_1\mathsf{U}(\mathsf{X}p_2) \equiv \mathsf{A}\mathsf{X}p_2 \vee (p_1 \wedge \mathsf{A}\mathsf{X}\mathsf{A}(p_1\,\mathsf{U}\,(p_2 \vee \mathsf{A}\mathsf{X}p_2)))$$

$$\mathsf{E}\,p_1\mathsf{U}(p_2\mathsf{U}p_3) \equiv \mathsf{E}(p_1\,\mathsf{U}\,\mathsf{E}(p_2\mathsf{U}p_3))$$

$$\mathsf{A}\,p_1\mathsf{U}(p_2\mathsf{U}p_3) \equiv \mathsf{A}(p_1\,\mathsf{U}(\mathsf{A}(p_2\mathsf{U}p_3)))$$

$$\mathsf{E}\,p_1\mathsf{U}\neg(p_2\mathsf{U}p_3) \equiv \mathsf{E}(p_1\,\mathsf{U}\,\neg\mathsf{A}(p_2\,\mathsf{U}\,p_3))$$

$$\mathsf{E}\,(\mathsf{X}p_1)\mathsf{U}p_2 \equiv p_2 \vee \mathsf{E}\mathsf{X}\,\mathsf{E}(p_1\,\mathsf{U}\,(p_1 \wedge p_2))$$

$$\mathsf{A}\,(\mathsf{X}p_1)\mathsf{U}p_2 \equiv \mathsf{A}(\mathsf{A}\mathsf{X}\,p_1)\mathsf{U}p_2$$

$$\mathsf{E}\,(p_1\mathsf{U}p_2)\mathsf{U}p_3 \equiv p_3 \vee \mathsf{E}((p_1 \vee p_2)\,\mathsf{U}((p_2 \wedge \mathsf{E}\mathsf{X}p_3) \vee (p_3 \wedge \mathsf{E}(p_1\mathsf{U}p_2))))$$

$$\mathsf{A}\,(p_1\mathsf{U}p_2)\mathsf{U}p_3 \equiv \mathsf{A}(\mathsf{A}(p_1\mathsf{U}p_2)\mathsf{U}p_3)$$

$$\mathsf{E}\,(\neg(p_1\mathsf{U}p_2))\mathsf{U}p_3 \equiv p_3 \vee \mathsf{E}(\neg p_2 \,\mathsf{U}\,((\neg p_1 \wedge \neg p_2 \wedge \mathsf{E}\mathsf{X}\,p_3) \vee (p_3 \wedge \neg\mathsf{A}(p_1\,\mathsf{U}\,p_2))))$$

$$\mathsf{A}\,(\neg(p_1\mathsf{U}p_2))\mathsf{U}p_3 \equiv \mathsf{A}(\neg\mathsf{E}(p_1\,\mathsf{U}\,p_2)\,\mathsf{U}\,p_3)$$

Figure 7.8 Expressing CTL^2 formulae in CTL.

outermost linear operators. Note that we have applied a few simplifications that do not affect the expressive power (for example, by using the duality between E and A), while providing a better and more operational definition for further analysis.

$$\varphi ::= \bot \mid p \mid (\varphi \wedge \varphi) \mid \neg\varphi \mid \mathsf{E}\vartheta_2 \mid \mathsf{A}\vartheta_2$$

$$\vartheta_2 ::= \vartheta_1 \mid \mathsf{X}\vartheta_1 \mid (\varphi\mathsf{U}\vartheta_1) \mid (\vartheta_1\mathsf{U}\varphi) \mid (\vartheta_1 \wedge \vartheta_1) \mid (\vartheta_1 \vee \vartheta_1)$$

$$\vartheta_1 ::= \mathsf{X}\varphi \mid (\varphi\mathsf{U}\varphi) \mid \neg(\varphi\mathsf{U}\varphi).$$

Many temporal connectives defined in CTL^2 have equivalents in CTL, which shall be explained next.

Expressive Power

In Figure 7.8, we present the translation of temporal connectives from CTL^2 into CTL (we omit the obvious ones obtained from path formulae of degree 1 that are already in CTL). Similarly, in Figure 7.8, we omit the temporal connectives obtained from the clauses '$\vartheta_1 \wedge \vartheta_1$' or '$\vartheta_1 \vee \vartheta_1$' since they can be handled in CTL thanks to the results for CTL^+ in Section 10.2.3. So, it is almost possible to translate CTL^2 into CTL. This is based on the observation that CTL^2 can be defined as a temporal logic of the form $BT(\vartheta_1, \ldots, \vartheta_M)$, possibly with about 36 temporal connectives. In that respect, the list of equivalences in Figure 7.8 is incomplete since we have not provided any equivalent CTL formula for the CTL^2 formula $A\, p_1 U \neg (p_2 U p_3)$. If we were able to provide such an equivalent formula, the temporal logic CTL^2 would be as expressive as CTL. However, we cannot do this because

$$\neg EGFq \equiv AFG\neg q \equiv A(TU\neg(TUq)).$$

Hence, if $A(TU\neg(TUq))$ was expressible in CTL then so would be its negation, and therefore also $EGFq$, which would contradict Proposition 7.4.1. This yields the following consequence.

Corollary 7.4.3. CTL is strictly weaker than CTL^2, i.e. $CTL \sqsubset CTL^2$. ■

On the other hand, CTL^2 is not that much more expressive than CTL.

Theorem 7.4.4. CTL^2 is equally expressive to the extension of CTL with the temporal connective EGU, i.e. to $BT(X, U, Gp_1Up_2)$. ■

Proof. It is easily checked that the equivalences in Figure 7.8 hold. They can be used to successively turn a CTL^2 formula into a $BT(X, U, Gp_1Up_2)$ formula. The temporal connectives obtained from the clauses '$\vartheta_1 \wedge \vartheta_1$' or '$\vartheta_1 \vee \vartheta_1$' can be handled in CTL thanks to the results for CTL^+ in Section 10.2.3. □

Model Checking

The translation of CTL^2 into CTL augmented with the binary temporal connective EGU opens a possibility for model checking CTL^2 based on an algorithm for CTL. Note that the translation increases the size of a formula linearly. Then one can extend the model-checking algorithm for CTL presented in Section 7.3.2, to formulae whose outermost connective is EGU. This amounts to looking for a simple property on the graph of the transition system.

Lemma 7.4.5. Let $T = (S, R, L)$ be a finite ITS and $s \in S$. Then $T, s \models EG(pUq)$ iff there is an s' that belongs to some nontrivial strongly connected component X from the graph (S', R') obtained by restricting T to states satisfying either p or q, there is a state in X satisfying q, and there is a path from s to s' such that all states on it satisfy p or q. ■

We leave the proof as Exercise 7.37. Strongly connected components can be computed in time linear in the number of edges of a graph, for instance using Tarjan's algorithm. Hence, we get the following result.

Theorem 7.4.6. The model-checking problem for CTL^2 can be solved in polynomial time. ■

A generalisation of this result is discussed in Exercise 7.35: the model-checking problem for $BT(\vartheta_1, \ldots, \vartheta_M)$ when $\vartheta_1, \ldots, \vartheta_M$ generates a fixed set of temporal connectives can be solved in polynomial time in a uniform way.

7.4.3 Boolean Combinations of Path Formulae

Here we assume that CTL has four temporal connectives, namely the unary temporal connectives EX and AX, and the binary temporal connectives EU and AU. Recall that while EX and AX are dual to each other, this is not the case for EU and AU.

Boolean Combinations of Path Formulae

CTL^+ extends CTL by allowing path quantification on any *Boolean combination* of path formulae starting with single temporal operators. More precisely, we define **state formulae** φ and **path formulae** ϑ of CTL^+ using the following grammar:

$$\varphi ::= \bot \mid p \mid \neg\varphi \mid (\varphi \wedge \varphi) \mid E\vartheta \mid A\vartheta$$
$$\vartheta ::= \neg\vartheta \mid (\vartheta \wedge \vartheta) \mid X\varphi \mid (\varphi U\varphi)$$

where $p \in \text{PROP}$. As usual, $\vee$, $\rightarrow$ and $\leftrightarrow$ are assumed definable and $F\varphi$ is a shortcut for $\top U\varphi$ and $G\varphi$ is a shortcut for $\neg F\neg\varphi$. In the context of CTL^+ we can assume further that $A\vartheta$ is defined as $\neg E\neg\vartheta$. While this equivalence cannot be used in CTL because $E\neg\vartheta$ would not be anymore a syntactically correct CTL formula, this is fine in CTL^+.

Examples of CTL^+ formulae which are not CTL formulae include $E(Fp \wedge Fq)$ and $A(pUq \vee \neg Fr)$. On the other hand, $E((AFp) \vee (pUq))$ and $A((pUq)Ur)$ are CTL^* formulae which are not CTL^+ formulae.

It is also easy to show that the fragment of CTL^* consisting of all LTL formulae prefixed by path quantifiers is not included in CTL^+. Actually, CTL^+ includes the union of all the temporal logics $BT(\vartheta)$ (see definition in Section 7.4.2) where ϑ is an LTL formula of modal depth 1, i.e. with no nestings of temporal operators.

Even though CTL^+ is syntactically much larger than CTL, the following holds.

Proposition 7.4.7. Every CTL^+ formula is equivalent to a CTL formula. Thus, CTL^+ is as expressive as CTL. ∎

We restate this claim as Theorem 10.2.12 in Chapter 10 and provide a detailed proof there.

An interesting question that arises with equi-expressiveness is that of **succinctness**. The translation from CTL^+ to CTL in the proof of Theorem 10.2.12 involves an exponential blow-up. Thus, there are CTL^+ formulae which get translated into relatively large CTL formulae. Succinctness asks whether this is necessary. The answer is *Yes*.

Theorem 7.4.8. There is a family $(\varphi_n)_{n \geq 1}$ of CTL^+ formulae, growing linearly in size, such that no family $(\psi_n)_{n \geq 1}$ of CTL formulae which grow polynomially is such that φ_n and ψ_n are equivalent for all $n \geq 1$. ∎

Proof. In the proof of Theorem 11.3.4 we construct such a family of CTL^+ formulae. It is easy to check that their size is only linear in n. It requires a little bit more insight into the constructions explained in this proof to see that these φ_n are in fact satisfiable (depending on the choice of the underlying *tiling system*) and that they cannot be satisfied in a model of size smaller than $2^n \cdot 2^{2^n}$. In Corollary 13.3.25 we will show that CTL, on the other hand, has the small model property of exponential size, i.e. every satisfiable CTL formula is satisfied in a model that is at most exponentially larger than the formula. Combining these yields the succinctness gap: any family $(\psi_n)_{n \geq 1}$ of CTL formulae which satisfies $\psi_n \equiv \varphi_n$ for all n must have an exponential growth in formula size in order to satisfy the requirement that their smallest models are doubly exponentially larger in n.   □

Model Checking

Given the expressive equivalence of CTL$^+$ and CTL, it turns out somewhat surprisingly that the satisfiability problem for CTL$^+$ has the same worst-case complexity as the satisfiability problem for the full CTL*, i.e. 2ExpTime-complete (see Section 11.4.2). On the other hand, the model-checking problem for CTL$^+$ is Δ_2^p-complete. The complexity class Δ_2^p belongs to the **polynomial-time hierarchy** and can be defined as the class of decision problems solvable by a deterministic polynomial-time Turing machine querying an NP set oracle (so it is equivalent to PTime ^{NP}). This complexity is likely to be strictly in between the complexity of model checking for CTL (PTime-complete) and that of CTL* (PSpace-complete), which confers upon CTL$^+$ a special status among the family of branching-time temporal logics.

Theorem 7.4.9. The model-checking problem for CTL$^+$ is in Δ_2^p.   ■

Proof. We have seen in Exercise 6.34 that MC(LTL^1(X, U)) can be solved in NP. By using the inductive bottom-up procedure from the proof of Theorem 7.3.1 for CTL* but applied to CTL$^+$ formulae, one can observe that the instances of the model-checking problem for LTL are indeed those for MC(LTL^1(X, U)). Since the number of calls to such a subroutine is polynomial in the size of the input formula and since MC(LTL^1(X, U)) is in NP, we can conclude that MC(CTL$^+$) is in PTime ^{NP}, i.e. in the complexity class Δ_2^p from the polynomial-time hierarchy.   □

Since CTL$^+$ allows Boolean combinations of path formulae, CTL$^+$ formulae might be more handy to express simple properties, even though CTL$^+$ is equally expressive with CTL. The natural price to pay would be to get a computationally more expensive model-checking problem. However, recall that for any fixed finite set $\vartheta_1, \ldots, \vartheta_M$ of LTL formulae of modal depth one, $B(\vartheta_1, \ldots, \vartheta_M)$ is a fragment of CTL* but with a polynomial-time model-checking problem (see Exercise 7.35).

Adding Fairness to CTL$^+$

An obvious shortcoming of ECTL is the lack of ability to express Boolean combinations of fairness properties of the form $E(F^\infty p_1 \wedge \ldots \wedge F^\infty p_n)$. This is a strong motivation to consider the extension ECTL$^+$, roughly obtained by augmenting the temporal patterns on which Boolean combinations can be path quantified in CTL$^+$ with the linear-time temporal operator F^∞, that is also present in ECTL. Similarly, **strong fairness** conditions can be expressed by formulae of the type $A(F^\infty$ enabled $\rightarrow F^\infty$ executed$)$.

We formally define **state formulae** φ and **path formulae** ϑ of ECTL$^+$ by mutual recursion using the grammar

$$\varphi ::= \bot \mid p \mid \neg\varphi \mid (\varphi \wedge \varphi) \mid \mathsf{E}\vartheta \mid \mathsf{A}\vartheta$$
$$\vartheta ::= \neg\vartheta \mid (\vartheta \wedge \vartheta) \mid \mathsf{X}\varphi \mid (\varphi\mathsf{U}\varphi) \mid \mathsf{F}^\infty\varphi$$

where $p \in \text{PROP}$. Note that the only difference with the definition for CTL$^+$ is the addition of the clause $\mathsf{F}^\infty\varphi$. Thus, formulae of CTL can be relativised in ECTL$^+$ with any kind of fairness conditions imposed as Boolean combinations of temporal path formulae.

It can be proved that ECTL$^+$ is strictly more expressive than CTL$^+$ and ECTL but less expressive than CTL*.

Theorem 7.4.10. The following strict inclusions hold with regards to expressive power.

  (I) CTL$^+$ $\sqsubset$ ECTL$^+$,
  (II) ECTL $\sqsubset$ ECTL$^+$,
 (III) ECTL$^+$ $\sqsubset$ CTL*.   ■

Proof. The inclusions are trivial. Regarding their strictness, (I) is an immediate consequence of the fact that CTL$^+$ is only as expressive as CTL (Proposition 7.4.7) and that it cannot express $\mathsf{EF}^\infty q$ (Proposition 7.4.1).

(II) It can be shown that the ECTL$^+$ property $\mathsf{E}(\mathsf{F}^\infty p \wedge \mathsf{F}^\infty q)$ cannot be expressed in ECTL. A formal proof is provide in Theorem 10.3.15 in Chapter 10.

(III) Theorem 10.3.16 in Chapter 10 shows that $\mathsf{AF}(q \wedge \mathsf{X}q)$ is not expressible in ECTL$^+$. □

Another example of a CTL* formula that cannot be expressed in ECTL$^+$ is $\mathsf{E}(p \vee (p'\mathsf{U}q'))\mathsf{U}r$.

The model-checking problem for ECTL$^+$ is of the same complexity as that for CTL$^+$. It can be solved using a polynomial algorithm that makes calls to a subroutine which solves a problem in NP.

Theorem 7.4.11. The model-checking problem for ECTL$^+$ is in Δ_2^p.   ■

The proof of Theorem 7.4.11 is similar to the proof of Theorem 7.4.9 by showing that $\text{MC}(\text{LTL}^1(\mathsf{X}, \mathsf{U}, \mathsf{F}^\infty))$ is NP, which extends the main result from Exercise 6.34.

7.4.4 Adding Operators for a Linear Past

We present a syntactic extension of CTL* with past-time operators 'Y' ('previous') and 'S' (since). Their interpretation is analogous to the one for LTL+Past, see Section 6.5. Whereas the past-time extension of LTL does not alter the class of models, adding past-time operators in a branching-time setting leads to several reasonable options for representing the past. Here we assume *tree-like representations* with a finite and linear past whereas the future is

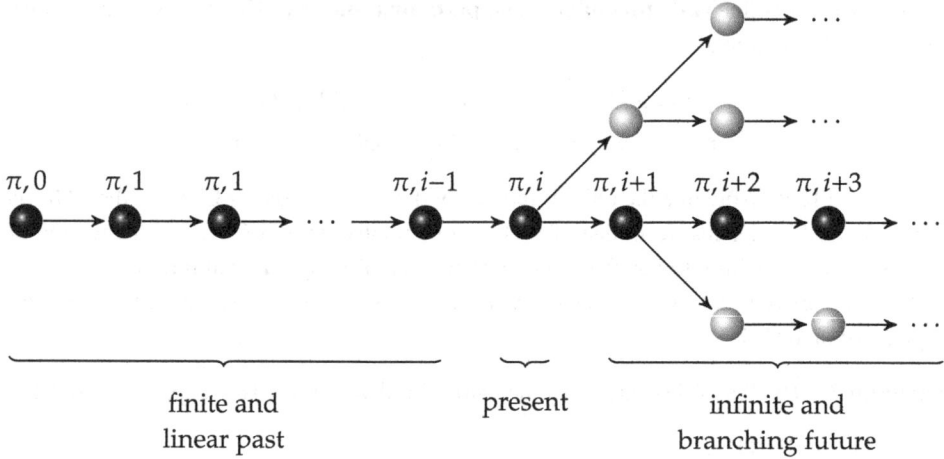

infinite and possibly branching. Usually this is referred to as **Ockhamist past**. Figure 7.9 illustrates how past is dealt with in the extension CTL$^*_{lp}$ of CTL* with linear past.

The formulae for CTL$^*_{lp}$ are defined according to the following grammar.

$$\varphi ::= \bot \mid p \mid (\varphi \wedge \varphi) \mid \neg\varphi \mid \mathsf{X}\varphi \mid (\varphi\mathsf{U}\varphi) \mid \mathsf{E}\varphi \mid \mathsf{A}\varphi \mid \mathsf{Y}\varphi \mid (\varphi\mathsf{S}\varphi)$$

where $p \in \text{PROP}$. As in LTL+Past, we use $\mathsf{F}^{-1}\varphi$ as an abbreviation for $\top\mathsf{S}\varphi$ and $\mathsf{G}^{-1}\varphi$ as an abbreviation for $\neg\mathsf{F}^{-1}\neg\varphi$.

The semantics for CTL$^*_{lp}$ is based again on transition systems but the truth of a CTL$^*_{lp}$ formula is evaluated relative to a path and a position in $\mathbb{N}$ along the path, as follows.

$\mathcal{T}, \pi, i \models p$	iff	$p \in L(\pi(i))$
$\mathcal{T}, \pi, i \models \neg\varphi$	iff	not $\mathcal{T}, \pi, i \models \varphi$
$\mathcal{T}, \pi, i \models \varphi \wedge \psi$	iff	$\mathcal{T}, \pi, i \models \varphi$ and $\mathcal{T}, \pi, i \models \psi$
$\mathcal{T}, \pi, i \models \mathsf{E}\varphi$	iff	there is a path $\mathcal{T}, \pi'$ such that $\mathcal{T}, \pi[0, i] = \pi'[0, i]$ and $\mathcal{T}, \pi', i \models \varphi$
$\mathcal{T}, \pi, i \models \mathsf{X}\varphi$	iff	$\mathcal{T}, \pi, i+1 \models \varphi$
$\mathcal{T}, \pi, i \models \varphi\mathsf{U}\psi$	iff	there is $j \geq i$ such that $\mathcal{T}, \pi, j \models \psi$ and for every $k \in [i, j-1]$ we have $\mathcal{T}, \pi, k \models \varphi$
$\mathcal{T}, \pi, i \models \mathsf{Y}\varphi$	iff	$i > 0$ and $\mathcal{T}, \pi, i-1 \models \varphi$
$\mathcal{T}, \pi, i \models \varphi\mathsf{S}\psi$	iff	there is $j \leq i$ such that $\mathcal{T}, \pi, j \models \psi$ and for every $k \in [j-1, i]$ we have $\mathcal{T}, \pi, k \models \varphi$.

Thus, while the satisfaction relation for CTL* only involves a path and a formula, the satisfaction relation for CTL$^*_{lp}$ also involves a position on that path. This semantics illustrates the idea that in CTL$^*_{lp}$, the past is finite, determined and cumulative, in the following sense. This reflects the fact that program computations have a definite starting time. A different semantics would be obtained on paths of order type similar to $\mathbb{Z}$. Determination of the past is given by the fact that it is linear. Finally, past is cumulative since nothing is forgotten along the path; it contains all the positions that have already been visited.

The next statement relates the semantics of CTL* formulae to their semantics when read as CTL^*_{lp} formulae. A formal proof is left as Exercise 7.37.

Lemma 7.4.12. For any CTL* state formula φ, ITS $\mathcal{T}$, path π in $\mathcal{T}$ and any position $i \in \mathbb{N}$ the following are equivalent.

(I) $\mathcal{T}, \pi, i \models \varphi$ in CTL^*_{lp}.
(II) $\mathcal{T}, \pi[i, \infty), 0 \models \varphi$ in CTL^*_{lp}.
(III) $\mathcal{T}, \pi[i, \infty) \models \varphi$ in CTL*. ∎

Consequently, a state formula in CTL* is satisfiable in CTL* iff it is satisfiable in CTL^*_{lp} which means that CTL^*_{lp} is a conservative extension of CTL*, i.e. does not change the set of validities of CTL*.

The addition of past-time operators to CTL* has a significant effect on the complexity of model checking as the following states.

Proposition 7.4.13. The model-checking problem for CTL^*_{lp} is in 2ExpTime. ∎

The proof is not presented here, see the bibliographic notes.

Expressiveness

In order to compare the expressiveness of CTL* and CTL^*_{lp} (more generally, between a temporal logic without past-time operators and its extension with past-time operators), it is necessary to align their semantics in a 'fair' way. Note that the notion of logical equivalence between two CTL^*_{lp} formulae φ and ψ induced by the semantics of CTL^*_{lp} would require that $\mathcal{T}, \pi, i \models \varphi$ iff $\mathcal{T}, \pi, i \models \psi$ for every ITS $\mathcal{T}$, for all paths π in $\mathcal{T}$ and for all positions $i \in \mathbb{N}$. Clearly, since CTL* formulae are indifferent to the past, it cannot be expected in general that a given CTL^*_{lp} formula is logically equivalent in that sense to a CTL* formula, so this notion is too strong and does not provide a good ground for comparing the expressiveness of CTL* and CTL^*_{lp}. A more suitable notion for that purpose is that of **initial equivalence**. We say that two formulae φ and ψ in CTL^*_{lp}, are **initially logically equivalent**, denoted $\varphi \equiv_0 \psi$, iff for every ITS $\mathcal{T}$ and for all paths π in $\mathcal{T}$, we have $\pi, 0 \models \varphi$ iff $\pi, 0 \models \psi$. Note that initial equivalence is quite adequate in the framework of computer systems, such as reactive systems, since specifications are usually defined from an initial configuration. It turns out that in terms of initial equivalence CTL^*_{lp} does not really add expressive power to CTL*, but it is more convenient for expressing some specifications.

Proposition 7.4.14. For every CTL^*_{lp} formula φ, there is a CTL* formula φ' which is initially equivalent to φ. ∎

The proof is long and tedious and will not be presented here; consult the bibliographic notes for a reference.

The Fragment CTL_{lp}

The extension CTL_{lp} of the logic CTL with past operators can be defined as the fragment of CTL_{lp}^* consisting of those formulae in which every occurrence of a temporal operator is immediately preceded by a path quantifier. More precisely, the set of CTL_{lp} formulae can be defined by the following grammar.

$$\varphi ::= p \mid \varphi \wedge \varphi \mid \neg\varphi \mid \mathsf{EX}\varphi \mid \mathsf{AX}\varphi \mid \mathsf{E}(\varphi\mathsf{U}\varphi) \mid \mathsf{A}(\varphi\mathsf{U}\varphi) \mid \mathsf{Y}\varphi \mid (\varphi\mathsf{S}\varphi).$$

Note that, since the past is linear and all formulae referring to the future are state formulae, there is no need to quantify over paths when applying past operators Y and S. In contrast to Proposition 7.4.14, adding past-time operators to CTL strictly increases its expressive power. For a pointer to a proof consider the bibliographic notes.

Proposition 7.4.15. Not every CTL_{lp} formula is initially equivalent to a CTL formula. ∎

Let us consider the CTL_{lp} formula

$$\mathsf{EG}(p \vee \mathsf{Y}p \vee \neg\mathsf{Y}\top).$$

It is initially logically equivalent to the CTL* formula $\mathsf{EG}(p \vee \mathsf{X}p)$ that is notoriously known not to have an equivalent formula in ECTL^+, and therefore in CTL. This is the idea to prove Proposition 7.4.15.

The following result indicates a (very likely) substantial increase of complexity of the model checking for CTL_{lp} over that for CTL.

Proposition 7.4.16. The model-checking problem for CTL_{lp} is in PSPACE. ∎

This bound is tight since the problem can also be shown to be PSPACE-hard, see Chapter 11 for a discussion on complexity-theoretic hardness. Hardness already occurs for the small fragment of CTL_{lp} using only F^{-1} and X.

7.5 Axiomatic Systems

For technical simplicity we will only consider a language for mono-transition systems. The extensions to the general case of many transitions of the axiomatic systems presented here are routine.

7.5.1 A Proof System for TLR

For the language of TLR we can now assume for technical convenience that the primitive temporal operators are AX, AG and the others are definable as usual.

An axiomatic system $\mathrm{AxSys_{TLR}}$ for the set of valid formulae of TLR extends $\mathrm{AxSys_{BML}}$ with one axiom needed to ensure seriality of the transition relation, as usually required, plus two axiom schemes and one rule of inference for the coverability operator AG. The axioms of $\mathrm{AxSys_{TLR}}$ are all instances of the following schemes.

(BML)	All axiom schemes of $\text{AxSys}_{\text{BML}}$
(K_{AX})	$AX(\varphi \rightarrow \psi) \rightarrow (AX\varphi \rightarrow AX\psi)$
(SER)	$EX\top$
(PostFP_{AG})	$AG\varphi \rightarrow \varphi \wedge AXAG\varphi$
(GFP_{AG})	$AG(\psi \rightarrow (\varphi \wedge AX\psi)) \rightarrow (\psi \rightarrow AG\varphi).$

The rules of inference are **Modus Ponens** (MP) and the rules of **Necessitation**:

$$\text{Nec}_{AX} \quad \frac{\vdash \varphi}{\vdash AX\varphi} \qquad \text{Nec}_{AG} \quad \frac{\vdash \varphi}{\vdash AG\varphi}.$$

The axiom PostFP_{AG} says that $AG\varphi$ is a **post-fixpoint** of the operator Γ_{AG} defined by '$\Gamma_{AG}(\vartheta) = \varphi \wedge AX\vartheta$', whereas GFP_{AG} says that $AG\varphi$ is (in terms of its extension) a **greatest post-fixpoint** of Γ_{AG}. As we show further, in Lemma 7.5.1, item (VII), the axioms imply something stronger, namely that $AG\varphi$ is a **greatest fixpoint** of the respective operators (recall Theorem 7.1.16). Note that GFP_{AG} generalises the following **induction axiom**.

(IND): $AG(\varphi \rightarrow AX\varphi) \rightarrow (\varphi \rightarrow AG\varphi)$.

In fact, the axiom GFP_{AG} can be replaced by the following induction rule, easily derivable in the axiomatic system:

IND-Rule: If $\vdash \psi \rightarrow \varphi \wedge AX\psi$ then $\vdash \psi \rightarrow AG\varphi$.

Note also that the rule **Nec$_{AX}$** can be replaced by an additional axiom scheme $AG\varphi \rightarrow AX\varphi$ which, in turn, is derivable in the system $\text{AxSys}_{\text{TLR}}$ (see Lemma 7.5.1).

All basic notions related to derivations and derivability, defined for $\text{AxSys}_{\text{BML}}$ in Section 5.7, apply likewise to $\text{AxSys}_{\text{TLR}}$. In particular, deductive consequence from a set of assumptions in $\text{AxSys}_{\text{TLR}}$ is defined likewise, where the rules **Nec** can be applied in derivations in $\text{AxSys}_{\text{TLR}}$ to any theorem (in particular, any axiom) of $\text{AxSys}_{\text{TLR}}$, but *not* to the other assumptions.

Since $\text{AxSys}_{\text{TLR}}$ is an extension of $\text{AxSys}_{\text{BML}}$, all derivable formulae and rules in $\text{AxSys}_{\text{BML}}$ listed in Section 5.7 are derivable in $\text{AxSys}_{\text{TLR}}$, as well. Besides, the Deduction Theorem, as stated for $\text{AxSys}_{\text{BML}}$ in Section 5.7 holds here likewise. Moreover, we list some additional useful facts about $\text{AxSys}_{\text{TLR}}$ in the following proposition, in the proof of which we will illustrate derivations in $\text{AxSys}_{\text{TLR}}$. Most of them are quite similar to those in $\text{AxSys}_{\text{LTL}}$, see Section 6.8.

Lemma 7.5.1. The following are derivable in $\text{AxSys}_{\text{TLR}}$.

(I) $AG\varphi \rightarrow AX\varphi$

(II) AG-monotonicity rule **AG-Mon**:
   if $\vdash_{\text{AxSys}_{\text{TLR}}} \varphi \rightarrow \psi$ then $\vdash_{\text{AxSys}_{\text{TLR}}} AG\varphi \rightarrow AG\psi$.

(III) $AXAG\varphi \rightarrow AGAX\varphi$

(IV) $\varphi \wedge AGAX\varphi \rightarrow AG\varphi$

(V) $AGAX\varphi \rightarrow AXAG\varphi$

(VI) K_{AG}: $AG(\varphi \to \psi) \to (AG\varphi \to AG\psi)$

(VII) FP_{AG}: $AG\varphi \leftrightarrow (\varphi \land AXAG\varphi)$

(VIII) FP_{EF}: $EF\varphi \leftrightarrow (\varphi \lor EXEF\varphi)$

(IX) LFP_{EF}: $AG((\varphi \lor EX\psi) \to \psi) \to (EF\varphi \to \psi)$.   ∎

Proof. We will sketch some of the derivations in $AxSys_{TLR}$, skipping some easy steps done in PL. We will omit the subscript $AxSys_{TLR}$.

(I) $\vdash AG\varphi \to AX\varphi$:

1.1	$\vdash AG\varphi \to (\varphi \land AXAG\varphi)$	by Axiom (PostFP$_{AG}$) and PL
1.2	$\vdash AG\varphi \to \varphi$	by 1.1 and PL
1.3	$\vdash AG\varphi \to AXAG\varphi$	by 1.1 and PL
1.4	$\vdash AX(AG\varphi \to \varphi)$	by 1.2 and **Nec$_{AX}$**
1.5	$\vdash AX(AG\varphi \to \varphi) \to (AXAG\varphi \to AX\varphi)$	by Axiom (K$_{AX}$)
1.6	$\vdash AXAG\varphi \to AX\varphi$	by 1.4, 1.5 and **MP**
1.7	$AG\varphi \vdash AXAG\varphi$	by 1.3 and the Deduction Theorem
1.8	$AG\varphi \vdash AX\varphi$	by 1.6, 1.7 and **MP**
1.9	$\vdash AG\varphi \to AX\varphi$	by 1.8 and the Deduction Theorem

(II) Assume $\vdash \varphi \to \psi$.

2.1	$\vdash AG\varphi \to \varphi$	by Axiom (PostFP$_{AG}$) and PL
2.2	$\vdash AG\varphi \to \psi$	by 1.1, assumption and PL
2.3	$\vdash AG\varphi \to AXAG\varphi$	by Axiom (PostFP$_{AG}$)
2.4	$\vdash AG\varphi \to \psi \land AXAG\varphi$	by 2.2, 2.3 and PL
2.5	$\vdash AG(AG\varphi \to \psi \land AXAG\varphi)$	by 2.4 and **Nec$_{AG}$**
2.6	$\vdash AG(AG\varphi \to \psi \land AXAG\varphi) \to (AG\varphi \to AG\psi)$	by Axiom (GFP$_{AG}$)
2.7	$\vdash AG\varphi \to AG\psi$	by 2.5, 2.6 and **MP**

(III) $\vdash AXAG\varphi \to AGAX\varphi$:

3.1	$\vdash AG\varphi \to \varphi \land AXAG\varphi$	by Axiom (PostFP$_{AG}$)
3.2	$\vdash AXAG\varphi \to AX(\varphi \land AXAG\varphi)$	by 3.1, Axiom (FP$_{AX}$), **Nec$_{AX}$** and PL
	(See also Proposition 5.7.2.)	
3.3	$\vdash AX(\varphi \land AXAG\varphi) \to (AX\varphi \land AXAXAG\varphi)$	by Axiom (FP$_{AX}$) and PL
	(See also Proposition 5.7.2.)	
3.4	$\vdash AXAG\varphi \to AX\varphi \land AXAXAG\varphi$	by 3.2, 3.3 and PL
3.5	$\vdash AG(AXAG\varphi \to AX\varphi \land AXAXAG\varphi)$	by 3.4 and **Nec$_{AG}$**
3.6	$\vdash AG(AXAG\varphi \to AX\varphi \land AXAXAG\varphi) \to (AXAG\varphi \to AGAX\varphi)$	
	by Axiom (GFP$_{AG}$)	
3.7	$\vdash AXAG\varphi \to AGAX\varphi$	by 3.5, 3.6 and **MP**

(IV) $\vdash \varphi \land AGAX\varphi \to AG\varphi$: this is left as Exercise 7.38.

(V) $\vdash AGAX\varphi \to AXAG\varphi$:

5.1	$\vdash \varphi \land AGAX\varphi \to AG\varphi$	by (IV)
5.2	$\vdash AX(\varphi \land AGAX\varphi \to AG\varphi)$	by 5.1 and **Nec$_{AX}$**
5.3	$\vdash AX(\varphi \land AGAX\varphi) \to AXAG\varphi$	by 5.2, Axiom (K$_{AX}$) and PL

5.4 $\vdash (\mathsf{AX}\varphi \wedge \mathsf{AXAGAX}\varphi) \to \mathsf{AX}(\varphi \wedge \mathsf{AGAX}\varphi)$ by Axiom ($\mathsf{K_{AX}}$) and PL

5.5 $\vdash (\mathsf{AX}\varphi \wedge \mathsf{AXAGAX}\varphi) \to \mathsf{AXAG}\varphi$ by 5.2, 5.3 and PL

5.6 $\vdash \mathsf{AGAX}\varphi \to \mathsf{AX}\varphi \wedge \mathsf{AXAGAX}\varphi$ by Axiom ($\mathsf{PostFP_{AG}}$)

5.7 $\vdash \mathsf{AGAX}\varphi \to \mathsf{AXAG}\varphi$ by 5.5, 5.6 and PL

(VI) $\mathsf{K_{AG}}$: $\mathsf{AG}(\varphi \to \psi) \to (\mathsf{AG}\varphi \to \mathsf{AG}\psi)$

    6.1 $\vdash \mathsf{AG}\varphi \to \varphi \wedge \mathsf{AXAG}\varphi$ by Axiom ($\mathsf{PostFP_{AG}}$)

    6.2 $\varphi \to \psi \vdash \mathsf{AG}\varphi \to \varphi \wedge \mathsf{AXAG}\varphi$ by 6.1

    6.3 $\varphi \to \psi \vdash \mathsf{AG}\varphi \to \psi \wedge \mathsf{AXAG}\varphi$ by 6.2 and PL

    6.4 $\vdash (\varphi \to \psi) \to (\mathsf{AG}\varphi \to \psi \wedge \mathsf{AXAG}\varphi)$ by 6.3 and Deduction Theorem

    6.5 $\vdash \mathsf{AG}(\varphi \to \psi) \to \mathsf{AG}(\mathsf{AG}\varphi \to \psi \wedge \mathsf{AXAG}\varphi)$ by AG-**Mon**

    6.6 $\vdash \mathsf{AG}(\mathsf{AG}\varphi \to \psi \wedge \mathsf{AXAG}\varphi) \to (\mathsf{AG}\varphi \to \mathsf{AG}\psi)$ by Axiom ($\mathsf{PostFP_{AG}}$)

    6.7 $\vdash \mathsf{AG}(\varphi \to \psi) \to (\mathsf{AG}\varphi \to \mathsf{AG}\psi)$ by 6.5, 6.6 and PL

We leave the last three derivations as Exercise 7.38. The derivation of (VII) is very similar to the derivation of $\mathsf{G}\varphi \leftrightarrow (\varphi \wedge \mathsf{XG}\varphi)$ in $\mathrm{AxSys_{LTL}}$, see Section 6.8. The remaining two derivations can easily be extracted from the respective axioms for AG by using the duality with EF. $\qquad\qquad\Box$

7.5.2 A Proof System for CTL

For the language of CTL we can assume that the primitive temporal operators are AX, EU, AU and the others are definable as usual. In particular, recall that $\mathsf{EF}\varphi := \mathsf{E}(\top\mathsf{U}\varphi)$, $\mathsf{AF}\varphi := \mathsf{A}(\top\mathsf{U}\varphi)$, $\mathsf{AG}\varphi := \neg\mathsf{EF}\neg\varphi$, $\mathsf{EG}\varphi := \neg\mathsf{AF}\neg\varphi$.

An axiomatic system $\mathrm{AxSys_{CTL}}$ for the valid formulae of CTL can be obtained by replacing the axioms $\mathsf{FP_{AG}}$ and $\mathsf{GFP_{AG}}$ in $\mathrm{AxSys_{TLR}}$ with the respective fixpoint axioms for EU and AU:

(BML)	All axiom schemes of $\mathrm{AxSys_{BML}}$
($\mathsf{K_{AX}}$)	$\mathsf{AX}(\varphi \to \psi) \to (\mathsf{AX}\varphi \to \mathsf{AX}\psi)$
(SER)	$\mathsf{EX}\top$
($\mathsf{PreFP_{EU}}$)	$(\psi \vee (\varphi \wedge \mathsf{EXE}(\varphi\mathsf{U}\psi))) \to \mathsf{E}(\varphi\mathsf{U}\psi)$
($\mathsf{PreFP_{AU}}$)	$(\psi \vee (\varphi \wedge \mathsf{AXA}(\varphi\mathsf{U}\psi))) \to \mathsf{A}(\varphi\mathsf{U}\psi)$
($\mathsf{LFP_{EU}}$)	$\mathsf{AG}((\psi \vee (\varphi \wedge \mathsf{EX}\chi)) \to \chi) \to (\mathsf{E}(\varphi\mathsf{U}\psi) \to \chi)$
($\mathsf{LFP_{AU}}$)	$\mathsf{AG}((\psi \vee (\varphi \wedge \mathsf{AX}\chi)) \to \chi) \to (\mathsf{A}(\varphi\mathsf{U}\psi) \to \chi).$

Note that the axioms for EU and AU can also be obtained by replacing the axioms for U in $\mathrm{AxSys_{LTL}}$ (see Section 6.8) with their path-quantified versions. The respective axioms for the definable operators EF and AF extracted from the axiomatic system $\mathrm{AxSys_{CTL}}$ are as follows:

($\mathsf{PreFP_{EF}}$)	$(\psi \vee \mathsf{EXEF}\psi) \to \mathsf{EF}\psi$
($\mathsf{PreFP_{AF}}$)	$(\psi \vee \mathsf{AXAF}\psi) \to \mathsf{AF}\psi$
($\mathsf{LFP_{EF}}$)	$\mathsf{AG}((\psi \vee \mathsf{EX}\chi) \to \chi) \to (\mathsf{EF}\psi \to \chi)$
($\mathsf{LFP_{AF}}$)	$\mathsf{AG}((\psi \vee \mathsf{AX}\chi) \to \chi) \to (\mathsf{AF}\psi \to \chi).$

The axiom PreFP$_{\mathsf{EU}}$ says that $\mathsf{E}(\varphi \mathsf{U} \psi)$ is a **pre-fixpoint** (see Definition 2.2.2) of the operator Γ_{EU} defined by '$\Gamma_{\mathsf{EU}}(\vartheta) := \psi \vee (\varphi \wedge \mathsf{EX}\vartheta)$', whereas LFP$_{\mathsf{EU}}$ says that $\mathsf{E}(\varphi \mathsf{U} \psi)$ is a least pre-fixpoint of Γ_{EU}. Likewise, the axioms PreFP$_{\mathsf{AU}}$ and LFP$_{\mathsf{AU}}$ state that $\mathsf{A}(\varphi \mathsf{U} \psi)$ is a least pre-fixpoint of the respective operator Γ_{AU} defined by '$\Gamma_{\mathsf{AU}}(\vartheta) := \psi \vee (\varphi \wedge \mathsf{AX}\vartheta)$'. As we indicate further, in Proposition 7.5.2, the axioms imply something stronger, namely that $\mathsf{E}(\varphi \mathsf{U} \psi)$ and $\mathsf{A}(\varphi \mathsf{U} \psi)$ are least fixpoints of the respective operators (recall Theorem 7.1.16).

Again, all basic notions related to derivations and derivability apply likewise to AxSys$_{\mathsf{CTL}}$. We will denote derivability in AxSys$_{\mathsf{CTL}}$ by $\vdash_{\mathrm{AxSys}_{\mathsf{CTL}}}$ and within this subsection we will sometimes omit the subscript.

We state some useful claims about AxSys$_{\mathsf{CTL}}$.

Proposition 7.5.2. The following are derivable in AxSys$_{\mathsf{CTL}}$.

$$
\begin{array}{ll}
\text{FP}_{\mathsf{EU}} & \mathsf{E}(\varphi \mathsf{U} \psi) \leftrightarrow (\psi \vee (\varphi \wedge \mathsf{EXE}(\varphi \mathsf{U} \psi))) \\
\text{FP}_{\mathsf{AU}} & \mathsf{A}(\varphi \mathsf{U} \psi) \leftrightarrow (\psi \vee (\varphi \wedge \mathsf{AXA}(\varphi \mathsf{U} \psi))) \\
\text{FP}_{\mathsf{AG}} & \mathsf{AG}\varphi \leftrightarrow (\psi \wedge \mathsf{AXAG}\varphi) \\
\text{GFP}_{\mathsf{AG}} & \psi \wedge \mathsf{AG}(\psi \rightarrow (\varphi \wedge \mathsf{X}\psi)) \rightarrow \mathsf{AG}\varphi \\
\text{FP}_{\mathsf{EG}} & \mathsf{EG}\varphi \leftrightarrow (\varphi \wedge \mathsf{EXEG}\varphi) \\
\text{GFP}_{\mathsf{EG}} & \psi \wedge \mathsf{EG}(\psi \rightarrow (\varphi \wedge \mathsf{X}\psi)) \rightarrow \mathsf{EG}\varphi.
\end{array}
$$

■

Proof. We will sketch the derivation of FP$_{\mathsf{EU}}$ in AxSys$_{\mathsf{CTL}}$, skipping some easy steps done in BML. In particular, we will use the following theorem of AxSys$_{\mathsf{BML}}$, derived in Example 5.7.3: $\vdash_{\mathrm{AxSys}_{\mathsf{BML}}} \mathsf{AX}(p \rightarrow q) \rightarrow (\mathsf{EX}p \rightarrow \mathsf{EX}q)$. Hereafter we omit the subscript AxSys$_{\mathsf{CTL}}$.

To derive $\mathsf{E}(\varphi \mathsf{U} \psi) \leftrightarrow (\psi \vee (\varphi \wedge \mathsf{EXE}(\varphi \mathsf{U} \psi)))$ it suffices to derive the implication from left to right, since the other is Axiom (PreFP$_{\mathsf{EU}}$). Let us denote $\chi := (\psi \vee (\varphi \wedge \mathsf{EXE}(\varphi \mathsf{U} \psi)))$. The idea is to apply Axiom (LFP$_{\mathsf{EU}}$) for this ϑ.

$$
\begin{array}{lll}
1 & \vdash \chi \rightarrow \mathsf{E}(\varphi \mathsf{U} \psi) & \text{by Axiom (PreFP}_{\mathsf{EU}}) \\
2 & \vdash \mathsf{AX}(\vartheta \rightarrow \mathsf{E}(\varphi \mathsf{U} \psi)) & \text{by 1 and } \mathbf{Nec_{AX}} \\
3 & \vdash \mathsf{AX}(\vartheta \rightarrow \mathsf{E}(\varphi \mathsf{U} \psi)) \rightarrow (\mathsf{EX}\vartheta \rightarrow \mathsf{EXE}(\varphi \mathsf{U} \psi)) & \text{by theorem of AxSys}_{\mathsf{BML}}, \\
 & & \text{Example 5.7.3} \\
4 & \vdash \mathsf{EX}\chi \rightarrow \mathsf{EXE}(\varphi \mathsf{U} \psi) & \text{by 2,3 and } \mathbf{MP} \\
5 & \vdash \varphi \wedge \mathsf{EX}\chi \rightarrow \varphi \wedge \mathsf{EXE}(\varphi \mathsf{U} \psi) & \text{by 4 and PL} \\
6 & \vdash \varphi \wedge \mathsf{EX}\chi \rightarrow \psi \vee (\varphi \wedge \mathsf{EXE}(\varphi \mathsf{U} \psi)), & \\
 & \quad \text{i.e.} \vdash \varphi \wedge \mathsf{EX}\chi \rightarrow \chi & \text{by 5 and PL} \\
7 & \vdash \psi \rightarrow \chi & \text{by PL} \\
8 & \vdash \psi \vee (\varphi \wedge \mathsf{EX}\chi) \rightarrow \vartheta & \text{by 6,7 and PL} \\
9 & \vdash \mathsf{AG}(\psi \vee (\varphi \wedge \mathsf{EX}\chi) \rightarrow \chi) & \text{by 8 and } \mathbf{Nec_{AG}} \\
10 & \vdash \mathsf{AG}(\psi \vee (\varphi \wedge \mathsf{EX}\vartheta) \rightarrow \chi) \rightarrow (\mathsf{E}(\varphi \mathsf{U} \psi) \rightarrow \chi) & \text{by Axiom (LFP}_{\mathsf{EU}}) \\
11 & \vdash \mathsf{E}(\varphi \mathsf{U} \psi) \rightarrow \chi & \text{by 9, 10 and } \mathbf{MP}
\end{array}
$$

The other derivations are similar and left as Exercise 7.38.   □

Proposition 7.5.3. The following rules of inference are derivable in AxSys$_{\text{CTL}}$:

(E-Ind) If $\vdash \psi \vee (\varphi \wedge \mathsf{EX}\chi) \rightarrow \chi$ then $\vdash \mathsf{E}(\varphi\mathsf{U}\psi) \rightarrow \chi$,
(A-Ind) If $\vdash \psi \vee (\varphi \wedge \mathsf{AX}\chi) \rightarrow \chi$ then $\vdash \mathsf{A}(\varphi\mathsf{U}\psi) \rightarrow \chi$.

Furthermore, the axioms LFP$_{\mathsf{EU}}$ and LFP$_{\mathsf{AU}}$ of AxSys$_{\text{CTL}}$ can be derived from the rest of AxSys$_{\text{CTL}}$ using these additional rules of inference. $\blacksquare$

Thus, the axioms LFP$_{\mathsf{EU}}$ and LFP$_{\mathsf{AU}}$ can be replaced in AxSys$_{\text{CTL}}$ by the respective rules of inference in the preceding proposition.

7.5.3 Properties of AxSys$_{TLR}$ and AxSys$_{CTL}$

Like for the previous axiomatic systems, the soundness and completeness for AxSys$_{\text{TLR}}$ and AxSys$_{\text{CTL}}$ can be stated in two different forms.

Proposition 7.5.4. The axiomatic systems AxSys$_{\text{TLR}}$ and AxSys$_{\text{CTL}}$ are sound and weakly complete, i.e.:

(I) For every finite set of TLR formulae $\{\varphi_1, \ldots, \varphi_n, \varphi\}$:

$$\varphi_1, \ldots, \varphi_n \vdash_{\text{AxSys}_{\text{TLR}}} \psi \text{ if and only if } \varphi_1, \ldots, \varphi_n \models \psi.$$

(II) For every finite set of CTL formulae $\{\varphi_1, \ldots, \varphi_n, \varphi\}$:

$$\varphi_1, \ldots, \varphi_n \vdash_{\text{AxSys}_{\text{CTL}}} \psi \text{ if and only if } \varphi_1, \ldots, \varphi_n \models \psi.$$

Equivalently, every set of TLR (respectively, CTL) formulae is satisfiable if and only if it is consistent in AxSys$_{\text{TLR}}$ (respectively, AxSys$_{\text{CTL}}$). $\blacksquare$

Remark 7.5.5. Like LTL, the logics TLR and CTL are **not compact**, meaning that TLR, and hence CTL too, contains infinite sets of formulae which are not satisfiable but every finite subset of them is satisfiable. Indeed, such a set of TLR formulae is $\{\mathsf{EF}\neg p, p, \mathsf{AX}p, \mathsf{AXAX}p \ldots \mathsf{AX}^n p, \ldots\}$. It is clearly unsatisfiable, but it is AxSys$_{\text{TLR}}$-consistent, because any derivation of a contradiction, say $\bot$, would only involve finitely many of these formulae, but every finite set of the type

$$\{\mathsf{EF}\neg p, p, \mathsf{AX}p, \mathsf{AXAX}p \ldots \mathsf{AX}^n p\}$$

is clearly satisfiable, and therefore must be AxSys$_{\text{TLR}}$-consistent. That is why only *weak completeness* with respect to a finite set of formulae holds for TLR and CTL.

Given the soundness of AxSys$_{\text{BML}}$, in order to prove the soundness of each of AxSys$_{\text{TLR}}$ and AxSys$_{\text{CTL}}$ it suffices to show that the new axiom scheme consists of valid formulae and that the necessitation rules preserve validity, which we leave as Exercise 7.39.

We are not going to prove the completeness part of Proposition 7.5.4 here. Both TLR and CTL are not canonical and, like for AxSys$_{\text{LTL}}$, the completeness proof starts with

building a canonical ITS but it does not validate the fixpoint axioms for the temporal operators, so additional constructions and further steps are needed. References to such proofs
of completeness can be found in the bibliographic notes. An alternative approach is to
reduce the proof of Proposition 7.5.4 to the proof of soundness and completeness of the
systems of semantic tableaux developed in Chapter 13, see Theorem 13.3.19 for TLR and
Theorem 13.3.24 for CTL. For such a reduction it suffices to show that the tableau for any
one of these logics closes if and only if the input set of formulae is inconsistent in the respective logic. This claim can be proved by modifying the respective proofs that the tableau
closes if and only if the input set of formulae is unsatisfiable, by replacing the semantic arguments there with syntactic ones, based on derivations in the respective deductive
systems.

7.5.4 *Towards a Proof System for CTL**

For capturing the validities in the semantics on generalised branching-time structures, the
axiomatic system $\text{AxSys}_{\text{CTL}^*(B)}$ for the full logic CTL* involves two types of axioms: the
axioms of $\text{AxSys}_{\text{LTL}}$ treated as path formulae here, additional axioms for the path quantifiers, plus a simple axiom for the interaction of A and X. The axioms of $\text{AxSys}_{\text{CTL}^*(B)}$ are
all instances of the following schemes.

1. All axioms of $\text{AxSys}_{\text{LTL}}$.
2. $A(\varphi \to \psi) \to (A\varphi \to A\psi)$.
3. $A\varphi \to AA\varphi$.
4. $A\varphi \to \varphi$.
5. $A\varphi \to AE\varphi$.
6. $p \to Ap$, for each atomic proposition p.
7. $AX\varphi \to XA\varphi$.

The rules of inference are **Modus Ponens** (MP) and the rules of **Necessitation**:

$$\text{Nec}_{AX} \; \frac{\vdash \varphi}{\vdash AX\varphi} \qquad \text{Nec}_{AG} \; \frac{\vdash \varphi}{\vdash AG\varphi} \qquad \text{Nec}_A \; \frac{\vdash \varphi}{\vdash A\varphi}.$$

The rule **Nec**$_{AX}$ can be replaced by an axiom scheme $G\varphi \to X\varphi$. Note that uniform substitutions are not allowed, but axiom schemes are being used.

Proposition 7.5.6. $\text{AxSys}_{\text{CTL}^*(B)}$ is sound and complete with respect to the class of all
generalised branching-time structures. ∎

See the references in the bibliographic notes for a proof. Note that every tree transition
system is a generalised branching-time structure and therefore $\text{AxSys}_{\text{CTL}^*(B)}$ is sound for
CTL* but completeness does not hold for CTL* with $\text{AxSys}_{\text{CTL}^*(B)}$.

For capturing the validities of CTL* on the class of complete trees, equivalently, the class of all transition systems, more axioms must be added, to enforce the limit closure property, in the form of the following additional 'limit closure axiom':

$$\textbf{LC} \quad \mathsf{AG}(\mathsf{E}\varphi \rightarrow \mathsf{EX}((\mathsf{E}\psi\mathsf{U}\mathsf{E}\varphi))) \rightarrow (\mathsf{E}\varphi \rightarrow \mathsf{EG}((\mathsf{E}\psi\mathsf{U}\mathsf{E}\varphi))).$$

Obtaining a complete axiomatisation for CTL* has turned out to be much more difficult than for CTL and the only one known so far involves, in addition to the axioms for $\mathrm{AxSys}_{\mathrm{CTL}^*}^B$ plus **LC**, a complicated inference rule, extracted from the use of **Rabin automata** in the proof of completeness. Interestingly, such a rule has turned out to be redundant in the extension of CTL* with past operators. See references in the bibliographic notes for further details.

7.6 Exercises

Exercises on CTL

Exercise 7.1. Draw a picture illustrating the operator EG of CTL.

Exercise 7.2. Consider the ITS $\mathcal{T} = (S, R, L)$, where

- $S = \{s, t, u, v, w\}$,
- $R = \{(s, w), (s, t), (s, v), (w, w), (t, u), (t, v)(u, u), (u, v), (v, u), (v, t), (v, s)\}$ and
- $L(u) = \{\}, L(s) = L(t) = \{q\}, L(w) = \{p\}, L(v) = \{p, q\}$.

Draw the graph of the ITS and check the truth at the state s of the following CTL formulae:

(a) $\mathsf{E}(q\mathsf{U}(p \wedge \neg q))$.
(b) $\mathsf{EX}\mathsf{A}(q\mathsf{U}(\neg p \wedge \neg q))$.

Exercise 7.3. Consider the following transition system $\mathcal{T}$.

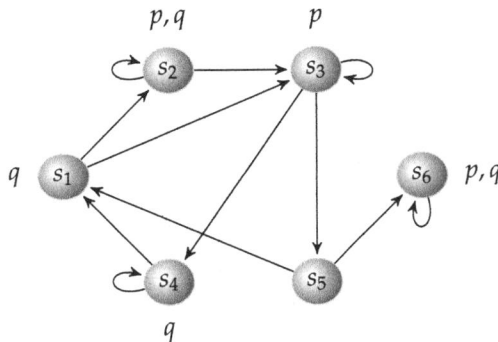

Check whether the following statements hold, using the semantic truth definition.

(a) $\mathcal{T}, s_2 \models \mathsf{EGEF}p$ (f) $\mathcal{T}, s_3 \models \mathsf{EGF}((\mathsf{EF}p)\mathsf{U}q)$

(b) $\mathcal{T}, s_3 \models \mathsf{AFEG}(p \vee q)$ (g) $\mathcal{T}, s_1 \models \mathsf{AGEF}q \rightarrow \mathsf{EGF}q$

(c) $\mathcal{T}, s_1 \models \mathsf{AF}(q \wedge \mathsf{EX}p)$ (h) $\mathcal{T}, s_3 \models \mathsf{EF}(\mathsf{A}(q\mathsf{U}p) \wedge \neg q \wedge \mathsf{EXE}\neg(q\mathsf{U}p))$

(d) $\mathcal{T}, s_1 \models \mathsf{AF}(q \wedge \mathsf{X}p)$ (i) $\mathcal{T}, s_4 \models (q \wedge \mathsf{AXE}(q\mathsf{U}p)) \rightarrow \mathsf{E}(q\mathsf{U}p)$.

(e) $\mathcal{T}, s_1 \models \mathsf{AXE}(p\,\mathsf{U}\,\mathsf{G}q)$

Exercise 7.4. Verify the logical equivalences and consequences in Theorem 7.1.17, by using the semantic truth definition. Verify those that involve the operators AF, EF, AG, EG as well by relating them to those for the operators AU and EU.

Exercise 7.5. Verify the logical equivalence in Lemma 7.1.2 expressing AU in terms of EG and EU.

Exercises on CTL*

Exercise 7.6. Find CTL formulae equivalent to each of the following CTL* formulae:

(a) $\mathsf{E}\,p_1\mathsf{U}(p_2\mathsf{U}p_3)$ (g) $\mathsf{A}\,(p_1\mathsf{U}p_2)\mathsf{U}p_3$

(b) $\mathsf{A}\,p_1\mathsf{U}(p_2\mathsf{U}p_3)$ (h) $\mathsf{A}\,p_1\mathsf{U}(\mathsf{X}p_2)$

(c) $\mathsf{E}\,p_1\mathsf{U}\neg(p_2\mathsf{U}p_3)$ (i) $\mathsf{E}\,(p_1\mathsf{U}p_2)\mathsf{U}p_3$

(d) $\mathsf{E}\,(\mathsf{X}p_1)\mathsf{U}p_2$ (j) $\mathsf{E}\,(\neg(p_1\mathsf{U}p_2))\mathsf{U}p_3$

(e) $\mathsf{A}\,(\mathsf{X}p_1)\mathsf{U}p_2$ (k) $\mathsf{E}(\neg(p\mathsf{U}q) \wedge \neg(p\mathsf{U}r) \wedge \mathsf{G}p)$.

(f) $\mathsf{A}\,(\neg(p_1\mathsf{U}p_2))\mathsf{U}p_3$

Exercise 7.7. Prove Lemma 7.1.2 and Lemma 7.1.13.

Exercise 7.8. Show that $\mathsf{A}(\mathsf{G}p \rightarrow \mathsf{AG}p)$ is not a valid CTL* formula.

Exercise 7.9. Formalise the following specifications as state formulae in the language of CTL*. Whenever possible, produce a CTL formula.

(a) 'On some computation starting from the current state every occurrence of p is eventually followed by an occurrence of q'.

(b) 'Every state on some computation starting from the current state which satisfies p will satisfy it until q becomes false'.

(c) 'From every state of every computation on which q is true infinitely often, a computation starts on which p will be eventually always true'.

(d) 'On every computation where p is eventually always true, every state where q is false starts a computation on which p is true infinitely often'.

(e) 'On every computation where p is eventually false, some state in which q is true starts no computations on which q holds immediately after every occurrence of p'.

(f) 'If φ is eventually true on every computation starting from the current state, then there is a computation starting from that state and leading to a state, on every computation starting from which ψ will remain false until φ becomes true'.

(g) 'There is a computation on which every state where `safe` does not hold starts a computation on which `alert` will hold until `safe` becomes true'.

(h) 'No computation starting from any reachable state satisfying `start` may eventually reach an `alert` state that also starts a computation satisfying `alert` eventually always'.

(i) 'φ is infinitely often true on every computation starting from the current state only if on some computation, starting from that state and eventually reaching a state satisfying ψ, the property φ holds until a state not satisfying ψ is reached'.

(j) 'Every computation on which the variable x eventually becomes positive branches infinitely often into (some) computations on which x is eventually always 0'.

(k) 'If on some computation starting from the current state the process Pr is enabled infinitely often, then on every computation starting from the current state, whenever Pr is enabled it will remain enabled until immediately before the process Pr' is disabled'.

Exercise 7.10. Show that the CTL formula

$$\mathsf{AGAF}(resourcerequested) \to \mathsf{AF}(resourcegranted)$$

is not equivalent to the CTL*-formula

$$\mathsf{A}(\mathsf{GF}(resourcerequested) \to \mathsf{F}(resourcegranted))$$

expressing fairness along every possible computation. Which of these formulae is logically stronger?

Exercise 7.11. Translate the following CTL* specifications into English. Simplify the translations as much as possible, up to logical equivalence. Then decide whether the formulae are valid, satisfiable (but not valid) or unsatisfiable. Give a brief reason, using semantic arguments.

(a) $\mathsf{AG}(q \to \mathsf{F}p)$

(b) $\mathsf{AF}(p \wedge \mathsf{AXG}\neg p)$

(c) $\mathsf{AFAGF}(p\mathsf{U}\neg p)$

(d) $\neg\mathsf{AG}q \to \mathsf{E}(q\,\mathsf{U}\,\neg q)$

(e) $\mathsf{AG}(q \wedge \neg p \to \mathsf{E}(q\,\mathsf{U}\,p))$

(f) $\mathsf{EFEG}^{\infty}(\neg p\mathsf{U}p)$

(g) $\neg p \wedge \mathsf{E}q\mathsf{U}p \to q \wedge \mathsf{EXE}(q\mathsf{U}p))$

(h) $\mathsf{EG}^{\infty}p \wedge \mathsf{AF}^{\infty}(\neg p\mathsf{U}q)$

(i) $\neg p \wedge \mathsf{AG}^{\infty}p \wedge \mathsf{EG}(\neg p \to \mathsf{FX}\neg p)$.

Exercise 7.12. Prove the equality of the two semantics for CTL* as stated in Proposition 7.1.6.

Exercise 7.13. Check the validity of each of the following CTL* formulae, by using semantic arguments. If not valid, give a countermodel: an ITS on which the formula is false.

(a) $\mathsf{XA}p \to \mathsf{AX}p$

(b) $\mathsf{GA}p \to \mathsf{AG}p$

(c) $\mathsf{AG}(p \to \mathsf{EX}p) \to (p \to \mathsf{EG}p)$

(d) $\mathsf{AFEG}p \to \mathsf{AFG}p$

(e) $\mathsf{AGEF}p \to \mathsf{EGF}p$

(f) $\mathsf{AGEF}p \to \mathsf{AGF}p$

(g) $\mathsf{AFG}p \to \mathsf{AFAG}p$

(h) $\mathsf{A}(\mathsf{G}p \to \mathsf{AG}p)$

(i) $\mathsf{AG}(p \to \mathsf{EXF}p) \to (p \to \mathsf{EFG}p)$.

Exercise 7.14. Verify the validities in Proposition 7.1.18 and Proposition 7.1.19.

Exercise 7.15. Verify the following logical equivalences in CTL*.

(a) $\mathsf{AGF}\varphi \equiv \mathsf{AGAF}\varphi$

(b) $\mathsf{EFG}\varphi \equiv \mathsf{EFEG}\varphi$

(c) $\neg(\mathsf{A}(p\mathsf{U}q)) \equiv \mathsf{E}(\mathsf{G}\neg q \vee ((\neg q)\mathsf{U}(\neg q \wedge \neg p)))$.

Exercise 7.16. Show that the following pairs of CTL* formulae are *not equivalent*, by constructing appropriate countermodels. Determine which implications are valid.

(a) $\mathsf{EGF}\varphi$ and $\mathsf{EGAF}\varphi$

(b) $\mathsf{EGF}\varphi$ and $\mathsf{EGEF}\varphi$

(c) $\mathsf{AFG}\varphi$ and $\mathsf{AFEG}\varphi$

(d) $\mathsf{EFG}\varphi$ and $\mathsf{EFAG}\varphi$

(e) $\mathsf{AFG}\varphi$ and $\mathsf{AFAG}\varphi$.

Exercise 7.17. Show that in every generalised branching-time structure fusion closure implies prefix closure, while suffix closure and prefix closure together imply fusion closure.

Exercise 7.18. For each of the validities in Proposition 7.1.19, determine whether it is valid in the generalised semantics, that is, on every generalised branching-time structure. If not, provide a countermodel. Which of the properties of suffix, prefix and limit closure need to be required for each of these to be valid? For instance, show that Burgess's formula $\mathsf{AGEF}\varphi \to \mathsf{EGF}\varphi$ fails in some suffix and fusion closed generalised branching-time structure.

Exercise 7.19. In the proof of Theorem 7.2.2, show that $\mathcal{T}, r \models \Phi_{[\mathcal{T},r]}$ for every $r \in \mathcal{T}$.

Exercise 7.20. Would it be sufficient for the proof of Theorem 7.2.2 to replace in the definition of the formulae $\Xi_{[\mathcal{T},r]}$ and $\Phi_{[\mathcal{T},r]}$ all subformulae $\chi_{[\mathcal{T},r]}$ by $\chi^0_{[\mathcal{T},r]}$? What if this was $\chi^n_{[\mathcal{T},r]}$ for some fixed n independent of $\mathcal{T}$?

Exercise 7.21. In the transition system defined in Figure 7.4, show that ω and $\omega + 1$ agree on all CTL* formulae.

Exercise 7.22.

(a) Show, by giving suitable countermodels, that the following pairs of formulae are not equivalent in general, where $\mathcal{Q} \in \{\mathsf{A}, \mathsf{E}\}$.
   - $\mathcal{Q}\mathsf{G}\varphi$ and $\mathsf{G}\mathcal{Q}\varphi$,
   - $\mathcal{Q}\mathsf{F}\varphi$ and $\mathsf{F}\mathcal{Q}\varphi$,
   - $\mathcal{Q}\mathsf{X}\varphi$ and $\mathsf{X}\mathcal{Q}\varphi$.

(b) Check whether these pairs become equivalent if φ is assumed to be a state formula.

Exercise 7.23. Write pseudocode describing both versions (top-down and bottom-up) of the algorithm $\mathrm{MC}_{\mathrm{CTL}^*}$ for global model checking of CTL*.

Exercise 7.24. Show Lemma 7.1.20, Lemma 7.1.21 and Proposition 7.1.9. Complete the proof of Theorem 7.2.6 and the details of the proof of Theorem 7.2.1. Prove Lemma 7.1.10 for the case of existential path quantification.

Exercise 7.25. Let φ be a CTL* state formula and φ' be the LTL formula obtained from φ by removing all the occurrences of the path quantifiers. For all LTL models σ, show that $\sigma, 0 \models \varphi$ (in CTL*) iff $\sigma, 0 \models \varphi'$ (in LTL).

Exercises on model-checking

Exercise 7.26. Extend the algorithm for global model checking of CTL formulae in Section 7.3.2 with each of the additional operators: $AG\varphi$ and $A\varphi U\psi$, EF^∞, EG^∞, AF^∞, AG^∞.

Exercise 7.27. This exercise refers to Dijkstra's mutual exclusion problem in Section 7.3.3.

(a) Run the labelling algorithm for GMC(CTL) on $\mathcal{T}^1_{MEP}$ and show that it satisfies *Safety* and *Nonblocking* at the initial state s_0, but does not satisfy any of the two *Liveness* conditions there.
(b) Run the labelling algorithm for GMC(CTL) on $\mathcal{T}^2_{MEP}$ and show that it satisfies all *Safety*, *Nonblocking* and *Liveness* conditions at the initial state s_0.
(c) Run the model-checking algorithm for GMC(CTL*) on $\mathcal{T}^2_{MEP}$ and show that it satisfies the conditions *Fair2-Fair4*, but not *Fair1*.
(d) Contemplate how the fairness conditions listed in the section are ordered in terms of their logical strength, i.e. which implies which of them, and also which of these conditions can be assumed reasonable and which of them are too strong to impose.
(e) Search for alternative protocols solving the MEP and satisfying all *Safety* and *Nonblocking* and *Liveness* conditions and possibly all fairness conditions conditions *Fair1-Fair4*. If you find that there are no such protocols, justify your claim.

Exercise 7.28. Consider the following transition system $\mathcal{T}$.

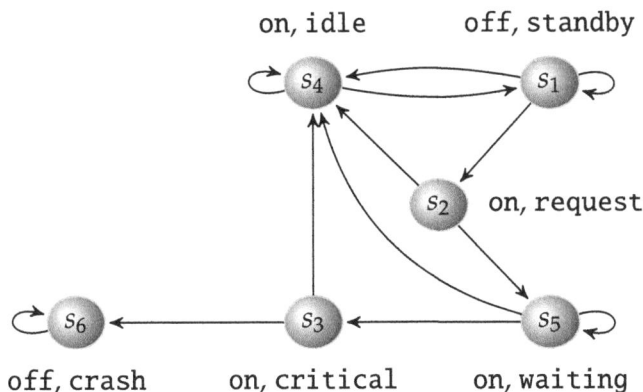

Determine, with brief argumentation the following. For global model checking of CTL or CTL* formulae run the respective recursive algorithms step by step and trace the steps.

(a) Does $\mathcal{T} \models \mathsf{AG}(\mathtt{request} \to \mathsf{EF\,critical} \land \mathsf{EG\,\lnot critical})$ hold?
(b) What is $[\![\lnot(\mathtt{on} \to \mathsf{AF}(\mathtt{idle} \lor \mathsf{AX\,on}))]\!]^{\mathcal{T}}$?
(c) What is $[\![\mathsf{EG}(\lnot\mathtt{crash} \to \mathsf{EXE}(\mathtt{on\,U\,critical}))]\!]^{\mathcal{T}}$?
(d) Does $\mathcal{T}, s_1 \models \mathsf{EG}(\lnot\mathtt{crash} \land \mathsf{AX}\lnot\mathtt{crash} \land \mathsf{F}^{\infty}\mathsf{EXEX\,crash})$ hold?
(e) What is $[\![\mathsf{EG}^{\infty}((\lnot\mathtt{off})\mathsf{U\,on}) \land \mathsf{F}^{\infty}\mathsf{EX\,crash}]\!]^{\mathcal{T}}$?

Exercise 7.29. Consider the following transition system $\mathcal{T}$ with state space $S = \{s_i \mid i \in [1, 8]\}$

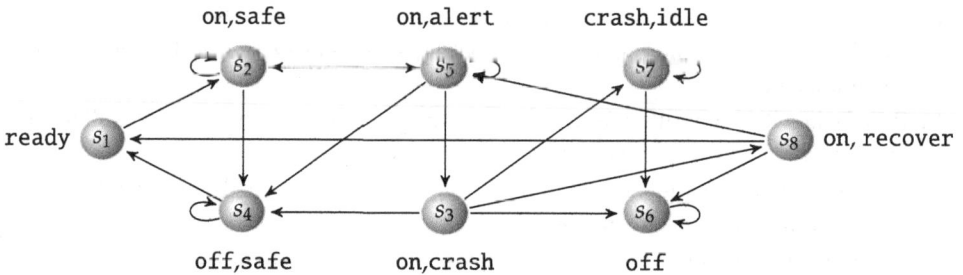

Determine for each of the following statements whether it is true.

(a) $\mathcal{T}, s_1 \models \mathsf{E}(\lnot\mathtt{crash} \lor \mathtt{off})\mathsf{U\,recover}$
(b) $\mathcal{T}, s_1 \models \mathsf{EF}^{\infty}(\mathtt{alert} \land \mathsf{X}\lnot\mathtt{crash}) \land \mathsf{F}^{\infty}\mathtt{recover}$
(c) $\mathcal{T}, s_1 \models \mathsf{EF}^{\infty}(\mathtt{alert\,U\,safe}) \land \mathsf{F}^{\infty}\mathtt{crash}$
(d) $\mathcal{T}, s_1 \models \mathsf{AF}^{\infty}(\mathtt{alert\,U\,safe}) \to \mathsf{G}^{\infty}\lnot\mathtt{crash}$.

Run the respective global model-checking algorithms step by step in order to compute the following sets.

(e) $[\![\mathsf{E}(\mathtt{safe\,U\,(EX\,crash)})]\!]^{\mathcal{T}}$
(f) $[\![\mathsf{EF}\lnot(\mathtt{alert} \to \mathsf{E}((\lnot\mathtt{crash})\mathsf{U\,ready}))]\!]^{\mathcal{T}}$
(g) $[\![\mathsf{EG\,safe} \lor \mathsf{E}(\mathtt{on\,U\,(EX\,crash)})]\!]^{\mathcal{T}}$
(h) $[\![\mathsf{AG}^{\infty}(\mathtt{alert} \to \mathtt{alert\,U\,safe}) \to \mathsf{G}^{\infty}\lnot\mathtt{crash}]\!]^{\mathcal{T}}$
(i) $[\![\mathsf{AGE}(\mathsf{G}^{\infty}\lnot\mathtt{crash} \land \mathsf{F}^{\infty}\lnot\mathtt{safe})]\!]^{\mathcal{T}}$
(j) $[\![\mathsf{AGEG}^{\infty}\mathtt{safe}]\!]^{\mathcal{T}}$.

Exercise 7.30. Show that GMC(ECTL) is in PTIME by adapting the labelling algorithm for GMC(CTL) (cf. Proposition 7.4.2).

Exercises on fragments and extensions

Exercise 7.31. Check for each of the following ECTL formulae whether it is valid by using semantic arguments. For those that are not valid, construct countermodels.

(a) $\text{EF}^\infty(p \vee q) \leftrightarrow \text{EF}^\infty p \vee \text{EF}^\infty q$

(b) $\text{AF}^\infty(p \wedge q) \leftrightarrow \text{AF}^\infty p \wedge \text{AF}^\infty q$

(c) $\text{EF}^\infty p \leftrightarrow \text{EF}^\infty \text{EF}^\infty p$

(d) $\text{AF}^\infty p \leftrightarrow \text{AF}^\infty \text{AF}^\infty p$

(e) $\text{AF}^\infty \text{EF}^\infty p \rightarrow \text{AF}^\infty p$

(f) $\text{AF}^\infty p \rightarrow \text{AF}^\infty \text{EF}^\infty p$.

Exercise 7.32. Show that $\text{MC}(\text{LTL}^1(\text{X}, \text{U}, \text{F}^\infty))$ and $\text{SAT}(\text{LTL}^1(\text{X}, \text{U}, \text{F}^\infty))$ are in NP by adapting the proof from Exercise 6.34.

Exercise 7.33. In reference to the fragments of CTL* defined in Section 7.4.2 show that $\text{BT}(\vartheta_1, \ldots, \vartheta_M)$ and $\text{BT}(\vartheta_1, \ldots, \vartheta_M, \neg\vartheta_1, \ldots, \neg\vartheta_M)$ are expressively equivalent.

Exercise 7.34. Verify the equivalences in Figure 7.8.

Exercise 7.35. Let $\vartheta_1, \ldots, \vartheta_M$ be a fixed set of pure path formulae (i.e. LTL formulae). Show that the model-checking problem for $\text{BT}(\vartheta_1, \ldots, \vartheta_M)$ can be solved in polynomial time.

Exercise 7.36. Show that the fragment of CTL* consisting of all LTL formulae prefixed by path quantifiers is not included in CTL^+.

Exercise 7.37. Prove Lemma 7.3.5, Lemma 7.4.5 and Lemma 7.4.12.

Exercises on axiomatic systems

Exercise 7.38. Complete the derivations left as exercises in Lemma 7.5.1. and in Proposition 7.5.2.

Exercise 7.39. Given the soundness of $\text{AxSys}_{\text{BML}}$, prove the soundness of each of $\text{AxSys}_{\text{TLR}}$ and $\text{AxSys}_{\text{CTL}}$.

Exercise 7.40. Verify the soundness of the limit closure axiom **LC** in Section 7.5.4.

Exercise 7.41. Prove Proposition 7.5.3.

7.7 Bibliographical Notes

In Figure 7.10, we present the hierarchy of the branching-time temporal logics considered in this chapter. Solid edges refer to syntactic inclusions whereas dashed edges are related to comparing the expressive powers. Some logics, such as UB (Universal Branching logic) and UB^-, are present in the figure because of their historical role in the development of branching-time temporal logics but we have not treated them in the chapter because they are subsumed by more expressive logics with the same computational cost.

Modal μ-calculus (Chapter 8)

ECTL* [VW83]

CTL^2 (Section 7.4.2)   ECTL$^+$ →   CTL* (Section 7.1.4)

ECTL   CTL$^+$ (Section 7.4.3)

CTL (Section 7.1.3)   LTL (Chapter 6)

UB = TLR + **EG, AG** [BAPM81]

TLR (Section 7.1.2) – a.k.a. UB$^-$ [BAPM81]

BML (Chapter 5)

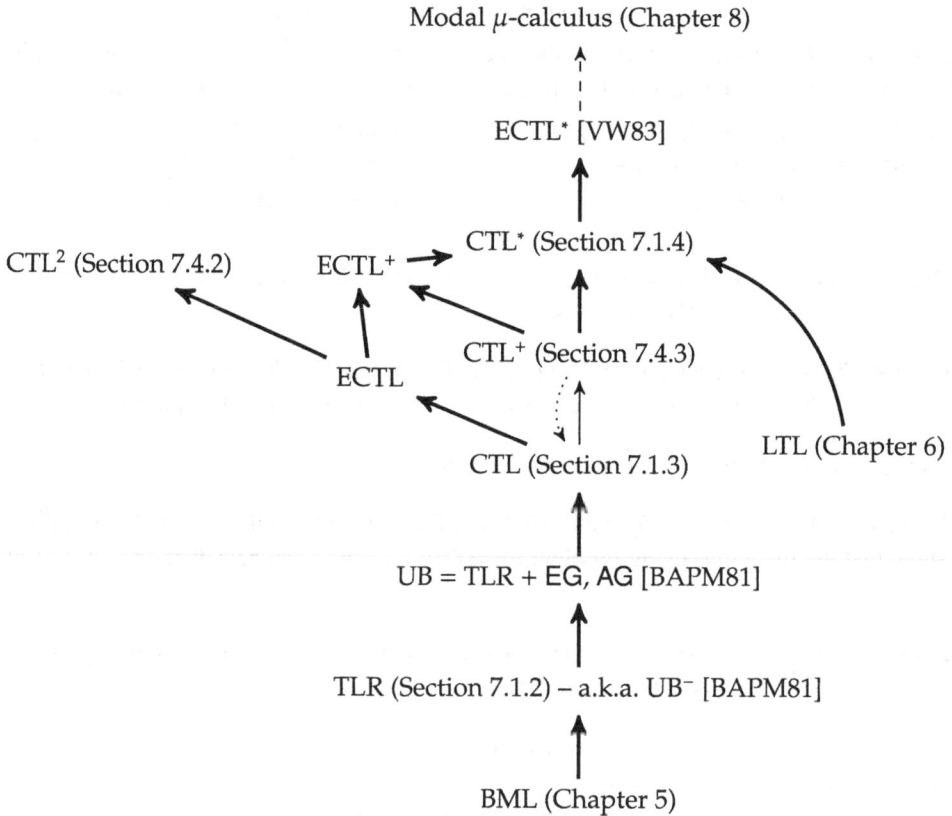

Figure 7.10 Branching-time logics.

Birth of computation tree logics. The use of branching-time logics in computer science started in the late 1970s to early 1980s when several similar branching-time logical systems were proposed in Abrahamson (1979), Lamport (1980), Ben-Ari et al. (1981, 1983) and Clarke and Emerson (1981). The latter paper introduced the computation tree logic CTL, which subsequently emerged as the most popular and practically useful among these. Of course, this follows the approach advocated in Pnueli (1977) where temporal logics are proposed as a framework for formal verification of programs and not only as a class of modal logics for reasoning about occurrences of events (Prior 1957, 1967).

Whereas linearity of time implies that each instant has only one future (see Chapter 6), when time has a tree-like nature, this is more adequate to deal with nondeterministic programs. Soon, a debate on the pros and cons of linear time (LTL) versus branching time (CTL) logics ensued, and in response to it the very expressive logic CTL*, encompassing both approaches, was introduced in Emerson and Halpern (1983, 1986). See the survey by Emerson (1990) and the bibliographic notes for more details and references.

Model checking. The model-checking approach to formal verification became very popular when efficient algorithms for model checking of CTL and some extensions of it were developed in the early 1980s (see e.g. Clarke and Emerson 1981; Queille and Sifakis 1982a). Gradually, research on model checking was extended to more expressive branching time logics such as CTL* and many others. The fact that model-checking problem for CTL* is PSPACE-complete is established in Clarke et al. (1983, 1986) (see also Emerson and Lei 1987). It was first shown in Emerson and Lei (1987) how model checking of CTL* formulae can be reduced to global model checking of LTL formulae. For more details on CTL* model checking, see also Baier and Katoen (2008). As an alternative approach, an efficient on-the-fly method for CTL* model checking has been developed in Bhat et al. (1995). Model checking of temporal logics was boosted enormously with the development of automata-based methods (see Chapter 14).

TLR and CTL. Extending TLR with operators EG and AG leads to a more expressive logic, introduced in the early 1980s by Ben Ari, Pnueli and Manna (1981) under the name of UB (universal branching) logic. However, it is subsumed by an even more expressive logic, introduced at about the same time by Clarke and Emerson (1981), called computation tree logic, abbreviated CTL, where the reachability operator is replaced by the more general Until operator, already known from LTL. As noted earlier, the logic CTL became a very popular formalism for specification and practical verification of properties of transition systems because of its tractable model checking. CTL is a key formalism in the class of branching-time temporal logics since it admits efficient model checking while being quite expressive. CTL extends the so-called 'Unified Branching-time logic' UB (Ben-Ari et al. 1981, 1983). The logic UB does not contain U, but only X and G. In Qucille and Sifakis (1982a), a branching-time temporal logic containing the temporal operators EF and AF (no next-time operator, no until operator) has been studied from the point of view of model checking. No complexity analysis is provided there. Theorem 7.3.6 and the ExpTime upper bound for CTL are due to Clarke and Emerson (1981). Note that the original version of CTL introduced in Emerson and Clarke (1980) contained the operators F^{∞} and G^{∞}.

Theorem 7.2.2 is from Browne et al. (1988). The characterisation of finite transition systems up to bisimulation equivalence with CTL formulae was first established in Browne et al. (1988) for CTL, but was essentially known earlier in the literature on modal logics.

CTL*. The logic CTL* was introduced by Emerson and Halpern (1983, 1986) as a unifying extension both of the linear-time logic LTL and the branching-time logic CTL. From a purely logical perspective, the logic CTL* is precisely the **Ockhamist logic** of the class of ω-trees, i.e. of the tree-like models where every path has the order type ω of the natural numbers, while CTL is the **Peircean logic** on the same class of models.

The introduction and results on the generalised semantics for CTL*, based on generalised and R-generated branching-time structures have been introduced in Emerson (1983), where Proposition 7.1.9 can be found. For more recent and detailed exposition, see Wolper (1989) and Emerson (1995). More discussion on the standard versus generalised semantics for CTL* is presented in Stirling (1992), as well as in Thomason (1984) and in Zanardo (1996), from the viewpoint of complete trees versus bundled trees in Ockhamist branching-time temporal logics.

The notion of bisimulation can be accordingly introduced as a relation between paths rather than states; see Stirling (1992) for details.

While CTL* is usually interpreted on transition systems with serial transition relations, generating only ω-paths, it can be also interpreted directly on $(\omega + 1)$-trees, i.e. trees in which every path has the order type of $\omega + 1$, where the last point can be regarded as marking the 'end' of the ω-path. This allows for reduction of the second-order quantification over paths to a first-order quantification in a more expressive *hybrid* language with reference pointers (see Goranko 2000). Note also that CTL* augmented with graded modalities stating that at least $n \geq 0$ states satisfies a subformula has been shown expressively equivalent to monadic path logic (monadic second-order logic in which quantifications are over paths) on trees (Moller and Rabinovich 2003). Similarly, CTL* is expressively equivalent to the monadic path logic over the full binary tree (Hafer and Thomas 1987). A property that cannot be expressed in CTL* is that a proposition holds true at every even state (Wolper 1983). Of course, this can be easily expressed in the modal μ-calculus, see Chapter 8. The satisfiability problem for CTL* is shown to be 2ExpTime-hard in Vardi and Stockmeyer (1985) and in 2ExpTime in Emerson and Jutla (2000).

A consequence of Pinchinat (1992, Theorem 5) is that ω and $\omega + 1$ agree on all CTL* formulae in the transition system defined in Figure 7.4. More specifically, the **distinguishing power** for temporal logics such as CTL* or CTL has been studied in Pinchinat (1992). The transition system in Figure 7.4 is a slight variant of an **ordinal process** (see e.g. Pinchinat 1992) in which the state 0 has a self-loop and it is labelled by the atomic proposition p.

The proof of Theorem 7.2.6 is due to Emerson and Sistla (1984, Theorem 3.2). For a detailed proof, see also Wolper (1989).

In Clarke and Draghicescu (1988, Theorem 1) it is shown that given a CTL* formula φ, it has an equivalent formula in LTL iff it is logically equivalent to A φ^d where φ^d is an LTL formula obtained from φ by removing all the path quantifiers. This is an interesting result that characterises the CTL* formulae that are equivalent to an LTL formula and this can be checked using a decision procedure for testing CTL* validity.

CTL^2. Most of the material presented in Section 7.4.2 comes from Kupferman and Grumberg (1996). We have presented here a variant of CTL^2 with the same expressive power. Nevertheless, as shown in Exercise 7.35, every fragment $BT(\vartheta_1, \ldots, \vartheta_M)$ in CTL* admits a model-checking problem solvable in polynomial time.

ECTL, ECTL$^+$ and ECTL*. In Emerson and Halpern (1983, Section 4), it is shown that CTL is strictly less expressive than ECTL, that is strictly less expressive than ECTL$^+$, that is strictly less expressive than CTL*. The fact that ECTL* (in the sense of Vardi and Wolper

1983) is strictly more expressive than ECTL has been shown in Emerson and Halpern (1986). We know that $E(p \vee (p'Uq'))Ur$ cannot be expressed in $ECTL^+$ from Laroussinie (1994) (in French), whereas $ECTL^+ \sqsubset CTL^*$ has been established in Emerson and Halpern (1986) with the formula $E(pUq \vee p'Uq')Ur$. Proofs of the expressiveness results can be found in Chapter 10.

The proof of Proposition 7.4.1 is essentially the proof of Emerson and Halpern (1986, Theorem 7). ECTL and $ECTL^+$ have been introduced in Emerson and Halpern (1983). $ECTL^*$ has been introduced in Vardi and Wolper (1983), and it is defined as for ETL by adding automata-based constraints on runs. It is known that $ECTL^*$ is strictly more expressive than CTL^* and still it can be translated into the modal μ-calculus (Dam 1994). The model-checking problem for $ECTL^+$ has been shown to be Δ_2^p-complete in Laroussinie et al. (2001).

A proof of Theorem 7.4.10 can be found in Emerson and Halpern (1986).

CTL$_{lp}^*$ The version of CTL_{lp}^* presented in Section 7.4.4 is taken from Kupferman and Pnueli (1995), where past is finite, linear and cumulative (other versions are possible and have been studied (see e.g. Hafer and Thomas 1987). Complexity results for model checking and satisfiability problems have been obtained in Bozzelli (2008). For instance, the model-checking problem for the existential fragment of CTL_{lp}^* is ExpSpace-complete (Bozzelli 2008), which makes a notable difference with CTL^*. Nevertheless, CTL^* and CTL_{lp}^* have the same expressive power (see e.g. Laroussinie and Schnoebelen 1995). The CTL restriction of CTL_{lp}^*, i.e. CTL_{lp}, is strictly more expressive than CTL (Laroussinie and Schnoebelen 1995). More results about the expressive power of branching-time temporal logics can be found in Chapter 10. Proposition 7.4.16 is due to Laroussinie and Schnoebelen (2000) (see also Schnoebelen 2003). See a good discussion about past in branching-time logics in Laroussinie and Schnoebelen (2000, Section 3). CTL^* with past presented in this chapter differs from the version introduced in Hafer and Thomas (1987), but Proposition 7.4.14 is essentially due to Hafer and Thomas (1987). See more details in Laroussinie and Schnoebelen (1995), whereas Proposition 7.4.15 is due to Laroussinie and Schnoebelen (1995, Theorem 4.1) (making use of results from Emerson and Halpern 1986, too). Proposition 7.4.13 is established in Bozzelli (2008).

Axiomatic systems. The first complete axiomatic system for CTL was proposed in Emerson and Halpern (1982), but see also the more detailed journal version in Emerson and Halpern (1985). The proof of completeness there is essentially done by constructing an open semantic tableau for any consistent formula; for details see also Emerson (1990). Here we have given a streamlined version of the axiomatic system for CTL presented in Emerson (1990), all original axioms in which are easily derivable in the system presented here. For a modal model-theoretic proof of another version of the axiomatic system for CTL presented here, see Goldblatt (1992).

While there are not so difficult completeness results (see Stirling 1992) for CTL* with respect to the generalised semantics introduced here, the first explicit complete axiomatisation of CTL* with respect to the standard semantics was only obtained in Reynolds (2001), by using a rather complex additional inference rule in the style of Gabbay's irreflexivity rule, the idea of which is based on the relation between CTL* and Muller automata, used in the proof of completeness. Reynolds (2000) announced that such a rule can be omitted for CTL* with past operators.

Books and surveys. There is abundant literature on branching-time logics and their applications to formal verification and model checking. We list here just a selection of references that have a more general, or survey nature and in which further bibliographical references can be found.

- Emerson (1990): a survey of temporal logics for specification of computing systems.
- Emerson (1995): a detailed survey on branching-time logics and automata, as well as discussion on expressiveness versus complexity.
- Wolper (1989): a survey on the relation of programs and computations to models of temporal logics, in particular from automata-theoretic perspective.
- Schnoebelen (2003): a survey on model checking of both branching-time and linear-time temporal logics.
- Classical books on model checking of temporal logics and formal verification include Clarke et al. (2000), Bérard et al. (2001) and Baier and Katoen (2008).

8

The Modal Mu-Calculus

We have noted that the basic modal logic BML suffers from the deficiency of not being able to make assertions about connectivity, i.e. every BML formula can only 'look' up to a certain depth into a transition system. This is of course not enough for many purposes, and this is why richer formalisms like reachability logic TLR and the computation tree logic CTL have been introduced. As we demonstrated in Chapter 7, these logics possess temporal operators which directly translate such assertions into the syntax of a logic. As we showed in Section 7.1.5, all temporal operators in CTL added on top of BML have simple and elegant characterisations in terms of least or greatest fixpoint solutions to certain equations.

The modal μ-calculus $\mathcal{L}_\mu$ uses this idea as a general principle in order to add expressive power to the basic modal logic BML. It only features two additional syntactic constructs: a least and a greatest fixpoint operator. Thus, it differs from the other logics studied here in the way that the fixpoint character of a formula is being made explicit in it. This has pros and cons: it allows *any* least or greatest fixpoint solution of an equation expressed with basic modal logic to be defined; on the other hand this results in a far less intuitive syntax of the logic when compared to the other temporal logics.

These two aspects determine the role that the modal μ-calculus plays in the world of temporal logics. The generic use of fixpoint quantifiers gives it a relatively high expressive power. Many other temporal logics can be embedded into the modal μ-calculus. The explicit use of fixpoint quantifiers come with a generic instruction for doing model checking using fixpoint iteration. Such algorithms can then be specialised to the embedded temporal logics. Thus, the modal μ-calculus is often called the *backbone* of temporal logics.

Structure of the chapter. In Section 8.1 we start by introducing the concept of fixpoint quantification which leads to the formal logic called the modal μ-calculus. Early on we show that it can embed CTL simply because this translation is helpful in understanding the use of fixpoint quantifiers for the specification of temporal behaviour. Section 8.2 essentially deals with model checking; it introduces fixpoint iteration as a method to compute the extension of formulae using fixpoint quantifiers. The model-checking problem is not the main focus, though. The methods and tools developed there from naïve global model checking – approximants and signatures – are essential for arguing about the correctness of methods to be presented later. Section 8.3 analyses the naïve global model-checking procedure with respect to what makes formulae hard to be evaluated and develops syntactic measures for formulae based on this. It is followed by a section on local model checking, presented as a game-theoretic framework. It extends the model-checking games for BML from Section 5.4.3 to the richer logic.

The following two sections look past the logic itself: Sections 8.5 and 8.6 analyse its relationship to bisimilarity and to monadic second-order logic. The latter acts as a yardstick outside of the world of temporal logics that they relate to. Finally, Section 8.7 finishes this chapter by considering some variants and extensions of $\mathcal{L}_\mu$.

8.1 Fixpoint Quantifiers

8.1.1 Syntax

We introduce the **modal μ-calculus** $\mathcal{L}_\mu$ by presenting its syntax and its semantics. As with other temporal logics, the latter interprets well-formed formulae in transition systems.

Unlike the temporal logics seen before, the logic $\mathcal{L}_\mu$ uses **propositional variables** in order to define the least and greatest fixpoints of arbitrary, modal-logic definable functions. The variables will serve the purpose of representing an argument to such functions.

As usual, let $\text{PROP} = \{p, q, \ldots\}$ be a set of atomic propositions, and $Act = \{a, b, \ldots\}$ be a set of actions. The modal μ-calculus is interpreted over transition systems with nodes labelled by subsets of PROP and the transitions labelled with elements of Act. Additionally, let $\text{VAR} = \{X, Y, Z, \ldots\}$ be a countably infinite set of propositional variables that is disjoint from PROP. The language of the modal μ-calculus can be represented by a context-free grammar as usual. However, there are some conditions that would require a slightly more complicated form than that given for other temporal logics. In order to preserve the simpler form, we take the following route. We first give a context-free grammar for formulae and then define the notion of a well-formed formula. From then on, we will only consider well-formed formulae.

Definition 8.1.1. Let PROP, Act, VAR as earlier. The language of (possibly non-well-formed) formulae of the modal μ-calculus $\mathcal{L}_\mu$ is given as follows.

$$\varphi ::= p \mid X \mid (\varphi \wedge \varphi) \mid \neg\varphi \mid \langle a \rangle\varphi \mid \mu X.\varphi$$

where $p \in \text{PROP}$, $a \in Act$ and $X \in \text{VAR}$.

As usual, we assume $\vee, \rightarrow, \leftrightarrow$ and $[a]$ to be definable.

The set $sub(\varphi)$ of **subformulae** of φ is defined in a straightforward way with $sub(\mu X.\psi) := \{\mu X.\psi\} \cup sub(\psi)$, etc. The **size** of a formula is measured as the number of its distinct subformulae: $|\varphi| := \text{card}(sub(\varphi))$.

The operator μ acts as a binder, i.e. every occurrence of X in $\mu X.\psi$ is **bound**. An occurrence of a variable in a formula is **free** if it is not bound. A **sentence** is a formula without free occurrences of any variable. Let $free(\varphi)$ denote the variables that have free occurrences in φ.

A formula φ is **well formed** if, for all $\mu X.\psi \in sub(\varphi)$,

- $X \notin free(\varphi)$, and
- for all $\mu X.\psi' \in sub(\varphi)$ we have $\psi = \psi'$ and
- every occurrence of X in the syntax DAG of ψ is under an even number of negation symbols in ψ. ∇

The operator μ is also called a **quantifier**, as we will see later that it acts like a special kind of (second-order) quantifier.

Example 8.1.2. The formula

$$\mu X.q \wedge \neg\langle a \rangle\mu X.\neg(X \wedge \langle a \rangle\neg X)$$

is clearly not well formed because the variable X gets quantified twice in it. It also shows why one may want to avoid this: it is not clear which of the two quantifications the two occurrences of X should belong to. We could introduce a convention as in predicate logics that the inner quantifiers overwrite the outer ones. This would result in the following formula

$$\mu X.q \wedge \neg \langle a \rangle \mu Y. \neg (Y \wedge \langle a \rangle \neg Y)$$

in which the second quantification uses a different variable. Given that variables are merely place-holders for arguments to modal functions it should be clear that renaming variables is a legal way to obtain well-formedness.

Now this formula is still not well formed because the first occurrence of what is now Y occurs under an odd number – namely once – of negation symbols under the corresponding quantifier. Note that it actually occurs under an even number of negation symbols in the whole formula, which is irrelevant to well-formedness, though.

Now note that Y is quantified over but never used further in the formula. So maybe one of the two original occurrences should have belonged to the first quantification, for instance the first occurrence. Then renaming the inner one to Y results in the following formula.

$$\mu X.q \wedge \neg \langle a \rangle (\mu Y. \neg X \vee \neg \langle a \rangle \neg Y).$$

This is indeed well formed because both X and Y occur an even number of negations under their respective quantifications.

Well-formedness guarantees two important properties: monotonicity of the modal functions for which fixpoints are being used, and existence of a unique mapping from fixpoint variables to its defining fixpoint formulae.

Definition 8.1.3. Let φ be a well-formed formula. It induces a **fixpoint map** which is a partial function $fp_\varphi : \text{VAR} \to sub(\varphi)$ such that $fp_\varphi(X) = \mu X.\psi$ for some ψ. ∇

Thus, fp_φ maps each variable that gets quantified over in φ to the subformula which is the scope of the quantification. This would not be well defined in case the underlying formula is not well formed because a variable would have to be mapped to more than one formula in its quantification. Furthermore, in the presence of greatest fixpoint operators (see definition further) as first-class objects in the syntax, the definition of fp_φ is extended so that a variable X can also get mapped to some $\nu X.\psi$.

From now on, let $\mathcal{L}_\mu$ denote the set of all well-formed formulae of the modal μ-calculus. Even more so, we will not consider non-well-formed formulae anymore and therefore just speak of formulae whenever we mean well-formed ones.

In this chapter we will use the more traditional notation for the modal operators, writing $\langle a \rangle \psi$ instead of $\text{EX}_a \psi$ and respectively $[a]\psi$ instead of $\text{AX}_a \psi$. This is standard for the modal μ-calculus, and it is mainly owed to the fact that its syntax uses second-order variables – often denoted using capital letters $X, Y, Z, \ldots$ – which is why it is helpful not to use capital letters for modal operators.

We also introduce the following abbreviations which may be used in cases when the underlying set Act of actions is finite:

$$\Diamond\varphi := \bigvee_{a\in Act} \langle a\rangle\varphi \qquad \Box\varphi := \bigwedge_{a\in Act} [a]\varphi.$$

We will use these convenient operators in examples, and one may have to derive the underlying actions from the context or the rest of the formula that they are used in. We also introduce a dual to μ operator – the **greatest fixpoint quantifier** ν – defined by

$$\nu X.\varphi := \neg\mu X.\neg\varphi[\neg X/X]$$

where $\varphi[\psi/X]$ denotes the formula that results from φ by simultaneously replacing every free occurrence of X by ψ. We leave as an exercise the formulation of the requirements on well-formedness in the presence of ν-operators as well.

In order to avoid ambiguity we introduce some precedence rules for the syntax of $\mathcal{L}_\mu$. The unary operators $\neg$, $\langle a\rangle$ and $[a]$ are the strongest, followed by the Boolean operators in their usual order with $\wedge$ strongest, etc. The fixpoint quantifiers have the weakest precedence even though they are also unary operators. This convention is made in order to save parentheses: typically, the formulae prefixed by a fixpoint quantifier use some Boolean operator which would require a pair of parentheses immediately. The dot after the fixpoint variable in $\mu X.\Box X$ for instance is there to remind us of this weak precedence.

Clearly, there is no ambiguity in $\mu X.\Box X$ regardless of which precedence rules. However, in $\mu X.p \vee \Box X$ for instance, the disjunction is stronger than the least fixpoint quantifier. If it was the other way round then the formula would be $(\mu X.p) \vee \Box X$ which is completely different for two reasons: now it has a free occurrence of X that is not under the binder μX anymore. The left disjunct also formalises a fixpoint of a constant function – see the definition of the following semantics – which is useless, and it could simply be written as $p \vee \Box X$.

8.1.2 Semantics

The extension of a formula in an ITS is a set of states, namely all the states in which the formula is true. Recall how the semantics of other temporal logics is given inductively by defining this set using some operations on the extensions of subformulae. This can also be done for the modal μ-calculus but it requires a little bit of extra input: variable assignments.

Consider the formula $\mu X.p \vee \Diamond X$. It has one maximal genuine subformula, namely $p \vee \Diamond X$. The essential difference between these two is that the former is a sentence whereas the latter is not. The set of states satisfying $p \vee \Diamond X$ should intuitively consist of all states that either satisfy p or have a successor that satisfies X. Thus, $p \vee \Diamond X$ describes a set of states in an ITS which depends on X in the sense that some set of states must be given for X, and only then is the set of states satisfying $p \vee \Diamond X$ well defined. This takes us to the definition of a variable assignment.

Definition 8.1.4. Let $T = (S, \rightarrow, L)$ be a transition system. A **variable assignment** for T is a mapping $\rho : \text{VAR} \rightarrow \mathcal{P}(S)$ where $\mathcal{P}(S)$ denotes the powerset of S.

We write $\rho[X \mapsto T]$ for some $X \in \text{VAR}$ and some $T \subseteq S$ to denote the **update** of ρ at X to T, i.e. the variable assignment that is defined as follows.

$$\rho[X \mapsto T](Y) := \begin{cases} T, & \text{if } X = Y \\ \rho(Y), & \text{otherwise.} \end{cases} \qquad \nabla$$

Definition 8.1.5. Let $T = (S, \rightarrow, L)$ be a transition system, ρ a variable assignment with regards to T. We write $[\![\varphi]\!]_\rho^T$ to denote the set of states in T that satisfy φ relative to ρ. It is inductively defined as follows.

$$[\![q]\!]_\rho^T := \{s \mid q \in L(s)\}$$
$$[\![X]\!]_\rho^T := \rho(X)$$
$$[\![\varphi \wedge \psi]\!]_\rho^T := [\![\varphi]\!]_\rho^T \cap [\![\psi]\!]_\rho^T$$
$$[\![\neg\varphi]\!]_\rho^T := S \setminus [\![\varphi]\!]_\rho^T$$
$$[\![\langle a\rangle\varphi]\!]_\rho^T := \texttt{pre}(a, [\![\varphi]\!]_\rho^T) = \{s \mid \exists t \in [\![\varphi]\!]_\rho^T \text{ with } s \xrightarrow{a} t\}$$
$$[\![\mu X.\varphi]\!]_\rho^T := \bigcap\{T \subseteq S \mid [\![\varphi]\!]_{\rho[X \mapsto T]}^T \subseteq T\}.$$

So, we get that $[\![[a]\varphi]\!]_\rho^T$ is equal to $\{s \mid t \in [\![\varphi]\!]_\rho^T \text{ for all } t \text{ such that } s \xrightarrow{a} t\}$.

A state s of a transition system T **satisfies** a formula φ relative to some variable assignment ρ, written $T, s \models_\rho \varphi$ iff $s \in [\![\varphi]\!]_\rho^T$.

Two $\mathcal{L}_\mu$-formulae are **equivalent**, written $\varphi \equiv \psi$, iff they are satisfied by the same states in any transition system relative to any variable assignment, i.e. if, for all T and all ρ, we have $[\![\varphi]\!]_\rho^T = [\![\psi]\!]_\rho^T$. $\qquad \nabla$

The semantics of the μ-operator may seem arbitrary at first sight but it incorporates the Knaster–Tarski Theorem (Theorem 2.2.3) which states that the least fixpoint of a monotone function on a powerset lattice is given as the intersection of all pre-fixpoints of that function.

For many purposes it is easier to have formulae in which negation does not occur at arbitrary positions in a formula because there it may violate monotonicity constraints.

Definition 8.1.6. A formula is in **negation normal form** if it is built from literals q, $\neg q$ for $q \in \text{PROP}$, and variables using the operators $\wedge$, $\vee$, $\langle a\rangle$, $[a]$, μ and ν. $\qquad \nabla$

Negation normal form is not a restriction in the sense of the following lemma. It is easily proved using the definition of the derived operators in terms of negation and the original operators $\wedge$, $\langle a\rangle$, μ.

The proof of the following lemma is left as Exercise 8.5.

Lemma 8.1.7. For every $\varphi \in \mathcal{L}_\mu$ there is a $\varphi' \in \mathcal{L}_\mu$ in negation normal form such that $\varphi' \equiv \varphi$ and $|\varphi'| \leq 2 \cdot |\varphi|$. $\qquad \blacksquare$

Definition 8.1.8. For a formula φ in negation normal form we assume that fp_φ maps variables to subformulae of the form $\mu X.\psi$ or $\nu X.\psi$. A bound variable X is then called μ-**bound**, respectively ν-**bound** is $fp_\varphi(X) = \mu X.\psi$, respectively $fp_\varphi(X) = \nu X.\psi$ for some ψ. $\hspace{1cm} \triangledown$

An immediate consequence of the use of fixpoint quantifiers is the fact that fixpoint formulae can be unfolded in order to obtain equivalent formulae.

Corollary 8.1.9. For all $X \in$ VAR and all φ we have $\mu X.\varphi \equiv \varphi[\mu X.\varphi/X]$ and $\nu X.\varphi \equiv \varphi[\nu X.\varphi/X]$. $\hspace{1cm} \blacksquare$

The second important property that is ensured by well-foundness is monotonicity.

Lemma 8.1.10. Let $\varphi \in \mathcal{L}_\mu$ and $X \in free(\varphi)$ is such that it only occurs under even numbers of negation symbols in φ. Then for any transition system $\mathcal{T}$ and any variable assignment ρ the map $\mathfrak{f}_\varphi : T \mapsto [\![\varphi]\!]^{\mathcal{T}}_{\rho[X \mapsto T]}$ is monotone with respect to $\subseteq$. $\hspace{1cm} \blacksquare$

Proof. Let $\mathcal{T} = (S, \{\xrightarrow{a}\}_{a \in Act}, L)$ and ρ be given.

This property can be proved by induction on the structure of φ. Note, however, that even if X only occurs under even numbers of negation symbols in φ, there may be subformulae ψ such that X occurs under an odd number of negation symbols in them. Hence, we need to strengthen the hypothesis and simultaneously show that the map $\mathfrak{f}_\varphi$ is antitone with respect to $\subseteq$ if X only occurs under such an odd number of negation symbols.

The base cases for the induction are simple: φ is either an atomic proposition q, or a variable Y different from X, or X itself. In all cases, X occurs under an even number of negation symbols, namely none. In the first two cases, $T \mapsto [\![\varphi]\!]^{\mathcal{T}}_{\rho[X \mapsto T]}$ is a constant function and therefore monotone, in the last case it is the identity function and therefore monotone, too.

Let $\varphi = \psi_1 \wedge \psi_2$. Take T_1 and T_2 such that $T_1 \subseteq T_2$. Suppose X occurs under an even number of negation symbols in φ. Then it does so in both ψ_1 and ψ_2. We have

$$
\begin{aligned}
[\![\varphi]\!]^{\mathcal{T}}_{\rho[X \mapsto T_1]} &= [\![\psi_1]\!]^{\mathcal{T}}_{\rho[X \mapsto T_1]} \cap [\![\psi_2]\!]^{\mathcal{T}}_{\rho[X \mapsto T_1]} \\
&\subseteq [\![\psi_1]\!]^{\mathcal{T}}_{\rho[X \mapsto T_2]} \cap [\![\psi_2]\!]^{\mathcal{T}}_{\rho[X \mapsto T_1]} \\
&\subseteq [\![\psi_1]\!]^{\mathcal{T}}_{\rho[X \mapsto T_2]} \cap [\![\psi_2]\!]^{\mathcal{T}}_{\rho[X \mapsto T_2]} \\
&= [\![\varphi]\!]^{\mathcal{T}}_{\rho[X \mapsto T_2]}
\end{aligned}
$$

by the hypothesis and monotonicity of set intersection. If X only occurs under an odd number of negation symbols then it does so in both ψ_1 and ψ_2. Then the corresponding functions for ψ_1 and ψ_2 are antitone by hypothesis, and antitonicity for φ is shown in the same way as monotonicity.

Let $\varphi = \langle a \rangle \psi$ and $T_1 \subseteq T_2$. Again, the number of occurrences of X in φ is the same as that in ψ. Hence, we have, for instance,

$$
\begin{aligned}
\llbracket \varphi \rrbracket^{\mathcal{T}}_{\rho[X \mapsto T_1]} &= \{ s \in S \mid \exists t \in \llbracket \psi \rrbracket^{\mathcal{T}}_{\rho[X \mapsto T_1]} \text{ with } s \xrightarrow{a} t \} \\
&\subseteq \{ s \in S \mid \exists t \in \llbracket \psi \rrbracket^{\mathcal{T}}_{\rho[X \mapsto T_2]} \text{ with } s \xrightarrow{a} t \} \\
&= \llbracket \varphi \rrbracket^{\mathcal{T}}_{\rho[X \mapsto T_2]}
\end{aligned}
$$

by hypothesis and the fact that increasing the number of possible target states for transitions can only increase the number of states that have some of them as successors. The case with an odd number of occurrences is proved in the same way.

The case of $\varphi = \neg \psi$ is particularly simple because $\llbracket \varphi \rrbracket^{\mathcal{T}}_{\rho[X \mapsto T]} = S \setminus \llbracket \psi \rrbracket^{\mathcal{T}}_{\rho[X \mapsto T]}$ and complementation turns a monotone function into an antitone one, and vice versa. Additionally, X only occurs under an even number of occurrences in φ iff it only occurs under an odd number in ψ, and vice versa.

For the remaining case let $\varphi = \mu Y.\psi$. Note that $Y \neq X$ for otherwise X would not have been a free variable. Then we have

$$
\begin{aligned}
\llbracket \varphi \rrbracket^{\mathcal{T}}_{\rho[X \mapsto T_1]} &= \bigcap \{ T \mid \llbracket \psi \rrbracket^{\mathcal{T}}_{\rho[X \mapsto T_1][Y \mapsto T]} \subseteq T \} \\
&= \bigcap \{ T \mid \llbracket \psi \rrbracket^{\mathcal{T}}_{\rho[Y \mapsto T][X \mapsto T_1]} \subseteq T \}.
\end{aligned}
$$

The hypothesis yields $\llbracket \psi \rrbracket^{\mathcal{T}}_{\rho[Y \mapsto T][X \mapsto T_1]} \subseteq \llbracket \psi \rrbracket^{\mathcal{T}}_{\rho[Y \mapsto T][X \mapsto T_2]}$. Thus, we get

$$
\{ T \mid \llbracket \psi \rrbracket^{\mathcal{T}}_{\rho[Y \mapsto T][X \mapsto T_2]} \subseteq T \} \subseteq \{ T \mid \llbracket \psi \rrbracket^{\mathcal{T}}_{\rho[Y \mapsto T][X \mapsto T_1]} \subseteq T \}
$$

and therefore

$$
\bigcap \{ T \mid \llbracket \psi \rrbracket^{\mathcal{T}}_{\rho[Y \mapsto T][X \mapsto T_1]} \subseteq T \} \subseteq \bigcap \{ T \mid \llbracket \psi \rrbracket^{\mathcal{T}}_{\rho[Y \mapsto T][X \mapsto T_2]} \subseteq T \}.
$$

But the latter equals $\llbracket \varphi \rrbracket^{\mathcal{T}}_{\rho[X \mapsto T_2]}$ which finishes the proof. Again, the case of antitonicity is proved in the same way. $\square$

Example 8.1.11. The computation of the extension of $\mathcal{L}_\mu$-formulae in an arbitrary transition system can be used to understand what properties are being formalised.

1. Let $\varphi = \mu Z.\Diamond Z$. By definition, $\llbracket \varphi \rrbracket_\rho = \bigcap \{ T \subseteq S \mid \{ s \mid R(s) \cap T \neq \varnothing \} \subseteq T \}$ when R is the union transition relation of the underlying transition system. This expression may not seem easy to analyse unless we notice that $\{ s \mid R(s) \cap \varnothing \neq \varnothing \} \subseteq \varnothing$ for any transition system. Hence, $\varnothing$ is one of those pre-fixpoints T occurring in the intersection. So, $\llbracket \varphi \rrbracket_\rho = \varnothing$, i.e. $\mu Z.\Diamond Z$ is equivalent to $\bot$.

2. Let $\varphi = \nu Z.\Box Z$. Note that $\{ s \mid R(s) \subseteq S \} = S$, which is a fixpoint. Hence, $\nu Z.\Box Z$ is equivalent to $\top$. Alternatively, we can use the previous example and duality: $\nu Z.\Box Z \equiv \neg \mu Z.\neg\Box\neg Z \equiv \neg \mu Z.\Diamond Z \equiv \neg\bot \equiv \top$.

8.1.3 Least versus Greatest Fixpoints

Explicit fixpoint quantification is typically not easy to understand, at least at the beginning. A particular question that normally arises concerns the difference between least and greatest fixpoints. One way to build some intuition is to see both as two kinds of recursion operators. Then μ starts a recursion that intuitively must terminate whereas a ν-recursion need not terminate. It may seem equally strange to think of temporal predicates as something that may or may not terminate.

Example 8.1.12. Let $\psi(X) := p \vee (q \wedge \Box X)$. As a formula with a free variable not occurring under any negation symbols, it induces a monotone map $\mathfrak{f} : T \mapsto \llbracket \psi \rrbracket^{\mathcal{T}}_{[X \mapsto T]}$ on the powerset lattice of any underlying transition system $\mathcal{T}$. For instance, consider the following one.

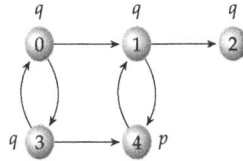

We have $\mathfrak{f}(\emptyset) = \{2, 4\}$, $\mathfrak{f}(\{2, 4\}) = \{1, 2, 4\}$, $\mathfrak{f}(\{0, \ldots, 4\}) = \{0, \ldots, 4\}$, etc. The latter simply means that the entire state set is a fixpoint of $\mathfrak{f}$, hence, it is the greatest fixpoint. So we have that all states satisfy $\nu X.\psi(X)$.

In order to find out what the least fixpoint is we can check that $\mathfrak{f}$ only has two pre-fixpoints – $\{0, \ldots, 4\}$ and $\{1, 2, 4\}$ – of which the latter is their intersection. Hence, only the states 1, 2 and 4 satisfy $\mu X.\psi(X)$.

The difference in the extension of these two fixpoint formulae can also be explained using the intuition of μ denoting a terminating recursion, and ν denoting a possibly non-terminating recursion. Note that $\psi(X)$ defines all states that satisfy p or satisfy q whilst also having all successors in X. This is the case for 1 and 4, regardless of what X is because we have $p \in L(4)$ and 2 has no successors.

Recall that $1 \models \mu X.\psi(X)$, too, but here the reason is a different one. We do not have $p \in L(1)$, and we only get $1 \models_\rho q \wedge \Box X$ if $\{2, 4\} \subseteq \rho(X)$. But we already established that 2 and 4 satisfy the property defined by ψ. Hence, 1 satisfies $\psi(\psi(X))$, regardless of what X stands for. In other words, it satisfies the property that is defined by recursion over ψ.

In order to get an idea of the difference between least and greatest fixpoints, we need to examine states 0 and 3 because they satisfy $\nu X.\psi(X)$ but not $\mu X.\psi(X)$. For both we note that the question of whether each of them satisfies $\psi(X)$ under some variable assignment ρ indeed depends on whether the other one is included in $\rho(X)$. Note that each of 0 and 3 has the other as one successor, and another one which is 1 or 4. Since 1 and 4 satisfy $\psi(X)$ regardless of the interpretation of X we can conclude that 0 and 3 only satisfy $\psi(X)$ if they are assumed to satisfy X. Equally speaking, in order for $0 \models_\rho \psi(X)$ to hold we need $3 \in \rho(X)$. Since we are interested in the property defined by recursing $\psi(X)$ we can read this as the necessity for 3 to satisfy $\psi(X)$ at the next recursion level. But this can only hold if 0 satisfies $\psi(X)$ at the next-next recursion level. This is exactly what is meant by ν defining a possibly nonterminating recursion: we have $0 \models \nu X.\psi(X)$ but $0 \not\models \mu X.\psi(X)$ because a μ-recursion requires a definite reason to be found after finitely many steps. This is the case for 2 and 4 at the first step and 1 at the second, but in order to argue that 0 should satisfy the property defined by recursion over ψ we would need infinitely many steps.

This, of course, also shows that there is no such thing as *the* property defined by recursion of some modal formula. Instead, μ- and ν-quantification define, in general, different recursive properties.

Example 8.1.13. The correspondence between ν-quantification and infinite behaviour is also seen in the following. Consider $\varphi := \nu X.\langle a \rangle X \wedge \nu Y.\langle b \rangle Y$. First we remark that $\nu Y.\langle b \rangle Y$ expresses 'there is an infinite b-path': it is satisfied by the largest set Y of states in an ITS such that each of them has a b-successor in Y. This is only possible if each state in this set Y is at the origin of an infinite b-path.

Then $\nu X.\langle a \rangle X \wedge \psi$ expresses 'there is an infinite a-path such that every state on this path satisfies ψ': consider the largest set X such that each state in it satisfies ψ and has an a-successor in X. Again, every state in this set X must be at the origin of an infinite a-path on which every state satisfies ψ.

Hence, φ postulates the existence of an infinite a-path on which every state is the origin of an infinite b-path.

Now consider $\varphi' := \nu X.\langle a \rangle X \wedge \nu Y.\langle b \rangle (Y \wedge X)$. Its meaning is not so easy to work out because $\psi(X) := \nu Y.\langle b \rangle (Y \wedge X)$ is not a closed formula. We do know, though, that – under any variable assignment ρ – it expresses that there is an infinite b-path such that all states starting from the second one must belong to $\rho(X)$. So, in order to infer the meaning of φ' we can attempt to figure out the shape of any post-fixpoint of the map $T \mapsto [\![\langle a \rangle X \wedge \psi(X)]\!]^{\mathcal{T}}_{[X \mapsto T]}$ for a set of states T in an arbitrary transition system $\mathcal{T}$. Suppose such a T was a post-fixpoint thereof. Hence, we have

$$T \subseteq [\![\langle a \rangle X \wedge \psi(X)]\!]^{\mathcal{T}}_{[X \mapsto T]}.$$

Then any state $t \in T$ must have an a-successor in T, and it satisfies $\psi(X)$ when X is interpreted by T as well. This is only possible, if t is the origin of an infinite a-path such that each state on it is the origin of an infinite b-path on which every state after the origin satisfies this property again, i.e. is the origin of an infinite a-path, etc.

8.1.4 Embedding CTL

As we stated in the introductory part to this chapter, the modal μ-calculus is often perceived as the backbone of temporal logics. Here we revisit the fixpoint characterisations of the temporal operators of CTL in Section 7.1.5 and show that CTL can be embedded into $\mathcal{L}_\mu$. The translation is conceptually very simple and needs no combinatorial machinery. All that is needed is the observation that the temporal operators of CTL can be seen as least or greatest fixpoints of certain modal equivalences.

Theorem 8.1.14. For every CTL formula φ there is an $\mathcal{L}_\mu$ formula $tr(\varphi)$ such that $tr(\varphi) \equiv \varphi$ and $|tr(\varphi)| = \mathcal{O}(|\varphi|)$. ∎

Proof. We construct $tr(\varphi)$ by induction on the structure of the CTL formula φ. The translation presented here actually only proves a weaker result: CTL can be embedded into $\mathcal{L}_\mu$ over total transition systems. It is possible to extend the translation such that it yields formulae that are equivalent over possibly nontotal transition systems, too. This is left as Exercise 8.9.

$$tr(q) := q$$
$$tr(\neg\varphi) := \neg tr(\varphi)$$
$$tr(\varphi \wedge \psi) := tr(\varphi) \wedge tr(\psi)$$
$$tr(\mathsf{EX}\varphi) := \Diamond tr(\varphi)$$
$$tr(\mathsf{E}(\varphi\mathsf{U}\psi)) := \mu X.tr(\psi) \vee (tr(\varphi) \wedge \Diamond X)$$
$$tr(\mathsf{E}(\varphi\mathsf{R}\psi)) := \nu X.tr(\psi) \wedge (tr(\varphi) \vee \Diamond X).$$

Note that in order to guarantee well-formedness, the last two clauses need to introduce a fresh variable each time. It is also not difficult to see that these variables always occur under an even number of negations inside their defining fixpoint subformula.

It is obvious that the constructed formulae are only linearly bigger in size than the original CTL formulae.

Finally, correctness of this translation is proved by induction on the structure of the CTL formula. It is trivial for atomic propositions and the Boolean cases and immediate for the case of the modal operators EX and AX. The remaining cases follow from the fact that, for example, $\mathsf{E}(\varphi\mathsf{U}\psi)$ is the least fixpoint of the equivalence $\chi \equiv \psi \vee (\varphi \wedge \mathsf{EX}\chi)$, see Theorem 7.1.17. ☐

This translation also reinforces the intuition of μ-recursion as something that needs to terminate as opposed to ν-recursion. Take for instance the CTL formula $\mathsf{E}(p\mathsf{U}q)$ which gets translated into the least fixpoint of the equivalence induced by the modal formula $p \vee (q \wedge \Diamond X)$. Now note that $\mathsf{E}(p\mathsf{U}q)$ can only be unfolded finitely many times in order to show that some state satisfies it; a state satisfying q must be reached after a finite number of times and this is where the recursion terminates in this sense.

On the other hand, take $\mathsf{EG}q$, logically equivalent to $\mathsf{E}(\bot \mathsf{R}\ q)$, which translates into $\nu X.q \wedge \Diamond X$. Showing that some state satisfies $\mathsf{EG}q$ using its unfolding requires infinitely many steps, namely the construction of an infinite path. Hence, its $\mathcal{L}_\mu$-equivalent uses ν-recursion.

8.2 Fixpoint Iteration

In order to prove statements about the modal μ-calculus – for instance existence of normal forms or correctness of decision procedures – it is useful to introduce approximants. Recall that the semantics of least (and also greatest) fixpoint formulae is given as the infimum, respectively, supremum of all pre-, respectively, post-fixpoints of the underlying modal function in the powerset lattice of a transition system. The use of the Knaster–Tarski Theorem has certain advantages, namely implies the existence and uniqueness of least and greatest fixpoints, which is not obvious otherwise. On the other hand, proofs by induction on the structure of formulae can be complicated by this fixpoint semantics. We therefore introduce a tool which makes such inductive proofs easier: approximants.

8.2.1 Approximants

Approximants can be defined syntactically or semantically; both comes with certain advantages and disadvantages. Here we choose the syntactic version. An approximant is a fixpoint formula annotated with an ordinal number. The advantage of this approach is the fact that this can be seen as an extension of the syntax of the modal μ-calculus, i.e. approximants can be treated like formulae. The disadvantage is the fact that many ordinals are infinite objects, which could raise questions after their representability. However, we will only use approximants in order to reason *about* the modal μ-calculus; these annotated formulae will never occur as inputs to decision problems associated with this logic. Thus, representability is not an issue. All we need is the distinction between 0, a successor ordinal $\alpha + 1$, and a limit ordinal κ.

Definition 8.2.1. Let α be an ordinal number, $\mu X.\varphi \in \mathcal{L}_\mu$. The αth **approximant** is $\mu^\alpha X.\varphi$. Likewise, the αth approximant to $\nu X.\varphi$ is $\nu^\alpha X.\varphi$. $\qquad \nabla$

The semantics of an approximant in a given transition system $\mathcal{T} = (S, \to, L)$ relative to some variable assignment ρ is given by transfinite induction for any ordinal α and any limit ordinal κ as follows.

$$\llbracket \mu^0 X.\varphi \rrbracket_\rho^{\mathcal{T}} := \emptyset$$
$$\llbracket \mu^{\alpha+1} X.\varphi \rrbracket_\rho^{\mathcal{T}} := \llbracket \varphi \rrbracket_{\rho[X \mapsto T]}^{\mathcal{T}} \text{ where } T = \llbracket \mu^\alpha X.\varphi \rrbracket_\rho^{\mathcal{T}}$$
$$\llbracket \mu^\kappa X.\varphi \rrbracket_\rho^{\mathcal{T}} := \bigcup_{\alpha < \kappa} \llbracket \mu^\alpha X.\varphi \rrbracket_\rho^{\mathcal{T}}$$
$$\llbracket \nu^0 X.\varphi \rrbracket_\rho^{\mathcal{T}} := S$$
$$\llbracket \nu^{\alpha+1} X.\varphi \rrbracket_\rho^{\mathcal{T}} := \llbracket \varphi \rrbracket_{\rho[X \mapsto T]}^{\mathcal{T}} \text{ where } T = \llbracket \nu^\alpha X.\varphi \rrbracket_\rho^{\mathcal{T}}$$
$$\llbracket \nu^\kappa X.\varphi \rrbracket_\rho^{\mathcal{T}} := \bigcap_{\alpha < \kappa} \llbracket \nu^\alpha X.\varphi \rrbracket_\rho^{\mathcal{T}}.$$

Thus, it should be clear that we have $\mu^0 X.\varphi \equiv \bot$, $\nu^0 X.\varphi \equiv \top$ and $\tau^{\alpha+1} X.\varphi \equiv \varphi[\tau^\alpha X.\varphi / X]$ for any $\tau \in \{\mu, \nu\}$.

The name approximant is derived from the fact that these formulae approximate least fixpoints from below and greatest fixpoints from above. Moreover, for all $\mathcal{T}$, ρ, φ and X we have

$$[\![\mu^0 X.\varphi]\!]_\rho^{\mathcal{T}} \subseteq [\![\mu^1 X.\varphi]\!]_\rho^{\mathcal{T}} \subseteq \ldots \subseteq [\![\mu^\omega X.\varphi]\!]_\rho^{\mathcal{T}} \subseteq \ldots\ldots \subseteq [\![\mu X.\varphi]\!]_\rho^{\mathcal{T}} \qquad (8.1)$$

$$[\![\nu^0 X.\varphi]\!]_\rho^{\mathcal{T}} \supseteq [\![\nu^1 X.\varphi]\!]_\rho^{\mathcal{T}} \supseteq \ldots \supseteq [\![\nu^\omega X.\varphi]\!]_\rho^{\mathcal{T}} \supseteq \ldots\ldots \supseteq [\![\nu X.\varphi]\!]_\rho^{\mathcal{T}}.$$

Lemma 8.2.2. Let $\mathcal{T}$ be a transition system, ρ a variable assignment and $\mu X.\varphi \in \mathcal{L}_\mu$. Then there is an ordinal α such that $[\![\mu^\alpha X.\varphi]\!]_\rho^{\mathcal{T}} = [\![\mu X.\varphi]\!]_\rho^{\mathcal{T}}$. ∎

Proof. First we show that there is indeed a chain of approximants below the least fixpoint as shown in (8.1). This is proved by transfinite induction on α. The base case of $\alpha = 0$ is trivial.

The case of a successor ordinal $\alpha + 1$ uses the fact that the function $T \mapsto [\![\varphi]\!]_{\rho[X \mapsto T]}^{\mathcal{T}}$ is monotone because X can only occur under an even number of negation symbols in φ. By induction hypothesis we have $[\![\mu^\alpha X.\varphi]\!]_\rho^{\mathcal{T}} \subseteq [\![\mu X.\varphi]\!]_\rho^{\mathcal{T}}$. By monotonicity we then obtain

$$[\![\mu^{\alpha+1} X.\varphi]\!]_\rho^{\mathcal{T}} = [\![\varphi]\!]_{\rho[X \mapsto [\![\mu^\alpha X.\varphi]\!]_\rho^{\mathcal{T}}]}^{\mathcal{T}} \subseteq [\![\varphi]\!]_{\rho[X \mapsto [\![\mu X.\varphi]\!]_\rho^{\mathcal{T}}]}^{\mathcal{T}} = [\![\mu X.\varphi]\!]_\rho^{\mathcal{T}}$$

because $[\![\mu X.\varphi]\!]_\rho^{\mathcal{T}}$ is a fixpoint of that monotone function.

The last case of a limit ordinal κ follows directly from the hypothesis and the fact that the supremum over any class of sets contained in some set T is still contained in that T.

Now we know that for any ordinal α we have $[\![\mu^\alpha X.\varphi]\!]_\rho^{\mathcal{T}} \subseteq [\![\mu X.\varphi]\!]_\rho^{\mathcal{T}}$. Hence, it suffices to show that there is some ordinal α for which the converse inclusion holds.

Consider the chain $\{[\![\mu^\alpha X.\varphi]\!]_\rho^{\mathcal{T}} \mid \alpha \text{ being some ordinal}\}$. It is linearly ordered by $\subseteq$ and this linear order is well founded, as shown. Then it must have some type which is represented by some ordinal β. We then have $[\![\mu^{\beta+1} X.\varphi]\!]_\rho^{\mathcal{T}} = [\![\mu^\beta X.\varphi]\!]_\rho^{\mathcal{T}}$. Indeed, otherwise β would be an ordinal smaller than itself because it would contain a chain of the type $0, 1, \ldots, \beta, \beta + 1, \ldots$. But then we have

$$[\![\mu^{\beta+1} X.\varphi]\!]_\rho^{\mathcal{T}} = [\![\varphi]\!]_{\rho[X \mapsto [\![\mu^\beta X.\varphi]\!]_\rho^{\mathcal{T}}]}^{\mathcal{T}} \subseteq [\![\mu^\beta X.\varphi]\!]_\rho^{\mathcal{T}}$$

which shows that $[\![\mu^\beta X.\varphi]\!]_\rho^{\mathcal{T}}$ is a pre-fixpoint of the map $T \mapsto [\![\varphi]\!]_{\rho[X \mapsto T]}^{\mathcal{T}}$. Since $[\![\mu X.\varphi]\!]_\rho^{\mathcal{T}}$ is the infimum of all its pre-fixpoints we also have $[\![\mu X.\varphi]\!]_\rho^{\mathcal{T}} \subseteq [\![\mu^\beta X.\varphi]\!]_\rho^{\mathcal{T}}$, hence $[\![\mu X.\varphi]\!]_\rho^{\mathcal{T}} = [\![\mu^\beta X.\varphi]\!]_\rho^{\mathcal{T}}$. □

The same statement holds for greatest fixpoints, with a very similar proof.

Lemma 8.2.3. Let $\mathcal{T}$ be a transition system, ρ a variable assignment and $\nu X.\varphi \in \mathcal{L}_\mu$. Then there is an ordinal α such that $[\![\nu^\alpha X.\varphi]\!]_\rho^{\mathcal{T}} = [\![\nu X.\varphi]\!]_\rho^{\mathcal{T}}$. ∎

Despite the very similarity in the statements about least and greatest fixpoints in the previous lemmas there is an essential difference between the two: the chain of approximants for a least fixpoint formula is increasing whereas that for a greatest fixpoint formula is decreasing. A consequence of this is the following.

Lemma 8.2.4. Let T be a transition system, s one of its states, ρ a variable assignment, $X \in \text{VAR}, \varphi \in \mathcal{L}_\mu$.

(I) If $T, s \models_\rho \mu X.\varphi$ then there is an ordinal α such that $T, s \models_\rho \mu^\alpha X.\varphi$.

(II) If $T, s \not\models_\rho \nu X.\varphi$ then there is an ordinal α such that $T, s \not\models_\rho \nu^\alpha X.\varphi$.   ∎

Together with the fact that the ordinal numbers are linearly ordered we obtain the following fact, characterising the difference between least and greatest fixpoint formulae: the satisfaction of a least fixpoint formula is witnessed by some least ordinal $\alpha \neq 0$ whereas it is the refutation of a greatest fixpoint formula that is witnessed by some least ordinal $\alpha \neq 0$. Remember that the 0th approximants are semantically equivalent to $\bot$, respectively $\top$ and hence cannot be satisfied, respectively refuted.

Example 8.2.5. We consider an arbitrary transition system.

1. Let us revisit the formula $\varphi = \mu Z.\Diamond Z$. Computing the successive approximants we obtain: $\text{pre}(\varnothing) = \{s \mid R(s) \cap \varnothing \neq \varnothing\} = \varnothing$ and we have reached the fixpoint.

2. Now consider $\varphi = \nu Z.\Diamond Z$ again. Note that $\text{pre}(S) = \{s \mid R(s) \cap S \neq \varnothing\} = \{s \mid R(s) \neq \varnothing\} = [\![\Diamond\top]\!]_\rho$. Likewise, $\text{pre}^2(S) = \text{pre}(\text{pre}(S)) = [\![\Diamond\Diamond\top]\!]_\rho = [\![\Diamond^2\top]\!]_\rho$. In general, we get $\text{pre}^m(S) = [\![\Diamond^m\top]\!]_\rho$, and this consists of all those states from which some a path of length at least m starts.

   Thus, $\text{pre}^\omega(S) = \bigcap_{m<\omega}\text{pre}^m(S)$ is the set of those states which initiate arbitrarily long finite runs. So, $\text{pre}^{\omega+1}(S)$ consists of the states which have a successor with that property (and hence have the property themselves), etc. With no assumptions on the transition system, the description of the fixpoint does not seem easy. However, assuming that it is *image finite*, i.e. every state has finitely many successors, then König's Lemma can be applied at the ω-step, implying that $\text{pre}^\omega(S)$ consists of all states which initiate an infinite run. This is easily seen to be a fixpoint.

   Actually, the assumption of image-finiteness is not necessary. Indeed, knowing the answer, let us show that the extension of $\nu Z.\Diamond Z$ is $S_\infty = \{s \mid$ there is an infinite run beginning at $s\}$ in an arbitrary transition system. For that, we simply apply the definition of a greatest fixpoint. Two facts must be proved.

   (i) S_∞ is a fixpoint of the map $T \mapsto \text{pre}(T)$. Indeed, every state in S_∞ has a successor in S_∞, so $S_\infty \subseteq \text{pre}(S_\infty)$; conversely, if a state has a successor in S_∞ then it is in S_∞ itself, hence $S_\infty \supseteq \text{pre}(S_\infty)$.

   (ii) Every fixpoint of this map is included in S_∞. Indeed, let $T = \text{pre}(T)$ and $s \in T$. Then $s \in \text{pre}(T)$, i.e. s has a successor s_1 in T. Applying the same argument to s_1 we obtain a successor s_2 in T, etc. Eventually, we obtain an infinite run beginning at s, i.e. $s \in S_\infty$. Thus, $T \subseteq S_\infty$.

3. Consider $\varphi = \mu Z.\Box Z$. Then we have $\varphi \equiv \neg\nu Z.\neg\Box\neg Z \equiv \neg\nu Z.\Diamond Z$. Hence, $\mu Z.\Box Z$ describes the set of all states which no infinite run begins from.

Example 8.2.6. Consider the transition system $\mathcal{T}$ given as

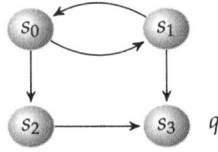

and the $\mathcal{L}_\mu$ formula $\nu X.\Diamond(\mu Y.q \vee \Box Y) \wedge \Diamond X$. Clearly, it contains two fixpoint formulae. The inner one expresses 'all paths eventually hit a state satisfying q' (AFq in CTL) and it is satisfied by s_2 and s_3 but not by s_0 or s_1. The states satisfying the corresponding approximants are the following.

$$[\![\mu^0 Y.q \vee \Box Y]\!]^{\mathcal{T}} = \emptyset$$
$$[\![\mu^1 Y.q \vee \Box Y]\!]^{\mathcal{T}} = \{s_3\}$$
$$[\![\mu^2 Y.q \vee \Box Y]\!]^{\mathcal{T}} = \{s_2, s_3\} = [\![\mu^3 Y.q \vee \Box Y]\!]^{\mathcal{T}}.$$

Thus, the fixpoint is reached at the second approximant level already. Let $\psi := \Diamond(\mu Y.q \vee \Box Y)$. It is satisfied by s_0, s_1 and s_2.

Now take the outer fixpoint formula $\nu X.\psi \wedge \Diamond X$. Its approximant levels are the following.

$$[\![\nu^0 X.\psi \wedge \Diamond X]\!]^{\mathcal{T}} = \{s_0, s_1, s_2, s_3\}$$
$$[\![\nu^1 X.\psi \wedge \Diamond X]\!]^{\mathcal{T}} = \{s_0, s_1, s_2\}$$
$$[\![\nu^2 X.\psi \wedge \Diamond X]\!]^{\mathcal{T}} = \{s_0, s_1\} = [\![\nu^3 X.\psi \wedge \Diamond X]\!]^{\mathcal{T}}.$$

So this fixpoint is reached at approximant level 2 as well.

Intuitively, on finite structures, every sequence of approximants must stabilise in a finite number of steps because in each step it either obtains the same result as before or increases, respectively decreases, the approximant, depending on whether the underlying fixpoint formula is of least or greatest type. The next theorem states this formally.

Definition 8.2.7. Let $\mathcal{T}$ be a transition system and $\varphi = \tau X.\psi$ be a fixpoint formula of $\mathcal{L}_\mu$ for some $\tau \in \{\mu, \nu\}$. The **closure ordinal** for φ and $\mathcal{T}$ (under some variable assignment ρ) is the least α such that $[\![\tau^\alpha X.\psi]\!]_\rho^{\mathcal{T}} = [\![\tau X.\psi]\!]_\rho^{\mathcal{T}}$. ▽

Theorem 8.2.8. Let $\mathcal{T}$ be a finite transition system and $\varphi = \tau X.\psi \in \mathcal{L}_\mu$ with some variable assignment ρ. Then the closure ordinal α for $\mathcal{T}$, φ and ρ is finite. ∎

Proof. Let n be the number of states in $\mathcal{T}$. It is not hard to see that $[\![\tau^{n+1} X.\psi]\!]_\rho^{\mathcal{T}} = [\![\tau^n X.\psi]\!]_\rho^{\mathcal{T}}$ because there can be at most $n+1$ different elements in a chain of approximants that is bounded by some set with n elements. □

It is possible to give better bounds on closure ordinals on finite structures. In the preceding example the closure ordinals are 2 but the number of states is 4. In fact, the number of different states on a longest path in a finite transition system is an upper bound to the closure ordinals in this structure.

8.2.2 Signatures

Signatures are special variable assignments which extend the idea of approximants from one fixpoint formula to arbitrary formulae with free variables. Thus, they provide a tool for reasoning about such formulae, for instance in proofs by induction on the formula structure or – as we will see in Section 8.4 – for showing correctness of certain decision procedures.

Example 8.2.9. Consider the formula $\varphi := \nu X.\langle a \rangle X \wedge \nu Y.\langle b \rangle (Y \wedge X)$ which formalises the recursive property 'there is an infinite a-path such that each state on it is the origin of an infinite b-path, and on every state (except the first one) on that path, the same holds again', see Exercise 8.13. It is satisfied by the following transition system, for instance.

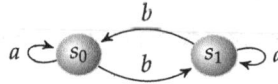

We can consider approximants for the outer fixpoint formulae represented by the variable X. However, the inner fixpoint formula, represented by Y, contains X as a free variable. Thus, we can consider its approximants only under some interpretation ρ which assigns a set of states in an underlying transition system to X. In other words, the approximants for Y depend on the value of X. If we use approximants to compute the value of a fixpoint formula then we are not interested in an arbitrary value for X but only in those which are approximants themselves.

Intuitively, a **signature** assigns approximant values to variables. We will only need them for variables of one fixpoint type; this leads to the definition of μ- and ν-signatures. Thus, signatures are partial mappings. Consider φ from the earlier example. The fixpoint formula for X does not depend on any variables, but the one for Y depends on X. Thus, a mapping which only provides a value for Y but not for X should not be considered a signature.

Definition 8.2.10. Let $\varphi \in \mathcal{L}_\mu$ and X, Y be some of its variables. We write $X \succeq_\varphi Y$ if there is a free occurrence of X in $fp_\varphi(Y)$. The **dependency order** on the variables in φ is the transitive closure of $\succeq_\varphi$. In the following we will only be interested in this transitive closure rather than its base. We will therefore not distinguish them notationally and simply write $\succeq_\varphi$ for this dependeny order. As usual, $\succ_\varphi$ is used to denote its strict version. ∇

The following demonstrates why the transitive closure of the immediate dependency relation is important.

Example 8.2.11. Consider $\nu X.\langle a \rangle X \wedge \nu Y.\langle b \rangle (Y \wedge X) \wedge \nu Z.\langle c \rangle (Z \wedge Y)$. We have $X \succeq Y$ and $Y \succeq Z$ and therefore $X \succeq Z$. However, X has no free occurrence inside of $fp_\varphi(Z)$ unlike

Y. An approximant for Z will depend on a value for Y, but approximant values for Y depend on a value for X. Thus, we can only give a meaningful approximant value for Z in a signature if we also give one to Y *and* one to X.

Definition 8.2.12. Let $\tau \in \{\mu, \nu\}$ and $\varphi \in \mathcal{L}_\mu$. A τ-**signature** for φ is a partial map η which assigns ordinal numbers to fixpoint variables of type τ in φ such that for all X, Y of type τ: if $\eta(Y)$ is defined and $X \succeq Y$ then $\eta(X)$ is defined.

The (strict) total ordering $<$ on ordinal numbers extends to a lexicographic ordering on τ-signatures for φ, which we also denote by $<$, as follows. We have $\eta < \eta'$ iff there is some τ-variable Y such that $\eta(Y)$ is defined and

- $\eta'(Y)$ is undefined or $\eta(Y) < \eta'(Y)$ and
- for all X with $X \succ_\varphi Y$ we have $\eta(X) \le \eta'(X)$.

As usual, let $\le$ denote its reflexive closure. $\qquad\qquad\qquad\qquad\qquad\qquad \nabla$

Lemma 8.2.13. The lexicographic ordering $\le$ on τ-signatures is well founded. $\qquad\blacksquare$

The proof is standard and is therefore left as Exercise 8.14.

Example 8.2.14. Reconsider the formula $\varphi := \nu X.\langle a\rangle X \wedge \nu Y.\langle b\rangle(Y \wedge X)$ and the 2-state transition system in Exercise 8.2.9. Clearly, since φ has no least fixpoint subformulae, μ-signatures are of no interest to it. We list all of its ν-signatures restricted to the ordinal values $0, 1, 2$ – note that on the 2-state transition system, fixpoints equal their approximants at level 2 according to Theorem 8.2.8. We denote a ν-signature η as a tuple of fixed arity and use '$-$' to mark those positions for which it is undefined, e.g. $(\eta(X), -)$ or $(\eta(X), \eta(Y))$. Recall that $X \succ_\varphi Y$ and therefore each ν-signature which defines a value for Y must also define a value for X, but not vice versa:

$$
\begin{aligned}
(-,-) \;>\; (2,-) \;>\; (2,2) \;>\; (2,1) \;>\; (2,0) \;>\; (1,-) \;>\; (1,2) \\
>\; (1,1) \;>\; (1,0) \;>\; (0,-) \;>\; (0,2) \;>\; (0,1) \;>\; (0,0).
\end{aligned}
$$

The signature $(-, \ldots, -)$ which is undefined on all arguments is always the largest.

Finally, we show that signatures are in fact just special variable assignments by defining the interpretation of a formula under a τ-signature for some $\tau \in \{\mu, \nu\}$. Intuitively, this interpretation gives values to variables of type τ which are free in subformulae and interprets the variables of the other type by the respective fixpoint.

Definition 8.2.15. Let $\mathcal{T}$ be a transition system and φ a closed formula of $\mathcal{L}_\mu$. Let η be a μ-signature for φ. We define a variable assignment ρ_η for the variables in φ recursively as follows.

$$
\rho_\eta(X) \;:=\; \begin{cases} [\![\mu^{\eta(X)} X.\psi]\!]^{\mathcal{T}}_{\rho_\eta}, & \text{if } fp_\varphi(X) = \mu X.\psi \\ [\![\nu X.\psi]\!]^{\mathcal{T}}_{\rho_\eta}, & \text{if } fp_\varphi(X) = \nu X.\psi. \end{cases}
$$

The variable assignment ρ_η for a ν-signature η is defined dually: ν-bound variables are interpreted by the respective approximant, μ-bound variables are interpreted by the respective fixpoint. ∇

Note that the preceding definition is indeed recursive but this recursion is well founded: the formulae $\mu^{\eta(X)}X.\psi$ do not contain X anymore. Thus, the definition of ρ_η at argument X needs the definition of the approximants for $fp_\varphi(X)$. They, however, only need ρ_η on arguments Y such that $Y \succ_\varphi X$. In particular, for a maximal, say, μ-bound variable X with respect to $\succeq_\varphi$, i.e. one that does not depend on any other, we have $[\![\mu^{\eta(X)}X.\psi]\!]^T_{\rho_\eta} = [\![\mu^{\eta(X)}X.\psi]\!]^T$. In other words, ρ_η can unambiguously be constructed from η (and the information of whether it is a μ- or a ν-signature) by recursion over the finite dependency order $\succeq$. We will simply write $T, s \models_\eta \varphi$ instead of $T, s \models_{\rho_\eta} \varphi$.

8.2.3 Global Model Checking

In this section we introduce **fixpoint iteration** as a method for solving the global model-checking problem for the modal μ-calculus. The formal semantics of the modal μ-calculus prescribes how to do this. For example, the set of states satisfying a conjunction can simply be obtained as the intersection of the two sets of states satisfying the two conjuncts.

Note that the set of states satisfying a least fixpoint operator on a finite transition system could equally be computed using the definition in the formal semantics: compute all pre-fixpoints and take their intersection. However, this is not very practical because there are $2^n - 1$ many sets to be checked for being a pre-fixpoint in a transition system with n states. Thus, such an algorithm would have a running time that is exponential in the size of the transition system. The theory of approximants to fixpoint formulae gives a better algorithm which is polynomial in the size of the underlying transition system. It is presented as FPITER in Algorithm 8.

Its correctness is easily established by induction using the theory of approximants. The formal proof is left as Exercise 8.16.

Theorem 8.2.16. Given a finite transition system T, a formula $\varphi \in \mathcal{L}_\mu$ and a variable assignment ρ for its free variables, Algorithm 8 correctly computes $[\![\varphi]\!]^T_\rho$.   ■

If we try to estimate its running time then we see that pure size of the input is not a very good measure. Note that all cases apart from fixpoint formulae can be computed in time linear in the size of the underlying transition system. Let n be the number of states in it. Each fixpoint formula induces an iteration which is – by monotonicity – can take at most n rounds. However, in each round the procedure FPITER is called recursively. Thus, each round of the iteration may entail further inner iterations which are being set off by nested fixpoint formulae. In order to measure the running time precisely, we need a parameter that measures this nesting.

Algorithm 8 FPITER for computing $\llbracket \varphi \rrbracket^{\mathcal{T}}_{\rho}$ with $\mathcal{T} = (S, \{\xrightarrow{a}\}_{a \in Act}, L)$.

1: **procedure** FPITER(φ, ρ)
2:     **case** φ **of**
3:         p: **return** $\{s \mid p \in L(s)\}$ ▷ some atomic proposition
4:         X: **return** $\rho(X)$ ▷ some variable
5:         $\neg\psi$: **return** $S \setminus$ FPITER(ψ, ρ)
6:         $\psi_1 \wedge \psi_2$: **return** FPITER(ψ_1, ρ) $\cap$ FPITER(ψ_2, ρ)
7:         $\langle a \rangle \psi$:
8:             $T \leftarrow$ FPITER(ψ, ρ)
9:             **return** $\{s \mid \exists t$ such that $t \in T$ and $s \xrightarrow{a} t\}$
10:       $\mu X.\psi$:
11:           $T \leftarrow \emptyset$
12:           **repeat**
13:              $T' \leftarrow T$
14:              $T \leftarrow$ FPITER($\psi, \rho[X \mapsto T']$)
15:           **until** $T = T'$
16:           **return** T
17:     **end case**
18: **end procedure**

Definition 8.2.17. The **quantifier depth** of an $\mathcal{L}_\mu$ formula is the maximal number of fixpoint quantifiers on each path of the syntax DAG. It is defined inductively as follows.

$$qd(q) = qd(X) := 0$$
$$qd(\varphi \wedge \psi) := \max\{qd(\varphi), qd(\psi)\}$$
$$qd(\neg\psi) = qd(\langle a \rangle \psi) := qd(\psi)$$
$$qd(\mu X.\psi) := 1 + qd(\psi). \qquad\qquad \nabla$$

Theorem 8.2.18. Given a finite transition system $\mathcal{T}$ with n states and m edges as well as a closed formula $\varphi \in \mathcal{L}_\mu$, Algorithm 8 terminates in time $\mathcal{O}(m \cdot |\varphi| \cdot n^{1+qd(\varphi)})$.   ■

The proof is left as Exercise 8.16.

8.3 The Structural Complexity of Formulae

8.3.1 Fixpoint Nestings

Algorithm FPITER is not optimal. Consider the following two formulae.

$$\varphi_1 := \mu X.\langle a \rangle \big(\mu Y.\langle a \rangle Y \vee p \vee \langle b \rangle X \big)$$
$$\varphi_2 := \mu X.\langle a \rangle \big(\mu Y.\langle a \rangle Y \vee p \big) \vee \langle b \rangle X.$$

The first one expresses 'there is a path with labels of the form $(a^+b)^*$ that ends in a state satisfying p'; the second one expresses 'there is a path with labels of the form b^*a^+ that ends in a state satisfying p' but these properties are irrelevant for the following consideration.

Note that we have $qd(\varphi_1) = qd(\varphi_2) = 2$. In order to evaluate φ_1 on a finite transition system with n states, algorithm FPITER runs two nested iterations, one for X and an inner one for Y. The same holds for the evaluation of φ_2. However, note that here, in each iteration of the outer loop the inner iteration yields the same value. The reason for this is the fact that the inner iteration computes $[\![\mu Y.\langle a\rangle Y \vee p]\!]$ which does not depend on a value for X because X has no free occurrence in this formula. Thus, it suffices to compute this value once and reuse it in each iteration of the outer loop. This reduces the number of possible iterations from n^2 to $2n$. In order to generalise this suitably we introduce a second parameter that measures the structural complexity of an $\mathcal{L}_\mu$ formula in a more refined way than the quantifier depth.

Definition 8.3.1. The **nesting depth** of a formula φ, written $nd(\varphi)$, is the maximal number n in a chain

$$X_1 \succ_\varphi X_2 \succ_\varphi \ldots \succ_\varphi X_n. \qquad\qquad \triangledown$$

Note that $nd(\varphi_1) = 2$ but $nd(\varphi_2) = 1$ for the two example formulae defined previously.

The optimisation for FPITER that reuses the values of formulae which do not depend on outer iterations leads to a better complexity bound. Note that for each φ we have $nd(\varphi) \leq qd(\varphi)$.

Theorem 8.3.2. Given a transition system $\mathcal{T}$ with n states and m edges, and a closed formula φ, it is possible to compute $[\![\varphi]\!]^{\mathcal{T}}$ in time $\mathcal{O}(m \cdot |\varphi| \cdot n^{nd(\varphi)})$. $\qquad$ ∎

The proof is left as Exercise 8.18.

8.3.2 The Bekić Lemma

Reconsider again the two example formulae φ_1 and φ_2. Since φ_2 has no true nesting between the two fixpoint formulae in the sense that the outer variable occurs in the inner fixpoint formula, it is possible to evaluate it using a linear number of iterations. The formula with true nesting in this sense requires a quadratic number of iterations – a linear number of the inner for each iteration of the outer. This is what the procedure FPITER would do, even in the optimised form according to Theorem 8.3.2. Still, it is possible to employ yet another trick about fixpoint iteration which makes a linear number of iterations suffice for formulae like φ_1.

Let $(\mathcal{P}(S), \subseteq)$ be the powerset lattice of some set S of states of some transition system. Then $(\mathcal{P}(S) \times \mathcal{P}(S), \sqsubseteq)$ is a complete lattice when $\sqsubseteq$ denotes the pointwise ordering defined by $(x, y) \sqsubseteq (x', y')$ iff $x \subseteq x'$ and $y \subseteq y'$. Let $F : \mathcal{P}(S)^2 \to \mathcal{P}(S)^2$ be defined by $F(x, y) = (f(x, y), g(x, y))$. Clearly, if f and g are monotone in both its arguments, so is F on $\mathcal{P}(S)^2$. In that case it possesses a unique least and a unique greatest fixpoint according to the Knaster–Tarski Theorem (see also Section 2.2.1). It can be found by iterating through its approximants

$$(\emptyset, \emptyset), \quad (f(\emptyset, \emptyset), g(\emptyset, \emptyset)), \quad (f(f(\emptyset, \emptyset), g(\emptyset, \emptyset)), g(f(\emptyset, \emptyset), g(\emptyset, \emptyset))), \ \ldots$$

Thus, in order to compute its nth approximant in $\mathcal{P}(S)^2$ one only has to compute $2n + 2$ values in $\mathcal{P}(S)$. We can easily generalise this to functions of type $\mathcal{P}(S)^k \to \mathcal{P}(S)^k$ for any fixed $k \geq 1$. In that case, the computation of the nth approximant in $\mathcal{P}(S)^k$ will require the computation of $k(n + 1)$ many values, i.e. linearly many in $\mathcal{P}(S)$ only.

Now, note that $\mathcal{L}_\mu$ formulae are not interpreted in such products of lattices but the interpretation of a formula $\psi(X, Y)$ with two free variables X and Y for instance behaves like one of the functions f or g of type $\mathcal{P}(S)^2 \to \mathcal{P}(S)$ used in the definition of the function F of type $\mathcal{P}(S)^2 \to \mathcal{P}(S)^2$. The extension of an $\mathcal{L}_\mu$ formula is not an element of such a product lattice, yet the simple computation of approximants in the product lattice can be used in order to speed up fixpoint iteration for $\mathcal{L}_\mu$. The reason for this is the following theorem, known as the **Bekić Lemma**, which states the equivalences between **simultaneous fixpoints** – i.e. defined by functions on product lattices – and **parametric fixpoints** – i.e. defined by polyadic functions on the underlying lattice. Here we formulate it for the case of $k = 2$ only. An explicit generalisation to arbitrary k is straightforwardly possible. It also follows by induction from associativity of the product operator: $\mathcal{P}(S)^{k+1} = \mathcal{P}(S)^k \times \mathcal{P}(S)$.

Here we need to deal with functions f of type $\mathcal{P}(S)^2 \to \mathcal{P}(S)$, and we write $\mu x. f(x, y)$ for the least fixpoints of the families of functions which take x as input and are parameterised by y.

Theorem 8.3.3 (Bekić Lemma). Let $(\mathcal{P}(S), \subseteq)$ be a powerset lattice, $f, g : \mathcal{P}(S)^2 \to \mathcal{P}(S)$ monotone in both their arguments, and $F : \mathcal{P}(S)^2 \to \mathcal{P}(S)^2$ defined by $F(x, y) = (f(x, y), g(x, y))$. Then

$$\mu(x, y). F(x, y) = \big(\mu x. f(x, \mu y. g(x, y)),\ \mu y. g(\mu x. f(x, \mu y. g(x, y)), y)\big). \qquad \blacksquare$$

Proof. We introduce the abbreviations $x^* := \mu x. f(x, \mu y. g(x, y))$ and $y^* := \mu y. g(x^*, y)$. Thus, we want to show that $\mu(x, y). F(x, y) = (x^*, y^*)$ holds in the powerset lattice $(\mathcal{P}(S)^2, \sqsubseteq)$. So we need to show two directions.

'$\sqsubseteq$' Since $\mu(x, y). F(x, y)$ is the infimum of all pre-fixpoints it suffices to show for this part that (x^*, y^*) is a pre-fixpoint of F. First note that we have $g(x^*, y^*) = y^*$ because y^* is the least fixpoint of the map g when its first argument is fixed to x^*. Hence it is also

- a post-fixpoint, which means that we have $y^* \subseteq g(x^*, y^*)$, as well as
- a pre-fixpoint, which means that we get $\mu y. g(x^*, y) \subseteq y^*$ because $\mu y. g(x^*, y)$ is the infimum over all such pre-fixpoints. By monotonicity of f in its second argument we then have $f(x^*, \mu y. g(x^*, y)) \subseteq f(x^*, y^*)$, i.e. $x^* \subseteq f(x^*, y^*)$.

Combining these two facts we get $(x^*, y^*) \sqsubseteq (f(x^*, y^*), g(x^*, y^*)) = F(x^*, y^*)$ which was to be proved.

'$\sqsupseteq$' For this direction we use F_1^* and F_2^* to denote that first and second component of the left-hand side, i.e. $\mu(x, y). F(x, y) = (F_1^*, F_2^*)$. Since this is a fixpoint, we get, in fact, $F_1^* =$

$f(F_1^*, F_2^*)$ and $F_2^* = g(F_1^*, F_2^*)$. The latter shows immediately that we have $\mu y.g(F_1^*, y) \subseteq F_2^*$ because F_2^* is obviously a fixpoint of the map that sends y to $g(F_1^*, y)$. We weaken the former to $f(F_1^*, F_2^*) \subseteq F_1^*$ and then use monotonicity of f in its second argument, to obtain $f(F_1^*, \mu y.g(F_1^*, y)) \subseteq F_1^*$. This completes half of the proof because now we know that F_1^* is a pre-fixpoint of the map that sends x to $f(x, \mu y.g(x, y))$, hence we get $F_1^* \supseteq \mu x.f(x, \mu y.g(x, y))$.

It remains to be seen that we also have $F_2^* \supseteq \mu y.g(\mu x.f(x, \mu y.g(x, y)), y)$. By the preceding observation, we have $F_2^* \supseteq g(F_1^*, F_2^*)$ and by monotonicity of g in its first argument, we have $F_2^* \supseteq g(\mu x.f(x, \mu y.g(x, y)), F_2^*)$. This means that F_2^* is a pre-fixpoint of the map that sends y to $g(\mu x.f(x, \mu y.g(x, y)), y)$ which gives us $F_2^* \supseteq \mu y.g(\mu x.f(x, \mu y.g(x, y)), y)$. This completes the second half of this claim.   □

In particular, consider an $\mathcal{L}_\mu$ formula of the form $\mu X.\varphi(X, \mu Y.\psi(X, Y))$. Then the Bekić Lemma states that it is possible to compute its value in a transition system simultaneously rather than in a parametric fashion. Thus, instead of an outer fixpoint iteration for X and a full inner iteration for Y at every stage of the outer one, it suffices to do a single iteration in which both X and Y are initially evaluated as $\emptyset$, and then one computes $[\![\psi]\!]_\rho^I$ as well as $[\![\varphi']\!]_\rho^I$ for $\rho = [X \mapsto \emptyset, Y \mapsto \emptyset]$ where φ' results from φ by replacing the inner fixpoint formula $\mu Y.\psi(X, Y)$ with just the variable Y. This iteration continues for as long as either the value of X or the value of Y changes. Finally, when both have stabilised, the value for X is the value of the nested fixpoint formula under consideration.

We remark that the analogue version of the Bekić Lemma exists for greatest fixpoints. Its essence is, again: greatest fixpoints can be computed simultaneously. It should be clear that these two iteration schemes lead to yet a further improvement of Algorithm FPITER. Besides taking the dependency relation between the fixpoint subformulae into account one can also use a single fixpoint iteration for several possibly nested formulae of the same type. Note, however, that the Bekić Lemma *does not* allow the fixpoint iterations for formulae of different fixpoint types to be combined into a single simultaneous iteration.

In order to measure the effect that this optimisation has on Algorithm FPITER we introduce yet another parameter which measures the structural complexity of formulae in an even more refined way than the nesting depth.

Definition 8.3.4. Let φ be a formula in negation normal form. The **type** of a variable X in it is μ if $fp_\varphi(X) = \mu X.\psi$ for some ψ. Otherwise its type is ν.

The **alternation depth** of a formula φ in negation normal form, written $ad(\varphi)$ is the maximal number n in a chain

$$X_1 \succ_\varphi X_2 \succ_\varphi \ldots \succ_\varphi X_n$$

such that adjacent variables in this chain have different types.

A formula φ is called **alternation-free** if $ad(\varphi) \leq 1$.   ▽

Note that in general we have $ad(\varphi) \leq nd(\varphi)$, and that for the two example formulae we have $ad(\varphi_1) = ad(\varphi_2) = 1$.

Theorem 8.3.5. Given a transition system $\mathcal{T}$ with n nodes and m edges, as well as a closed formula φ, it is possible to compute $[\![\varphi]\!]^{\mathcal{T}}$ in time $\mathcal{O}(m \cdot |\varphi| \cdot n^{1+ad(\varphi)})$. ■

The proof is left as Exercise 8.20.

8.3.3 Fixpoint Alternation

Finally, we consider a refinement of the alternation depth measure. It distinguishes between different kinds of alternation, for example a least fixpoint nested within a greatest fixpoint is a different kind of alternation than a greatest fixpoint nested within a least fixpoint, although both would lead to alternation depth at least 2. This finer distinction does not necessarily lead to better upper bounds for model checking but it has important applications in the study of $\mathcal{L}_\mu$'s expressive power. Further we assume all formulae to be in negation normal form.

Definition 8.3.6 (Alternation hierarchy). Let Σ_0 and Π_0 consist of all formulae which do not contain fixpoint subformulae. Based on this we define sets of formulae Σ_n, Π_n and Δ_n for $n \geq 1$ inductively as follows.

- Σ_n is the least set of formulae that contains $\Sigma_{n-1} \cup \Pi_{n-1}$ and is closed under the following operations.
  - If $\varphi, \psi \in \Sigma_n$ then $\{\varphi \wedge \psi, \varphi \vee \psi\} \subseteq \Sigma_n$.
  - If $\varphi \in \Sigma_n$ and $a \in Act$ then $\{\langle a \rangle \varphi, [a]\varphi\} \subseteq \Sigma_n$.
  - If $\varphi \in \Sigma_n$ and $X \in \text{VAR}$ then $\mu X.\varphi \in \Sigma_n$.
  - If $\varphi, \psi \in \Sigma_n$ and $Z \in \text{VAR}$ then $\varphi[\psi/Z] \in \Sigma_n$ provided that this substitution does not bind any free variable of ψ.
- Π_n is defined in the same way with ν instead of μ.
- $\Delta_n := \Sigma_n \cap \Pi_n$. $\triangledown$

The term alternation hierarchy refers to the hierarchical structure that these sets impose on $\mathcal{L}_\mu$. The $\subseteq$-relation is depicted using lines that go from left to right.

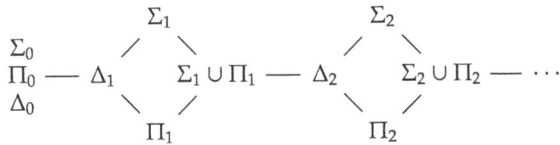

$$
\begin{array}{ccccccc}
 & & \Sigma_1 & & & \Sigma_2 & \\
 & & \diagup \quad \diagdown & & & \diagup \quad \diagdown & \\
\begin{matrix}\Sigma_0 \\ \Pi_0 \\ \Delta_0\end{matrix} & \!\!\!\!-\! \Delta_1 - \!\!\!\! & \Sigma_1 \cup \Pi_1 & \!\!\!\!-\! \Delta_2 -\!\!\!\! & \Sigma_2 \cup \Pi_2 & -\cdots & \\
 & & \diagdown \quad \diagup & & & \diagdown \quad \diagup & \\
 & & \Pi_1 & & & \Pi_2 &
\end{array}
$$

Example 8.3.7. Consider $\varphi = \mu X.\Diamond(\nu Y.\mu Z.(q \wedge \Diamond Y) \vee \Diamond Z) \vee \Diamond X$. We have $\varphi \in \Pi_2$ for the following reason. Clearly, $(q \wedge \Diamond Y) \vee Z \in \Sigma_0$ because it does not contain any fixpoint operator. Since $\Sigma_0 \subseteq \Sigma_1$ and Σ_1 is closed under introducing μ-operators we have $\mu Z.(q \wedge \Diamond Y) \vee \Diamond Z \in \Sigma_1$. Now $\Sigma_1 \subseteq \Pi_2$ and Π_2 is equally closed under introducing ν-operators. Therefore we have $\nu Y.\mu Z.(q \wedge \Diamond Y) \vee \Diamond Z \in \Pi_2$.

On the other hand, $X' \vee \Diamond X \in \Sigma_0$ and therefore $\mu X.X' \vee \Diamond X \in \Sigma_1 \subseteq \Pi_2$. Since Π_2 is closed under substitutions that do not introduce new variable bindings, we get that $\varphi \in \Pi_2$

because it results from $\mu X.X' \vee \Diamond X$ by replacing X' with the closed Π_2-formula $\nu Y.\mu Z.(q \wedge \Diamond Y) \vee \Diamond Z$.

The next two lemmas state how the notion of alternation depth relates to the alternation hierarchy.

Lemma 8.3.8. For all $n \geq 1$, for all formulae $\varphi \in \Sigma_{n+1} \cup \Pi_{n+1}$, we have $ad(\varphi) \leq n$. ■

The proof is left as Exercise 8.22 and can be done by induction on n.

Lemma 8.3.9. For any φ, if $ad(\varphi) = n$, then $\varphi \in \Sigma_{n+1} \cup \Pi_{n+1}$. ■

The proof is left as Exercise 8.22.

8.3.4 Modal Equation Systems

The modal μ-calculus uses fixpoints of monotone functions given by modal terms in order to define temporal properties. Fixpoints are usually associated with equation systems, i.e. an equation system is used in order to define some concept which is given as a solution to this system, and a solution is typically a fixpoint. It is in fact possible to define a different syntax for the modal μ-calculus in terms of systems of equations of modal terms. We present this alternative syntax here because it sometimes proves to be beneficial, in particular when one needs to define properties by simultaneous fixpoints as is done by automata for instance.

Before we define this syntax – called Modal Equation Systems (MES) – formally, we give an example which shows that one has to take a little bit of care in defining such systems in order to guarantee unique solutions.

Example 8.3.10. Consider the two equations

$$X = Y$$
$$Y = \Diamond(p \wedge X) \vee \Diamond(\neg p \wedge Y)$$

and the following transition system $\mathcal{T}$.

A solution to the equation system is a pair (S_X, S_Y) of sets of states of $\mathcal{T}$ satisfying the following. Let $\rho = [X \mapsto S_X, Y \mapsto S_Y]$ and φ_X, respectively φ_Y, denote the two right-hand sides of the defining equation for X, respectively Y. Then (S_X, S_Y) is a solution if $[\![\varphi_X]\!]_\rho^{\mathcal{T}} = S_X$ and $[\![\varphi_Y]\!]_\rho^{\mathcal{T}} = S_Y$.

Intuitively, a solution is a tuple of state sets which can be put into the variables in right-hand sides such that these evaluate to the same tuple of state sets, i.e. it is a fixpoint of this equation system.

It is easy to see that any solution (S_X, S_Y) of the system must satisfy $S_X = S_Y$ because of the first equation. Thus, we can restrict our attention to single sets of states when trying to find solutions of this particular system. One may verify that all of the following are in fact solutions: $\emptyset$, $\{2\}$, $\{3\}$, $\{0, 1, 2\}$, $\{0, 1, 3\}$ and $\{0, 1, 2, 3\}$. These are clearly ordered by $\subseteq$ with $\emptyset$ and $\{0, 1, 2, 3\}$ being the least and greatest possible solutions. In fact, $\emptyset$ is obtained as the simultaneous least fixpoint for both X and Y of this MES. In more detail, $(\emptyset, \emptyset)$ is the solution that is least with respect to the pointwise extension $\subseteq \times \subseteq$ of $\subseteq$ onto pairs of states sets. Equally, $\{0, 1, 2, 3\}$ is obtained as the simultaneous greatest fixpoint for X and Y. In both cases, this solution would have also been found with the simpler MES in which the equation $X = Y$ is being inlined in the second, resulting in a MES with the single equation $Y = \Diamond(p \wedge Y) \vee \Diamond(\neg p \wedge Y)$. Note that in this case, the right-hand side is equal to $\Diamond Y$.

An interesting question asks whether it is possible to characterise the four other solutions of the MES with the two equations as being least or greatest in some sense. This is indeed the case, and it shows that one cannot always eliminate equations of the form $X = Y$, since we can consider solutions that are least with respect to one variable and greatest with respect to another. This still does not yield a unique classification: take for instance $\{2\}$ and $\{0, 1, 2\}$. Both are being obtained as the least solution for Y and the greatest for X. They differ in the order between X and Y in which one obtains the solution. For instance, if we set Y to be $\emptyset$ – which is clearly least – and then try to find the largest X that is a solution, and then continue with this value for Y again, etc., then the result is $\{2\}$. If, on the other hand, we set X to the largest value first and then compute the least value for Y, etc., then the result will be $\{0, 1, 2\}$. Formally, $\{0, 1, 2\}$ is the largest solution for X that is parametrised by the least solution for Y. The value $\{2\}$ is obtained as the least solution for Y that is parametrised by the largest solution for X.

Equally, $\{0, 1, 3\}$ is obtained as the largest solution for Y parametrised by the least solution for X, and $\{3\}$ when the order of parametrisation is reversed.

Note that the modal μ-calculus is capable of expressing all of these solutions; the vague notion of parametrisation is simply given by the subformula ordering. In fact, let $\varphi = \Diamond(p \wedge X) \vee \Diamond(\neg p \wedge Y)$. Then we have the following.

$$
\begin{aligned}
\llbracket \mu X.\mu Y.\varphi \rrbracket^T &= \llbracket \mu Y.\mu X.\varphi \rrbracket^T = \emptyset \\
\llbracket \mu X.\nu Y.\varphi \rrbracket^T &= \{3\} \\
\llbracket \nu X.\mu Y.\varphi \rrbracket^T &= \{0, 1, 2\} \\
\llbracket \mu Y.\nu X.\varphi \rrbracket^T &= \{2\} \\
\llbracket \nu Y.\mu X.\varphi \rrbracket^T &= \{0, 1, 3\} \\
\llbracket \nu X.\nu Y.\varphi \rrbracket^T &= \llbracket \nu Y.\nu X.\varphi \rrbracket^T = \{0, 1, 2, 3\}.
\end{aligned}
$$

This example shows in particular that one needs to take care of two problems when defining Modal Equation Systems in order not to obtain an ambiguous semantics: we need to specify the kind of fixpoint we want to define (least, greatest, possibly others) for each variable, and we need to provide an order of parametrisation between the variables. We will do so implicitly by assigning natural numbers to each variable that naturally provide a total ordering, as well as the information on least or greatest fixpoints through their parity (even or odd).

Definition 8.3.11. Let $V = \{X_1, \ldots, X_n\} \subseteq \text{VAR}$ be a finite set of variables. A **Modal Equation System** (MES) over V (and sets of atomic propositions PROP and action names *Act*) is a pair $(\mathcal{E}, i)$ such that $1 \leq i \leq n$ and $\mathcal{E}$ is a set of n equations of the form

$$\{X_1 =_{\mathsf{p}_1} \varphi_1, \ldots, X_n =_{\mathsf{p}_n} \varphi_n\}$$

where, for $j = 1, \ldots, n$,

- φ_j is a formula of $\mathcal{L}_\mu$ built from the variables in V and literals over atomic propositions in PROP using the operators $\wedge$, $\vee$, $\langle a \rangle$ and $[a]$ for some $a \in Act$ only;
- $\mathsf{p}_j \in \mathbb{N}$.

The annotations p_j are also called **priorities**.   ▽

The index i singles out a particular variable; it is used in order to define sets of states in a transition system rather than n-tuples thereof. Intuitively, the solution of a MES is an n-tuple of such states, and in the end it gets projected onto its ith component. We use the convention that the first variable (in a list presentation for instance) defines this value i when it is not given explicitly.

Example 8.3.12. The equations of the preceding example can be turned into a MES by assigning priorities, for example

$$X =_2 Y, \quad Y =_1 \Diamond(p \wedge X) \vee \Diamond(\neg p \wedge Y).$$

Even priorities define greatest fixpoints, odd ones define least fixpoints. Thus, the solution of this equation system with respect to the transition system of the previous example should be $\{0, 1, 2\}$ for both X and Y. On the other hand, the solution of

$$X =_{17} Y, \quad Y =_{2098} \Diamond(p \wedge X) \vee \Diamond(\neg p \wedge Y)$$

should be $\{0, 1, 3\}$ because now X has received an odd priority, Y an even one and that is also higher now than the one for X. That is, the solution is supposed to be the greatest one for Y parametrised by the least one for X. Intuitively, this MES is clearly equivalent to

$$X =_1 Y, \quad Y =_2 \Diamond(p \wedge X) \vee \Diamond(\neg p \wedge Y).$$

We provide a semantics for MES by a syntactic translation into formulae of $\mathcal{L}_\mu$. Let $(\mathcal{E}, i)$ be a MES with equations of the form $X_j =_{\mathsf{p}_j} \varphi_j$ for $j = 1, \ldots, n$. It abbreviates the $\mathcal{L}_\mu$ formula $tr_\emptyset(X_i)$, recursively defined as follows. Intuitively, *tr* flattens the equation system into a single formula. It takes two parameters: the variable or formula to be translated and a set of indices of variables which have already been traversed. This is needed in order to map the order of parametrisation given by the priorities into the nesting order of fixpoints in the resulting formula. The translation is straightforward for all operators occurring on right-hand sides of a MES.

$$tr_T(p) := p \qquad\qquad tr_T(\neg p) := \neg p$$
$$tr_T(\varphi \wedge \psi) := tr_T(\varphi) \wedge tr_T(\psi) \qquad\qquad tr_T(\varphi \vee \psi) := tr_T(\varphi) \vee tr_T(\psi)$$
$$tr_T(\langle a \rangle \varphi) := \langle a \rangle tr_T(\varphi) \qquad\qquad tr_T([a]\varphi) := [a]tr_T(\varphi).$$

The only interesting case is that of a variable X. The parameter T collects variables that have been quantified already. Thus, if X does not occur in T then we need to introduce a new quantification for X matching the fixpoint type given by its priority in $\mathcal{E}$. Otherwise, we can simply leave the variable at this place in the resulting formula. However, when we introduce a new quantification for a variable with some priority $\mathfrak{p}$ then inside this fixpoint formula we must not use variables with smaller priorities that occur in T already. This is because their fixpoint quantification will occur on an outer level in the resulting formula which would give them a higher priority over inner ones in the usual semantics of $\mathcal{L}_\mu$. Hence, the remaining clause for the translation function is

$$tr_T(X_j) := \begin{cases} X_j, & \text{if } X_j \in T \\ \tau X_j.tr_{T'}(\varphi_j), & \text{if } X_j \notin T \end{cases}$$

where $\tau := \mu$ if $\mathfrak{p}_j$ is odd and $\tau = \nu$ otherwise, and $T' := (T \setminus \{X_i \mid \mathfrak{p}_i < \mathfrak{p}_j\}) \cup \{X_j\}$.

It should be clear that the translation of a MES into a plain formula can cause an exponential blow-up.

Example 8.3.13. Consider the equation system

$$X_1 =_1 (p \wedge \Diamond X_2) \vee \Diamond X_1 \qquad X_2 =_2 X_1$$

with initial variable X_1. Its translation into a plain $\mathcal{L}_\mu$ formula is

$$tr_\emptyset(X_1) = \mu X_1.tr_{\{X_1\}}((p \wedge \Diamond X_2) \vee \Diamond X_1) = \mu X_1.(p \wedge \Diamond tr_{\{X_1\}}(X_2)) \vee \Diamond X_1.$$

Now suppose that in order to further evaluate $tr_{\{X_1\}}(X_2)$ we would simply introduce a ν-quantification, since X_2 has an even priority, and remember that we have seen that variable as well. Thus, we would replace it by $\nu X_2.tr_{\{X_1, X_2\}}(X_1) = \nu X_2.X_1$ which is easily seen to be equivalent to X_1. Thus, the resulting formula would be $\mu X_1.(p \wedge \Diamond X_1) \vee \Diamond X_1$ which is clearly equivalent to $\mu X_1.\Diamond X_1$. This, however, is unsatisfiable and therefore does not express the aforementioned property.

The mistake that has happened here is the ignoring of the fact that X_2 has a greater priority than X_1, and therefore it must not be quantified inside of the quantification for X_1. A solution could be to re-order subformulae cleverly but it is not clear how one could do this in general. That is why the correct definition of *tr* requires variables in the T-parameter to be deleted. This has the essential effect that the subformula relation between fixpoint quantifications in the resulting formula reflects the order on priorities. The price to pay for this is possible multiple occurrences of variables.

The correct way to build the corresponding formula uses

$$tr_{\{X_1\}}(X_2) = \nu X_2.tr_{\{X_2\}}(X_1) = \nu X_2.\mu X_1.tr_{\{X_1,X_2\}}((p \wedge \Diamond X_2) \vee \Diamond X_1$$
$$= \nu X_2.\mu X_1.(p \wedge \Diamond X_2) \vee \Diamond X_1.$$

Thus, the formula that the MES represents is

$$\mu X_1.(p \wedge \Diamond(\nu X_2.\mu X_1.(p \wedge \Diamond X_2) \vee \Diamond X_1)) \vee \Diamond X_1$$

which can easily be made well formed by renaming the inner or outer X_1 to X_3 for instance.

MES can indeed provide succinct representations of $\mathcal{L}_\mu$ formulae. This is hinted at by the facts that the translation from a MES into a formula involves an exponential blow-up whereas the translation in the other direction is linear. An $\mathcal{L}_\mu$ formula can easily be read as a MES in the following way.

Definition 8.3.14. Let φ be an $\mathcal{L}_\mu$ formula. W.l.o.g. we can assume φ's topmost operator to be a fixpoint quantifier, i.e. $\varphi = \tau X.\psi$ for some ψ and some $\tau \in \{\mu, \nu\}$. This assumption can be made because of the equivalence $\tau X.\psi \equiv \psi$ if X has no free occurrence in ψ.

Let $\tau_1 X_1.\psi_1, \ldots, \tau_n X_n.\psi_n$ be all fixpoint formulae in $sub(\varphi)$ in ascending order of size. That is, for all $i \neq j$: if $\tau_i X_i.\psi_i \in sub(\psi_j)$ then we have $i < j$. This entails $\varphi = \tau_n X_n.\psi_n$.

We assign to each variable X_i a priority p_i as follows: $p_i = 2i$ if $\tau_i = \nu$, and $p_i = 2i + 1$ otherwise. Hence, variables bound by a greatest fixpoint quantifer receive even priorities, those bound by a least fixpoint quantifer receive odd ones. Moreover, variables quantified in outer formulae receive greater priorities and those of inner formulae.

The **MES representation** of φ is $(\{X_i -_{p_i} \psi_i' \mid i = 1, \ldots, n\}, n)$ where for each $i = 1, \ldots, n$, ψ_i' is obtained from ψ_i by replacing every subformula of the form $\tau_j X_j.\psi_j$ with X_j. It should be clear that the result is indeed a MES. We leave it as Exercise 8.28 to show that translating a formula into a MES and then back produces the original formula again. ▽

Some work on $\mathcal{L}_\mu$ uses the cardinality of the Fischer–Ladner closure as a size measure for a formula.

Definition 8.3.15. Let φ be an $\mathcal{L}_\mu$ formula in negation normal form. Its **Fischer–Ladner closure** is the least set $fl(\varphi)$ that contains φ and is closed under the following operations.

- If $\psi_1 \wedge \psi_2 \in fl(\varphi)$ or $\psi_1 \vee \psi_2 \in fl(\varphi)$ then $\{\psi_1, \psi_2\} \subseteq fl(\varphi)$.
- If $\langle a \rangle \psi \in fl(\varphi)$ or $[a]\psi \in fl(\varphi)$ then $\psi \in fl(\varphi)$.
- If $\tau X.\psi \in fl(\varphi)$ for some $\tau \in \{\mu, \nu\}$ then $\psi[\tau X.\psi/X] \in fl(\varphi)$. ▽

Similar to the set $sub(\varphi)$ of subformulae, using $fl(\varphi)$ is an attempt at collecting all formulae that are relevant in an evalutation of φ in some transition system. It just applies a slightly different principle when it comes to handling fixpoint formulae: instead of using a recursion variable X and explicitly linking it to $fp_\varphi(X)$, we immediately eliminate variables by unfolding fixpoint formulae, as it is done in the last clause of Definition 8.3.15.

It may not be immediately clear that the Fischer–Ladner closure is finite, since one cannot argue that the membership of one formula in this set only entails the membership of strictly smaller formulae, as it can be done for the subformula set. However, it is indeed finite which follows from the following fact, the proof of which is left as Exercise 8.29.

Lemma 8.3.16. For every φ we have $\mathrm{card}(fi(\varphi)) \leq \mathrm{card}(sub(\varphi))$. ∎

It is worth noting that the cardinality of the Fischer–Ladner closure can be smaller than the number of subformulae, take for instance $\varphi = \Diamond \nu X.\Diamond X$. Then we have $\mathrm{card}(fi(\varphi)) = 2$ and $\mathrm{card}(sub(\varphi)) = 4$. Note that there is only one formula in $fi(\varphi)$ which starts with $\Diamond$, even though there are two such operators in φ. The reason for this phenomenon is the fact that the Fischer–Ladner closure identifies a fixpoint variable with its quantifying formula; and if X and $\nu X.\Diamond X$ are not being distinguished then so are $\Diamond X$ and $\Diamond \nu X.\Diamond X$. This principle can be used to construct formulae for which the cardinalities of the Fischer–Ladner closure and the subformula set differ notably.

Theorem 8.3.17. There is a family of formulae $(\varphi_n)_{n \geq 1}$ such that $\mathrm{card}(fi(\varphi_n)) = \mathcal{O}(n^2)$ and $\mathrm{card}(sub(\varphi_n)) = \Omega(2^n)$. ∎

Proof. Consider the following family of MES $\mathcal{E}_n$.

$$X_n =_1 \Diamond (X_1 \vee \ldots \vee X_n)$$
$$X_{n-1} =_1 \Diamond (X_1 \vee \ldots \vee X_n) \vee X_n$$

$$\vdots$$

$$X_2 =_1 \Diamond (X_1 \vee \ldots \vee X_n) \vee X_n \vee \ldots \vee X_3$$
$$X_1 =_1 \Diamond (X_1 \vee \ldots \vee X_n) \vee X_n \vee \ldots \vee X_3 \vee X_2.$$

Define $\varphi_n = tr_\emptyset(X_n)$. We leave it as Exercise 8.30 to verify the claims about the cardinalities of Fischer–Ladner closure and subformula set of φ_n. □

The actual priorities in these MES need not be 1; they are in fact irrelevant. Here they are just chosen as 1 to be consistent with Example 8.3.22 because these are the MES representations of the formulae in that example after the procedure in the next section has been applied to them.

The proof of Theorem 8.3.17 indicates what a good measure for the size of a formula representation is: the cardinality of the subformula set measures the number of nodes in the syntax DAG representation of a formula, i.e. the syntax tree with sharing of equal subtrees. The cardinality of the Fischer–Ladner closure, however, measures the size of a MES representation of a formula. This is why it can be significantly smaller.

8.3.5 Guardedness

The unfolding equivalences stated in Corollary 8.1.9 are being used in basically all algorithms for any logical problem regarding $\mathcal{L}_\mu$. For instance, in model checking, when one wants to determine whether a state s satisfies a formula of the form $\mu X.\varphi$, one can equivalently check the formula $\varphi[\mu X.\varphi/X]$ in s. This reduces the check in the sense that φ is a smaller formula than $\mu X.\varphi$. However, note that it is not φ that is being checked in s but $\varphi[\mu X.\varphi/X]$. Hence, by continuously reducing the checks to subformulae it may become necessary to check $\mu X.\varphi$ again – in some state r. Guardedness of φ is a syntactic property that ensures that between s and r at least one transition has been traversed. In other words, when model checking guarded formulae one does not recurse inside a state without progressing along transitions in a transition system.

For the sake of simplicity we will assume that all formulae are given in negation normal form.

Definition 8.3.18. Let $\varphi \in \mathcal{L}_\mu$ be in negation normal form. We say that an occurrence of a variable X is **guarded** in φ if it is under the scope of a $\langle a \rangle$- or $[a]$-operator within $fp_\varphi(X)$. The variable X itself is **guarded** if all of its occurrences are guarded. Finally, the formula φ itself is **guarded** if every bound variable is guarded in φ.

An occurrence of X in φ is **weakly guarded** if it is under the scope of a $\langle a \rangle$-, $[a]$-, or a fixpoint quantifier that binds a different variable within $fp_\varphi(X)$. ∇

Example 8.3.19. Consider $\varphi = \mu X.Z \vee \mu Y.X \vee \Diamond Y$. Then the single occurrence of Y – and therefore Y itself – is guarded in φ but X is not. Hence, φ is not guarded. However, the single occurrence of X is weakly guarded.

On the other hand, $\psi = \mu X.Z \vee \Diamond(\mu Y.X \vee \Diamond Y)$ is guarded. Note that Z does not occur under the scope of modalities but Z is a free variable of ψ.

We will present a procedure that transforms an arbitrary formula into an equivalent guarded one. It only requires two principles, the first one being the unfolding equivalence $\tau X.\varphi \equiv \varphi[\tau X.\varphi/X]$ stated in Corollary 8.1.9. The second principle is the fact that variables which are not even weakly guarded can be replaced by constants. In order to formalise this we introduce the notation $\varphi[\psi/X]^{\mathsf{nwg}}$ which denotes the formula that results from φ by replacing every free occurrence of X which is not weakly guarded by ψ.

Lemma 8.3.20. Let $\mu X.\varphi \in \mathcal{L}_\mu$. Then $\mu X.\varphi[\bot/X]^{\mathsf{nwg}} \equiv \mu X.\varphi$.   ∎

Proof. Let $\mathcal{T} = (S, \rightarrow, L)$ be a transition system and ρ a variable assignment. We need to show $[\![\mu X.\varphi[\bot/X]^{\mathsf{nwg}}]\!]_\rho^{\mathcal{T}} = [\![\mu X.\varphi]\!]_\rho^{\mathcal{T}}$. The '$\subseteq$'-part is a direct consequence of Lemma 8.1.10 because the replacement only operates on variable occurrences which are under an even number of negation symbols, and these get replaced by $\bot$ whose semantics is $\emptyset$ in any transition system.

For the '$\supseteq$'-part we first want to establish that for any $T \subseteq S$ we have

$$[\![\varphi[\bot/X]^{\mathsf{nwg}}]\!]_{\rho[X \mapsto T]}^{\mathcal{T}} \subseteq T \implies [\![\varphi]\!]_{\rho[X \mapsto T]}^{\mathcal{T}} \subseteq T . \tag{8.2}$$

This cannot be proved by induction on the structure of φ, in fact it is the case of conjunctions which poses a difficulty. We therefore consider a stronger statement: for any $T \subseteq S$ we have

$$\llbracket \varphi \rrbracket^T_{\rho[X \mapsto T]} \subseteq \llbracket \varphi[\bot/X]^{\mathsf{nwg}} \rrbracket^T_\rho \cup T.$$

It should be clear that (8.2) follows from this.

Now this can be proved by induction on the structure of φ. Note that we only need to consider the cases of the variable X itself and Boolean operators $\wedge$ and $\vee$. The cases of literals q and $\neg q$, variables Y other than X itself, modal and fixpoint operators are trivial because, in each of these cases we have $\varphi[\bot/X]^{\mathsf{nwg}} = \varphi$.

The case of $\varphi = X$ is very simple because it boils down to $T \subseteq \emptyset \cup T$ which is clearly true.

Now let $\varphi = \psi_1 \vee \psi_2$. Note that $\varphi[\bot/X]^{\mathsf{nwg}} = \psi_1[\bot/X]^{\mathsf{nwg}} \vee \psi_2[\bot/X]^{\mathsf{nwg}}$. Then we have

$$
\begin{aligned}
\llbracket \varphi \rrbracket^T_{\rho[X \mapsto T]} &= \llbracket \psi_1 \rrbracket^T_{\rho[X \mapsto T]} \cup \llbracket \psi_2 \rrbracket^T_{\rho[X \mapsto T]} \\
&\subseteq (\llbracket \psi_1[\bot/X]^{\mathsf{nwg}} \rrbracket^T_{\rho[X \mapsto T]} \cup T) \cup (\llbracket \psi_2[\bot/X]^{\mathsf{nwg}} \rrbracket^T_{\rho[X \mapsto T]} \cup T) \\
&= (\llbracket \psi_1[\bot/X]^{\mathsf{nwg}} \rrbracket^T_{\rho[X \mapsto T]} \cup \llbracket \psi_2[\bot/X]^{\mathsf{nwg}} \rrbracket^T_{\rho[X \mapsto T]}) \cup T \\
&= \llbracket \psi_1[\bot/X]^{\mathsf{nwg}} \vee \psi_2[\bot/X]^{\mathsf{nwg}} \rrbracket^T_{\rho[X \mapsto T]} \cup T \\
&= \llbracket \varphi[\bot/X]^{\mathsf{nwg}} \rrbracket^T_\rho .
\end{aligned}
$$

The remaining case of $\varphi = \psi_1 \wedge \psi_2$ is very similar to the last case of a disjunction. Finally, now that (8.2) is established we obtain

$$
\begin{aligned}
\llbracket \mu X.\varphi \rrbracket^T_\rho &= \bigcap \{ T \mid \llbracket \varphi \rrbracket^T_{\rho[X \mapsto T]} \} \subseteq \bigcap \{ T \mid \llbracket \varphi[\bot/X]^{\mathsf{nwg}} \rrbracket^T_{\rho[X \mapsto T]} \} \\
&= \llbracket \mu X.\varphi[\bot/X]^{\mathsf{nwg}} \rrbracket^T_\rho .
\end{aligned}
$$

which finishes the proof. $\qquad \square$

In very much the same way it is possible to prove the dual statement for greatest fixpoint formulae.

Lemma 8.3.21. Let $\nu X.\varphi \in \mathcal{L}_\mu$. Then $\nu X.\varphi[\top/X]^{\mathsf{nwg}} \equiv \nu X.\varphi$. $\qquad \blacksquare$

Note that Lemma 8.3.20 and Lemma 8.3.21 are not sufficient for a guarded transformation. Consider for instance the formula $\mu X.Z \vee \mu Y.X \vee \Diamond Y$ from Example 8.3.19. It is not guarded but no variable is not weakly guarded. In effect, Y is guarded, and X is weakly guarded. These two lemmas however only get rid of occurrences which are not weakly guarded. The solution lies in the combination of these two lemmas with the aforementioned unfolding equivalence.

Let φ be an arbitrary formula of the modal μ-calculus. Consider the innermost fixpoint subformulae in it, i.e. those that do not contain other fixpoint subformulae. The occurrences of the variables that get bound in these are either guarded or not even weakly guarded – just weakly guarded but not guarded is impossible because it would require smaller fixpoint formulae. By Lemma 8.3.20 and 8.3.21 the occurrences that are not even weakly guarded can be replaced, leaving only guarded occurrences.

Now consider an arbitrary fixpoint subformula $\tau X.\psi$ in φ. Then X can occur in three different forms: not even weakly guarded, just weakly guarded or guarded. Obviously, the guarded occurrences are harmless, and those that are not even weakly guarded can be replaced using the aforementioned lemmas. This only leaves the occurrences that are weakly guarded, i.e. that occur under the scope of some inner fixpoint formula $\tau'Y.\chi$. Since it is genuinely smaller we can assume that it is guarded already. Now, we can use the unfolding principle and replace it by $\chi[\tau'Y.\chi/Y]$. Since Y in particular is guarded within $\tau'Y.\chi$, every occurrence of X in $\tau'Y.\chi$ will be guarded in $\chi[\tau'Y.\chi/Y]$. Thus, this ensures that $\tau X.\psi$ becomes guarded.

Altogether this can be turned into a simple procedure which handles the fixpoint subformulae $\tau X.\psi$ of some input φ in increasing order of size and:

1. replaces all occurrences which are not even weakly guarded by the corresponding constants I or $\bot$ and
2. unfolds the maximal fixpoint formulae within ψ.

Note that the outermost fixpoint subformulae need not be unfolded.

Correctness of this procedure is given by the preceding argumentation using the appropriate lemmas. Another important issue is the blow-up in formula size. Unfortunately, it is exponential because of subsequent unfoldings. This even concerns the number of subformulae, not just the syntactic length of formulae which can grow exponentially when variables occur more than once. Suppose that a variable occurs twice in a formula, once guarded and once unguarded. Then, unfolding the corresponding fixpoint formula does not double the number of subformulae because it only gets inserted twice into the two occurrences. However, note that the replacement of variables in the other step is restricted to occurrences that are not even weakly guarded. Hence, such a replacement step can turn these two copies into different subformulae thus essentially doubling the number of subformulae.

Example 8.3.22. Consider the Friedmann formulae φ_n, $n \in \mathbb{N}$, defined by

$$\varphi_n := \mu X_n \ldots \mu X_1.X_1 \vee \ldots \vee X_n \vee \Diamond(X_1 \wedge \ldots \wedge X_n).$$

Note that $|\varphi_n| = \mathcal{O}(n)$. Executing the procedure described earlier will result in formulae of size exponential in n.

Theorem 8.3.23. For every $\varphi \in \mathcal{L}_\mu$ there is a guarded φ' such that $\varphi' \equiv \varphi$ and $|\varphi'| = 2^{\mathcal{O}(|\varphi|)}$. ∎

The exponential blow-up can be avoided when the transformation is formulated so that it creates a MES instead of a plain formula directly. Here, one can simply share inner fixpoint formulae by a variable, and the replacement of variables that are not weakly guarded does not create multiple subformulae from single ones. However, this transformation comes at a

$$(\vee) \ \frac{s \vdash \psi_1 \vee \psi_2}{s \vdash \psi_i} \ \mathbf{V} \qquad\qquad (\wedge) \ \frac{s \vdash \psi_1 \wedge \psi_2}{s \vdash \psi_i} \ \mathbf{R}$$

$$(\Diamond) \ \frac{s \vdash \langle a \rangle \psi}{t \vdash \psi} \ \mathbf{V}, s \xrightarrow{a} t \qquad\qquad (\Box) \ \frac{s \vdash [a]\psi}{t \vdash \psi} \ \mathbf{R}, s \xrightarrow{a} t$$

$$(\text{FP}) \ \frac{s \vdash \tau X.\psi}{s \vdash X} \qquad\qquad (\text{Var}) \ \frac{s \vdash X}{s \vdash \psi} \ \text{if } fp_\varphi(X) = \tau X.\psi$$

Figure 8.1 The rules for the $\mathcal{L}_\mu$ model-checking game on some formula φ.

price as well: the resulting MES does not have a structure which would guarantee a polynomial translation into plain formulae anymore.

8.4 Model-Checking Games

We present a game-theoretic characterisation of the local model-checking problem. We define a game $\mathcal{G}^{\mathcal{T}}(s, \varphi)$ that is played on a transition system $\mathcal{T}$ with root s and a formula φ between two players $\mathbf{V}$ and $\mathbf{R}$ ('verifier' and 'refuter') with the following aims: $\mathbf{V}$ wants to show that $\mathcal{T}, s \models \varphi$ holds whereas $\mathbf{R}$ wants to show that it does not hold. We will prove that the game characterisation is sound and complete, i.e. $\mathbf{V}$ has a winning strategy for $\mathcal{G}^{\mathcal{T}}(s, \varphi)$ if and only if $\mathcal{T}, s \models \varphi$. Thus, any procedure that decides the existence of such winning strategies can be used as a model-checking algorithm for the modal μ-calculus. Here we restrict our attention to the game-theoretic characterisation of the model-checking problem. An algorithmic solution for solving these games – i.e. deciding the existence of winning strategies – will be given in Chapter 15.

We fix a transition system $\mathcal{T} = (S, \{\xrightarrow{a}\}_{a \in Act}, L)$ with a particular $s_0 \in S$, and a closed formula $\varphi \in \mathcal{L}_\mu$ in negation normal form.

Definition 8.4.1. The **model-checking game** on $\mathcal{T}$, s_0 and φ is played on the arena (V, Own, E) where $V = S \times sub(\varphi)$, and the ownership function is given by the partition $V_{\mathbf{V}} = \{(s, \chi) \mid \chi \text{ is of the form } \psi_1 \vee \psi_2 \text{ or } \langle a \rangle \psi\}$ and $V_{\mathbf{R}} = V \setminus V_{\mathbf{V}}$.

The starting configuration of the game is $C_0 = (s_0, \varphi)$. The game rules are shown in Figure 8.1. In particular, configurations of the form (s, q) or $(s, \neg q)$ have no successors, and the same holds for configurations of the form $(s, \langle a \rangle \psi)$, respectively $(s, [a]\psi)$ if s has no a-successors in $\mathcal{T}$. All other configurations have at least one successor. $\qquad \nabla$

Thus, the game $\mathcal{G}^{\mathcal{T}}(s_0, \varphi) = (G, W)$ can have finite and infinite plays.

Definition 8.4.2. The **winning conditions** are given as follows. A finite play $C_0, \ldots, C_n$ with ...

- $C_n = s \vdash q$ such that $q \in L(s)$ is won by player **V**,
- $C_n = s \vdash q$ such that $q \notin L(s)$ is won by player **R**,
- $C_n = s \vdash \neg q$ such that $q \in L(s)$ is won by player **R**,
- $C_n = s \vdash \neg q$ such that $q \notin L(s)$ is won by player **V**,
- $C_n = s \vdash \langle a \rangle \psi$ such that there is no r with $s \xrightarrow{a} r$ is won by player **R**,
- $C_n = s \vdash [a] \psi$ such that there is no r with $s \xrightarrow{a} r$ is won by player **V**.

A variable is called **outermost** among a set of variables from φ if it is maximal with respect to the dependency order $\succeq_\varphi$.

An infinite play $C_0, C_1, \ldots$ in which the outermost variable X that occurs infinitely often ...

- is of type μ is won by player **R**,
- is of type ν is won by player **V**. $\triangledown$

The two last conditions on finite plays simply say that a player who is to make a move with some rule – player **V** with ($\Diamond$) or player **R** with ($\Box$) – but cannot move loses.

It is not obvious that the winning conditions capture all possible infinite plays. We will show in the context of the next lemma that this is indeed the case, namely that there is always a (unique) outermost variable which occurs infinitely often.

Lemma 8.4.3. Every play has a unique winner.   ■

Proof. It is easy to see that finite plays can only end in one of the six situations described earlier, and that these are mutually exclusive. Thus, every finite play has a unique winner.

Consider an infinite play. Note that the game rules for all formulae, apart from variables, genuinely decrease the size of the formula in a configuration. The rule for variables genuinely increases them. Thus, every infinite play must have infinitely many configurations of the form $s \vdash X$. Since $sub(\varphi)$ only contains finitely many variables, one of them must occur like this infinitely often. This guarantees that every infinite play has at least one winner. Suppose that the winning conditions for infinite plays and both players applied to some play. Then there would be variables X and Y (of different fixpoint type) which occur infinitely often. Now note that the game rules follow the syntactic structure of the input formula. In particular, after X we see, say, a formula ψ because $fp_\varphi(X) = \mu X.\psi$. In order to reach Y after that, it must be a subformula of ψ. If $fp_\varphi(Y)$ is actually a subformula of ψ then we have $X >_\varphi Y$ because X must have a free occurrence in $fp_\varphi(Y)$ for otherwise X could not occur in the play after Y. If $fp_\varphi(Y)$ is not a subformula of ψ then Y must have a free occurrence in ψ, i.e. we have $Y >_\varphi X$. Thus, only one of them can be outermost, and it determines the winner uniquely. $\Box$

It is our goal to prove soundness and completeness of the model-checking games. In particular, we need to derive a winning strategy for player **V** from the fact that the input formula is satisfied in $\mathcal{T}$'s starting state. It is tempting to use the simple strategy of preserving satisfaction of the formula in a configuration by the configuration's state component as an invariant, i.e. player **V** should play such that only configurations of the form (s, ψ) are being reached in which $\mathcal{T}, s \models \psi$ holds. However, this is not sufficient, as the next example shows.

Example 8.4.4. Consider $\varphi = \mu X.p \vee \Diamond X$, expressing 'a state in which p holds is reachable', and the following transition system.

We leave it as an exercise to construct the game graph of this model-checking problem. Note that $s_0 \models \varphi$. The starting configuration requires an unfolding of the fixpoint formula, and after that player **V** will have to choose the disjunct other than p because $p \notin L(s_0)$. This yields the configuration $s_0 \vdash \Diamond X$ in which player **V** needs to choose a successor state to s_0. Clearly, there are only two choices, s_0 itself and s_1. Note that $s_i \models \mu X.p \vee \Diamond X$ for both $i \in \{0, 1\}$. On the other hand, if **V** chooses s_0 then the play continues like it did after the initial configuration. If this was part of a memoryless strategy then she would always get back there and the strategy would not be winning because it infinitely often leads to the unfolding of a fixpoint formula of type μ. Thus, she has to choose a particular successor configuration despite the fact that both choices allow her to preserve the truth of the current configuration.

The necessary refinement for a winning strategy will be based on approximants and μ-signatures. Note that in the preceding example we have $s_0 \models \mu X.p \vee \Diamond X$ because $s_0 \models \mu^2 X.p \vee \Diamond X$. Furthermore, $s_1 \models \mu X.p \vee \Diamond X$ because $s_1 \models \mu^1 X.p \vee \Diamond X$. Thus, it is only the choice of the transition from s_0 to s_1 which decreases the index of the approximant, that witnesses the truth of the configuration and thus takes her closer to actually showing that the configuration is true. The choice of the transition from s_0 to s_0 does not decrease that index, which intuitively can be understood as not providing a proof for the truth of the input configuration.

Before we proceed to showing completeness of the model-checking games we need to formalise this properly and prove some results about the preservation of truth along a play.

Definition 8.4.5. Let η be a μ-signature. A configuration $s \vdash \psi$ in the game $\mathcal{G}^\mathcal{T}(s_0, \varphi)$ is called **true under** η if $\mathcal{T}, s \models_\eta \psi$. $\qquad\qquad \triangledown$

An important observation is the fact that player **V** *can* preserve truth under signatures, while player **R** *must* preserve it.

Lemma 8.4.6. A configuration that is true under some η and which requires player **V** to make a choice has at least one successor configuration that is true under η. $\qquad \blacksquare$

Proof. By a simple case inspection. Player **V** chooses disjuncts, for instance. If $s \vdash \psi_1 \vee \psi_2$ is true under η, i.e. $\mathcal{T}, s \models_\eta \psi_1 \vee \psi_2$ then $\mathcal{T}, s \models_\eta \psi_i$ for at least some $i \in \{1, 2\}$ which means that one of the two choices in this case must lead to a successor configuration that is true under η.

The other case in which player **V** makes a choice is that of $s \vdash \langle a \rangle \psi$. Again, it is true under η only if $\mathcal{T}, s \models_\eta \langle a \rangle \psi$ which is only the case if there is a $r \in S$ with $s \xrightarrow{a} r$ and $\mathcal{T}, r \models_\eta \psi$. Thus, player **V** can choose this particular r and preserve truth. $\square$

Lemma 8.4.7. All successors of a configuration that is true under some η and in which player **R** makes a choice are true under this η.   ∎

The cases of conjunctions and $[a]$-formulae are very similar to those of the previous lemma and therefore left as Exercise 8.32.

Finally, we consider how truth is being preserved in the cases of unfolding a fixpoint formula.

Lemma 8.4.8. Suppose that $s \vdash \tau X.\psi$ is true under some η. Then its unique successor $s \vdash X$ is true under η as well.   ∎

Proof. If $\tau = \nu$ then this is trivial because μ-signatures interpret free ν-variables as the corresponding greatest fixpoints. In the case of $\tau = \mu$ the statement follows immediately from Lemma 8.2.4 which states that a least fixpoint formula can only be satisfied if it is satisfied at some approximant level. $\square$

Finally, we need to consider the case of the unfolding of a fixpoint variable.

Lemma 8.4.9. Suppose that $s \vdash X$ is true under some η.

a) If X is ν-bound then its unique successor $s \vdash \psi$ is true under η as well.
b) If X is μ-bound then there is a μ-signature η' such that $\eta' < \eta$ and the unique successor configuration $s \vdash \psi$ is true under η'.   ∎

Proof. (a) Again, this simply follows from the fact that μ-signatures interpret greatest fixpoint variables as the corresponding greatest fixpoints. Since they are fixpoints we have $s \models_\eta X$ iff $s \models_\eta \psi(X)$ iff $s \models_\eta \nu X.\psi(X)$.

(b) Suppose X is μ-bound and $s \vdash X$ is true under η. Thus, $s \models_\eta \mu^{\eta(X)} X.\psi$. There are two cases to consider. If $\eta(X)$ is a limit ordinal κ then there is an $\alpha < \kappa$ such that $s \models_\eta \mu^\alpha X.\psi$. Without any loss of generality, we can assume α not to be a limit ordinal itself for otherwise we could just repeat the argument. Well-foundedness of the ordinals eventually will yield such an α which is a successor ordinal, i.e. $\alpha = \beta + 1$ for some ordinal β. Let $\eta'' := \eta[X \mapsto \alpha]$. Note that $\eta'' < \eta$. By the definition of the semantics for limit ordinals we have $s \models_\eta \mu^\alpha X.\psi$. Note that η and η'' agree on all variables apart from X, but X is not a free variable in $\mu^\alpha X.\psi$. Thus we also have $s \models_{\eta''} \mu^\alpha X.\psi$. Since $\alpha = \beta + 1$ we also have $s \models_{\eta''} \psi[\mu^\beta X.\psi / X]$. This, however means that $s \vdash \psi(X)$ is true under η' which is defined as $\eta''[X \mapsto \beta]$. Note that $\eta' < \eta$. $\square$

Theorem 8.4.10. Player **V** has a memoryless winning strategy for $\mathcal{G}^{\mathcal{T}}(s_0, \varphi)$ if $\mathcal{T}, s_0 \models \varphi$.   ∎

Proof. Suppose $\mathcal{T}, s_0 \models \varphi$. Hence, the initial configuration in $\mathcal{G}^{\mathcal{T}}(s_0, \varphi)$ is true. We will describe a winning strategy for player **V** in this game. She keeps a record of a μ-signature with every configuration, starting with the empty signature () in the initial configuration. We denote this as $s_0 \vdash_{()} \varphi$. It is not hard to see in the following that she does so maintaining the invariant that in any configuration $s \vdash_\eta \psi$, we have that $\eta(X)$ is defined for any $X \in$ *free*(ψ).

Whenever she has to make a choice in a configuration $s \vdash_\eta \varphi$ then she preserves truth of this configuration under η according to Lemma 8.4.6. If there is more than one option which will allow her to preserve truth under this η then she chooses a best one in the sense of a minimal μ-signature under which the corresponding successor configuration is true.

Whenever player **R** has to make a choice it will preserve truth under this μ-signature according to Lemma 8.4.7. Unfolding fixpoint formulae in general and greatest fixpoint variables in particular preserves truth under this μ-signature as well, according to Lemma 8.4.8 and 8.4.9. In the case of a configuration $s \vdash_\eta X$ for some μ-bound X Lemma 8.4.9 we obtain an $\eta' < \eta$ such that the unique successor is true under η'.

This defines a strategy for player **V**. Note that it is memoryless because the choices prescribed by this strategy do not depend on the history of a play but can be made for a single configuration only. It remains to be seen that it is a winning strategy. Let $\lambda = C_0, C_1, \ldots$ be a play that conforms to this strategy. If it is a finite play ending in some C_n then it cannot by won by player **R** because he only wins finite plays that end in configurations which are not true under any μ-signature. According to Lemma 8.4.3 these must be won by player **V**. So suppose that it is infinite and was won by player **R**. Then there would be an outermost fixpoint variable X of type μ which occurs infinitely often in the play. Together with its recorded annotations it is of the following form.

$$s_0 \vdash_{()} \varphi, \ldots, s_1 \vdash_{\eta_1} X, \ldots, s_2 \vdash_{\eta_2} X, \ldots, s_3 \vdash_{\eta_3} X, \ldots$$

Note that $s_1 \vdash_{\eta_1} X$ can be chosen such that no variable Y with $Y \succ_\varphi X$ occurs after this anymore. The preservation of truth only yields $\eta_1 \geq \eta_2 \geq \eta_3 \geq \ldots$. However, since it is the rule for variables which is being played in each such configuration we have $\eta_1 > \eta_2 > \eta_3 > \ldots$ indeed. Since no outer variable occurs after $s_1 \vdash_{\eta_1} X$ anymore, we have $\eta_i(Y) = \eta_1(Y)$ for all such Y and all $i \geq 1$. Thus, we must have $\eta_1(X) > \eta_2(X) > \ldots$. Since the ordinals are well founded, there must be an $i \in \mathbb{N}$ with $\eta_i(X) = 0$. But then $s_i \models_{\eta_i} X$ would be impossible in this case because $\mu^0 X.\psi \equiv \bot$. We conclude that it cannot be the case that player **R** wins such a play and, using Lemma 8.4.3 again, player **V** must indeed be the winner. Thus, she wins any play that conforms to this memoryless strategy. In other words, she has a memoryless winning strategy for $\mathcal{G}^{\mathcal{T}}(s_0, \varphi)$. $\square$

For the converse direction we need the dual notion of preserving truth, namely preservation of falsity.

Definition 8.4.11. Let η be a ν-signature. A configuration $s \vdash \psi$ in the game $\mathcal{G}^{\mathcal{T}}(s_0, \varphi)$ is called **false under** η if $\mathcal{T}, s \not\models_\eta \psi$. $\triangledown$

The following lemma is proved in the same way as Lemmas 8.4.6–8.4.9.

Lemma 8.4.12. Player **V** must preserve falsity under some ν-signature with his choices; player **R** can preserve falsity under a ν-signature; unfolding least fixpoint variables preserves falsity under a ν-signature; unfolding greatest fixpoint variables decreases the ν-signature under which the configurations are false. ∎

Theorem 8.4.13. Player **V** has a winning strategy for $\mathcal{G}^T(s_0, \varphi)$ only if $T, s_0 \models \varphi$. ∎

Proof. Suppose that **V** has a winning strategy $\mathfrak{str}_\mathbf{V}$ for $\mathcal{G}^T(s_0, \varphi)$ but that $T, s_0 \not\models \varphi$. Consider the strategy $\mathfrak{str}_\mathbf{R}$ for player **R** which is defined dually to player **V**'s winning strategy in the proof of Theorem 8.4.10: he preserves falsity under ν-signatures.

Let $\lambda = C_0, C_1, \ldots$ be the play that results from the interaction of these two strategies. Formally: for all $i \geq 0$ and $\mathbf{P} \in \{\mathbf{V}, \mathbf{R}\}$, if $C_i \in V_\mathbf{P}$ then $C_{i+1} = \mathfrak{str}_\mathbf{P}(C_0 \ldots C_i)$. According to Lemma 8.4.12, there are ν-signatures $\eta_0 \geq \eta_1 \geq \ldots$ such that C_i is false under η_i for all $i \geq 0$.

Since $\mathfrak{str}_\mathbf{V}$ is supposed to be a winning strategy, **V** must win λ. It is easy to see that λ cannot be a finite play because those finite ones that are being won by player **V** only end in configurations which are true under any ν-signature. Suppose therefore that λ is an infinite play. Then its outermost fixpoint variable X that gets seen infinitely often in this play is of type ν. Dually to the proof of Theorem 8.4.10 we consider the part of λ in which no variable Y with $Y \succ_\varphi^+ X$ is seen anymore. Since X gets unfolded infinitely often, the ν-signatures under which the configurations are false are decreasing infinitely often. By well-foundedness of ν-signatures, there must be some configuration (s, X) which is false under some η with $\eta(X) = 0$. This is impossible though if X is of type ν because $\nu^0 X. \psi \equiv \top$. Thus, the assumption $T, s_0 \not\models \varphi$ must have been wrong. ☐

Combining Theorem 8.4.10 and 8.4.13 shows that memoryless winning strategies suffice for these local model-checking games: player **V** has a winning strategy iff she has a memoryless winning strategy. By completely dualising the proofs of the two theorems – i.e. using preservation of falsity under ν-signatures and swapping the roles of the two players – one can equally characterise nonsatisfaction of a formula in terms of the existence of a winning strategy for player **R**.

Theorem 8.4.14. Player **R** has a memoryless winning strategy for the game $\mathcal{G}^T(s_0, \varphi)$ iff $T, s_0 \not\models \varphi$. ∎

Combining this with the two previous theorems yields determinacy of the local model-checking games.

Corollary 8.4.15. Player **P** has a memoryless winning strategy for $\mathcal{G}^T(s_0, \varphi)$ if player $\bar{\mathbf{P}}$ does not have a winning strategy for this game. ∎

8.5 Bisimulation Invariance

8.5.1 Closure under Bisimulation

The goal of this section is to show that properties defined in the modal μ-calculus (and therefore any other logic that can be embedded into it) are bisimulation-invariant in the following sense. Suppose that $\mathcal{T}, s \models \varphi$ holds for some state s of some transition system $\mathcal{T}$ and some property expressed by the formula φ. Suppose furthermore that $\mathcal{T}, s \sim \mathcal{T}', s'$, i.e. state s' of some other transition system $\mathcal{T}'$ is equivalent to s with respect to bisimilarity, see Definition 3.3.1. Then $\mathcal{T}', s' \models \varphi$ should also hold, i.e. one cannot refute a property of a system by replacing it with a bisimilar one. Note that first-order logic is not bisimulation-invariant because it is easy to express in it that, e.g. 'there are exactly 17 successor states' which is not a bisimulation-invariant property in this sense.

Before we can proceed to show bisimulation-invariance we need to introduce the simple notion of a set of states being bisimulation-closed.

Definition 8.5.1. Let $\mathcal{T} = (S, \{\xrightarrow{a}\}_{a \in Act}, L)$ be a transition system and $T \subseteq S$. We say that T is **bisimulation-closed** if, for all $s, s' \in S$ such that $s \sim s'$ and $s \in T$, we also have $s' \in T$.

A variable assignment ρ is bisimulation-closed if $\rho(X)$ is bisimulation-closed for every variable X in its domain. $\qquad \triangledown$

Theorem 8.5.2. For all closed $\varphi \in \mathcal{L}_\mu$ and all transition systems $\mathcal{T}$ we have that $[\![\varphi]\!]^{\mathcal{T}}$ is bisimulation-closed. $\qquad \blacksquare$

Proof. Suppose that $\mathcal{T} = (S, \{\xrightarrow{a}\}_{a \in Act}, L)$. It should be clear that the claim is too weak to be proved by induction on the structure of the formula; a proof by induction will require a suitable handling of free variables. Hence, we will show a stronger statement by induction on the structure of φ, namely that $[\![\varphi]\!]^{\mathcal{T}}_\rho$ is bisimulation-closed provided that ρ is bisimulation-closed. Note that this requirement is necessary, consider for instance $\varphi = X$ with $\rho(X)$ not being bisimulation-closed.

The base case of $\varphi = X$ for some variable X follows immediately from this additional requirement. The other base case is $\varphi = p$ for some $p \in \text{PROP}$. Suppose that $s \models_\rho p$ and $s \sim s'$. Thus, there is a bisimulation $\beta \subseteq S \times S$ with $(s, s') \in \beta$. By the definition of a bisimulation, we have $L(s) = L(s')$ and therefore $s' \models_\rho p$ as well.

The cases of $\varphi = \neg \psi$ and $\varphi = \psi_1 \vee \psi_2$ follow from the observation that the complement of a bisimulation-closed set is again bisimulation-closed, and so is the union of two bisimulation-closed sets. We leave the details as Exercise 8.37.

Now let $\varphi = \langle a \rangle \psi$. Assume $\mathcal{T}, s \models_\rho \langle a \rangle \psi$ and $s \sim s'$. Again, there is a bisimulation β with $(s, s') \in \beta$. By the semantics of the modal operator there is a $r \in S$ such that $s \xrightarrow{a} r$ and $\mathcal{T}, r \models_\rho \psi$. Since β is a bisimulation, there must be a $r' \in S$ with $s' \xrightarrow{a} r'$ and $(r, r') \in \beta$. In particular, $r \sim r'$. The hypothesis yields bisimulation-closure of $[\![\psi]\!]^{\mathcal{T}}_\rho$, thus we have $\mathcal{T}, r' \models_\rho \psi$ as well. This implies $\mathcal{T}, s' \models_\rho \varphi$ which establishes bisimulation-closure of $[\![\varphi]\!]^{\mathcal{T}}_\rho$.

The last case is that of $\varphi = \mu X.\psi$. In a separate induction on all ordinals we will show that $[\![\mu^\alpha X.\psi]\!]_\rho^T$ is bisimulation-closed for any α. Thus, if $s \sim s'$ and $s \models_\rho \mu^\alpha X.\psi$ then $s' \models_\rho \mu^\alpha X.\psi$ which suffices to establish that $[\![\mu X.\psi]\!]_\rho^T$ is bisimulation-closed, as well, since it is just the union over all $[\![\mu^\alpha X.\psi]\!]_\rho^T$.

The base case of $\alpha = 0$ is trivial because $\emptyset$ is clearly bisimulation-closed. The case of α being some limit ordinal κ is not difficult – as just noted, the union of bisimulation-closed sets is still bisimulation-closed. Finally, let $\alpha = \beta + 1$ for some β. We have

$$[\![\mu^{\beta+1}X.\psi]\!]_\rho^T \;=\; [\![\psi]\!]_{\rho[X \mapsto [\![\mu^\beta X.\psi]\!]_\rho^T]}^T .$$

By the hypothesis of the inner induction, $\rho' := \rho[X \mapsto [\![\mu^\beta X.\psi]\!]_\rho^T]$ is bisimulation-closed. The hypothesis of the outer induction then yields that $[\![\psi]\!]_{\rho'}^T$ is also bisimulation-closed, which clearly transfers to the left side of the equation. This finishes the claim. $\square$

8.5.2 Characteristic Formulae

We have already seen that $\mathcal{L}_\mu$ supersedes CTL with respect to expressive power, i.e. every CTL-definable property is also $\mathcal{L}_\mu$-definable (cf. Theorem 8.1.14). An immediate consequence of this and Theorem 8.5.2 is bisimulation-invariance of CTL: clearly, if there was CTL formula that defined a property which was not bisimulation-invariant then so would there be an $\mathcal{L}_\mu$ formula, but this is excluded by Theorem 8.5.2. In Chapter 10 we will see that $\mathcal{L}_\mu$ also supersedes CTL* and therefore also LTL interpreted over transition systems. Hence, we get bisimulation-invariance for all these temporal logics.

There is one feature of $\mathcal{L}_\mu$ with respect to bisimulation that distinguishes it from these other logics: it is able to express bisimilarity in the following sense.

Definition 8.5.3. Let $\approx$ be an equivalence relation on states of transition system and s be some state of a transition system $\mathcal{T}$. A **characteristic formula** for s with respect to $\approx$ is a formula $\varphi_\approx^s$ such that for all $\mathcal{T}'$ and all s' we have $\mathcal{T}', s' \models \varphi_\approx^s$ iff $\mathcal{T}', s' \approx \mathcal{T}, s$.

We say that a logic $\mathcal{L}$ **admits** characteristic formulae for $\approx$ and a class $\mathfrak{T}$ of transition systems if, for all $\mathcal{T} \in \mathfrak{T}$ and all its states s, there is a characteristic $\mathcal{L}$-formula $\varphi_\approx^s$ for s with respect to $\approx$. $\triangledown$

Theorem 8.5.4. $\mathcal{L}_\mu$ admits characteristic formulae for bisimilarity $\rightleftarrows$ and the class of all finite transition systems.   ■

Proof. Let $\mathcal{T} = (S, \{\xrightarrow{a}\}_{a \in Act}, L)$ be a transition system with a finite set of states S. We construct an MES $\mathcal{E}_\mathcal{T}$ with one variable per state; the characteristic formula $\varphi_\rightleftarrows^s$ for a state s is obtained by unfolding it into $tr_\emptyset(X_s)$. $\mathcal{E}_\mathcal{T}$ contains, for every $s \in S$ an equation of the form

$$X_s =_0 \Big(\bigwedge_{p \in L(s)} p \Big) \wedge \Big(\bigwedge_{p \notin L(s)} \neg p \Big) \wedge \bigwedge_{a \in Act} \Big(\big(\bigwedge_{r \in R_a(s)} \langle a \rangle X_r \big) \wedge [a]\big(\bigvee_{r \in R_a(s)} X_r \big) \Big)$$

where $R_a(s)$ abbreviates $\{r \in S \mid s \xrightarrow{a} r\}$.

It remains to be seen that this construction is sound and complete.

Soundness. We need to show that for any state $\mathcal{T}'$ with state s' with $\mathcal{T}', s' \models \varphi^s_{\rightleftarrows}$ we have $\mathcal{T}', s' \rightleftarrows \mathcal{T}, s$. Let $\mathcal{T}'$ with state space S' be fixed and consider the variable mapping ρ defined by $\rho(X_s) = \{s' \mid \mathcal{T}', s' \models \varphi^s_{\rightleftarrows}\}$. In other words, ρ simply represents, read as an n-tuple, the simultaneous greatest solution of $\mathcal{E}_\mathcal{T}$. It is greatest because all priorities in $\mathcal{E}_\mathcal{T}$ are even. Then consider the relation $\beta \subseteq S' \times S$, defined by $(s', s) \in \beta$ iff $s' \in \rho(X_s)$. Then β satisfies the Forth-and-Back property:

- If $(s', s) \in \beta$ then s' is a model of the right-hand side of X_s. Because of the first two conjunctions they are atom equivalent.
- Let $(s', s) \in \beta$ and suppose there are a and t' such that $s' \xrightarrow{a} t'$. Since $s' \in \rho(X_s)$, it must satisfy $[a] \bigvee_{r \in R_a(s)} X_r$, i.e. there must be a r with $s \xrightarrow{a} r$ and $r' \in \rho(X_r)$, resp. $(r', r) \in \beta$.
- If $(s', s) \in \beta$ and $s \xrightarrow{a} r$ for some a and r then remember that $s' \models \bigwedge_{r \in R_a(s)} \langle a \rangle X_r$, i.e. there must be some r' with $s' \xrightarrow{a} r'$. Analogously to the previous case we get $(r', r) \in \beta$.

Completeness. Suppose there are $\mathcal{T}', s'$ with $\mathcal{T}', s' \rightleftarrows \mathcal{T}, s$. Hence, there is a bisimulation relation β between the state spaces of $\mathcal{T}'$ and $\mathcal{T}$ that contains (s', s). This can be used to obtain a winning strategy for player $\mathbf{V}$ in the model-checking game $\mathcal{G}^{\mathcal{T}'}(s', \varphi^s_{\rightleftarrows})$. For the sake of simplicity we imagine that this game is being played directly on $\mathcal{E}_\mathcal{T}$ rather than its unfolding to a formula; than it visits variables X_t instead of formulae $tr_\mathcal{T}(X_t)$ for various sets T.

Player $\mathbf{V}$'s strategy consists of making choices such that whenever a play reaches a configuration $t' \vdash X_t$ then we have $(t', t) \in \beta$. This is clearly given at the beginning, and player $\mathbf{V}$ can always preserve this invariant: suppose a play has reached such a configuration. Note that the right-hand sides of $\mathcal{E}_\mathcal{T}$ mainly consist of conjunctions. Player $\mathbf{R}$ cannot choose any conjunction with an atomic proposition because $(t', t) \in \beta$ implies atom equivalence of them, and hence he would lose immediately.

Suppose he chooses a conjunct $\langle a \rangle X_r$. According to the construction of $\mathcal{E}_\mathcal{T}$ we must have $t \xrightarrow{a} r$, and by β's Back-property there is some r' with $t' \xrightarrow{a} r'$ and $(r', r) \in \beta$. Player $\mathbf{V}$ can choose this r' in her subsequent move with rule $(\Diamond)$.

If player $\mathbf{R}$ chose the conjunct $[a] \bigvee_{r \in R_a(t)}$ then he would have to continue by proposing an a-successor r' of t'. By β's Forth-property, there is an a-successor r of t with $(r', r) \in \beta$. Player $\mathbf{V}$ can choose this successor symbolically by picking the disjunct X_r in her subsequent moves with rule $(\vee)$.

This is indeed a winning strategy for player $\mathbf{V}$ since she can never get stuck with rule $(\Diamond)$, nor will an atomic proposition be reached that is false in the corresponding state. Moreover, all priorities are even, i.e. all infinite plays only see greatest fixpoint variables which makes her the winning of those plays, too. □

The following gives one of the reasons why characteristic formulae are interesting objects of study: characteristic formulae and model checking put together yield an algorithm for checking the underlying behavioural equivalence.

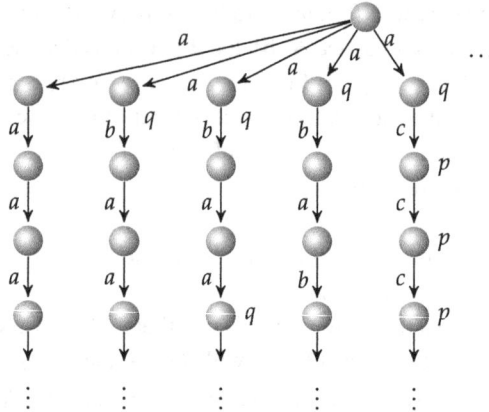

Figure 8.2 Forking all traces of a transition system.

Corollary 8.5.5. Bisimilarity between finite transition systems can be checked in polynomial time. ∎

A stronger result was presented in Section 3.4.5 already using explicit algorithms for bisimilarity checking. We state it here again because of some subtleties involved in it. A bisimilarity checking algorithm can be obtained as follows. Take two transition systems T and T' with states s and s'. Construct $\varphi_{\rightleftarrows}^{s}$ and check whether it is satisfied by T', s'. Since it is alternation-free, it can be checked in time that is linear in $|T'|$ and $|\varphi_{\rightleftarrows}^{s}|$ according to Theorem 8.3.5. Unfortunately, $|\varphi_{\rightleftarrows}^{s}|$ is in general exponentially larger than $|T|$ because we required it to be a *formula*. As the proof of Theorem 8.5.4 shows, it has a MES representation of size $\mathcal{O}(|T|)$, though. Hence, the question arises whether $\mathcal{L}_\mu$ properties represented as such MES can be model-checked in linear time. The answer is 'Yes', and it is possible to show this using techniques developed in Section 15.1.

Now, we want to ask whether $\mathcal{L}_\mu$ also admits characteristic formulae for trace equivalence $\leftrightsquigarrow$. The answer is 'No' in general, and the proof is not difficult. It needs a construction on transition systems similar to the unfolding operation (cf. Definition 3.3.10).

If T is a transition system and s a state of it then we denote by $\text{fork}_T(s)$ the rooted transition system which has a path for every $\sigma \in \text{traces}_T(s)$ that are joined at a common root node and are otherwise disjoint. Figure 8.2 shows $\text{fork}_T(s)$ for the following transition system.

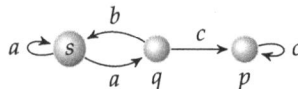

Theorem 8.5.6. For any transition system T with root s such that $\text{traces}_T(s)$ is an infinite set, there is no formula $\varphi \in \mathcal{L}_\mu$ such that $T', s' \models \varphi$ iff $T', s' \leftrightsquigarrow T, s$. ∎

Proof. Take any $\mathcal{T}$ with state s from which there are infinitely many traces. Since there is only a single trace of length 0 starting in s, we must have infinitely many different ones of length at least 1. Now suppose there was such a formula φ characterising s in $\mathcal{T}$ up to trace equivalence. Since $\mathrm{fork}_{\mathcal{T}}(s) \rightsquigarrow \mathcal{T}, s$ we would have $\mathrm{fork}_{\mathcal{T}}(s) \models \varphi$.

Using Theorem 8.3.23 we can assume φ to be guarded, and using Corollary 8.1.9 we can unfold the topmost fixpoint subformulae in it. Every Boolean formula can equivalently be transformed into disjunctive normal form and conjunctions can be pushed below $[a]$-operators via $[a]\psi_1 \wedge [a]\psi_2 \equiv [a](\psi_1 \wedge \psi_2)$. Hence, φ is equivalent to an $\mathcal{L}_\mu$ formula φ' of the form

$$\bigvee_{i=1}^{n} \left(\Lambda_i \wedge \left(\bigwedge_{j=1}^{m_i} \langle a_j \rangle \varphi_{i,j} \right) \wedge \left(\bigwedge_{a \in Act} [a]\psi_a \right) \right)$$

for some $n, m_i, k_i \geq 0$ and the Λ_i being conjunctions of atomic literals.

Since $\varphi' \equiv \varphi$ we also have $\mathrm{fork}_{ts}(s) \models \varphi'$. That is, there is an i such that $\mathrm{fork}_{\mathcal{T}}(s)$ satisfies the ith disjunct of φ'. Now this ith disjunct demands that the label root of the root of $\mathrm{fork}_{\mathcal{T}}(s)$ satisfies Λ_i, and that it has m_i successors satisfying $\varphi_{i,1}, \ldots, \varphi_{i,m_i}$ respectively. Moreover, every a-successor satisfies ψ_a.

It then should be clear that φ' also has a model with m_i traces only: simply take $\mathrm{fork}_{\mathcal{T}}(s)$ and throw away everything apart from the m_i traces that are needed to satisfy $\varphi_{i,1}, \ldots, \varphi_{i,m_i}$. Since $\mathcal{T}$ was assumed to have infinitely many different traces, the transition system obtained in this way cannot be trace equivalent to it. Hence, φ would also have to have models with strictly fewer traces than $\mathcal{T}$. $\qquad\square$

8.6 The Second-Order Nature of Temporal Logics

8.6.1 Monadic Second-Order Logic

Monadic second-order logic (MSO) is an extension of first-order logic which has turned out to be an important yardstick when considering the expressive power of temporal logics. Recall that the defining feature of first-order logic is the ability to quantify – in an existential or universal way – over elements of the universe. Second-order logic then extends first-order logic by adding the ability to quantify over relations on the universe. Monadic second-order logic is its fragment in which this additional quantification is restricted to *unary* relations, i.e. subsets of the universe. Here we consider MSO interpreted over ITS over atomic propositions PROP and actions *Act*. In order to access them, we assume to have a unary predicate P_q for every $q \in$ PROP, and a binary predicate R_a for every $a \in Act$.

Definition 8.6.1. Let $\mathrm{VAR}_1 = \{x, y, \ldots\}$ be a countably infinite set of first-order variables, and $\mathrm{VAR}_2 = \{X, Y, \ldots\}$ a countably infinite set of monadic second-order variables (as with $\mathcal{L}_\mu$). The syntax of MSO on transition systems is given as follows.

$$\varphi := P_q(x) \mid X(x) \mid R_a(x, y) \mid (\varphi \wedge \varphi) \mid \neg\varphi \mid \exists x.\varphi \mid \exists X.\varphi$$

where $q \in$ PROP, $x, y \in \mathrm{VAR}_1$ and $X \in \mathrm{VAR}_2$. $\qquad\nabla$

As usual, we allow derived Boolean operators like $\vee$ and universal quantification is defined in the usual way too: $\forall x.\varphi := \neg\exists x.\neg\varphi$ and $\forall X.\varphi := \neg\exists X.\neg\varphi$.

Definition 8.6.2. MSO is interpreted over ITS $\mathcal{T} = (S, \{\xrightarrow{a}\}_{a \in Act}, L)$ using variable assignments $\rho : (\text{VAR}_1 \to S) + (\text{VAR}_2 \to \mathcal{P}(S))$ as follows:

$$
\begin{aligned}
\mathcal{T} \models_\rho P_q(x) \quad &\text{iff} \quad q \in L(\rho(x)) \\
\mathcal{T} \models_\rho X(x) \quad &\text{iff} \quad \rho(x) \in \rho(X) \\
\mathcal{T} \models_\rho R_a(x, y) \quad &\text{iff} \quad \rho(x) \xrightarrow{a} \rho(y) \\
\mathcal{T} \models_\rho \varphi \wedge \psi \quad &\text{iff} \quad \mathcal{T} \models_\rho \varphi \text{ and } \mathcal{T} \models_\rho \psi \\
\mathcal{T} \models_\rho \neg\varphi \quad &\text{iff} \quad \mathcal{T} \not\models_\rho \varphi \\
\mathcal{T} \models_\rho \exists x.\varphi \quad &\text{iff} \quad \text{there is } s \in S \text{ such that } \mathcal{T} \models_{\rho[x \mapsto s]} \varphi \\
\mathcal{T} \models_\rho \exists X.\varphi \quad &\text{iff} \quad \text{there is } T \subseteq S \text{ such that } \mathcal{T} \models_{\rho[X \mapsto T]} \varphi.
\end{aligned}
$$

∇

The standard notions like that of a free variable, a sentence, etc., are defined as usual.

Example 8.6.3. Monadic second-order logic can define equality. Note that two states of a transition system must be equal if they belong to exactly the same subsets of the state space. In other words, if they are not equal, then it is always possible to find a subset that contains one of them but not the other:

$$x = y := \forall X.X(x) \leftrightarrow X(y).$$

It is then possible to assert for instance that a state interpreting the variable x has two distinct a-successors:

$$\exists y.\exists z.\neg(y = z) \wedge R_a(x, y) \wedge R_a(x, z).$$

8.6.2 A Translation into MSO

Note an essential difference between temporal logics and MSO: an MSO sentence holds in a transition system or it does not; the truth of a sentence of $\mathcal{L}_\mu$ in a transition system depends on the actual state in which it is interpreted. There is no way to model the predicate logic interpretation (truth independent of a single state) in $\mathcal{L}_\mu$; this would require the so-called **universal modality** which cannot be defined in $\mathcal{L}_\mu$. On the other hand, MSO can easily mimic a temporal interpretation (truth in a single state). As usual, the truth of an MSO formula in a transition system relative to some variable assignment ρ only depends on the restriction of ρ to the free variables in the formula. Thus, a formula $\varphi(x)$ with one free first-order variable x can be interpreted in a transition system just like a temporal formula by intuitively understanding this as 'φ holds in the state x'.

Theorem 8.6.4. For every $\mathcal{L}_\mu$-sentence φ there is an MSO formula $\text{ST}(\varphi, x)$ with a single free variable x such that for all transition systems and all its states s we have $\mathcal{T}, s \models \varphi$ iff $\mathcal{T} \models_{[x \mapsto s]} \text{ST}(\varphi, x)$ and $|\text{ST}(\varphi, x)| = \mathcal{O}(|\varphi|)$.   ∎

Proof. We simply need to express the semantics of $\mathcal{L}_\mu$ in MSO. Monadic second-order quantifiers are needed and in order to translate least fixpoints. Without them, $\mathcal{L}_\mu$ just boils down to BML which can be translated into first-order logic (cf. Lemma 5.1.4). The translation of $\mathcal{L}_\mu$ into MSO is just an extension of that one with a new clause for fixpoint quantifiers.

$$\mathrm{ST}(q, x) := P_q(x)$$
$$\mathrm{ST}(X, x) := X(x)$$
$$\mathrm{ST}(\varphi \wedge \psi, x) := \mathrm{ST}(\varphi, x) \wedge \mathrm{ST}(\psi, x)$$
$$\mathrm{ST}(\neg\varphi, x) := \neg\mathrm{ST}(\varphi, x)$$
$$\mathrm{ST}(\langle a\rangle\varphi, x) := \exists y(R_a(x, y) \wedge \mathrm{ST}(\varphi, y)) \quad \text{for some fresh variable } y$$
$$\mathrm{ST}(\mu X.\varphi, x) := \forall X.(\forall y.\mathrm{ST}(\varphi, y) \to X(y)) \to X(x).$$

The last clause simply states that x belongs to any pre-fixpoint of φ. Hence, it belongs to the intersection of all these pre-fixpoints and therefore – according to Theorem 2.2.3 – to the least fixpoint.

It is obvious that the translation produces formulae of linear size. Correctness is not difficult to prove by strengthening the statement of the theorem such that it can be used as an inductive hypothesis: for all $\mathcal{T}$, all states s, all first-order variables x and all variable assignments ρ we have $\mathcal{T}, s \models \varphi$ iff $\mathcal{T} \models_{\rho[x\mapsto s]} \mathrm{ST}(\varphi, x)$. $\qquad\square$

Thus, $\mathcal{L}_\mu$ is not more expressive than MSO. It is not hard to see that MSO is strictly more expressive then $\mathcal{L}_\mu$, see Exercise 8.40.

Proposition 8.6.5. There are MSO properties that cannot be formalised in $\mathcal{L}_\mu$. ∎

8.7 Variants

8.7.1 The Linear-Time Mu-Calculus

The modal μ-calculus, as an extension of modal logic, is naturally a branching-time temporal logic. It can make assertions like 'wherever we go, it will always be possible to reach a state satisfying p from there'. This uses both modal operators $\Diamond$ and $\square$ (cf. $\nu X.(\mu Y.p \vee \Diamond Y) \wedge \square X$). The branching-time nature of $\mathcal{L}_\mu$ is also seen in the fact that it is interpreted over arbitrary ITS. Recall that linear-time temporal logics are interpreted over computation paths. It is, of course, possible to see an LTL formula for instance as a CTL* formula which can then be translated into a formula of $\mathcal{L}_\mu$ (see Chapter 10), and this is why $\mathcal{L}_\mu$ can also express linear-time properties. However, this uses the convention of simply adding a (universal) path quantifier which turns a linear-time property into a branching-time one with little branching expressed in the formulae. An interesting question is whether the technical framework of extremal fixpoint quantifiers can also be used in the pure linear-time setting in order to obtain a logic which is for the linear-time world what the modal μ-calculus is for the branching-time world. The answer is 'Yes' – we speak of the **linear-time μ-calculus** LT_μ, which is the modal μ-calculus interpreted over computation paths, i.e. interpreted transition systems built over the transition system $(\mathbb{N}, \texttt{succ})$. Because of the following observation we use a slightly modified syntax.

Lemma 8.7.1. Let σ be a linear ITS and s be a state on it. For every $\mathcal{L}_\mu$ formula φ and every variable assignment ρ we have $\sigma, s \models_\rho \Diamond\varphi$ iff $\sigma, s \models_\rho \Box\varphi$.   ∎

Proof. This is simply a consequence of the fact that every state on an (infinite) computation path has a unique successor. Hence, there is a successor satisfying φ iff all its successors do so.   □

For this reason, we use the symbol $\bigcirc$ as the only modal operator in LT_μ. It can either be seen as a $\Diamond$ or $\Box$ from $\mathcal{L}_\mu$ when these coincide, or as the 'next-time' operator X in linear-time temporal logics. In order to avoid confusion with variables, we do not want to use X as a modal operator in this setting.

Example 8.7.2. The LTL formula $\mathsf{G}q$ – 'q holds everywhere' – can be expressed in LT_μ as $\nu X.\, q \wedge \bigcirc X$. Consider now $\nu X.q \wedge \bigcirc\bigcirc X$. It expresses '$q$ holds now in every second moment from now on'. Recall that this property is not LTL-definable, hence, LT_μ cannot be embedded into LTL (cf. Theorem 10.3.3).

Example 8.7.3. Recall the $\mathcal{L}_\mu$ properties $\mu Y.q \vee \Diamond Y$ for 'some state with q is reachable' and $\nu X.\psi \wedge \Box X$ for 'all reachable states satisfy ψ'. Since in a linear model every state has only one immediate successor, so $\nu X.(\mu Y.q \vee \bigcirc Y) \wedge \bigcirc X$ expresses the same, namely 'from every reachable state a state satisfying q is reachable'. On such linear structures, this requires that for every future state there is a future state (possible itself) that satisfies q. In other words, q must hold infinitely often on the path ahead.

The same property is formalised using $\varphi := \nu X.\mu Y.(q \wedge \bigcirc X) \vee \bigcirc Y$ but this is a little bit more difficult to see because it uses proper alternation between the two fixpoint operators. Consider for instance the following linear ITS σ.

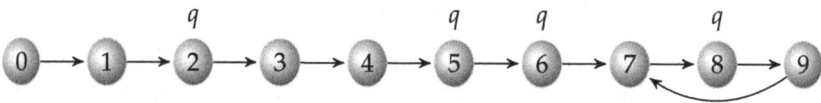

We use fixpoint iteration to compute the set of states that satisfies this formula. Starting with $\rho(X) = \{0, \ldots, 9\}$ we find that $[\![\mu^i Y.(q \wedge \bigcirc X) \vee \bigcirc Y]\!]^\sigma_{[X \mapsto \{0,\ldots,9\}]}$ contains all nodes that can reach a q-node in at most $i - 1$ steps. If X was mapped to an arbitrary set then it would contain all nodes that reach, in at most $i - 1$ steps, a q-node whose successor belongs to X. Thus, we get that the fixpoint is reached at approximant level 3, and it is $\{0, \ldots, 9\}$ since every state can reach a q-state in at most 2 steps. In particular, 3 and 9 are the last to be found in this iteration for the inner fixpoint. But then the iteration for the outer fixpoint is finished, too, since the $\{0, \ldots, 9\}$ is obviously a fixpoint for X, i.e. all states satisfy φ.

In order to better understand how it expresses 'q holds infinitely often', consider the path σ' which is obtained from the earlier one by removing q from the label of 8. Then the first inner fixpoint iteration terminates with $\{0, \ldots, 6\}$ at approximant level 3. Hence, the fixpoint in the outer iteration is not reached yet and we need to re-do an inner iteration with $X \mapsto \{0, \ldots, 6\}$. Knowing what this inner fixpoint formula expresses, we see that it eventually terminates with $\{0, \ldots, 5\}$ since 6 now does not have a successor satisfying X anymore. Again, the outer fixpoint is not reached, and the inner iteration needs to be repeated with $X \mapsto \{0, \ldots, 5\}$ which yields $\{0, \ldots, 2\}$. At last, these are also eliminated because 2 then has no successor in X anymore, and the fixpoint $\emptyset$ is reached, i.e. no state satisfies φ in this case.

The first examples suggest that LTL can be embedded into LT_μ. This is indeed the case, and the translation is rather straightforward. In fact, it uses just the same simple principles as the translation from CTL into $\mathcal{L}_\mu$ in Theorem 8.1.14.

Theorem 8.7.4. For every LTL-formula φ there is a $tr(\varphi) \in LT_\mu$ such that $tr(\varphi) \equiv \varphi$ and $|tr(\varphi)| = \mathcal{O}(|\varphi|)$. ∎

Proof. We construct $tr(\varphi)$ by induction on the structure of φ.

$$tr(p) := p$$
$$tr(\varphi \wedge \psi) := tr(\varphi) \wedge tr(\psi)$$
$$tr(\neg\varphi) := \neg tr(\varphi)$$
$$tr(\mathsf{X}\varphi) := \bigcirc tr(\varphi)$$
$$tr(\varphi \mathsf{U} \psi) := \mu X.tr(\psi) \vee (tr(\varphi) \wedge \bigcirc X).$$

In order to guarantee well-formedness, each application of the clause for the U-formulae requires the use of a fresh variable X. The size bound is easily verified. Correctness of this translation is a simple consequence of the fact that $\varphi \mathsf{U} \psi$ can be characterised as the least fixpoint of the corresponding unfolding equivalence. This least fixpoint is definable in LT_μ. A formal argument can proceed by induction on the structure of the formula. □

As shown earlier, LT_μ is strictly more expressive than LTL. A thorough study of LT_μ's expressive power is deferred to Chapter 10. Moreover, LT_μ's satisfiability problem is also slightly easier to decide than that of $\mathcal{L}_\mu$, see Section 15.4.1. Finally, we note that the alternation-hierarchy in LT_μ collapses, unlike the one in $\mathcal{L}_\mu$, i.e. on computation paths more fixpoint alternation does not yield higher expressiveness whereas on arbitrary ITS it does, see Chapter 10.

8.7.2 Adding Past-Time Operators

Temporal operators that speak about the past can be useful in specifications like 'every cash withdrawal is preceded by an entering of the correct PIN' (see e.g. Section 5.6 for the introduction of BTL). Here we will briefly consider an extension of the modal μ-calculus with past modalities which would allow such statements to be formalised directly without

re-writing it into one that solely speaks about the future, e.g. 'it is not possible to continuously not enter a correct PIN and then withdraw some cash'. Such a rewriting is always
possible on certain linear structures (cf. Corollary 10.1.23). Here we briefly study the effect
of adding past-time operators to a branching-time formalism.

The most straightforward way to extend the modal μ-calculus with operators for the past
is to add **converse modalities**. These act like the usual diamond- and box-modalities but
for the converse transition relation.

The syntax of the **modal μ-calculus with past**, $\mathcal{L}_\mu$+Past , is that of $\mathcal{L}_\mu$ with the two
additional operators $\langle a^{-1}\rangle\varphi$ and $[a^{-1}]\varphi$ for any action name $a \in Act$. They are interpreted
just like the corresponding future modalities but over the inverse transition relation:

$$[\![\langle a^{-1}\rangle\varphi]\!]_\rho^T := \{r \mid \exists\, s \in [\![\varphi]\!]_\rho^T \text{ with } s \xrightarrow{a} r\}.$$

The semantics of the converse-box-modality is defined by the duality law $[a^{-1}]\varphi :=$
$\neg\langle a^{-1}\rangle\neg\varphi$. Hence, $\langle a^{-1}\rangle\varphi$ reads as 'there is a *predecessor* that satisfies φ', and $[a^{-1}]\varphi$
reads like 'all predecessors satisfy φ'.

We will also use converse modalities for an unspecified transition, i.e. the past-
counterparts of $\Diamond\varphi$ and $\Box\varphi$ which will be written as $\langle-\rangle\varphi$ and $[-]\varphi$.

The present is the past of the future and the future of the past, so there are fundamental
correlations between past and future which should lead to valid principles in temporal logics
that can speak about both. Similar to LTL+Past and various branching-time temporal logics
extended with past, $\mathcal{L}_\mu$+Past features validities that formulate these principles, e.g. $\varphi \to$
$[a]\langle a^{-1}\rangle\varphi$ and $\varphi \to [a^{-1}]\langle a\rangle\varphi$.

Recall that $\mathcal{L}_\mu$ is bisimulation-invariant (Theorem 8.5.2). It has the finite model property
(Theorem 15.4.33). The addition of past-modalities does not preserve either of these.

First we consider bisimulation-invariance. It is in fact not surprising that $\mathcal{L}_\mu$+Past can
distinguish bisimilar structures as the following example shows.

Example 8.7.5. Consider the states s_0 and r_0 of this transition system:

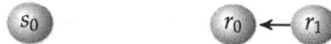

Clearly, they are (locally) bisimilar because they both have no successors. On the other
hand, they can easily be distinguished by the $\mathcal{L}_\mu$+Past formula $\langle-\rangle\top$.

Thus, while it is technically correct that $\mathcal{L}_\mu$+Past can distinguish bisimilar models and
therefore is not bisimulation-invariant it is clearly a relative weakness of the definition of
bisimilarity which is being exploited for this observation: bisimulation is only concerned
with forward edges. An equivalence notion that would be better suited as a relation that
could capture logical equivalence in $\mathcal{L}_\mu$+Past would clearly have to consider backward
edges as well. We leave it as Exercise 8.44 to define such a refined equivalence called
2-way bisimulation and to show that $\mathcal{L}_\mu$+Past cannot distinguish structures which are
related by this equivalence.

The loss of the finite model property is of more serious nature; it is not just an artefact of applying some notion to temporal logics with past that does not consider the past adequately. Finiteness of transition systems is not just a property of the future view onto transition systems.

Example 8.7.6. Consider the formula $\mu X.\Box X$ of $\mathcal{L}_\mu$, and therefore also of $\mathcal{L}_\mu$+Past, interpreted over transition systems with a single accessibility relation. It expresses well-foundedness of this relation in a state, i.e. the impossibility of an infinite path starting in this state. This can be seen by considering its approximants $\bot, \Box\bot, \Box\Box\bot, \ldots$. The nth in this order (starting at 0) expresses 'there is no path of length n' or, equivalently, 'every path has length at most $n-1$' if $n \geq 1$.

Further approximants at transfinite ordinal level then express for instance 'all paths have finite length', 'all paths starting from any successor have finite length', and so on. Altogether this formula does not permit any path of infinite length.

Not surprisingly, its logical complement, which can be written as $\nu Y.\Diamond Y$, expresses 'there is a path of infinite length'.

The converse version $\nu Y.\langle-\rangle Y$ then expresses that there is an infinite backwards path. Moreover, take any closed $\mathcal{L}_\mu$+Past formula ψ and consider $\nu Y.\psi \wedge \langle-\rangle Y$. This states that there is an infinite backwards path on which every state satisfies ψ.

Now take as ψ the formula which states that there are no infinite paths, i.e. consider $\nu Y.(\mu X.\Box X) \wedge \langle-\rangle Y$. It is satisfiable; the leftmost state in the transition system has an infinite backwards path such that at every moment there is no infinite forwards path. This model is clearly of infinite size, and it remains to see that this formula cannot have a finite model.

Theorem 8.7.7. $\mathcal{L}_\mu$+Past does not have the finite model property. ∎

Proof. The preceding example shows that the $\mathcal{L}_\mu$+Past formula $\varphi := \nu Y.(\mu X.\Box X) \wedge \langle-\rangle Y$ is satisfiable. Suppose there was a transition system $\mathcal{T}$ with some state s_0 such that $\mathcal{T}$ has n states for some $n \in \mathbb{N}$ and $\mathcal{T}, s_0 \models \varphi$. Then we would, in particular, have $\mathcal{T}, s_0 \models \nu^n Y.(\mu X.\Box X) \wedge \langle-\rangle X)$, i.e. there would have to be states $s_1, \ldots, s_n$ such that $s_i \rightarrow s_{i-1}$ for all $i = n, \ldots, 1$ and $\mathcal{T}, s_i \models \mu X.\Box X$ for all $i = n, \ldots, 0$.

Since $|\mathcal{T}| = n$, there are i, j with $i < j$ but $s_i = s_j$. Thus, the transition relation in $\mathcal{T}$ forms a loop:

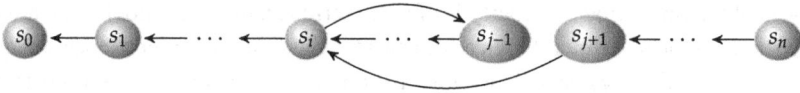

In particular there is an obvious infinite forwards path starting in s_i so we have $\mathcal{T}, s_i \not\models \mu X.\Box X$ which contradicts the assumption, and we conclude that φ cannot have a finite model. $\Box$

8.8 Exercises

Exercises on the syntax and semantics

Exercise 8.1. Extend the definition of well-formedness to formulae in negation normal form.

Exercise 8.2. Define $free(\varphi)$ by induction on the structure of φ.

Exercise 8.3. Let $\mathcal{T} = (S, \rightarrow, L)$. Show that $[\![\nu X.\varphi]\!]^{\mathcal{T}}_\rho = \bigcup \{T \subseteq S \mid [\![\varphi]\!]^{\mathcal{T}}_{\rho[X \mapsto T]} \supseteq T\}$.

Exercise 8.4. Suppose $\mathfrak{f} : \mathcal{P}(S) \rightarrow \mathcal{P}(S)$ is a monotone function on some powerset lattice. Define its dual $\hat{\mathfrak{f}} : \mathcal{P}(S) \rightarrow \mathcal{P}(S)$ via $\hat{\mathfrak{f}}(X) := S \setminus \mathfrak{f}(S \setminus X)$.

(a) Show that $\hat{\mathfrak{f}}$ is monotone as well.
(b) Show that $\bigcup \{X \mid X \subseteq \mathfrak{f}(X)\} = S \setminus \bigcap \{X \mid \hat{\mathfrak{f}}(X) \subseteq X\}$.

Exercise 8.5. Prove Lemma 8.1.7.

Exercise 8.6. Let $\mathcal{T}$ be some transition system, $\varphi \in \mathcal{L}_\mu$ and ρ, ρ' be two variable assignments such that $\rho(X) = \rho'(X)$ for all $X \in free(\varphi)$. Show that $[\![\varphi]\!]^{\mathcal{T}}_\rho = [\![\varphi]\!]^{\mathcal{T}}_{\rho'}$. This formalises the intuition that the extension of a formula in a structure only depends on the valuation of the formula's free variables.

Exercise 8.7. Prove the equivalence of the following formulae for arbitrary φ by showing that their semantics coincide on any transition system.

$$\mu X.\mu Y.\varphi(X, Y) \equiv \mu X.\varphi(X, X) \equiv \mu Y.\mu X.\varphi(X, Y).$$

Exercise 8.8. Prove that the following implications hold in $\mathcal{L}_\mu$ for arbitrary φ, using $\mathcal{L}_\mu$'s semantics.

(a) $\mu X.\varphi(X) \rightarrow \nu X.\varphi(X)$.
(b) $\mu X.\nu Y.\varphi(X, Y) \rightarrow \nu Y.\mu X.\varphi(X, Y)$.

Exercise 8.9. Show that CTL can be embedded into $\mathcal{L}_\mu$ over the class of all transition systems. *Hint:* Check how the construction in the proof of Theorem 8.1.14 needs to be amended to work for possibly nontotal systems, too.

Exercises on approximants and signatures

Exercise 8.10. Prove Lemma 8.2.3.

Exercise 8.11. Let $\varphi = \mu X.q \vee \square X$. Compute for each state s of the two transition systems below the least ordinal α such that s satisfies the αth approximant of φ. Why is it clear that, for the transition system on the left, α must in fact be a natural number if it exists?

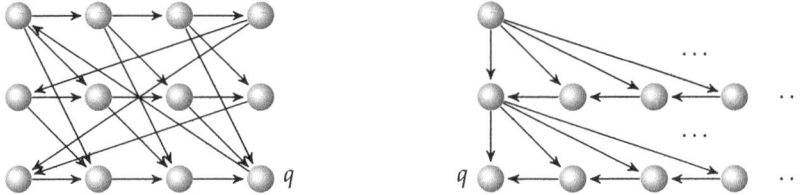

Now do the same for the formula $\mu X.\square(q \vee X)$.

Exercise 8.12. Show that the number of different states on a longest path in a finite transition system is an upper bound on the closure ordinals in this transition system.

Exercise 8.13. Show that the formula $\nu X.\langle a \rangle X \wedge \nu Y.\langle b \rangle (Y \wedge X)$ formalises the property 'there is an infinite a-path such that each state on it is the origin of an infinite b-path, and on every state (except the first one) on that path, the same holds again'.

Exercise 8.14. Prove Lemma 8.2.13.

Exercises on global model checking

Exercise 8.15. Execute the global model-checking algorithm (Algorithm 8) with the formula $\nu X.\langle a \rangle X \wedge \nu Y.\langle b \rangle (Y \wedge X)$ and the transition system from Example 8.2.9.

Exercise 8.16. Prove Theorem 8.2.16 and Theorem 8.2.18.

Exercises on the structural complexity of formulae

Exercise 8.17. Compute the nesting depth, the quantifier depth and the alternation depth for the following formulae:

- $\mu Z.(\nu X.(\square Z \wedge p \wedge (\mu Y.(X \wedge \Diamond Y))))$.
- $\mu Z.(\mu X.(\square Z \wedge p \wedge (\mu Y.(q \vee \Diamond Y)) \wedge \Diamond X))$.

Exercise 8.18. Prove Theorem 8.3.2. *Hint:* Reformulate Algorithm FPITER such that it avoids unnecessary fixpoint iterations for inner fixpoint formulae which do not depend on the stages of outer ones.

Exercise 8.19. Compute the alternation depth of the $\mathcal{L}_\mu$ formulae resulting from the translation of CTL into $\mathcal{L}_\mu$ in Theorem 8.1.14.

Exercise 8.20. Prove Theorem 8.3.5. *Hint:* Reformulate Algorithm FPITER such that it combines fixpoint iterations of the same type whenever possible according to the Bekič Lemma.

Exercise 8.21. Show that $\nu X.\mu Y(\Diamond Y \vee (p \wedge \Diamond X))$ belongs to $\Sigma_3 \cap \Pi_2$.

Exercise 8.22. Prove Lemma 8.3.9.

Exercise 8.23. Transform φ_1, φ_2 and φ_3 from Example 8.3.22 into guarded form using the procedure described in Section 8.3.5.

Exercise 8.24. Formulate the guarded transformation procedure such that it produces polynomially sized MES instead of exponentially sized formulae.

Exercises on modal equation systems

Exercise 8.25. Translate the following MES with starting variable 1 into an equivalent $\mathcal{L}_\mu$ formula.

$$X_1 =_1 \Diamond(X_1 \wedge X_2 \wedge X_3) \quad X_2 =_2 \Box(X_1 \vee X_2 \vee X_3) \quad X_3 =_3 X_1.$$

Exercise 8.26. Let $(\mathcal{E}, i)$ be a MES and φ be its translation into an $\mathcal{L}_\mu$ formula.

(a) Show that the size of φ is at most exponential in the size of $\mathcal{E}$.
(b) Find a family of MES such that the size of their corresponding formulae grows at least exponentially in their size.

Exercise 8.27. Consider the translation function from MES to $\mathcal{L}_\mu$ from Section 8.3.4. Show that it is well founded. *Hint:* Consider the definition as a recursive function *tr*. Find an argument which shows that this function terminates for all input parameters. Note that this is not obvious because the size of the formula parameter can shrink and grow by translating further equations, and so can the size of the variable set parameter.

Exercise 8.28. Show that the formula obtained by translating an arbitrary $\mathcal{L}_\mu$ formula φ into a MES according to Definition 8.3.14 and then back into a formula equals φ.

Exercise 8.29. Prove Lemma 8.3.16.

Exercise 8.30. Finish the proof of Theorem 8.3.17 by verifying the cardinality estimations.

Exercises on model-checking games

Exercise 8.31. Construct the model-checking game graph for the transition system and the formula given in Example 8.4.4.

Exercise 8.32. Spell out the details of the proof for Lemma 8.4.7.

Exercise 8.33. Prove Lemma 8.4.12.

Exercise 8.34. Formulate games that characterise the local model-checking problem for CTL. *Hint:* Consider the definition of the $\mathcal{L}_\mu$ games on formulae which result from a translation of CTL formulae into $\mathcal{L}_\mu$. In particular, try to define the winning conditions without referring to the infinite occurrences of some outermost subformula. Instead consider which formulae the plays must eventually get trapped in.

Exercise 8.35. Use the model-checking games in order to prove the equivalence of the following formulae for arbitrary φ (cf. Exercise 8.7.):

$$\mu X.\mu Y.\varphi(X,Y) \equiv \mu X.\varphi(X,X) \equiv \mu Y.\mu X.\varphi(X,Y).$$

Hint: Transform a winning strategy for player **V** in a game on a transition system and one of these formulae into a winning strategy on the same transition system an the other formulae.

Exercise 8.36. Use game-theoretical arguments in order to show that the following implications hold in $\mathcal{L}_\mu$ for arbitrary φ (cf. Exercise 8.8.):

(a) $\mu X.\varphi(X) \rightarrow \nu X.\varphi(X)$.
(b) $\mu X.\nu Y.\varphi(X,Y) \rightarrow \nu Y.\mu X.\varphi(X,Y)$.

Exercises on bisimulation invariance and MSO

Exercise 8.37. Show that the complement of a bisimulation-closed set is bisimulation-closed. Show that the union, respectively intersection of an arbitrary (not necessarily finite) family of bisimulation-closed sets is again bisimulation-closed.

Exercise 8.38. Can Theorem 8.5.6 be extended to transition systems with finitely many different traces only? *Hint:* It is helpful to distinguish two cases depending on whether they are all finitely representable.

Exercise 8.39. Theorem 8.5.6 states that it is impossible to characterise transition systems with infinitely many traces in $\mathcal{L}_\mu$ up to trace equivalence. The proof shows an even stronger result: it is not possible to construct a formula for any such system $\mathcal{T}$ that demands existence of *all* traces that occur in $\mathcal{T}$.

Is it possible to construct, for any finite transition system $\mathcal{T}$ and root s, a formula φ which characterises trace inclusion in the sense that its models are exactly those transition systems whose traces are included in $\text{traces}_{\mathcal{T}}(s)$?

Exercise 8.40. Give MSO formulae for the following properties.

(a) 'There are two different a-successors'.
(b) 'There is an a-loop'.
(c) 'The relation $\xrightarrow{a}$ is the transitive closure of the relation $\xrightarrow{b}$'.

In case of (a) and (b), also give an argument that shows why these properties are not formalisable in $\mathcal{L}_\mu$. In case of (c), argue intuitively.

Exercises on variants of $\mathcal{L}_\mu$

Exercise 8.41. Give LT_μ formulae which define the following linear-time properties.

(a) 'p holds exactly in every second position from now on'
(b) 'p only holds finitely often'
(c) 'p holds infinitely often at even positions'
(d) 'every p is preceded by some q that occurs strictly before that p'
(e) 'every p is preceded by some q that occurs strictly before that p and strictly after any previous p'

Exercise 8.42. Prove or refute: if some $\varphi \in LT_\mu$ is equivalent to some $\psi \in LTL$ then $\mathit{free}(\varphi) = \emptyset$.

Exercise 8.43. Devise a translation from nondeterministic Büchi automata into equivalent LT_μ-formulae. *Hint:* Consider the states as propositional variables. Nondeterministic Büchi automata are defined in Chapter 14.

Exercise 8.44. Extend the notion of bisimulation to a 2-way bisimulation which also considers predecessors of related states of a transition system and show that $\mathcal{L}_\mu$+Past cannot distinguish states that are 2-way bisimilar.

8.9 Bibliographical Notes

The modal μ-calculus in its present form was introduced by Kozen (1983). It was designed in order to generalise ideas used in program logics like PDL (Fischer and Ladner 1979), which puts some restricted form of second-order quantification (here: reflexive-transitive closures) on top of multimodal logic. It was then natural to consider logics that combine modal logic with the more general concept of a least fixpoint operator. This had in fact already been done before Kozen's work in one form or the other, for instance with Park's (1970) *least-fixpoint calculus*, Pratt's (1981) *μ-calculus* as well as Bakker and de Roever's (1972) *calculus for recursive program schemes*.

Model checking. While early work on program logics mainly focused on validity and therefore also satisfiability problems in order to model program behaviours logically, it was not long after the introduction of temporal or modal fixpoint logics in computer science that model checking had been proposed for program verification (Clarke and Emerson 1981; Queille and Sifakis 1982a). With $\mathcal{L}_\mu$ as a generalisation of various logics around, it was natural to consider its model-checking problem, too. A lot of effort has been made in order to find efficient procedures, for instance through local model checking by Stirling and Walker (1989) and Cleaveland (1989), or simply by designing specialised algorithms for parts of $\mathcal{L}_\mu$ like its alternation-free fragment only (Emerson and Lei 1986; Cleaveland and Steffen 1991; Bhat and Cleaveland 1996a).

Different, yet similar techniques have been introduced to reduce the model-checking problem to some sort of graph-theoretic one, for instance through *Boolean* graphs by Andersen (1994a) which are close to alternating tree automata. A clear automata-theoretic approach has also been taken by Emerson et al. (2001) and Kupferman et al. (2000).

The model-checking games presented here were invented by Stirling (1995). As it turned out, they are in fact just special cases of *parity games* which will be treated to some extend in Chapter 15.

Nested and alternating fixpoints. The main obstacle for efficiency in $\mathcal{L}_\mu$ model checking is the logic's ability to formalise temporal properties by nesting and intertwining fixpoint quantifiers. It is a simple exercise to devise a naïve model-checking algorithm that simply calculates the extension of a formula in an ITS by induction on the formula structure and uses fixpoint iteration for fixpoint quantifiers. It was observed by Emerson and Lei (1986) that this can be optimised so that fixpoints of the same type that are adjacent to each other in the syntax DAG of the formula do not add to the exponential complexity. This exploits the Bekić Lemma (1984) resulting in a complexity that is only exponential in the alternation depth of the formula. Browne et al. (1997) have taken this idea further and were able to reduce the complexity to half of the alternation depth, also found by Seidl (1996) in a more general setting.

Since fixpoint alternation proved to be the main obstacle against a polynomial-time model-checking algorithm, it has been analysed thoroughly as well. Emerson and Lei's (1986) improvisation over the completely naïve model-checking algorithm by fixpoint iteration has led to the definition of the Emerson–Lei alternation hierarchy. The version presented here is the more refined Niwiński hierarchy (Niwiński 1986, 1997; Arnold and Niwiński 2001), i.e. it assigns in general a lower index of alternation to formulae than the Emerson–Lei definition does. A short dicussion on the differences can be found in Bradfield and Stirling's (2007) handbook article. We refer the reader to the bibliographic notes in the expressiveness chapter (Section 10.5) for a more detailed description on results regarding fixpoint alternation.

Syntactical variants and guardedness. Modal equation systems have been studied as a convenient syntactical variant of $\mathcal{L}_\mu$ formulae for various purposes, for instance for verification questions (Mader 1997a,b; Bhat and Cleaveland 1996b). An intermediate formalism is known as the *μ-calculus with vectorial form* which allows multiple fixpoints of the same kind to be grouped together. Semantically, its components are interpreted by tuples of sets of states rather than sets of states alone (Arnold and Niwiński 2001).

Some of the literature on $\mathcal{L}_\mu$ may give the impression that these different forms are really just syntactical variants. While this is true with respect to expressive power it seems like modal equation systems are more compact than formulae which has effects on complexity results. The only known translations from equation systems to formulae are exponential; it is not known whether polynomial translations exists. Interestingly, the question is tightly linked to the question of whether a polynomial guarded transformation procedure exists (Bruse et al. 2015).

The problem of guardedness had already been mentioned by Kozen (1983); an explicit guarded transformation procedure was presented by Walukiewicz (2000). This is clearly exponential because it uses transformation of Boolean formulae into conjunctive or disjunctive normal form successively. It was observed by Kupferman et al. (2000) and Mateescu (2002) that this unfolding of Boolean formulae is unnecessary; the procedure sketched here is essentially the one given by them. However, both independently misjudge the complexity of their procedures and miss that it is still exponential in the size of the formula in the worst case which was shown recently by Bruse et al. (2015) using the Friedmann formulae of Example 8.3.22. They carry out a detailed analysis on the problem of guarded transformation and show that it is not easy for vectorial formulae, namely at least as hard as solving parity games (cf. Section 15.1), and therefore not currently known to be in PTime. They also reveal an exponential gap between a formula's DAG size and the size of its Fischer–Ladner closure which is often used interchangeably in the literature. In fact, it is a measure for the size of an equivalent modal equation system.

Neumann and Seidl (1999) studied the problem of guarded transformation in such systems and present a procedure which uses the same principles as the other procedures mentioned earlier. It is exponential in general but, as they claim, polynomial on a class of equation systems that supersedes formulae. This claim needs to be considered carefully, though. While the procedure is seemingly correct and polynomial, it does not produce equation systems that correspond to formulae anymore. Hence, existence of a guarded transformation procedure for formulae (or even equation systems) is still an open problem, and so is the question after a polynomial translation from equation systems to formulae.

The problem of axiomatisation. Axiomatisability was one of the key logical problems considered in the time when temporal logics arose in computer science. Kozen managed to give a complete axiomatisation for a syntactic fragment of $\mathcal{L}_\mu$. In terms of the satisfiability games introduced in Section 15.4.1, the fragment is such that there is a unique path from any fixpoint variable to its unfolding in the context of such games. This is weaker than demanding single occurrences of fixpoint variables; it relaxes this with respect to disjunctions, hence the name *aconjunctive fragment*. Walukiewicz (2000) then managed to show that every formula is provably (in this axiomatisation) equivalent to an aconjunctive one which yields completeness for the entire $\mathcal{L}_\mu$.

On the other hand, the linear-time μ-calculus poses less problems for axiomatisability (Kaivola 1995a).

Decision procedures. A procedure for deciding satisfiability of validity in $\mathcal{L}_\mu$ has not been given in this chapter; this is being done in Chapter 15. Decidability of these problems is not obvious but was established quite early on by Kozen and Parikh (1983). They observed that it can be reduced to the satisfiability problem of second-order logic over trees of fixed branching degree whose decidability was shown by Rabin (1969) before. This is essentially what we called MSO in Section 8.6 in this chapter.

The complexity of the resulting procedure is nonelementary and therefore highly non-optimal. Decision procedures of elementary complexity have been found subsequently, starting with work by Streett and Emerson (1984), who reduced $\mathcal{L}_\mu$ satisfiability directly to the nonemptiness problem of tree automata (rather than going through MSO) resulting in a triply exponential time procedure. This not yet optimal complexity is mainly due to the non-optimal procedures for emptiness of tree automata available at that time (e.g. Streett 1982). Improved methods have been found resulting in a singly exponential decision procedure based on such a reduction given by Emerson and Jutla (1988, 2000).

Related to the question of (semi-)decidability is the finite and small model property for a logic. Since model checking is easily seen to be decidable, a small model theorem can be used to derive decidability by either guessing and verifying a suitable model or simply enumerating all possible models up to the size determined by the small model property. Since finite models are enumerable, a finite model property together with decidability of model checking at least establishes semi-decidability of satisfiability. Kozen (1988) managed to refine a filtration method, which otherwise fails on logics like $\mathcal{L}_\mu$, thus establishing a finite model property but not necessarily the small model property. That was first obtained through the automata constructions (Streett and Emerson 1984).

More decision procedures have been designed, for example a game-based one by Niwiński and Walukiewicz (1996). The procedure given later in Chapter 15 uses the same principles but makes use of the more modern and more suitable parity games. A tableau-based decision procedure has been given by Jungteerapanich (2009). Its complexity is non-optimal since it involves guessing of names and therefore only yields a nondeterministic exponential time procedure, assuming that the input formulae are guarded. See Chapter 13 for further material on tableau-based decision procedures, even though we do not give a tableau-based procedure for $\mathcal{L}_\mu$ there. Friedmann and Lange (2013) have shown how such approaches, in particular the game-based one, can be rendered to cope with unguarded formulae directly, thus avoiding a possibly costly transformation into guarded form.

Variants and extensions. The linear-time μ-calculus LT_μ had been proposed as a generalisation of linear-time temporal logics just like the modal μ-calculus generalised branching-time logics suitably via the fixpoint characterisations of their temporal operators (Barringer et al. 1986; Banieqbal and Barringer 1989). Vardi (1988) considered an extension with past operators and used 2-way automata to show its decidability.

While $\mathcal{L}_\mu$ plays the role of a most general logic for temporal property specification, see for instance Chapter 10, it is also quite useful as a basis for further extensions, of which many exist but have not been dealt with in this book, e.g. the *alternating-time* μ-calculus (Alur et al. 2002; Schewe and Finkbeiner 2006), the *polyadic* μ-calculus (Andersen 1994b; Otto 1999; Lange and Lozes 2012), the *hybrid* μ-calculus (Sattler and Vardi 2001), the *inflationary* fixpoint logic (Dawar et al. 2004), some *higher-order* fixpoint logics (Müller-Olm 1999; Viswanathan and Viswanathan 2004) and so on.

Characteristic formulae. The modal μ-calculus can define characteristic formulae for many more equivalence relations and preorders than just bisimilarity, for instance, simulation, simulation equivalence, or 2-nested bisimulation (Aceto et al. 2012b). A better link between behavioural equivalences and modal fixpoint logics is given with the aforementioned polyadic μ-calculus (Andersen 1994b; Otto 1999), though. It captures bisimilarity in the much stronger sense of *defining* these relations by a formula interpreted over *pairs* of transition system states. This is not restricted to finite-state systems only, and it admits fully symbolic algorithms for checking behavioural equivalences (Lange et al. 2014).

9

Alternating-Time Temporal Logics

The transitions in the transition systems that we have studied so far are primitive and abstract objects. The nature of the possible transitions between states and the mechanisms that generate and determine them have not been essential in the context of the linear and branching time temporal logics we have studied in the previous chapters.

Here we introduce and study a more involved type of transition system, called *concurrent game structures*, for modelling scenarios that typically arise in **open** or **multiagent systems**. An **open system** is a system (computer, device, agent) interacting with an environment. The properties and behaviour of such open systems can be modelled by 2-player games. More generally, a multiagent system may involve several interacting (possibly, cooperating or competing) agents, each pursuing their own goals or acting randomly (like nature or the environment). Concurrent game structures are special types of *multiagent transition systems*, where the transitions are determined by tuples of simultaneous actions performed by a fixed set of agents. Various logical formalisms extending linear and branching-time temporal logics can be used for the specification, verification and reasoning about dynamic properties of open and multiagent systems.

In this chapter we present and study concurrent game structures as models for the family of so-called *alternating-time temporal logics*. They are the most popular and influential logics for strategic reasoning in multiagent systems and are multiagent versions of branching-time temporal logics which correspond to closed or single-agent systems in a sense that we will discuss in the chapter.

Structure of the chapter. We introduce concurrent multiagent transition systems and models in Section 9.1 and then the logics ATL* and ATL in Section 9.2. We then discuss model checking and satisfiability testing for these logics in Section 9.3. As usual, the chapter ends with exercises and bibliographic notes.

9.1 Concurrent Multiagent Transition Systems

9.1.1 Concurrent Game Structures and Models

We begin with a motivating example. Figure 9.1 depicts two transition systems. The one on top involves two robots, Robot_1 and Robot_2, and a carriage. There are three different positions of the carriage, denoted by states s_0, s_1 and s_2. Each robot has two possible actions at any of the states: push and wait. Robot_1 can only push the carriage in clockwise direction, whereas Robot_2 can only push it in anticlockwise direction. As a result of their joint action at any state the carriage can move clockwise or anticlockwise, or – if both robots wait or push at the same time – it can remain in the same place. The possible joint actions (an action for Robot_1 and an action for Robot_2) and the respective transitions between states are indicated in this figure.

The transition system at the bottom involves only one robot, Robot_1 that can push the carriage in any direction (clockwise, by performing action push+ or anti-clockwise, by action push−) or can do nothing (action wait).

Note that these two transition systems look the same, except for the labelling of their transitions. In fact, with respect to any temporal properties expressible in CTL*, these transition systems are equivalent. On the other hand, they are essentially different in terms of what the agents (robots) involved in them can achieve in each of them: in the latter, Robot_1 has full control over where to position the carriage starting from any initial state, whereas in the former one its abilities are limited by the respective actions that Robot_2 may perform from the initial state.

Thus, what makes these transition systems different is the nature of the transitions: they are not abstract but are explicitly determined and labelled by the actions of the agents (robots) involved in each of them.

We are now going to enrich the notion of transition system to enable more adequate modelling of those transition systems arising in the context of multiagent systems where

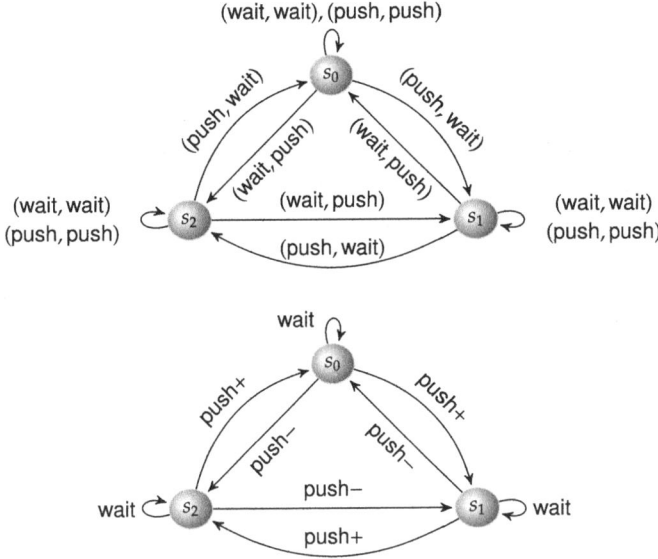

Figure 9.1 (top) Two robots pushing a carriage; (bottom) one robot pushing a carriage.

agents take simultaneous actions in discrete steps. Throughout this chapter we use the terms 'agent' and 'player' as synonyms.

Definition 9.1.1. A **concurrent game structure** (CGS) is a tuple

$$\mathcal{S} = (\mathbb{AG}, S, Act, \mathrm{act}, \delta)$$

which consists of:

- a finite, nonempty set of **players** or **agents** $\mathbb{AG}$. The subsets of $\mathbb{AG}$ are often called **coalitions**. We often assume for convenience that $\mathbb{AG} = \{1, \ldots, k\}$ and therefore implicitly assume a linear ordering on the set of agents.
- a nonempty set of **states** or **game positions** S.
- a nonempty set of **actions**, or **moves** Act.
- an **action manager** function $\mathrm{act} : \mathbb{AG} \times S \to \mathcal{P}(Act)$ assigning nonempty sets of actions available for execution to each player at each state,
- a deterministic **transition function** δ that assigns to every state s and every **action profile** $\alpha = (\alpha_1, \ldots, \alpha_k)$, such that $\alpha_{\mathbf{a}} \in \mathrm{act}(\mathbf{a}, s)$ for every $\mathbf{a} \in \mathbb{AG}$, a unique **successor (outcome) state** $\delta(s, \alpha)$. ∇

We denote by $\mathrm{act}_{\mathcal{S}}(s)$ the set $\prod_{\mathbf{a} \in \mathbb{AG}} \mathrm{act}(\mathbf{a}, s)$ of all action tuples executable from the state s. When $\mathcal{S}$ is fixed by the context, we omit it and write $\mathrm{act}(s)$.

An **interpreted concurrent game structure** (ICGS), also known as a **concurrent game model** (CGM), is a CGS endowed with a labelling $L : S \to \mathcal{P}(\mathrm{PROP})$ of game states with sets of atomic propositions from a fixed set PROP. As usual, that labelling describes which atomic propositions are true at any given state.   ▽

Thus, in a CGS all players execute their actions independently and synchronously from a given current state of the system and the combination of these actions, together with the current state, determines the transition to a successor state in the CGS.

Note that the actions in concurrent game structures are of local nature: the 'same action' when applied at different states has unrelated effects. Therefore, we can assume that every state has its own set of associated actions. Then, the function act can be re-defined to assign a number $act_a(s)$ greater than 1 of actions to every player $a \in \mathbb{AG}$ and every state $s \in S$, available to player a at state s; these actions can be named with the integers $0, \ldots, d_a(s) - 1$. Then, for every state $s \in S$, an **action vector** is a k-tuple $(\alpha_1, \ldots, \alpha_k)$, where $k = card(\mathbb{AG})$, such that $0 \le \alpha_a < d_a(s)$ for every $a \in [1, k]$.

Example 9.1.2. The two-robot example in Figure 9.1 can be formally defined as a concurrent game structure as follows:

- $\mathbb{AG} = \{Robot_1, Robot_2\}$.
- $S = \{s_0, s_1, s_2\}$; $Act = \{push, wait\}$.
- the action manager function act is defined so that both actions are available to each agent at every state.
- the outcome function δ is defined as in the figure.

It can then be expanded to a concurrent game model, e.g. by defining PROP = $\{pos_0, pos_1, pos_2\}$ and $L : S \to \mathcal{P}(PROP)$ defined by $L(s_i) = \{pos_i\}$, for $i = 0, 1, 2$. Thus, one can refer directly to each state of the model in the language.

Example 9.1.3. Two agents share a file in the cyberspace. The file can be updated only at designated moments (e.g. only on the hour). At every such moment each of the agents can apply action Update (U) if they are enabled to do so, or Skip (N). Both agents act simultaneously. Initially (at state E), both agents are enabled to apply Update. If at any moment both apply Update, the file is locked forever and none of the agents can apply Update any longer. If one agent applies Skip while the other applies Update at the same moment, the file gets updated by the updating agent i (state U_i). If that agent i applies Update again before the other has applied Update, then the process goes to a state D_i where they are disabled from updating and can only apply Skip. At that state the other agent can enable i to apply further updates by applying Skip, too, as the procedure then goes back to state U_i, for $i = 1, 2$; alternatively, each one of them can decide to apply Update themselves. If both agents apply Skip at any state but D_i, then nothing happens. After, if ever, the non-i agent applies Update at state U_i or D_i, while agent i applies Skip the procedure goes to a state Processed (P), where both agents are disabled from making further updates. From that state, agent 1 can reset the process from state E, by applying action Reset (R).

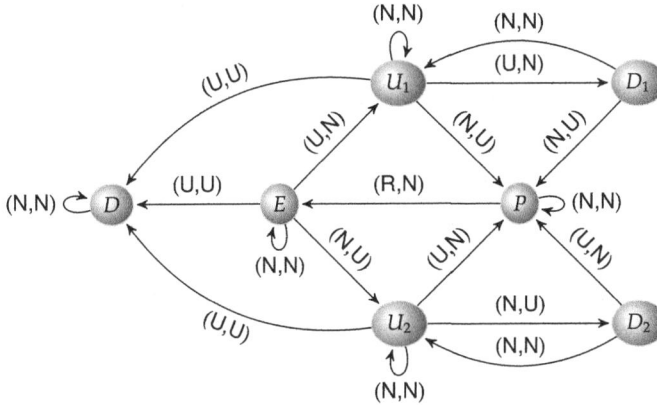

Figure 9.2 A concurrent game model encoding the shared file updating procedure.

The procedure is encoded as a concurrent game model in Figure 9.2, where the atomic propositions are then identified with the names of the states where they hold. The actions of agent 1 and 2 are again shown as pairs.

9.1.2 Plays, Computations and Strategies

We start with the intuitive notions and then we provide the formal definitions. A **play** in a CGS/CGM $\mathcal{M}$ is just a path in $\mathcal{M}$, that is, an infinite sequence of states that can result from subsequent transitions in $\mathcal{M}$ affected by sequences of joint moves (action profiles) of all players. Here we will use the term 'play' to emphasise the game-theoretic nature of the paths arising in concurrent game models. A computation in $\mathcal{M}$ is, as usual, the observable effect of a play, that is, the corresponding sequence of labels of states. A strategy of a player **a** in $\mathcal{M}$ is a conditional plan that specifies what **a** should do in each possible situation given the history of the play. There can be different types of strategies, depending on the amount of memory that we assume the players can use. At one end of the spectrum are **positional strategies**, for players whose memory, if any, is entirely encoded in the current state of the system. Thus, a positional strategy can only use that current state to determine the prescribed action. At the other extreme are **memory-based strategies**, which at every position of a play can use the entire history of that play in order to determine the prescribed action. In between there is a range of 'bounded memory' strategies that we will not discuss here.

Remark 9.1.4. By a 'history' of the play here we mean the sequence of game states in the play. One can consider richer notions of history, also including the sequence of action profiles affecting the transitions. However, by reproducing every state in sufficiently many copies, every CGM can be transformed to an 'equivalent' (bisimilar, see further) one where different action profiles applied at the same state lead to different successor states. Every play in the resulting CGM is affected by a unique sequence of action profiles, hence the two notions of history in such systems essentially coincide. We leave the details to the reader.

Hereafter we fix a concurrent game structure $\mathcal{S} = (\mathbb{AG}, S, Act, \text{act}, \delta)$. All notions defined here apply to concurrent game models likewise.

Definition 9.1.5. A **play** in $\mathcal{S}$ is an infinite sequence $\lambda = s_0, s_1, \ldots$ of states in S such that, for all $i \geq 0$, the state s_{i+1} is a successor of the state s_i. The elements of the domain of λ will be called **positions**.

For a play λ and positions $i, j \geq 0$, we use $\lambda[i]$, $\lambda[j, i]$ and $\lambda[j, \infty)$ to denote the ith state of λ, the finite segment $s_j, s_{j+1} \ldots, s_i$, and the suffix $s_j, s_{j+1}, \ldots$ of λ, respectively. A play with $\lambda[0] = s$ will be called an s-**play**.

The initial segments $\lambda[0, i]$ of plays λ will be called **histories** in $\mathcal{S}$. A typical history will be denoted by h and the last state of h will be denoted by $\texttt{last}(h)$.

A **computation** in $\mathcal{S}$ is an infinite sequence $L(\lambda[0]), L(\lambda[1]), \ldots$ where λ is a play in $\mathcal{S}$.   ∇

Note that if the action profiles affecting the transitions are taken as abstract labels then the notions of play and computation correspond to the standard notions of path and computation in labelled transition systems, as defined in Chapter 3.

Definition 9.1.6. Let $\mathbf{a} \in \mathbb{AG}$ and $C \subseteq \mathbb{AG}$.

- A **positional strategy** (also known as **memoryless strategy**) in $\mathcal{S}$ for the player $\mathbf{a}$ is a function $\mathfrak{str}_\mathbf{a} : S \to Act$, such that $\mathfrak{str}_\mathbf{a}(s) \in \text{act}(\mathbf{a}, s)$.
- A **memory-based strategy** (also known as **perfect recall strategy**) in $\mathcal{S}$ for the player $\mathbf{a}$ is a function $\mathfrak{str}_\mathbf{a} : S^+ \to Act$ such that $\mathfrak{str}_\mathbf{a}(h) \in \text{act}(\mathbf{a}, \texttt{last}(h))$, where S^+ is the set of all finite sequences of states in $\mathcal{S}$. (It suffices to define memory-based strategies only on the set of all *histories* of plays in $\mathcal{S}$.)

A positional (resp. memory-based) strategy in $\mathcal{S}$ for the coalition C is a tuple of positional (resp. memory-based) strategies, one for each player in C.   ∇

Clearly, every positional strategy is a memory-based strategy, too.

Definition 9.1.7. Let $s \in S$ and let $C \subseteq \mathbb{AG}$. We denote the complementary coalition $\mathbb{AG} \setminus C$ by $\overline{C}$.

- A C-**action** at state s is a tuple α_C such that $\alpha_C(\mathbf{a}) \in \text{act}(\mathbf{a}, s)$ for every $\mathbf{a} \in C$ and $\alpha_C(\mathbf{a}') = \sharp_{\mathbf{a}'}$ for every $\mathbf{a}' \notin C$, where $\sharp_{\mathbf{a}'}$ is a fixed symbol used as a placeholder for an arbitrary action of player $\mathbf{a}'$. We denote by $\text{act}(C, s)$ the set of all C-actions at state s.
  Alternatively, C-actions at s can be defined as equivalence classes on the set of all action profiles at s, where each equivalence class is determined by the choices of actions of players in C.
- An action profile $\alpha \in \text{act}(s)$ extends a C-action α_C, denoted $\alpha_C \sqsubseteq \alpha$, if $\alpha(\mathbf{a}) = \alpha_C(\mathbf{a})$ for every $\mathbf{a} \in C$.

- Given a C-action $\alpha_C \in \mathrm{act}(C, s)$ and a $\overline{C}$-action $\alpha_{\overline{C}} \in \mathrm{act}(\overline{C}, s)$, we denote by $\alpha_C \oplus \alpha_{\overline{C}}$ the unique action profile $\alpha \in \mathrm{act}(s)$ such that both $\alpha_C \sqsubseteq \alpha$ and $\alpha_{\overline{C}} \sqsubseteq \alpha$. $\qquad\qquad \nabla$

Definition 9.1.8. Let $s \in S$, $C \subseteq \mathbb{AG}$ and $\alpha_C \in \mathrm{act}(C, s)$. The **outcome set** of the C-action α_C at s in S is the set of states

$$\mathrm{post}_S(s, \alpha_C) := \{\delta(s, \alpha) \mid \alpha \in \mathrm{act}(s) \text{ and } \alpha_C \sqsubseteq \alpha\}. \qquad\qquad \nabla$$

The outcome set function $\mathrm{post}(\cdot)$ can naturally be extended to act not just on collective actions but on all collective strategies applied at a given state (resp. history) in a given CGS. Then $\mathrm{post}_S(s, \mathfrak{str}_C)$ (resp. $\mathrm{post}_S(h, \mathfrak{str}_C)$) returns the set of all possible successor states that can result from applying a given positional (resp. memory-based) joint strategy $\mathfrak{str}_C$ of the coalition C at the state s (resp. the history h).

Further, we extend the function $\mathrm{post}(\cdot)$ to $\mathrm{Plays}(\cdot)$ returning the set of all *plays* that can be realised when the players in C follow the strategy $\mathfrak{str}_C$ from a given state s (respectively, history h) in S onwards. Formally, for positional strategies, it is defined as $\mathrm{Plays}_S^{\mathrm{pos}}(s, \mathfrak{str}_C) :=$

$$\{\lambda \in S^\omega \mid \lambda[0] = s \text{ and } \lambda[j + 1] \in \mathrm{post}_S(\lambda[j], \mathfrak{str}_C) \text{ for each } j \in \mathbb{N}\}.$$

Respectively, for memory-based strategies, $\mathrm{Plays}_S^{\mathrm{mem}}(s, \mathfrak{str}_C) :=$

$$\{\lambda \in S^\omega \mid \lambda[0] = s \text{ and } \lambda[j + 1] \in \mathrm{post}_S(\lambda[0, j], \mathfrak{str}_C) \text{ for each } j \in \mathbb{N}\}.$$

More generally, for memory-based strategies we define $\mathrm{Plays}_S(h, \mathfrak{str}_C)$ for any finite history h to consist of all plays in S that extend h and can be realised as a result of each player in C following its individual memory-based strategy in $\mathfrak{str}_C$, while the remaining players act in any way that is admissible in S. Formally, if $h = s_0, \dots, s_i$, then $\mathrm{Plays}_S^{\mathrm{mem}}(h, \mathfrak{str}_C) :=$

$$\{\lambda \in S^\omega \mid \lambda[0, i] = h \text{ and } \lambda[j + 1] \in \mathrm{post}_S(\lambda[0, j], \mathfrak{str}_C) \text{ for each } j \in \mathbb{N}, j \geq i\}.$$

Since all positional strategies are trivially memory-based, the definition of $\mathrm{Plays}_S^{\mathrm{mem}}(h, \mathfrak{str}_C)$ applies when $\mathfrak{str}_C$ is a positional strategy, too. In that case, $\mathrm{Plays}_S^{\mathrm{mem}}(h, \mathfrak{str}_C) = \mathrm{Plays}_S^{\mathrm{pos}}(\mathrm{last}(h), \mathfrak{str}_C)$.

We say that a given path λ in a CGS S is **enabled** by a given positional strategy $\mathfrak{str}_C$ of a coalition C from a given current state s in S if $\lambda \in \mathrm{Plays}_S^{\mathrm{pos}}(s, \mathfrak{str}_C)$. Likewise, λ is **enabled** by a given memory-based strategy $\mathfrak{str}_C$ of a coalition C from a given current history h if $\lambda \in \mathrm{Plays}_S^{\mathrm{mem}}(h, \mathfrak{str}_C)$. If we do not wish to specify the type of strategies we consider, we simply write $\mathrm{Plays}_S(s, \mathfrak{str}_C)$ and say that λ is **currently enabled** by that strategy.

Hereafter, when the CGS S is fixed in the context, we may omit the subscript in $\mathrm{post}_S(\cdot)$ and $\mathrm{Plays}_S(\cdot)$.

Example 9.1.9. In the two-robot CGS in Figure 9.1 we have the following.

- $\mathrm{post}(s_0, (\mathsf{push}, \mathsf{push})) = \{s_0\}$, $\mathrm{post}(s_0, (\mathsf{push}, \#_2))) = \{s_0, s_1\}$, $\mathrm{post}(s_0, (\#_1, \mathsf{push}))) = \{s_0, s_2\}$ and $\mathrm{post}(s_0, (\#_1, \#_2)))) = \{s_0, s_1, s_2\}$.

- Let Robot_1 adopt the positional strategy $\mathfrak{str}_{\mathsf{Robot}_1}$ such that $\mathfrak{str}_{\mathsf{Robot}_1}(s_0) = \mathsf{push}$, $\mathfrak{str}_{\mathsf{Robot}_1}(s_1) = \mathsf{push}$, $\mathfrak{str}_{\mathsf{Robot}_1}(s_2) = \mathsf{wait}$. Then the set of outcome plays from s_0, given as an ω-regular expression (see definition of ω-regular expressions in Section 10.1.1) in the alphabet S, is:

$$\mathsf{Plays}^{\mathrm{pos}}(s_0, \mathfrak{str}_{\mathsf{Robot}_1}) = \{s_0^\omega\} \cup s_0^+(s_1^*s_2^*)^\omega.$$

- Let Robot_1 adopt the memory-based strategy $\mathfrak{str}_{\mathsf{Robot}_1}^m$ which we describe in the following by using the notation '$\mathfrak{str}(E) = \mathsf{a}$' for a regular expression E to indicate that the value of $\mathfrak{str}$ for every element of E is a.
  - $\mathfrak{str}_{\mathsf{Robot}_1}^m(s_0S^*) = \mathsf{push}$,
  - $\mathfrak{str}_{\mathsf{Robot}_1}^m(s_1S^*) = \mathsf{push}$,
  - $\mathfrak{str}_{\mathsf{Robot}_1}^m(s_2\{s_0, s_1\}^*) = \mathsf{push}$,
  - $\mathfrak{str}_{\mathsf{Robot}_1}^m(s_2\{s_0, s_1\}^*s_2S^*) = \mathsf{wait}$.

  That is, the strategy prescribes pushing forever if the play starts from s_0 or s_1 and pushing until visiting s_2 for a second time and then waiting forever if the play starts from s_2.

  Then the set of outcome plays starting from s_0 is:

$$\mathsf{Plays}^{\mathrm{mem}}(s_0, \mathfrak{str}_{\mathsf{Robot}_1}^m) = (s_0^+s_1^+s_2^+)^\omega \cup (s_0^+s_1^+s_2^+)^*(s_0^\omega \cup s_0^+s_1^\omega \cup s_0^+s_1^+s_2^\omega).$$

  Respectively, if $h = s_2, s_0$ then

$$\mathsf{Plays}^{\mathrm{mem}}(h, \mathfrak{str}_{\mathsf{Robot}_1}^m) = \{hs_0^\omega\} \cup hs_0^*(s_1^+s_2^+)^\omega \cup hs_0^*(s_1^+s_2^+)^*s_1^\omega \cup hs_0^*(s_1^+s_2^+)^*s_2^\omega.$$

In the shared file update CGM in Figure 9.2 we have the following.

- $\mathsf{post}(E, (\mathsf{U}, \mathsf{N})) = \{U_1\}$, $\mathsf{post}(E, (\mathsf{U}, \#_2)) = \{D, U_1\}$,
  $\mathsf{post}(E, (\#_1, \mathsf{N})) = \{U_1, E\}$, $\mathsf{post}(E, (\#_1, \#_2)) = \{D, E, U_1, U_2\}$.
- Let Agent_1 adopt the positional strategy $\mathfrak{str}_{\mathsf{Agent}_1}$ such that:
  - $\mathfrak{str}_{\mathsf{Agent}_1}(X) = \mathsf{U}$ for every state X where action U is available to Agent_1,
  - $\mathfrak{str}_{\mathsf{Agent}_1}(P) = \mathsf{R}$ and
  - $\mathfrak{str}_{\mathsf{Agent}_1}(X) = \mathsf{N}$ for all other states X.

  Then the set of outcome plays from E, given as an ω-regular expression in the alphabet S, is $\mathsf{Plays}^{\mathrm{pos}}(E, \mathfrak{str}_{\mathsf{Agent}_1}) =$

$$(E(U_1D_1)^+P)^*\{ED^\omega \cup EU_1D^\omega \cup E(U_1D_1)^\omega\} \cup (E(U_1D_1)^+P)^\omega.$$

- Let Agent_1 adopt the memory-based strategy $\mathfrak{str}_{\mathsf{Agent}_1}^m$ such that:
  - $\mathfrak{str}_{\mathsf{Agent}_1}^m(S^*PE) = \mathsf{U}$,
  - $\mathfrak{str}_{\mathsf{Agent}_1}^m(S^*EU_1) = \mathsf{U}$,
  - $\mathfrak{str}_{\mathsf{Agent}_1}^m(S^*D_1P) = \mathsf{R}$.

  In all other cases, the strategy prescribes N. We leave it as Exercise 9.2 to compute the set of outcome plays $\mathsf{Plays}^{\mathrm{mem}}(s_0, \mathfrak{str}_{\mathsf{Agent}_1}^m)$.

A fundamental question about a concurrent game model is: *what can a given player or coalition achieve in that game?* So far the objectives of players and coalitions are not formally specified, but a typical such objective would be to reach a state satisfying a given property expressed in terms of the atomic propositions, e.g. a *winning* state. Generally, an objective is a property of plays, e.g. one can talk about winning or losing plays for the given player or coalition. More precisely, if the current state of the game is *s* we say that a coalition of players *C* can (is guaranteed to) achieve an objective *Win* from that state if there is a joint strategy $\mathfrak{str}_C$ for *C* such that every play from $\mathtt{Plays}(s, \mathfrak{str}_C)$ satisfies the objective *Win*. In the rest of this chapter we will show how to use logic to formally specify strategic objectives of players and coalitions and how to formally determine their abilities to achieve such objectives.

9.2 Temporal Logics for Concurrent Game Models

The alternating-time temporal logic ATL* is a multiagent extension of CTL*, designed for specifying temporal properties of computations in multiagent systems that different players and coalitions can enforce by adopting suitable strategies. Likewise, ATL is the syntactic fragment of ATL* that corresponds to CTL, in a sense explained further.

9.2.1 The Syntax of ATL* and ATL

The language of ATL* extends that of CTL* with path quantifiers indexed by all subsets of the fixed set $\mathbb{AG} = [1, k]$ of (names of) agents.

Definition 9.2.1. The formulae of ATL* are defined with respect to the set of agents $\mathbb{AG}$ and a countably infinite set PROP of atomic propositions, recursively by the following grammar:

$$\varphi ::= p \mid \bot \mid \neg\varphi \mid (\varphi \wedge \varphi) \mid \mathsf{X}\varphi \mid \mathsf{G}\varphi \mid (\varphi\mathsf{U}\varphi) \mid \langle\!\langle C \rangle\!\rangle \varphi,$$

where *p* ranges over PROP and *C* ranges over $\mathcal{P}(\mathbb{AG})$, the powerset of $\mathbb{AG}$. We denote the set of these formulae by ATL*($\mathbb{AG}$, PROP). $\triangledown$

The other Boolean connectives and the propositional constant $\top$ are defined in the usual way. Just like in LTL and CTL*, $\mathsf{F}\varphi$ can be defined as $\top\mathsf{U}\varphi$. Besides, we will use dual strategic path quantifiers $[\![C]\!]$ defined as

$$[\![C]\!]\,\varphi := \neg\langle\!\langle C \rangle\!\rangle \neg\varphi.$$

As in CTL*, the formulae of ATL* can be classified in two sorts: **state formulae**, which are evaluated at game states, and **path formulae**, which are evaluated on game plays. These are respectively defined by the following grammars, where $C \subseteq \mathbb{AG}$, $p \in$ PROP:

$$\begin{aligned}\text{State formulae:} \quad & \varphi ::= p \mid \neg\varphi \mid (\varphi \wedge \varphi) \mid \langle\!\langle C \rangle\!\rangle \gamma \\ \text{Path formulae:} \quad & \gamma ::= \varphi \mid \neg\gamma \mid (\gamma \wedge \gamma) \mid \mathsf{X}\gamma \mid \mathsf{G}\gamma \mid (\gamma\mathsf{U}\gamma).\end{aligned}$$

There are two ways that ATL* can be regarded as an extension of CTL*, respectively, ATL as an extension of CTL:

1. CTL* can be regarded as the fragment of ATL*, where the existential path quantifier E is identified with $\langle\!\langle \mathbb{A}\mathbb{G} \rangle\!\rangle$ and the universal path quantifier A is identified with $\langle\!\langle \emptyset \rangle\!\rangle$.
2. Likewise, CTL* can be regarded as a 1-agent case of ATL*, i.e. where $\mathbb{A}\mathbb{G} = \{1\}$. Then E is identified with $\langle\!\langle 1 \rangle\!\rangle$ and A is identified with $\langle\!\langle \emptyset \rangle\!\rangle$.

Later we will see that these interpretations of the path quantifiers indeed match the semantics of ATL*. By analogy with CTL, we can formally define the 'purely-state-formulae' fragment ATL consisting of those ATL* formulae where every temporal operator is in the immediate scope of a strategic path quantifier.

Definition 9.2.2. The subset ATL($\mathbb{A}\mathbb{G}$, PROP) of formulae of ATL*($\mathbb{A}\mathbb{G}$, PROP) is defined by the following grammar:

$$\varphi := p \mid \neg\varphi \mid (\varphi \wedge \varphi) \mid \langle\!\langle C \rangle\!\rangle \mathsf{X}\varphi \mid \langle\!\langle C \rangle\!\rangle \mathsf{G}\varphi \mid \langle\!\langle C \rangle\!\rangle(\varphi\mathsf{U}\varphi),$$

where p ranges over PROP and C ranges over $\mathcal{P}(\mathbb{A}\mathbb{G})$. ▽

9.2.2 *Introducing the Semantics Intuitively*

The key new feature in ATL* is the strategic path operator $\langle\!\langle \rangle\!\rangle$ which has the following intuitive interpretation of $\langle\!\langle C \rangle\!\rangle\varphi$:

'The coalition C has a collective strategy that ensures that every path/play currently enabled by that strategy satisfies φ'.

In particular, the ATL operators can intuitively be interpreted as follows:

- $\langle\!\langle C \rangle\!\rangle \mathsf{X}\varphi$: 'The coalition C has a collective action ensuring that any outcome (state) satisfies φ'.
- $\langle\!\langle C \rangle\!\rangle \mathsf{G}\varphi$: 'The coalition C has a collective strategy to maintain forever outcomes satisfying φ on every play currently enabled by that strategy'.
- $\langle\!\langle C \rangle\!\rangle \psi\mathsf{U}\varphi$: 'The coalition C has a collective strategy to eventually reach an outcome satisfying φ, while maintaining the truth of ψ on every play currently enabled by that strategy'.

Respectively, the intuitive meaning of $[\![C]\!]\,\varphi$ is: 'The coalition C cannot prevent an outcome satisfying φ'. Note that the semantic definitions involve an *existential quantification* over strategies – that is, functions from the set of histories to the set of actions – followed by *universal quantification* over all plays enabled by the chosen strategy. Also, note that while the actions and strategies defined in terms of them are crucial in the semantics, they cannot explicitly be referred to in the language of ATL*.

We will list some properties expressed in ATL*. Actually, all but the last of the following formulae are in ATL. The reader might contemplate for each of them whether they are satisfiable, valid, or neither.

- 'If agent **a** has an action to guarantee a successor state where she is rich and has an action to guarantee a successor state where she is happy then she has an action to guarantee a successor state where she is both rich and happy'.

$$(\langle\!\langle \mathbf{a} \rangle\!\rangle \mathsf{X}\, \mathtt{Rich} \wedge \langle\!\langle \mathbf{a} \rangle\!\rangle \mathsf{X}\, \mathtt{Happy}) \rightarrow \langle\!\langle \mathbf{a} \rangle\!\rangle \mathsf{X}\, (\mathtt{Rich} \wedge \mathtt{Happy}).$$

- 'None of the agents 1 and 2 has an action ensuring an outcome state satisfying Goal, but they both have a collective action ensuring such an outcome state':

$$\neg\langle\!\langle 1 \rangle\!\rangle \mathsf{X}\, \mathtt{Goal} \wedge \neg\langle\!\langle 2 \rangle\!\rangle \mathsf{X}\, \mathtt{Goal} \wedge \langle\!\langle 1, 2 \rangle\!\rangle \mathsf{X}\, \mathtt{Goal}.$$

- 'If the system has a strategy to eventually reach a safe state, then the environment cannot prevent it from reaching a safe state':

$$\langle\!\langle \mathbf{System} \rangle\!\rangle \mathsf{F}\, \mathtt{Safe} \rightarrow [\![\mathbf{Environment}]\!]\, \mathsf{F}\, \mathtt{Safe}.$$

- 'If the system has a strategy to stay in a safe state forever and has a strategy to eventually achieve its goal, then it has a strategy to stay in a safe state until it achieves its goal':

$$(\langle\!\langle \mathbf{System} \rangle\!\rangle \mathsf{G}\, \mathtt{Safe} \wedge \langle\!\langle \mathbf{System} \rangle\!\rangle \mathsf{F}\, \mathtt{Goal}) \rightarrow \langle\!\langle \mathbf{System} \rangle\!\rangle (\mathtt{Safe}\, \mathsf{U}\, \mathtt{Goal}).$$

- 'The coalition C has a collective action to ensure that the coalition C' cannot prevent Win(C) from happening eventually':

$$\langle\!\langle C \rangle\!\rangle [\![C']\!]\, \mathsf{F}\, \mathrm{Win}(\mathrm{C}).$$

9.2.3 The Formal Semantics

The formal definition of truth of ATL* formulae on plays of concurrent game models essentially repeats the truth definition of CTL* formulae in interpreted transition systems, but with the standard path quantifiers refined to strategic path quantifiers, according to the preceding intuition.

Definition 9.2.3. Let $\mathcal{M} = (\mathbb{AG}, S, Act, \mathsf{act}, \delta, L)$ be a concurrent game model over a fixed set of atomic propositions PROP. **Truth** of ATL* formulae is defined by mutual induction on state and path formulae as follows. For state formulae, at a state $s \in S$:

$$
\begin{aligned}
\mathcal{M}, s \models p \quad &\text{iff} \quad p \in L(s), \text{ for all } p \in \mathrm{PROP} \\
\mathcal{M}, s \models \neg\varphi \quad &\text{iff} \quad \mathcal{M}, s \not\models \varphi \\
\mathcal{M}, s \models \varphi \wedge \psi \quad &\text{iff} \quad \mathcal{M}, s \models \varphi \text{ and } \mathcal{M}, s \models \psi \\
\mathcal{M}, s \models \langle\!\langle C \rangle\!\rangle \varphi \quad &\text{iff} \quad \text{there exists a } C\text{-strategy } \mathfrak{str}_C \text{ such that} \\
&\qquad \mathcal{M}, \lambda \models \varphi \text{ holds for all } \lambda \in \mathrm{Plays}^{\mathrm{mem}}(s, \mathfrak{str}_C).
\end{aligned}
$$

Note that strategies can be memory-based. For path formulae, at a path $\lambda \in S^\omega$:

$$
\begin{aligned}
\mathcal{M}, \lambda \models \varphi &\quad \text{iff} \quad \mathcal{M}, \lambda[0] \models \varphi, \text{ for every state formula } \varphi \\
\mathcal{M}, \lambda \models \neg\psi &\quad \text{iff} \quad \mathcal{M}, \lambda \not\models \psi \\
\mathcal{M}, \lambda \models \psi_1 \wedge \psi_2 &\quad \text{iff} \quad \mathcal{M}, \lambda \models \psi_1 \text{ and } \mathcal{M}, \lambda \models \psi_2 \\
\mathcal{M}, \lambda \models \mathsf{X}\psi &\quad \text{iff} \quad \mathcal{M}, \lambda[1, \infty) \models \psi \\
\mathcal{M}, \lambda \models \mathsf{G}\psi &\quad \text{iff} \quad \mathcal{M}, \lambda[i, \infty) \models \psi \text{ holds for all positions } i \geq 0 \\
\mathcal{M}, \lambda \models \psi_1 \mathsf{U} \psi_2 &\quad \text{iff} \quad \text{there exists a position } i \geq 0 \text{ such that} \\
&\qquad\quad \mathcal{M}, \lambda[i, \infty) \models \psi_2 \text{ and } \mathcal{M}, \lambda[j, \infty) \models \psi_1 \\
&\qquad\quad \text{holds for all positions } 0 \leq j < i.
\end{aligned}
$$

∇

Since all state formulae of ATL* are also path formulae, the truth definition for the former can be subsumed into the latter, by declaring, just like in CTL*, every state formula to be true at a path iff it is true at its initial state.

Note that every path in a given CGM is produced by an infinite sequence of $\mathbb{AG}$-actions that can be regarded as generated by a suitable memory-based strategy for $\mathbb{AG}$. Conversely, starting at any fixed initial state r, every memory-based strategy for $\mathbb{AG}$ generates a unique play, i.e. unique path starting from r. Therefore, quantifying over paths in a CGM is equivalent to quantifying over memory-based strategies for $\mathbb{AG}$. This explains why the existential path quantifier E can be identified with $\langle\!\langle \mathbb{AG} \rangle\!\rangle$. Since the empty coalition has only one (vacuous) strategy, against which the complementary coalition $\mathbb{AG}$ can act to generate any possible path as a play, that also explains the identification of the universal path quantifier A with $\langle\!\langle \emptyset \rangle\!\rangle$.

Now we focus on the semantics of ATL formulae. Because ATL only involves state formulae, the memory used in the strategies required to satisfy $\langle\!\langle \rangle\!\rangle$-formulae becomes redundant and these can be replaced with positional strategies. Formally, let us denote by $\models^p$ the truth definition for ATL*-formulae given earlier, where memory-based strategies are replaced by positional strategies throughout. The restriction to positional strategies results in an essential difference in the satisfaction relation, as shown in the following example.

Example 9.2.4. Let us consider the following CGM in which we have omitted to represent the action profiles on edges since the formula we consider uses the full set of agents: $\langle\!\langle \mathbb{AG} \rangle\!\rangle (\mathsf{F}p \wedge \mathsf{F}q)$.

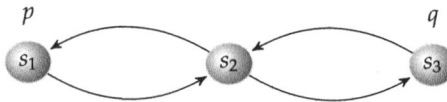

$$p \qquad\qquad\qquad\qquad\qquad\qquad q$$
$$s_1 \rightleftarrows s_2 \rightleftarrows s_3$$

One can show that $s_2 \models \langle\!\langle \mathbb{AG} \rangle\!\rangle (\mathsf{F}p \wedge \mathsf{F}q)$ but not $s_2 \models^p \langle\!\langle \mathbb{AG} \rangle\!\rangle (\mathsf{F}p \wedge \mathsf{F}q)$ since any positional strategy decides once and for all whether from s_2, the next state is s_1 or s_3 (without any possibility of alternation).

For ATL formulae, the restriction to positional strategies does not make any difference, which is stated formally as follows.

Lemma 9.2.5. For every concurrent game model $\mathcal{M}$, ATL-formula φ and a state $s \in \mathcal{M}$: $\mathcal{M}, s \models \varphi$ iff $\mathcal{M}, s \models^p \varphi$. ∎

The proof is left as Exercise 9.6. Note, however, that restricting the strategies of $\mathbb{A}\mathbb{G}$ to only positional strategies does not generate all paths in the model, so the embedding of CTL into ATL formally requires using all memory-based strategies.

Example 9.2.6. The following hold in the CGM defined from the CGS at the top of Figure 9.1 but augmented with the atomic propositions pos_i's.

- $\mathcal{M}, s_0 \not\models \langle\!\langle 1 \rangle\!\rangle \mathsf{X} \, \mathrm{pos}_1$.
- $\mathcal{M}, s_0 \not\models \langle\!\langle 2 \rangle\!\rangle \mathsf{X} \, \mathrm{pos}_1$.
- $\mathcal{M}, s_0 \models \langle\!\langle 1, 2 \rangle\!\rangle \mathsf{X} \, \mathrm{pos}_0 \wedge \langle\!\langle 1, 2 \rangle\!\rangle \mathsf{X} \, \mathrm{pos}_1 \wedge \langle\!\langle 1, 2 \rangle\!\rangle \mathsf{X} \, \mathrm{pos}_2$.
- $\mathcal{M}, s_0 \not\models \langle\!\langle 1 \rangle\!\rangle \mathsf{F} \, \mathrm{pos}_1$.
- $\mathcal{M}, s_1 \models \langle\!\langle 1 \rangle\!\rangle \mathsf{F} \, (\mathrm{pos}_1 \vee \mathrm{pos}_2)$.
- $\mathcal{M}, s_0 \models \langle\!\langle 1 \rangle\!\rangle \mathsf{G} \, \neg \mathrm{pos}_1$.
- $\mathcal{M} \models \langle\!\langle 1, 2 \rangle\!\rangle \mathsf{X} \langle\!\langle 1 \rangle\!\rangle (\mathrm{pos}_0 \, \mathsf{U} \, \mathrm{pos}_2)$.

Example 9.2.7. Consider the shared file updates in Figure 9.2. Denote the model by $\mathcal{M}$. With a slight abuse we use the same notation for states and for the atomic propositions that refer to them. We leave it to the reader to verify the following (cf. Exercise 9.7).

- $\mathcal{M}, E \models \neg \langle\!\langle 1 \rangle\!\rangle \mathsf{X} D \wedge \langle\!\langle 1 \rangle\!\rangle \mathsf{X} \neg D \wedge \langle\!\langle 1 \rangle\!\rangle \mathsf{X} (E \vee U_2) \wedge \neg \langle\!\langle 2 \rangle\!\rangle \mathsf{X} (E \vee U_2)$.
- $\mathcal{M}, E \models \neg \langle\!\langle 1 \rangle\!\rangle \mathsf{F} D \wedge \neg \langle\!\langle 2 \rangle\!\rangle \mathsf{F} D \wedge \langle\!\langle 1, 2 \rangle\!\rangle \mathsf{G} \neg D$.
- $\mathcal{M}, U_1 \models \neg \langle\!\langle 1 \rangle\!\rangle \mathsf{F} P \wedge \langle\!\langle 1, 2 \rangle\!\rangle \mathsf{G} \mathsf{F} P$.
- $\mathcal{M}, U_2 \models \langle\!\langle 1, 2 \rangle\!\rangle ((\neg D_2 \, \mathsf{U} \, U_1) \wedge \neg \langle\!\langle 1 \rangle\!\rangle ((\neg D_2) \, \mathsf{U} \, P)$.
- $\mathcal{M}, E \models \langle\!\langle 1, 2 \rangle\!\rangle \mathsf{F} (P \wedge \mathsf{X} (E \wedge \mathsf{G} \neg P))$.

    (NB: the truth of this formula requires a strategy for 1 and 2 using memory.)

The semantic definitions of satisfiability, validity in a model, logical validity and the other related notions are naturally transferred from Section 4.2 but instantiated for the logic ATL*.

9.2.4 A Fixpoint Characterisation

The strategic operators $\langle\!\langle C \rangle\!\rangle \mathsf{G}$ and $\langle\!\langle C \rangle\!\rangle \mathsf{U}$ in ATL have natural fixpoint characterisations very similar to the respective operators in CTL. These characterisations, presented here, are instrumental in designing algorithmic methods for model checking and satisfiability testing in ATL.

The Operator `pre`

Given a CGM $\mathcal{M} = (\mathbb{A}\mathbb{G}, S, Act, \mathrm{act}, \delta, L)$ a coalition $C \subseteq \mathbb{A}\mathbb{G}$ and a set $Z \subseteq S$, we define $\mathrm{pre}(\mathcal{M}, C, Z)$ as the set of states from which the coalition C has a collective move that guarantees the outcome to be in Z, no matter how the remaining agents act.

Definition 9.2.8. Let $\mathcal{M} = (\mathbb{AG}, S, Act, \text{act}, \delta, L)$ be a CGM and let $Z \subseteq S$. Then, $\text{pre}(\mathcal{M}, C, Z)$ is an operator from $\mathcal{P}(S)$ to $\mathcal{P}(S)$ defined as follows:

$$\text{pre}(\mathcal{M}, C, Z) := \{s \in S \mid \text{there is } \alpha_C \in \text{act}(C, s) \text{ such that } \text{post}(s, \alpha_C) \subseteq Z\}. \qquad \nabla$$

Recall that, for a state formula φ and a model $\mathcal{M}$, we denote

$$[\![\varphi]\!]^{\mathcal{M}} := \{s \mid \mathcal{M}, s \models \varphi\}.$$

Thus, the following holds.

Lemma 9.2.9. For any CGM $\mathcal{M}$ and ATL formula φ:

$$[\![\langle\!\langle C \rangle\!\rangle \mathsf{X}\varphi]\!]^{\mathcal{M}} = \text{pre}\left(\mathcal{M}, C, [\![\varphi]\!]^{\mathcal{M}}\right). \qquad \blacksquare$$

The formal proof of this claim is left as Exercise 9.16.

The Strategic-Temporal Operators in ATL as Fixpoints

The following proposition claims equivalences providing fixpoint characterisations (see Chapter 8) of the ATL operators.

Lemma 9.2.10. The following formulae are valid for every $C \subseteq \mathbb{AG}$:

(I) $\langle\!\langle C \rangle\!\rangle \mathsf{G}\varphi \leftrightarrow \varphi \wedge \langle\!\langle C \rangle\!\rangle \mathsf{X}\langle\!\langle C \rangle\!\rangle \mathsf{G}\varphi$.

(II) $\langle\!\langle \emptyset \rangle\!\rangle \mathsf{G}(\psi \rightarrow (\varphi \wedge \langle\!\langle C \rangle\!\rangle \mathsf{X}\psi)) \rightarrow \langle\!\langle \emptyset \rangle\!\rangle \mathsf{G}(\psi \rightarrow \langle\!\langle C \rangle\!\rangle \mathsf{G}\varphi)$.

(III) $\langle\!\langle C \rangle\!\rangle \varphi \mathsf{U}\psi \leftrightarrow \psi \vee (\varphi \wedge \langle\!\langle C \rangle\!\rangle \mathsf{X}\langle\!\langle C \rangle\!\rangle \varphi \mathsf{U}\psi)$.

(IV) $\langle\!\langle \emptyset \rangle\!\rangle \mathsf{G}((\psi \vee (\varphi \wedge \langle\!\langle C \rangle\!\rangle \mathsf{X}\chi)) \rightarrow \chi) \rightarrow \langle\!\langle \emptyset \rangle\!\rangle \mathsf{G}(\langle\!\langle C \rangle\!\rangle \varphi \mathsf{U}\psi \rightarrow \chi)$. $\qquad \blacksquare$

The first validity essentially means that $[\![\langle\!\langle C \rangle\!\rangle \mathsf{G}\varphi]\!]^{\mathcal{M}}$ is a *fixpoint* of the operator

$$\mathbf{G}_{C,\varphi}(Z) := [\![\varphi]\!]^{\mathcal{M}} \cap \text{pre}(\mathcal{M}, C, Z).$$

The second validity essentially means that $[\![\langle\!\langle C \rangle\!\rangle \mathsf{G}\varphi]\!]^{\mathcal{M}}$ is the greatest (post)-fixpoint of $\mathbf{G}_{C,\varphi}$. Indeed, it says (noting that $\langle\!\langle \emptyset \rangle\!\rangle \mathsf{G}$ refers to all reachable states from the current one) that if $[\![\psi]\!]^{\mathcal{M}}$ is a post-fixpoint of $\mathbf{G}_{C,\varphi}$ then it is included in $[\![\langle\!\langle C \rangle\!\rangle \mathsf{G}\varphi]\!]^{\mathcal{M}}$.

Likewise, the third validity means that $[\![\langle\!\langle C \rangle\!\rangle \varphi \mathsf{U}\psi]\!]^{\mathcal{M}}$ is a fixpoint of the operator

$$\mathbf{U}_{C,\varphi,\psi}(Z) := [\![\psi]\!]^{\mathcal{M}} \cup \left([\![\varphi]\!]^{\mathcal{M}} \cap \text{pre}(\mathcal{M}, C, Z)\right)$$

and the last validity means that $[\![\langle\!\langle C \rangle\!\rangle \varphi \mathsf{U}\psi]\!]^{\mathcal{M}}$ is the least (pre)-fixpoint of $\mathbf{U}_{C,\varphi,\psi}$.

We formally represent and summarise these observations in the following theorem, where μZ and νZ denote least and greatest fixpoint operators respectively. The reader unfamiliar with these is referred to Chapter 2 and Chapter 8. We leave the proof of these as part of Exercise 9.11.

Proposition 9.2.11. Let $\mathcal{M} = (\mathbb{AG}, S, Act, \text{act}, \delta, L)$ be a CGM over a fixed set of atomic propositions PROP. Then, for any formulae φ, ψ:

(I) $[\![\langle\!\langle C\rangle\!\rangle G\varphi]\!]^{\mathcal{M}} = \nu Z. \left([\![\varphi]\!]^{\mathcal{M}} \cap \mathtt{pre}(\mathcal{M}, C, Z)\right)$

(II) $[\![\langle\!\langle C\rangle\!\rangle \varphi U\psi]\!]^{\mathcal{M}} = \mu Z. \left([\![\psi]\!]^{\mathcal{M}} \cup \left([\![\varphi]\!]^{\mathcal{M}} \cap \mathtt{pre}(\mathcal{M}, C, Z)\right)\right).$ ∎

Claim (I) intuitively says that the set of states from which coalition C can make sure that φ is globally true is the largest set of states such that φ is true in every state of the set and from every state in the set coalition C can make sure to stay in the set in the next step. Likewise, claim (II) states the least fixpoint characterisation of Until, explained previously.

9.2.5 A Complete Axiomatic System for ATL

Adding the validities from Lemma 9.2.10 providing fixpoint characterisations of the ATL operators to several axioms describing the local behaviour of the operator X yields a complete axiomatic system for ATL.

Proposition 9.2.12. The following system of axioms and inference rules, added to any sound and complete axiomatic system for the classical propositional logic provides a sound and complete axiomatic system for ATL.

(I) Axioms (where $C, C_1, C_2 \subseteq \mathbb{AG}$):

(⊥) $\neg\langle\!\langle C\rangle\!\rangle X\bot$

(⊤) $\langle\!\langle C\rangle\!\rangle X\top$

($\mathbb{AG}$) $\neg\langle\!\langle\emptyset\rangle\!\rangle X\neg\varphi \rightarrow \langle\!\langle\mathbb{AG}\rangle\!\rangle X\varphi$

(S) $\langle\!\langle C_1\rangle\!\rangle X\varphi \wedge \langle\!\langle C_2\rangle\!\rangle X\psi \rightarrow \langle\!\langle C_1 \cup C_2\rangle\!\rangle X(\varphi \wedge \psi)$, for disjoint C_1 and C_2

(FP$_G$) $\langle\!\langle C\rangle\!\rangle G\varphi \leftrightarrow \varphi \wedge \langle\!\langle C\rangle\!\rangle X\langle\!\langle C\rangle\!\rangle G\varphi$

(GFP$_G$) $\langle\!\langle\emptyset\rangle\!\rangle G(\psi \rightarrow (\varphi \wedge \langle\!\langle C\rangle\!\rangle X\psi)) \rightarrow \langle\!\langle\emptyset\rangle\!\rangle G(\psi \rightarrow \langle\!\langle C\rangle\!\rangle G\varphi)$

(FP$_U$) $\langle\!\langle C\rangle\!\rangle \varphi U\psi \leftrightarrow \psi \vee (\varphi \wedge \langle\!\langle C\rangle\!\rangle X\langle\!\langle C\rangle\!\rangle \varphi U\psi)$

(LFP$_U$) $\langle\!\langle\emptyset\rangle\!\rangle G((\psi \vee (\varphi \wedge \langle\!\langle C\rangle\!\rangle X\chi)) \rightarrow \chi) \rightarrow \langle\!\langle\emptyset\rangle\!\rangle G(\langle\!\langle C\rangle\!\rangle \varphi U\psi \rightarrow \chi).$

(II) Inference rules:

- $\langle\!\langle C\rangle\!\rangle$X-**Monotonicity:** $\dfrac{\varphi \rightarrow \psi}{\langle\!\langle C\rangle\!\rangle X\varphi \rightarrow \langle\!\langle C\rangle\!\rangle X\psi}$

- $\langle\!\langle\emptyset\rangle\!\rangle$G-**Necessitation:** $\dfrac{\varphi}{\langle\!\langle\emptyset\rangle\!\rangle G\varphi}.$ ∎

Axiom ($\mathbb{AG}$) says that the grand coalition $\mathbb{AG}$ has complete control over the system and can realise any possible play, whereas the **Superadditivity axiom** (S) says that two disjoint coalitions, each of which has the power to achieve its own objective, can always join forces to achieve both objectives.

9.2.6 Alternating Bisimulations

The notion of alternating bisimulation between concurrent game models is an adaptation of the notion of bisimulation between transition systems introduced in Section 3.3. It characterises equivalence of concurrent game models with respect to properties definable in ATL*.

For the sake of a simpler exposition, we will restrict our attention to ATL for the rest of this section.

Definition 9.2.13. Let $\mathcal{M}_1 = (\mathbb{AG}, S_1, Act_1, \mathrm{act}_1, \delta_1, L_1)$ and $\mathcal{M}_2 = (\mathbb{AG}, S_2, Act_2, \mathrm{act}_2, \delta_2, L_2)$ be two concurrent game models over the same set of atomic propositions PROP and over the same set of agents, and $C \subseteq \mathbb{AG}$. A relation $\beta \subseteq S_1 \times S_2$ is an **alternating C-bisimulation** between $\mathcal{M}_1$ and $\mathcal{M}_2$, denoted $\mathcal{M}_1 \overset{\beta}{\rightleftharpoons}_C \mathcal{M}_2$, iff for all $s_1 \in S_1$ and $s_2 \in S_2$, $s_1 \beta s_2$ implies that the following holds:

Local harmony: $L_1(s_1) = L_2(s_2)$.

Forth: For any $\alpha_1(C) \in \mathrm{act}_1(s_1, C)$, there exists $\alpha_2(C) \in \mathrm{act}_2(s_2, C)$ such that for every $s_2 \in \mathrm{post}_{\mathcal{M}_2}(s_2, \alpha_2(C))$, there exists $s_1 \in \mathrm{post}_{\mathcal{M}_1}(s_1, \alpha_1(C))$ such that $s_1 \beta s_2$. Intuitively: for every collective action $\alpha_1(C)$ of C at s_1 in $\mathcal{M}_1$ there is a corresponding collective action $\alpha_2(C)$ of C at s_2 in $\mathcal{M}_2$ such that every successor state enabled by that collective action is β-related to a successor state enabled by $\alpha_1(C)$.

Back: Likewise, with 1 and 2 swapped.

If β is an alternating C-bisimulation between $\mathcal{M}_1$ and $\mathcal{M}_2$ for every $C \subseteq \mathbb{AG}$, we call it a **(full) alternating bisimulation** between $\mathcal{M}_1$ and $\mathcal{M}_2$, denoted $\mathcal{M}_1 \overset{\beta}{\rightleftharpoons} \mathcal{M}_2$. If β links every state in $\mathcal{M}_1$ to some state of $\mathcal{M}_2$ and vice versa, it is a **global alternating bisimulation** between $\mathcal{M}_1$ and $\mathcal{M}_2$. $\qquad \nabla$

Given a pointed CGM $(\mathcal{M}, s)$, $C \subseteq \mathbb{AG}$ and a joint strategy $\mathfrak{str}_C$, we define the set $\mathrm{reach}(\mathcal{M}, s, \mathfrak{str}_C)$ of all states in $\mathcal{M}$ which occur in plays that are enabled by $\mathfrak{str}_C$ at s, i.e.:

$$\mathrm{reach}(\mathcal{M}, s, \mathfrak{str}_C) := \{\lambda[i] \mid \lambda \in \mathrm{Plays}_{\mathcal{M}}(s, \mathfrak{str}_C), i \in \mathbb{N}\}.$$

The meaning of $\mathrm{reach}(\mathcal{M}, s, \mathfrak{str}_C)$ is analogous to that of $\mathrm{post}^\star(s)$, as defined in Chapter 3. In particular, we write $\mathrm{reach}(\mathcal{M}, s)$ for $\mathrm{reach}(\mathcal{M}, s, \mathfrak{str}_\emptyset)$, where $\mathfrak{str}_\emptyset$ is the (only) strategy for the empty coalition. Note that it enables every successor state affected by any action profile for $\mathbb{AG}$.

Likewise, given a CGM $\mathcal{M}$, a history h in it, $C \subseteq \mathbb{AG}$ and a joint strategy $\mathfrak{str}_C$, we put

$$\mathrm{reach}(\mathcal{M}, h, \mathfrak{str}_C) := \{\lambda[i] \mid \lambda \in \mathrm{Plays}_{\mathcal{M}}(h, \mathfrak{str}_C), i \in \mathbb{N}\}.$$

Note that a CGM $\mathcal{M}$ can naturally be restricted to a CGM over the subset $\mathrm{reach}(\mathcal{M}, s)$ of S. We denote that CGM by $\mathcal{M}[s]$.

Lemma 9.2.14. For any pointed CGM $(\mathcal{M}, s)$, the identity relation in $\mathcal{M}$ restricted to $\mathrm{reach}(\mathcal{M}, s)$ is a bisimulation between $(\mathcal{M}, s)$ and $(\mathcal{M}[s], s)$. $\qquad\blacksquare$

The easy proof is left as Exercise 9.17.

Lemma 9.2.15. Given pointed CGMs $(\mathcal{M}_1, s_1)$ and $(\mathcal{M}_2, s_2)$ and a relation $\beta \subseteq \mathrm{reach}(\mathcal{M}_1, s_1) \times \mathrm{reach}(\mathcal{M}_2, s_2)$ we have

$$(\mathcal{M}_1, s_1) \overset{\beta}{\rightleftharpoons} (\mathcal{M}_2, s_2) \quad \text{iff} \quad (\mathcal{M}_1[s_1], s_1) \overset{\beta}{\rightleftharpoons} (\mathcal{M}_2[s_2], s_2).$$

Proof. This follows from Lemma 9.2.14 and the fact that a composition of alternating bisimulations is an alternating bisimulation (Exercise 9.13). □

For a fixed $C \subseteq \mathbb{AG}$ we denote the fragment of the logic ATL($\mathbb{AG}$, PROP) where C is the only coalition occurring in the formulae by ATL$_C$($\mathbb{AG}$, PROP).

Theorem 9.2.16.

(I) If $\mathcal{M}_1 \overset{\beta}{\rightleftharpoons}_C \mathcal{M}_2$ and $s_1 \beta s_2$, then $\mathcal{M}_1, s_1 \models \varphi$ iff $\mathcal{M}_2, s_2 \models \varphi$, for every $\varphi \in$ ATL$_C$($\mathbb{AG}$, PROP).

(II) If $\mathcal{M}_1 \overset{\beta}{\rightleftharpoons} \mathcal{M}_2$ and $s_1 \beta s_2$, then $\mathcal{M}_1, s_1 \models \varphi$ iff $\mathcal{M}_2, s_2 \models \varphi$ for every formula $\varphi \in$ ATL($\mathbb{AG}$, PROP).

(III) If, furthermore, $\mathrm{dom}(\beta) = S_1$ and $\mathrm{ran}(\beta) = S_2$, then $\mathcal{M}_1 \models \varphi$ iff $\mathcal{M}_2 \models \varphi$ for every formula $\varphi \in$ ATL($\mathbb{AG}$, PROP). ■

Proof. Claim (I). The proof is by induction on the formulae from the set ATL$_C$($\mathbb{AG}$, PROP). The case of atomic propositions is immediate from the definition of alternating bisimulation. The Boolean cases are straightforward. For the case of $\langle\!\langle C \rangle\!\rangle X\varphi$, the claim follows immediately from the definition of alternating bisimulation, the semantics of $\langle\!\langle C \rangle\!\rangle X$ and the inductive hypothesis.

For the cases of $\langle\!\langle C \rangle\!\rangle G\varphi$ and $\langle\!\langle C \rangle\!\rangle \psi U\varphi$, the key step will be to show that every positional strategy for C on the set reach($\mathcal{M}_1, s_1$) can be 'simulated' by a positional strategy on reach($\mathcal{M}_2, s_2$) and vice versa.

First, consider the case of $\langle\!\langle C \rangle\!\rangle G\varphi$, assuming the claim holds for φ. Suppose $\mathcal{M}_1, s_1 \models \langle\!\langle C \rangle\!\rangle G\varphi$ and let $\mathfrak{str}_C^1$ be a joint strategy for C in $\mathcal{M}_1$ that ensures $\mathcal{M}, s \models \varphi$ for every $s \in$ reach($\mathcal{M}_1, s_1, \mathfrak{str}_C^1$). Assuming, for convenience, that the set of actions in $\mathcal{M}_1$ is at most countable, the set reach($\mathcal{M}_1, s_1, \mathfrak{str}_C^1$) will be at most countable, too; then we fix an enumeration of it. (In general, the construction in the proof would require transfinite induction and the application of the Axiom of Choice.)

We will define a joint strategy $\mathfrak{str}_C^2$ for C in $\mathcal{M}_2$ that ensures $\mathcal{M}_2, s \models \varphi$ for every $s \in$ reach($\mathcal{M}_2, s_2, \mathfrak{str}_C^2$). We define the following by simultaneous induction on n.

(i) a chain of sets reach$_0$($\mathcal{M}_2, s_2$) $\subseteq \ldots \subseteq$ reach$_n$($\mathcal{M}_2, s_2$) $\subseteq \ldots \subseteq$ reach($\mathcal{M}_2, s_2$), where reach$_n$($\mathcal{M}_2, s_2$) will be the set of states in $\mathcal{M}_2$ reachable in at most n steps from s_2 if the agents in C follow the joint strategy $\mathfrak{str}_C^2$;

(ii) a chain of mappings $\zeta_0 \subseteq \ldots \subseteq \zeta_n \subseteq \ldots$, such that $\zeta_n :$ reach$_n$($\mathcal{M}_2, s_2$) $\rightarrow$ reach($\mathcal{M}_1, s_1, \mathfrak{str}_C^1$) and $\zeta_n(s)\beta s$ for every $s \in$ reach$_n$($\mathcal{M}_2, s_2$);

(iii) and a chain of partial joint strategies for C in $\mathcal{M}_2$: $\mathfrak{str}_0(C) \subseteq \ldots \subseteq \mathfrak{str}_n(C) \subseteq \ldots$, where the domain of $\mathfrak{str}_n(C)$ is reach$_{n-1}$($\mathcal{M}_2, s_2$) (reach$_{-1}$($\mathcal{M}_2, s_2$) = $\emptyset$ by convention).

First, we put reach$_0$($\mathcal{M}_2, s_2$) := $\{s_2\}$, $\zeta_0(s_2) = s_1$, and $\mathfrak{str}_0(C) := \emptyset$. Now, assuming that reach$_n$($\mathcal{M}_2, s_2$), ζ_n and $s_n(C)$ are defined accordingly, we define reach$_{n+1}$($\mathcal{M}_2, s_2$), ζ_{n+1} and $\mathfrak{str}_{n+1}(C)$ as follows.

Let $S_n := \text{reach}_n(\mathcal{M}_2, s_2) \setminus \text{reach}_{n-1}(\mathcal{M}_2, s_2)$. For every $s \in S_n$, let $s' = \zeta_n(s)$. Since $s' \beta s$, we can choose a joint action $\alpha(s, C)$ for C from s in $\mathcal{M}_2$, corresponding to the joint action for C from s' in $\mathcal{M}_1$ determined by $\mathfrak{str}_C^1$, so as to ensure that for every $t \in \text{post}_{\mathcal{M}_2}(s, \alpha(s, C))$ there is a β-bisimilar state $\zeta_{n+1}(t) \in \text{post}_{\mathcal{M}_1}(s', \mathfrak{str}_C^1)$. In case $t \in \text{reach}_n(\mathcal{M}_2, s_2)$ we put $\zeta_{n+1}(t) = \zeta_n(t)$, otherwise – the first suitable (i.e. β-related to t) state in the enumeration of $\text{reach}(\mathcal{M}_1, s_1, \mathfrak{str}_C^1)$ (such state exists since $s' \beta s$). Note, that $\zeta(t)$ does not depend on s. Now we define

$$\text{reach}_{n+1}(\mathcal{M}_2, s_2) := \text{reach}_n(\mathcal{M}_2, s_2) \cup \bigcup_{s \in S_n} \text{post}_{\mathcal{M}_2}(s, \alpha(s, C)),$$

$$\mathfrak{str}_{n+1}(C) := \mathfrak{str}_n(C) \cup \bigcup_{s \in S_n} \alpha(s, C).$$

It is immediate from the construction that $\text{reach}_{n+1}(\mathcal{M}_2, s_2)$, ζ_{n+1}, and $\mathfrak{str}_{n+1}(C)$ satisfy the requirements set earlier. This completes the inductive definition.

Finally, we define $\mathfrak{str}^2(C) := \bigcup_{n \in \omega} \mathfrak{str}_n(C)$ and extend it arbitrarily (but constructively) to all states in $\mathcal{M}_2$ where it is not defined, to obtain the desired $\mathfrak{str}_C^2$. It follows from the definition, and from the main inductive hypothesis of the proof (applied to φ), that $\text{reach}(\mathcal{M}_2, s_2, \mathfrak{str}_C^2) = \bigcup_{n \in \omega} \text{reach}_n(\mathcal{M}_2, s_2)$ and that $\mathcal{M}_2, s \models \varphi$ for every $s \in \text{reach}(\mathcal{M}_2, s_2, \mathfrak{str}_C^2)$. Thus, $\mathcal{M}_2, s_2 \models \langle\!\langle C \rangle\!\rangle G\varphi$. The converse direction is completely symmetric.

The proof for the case $\langle\!\langle C \rangle\!\rangle \varphi_1 U \varphi_2$ is similar and the details are left to the reader as Exercise 9.17. The preceding proof can easily be adapted to the memory-based semantics. Claim (II) is an immediate consequence of Claim (I) and Claim (III) follows, again immediately, from Claim (II). □

Example 9.2.17. Consider the 2-player CGMs $\mathcal{M}$ and $\mathcal{M}'$ shown in Figure 9.3. We claim (Exercise 9.14) that $\mathcal{M} \overset{\beta}{\rightleftarrows} \mathcal{M}$, because of the alternating bisimulation β shown in dotted lines. Note that the actions in $\mathcal{M}'$ are suitably renamed.

For any concurrent game model $\mathcal{M}$ and a state $s \in \mathcal{M}$ the **tree unfolding** $\widehat{\mathcal{M}}[s]$ of $\mathcal{M}$ from s can naturally be defined and there is a canonically defined global alternating bisimulation between $\text{reach}(\mathcal{M}, s)$ and $\widehat{\mathcal{M}}[s]$. We leave these as Exercise 9.15.

9.3 Logical Decision Problems

9.3.1 Satisfiability and Validity

There are two essential differences between satisfiability and validity for ATL/ATL* on one hand and CTL/CTL* on the other. These have to do with the agents and coalitions mentioned in the formula.

1. There are two variants of this satisfiability problem for ATL/ATL*: **tight**, where it is assumed that all agents in the required model are mentioned in the formula, and **loose**, where additional agents, not mentioned in the formula, are allowed in the model. These

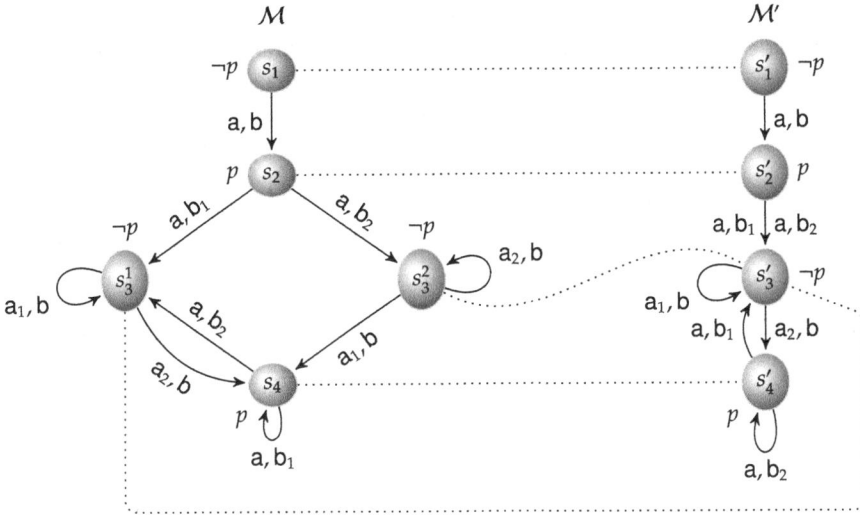

Figure 9.3 An alternating bisimulation between concurrent game models.

variants are essentially different, as they generated different sets of valid formulae, but the latter one is easily reducible to the former by adding just one extra agent $\mathbf{a}_{new}$ to the language (Exercise 9.9). Furthermore, this extra agent can easily be added superfluously to the formula, e.g. by adding a conjunct $\langle\!\langle\mathbf{a}_{new}\rangle\!\rangle\mathsf{X}\top$, so hereafter we only consider the tight satisfiability version.

2. The issue of the cardinality of the set of players $\mathbb{A}\mathbb{G}$ is more subtle, as even infinite coalitions can be *named* within a single formula, which would imply certain technical complications. Nevertheless, when interested in satisfiability of single formulae, the finiteness of $\mathbb{A}\mathbb{G}$ does not result in a loss of generality. Indeed, as every formula φ mentions only *finitely many coalitions*, we can define an equivalence relation of finite index on the set of players, that is naturally induced by φ, viz. two players are considered 'equivalent' if they always occur, or otherwise, together in all the coalitions mentioned in φ (i.e. $\mathbf{a} \cong_\varphi \mathbf{a}'$ if $\mathbf{a} \in C$ iff $\mathbf{a}' \in C$ holds for every coalition C mentioned in φ). Then φ can be rewritten into a formula φ' in which equivalence classes with respect to $\cong_\varphi$ are treated as single players. It is not hard to show that φ' is satisfiable iff φ is, and thus the satisfiability of the latter can be reduced to the satisfiablity of the former.

As with the other logics studied here, we will specifically be interested in the **constructive satisfiability-testing** problem: given an ATL formula φ, determine whether φ is satisfiable, and if so, construct a CGM $\mathcal{M}$ and a state s in $\mathcal{M}$ such that $\mathcal{M}, s \vDash \varphi$. The following results tell us that ATL and ATL* preserve the good properties of CTL and CTL* that guarantee their decidability of satisfiability. A CGM is **tree-like** if its underlying transition graph is a directed tree, i.e. every state can be reached by a unique path from a designated state (the root).

Proposition 9.3.1 (Bounded-branching model property for ATL). For every satisfiable ATL formula φ there is a tree-like CGM Tr_φ of a fixed branching degree m^n, such that $\text{Tr}_\varphi \models \varphi$, where n is the number of agents mentioned in φ and $m \in \mathcal{O}(|\varphi|)$. ∎

We state the next complexity results without proofs (see references in Section 9.5). In Theorem 9.3.6 (for SAT(ATL)) and Theorem 10.2.9 (for SAT(ATL*)) we provide alternative arguments, based on translations to the μ-calculus, leading to such results, but under the assumption of an explicitly fixed number of agents and actions which, in view of the earlier comments and Proposition 9.3.1 are not restrictions of essential importance.

Theorem 9.3.2. The satisfiability-testing problem SAT(ATL) is decidable and in EXPTIME. ∎

Theorem 9.3.3. The satisfiability-testing problem SAT(ATL*) is decidable and in 2EXPTIME. ∎

9.3.2 Model Checking

The main model-checking problems for ATL and ATL* are like those for CTL and CTL*. We distinguish local and global model checking again.

Proposition 9.3.4.

(I) The global model-checking problem for ATL can be solved in time linear both in the size of the formula and in the size of the model.
(II) The model-checking problem for ATL* is in 2EXPTIME. ∎

The procedure for global model checking of ATL, given in pseudocode in Algorithm 9, is an extension of the labelling algorithm for global model checking of CTL.

Example 9.3.5. We informally illustrate the global model-checking procedure for ATL in the CGM $\mathcal{M}$ in Figure 9.4 to determine $[\![\langle\!\langle\{2\}\rangle\!\rangle \mathsf{X}q \wedge \langle\!\langle\{1\}\rangle\!\rangle p\mathsf{U}q]\!]^{\mathcal{M}}$. First, we have $[\![q]\!]^{\mathcal{M}} = \{s_3\}$ and $[\![p]\!]^{\mathcal{M}} = \{s_1, s_2\}$. For the first conjunct we get

$$[\![\langle\!\langle\{2\}\rangle\!\rangle\mathsf{X}q]\!]^{\mathcal{M}} = \text{pre}(\mathcal{M}, \{2\}, [\![q]\!]^{\mathcal{M}}) = \text{pre}(\mathcal{M}, \{2\}, \{s_3\}) = \{s_3, s_4\}$$

since player 2 can force the play to s_3 in the next step exactly when the play is in s_3 or s_4. Next, we have $[\![\langle\!\langle\{1\}\rangle\!\rangle p\mathsf{U}q]\!]^{\mathcal{M}} = \{s_3, s_2, s_1\}$. In this step, s_3 is added first since $[\![q]\!]^{\mathcal{M}} = \{s_3\}$. Then s_2 is added since $s_2 \in [\![p]\!]^{\mathcal{M}}$ and $s_2 \in \text{pre}(\mathcal{M}, \{1\}, \{s_3\})$. Finally, s_1 is added since $s_1 \in [\![p]\!]^{\mathcal{M}}$ and $s_1 \in \text{pre}(\mathcal{M}, \{1\}, \{s_2, s_3\})$. This leads us to

$$[\![\langle\!\langle\{2\}\rangle\!\rangle\mathsf{X}q \wedge \langle\!\langle\{1\}\rangle\!\rangle p\mathsf{U}q]\!]^{\mathcal{M}} = [\![\langle\!\langle\{2\}\rangle\!\rangle\mathsf{X}q]\!]^{\mathcal{M}} \cap [\![\langle\!\langle\{1\}\rangle\!\rangle p\mathsf{U}q]\!]^{\mathcal{M}} = \{s_3\}.$$

Thus, s_3 is the only state from which player 1 can make sure that p is true until q is true and from which player 2 can make sure that q is true in the next state.

Algorithm 9 An algorithm for global ATL model checking.

1: **procedure** GLOBALMC($\mathcal{M}, \varphi$)

2:     **case** φ **of**

3:       p: **return** $\{s \in S \mid p \in L(s)\}$ ▷ some atomic proposition

4:       $\neg\psi$: **return** $S \setminus$ GLOBALMC($\mathcal{M}, \psi$)

5:       $\psi_1 \vee \psi_2$: **return** GLOBALMC($\mathcal{M}, \psi_1$) $\cup$ GLOBALMC($\mathcal{M}, \psi_2$)

6:       $\langle\!\langle C \rangle\!\rangle \mathsf{X}\psi$: **return** pre($\mathcal{M}, C$, GLOBALMC($\mathcal{M}, \psi$))

7:       $\langle\!\langle C \rangle\!\rangle \mathsf{G}\psi$:

8:           $X \leftarrow S; Y \leftarrow$ GLOBALMC($\mathcal{M}, \psi$);

9:           **while** $X \nsubseteq Y$ **do**

10:             $X \leftarrow Y; Y \leftarrow$ pre($\mathcal{M}, C, X$) $\cap$ GLOBALMC($\mathcal{M}, \psi$)

11:           **end while**; **return** Y

12:       $\langle\!\langle C \rangle\!\rangle \psi_1 \mathsf{U}\psi_2$:

13:           $X \leftarrow \emptyset; Y \leftarrow$ GLOBALMC($\mathcal{M}, \psi_2$);

14:           **while** $Y \nsubseteq X$ **do**

15:             $X \leftarrow Y$

16:             $Y \leftarrow$ GLOBALMC($\mathcal{M}, \psi_2$) $\cup$ (pre($\mathcal{M}, C, X$) $\cap$ GLOBALMC($\mathcal{M}, \psi_1$))

17:           **end while**; **return** Y

18:     **end case**

19: **end procedure**

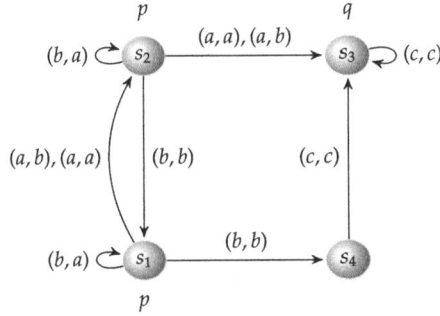

Figure 9.4 Global model checking of ATL: an example.

9.3.3 From ATL to the Modal μ-Calculus

Let $\mathcal{M} = (\mathbb{AG}, S, Act, \mathsf{act}, \delta, L)$ be a finite CGM. Naturally, finiteness of $\mathcal{M}$ implies that $\mathbb{AG}$, S and Act are nonempty finite sets. Recall that we have assumed $\mathbb{AG} = \{1, \ldots, k\}$, hereafter denoted $[1, k]$. Obviously, the structure $\mathcal{M}$ can be viewed as a transition system by omitting $\mathbb{AG}$ and by encoding the maps act and δ. Let $\mathfrak{T}(\mathcal{M})$ be the transition system sharing the set of states S with $\mathcal{M}$ and extending the labelling function L such that

$$\mathfrak{T}(\mathcal{M}) := (S, \{\xrightarrow{a}\}_{a \in Act'}, L')$$

where the following hold.

- $Act' = Act \times \cdots \times Act$ (k times).
- For all states $s, r \in S$, for all actions $(a_1, \ldots, a_k) \in Act'$, we have $s \xrightarrow{(a_1, \ldots, a_k)} r$ iff
  1. for all $i \in [1, k]$, we have $a_i \in \text{act}(i, s)$,
  2. $\delta((a_1, \ldots, a_k), s) = r$.
- L' is a conservative extension of L by addition of the atomic propositions $\{\text{act}_{i,a} \mid i \in \mathbb{AG}, a \in Act\}$ (used to encode the action manager act) so that for all states s,

$$L'(s) := L(s) \cup \{\text{act}_{i,a} \mid i \in \mathbb{AG}, a \in \text{act}(i, s)\}.$$

Obviously, each transition relation $\xrightarrow{(a_1, \ldots, a_k)}$ is deterministic but not necessarily total. Totality of all the transition relations is guaranteed when for all agents $i \in [1, k]$ and for all states $s \in S$, we have that $\text{act}(i, s) = Act$.

The reduction from $\mathcal{M}$ to $\mathfrak{T}(\mathcal{M})$ is quite elementary and can be viewed as making the transition system underlying the semantical structure $\mathcal{M}$ explicit. We show how it can be used to polynomially reduce the model-checking problem for ATL to the model-checking problem for the alternation-free fragment of the modal μ-calculus $\mathcal{L}_\mu$.

Let ψ be an ATL formula such that all the coalitions C occurring in ψ are subsets of $\mathbb{AG}$. We build a formula $tr(\varphi)$ such that for all states $s \in S$, we have $\mathcal{M}, s \models \varphi$ iff $\mathfrak{T}(\mathcal{M}), s \models tr(\varphi)$. Since $\mathfrak{T}(\mathcal{M})$ and $tr(\varphi)$ can be constructed in polynomial time in the respective sizes of $\mathcal{M}$ and φ, and since the model-checking problem for the alternation-free fragment of $\mathcal{L}_\mu$ is in PTIME (see Theorem 8.3.5), this provides an alternative argument establishing that the model-checking problem for ATL is in PTIME. We define the reduction map tr as follows.

$$tr(p) := p$$

$$tr(\neg\varphi) := \neg tr(\varphi)$$

$$tr(\varphi \wedge \psi) := tr(\varphi) \wedge tr(\psi)$$

$$tr(\langle\!\langle C \rangle\!\rangle \mathsf{X}\varphi) := \bigvee_{\alpha_C} \left(\psi_{\alpha_C} \wedge \bigwedge_{\alpha_C \sqsubseteq \alpha} (\psi_\alpha \to [(\alpha(1), \ldots, \alpha(k))]tr(\varphi)) \right)$$

$$tr(\langle\!\langle C \rangle\!\rangle \mathsf{G}\varphi) := \nu Z.\, tr(\varphi) \wedge \bigvee_{\alpha_C} \left(\psi_{\alpha_C} \wedge \bigwedge_{\alpha_C \sqsubseteq \alpha} (\psi_\alpha \to [(\alpha(1), \ldots, \alpha(k))]\, Z) \right)$$

$$tr(\langle\!\langle C \rangle\!\rangle \varphi\mathsf{U}\psi) := \mu Z.\, \Bigg(tr(\psi) \vee$$

$$\left(tr(\varphi) \wedge \bigvee_{\alpha_C} \left(\psi_{\alpha_C} \wedge \bigwedge_{\alpha_C \sqsubseteq \alpha} (\psi_\alpha \to [(\alpha(1), \ldots, \alpha(k))]\, Z) \right) \right) \Bigg)$$

where α_C is a map $C \to Act$, α is a map $\mathbb{AG} \to Act$ and $\alpha_C \sqsubseteq \alpha$ means that α is an extension of α_C. Moreover, the formula ψ_{α_C} expresses that all the actions chosen by the agents in C respect the map act, which can be expressed as follows:

$$\bigwedge_{i \in C} \text{act}_{i, \alpha_C(i)}.$$

The formula ψ_α is defined similarly to check the consistency with δ but for all the agents in $\mathbb{AG}$. The formulae ψ_{α_C} and ψ_α become redundant if, for all agents $i \in [1, k]$ and for all states $s \in S$, we assume that $\mathsf{act}(i, s) = Act$.

The correctness proof for the equivalence between $\mathcal{M}, s \models \varphi$ and $\mathfrak{T}(\mathcal{M}), s \models tr(\varphi)$ relies on the fixpoint characterisation of the operators in ATL, see Proposition 9.2.11 and Lemma 9.2.10. At this point, it is worth noting that each formula $tr(\psi)$ is guarded and belongs to the alternation-free fragment of $\mathcal{L}_\mu$ and its size is polynomial in the sum of the respective sizes of $\mathcal{M}$ and φ. This may come as a surprise in view of the generalised disjunctions or conjunctions indexed by sets of maps of the form $C \to Act$ but the encoding of δ is already of size in $\mathcal{O}(\mathrm{card}(S) \cdot \mathrm{card}(Act)^k)$.

The reduction between the model-checking problems can be lifted to satisfiability but we need to make a few more assumptions. Even though the extension does not yield an optimal upper complexity bound for ATL, still it can establish this bound for a nontrivial variant of ATL and it illustrates the interplay between operators in ATL and the fixpoint operators in $\mathcal{L}_\mu$.

Let ATL($[1, k], Act$) be the variant of ATL obtained by explicitly fixing the set of agents to $[1, k]$ and restricting the set of actions that can be used in the concurrent game models to a fixed nonempty finite set of actions Act. The latter restriction modifies the satisfiability problem accordingly to one where only models satisfying it are searched. Due to Proposition 9.3.1, such a restriction can be imposed for any fixed number of agents with a suitably large set Act without affecting the solution of the satisfiability problem.

Theorem 9.3.6. The satisfiability problem for ATL($[1, k], Act$) can be solved in exponential time. ∎

Proof. Using reasoning similar to that done for model checking, and actually by reusing the map tr relatively to the sets $[1, k]$ and Act, one can show that φ in ATL is satisfiable iff the formula φ' defined by

$$\varphi' := tr(\varphi) \wedge \nu Z. \left(\left(\bigwedge_{(a_1, \dots, a_k) \in Act'} \left(\left(\bigwedge_{i \in \mathbb{AG}} \mathsf{act}_{i, a_i} \right) \leftrightarrow \langle (a_1, \dots, a_k) \rangle \top \right) \right) \wedge \right.$$
$$\left. \bigwedge_{(a_1, \dots, a_k) \in Act} [(a_1, \dots, a_k)] Z \right)$$

is satisfiable in the deterministic version of the modal μ-calculus. The second conjunct simply states that

$$\bigwedge_{(a_1, \dots, a_k) \in Act'} \left(\bigwedge_{i \in \mathbb{AG}} \mathsf{act}_{i, a_i} \right) \leftrightarrow \langle (a_1, \dots, a_k) \rangle \top$$

holds in all reachable states. In Theorem 15.4.15, we establish that the satisfiability problem for the modal μ-calculus $\mathcal{L}_\mu$ restricted to transition systems with deterministic transition relations only can be solved in EXPTIME.

Note that k and *Act* are constant parameters of the language ATL$([1, k], Act)$ and therefore the reduction is in polynomial time. By Theorem 15.4.15, we conclude that the satisfiability problem for ATL$([1, k], Act)$ is in EXPTIME. Indeed, let $\mathcal{T} = (S, \{\xrightarrow{a}\}_{a \in Act'}, L')$ be a transition system satisfying the second conjunct in φ'. Since $\mathcal{T}$ has only deterministic transition relations it is quite easy to build a concurrent game model $\mathcal{M}$ such that $\mathfrak{T}(\mathcal{M}) = \mathcal{T}$. Indeed, L is a restriction of L' obtained by discarding the atomic propositions from $\{act_{i,a} \mid i \in \mathbb{AG}, a \in Act\}$, act is defined thanks to the atomic propositions from the latter set, and δ can be read directly from the transition relations. The second conjunct guarantees that act and δ agree. □

A translation working likewise for ATL* can be found in the forthcoming Section 15.4.3.

9.4 Exercises

Exercise 9.1. Consider the CGM from Example 9.1.2 with state space S.

(a) Let $\alpha_{\{Robot_1\}} = $ push and $\alpha_{\{Robot_2\}} = $ wait. Then determine $post(s_1, \alpha_{\{Robot_1\}})$ and $post(s_1, \alpha_{\{Robot_2\}})$.

(b) Let Robot$_1$ adopt the positional strategy $\mathfrak{str}_{Robot_1}$ such that $\mathfrak{str}_{Robot_1}(s_0) = $ wait, $\mathfrak{str}_{Robot_1}(s_1) = $ push, $\mathfrak{str}_{Robot_1}(s_2) = $ wait. Then determine the sets of outcome plays

$$\text{Plays}^{pos}(s_0, \mathfrak{str}_{Robot_1}), \quad \text{Plays}^{pos}(s_1, \mathfrak{str}_{Robot_1}), \quad \text{Plays}^{pos}(s_2, \mathfrak{str}_{Robot_1}).$$

(c) Let Robot$_1$ adopt the following memory-based strategy $\mathfrak{str}^m_{Robot_1}$. (Recall the notation '$\mathfrak{str}(E) = $ a' for a regular expression E, meaning to indicate that the value of $\mathfrak{str}$ for every element of E is a.)

$$\mathfrak{str}^m_{Robot_1}(\{s_0, s_1\}^*) = \text{wait}, \quad \mathfrak{str}^m_{Robot_1}(\{s_0, s_1\}^* s_2 S^*) = \text{push}.$$

That is, the strategy prescribes waiting until the state s_2 is visited, if ever, and then pushing forever. Determine the set of outcome plays starting from each of the following histories.

$$s_1 \qquad s_2 \qquad s_1, s_0 \qquad s_1, s_0, s_1 \qquad s_2, s_0, s_1 \qquad s_2, s_1, s_0$$

Which of these histories are consistent with the strategy $\mathfrak{str}^m_{Robot_1}$?

Exercise 9.2. Consider the following memory-based strategy for Agent$_1$ in the CGM in Figure 9.1, defined in the last item of Example 9.1.9:

$$\mathfrak{str}^m_{Agent_1}(S^* PE) = \text{U}, \quad \mathfrak{str}^m_{Agent_1}(S^* EU_1) = \text{U}, \quad \mathfrak{str}^m_{Agent_1}(S^* D_1 P) = \text{R}.$$

In all other cases, the strategy prescribes N.
Compute the set of outcome plays $\text{Plays}^{mem}(s_0, \mathfrak{str}^m_{Agent_1})$.

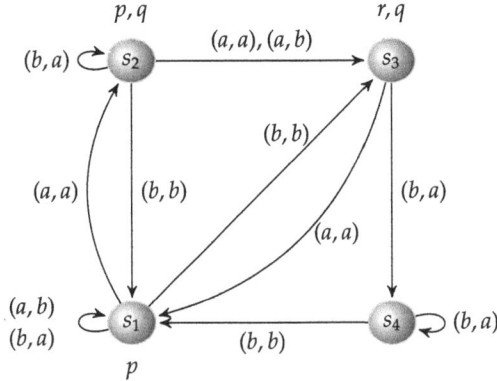

Figure 9.5 An abstract concurrent game model.

Exercise 9.3. Consider the CGM in Figure 9.5. It involves two players 1 and 2; two types of actions a, b, and three atomic propositions: PROP $= \{p, q, r\}$. Note that at state s_3 player 2 has only action a available, while at state s_4 player 1 has only action b available.

(a) Let $\alpha_1 = a$ and $\alpha_2 = b$. Then determine $\text{post}(s, \alpha_1)$ and $\text{post}(s, \alpha_2)$ for every state s where the respective move is admissible.
(b) Let player 1 adopt the positional strategy $\mathfrak{str}_1$ such that $\mathfrak{str}_1(s) = b$ for every state s. Then determine the set of outcome plays $\text{Plays}^{\text{pos}}(s_1, \mathfrak{str}_1)$ and $\text{Plays}^{\text{pos}}(s_2, \mathfrak{str}_1)$.
(c) Let player 2 adopt the positional strategy $\mathfrak{str}_2$ such that $\mathfrak{str}_2(s) = a$ for every state q. Then determine the set of outcome plays $\text{Plays}^{\text{pos}}(s_1, \mathfrak{str}_2)$.
(d) Let player 1 adopt the following memory-based strategy $\mathfrak{str}_1^m$:
  • $\mathfrak{str}_1^m(\{s_1, s_2\}^*) = a$,
  • $\mathfrak{str}_1^m(w) = b$, for all other words $w \in S^*$.
  That is, the strategy prescribes playing a until any of the states s_3, s_4 is visited, if ever, and then playing b forever. Determine the set of outcome plays starting from each of the following histories:

$$s_1 \qquad s_3 \qquad s_3, s_1 \qquad s_4, s_1 \qquad s_4, s_1, s_2$$

Which of these histories are consistent with the strategy $\mathfrak{str}_1^m$?

Exercise 9.4. Show that the ATL operators $\langle\!\langle C \rangle\!\rangle F$ and $\langle\!\langle C \rangle\!\rangle G$ are not interdefinable. (Hint: restrict the notion of alternating bisimulation suitably to preserve only one of these.)

Exercise 9.5. Formalise the following specifications in ATL.

(a) 'If Player 1 has an action to guarantee a winning successor state, then Player 2 cannot prevent from reaching a winning successor state'.

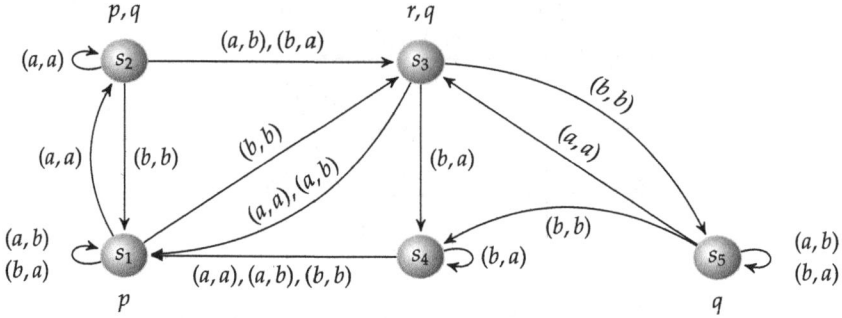

Figure 9.6 A concurrent game model.

(b) 'Player **a** has an action to guarantee a successor state where he is rich, and has an action to guarantee a successor state where he is happy, but does not have an action to guarantee a successor state where he is both rich and happy'.

(c) 'Agent 1 has a strategy to keep the system in states from which agent 2 cannot force the system to ever crash, until a state is reached from which agent 1 can ensure that the system will reach a safe successor state'.

(d) 'The coalition of all agents $\mathbb{A}\mathbb{G}$ has no collective move preventing the environment from eventually getting the system into a state of alert'.

(e) 'The agent 1 has a strategy that can maintain his control on the resource a until agent 2 releases control on resource b, while agent 3 can cooperate with 2 to eventually force agent 1 to release control on resource a'.

(f) 'None of the coalitions C and C' has a strategy to maintain the system in a safe state forever, but the two coalitions C and C' have a collective strategy that will eventually get the system into a safe state while meanwhile maintaining a state of alert, and to enable C from that safe state to ensure that the system will never crash thereafter'.

Exercise 9.6. Prove Lemma 9.2.5 by showing that perfect-recall strategies can be replaced by positional strategies in the truth definitions of $\langle\!\langle C \rangle\!\rangle G\varphi$ and $\langle\!\langle C \rangle\!\rangle \varphi U\psi$, and then doing induction on the formula φ.

Exercise 9.7. Consider the shared file updates in Example 9.2.7 and verify the claims made there.

Exercise 9.8. Consider the concurrent game model in Figure 9.6. It involves two agents 1 and 2; two types of actions a, b; and atomic propositions $\text{PROP} = \{p, q, r\}$. Determine which of the following statements hold.

(a) $s_1 \models p \wedge \langle\!\langle 1 \rangle\!\rangle Xq$

(b) $s_2 \models \langle\!\langle 1 \rangle\!\rangle (p \vee r)U\neg q$

(c) $s_1 \models \langle\!\langle 1 \rangle\!\rangle F\neg\langle\!\langle 2 \rangle\!\rangle \neg Xp$

(d) $s_1 \models \langle\!\langle 1 \rangle\!\rangle Gp \wedge \langle\!\langle 2 \rangle\!\rangle Gp \wedge \langle\!\langle 1, 2 \rangle\!\rangle F\neg p$

(e) $s_2 \models \neg\langle\!\langle 1 \rangle\!\rangle X(q \wedge r) \wedge \neg\langle\!\langle 2 \rangle\!\rangle Xp \wedge \neg\langle\!\langle 1, 2 \rangle\!\rangle X(p \vee r)$

(f) $s_3 \models \langle\!\langle 1 \rangle\!\rangle G\langle\!\langle 1, 2 \rangle\!\rangle (\neg qUp)$

Exercise 9.9. Show that loose satisfiability can be reduced to tight satisfiability by adding just one extra agent $\mathbf{a}_{new}$, not mentioned in the formula, to the language, respectively to the set of agents in the required model.

Exercise 9.10. Judge whether each of the following ATL formulae is tightly satisfiable, using the semantic definition. If claimed satisfiable, provide a model that satisfies it.

(a) $\langle\!\langle 1\rangle\!\rangle Xp \wedge \langle\!\langle 1\rangle\!\rangle G\neg p$

(b) $\langle\!\langle 1, 2\rangle\!\rangle Xp \wedge \langle\!\langle 1, 3\rangle\!\rangle G\neg p$

(c) $\langle\!\langle 1, 2\rangle\!\rangle (pUq) \wedge \langle\!\langle 3\rangle\!\rangle G\neg q$

(d) $\neg\langle\!\langle 1, 2\rangle\!\rangle Xp \wedge \neg\langle\!\langle 2\rangle\!\rangle G\neg p$

(e) $\langle\!\langle 1\rangle\!\rangle (pU\langle\!\langle 2\rangle\!\rangle Xq) \wedge \langle\!\langle 2\rangle\!\rangle G\neg q$

(f) $\langle\!\langle 1\rangle\!\rangle (pU\langle\!\langle 2\rangle\!\rangle Xq) \wedge \langle\!\langle 2\rangle\!\rangle ((\neg q)U\langle\!\langle 1\rangle\!\rangle G\neg p)$

(g) $\neg\langle\!\langle 1, 2\rangle\!\rangle Xp \wedge \neg\langle\!\langle 2, 3\rangle\!\rangle Xp \wedge \neg\langle\!\langle 1, 3\rangle\!\rangle Xp \wedge \langle\!\langle 1, 2, 3\rangle\!\rangle Gp$

Exercise 9.11. Check the validity of each of the axioms and the correctness of each of the inference rules for ATL listed in Section 9.2.5, by using the semantic definition.

Exercise 9.12. Show that the algorithm for global model checking of ATL formulae given in Section 9.3.2 works in time linear both in the size of the formula and in the size of the model.

Exercise 9.13. Show that the composition of two alternating bisimulations is an alternating bisimulation.

Exercise 9.14. Verify the claimed alternating bisimulation in Example 9.2.17.

Exercise 9.15. For any concurrent game model $\mathcal{M}$ and a state $s \in \mathcal{M}$ define the tree unfolding $\widehat{\mathcal{M}}[s]$ of $\mathcal{M}$ from s. Show that there is a global alternating bisimulation between reach$(\mathcal{M}, s)$ and $\widehat{\mathcal{M}}[s]$.

Exercise 9.16. Show that $\mathtt{pre}(\mathcal{M}, C, [\![\varphi]\!]^{\mathcal{M}}) = [\![\langle\!\langle C\rangle\!\rangle X\varphi]\!]^{\mathcal{M}}$.

Exercise 9.17. Prove Proposition 9.2.11, Lemma 9.2.14 and Lemma 9.2.15. Complete the proof for the case of $\langle\!\langle C\rangle\!\rangle \psi U\varphi$ in Claim 1 of Theorem 9.2.16.

9.5 Bibliographical Notes

Multiagent transition systems of the type studied here come from game theory, built on the notions of '(coalitional) α-effectivity functions' (Abdou and Keiding 1991) and 'playable coalition frames' (Pauly 2001a,b). They were introduced as models for multiagent logics apparently independently by Pauly (2002) as '(multiplayer) game frames/models', and by Alur, Henzinger and Kupferman (2002) as 'concurrent game models'; see also Goranko (2001). The initial motivation in Alur et al. (1997) and its following versions was to design a logical formalism to reason about *open systems*, but ATL* more naturally applies to the case of multiagent systems. Note that the set of states was originally assumed finite in Alur et al. (2002), but that restriction is not necessary.

Pauly introduced his Coalition Logic CL in Pauly (2002) and then the Extended Coalition Logic ECL in Pauly (2001a) to reason about the power of agents and coalition in effectivity models, whereas Alur et al. (1997, 1998b, 2002) introduced ATL* and its fragment ATL in the series.

Alur, Henzinger and Kupferman originally proposed a semantics for ATL* and ATL based on a more restricted class of models, called 'alternating transition systems' in Alur et al. (1997, 1998b), later replaced by concurrent game models in the journal version (Alur et al. 2002). Meanwhile, it was shown in Goranko (2001) that Pauly's CL embeds into ATL as its X-fragment (while ECL embeds as its XG-fragment) and that multiplayer game models and alternating transition systems provide equivalent semantics for ATL in terms of validities. For further and more detailed semantic comparisons of these semantics, see also Goranko and Jamroga (2004). ATL was considered in Alur et al. (2002) on some special types of CGS: Moore synchronous, lock step, turn based, etc. Fair ATL (ATL with fairness constraints) was considered there, too.

The example in Figure 9.1 is due to Wojtek Jamroga.

For further details on the issue of tight versus loose satisfiability, see e.g. Walther et al. (2006), Goranko and van Drimmelen (2006) and Goranko and Shkatov (2009c).

Fragments and expressiveness. Several fragments of ATL* have been studied and shown to be expressively distinct. In particular, by analogy with CTL$^+$, ATL$^+$ is the fragment of ATL* where the subformulae following the strategic operators, i.e. expressing the objectives of the coalitions, can be any Boolean combination of unnested temporal operators followed by state formulae. Expressiveness results about ATL$^+$ and ATL are presented in Laroussinie et al. (2008), Bulling and Jamroga (2014). For instance, Bulling and Jamroga (2014) show that, unlike ATL, the semantics of ATL$^+$ differs when strategies are restricted to positional ones only. Also, a hierarchy of flat fragments of ATL* were introduced in Goranko and Vester (2014).

Axiomatisations. The first four axioms in the axiomatic system in Section 9.2.5 were first proposed by Pauly (2001a,b) and shown there to provide a sound and complete axiomatisation for the Coalition Logic CL. The full axiomatic system for ATL presented in Section 9.2.5 was first proposed in Goranko (2001) and proved sound and complete in Goranko and van Drimmelen (2006), where Proposition 9.2.11 was proved. No explicit complete axiomatisation for ATL* is currently known yet.

Alternating bisimulations. Alternating simulations and other alternating refinement relations were defined and studied in Alur et al. (1998a). Alternating bisimulations, as presented here, were defined in Ågotnes et al. (2007), where a version of Theorem 9.2.16 was proved.

Model checking of ATL and extensions. The model-checker Mocha for ATL was developed and described in Alur et al. (1998c). Alur et al. (2002) extend the labelling algorithm for model checking for CTL to ATL and show that:

- The model-checking problem for ATL is solvable in time linear both is the length of the formula and the size of the model (given explicitly by its transition table), and is PTime-complete.
- The model-checking problem for Fair ATL (ATL with fairness constraints) is PSpace-complete.
- The model-checking problem for ATL* is 2ExpTime-complete (even in the special case of turn-based models).

Van der Hoek et al. (2006) revisit the model-checking problem for ATL with respect to practically more efficient representations of the models. Further complexity analyses of that problem, also taking into account the number of agents as parameter, as well as memory and perfect versus imperfect information, can be found in Bulling et al. (2010), Jamroga and Dix (2008), Laroussinie (2010) and Laroussinie et al. (2008).

Satisfiability and decision methods. The proofs of Proposition 9.3.1 and Theorem 9.3.2 can be found in van Drimmelen (2003), where a first decision procedure, using alternating tree automata and working in ExpTime (for a fixed number of agents), was proposed. It was further refined in Goranko and van Drimmelen (2006) and in Walther et al. (2006), where the ExpTime upper bound was proved without fixing the number of agents. A 2ExpTime-complete satisfiability-testing algorithm for ATL* was first presented in Schewe (2008a), where Theorem 9.3.3 was proved. The complexity of satisfiability in various flat fragments of ATL* is analysed in Goranko and Vester (2014), where all of them are shown to be in PSpace, and the full flat fragment of ATL* (with no nesting of strategic quantifiers but any nesting of temporal operators) to be PSpace-complete.

An ExpTime, optimal, constructive and practically usable tableau-based decision procedure for ATL was developed in Goranko and Shkatov (2009c) and further extended to ATL$^+$ in Cerrito et al. (2014) and to the full ATL* in David (2015). An implementation of the tableaux method for ATL is presented in David (2013) and its extension to ATL* in David (2015).

ATL* with incomplete information and with memory. Schobbens (2004) considered four variations of the semantics of ATL: with perfect or imperfect information and with no recall (memoryless) or perfect recall strategies. It was shown in Jamroga and Bulling (2011) that those semantic variations generate different sets of validities. Under assumptions of incomplete information and perfect memory, model checking of ATL becomes undecidable, as stated without explicit proof in Alur et al. (2002) and proved later in Dima and Tiplea (2011).

Strategy logics and ATL with strategy contexts. Some conceptual problems with the original semantics of ATL*/ATL, arising when strategic operators are nested, were identified and discussed in Ågotnes et al. (2007) and some solutions were proposed in Ågotnes et al. (2008) and Brihaye et al. (2009). The latter proposed a modified semantics for ATL, involving a **strategy context** (see also Lopes et al. 2010). A proof of the undecidability of the satisfiability problem for ATL with strategy contexts was presented in Troquard and Walther (2012).

Extensions of ATL* and strategy logics. Various extensions of ATL* have been proposed, starting with the alternating μ-calculus (AMC) introduced already in Alur et al. (2002); see Schewe and Finkbeiner (2006) on satisfiability and finite model property for AMC. A timed version of ATL was introduced in Henzinger and Prabhu (2006) and timed concurrent game structures were studied in Brihaye et al. (2007). Alternating-time temporal logic with explicit reference to strategies in the language was proposed in Walther et al. (2007). Another version, called Strategy Logic, was introduced in Chatterjee et al. (2010). Several extensions and generalisations of Strategy Logic were developed in Mogavero et al. (2010a,b, 2012).

Part III

Properties

10

Expressiveness

A formula of a temporal logic expresses a temporal property of interpreted transition systems, for instance in order to specify formally some wanted or some unwanted behaviour of the system. With several logics at hand, a natural question arises that has already been introduced in Chapter 7 with the definition of several syntactic fragments of CTL*: what are the properties that can be formalised in a particular logic? And which ones cannot be formalised? The first question is answered, in a way, by all formulae of that logic, but this answer is pretty much useless for getting an idea of what is possible with that logic. A better way to address these questions is to look at the whole picture of *all* temporal logics. We can naturally compare two logics $\mathcal{L}_1$ and $\mathcal{L}_2$ by asking whether every property that is formalisable in $\mathcal{L}_1$ can also be formalised in $\mathcal{L}_2$. It is easily seen that this yields a preorder on all temporal logics of the same kind, for example all linear-time temporal logics or all

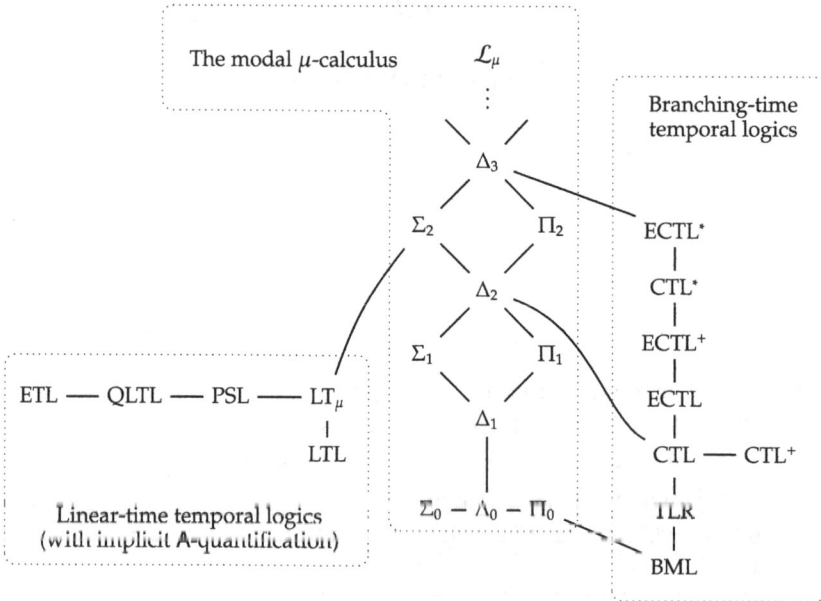

Figure 10.1 The hierarchy of temporal logics with respect to expressiveness.

branching-time temporal logics. Note that a temporal property can be identified with the class of (rooted) interpreted transition systems that possess this property. Thus, a formula from one logic being expressible by a formula in another logic simply amounts to the two formulae being equivalent in the usual logical sense, i.e. having the same families of models. For linear-time logics this is a family of computation paths, while for branching-time logics it is a family of rooted interpreted transition systems.

A careful analysis of what is possible in which logic should thus give us two hierarchies, of linear-time logics and of branching-time logics. Obviously, it would be nice to unify them in one big picture which shows the expressive power of every temporal logic. For this we need to be able to compare a linear-time and a branching-time logic, and this can be done by regarding the former as a latter with implicit quantification over computation paths. When we identify a linear-time formula φ with the branching-time property $A\varphi$ or $E\varphi$ then we should be able to study the relative expressive power of all temporal logics in one big picture.

This picture is shown in Figure 10.1, and the rest of this chapter is devoted to the study of all the relationships between temporal logics depicted there. A line going upwards indicates that the upper logic is strictly more expressive than the lower one; a horizontal line denotes equi-expressiveness amongst two (or more) logics. Note that the comparison relation is transitive. Not every logic that has been mentioned in the previous part is shown in this picture; in particular various fragments of CTL* have been left out purely to avoid an overcrowded picture. See Figure 7.10.

Structure of the chapter. The division of this chapter into sections reflects the two kinds of results that are being presented here. The first two sections contain translations from some logic to another, the two different worlds of linear time and branching time are being handled in separate sections. Section 10.1 mainly shows that several different extensions of LTL introduced in Chapter 6 share the same expressiveness. Section 10.2 is then concerned with results in branching-time logics, for instance the embedding of CTL* into $\mathcal{L}_\mu$.

At last, Section 10.3 presents results of the other kind: what is *not* possible in some logic, for instance the relative weakness of LTL in comparison to its extensions. It also pinpoints CTL's expressive power by separating it from other branching-time logics, and it proves that higher degree of fixpoint alternation in $\mathcal{L}_\mu$ yields greater expressiveness.

10.1 Embeddings among Linear-Time Logics

We introduce a formalism for specifying sets of computations: ω-regular expressions. These will serve two purposes. First, while we mainly focus on the *relative* expressive power among temporal logics it is equally worthwhile to link this to the outside world which – in a sense – yields a notion of *absolute* expressive power. These ω-regular expressions are a natural formalism for the specification of languages of infinite words and – not surprisingly – they characterise exactly the ω-regular languages. In Chapter 14 we present a specification formalism of finite automata and show that its expressive power coincides with that of ω-regular expressions.

Second, some of the embeddings between temporal logics are tricky to prove, in particular the translation from CTL* into the modal μ-calculus. We solve this problem by considering a specification formalism for linear-time properties that does not have conjunctive operators. Büchi automata would suffice for this, but we would like to defer their introduction to the chapter where they are being used in order to obtain decision procedures for temporal logics. For the study of expressiveness that we conduct here, ω-regular expressions are equally suitable and they also add to the variety of linear-time specification formalisms presented in this book.

On the other hand, automata are too fundamental to the questions of expressiveness to get by without them entirely. Translations from linear-time logics into Büchi automata and back are crucial to the results that we present here. Thus, ω-regular expressions only act as an easily understandable surrogate for Büchi automata which are to be introduced later on. At this point we will have to accept for granted that extensions of LTL like ETL, QLTL, PSL and the linear-time μ-calculus LT_μ can be translated into Büchi automata which in turn can be translated into ω-regular expressions. The technicalities of these results – going via Büchi automata – will be dealt with in Chapter 14.

The following picture shows how the equi-expressiveness of all these formalisms is being obtained with nondeterministic Büchi automata (NBA), respectively alternating Büchi automata (ABA), to be introduced in Chapter 14, and ω-regular expressions (ω-REG), to be introduced in the following section.

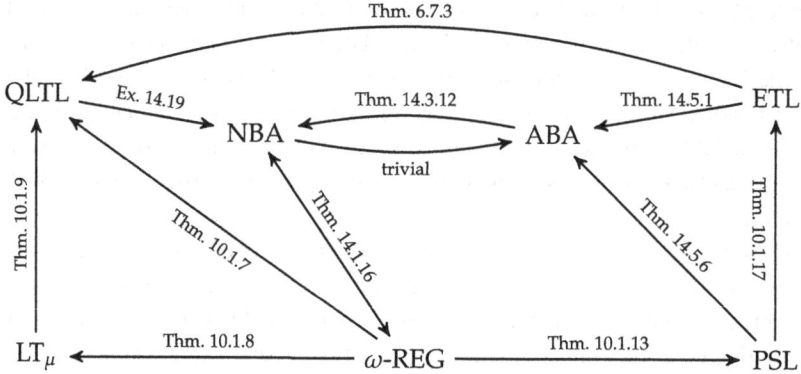

Clearly, not all translations are necessary in order to obtain expressive equivalence for all these formalisms. For instance, the translation from ω-regular expressions into QLTL is made redundant by the translations from ω-REG to LT_μ and then on to QLTL. However, the translation from ω-REG to QLTL obtained from the composition of these two is not necessarily easy to grasp and also differs from the direct one presented here. For such reasons we include some redundant translations, as well.

10.1.1 A Yardstick: ω-Regular Expressions

We start by recalling regular expressions for the specification of finite parts of computations. They use Boolean expressions over atomic propositions to describe properties of single states in a computation.

Definition 10.1.1. Let PROP be a set of atomic propositions. The language of ω-regular expressions is built from **Boolean expressions** (in negation normal form) over PROP which are given by the following grammar.

$$b ::= p \mid \neg p \mid b \vee b \mid b \wedge b.$$

A **regular expression** is given by

$$E := \bot \mid b \mid E \cup E \mid E \cdot E \mid E^*$$

where b is a Boolean expression as previously defined. $\qquad \nabla$

We will often drop the dot in denoting concatenations and simply write $p\,\neg p$ for instance instead of $p \cdot \neg p$ when there is no risk of confusion or ambiguity.

Regular expressions are interpreted in finite computations as follows.

Definition 10.1.2. Let PROP be as earlier and b be a Boolean expression. The **language of** b is the set of all sets of atomic propositions that are described by b in the usual way, where $\Pi \subseteq$ PROP:

- $L(p) := \{\Pi \mid p \in \Pi\}; L(\neg p) := \{\Pi \mid p \notin \Pi\};$
- $L(b \vee b') := L(b) \cup L(b'); L(b \wedge b') := L(b) \cap L(b').$

The **language** of a regular expression E is the set of all finite parts of computations, i.e. finite sequences of sets of atomic propositions, which are described by E in the following way. Note that every Boolean expression is a regular expression by Definition 10.1.1, and every set of atomic propositions can naturally be seen as such a sequence of length 1. Hence, the semantics of a Boolean expression as a regular expression is already defined.

$$L(\bot) := \emptyset$$

$$L(E \cup F) := L(E) \cup L(F)$$

$$L(E \cdot F) := \{\rho\rho' \mid \rho \in L(E), \rho' \in L(F)\}$$

$$L(E^*) := \{\rho_1 \ldots \rho_n \mid n \geq 0 \text{ and } \rho_i \in L(E) \text{ for all } i = 1, \ldots, n\}.$$

Note that the last clause includes the case of $n = 0$, i.e. the empty sequence which is denoted by ε. We call a regular expression E ε-**free** if $\varepsilon \notin L(E)$. $\qquad\qquad$ ∇

Before we can introduce ω-regular expressions we need the notion of an ε-free regular expression, that is one that does not include ε in its language. Fortunately, it is quite easy to 'see' whether a regular expression describes ε as well. We leave it as Exercise 10.1 to prove the following lemma and turn it into an algorithm which decides, given a regular expression, whether or not it is ε-free.

Lemma 10.1.3. For all Boolean expressions b and regular expressions E, F we have:

  (I) $\bot$ and b are ε-free,
  (II) E^* is not ε-free,
 (III) $E \cup F$ is ε-free if so are E and F,
 (IV) $E \cdot F$ is ε-free if so is E or F. $\qquad\qquad\qquad\qquad\qquad\qquad$ ■

With this at hand we are ready to define ω-regular expressions.

Definition 10.1.4. An ω-**regular expression** E is of the form

$$\bigcup_{i=1}^{n} E_i \cdot F_i^{\omega}$$

where $n \geq 0$ and the E_i and F_i are regular expressions such that each F_i is ε-free. In case of $n = 0$ we may also simply write $\bot$ for this ω-regular expression.

Such an ω-regular expression E describes a **language** $L(E)$ of infinite computations as follows.

$$L(E) := \bigcup_{i=1}^{n} L(E_i) \cdot L(F_i)^{\omega}$$

where $L^{\omega} := \{\rho_0 \rho_1 \rho_2 \ldots \mid \rho_i \in L \text{ for all } i \in \mathbb{N}\}$. $\qquad\qquad\qquad\qquad\qquad$ ∇

Example 10.1.5. Let PROP $= \{p, q\}$. The language of all words containing infinitely many positions in which q hold can be described by $((\neg q)^* q)^\omega$ for instance. Stating that q holds at every even moment can be done with the ω-regular expression $(\top q)^\omega$ where $\top$ abbreviates $q \vee \neg q$ for instance. The natural combination of these two properties, viz. 'q holds infinitely often in even positions', can be described by $((\top \top)^* \top q)^\omega$.

The property 'if p holds infinitely often then q holds infinitely often' can be read as 'p holds only finitely often or q holds infinitely often' and is therefore easily formalised as an ω-regular expression as follows.

$$\top^* (\neg p)^\omega \cup ((\neg q)^* q)^\omega.$$

10.1.2 Different Extensions, Same Expressiveness

It is not easy to obtain direct translations between the various extensions of LTL that have been introduced in Chapter 6 and Section 8.7.1. For instance, ETL, QLTL and PSL have no direct means for expressing the nesting of fixpoint operators that occur in LT_μ formulae. It is equally unclear how ETL, PSL and LT_μ should cope with the quantification over atomic proposition that QLTL provides. Yet, all these formalisms turn out to be equally expressive, and the first step towards this result is the statement that all of them are not more powerful than ω-regular expressions.

Theorem 10.1.6. For every (closed) formula φ of LTL, ETL, QLTL, PSL or LT_μ there is an ω-regular expression E_φ such that $L(E_\varphi) = \text{Mod}(\varphi)$.   ∎

The proof of this result is deferred to Chapter 14 where for each of these logics it is shown that their formulae can be equivalently translated into Büchi automata which in turn can be translated into ω-regular expressions. Without going into further details at this point we remark that the translation is exponential in all cases; in the case of QLTL it is even nonelementary.

The rest of this section is devoted to showing that all of these logics are at least as powerful as ω-regular expressions. We will start with QLTL.

The Power of Propositional Quantification

Quantification over new atomic propositions that do not occur in the underlying computations gives us the ability to 'mark' positions in a computation and use these markers to postulate that the parts in between are defined by regular expressions of finite words.

Theorem 10.1.7. For every ω-regular expression E there is a formula $\varphi_E \in$ QLTL such that $\text{Mod}(\varphi_E) = L(E)$.   ∎

Proof. First we note that every Boolean expression is, syntactically, already a QLTL formula but their semantics differ slightly. Given such a Boolean expression b, when considered as such, it is interpreted in a single state of a computation, while when considered to be a QLTL formula it is interpreted in an infinite computation. The connection is as follows: $\sigma \models b$ (as a QLTL formula) iff $\sigma(0) \models b$ (as a Boolean expression).

Keeping this in mind we devise a translation function tr_p for any atomic proposition p which takes a regular expression E not containing p, and returns a QLTL formula $tr_p(E)$ that satisfies $\sigma \models tr_p(E)$ for any infinite computation σ iff $\sigma = \rho\sigma'$ for some finite computation part ρ and some infinite computation σ' such that $\rho \in L(E)$ and $\sigma' \models p$. This translation can easily be defined by induction on the structure of E.

$$tr_p(\bot) := \bot$$
$$tr_p(b) := b \wedge \mathsf{X}p$$
$$tr_p(E \cup F) := tr_p(E) \vee tr_p(F)$$
$$tr_p(E \cdot F) := tr_p(E)[tr_p(F)/p].$$

The latter denotes the replacement of every occurrence of p by $tr_p(F)$. It is important that p does not occur in E for otherwise this translation does not preserve equivalence.

Finally, we use existential quantification to mark segments in a finite computation path in order to translate regular expressions with a Kleene star.

$$tr_p(E^*) := p$$
$$\vee\; tr_p(E)$$
$$\vee\; \exists\, \mathrm{mark}.\, \mathrm{mark} \wedge \mathsf{F}(\mathrm{mark} \wedge p \wedge \mathsf{X}\mathsf{G}\neg\mathrm{mark}) \wedge$$
$$\mathsf{G}(\mathrm{mark} \wedge \mathsf{X}\mathsf{F}p \rightarrow tr_{\mathrm{mark}}(E)).$$

The first line is for the case in which a computation part satisfies E^* because of no iterations of E, the second line is for exactly one iteration of E, and the third disjunct handles the case of more than one iteration.

Finally, in order to translate the ω-regular expression $E = \bigcup_{i=1}^{n} E_i F_i^{\omega}$, we take a fresh atomic proposition mid that does not occur anywhere in E. It is only used as an auxiliary proposition to handle the top-level concatenations in E. It does not occur anywhere in the resulting QLTL formula which is

$$\bigvee_{i=1}^{n} tr_{\mathrm{mid}}(E_i)[tr(F_i^{\omega})/\mathrm{mid}]$$

where, as earlier, we use the replacement of every occurrence of mid. All that remains is to show how to translate the operator for infinite concatenations. This uses the same trick as the translation of the Kleene-star operator. In fact, it is much simpler.

$$tr(F^{\omega}) := \exists\, \mathrm{mark}.\, \mathrm{mark} \wedge \mathsf{G}\mathsf{F}\mathrm{mark} \wedge \mathsf{G}(\mathrm{mark} \rightarrow tr_{\mathrm{mark}}(F)). \qquad \square$$

Regular Languages via Fixpoints

The next translation we consider is that of ω-regular expressions into the linear-time μ-calculus because it is conceptually very similar to the previous one.

Theorem 10.1.8. For every ω-regular expression E there is a formula $\varphi_E \in \mathrm{LT}_{\mu}$ such that $\mathrm{Mod}(\varphi_E) = L(E)$. ∎

Proof. Again, we first devise a translation function tr_p that handles an ordinary regular expression of finite words and uses a fresh atomic proposition p as its 'continuation'. Recall that LT_μ is interpreted over infinite computations. The translation is, again, defined by induction on the structure of a regular expression in exactly the same way as in the previous proof for the target logic QLTL. The only, very minor, difference is the different notation for the next-time operator: while it is written X in LTL-like logics, we use $\bigcirc$ in LT_μ in order to avoid confusion with a second-order variable X.

Clearly, the Kleene-star or infinite-concatenation operators must be handled differently because LT_μ does not feature propositional quantification. Instead, we can use least fixpoints for finite iterations in

$$tr_p(E^*) := \mu X.p \vee tr_X(E).$$

Note that there is no syntactical (and not even semantical) difference between atomic propositions p and second-order variables X. This is why we can use X to 'mark' those moments in a computation at which a part that satisfies E starts. Finally, infinite concatenations can be expressed using greatest fixpoints via

$$tr_p(E^\omega) := \nu Y.tr_Y(E).$$

These ingredients are sufficient to translate an entire ω-regular expression $E = \bigcup_{i=1}^n E_i F_i^\omega$ such that $L(E) = \text{Mod}(tr(E))$. We leave it as Exercise 10.3 to show that this translation is correct. $\qquad\square$

The next result – an embedding of LT_μ into QLTL – is included here for two reasons. First of all, it saves us the effort of showing that LT_μ can be translated back into ω-regular expressions, as in Chapter 14 this will be done for QLTL (see Exercise 14.19). Second, it helps to understand the power of propositional quantification which can easily be used to express fixpoints. In fact, this is not the first place where this is being done; recall the translation of $\mathcal{L}_\mu$ into MSO in Theorem 8.6.4. The same principles are being used here.

Theorem 10.1.9. For every closed formula $\varphi \in LT_\mu$ there is a formula $\varphi' \in$ QLTL such that $\varphi' \equiv \varphi$. $\qquad\blacksquare$

Proof. The translation is entirely modular, by induction on the structure of LT_μ formulae. We only present the cases of quantified formulae. They are based on the characterisation of a least fixpoint as the intersection of all pre-fixpoints, and that of a greatest as the union over all post-fixpoints (cf. Theorem 2.2.3).

$$tr(\mu X.\psi) := \forall X.\big(\mathsf{G}(tr(\psi) \to \psi) \to X\big)$$
$$tr(\nu X.\psi) := \exists X.\big(\mathsf{G}(\psi \to tr(\psi)) \wedge X\big).$$

Correctness of this translation can be shown by induction on the structure of the LT_μ formula with a suitable interpretation of the free variables. $\qquad\square$

The presumption of φ being closed is, in fact, not necessary. The translation can be carried out for open formulae as well; the resulting QLTL formulae use propositional variables as quantified propositions anyway. At first sight this may look like a syntactical mismatch. In fact it is not, as there is no essential difference between an atomic proposition in a formula and a free propositional variable. Both need to be interpreted externally in order to provide meaning to the formula. For atomic propositions this is being done through their interpretation in an interpreted transition system, for free variables this is done through a variable assignment which can be regarded as an extension of the interpretation function in such an interpreted transition system. Technically it would have been easy not to introduce variables explicitly in $\mathcal{L}_\mu$, but simply (re-)use atomic propositions. The only reason for not doing so is the fact that quantification would override the interpretation in an interpreted transition system which may look confusing. It is certainly cleaner to distinguish between those propositions in an interpreted transition system that a formula has access to and those auxiliary ones, then called variables, that the formula only uses to formalise certain temporal properties.

Regular Expressive Power for PSL

Next we turn to PSL. Its operators cannot directly capture ω-regular expressions; in particular, there is no direct operator for limit construction in PSL as is needed for infinite repetitions. The closure operator of PSL would be a candidate for expressing properties that explicitly mention infinite behaviour but this one is, indeed, too weak. Still, PSL can express all ω-regular properties but the proof needs ω-regular expressions with some special property that allows the $\Diamond\!\!\!\rightarrow$ -operator to express an infinite behaviour.

Definition 10.1.10. Given two languages L and L$'$, let $L \setminus L'$ denote its **left quotient**, defined as $\{v \mid$ there is $u \in L$ with $uv \in L'\}$. Thus, it contains all leftovers of words in L$'$ when a prefix that belongs to L has been removed from them.

A language L is called **left-deletable** if $L \setminus L \subseteq L$. A regular expression is called **left-deletable** if its language is. We may also simply write $E \setminus F$ instead of $L(E) \setminus L(F)$ for the left quotient of the languages defined by the regular expressions E and F. $\qquad \nabla$

Example 10.1.11. Consider the regular expression $E := \mathsf{ba} + \mathsf{baa}$. It is not left-deletable because $E \setminus E$ is $\{\mathsf{a}\}$ which is not contained in E in itself. Note that there is a similarity to idempotency in the definition but it is still a different concept because $(\mathsf{ba} + \mathsf{baa})^*$ is idempotent but still not left-deletable because its left quotient with itself is $(\mathsf{ba} + \mathsf{baa})^*(\varepsilon + \mathsf{a})$ which is not contained in $(\mathsf{ba} + \mathsf{baa})^*$ either.

On the other hand, for instance, $(\mathsf{ba} + \mathsf{ab})^*$ is left-deletable.

Left-deletability has an important consequence: it allows the infinite repetition of a language to be expressed locally in terms of what follows after a finite repetition of this language.

Lemma 10.1.12. Let L be left-deletable with $\varepsilon \notin L$. Then $L^\omega = L_{\mathsf{init}} \cap L_{\mathsf{ind}}$ where

$$L_{\mathsf{init}} := \{\sigma \in (\mathcal{P}(\mathrm{PROP}))^\omega \mid \text{ there is } i > 0 \text{ such that } \sigma[0 \ldots i] \in L\},$$

$$L_{\mathsf{ind}} := \{\sigma \in (\mathcal{P}(\mathrm{PROP}))^\omega \mid \text{ for all } i > 0,$$

$$(\sigma[0 \ldots i] \in L^+ \text{ implies there is } j > i \text{ such that } \sigma[i+1 \ldots j] \in L\}. \qquad \blacksquare$$

Proof. '⊇' This direction is simple and does not even need the assumption of L being left-deletable. Suppose that $\sigma \in L_{\text{init}}$. Hence, $\sigma = \rho_1\sigma_1$ for some $\rho_1 \in L$ and some σ_1. Suppose that also $\sigma \in L_{\text{ind}}$. Since σ has the prefix ρ_1 which belongs to L and therefore in particular to L^+ it must be followed by a part in L, i.e. $\sigma = \rho_1\rho_2\sigma_2$ for some $\rho_2 \in L$. This can be iterated ad infinitum to show that $\sigma = \rho_1\rho_2\rho_3 \dots$ with $\rho_i \in L$ for all $i \in \mathbb{N}$. Thus, we get that $\sigma \in L^\omega$.

'⊆' Now suppose that $\sigma \in L^\omega$. Then there are $i_0 < i_1 < i_2 \dots$ with $i_0 = 0$ such that $\sigma[i_j \dots i_{j+1} - 1] \in L$ for all $j \in \mathbb{N}$. Since L is presumed to be left-deletable we can assume this chain of positions in σ to be maximal. In particular, for every $j \in \mathbb{N}$ there is no k with $i_j < k < i_{j+1}$ such that $\sigma[i_j \dots k - 1] \in L$. For, if this was the case, then by left-deletability we would also have that $\sigma[k \dots i_{j+1} - 1] \in L$ and therefore k could have been included in the chain $i_0 < i_1 \dots$. In other words, for every $i \in \mathbb{N}$ we have that $\sigma[0 \dots i] \notin L^+$ or $i = i_j$ for some $j \geq 1$ and then $\sigma[i \dots i_{j+1} - 1] \in L$. This shows that $\sigma \in L_{\text{ind}}$. Since $\sigma[0 \dots i_1 - 1] \in L$ we also have $\sigma \in L_{\text{init}}$.   □

It should be clear that the ω-iteration of a left-deletable regular expression E can therefore be expressed in PSL via $(E \diamondsuit\!\!\rightarrow \top) \wedge (E^+ \square\!\!\rightarrow X(E \diamondsuit\!\!\rightarrow \top))$. Thus, the only part that is missing in order to show that PSL can express all ω-regular properties is a result which states that every ω-regular language can be described by ω-regular expressions in which the ω-operator is only applied to left-deletable regular expressions. This is, in fact, true but its proof relies on some automata-theoretic constructions which are mainly used in Chapter 15 on games for temporal logics. This result is therefore presented as Theorem 15.2.12.

Theorem 10.1.13. For every ω-regular expression E there is a formula $\varphi_E \in$ PSL such that $\text{Mod}(\varphi_E) = L(E)$.   ∎

Proof. Every ω-regular expression E can be translated into a nondeterministic Büchi automaton, see Chapter 14. It can be translated into a deterministic parity automaton from which we can translate back into an ω-regular expression of the form $\bigcup_{i=1}^n E_iF_i^\omega$ such that each F_i is left-deletable (cf. Theorem 15.2.12). Then this language is described by the PSL formula

$$\varphi_E := \bigvee_{i=1}^n E_i \diamondsuit\!\!\rightarrow X\big((F_i \diamondsuit\!\!\rightarrow \top) \wedge (F_i^+ \square\!\!\rightarrow X(F_i \diamondsuit\!\!\rightarrow \top))\big)$$

using Lemma 10.1.12.   □

From One Automata-Based Logic to the Other

Let E be a semi-extended regular expression (SERE, recall the definition from Section 6.7.3) built over Boolean expressions with atomic propositions in Π. Operators in such expressions include union, composition, Kleene star operator and intersection (see Section 6.7.3). We write $L(E)$ to denote the set of finite parts of a computation $\rho : [n] \rightarrow \mathcal{P}(\Pi)$ for some $n \geq 0$ such that $\rho \models E$.

Proposition 10.1.14. Given a semi-extended regular expression E built over Boolean expressions with atomic propositions in Π, there is a finite-state automaton $\mathcal{A}$ such that $\mathrm{L}(\mathcal{A}) = \mathrm{L}(E)$ and $\mathcal{A}$ has a number of states exponential in the size of E. ∎

If we discard the intersection operator in SEREs (leading to standard regular expressions), we know that such an automaton exists and it can have at most a number of states that is polynomial in the size of E. Products of finite-state automata need to be considered when the intersection operator is allowed, which explains the potential exponential amount of states in $\mathcal{A}$.

Let $E \Diamond\!\!\rightarrow \psi$ be a PSL formula such that $\varepsilon \in \mathrm{L}(E)$. It is easy to show that $E \Diamond\!\!\rightarrow \psi$ is logically equivalent to the formula $\psi \vee ((E \cap (p \vee \neg p)(p \vee \neg p)^*) \Diamond\!\!\rightarrow \psi$ where p occurs in E (for instance). Note that $\varepsilon \notin \mathrm{L}((E \cap (p \vee \neg p)(p \vee \neg p)^*)$. That is why, in the sequel, without any loss of generality, we can assume that if $E \Diamond\!\!\rightarrow \psi$ occurs as a subformula, then $\varepsilon \notin \mathrm{L}(E)$ (otherwise we apply the preceding transformation as many times as necessary).

Similarly, note that $\mathrm{Cl}(E)$ is equivalent to $\top$ as soon as ε belongs to $\mathrm{L}(E)$. That is why, in the sequel, without any loss of generality, we can assume that if $\mathrm{Cl}(E)$ occurs as a subformula, then $\varepsilon \notin \mathrm{L}(E)$.

Lemma 10.1.15. Let E be a semi-extended regular expression built over the atomic propositions in $\Pi = \{p_1, \ldots, p_n\}$ such that $\varepsilon \notin \mathrm{L}(E)$ and p be an atomic proposition. There exist a finite-state automaton $\mathcal{A}_E$ over an alphabet of cardinality 2^{n+1} and 2^{n+1} formulae ψ_0, $\ldots, \psi_{2^n-1}, \psi'_0, \ldots, \psi'_{2^n-1}$ that are conjunctions of literals from $\Pi \cup \{p\}$ such that $E \Diamond\!\!\rightarrow p$ and the ETL formula $\psi = \mathcal{A}_E(\psi_0, \ldots, \psi_{2^n-1}, \psi'_0, \ldots, \psi'_{2^n-1})$ are equivalent, i.e. for all the models σ and positions $i \in \mathbb{N}$, we have $\sigma, i \models E \Diamond\!\!\rightarrow p$ iff $\sigma, i \models \psi$. ∎

Proof. Let $\mathcal{A} = (\Sigma, Q, Q_0, \delta, F)$ be a nondeterministic finite-state automaton such that $\mathrm{L}(\mathcal{A}) = \mathrm{L}(E)$ (by application of Proposition 10.1.14). Without any loss of generality, we can assume that no state in F has an outgoing transition and $Q_0 \cap F = \emptyset$ (since by assumption $\varepsilon \notin \mathrm{L}(E)$). So, whenever a transition is visited and it leads to a state in F, this is the last transition to be fired.

Let $\mathcal{A}_E := (\Sigma', Q, Q_0, \delta', F)$ be the finite-state automaton defined from $\mathcal{A}$ as follows:

- $\Sigma' := \{a_0, \ldots, a_{2^n-1}, b_0, \ldots, b_{2^n-1}\}$ and the letters of Σ' are linearly ordered according to the preceding presentation,
- $q \xrightarrow{a_i} q' \in \delta'$ iff $q' \notin F$, $q \xrightarrow{\Pi_i} q' \in \delta$ where Π_i is the unique subset of Π that contains exactly the atomic proposition p_j such that the jth bit of i is equal to 1,
- $q \xrightarrow{b_i} q' \in \delta'$ iff $q' \in F$ and $q \xrightarrow{\Pi_i} q' \in \delta$ and Π_i satisfies the preceding condition too.

So, the difference between a transition labelled by a_i and a transition labelled by b_i is not related to the truth of atomic propositions but rather to the fact that a transition labelled by b_i is the last transition to be fired. And precisely, the atomic proposition p should hold at the last position of the pattern from $\mathrm{L}(E)$. For every $i \in [0, 2^n - 1]$, we denote $i|0 := \{j \mid$ the jth bit of i is 0 $\}$ and $i|1 := \{j \mid$ the jth bit of i is 1 $\}$. Then we have:

1. $\psi_i := (\bigwedge_{j \in i|1} p_j) \wedge (\bigwedge_{j \in i|0} \neg p_j)$,
2. $\psi'_i := \psi_i \wedge p$.

It is easy to show that $E \diamondsuit\!\rightarrow p$ is equivalent to the ETL formula

$$\psi = \mathcal{A}_E(\psi_0, \ldots, \psi_{2^n-1}, \psi'_0, \ldots, \psi'_{2^n-1})$$

(this is left as Exercise 10.4). It is worth noting that there is an exponential blow-up from the size of $E \diamondsuit\!\rightarrow p$ to the size of ψ. Furthermore, the formulae $\psi_0, \ldots, \psi_{2^n-1}, \psi'_0, \ldots, \psi'_{2^n-1}$ are indeed conjunctions of literals from $\Pi \cup \{p\}$. $\square$

Now we deal with the closure operator.

Lemma 10.1.16. Let E be a semi-extended regular expression built over the atomic propositions in $\Pi = \{p_1, \ldots, p_n\}$ such that $\varepsilon \notin L(E)$. There is a finite-state automaton $\mathcal{B}_E$ over an alphabet of cardinality 2^n and 2^n formulae $\psi_0, \ldots, \psi_{2^n-1}$ that are conjunctions of literals from Π such that $\neg Cl(E)$ and the ETL formula $\psi = \mathcal{B}_E(\psi_0, \ldots, \psi_{2^n-1})$ are equivalent, i.e. for all the models σ and positions $i \in \mathbb{N}$, we have $\sigma, i \models \neg Cl(E)$ iff $\sigma, i \models \psi$.   ∎

Proof. Let $\Sigma = \mathcal{P}(\Pi)$.

(a) We start with a few definitions and observations. Given a language $L \subseteq \Sigma^*$ we write $\mathrm{pref}(L)$ to denote its set of **prefixes**. Formally, we have:

$$\mathrm{pref}(L) := \{u \in \Sigma^* \mid \exists v \text{ such that } u \cdot v \in L\}.$$

Let $\mathcal{A} = (\Sigma, Q, Q_0, \delta, F)$ be a finite-state automaton and $Q' \subseteq Q$ be the set of states for which there is a path to a state in F. Let $\mathcal{A}' = (\Sigma, Q', Q'_0, \delta', Q')$ be the finite-state automaton obtained from $\mathcal{A}$ by removing the states in $Q \setminus Q'$ and by requiring that the set of final states is precisely Q'. One can show that $\mathrm{pref}(L(\mathcal{A})) = L(\mathcal{A}')$. Since regular languages are (effectively) closed under complementation, and by using Proposition 10.1.14, one can build a finite-state automaton $\mathcal{B}_1$ such that $L(\mathcal{B}_1) = \Sigma^* \setminus \mathrm{pref}(L(E))$.

(b) Let $\mathcal{A} = (\Sigma, Q, q_0, \delta, F)$ be a complete and deterministic finite-state automaton with $q_0 \notin F$ and $Q' \subseteq Q$ be the set of states q for which there is a path from q_0 to q without passing via a state in F. As usual, completeness and determinism means that from any state, there is exactly one transition labelled by a given letter. Let $\mathcal{B}_2 = (\Sigma, Q', Q'_0, \delta', Q')$ be the finite-state automaton obtained from $\mathcal{A}$ by removing the states in $Q \setminus Q'$ and by requiring that the set of final states is equal to Q'. One can show that $L(\mathcal{B}_2)$ is precisely the words in Σ^* such that none of the prefixes belongs to $L(\mathcal{A})$. We will write $\mathcal{B}_2$ to denote the finite-state automaton that accepts the words such that none of the prefixes belongs to $L(E)$.

(c) Further, we show how the nonsatisfaction of $Cl(E)$ is related to the automaton constructions in (a) and (b). Let σ be a linear model and $i \in \mathbb{N}$. The following conditions are equivalent:

1. $\sigma, i \models \neg Cl(E)$,
2. not $(\sigma, i \models Cl(E))$,

3. not (for all $j \geq i$, there is σ' such that $\sigma[i, j]\sigma' \models E \diamondsuit\!\!\rightarrow \top$),
4. not (for all $j \geq i$, either there is $j' \in [i, j]$ such that $\sigma[i, j'] \in L(E)$ or $\sigma[i, j] \in$ pref(L(E))),
5. there is $j \geq i$ such that (for all $j' \in [i, j]$, we have $\sigma[i, j'] \notin L(E)$) and $\sigma[i, j] \notin$ pref(L(E))).

That is why, we need the constructions introduced in (a) and (b). Now, it is time to define $\mathcal{B}_E$ formally.

(d) Since regular languages are (effectively) closed under intersection, let $\mathcal{B} = (\Sigma, Q, Q_0, \delta, F)$ be the finite-state automaton such that $L(\mathcal{B}) = L(\mathcal{B}_1) \cap L(\mathcal{B}_2)$ where the respective finite-state automata from which $\mathcal{B}_1$ and $\mathcal{B}_2$ are built both accept $L(E)$. Let $\mathcal{B}_E := (\Sigma', Q, Q_0, \delta', F)$ be the finite-state automaton obtained from $\mathcal{B}$ defined as follows:

- $\Sigma' := \{a_0, \ldots, a_{2^n-1}\}$ and the letters of Σ' are linearly ordered according to the earlier presentation,
- $q \xrightarrow{a_i} q' \in \delta'$ iff $q \xrightarrow{\Pi_i} q' \in \delta$ where Π_i is the unique subset of Π that contains exactly the atomic proposition p_j such that the jth bit of i is equal to 1.

Moreover, for every $i \in [0, 2^n - 1]$,

$$\psi_i := \left(\bigwedge_{j \in i|1} p_j \right) \wedge \left(\bigwedge_{j \in i|0} \neg p_j \right).$$

It is easy to show that $\neg\mathrm{Cl}(E)$ is equivalent to $\psi = \mathcal{B}_E(\psi_0, \ldots, \psi_{2^n-1})$. □

Theorem 10.1.17. *For every formula $\varphi \in \mathrm{PSL}$ there is a $\varphi' \in \mathrm{ETL}$ such that $\varphi' \equiv \varphi$.* ∎

Proof. Let us define the map *tr* as follows:

- $tr(p) := p$ for every atomic proposition p,
- *tr* is homomorphic for Boolean connectives,
- $tr(\mathsf{X}\varphi) := \mathcal{A}_\mathsf{X}(\top, tr(\varphi))$ with $L(\mathcal{A}_\mathsf{X}) = a \cdot b$,
- $tr(\varphi\mathsf{U}\psi) := \mathcal{A}_\mathsf{U}(tr(\varphi), tr(\psi))$ with $L(\mathcal{A}_\mathsf{U}) = a^* \cdot b$,
  (The translation for X-formulae and U-formulae is quite standard and it simply witnesses that LTL can be viewed as a fragment of ETL.)
- $tr(E \diamondsuit\!\!\rightarrow \varphi) := tr(\varphi) \vee \mathcal{A}_E(\psi_0, \ldots, \psi_{2^n-1}, \psi'_0, \ldots, \psi'_{2^n-1})$ when $\varepsilon \in L(E)$, E contains the atomic propositions $p_1, \ldots, p_n$ and $\mathcal{A}_E$ is the finite-state automaton built from the proof of Lemma 10.1.15. Moreover, for every $i \in [0, 2^n - 1]$, $\psi_i := (\bigwedge_{j \in i|1} p_j) \wedge (\bigwedge_{j \in i|0} \neg p_j)$ and $\psi'_i := \psi_i \wedge tr(\varphi)$.
- Similarly, $tr(E \diamondsuit\!\!\rightarrow \varphi) := \mathcal{A}_E(\psi_0, \ldots, \psi_{2^n-1}, \psi'_0, \ldots, \psi'_{2^n-1})$ when $\varepsilon \notin L(E)$ and E contains the atomic propositions $p_1, \ldots, p_n$.
- $tr(\mathrm{Cl}(E)) := \neg\mathcal{B}_E(\psi_0, \ldots, \psi_{2^n-1})$, if $\varepsilon \notin L(E)$ and E contains the atomic propositions $p_1, \ldots, p_n$ and $\mathcal{B}_E$ is the finite-state automaton built from the proof of Lemma 10.1.16. Each formula ψ_i is defined as earlier.
- $tr(\mathrm{Cl}(E)) := \top$ if $\varepsilon \in L(E)$.

The proof is then by structural induction on the formulae by using Lemmas 10.1.15 and 10.1.16.   □

Summing up the translations from ω-regular expressions into various linear-time temporal logics (and back using nondeterministic Büchi automata in Chapter 14) we obtain that these all share the same expressive power. Note that LTL can be translated into ω-regular expressions but the converse does not hold.

Corollary 10.1.18. The linear-time logics ETL, QLTL, PSL and LT$_\mu$ are expressively equivalent.   ■

10.1.3 Eliminating Past Operators

As a final result in the world of linear-time logics we establish the expressive equivalence of LTL and LTL+Past on linear models based on $\mathbb{N}$. This is just the final goal, though. We will develop the technicalities that lead to this based on an interpretation of these logics on $\mathbb{Z}$-models. Thus, all the equivalences stated in the following are to be understood with respect to such models (and in fact some do not hold on models that are based on $\mathbb{N}$).

Definition 10.1.19. A **pure future formula** is an LTL+Past formula built from atomic propositions using Boolean operators and the temporal operators X and U only – i.e. just an LTL formula. A **pure past formula** is any formula of LTL+Past built up from atomic propositions using Boolean operators and only past-time temporal operators, Y and S (and those definable in terms of them).   ∨

First, we observe some equivalences in LTL+Past. We leave it to the reader to verify that these hold indeed. The first one shows how the X-operator and the Y-operator commute with other temporal operators, the second one shows how the temporal operators commute with Boolean operators.

Lemma 10.1.20. The following are equivalences in LTL+Past.

- $X(\varphi U\psi) \equiv (X\varphi)UX\psi$ and $X(\varphi S\psi) \equiv (X\varphi)SX\psi$,
- $Y(\varphi U\psi) \equiv (Y\varphi)U(Y\psi)$ and $Y(\varphi S\psi) \equiv (Y\varphi)S(Y\psi)$,
- $XG\varphi \equiv GX\varphi$ and $XG^{-1}\varphi \equiv G^{-1}X\varphi$,
- $YG\varphi \equiv GY\varphi$ and $YG^{-1}\varphi \equiv G^{-1}Y\varphi$,
- $XY\varphi \equiv \varphi$ and $YX\varphi \equiv \varphi$.   ■

Proofs are omitted and are left as Exercise 6.38. Some more equivalences can be established dealing with Boolean connectives.

Lemma 10.1.21. The following are also equivalences in LTL+Past.

- $(\varphi_1 \wedge \varphi_2)U\psi \equiv (\varphi_1 U\psi) \wedge (\varphi_2 U\psi)$ and $(\varphi_1 \wedge \varphi_2)S\psi \equiv (\varphi_1 S\psi) \wedge (\varphi_2 S\psi)$,
- $\psi U(\varphi_1 \vee \varphi_2) \equiv (\psi U\varphi_1) \vee (\psi U\varphi_2)$ and $\psi S(\varphi_1 \vee \varphi_2) \equiv (\psi S\varphi_1) \vee (\psi S\varphi_2)$,
- $G(\varphi_1 \wedge \varphi_2) \equiv G\varphi_1 \wedge G\varphi_2$ and $G^{-1}(\varphi_1 \wedge \varphi_2) \equiv G^{-1}\varphi_1 \wedge G^{-1}\varphi_2$.   ■

Proofs are omitted and are left as Exercise 6.39. The key result for the inspired equivalence proof is the following theorem.

Theorem 10.1.22 (Gabbay's Separation Theorem). Every formula of LTL+Past is equivalent to a Boolean combination of pure future and pure past formulae. ∎

Proof. (Sketch) The separation of an arbitrary LTL+Past formula into pure future and pure past parts is achieved by applying several equivalence-preserving replacements of subformulae. The purpose of these replacements is to reduce the nesting of future and past operators. We will illustrate the reduction with one such case; the others are similar and left to the reader as exercises.

Let $\varphi \in$ LTL+Past. According to Lemma 6.5.2 we can assume it to be in negation normal form. According to Lemma 10.1.20 we can even assume that φ is built from atomic formulae of the form $X^k \ell$ and $Y^k \ell$ where ℓ is a literal and $k \in \mathbb{N}$, using the temporal operators U, G and their counterparts for the past only.

Next one can transform Boolean combinations inside φ into disjunctive or conjunctive normal form and push temporal operators further inwards via the equivalences given in Lemma 10.1.21 such that every U-formula and every S-formula does not have a disjunction as their right argument and not a conjunction as their left argument, and the arguments of G- and G^{-1}-formulae are no conjunctions either.

If φ is not in the required form already, then it contains a subformula of the form $\varphi_1 U(\varphi_2 \wedge (\varphi_3 S\varphi_4))$ for instance. Now consider any model σ, i for this subformula. Clearly, there must be a position $i' \geq i$ such that the U-formula gets fulfilled at the position i'. Furthermore, there must be a position $i'' \leq i'$ such that the S-formula gets fulfilled at the position i''. We can distinguish three cases depending on the order of i'' relative to i and i'.

The simplest case is that of $i \leq i' = i''$ which is shown as follows.

If we have $i'' < i \leq i'$ then a model looks as follows.

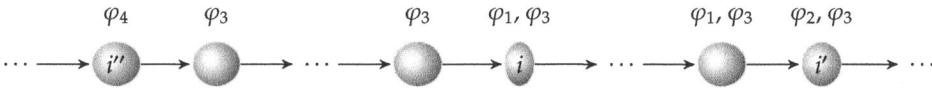

Finally, if we have $i \leq i'' < i'$ then it looks as follows.

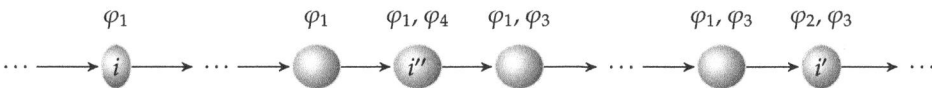

Hence, we have the equivalence

$$\varphi_1 \cup (\varphi_2 \wedge (\varphi_3 S \varphi_4)) \equiv \varphi_1 \cup (\varphi_2 \wedge \varphi_4)$$
$$\vee \left(((\varphi_1 \wedge \varphi_3) \cup (\varphi_2 \wedge \varphi_3)) \wedge (\varphi_3 \ S \ \varphi_4) \right)$$
$$\vee \varphi_1 \cup \left(\varphi_1 \wedge \varphi_4 \wedge \ X \ ((\varphi_1 \wedge \varphi_3) \cup (\varphi_2 \wedge \varphi_3)) \right).$$

A well-founded measuring function can be defined showing that rewriting according to such equivalences eventually yields a formula without any nesting of future with past temporal operators. The remaining cases are left as exercises.   □

We now obtain the expressive equivalence of LTL and LTL+Past as a simple consequence of this theorem.

Corollary 10.1.23 (Equivalence of LTL and LTL+Past). For every LTL+Past formula φ there is a pure LTL formula ψ such that $\varphi \equiv_0 \psi$ (initial equivalence) over every linear model based on $\mathbb{N}$.   ■

Proof. Using Theorem 10.1.22 one can separate φ into a Boolean combination of pure future and pure past formulae. Interpreting such a formula over a linear model based on $\mathbb{N}$ requires the pure past formulae to hold at the initial position 0 of the model. It is not hard to see that each $\psi S \psi'$ can – in such a case – be replaced by ψ', every $Y^k \psi$ with $k > 0$ can be replaced by $\bot$, etc., thus eliminating all occurrences of past operators whilst preserving equivalence.   □

Clearly, this equivalence cannot hold over models based on $\mathbb{Z}$ (see its definition in Section 6.5.2), where past-time operators clearly add more expressive power because formulae of LTL are clearly insensitive to the part of the model in the past of the point of evaluation.

10.2 Embeddings among Branching-Time Logics

10.2.1 From Linear to Branching Time

The purpose of this section is to link linear-time to branching-time temporal logics with respect to expressive power. Recall that according to Theorem 10.1.6 every formula of the linear-time logics LTL, ETL, PSL and QLTL can be translated into an ω-regular expression, and according to Theorem 10.1.8 each of these can be translated into a formula of the linear-time μ-calculus again. LT_μ is a fragment of the modal μ-calculus, so does this mean that every linear-time property expressible in either of these logics is also expressible in the modal μ-calculus? The answer is yes, but the reasoning in the last two sentences is misleading. LT_μ is a *semantical* fragment of $\mathcal{L}_\mu$ which is obtained by restricting the class of structures that it is interpreted over. So every such linear-time property – interpreted on linear-time models – is of course expressible in the modal μ-calculus because it is expressible in the linear-time μ-calculus according to Corollary 10.1.18.

A more difficult question asks for the expressive power of linear-time temporal logics, relative to branching-time logics, on the class of all interpreted transition systems. This of course only makes sense using the implicit universal or existential path semantics, i.e. we say that a state s of an ITS $\mathcal{T}$ satisfies a linear-time property φ if *all*, respectively *some* computation starting in s satisfies φ under the usual linear-time semantics. First of all we observe that the linear-time logics considered here are all closed under negation, and so is the modal μ-calculus. Thus, it does not matter whether we choose the universal or existential path semantics; either a translation is possible for both or for none. Borrowing notation from CTL* we see that $\mathcal{T}, s \models \mathsf{A}\varphi$ iff $\mathcal{T}, s \models \neg\mathsf{E}\neg\varphi$ holds for any $\mathcal{T}$, s and linear-time property φ. Thus, suppose it was possible to find an $\mathcal{L}_\mu$ formula φ' that is equivalent (over all ITS) to $\mathsf{E}\varphi$, then one could translate the same logic under the universal path semantics into $\mathcal{L}_\mu$ by translating $\neg\varphi$ under the existential path semantics and then negating the result.

For convenience we will carry out the translations under the existential path semantics, unless otherwise specified. We will also sometimes be harmlessly imprecise and write $\mathsf{E}\varphi$ with φ being some linear-time property, even though we may not have formally defined the extension of that logic with branching-time path quantifiers. This will not be necessary in the subsequent contexts; we only use it to denote the property of ITS that is derived from this linear-time property under the existential path semantics.

According to the preceding comments, it would suffice to translate a formula $\varphi \in \mathrm{LT}_\mu$ into a $\varphi' \in \mathcal{L}_\mu$ such that for all $\mathcal{T}$ and s we have $\mathcal{T}, s \models \varphi'$ iff $\mathcal{T}, s \models \mathsf{E}\varphi$, i.e. there is a computation σ starting in s such that $\sigma \models \varphi$. It is tempting to construct φ' by simply replacing every modality $\bigcirc$ by $\Diamond$. This is not correct in general, though.

Example 10.2.1. Consider the LT_μ formula $\bigcirc q \wedge \bigcirc \neg q$. It is clearly unsatisfiable. This also carries over to the existential or universal path semantics; there is no ITS state such that some or all of its computations satisfy both q and $\neg q$ after one step.

On the other hand, the $\mathcal{L}_\mu$ formula $\Diamond q \wedge \Diamond \neg q$ is satisfiable in a state that has two different successors.

This simple translation from LT_μ to $\mathcal{L}_\mu$ under the existential path semantics works for a fragment of LT_μ, though.

Definition 10.2.2. An LT_μ formula φ in negation normal form is called **separated** if for every $\psi \wedge \psi' \in sub(\varphi)$ at least one of ψ and ψ' does not contain any $\bigcirc$-operator. $\qquad\triangledown$

This concept should be easy to grasp, yet we consider some simple examples with the original task of translating LT_μ into $\mathcal{L}_\mu$ in mind.

Example 10.2.3. The LT_μ formula $\bigcirc q \wedge \bigcirc \neg q$ of the previous example is not separated. The formula $\varphi := \bigcirc q \vee \bigcirc \neg q$ is separated, and note that $\mathsf{E}\varphi$ is indeed equivalent to $\Diamond q \vee \Diamond \neg q$. This is easy to verify, but it can also be seen as follows: the E-operator commutes with disjunctions so we have

$$\mathsf{E}(\bigcirc q \vee \bigcirc \neg q) \equiv \mathsf{E}\bigcirc q \vee \mathsf{E}\bigcirc \neg q \equiv \Diamond q \vee \Diamond \neg q.$$

$\bigcirc q \wedge \bigcirc \bigcirc \neg q$ is not separated but it can easily be transformed into a separated formula because the $\bigcirc$-operator commutes with all Boolean operators. Hence, it is equivalent to $\bigcirc (q \wedge \bigcirc \neg q)$, and we leave it as an exercise to verify that replacing every $\bigcirc$ by $\Diamond$ yields a $\mathcal{L}_\mu$ formula that is equivalent to it under the existential path semantics.

In order to complete the link from linear-time logics to the modal μ-calculus, we only need two more steps. The first one is an observation about the formulae that the translation from ω-regular expressions into LT_μ produces. The straightforward check is left as Exercise 10.11.

Lemma 10.2.4. Let E be an ω-regular expression and let φ_E be its translation into LT_μ according to the construction in Theorem 10.1.8. Then φ_E is separated. ∎

The second step consists of showing that the simple replacement of $\bigcirc$-operators by $\Diamond$-operators is correct for separated formulae.

Lemma 10.2.5. Let ψ be a separated LT_μ formula and $\widehat{\varphi}$ result from it by replacing every $\bigcirc$-operator in it with $\Diamond$. Then for every ITS $\mathcal{T}$ and all of its states s we have $\mathcal{T}, s \vdash \mathrm{E}\varphi$ iff $\mathcal{T}, s \models \widehat{\varphi}$. ∎

Proof. We will argue using model-checking games. For $\mathcal{L}_\mu$ they have been defined in Section 8.4. This can be used to characterise whether $\mathcal{T}, s \models \widehat{\varphi}$ holds. In order to characterise the truth value of $\mathcal{T}, s \models \mathrm{E}\varphi$, we need a similar model-checking game. We avoid a formal introduction and correctness proof; instead we introduce it briefly as a variant of the $\mathcal{L}_\mu$ model-checking games and leave the correctness proof as an exercise. Remember that the property of being separated implies negation normal form.

In the game on $\mathcal{T}$, s and $\mathrm{E}\varphi$ – denoted $\mathcal{G}^\mathcal{T}(s, \mathrm{E}\varphi)$ – player **V** first chooses an entire computation path σ starting in s. Then the two players proceed to play the ordinary model-checking game $\mathcal{G}^\sigma(s, \varphi)$. Whenever this game reaches a position with a formula of the form $\bigcirc \psi$ then it proceeds deterministically to the next state in σ and ψ.

First of all we observe the following. If player **V** has a winning strategy in $\mathcal{G}^\mathcal{T}(s, \mathrm{E}\varphi)$ then she has a winning strategy in $\mathcal{G}^\mathcal{T}(s, \widehat{\varphi})$: if it is possible for her to reveal the entire path at the beginning and then win against the remaining choice, then it surely is possible for her to do the same and only choose this path stepwise whenever needed because of a modal $\Diamond$-operator. This yields direction '$\Rightarrow$' of this lemma, and it does not even need the requirement of φ being separated.

For the direction '$\Leftarrow$' suppose she has a winning strategy $\mathfrak{str}$ for the game $\mathcal{G}^\mathcal{T}(s, \widehat{\varphi})$. Consider the tree of all plays won by her. That is, the root is the starting configuration $(s, \widehat{\varphi})$, and every node in which player **V** chooses has a unique successor whereas player **R** nodes have all possible successors in this tree. Furthermore, every path forms a play that conform to the winning strategy $\mathfrak{str}$ and is therefore won by player **V**. Next we note that player **R**'s choices in this tree are restricted: $\widehat{\varphi}$ does not contain any $\Box$-operators; hence, player **R** never makes any choices with rule ($\Box$). Thus, whenever **R** makes a choice, it is done for rule ($\wedge$), i.e. he chooses one of two conjuncts in a subformula $\psi_1 \wedge \psi_2$ of $\widehat{\varphi}$. Now that φ was assumed to be separated, at least one of them does not contain any $\Diamond$-operators. Since such operators are the only ones that trigger the choice of a new state in $\mathcal{T}$, the tree of all plays conforming to $\mathfrak{str}$ contains exactly one path such that all others traverse a prefix of its underlying path in $\mathcal{T}$. In other words, the entire game restricted to the strategy $\mathfrak{str}$ is only being played on a single path through $\mathcal{T}$, and player $\mathbf{R}$ can at most choose to refute subformulae in a single state of this path.

This suffices to define a winning strategy for player $\mathbf{V}$ in $\mathcal{G}^{\mathcal{T}}(s, \mathsf{E}\varphi)$: at the beginning choose this determined infinite path, then play according to the strategy $\mathfrak{str}$ in $\mathcal{G}^{\mathcal{T}}(s, \widehat{\varphi})$. It should be clear that any play conforming to this strategy is also winning because it corresponds directly to a play in $\mathcal{G}^{\mathcal{T}}(s, \widehat{\varphi})$ that conforms to $\mathfrak{str}$. $\qquad\square$

Putting these observations together we obtain a translation from the linear-time to the modal μ-calculus under the existential path semantics. Once again, this may seem like a trivial result but it is not. It is not clear whether a simple translation based purely on syntactic principles exists; instead it seems like one needs semantical machinery like ω-regular expressions as were used here or Büchi automata for instance.

The following result places the translation of the linear-time temporal logic LT_μ into a low level of the alternation hierarchy in the modal μ-calculus (cf. Definition 8.3.6 for the definition of Π_2).

Theorem 10.2.6. For every $\varphi \in \mathrm{LT}_\mu$ there is a $\psi \in \Pi_2$ such that for all $\mathcal{T}$ and all its states s we get $\mathcal{T}, s \models \mathsf{E}\varphi$ iff $\mathcal{T}, s \models \psi$. $\qquad\blacksquare$

Proof. Take a formula $\varphi \in \mathrm{LT}_\mu$. According to Theorem 10.1.6 whose proof needs techniques that are being introduced in Chapter 14 there is an equivalent ω-regular expression E. According to Lemma 10.2.4 it can be translated back into LT_μ such that the resulting formula φ' is separated. Moreover, a close inspection of the underlying construction reveals that φ' belongs to Π_2. Finally, according to Lemma 10.2.5 it can be translated into a $\mathcal{L}_\mu$ formula that is equivalent to it under the existential path semantics. Again, an easy inspection of that translation, which only replaces modal operators, reveals that the resulting formula $\psi := \widehat{\varphi'}$ belongs to Π_2 if φ' does so. $\qquad\square$

The fact that the translation from LT_μ into the modal μ-calculus is far less trivial than the similarity of the two logics' names suggests is also hinted at by complexity considerations. We give upper bounds on these translations and leave it as Exercise 10.12 to verify that they are correct.

- An LT_μ formula of size n and alternation depth k can be translated into an equivalent (under the existential path semantics) $\mathcal{L}_\mu$ formula of size $2^{\mathcal{O}(n^2 k \log n)}$.
- As a consequence, an LTL formula can be translated like that into an $\mathcal{L}_\mu$ formula of size $2^{\mathcal{O}(n^2 \log n)}$.

10.2.2 Translating CTL* and ATL* into the Modal Mu-Calculus

With the instruments of the previous section at hand it is possible to provide a very simple
proof for an important embedding in the world of branching-time logics, namely that of the
full branching-time logic CTL* into the modal μ-calculus.

Theorem 10.2.7. For every state formula $\varphi \in$ CTL* there is a formula $\psi \in \mathcal{L}_\mu$ such that
$\psi \equiv \varphi$ and $|\psi| = 2^{\mathcal{O}(|\varphi| \cdot \log |\varphi|)}$.   ∎

Proof. Recall that any CTL* formula can be equivalently written using no universal path
quantifiers A but only existential ones E and negation. We translate such formulae inductively into $\mathcal{L}_\mu$ as follows. The induction is on the nesting depth of existential path quantifiers. Suppose that φ is of the form $\mathsf{E}\varphi'$ such that φ' contains no existential path quantifiers
(and therefore no path quantifiers at all). Then φ' is an LTL formula, and according to
Theorem 10.2.6 there is an $\mathcal{L}_\mu$ formula ψ that is equivalent to φ, and its size is bounded
accordingly by the remark after this theorem.

For the inductive step we can assume that φ – being a state formula – is of the form
$\mathsf{E}\varphi'$ or $\neg\mathsf{E}\varphi'$ for some φ'. Clearly, its nesting depth of existential path quantifiers is strictly
smaller than that of φ. We only consider the former case; the latter is carried out identically.
Take a maximal genuine subformula of the form $\mathsf{E}\varphi''$ in φ'. By the hypothesis it can be
translated into an equivalent $\mathcal{L}_\mu$ formula ψ''. Take a new atomic proposition r_1 and replace
$\mathsf{E}\varphi''$ by it in φ'. This is iterated until φ'' contains no more existential path quantifiers but
additional atomic propositions $r_1, \ldots, r_m$. Again, we can use Theorem 10.2.6 to translate
$\mathsf{E}\varphi'(r_1, \ldots, r_m)$ into $\mathcal{L}_\mu$. The resulting formula will of course feature the new atomic propositions $r_1, \ldots, r_m$ in general but they were only used temporarily and can now be replaced
by the $\mathcal{L}_\mu$ formulae for the original CTL* formulae of the form $\mathsf{E}\varphi''$ that they substituted
in the first place. Note that each $\mathcal{L}_\mu$ formula used in this way is closed, and therefore this
substitution is sound.

The size estimation follows from the remark after Theorem 10.2.6.   □

It is worth noting that the formulae obtained in this way by translating CTL* into $\mathcal{L}_\mu$
have bounded alternation depth. We leave it as Exercise 10.13 to verify that this is indeed
the case. We also leave it as Exercise 10.14 to extend this translation to ECTL*.

We can combine the techniques used in Theorem 9.3.6 (translating ATL into $\mathcal{L}_\mu$) and
Theorem 10.2.7 in order to obtain a translation from the alternating-time temporal logic
ATL* into $\mathcal{L}_\mu$. Since ATL* is interpreted over special transition systems, namely CGMs, this
translation is not equivalence preserving in a strict sense. However, if we fix the canonical
encoding of CGMs as transition systems then $\mathcal{L}_\mu$ can be interpreted over them as well and
such a translation becomes possible.

First we need to establish Lemma 10.2.8 along the lines of Lemma 10.2.5 which trans-
lates a separated LT_μ formula φ into $\mathcal{L}_\mu$ by replacing every $\bigcirc$ with $\Diamond$. The resulting $\mathcal{L}_\mu$
formula, interpreted on genuine transition systems, then expresses $\mathsf{E}\varphi$, and this is enough
to translate the whole of CTL* modularly, see Theorem 10.2.7.

In Section 9.3.3, we have shown how to simply build a transition system $\mathfrak{T}(\mathcal{M})$ from a finite CGM $\mathcal{M} = (\mathbb{AG}, S, Act, \text{act}, \delta, L)$ assuming that $\mathbb{AG} = \{1, \ldots, k\}$ and the set of actions Act' in $\mathfrak{T}(\mathcal{M})$ is equal to the product set Act^k. Additional atomic propositions are present in $\mathfrak{T}(\mathcal{M})$ in order to easily encode the action manager from $\mathcal{M}$. Note that the finiteness of S is not required to define $\mathfrak{T}(\mathcal{M})$ from $\mathcal{M}$ and therefore we use this map even in the case S is infinite.

Lemma 10.2.8. Let $\mathbb{AG}$ be a fixed set of agents and Act be a fixed finite set of actions. Let $\varphi \in \text{LT}_\mu$ be separated and C be any coalition of agents. Then there is a $\widehat{\varphi}_C \in \mathcal{L}_\mu$ such for any CGM $\mathcal{M}$ built over $\mathbb{AG}$ and Act, and for any state s, we have $\mathcal{M}, s \models \langle\!\langle C \rangle\!\rangle \varphi$ iff $\mathfrak{T}(\mathcal{M}), s \models \widehat{\varphi}_C$. ∎

Proof. As recalled, Lemma 10.2.5 states that for any separated LT_μ formula φ, the formula φ' obtained from φ by replacing every occurrence of $\bigcirc$ by $\Diamond$ satisfies that for all transition systems $\mathcal{T}$ and states s, we have $\mathcal{T}, s \models \mathsf{E}\varphi$ iff $\mathcal{T}, s \models \varphi'$.

Consequently, for any separated LT_μ formula φ, there is a formula ψ' in negation normal form and with no occurrences of $\Diamond$ such that for all transition systems $\mathcal{T}$ and states s, we have $\mathcal{T}, s \models \mathsf{A}\varphi$ iff $\mathcal{T}, s \models \psi'$. Indeed, every LT_μ formula is equivalent to a separated LT_μ formula (first translate the formula into an equivalent ω-regular expression and then use Theorem 10.1.8). So, let ψ be a separated LT_μ formula logically equivalent to $\neg\varphi$ and χ be the $\mathcal{L}_\mu$ formula obtained from ψ by replacing every occurrence of $\bigcirc$ by $\Diamond$. For all transition systems $\mathcal{T}$ and states s, we have $\mathcal{T}, s \models \mathsf{E}\psi$ iff $\mathcal{T}, s \models \chi$, i.e. $\mathcal{T}, s \models \mathsf{A}\varphi$ iff $\mathcal{T}, s \models \neg\chi$. So, the previously mentioned formula ψ' is precisely the negation normal form of $\neg\chi$ (and every occurrence of $\Diamond$ is replaced by $\square$).

The strategy quantifier $\langle\!\langle C \rangle\!\rangle$ performs a double quantification: first an existential quantification over strategies and then a universal quantification over plays. That is why it is helpful to build a $\mathcal{L}_\mu$ formula equivalent to $\mathsf{A}\varphi$. Let φ be a separated LT_μ formula and ψ' be a $\mathcal{L}_\mu$ formula so that for all $\mathcal{T}$ and s, we have $\mathcal{T}, s \models \mathsf{A}\varphi$ iff $\mathcal{T}, s \models \psi'$. This is not exactly what we need, since we would like to quantify over CGMs built over $\mathbb{AG} = \{1, \ldots, k\}$ and Act. Let $\widehat{\varphi}_C$ be the formula obtained from ψ' via the translation map tr that is homomorphic for all Boolean and fixpoint operators such that $\widehat{\varphi}_C = tr(\psi')$ and

$$tr(\square\psi) := \bigvee_{\alpha_C} (\psi_{\alpha_C} \wedge \bigwedge_{\alpha_C \sqsubseteq \alpha} (\psi_\alpha \rightarrow [(\alpha(1), \ldots, \alpha(k))]tr(\psi)))$$

where α_C is a map $C \rightarrow Act$, α is a map $\mathbb{AG} \rightarrow Act$ and $\alpha_C \sqsubseteq \alpha$ means that α is a conservative extension of α_C. A similar encoding can be found in Section 9.3.3 (see the definitions for ψ_{α_C} and ψ_α there). Remember that $(\alpha(1), \ldots, \alpha(k))$ is an action from $Act' = Act^k$. The correctness proof for the equivalence between $\mathcal{M}, s \models \langle\!\langle C \rangle\!\rangle \varphi$ and $\mathfrak{T}(\mathcal{M}), s \models \widehat{\varphi}$ mainly relies on Lemma 10.2.5 since the map tr is homomorphic for Boolean and fixpoint operators. □

Theorem 10.2.9. Let $\mathbb{AG}$ be a fixed set of agents and Act be a fixed finite set of actions. For every state formula $\varphi \in \text{ATL}^*$ there is a formula $\psi \in \mathcal{L}_\mu$ such that for all CGMs $\mathcal{M}$ built over $\mathbb{AG}$ and Act and for any state s, we have $\mathcal{M}, s \models \varphi$ iff $\mathfrak{T}(\mathcal{M}), s \models \psi$. ∎

Proof. Let $\varphi \in$ ATL* be such that it only uses the strategy quantifier $\langle\!\langle \cdot \rangle\!\rangle$ and negation. We translate its state subformulae modularly starting with the smallest ones. Since all Boolean operators are present in $\mathcal{L}_\mu$ we can restrict our attention to formulae of the form $\langle\!\langle C \rangle\!\rangle \varphi'$ where φ' is an LTL formula. According to Theorem 10.1.6 and Lemma 10.2.4 it can be translated into a separated LT$_\mu$ formula φ''. Clearly, $\langle\!\langle C \rangle\!\rangle \varphi \equiv \langle\!\langle C \rangle\!\rangle \varphi''$, and using Lemma 10.2.8 we can translate the latter into a (closed) formula of $\mathcal{L}_\mu$.

This can now be iterated using the standard trick of replacing inner state subformulae which have been translated already by new atomic propositions. Then the state formulae on the next-higher level of the form $\langle\!\langle C \rangle\!\rangle \varphi$ can be translated using the same scheme because φ is again an LTL formulae (over possibly more atomic propositions). Finally, one replaces the new atomic propositions in the resulting $\mathcal{L}_\mu$ formulae by the $\mathcal{L}_\mu$ formulae for the inner quantified state formulae.   □

We leave it as Exercise 10.15 to estimate the blow-up that this translation produces.

10.2.3 *CTL$^+$ Is Only as Expressive as CTL*

Recall that CTL is the fragment of CTL* in which every temporal operator is immediately preceded by a path quantifier, and that CTL$^+$ relaxes this requirement by allowing Boolean combinations right after path quantifiers (but disallowing the nesting of temporal operators not separated by path quantifiers). Thus, CTL is a fragment of CTL$^+$ and therefore CTL$^+$ is at least as expressive as CTL. Later we will prove that CTL is strictly less expressive than CTL*. The purpose of this section is to determine the exact expressive power of CTL$^+$ in the range between CTL and CTL*. It may come as a surprise to see that it does not lie somewhere in between but in fact right at one edge of this range: CTL$^+$ is 'only' as expressive as CTL. We will prove this by transforming every CTL$^+$ formula equivalently into a CTL formula. The main underlying principle is explained in the following example.

Example 10.2.10. The following CTL$^+$ formula states that there is a path such that p_1 holds true at some position and p_2 holds true at some position (possibly the same position).

$$\mathsf{E}(\mathsf{F}p_1 \wedge \mathsf{F}p_2).$$

It is not difficult to show that CTL has an equivalent formula of a slightly longer length:

$$\mathsf{EF}(p_1 \wedge \mathsf{EF}p_2) \vee \mathsf{EF}(p_2 \wedge \mathsf{EF}p_1).$$

The disjunction only witnesses the fact that p_1 may occur before p_2 along the path or afterwards. This simple reasoning can be generalised to the CTL$^+$ formula

$$\mathsf{E}(\mathsf{F}p_1 \wedge \ldots \wedge \mathsf{F}p_n)$$

which is equivalent to the CTL formula

$$\bigvee_{\pi \in \mathrm{PERM}_n} \mathsf{EF}(p_{\pi(1)} \wedge \mathsf{EF}(p_{\pi(2)} \wedge \mathsf{EF}(p_{\pi(3)} \cdots \wedge \mathsf{EF}p_{\pi(n)})))$$

where PERM_n stands for the set of all permutations of $[1, n]$. Admittedly, the resulting CTL formula is significantly bigger; its size is $\mathcal{O}(n!)$ whereas the size of the original CTL^+ formula is only $\mathcal{O}(n)$. This is the price to pay for expressing the fact that several atomic propositions hold along some path by the disjunction over all possible orders in which they may occur.

Example 10.2.11. Now consider the CTL^+ formula $\mathsf{E}(p_1\mathsf{U}q_1 \wedge p_2\mathsf{U}q_2)$. Again, there are essentially only two possibilities for how an ITS can be a model of this formula. It must possess a path of the form

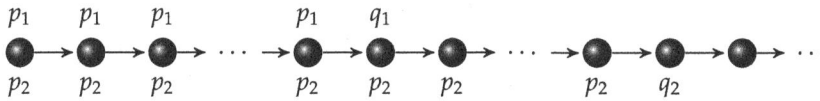

or of the form

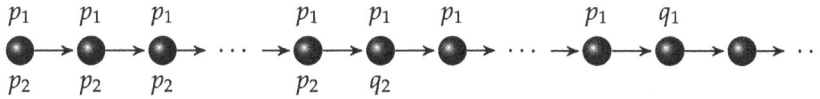

Of course there is also a third case in which both U formulae are being fulfilled at the same time but we can see this as a special case of these two. Then this CTL^+ formula is equivalent to

$$\mathsf{E}((p_1 \wedge p_2)\mathsf{U}(q_1 \wedge \mathsf{E}(p_2\mathsf{U}q_2))) \vee \mathsf{E}((p_1 \wedge p_2)\mathsf{U}(q_2 \wedge \mathsf{E}(p_1\mathsf{U}q_1))).$$

A similar reasoning shows that the CTL^+ formula $\mathsf{E}(p_1\mathsf{U}p_2 \wedge \mathsf{G}p_3)$ is equivalent to the CTL formula

$$\mathsf{E}((p_1 \wedge p_3)\mathsf{U}(p_2 \wedge \mathsf{EG}p_3)).$$

These examples show that several CTL^+ state formulae admit logically equivalent CTL formulae, possibly with an exponential blow-up. We can now show that CTL^+ is as expressive as CTL by generalising the earlier observations and by using a few more simple properties.

Theorem 10.2.12. For every CTL^+ state formula ϑ of size n there is a logically equivalent CTL formula ψ of size $\mathcal{O}(n!)$. ∎

Proof. We describe how to gradually transform a CTL^+ formula ϑ into an equivalent CTL formula by rewriting it according to some equivalences. Using $\mathsf{A}\varphi \equiv \neg\mathsf{E}\neg\varphi$, the De Morgan laws, $\neg\neg\varphi \equiv \varphi$, $\neg\mathsf{X}\varphi \equiv \mathsf{X}\neg\varphi$ and $\neg(\varphi\mathsf{U}\psi) \equiv (\neg\psi\mathsf{U}(\neg\varphi \wedge \neg\psi)) \vee \mathsf{G}\neg\psi$ we can eliminate universal path quantifiers and push negation inwards such that X, U and G are the only temporal operators occurring in ϑ.

Note that existential quantification commutes with disjunctions, i.e. $\mathsf{E}(\varphi \vee \psi) \equiv \mathsf{E}\varphi \vee \mathsf{E}\psi$. Hence we can assume that ϑ contains existentially path quantified subformulae of the form

$$\mathsf{E}(\bigwedge_{i \in I_1} \ell_i \wedge \bigwedge_{i \in I_2} \mathsf{X}\chi_i \wedge \bigwedge_{i \in I_3} \varphi_i \mathsf{U}\psi_i \wedge \bigwedge_{i \in I_4} \mathsf{G}\xi_i)$$

for some index sets $I_1, \ldots, I_4$ where the ℓ_i are literals and the χ_i, φ_i, ψ_i and ξ_i are appropriate temporal formulae such that the entire formula is still part of the syntax of CTL^+.

Note that existential path quantifiers commute with conjunctions if one conjunct is a state formula. This applies in particular to literals over the atomic proposition, i.e. we have $\mathsf{E}(\ell \wedge \varphi) \equiv \ell \wedge \mathsf{E}\varphi$. Moreover, the temporal operator G commutes with conjunctions in general (which we apply here in order to push it upwards rather than downwards), i.e. $\mathsf{G}\varphi \wedge \mathsf{G}\psi \equiv \mathsf{G}(\varphi \wedge \psi)$. We can do the same with the operator X because of $\mathsf{X}\varphi \wedge \mathsf{X}\psi \equiv \mathsf{X}(\varphi \wedge \psi)$. Hence, we can assume path quantified subformulae in ϑ to be of the form

$$\mathsf{E}\big(\mathsf{X}\chi \wedge \big(\bigwedge_{i \in I} \varphi_i \mathsf{U}\psi_i\big) \wedge \mathsf{G}\xi\big).$$

Note that the conjunctions over X- or G-formulae might have been empty. In this case the X- and G-parts would be missed. Instead of considering these special cases we note that they are covered when $\chi = \top$ or $\xi = \top$. Thus, such a subformula requires the existence of a path on which

- ξ holds at the beginning and
- χ and ξ hold after one step.
- There is some set $I' \subseteq I$ of those indices for which the corresponding U-formulae are *not* fulfilled in the first moment already, i.e. all ψ_i hold in the first moment for $i \notin I'$.
- For the other $i \in I'$ that represent the U-formulae which are not getting fulfilled in the first moment already, their left arguments must hold in that moment, i.e. φ_i for $i \in I'$ hold in the first moment.
- There is an order $i_i < i_2 < \ldots < i_m$ on I' such that from step one on all φ_{i_j} and ξ hold until ψ_{i_1} and ξ hold, then ξ and the φ_{i_j} hold for all $j = 2, \ldots, m$ until ψ_{i_2} holds, and so on.
- At the end, when the moment at which ψ_{i_m} holds is reached, ξ still holds and continues to hold on the infinite rest of the path.

All this can be expressed in CTL as follows. Again we use the trick of separating the path into pieces and using several existential path quantifiers for each piece. As a consequence, we require the existence of several paths such that the desired path is obtained by concatenating pieces of these. It suffices to require a path structure as it is depicted in the following for a very particular situation in which $I = \{1, \ldots, 5\}$ and $I' = \{1, 2, 4, 5\}$ with the order $2 < 4 < 1 < 5$.

The CTL formula describing this in general is

$$\xi \wedge \bigvee_{I' \subseteq I} \Big(\bigwedge_{i \notin I'} \psi_i\Big) \wedge \Big(\bigwedge_{i \in I'} \varphi_i\Big) \wedge$$

$$\mathsf{EX}\Big(\chi \wedge \bigvee_{\pi \in \mathrm{PERM}(I')} \mathsf{E}\Big((\xi \wedge \bigwedge_{j=1}^{\mathrm{card}(I')} \varphi_{\pi(j)})\mathsf{U}\Big(\psi_{\pi(1)} \wedge$$

$$\mathsf{E}\Big((\xi \wedge \bigwedge_{j=2}^{\mathrm{card}(I')} \varphi_{\pi(j)})\mathsf{U}\Big(\psi_{\pi(2)} \wedge$$

$$\mathsf{E}\Big((\xi \wedge \bigwedge_{j=3}^{\mathrm{card}(I')} \varphi_{\pi(j)})\mathsf{U}\Big(\psi_{\pi(3)} \wedge$$

$$\vdots$$

$$\mathsf{E}\big((\xi \wedge \varphi_{\pi(\mathrm{card}(I'))})\mathsf{U}(\psi_{\pi(\mathrm{card}(I'))} \wedge \mathsf{EG}\xi)\big) \dots \Big)\Big)\Big)\Big)\Big)\Big)\Big)\Big)$$

where $\mathrm{PERM}(I')$ denotes the set of all permutations of elements in I'.

We leave it to the reader to verify that this is indeed a CTL formula, in particular that all ξ, φ_i, ψ_i and χ could have been assumed to be CTL formulae. Also, the estimation of the occurring blowup is left as Exercise 10.16. ☐

It is worth noting that equivalence in terms of expressive power does not come with equal conciseness: it can be shown that certain CTL$^+$ formulae do require a blowup in translation into CTL of the order $\mathcal{O}(n!)$. This is the case for instance with the aforementioned $\mathsf{E}(\mathsf{F}p_1 \wedge \dots \wedge \mathsf{F}p_n)$. In Chapter 11 we will find another reason for the necessity of such a **succinctness gap**: the satisfiability problem for CTL$^+$ is exponentially harder than that for CTL. Consequently, there cannot be a polynomial-time translation from CTL$^+$ to CTL which preserves satisfiability, let alone equivalence.

10.3 Separation Results

In order to show that a logic $\mathfrak{L}$ is strictly stronger in expressive power than a logic $\mathfrak{L}'$ over a class of structures we need to find some property of structures in this class which can be formalised in $\mathfrak{L}$ but not in $\mathfrak{L}'$. Before we get to the point of explaining how to do this we need to clarify a few things. First, this is a general concept for separating the relative expressive power of two logics; here we only use it for temporal logics but it is just as applicable beyond them. Thus, we only consider the class of interpreted transition systems when comparing different branching-time logics or branching-time logics to linear-time logics with implicit universal or existential quantification over all its computations, or just the class of all computations when doing comparisons between linear-time temporal logics. The properties of such structures are typical temporal properties like those that have been used in examples of the previous chapters.

Second, finding a property which can be formalised in $\mathcal{L}$ but not in $\mathcal{L}'$ does actually not show that $\mathcal{L}$ is *more expressive* than $\mathcal{L}'$; it only shows that it *not* the case that $\mathcal{L}'$ is *at least as expressive* as $\mathcal{L}$. In general, this is an important distinction because there could be other properties which are formalisable in $\mathcal{L}'$ but not in $\mathcal{L}$ which would make the two logics incomparable in expressive power, e.g. CTL and LTL. Quite often, though, one already knows that $\mathcal{L}'$ can be embedded into $\mathcal{L}$, i.e. $\mathcal{L}$ is at least as expressive as $\mathcal{L}'$. When this is known and there is a property which can be formalised in $\mathcal{L}$ but not in $\mathcal{L}'$ then together we get that $\mathcal{L}$ is *strictly more expressive* than $\mathcal{L}'$.

In this section we will show two kinds of results: incomparability (between CTL and LTL for instance), and strict inclusion (in most cases). For both kinds we will use the same technique of presenting one property which is formalisable in one logic but not in another. Depending on whether the other can be embedded into the former we achieve strict inclusion or incomparability.

Before we present concrete results in this context we turn our attention to how this is done. Surely it is not hard to show that some property is formalisable in some logic: it suffices to write down any formula for it (NB: a property can be formalised by infinitely many equivalent formulae).

The other part of this proof technique is undoubtedly the harder one: showing that *no* formula formalises this particular property. A naïve (and therefore failing) attempt works as follows. Suppose we have a property specified by some formula $\varphi \in \mathcal{L}$ and want to show that no formula of $\mathcal{L}'$ is equivalent to it, i.e. formalises the same property. We could take two ITS $\mathcal{T}$ and $\mathcal{T}'$ such that $\mathcal{T} \models \varphi$ but $\mathcal{T}' \not\models \varphi$ and then try to prove by induction on the structure of formulae in $\mathcal{L}'$ that no $\psi \in \mathcal{L}'$ distinguishes $\mathcal{T}$ and $\mathcal{T}'$, i.e. that for all such ψ we have $\mathcal{T} \models \psi$ iff $\mathcal{T}' \models \psi$. This tempting idea is doomed to fail as the following example shows.

Example 10.3.1. Take the logic LTL over some set of atomic propositions containing a fixed q, and consider the property 'q holds at some even moment'. This is, in fact, not formalisable in LTL and a formal proof will follow further. However, now we take two computation paths σ and σ' such that one of them satisfies this property whereas the other does not, for instance these two.

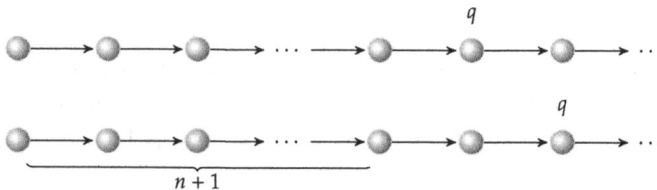

Clearly, regardless of what n is, exactly one of them has the property under consideration. But now the attempt to show that no LTL formula distinguishes between them must fail because they can clearly be distinguished by the formula $X^{n+1}q$.

The problem is the fact that these two computation paths are fixed. Clearly, if one of them has a property and the other does not then they must not be identical, i.e. must differ somewhere. But then this difference can typically be captured by a formula, here a very simple LTL formula. This is a consequence of the characterisation of indistiguishability in LTL by trace equivalence, and this problem is not restricted to linear-time logics only. Two ITS that differ in a way such that one satisfies a temporal property and the other does not must necessarily be non-bisimilar, unless the property under consideration is not bisimulation-invariant (but then it would arguably not be a 'temporal' property, either). On the other hand, two non-bisimilar ITS can always be distinguished by a simple CTL formula. In fact one only needs the operators EX and AX (see e.g. Section 5.3.3). Thus, the distinction is even possible in a fragment of TLR (actually in BML) which shows that this technique cannot prove inexpressibilty for logics from TLR upwards.

It is worth noting that the distinguishing formula $X^{n+1}q$ in the earlier example clearly has little to do with the property at hand. With just the operator X one can only separate computation paths that differ on a prefix of fixed length given by the nesting depth of such operators. This is what enables a refinement of the aforementioned technique with which inexpressibility can successfully be shown. The trick is to introduce a rank function on formulae and then not to consider two *fixed* structures (ITS or computation paths) but two *families* of structures such that (1) all structures in the one family have the underlying property, (2) all structures in the other do not and (3) formulae with rank at most n can distinguish at most the first n members of these families. This suffices to show inexpressibility in general. The following lemma introduces this technique formally and proves that it yields the desired result. We present it for ITS as structures but it can equally be used for computation paths (which are of course specialised ITS). The proof is left as Exercise 10.17.

Lemma 10.3.2 (Inexpressibility Lemma). Let $\mathcal{L}$ be a logic interpreted over ITS. Let P be a property of ITS, and let $\mathfrak{w} : \mathcal{L} \to \mathbb{N}$ be an arbitrary function. If there are two families $(\mathcal{T}_n)_{n \in \mathbb{N}}$ and $(\mathcal{T}'_n)_{n \in \mathbb{N}}$ of rooted ITS such that

- $\mathcal{T}_n \in P$ iff $\mathcal{T}'_n \notin P$ for all $n \in \mathbb{N}$ and
- for all $n \in \mathbb{N}$ and all $\varphi \in \mathcal{L}$ with $\mathfrak{w}(\varphi) \leq n$: $\mathcal{T}_n \models \varphi$ iff $\mathcal{T}'_n \models \varphi$,

then there is no $\mathcal{L}$-formula φ that formalises P. ∎

While this lemma's proof is pretty much straightforward, applying the lemma may not be. In particular it may not be easy to design these two families of structures right. Moreover, the lemma still requires a formal proof of indistinguishability by all formulae up to a certain rank. This is usually done by induction on the formula structure which then means that the rank function has to be monotone in the formula structure as well. As indicated, one typically considers the nesting depth of temporal operators in formulae as their rank. The next section uses this technique for a formal proof of the aforementioned fact that LTL cannot express that something holds eventually at an even position.

10.3.1 LTL Cannot Count

In this section let P_{even} denote the property of computation paths that the atomic proposition q holds eventually at some even moment on the path.

Theorem 10.3.3. P_{even} is not formalisable in LTL. ∎

Proof. Consider the two families of computation paths $(\sigma_n)_{n \in \mathbb{N}}$ and $(\sigma'_n)_{n \in \mathbb{N}}$ as depicted in Example 10.3.1, i.e. we get $\sigma_n, j \models q$ iff $j = n + 1$ and $\sigma'_n, j \models q$ iff $j = n + 2$ (the leftmost position is zero). It should be clear that we get $\sigma_n \in P_{even}$ iff $\sigma'_n \notin P_{even}$.

Next we need to choose a suitable rank function such that it is possible to show that σ_n and σ'_n are indistinguishable by formulae of rank at most i. As mentioned, we take the rank of a formula φ to be the maximal number of nested temporal operators, i.e. the modal depth $mdeg(\varphi)$, c.f. Definition 6.1.1.

We will prove by induction on the structure of LTL formulae that for all φ and all $n \geq mdeg(\varphi)$ we get $\sigma_n \models \varphi$ iff $\sigma'_n \models \varphi$. For atomic propositions this should be clear; their nesting depth is 0, but σ_n and σ'_n for $n \geq 0$ do not differ in their first states. The cases of φ starting with a Boolean operator follow immediately from the hypothesis. The only two interesting cases are those of the two temporal operators.

Suppose that $\varphi = X\psi$. Note that we have $mdeg(\psi) = mdeg(\varphi) - 1$. Take some $n \geq mdeg(\varphi) > 0$ and suppose we have $\sigma_n \models \varphi$, i.e. $\sigma_n \models X\psi$. This means we get $\sigma_{n-1} \models \psi$ because the first genuine suffix of σ_n is the same as σ_{n-1}. By the hypothesis, this entails $\sigma'_{n-1} \models \psi$ and therefore we have $\sigma'_n \models \varphi$. The converse implication is shown in the same way.

For the last case suppose that $\varphi = \psi_1 U \psi_2$. Then we have $mdeg(\varphi) > mdeg(\psi_i)$ for all $i \in \{1, 2\}$. Suppose we have $\sigma_n \models \varphi$ for some $n \geq mdeg(\varphi)$. Then there is some k such that $\sigma_n, k \models \psi_2$ and for all $j < k$ we have $\sigma_n, j \models \psi_1$. We need to distinguish two cases depending on whether $k = 0$. If $k = 0$ then the induction hypothesis immediately yields $\sigma'_n \models \psi_2$ and therefore also $\sigma'_n \models \varphi$. The most interesting case is that of $k > 0$. Then we have $\sigma_n \models \psi_1$ and the induction hypothesis yields $\sigma'_n \models \psi_1$, too. On the other hand, σ_i and σ'_{i-1} are trace equivalent and therefore no LTL formula can distinguish σ_i from σ'_{i-1} no matter what i is. Thus, since we have $\sigma_n, j \models \psi_1$ for all $j < k$ we also get $\sigma'_{n-1}, j \models \psi_1$ for all $j < k$. This, however, also means $\sigma'_n, j + 1 \models \psi_1$ for all $j < k$. In the same way we get that $\sigma'_n, k + 1 \models \psi_2$. This transferring of satisfaction of ψ_1 and ψ_2 from moments in σ_n to moments in σ'_n is shown as follows:

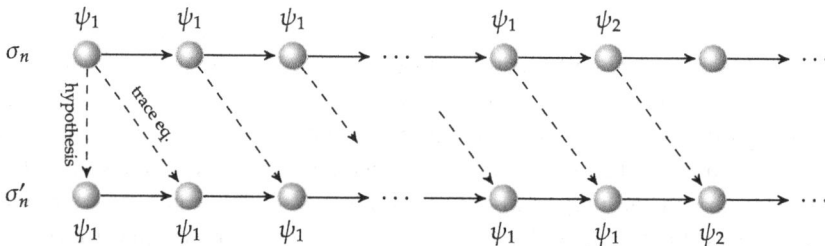

As it can be seen from this picture, we also have $\sigma'_n \models \psi_1 \cup \psi_2$. Again, the converse implication is proved in the same way.

This completes the premises for the application of the Inexpressibility Lemma 10.3.2 from which we can conclude that P_{even} is not formalisable in LTL. ☐

As a consequence we get that LTL is strictly less expressive than the four linear-time logics discussed in Section 10.1.2.

Corollary 10.3.4. LTL is strictly less expressive than ETL, QLTL, PSL and LT_μ. ■

Exercise 10.25 asks for formalisations of the property P_{even} in these four logics. For example, P_{even} can be expressed in LT_μ with the formula $\mu X. \, p \vee \bigcirc \bigcirc X$.

Corollary 10.3.5. There is a formula in $\mathcal{L}_\mu$ that has no equivalent formula in CTL*, thus we have $\mathcal{L}_\mu \not\sqsubseteq$ CTL*. ■

Indeed, let $\varphi = \mu X. p \vee \Diamond\Diamond X$ be the formula in $\mathcal{L}_\mu$ that states that the atomic proposition p holds on a state that can be reached from the current state by a path of even length. For *reductio ad absurdum*, suppose that there is a CTL* formula φ' that is equivalent to φ. On LTL models (linear transition systems of length ω), φ characterises the models satisfying the property P_{even} from Theorem 10.3.3. Similarly, on LTL models, φ' is equivalent to the LTL formula ψ' obtained from φ' by removing all the occurrences of the path quantifiers (due to linearity; see also Exercise 7.25). So, there is an LTL formula ψ' that characterises the linear models in P_{even}, which is in contradiction with Theorem 10.3.3.

10.3.2 LTL and CTL Are Incomparable

The next goal is to prove that there are properties in either LTL or CTL which are not formalisable in the other, i.e. the two logics are incomparable with respect to expressive power. At least one direction should intuitively be clear: when comparing linear-time logics with an implicit universal quantification over all computation paths to branching-time logics, it is not surprising that existentially path quantified properties cannot be expressed in general. For this part we do not even need to employ the Inexpressibility Lemma.

Theorem 10.3.6. The CTL property EXq is not expressible in LTL. ■

Proof. Recall the convention about comparing linear-time to branching-time properties and logics: so we assume that there was an LTL formula φ such that Aφ was equivalent to EXq. First of all we convince ourselves that φ cannot be valid because then any ITS in which q holds nowhere would be a model for Aφ but such an ITS cannot be a model for EXq. Thus, it must be the case that $\neg\varphi$ is satisfiable. Let σ (as a computation path) be a model for $\neg\varphi$. We use this to form the ITS $\mathcal{T}_\sigma$ as follows.

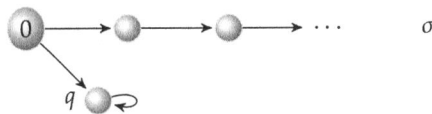

It should be clear that we have $\mathcal{T}_\sigma, 0 \models \mathsf{EX}q$. On the other hand, we must also have $\mathcal{T}_\sigma, 0 \not\models \mathsf{A}\varphi$ because there is a path starting from state 0 which does not satisfy φ. From this contradiction, we conclude that no such φ can exist.   □

The other direction is slightly more involved and uses the Inexpressibility Lemma again. One LTL property that cannot be expressed in CTL is $\mathsf{AFG}q$ – on all paths there comes a moment from which on q holds all the time. For technical convenience we consider the dual property – existence of a fair path – specified by $\mathsf{EGF}q$, and show that it cannot be formalised in CTL. This result carries over to the dual property because CTL is closed under negations, so if $\mathsf{AFG}q$ was expressible in CTL then so would be $\mathsf{EGF}q$. It is necessary to take some care in these distinctions because LTL is not closed under negations when using implicit universal path quantification, and in fact $\mathsf{EGF}q$ is also not expressible in LTL for this simple reason (when LTL formulae are implicitly universally quantified).

The rank function we use here for CTL formulae is, again, the maximal nesting depth of temporal operators, defined as follows.

$$nd(p) := 0 \text{ for any atomic proposition } p$$
$$nd(\neg\varphi) := nd(\varphi)$$
$$nd(\varphi \vee \psi) := \max\{nd(\varphi), nd(\psi)\}$$
$$nd(\mathsf{EX}\varphi) := 1 + nd(\varphi)$$
$$nd(\mathsf{E}(\varphi\mathsf{U}\psi)) := 1 + \max\{nd(\varphi), nd(\psi)\}$$
$$nd(\mathsf{E}(\varphi\mathsf{R}\psi)) := 1 + \max\{nd(\varphi), nd(\psi)\}.$$

Theorem 10.3.7. There is no CTL formula that is equivalent to $\mathsf{EGF}q$.   ■

Proof. The Inexpressibility Lemma requires the construction of two families of ITS in order to prove this. We will do something slightly different which results in essentially the same: we construct a single ITS; the two families are given by considering different starting states in this ITS $\mathcal{T}$.

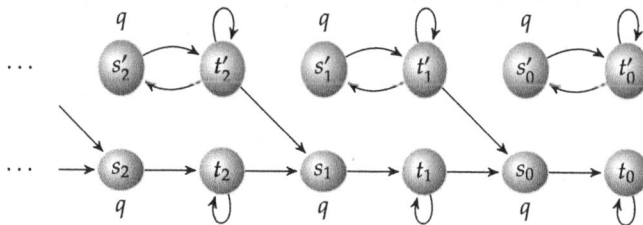

First of all we note that for all $n \in \mathbb{N}$ we have $\mathcal{T}, s'_n \models \mathsf{EGF}q$ and $\mathcal{T}, t'_n \models \mathsf{EGF}q$ whereas $\mathcal{T}, s_n \not\models \mathsf{EGF}q$ and $\mathcal{T}, t_n \not\models \mathsf{EGF}q$. This establishes the first premise for the application of Lemma 10.3.2.

For the second premise we show that the pair s_n and s'_m, as well as the pair t_n and t'_m, cannot be distinguished by any CTL formula φ for as long as $nd(\varphi) \leq \min\{n, m\}$. This should be obvious for the base case with φ being some atomic proposition because all s_n and s'_m, as well as t_n and t'_m respectively are labelled with the same atomic propositions.

The cases of φ being a Boolean combination immediately follow from the hypothesis. There are only three interesting cases.

Suppose $\varphi = \mathsf{EX}\psi$, and $n, m \geq nd(\varphi)$. Suppose that $s_n \models \varphi$. This is only possible when $t_n \models \psi$. Since $nd(\psi) < nd(\varphi)$ we can apply the hypothesis and get that $t'_m \models \psi$ for any $m \geq nd(\psi)$ and in particular those m for which we have $m \geq nd(\varphi)$ including n. Therefore we have $s'_n \models \varphi$.

There are three more implications to show in this case: one more to show that whenever $s'_n \models \varphi$ then we also have $s_m \models \varphi$ for suitable n, m. It is not hard to see that this is done in exactly the same way as the previous implication. The two others concern the way that t_n and t'_m cannot be distinguished by φ. We will only carry out the slightly more complicated direction, assuming that $t'_m \models \varphi$ and $m \geq nd(\varphi)$. Then there are three possibilities because t'_m has three successors if $m > 0$.

1. $t'_m \models \psi$. Then we apply the hypothesis to this and get $t_n \models \psi$ for all $n \geq nd(\psi)$ and therefore also $t_n \models \varphi$ since t_n is also a successor of t_n itself.

2. $s_{m-1} \models \psi$. From the hypothesis we get that $s'_{m'} \models \psi$ for every $m' \geq nd(\psi)$. Note that we want to show that t_n satisfies φ for suitable n but the hypothesis only lets us transfer satisfaction between some s_i and s'_j and not from some s_i to some s_j. However, applying it a second time gives us $s_n \models \psi$ for every $n \geq nd(\psi)$. Since t_{n+1} is a predecessor of s_n we then have $t_{n+1} \models \varphi$ for all n with $n \geq nd(\psi)$. Since $nd(\varphi) = nd(\psi) + 1$ we have $t_n \models \varphi$ for all $n \geq nd(\varphi)$.

3. $s'_m \models \psi$. By the hypothesis we get $s_n \models \psi$ for all n with $n \geq nd(\psi)$ and, as in the previous case, $t_{n+1} \models \varphi$ for all such n and therefore also $t_n \models \varphi$ for all $n \geq nd(\varphi)$.

We leave the remaining two cases of $\varphi = \mathsf{E}(\psi_1 \mathsf{U} \psi_2)$ or $\varphi = \mathsf{E}(\psi_1 \mathsf{R} \psi_2)$ as Exercise 10.19. They boil down to several subcases since in each of them we need to show four implications, and for each of them there can be different reasons for why φ holds. For instance when we suppose $s'_n \models \mathsf{E}(\psi_1 \mathsf{U} \psi_2)$ then we can have either of $s'_n \models \psi_2$ or $t'_n \models \psi_2$, or $s_{n'} \models \psi_2$ or $t_{n'} \models \psi_2$ for some $n' < n$.

This concludes the second premise of the Inexpressibility Lemma 10.3.2 which then shows that $\mathsf{EGF}q$ cannot be expressed in CTL. $\qquad\Box$

As mentioned, as a consequence we immediately get that $\mathsf{AFG}q$ is equally not expressible in CTL but it is obviously expressible in LTL. Putting this together with Theorem 10.3.6 we obtain their incomparability with respect to expressive power.

Corollary 10.3.8. LTL and CTL are incomparable with respect to expressive power. $\blacksquare$

A close inspection of the proof that shows that CTL cannot be embedded into LTL reveals that nothing that is particular to LTL has been used. Instead, this is a general result on linear-time logics. We leave it as Exercise 10.22 to prove the following statement.

Theorem 10.3.9. Let $\mathcal{L}$ be any linear-time temporal logic that can express the LTL property FGq. Then $\mathcal{L}$ and CTL are incomparable with respect to expressive power. ■

Since LTL and CTL are both sublogics of CTL*, their incomparability immediately shows that CTL* is more expressive then either of these.

Corollary 10.3.10. CTL* is strictly more expressive than CTL and than LTL. ■

10.3.3 Separating CTL from Above and Below

In this section we work out two separation results around CTL, namely we show that it is strictly more expressive than TLR but strictly less expressive than the alternation-free fragment of the modal μ-calculus.

A natural candidate of a CTL property that cannot be expressed in TLR is an Until formula. In fact, $E(pUq)$ is not expressible in TLR which we will show by application of the Inexpressibility Lemma. We are going to make things easy by considering ITS with a single computation path only. The two families are indexed by two parameters n and m in order to enable a proof by induction.

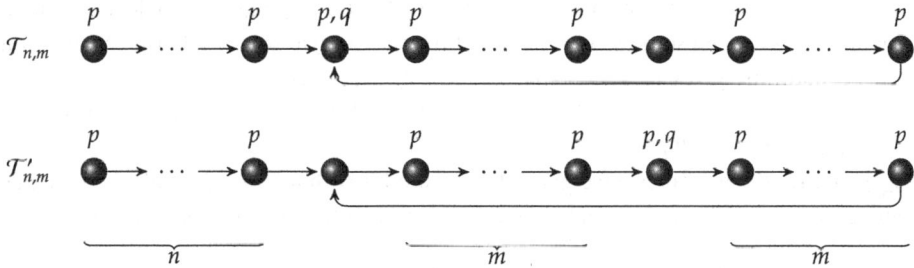

Thus, $\mathcal{T}_{n,m}$ consists of a loop which has two parts; the first one is started with a state satisfying p and q, the second one is started with a state satisfying neither of them. Both are followed by m states satisfying p only. In addition, there is a prefix of length n which leads into these loops. $\mathcal{T}'_{n,m}$ is built similarly but the two parts of the main loop are swapped around. By convention we call 0 the first state in each of these, depicted leftmost; 1 is the name for the next state, etc.

Before we consider which temporal properties the ITS of these two families possess we notice that we can completely discard path quantifiers from our considerations because on structures with a single computation path only we have $E\varphi \equiv A\varphi$. In fact, CTL and LTL have the same expressive power over such ITS. Hence, we will simply ignore path quantifiers and use LTL formulae instead of CTL formulae. Note that this is only valid in the context of properties interpreted on $\mathcal{T}_{n,m}$ and $\mathcal{T}'_{n,m}$ since each of them consists of a single computation path only.

It is easy to see that $\mathcal{T}_{n,m}, 0 \models pUq$ whereas $\mathcal{T}'_{n,m}, 0 \not\models pUq$ for all $n, m \in \mathbb{N}$. Moreover, there are connections between members of these families that allow inexpressibility to be shown inductively:

- Fact 1: $\mathcal{T}_{n,m}, 0 \models \varphi$ iff $\mathcal{T}_{n+1,m}, 1 \models \varphi$ iff $\mathcal{T}_{n+1,m}, 0 \models \mathsf{X}\varphi$ for all $n, m \in \mathbb{N}$ and any φ.
- Fact 2: Due to the loops we have $\mathcal{T}_{n,m}, i \models \varphi$ iff $\mathcal{T}_{n,m}, i+2m+2 \models \varphi$ for any $n, m, i \in \mathbb{N}$ with $i \geq n$ and any φ.
- Fact 3: $\mathcal{T}_{n,m}, i \models \varphi$ iff $\mathcal{T}'_{n,m}, i + m + 1 \models \varphi$ for all $n, m, i \in \mathbb{N}$ with $i \geq n$ and any φ.

Lemma 10.3.11. For all $n, m \in \mathbb{N}$ with $m \geq n$ and all $\varphi \in \text{TLR}$ with $nd(\varphi) < n$ we have $\mathcal{T}_{n,m}, 0 \models \varphi$ iff $\mathcal{T}'_{n,m}, 0 \models \varphi$. ∎

Proof. As mentioned, we will show this by induction on the structure of φ. Note that – even though φ is officially a TLR formula – we can assume it to be built from atomic propositions using Boolean operators and the temporal operators X, F and G only. Since negation is available we can even assume that it just uses $\wedge$, $\neg$, X and F. This reduces the number of cases in the induction step compared to considering full TLR syntax.

In the base case, φ is an atomic proposition and the claim is evident because its temporal nesting depth is 0 in which case $\mathcal{T}_{n,m}$ and $\mathcal{T}'_{n,m}$ do not differ in the labelling of their first state when $n > 0$.

In the step case, the claim follows immediately from the hypothesis for formulae of the form $\psi_1 \wedge \psi_2$, respectively $\neg\psi$. So suppose that $\varphi = \mathsf{X}\psi$. Note that $nd(\varphi) > 0$ in that case and remember the assumption of $m \geq n > nd(\varphi)$, i.e. $n > 1$. Then we have

$$\mathcal{T}_{n,m}, 0 \models \varphi \iff \mathcal{T}_{n,m}, 1 \models \psi \iff \mathcal{T}_{n-1,m}, 0 \models \psi$$
$$\iff \mathcal{T}'_{n-1,m}, 0 \models \psi \iff \mathcal{T}'_{n,m}, 0 \models \varphi.$$

The second and fourth equivalences hold because of Fact 1 bearing in mind that we have $n > 1$. The third one is the induction hypothesis applied to ψ. Note that $nd(\psi) < nd(\varphi)$, hence, we get that $m \geq n - 1 > nd(\psi)$ which is why the hypothesis can be applied at this moment.

Finally, consider the case of $\varphi = \mathsf{F}\psi$. This case is similar to the previous one yet a little tricker, and it is also this case that demands the second parameter in the indices of the families $\mathcal{T}_{n,m}$ and $\mathcal{T}'_{n,m}$. We will only show one direction of the 'iff'. The other direction is entirely symmetrical – simply swap $\mathcal{T}_{n,m}$ with $\mathcal{T}'_{n,m}$.

Again, note that we have $nd(\varphi) = nd(\psi) + 1$, hence we have $m \geq n > 1$. Suppose that $\mathcal{T}_{n,m}, 0 \models \mathsf{F}\psi$. Hence, there is some state i such that $\mathcal{T}_{n,m}, i \models \psi$. By Fact 2 we could actually assume $i \leq n + 2m + 3$ but this is not necessary for what follows. Instead, we need to distinguish two cases.

- Case $i < n$. Then we get $\mathcal{T}'_{n,m}, 0 \models \varphi$ in just the same way as in the previous case where φ was assumed to be of the form $\mathsf{X}\psi$.
- Case $i \geq n$. According to Fact 3 we have $\mathcal{T}'_{n,m}, i + m + 1 \models \psi$ and therefore $\mathcal{T}'_{n,m}, 0 \models \mathsf{F}\psi$.

This finishes the proof. □

A simple application of the Inexpressibility Lemma to this proves the separation between TLR and CTL.

Theorem 10.3.12. TLR is strictly less expressive than CTL.   ■

Not surprisingly, the proof can actually be used to separate LTL from its fragment with unary operators only; just like CTL and LTL coincide semantically on structures with a single computation path, so do TLR and LTL(X, F).

Theorem 10.3.13. LTL(X, F) is strictly less expressive than LTL.   ■

The second announced goal of this section is to provide a separation between CTL and the alternation-free modal μ-calculus. This is now particularly simple. We can actually reuse the proof of Theorem 10.3.3 which shows that the property 'p holds at some even moment' is not expressible in LTL. Recall the trick of using ITS with a single computation for the application of the Inexpressibility Lemma which allows results about CTL to be proved using LTL. Now note that the proof of Theorem 10.3.3 naturally uses such ITS because it was formalised as a result about LTL. In any case, on these structures path quantifiers are redundant and therefore the result equally holds for CTL*, i.e. 'p holds at some even moment' is not expressible in CTL* either.

It is expressible in the linear-time μ-calculus as $\mu Z.p \vee \bigcirc \bigcirc Z$, or when interpreted on branching structures in the modal μ-calculus as $\mu Z.p \vee \Diamond \Diamond Z$ stating 'p holds on *some* path at an even moment'. Clearly, this formula is alternation-free. Recall that the entire CTL can be translated into alternation-free $\mathcal{L}_\mu$, see the construction in the proof of Theorem 8.1.14.

Corollary 10.3.14. CTL is strictly weaker than the alternation-free modal μ-calculus.   ■

10.3.4 Extensions with Fairness Operators

As stated in Theorem 7.4.10, Boolean combinations of fairness operators, as formalisable in ECTL$^+$, increase the expressive power over formulae with simple fairness operators in ECTL.

Theorem 10.3.15. There is no ECTL formula that is equivalent to $\mathsf{E}(\mathsf{F}^\infty p \wedge \mathsf{G}q)$.   ■

Proof. We show that the formula $\mathsf{E}(\mathsf{F}^\infty p \wedge \mathsf{G}q)$ has no equivalent formula in ECTL by application of the Inexpressibility Lemma 10.3.2. We consider the two families of transition systems $(\mathcal{T}_i)_{i \geq 1}$ and $(\mathcal{T}_i')_{i \geq 1}$ as defined in Figure 10.2.

One can easily show that for all $i \geq 1$, we have

$$\mathcal{T}_i', s_i' \models \mathsf{E}(\mathsf{F}^\infty p \wedge \mathsf{G}q) \qquad \mathcal{T}_i, s_i \not\models \mathsf{E}(\mathsf{F}^\infty p \wedge \mathsf{G}q).$$

The infinite path that witnesses the satisfaction of the formula for $\mathcal{T}_i', s_i'$ is simply $(s_i' t_i')^\omega$. The following properties can be also proved for all ECTL formulae φ (see Exercise 10.23):

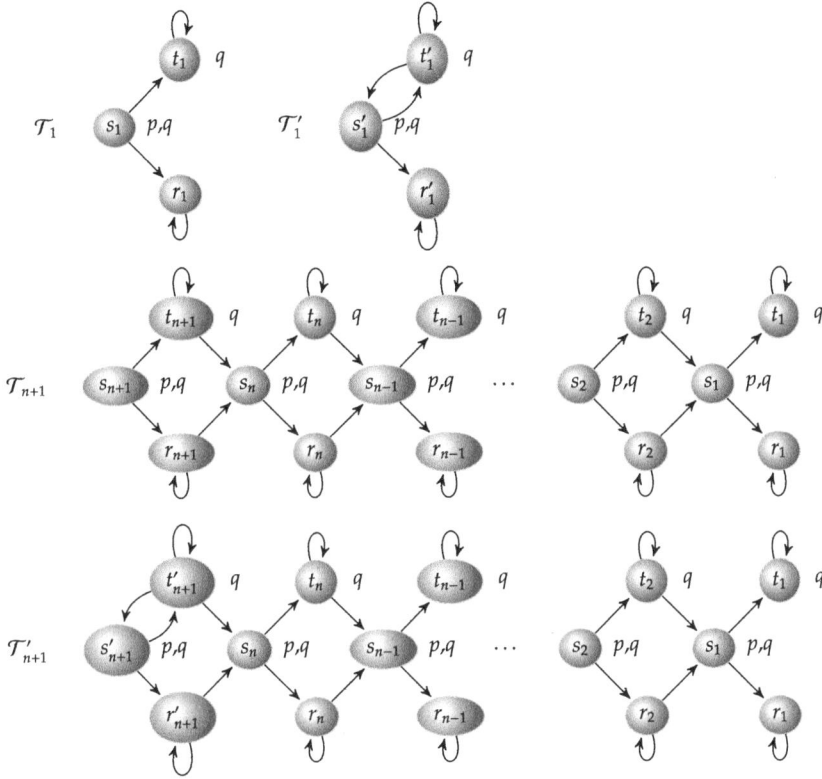

Figure 10.2 Two families of transition systems $(\mathcal{T}_i)_{i\geq 1}$ and $(\mathcal{T}'_i)_{i\geq 1}$.

1. There is $i > |\varphi|$ such that $\mathcal{T}_i, s_i \models \varphi$ iff for all $i' \geq |\varphi|$, we have $\mathcal{T}_{i'}, s_{i'} \models \varphi$.
2. There is $i > |\varphi|$ such that $\mathcal{T}_i, r_i \models \varphi$ iff for all $i' \geq |\varphi|$, we have $\mathcal{T}_{i'}, r_{i'} \models \varphi$.
3. There is $i > |\varphi|$ such that $\mathcal{T}_i, t_i \models \varphi$ iff for all $i' \geq |\varphi|$, we have $\mathcal{T}_{i'}, t_{i'} \models \varphi$.

With these properties, one can then show by structural induction that for all ECTL formulae φ and for all $i \geq |\varphi|$, we have

1. $\mathcal{T}_i, s_i \models \varphi$ iff $\mathcal{T}'_i, s'_i \models \varphi$,
2. $\mathcal{T}_i, r_i \models \varphi$ iff $\mathcal{T}'_i, r'_i \models \varphi$,
3. $\mathcal{T}_i, t_i \models \varphi$ iff $\mathcal{T}'_i, t'_i \models \varphi$.

The proof by induction is left as Exercise 10.23. Consequently, by Lemma 10.3.2, we conclude that $\mathsf{E}(\mathsf{F}^\infty p \wedge \mathsf{G}q)$ cannot be expressed in ECTL. $\qquad\square$

On the other hand, Boolean combinations of fairness formulae are not enough to express all of CTL*.

Theorem 10.3.16. *There is no* ECTL$^+$ *formula that is equivalent to* $\mathsf{AF}(p \wedge \mathsf{X}p)$. $\qquad\blacksquare$

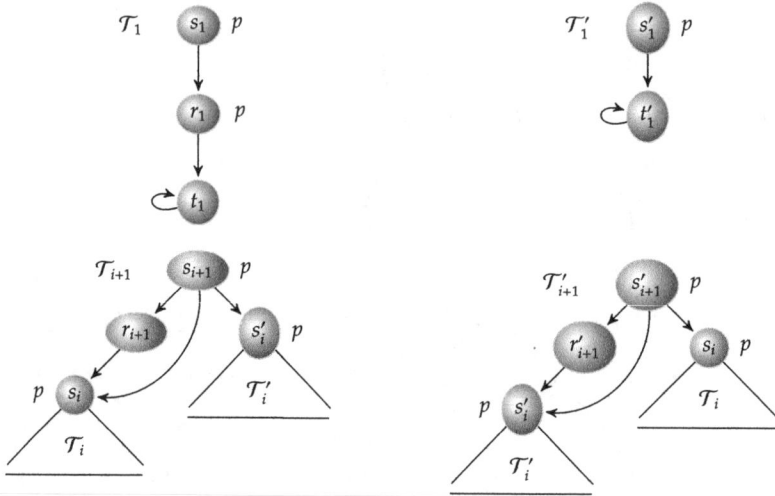

Figure 10.3 Two families of transition systems $(\mathcal{T}_i)_{i \geq 1}$ and $(\mathcal{T}_i')_{i \geq 1}$.

Proof. We show that the formula $\mathsf{AF}(p \wedge \mathsf{X}p)$ has no equivalent formula in ECTL^+ by application of the Inexpressibility Lemma 10.3.2. We consider the two families of transition systems $(\mathcal{T}_i)_{i \geq 1}$ and $(\mathcal{T}_i')_{i \geq 1}$ as defined in Figure 10.3.

So, the states in $\mathcal{T}_i$, $i \geq 2$, are precisely in the set

$$\{t_1, t_1'\} \cup \{s_j, r_j \mid j \in [1, i-1]\} \cup \{s_j', r_j' \mid j \in [1, i-1]\} \cup \{s_i, r_i\}$$

whereas the states in $\mathcal{T}_i'$, $i \geq 2$, are precisely in the set

$$\{t_1, t_1'\} \cup \{s_j, r_j \mid j \in [1, i-1]\} \cup \{s_j', r_j' \mid j \in [1, i-1]\} \cup \{s_i', r_i'\}.$$

One can easily show that for all $i \geq 1$, we have

$$\mathcal{T}_i, s_i \models \mathsf{AF}(p \wedge \mathsf{X}p) \qquad \mathcal{T}_i', s_i' \not\models \mathsf{AF}(p \wedge \mathsf{X}p).$$

The infinite path that invalidates the preceding formula on $\mathcal{T}_i'$, s_i' is equal to

$$s_i' r_i' s_{i-1}' r_{i-1}' \cdots s_2' r_2' s_1' \cdot (t_1')^\omega.$$

The rest of the proof consists of checking the following two properties:

(1) For every ECTL^+ formula φ, there is a CTL^+ formula φ' such that for all $i \geq 1$,
  - for all states s in $\mathcal{T}_i$, we have $\mathcal{T}_i, s \models \varphi$ iff $\mathcal{T}_i, s \models \varphi'$,
  - for all states s in $\mathcal{T}_i'$, we have $\mathcal{T}_i', s \models \varphi$ iff $\mathcal{T}_i', s \models \varphi'$,
(2) For all CTL formulae φ such that $|\varphi| \leq i$, we have $\mathcal{T}_i, s_i \models \varphi$ iff $\mathcal{T}_i', s_i' \models \varphi$.

By Theorem 10.2.12, CTL^+ and CTL have the same expressiveness and there is a computable function $\mathfrak{f}$ bounded by some exponential such that for every CTL^+ formula φ, there is an equivalent CTL formula of size bounded by $\mathfrak{f}(|\varphi|)$. Similarly, from the proof of (1.)

for every ECTL$^+$ formula φ, the CTL$^+$ formula φ' equivalent to φ in the transition systems $\mathcal{T}_i$ and $\mathcal{T}_i'$ has a size bounded by $\mathfrak{f}'(|\varphi|)$ for some computable map $\mathfrak{f}'$. Therefore, for all $i \in \mathbb{N}$, for all ECTL$^+$ formulae φ such that $\mathfrak{f}(\mathfrak{f}'(|\varphi|)) \leq i$, we have $\mathcal{T}_i, s_i \models \varphi$ iff $\mathcal{T}_i', s_i' \models \varphi$. By application of the Inexpressibility Lemma 10.3.2 (with the rank function equal to the composition of $\mathfrak{f}$ with $\mathfrak{f}'$), we conclude that $\mathsf{AF}(p \wedge \mathsf{X}p)$ cannot be expressed in ECTL$^+$. It remains to prove the preceding two properties.

Proof of (1.) For every ECTL$^+$ formula φ, we shall build a formula φ' in CTL$^+$ such that φ and φ' are equivalent in all the transition systems $\mathcal{T}_i$ and $\mathcal{T}_i'$ and $|\varphi'|$ is at most nonelementary in $|\varphi|$ (i.e. $|\varphi'|$ is bounded by a tower of exponentials of height at most a polynomial in $|\varphi|$ and the final exponent is also polynomial in $|\varphi|$). The only difference between ECTL$^+$ and CTL$^+$ is the use of subformulae of the form $\mathsf{F}^\infty \psi$ in Boolean combinations appearing under the immediate scope of the path quantifier E. As usual, we write $\mathsf{G}^\infty \psi$ to denote the formula $\neg \mathsf{F}^\infty \neg \psi$. However, in the transition systems of the form of either $\mathcal{T}_i$ or $\mathcal{T}_i'$, infinite paths end either by the self-loop on t_1 (from $\mathcal{T}_1$) or by the self-loop on t_1' (from $\mathcal{T}_1'$). So, when ψ is a CTL$^+$ formula and s is a state in either $\mathcal{T}_i$'s or $\mathcal{T}_i'$, the satisfaction of $s \models \mathsf{F}^\infty \psi$ is equivalent to either $t_1 \models \psi$ (and t_1 is reachable from s) or $t_1' \models \psi$ (and t_1' is reachable from s). Note that the underlying transition system is not specified before the symbol '$\models$' since this applies to any transition system from the two considered families. A similar analysis can be done with formulae of the form $\mathsf{G}^\infty \psi$ when ψ is a CTL$^+$ formula. In order to express the conditions on t_1 or on t_1', one can then observe that $s \models \mathsf{F}^\infty \psi$ iff $s \models \mathsf{G}^\infty \psi$ iff $s \models \mathsf{AGEF}\psi$ and $\mathsf{AGEF}\psi$ is a CTL$^+$ formula whenever ψ is also in CTL$^+$.

The translation of φ into φ' consists of replacing the innermost subformulae of the form $\mathsf{E}\psi$ where ψ has no subformulae of the form $\mathsf{F}^\infty \psi'$ in the scope of E (in ψ) and to replace $\mathsf{E}\psi$ by a CTL$^+$ formula that is equivalent to $\mathsf{E}\psi$ on the transition systems $\mathcal{T}_i$'s and $\mathcal{T}_i'$'s. This transformation is performed until we get a formula in CTL$^+$.

The subformula ψ can be written in disjunctive normal form $\psi_1 \vee \cdots \vee \psi_k$ where each ψ_i is of the form $\psi_i^0 \wedge \mathsf{F}^\infty \chi_i^1 \wedge \cdots \wedge \mathsf{F}^\infty \chi_i^\gamma \wedge \mathsf{G}^\infty \chi_i$ and all the subformulae $\mathsf{E}\psi_i^0, \chi_i^1, \ldots,$ χ_i^γ are in CTL$^+$. One has to use that $\mathsf{G}^\infty(\chi_1 \wedge \chi_2)$ is equivalent to $\mathsf{G}^\infty \chi_1 \wedge \mathsf{G}^\infty \chi_2$ in all rooted ITS. So, $\mathsf{E}\psi$ is equivalent to $\mathsf{E}\psi_1 \vee \cdots \vee \mathsf{E}\psi_k$, since $\mathsf{E}(\chi_1 \vee \chi_2)$ is equivalent to $\mathsf{E}\chi_1 \vee \mathsf{E}\chi_2$ in all rooted ITS. It remains to find a formula equivalent to $\mathsf{E}(\psi_i^0 \wedge \mathsf{F}^\infty \chi_i^1 \wedge \cdots \wedge \mathsf{F}^\infty \chi_i^\gamma \wedge \mathsf{G}^\infty \chi_i)$ in the $\mathcal{T}_i$'s and $\mathcal{T}_i'$'s. Here it is:

$$\chi := \mathsf{E}(\psi_i^0) \wedge \mathsf{EFAG}(\chi_i^0 \wedge \cdots \wedge \chi_i^\gamma \wedge \chi_i).$$

One can check that for all states s in either $\mathcal{T}_i$ and $\mathcal{T}_i'$, we have $s \models \mathsf{E}\psi$ iff $s \models \chi$. So, we replace $\mathsf{E}\psi$ by χ in φ and we do so for each disjunct of the form $\mathsf{E}\psi_i$. In the worst case, the translation may produce a formula φ' of nonelementary size because of the way inductive disjunctive normal forms are produced. Nevertheless, at each step of replacing the subformulae $\mathsf{E}\psi_1, \ldots, \mathsf{E}\psi_k$ the number of occurrences of F^∞ decreases strictly, which guarantees termination.

Proof of 2. The proof is by structural induction with an induction hypothesis of the form:

(IH) if $|\varphi| \leq i$, then $\mathcal{T}_i, s_i \models \varphi$ iff $\mathcal{T}_i', s_i' \models \varphi$.

This also implies that (IH') if $|\varphi| \leq i$, then $\mathcal{T}_{i+1}, s_i \models \varphi$ iff $\mathcal{T}_{i+1}', s_i' \models \varphi$. Indeed, the reachability graph from s_i in $\mathcal{T}_i$ is identical to the reachability graph from s_i in $\mathcal{T}_{i+1}$. Similarly, the reachability graph from s_i' in $\mathcal{T}_i'$ is identical to the reachability graph from s_i' in $\mathcal{T}_{i+1}'$. Moreover, this implies:

(IH'') if $|\varphi| \leq i$, then $\mathcal{T}_{i+1}, r_{i+1} \models \varphi$ iff $\mathcal{T}_{i+1}', r_{i+1}' \models \varphi$.

A proof that (IH) and (IH') imply (IH'') consists of assuming that there is a formula ψ of minimal size that distinguishes $\mathcal{T}_{i+1}, r_{i+1}$ from $\mathcal{T}_{i+1}', r_{i+1}'$ and leads to a contradiction with (IH) and (IH'). One takes advantage of the facts that the only successor of r_{i+1} is s_i and the only successor of r_{i+1}' is s_i'. Details are left to the reader.

The proof of (2.) is by structural induction based on the temporal operators EX, EU and AU. The base case with atomic propositions and the cases in the induction step dealing with Boolean connectives are by an easy verification. Let us consider the remaining and only interesting cases. In the following we provide the cases for EX and EU, the case for AU is left as Exercise 10.24.

Case: $\varphi = \text{EX}\varphi'$: we have the following equivalences:

$$\mathcal{T}_{i+1}, s_{i+1} \models \text{EX}\varphi' \quad \text{iff} \quad \mathcal{T}_{i+1}, r_{i+1} \models \varphi' \text{ or } \mathcal{T}_i, s_i \models \varphi' \text{ or } \mathcal{T}_i', s_i' \models \varphi'$$
$$\text{iff} \quad \mathcal{T}_{i+1}', r_{i+1}' \models \varphi' \text{ or } \mathcal{T}_i, s_i \models \varphi' \text{ or } \mathcal{T}_i', s_i' \models \varphi' \text{ (by (IH''))}$$
$$\text{iff} \quad \mathcal{T}_{i+1}', s_{i+1}' \models \text{EX}\varphi'.$$

Case: $\varphi = \text{E}(\varphi_1 \text{U} \varphi_2)$: we have that $\mathcal{T}_{i+1}, s_{i+1} \models \text{E}(\varphi_1 \text{U} \varphi_2)$ is equivalent to one of the following conditions:

1. $\mathcal{T}_{i+1}, s_{i+1} \models \varphi_2$,
2. $\mathcal{T}_{i+1}, s_{i+1} \models \varphi_1$ and $\mathcal{T}_{i+1}, r_{i+1} \models \varphi_2$,
3. $\mathcal{T}_{i+1}, s_{i+1} \models \varphi_1$ and $\mathcal{T}_i, s_i \models \text{E}(\varphi_1 \text{U} \varphi_2)$,
4. $\mathcal{T}_{i+1}, s_{i+1} \models \varphi_1$ and $\mathcal{T}_i', s_i' \models \text{E}(\varphi_1 \text{U} \varphi_2)$.

So, $\mathcal{T}_{i+1}, s_{i+1} \models \text{E}(\varphi_1 \text{U} \varphi_2)$ is equivalent to one of the following conditions:

1. $\mathcal{T}_{i+1}', s_{i+1}' \models \varphi_2$ (by (IH')),
2. $\mathcal{T}_{i+1}', s_{i+1}' \models \varphi_1$ and $\mathcal{T}_{i+1}', r_{i+1}' \models \varphi_2$ (by (III') and (III'')),
3. $\mathcal{T}_{i+1}', s_{i+1}' \models \varphi_1$ (by (IH')) and $\mathcal{T}_i, s_i \models \text{E}(\varphi_1 \text{U} \varphi_2)$,
4. $\mathcal{T}_{i+1}', s_{i+1}' \models \varphi_1$ (by (IH')) and $\mathcal{T}_i', s_i' \models \text{E}(\varphi_1 \text{U} \varphi_2)$,

which is equivalent to $\mathcal{T}_{i+1}', s_{i+1}' \models \text{E}(\varphi_1 \text{U} \varphi_2)$. The best way to convince oneself of the correctness of this analysis is to carefully have a look at the transition systems in Figure 10.3. □

10.3.5 *The Fixpoint Alternation Hierarchy*

We have seen that TLR is less expressive than CTL which is less expressive not only than the modal μ-calculus but already less expressive than its fragment in which no fixpoint alternation occurs. This raises naturally the question of whether such inexpressibility results can be extended to fragments of restricted alternation, i.e. whether more alternation gives strictly higher expressive power. The answer is 'yes' but the proof technique deviates slightly from those of previous inexpressibility results. It will be based on Banach's Fixpoint Theorem, which claims the existence of unique fixpoints of contracting maps on complete metric spaces. Note that the fixpoint in this theorem does not refer to the fixpoint quantifiers in the modal μ-calculus. We will see that certain ITS form such spaces and that each $\mathcal{L}_\mu$ formula induces such a contracting map on them. Their fixpoints, according to Banach's Theorem, are then used to prove that certain properties expressible in $\mathcal{L}_\mu$ require a certain amount of fixpoint alternation.

The Metric Space of Infinite Binary Trees

Definition 10.3.17. A **metric space** is a pair (M, δ) where M is an arbitrary set and $\delta : M^2 \to \mathbb{R}^{\geq 0}$ intuitively measures the **distance** between two elements of M in terms of non-negative real numbers such that for all $x, y, z \in M$:

- $\delta(x, y) = 0$ iff $x = y$, i.e. the distance between different elements can never be zero,
- $\delta(x, y) = \delta(y, x)$, i.e. the distance function is symmetric,
- $\delta(x, y) + \delta(y, z) \geq \delta(x, z)$, i.e. one can never decrease distances by going via a third element. This is also known as the **triangle inequality**. $\qquad \triangledown$

Some of the most standard examples of metric spaces are the real or the rational numbers with the usual distance: $(\mathbb{R}, \delta)$ or $(\mathbb{Q}, \delta)$ with $\delta(x, y) = |x - y|$. A not so well-known example is that of Σ^ω for any alphabet Σ. It is also possible to make it a metric space with the metric function

$$\delta(v, w) := \inf \left\{ \frac{1}{2^k} \mid \forall i < k : v(i) = w(i) \right\}.$$

It is easy to see that this function is symmetric. Checking the remaining properties of being a metric space is left as Exercise 10.28. Intuitively, the distance between two words is determined by the longest common prefix of the two words: the longer that is, the smaller their distance.

An important property that distinguishes this metric space and that of the real numbers from the one of the rational numbers, for instance, is *completeness*, to be defined later. For example, consider the sequence $(x_n)_{n \geq 1}$ with

$$x_n := \sum_{i=1}^{n} \frac{6}{i^2}.$$

It is obviously a sequence of rational numbers but it has been proved to converge with

$$\lim_{n \to \infty} x_n = \pi^2,$$

which is not rational. It is beyond the scope of this book to provide a formal proof of this result in mathematical analysis, so we will just accept it as given. What we can see more easily, however, is the fact that its terms get closer and closer to each other. For instance, consider $x_1 = 6$, $x_2 = 7.5$, $x_3 = 8.1666\ldots$, $x_4 = 8.541666\ldots$, and so on. In fact, if we fix any positive distance ε we can show that from some index on, all terms of the sequence are within that distance. For instance, for all i, $j \geq 3$ we have that $\delta(x_i, x_j) \leq 0.5$. Likewise, for any, arbitrarily small positive value ε one would still find some threshold of indices such that all distances between elements with larger indices in this sequence are bounded by ε. Sequences with such property are called **Cauchy sequences**, and the existence of limits of all such sequences in a given metric space makes it complete. The formal definitions follow.

Definition 10.3.18. Let (M, δ) be a metric space. A sequence $(x_n)_{n \geq 1}$ of elements in M is called a **Cauchy sequence** if for every $\varepsilon > 0$ there is an $n_0 \in \mathbb{N}$ such that for all i, j with $n_0 \leq i \leq j$ we have $\delta(x_i, x_j) < \varepsilon$.

The space (M, δ) is called **complete** if every Cauchy sequence $(x_n)_{n \geq 1}$ in M has a limit $\lim_{n \to \infty} x_n$ in M. ▽

Intuitively, any Cauchy sequence has a *limit point* given the fact that the elements of that sequence get closer and closer to each other, but that limit point may not exist in the space. The property of a metric space being complete is therefore about its closure under all limit points of its Cauchy sequences.

The metric space of rational numbers with the usual metric is not complete, as the earlier example shows. The metric space of real numbers, however, is complete, and so is the space of infinite words with the metric defined previously. Indeed, let $(w_n)_{n \geq 1}$ be a Cauchy sequence of infinite words. We can construct its limit $\hat{w}$ as follows. To determine its nth letter, take $\varepsilon = 2^{-n}$. Now, since $(w_n)_{n \geq 1}$ is a Cauchy sequence, there is some n_0 such that for all i, $j \geq n_0$ we have $\delta(w_i, w_j) < 2^{-n}$. This means that all such w_i and w_j must coincide on at least the first n letters. In other words, all but finitely many words in this sequence have a uniquely determined letter at position i. We take this to be the letter at position i in $\hat{w}$ as well. This can be done for every position in $\hat{w}$ which determines this infinite word uniquely, and it is obvious that it is part of Σ^ω which makes this a complete metric space.

Example 10.3.19. Let Σ be an alphabet, and let $T_2^\Sigma := \{0, 1\}^* \to \Sigma$ be the set of all functions that map each word over 0 and 1 to a letter in Σ. Note that each such function t can be seen as an infinite binary, Σ-labelled tree:

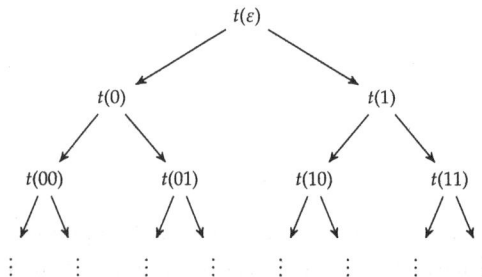

T_2^Σ can be made into a complete metric space using the same idea as in the case of infinite words (which are special infinite 'trees'). The corresponding metric function is

$$\delta(t, t') := \inf \left\{ \frac{1}{2^k} \mid \forall u \in \{0, 1\}^{<k} : t(u) = t'(u) \right\},$$

where $\{0, 1\}^{<k}$ denotes the set of all $\{0, 1\}$-words of length strictly smaller than k. In other words, the distance between two infinite binary trees is at most 2^{-k-1} unless they differ somewhere on the first k levels. Again, it is possible to prove formally that (T_2^Σ, δ) is a complete metric space (cf. Exercise 10.29).

Later, we will need the fact that a certain sequence in the metric space of infinite binary trees is indeed a Cauchy sequence. For this purpose it is helpful to derive a sufficient criterion for such a sequence to be Cauchy. The proof is left as Exercise 10.30.

Lemma 10.3.20. Let (M, δ) be a metric space and $(x_n)_{n\geq 1}$ a sequence such that there are $e, d \in \mathbb{R}^+$ with $d < 1$ and for all $n \geq 1$: $\delta(x_n, x_{n+1}) \leq e \cdot d^n$. Then the sequence $(x_n)_{n\geq 1}$ is a Cauchy sequence. ∎

The next technical notion we need is that of a contracting map.

Definition 10.3.21. Let (M, δ) be a metric space and $\mathfrak{f} : M \to M$. Then $\mathfrak{f}$ is said to be a **contracting map**, or just a **contraction**, if there is some $d \in \mathbb{R}$ with $d < 1$ such that for all $x, y \in M$: $\delta(\mathfrak{f}(x), \mathfrak{f}(y)) \leq d \cdot \delta(x, y)$. Then, d is also called a **contraction factor**. ▽

Thus, a contracting map intuitively moves elements closer to each other in this metric space. For instance, $\mathfrak{f}(x) = x/2$ is a contracting map on $\mathbb{R}$ and $\mathbb{Q}$ with their usual metrics since the distance between the halves of two elements is just half the distance between them. A similar example in the metric space of infinite words is the function that appends an additional symbol at the beginning, i.e. $\mathfrak{f}(w) = \mathsf{a}w$ for some fixed $\mathsf{a} \in \Sigma$. It is easily checked that it is also contracting with a factor of $1/2$. However, deletion of symbols at the beginning or elsewhere is not contracting in general; for instance we have $\delta(\mathsf{ab}^\omega, \mathsf{a}^\omega) = 1/2$ but $\delta(\mathsf{b}^\omega, \mathsf{a}^\omega) = 1$. Thus, a metric contraction rather expands words. However, not every operation that expands parts in a word is a metric contraction. Take for instance the map $rep : \Sigma^\omega \to \Sigma^\omega$ that repeats symbols, recursively defined as

$$rep(\mathsf{a}w) := \mathsf{aa} \cdot rep(w).$$

This is not a contraction on Σ^ω because the distance between two words that differ in the first symbol is not decreased by some constant factor <1. It is a contraction on $\mathsf{a}\Sigma^\omega$, though for every fixed $\mathsf{a} \in \Sigma$.

Equally, the map $\mathfrak{f}_\mathsf{a} : T_2^\Sigma \to T_2^\Sigma$ for any $\mathsf{a} \in \Sigma$, defined by $\mathfrak{f}_\mathsf{a}(t) = \mathsf{a}(t, t)$ is a contraction, where $\mathsf{a}(t, t)$ denotes the binary tree whose root is labelled with a and whose two immediate subtrees are each t. In order to check that this is the case, take two different trees t and t' and suppose that their distance is 2^{-k-1}, i.e. they do not differ on the first k levels. Then the distance between $\mathsf{a}(t, t)$ and $\mathsf{a}(t', t')$ is 2^{-k} because they do not differ on the first $k + 1$ levels. Thus, this map has halved the distances, too.

Later we will need the fact that contracting functions are *continuous* in the following sense.

Lemma 10.3.22. Let (M, δ) be a complete metric space, $\mathfrak{f} : M \to M$ be a contraction and $(x_n)_{n \geq 1}$ a Cauchy sequence. Then we have $\lim_{n \to \infty} \mathfrak{f}(x_n) = \mathfrak{f}(\lim_{n \to \infty} x_n)$. ■

Proof. Since (M, δ) is assumed to be complete, and $(x_n)_{n \geq 1}$ is Cauchy, $x^* := \lim_{n \to \infty} x_n$ exists in M. By the definition of a contraction, there is a constant $d < 1$ such that $\delta(\mathfrak{f}(x^*), \mathfrak{f}(x_n)) \leq d \cdot \delta(x^*, x_n)$ for every $n \geq 1$. Since $x^* = \lim_{n \to \infty} x_n$ we have $\lim_{n \to \infty} \delta(x^*, x_n) = 0$ and then also $\lim_{n \to \infty} d \cdot \delta(x^*, x_n) = 0$ and therefore

$$\lim_{n \to \infty} \delta(\mathfrak{f}(x^*), \mathfrak{f}(x_n)) = 0.$$

In other words, $\mathfrak{f}(x^*) = \lim_{n \to \infty} \mathfrak{f}(x_n)$. □

Model-Checking Games as Contracting Maps

We are particularly interested in a more elaborate mapping on infinite binary trees, induced by the μ-calculus model-checking games. It is contracting for the very same reason, though.

For the following we fix a set of atomic propositions $\text{PROP} := \{\mathbf{V}, \mathbf{R}\} \cup \mathbb{N}$. This would naturally lead to an uncountable alphabet which is not needed for our purposes. We only ever need node labels that contain exactly one proposition from $\{\mathbf{V}, \mathbf{R}\}$ and exactly one natural number. Clearly, every infinite binary tree t over such symbols is an ITS and so the satisfaction relation between such a tree and a μ-calculus formula over PROP is defined. We write $t \models \varphi$ to denote that the root of the tree t satisfies the formula φ.

Now take a tree t (seen as an ITS) and a μ-calculus formula φ. The model-checking game $\mathcal{G}^t(\varepsilon, \varphi)$ on t and φ, when started in the root ε of t, can naturally be seen as a binary tree again:

- The root position is given by the initial model-checking game configuration (ε, φ).
- If a position is given by some configuration $(v, \psi_1 \vee \psi_2)$, respectively $(v, \psi_1 \wedge \psi_2)$, then its label contains $\mathbf{V}$, respectively $\mathbf{R}$, and it has two successors formed by (v, ψ_1) and (v, ψ_2).
- If a position is given by some configuration $(v, \Diamond \psi)$, respectively $(v, \Box \psi)$, then its label contains $\mathbf{V}$, respectively $\mathbf{R}$, and it has two successors formed by $(v0, \psi)$ and $(v1, \psi)$. Note that these are the only two successors of v in the binary tree t.
- If a position is given by some configuration $(v, \tau X.\psi)$ then both its successors are formed by (v, X). Likewise, the two successors of such a configuration are both of the form (v, ψ), assuming that $fp_\vartheta(X) = \tau X.\psi$. The proposition in the label indicating the player who makes a choice in this configuration is irrelevant since the only two choices are equal. Thus, we arbitrarily say that these nodes are labelled with $\mathbf{V}$.
- Finally, we are left with configurations of the form (v, p) or $(v, \neg p)$ for some atomic proposition p. In the model-checking games, these configurations have no successors but

here we want $\mathcal{G}^t(\varepsilon, \varphi)$ to form an infinite binary tree so we simply let the model-checking games stay in these forever: their two successors are given by themselves, and their label contains, again arbitrarily chosen, the proposition **V**.

It remains to determine which natural number is contained in the label of each node. Just like the propositions **V** and **R** are used to mark which player makes a choice in the underlying node of the model-checking game, the natural numbers as propositions are used to signal the 'alternation index' of a variable that is encountered or, in case of an atomic proposition, whether or not it is satisfied in the corresponding node. Every node that is not given by a configuration of the form (v, X), (v, p) or $(v, \neg p)$ for some variable X, some atomic proposition p and some tree node v, contains the number 0 in its label. A node given by (v, p) contains 0 in its label if $v \models p$ and 1 otherwise. Likewise, a node of the form $(v, \neg p)$ contains 0 in its label if $v \not\models p$ and 1 otherwise. Thus, the value 0 is used to indicate that a configuration with a literal is obviously true; 1 is used in the case that it is false.

It may seem odd to use 0 for truth and 1 for falsity. The reason is the following. The atomic value $\top$ is equivalent to $\nu X.X$ whereas $\bot$ is equivalent to $\mu X.X$. The game trees implicitly 'behave' as if they encountered $\tau X.X$ in such a situation – the current configuration simply gets copied onto all nodes of the underlying subtree. Natural numbers are used in the following way to indicate which kind of fixpoint variable occurs in these configurations. To determine in general the labels of the variable-containing nodes, let ai_φ be the pointwise least function that assigns to each fixpoint variable $X \in sub(\varphi)$ a value $ai_\varphi(X)$ such that

- $ai_\varphi(X)$ is even if $fp_\varphi(X) = \nu X.\psi$ for some ψ;
- $ai_\varphi(X)$ is odd if $fp_\varphi(X) = \mu X.\psi$ for some ψ;
- $ai_\varphi(X) \geq ai_\varphi(Y)$ if $X \succeq_\varphi Y$.

Then, a configuration of the form (v, X) contains in its label the value $ai_\varphi(X)$.

Example 10.3.23. Take the formula

$$\varphi := \mu Y.\Diamond Y \vee \nu X.\mu Z.p \wedge ((q \wedge \Diamond X) \vee \Diamond Z))$$

expressing that 'there is a path on which p holds eventually always and q holds infinitely often'.

We have $X \succ_\varphi Z$ and no other dependency relations between any two different variables. Thus, we get $ai_\varphi(Z) = 1$, $ai_\varphi(X) = 2$ and $ai_\varphi(Y) = 1$.

Take $\varphi' := \mu Y.\nu X.((p \wedge \Diamond X) \vee \Diamond Y)$ expressing 'there is a path on which eventually p always holds'. Then we get $ai_{\varphi'}(X) = 0$ and $ai_{\varphi'}(Y) = 1$ because of $Y \succ_{\varphi'} X$. Interestingly, take $\varphi'' := \mu Y.(\nu X.(p \wedge \Diamond X)) \vee \Diamond Y$. It expresses the same property without alternation, i.e. there is no dependency between Y and X but we still have $ai_{\varphi''}(X) = 0$ and $ai_{\varphi''}(Y) = 1$.

Example 10.3.24. Consider $\varphi := \mu Y.\Diamond Y \vee \nu X.\mu Z.\mathbf{V} \wedge ((1 \wedge \Diamond X) \vee (\neg 2 \wedge \Diamond Z))$ which has a similar shape to the formula from the previous example. Again, we get $ai_\varphi(Z) = 1$, $ai_\varphi(X) = 2$ and $ai_\varphi(Y) = 1$. It is obviously defined over the aforementioned alphabet that is used to abstract model-checking games into infinite binary trees. Assume that it only uses the numbers 0, 1, 2. Then φ demands the existence of a path on which eventually all nodes are owned by **V** and 1 is the highest such alternation index that occurs infinitely often.

Consider the following tree t.

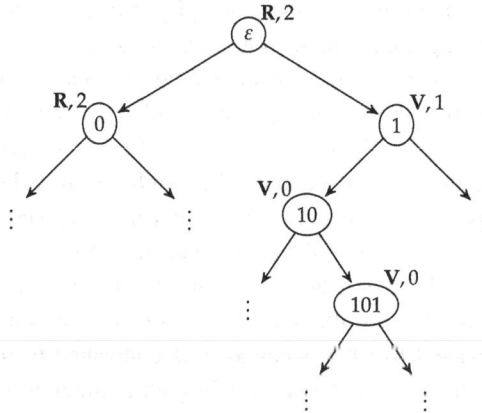

The infinite binary tree over the same alphabet that represents the model-checking game $\mathcal{G}^t(\varepsilon, \varphi)$ is shown in Figure 10.4. In order to make the construction more comprehensible we show the model-checking game configurations that are used to form the nodes rather than the tree positions $\varepsilon, 0, 1, 00, \ldots$ which can easily be inferred. We also abbreviate the formulae in the configurations as much as possible.

Note that natural numbers in this tree occur in three different roles:

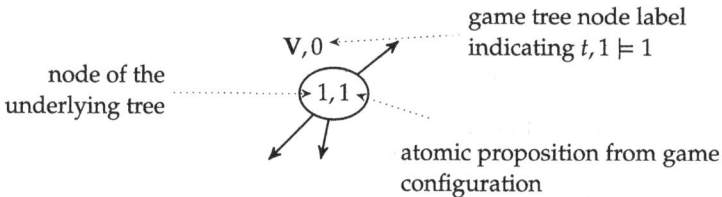

Now imagine what the two game trees $\mathcal{G}^t(\varepsilon, \varphi)$ and $\mathcal{G}^{t'}(\varepsilon, \varphi)$ look like for a fixed formula φ and two possibly different infinite binary trees t and t'. Since their construction can be seen as a deterministic top-down process we get that the two game trees will be equal on a prefix if t and t' equal on some prefix. More specifically, if t and t' do not differ on the first k levels, then $\mathcal{G}^t(\varepsilon, \varphi)$ and $\mathcal{G}^{t'}(\varepsilon, \varphi)$ do not differ on at least the first $k + 1$ levels. This gives us the following result.

Lemma 10.3.25. Let $\varphi \in \mathcal{L}_\mu$ be closed and consider the mapping $\mathfrak{f}_\varphi : T_2^\Sigma \to T_2^\Sigma$ defined by $\mathfrak{f}_\varphi(t) = \mathcal{G}^t(\varepsilon, \varphi)$. Then $\mathfrak{f}_\varphi$ is a contraction. ∎

We leave the proof as Exercise 10.30. It can be achieved by formalising the ideas described earlier about coinciding on at least the first $k + 1$ levels.

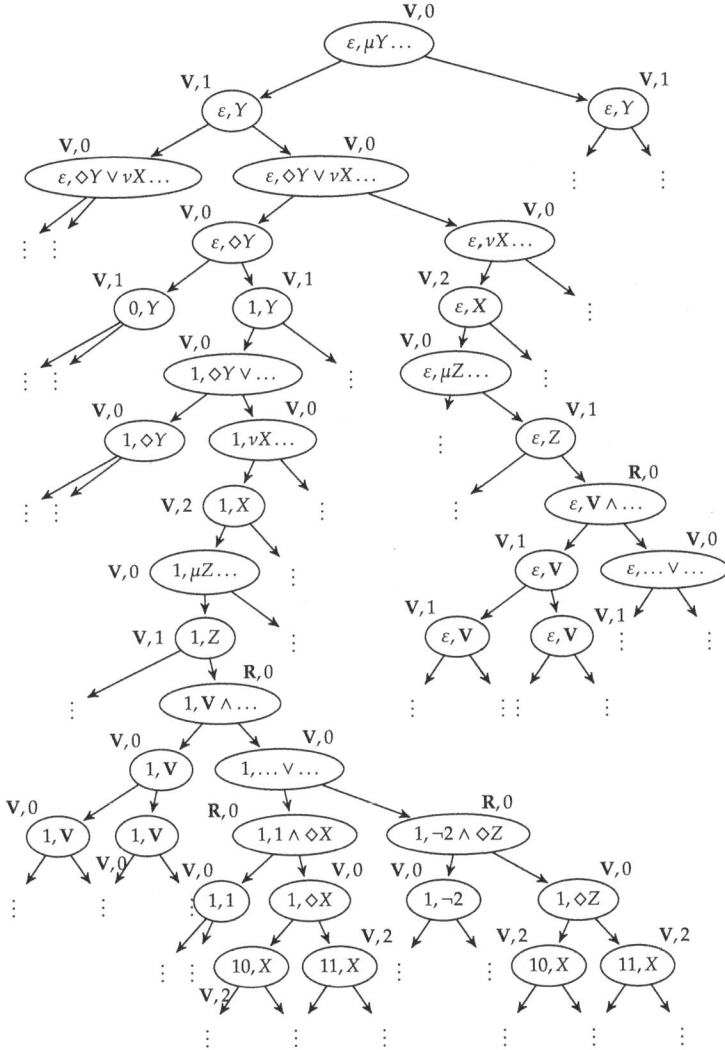

Figure 10.4 A model-checking game represented as an infinite binary tree.

The Walukiewicz Formulae

The previous section has shown how the model-checking game on an infinite binary tree and a μ-calculus formula φ can again be represented as an infinite binary tree. This is not very surprising; the connection between $\mathcal{G}^t(\varepsilon, \varphi)$ on one hand and t and φ on the other is purely syntactic so far. In this section we provide a semantic connection: these game trees carry the information about whether $t \models \varphi$ holds. This information is not obviously visible in most cases but the modal μ-calculus is strong enough to extract this information from these game trees. We present formulae which hold true in a game tree $\mathcal{G}^t(\varepsilon, \varphi)$ iff $t \models \varphi$, i.e. they define the model-checking problem of $\mathcal{L}_\mu$.

Definition 10.3.26. Let $k \geq 1$. The kth **Walukiewicz formula** is

$$\Phi_k := \tau X_{k-1} \ldots \mu X_1.\nu X_0. \bigvee_{i=0}^{k-1} i \wedge \left((\mathbf{V} \wedge \Diamond X_i) \vee (\mathbf{R} \wedge \Box X_i)\right)$$

where $\tau = \mu$ if k is even (and therefore $k - 1$ is odd), and $\tau = \nu$ otherwise. $\triangledown$

Note that Φ_k uses the propositions $\mathbf{V}$, $\mathbf{R}$ and $0, \ldots, k - 1$. Thus it can be interpreted over model-checking game trees.

Lemma 10.3.27. Let $k \geq 1, t \in T_2^\Sigma$ and $\varphi \in \mathcal{L}_\mu$ be closed such that $ai_\varphi(X) \in \{0, \ldots, k - 1\}$ for every $X \in sub(\varphi)$. Then $\mathcal{G}^t(\varepsilon, \varphi) \models \Phi_k$ iff $t \models \varphi$.   ∎

Proof. '$\Leftarrow$' Suppose that $t \models \varphi$. According to Theorem 8.4.10, player $\mathbf{V}$ has a winning strategy $\mathfrak{str}$ for the model-checking game $\mathcal{G}^t(\varepsilon, \varphi)$. Let t' be this model-checking game tree. We describe a strategy $\mathfrak{str}'$ for player $\mathbf{V}$ in the model-checking game $\mathcal{G}^{t'}(\varepsilon, \Phi_k)$. Consider how this game proceeds: starting in the root node ε of t', we generally reach a configuration (v, Φ_k) and then deterministically unfold the fixpoint formulae until we reach the body of the Walukiewicz formula which starts with a disjunction. Now $t(v)$ contains exactly one natural number i in its label, and player $\mathbf{V}$ chooses the ith disjunct of this body. If $\mathbf{R}$ chooses the conjunct i then he has lost immediately.

So, suppose he chooses the disjunction $(\mathbf{V} \wedge \Diamond X_i) \vee (\mathbf{R} \wedge \Box X_i)$. Again, $t(v)$ contains exactly one of the propositions $\mathbf{V}$ and $\mathbf{R}$, so $\mathbf{V}$ chooses the corresponding disjunct and $\mathbf{R}$ will have to answer with the modal formula if he wants to avoid immediate defeat. If it is $\Box X_i$ then $\mathbf{R}$ chooses some successor vj of v and the game continues with (vj, X_i). If it is $\Diamond X_i$ then player $\mathbf{V}$ consults his strategy in the model-checking game $\mathcal{G}^t(\varepsilon, \varphi)$. Note that the path $\varepsilon, \ldots, v$ in the tree t' that has been followed is a partial play in $\mathcal{G}^t(\varepsilon, \varphi)$ ending in the configuration $(v, \Diamond X_i)$. By assumption, $\mathbf{V}$'s winning strategy in this game lets him choose some successor which is vj for some $j \in \{0, 1\}$. In the game $\mathcal{G}^{t'}(\varepsilon, \Phi_k)$, player $\mathbf{V}$ chooses (vj, X_i), and the unfolding of a fixpoint prefix starts all over.

It remains to be seen that this informally described strategy $\mathfrak{str}'$ is winning for $\mathbf{V}$. Take any play that conforms to this strategy. It is of the form

$$\lambda := (v_0, \Phi_k), (v_0, X_{k-1}), \ldots, (v_0, X_{i_1}), \ldots, (v_1, X_{i_2}), \ldots, (v_2, X_{j_2}), \ldots$$

It is important to note that the sequence $v_0, v_1, v_2, \ldots$ is a play of $\mathcal{G}^t(\varepsilon, \varphi)$ that conforms to $\mathbf{V}$'s winning strategy $\mathfrak{str}$. Hence, it must have been won by her by either reaching a configuration with a literal that is true in the corresponding tree node, or the outermost fixpoint variable that is seen infinitely often is of type ν. In the first case, the labels of the nodes in λ eventually all contain 0. In the second case, the largest number that occurs infinitely often on their labels is even because ν-bound variables have even alternation index. In any case, the outermost variable in Φ_k that is seen infinitely often in the play λ is ν-bound, too. Hence, λ is won by $\mathbf{V}$ which means that $\mathfrak{str}'$ is indeed a winning strategy for her in the game $\mathcal{G}^{t'}(\varepsilon, \Phi_k)$. According to Theorem 8.4.13, we have $t' \models \Phi_k$.

'⇒' This direction can be shown in exactly the same way by assuming $t \not\models \varphi$ and then lifting a winning strategy for player **R** in $\mathcal{G}^t(\varepsilon, \varphi)$ to a winning strategy for him in $\mathcal{G}^{t'}(\varepsilon, \Phi_k)$. □

Banach's Fixpoint Theorem

The last vital ingredient to the proof of the alternation hierarchy in the modal μ-calculus is Banach's Fixpoint Theorem. It states that contracting maps on complete metric spaces have unique fixpoints. Intuitively, such a fixpoint is reached by starting at any point x in the metric space and then simply iterating this map $\mathfrak{f}$. The first iterations yield $\mathfrak{f}(x)$ and $\mathfrak{f}(\mathfrak{f}(x))$. Consider the distances between x and $\mathfrak{f}(x)$ on one hand, and $\mathfrak{f}(x)$ and $\mathfrak{f}(\mathfrak{f}(x))$ on the other. Since $\mathfrak{f}$ is assumed to be contracting we have $\delta(\mathfrak{f}(x), \mathfrak{f}(\mathfrak{f}(x))) < \delta(x, \mathfrak{f}(x))$ for the corresponding metric δ. That is, the third point in this sequence is closer to the second than the second is to the first. This continues making the distances between successive points in this sequence smaller and smaller. The limit point is then a fixpoint.

Theorem 10.3.28 (Banach's Fixpoint Theorem). Let (M, δ) be a nonempty complete metric space and $\mathfrak{f} : M \to M$ be a contraction. Then $\mathfrak{f}$ has a unique fixpoint $\mathfrak{f}^*$. ∎

Proof. First we show that $\mathfrak{f}$ has at least one fixpoint. Since M is assumed to be nonempty we can take some $x \in M$ and form a sequence

$$x, \mathfrak{f}(x), \mathfrak{f}(\mathfrak{f}(x)), \ldots, \mathfrak{f}^i(x), \ldots$$

of elements in M. Since $\mathfrak{f}$ is assumed to be contracting, there is some $d < 1$ such that $\delta(\mathfrak{f}^{i+1}(x), \mathfrak{f}^{i+2}(x)) \leq d \cdot \delta(\mathfrak{f}^i(x), \mathfrak{f}^{i+1}(x))$ for every $i \geq 0$. Thus, $\delta(\mathfrak{f}^i(x), \mathfrak{f}^{i+1}(x)) \leq d^i \cdot \delta(x, \mathfrak{f}(x))$ for every $i \geq 0$. According to Lemma 10.3.20, the sequence $(\mathfrak{f}^i(x))_{i \geq 0}$ is Cauchy and, since (M, δ) is assumed to be complete, it has a limit point $\mathfrak{f}^* := \lim_{i \to \infty} \mathfrak{f}^i(x)$ in M.

The fact that $\mathfrak{f}^*$ is a fixpoint of f is a direct consequence of Lemma 10.3.22: we have

$$\mathfrak{f}(\mathfrak{f}^*) = \mathfrak{f}(\lim_{i \to \infty} \mathfrak{f}^i(x)) = \lim_{i \to \infty} \mathfrak{f}(\mathfrak{f}^i(x)) = \lim_{i \to \infty} \mathfrak{f}^{i+1}(x) = \mathfrak{f}^*.$$

Finally, we show that there is no other fixpoint. Suppose there were two, called x^* and y^*. Then, by the triangle inequality, we have

$$\delta(x^*, y^*) \leq \delta(x^*, \mathfrak{f}(x^*)) + \delta(\mathfrak{f}(x^*), \mathfrak{f}(y^*)) + \delta(\mathfrak{f}(y^*), y^*)$$
$$\leq \delta(x^*, x^*) + d \cdot \delta(x^*, y^*) + \delta(y^*, y^*) = d \cdot \delta(x^*, y^*)$$

because $\mathfrak{f}(x^*) = x^*$ and $\mathfrak{f}(y^*) = y^*$ by assumption. Note that we could therefore also have replaced the term $\delta(\mathfrak{f}(x^*), \mathfrak{f}(y^*))$ by $\delta(x^*, y^*)$ instead of $d \cdot \delta(x^*, y^*)$ using these fixpoint properties. This would however only result in $\delta(x^*, y^*) \leq \delta(x^*, y^*)$ which is trivially true. Using the contraction property instead we now get $\delta(x^*, y^*) \leq d \cdot \delta(x^*, y^*)$ which implies $\delta(x^*, y^*) = 0$ because $d < 1$. By the definition of a metric space, we thus have $x^* = y^*$ which completes the proof. □

The Alternation Hierarchy Is Strict

Recall the μ-calculus alternation hierarchy formed by the fragments Σ_k and Π_k of formulae that, intuitively, use at most $k-1$ fixpoint alternations and least, respectively greatest fixpoint quantifiers as their outermost ones (cf. Definition 8.3.6). In particular we have $\Sigma_{k+1} \supseteq \Sigma_k \cup \Pi_k \subseteq \Pi_{k+1}$ for every $k \geq 0$. Our goal is to show that this syntactic hierarchy is semantically strict, i.e. more fixpoint alternation gives higher expressive power. Thus, we need to show that there are infinitely many levels of this hierarchy which contain formulae that are not equivalent to any formulae which syntactically fall into lower levels. With all the ingredients worked out in the previous sections, this is not too difficult anymore.

Candidates for such formulae that witness the strictness of the hierarchy are the Walukiewicz formulae Φ_k. We write $\overline{\varphi}$ for the formula that is obtained from $\neg\varphi$ by putting it into negation normal form according to the usual procedure. The first observation about them is easily checked.

Lemma 10.3.29. Let $k \geq 1$. If k is even then $\Phi_k \in \Pi_k$ and $\overline{\Phi_k} \in \Sigma_k$. If k is odd then $\Phi_k \in \Sigma_k$ and $\overline{\Phi_k} \in \Pi_k$. ∎

Theorem 10.3.30. For every odd $k \geq 1$ we have that Φ_k is not equivalent to any $\Psi \in \Pi_k$; for any even k it is not equivalent to any $\Psi \in \Sigma_k$. ∎

Proof. Let $k \geq 1$ be odd. The case of k being even can be shown in exactly the same way by swapping the roles of Σ_i and Π_i for any i.

As just observed in the previous lemma, we have $\Phi_k \in \Sigma_k$. So, suppose there was some $\Psi \in \Pi_k$ such that $\Psi \equiv \Phi_k$, i.e. for any infinite binary tree t we get that $t \models \Phi_k$ iff $t \models \Psi$. Consider $\overline{\Psi}$ which then belongs to Σ_k. Clearly, for any such tree t we also get that $t \models \overline{\Psi}$ iff $t \not\models \Psi$.

According to Lemma 10.3.25, the mapping $t \mapsto \mathcal{G}^t(\varepsilon, \overline{\Psi})$ is a contraction, and according to Theorem 10.3.28 it has a fixpoint t^*, i.e. $t^* = \mathcal{G}^{t^*}(\varepsilon, \overline{\Psi})$. Now all we need is Lemma 10.3.27, which yields the following:

$$t^* \models \overline{\Psi} \quad \text{iff} \quad \mathcal{G}^{t^*}(\varepsilon, \overline{\Psi}) \models \Phi_k \quad \text{iff} \quad t^* \models \Phi_k \quad \text{iff} \quad t^* \models \Psi \quad \text{iff} \quad t^* \not\models \overline{\Psi}.$$

This is obviously a contradiction, and we conclude that Ψ cannot exist. □

Thus, we get that the alternation hierarchy in the modal μ-calculus is strict over the class of interpreted transition systems that form infinite binary trees. This may not be such an interesting class for all sorts of purposes; however, the result easily transfers to any superclass.

Corollary 10.3.31. The alternation hierarchy is strict over the classes of all interpreted transition systems and the class of all trees. ∎

Proof. This is a direct consequence of the simple fact that these two classes contain the class of all infinite binary trees. Suppose that the hierarchy did collapse at some level, e.g. every formula was equivalent to a formula in Σ_k for some k over the class of, say, all trees.

Then this would hold, in particular, for the Walukiewicz formula Φ_{k+1}, which agrees with some Σ_k formula on all trees. This, of course, contradicts the fact that it does not agree with any Σ_k formula on all binary infinite trees. □

Another strictness result that is not directly obtained concerns the class of all finite models.

Theorem 10.3.32. The alternation hierarchy is strict over the classes of all finite interpreted transition systems. ■

Proof. This uses $\mathcal{L}_\mu$'s finite model property which is proved later on in Section 15.4.3. Note that logical equivalence between φ and ψ on a class $\mathcal{C}$ of models is itself equivalent to the unsatisfiability of the formula $\neg(\varphi \leftrightarrow \psi)$ over this class. Hence, suppose that the hierarchy did collapse over the class of all finite models, i.e. that there is some k such that every $\mathcal{L}_\mu$ formula is equivalent to some formula in Σ_k over all finite models. From Theorem 10.3.30 and Corollary 10.3.31 we know that the Walukiewicz formula Φ_k is not equivalent to any formula $\psi \in \Sigma_{k-1}$ for any $k \geq 1$. With the preceding remark we get that $\neg(\Phi_k \leftrightarrow \psi)$ is unsatisfiable. Since every satisfiable $\mathcal{L}_\mu$ formula is already satisfied in a finite model (Theorem 15.4.33), $\neg(\Phi_k \leftrightarrow \psi)$ is already unsatisfiable over the class of all finite models for any such ψ. In other words, Φ_k is not equivalent to ψ over the class of all finite models, i.e. those formulae that witness the strictness of the hierarchy in general also witness its strictness over finite models. □

10.4 Exercises

Exercises on equi-expressiveness of linear-time formalisms

Exercise 10.1.

(a) Prove Lemma 10.1.3.
(b) Give an algorithm that checks in linear-time whether a given regular expression is ε-free.

Exercise 10.2. Give an estimation on the size of the QLTL formulae that are produced by the translation from ω-regular expressions in Theorem 10.1.7. What is the maximal nesting of propositional quantifiers in these formulae? Do they contain quantifier alternation, i.e. nestings of existential and universal quantifiers when re-written into negation normal form?

Exercise 10.3. Consider the translation from ω-regular expressions into LT_μ as given in Theorem 10.1.8. The aim of this exercise is to show that it is correct, i.e. that for every ω-regular expression E we have $\mathrm{L}(E) = \mathrm{Mod}(tr(E))$.

(a) Give the full inductive definition of the two translation functions tr_p for regular expressions and tr for ω-regular expressions – in particular those of the form E^ω. *Hint:* This simply boils down to understanding the structure of ω-regular expressions properly and then assembling the already given translation clauses for each operator in each possible syntactic position.

(b) Prove by induction on the structure of (ω)-regular expressions E that the translation is correct, i.e. that for all computations σ we have $\sigma \in L(E)$ iff $\sigma \models tr(E)$. *Hints:*

- This needs a suitable generalisation for regular expressions; here we need to show that for each computation σ and every atomic proposition p we have $\sigma \models tr_p(E)$ iff $\sigma = \rho\sigma'$ for some finite computation path ρ and some infinite computation σ' such that $\rho \in L(E)$ and $\sigma' \models p$.

- Note that the Kleene star gets translated into a least fixpoint. For the direction '$\Leftarrow$' it may be helpful to argue using the model-checking games for the model and linear-time μ-calculus. For the direction '$\Rightarrow$' one can use fixpoint induction. It suffices to show that the set S of all infinite computations σ which can be decomposed into $\sigma = \rho\sigma'$ such that $\rho \in L(E)$ is a pre-fixpoint of the map $X \mapsto \mathrm{Mod}(p \vee tr_X(E))$. That is, whenever some infinite computation σ belongs to $\mathrm{Mod}(p \vee tr_X(E))$ under the assumption that X is assigned to S, then it must also belong to S. It follows from the Knaster–Tarski Theorem that the least fixpoint of this map, i.e. $\mathrm{Mod}(\mu X.p \vee tr_X(E))$, is included in S which is what is to be shown for the direction '$\Rightarrow$'.

- The case of the infinite-concatenation operator is handled similarly. However, note that it gets translated into a *greatest* fixpoint. Hence, fixpoint induction can be used to prove direction '$\Leftarrow$' by showing that the aforementioned set S is a post-fixpoint of the map $Y \mapsto \mathrm{Mod}(tr_Y(E))$, for then it is included in its greatest fixpoint. For the other direction '$\Rightarrow$' it may be useful to consider model-checking games again.

Exercise 10.4. Show that $E \diamondsuit\!\!\rightarrow p$ is equivalent to

$$\mathcal{A}_E(\psi_0, \ldots, \psi_{2^n-1}, \psi'_0, \ldots, \psi'_{2^n-1})$$

in the proof of Lemma 10.1.15.

Exercise 10.5. Give a direct translation from ETL into the linear-time μ-calculus.

Exercise 10.6. Show that the PSL formula $(E \diamondsuit\!\!\rightarrow \top) \wedge (E^+ \Box\!\!\rightarrow X(E \diamondsuit\!\!\rightarrow \top))$ defines less infinite computations than E^ω when E is not left-deletable.

Exercises on logics with past operators

Exercise 10.7. Prove Lemma 10.1.20 and 10.1.21. *Hint:* In order to save half the work, define inductively a translation $tr : \text{LTL+Past} \to \text{LTL+Past}$ first, such that for every model σ based on $\mathbb{Z}$, every $i \in \mathbb{Z}$, and every $\varphi \in \text{LTL+Past}$ we have: $\sigma, i \models \varphi$ iff $\sigma, -i \models tr(\varphi)$. Then argue that half of the equivalences in these lemmata follow from the other half and this principle.

Exercise 10.8. Complete the details in the proofs of Theorem 10.1.22. and Corollary 10.1.23.

Exercise 10.9. The elimination of past-time operators (Theorem 10.1.22) guarantees that there is a formula φ in LTL that is initially equivalent to

$$G(\text{grant} \to F^{-1} \text{ request}).$$

Find one.

Exercise 10.10. Find Boolean combinations of pure past and pure future formulae that are equivalent to the following formulae:

- $\varphi_1 S(\varphi_2 \wedge (\varphi_3 U \varphi_4))$ and develop a general correspondence between formulae and their duals in which each future operator is replaced by a certain past operator and vice versa. (Hint: consider the proof sketch of Theorem 10.1.22.)
- $(\varphi_1 \vee (\varphi_2 S \varphi_3)) U \varphi_4$.
- $G(\varphi_1 \vee (\varphi_2 S \varphi_3))$. (Hint: consider its negation.)

Exercises on the connections between linear- and branching-time formulae

Exercise 10.11. Verify that the claim in Lemma 10.2.4 is correct.

Exercise 10.12. Verify the claim that an LT_μ formula φ of size n and alternation depth k can be translated into a $\mathcal{L}_\mu$ formula of size $2^{\mathcal{O}(n^2 k \log n)}$ that is equivalent to φ under the existential path semantics.

Hint: This needs concepts from Chapters 14 and 15 and can be seen as follows. An LT_μ formula is essentially an alternating parity automaton. Alternating *Büchi* automata – a subclass thereof – can be translated into nondeterministic Büchi automata using the Miyano–Hayashi construction (cf. Section 15.2.1, where it is used for an equivalent problem, namely the determinisation of co-Büchi automata). This construction cannot be used as such on alternating *parity* automata, but the underlying principles can. A nondeterministic parity automaton can be obtained as follows: one overapproximates the language of the alternating parity automaton by a powerset construction. This is done by a nondeterministic automaton with all states final (also called safety automaton) that simply guesses in each step the next layer of a level of a run of the alternating automaton. This simple automaton is paired with a deterministic parity automaton which checks that no path in this run sees as its maximal priority occurring infinitely often an odd one. This deterministic parity automaton can be obtained by determinising and complementing a suitable nonderministic Büchi automaton which guesses such a path in the run DAG. Section 15.2.2 shows how to do this in the context of games rather than nondeterministic Büchi automata but the principles are equally applicable here.

Then Chapter 14 also shows how a nondeterministic Büchi automaton can be translated into an ω-regular expression, and the rest is done by inspecting the corresponding translations in this chapter.

Exercises on translations among branching-time logics

Exercise 10.13. Consider the translation from CTL* into $\mathcal{L}_\mu$ that is presented in Theorem 10.2.7. Estimate the alternation depth of the resulting formulae. Which class in the alternation hierarchy do they fall into?

Exercise 10.14. Extend the translation from CTL* into $\mathcal{L}_\mu$ from Theorem 10.2.7 to ECTL*.

Exercise 10.15. Estimate the size of the resulting $\mathcal{L}_\mu$ formula in the translation from ATL* in Theorem 10.2.9.

Exercise 10.16. Estimate the blowup in the translation from CTL$^+$ into CTL as presented in the proof of Theorem 10.2.12.

Exercises on separation results

Exercise 10.17. Prove the Inexpressibility Lemma 10.3.2.

Exercise 10.18. Show that BML cannot express the TLR property EFp.

Exercise 10.19. Spell out the missing details in the proof of Theorem 10.3.7.

Exercise 10.20. Show that there is no LTL formula φ such that A$\varphi \equiv$ AFG$p \wedge$ EGp.

Exercise 10.21. Show that in each case there is no CTL formula φ such that

(a) $\varphi \equiv$ A(FG$p \wedge$ GFq),
(b) $\varphi \equiv$ AF($p \wedge$ Xp),
(c) $\varphi \equiv$ EGFq.

Show furthermore that there is also no LTL formula in each case such that

(d) A$\varphi \equiv$ EXq,
(e) A$\varphi \equiv$ AGF$p \wedge$ EGp.

Exercise 10.22. Show that EGq is not expressible in the branching-time logic that only has the operators EX and EF. *Hint:* You can use the following two families of transition systems $\mathcal{T}_n$ and $\mathcal{T}'_n$.

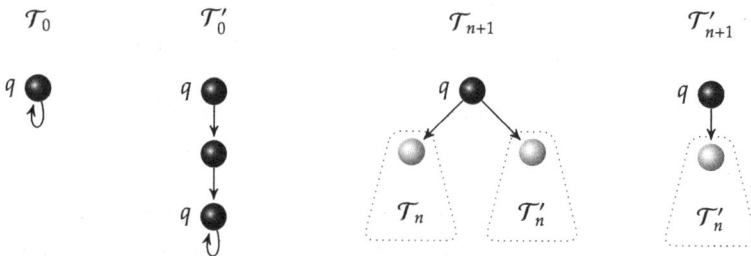

Exercise 10.23. Let us consider the two families of transition systems $(\mathcal{T}_i)_{i \geq 1}$ and $(\mathcal{T}_i')_{i \geq 1}$ from Figure 10.2.

(a) Show that for all $1 \leq i < i'$, we have

$$\mathcal{T}_i, s_i \rightleftarrows \mathcal{T}_{i'}, s_i \quad \mathcal{T}_i, r_i \rightleftarrows \mathcal{T}_{i'}, r_i \quad \mathcal{T}_i, t_i \rightleftarrows \mathcal{T}_{i'}, t_i.$$

(b) Show that for all $1 \leq i < i'$, we have

$$\mathcal{T}_i, s_i \rightleftarrows \mathcal{T}_{i'}', s_i \quad \mathcal{T}_i, r_i \rightleftarrows \mathcal{T}_{i'}', r_i \quad \mathcal{T}_i, t_i \rightleftarrows \mathcal{T}_{i'}', t_i.$$

(c) Let φ be an ECTL formula. In the following, we write $s_i \models \varphi$ to mean that the state s_i satisfies φ in any transition system $\mathcal{T}_{i'}$ with $i' \geq i$ or $\mathcal{T}_{i'}'$ with $i' > i$. A similar simplified notation is used for r_i and t_i. Show the properties for all i and for all φ in ECTL:
   (a) $s_i \models \varphi$ implies $s_{i+1} \models \varphi$ and $s_i \models \varphi$ and $i > |\varphi|$ imply $s_{i-1} \models \varphi$.
   (b) $r_i \models \varphi$ implies $r_{i+1} \models \varphi$ and $r_i \models \varphi$ and $i > |\varphi|$ imply $r_{i-1} \models \varphi$.
   (c) $t_i \models \varphi$ implies $t_{i+1} \models \varphi$ and $t_i \models \varphi$ and $i > |\varphi|$ imply $t_{i-1} \models \varphi$.
(d) Conclude that the following properties hold for all ECTL formulae φ:
   (a) There is $i > |\varphi|$ such that $\mathcal{T}_i, s_i \models \varphi$ iff for all $i' \geq |\varphi|$, we have $\mathcal{T}_{i'}, s_{i'} \models \varphi$.
   (b) There is $i > |\varphi|$ such that $\mathcal{T}_i, r_i \models \varphi$ iff for all $i' \geq |\varphi|$, we have $\mathcal{T}_{i'}, r_{i'} \models \varphi$.
   (c) There is $i > |\varphi|$ such that $\mathcal{T}_i, t_i \models \varphi$ iff for all $i' \geq |\varphi|$, we have $\mathcal{T}_{i'}, t_{i'} \models \varphi$.
(e) Show that for all ECTL formulae φ and for all $i \geq |\varphi|$, we have
   (a) $\mathcal{T}_i, s_i \models \varphi$ iff $\mathcal{T}_i', s_i' \models \varphi$.
   (b) $\mathcal{T}_i, r_i \models \varphi$ iff $\mathcal{T}_i', r_i' \models \varphi$.
   (c) $\mathcal{T}_i, t_i \models \varphi$ iff $\mathcal{T}_i', t_i' \models \varphi$.

Exercise 10.24. Complete the proof of Theorem 10.3.16.

Exercise 10.25. Find formulae in ETL, QLTL, PSL and LT_μ that formalise the linear-time property 'p holds at an even moment'. Give an ω-regular expression of it, too.

Exercise 10.26. Why does $\mu Z.p \vee \Box\Box Z$ not express 'p holds on *all* paths at some even moment'? How can the formula be fixed to state this property?

Exercise 10.27. Consider the (infinite) interpreted transition system $\mathcal{T} = (S, R, L)$ in Figure 10.5 where each state s_i or r_i satisfies $p \wedge \neg q$, the state $s^\star$ satisfies $\neg p \wedge \neg q$ and the state $r^\star$ satisfies $\neg p \wedge q$. Let $\mathcal{L}$ be the fragment of CTL restricted to the temporal operators AU, EF and EX.

(a) Show that for all $k \geq 0$ and $j \geq k$, the states s_j and r_j agree on all the formulae of $\mathcal{L}$ with height of nested temporal operators bounded by k.
(b) Conclude that there is no formula in $\mathcal{L}$ equivalent to the CTL formula $\mathsf{E}(p\mathsf{U}q)$. *Hint*: Note that $\mathcal{T}, s_j \not\models \mathsf{E}(p\mathsf{U}q)$ and $\mathcal{T}, r_j \models \mathsf{E}(p\mathsf{U}q)$.

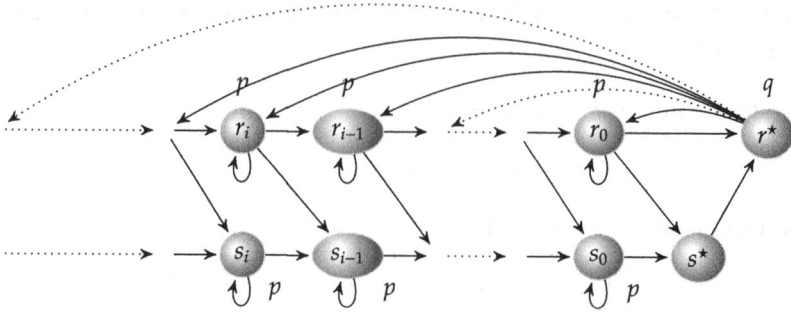

Figure 10.5 ITS showing that EU is not definable in terms of AU, EF and EX.

Exercises on the $\mathcal{L}_\mu$ alternation hierarchy

Exercise 10.28. Check that (Σ^ω, δ) with $\delta(v, w) := 2^{-pr(v,w)}$ where $pr(v, w) = \sup\{k \mid \forall i < k ; v(i) = w(i)\}$ forms a complete metric space.

Exercise 10.29. Show that (T_2^∞, δ) is a complete metric space where δ is given as in Example 10.3.19.

Exercise 10.30. Prove Lemma 10.3.20 and Lemma 10.3.25.

10.5 Bibliographical Notes

Expressiveness has always been one of the central issues of study around temporal logics, perhaps because temporal logics serve a very clear purpose in the specification and verification of systems, and the formal study of expressiveness (partly) answers questions about how usable logics are.

Expressiveness is a unit-less and therefore vague notion that becomes meaningful through the relationships between different logics with respect to expressive power. In this chapter we have built a picture from temporal logics alone; we do not consider other kinds of logics which can be interpreted over ITS and therefore be compared to temporal logics as well. In fact, this neglects a large historical part of the study of temporal logics.

Temporal versus first-order logics. One of the reasons for introducing the perhaps seemingly arbitrary until operator in LTL was the goal of obtaining a logic that would be equi-expressive to first-order logic on linear structures. The claim that this is the case for LTL is known as Kamp's Theorem (Kamp 1968; Hodkinson 1999; Rabinovich 2014), which proves this equi-expressiveness over all Dedekind-complete total orders. Clearly, LTL can be embedded, in terms of its semantics on interpreted transition systems, into first-order logic on any class of such structures, because the semantics of LTL can be formalised in first-order logic. The other direction is everything but simple. A proof for the equi-expressiveness on all linear orders – and therefore in particular also the computation paths we are interested here – was given by Gabbay et al. (1980). On the other hand, Gabbay et al. (1994) has shown that no finite number of new temporal operators can make the temporal language functionally complete on all partial orderings.

A close inspection of the formulation of LTL's semantics in first-order logic shows that three first-order variables suffice for expressing every LTL property. It is known that first-order logic with unary relation symbols (also known as atomic propositions in the temporal world) over linear orders is equi-expressiveness to its three-variable fragment (Poizat 1982; Dawar 2005). This at least gives some evidence that LTL is not much weaker than first-order logic on such structures. It also raises the question to identify a temporal logic that captures the two-variable fragment. This has indeed been found as the fragment of LTL with unary temporal operators (Etessami et al. 1997).

Temporal versus second-order logics. In very much the same spirit as the correspondence of LTL to first-order logic on the temporal side on linear structures, one can ask for correspondences to natural predicate logics on general ITS. As stated in Chapter 8 already, the modal μ-calculus is almost as expressive as monadic second-order logic on ITS. It cannot have exactly the same expressive power because it is limited to bisimulation-invariant properties. Predicate logics can easily express non-bisimulation-invariant properties like 'there are two successors'. So the weakness in expressiveness only concerns properties which are not necessarily interesting for the specification of the behaviour of dynamic systems. Hence, one can regard $\mathcal{L}_\mu$ as the logic that corresponds to monadic second-order logic in the temporal world on general ITS. The direction from $\mathcal{L}_\mu$ to MSO is easily seen, purely by the formulation of $\mathcal{L}_\mu$'s semantics. The other direction is a lot more difficult and was finally proved by Janin and Walukiewicz (1996).

This raises the question of a natural correspondence for something like CTL*. It has, in fact, been identified as the **monadic path logic**, which is the fragment of MSO in which second-order quantification is over paths only (Hafer and Thomas 1987).

Temporal logics with past-time operators. Gabbay's Separation Theorem (see herein Theorem 10.1.22) is stated in Gabbay et al. (1980) but this paper does not contain a proof. Instead, it points to an unpublished work of Gabbay's from 1979 under the title 'The Separation Property of Tense Logic' which is supposed to contain a syntactic proof. A proof is included in Gabbay (1989), which was only published much later. The chapter by Hodkinson and Reynolds (2005) is dedicated to Gabbay's separation property, to the main existing results and to directions for future work.

Temporal logics with past operators have also been studied with respect to expressiveness in Laroussinie and Schnoebelen (1995).

Similar questions can be asked for branching-time logics, but then one needs to distinguish two kinds of past: linear past (i.e. interpretation on trees only) and branching past (i.e. interpretation on arbitrary ITS). For instance, adding linear-time past operators to CTL* does not increase the expressive power (Kupferman and Pnueli 1995). Further results in this direction can be found there as well.

Linear versus branching-time logics. A comparison between LTL, CTL and CTL* can be found in Grumberg and Kurshan (2001). The question of whether temporal logics should be linear-time or branching-time ones had been discussed for a while with expressive power as one of the deciding criteria (Stirling 1987). The other deciding issue is complexity of their decision problems, see the following chapter for a discussion thereof.

Fragments of CTL*. Much has been debated about the pros and cons of linear-time or branching-time temporal logics (Lamport 1980; Emerson and Halpern 1986; Stirling 1987; Vardi 2001), and expressiveness issues have played a major role in this. CTL* has been proposed as a unifying framework for the two previously separated streaks of temporal logics. One major reason for dispute was the fact that expressive power opposes computational efficiency, in particular the fact that a logic like CTL has polynomial-time model checking (Clarke et al. 1986) but cannot express important properties like fairness (Emerson and Halpern 1985) (though, its extension with EF^∞ was considered already in the paper by Clarke and Emerson 1981 introducing CTL). This has led to the study of fragments like CTL^+, ECTL and $ECTL^+$ (Emerson and Halpern 1985, 1986).

The fact that CTL^+ is only as expressive as CTL was shown in Emerson and Halpern (1985). Recall that ECTL is equal to CTL with EF^∞ whereas $ECTL^+$ is equal to CTL^+ with EF^∞. The separation of ECTL from CTL can be found in Emerson and Halpern (1983). Another proof can be found in Laroussinie (1994, Lemma 2.8.4) (in French), using the $ECTL^1$ formula $E(F^\infty p \wedge Gq)$ as a separator (Theorem 10.3.15). Exercise 10.27 follows the work Laroussinie (1995). The proof of Theorem 10.3.16 is due to Emerson and Halpern (1986, Theorem 5).

CTL^+. Even though CTL^+ is not more expressive than CTL (Emerson and Halpern 1985) (see Theorem 10.2.12), CTL^+ is exponentially more succinct than CTL, i.e. there are properties that can be expressed in CTL only with formulae that are exponentially bigger than some CTL^+ counterparts (see Theorem 7.4.8). This was first stated by Wilke (1999) for the simple witnessing family of formulae $E(Fp_1 \wedge \cdots \wedge Fp_n)$. Unfortunately, the argument contains a small flaw since it relies on the elimination of ε-transitions in alternating automata. Wilke states that this can be done without considering additional states. This only seems to be true for automata with a trivial acceptance condition. For alternating parity automata it is not clear how to avoid a quadratic blowup that is needed in order to keep track of priorities of states that can be reached via ε-transitions. Thus, Wilke (1999) 'only' shows a succinctness gap of $n^4 \cdot 2^{\Omega(\sqrt{n})}$. Also, Wilke's result is stated for formula length, not size, i.e. number of nodes in a syntax tree rather than number of nodes in a syntax DAG which can be exponentially less. It seems, however, that the argument does not crucially rely on this measure.

Adler and Immerman (2001) have given an alternative proof for the same witnessing family of formulae with a better lower bound of $2^{\Omega(n \log n)}$ matching the upper bound from Emerson and Halpern (1985). This uses EF-games and really only shows the exponential succinctness gap with respect to formula length. Another proof of the exponential gap was given in Lange (2008). It is, on one hand, stronger because it shows the result for formula size rather than length, and, on the other hand, weaker because it only proves an asymptotic gap of $2^{\Omega(n)}$ and the witnessing formulae are by no means as simple as the ones used in Adler and Immerman (2001).

CTL* and the modal μ-calculus. The embedding of CTL* into $\mathcal{L}_\mu$ is attributed to Dam (1994), who used the expressibility of some tableau calculus for CTL* in $\mathcal{L}_\mu$. This results in a doubly exponential translation when resulting in plain formulae, or singly exponential when using modal equation systems instead (Bhat and Cleaveland 1996b). Dam's translation also works for ECTL*. The translation presented here is conceptionally much simpler and builds upon the known correspondence between LTL and Büchi automata (Vardi and Wolper 1986a) and formulae of the linear-time μ-calculus (Kaivola 1995b).

The μ-calculus alternation hierarchy. There are two kinds of results on the $\mathcal{L}_\mu$ alternation hierarchy: *strictness*, i.e. unexpressibility of certain properties with less alternation; and *collapse* results, i.e. equivalence of all formulae with high alternation index to some of lower index. The strictness of the Niwiński alternation hierarchy over the class of all structures was first proved by Bradfield (1996), who reduced it to the known strictness of the alternation hierarchy of arithmetic with least and greatest fixpoints (Lubarsky 1993). Lenzi (1996) showed strictness of the Emerson–Lei alternation hierarchy – which is superseded by Bradfield's result – for the fragment that consists of purely positive formulae only. Later, Bradfield (1998) gave a strictness proof that does not need arithmetic with fixpoints anymore.

Strictness over some class of structures implies strictness over any superclass. This is why the results of Bradfield and Lenzi extend to the class of all interpreted transition systems. Strictness, unlike collapse, does not carry over to subclasses. This is why the interesting cases of classes of structures need to be considered separately. Strictness over the class of all *finite* interpreted transition systems follows from the strictness over all interpreted transition systems because of $\mathcal{L}_\mu$'s finite model property (Kozen 1988). Something that does not follow that easily is strictness over the class of all interpreted transition systems of bounded branching degree or, equivalently – because of bisimulation-invariance and the fact that structures of any fixed branching degree can be encoded by degree 2 – over the class of all binary trees. Bradfield (1999) managed to improve his strictness proof to this class. Independently, Arnold (1999) found the proof presented here based on Banach's (1922) Fixpoint Theorem and topological arguments (Arnold and Nivat 1980). Walukiewicz (1996) defined the formulae that witness the hierarchy's strictness.

On linear models, the situation is different. It was observed early on that the hierarchy collapses because on linear models – unlike trees – Büchi automata suffice to define all regular languages (Kaivola 1995a). The acceptance condition in Büchi automata, written as a formula in LTL is simply GFfin assuming that the atomic proposition fin holds on particular states of the automaton. It is a simple exercise to see that this can be expressed using two fixpoints – an outer greatest fixpoint and an inner least one.

This gives a general recipe for obtaining collapse results: $\mathcal{L}_\mu$ formulae can be translated into alternating parity automata (Emerson and Jutla 1991), and Büchi automata can be translated into $\mathcal{L}_\mu$ formulae of low alternation depth. Thus, if a class admits an equivalence-preserving translation from alternation parity automata to Büchi automata (nondeterministic or even alternating), then the $\mathcal{L}_\mu$ alternation hierarchy collapses over this class. This is, of course, not restricted to Büchi automata but can be used for any kind of automata that translate into $\mathcal{L}_\mu$ of fixed alternation depth. Kaivola's work on LT_μ in fact showed that the hierarchy collapses to the even lower level of Δ_2, i.e. every formula is equivalent to an alternation-free one. Note that the translation via Büchi automata only yields collapse at Π_2 (Kaivola 1995b). For this he showed that LT_μ can be translated into weak alternating automata. (Note that the term 'alternation' here refers to the availability of both existential and universal choices in their transition function (see Section 14.3) and is different from the concept of fixpoint alternation, which corresponds to the index of the acceptance condition when seen as a parity condition.)

Stronger collapse results have been found along these lines, for example for nested words (Arenas et al. 2011), a class of transition systems that is useful in modelling runs of recursive programs (Alur et al. 2004). This has been strengthened later both with respect to an even lower collapse at alternation-free formulae, as well as by proving it for the larger class of bottlenecked graphs (Gutierrez et al. 2014). Using different techniques, collapse results have been found for other classes of graphs (Alberucci and Facchini 2009; D'Agostino and Lenzi 2010).

11

Computational Complexity

This chapter is devoted to the study of the computational complexity of the standard decision problems – satisfiability, validity and model checking – for temporal logics that have been introduced earlier.

Complexity theory is the classification of problems according to the resources needed to solve (or define) them, not just the resources needed to run a particular algorithm for a given problem. This classification leads to a hierarchy of complexity classes, the important ones have been recalled in Section 2.2.2. Our general aim is, of course, to pinpoint the exact location of a given decision problem for any given temporal logic within this hierarchy. The purpose of this chapter, though, is to focus on *lower bounds* on these positions.

A decision problem, like the satisfiability problem for LTL, for instance, is classified in a complexity-theoretic sense when matching lower and upper bounds have been found. Upper bounds are often given by the analysis of the resource consumption of a particular algorithm for that problem. Part IV of this book presents different methodologies that can be used to solve these problems for temporal logics. Tight upper bounds on their complexities will be established there. The developments in this chapter underline the notion of *optimal* complexity used in previous chapters: that no algorithm with considerably less resource consumption can be found for the underlying problem (unless such algorithms could be found for an entire class of problems).

The concept of lower bound is easy to grasp when the complexity hierarchy is not seen as a system measuring absolute but relative values; the complexity of a decision problem is measured by relating it to the complexity of other decision problems. A lower bound of a complexity class C is then simply to be understood as 'this problem is (provably) as difficult as all problems in the class C'. Difficulty is, of course, measured in a formal way, meaning that one would be able to find better algorithms for all problems in class C if one could find a better algorithm for that particular problem. This decision problem is then said to be C-**hard**.

How are such lower bounds established? Take a complexity class C, and suppose we already knew that some decision problem A (understood as a formal language over some alphabet Σ) is C-hard. Some given problem B (also understood as a formal language over some alphabet Δ) will then also be C-hard if there is a **reduction** f from A to B which is a mapping $f : \Sigma^* \to \Delta^*$ such that

- for all $u \in \Sigma^*$, we have $u \in A$ iff $f(u) \in B$ and
- f is computable using, vaguely said, only resources under which the complexity class C is closed.

The vagueness in the second clause is eliminated by allowing certain specific resources only, for example polynomial-time or logarithmic-space reducibility. For this general introduction which is supposed to build intuition we can live with the vague definition, though. Note that the second requirement is stronger than saying that the reduction can be carried out using less resources than C admits. For instance, a reasonable notion of hardness for the class 2ExpTime cannot be given under reductions that can use exponential time. Instead one needs to consider polynomial-time bounded reductions because 2ExpTime is closed under composition with polynomials but not under composition with an exponential function.

Now suppose that one would find a very clever algorithm for problem B. Then we would immediately have a clever algorithm for problem A, as well, which would take an input u, compute $f(u)$, call the algorithm for B on it as a subroutine and return its answer. Now, by assumption any clever algorithm for A would already yield a clever algorithm for any problem in C; thus having such a reduction makes B also C-hard in the same sense.

This yields a recipe for bounding the complexity of a temporal logic problem from below: define a corresponding reduction from a problem that is already known to be hard for a certain class. So, how do we obtain such a problem in the first place? The solution is sometimes called a **master reduction**. It is only special in the sense that the problem *A* from which it reduces is a very particular one which is easily seen to be hard for that class: it is the word problem for a machine used to define this class. For instance, NP-hardness of the satisfiability problem for propositional logic (**SAT**) is usually established through a reduction from the word problem for arbitrary nondeterministic, polynomial-time bounded Turing machines to SAT.

Structure of the chapter. This chapter is structured as follows. In the first Section 11.1 we develop a generic framework for complexity-theoretic lower bounds based on tiling (game) problems. These are being used in the subsequent Section 11.2 and 11.3 in order to give complexity-theoretic lower bounds on the model-checking and satisfiability problems for linear-time, respectively branching-time temporal logics. Section 11.4 gives a brief summary of completeness results, i.e. it states that these lower bounds are tight in the sense that they match the known upper bounds for these problems. It contains pointers to the places in Part IV where algorithms with the corresponding complexity are given.

11.1 Proving Lower Bounds

In this chapter we will present lower complexity bounds for certain logical decision problems. Using master reductions for the proofs has an advantage and a disadvantage: on the positive side, we would be able to show the true inherent complexity of a logic's decision problem by encoding computations of Turing machines in such a problem. A reduction from a problem which is already known to be hard for a certain class only yields a transformation: the reader who is not familiar with this particular problem would simply have to believe that it is hard for the corresponding class. On the other hand, master reductions tend to be technically tedious because they reduce from very technical and artificial problems while reductions from other problems may be a lot more elegant and easy to understand in detail. We therefore choose the middle way: we introduce a generic framework of decision problems which are:

- abstract enough to be encoded in temporal logics' decision problems without too much technical clutter,
- close enough to the artificial word problems so that using these problems still captures the essence of the corresponding complexity classes.

These abstract problems are *tiling problems* and *tiling game problems*. We will first introduce them and state for which complexity classes they are hard. Then we argue intuitively why they are only abstract versions of certain word problems for certain resource bounded Turing machines. Later, we will use these problems to establish hardness results for the logical decision problems. Those readers who only want to know how to do the latter and are happy to believe some problems to be complete for certain complexity class without seeing an actual proof, can skip this section.

11.1.1 A Generic Framework

The problems in this tiling framework are all concerned with the question of whether a certain structure can be labelled with elements of a finite set (of tiles) which need to obey certain adjacency restrictions.

Definition 11.1.1. A **tiling system** is a triple (T, H, V, t_0) where T is a finite set of objects that will be called **tiles**, including the designated tile t_0, and $H, V \subseteq T \times T$ are two relations referred to as the **horizontal**, resp. **vertical matching relation**. $\triangledown$

It is helpful to imagine such tiles as having coloured edges. The relation H then, for instance, consists of all pairs (t, t') of tiles such that the right edge of t has the same colour as the left edge of t'. Likewise, $(t, t') \in V$ means that the upper edge of t and the lower edge of t' are coloured in the same way.

Example 11.1.2. For visual clarity we will use natural numbers as colours, i.e. a set of tiles is the same as a finite subset of $\mathbb{N}^4$: the four numbers represent the colours of the upper, right, lower and left edge. For example, the following represents a (T, H, V) where $T = \{t_1, t_2, t_3, t_4\}$, the horizontal matching relation is $H = \{(t_1, t_3), (t_1, t_4), (t_2, t_1), (t_3, t_2), (t_4, t_1)\}$ and the vertical matching relation is $V = \{(t_1, t_2), (t_1, t_4), (t_2, t_3), (t_4, t_1), (t_4, t_2)\}$.

$$t_1 = \boxed{\begin{smallmatrix} & 2 & \\ 1 & & 0 \\ & 2 & \end{smallmatrix}} \qquad t_2 = \boxed{\begin{smallmatrix} & 1 & \\ 2 & & 1 \\ & 2 & \end{smallmatrix}} \qquad t_3 = \boxed{\begin{smallmatrix} & 0 & \\ 0 & & 2 \\ & 1 & \end{smallmatrix}} \qquad t_4 = \boxed{\begin{smallmatrix} & 2 & \\ 0 & & 1 \\ & 2 & \end{smallmatrix}}$$

We will consider two classes of decision problems about tiling systems. The first one asks whether a given part of the plane can be labelled with tiles in a consistent way, the second class – to be handled in Section 11.1.3 – considers tree-like structures.

Definition 11.1.3. As usual, we write $[m]$ to denote $\{0, \ldots, m-1\}$ when $m \in \mathbb{N}$. Let $w, h : \mathbb{N} \to \mathbb{N}$ be two functions on natural numbers. The $(w \times h)$**-tiling problem** is the following. Given a tiling system (T, H, V, t_0) and a natural number $n \in \mathbb{N}$, decide whether there is a mapping $\tau : [w(n)] \times [h(n)] \to T$ such that

- $\tau(0, 0) = t_0$,
- for all i with $0 \le i < w(n) - 1$ and all $j \in [h(n)]$ we have $\big(\tau(i, j), \tau(i+1, j)\big) \in H$ and
- for all $i \in [w(n)]$ and all j with $0 \le j < h(n) - 1$ we have $\big(\tau(i, j), \tau(i, j+1)\big) \in V$. $\triangledown$

Such a map τ is of course nothing other than a tiling of the plane consisting of $w(n)$ columns and $h(n)$ rows such that tiles are placed in a way that only edges of the same colour touch each other. Note that for this intuition, tiles may not be turned around, etc., i.e. a tile can only ever be placed with one fixed alignment into the plane.

Example 11.1.4. Consider the set of tiles T with corresponding relations H, V shown in Example 11.1.2. A tiling of the $([4] \times [3])$-plane with this set is the following.

Hence, suppose that w, h are two functions such that $w(n) = n + 1$ and $h(n) = n$. Then the pair consisting of (T, H, V, t_4) and 3 forms an instance of the $(w \times h)$-tiling problem as the picture shows.

There is no need to restrict the attention to finite planes only. The following definition introduces tiling problems of certain infinite planes.

Definition 11.1.5. Let $w : \mathbb{N} \to \mathbb{N}$. The $(w \times \infty)$-**tiling problem** is the following: given a tiling system (T, H, V, t_0), a designated tile $t_0 \in T$ and an $n \in \mathbb{N}$, decide whether there is a function $\tau : [w(n)] \times \mathbb{N} \to T$ such that

* $\tau(0, 0) = t_0$,
* for all i with $0 \le i < w(n) - 1$ and all $j \in \mathbb{N}$ we have $\big(\tau(i, j), \tau(i + 1, j)\big) \in H$ and
* for all $i \in [w(n)]$ and all $j \in \mathbb{N}$ we have $\big(\tau(i, j), \tau(i, j + 1)\big) \in V$. $\qquad\qquad \nabla$

We leave as an exercise to the reader to verify that it is possible to find tilings of the $([n] \times \mathbb{N})$-plane for every n using the tile set in Example 11.1.2 and starting with either t_1 or t_4.

Since we are concerned with complexity of such problems we need to define the size of an instance of a tiling problem is. Clearly, the size of a quadruple (T, H, V, t_0) can be estimated as $(\mathrm{card}(T) + \mathrm{card}(H) + \mathrm{card}(V) + 1) \cdot \log \mathrm{card}(T)$ which is at most $\mathcal{O}(\mathrm{card}(T)^2 \log \mathrm{card}(T))$. All the decision problems for temporal logics we consider here fall into classes which are closed under polynomial-time reductions, though. This means that the results are invariant under polynomial transformations of the input size, and it therefore does not matter whether we consider $\mathrm{card}(T)$ as the size of a set of tiles instead.

However, recall that such an instance consists of a set of tiles and a natural number. The standard way of measuring the size of a natural number in computer science is via binary encodings. Thus, the size of n is $\lfloor \log(n + 1) \rfloor$, or simply $\mathcal{O}(\log n)$. We will consider a different encoding though, namely the unary one. Clearly, the size of n in this encoding is $\mathcal{O}(n)$. It is worth noting that this does not mean that the complexity results achieved in the following are unrealistic because they are not based on the most natural encoding of natural numbers. Recall that the tiling problems are introduced in order to show hardness of certain logical decision problems for certain complexity classes. The choice of natural number encoding and thus the choice of tiling problem used to prove such results does not affect the computational complexity of the logical decision problem. Simply, different tiling problems need to be chosen to prove this for different encodings of natural numbers: we can, for instance, either take the $(n \times n)$-tiling problem with unarily encoded input parameter n or the $(2^n \times 2^n)$-tiling problem with binarily encoded input parameter n in order to obtain the same complexity results. We choose the unary encoding because it is more intuitive since then the bounds on the plane to be tiled correspond more closely to the values of the input parameter.

11.1.2 Tiling Problems

As explained, we will use tiling problems as a general framework for proving lower complexity bounds for temporal logics' decision problems. We will argue that the tiling problems are in fact just abstract versions of word problems for nondeterministic time-bounded or space-bounded Turing machines. In this way, the lower bound proofs are essentially based on master reductions without unnecessary technical clutter.

Reducing the Word Problem

Consider a **nondeterministic Turing machines** with state set Q, starting state q_0, tape alphabet Γ containing a special empty cell symbol $\square$, input alphabet $\Sigma \subseteq \Gamma$ and transition function $\delta : Q \times \Gamma \to Q \times \Gamma \times \{-1, 0, 1\}$. For the moment we do not consider accepting or rejecting states, etc. The machine is called $\mathfrak{f}$-**space-bounded** for a function $\mathfrak{f} : \mathbb{N} \to \mathbb{N}$, if any computation an any input word of length n visits at most the first $\mathfrak{f}(n)$ many cells of the machine's tape. Note that at any moment in a configuration, at most finitely many tape cells can have been visited so far, and we are mostly interested in finite computations of such Turing machines.

A **configuration** of an $\mathfrak{f}$-space-bounded machine in a computation on a word of length n therefore consists of a sequence of $\mathfrak{f}(n)$ tape cell contents $c_0, \ldots, c_{\mathfrak{f}(n)-1}$, a head position $h \in \{0, \ldots, \mathfrak{f}(n) - 1\}$ and a state $q \in Q$. We will represent such configurations in the following way.

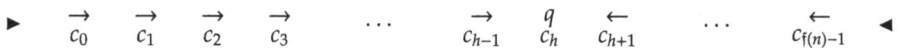

Thus, it can be represented by a word of length $\mathfrak{f}(n) + 2$ in the regular language

$$\{\blacktriangleright\} \, (\Gamma \times \{\to\})^* \, (\Gamma \times Q) \, (\Gamma \times \{\leftarrow\})^* \, \{\blacktriangleleft\}$$

over an obviously finite alphabet. Clearly, the set of pairs of symbols over this alphabet is also finite, and the following picture should show that a configuration can be represented as a sequence of tiles derived as pairs from this alphabet with a horizontal matching relation.

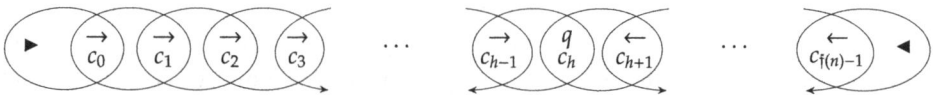

The horizontal matching relation is therefore simply given by agreement on a tape symbol and an arrow pointing into the direction of the tape head, respectively the current state.

A **computation** of this machine on an input word w is a sequence of configurations $C_0, C_1, \ldots$ such that adjacent configurations only differ by means of the transition relation. If the current state in C_i is q, the head position is h, the symbol at position h is a, and in C_{i+1} they are q' and h' with symbol b in position h', then we must have $(q, a, q', b, h' - h) \in \delta$ for the transition relation δ of the Turing machine. Furthermore, the tape contents must agree on all positions other than h.

It should be clear that a sequence of configurations can be modelled by – intuitively speaking – putting the corresponding words on top of each other, for instance as follows where a move of the tape head to the right with state change from q to q' and replacement of c_h with c'_h is depicted.

$$\vdots$$

$$\blacktriangleright \quad \overset{\rightarrow}{c_0} \quad \overset{\rightarrow}{c_1} \quad \overset{\rightarrow}{c_2} \quad \cdots \quad \overset{\rightarrow}{c_{h-1}} \quad \overset{\rightarrow}{c'_h} \quad \overset{q'}{c_{h+1}} \quad \cdots \quad \overset{\leftarrow}{c_{f(n)-1}} \quad \blacktriangleleft$$

$$\blacktriangleright \quad \overset{\rightarrow}{c_0} \quad \overset{\rightarrow}{c_1} \quad \overset{\rightarrow}{c_2} \quad \cdots \quad \overset{\rightarrow}{c_{h-1}} \quad \overset{q}{c_h} \quad \overset{\leftarrow}{c_{h+1}} \quad \cdots \quad \overset{\leftarrow}{c_{f(n)-1}} \quad \blacktriangleleft$$

$$\vdots$$

Note that the condition on configurations of being adjacent to each other can easily be expressed in terms of a vertical matching relation on tiles which are pairs of tape cells now. A vertical match only occurs when there is no tape head in the lower configuration and the two configurations agree at this part, or there is the tape head in the lower one and the transition to the upper one agrees with the machine's transition relation at this part.

Finally, two more points need to be clarified: starting of a computation and its finishing with acceptance. Regarding the former, we leave it to reader to see that it is possible to use the designated starting tile t_0 in a tiling problem in order to enforce the first configuration (i.e. bottom row of the plane) to contain (tile encodings of) the input word followed by blank symbols.

Regarding acceptance, we will distinguish the two cases in which the nondeterministic Turing machine is time-bounded, respectively space-bounded. For an $\mathfrak{f}(n)$-space-bounded machine we assume that it rejects by entering a designated state q_{rej}, and it accepts by running forever. Then an accepting computation of such a machine is an infinite sequence of configurations of length $\mathfrak{f}(n)$, and the question of whether such a machine accepts a given input can be abstractly transformed into the $((\mathfrak{f}(n) + 1) \times \infty)$-tiling problem. One has to make sure that no tile containing the rejecting state can be matched from above.

A Turing machine is called $\mathfrak{f}$-**time-bounded** for a function $\mathfrak{f} : \mathbb{N} \to \mathbb{N}$ if every computation on an input of size n hits an accepting or rejecting configuration after at most $\mathfrak{f}(n)$ many steps.

Now consider an $\mathfrak{f}(n)$-time-bounded nondeterministic Turing machine. Clearly, we cannot assume that it accepts by running forever but its computation should terminate after $\mathfrak{f}(n)$ many steps. In fact, it is always possible to assume that it is equipped with a counter such that it stops after exactly $\mathfrak{f}(n)$ steps for every input of length n. Then we can assume that

426   *Computational Complexity*

every computation that completes $\mathfrak{f}(n)$ many steps is accepting whereas any nonaccepting computation would reach a rejecting configuration, i.e. one with a designated state q_{rej}, after at most $\mathfrak{f}(n) - 1$ many steps. Again, the word problem for such machines can easily be considered as a tiling problem for a set of tiles in which no tile containing a rejecting state can be matched from above.

With the explanations of how to view word problems for space- or time-bounded nondeterministic Turing machines as tiling problems we can establish hardness of the latter easily. There is only one more point to consider. Suppose we wanted to establish NP-hardness of a tiling problem under polynomial-time reductions. Which one could this be? A language L is in NP iff there is a polynomial $\mathfrak{f}(n)$ and a nondeterministic, $\mathfrak{f}(n)$-time-bounded Turing machine that accepts L. Using the assumption on time-bounded Turing machines, a candidate would be the $(\mathfrak{f}(n) \times \mathfrak{f}(n))$-tiling problem. This would ignore the fact that different languages in NP may be solved by different machines with different polynomials bounding their running time. A polynomial reduction to such a tiling problem can simply produce the polynomial $\mathfrak{f}(n)$ as the size parameter to the tiling problem. Hence, the $(n \times n)$-tiling problem is NP-hard under polynomial time reductions already. It is not hard to see that such reductions are also implementable using logarithmic space only.

Nondeterministic Space Complexity

We apply the preceding considerations to obtain hardness results of certain tiling problems for various nondeterministic and – by Savitch's Theorem – also deterministic complexity classes. Recall that space-bounded machines were assumed to run forever in the accepting case. Hence, the resulting problems all consider the $([\mathfrak{f}(n)] \times \mathbb{N})$-plane.

The word problem for nondeterministic, logarithmic space bounded Turing machines can be seen as a tiling problem for the $([\log n] \times \mathbb{N})$-plane.

Proposition 11.1.6. The $(\log n \times \infty)$-tiling problem is NLogSpace-hard under LogSpace-reductions.   ■

Similarly, the word problem for a nondeterministic, polynomial space bounded Turing machine gives rise to the following tiling problem. Recall (Savitch's Theorem) that NPSpace = PSpace.

Proposition 11.1.7. The $(n \times \infty)$-tiling problem is PSpace-hard under LogSpace-reductions.   ■

Finally, this can be generalised. Let $2_0^n := n$ and $2_{k+1}^n := 2^{2_k^n}$ for any $k \in \mathbb{N}$ describe the k-fold exponential functions. We can then consider the word problems for k-fold exponentially space-bounded Turing machines and transfer hardness to the following tiling problems.

Proposition 11.1.8. The $(2_k^n \times \infty)$-tiling problem is k-ExpSpace-hard under LogSpace-reductions.   ■

Nondeterministic Time Complexity

Likewise, we can consider $\mathfrak{f}(n)$-time-bounded Turing machines and apply the trick of reducing polynomials which gives us the following hardness results.

Proposition 11.1.9. The $(n \times n)$-tiling problem is NP-hard under LOGSPACE-reductions. ∎

The same generalisation as earlier yields the following.

Proposition 11.1.10. The $(2_k^n \times 2_k^n)$-tiling problem is k-NEXPTIME-hard under LOGSPACE-reductions. ∎

11.1.3 Tiling Game Problems

Note that the results obtained earlier are only usable for hardness results for nondeterministic time or space classes, with the exception of such classes which actually equal some deterministic class, like NPSPACE. However, there are no nondeterministic characterisations of standard complexity classes like PTIME or EXPTIME which could be used to show hardness of any problem for such a class via a reduction from a tiling problem. It should also be clear that the tiling problems defined earlier are inherently nondeterministic. A deterministic variant in the light of encoding deterministic Turing machines would lose its intuitive character because it would require that any tile is matched by at most one other tile.

There are, however, characterisations of deterministic complexity classes in terms of **alternating Turing machines**. We will use these characterisations in order to present a generalisation of the tiling problem framework which can be used to show hardness for deterministic complexity classes.

Alternating Turing Machines

Note that the computation of a nondeterministic machine can be seen as a search through a graph for an accepting configuration. At any configuration, one may guess which successor leads to acceptance. Alternation then adds the dual concept to this: the state space of such a machine is partitioned into **existential** and **universal** states. In an existential state the machine behaves nondeterministically, i.e. one successor configuration must lead to acceptance; while from a universal state all successor configurations must lead to an accepting state.

Definition 11.1.11. An **alternating Turing machine** is a tuple $\mathcal{M} = (Q, Q_\exists, Q_\forall, \Sigma, \Gamma, \Box, q_0, \delta, q_{acc}, q_{rej})$ where state set Q, input alphabet Σ, tape alphabet $\Gamma \supseteq \Sigma$, empty tape symbol $\Box \in \Gamma$, starting state $q_0 \in Q$, transition relation $\delta : Q \times \Gamma \times Q \times \Gamma \times \{-1, 0, 1\}$, accepting and rejecting states $q_{acc}, q_{rej} \in Q$ are the same as they are for nondeterministic Turing machines. Additionally, the state set Q is partitioned into $Q = Q_\exists \cup Q_\forall \cup \{q_{acc}, q_{rej}\}$ with $\{q_{acc}, q_{rej}\} \cap (Q_\exists \cup Q_\forall) = Q_\exists \cap Q_\forall = \emptyset$.

A **configuration** is, as usual, a word in $\Gamma^*(Q \times \Gamma)\Gamma^*$. An **accepting**, resp. **rejecting** configuration is of the form $u(q_{acc}, a)v$, resp. $u(q_{rej}, a)v$ for some $u, v \in \Gamma^*$, $a \in \Gamma$. The **initial configuration** for input $w = aw' \in \Sigma^*$ is $(q_0, a)w'$ and $(q_0, \square)$ if $w = \varepsilon$. A configuration $u(q, a)v$ is called **existential**, if $q \in Q_\exists$, and **universal**, if $q \in Q_\forall$.

The transition relation on configurations is defined in the usual way: we have

$$ua(q, b)w \quad \curvearrowright \quad \begin{cases} ua(q', c)w, & \text{if } (q, b, q', c, 0) \in \delta \\ u(q', a)cw, & \text{if } (q, b, q', c, -1) \in \delta \\ uac(q', d)w', & \text{if } (q, b, q', c, 1) \in \delta \text{ and } w = dw' \\ uac(q', \square), & \text{if } (q, b, q', c, 1) \in \delta \text{ and } w = \varepsilon. \end{cases} \qquad \nabla$$

There are various equivalent ways of giving alternating Turing machines a semantics, for instance via games. Here we prefer the natural extension of computations as sequences of configurations to computations as trees of configurations.

Definition 11.1.12. A **computation** of an alternating Turing machine $\mathcal{M}$ on an input word $w \in \Sigma^*$ is a possibly infinite tree labelled with configurations satisfying the following properties.

- The root of the tree is the initial configuration for w.
- If a node is labelled with some configuration C and $C_1, \ldots, C_m$ are all the configurations C' such that $C \curvearrowright C'$ then this node has m successors which are labelled with $C_1, \ldots, C_m$. $\qquad \nabla$

Thus, the branches of a computation (tree) are all possible sequences of configurations starting in the initial one.

We will use the same principles regarding acceptance as defined for nondeterministic machines, assuming that rejection is signalled by reaching the state q_{rej} whereas the state q_{acc} is obsolete: successful runs of a space bounded machine are simply supposed to go on forever, and for time bounded machines we assume a run to be successful when it has reached the time limit without hitting the rejecting state. The reason for this assumption is, again, the fact that we are ultimately interested in complexity bounds for temporal logics. These are obtained by regarding successful computations as models for temporal formulae, and often these models are supposed to be nonterminating, e.g. for LTL or CTL.

Intuitively, alternation means that from an existential configuration it is possible to guess the next step leading to acceptance whereas from a universal configuration all steps must lead to acceptance. This can be formalised easily as follows.

Definition 11.1.13. The **accepting core** of a computation is the greatest set of configurations which obeys the following conditions.

- No rejecting configuration belongs to the accepting core.
- A node labelled with an existential configuration does not belong to the accepting core if all its successors do not.

$\cdots q_\forall \cdots$ $\cdots q_\exists \cdots$ $\cdots q_{rej} \cdots$ $\cdots q_{rej} \cdots$ $\cdots$

$\cdots q_\exists \cdots$ $\cdots q_\exists \cdots$ $\cdots q_\exists \cdots$ $\cdots$ $\cdots q_{rej} \cdots$

$\cdots q_\forall \cdots$ $\cdots q_\exists \cdots$ $\cdots$ $\cdots q_\forall \cdots$ $\cdots$

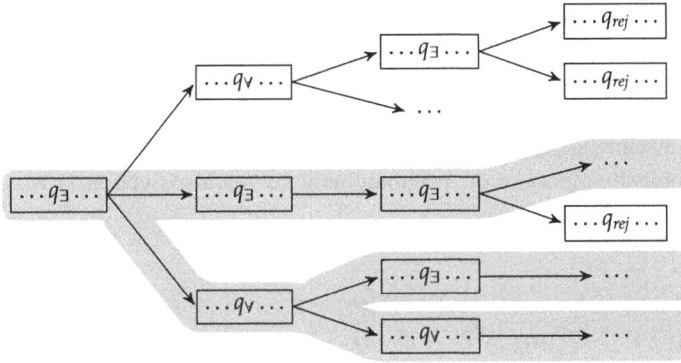

Figure 11.1 Sketch of the accepting core of an alternating Turing machine's computation.

- A node labelled with a universal configuration does not belong to the accepting core if some of its successors does not.   ∇

We call a computation **accepting** if its root belongs to the accepting core.

As usual, the **language** $L(\mathcal{M})$ of an alternating Turing machine $\mathcal{M}$ consists of all words for which there is an accepting computation.

Example 11.1.14. Consider an alternating Turing machine with states $q_\exists \in Q_\exists$, $q_\forall \in Q_\forall$ and q_{rej}. A computation tree is sketched in Figure 11.1; only the states in the configurations are depicted since concrete tape contents and head positions are irrelevant for the concept of the accepting core. It is shown shaded.

It should be clear that the concept of being space bounded can easily be adopted for alternating machines: $\mathcal{M}$ is $\mathfrak{f}(n)$-space-bounded if every configuration in every computation on an input of length n is of length at most $\mathfrak{f}(n)$. Regarding the different choices in an alternating computation as a kind of parallelism also yields a sensible notion of being time-bounded: $\mathcal{M}$ is $\mathfrak{f}(n)$-time-bounded if every computation tree on an input of length n has height at most $\mathfrak{f}(n)$. It is not too hard to see that every resource-bounded alternating Turing can be normalised such that computations are finite trees, i.e. on every path either no rejecting configuration is reached, and accepting infinite paths can be truncated when a configuration occurs repeatedly.

This allows us to define elementary complexity classes $\mathrm{ATIME}(\mathfrak{f}(n))$ and $\mathrm{ASPACE}(\mathfrak{f}(n))$ consisting of all languages which can be accepted by $\mathfrak{f}(n)$-time-, resp. $\mathfrak{f}(n)$-space-bounded alternating Turing machines. On top of that we define the following classes.

$$\mathrm{ALOGSPACE} := \mathrm{ASPACE}(\mathcal{O}(\log n))$$
$$k-\mathrm{AEXPTIME} := \mathrm{ATIME}(2_k^{n^{\mathcal{O}(1)}})$$
$$k-\mathrm{AEXPSPACE} := \mathrm{ASPACE}(2_k^{n^{\mathcal{O}(1)}})$$
$$\mathrm{APTIME} := 0-\mathrm{AEXPTIME}$$
$$\mathrm{APSPACE} ::= 0-\mathrm{AEXPSPACE}$$
$$\mathrm{AEXPSPACE} := 1-\mathrm{AEXPSPACE}.$$

Thus, APTIME for instance consists of all problems that can be solved in polynomial time on an alternating Turing machine.

There are two constructions that yield a relationship between alternating and deterministic complexity classes. These state what resources a machine of one kind need in order to simulate a machine of the other kind. For details on these constructions we refer to textbooks on complexity theory or the original literature, see also Section 11.6.

Proposition 11.1.15.

(I) $\text{ATIME}(\mathfrak{f}(n)) \subseteq \text{DSPACE}(\mathcal{O}(\mathfrak{f}(n)^2))$ if $\mathfrak{f}(n) \geq n$.

(II) $\text{ASPACE}(\mathfrak{f}(n)) \subseteq \text{DTIME}(2^{\mathcal{O}(\mathfrak{f}(n))})$ if $\mathfrak{f}(n) \geq \log n$.   ■

The first simulation in (I) is simply done by generating all possible computations of an alternating machine with a deterministic machine. The trick though is not to store the entire computation tree but to store at most one path in it and then use backtracking in order to check whether all the tree's branches end in an accepting configuration. Note that each such path has length at most $\mathfrak{f}(n)$, and each node in this path is a configuration which, again, can have length at most $\mathfrak{f}(n)$.

The second simulation in (II) relies on the same principle, with the observation that the height of a computation tree of an $\mathfrak{f}(n)$-space bounded Turing machine can be bounded exponentially in $\mathfrak{f}(n)$ for there are only that many different configurations.

Proposition 11.1.16.

(I) $\text{DSPACE}(\mathfrak{f}(n)) \subseteq \text{ATIME}(\mathcal{O}((\mathfrak{f}(n))^2))$ if $\mathfrak{f}(n) \geq \log n$.

(II) $\text{DTIME}(\mathfrak{f}(n)) \subseteq \text{ASPACE}(\mathcal{O}(\log \mathfrak{f}(n)))$ if $\mathfrak{f}(n) \geq n$.   ■

For (I) we can assume that the deterministic Turing machine clears its tape at the end of each configuration such that there is a unique accepting configuration. We can then simulate its computation by an alternating machine which stores two configurations of the deterministic machine, starting with the pair of the initial and the accepting one. In general, when faced with the pair (C, C'), it nondeterministically chooses to either check that $C \curvearrowright C'$ holds, or it guesses an intermediate configuration C'' and then uses universal branching to continue with both pairs (C, C'') and (C'', C'). This is in fact divide-and-conquer, and it should be clear that splitting the computation of the deterministic machine successively into halves results in a number of recursive descends that is at most logarithmic in the distance between the initial and the accepting configuration. Since this can be exponential in $\mathfrak{f}(n)$, this number is bounded by $\mathfrak{f}(n)$ as well. However, each iteration may require an inspection of a configuration of length $\mathfrak{f}(n)$, which yields the second factor in the time estimation.

Simulation (II) uses the same principle. However, here the distance is only $\mathfrak{f}(n)$.

Combining Proposition 11.1.15 and 11.1.16 yields the following characterisations of deterministic complexity classes in terms of alternating Turing machines.

Corollary 11.1.17. The following equalities hold for $k \geq 1$.

$$\text{PTime} = \text{ALogSpace} \qquad\qquad \text{PSpace} = \text{APTime}$$
$$\text{ExpTime} = \text{APSpace} \qquad\qquad \text{ExpSpace} = \text{AExpTime}$$
$$2\text{-ExpTime} = \text{AExpSpace} \qquad\qquad 2\text{-ExpSpace} = \text{AExpTime}$$
$$k\text{-ExpTime} = (k-1)\text{-AExpSpace} \qquad\qquad k\text{-ExpSpace} = k\text{-AExpTime}. \qquad \blacksquare$$

Acceptance as a Game

Now, we will describe the problem of determining whether an alternating Turing machine accepts an input word as a game. Naturally, it can be described as a game in which players make choices on configuration. This, however, cannot be translated into the setting of tilings without incurring more than a polynomial blowup. Hence, we need a slightly different kind of game between players 1 and 2 in which player 2's objective is to convince player 1 of the existence of an accepting core of the machine's computation that contains the initial configuration. To this end, we will enumerate successor configurations in a slightly strange way.

Suppose that $\delta \subseteq Q \times \Gamma \times Q \times \Gamma \times \{-1, 0, 1\}$ is the transition relation of the machine at hand. Since it is finite, it can be regarded as a function $\delta : Q \times \Gamma \to (Q \times \Gamma \times \{-1, 0, 1\})^*$, i.e. for every pair of state $q \in Q$ and tape symbol $c \in \Gamma$ we can list the finitely many transitions $(q_1, c_1, d_1), \ldots, (q_k, c_k, d_k)$ that are possible in a configuration with state q and the tape head on the symbol c. This naturally provides an enumeration of the possible successors of such a configuration; the one that is obtained by writing down c_i, switching to state q_i and moving the head in direction d_i will simply be seen as the ith successor, if $q \in Q_\forall$. That is, the numbering of successors of a universal configuration is just straightforwardly derived from the transition table. If $q \in Q_\exists$ however, then any successor configuration will be seen as the ith one for any i. Thus, the numbering of successors is a relation in general, for universal configurations only it is a function, and for existential ones it is the full relation. The reason for doing so is very simple: in the acceptance game to be defined formally later, it is not the case that a universal player chooses successors of universal configurations, and an existential player chooses successors of an existential configuration. Instead, the universal player announces at the beginning which successor should be constructed, and the existential player carries out the construction. This allows us to use a more convenient tiling game problem – see the following – in order to prove lower bounds for the corresponding temporal logics' decision problems.

Now, with this strange numbering scheme we mimic a game in which each player chooses successors of 'their' configurations: suppose we are in a universal configuration and the universal player demands to see the 5th successor of that. Since this is uniquely defined, the existential player has no choice but to construct the configuration that is obtained by applying the 5th transition to the current one. However, if we are in an existential configuration and the universal player now demands to see the 5th successor, then any successor counts as the 5th so the existential player is free to construct any.

Definition 11.1.18. The **acceptance game** for an alternating Turing machine $\mathcal{M}$ and an input word w is played between players 1 and 2 in several rounds as follows. At the beginning of each round player 1 writes down a value k, and then player 2 constructs a configuration in the encoding shown earlier in which k is carried through to the cell with the tape head.

Player 1 wins a play if

- its first configuration is not the initial configuration of $\mathcal{M}$ on w, or
- player 2 produces a configuration that does not match the preceding one in the preceding sense, or
- it reaches a rejecting configuration.

Player 2 wins a play if

- player 1 writes down an illegal value at the beginning of a round,
- it continues forever with none of the other conditions getting satisfied. ∇

It should be clear that player 2 has a winning strategy for this game if $w \in L(\mathcal{M})$. Her strategy consists of writing down the configurations as they are given in an accepting computation whilst staying within the accepting core. By assumption, the initial configuration belongs to this core, and player 1 can only use his choices to select successors of universal configurations, and thus cannot leave the accepting core.

Now suppose that $w \notin L(\mathcal{M})$. Then the initial configuration does not belong to the accepting core. Furthermore, every existential configuration in the computation tree that does not belong to it cannot have a successor belonging to it. Thus, whenever the play reaches an existential configuration, player 2 can either lose by constructing nonmatching or nonvalid encodings of configurations, or she remains outside the accepting core with her choices of successor configurations. If the play reaches a universal configuration then one of its successors does not belong to the accepting core. In the beginning of the next round, player 1 can request the construction of this particular successor by starting with the corresponding index of the transition that is used in order to obtain that successor. If a play remains invariably outside of the accepting core, then player 1 must win eventually by reaching a rejecting configuration.

We use the encoding techniques introduced in the previous section in order to obtain a tiling game that mimics the acceptance game for resource-bounded alternating Turing machines. We require that a valid encoding of a configuration passes the value k chosen by player 1 through to the cell that carries the tape head. This then also serves the purpose of marking the part of the configuration which is to the left of the tape head. We can therefore get rid of the marker $\rightarrow$, as well as the left boundary marker $\blacktriangleright$. Two successive configurations may then look as follows.

$$
\begin{array}{ccccccccccc}
 & & & & & & & & \vdots & & \\
k' & {k' \atop c_0} & {k' \atop c_1} & {k' \atop c_2} & \cdots & {k' \atop c_{h-1}} & {k' \atop c'_h} & {k'q' \atop c_{h+1}} & \cdots & {\leftarrow \atop c_{\mathfrak{f}(n)-1}} & \blacktriangleleft \\[2ex]
k & {k \atop c_0} & {k \atop c_1} & {k \atop c_2} & \cdots & {k \atop c_{h-1}} & {kq \atop c_h} & {\leftarrow \atop c_{h+1}} & \cdots & {\leftarrow \atop c_{\mathfrak{f}(n)-1}} & \blacktriangleleft \\[2ex]
 & & & & & & & & \vdots & &
\end{array}
$$

Again, it is not hard to imagine that every pair of adjacent tape cells can be seen as a tile with corresponding horizontal and vertical matching relations. A little bit more information needs to be put into the tiles of the first row such that the leftmost tile can only be used to create the initial configuration of this machine on the input word at hand. With all this being done, it should be clear that the acceptance game for such machines can abstractly be reformulated as a tiling game.

Tiling Game Problems

All that we need to do now in order to have a fairly abstract and simple problem that captures the complexity of certain complexity classes obtained by simulating alternating by deterministic machines, and vice versa, is to formulate the acceptance game sketched earlier without the technical details arising from encoding Turing machine configurations.

Definition 11.1.19. Let $w, h : \mathbb{N} \to \mathbb{N}$ and (T, H, V, t_0) be a tiling system as introduced in Definition 11.1.1. The $(w \times h)$-**tiling game** on (T, H, V, t_0) and $n \in \mathbb{N}$ is played for $h(n)$ rounds between players 1 and 2 in order to construct a mapping $\tau : [w(n)] \times [h(n)] \to T$ as follows. In the jth round, player 1 chooses $\tau(0, j)$, then player 2 chooses $\tau(1, j), \ldots, \tau(w(n) - 1, j)$.

Player 1 loses immediately in

- round 0, if $\tau(0, 0) \neq t_0$;
- round $j > 0$, if $\big(\tau(0, j - 1), \tau(0, j)\big) \notin V$.

Player 2 loses immediately in

- round $j \geq 0$, if there is an $i < w(n) - 1$ such that $\big(\tau(i, j), \tau(i + 1, j)\big) \notin H$;
- round $j > 0$, if there is an i with $0 < i < w(n)$ and $\big(\tau(i, j - 1), \tau(i, j)\big) \notin V$.

A player wins if the opponent loses.

The $(w \times \infty)$-tiling game is its natural extension to infinitely many rounds constructing a mapping $\tau : [w(n)] \times \mathbb{N} \to T$. Again, either player loses once she places a tile that does not match its horizontal or vertical predecessor. ∇

Note how the players changed their roles when moving from the acceptance game for alternating Turing machines to the tiling games: player 2 in the tiling game, who completes a row, mimics the role of player 1 in the acceptance game where he produces a configuration. Likewise, player 1 in the tiling game simulates the role of player 2 in the acceptance game by choosing the first tile which implicitly asks for a particular successor configuration.

Definition 11.1.20. Let $w, h : \mathbb{N} \to \mathbb{N}$ be two functions on natural numbers. The $(w \times h)$-**tiling game problem** is the following. Given a tiling system (T, H, V, t_0) and a unarily encoded $n \in \mathbb{N}$, decide whether player 2 has a winning strategy for the $(w \times h)$-tiling game on (T, H, V, t_0) and n. ∇

This change of roles among the players implies that we reduce the acceptance problem for time- and space-bounded alternating Turing machines to the *complement* of the tiling game problems, i.e. the question of whether player 1 has a winning strategy. Luckily, we only use these to obtain hardness results for complexity classes that are closed under complementation. Hence, it makes no difference for these results which player's winning strategies we are looking for.

Deterministic Time Complexity

It should be clear that the tiling game problems are only abstract versions of the acceptance game problem for alternating Turing machines. It is easy to reduce the latter to the former since there are only finitely many tape cells in the encoding presented previously. Combining this observation with the characterisations of deterministic complexity classes via alternating Turing machines in Corollary 11.1.17 yields the following hardness results.

Proposition 11.1.21.

(I) The $(\log n \times \infty)$-tiling game problem is PTIME-hard.

(II) The $(n \times \infty)$-tiling game problem is EXPTIME-hard.

(III) The $(2_k^n \times \infty)$-tiling game problem is $(k+1)$-EXPTIME-hard for any $k \geq 0$.   ■

Deterministic Space Complexity

It is shown that (most) deterministic space complexity classes can be characterised by tiling problems thanks to Savitch's Theorem because such classes like PSPACE and above equal their nondeterministic counterpart. This does not necessarily mean though that any problem which is hard for a deterministic space complexity class can easily be shown to be so by using a reduction from a tiling problem. An example is the satisfiability problem for BML shown later. It is much more suitable for a tiling game problem. Note that deterministic space complexity classes have characterisations as alternating time complexity classes which immediately give us hard tiling game problems for such classes as well.

Proposition 11.1.22.

(I) The $(n \times n)$-tiling game problem is PSPACE-hard.

(II) The $(2_k^n \times 2_k^n)$-tiling game problem is k-EXPSPACE-hard.   ■

Before we move on to use these results in order to show complexity-theoretic hardness results for decision problems of temporal logics we remark that the lower bounds stated so far are tight: corresponding upper bounds also hold, i.e. the $(n \times n)$-tiling game problem is indeed PSPACE-complete, etc. We leave it as Exercise 11.1 to give algorithms for solving tiling (game) problems and to show that it can be run within the corresponding resource bounds.

11.2 Linear-Time Temporal Logics

In order to show that the satisfiability problem for some linear-time temporal logic is hard for some complexity class, we need to provide a reduction from a suitable other problem which turns positive instances of that problem into satisfiable formulae. Recall that a model of a linear-time formula can be viewed as an infinite sequence of sets of atomic propositions. Thus, creating such reductions will be particularly easy if the positive instances of the corresponding problems to reduce from are already closely related to infinite sequences of some kind. This is provided by $(w \times \infty)$-tiling problems for some function $w : \mathbb{N} \to \mathbb{N}$. Note that a tiling τ of the $([w(n)] \times \infty)$-corridor can easily be regarded as an infinite sequence of tiles, concatenated row-wise:

$$\tau(0,0), \ldots, \tau(0, w(n) - 1), \tau(1, 0), \ldots, \tau(1, w(n) - 1), \ldots$$

Suitable tiling problems are of type $(n \times \infty)$ for PSPACE-hardness, $(2^n \times \infty)$ for EXPSPACE-hardness, etc. The $(\log n \times \infty)$-tiling problem is only NLOGSPACE-hard which is of course way less than NP-hardness which is trivially obtained for linear-time temporal logics since they subsume propositional logic.

11.2.1 From Satisfiability to Model Checking

Before we present complexity-theoretic lower bounds for the satisfiability problem of linear-time temporal logics, we remark that there is no need to consider the model-checking problems for such logics separately. In fact, the lower bounds for satisfiability immediately carry over to the existential model-checking problem – and thus also to the universal model-checking problem via complementation – as stated in the following theorem.

Theorem 11.2.1. Let $\mathfrak{L}$ be a linear-time temporal logic that admits the next-time modality such that its satisfiability problem is hard for some complexity class $\mathcal{C}$ under LOGSPACE-reductions. Then the existential model-checking problem for $\mathfrak{L}$ and finite transition systems over at least two atomic propositions is also hard for $\mathcal{C}$ under LOGSPACE-reductions, and the universal model-checking problem is hard for co$\mathcal{C}$ under LOGSPACE-reductions. ∎

Proof. First we consider the case that satisfiability for $\mathfrak{L}$ is hard for $\mathcal{C}$ over a fixed set of atomic propositions PROP already. Then consider the equally fixed transition system $\mathcal{T} = (\mathcal{P}(\text{PROP}), \mathcal{P}(\text{PROP}) \times \mathcal{P}(\text{PROP}), L)$ with $L(s) = s$ for all $s \in \mathcal{P}(\text{PROP})$. Note that any possible computation over PROP exists as some path in $\mathcal{T}$. Furthermore, any possible computation over PROP exists as the first proper suffix of some path in $\mathcal{T}$ starting in state $\emptyset$ (or any other state). Thus we have that φ is satisfiable iff $\mathcal{T}, \emptyset \models_\exists X\varphi$.

Hardness for co$\mathcal{C}$ of the universal model-checking problem then immediately follows from this because of $\mathcal{T}, \emptyset \models_\forall \neg X\varphi$ iff φ is not satisfiable.

Next we consider the case that $\mathcal{C}$-hardness requires an unbounded number of atomic propositions, i.e. there is a family φ_i, $i \in \mathbb{N}$, of formulae in $\mathfrak{L}$ such that checking satisfiability of these is $\mathcal{C}$-hard, and for every $m \in \mathbb{N}$ there is an i such that φ_i uses at least

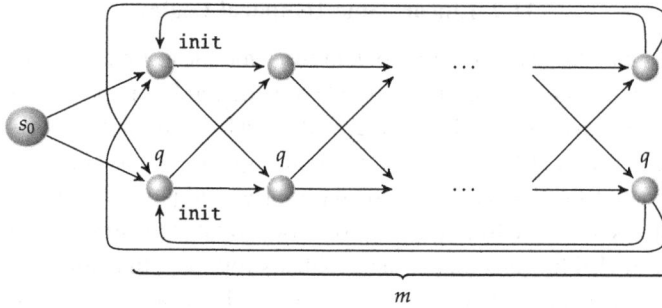

Figure 11.2 Transition system used to reduce satisfiability to model checking.

m atomic propositions. Note that in the preceding reduction, every possible set of atomic propositions – i.e. every possible state in a model – is realised by some state in $\mathcal{T}$. Since every formula only contains a finite number of atomic proposition, it would be possible to make $\mathcal{T}$ dependent on the formula φ whose satisfiability should be reduced to a model-checking instance. However, this would result in an exponential reduction since $\mathcal{T}$ would have to contain $\mathcal{P}(\mathrm{PROP})$ many states. The trick is to use a binary encoding of such sets.

Let φ be given. We construct a transition system $\mathcal{T}_\varphi$ with some state s_0 and a formula φ' of the same linear-time temporal logic such that $\mathcal{T}_\varphi, s_0 \models_\exists \varphi'$ iff φ is satisfiable. The construction of φ' depends on the actual logic $\mathcal{L}$, and here we give the reduction for LTL. An adaptation to extensions of LTL is left as an exercise. First of all, suppose that $q_0, \ldots, q_{m-1}$ are all the atomic propositions occurring in φ. Define the transition system $\mathcal{T}_\varphi$ over the atomic propositions init, q as shown in Figure 11.2. Now every path of length m starting in a state that satisfies init uniquely determines a valuation of the m atomic propositions as follows. If the ith node on this finite path satisfies q then q_i is included in this evaluation, otherwise it is not. All that remains to do is to intuitively stretch out a possible model of φ by starting in the second state of a path beginning in s_0 and using up m states in $\mathcal{T}_\varphi$ for every state in this possible model. This can be achieved by restricting the temporal operators in φ to those positions satisfying init, done by the following translation.

$$tr(q_i) := \mathsf{X}^i\, q$$
$$tr(\neg\psi) := \neg tr(\psi)$$
$$tr(\psi_0 \wedge \psi_1) := tr(\psi_0) \wedge tr(\psi_1)$$
$$tr(\mathsf{X}\psi) := \mathsf{X}^{m+1}\, tr(\psi)$$
$$tr(\psi_0 \mathsf{U}\psi_1) := \big(\mathrm{init} \to tr(\psi_0)\big)\, \mathsf{U}\, \big(\mathrm{init} \wedge tr(\psi_1)\big).$$

Finally, let $\varphi' := \mathsf{X}\, tr(\varphi)$. Note that the reduction from φ to $\mathcal{T}_\varphi$ and φ' is computable using at most logarithmic space. Furthermore, every model of φ induces a path in $\mathcal{T}_\varphi$ that satisfies φ', and vice versa. $\qquad\square$

11.2.2 PSPACE-*Hardness of LTL and Some Fragments*

LTL can be shown to be PSPACE-hard by a reduction form the $(n \times \infty)$-tiling problem.

Theorem 11.2.2. The satisfiability problem for LTL is PSPACE-hard. ∎

Proof. Suppose $T = (T, H, V, t_0)$ is a tiling system and $n \in \mathbb{N}$. We will construct an LTL formula φ_T^n that is satisfiable iff there is a T-tiling of the $(n \times \infty)$-corridor. This is a simple consequence of the fact that φ_T^n will be constructed such that every successful tiling induces a model under the row-wise representation mentioned earlier, and vice versa. Thus, it uses T as the underlying set of atomic propositions.

The formula φ_T^n will be the conjunction of several parts. The first one states that at every position there is exactly one tile.

$$\varphi_{\mathsf{uni}} := \mathsf{G}\Big(\bigvee_{t \in T}\big(t \wedge \bigwedge_{t' \neq t} \neg t'\big)\Big).$$

We need to state that the tile in the first cell of the first row, i.e. the first state in the row-wise representation, is t_0. This is particularly simple.

$$\varphi_{\mathsf{init}} := t_0.$$

We need to ensure that the vertical matching relation is respected. Note that each cell's vertical neighbour can be accessed in the row-wise representation as the nth successor since each row has width n.

$$\varphi_{\mathsf{vert}}^n := \mathsf{G}\big(\bigwedge_{(t,t')\notin V} t \to \underbrace{\mathsf{X}\ldots\mathsf{X}}_{n \text{ times}} \neg t'\big).$$

Finally, we can use the same principle in order to state that every cell matches its right neighbour. However, note that the right neighbour of the last cell in a row is the first cell of the next row in the encoding of the $(n \times \infty)$-plane as an infinite sequence of cells. Clearly, the tiles placed on these do not need to match in the horizontal matching relation. Thus, we mark each first cell of a row with a special proposition $\mathtt{f}$ which is required only to hold in the first states of each row.

$$\varphi_{\mathsf{first}}^n := \mathtt{f} \wedge \mathsf{G}\big(\mathtt{f} \to \mathsf{X}(\underbrace{\neg\mathtt{f} \wedge \mathsf{X}(\neg\mathtt{f} \wedge \ldots \mathsf{X}(\neg\mathtt{f}}_{n-1 \text{ times}} \wedge \mathsf{X}\mathtt{f})\ldots))\big).$$

Then the following formula expresses correct tile placement with regard to the horizontal matching relation H.

$$\varphi_{\mathsf{horiz}} := \mathsf{G}\big(\mathsf{X}\neg\mathtt{f} \to \bigwedge_{(t,t')\notin H} t \to \mathsf{X}\neg t'\big).$$

Now let $\varphi_T^n := \varphi_{\mathsf{uni}} \wedge \varphi_{\mathsf{init}} \wedge \varphi_{\mathsf{vert}}^n \wedge \varphi_{\mathsf{first}}^n \wedge \varphi_{\mathsf{horiz}}$. It should be clear that its size is linear in the value of n, i.e. the size of the unary representation of n, as well as $|T|$. Furthermore, it can be constructed using additional space that is at most logarithmic in the sizes of n and T. Finally, every tiling of the $(n \times \infty)$-plane that is valid with respect to T represents a model of φ_T^n when read row-wise, and vice versa. Thus, this forms a logarithmic-space computable reduction from the $(n \times \infty)$-tiling problem to the satisfiability problem for LTL. □

A simple inspection of the formulae that have been constructed in this proof shows that one obtains PSPACE-hardness already for a fragment of LTL. Note that these formulae only use unary temporal operators.

Corollary 11.2.3. The satisfiability problem for LTL(X, G) is PSPACE-hard. ∎

It is fair to ask whether one can restrict the use of temporal operators any further whilst still maintaining PSPACE-hardness. The answer is given in the next theorem.

Theorem 11.2.4. The satisfiability problem for LTL(U) is PSPACE-hard. ∎

Proof. We define a logarithmic-space reduction from the satisfiability problem for LTL(X, F) – which is of course the same as LTL(X, G) – to the satisfiability problem for LTL(U). Given a formula φ in LTL(X, F) built over the atomic propositions $p_1, \ldots, p_n$, we construct a formula φ' in LTL(U) over the atomic propositions $p_0, p_1, \ldots, p_n$ (we add the atomic proposition p_0) such that φ is satisfiable iff φ' is satisfiable.

We define a formula φ'_{shape} that enforces models with a certain shape:

$$p_0 \wedge (\mathsf{GF}p_0) \wedge (\mathsf{GF}\neg p_0) \wedge (\mathsf{G}(p_0 \rightarrow (\neg p_1 \wedge \cdots \wedge \neg p_n)))\wedge$$

$$\bigwedge_{i \in [1,n]} (\mathsf{G}((\neg p_0 \wedge p_i) \rightarrow p_i \mathsf{U} p_0)) \wedge (\mathsf{G}((\neg p_0 \wedge \neg p_i) \rightarrow (\neg p_i)\mathsf{U}p_0)).$$

Every LTL model satisfying φ'_{shape} has the form

$$\{p_0\}^{n_0} P_0^{m_0} \{p_0\}^{n_1} P_1^{m_1} \{p_0\}^{n_2} P_2^{m_2} \cdots,$$

where $n_i, m_i > 0$ and each $P_i \subseteq \{p_1, \ldots, p_n\}$. Note also that φ'_{shape} can be built in logarithmic space in the size of φ. Such models, when evaluated by formulae in LTL(U), encode models of the form $P_0 P_1 \cdots$, when evaluated by formulae in LTL(X, F). We also define a logarithmic-space map $\mathfrak{f}(\cdot)$ that reflects this encoding at the syntactic level:

$$
\begin{aligned}
\mathfrak{f}(p_i) &:= p_0 \mathsf{U}(\neg p_0 \wedge p_i) \\
\mathfrak{f}(\psi_1 \wedge \psi_2) &:= \mathfrak{f}(\psi_1) \wedge \mathfrak{f}(\psi_2) \\
\mathfrak{f}(\neg\psi) &:= \neg\mathfrak{f}(\psi) \\
\mathfrak{f}(\mathsf{X}\psi) &:= p_0 \mathsf{U}(\neg p_0 \wedge (\neg p_0)\mathsf{U}(p_0 \wedge \mathfrak{f}(\psi))) \\
\mathfrak{f}(\mathsf{F}\psi) &:= \mathsf{F}(p_0 \wedge \mathfrak{f}(\psi)).
\end{aligned}
$$

Now we prove that φ is satisfiable iff $\varphi'_{\text{shape}} \wedge \mathfrak{f}(\varphi)$ is satisfiable. Note that $\varphi'_{\text{shape}} \wedge \mathfrak{f}(\varphi)$ belongs to LTL(U).

Let $\sigma_0 : \mathbb{N} \rightarrow \mathcal{P}(\{p_1, \ldots, p_n\})$ be an LTL model for φ, that is $\sigma_0, 0 \models \varphi$. Consider the model $\sigma'_0 : \mathbb{N} \rightarrow \mathcal{P}(\{p_0, p_1, \ldots, p_n\})$ such that for every $i \in \mathbb{N}$, $\sigma'_0(2i) := \{p_0\}$ and $\sigma'_0(2i+1) := \sigma_0(i)$. Note that $\sigma'_0, 0 \models \varphi'_{\text{shape}}$. Moreover, one can show that $(\star)$ $\sigma'_0, 0 \models \mathfrak{f}(\varphi)$. Figure 11.3 presents a model σ_0 and its counterpart σ'_0.

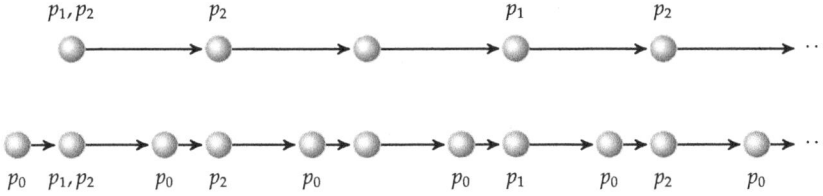

Figure 11.3 σ_0 and its counterpart σ_0'.

Similarly, let $\sigma_1' : \mathbb{N} \to \mathcal{P}(\{p_0, p_1, \ldots, p_n\})$ be an LTL model such that $\sigma_1', 0 \models \varphi_{\text{shape}}' \wedge \mathfrak{f}(\varphi)$. By satisfaction of the formula φ_{shape}', the LTL model σ_1' can be written in the form

$$\{p_0\}^{n_0} P_0^{m_0} \{p_0\}^{n_1} P_1^{m_1} \{p_0\}^{n_2} P_2^{m_2} \cdots,$$

where $n_i, m_i > 0$ and each $P_i \subseteq \{p_1, \ldots, p_n\}$. Let $\sigma_1 : \mathbb{N} \to \mathcal{P}(\{p_1, \ldots, p_n\})$ be the LTL model such that for every $i \in \mathbb{N}$, $\sigma_1(i) := P_i$. One can show that $(\star\star)$ $\sigma_1, 0 \models \varphi$.

In order to prove that $(\star)$ and $(\star\star)$ hold, we establish a more general property stated later. Given an LTL model $\sigma : \mathbb{N} \to \mathcal{P}(\{p_1, \ldots, p_n\})$ and an LTL model $\sigma' : \mathbb{N} \to \mathcal{P}(\{p_0, p_1, \ldots, p_n\})$ satisfying φ_{shape}', we say that σ' is **equivalent** to σ whenever σ' can be decomposed as follows:

$$\{p_0\}^{n_0} \sigma(0)^{m_0} \{p_0\}^{n_1} \sigma(1)^{m_1} \{p_0\}^{n_2} \sigma(2)^{m_2} \cdots.$$

Note that in the statements to prove the two directions, σ_ℓ' is indeed equivalent to σ_ℓ ($\ell \in \{0, 1\}$), see also Figure 11.3. Given $i \in \mathbb{N}$, we write $\mathcal{I}_i$ to denote the interval $[\sum_{j<i}(n_j + m_j), \sum_{j<i}(n_j + m_j) + n_i - 1]$. One can show that $(\dagger)$ for every formula ψ built over $p_1, \ldots, p_n$, for all $i \in \mathbb{N}$ and $i' \in \mathcal{I}_i$, we have $\sigma, i \models \psi$ iff $\sigma', i' \models \mathfrak{f}(\psi)$. This is sufficient to show $(\star)$ and $(\star\star)$ since $0 \in \mathcal{I}_0$. The proof is by structural induction and uses arguments analogous to those for establishing that formulae in LTL(U) are invariant modulo stuttering (see Theorem 6.6.5). $\square$

Thus, the logic remains PSPACE-hard if the next-time operator X is forbidden but binary temporal operators like U are allowed, or if binary operators are forbidden but both the next-time and the unary temporal operators like G or F are allowed. This immediately raises the question after the complexity of satisfiability checking for the two even smaller fragments LTL(X) and LTL(F). Note, though, that Theorem 11.2.1 does not imply that MC(LTL(U)) is PSPACE-hard since it requires the presence of the X-operator. It is not hard to see that PSPACE-hardness of MC(LTL(U)) still holds; the construction in the proof of Theorem 11.2.4 can easily be amended to a reduction from MC(LTL(X, F)) to MC(LTL(U)). We leave the details as Exercise 11.6.

Theorem 11.2.5. The model-checking problem for LTL(U) is PSPACE-hard. ∎

11.2.3 NP-*Hardness of Simpler Fragments of LTL*

PSPACE-hardness of an important specification language like LTL can be seen as disappointing. It is therefore fair to ask whether there are at least some easier fragments of LTL. In other words: what in LTL is it that causes PSPACE-hardness? We cannot answer this question formally by giving more lower bounds, but we can at least find hints by considering fragments in which the formulae produced in the PSPACE-hardness proofs cannot be constructed.

Clearly, NP is a general lower bound for any fragment containing the Boolean operators since the satisfiability for purely Boolean formulae is already NP-hard. We therefore know that satisfiability of LTL(X) or LTL(F) cannot be easier than that. Still, we give a proof of these facts using tiling problems because it yields a stronger result, namely NP-hardness of these fragments over a fixed set of atomic propositions. The proof presented in the following uses a nonfixed set; Exercise 11.8 then asks for it to be modified such that a fixed set is sufficient.

Theorem 11.2.6. The satishability problems for LTL(X) and LTL(F) are NP-hard. ∎

Proof. We will only prove NP-hardness for the case of LTL(F). The case of LTL(X) is simpler and left as an exercise. The proof proceeds by reduction from the $(n \times n)$ tiling problem. Let $T = (T, H, V, t_0)$ be a tiling system and $n \in \mathbb{N}$. Note that the entire $([n] \times [n])$-plane can easily be enumerated using n^2 many atomic propositions $c_0, \ldots, c_{n^2-1}$. First we require that every state in a possible model is labelled with a unique tile and a unique number represented by these propositions, or it is labelled by a distinct atomic proposition # denoting that the state is not used to model a cell:

$$\varphi_{\text{uni}}^n := \mathsf{G}\left(\# \vee \left(\left(\bigvee_{t \in T} t \wedge \bigwedge_{\substack{t' \in T \\ t' \neq t}} \neg t' \right) \wedge \left(\bigvee_{i=0}^{n^2-1} c_i \wedge \bigwedge_{j=i+1}^{n^2-1} \neg c_j \right) \right) \right).$$

We need to make sure that every cell is represented by some state in the model. It is convenient (but not strictly necessary) to also require them to occur in an order that respects the row-wise enumeration of the plane, and that there are not too many states representing any particular cell:

$$\varphi_{\text{enum}}^n := c_0 \wedge \mathsf{G}\left(\bigwedge_{i=0}^{n^2-2} c_i \rightarrow \mathsf{F}(c_{i+1} \wedge \mathsf{G}\neg c_i) \right).$$

It is then very simple to create a single formula which requires a model to contain n^2 many (not necessarily adjacent) states that represent the cells of the $([n] \times [n])$-plane. Furthermore, it is easy to require that their labellings obey respectively both the horizontal and vertical matching relation:

$$\varphi_{\text{horiz}}^n := \mathsf{G}\left(\bigwedge_{i=0}^{n-1} \bigwedge_{j=0}^{n-2} c_{i \cdot n + j} \rightarrow \bigvee_{(t,t') \in H} t \wedge \mathsf{G}(c_{i \cdot n + j + 1} \rightarrow t') \right)$$

$$\varphi_{\text{vert}}^n := \mathsf{G}\left(\bigwedge_{i=0}^{n^2-n-1} c_i \rightarrow \bigvee_{(t,t') \in V} t \wedge \mathsf{G}(c_{i+n} \rightarrow t') \right).$$

Now, note that $\varphi_T^n := \varphi_{\mathsf{uni}}^n \wedge \varphi_{\mathsf{horiz}}^n \wedge \varphi_{\mathsf{vert}}^n$ is constructible in space that is logarithmic in $|T|$ and n, and it is satisfiable iff there is a valid tiling of the $([n] \times [n])$-plane. Such a tiling can easily be constructed from a model of this formula by placing tile t into the jth cell of the i-row iff the last node that is labelled with $c_{i \cdot n + j}$ is also labelled with t. Conversely, a matching tiling of the plane at hand can easily be converted into a model for φ_T^n through the usual row-wise encoding. □

Theorem 11.2.1 can be used to transfer the result to MC(LTL(X)) but not MC(LTL(F)). On the other hand, it is also possible to carry out the ideas in the previous proof to show hardness of the corresponding model-checking results directly. Then the constructed ITS needs to generate all paths that encode successions of valid rows of length n. This simply uses $n \times \mathrm{card}(T)$ states for a tiling set T with edges from a state in 'position' i with tile t to any state in position $i + 1$ with tile t' if t and t' match horizontally. Equally, one puts edges from the 'last' states in this structure back to the first ones to generate the next row. This enforces horizontal matching in the ITS; vertical matching can be enforced in the formula as done in the previous proof. The details are left as Exercise 11.9.

11.2.4 Extensions of LTL beyond PSPACE

As a consequence of Theorem 11.2.2 and Theorem 11.2.1 the satisfiability and model-checking problems for any extension of LTL are at least PSPACE-hard as well. Among those extensions, PSL is worth considering because its satisfiability problem is more difficult than that of LTL. We will show that it is ExpSpace-hard, i.e. it is in fact exponentially more difficult than the satisfiability problem for LTL. The reason for this is simply the use of semi-extended regular expressions, namely the intersection operator.

The proof follows the same lines as the PSPACE-hardness proof for LTL. The source problem is now the $(2^n \times \infty)$-tiling problem rather than the $(n \times \infty)$-tiling problem. Again, a valid tiling of this plane can be represented row-wise as an infinite sequence of states. However, one cannot simply amend the LTL formulae given in the proof of Theorem 11.2.2 which express valid tilings with respect to the vertical matching relations because the vertical neighbour of a cell is then being found 2^n steps further away in this representation. Clearly, a formula of the form $X^{2^n} \psi$ cannot be produced using logarithmic space only when n is unarily encoded. However, it is possible to introduce further atomic propositions which act like bits of a counter, and a semi-extended regular expression can easily be defined which represents path pieces of length 2^n.

Theorem 11.2.7. The satisfiability problem for PSL is ExpSpace-hard under LogSpace-reductions. ∎

Proof. Let $T = (T, H, V, t_0)$ and $n \in \mathbb{N}$. We will construct a PSL formula φ_T^n which is satisfiable iff there is a T-tiling of the $(2^n \times \infty)$-corridor. As in the construction of the corresponding LTL formula (Theorem 11.2.2), φ_T^n will consist of the conjunction of several parts; φ_{uni} and φ_{init} are as defined in the proof of Theorem 11.2.2.

We introduce new atomic propositions $c_0, \ldots, c_{n-1}$ and state that they represent a counter starting with the value 0 (all bits unset) and successively increasing such that it counts modulo 2^n:

$$\varphi^n_{\text{count}} := \left(\bigwedge_{i=0}^{n-1} \neg c_i \right) \wedge \mathsf{G}\left((c_0 \leftrightarrow \mathsf{X}\neg c_0) \wedge \bigwedge_{i=1}^{n-1} (c_i \leftrightarrow \mathsf{X}c_i) \leftrightarrow (c_{i-1} \to \mathsf{X}c_{i-1}) \right).$$

Since the length of a row in the corridor under consideration is exactly 2^n we have that two vertically neighbouring cells can be recognised by having the same counter value (with no other state with the same value in between). Furthermore, the first cell of each row can be recognised by having all these bits unset. Thus, we can easily express the horizontal matching relation as follows:

$$\varphi^n_{\text{horiz}} := \mathsf{G}\left((\mathsf{X}\bigvee_{i=0}^{n-1} c_i) \to \bigwedge_{(t,t') \notin H} t \to \mathsf{X}\neg t' \right).$$

For the vertical matching relation we first introduce a semi-extended regular expression whose models are words that start and end with the same counter value and do not repeat another value. Thus the lengths of such words are exactly $2^n + 1$:

$$E^n_{\text{exp}} := \left(\bigcap_{i=0}^{n-1} (c_i; \mathsf{T}^*; c_i) \cup (\neg c_i; \mathsf{T}^*; \neg c_i) \right) \cap$$

$$\left((c_{n-1}^+; (\neg c_{n-1})^+; c_{n-1}^+) \cup ((\neg c_{n-1})^+; c_{n-1}^+; (\neg c_{n-1})^+) \right).$$

With this at hand, it is easy to express the vertical matching relation:

$$\varphi^n_{\text{vert}} := \mathsf{G}\left(\bigwedge_{(t,t') \notin V} t \to \neg(E^n_{\text{exp}} \diamondsuit\!\!\to t') \right).$$

Now let $\varphi^n_{\mathsf{T}} := \varphi_{\text{uni}} \wedge \varphi_{\text{init}} \wedge \varphi^n_{\text{count}} \wedge \varphi^n_{\text{horiz}} \wedge \varphi^n_{\text{vert}}$. Again, this formula is constructible using at most space that is logarithmic in $|\mathsf{T}|$ and n, and its models are exactly the row-wise encodings (enhanced with counter values) of valid T-tilings of the $(2^n \times \infty)$-plane. $\qquad\square$

Another extension that adds more computational complexity to LTL is quantification over atomic propositions as done in QLTL. It turns out that its satisfiability problem cannot be solved by an algorithm that uses time or space which is bounded by a tower of exponentials of fixed height. This can be shown by proving it to be k-ExpTime-hard or k-ExpSpace-hard for any $k \in \mathbb{N}$. According to Proposition 11.1.8 it would suffice to reduce the $(2^n_k \times \infty)$-tiling problems to satisfiability in QLTL. Note that k-ExpSpace $\subsetneq (k+1)$-ExpSpace for any $k \in \mathbb{N}$. Thus, these complexity classes form a strict hierarchy, and if a problem is hard for any level of this hierarchy then it cannot be contained in a fixed level of the hierarchy.

For technical convenience we consider tiling problems of slightly different dimension. Let $F_0(n) := n$ and $F_{k+1}(n) := F_k(n) \cdot 2^{F_k(n)}$. Clearly, we have $F_k(n) \geq 2^n_k$ for all $k, n \in \mathbb{N}$. Furthermore, a Turing machine that uses space 2^n_k for some fixed k can easily be regarded as a Turing machine which uses space $F_k(n)$ but simply does not touch the rightmost $(F_k(n) - 2^n_k)$ many tape cells. Thus, it should be clear that the $(F_k(n) \times \infty)$-tiling problem is k-EXPSPACE hard, as well.

In order to reduce these problems to satisfiability in QLTL, we use the same row-wise representation of the $(F_k(n) \times \infty)$-corridor as done in the previous proofs. The most difficult part is then to enforce the vertical matching relation which requires to relate states in a model to states at distance $F_k(n)$, which is clearly a very large number for most values of k and n. Thus, what is needed is a family of operators which express that something holds after $F_k(n)$ many steps. The most obvious choice would be $\mathsf{X}^{F_k(n)}\psi$ which is, of course, useless for $k > 0$ because $F_k(n)$ is not polynomially bounded in these cases, and the reduction could not be computed in logarithmic space. However, for $k = 0$ this is already a good choice. For technical convenience it is better to introduce a stronger operator which does not only require something to hold after $F_k(n)$ many steps but also requests something else to hold on all states before that apart from the current state. Note that this is very reminiscent of the usual Until operator in LTL, and that is why we use a similar symbol for this operator.

$$\varphi \hat{\mathsf{U}}^n_0 \psi := \underbrace{\mathsf{X}(\varphi \wedge \mathsf{X}(\varphi \wedge \ldots \mathsf{X}(\varphi \wedge \mathsf{X}\,\psi)\ldots)).}_{n \text{ occurrences of } \mathsf{X}}$$

For larger k, we construct these operators by induction on k. Suppose therefore that we already have defined $\hat{\mathsf{U}}^n_k$. Note that $F_{k+1}(n) = F_k(n) \cdot 2^{F_k(n)}$ is exactly the length that one would obtain if one wrote down in successive order all possible values of a counter that uses $F_k(n)$ many bits, here depicted with least-valued bits on the left.

$$\underbrace{\underbrace{000\ldots0}_{F_k(n)}\underbrace{100\ldots0}_{F_k(n)}\underbrace{010\ldots0}_{F_k(n)}\underbrace{110\ldots0}_{F_k(n)}\quad\ldots\quad\underbrace{111\ldots1}_{F_k(n)}.}_{F_{k+1}(n)}$$

Now these bit values can be seen as values of a propositional variable along the states of a computation, and it is not too difficult to express in LTL that the bits form the successive values of an $F_k(n)$-bit counter. Thus, in order to take $F_{k+1}(n)$ many steps in such a computation, one can simply request such an additional track of bits in the form of one atomic proposition c. Again, for technical convenience we request a second atomic proposition # which is used to mark the beginning of each block of length $F_k(n)$. Furthermore, let $\hat{\mathsf{F}}^n_k\psi := \top\hat{\mathsf{U}}^n_k\psi$.

$$\varphi\hat{\mathsf{U}}^n_{k+1}\psi := \exists c.\exists \#.\ \# \wedge\ \mathsf{G}(\# \to (\neg\#)\hat{\mathsf{U}}^n_k\#) \wedge$$
$$\neg c \wedge (\neg c)\hat{\mathsf{U}}^n_k\# \wedge$$
$$\mathsf{G}\big(\# \to (c \to \hat{\mathsf{F}}^n_k\neg c) \wedge (\neg c \to \hat{\mathsf{F}}^n_k c)\big) \wedge$$
$$\mathsf{G}\Big(\neg\mathsf{X}\# \to \big(((\neg c \wedge \hat{\mathsf{F}}^n_k\neg c) \vee (\neg c \wedge \hat{\mathsf{F}}^n_k c) \vee (c \wedge \hat{\mathsf{F}}^n_k c)) \to$$
$$((\mathsf{X}c \to \mathsf{X}\hat{\mathsf{F}}^n_k c) \wedge (\mathsf{X}\neg c \to \mathsf{X}\hat{\mathsf{F}}^n_k\neg c))\big)$$
$$\wedge\ \big((c \wedge \hat{\mathsf{F}}^n_k\neg c) \to ((\mathsf{X}c \to \mathsf{X}\hat{\mathsf{F}}^n_k\neg c) \wedge (\mathsf{X}\neg c \to \mathsf{X}\hat{\mathsf{F}}^n_k c))\big)\Big) \wedge$$
$$\mathsf{X}\Big(\varphi\mathsf{U}\big(\# \wedge c \wedge (c\hat{\mathsf{U}}^n_k\psi)\big)\Big).$$

The first line states that the beginning-of-block marker # holds now and whenever it holds anywhere then it holds after $F_k(n)$ many steps again but not in between. Thus, it really marks the beginning of every block.

The second line initialises the counter by setting all its bits in the first block to 0 ($\neg c$).

The two conjuncts starting with a G-operator formalise the successive increment of the counter values. The third line states that the first bit in each block changes its value when moving on to the next block. Note that in binary counting, the least significant bit, i.e. the first in the blocks here, is always flipped in each step that the counter is increased. The part in lines 4–6 formalises the way that all other bits get set when incrementing the counter. Note that the value of the next highest bit in the next step (as accessed by $\mathsf{X}\hat{\mathsf{F}}_k^n$) is uniquely determined by its current value (as accessed by X), the value of the bit below it now (represented by the literals c and $\neg c$ without temporal operators) and its value in the next step (as accessed by $\hat{\mathsf{F}}_k^n$). Thus, the lines 4–6 state that for every bit apart from the highest (as recognised by $\neg\mathsf{X}\#$) we have that if its value is less or equal than its value in the next step then the bit above that does not change its value when doing an increment (lines 4–5), but if it is set now and not set after the increment then the next highest bit will be flipped in the increment (line 6).

Finally, line 7 expressed that ψ holds after $F_{k+1}(n)$ many steps and φ holds before that apart from the current state. The distance $F_{k+1}(n)$ is simply recognised by searching for the last block in the increment of the $F_k(n)$-bit counter which consists of set bits only.

Theorem 11.2.8. The satisfiability problem for QLTL is k-ExpSpace-hard under LogSpace-reductions for every $k \in \mathbb{N}$. ∎

Proof. Let $k \in \mathbb{N}$. Hardness is established by a reduction from the $(F_k(n) \times \infty)$-tiling problem which works in just the same way is it does for LTL. Let $\mathsf{T} = (T, H, V, t_0)$ be a tiling system and $n \in \mathbb{N}$. We construct a formula φ_{T}^n which is satisfiable iff there is a valid tiling of the $([F_k(n)] \times \infty)$-corridor. The conjuncts φ_{uni}, φ_{init} and φ_{horiz} are just like they are in the proof of PSpace-hardness for LTL (Theorem 11.2.2). All we need to do is to say that the atomic proposition $\mathtt{f}$ holds at every $F_k(n)$th state which is particularly simple given the operators $\hat{\mathsf{U}}_k^n$ which are definable in QLTL:

$$\varphi_{\mathsf{first}}^n := \mathtt{f} \wedge \mathsf{G}(\mathtt{f} \to (\neg\mathtt{f})\hat{\mathsf{U}}_k^n \mathtt{f}).$$

The only other part that needs to be changed is the one that requires the vertical matching relation to be respected:

$$\varphi_{\mathsf{vert}}^n := \mathsf{G}(\bigwedge_{(t,t')\notin V} t \to \hat{\mathsf{F}}_k^n \neg t).$$

Then let $\varphi_{\mathsf{T}}^n := \varphi_{\mathsf{uni}} \wedge \varphi_{\mathsf{init}} \wedge \varphi_{\mathsf{horiz}} \wedge \varphi_{\mathsf{first}}^n \wedge \varphi_{\mathsf{vert}}^n$. Again, its models are exactly the row-wise encodings of valid tilings of the aforementioned corridor. Also note that φ_{T}^n can be constructed in space that is logarithmic in n and $|T|$. This holds for every fixed $k \in \mathbb{N}$. □

11.3 Branching-Time Temporal Logics

For branching-time temporal logics the satisfiability and model-checking problems often have different complexities. Clearly, determining whether there is a model is generally more difficult than checking whether a given structure is a model. We consider the satisfiability problems first, starting with the basic modal logic BML.

We use the same framework as is used in the previous section: reductions from suitable problems on tiling systems. However, note that a model of a linear-time temporal formula is an infinite word, and these words can easily be used to encode the plane of fixed width which is to be tiled. The models of branching-time temporal formulae, however, are trees (up to bisimulation). Since every infinite word is also an infinite tree, one could also reduce such tiling problems to the satisfiability problems of branching-time logics but this would not use the full power of these logics, and the obtained results would be suboptimal. In order to get optimal results, i.e. results that match the corresponding upper bounds, one generally has to consider tiling game problems. The reason for this is the fact that the arenas for tiling game problems are not just simple fixed-width planes anymore. A winning strategy for player 2 in a tiling game can be represented by a tree in which every node carries a row of the plane. Each node can have several successors, each one corresponding to one of player 1's choices for the starting tile of the next row. Note that player 1 does not have any choices in the first row because he has to play the initial tile for otherwise he would lose immediately.

Example 11.3.1. Consider the $(n \times n{+}1)$-tiling game played on the tiling system from Example 11.1.2, as shown below with initial tile t_1, and take $n = 2$.

$$t_1 = \begin{array}{c} 2 \\ 1 \times 0 \\ 2 \end{array} \qquad t_2 = \begin{array}{c} 1 \\ 2 \times 1 \\ 2 \end{array} \qquad t_3 = \begin{array}{c} 0 \\ 0 \times 2 \\ 1 \end{array} \qquad t_4 = \begin{array}{c} 2 \\ 0 \times 1 \\ 2 \end{array}$$

Player 2 has a winning strategy for this game, and the tree representation of the game on the $([2] \times [3])$-arena is shown in Figure 11.4.

Note that the exact structure of such trees cannot be enforced by the branching-time temporal logics considered here because of bisimulation invariance. However, satisfiability is only about *existence* of a model. It is not necessary to require that all models of a constructed formula represent a winning strategy in the way shown in the example. Instead, it suffices if such a tree can be inferred from a model.

11.3.1 PSPACE-*Hardness of BML*

Theorem 11.3.2. The satisfiability-checking problem for BML is PSPACE-hard under LOGSPACE-reductions. ∎

Proof. By a reduction from the $(n \times n)$-tiling game problem. Let $T = (T, H, V, t_0)$ be a tiling system and $n \in \mathbb{N}$. We construct a BML formula φ_T^n which is satisfiable iff

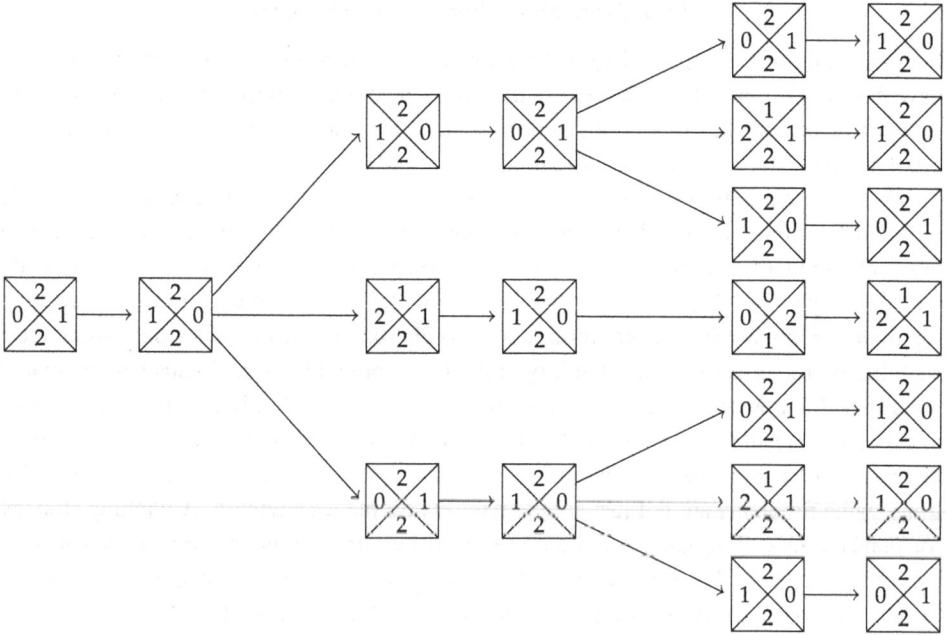

Figure 11.4 Tree representing the game of Example 11.3.1.

player 2 has a winning strategy for the tiling game on T and the $(n \times n)$-plane. Note that such a strategy can be represented by a tree – as described above – of depth n^2. Again, φ_T^n will be composed of several constructs.

The first part expresses that every node in the tree is occupied by a unique tile, using T as atomic propositions again. Let $uni := \bigvee_{t \in T}(t \wedge \bigwedge_{t' \neq t} \neg t')$. At the same time we can require the very first cell to carry the initial tile.

$$\varphi_{uni}^n := t_0 \wedge \bigwedge_{t \neq t_0} \neg t \wedge \underbrace{\mathsf{AX}(uni \wedge \mathsf{AX}(uni \wedge \ldots \mathsf{AX}(uni \wedge \mathsf{AX}\, uni)\ldots))).}_{n^2-1 \text{ occurrences of AX}}$$

Next we assert that the horizontal matching relation is being respected. Let $hm := \bigwedge_{(t,t') \notin H} t \to \mathsf{AX}\neg t'$. The formula φ_{horiz}^n is equal to

$$hm \wedge \underbrace{\overbrace{\mathsf{AX}(hm \wedge \ldots \mathsf{AX}}^{n-2 \text{ occurrences of AX}}(hm \wedge \mathsf{AXAX}(hm \wedge \mathsf{AX}(hm \wedge \ldots \mathsf{AX}(hm \wedge \mathsf{AX}\, hm)\ldots)))).}_{n^2-1 \text{ occurrences of AX}}$$

Thus, φ_{horiz}^n requires *hm* to hold everwhere up to depth $n^2 - 1$ (starting with 0), apart from those states that are at distance $n - 1, 2n - 1, \ldots, n^2 - n - 1$, i.e. all states representing a cell that is last in its row.

The vertical matching relation can be enforced in the same way. Note that with respect to vertical matching, it is all the cells in the last row which do not need to match anything above them anymore. This makes it slightly simpler than the formula for the horizontal matching relation. Let $vm := \bigwedge_{(t,t') \notin V} t \to \mathsf{AX}^n \neg t$:

$$\varphi_{\mathsf{vert}}^n := vm \wedge \underbrace{\mathsf{AX}(vm \wedge \mathsf{AX}(vm \wedge \ldots \mathsf{AX}(vm \wedge \mathsf{AX}\, vm) \ldots))}_{n^2-n-1 \text{ occurrences of } \mathsf{AX}}.$$

Now note that the conjunction of these formulae can be easily satisfied in a model of a single state without any successors because the only modal operators occurring in it are universal. This also does not yet require the structure of a tree representing player 2's winning strategy as sketched. The last formula will do exactly that. Remember that the tree is defined by (I) having at least one successor node representing a cell that is tiled by player 2, and (II) having all possible successor nodes for all choices that player 1 can make. It suffices to require that every first cell of a row (besides the last one) has a chain of $n-2$ successors that represent the rest of the row, such that the last of these has a successor for every possible matching choice of player 1's. Let $ch := \bigwedge_{t \in T} t \to \mathsf{EX}^{n-2}(\bigwedge_{(t,t') \in V} \mathsf{EX} t')$:

$$\varphi_{\mathsf{struct}}^n := ch \wedge \underbrace{\mathsf{AX}^n(ch \wedge \ldots \mathsf{AX}^n(ch \wedge \mathsf{AX}^n\, ch) \ldots)}_{n-2 \text{ occurrences of } \mathsf{AX}^n}.$$

Finally, let $\varphi_{\mathsf{T}}^n := \varphi_{\mathsf{uni}}^n \wedge \varphi_{\mathsf{horiz}}^n \wedge \varphi_{\mathsf{vert}}^n \wedge \varphi_{\mathsf{struct}}^n$. It is not hard to see that φ_{T}^n can be constructed in space that is logarithmic in n and $|\mathsf{T}|$. Furthermore, every winning strategy for player 2 in the tiling game on T and the $([n] \times [n])$-arena induces a model via the encoding of such strategies as trees as sketched, and every model of φ_{T}^n bears such a winning strategy. Thus, φ_{T}^n is satisfiable iff player 2 has such a winning strategy. □

It is worth noting that this reduction intuitively shows that the satisfiability problem for BML cannot be proved to be harder than PSPACE. For this to work, it would have to be able to capture the $(w \times h)$-tiling game problems for functions h, w that grow faster than polynomials. However, BML needs a single operator in order to make one modal step in an ITS, and the modal depth of the constructed formulae will therefore roughly be $h(n) \cdot w(n)$. Thus, if either of h or w was not polynomially bounded then the reduction would not be computable in polynomial time, let alone logarithmic space.

11.3.2 EXPTIME-*Hardness of TLR*

The satisfiability problem for CTL is more difficult than that of BML: it turns out to be EXPTIME-hard. Recall that a typical EXPTIME-hard problem is the $(n \times \infty)$-tiling game problem which only differs from the PSPACE-hard $(n \times n)$-tiling game problem in the fact that the arena is not height-bounded but of infinite height. Clearly, the proof of PSPACE-hardness for BML (Theorem 11.3.2) could not simply be amended to capture such tiling games of infinite height because it would require formulae with infinitely many nested AX-operators for instance. In CTL and even in the simpler reachability logic TLR, though, there is the operator AG which can express that something holds everywhere including the case of infinitely many successor states.

We prove that satisfiability for TLR is ExpTime-hard by reduction from the $(n \times \infty)$-tiling game problem. The proof proceeds along the same lines as the PSPACE-hardness proof for BML: a winning strategy for player 2 in a tiling game is represented by a tree of cells which has the same structural properties as said earlier.

Theorem 11.3.3. The satisfiability problem for TLR is ExpTime-hard under LogSpace-reductions.   ∎

Proof. Let $T = (T, H, V, t_0)$ be a tiling system and $n \in \mathbb{N}$. Again, we construct a formula φ_T^n as the conjunction of several parts. The first one states that every node carries a unique tile, and that the initial tile is placed onto the first cell of the first row, i.e. the root node of any model of φ_T^n:

$$\varphi_{\text{uni}} := t_0 \wedge \text{AG}\left(\bigvee_{t \in T} t \wedge \bigwedge_{t' \neq t} \neg t' \right).$$

We use a proposition f to mark the first cell of each row in this encoding:

$$\varphi_{\text{mark}}^n := f \wedge \text{AG}\big(f \to \underbrace{\text{AX}(\neg f \wedge \text{AX}(\neg f \wedge \ldots \text{AX}(\neg f \wedge \text{AX } f)\ldots))}_{n \text{ occurrences of AX}}\big).$$

Expressing that the horizontal and vertical matching relations are respected is particularly simple:

$$\varphi_{\text{horiz}} := \text{AG}\left(\bigwedge_{(t,t') \notin H} t \to \text{AX}(\neg t' \vee f) \right), \quad \varphi_{\text{vert}}^n := \text{AG}\left(\bigwedge_{(t,t') \notin V} t \to \text{AX}^n \neg t' \right).$$

Finally, the correct tree structure is required by the following formula:

$$\varphi_{\text{struct}}^n := \text{AG}\left(f \to \bigwedge_{t \in T} t \to \text{EX}^{n-1}(\bigwedge_{\substack{t' \in T \\ (t,t') \in V}} \text{EX} t') \right).$$

Now let $\varphi_T^n := \varphi_{\text{uni}} \wedge \varphi_{\text{mark}}^n \wedge \varphi_{\text{horiz}} \wedge \varphi_{\text{vert}}^n \wedge \varphi_{\text{struct}}^n$. Again, it can be constructed using at most logarithmic space, and it is satisfiable iff player 2 has a winning strategy for the tiling game on T and the $([n] \times \infty)$-arena.   □

11.3.3 2ExpTime-*Hardness of* CTL$^+$

The best upper bound on the complexity of satisfiability checking for CTL$^+$ is inherited from its extension CTL*, and it is doubly exponential deterministic time. It turns out that this is optimal, i.e. the satisfiability problem for CTL$^+$ is already 2ExpTime-hard (and then, trivially, so is that of CTL*). Recall that the $(2^n \times \infty)$-tiling game problem is a typical 2ExpTime-hard decision problem. The ExpTime lower bound for the simple reachability logic – a fragment of CTL which in turn is a fragment of CTL$^+$ – was obtained by a reduction from the $(n \times \infty)$-tiling game problem. Thus, it is fair to ask whether the proof for the lower bound for TLR can be extended to show 2ExpTime-hardness for CTL$^+$. Note that this is very similar to the situation with LTL (PSPACE-hard via reduction from the $(n \times \infty)$-tiling problem) and PSL (ExpSpace-hard via the $(2^n \times \infty)$-tiling problem). In order to extend the proof from the former to the latter, we introduced n atomic propositions $c_0, \ldots, c_{n-1}$ and required them to act like an n-bit counter which is successively increased along any path in a possible model. Then it became possible to require that something holds after 2^n many steps by requiring that it holds as soon as these bits have the same value as they have in the current state. Such assertions were necessary in order to formulate the requirements on the vertical matching condition in the tiling games. However, it is not easily possible to express, in CTL^+, that something holds on all paths after 2^n many steps, even in the presence of such counter bits. This is because the temporal operators in CTL^+, in particular F and G only make assertions about some or all states along a path, and forming Boolean combinations of them does not necessarily require them to make assertions about some particular moment. We therefore extend the encoding of winning strategies in tiling games as trees with tile-labelled nodes as follows. Again, we will construct a formula φ_T^n which is satisfiable iff player 2 has a winning strategy for the $(2^n \times \infty)$-tiling game on T. However, this time such a strategy will be found as a particular subtree of a tree model of φ_T^n. In detail, we extend the tree encodings shown previously so that:

1. every node in these trees corresponding to such a strategy is marked by an atomic proposition s and
2. every such node has at least one successor node which does not encode a cell and therefore is not marked by s. These nodes will be called **cache** nodes because they will not be distinguishable from their parent nodes by any atomic proposition other than s. Furthermore, the successors of cache nodes also have the same labelling in terms of atomic proposition as their parents.
3. Every sequence of 2^n nodes in the strategy tree that forms an even row will be marked by an atomic proposition e.

A schematic example for the case of $n = 2$, i.e. row length 4, is shown in Figure 11.5. Cache nodes are shown darker, and they are also recognisable by the fact that they do not satisfy the atomic proposition s. We use $\underline{i}$ to denote the value of i represented by the atomic propositions $c_0, \ldots, c_{n-1}$ in binary encoding. On tree models obeying these conditions it is very simple to require something to hold after 2^n many steps: note that every path that leaves the s-subtree will eventually be trapped in (black-circled) states which have the same atomic labelling as the last s-state on this path. Thus, in order to require that some atomic proposition holds on a path in 2^n many steps, it suffices to require that it holds eventually forever and the same holds for all literals that hold in the current state because 2^n many steps through the s-part lead to a state with the same number $\underline{i}$. However, note that this also holds for nodes at distance $k \cdot 2^n$ for any $k \geq 1$. The atomic proposition e which marks every even row can then be used to ensure that a path leaves the s-part after exactly 2^n many steps which happens only when the e-value changes exactly once along that path.

Theorem 11.3.4. The satisfiability problem for CTL^+ is 2ExpTime-hard under LogSpace-reductions. ∎

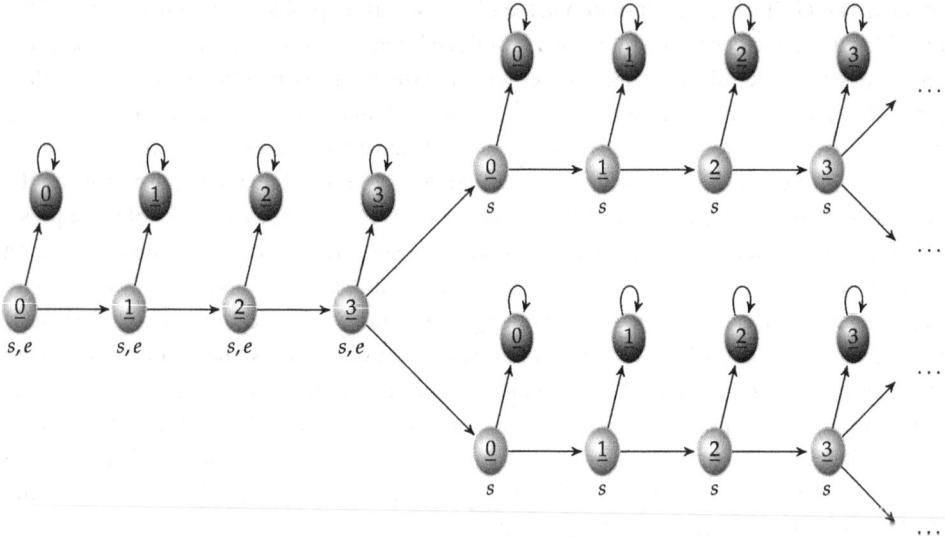

Figure 11.5 Structure of the intended models used in the 2EXPTIME-hardness proof for CTL$^+$.

Proof. By reduction from the $(2^n \times \infty)$-tiling game problem using the encoding of winning strategies as described in Example 11.3.1 and earlier. Let $T = (T, H, V, t_0)$ be a tiling system and $n \in \mathbb{N}$. First we describe the structure of the trees representing winning strategies and using cache nodes. Let PROP $= T \cup \{s, e\} \cup \{c_0, \ldots, c_{n-1}\}$ and PROP$'$ = PROP $\setminus \{s\}$:

$$\varphi_{\text{tree}} := t_0 \wedge s \wedge \mathsf{AG}\left(\left(\bigvee_{t \in T} t \wedge \bigwedge_{\substack{t' \in T \\ t' \neq t}} \neg t' \right) \wedge (s \rightarrow \mathsf{EX} \neg s) \wedge \mathsf{A}\left(\mathsf{X} \neg s \rightarrow \bigwedge_{q \in \text{PROP}'} q \leftrightarrow \mathsf{X} q\right) \right).$$

Note that this includes the requirements that every cell is occupied by a single tile starting with the initial tile t_0 in the first node.

We use an n-bit counter that increments along the noncache nodes in order to identify nodes that represent vertically adjacent cells:

$$\varphi_{\text{count}}^n := \left(\bigwedge_{i=0}^{n-1} \neg c_i \right) \wedge \mathsf{AGA}(\mathsf{G} s \rightarrow (c_0 \leftrightarrow \mathsf{X} \neg c_0) \wedge \bigwedge_{i=1}^{n-1} (c_i \leftrightarrow \mathsf{X} c_i) \leftrightarrow (c_{i-1} \rightarrow \mathsf{X} c_{i-1})).$$

With this counter in place it is easy to require that every even row is marked with e and every odd row is not. Note that each last cell of a row is recognised by having all c_i set. Let $last := \bigwedge_{i=0}^{n-1} c_i$. Then:

$$\varphi_{\text{even}}^n := e \wedge \mathsf{AGA}\left(\mathsf{G} s \rightarrow \left(\neg last \rightarrow (e \leftrightarrow \mathsf{X} e)\right) \wedge \left(last \rightarrow (e \leftrightarrow \mathsf{X} \neg e)\right)\right).$$

The horizontal matching relation is, again, easily formalised:

$$\varphi_{\text{horiz}}^n := \mathsf{AG}\left(s \wedge \bigvee_{i=0}^{n-1} \neg c_i \rightarrow \bigwedge_{(t,t') \in H} t \wedge \mathsf{EX}(s \wedge t')\right).$$

Note that this also requires each nonlast cell of a row to have at least one successor.

Finally, we need to formalise the vertical matching relation. As with the horizontal one, we include the requirement on every last cell of a row having some successor for any tile that matches the first cell of that row vertically. This models player 1's choice at the beginning of each row. We separate this case from the vertical matching for the other cells because those do not need that extract requirement and the vertical matching relation in the first cells per row do not need the counter bits directly. Let $start := \bigwedge_{i=0}^{n-1} \neg c_i$. Then:

$$\varphi_{\text{vert},1}^n := \mathsf{AGA}\Bigg((\mathsf{G}s \wedge start) \rightarrow \bigwedge_{t \in T} t \rightarrow e\mathsf{U}\Big(e \wedge \bigwedge_{\substack{t' \in T \\ (t,t') \in V}} \mathsf{EX}(s \wedge \neg e \wedge t')\Big)$$

$$\vee \neg e\mathsf{U}\Big(\neg e \wedge \bigwedge_{\substack{t' \in T \\ (t,t') \in V}} \mathsf{EX}(s \wedge e \wedge t')\Big)\Bigg).$$

The vertical matching relation for the other cells can use the cache states and the marker e in order to quantify over paths that stay in the s-part for exactly 2^n many steps and then divert into the cache states:

$$\varphi_{\text{vert},2}^n := \mathsf{AG}\Bigg(s \wedge \neg start \rightarrow \bigvee_{(t,t') \in V} t \wedge \mathsf{A}\Bigg(\Big(\bigwedge_{i=0}^{n-1}(c_i \wedge \mathsf{FAG}c_i) \vee (\neg c_i \wedge \mathsf{FAG}\neg c_i)\Big) \wedge$$

$$\neg\big(\mathsf{F}(e \wedge start) \wedge \mathsf{F}(\neg e \wedge start)\big) \rightarrow \mathsf{FAG}t'\Bigg)\Bigg).$$

Now let $\varphi_{\mathsf{T}}^n := \varphi_{\text{tree}} \wedge \varphi_{\text{count}}^n \wedge \varphi_{\text{even}}^n \wedge \varphi_{\text{horiz}}^n \wedge \varphi_{\text{vert},1}^n \wedge \varphi_{\text{vert},2}^n$. It is easy to verify that φ_{T}^n is constructible using space that is logarithmic in $|\mathsf{T}|$ and n. Furthermore, it is satisfiable iff player 2 has a winning strategy for the T-tiling game on the $(2^n \times \infty)$-game board. $\square$

11.3.4 Model Checking

The model-checking problem for CTL is solvable in polynomial time. It is therefore fair to ask whether it is PTIME-hard as well. The answer is yes; PTIME-hardness can even be achieved for the much simpler basic modal logic BML already. A natural candidate for a reduction is the $(\log n \times \infty)$-tiling game problem using a similar technique as in the section on satisfiability problems: winning strategies can be represented as trees in which nodes are labelled with tiles. Now, instead of modelling the existence of such a tree as a satisfiability problem we construct a transition system $\mathcal{T}_\mathsf{T}$ and a formula φ such that the transition system is a model of the formula iff such a tree exists. Satisfaction of the formula will be given by a subtree of the unravelling of $\mathcal{M}$.

For the case of BML and PTime-hardness via a reduction from the $(\log n \times \infty)$-tiling game problem there is a little problem to overcome. Note that a winning strategy for such a game is an infinite tree. However, a formula of BML can only make requirements on nodes at distance at most its modal depth. Thus, for any such formula φ there is a fixed m such that φ_m would not be able to ensure correct matchings in rows after the mth one. A little observation, formalised in the following lemma, shows though that mismatches occur in rows of small index if there are any at all.

Lemma 11.3.5. Let $T = (T, H, V, t_0)$ be a tiling system and $n \in \mathbb{N}$. Player 2 has a winning strategy for the $(w(n) \times \infty)$-tiling game iff she has a winning strategy for the $(w(n) \times (1 + \mathrm{card}(T)^{w(n)}))$-tiling game. ∎

Proof. The 'only if' part is trivial because player 2 can simply play according to the strategy for the $(w(n) \times \infty)$ tiling game for the first $1 + \mathrm{card}(T)^{w(n)}$ rounds.

The 'if'-part holds because there are at most $|T|^{w(n)}$ many different rows in a tiling of width $w(n)$. Thus, if player 2 manages to survive $1 + |T|^{w(n)}$ many rounds then each play of this game must have seen at least one row twice, and player 2 can simply repeat forever what they have done before. □

Thus, it suffices to consider a finite number of rows in the $(\log n \times \infty)$-tiling game only. Next we describe the construction of the transition system $\mathcal{T}_T^k$ for some tiling system $T = (T, H, V, t_0)$ and some $k \in \mathbb{N}$. We have $\mathcal{T}_T^k := (\{\bullet\} \cup Rows_H^k, \to, L)$ where:

- $Rows_H^k := \{t_1 \ldots t_k \mid \forall i = 1, \ldots, k-1 : (t_i, t_{i+1}) \in H\}$,
- $t_1 \ldots t_k \to t_1' \ldots t_k'$ iff $(t_i, t_i') \in V$ for all $i = 1, \ldots, k$,
- $\bullet \to t_1 \ldots t_k$ iff $t_1 = t_0$,
- $L(t_1 \ldots t_k) := t_1$.

Thus, the states of $\mathcal{T}_T^k$ are sequences of length k of tiles that match horizontally, and an edge between two such states exists iff the target matches the source when seen as a row in a tiling game. The additional state $\bullet$ is only used to have a unique starting state. The tiles are also used as labels on the states: each sequence, respectively row, is labelled with its first tile.

Theorem 11.3.6. The model-checking problem for BML is PTime-hard under LogSpace-reductions. ∎

Proof. By a reduction from the $(\log n \times \infty)$-tiling game problem. Let $T = (T, H, V, t_0)$ be a tiling system and $n \in \mathbb{N}$. Let $k := \lceil \log n \rceil$ and $m := \mathrm{card}(T)^k$. Consider $\mathcal{T}_T^k$ and

$$\varphi_m := \mathsf{EX}\left(t_0 \wedge \bigwedge_{\substack{t_1 \in T \\ (t_0, t_1) \in V}} \mathsf{EX}\left(t_1 \wedge \bigwedge_{\substack{t_2 \in T \\ (t_1, t_2) \in V}} \mathsf{EX}\left(t_2 \wedge \ldots \bigwedge_{\substack{t_{m-1} \in T \\ (t_{m-2}, t_{m-1}) \in V}} \mathsf{EX}\left(t_{m-1} \wedge \bigwedge_{\substack{t_m \in T \\ (t_{m-1}, t_m) \in V}} \mathsf{EX} t_m\right) \ldots\right)\right)\right).$$

Both are constructible using logarithmic space in $|T|$ and n. Furthermore, we have $\mathcal{T}_T^k, \bullet \models \varphi_m$ iff player 2 has a winning strategy for the $(\log n \times (1 + m))$-tiling game on T, which, according to Lemma 11.3.5, is sufficient to have a winning strategy for the $(\log n \times \infty)$-tiling game. $\qquad\qquad\square$

11.4 An Overview of Completeness Results

The aim of this section is to give a complete picture of the computational complexity of model checking and satisfiability checking for all the temporal logics considered in this book. We put together the lower bounds that have been obtained in the previous sections for satisfiability and model-checking problems as well as the upper bounds on these problems that will be obtained in detail in the chapters of the part on methods. Furthermore, we will derive lower and upper bounds for further logics as simple consequences of the explicitly given ones. Suppose that some logic $\mathfrak{L}$ is a syntactical fragment of some other logic $\mathfrak{L}'$. Then it should be clear that lower bounds for $\mathfrak{L}$ also hold for the extension (superlogic) $\mathfrak{L}'$, and upper bounds for $\mathfrak{L}'$ also hold for the sublogic $\mathfrak{L}$. Finally, we state some known results which have not been considered explicitly or cannot simply be derived from the ones presented here. Lower bounds should implicitly be understood with respect to LogSpace-reductions unless stated otherwise.

A summary of the results stated here is also given in tabular form in Figure 11.6 at the end of this section.

11.4.1 Linear-Time Logics

Recall Theorem 11.2.1 that shows how the satisfiability problem for a linear-time temporal logic can be reduced to the existential model-checking problem for the same logic – provided that the X-modality can be used. Thus, the universal path model-checking problem is just complementary to satisfiability checking. It is also possible to obtain a reduction in the other direction (cf. Corollary 6.2.7). Thus, existential model checking and satisfiability checking for linear-time temporal logics are, from a complexity-theoretic point of view, the same problems, while universal path model checking and satisfiability are complementary to each other. Of course, this complementation only shows up for nondeterministic complexity classes that are not, or are not known to be, closed under complementation. Deterministic complexity classes (and nondeterministic space) are closed under complements.

Theorem 11.4.1. The existential model-checking and the satisfiability-checking problems for LTL(X) and LTL(F) are NP-complete. The universal path model checking problem for these logics are coNP-complete. ∎

Proof. The lower bound for the satisfiability problem LTL(F) is shown in Theorem 11.2.6 whereas for LTL(X) it can be proved in an even simpler way, and it is therefore left as Exercise 11.5. The upper bound for SAT(LTL(F)) is shown in Exercise 6.33 whereas for SAT(LTL(X)) it is again left as an exercise. The lower bound for MC(LTL(X))

follows from that of SAT(LTL(X)) using Theorem 11.2.1. For MC(LTL(F)) it is shown
in Exercise 11.9.   □

Theorem 11.4.2. The model-checking and satisfiability-checking problems for LTL,
LTL(U), LTL(X, G) and ETL are PSPACE-complete.   ■

Proof. For satisfiability, the lower bound for LTL(X, G) (and therefore for LTL) is established in Corollary 11.2.3. For LTL(U) it is given in Theorem 11.2.4. The upper bound
for ETL and therefore all the other mentioned logics is given in Chapter 14. For the model-
checking problem, the lower bound for LTL, LTL(X, G) and ETL is obtained by application
of Theorem 11.2.1. For LTL(U), it is shown in Exercise 11.6.   □

The decision problems for PSL are exponentially harder than those for LTL, etc. This is
the price to pay for using semi-extended regular expressions in its temporal operators. With
ordinary regular expressions, the complexity would also only be PSPACE.

Theorem 11.4.3. The model checking and satisfiability-checking problems for PSL are
EXPSPACE-complete.   ■

Proof. For satisfiability, the lower bound is given in Theorem 11.2.7. The upper bound
can be derived from an exponential translation of PSL formulae into alternating Büchi
automata, see Section 14.5.2 for which the emptiness problem can be solved in PSPACE.
The model-checking problem for PSL is EXPSPACE-hard by application of Theorem 11.2.1.
The EXPSPACE upper bound is obtained by building an alternating Büchi automaton synchronising the ITS and the alternating Büchi automaton from the formula, again see
Section 14.5.2.   □

Finally, the computationally hardest linear-time temporal logic considered here is LTL
extended with quantification over atomic propositions. Roughly speaking, two additional
existential quantifications suffice to increase the complexity by one exponential. Thus, for
arbitrary formulae, there is no elementary function that bounds the space consumption
needed for satisfiability testing, and therefore also the model checking.

Theorem 11.4.4. The model-checking and satisfiability problems for QLTL are nonelementary.   ■

Proof. Lower bounds of k-EXPSPACE for any $k \in \mathbb{N}$ are given in Theorem 11.2.8. Upper
bounds are direct consequences from Exercise 14.19.   □

11.4.2 Satisfiability of Branching-Time Logics

Theorem 11.4.5. The satisfiability problem for BML is PSPACE-complete.   ■

Proof. The lower bound is given in Theorem 11.3.2, the corresponding upper bound is
given in Section 5.5.2.   □

Having temporal operators that can formalise reachability questions makes a difference in the computational complexity.

Theorem 11.4.6. The satisfiability problems for TLR, CTL and $\mathcal{L}_\mu$ are EXPTIME-complete. ∎

Proof. The lower bound for TLR is proved in Theorem 11.3.3 and it immediately carries over to CTL and then to $\mathcal{L}_\mu$ via their linear translations, see for instance Theorem 8.1.14. The upper bound for CTL is obtained in Section 13.3.4, and hence for its fragment TLR, too. An EXPTIME upper bound for $\mathcal{L}_\mu$ is obtained in Theorem 15.4.12. □

Finally, allowing Boolean combinations of linear-time temporal operators under a path quantifier makes a real difference to the complexity of satisfiability checking, causing it to increase by one exponential.

Theorem 11.4.7. The satisfiability problems for CTL$^+$ and CTL* are 2EXPTIME-complete. ∎

Proof. The lower bound for CTL$^+$ is proved in Theorem 11.3.4. The upper bound for CTL*, and hence for CTL$^+$, can be obtained using a doubly exponential reduction to the problem of solving a parity game for instance (cf. Corollary 15.4.32). □

11.4.3 Model Checking of Branching-Time Logics

Model checking for simple branching-time temporal logics up to CTL turns out to be PTIME-complete.

Theorem 11.4.8. The model-checking problems for BML, TLR and CTL are PTIME-complete. ∎

Proof. Recall that BML is a syntactic fragment of TLR, which itself is a fragment of CTL. PTIME-hardness of model checking BML is proved in Theorem 11.3.6. A polynomial-time algorithm for model checking CTL is given in Section 7.3.2. □

The full branching-time temporal logic CTL* has higher complexity.

Theorem 11.4.9. The model-checking problem for CTL* is PSPACE-complete. ∎

Proof. The lower bound follows from the complexity of existential path model checking for LTL (cf. Theorems 11.2.2 and 11.2.1). Recall that, for any LTL formula φ, we have that $\mathsf{E}\varphi$ is a CTL* state formula which holds in a state of a transition system iff that transition system has a path on which φ holds.

The upper bound uses the fact that an LTL model-checking procedure can be used successively to solve a CTL* model-checking problem. This is done in Section 7.3 and, in a game-theoretic setting, also in Section 15.3.3. □

logic	model checking	satisfiability
BML	PTIME	PSPACE
TLR, CTL	PTIME	EXPTIME
CTL$^+$	Δ_2^P	2EXPTIME
CTL*	PSPACE	2EXPTIME
LTL(F), LTL(X)	coNP	NP
ETL, LTL, LTL(U), LTL(X, G)	PSPACE	
PSL	EXPSPACE	
QLTL	non elementary	

Figure 11.6 Complexity-theoretic completeness results for model checking and satisfiability checking of temporal logics.

Recall that CTL is a syntactic fragment of CTL$^+$, which itself is a fragment of CTL*. Note that regarding expressive power the first inclusion collapses, whereas regarding the complexity of satisfiability checking the second inclusion collapses in the sense that CTL$^+$ and CTL* are both 2EXPTIME-complete, as opposed to CTL which is only EXPTIME-complete. It is a curious fact that, regarding model checking neither of these happens: the model-checking problem for CTL$^+$ is (presumably) harder than that of CTL and easier than that of CTL*.

Proposition 11.4.10. The model-checking problem for CTL$^+$ is Δ_2^P-complete. ■

The Δ_2^P upper bound is obtained from Theorem 7.4.9. A bibliographical reference where the lower bound is established can be found in Section 11.6.

11.4.4 Satisfiability and Model Checking for Alternating-Time Logics

Proposition 11.4.11. The satisfiability problem SAT(ATL) is EXPTIME-complete. ■

The EXPTIME upper bound is established in Theorem 9.3.2 (see also the bibliographical references) whereas the lower bound follows from the EXPTIME-hardness of SAT(TLR). Indeed, formally, one can design a logarithmic-space reduction from the satisfiability problem for TLR (see Theorem 11.4.6) into the satisfiability problem for ATL, by translation map *tr*, as follows:

$$tr(p) := p$$
$$tr(\neg\varphi) := \neg tr(\varphi)$$
$$tr(\varphi \wedge \psi) := tr(\varphi) \wedge tr(\psi)$$
$$tr(\mathsf{AX}\varphi) := \langle\!\langle\emptyset\rangle\!\rangle\mathsf{X}\, tr(\varphi)$$
$$tr(\mathsf{AG}\varphi) := \langle\!\langle\emptyset\rangle\!\rangle\mathsf{G}\, tr(\varphi).$$

One can show that any TLR formula φ is satisfiable iff $tr(\varphi)$ is a satisfiable ATL formula (see Theorem 11.4.6).

Proposition 11.4.12. The satisfiability problem SAT(ATL*) is 2ExpTime-complete. ■

The 2ExpTime upper bound is established in Theorem 9.3.3 (see also the bibliographical references) whereas the lower bound follows from the 2ExpTime-hardness of SAT(CTL*).

Proposition 11.4.13.

(I) The model-checking problem for ATL can be solved in time linear both in the size of the formula and in the size of the model. Furthermore, it is PTime-complete.
(II) The model-checking problem for ATL* is 2ExpTime-complete, even in the special case of turn-based models (where at each state only one of the players has a choice of more than one actions). ■

The PTime upper bound for Proposition 11.4.13 is from Proposition 9.3.4 whereas the PTime lower bound is inherited from CTL. The 2ExpTime upper bound is established in Proposition 9.3.4; see also the bibliographical references.

11.5 Exercises

Exercise 11.1. Give algorithms that solve the tiling problem and the tiling game problem within the resource bounds for which they are hard according to Proposition 11.1.6 – 11.1.22. In other words: show that we may just as well have stated that these problems are complete rather than just hard for the corresponding complexity classes.

Exercise 11.2. Show (†) in the proof of Theorem 11.2.4.

Exercise 11.3. Show how to reduce the satisfiability problem for ETL and PSL to their existential model-checking problems in logarithmic space.

(Hint: All that is required is to define the translation as given in the proof of Theorem 11.2.1 for these logics. The ITS defined there can be used as it is.)

Exercise 11.4. Show how to reduce the satisfiability problem for LTL over an unbounded set of atomic propositions to the satisfiability problem for LTL over two propositions.

(*Hint:* Follow the lines of the reduction from satisfiability to model checking in the proof of Theorem 11.2.1. Find an LTL formula which describes exactly the paths that exist in the ITS $\mathcal{T}_\varphi$ given there.)

Exercise 11.5. Show that SAT(LTL$_1$(X)) is NP-complete, where LTL$_1$(X) is the restriction of LTL(X) to a unique atomic proposition.

Exercise 11.6. Prove Theorem 11.2.5 by a reduction from MC(LTL(X, F)).

Exercise 11.7. Consider the reduction used to show PSPACE-hardness of LTL in Theorem 11.2.2. Note that the formulae constructed there have unbounded modal depth. In detail: their modal depth is $\mathcal{O}(n)$, and n is part of the input to the reduction.

Show that satisfiability for LTL is already PSPACE-hard for formulae of some fixed modal depth.

(*Hint:* Use additional atomic propositions to define a counter that is then used to identify cells in each row of the tiling. Then express the properties for which an unbounded modal depth is currently being needed by some with fixed modal depth that use the counter values to express the same thing.)

Exercise 11.8. Modify the proof of Theorem 11.2.6 so that it creates formulae of LTL(X) or LTL(F) over a *fixed* set of atomic propositions.

Exercise 11.9. Show that the existential model-checking problem for LTL(F) is NP-hard, by using a reduction from the $(n \times n)$-tiling problem.

Exercise 11.10. An interpreted transition system $\mathcal{T} = (S, R, I)$ is **flat** whenever every state s in S belongs to at most one simple cycle (no repetition of transitions). Show that MC$^\exists$(LTL(F)) restricted to flat interpreted transition systems is NP-hard.

Exercise 11.11. We write LTL+O to denote the extension of LTL by adding a single operator O of arity $n \geq 1$ with semantics defined as follows. (In this exercise, we assume that the size of a formula in LTL+O is defined as the size of its syntactic tree.) Let t be the mapping from the set of LTL+O formulae into the set of LTL formulae such that t is homomorphic for $\neg$, $\wedge$, X and U, and

- $t(O(\varphi_1, \ldots, \varphi_n)) := \varphi_0[t(\varphi_1)/p_1, \ldots, t(\varphi_n)/p_n]$
  (recall that $\varphi_0[\psi_1/p_1, \ldots, \psi_n/p_n]$ is the formula obtained from $\varphi_0(p_1, \ldots, p_n)$, by simultaneously replacing every occurrence of p_i by ψ_i),
- $t(p) := p$ for the propositional variable p.

By definition, $w, i \models \varphi$ in LTL+O $\stackrel{\text{def}}{\Leftrightarrow} w, i \models t(\varphi)$ in LTL. By way of example, the 'weak until' operator is usually defined by $\varphi W \psi := (G\varphi) \vee \varphi U \psi$ and the formula φ_W takes the value $(Gp_1) \vee p_1 U p_2$.

(a) From the preceding definition, what can be said about the complexity of model-checking and satisfiability problems for LTL+O?

(b) Define a family of formulae $(\varphi_i)_{i\in\mathbb{N}}$ in LTL+W such that for every $i \geq 1$, $|\varphi_i|$ is in order i and $|t(\varphi_i)|$ is in order 2^i.

(c) Provide a syntactic condition on φ_O that guarantees that $t(\varphi)$ can be computed in polynomial-time in $|\varphi|$.

(d) For every formula φ in LTL+O, we write $\text{cl}_O(\varphi)$ to denote the smallest set of formulae satisfying the clauses for defining $\text{cl}(\cdot)$ in LTL plus the following one: $O(\varphi_1, \dots, \varphi_n) \in \text{cl}_O(\varphi)$ implies $\varphi_O[\varphi_1/p_1, \dots, \varphi_n/p_n] \in \text{cl}_O(\varphi)$. Evaluate the cardinality of $\text{cl}_O(\varphi)$ with respect to the sizes of φ and φ_O.

(e) Determine the complexity of model-checking and satisfiability problems for LTL+O.

Exercise 11.12. In this exercise, we study the complexity of the satisfiability problem for $\text{LTL}_1(U)$. As defined in Section 6.1.2, $\text{LTL}_1(U)$ is the set of LTL formulae with at most one distinct atomic proposition and restricted to the temporal operator U (apart from all the Boolean connectives). For $n \geq 0$, let us consider the following LTL models restricted to the atomic proposition p:

$$\sigma_1^n := (\{p\} \cdot \emptyset)^n \cdot \{p\}^\omega$$
$$\sigma_2^n := \emptyset \cdot (\{p\} \cdot \emptyset)^n \cdot \{p\}^\omega$$
$$\sigma_3^n := (\{p\} \cdot \emptyset)^\omega.$$
$$\sigma_4^n := (\emptyset \cdot \{p\})^n \cdot \emptyset^\omega$$
$$\sigma_5^n := \{p\} \cdot (\emptyset \cdot \{p\})^n \cdot \emptyset^\omega$$
$$\sigma_6^n := (\emptyset \cdot \{p\})^\omega.$$

(a) Show that for every model $\sigma : \mathbb{N} \to \{\emptyset, \{p\}\}$ there is $n \geq 0$ and $j \in [1, 6]$ such that $\sigma \approx \sigma_j^n$ in the sense of Definition 6.6.4.

(b) Show that for all $j \in [1, 6]$, $n \geq 0$ and φ in $\text{LTL}_1(U)$ such that its modal depth is bounded by n, we have $\sigma_j^n, 0 \models \varphi$ iff $\sigma_j^{n+1}, 0 \models \varphi$.

(c) Conclude that the satisfiability problem for $\text{LTL}_1(U)$ is in PTIME.

Exercise 11.13. In the following, we show that the satisfiability problem for $\text{LTL}_2(U)$ is PSPACE-hard by reduction from the satisfiability problem for $\text{LTL}(U)$. Given a formula φ in $\text{LTL}(U)$ built over the atomic propositions $p_1, \dots, p_n$, we construct a formula φ' in $\text{LTL}_2(U)$ over the atomic propositions p_0, p_1 such that φ is satisfiable iff φ' is satisfiable.

(a) Let φ'_{shape} be the formula

$$\texttt{start} \wedge (G((\neg p_0 \wedge p_1) \to p_1 U p_0)) \wedge (G((\neg p_0 \wedge \neg p_1) \to (\neg p_1) U p_0)) \wedge$$

$$G(\texttt{start} \to \texttt{start} U(\neg p_0 \wedge \neg p_1 \wedge (\neg p_0 \wedge \neg p_1 U \chi^n))),$$

where the formulae $\texttt{start}$ and χ^n are defined as follows:

- $\texttt{start} := p_0 \wedge p_1$,
- $\chi^0 := \texttt{start}$,
- $\chi^{k+1} := (p_0 \wedge \neg p_1) \wedge (p_0 U(\neg p_0 \wedge (\neg p_0 U \chi^k)))$.

Show that for any LTL model $\sigma : \mathbb{N} \to \mathcal{P}(\{p_0, p_1\})$, $\sigma, 0 \models \varphi'_{\text{shape}}$ iff σ can be written in the form

$$\{p_0, p_1\}^{\alpha_0^1} \, \emptyset^{\alpha_0^2} \, \{p_0\}^{\alpha_0^3} \, (X_0^1)^{\alpha_0^4} \, \{p_0\}^{\alpha_0^5} \, (X_0^2)^{\alpha_0^6} \cdots \{p_0\}^{\alpha_0^{1+2n}} \, (X_0^n)^{\alpha_0^{2+2n}}$$

$$\{p_0, p_1\}^{\alpha_1^1} \, \emptyset^{\alpha_1^2} \, \{p_0\}^{\alpha_1^3} \, (X_1^1)^{\alpha_1^4} \, \{p_0\}^{\alpha_1^5} \, (X_1^2)^{\alpha_1^6} \cdots \{p_0\}^{\alpha_1^{1+2n}} \, (X_1^n)^{\alpha_1^{2+2n}} \cdots$$

where each $X_i^j \in \{\emptyset, \{p_1\}\}$ and each $\alpha_i^j > 0$.

(*Hint*: Start by showing that for $\ell \in [1, n]$, for every $i > 0$, $\sigma, (2 + 2n)(i - 1) + 2\ell \models \chi^{n+1-\ell}$.)

(b) Define the map $\mathfrak{f}(\cdot)$ as follows:

$$\begin{aligned}
\mathfrak{f}(p_i) &:= p_0 \, \mathsf{U} \, (\neg\mathsf{start} \wedge \neg\mathsf{start} \, \mathsf{U} \, (\chi^{n+1-i} \wedge p_0 \mathsf{U} p_1)) \\
\mathfrak{f}(\psi_1 \wedge \psi_2) &:= \mathfrak{f}(\psi_1) \wedge \mathfrak{f}(\psi_2) \\
\mathfrak{f}(\neg\psi) &:= \neg\mathfrak{f}(\psi) \\
\mathfrak{f}(\psi_1 \mathsf{U} \psi_2) &:= ((\mathsf{start} \wedge \mathfrak{f}(\psi_1)) \, \mathsf{U} \, (\mathsf{start} \wedge \mathfrak{f}(\psi_2))).
\end{aligned}$$

Given a formula φ in LTL(U) built over the atomic propositions $p_1, \ldots, p_n$, show that φ is satisfiable iff $\varphi'_{\text{shape}} \wedge \mathfrak{f}(\varphi)$ is satisfiable.

(c) Conclude that the satisfiability and model-checking problems for $\text{LTL}_2(\mathsf{U})$ are PSPACE-hard.

11.6 Bibliographical Notes

The origins of complexity theory (see Johnson 2012) apparently go back to a long lost and then recovered letter of Gödel to von Neumann in 1956, where he essentially raised the question of the complexity of finding proofs in a given proof system. At about the same time Trakhtenbrot had ideas of introducing what can now be called 'complexity measure' for certain problems. The earliest published references are papers by Cobham, Edmond, Myhill and Yamada in the early 1960s, but the field of complexity theory is widely regarded to be explicitly founded in Hartmanis and Stearns's paper (Hartmanis and Stearns 1965). However, its active development as the study of computational resources that are needed in order to solve a problem, started in real in the early 1970s, with the pioneering works of Cook and Levin, who independently defined the class of NP-problems and the notion of NP-completeness, and proved the NP-completeness of the satisfiability problem for propositional logic SAT. In particular, Cook (1971) showed that SAT is at least as hard as solving any problem that is in NP, thus also establishing the notion of NP-hardness. Then Karp (1972) in his seminal paper proved NP-hardness of many other problems, by developing the technique of polynomial reduction from one NP-hard problem to another.

Nowadays, establishing computational completeness – and therefore, in particular, hardness – for some class of problems is a task routinely taken on when studying any kind of decision problem in computer science. It is nearly impossible to give a complete overview of problems that are known to be complete for popular and important complexity classes like NP or PSPACE. We refer to standard textbooks in complexity theory for some examples (Papadimitriou 1994; Arora and Barak 2009; Goldreich 2008). Such textbooks will also draw a better picture of the hierarchy of complexity classes than can be done here.

Deterministic and nondeterministic time and space classes are so natural so that it is difficult to attribute their invention to a particular piece of work. The alternating time and space classes were introduced by Chandra et al. (1981), where the results on the relationship between alternating and other complexity classes, stated in Section 11.1, were established.

Complexities of temporal logics have been extensively developed in the literature but rarely in a uniform way in textbooks or monographs as done in this chapter. There is at least one exception with (Blackburn et al., 2001, Chapter 6) that is dedicated to (computability and) computational complexity of the satisfiability problem for modal logics by using reductions from tiling problems, as done also here. A notable difference is certainly that the current chapter also deals with model-checking problems for temporal logics and it is mainly focused on proving lower bounds, while upper bounds are established in other chapters.

Tiling systems. The tiling problems and tiling game problems for which we have sketched master reductions are very natural in the sense that they can be seen as word problems for nondeterministic or alternating time or space bounded Turing machines with most unimportant technicalities removed. Because of their naturalness and simplicity they have been advocated as a means for proving lower bounds. Harel (1983, 1985) presented a uniform view on tiling problems and how they are useful to establish complexity lower bounds or undecidability results. A survey of tiling problems was also given by van Emde Boas (1997).

Complexity of linear-time logics. PSPACE-hardness of satisfiability for LTL and some of its fragments was proved by Sistla and Clarke (1982, 1985) and by Halpern and Reif (1981, 1983). They also obtained a matching upper bound by considering LTL as a fragment of deterministic PDL with well-structured programs (also known as SDPDL) (Halpern and Reif, 1983, Theorem 5.3). Sistla and Clarke (1985) also proved inclusion in PSPACE, even for the extension of LTL with past-time operators (see also Markey (2004) for work on the complexity of that extension).

The complexity of LTL fragments, including LTL with unary operators only, has been actively studied (see e.g. Chen and Lin 1993; Sistla and Clarke 1985; Demri and Schnoebelen 2002; Markey 2004; Nakamura and Ono 1980). The latter establishes a small model property in order to prove inclusion in NP. In Bauland et al. (2009, 2011), the complexity of the satisfiability and model-checking problems for fragments of LTL obtained by restricting the set of propositional connectives, has been systematically investigated.

A PSPACE upper bound for the ETL satisfiability problem has been established in different sources, for instance by Wolper, using a tableaux-based decision procedure (Wolper, 1983, Lemma 8.2), by Halpern and Reif, viewing it as a fragment of SDPDL (Halpern and Reif, 1983, Theorem 5.3), as well as by Sistla and Clarke (1985). The first decision procedure with an elementary complexity was designed by Wolper (1981), but it required exponential space.

The complexity of certain extensions of LTL with regular expressions and fixpoints was studied in Lange (2007), including the EXPSPACE-completeness of PSL which was also obtained beforehand by considering preceding specification languages like SystemVerilog (e.g. Bustan and Havlicek 2006).

The nonelementary complexity of QLTL can be obtained as a direct consequence of the nonelementary complexity of the second-order theory of one successor, as shown by Meyer (1973, 1975). The latter theory can naturally be embedded into QLTL. A nonelementary upper bound for the satisfiability problem of QLTL was established by Sistla, Vardi and Wolper (Sistla et al. 1987, Lemma 4.2; see also Sistla 1983 PhD thesis).

Basic modal logic BML. PSPACE-completeness of BML satisfiability was shown by Ladner (1977). The lower bound uses a reduction from QBF, the upper bound is obtained via a tableaux-based decision procedure. This PSPACE-completeness result has been extended and refined in many directions since then (see e.g. Spaan 1993a; Hemaspaandra 1994). For example, the satisfiability problem for BML without atomic propositions but with logical constants was shown to be PSPACE-hard too (Hemaspaandra 2001), refining the PSPACE-hardness for BML restricted to a single atomic proposition (Halpern 1995).

Branching-time temporal logics. EXPTIME-hardness of TLR and CTL was first established by Fischer and Ladner (1979) who actually considered the closely related propositional dynamic logic PDL and proved EXPTIME-hardness of its satisfiability problem by a reduction from the word problem for alternating polynomially space-bounded Turing machines. A close inspection of that proof shows that the only operators which are needed in this reduction are those that are already available in TLR. Moreover, the reduction from the corresponding tiling game problem used here can be seen as a simplification of the reduction from the corresponding word problem.

The 2-EXPTIME-hardness of CTL* was shown by Vardi and Stockmeyer (1985) using similar techniques, in fact much before a matching upper bound could be found. Johannsen and Lange (2003) showed that the encoding of the word problem for exponentially space-bounded Turing machines could be improved such that the resulting formulae fall into CTL$^+$ already.

Most lower bounds on model-checking problems are either folklore (BML), or follow immediately from results about some of their fragments (TLR, CTL, CTL*), or – in the linear-time case – from corresponding satisfiability-checking problems (LTL and all its fragments and extensions). The only temporal logic whose model-checking problem is not covered by either of these cases is CTL$^+$, see further the relevant references on it.

A PTIME upper bound for CTL model checking was first established by Clarke and Emerson (1981); a bilinear time upper bound is due to Clarke et al. (1986). Queille and Sifakis also gave an algorithm for model checking CTL without the until operator (Queille and

Sifakis 1982a; Grumberg and Veith 2008), even though complexity issues were not considered in that work.

Emerson and Lei (1987) showed why LTL model checking and CTL* model checking have the same complexity. Sistla and Clarke (1985) also transferred bounds between satisfiability and model checking for LTL.

An extensive survey on the complexity of model checking temporal logics was produced by Schnoebelen (2003).

Here we have not touched upon branching-time temporal logics extended with past-time operators. The complexities of satisfiability and model checking for such logics have been investigated in several papers, too (Kupferman and Pnueli 1995; Laroussinie and Schnoebelen 2000; Kupferman et al. 2012; Bozzelli 2008).

CTL$^+$. There is also a consequence related to succinctness that follows from complexity-theoretic observations. Since CTL can be decided in exponential time (Emerson and Halpern 1985) and CTL$^+$ is hard for doubly exponential time (Johannsen and Lange 2003), and it is known from the time hierarchy theorem in complexity theory (Hartmanis and Stearns 1965) that these two classes are different, there can be no polynomial reduction from CTL$^+$ satisfiability to CTL satisfiability. This is, on one hand, stronger and, on the other hand, weaker than the question of succinctness of CTL$^+$ over CTL. It is weaker because it does not preclude the existence of short formulae in CTL; it only precludes the possibility to compute them in short time. On the other hand it is stronger because it shows that this holds not only for translations that preserve equivalence but even for the much larger class of translations that only preserve satisfiability.

Regarding the decision problems for CTL$^+$, the fact that satisfiability can be decided in 2ExpTime is inherited from CTL* (Emerson and Jutla 1988, 2000). It can also be obtained from an exponential translation into CTL which can be decided in ExpTime (Emerson and Halpern 1985). In Emerson and Halpern (1985) it is established that for any CTL$^+$ formula of length n, there is a logically equivalent CTL formula of length at most $2^{\mathcal{O}(n \log(n))}$. The model-checking problem for CTL$^+$ is Δ_2^p-complete: the lower bound was established by Laroussinie et al. (2001), whereas the upper bound is from Clarke et al. (1986, Theorem 6.2). The paper by Laroussinie et al. (2001) also shows that the model-checking problems of other temporal logics between CTL and CTL*, like CTL with fairness constraints, belong to that class as well.

Flat and other fragments. The complexity of satisfiability of the flat (with no nesting of temporal operators) fragment of LTL was proved NP-complete in Halpern (1995) (see also Demri and Schnoebelen 2002), and for the flat fragments of CTL and CTL$^+$ the same complexity was established in Goranko and Vester (2014), where the satisfiability in the fragment of CTL* with no nesting of path quantifiers was shown to be PSpace-complete. For more complexity results of fragments of temporal logics obtained by restricting the number of atomic propositions, see Halpern (1995).

ATL* and fragments. The PTIME-completeness of the model-checking problem for ATL and the 2EXPTIME-completeness of that problem for ATL* were established in Alur et al. (2002). Further complexity analyses of these problems, also taking into account the number of agents as parameter, as well as memory and perfect versus imperfect information, can be found in Bulling et al. (2010), Jamroga and Dix (2008), Laroussinie (2010) and Laroussinie et al. (2008). The EXPTIME-completeness of the satisfiability problem for ATL was first established, assuming a fixed number of agents, in van Drimmelen (2003) and further refined in Goranko and van Drimmelen (2006) and in Walther et al. (2006), where the EXPTIME upper bound was proved without fixing the number of agents. 2EXPTIME-completeness of satisfiability testing for ATL* was obtained by Schewe (2008a). The complexity of satisfiability in various flat fragments of ATL* was established in Goranko and Vester (2014), where all of them are shown to be in PSPACE; more precisely, Σ_3^P-complete for the flat (with no nesting of strategic operators) fragments of ATL and ATL$^+$, and PSPACE-complete for the full flat fragment of ATL*.

Part IV
Methods

12

Frameworks for Decision Procedures

This fourth and last part of the book provides algorithmic methods for the main decision problems that come with temporal logics: satisfiability, validity and model checking. Model checking is typically easier, particularly for branching-time logics, and therefore admits simpler solutions that have been presented in the chapters of Part II already. Since temporal logics are usually closed under complementation, satisfiability and validity are very closely related and methods dealing with one of them can easily be used to solve the other, so we will not consider them separately. Indeed, in order to check a formula φ for validity, one can check $\neg\varphi$ for satisfiability and invert the result since φ is valid iff $\neg\varphi$ is unsatisfiable. Satisfiability is reducible to validity likewise. Furthermore, a satisfiability-checking procedure would typically yield not only the answer but also, in the positive case, a model *witnessing* the satisfiability of the input formula. Such an interpreted transition system would *refute* validity of $\neg\varphi$, i.e. be a countermodel for its validity. Hence, the focus of this part is on satisfiability checking.

The methods presented here are closely linked to Chapter 11, which provided lower bounds on the computational complexity of these decision problems, i.e. it explained how difficult these problems are from a computational perspective. The following chapters provide the missing halves to an exact analysis of temporal logics' computational complexities: by estimating the time and space consumption that these methods need in order to check for satisfiability, satisfaction, etc., we obtain upper bounds on these decision problems. Thus, while Chapter 11 showed how hard *at least* these problems are, the following chapters show how hard they are *at most*, by presenting concrete algorithmic solutions for these decision problems.

The methods presented in the following three chapters are in fact *methodologies* in the sense that each chapter introduces a particular framework for obtaining methods for certain temporal logics. Each of these frameworks – tableaux, automata and games – has its own characteristics, strengths and weaknesses and may or may not be particularly suited for particular temporal logics. Axiomatic systems, presented in the respective chapters of Part II, provide an alternative methodology that historically appeared first, but they can only be used to establish validity (resp. nonsatisfiability) when it is the case, and provide no answer otherwise, so they are not really decision methods. That is why they are not treated in this part, which studies *model-theoretic* methodologies based respectively on tableaux, automata and games to fully solve the logical decision problems, by providing an answer in either case.

This chapter contains two sections. The first one gives a brief introduction into the three methodologies that are studied in detail in the following three chapters. It is not necessary in order to understand those methods, but it is useful to read Section 12.1 first because it puts Chapters 13–15 into the perspective of (often) having choices when designing decision methods for temporal logics.

Section 12.2 tries to give an account of similarities and differences between these methodologies. A natural place for that section would be the very end of Part IV. However, we also want to encourage the reader to come to their own conclusions about the usefulness, disadvantages, similarities, etc., between tableaux, automata and games. In this sense, Section 12.2 will simply prepare the reader to look out for certain aspects when reading the following Chapters 13–15.

12.1 A Brief Introduction to Three Methodologies

12.1.1 Tableaux

A tableau for classical logic is a tree- or DAG-like graph that represents a systematic search for a model of the formula (or set of formulae) at its root. A fundamental notion here is that of an open node which is used to indicate success of the search for a model. It provides sufficient information for building a satisfying model, and in that sense an open tableau witnesses satisfiability of the input formula.

Tableaux for modal and temporal logics follow that idea, so naturally there is a direct correspondence between the shape of an open tableau and the shape of a model for the input formula if it is satisfiable, but it need not be a tree or a DAG anymore, because the more expressive temporal logics do not have a finite tree-model property. If a satisfying model does not exist, a sound and complete tableau-building procedure should end up with a closed tableau which can be regarded as a proof that the input formula is not satisfiable.

Thus, tableaux can be 'successful' or not, and that distinguishes tableau methods from the two other methodologies to be discussed later. Automata and games are not supposed to be successful – it is a method that works on the automaton or on the game that is to be successful.

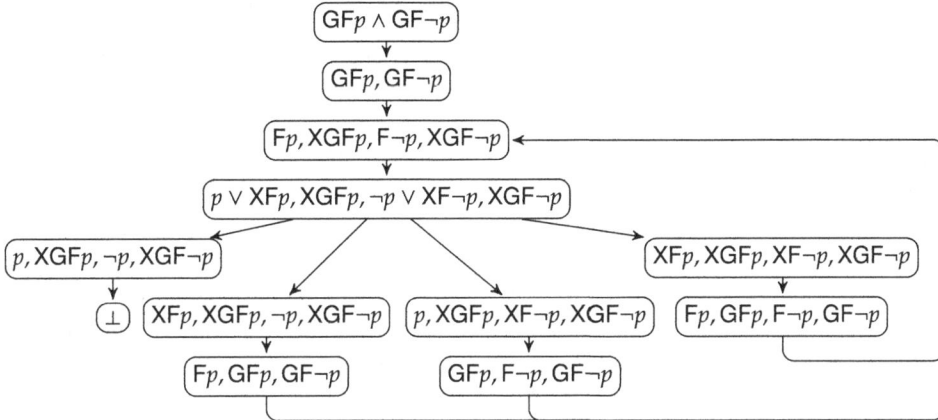

Figure 12.1 An example tableau.

The tableau search builds a graph step by step, following the syntactic structure of the formula and decomposing or unfolding it into 'simpler' formulae, until all requirements corresponding to the truth of the formulae in the labels are fulfilled. This is similar to proof search procedures for other, Gentzen-style deductive systems, which also build proof trees. However, when building a tableau for temporal formulae and using unfolding principles one may arrive at nodes which carry the same list of formulae in the label as nodes encountered before. In order to terminate the procedure, one has to decide how to interpret such situations in terms of satisfiability and how to define the notions of closed and open tableau in order to determine whether a model representation has been found. We give an example (see Figure 12.1) which does not follow exactly the tableaux-building procedure presented in Chapter 13 but is rather intended to give an intuitive idea of such a construction.

Example 12.1.1. Consider the LTL formula $GFp \land GF\neg p$. We build a tableau graph for it whose nodes are sets of formulae from its 'extended closure', starting with the singleton set only containing the input formula. The tableau grows as a directed graph, following rules for generating new nodes from existing ones. These rules, which we will not formally present here, follow the formula decomposition rules for the Boolean connectives, also taking into account the unfoldings of the temporal operators, plus an extra rule for creating a successor of the current state, with a label collecting all X-prefixed subformulae in the label of that state. When a state with an already existing label is to be created, the construction loops back to the existing state with that label. When a label with a contradictory pair of formulae is created, the branch terminates with a label $\bot$. The resulting tableau graph is shown in Figure 12.1. From that tableau one can conclude that the input formula is satisfiable, and moreover can extract a satisfying linear model, e.g. one that loops by passing alternatively through the two middle branches at the bottom. We leave it as an exercise to see that it is indeed a model for $GFp \land GF\neg p$.

12.1.2 Automata

The automata-theoretic framework, as well as the game-theoretic one described further, differs from the tableau framework by separating the characterisation of a logical property like satisfiability from the algorithms that decide this property on the basis of this characterisation. Note that these two aspects are intertwined in tableaux: building a tableau means searching for a witness of satisfiability.

Designing a decision procedure for temporal logics in the automata-theoretic framework is separated into two parts. The first is finding an effective translation from logical formulae to automata of a certain kind, depending on the kind of temporal logic at hand. The second part consists of the design of decision procedures for automata-theoretic or language-theoretic problems like nonemptiness or universality of the language of a given automaton. Thus, the central aspect of the automata-theoretic framework is the transfer from deciding logical properties to language-theoretic properties, by forming connections between temporal formulae and certain types of automata. What makes such connections useful in transferring decision problems is the fact that they preserve models or their representations. As noted earlier, there is no notion of a 'successful' automaton, unlike tableaux. Instead it is the algorithm operating on the automaton that terminates with success or not.

These principles are most easily explained for linear-time temporal logics. A formula of, say, LTL describes a set of computation paths, i.e. infinite words over an alphabet obtained as the powerset of a finite set of atomic propositions. Sets of such computation paths are just languages of infinite words over this powerset alphabet. The automata-theoretic approach to temporal logic seeks for transformations of formulae – in this case from LTL – into automata that recognise languages over such words, for instance Büchi automata – finite-state automata that recognise an infinite word by visiting accepting states infinitely often.

Preservation of models in this simple example just means that the language of the automaton $\mathcal{A}_\varphi$ constructed from the temporal formula φ recognises exactly those computation paths that are models of φ. Then satisfiability of φ reduces to the nonemptiness of the language of $\mathcal{A}_\varphi$, and the combination of the effective translation from φ to $\mathcal{A}_\varphi$ together with an algorithm for checking $\mathcal{A}_\varphi$ for nonemptiness yields a decision procedure for satisfiability of the underlying temporal logic. Likewise, validity of φ corresponds to universality of $\mathcal{A}_\varphi$.

Example 12.1.2. Consider the LTL formula $\varphi := \mathsf{GF}p \wedge \mathsf{GF}\neg p$ that was used in the tableau example. It expresses 'p must hold infinitely often but also infinitely often p must not hold'. We will transfer the satisfiability problem for that formula to a question about a *Büchi automaton* associated with it. Figure 12.2 presents a Büchi automaton for the language of φ. We leave it to the reader to check that it accepts exactly those computation paths seen as infinite words over the alphabet $\{\emptyset, \{p\}\}$ that satisfy the condition expressed by that formula. We leave it as an exercise to verify that, for example, the trace

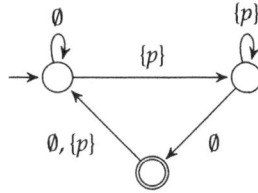

Figure 12.2 A Büchi automaton.

$\{p\}\,\emptyset\,\emptyset\,\{p\}\,\emptyset\,\emptyset\,\{p\}\,\emptyset\,\ldots$ is accepted by this automaton and that, in general, its language is exactly $\mathrm{Mod}(\varphi)$.

12.1.3 Games

The last methodology for designing decision procedures for temporal logics that we present in this book is based on the framework of games. It is similar to the automata-theoretic framework in that it separates the characterisation of a logical decision problem from the algorithm that is employed for solving it. Thus, it also differs from tableaux in this respect.

Some game-based characterisations of model-checking problems have been presented in the chapters of Part II already. The model checking and satisfiability-checking games presented in Chapter 15 work along the same lines: two players play with opposing objectives that are based on the underlying logical decision problem. In *model checking games* the input is again an interpreted transition system and a temporal formula, and the two players Verifier and Refuter want to verify, respectively refute, the claim that the given interpreted transition system is a model of the formula. In *satisfiability games*, the two players want to verify, respectively refute, the claim that the input formula is satisfiable. Such games are typically played on the closure set of the input formula.

The central algorithmic concept in the game-theoretic approach to temporal logics is *solving a game*: given a game represented as a graph, decide whether the player Verifier has a *winning strategy* for it, i.e. is able to enforce a winning play against any possible behaviour or her opponent. This is a purely graph-theoretic problem, so game solving is independent of properties of the temporal logics that one is interested in.

The games that we will use in Chapter 15 are **parity games** which are being played on directed graphs whose nodes carry priorities that determine the winner of an infinite play by inspecting the *limes superior*, i.e. the highest ranking state that occurs infinitely often on the play. This may seem at first sight like an odd and arbitrary choice, but a closer look reveals that it captures exactly the nature of the unfolding principle for (possibly nested and alternating) fixpoint operators of least and greatest type. Thus, these games turn out to be a natural choice as the backbone in the game-theoretic framework for temporal logics.

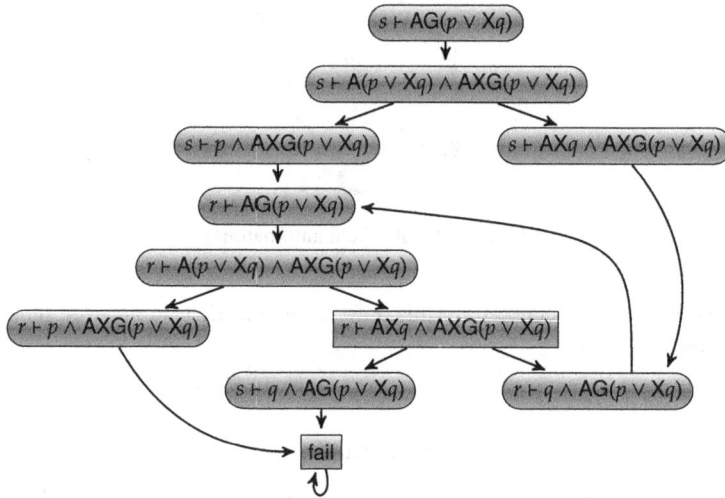

Figure 12.3 The idea of model-checking games.

Example 12.1.3. Consider the interpreted transition system

and the CTL* formula $\mathsf{AG}(p \vee \mathsf{X}q)$. A game capturing the essence of the model-checking question of whether s satisfies this property is shown in Figure 12.3. The two kinds of nodes represent the players' choice points: Verifier chooses in oval nodes while Refuter chooses in rectangular nodes. The node labelled fail indicate that the property to be checked locally in this node fails to hold, and therefore Refuter wins at this point. The formulae and state annotations in the nodes reflect the decomposition of the original property by players' choices in order to establish or refute satisfaction in the node s of the interpreted transition system.

It is not too hard to see that Refuter has a winning strategy, as he can force any play to reach the node fail: he selects a path in the interpreted transition system which is obtained by simply following the state annotations in the earlier game on the way to the node fail. Not surprisingly, the last two states on this path must be r and s in this order, and they give a counterexample to the truth of $\mathsf{AG}(p \vee \mathsf{X}q)$ which requires all successive pairs of states to satisfy p in the first one or q in the second one.

12.2 The Frameworks Compared

Besides some apparently essential differences between tableaux, automata and games – like the separation between characterisation and decision procedure – there are also many commonalities between these methodologies. In this section we compare them with respect to different aspects, thus trying to build a picture of what the pros and cons of each of these methodologies are.

We will only make some general observations here. The exact differences and commonalities may depend on the underlying temporal logics for which a decision procedure is being designed, and depending on this logic some methodologies may be more or less similar.

12.2.1 Particular Advantages

Tableaux are often seen as particularly flexible and efficient for decision procedures. It is tempting to explain this with their direct algorithmic attack on the logical decision problem. As a consequence, tableaux techniques often perform very well for simple logics because they focus directly on establishing satisfiability, and satisfiability only. The price to pay for this, however, shows up when considering logics of higher computational and combinatorial complexity. That is why, in Chapter 13 we focus on tableaux for 'easy' temporal logics like LTL and CTL but do not design direct satisfiability-checking procedures for $\mathcal{L}_\mu$ and CTL*, because the decision problems for such logics do require greater combinatorial effort, and this is where the frameworks of automata and games work generally better. We present satisfiability-checking procedures for such logics in terms of games in Chapter 15, yet the combinatorics also involves a fair amount of automata theory. It is exactly the separation of a characterisation – here in terms of an abstract game – from the algorithmic question that allows these more difficult decision problems to be tackled.

The major advantage of the automata-theoretic framework is also such a separation between the *characterisation* of the set of models of a temporal formula and the *algorithm* that analyses this set. The automata-theoretic framework hence provides a computational semantics for temporal logics through a correspondence between temporal formulae as declarative objects and automata as computational devices. This makes it particularly interesting in the context of computer science.

Both automata and games are prone to benefit from improvements on the outside by using algorithms as black-boxes, for instance emptiness tests on the automata side and solving algorithms for games.

The main advantage of the game-theoretic approach, though, is its interactive nature which can be used to illustrate logical decision problems, such as the unsatisfiability of a temporal formula or its unsatisfaction in a particular state of an interpreted transition system, by means of winning strategies. These can be used directly in a tool not only in order to tell the user that a formula is not satisfiable but also to convince him why it is not satisfiable. In order to gain this insight, the user could play a satisfiability game against the tool which simply follows the already computed winning strategy for player Refuter.

Summing up, as a rule of thumb, the particular advantage of the automata-theoretic framework is that of a computational semantics for temporal logics, while the one of the game-theoretic framework is that of an interactive semantics, and the one of the tableaux framework is the aim for direct and efficient decision procedures.

12.2.2 Common Features and Differences

Some of the advantages of certain frameworks surely carry over to others simply because they share certain features. The aforementioned separation of a syntactic characterisation from the algorithmic question that is shared by automata and games is an example of such features. However, there is also a clear difference between these two frameworks.

The automata-theoretic framework typically provides a *single* syntactic object, namely an automaton, representing the given temporal formula. Different logical decision problems are then tackled by *different* algorithms that work on that automaton. Thus, in order to decide satisfiability, respectively validity, of an LTL formula φ, one can consider the same Büchi automaton $\mathcal{A}_\varphi$ and analyse emptiness, respectively universality, of its language. But these are essentially different problems that require different algorithms. Also, one can use this automaton to do model checking with yet another algorithm which, in this case, couples this automaton with the input interpreted transition system and analyses the resulting automaton for universality. Note that these do not yield optimal solutions for validity and model checking.

The game-theoretic framework on the other hand provides *different* games for different logical decision problems: while the model checking and satisfiability-checking games for LTL still look very similar, the differences become very apparent when considering branching-time logics. However, it is possible to reduce all these decision problems to the same type of games and therefore always use a *single* solving mechanism for all of them.

There are similarities between tableaux on one hand and automata and games on the other hand, too. Tableaux and games typically work rule-based by decomposition of the input formula. This preserves a close relationship between the input formula and the syntactic object (tableau or game) that is being created in order to decide a logical property. This is a vital ingredient for such methods to be able to provide more than just a simple yes/no answer but also comprehensible witnesses or counterexamples to this answer.

12.2.3 Going from One Method to Another

A fair question to ask is whether it is possible to design a decision procedure for a particular temporal logic in one of these frameworks, when a procedure in another framework already exists, i.e. whether it is possible to transfer decision procedures and thus benefit from particular advantages in more than one methodology. Here we try to give some high-level guidelines of how to turn one procedure into another.

From Tableaux to Games and Back

Tableau procedures can easily be seen as games: the OR-branching in tableaux can simply be seen as choices for Verifier in the game whose objective is to decide whether a successful tableau exists, whereas Refuter handles the AND-branchings, and the winning conditions in this game correspond to the success conditions on the tableau branches.

On the other hand, a game in the sense defined in Chapter 15 is just a graph with nodes as game states and edges as choices. The search for a winning strategy in such a game graph can be seen as building a tableau: Verifier's choices become OR-branchings and Refuter's choices become AND-branchings. The winning conditions in games generally correspond to the conditions of successful (open) tableaux.

The transformation from games to tableaux becomes more subtle, though, when winning strategies are not history-free. Simple types of games that admit history-free winning strategies like reachability and safety games can easily be translated into tableaux where the question of whether a branch is open solely depends on the last node of the branch. Slightly more complex winning conditions that, for instance, refer to the repetition of a configuration can then also be translated into relatively simple conditions of openness in tableaux. The handling of very general winning conditions, for instance of full ω-regularity (as is needed in satisfiability games for $\mathcal{L}_\mu$ and CTL* for example) becomes difficult though and would typically require automata determinisation techniques to be encoded in tableau rules.

Automata and Games

The evaluation of a property on automata can often be seen as a game, for instance the question of whether an automaton accepts a given word.

In the case of a nondeterministic automaton, this results in a rather uninteresting 1-player game, where the single player mimics the automaton's nondeterminism to produce an accepting run. The winning conditions in such games are directly obtained from the automata's acceptance condition. If the automata are deterministic then this game becomes even more simple: no player has a choice in it.

The full beauty of this correspondence is only seen when considering stronger types of automata, namely *alternating automata*, that not only can guess what the next right transition for accepting some input is, but also what a wrong choice would be. Seen differently, they offer a second mode of operation besides nondeterministic choice: forking several copies that simultaneously read the remaining input. These two modes then translate into choices of the players in 2-player games. Interestingly, alternating automata also often provide a much more natural computational counterpart to temporal formulae than nondeterministic ones do. The price to pay for this, however, is the increased complexity of decision procedures on alternating automata.

13

Tableaux-Based Decision Methods

The underlying idea of the method of semantic tableaux for testing satisfiability of logical formulae is to organise a systematic search for a satisfying model of the input formula, or set of formulae. Both the entire procedure and the search tree itself are usually called 'tableau'. The tableau search follows the logical structure of the formulae to be satisfied and consists of repeated application of specific *formula decomposition rules* associated with the logical connectives in the given logical language. If the search for a satisfying model terminates without success, the tableau is pronounced 'closed' and the input set of formulae is declared unsatisfiable. If the tableau method is *sound*, closure of the tableau search must imply that the input set of formulae is indeed unsatisfiable. If the search succeeds, or never terminates, the tableau is pronounced 'open'. If the input is not satisfiable, a *complete* tableau procedure is supposed to terminate and establish that the input is not satisfiable, indeed.

Traditionally tableaux are regarded as logical deductive systems, built in a formal, declarative, rule-based manner. Tableaux for classical logic use only *local decomposition* rules, while tableaux for modal and temporal logics also involve *successor rules* and in the traditional versions both types of rules are treated on a par and the control mechanisms are built in as provisos for the application of these rules. While soundness and completeness are *sine qua non*, termination is not a common requirement. Indeed, in case of logics with undecidable but recursively axiomatisable validity, such as first-order logic, a sound and complete tableau cannot be always terminating, so it can only be used as a deductive system, but not as a decision procedure. In this book we use tableaux as *decision procedures*, hence in our context termination is a requirement that is as essential as soundness and completeness. Moreover, if a tableau-based search terminates successfully (as open tableau) it usually provides sufficient information to build a model satisfying the input. Thus, a sound, complete and always terminating tableau for a given logic provides not only a decision procedure for testing satisfiability (respectively, validity) in it, but also a constructive method for *model building*, whenever a model for the input set of formulae exists. That is why tableau-based methods are particularly useful, both theoretically and for practical use. Furthermore, tableau-based procedures can often be adapted (though, not always optimally) to other logical tasks, such as model checking.

In this chapter we first sketch a generic tableaux construction for testing satisfiability of temporal logics, which we will illustrate with our basic logic BML. Then, building on that generic construction, we develop in detail, in a relatively independent but uniform way, the tableau constructions for each of the logics LTL and CTL (subsuming the case of TLR) and give proofs of their soundness and completeness. Thus, while seeing the common methodology, the reader should be able to follow each of these cases fairly independently, though this comes at the expense of some inevitable repetitions, *mutatis mutandis*, of technical details. All these tableau-based decision procedures for testing satisfiability run in Exp-Time, which is optimal in the cases of TLR and extensions, but not in the cases of BML and LTL. In these cases we will show how the procedure can be optimised to PSpace. For each of these logics we also show how the tableau procedure can be adapted for model checking.

In the case of modal and temporal logics the tableau search for a satisfying model essentially alternates between *local steps*, applying local decomposition rules corresponding to the classical logical connectives and reflecting reasoning within a state (possible world) and *successor steps*, applying modal decomposition rules corresponding to the modal operators and reflecting transitions from a state to its successor states. In the traditional style of tableau systems, all steps are presented by formal tableau-building rules which treat both types of steps on a par. This approach makes the internal structure of the search less transparent, so here we adopt a less formalised but better structured approach, where the local steps are encapsulated in a separate sub-procedure, alternating with the successor-building rules.

In the case of simple logics like BML, the tableau building procedure terminates naturally because every time a successor step is performed the maximal modal depth of the set of formulae under consideration decreases. When fixpoint operators are added to the language, i.e. in the cases of LTL, TLR and their extensions, some complications in the tableau procedure arise because these logics need special mechanisms for checking *realisation of eventualities*. Other types of complications arise when past modalities are involved, too, which typically require either using a suitably restricted (analytic) cut rule, or a mechanism for backtracking and expanding the labels of already constructed nodes of the tableau. Since we do not consider logics with past modalities in this chapter, these complications will not be treated here, but the interested reader can find references where they are dealt with in the bibliographic notes.

One can distinguish two types of tableau constructions for temporal logics, viz. *declarative* (a.k.a., *top-down*) and *incremental* (or, *bottom-up*). They differ in the strategy of building the tableau graph: the declarative approach takes as nodes all 'atoms' (suitably saturated sets of formulae) under consideration and then constructs transition arcs between them according to their content and the semantics of the temporal operators, while the incremental approach starts with only one atom, containing the input formula or set of formulae, and then expands the tableau 'on demand', by adding step by step only those atoms that are needed for the necessary successor nodes of the nodes that have already been added. While both approaches usually yield the same worst case complexity, the declarative approach *always* performs as in the worst case, while the incremental approach is practically much more efficient in most cases. That is why here we develop the incremental tableau-building methodology.

The most distinctive features of the tableaux building methodology that we present are uniformity, conceptual simplicity, intuitive clarity and flexibility. The price to pay for these is that, because of following a breadth-first search approach, the generic construction is not always worst-case optimal and needs additional optimisation for the cases of BML and LTL where satisfiability is PSPACE-complete (see Chapter 11). Also, the adaptation of this methodology for more expressive logics like CTL* and the modal μ-calculus is non-trivial and not covered here; instead, we present satisfiability-checking games for these in Chapter 15.

For simplicity of the exposition, we only consider languages for mono-transition systems. In the case of many transition relations the same procedures apply, again *mutatis mutandis*, by treating all temporal operators over the different transitions in the same way.

Chapter structure. We begin with a detailed exposition of a generic methodology for the construction of incremental tableaux in Section 13.1, illustrated on the basic modal logic BML. In particular, we define and illustrate with several running examples the basic concepts underpinning that methodology: components and closure of a formula, full expansion of a set of formulae, local tableaux (essentially, side application of classical propositional tableaux), Hintikka structures, pre-tableaux construction, prestate elimination and state elimination phases, eventually yielding the final tableaux. We then prove the termination, soundness and completeness of the procedure and analyse its complexity.

In Section 13.2 we apply this methodology to tableaux for satisfiability testing in the linear-time temporal logic LTL and again illustrate it with several running examples. The main new element in the construction of tableaux for LTL is the dealing with eventualities and checking their realisation in the construction of the tableaux. We prove the termination, soundness and completeness of the procedure, explain how satisfying linear models are extracted from open final tableaux and analyse the complexity of the procedure. We also demonstrate how the tableaux-based procedure can be adapted for model checking of LTL formulae.

In Section 13.3 we apply the same approach to the development of tableaux for the branching-time logic CTL and again illustrate it with several running examples. Inter alia, we demonstrate how to deal with the two types of eventualities arising here: existential and universal. Again, we prove the termination, soundness and completeness of the procedure, explain how satisfying interpreted transition systems are extracted from open final tableaux, and analyse the complexity of the procedure.

13.1 A Generic Incremental Tableau Construction

First, we give an informal outline of a generic incremental tableaux construction for modal and temporal logics, beginning with some preliminaries.

13.1.1 Preliminaries

Recall that the set of all subformulae of a formula η is denoted by $sub(\eta)$, while the set of all subformulae of a set of formulae Γ is denoted by $sub(\Gamma)$.

Types and Components of Formulae

For the sake of presenting the tableau rules for all basic logical connectives in BML, within this section we will assume each of $\top, \bot, \neg, \wedge, \vee, \rightarrow, \mathsf{EX}, \mathsf{AX}$ as a primitive connective in the language, while $\varphi \leftrightarrow \psi$ will be regarded as an abbreviation of $(\varphi \rightarrow \psi) \wedge (\psi \rightarrow \varphi)$.

We will distinguish four **types** of formulae:

Definition 13.1.1.

1. *Conjunctive formulae.* Every conjunctive formula, typically denoted by α, is associated with several (in all our cases at most two) formulae, called its **conjunctive components**, such that α is equivalent to the conjunction of its conjunctive components.

    For instance, the conjunctive components of $\alpha = \varphi \wedge \psi$ are $\alpha_1 = \varphi$ and $\alpha_2 = \psi$, and the only conjunctive component of $\neg\neg\varphi$ is $\alpha_1 = \varphi$.

conjunctive		disjunctive		successor	
formula	components	formula	components	formula	components
$\neg\neg\varphi$	φ, φ	$\varphi \vee \psi$	φ, ψ	$\mathsf{EX}\varphi$	φ
$\varphi \wedge \psi$	φ, ψ	$\varphi \rightarrow \psi$	$\neg\varphi, \psi$	$\mathsf{AX}\varphi$	φ
$\neg(\varphi \vee \psi)$	$\neg\varphi, \neg\psi$	$\neg(\varphi \wedge \psi)$	$\neg\varphi, \neg\psi$	$\neg\mathsf{EX}\varphi$	$\neg\varphi$
$\neg(\varphi \rightarrow \psi)$	$\varphi, \neg\psi$			$\neg\mathsf{AX}\varphi$	$\neg\varphi$

Figure 13.1 Types and components of formulae in BML.

2. *Disjunctive formulae.* Every disjunctive formula, typically denoted by β, is associated with several (in all our cases at most two) formulae, called its **disjunctive components**, such that β is equivalent to the disjunction of its disjunctive components.

   For instance, the disjunctive components of $\beta = \varphi \vee \psi$ are $\beta_1 = \varphi$ and $\beta_2 = \psi$.

3. *Successor formulae.* These are formulae referring to truth in (some, or all) successor states. Typically, they are of the type $\mathsf{O}\varphi$ or $\neg\mathsf{O}\varphi$, where O is a 'local' modal operator: the operators EX and AX in case of BML, TLR and CTL, and X in case of LTL.

   In particular, formulae of the type $\mathsf{EX}\varphi$ and $\neg\mathsf{AX}\varphi$ are called **existential successor formulae** while formulae of the type $\mathsf{AX}\varphi$ and $\neg\mathsf{EX}\varphi$ are called **universal successor formulae**.

   The only component of a successor formula $\chi = \mathsf{O}\varphi$ is its **successor component** φ, while the only component of $\chi = \neg\mathsf{O}\varphi$ is its **successor component** $\neg\varphi$. We write $scomp(\chi)$ to denote the successor component of the formula χ. Hereafter we use the term X-**components** for the successor components.

4. *Literals*: I, $\perp$, atomic propositions and negations of these. They have no components.

   The literals and the successor formulae are commonly called **primitive formulae**. ∇

   In Figure 13.1 we summarise the types and components of the formulae in BML.

Lemma 13.1.2.

(I) Every conjunctive formula φ of BML is equivalent to the conjunction of its conjunctive components.

(II) Every disjunctive formula φ of BML is equivalent to the disjunction of its disjunctive components.   ∎

The proof is left as Exercise 13.10.

Extended Closure of a Formula

In order to determine the truth of a formula η, one has to consider a number of 'simpler' formulae which appear in the process of the truth evaluation of η. Some of these are not really simpler, because they come from the fixpoint unfoldings of the temporal operators, and may not belong to the closure $cl(\eta)$ as defined in Chapter 4.

Thus, the notion of **extended closure** of the formula η, denoted $ecl(\eta)$, emerges. The term 'extended' refers to the fact that, besides the formulae obtained by applying local tableau rules, for the logics TLR, LTL and CTL, $ecl(\eta)$ may contain formulae that are not in the closure as defined in Definition 4.1.2 but are needed in the tableaux construction, because they are obtained by unfoldings of fixpoint operators occurring in η. However, while for the logic BML, any formula in $ecl(\varphi)$ is either a subformula of φ or the negation of a subformula of φ, $ecl(\cdot)$ is not a closure in the sense of Definition 4.1.2 because it is not required to be closed under negations or subformulae. This might be a bit confusing at first glance, but we have to reuse the closure terminology for several somewhat different purposes. Instead, the extended closure of a formula is obtained by closing it under taking components of already added formulae, defined generically as follows.

Definition 13.1.3. The **extended closure** $ecl(\varphi)$ of the formula φ is the least set of formulae such that:

1. $\varphi \in ecl(\varphi)$,
2. $ecl(\varphi)$ is closed under taking all conjunctive, disjunctive, successor components of the respective formulae in $ecl(\varphi)$. $\qquad\qquad\qquad\qquad\qquad\qquad\qquad \triangledown$

The term 'closure' is quite appropriate here because $ecl(\cdot)$ satisfies the three fundamental properties for closure operators:

1. $\{\varphi\} \subseteq ecl(\{\varphi\})$,
2. $\Gamma \subseteq \Gamma'$ implies $ecl(\Gamma) \subseteq ecl(\Gamma')$,
3. $ecl(ecl(\Gamma)) = ecl(\Gamma)$.

Definition 13.1.4. For any set of formulae Γ we define

$$ecl(\Gamma) := \bigcup \{ ecl(\varphi) \mid \varphi \in \Gamma \}.$$

A set of formulae Γ is **closed** if $\Gamma = ecl(\Gamma)$. $\qquad\qquad\qquad\qquad\qquad\qquad \triangledown$

In this section we present several examples with the two formulae η_1, η_2 and with the set of formulae Δ, defined as follows. The running examples related to these formulae are indicated by explanatory labels at the beginning.

η_1	$\neg(\mathsf{AX}p \to \mathsf{AXAX}p)$
η_2	$\neg(\mathsf{AX}(p \to q) \to (\mathsf{AX}p \to \mathsf{AX}q))$
Δ	$\{\mathsf{EX}(\neg p \wedge \mathsf{EX}(p \wedge q)), \mathsf{AX}(\mathsf{AX}p \to \neg\mathsf{EX}q)\}$

Example 13.1.5 (Extended closure for η_1, η_2 and Δ).

1. The extended closure of η_1 is

$$ecl(\eta_1) = \{\eta_1, \mathsf{AX}p, p, \neg\mathsf{AXAX}p, \neg\mathsf{AX}p, \neg p\}.$$

2. The extended closure of η_2 is

$$ecl(\eta_2) = \{\eta_2, \mathsf{AX}(p \to q), p \to q, \neg p, q, \neg(\mathsf{AX}p \to \mathsf{AX}q), \mathsf{AX}p, p, \neg\mathsf{AX}q, \neg q\}.$$

3. The extended closure of Δ is

$$ecl(\Delta) = \{\mathsf{EX}(\neg p \wedge \mathsf{EX}(p \wedge q)), \neg p \wedge \mathsf{EX}(p \wedge q), \neg p, \mathsf{EX}(p \wedge q), p \wedge q,$$
$$p, q, \mathsf{AX}(\mathsf{AX}p \to \neg\mathsf{EX}q), \mathsf{AX}p \to \neg\mathsf{EX}q, \neg\mathsf{AX}p, \neg\mathsf{EX}q, \neg q\}.$$

The following are straightforward to check for each of the logics BML, TLR, LTL, CTL we will consider in this chapter.

Lemma 13.1.6. For every formula φ, $ecl(\varphi)$ is finite and its cardinality is polynomial in the size of φ. ∎

The latter holds essentially because all logical connectives in our logics, except $\neg$, are 'positive' in each argument.

13.1.2 Local Tableau for Modal Logics

Here we introduce a restricted generic version of the tableau construction, that only processes formulae 'locally', i.e. at the current state, by treating all primitive formulae as atomic propositions. We will illustrate this local tableau with our basic logic BML.

Rules for the Classical Propositional Tableau

We begin by recalling a standard version of tableau for classical propositional logic PL. It is a formal system for systematic search for a falsifying truth-assignment of an input set of formulae, based on *formula-decomposition rules* which reduce the truth of a formula to the truth of its components. These rules can be extracted from the truth tables of the propositional connectives and some basic equivalences (double negation, de Morgan's laws, etc.) used for importing the negation inwards and transforming a formula into negation normal form, as follows:

Non-branching rules   Branching rules

$(\wedge)$ $\quad \dfrac{\varphi \wedge \psi}{\varphi, \psi}$ $\qquad (\neg\wedge)$ $\quad \neg(\varphi \wedge \psi) \swarrow \searrow \; \neg\varphi \quad \neg\psi$

$(\neg\vee)$ $\quad \dfrac{\neg(\varphi \vee \psi)}{\neg\varphi, \neg\psi}$ $\qquad (\vee)$ $\quad \varphi \vee \psi \swarrow \searrow \; \varphi \quad \psi$

$(\neg\to)$ $\quad \dfrac{\neg(\varphi \to \psi)}{\varphi, \neg\psi}$ $\qquad (\to)$ $\quad \varphi \to \psi \swarrow \searrow \; \neg\varphi \quad \psi$

The tableau method for PL consists of a systematic decomposition of the input formula (or, set of formulae) applying these rules, and thus producing a tree (called itself **tableau**) with nodes labelled by sets of formulae, until saturation, i.e. until reaching a stage where no new formula can appear on any **branch** of the tableau as a result of applying a rule to any of the formulae in the labels of the nodes on that branch.

A branch of the tableau is **closed** if either of $\bot$, $\neg\top$, or a *complementary pair* of formulae φ, $\neg\varphi$ appears on it; otherwise it remains **open**. Upon saturation, the tableau may have several (possibly none) open branches. If the saturated tableau has at least one open branch, it is declared *open*, otherwise it is *closed*.

The tableau system for PL presented earlier is sound and complete, in a sense that any saturated tableau is closed if and only if the input formula is not satisfiable.

Local Tableaux

In order to process all temporal formulae locally, as much as possible, the unlabelled tableau for PL presented previously must be extended with respective rules for all *temporal* conjunctive and disjunctive formulae or their negations in the language. In the case of BML, there are no such formulae.

The resulting tableau can be applied to all formulae of the logic, where the primitive formulae are treated as literals and not processed further. This tableau only represents *local reasoning*, within the current state, so we call it **local tableau** for the respective logic. Note that all formulae appearing on the local tableau with an input set of formulae Γ belong to $ecl(\Gamma)$.

It is easy to see that if a local tableau closes on a given input set of formulae, then that set is not satisfiable – essentially by a purely propositional reasoning.

On the other hand, however, *existence of open branches in a saturated local tableau does not imply existence of a model satisfying the input set of formulae*. For example, no rule of the local tableau for BML applies to the set

$$\Gamma = \{\mathsf{EX}\top, \mathsf{AX}p, \neg\mathsf{EX}p\}.$$

Hence, the local tableau for BML with the input set Γ immediately produces one open branch. However, it is easy to see that Γ is not satisfiable in any interpreted transition systems.

13.1.3 Full Expansions

Definition 13.1.7. A set of formulae is **patently inconsistent** if it contains $\bot$, or $\neg\top$, or a contradictory pair of formulae φ and $\neg\varphi$. $\qquad\qquad \nabla$

Here we give a generic definition of a fully expanded set, that applies to each of the particular logics which we study here. This is a variant of Definition 4.1.4 except that classical negation is used instead of the operation $\sim$.

Definition 13.1.8. A set of formulae Γ is **fully expanded** iff

1. it is not patently inconsistent,
2. for every conjunctive formula in Γ, all of its conjunctive components are in Γ,
3. for every disjunctive formula in Γ, at least one of its disjunctive components is in Γ.

$$\nabla$$

Thus, a nonpatently inconsistent set is fully expanded if it is closed under applications of all *local* (i.e. applying to the same state of the model) formula decomposition rules. Note that the empty set is fully expanded, too.

Definition 13.1.9. A fully expanded set of formulae Δ is a **full expansion** of a set of formulae Γ, if Δ can be obtained from Γ by repeated application of the following rules, where initially no formula is marked as 'used':

(C-comp) for every conjunctive formula φ in the current set Γ that has not been marked as 'used', add all of its conjunctive components to Γ and mark φ as 'used'.
(D-comp) for every disjunctive formula in the current set Γ that has not been marked as 'used', add one of its disjunctive components to Γ and mark φ as 'used'. ∇

Note that the rule (D-comp) is nondeterministic, so a set Γ may have several (or no) full expansions. Intuitively, a full expansion of a set of formulae Γ consists of all formulae appearing on some open branch in the saturated local tableau for input set Γ.

Remark 13.1.10. Note that *not* every fully expanded set may be obtained as a full expansion of a given set of formulae Γ. For instance, if $\Gamma = \{p \vee q\}$ then $\{p \vee q, p, q\}$ is a fully expanded set containing Γ, but it is not a full expansion of Γ because the preceding rules would only allow one of the disjuncts to be added before the formula $p \vee q$ is marked as 'used', thus disabling addition of the other disjunct.

Remark 13.1.11. A closer look at the construction of full expansions suggests a simple optimisation of that notion: if at least one component of a disjunctive formula φ in a set of formulae Γ already belongs to that set, it seems that there is no need to consider the extensions of Γ with other components of φ in order to establish satisfiability of Γ. Indeed, one can argue that if any such extension leads to a satisfiable full expansion Δ of Γ by applying all other possible expansion steps, the same steps applied to Γ itself will produce a satisfiable full expansion, too, since it will be contained in Δ. This is indeed the case for the logic BML, but *not always* the case for extended logics containing eventualities. We will discuss this issue and present an optimised version of the notion of full expansion later, in Section 13.1.8.

To summarise: in classical propositional logic every open branch in the saturated tableau yields at least one satisfying truth-assignment. Therefore, every fully expanded set of propositional formulae is satisfiable. On the other hand, in temporal logics *not every fully expanded set is satisfiable*, because a contradiction may occur not locally, at the current state, but somewhere deeper in the model, or globally, across it. The purpose of the tableaux for temporal logics is to determine whether at least one full expansion of the input formula set is satisfiable.

Computing full expansions by saturation under closure operations. One of the node construction rules in the tableau procedures calls the procedure FULLEXPANSION, described as follows, for computing the family $FE(\Gamma)$ of full expansions of a given set of formulae Γ obtained by saturation under the closure operations from the definition of full expansion. The procedure FULLEXPANSION essentially represents the local tableau, performing the local decomposition steps on the side of the main tableau procedure. That procedure nondeterministically uses the following **set replacement operations** applied to a set of formulae Γ in a family of sets of formulae $\mathcal{F}$:

(α): If $\varphi \in \Gamma$ for a conjunctive formula φ, not yet marked as 'used', with conjunctive components, say, φ_1 and φ_2, replace Γ by $\Gamma \cup \{\varphi_1, \varphi_2\}$ and mark in it φ as 'used'.

(β): If $\varphi \in \Gamma$ for a disjunctive formula φ, not yet marked as 'used', with disjunctive components, say, φ_1 and φ_2, replace Γ by $\Gamma \cup \{\varphi_1\}$ and $\Gamma \cup \{\varphi_2\}$ and mark in each of them φ as 'used'.

An **expansion step** consists of choosing a set Γ from the current family of sets $\mathcal{F}$, and then choosing a conjunctive or disjunctive formula $\varphi \in \Gamma$ (if there is any) and applying the respective set replacement operation for φ to Γ, with the following proviso: if a patently inconsistent set is added to $\mathcal{F}$ as a result of such application, it is removed immediately after the replacement.

Now, given a finite set of formulae Γ, the procedure FULLEXPANSION starts with the singleton family $\{\Gamma\}$ and checks if its only member is patently inconsistent. If so, it returns $FE(\Gamma) = \emptyset$. Otherwise, it applies repeatedly expansion steps to the current family $\mathcal{F}$ until saturation, i.e. until no application of a set replacement operation can change $\mathcal{F}$. At that stage, the family $FE(\Gamma)$ of sets of formulae is produced and returned. The stage of saturation is guaranteed to occur because all sets of formulae produced during the procedure FULLEXPANSION are subsets of the finite set $ecl(\Gamma)$.

Proposition 13.1.12. For any finite set of BML-formulae Γ:

$$\bigwedge \Gamma \equiv \bigvee \left\{ \bigwedge \Delta \mid \Delta \in FE(\Gamma) \right\}.$$

Proof. Lemma 13.1.2 implies that every set replacement operation applied to a family $\mathcal{F}$ preserves the formula $\bigvee \left\{ \bigwedge \Delta \mid \Delta \in \mathcal{F} \right\}$ up to logical equivalence. At the beginning, that formula is $\bigwedge \Gamma$. $\square$

Example 13.1.13.

1. The (singleton set of) formula $\eta_1 = \neg(\mathsf{AX}p \to \mathsf{AXAX}p)$ has only one full expansion:

$$\Gamma_1^1 = \{\eta_1, \mathsf{AX}p, \neg\mathsf{AXAX}p\}.$$

2. The formula $\eta_2 = \neg(\mathsf{AX}(p \to q) \to (\mathsf{AX}p \to \mathsf{AX}q))$ has only one full expansion, too:

$$\Gamma_2^1 = \{\eta_2, \mathsf{AX}(p \to q), \neg(\mathsf{AX}p \to \mathsf{AX}q), \mathsf{AX}p, \neg\mathsf{AX}q\}.$$

3. The full expansions of $\eta_3 = (\mathsf{EX}p \to \mathsf{AX}q) \wedge \mathsf{AX}\neg q$ are:

$$\Gamma_3^1 = \{\eta_3, \mathsf{EX}p \to \mathsf{AX}q, \neg\mathsf{EX}p, \mathsf{AX}\neg q\} \quad \Gamma_3^2 = \{\eta_3, \mathsf{EX}p \to \mathsf{AX}q, \mathsf{AX}q, \mathsf{AX}\neg q\}.$$

4. Computing the full expansions of $\eta_4 = (\mathsf{EX}p \to \mathsf{AX}q) \wedge (\mathsf{EXEX}p \vee \mathsf{EX}p)$ produces:
   - $\Gamma_4^1 = \{\eta_4, \mathsf{EX}p \to \mathsf{AX}q, \mathsf{EXEX}p \vee \mathsf{EX}p, \neg\mathsf{EX}p, \mathsf{EXEX}p\}$.
   - $\Gamma_4^2 = \{\eta_4, \mathsf{EX}p \to \mathsf{AX}q, \mathsf{EXEX}p \vee \mathsf{EX}p, \neg\mathsf{EX}p, \mathsf{EX}p\}$: patently inconsistent, removed.
   - $\Gamma_4^3 = \{\eta_4, \mathsf{EX}p \to \mathsf{AX}q, \mathsf{EXEX}p \vee \mathsf{EX}p, \mathsf{AX}q, \mathsf{EXEX}p\}$.
   - $\Gamma_4^4 = \{\eta_4, \mathsf{EX}p \to \mathsf{AX}q, \mathsf{EXEX}p \vee \mathsf{EX}p, \mathsf{AX}q, \mathsf{EX}p\}$.

Eventualities

Recall that, intuitively, **eventualities** are formulae stating that something will happen eventually in the future, but without specifying exactly when. In particular:

- the language BML has no eventualities;
- the eventualities in TLR are the formulae of the type $\mathsf{EF}\varphi$ and $\neg\mathsf{AG}\varphi$;
- the eventualities in LTL are the formulae of the type $\varphi \mathsf{U}\psi$ (in particular, $\mathsf{F}\varphi$, and $\neg\mathsf{G}\varphi$);
- the eventualities in CTL are two types:
  - **existential eventualities**, of the type $\mathsf{E}\varphi\mathsf{U}\psi$ and $\neg\mathsf{AG}\varphi$, referring to a single path on which such eventualities must be realised,
  - **universal eventualities**, of the type $\mathsf{A}\varphi\mathsf{U}\psi$ and $\neg\mathsf{EG}\varphi$, where the eventuality must be realised on every path.

13.1.4 Hintikka Structures

Here we will introduce the notion of *Hintikka structure*, analogous to Hintikka sets for propositional logic. It is not an explicit part of the tableaux construction, but it is fundamental for its understanding, because the purpose of that construction is to check for existence of a Hintikka structure 'satisfying' the input formula.

Intuitively, a Hintikka structure represents a partly defined rooted ITS satisfying the input formula. It is a graph, every node of which is labelled by a set of formulae. These labels are fully expanded subsets of the extended closure of a designated input formula (in the satisfiability of which we are interested). All desired properties of the transition relations in a Hintikka structure are encoded by means of the labels of the states. Membership in the label of the state of a Hintikka structure simulates the notion of truth of a formula at a state of an ITS, and the labelling of states must ensure that the Hintikka structure can generate a (sometimes nonstandard) model of the input formula.

Here is the formal definition of Hintikka structures for the logic BML.

Definition 13.1.14. Given a closed set of BML-formulae Γ, a **Hintikka structure (HS)** **for** Γ is a tuple $\mathcal{H} = (S, R, H)$ such that (S, R) is a transition system (without a labelling function), and $H : S \to \mathcal{P}(\Gamma)$ is a labelling of the states in S with sets of formulae from Γ satisfying the following conditions for every $s \in S$:

(H1) $H(s)$ is fully expanded (in the sense of Definition 13.1.8).
(H2) If $\varphi \in H(s)$ is an existential successor formula, then $scomp(\varphi) \in H(s')$ for some s' such that sRs'.
(H3) If $\varphi \in H(s)$ is a universal successor formula, then $scomp(\varphi) \in H(s')$ for every s' such that sRs'. ∇

Definition 13.1.15. A formula $\varphi \in$ BML is **satisfiable in a Hintikka structure** $\mathcal{H} = (S, R, H)$ for a set Γ if $\varphi \in H(s)$ for some $s \in S$. A set of formulae $\Delta \subseteq \Gamma$ is **satisfiable in** $\mathcal{H}$ if $\Delta \subseteq H(s)$ for some state s in $\mathcal{H}$. ∇

Note that every rooted ITS uniformly generates a rooted Hintikka structure for any closed set of formulae Γ by labelling each state of the ITS with the set of all formulae from Γ that are true at that state.

Lemma 13.1.16. For any closed set of BML-formulae Γ (in the sense of Definition 13.1.3) and for every ITS $\mathcal{T} = (S, R, L)$ the structure $\mathcal{H}(\mathcal{T}) = (S, R, H)$, where $H(s) = \{\varphi \in \Gamma \mid \mathcal{T}, s \models \varphi\}$ for every $s \in S$, is a Hintikka structure for Γ. ∎

However, an essential difference between interpreted transition systems and Hintikka structures is that, while an ITS determines the truth value of every formula at every state, a Hintikka structure only contains just enough information to determine the truth values of those formulae that are directly involved in the evaluation of the input formula η at the root state.

Given a formula φ for which we want to find a model, we will be interested in Hintikka structures for the set $ecl(\varphi)$. For a class of Hintikka structures to be suitable for the tableau procedure, it must be the case that every formula satisfiable in such a Hintikka structure is satisfiable in an ITS, so the two notions of satisfiability are equivalent. Thus, the following result is required.

Theorem 13.1.17. A formula η is satisfiable iff it is satisfiable in a Hintikka structure for $ecl(\eta)$. ∎

Proof. The proof follows the same scheme, *mutatis mutandis*, for all logics studied here, and we will present it now for the case of BML.

One direction is immediate by Lemma 13.1.16, for $\Gamma = ecl(\eta)$. For the converse, suppose $\eta \in H(s_0)$ for some state s_0 in some Hintikka structure $\mathcal{H} = (S, R, H)$. We define the ITS $\mathcal{T} = (S, R, L)$ where L is a state description in S defined as follows: $L(s) :=$ PROP $\cap H(s)$.

We now show by induction on the main components of $\varphi \in ecl(\eta)$ that for every $s \in S$:
$$\text{if } \varphi \in H(s) \text{ then } \mathcal{T}, s \models \varphi.$$

Suppose $\varphi \in H(s)$ and assume that the claim holds for all main components of φ and all states $s \in S$.

- When $\varphi \in \text{PROP} \cup \{\top, \bot\}$ the claim is immediate by definition of L.
- For $\varphi = \neg\psi$ we do a nested induction on ψ:
  - If $\psi \in \text{PROP} \cup \{\top, \bot\}$ then the claim follows from the definition of L and the fact that $\psi \notin H(s)$ since $H(s)$ is not patently inconsistent.
  - If $\psi = \neg\chi$ then $\chi \in H(s)$ by (H1) and the claim holds for χ by the inductive hypothesis, so $\mathcal{T}, s \models \chi$, hence $\mathcal{T}, s \models \varphi$.
  - If $\psi = \chi_1 \wedge \chi_2$ then $\neg\chi_1 \in H(s)$ or $\neg\chi_2 \in H(s)$ by (H1), and the inductive hypothesis applies to both of them, hence the claim follows.
  - The cases of $\psi = \chi_1 \vee \chi_2$ and $\psi = \chi_1 \to \chi_2$ are analogous.
  - If $\psi = \text{AX}\chi$ then $\neg\chi \in H(s')$ for some s' such that sRs', by (H2). The inductive hypothesis applies to $\neg\chi$ and $H(s')$, hence $\mathcal{T}, s' \models \neg\chi$. Therefore, $\mathcal{T}, s \models \neg\text{AX}\chi$.
    The case of $\psi = \text{EX}\chi$ is analogous.
- The cases $\varphi = \psi_1 \wedge \psi_2$, $\varphi = \psi_1 \vee \psi_2$ and $\varphi = \psi_1 \to \psi_2$ are immediate from (H1) and the inductive hypothesis.
- The case $\varphi = \text{EX}\psi$ follows from (H2) and the inductive hypothesis.
- The case $\varphi = \text{AX}\psi$ follows from (H3) and the inductive hypothesis.

Now, since $\eta \in H(s_0)$ we have that $\mathcal{T}, s_0 \models \eta$. $\square$

Corollary 13.1.18. A finite set of BML-formulae Γ is satisfiable iff it is satisfiable in a Hintikka structure for $ecl(\Gamma)$.   ∎

13.1.5 Constructing Tableaux

A Sketch of a Generic Tableaux Construction for Testing Satisfiability

The tableau procedure for a given input formula η attempts to construct a nonempty graph $\mathcal{T}^\eta$, called a **tableau**, representing in a way sufficiently many possible Hintikka structures for η. The procedure usually consists of three major phases:

1. **Construction phase.** In that phase a finite directed graph with labelled vertices $\mathcal{P}^\eta$, called the **pretableau** for η, is produced, following prescribed **construction rules**. The set of nodes of the pretableau properly contains the set of nodes of the tableau $\mathcal{T}^\eta$ that is to be ultimately built.

   The pretableau has two types of nodes: **states** and **prestates**. The states are labelled with fully expanded subsets of $ecl(\eta)$ and represent states of a Hintikka structure, while the prestates can be labelled with any subsets of $ecl(\eta)$ and they play only an auxiliary and temporary role.

In our tableau construction states and prestates with existing label are not created again but re-used. So, when there is no danger of confusion, we will identify prestates or states with their labels.

2. **Prestate elimination phase**. The prestates are removed during this phase, using the **prestate elimination rule**, and the result is a smaller graph $\mathcal{T}_0^\eta$, called the **initial tableau** for η.

3. **State elimination phase**. During this phase we remove, using **state elimination rules**, all states, if any, from $\mathcal{T}_0^\eta$ that cannot be satisfied in any Hintikka structure. Typically, this can happen for one of the following reasons: either their labels contain **unrealisable eventualities**, or some of the successor states they need for the satisfaction of successor formulae have been removed in the process.

The state elimination phase results in a (possibly empty) subgraph $\mathcal{T}^\eta$ of $\mathcal{T}_0^\eta$, called the **final tableau** for η.

If there is a state in the final tableau $\mathcal{T}^\eta$ containing η in its label, the tableau is declared **open** and the input formula η is pronounced satisfiable; otherwise, the tableau is declared **closed** and η is pronounced unsatisfiable.

The Pretableau Construction Phase for BML

The pretableau construction phase consists in alternating applications of two rules:

$\mathrm{PREXP}^{\mathrm{BML}}$: producing all **offspring states** of a given prestate;
$\mathrm{NEXT}^{\mathrm{BML}}$: producing the **successor prestate** of a given state.

The rule $\mathrm{PREXP}^{\mathrm{BML}}$ involves the procedure FULLEXPANSION, described in Section 13.1, for computing the family $\mathrm{FE}(\Gamma)$ of full expansions of a given subset Γ of $ecl(\eta)$ obtained by saturation under the closure operations corresponding to the definition of full expansion.

Rule $\mathrm{PREXP}^{\mathrm{BML}}$ Given a prestate Γ to which the rule has not yet been applied, do the following:

1. Compute the family $\mathrm{FE}(\Gamma)$ of full expansions of Γ and add these as (labels of) new states in the pretableau, called the **offspring states** of Γ.
2. For each newly introduced state Δ, create an edge $\Gamma \dashrightarrow \Delta$.
3. If, however, the pretableau already contains a state with label Δ then do not create a new state with that label, but create an edge $\Gamma \dashrightarrow \Delta$ to that state.

We denote the set $\{ \Delta \mid \Gamma \dashrightarrow \Delta \}$ of offspring states of Γ by $\mathsf{states}(\Gamma)$.

Hereafter we use the following notation, for any set of BML-formulae Δ:

$$\mathsf{X}(\Delta) := \{ \psi \mid \mathsf{AX}\psi \in \Delta \} \cup \{ \neg\psi \mid \neg\mathsf{EX}\psi \in \Delta \}.$$

Rule $\mathrm{NEXT}^{\mathrm{BML}}$ Given a state with label Δ, to which the rule has not yet been applied, for each existential successor formula $\varphi \in \Delta$ (i.e. $\varphi = \mathsf{EX}\chi$ or $\varphi = \neg\mathsf{AX}\chi$) do the following:

1. Add a successor prestate Γ of Δ with label $X(\Delta) \cup \{scomp(\varphi)\}$.
2. For each newly introduced prestate Γ, create an edge $\Delta \xrightarrow{\varphi} \Gamma$.
3. If, however, the pretableau already contains a prestate Γ' with the label of Γ then do not create a new prestate with that label, but extend an arrow $\Delta \xrightarrow{\varphi} \Gamma'$ to that prestate.

The construction phase of building a pretableau for η begins with creating a single prestate $\{\eta\}$, followed by alternating applications of the rules PREXP^{BML} and NEXT^{BML}, respectively to the prestates and the states created at a previous stage of the construction. The construction phase ends when none of these rules can add any new states or prestates to the current graph. The resulting graph is the pretableau $\mathcal{P}^\eta$.

Note that there are two types of branching in the pretableau: **tableau search branching**, from a prestate to its offspring states, indicated by $--\!\!\rightarrow$, and **structural branching**, from a state to its successor prestates, indicated by $\xrightarrow{\chi}$ where χ is an EX-formula. The tableau search branching is the type of branching of the search tree, thus it is **disjunctive**, or **existential** – only one offspring state of every prestate is eventually needed to build a satisfying structure, while the structural branching is **conjunctive**, or **universal**, as it represents branching in the satisfying structure to be built, so *all* successors prestates of every state are needed in the construction.

In all subsequent figures illustrating the tableaux examples, the prestates are indicated with shaded square boxes and labelled by P with indices, while the states are indicated with transparent boxes with rounded corners and labelled by S with indices.

Example 13.1.19 (Pretableaux for η_1, η_2 and Δ).

1. The pretableau for η_1 is presented as follows:

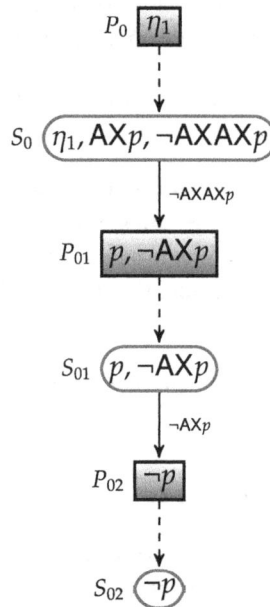

2. The pretableau for η_2 is presented as follows:

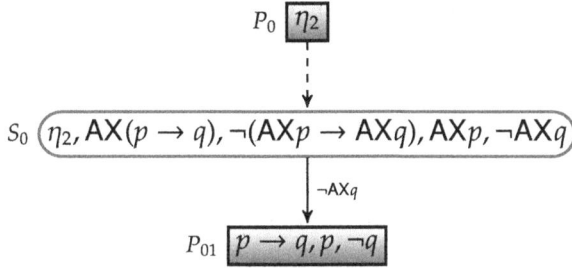

$$P_0 \quad \boxed{\eta_2}$$

$$S_0 \quad \left(\eta_2, \mathsf{AX}(p \to q), \neg(\mathsf{AX}p \to \mathsf{AX}q), \mathsf{AX}p, \neg\mathsf{AX}q \right)$$

$$\xrightarrow{\neg\mathsf{AX}q}$$

$$P_{01} \quad \boxed{p \to q, p, \neg q}$$

(Note that the last prestate does not have any full expansions because of the patent inconsistency arising in the execution of the procedure FULLEXPANSION.)

3. Clearly, the only full expansion of Δ is Δ itself, which labels the only offspring state of the input prestate. It has one successor prestate, corresponding to $\mathsf{EX}(\neg p \land \mathsf{EX}(p \land q))$. That prestate has label $\Gamma = \{\neg p \land \mathsf{EX}(p \land q), \mathsf{AX}p \to \neg\mathsf{EX}q\}$. It has two full expansions. The resulting pretableau is given as follows, where we have also indicated the patent inconsistent attempt to produce a full expansion of the prestate p_{21}.

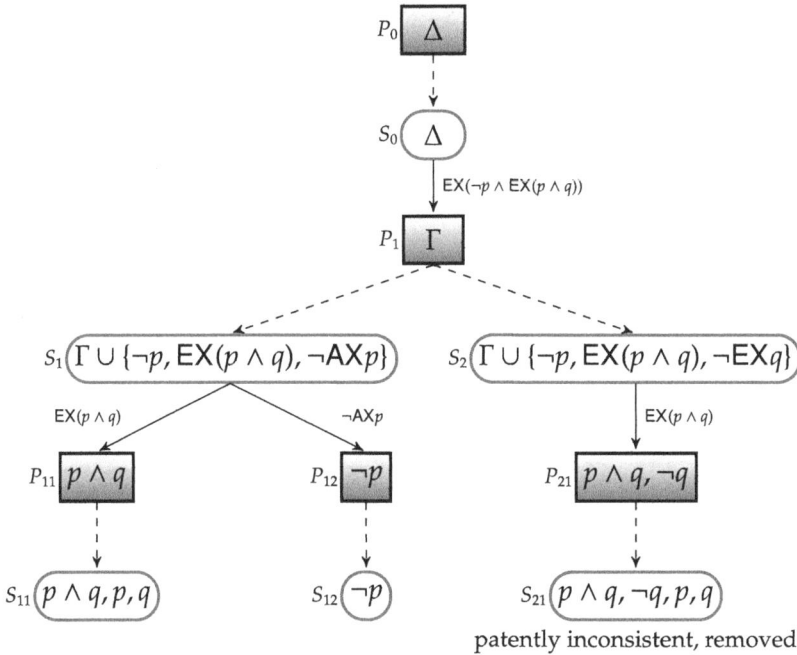

$$P_0 \quad \boxed{\Delta}$$

$$S_0 \quad \left(\Delta \right)$$

$$\xrightarrow{\mathsf{EX}(\neg p \land \mathsf{EX}(p \land q))}$$

$$P_1 \quad \boxed{\Gamma}$$

$$S_1 \left(\Gamma \cup \{\neg p, \mathsf{EX}(p \land q), \neg\mathsf{AX}p\} \right) \qquad S_2 \left(\Gamma \cup \{\neg p, \mathsf{EX}(p \land q), \neg\mathsf{EX}q\} \right)$$

$$\xrightarrow{\mathsf{EX}(p \land q)} \qquad \xrightarrow{\neg\mathsf{AX}p} \qquad \qquad \xrightarrow{\mathsf{EX}(p \land q)}$$

$$P_{11} \; \boxed{p \land q} \qquad P_{12} \; \boxed{\neg p} \qquad\qquad P_{21} \; \boxed{p \land q, \neg q}$$

$$S_{11} \left(p \land q, p, q \right) \qquad S_{12} \left(\neg p \right) \qquad\qquad S_{21} \left(p \land q, \neg q, p, q \right)$$

$$\text{patently inconsistent, removed}$$

Prestate Elimination Phase and Initial Tableaux

In this phase, all prestates are removed from $\mathcal{P}^\eta$, together with their incoming and outgoing arrows, by applying the following generic **prestate elimination rule**:

Rule PrestateElim For every prestate Γ in $\mathcal{P}^\eta$, do the following:

1. Remove Γ from $\mathcal{P}^\eta$ together with its outgoing arrows;
2. If there is a state Δ in $\mathcal{P}^\eta$ with $\Delta \to \Gamma$, then for every state $\Delta' \in \mathsf{states}(\Gamma)$, create an edge $\Delta \to \Delta'$.

The resulting graph is called the **initial tableau** for η, denoted $\mathcal{T}_0^\eta$. The offspring states of the input prestate $\{\eta\}$ are called **input states** of $\mathcal{T}_0^\eta$.

Example 13.1.20 (Initial tableaux for η_1, η_2 and Δ).

1. The initial tableau for η_1 is given as follows:

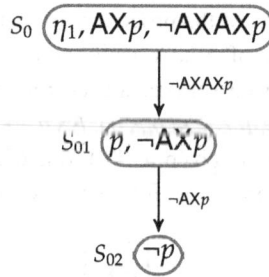

2. The initial tableau for η_2 is given as follows:

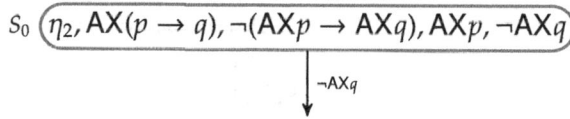

3. The initial tableau for Δ is given as follows:

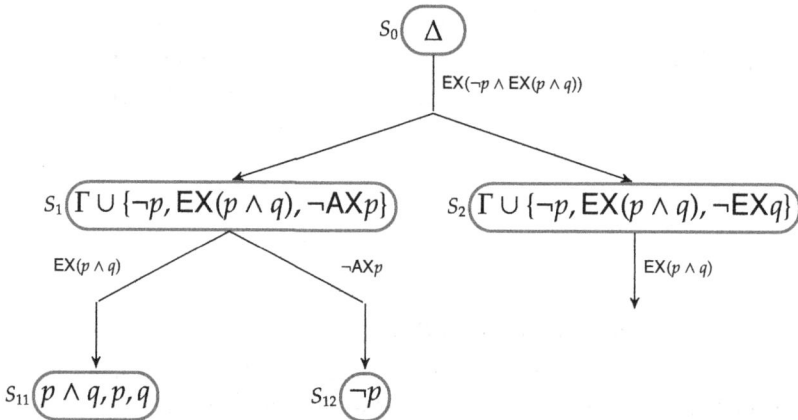

State Elimination Phase

The purpose of the state elimination phase is to remove all 'bad' states from the tableaux, the labels of which are not satisfiable in any Hintikka structure, and hence in any model. This will be done using **state elimination rules**; the only such rule for BML is introduced in the following. The state elimination phase is carried out in a sequence of stages, starting at stage 0 with the initial tableau T_0^η, and eliminating at every stage n at most one state for the current tableau T_n^η, by applying one of the state elimination rules, to produce the new current tableau T_{n+1}^η.

In the case of BML, the only possible reason for existence of a 'bad' state in a current tableau is that it may lack a successor state it needs. Such states can arise because some prestates may have no full expansions, and hence may yield no offspring states. Once such bad states are removed, some of their predecessor states may be left without needed successors, so they must be removed, too, etc., until stabilisation. Formally, the elimination of states with no successors is done by applying the following rule.

Rule STATEELIM^{BML} *If a state Δ, containing an existential successor formula $\mathsf{EX}\psi$ (respectively, $\neg\mathsf{AX}\psi$), has no successor states containing ψ (respectively, $\neg\psi$) in the current tableau, then remove Δ from the tableau.*

Here is an equivalent version of that rule:

Rule STELIM^{BML}: *If a state Δ, containing an existential successor formula $\mathsf{EX}\psi$ (resp. $\neg\mathsf{AX}\psi$), has no successor state along an outgoing arrow labelled with that formula, then remove Δ from the tableau.*

The rule STATEELIM^{BML} is applied repeatedly until reaching a stage when no further elimination of states by an application of any of the rules is possible.

The Final Tableau

When the state elimination phase reaches a stabilisation stage, the current tableau at that stage is the **final tableau for** η, denoted by T^η, with a set of states denoted by S^η.

Definition 13.1.21. The final tableau T^η is **open** if $\eta \in \Delta$ for some $\Delta \in S^\eta$; otherwise, T^η is **closed**. $\qquad\qquad \nabla$

The tableau procedure returns 'not satisfiable' if the final tableau is closed; otherwise, it returns 'satisfiable' and, moreover, provides sufficient information for producing a finite Hintikka structure satisfying η, as described further in the completeness proof.

Example 13.1.22 (Final tableaux for η_1, η_2 and Δ).

1. No states are eliminated from the initial tableau for η_1: the final tableau is the same as the initial tableau, hence it is open. Therefore, the formula η_1 is declared satisfiable. Hence, $\mathsf{AX}p \to \mathsf{AXAX}p$ is declared nonvalid. A 3-state linear model for η_1 can be extracted from that tableau.

2. The only state in the initial tableau for η_2 is eliminated. The final tableau is empty, therefore closed. Therefore, the formula η_2 is declared unsatisfiable. Hence, $\mathsf{AX}(p \to q) \to (\mathsf{AX}p \to \mathsf{AX}q)$ is declared valid.

3. The state S_2 in the initial tableau for Δ is eliminated because it has no successor corresponding to $\mathsf{EX}(p \wedge q)$. All other states survive. Thus, the final tableau looks as follows:

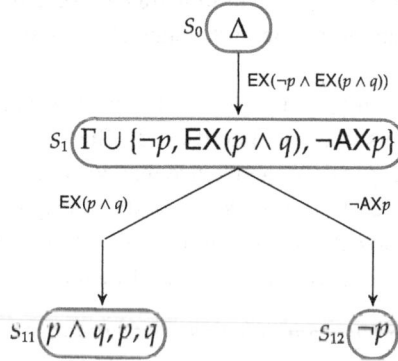

It is open because it contains the initial state. Hence, the input set of formulae Δ is declared satisfiable. We leave the extraction of a model from the final tableau as an exercise.

13.1.6 Termination, Soundness and Completeness

Termination

Each of the phases of the described procedure terminates:

1. The **termination** of the construction phase follows from the fact that there are only finitely many possible labels of states and prestates to be created in the tableau, and each of them is created at most once.

2. The prestate elimination phase terminates because the elimination of each of the finitely many prestates is a one-step act.

3. The state elimination phase terminates because there are only finitely many eventualities to be checked for realisation, each in finitely many state labels, and if any round of testing realisation of all eventualities at all states in the labels of which they occur ends without elimination of any state, the construction is completed.

Later we will compute estimates for the maximal number of steps needed for the construction of the tableau, in all particular cases, thus obtaining an upper bound for the time complexity of the decision procedures.

Soundness

Soundness of the tableau procedure means that if the input formula η is satisfiable, then the final tableau T^η is open, so the tableau procedure is guaranteed to establish the satisfiability.

A generic proof of soundness consists of showing that at least one tableau state containing η will survive until the end of the procedure. Note that if η is satisfiable, and hence propositionally consistent, there will be at least one offspring state of the initial prestate containing η. Moreover, for every rooted ITS $(\mathcal{T}, s)$ satisfying η, the set $\{\psi \in ecl(\eta) \mid \mathcal{T}, s \models \psi\}$ contains at least one such state.

Thereafter, it suffices to show that *only unsatisfiable states* get eliminated in the state elimination phase. The proof of that claim is done by induction on the applications of state elimination rules.

Soundness of the Tableau for BML

We will establish the soundness of the tableau for BML by proving that every state elimination rule is 'sound' in a sense that it never eliminates a state with a satisfiable label. The soundness of the overall procedure is then an immediate consequence.

Lemma 13.1.23. Let Γ be a prestate of $\mathcal{P}^\eta$ such that $\mathcal{T}, s \models \Gamma$ for some rooted ITS $(\mathcal{T}, s)$. Then $\mathcal{T}, s \models \Delta$ for at least one $\Delta \in \mathsf{states}(\Gamma)$. ∎

Lemma 13.1.23 follows from Proposition 13.1.12.

Lemma 13.1.24. No satisfiable state $\Delta \in \mathcal{T}_0^\eta$ is removed by any application of Rule STATEELIM^{BML} during the state elimination phase. ∎

Proof. It suffices to show, by induction on $n \in \mathbb{N}$, that no satisfiable state $\Delta \in \mathcal{T}_n^\eta$ is removed by an application of Rule STATEELIM^{BML} to $\mathcal{T}_n^\eta$. For that purpose we will prove a somewhat stronger inductive claim, viz. that for every $n \in \mathbb{N}$:

1. If $\Delta \in \mathcal{T}_n^\eta$ is satisfiable then for any $\mathsf{EX}\varphi \in \Delta$ there is a satisfiable state $\Delta_\varphi \in \mathcal{T}_n^\eta$ such that $\Delta \xrightarrow{\mathsf{EX}\varphi} \Delta_\varphi$ in $\mathcal{T}_n^\eta$.
2. If $\Delta \in \mathcal{T}_n^\eta$ is satisfiable then for any $\neg\mathsf{AX}\varphi \in \Delta$ there is a satisfiable state $\Delta_{\neg\varphi} \in \mathcal{T}_n^\eta$ such that $\Delta \xrightarrow{\neg\mathsf{AX}\varphi} \Delta_{\neg\varphi}$ in $\mathcal{T}_n^\eta$.
3. All satisfiable states in $\mathcal{T}_0^\eta$ are still present in $\mathcal{T}_n^\eta$.

Note that the inductive hypothesis refers simultaneously to all satisfiable $\Delta \in \mathcal{T}_n^\eta$ and all successor formulae $\mathsf{EX}\varphi \in \Delta$ and $\neg\mathsf{AX}\varphi \in \Delta$.

We will only give the proof of claim 1; claim 2 is completely analogous, and then claim 3 follows immediately from these.

Let $n = 0$. Take any satisfiable $\Delta \in \mathcal{T}_0^\eta$ and $\mathsf{EX}\varphi \in \Delta$. Then, $\mathcal{T}, s \models \Delta$ for some rooted ITS $(\mathcal{T}, s)$. Recall, that all states $\Delta' \in \mathcal{T}_0^\eta$ such that $\Delta \xrightarrow{\mathsf{EX}\varphi} \Delta'$ in $\mathcal{T}_0^\eta$ are obtained as full expansions of the prestate $\Gamma = \{\varphi\} \cup \{\psi \mid \mathsf{AX}\psi \in \Delta\} \cup \{\neg\psi \mid \neg\mathsf{EX}\psi \in \Delta\}$.

Since $\mathsf{EX}\varphi \in \Delta$, we have that $\mathcal{T}, s \models \mathsf{EX}\varphi$, hence there is an R-successor r of s in $\mathcal{T}$ such that $\mathcal{T}, r \models \varphi$. By the truth definition for successor formulae, it follows that $\mathcal{T}, r \models \Gamma$ because $\{\psi \mid \mathsf{AX}\psi \in \Delta\} \cup \{\neg\psi \mid \neg\mathsf{EX}\psi \in \Delta\}$ is satisfied at every R-successor of s in $\mathcal{T}$. Then, by Lemma 13.1.23, at least one full expansion Δ_φ of Γ is satisfied by $(\mathcal{T}, r)$, and, by construction of the initial tableau, there is a state (with label) Δ_φ in $\mathcal{T}_0^\eta$ such that

$\Delta \xrightarrow{\text{EX}\varphi} \Delta_\varphi$. Therefore, the state Δ cannot be removed from $\mathcal{T}_0^\eta$ by an application of the rule STATEELIM^{BML}.

Now, assuming the claim holds for all $n < m$, take a satisfiable $\Delta \in \mathcal{T}_m^\eta$. For any $\text{EX}\varphi \in \Delta$, by the argument for $n = 0$ there is a satisfiable state Δ_φ in $\mathcal{T}_0^\eta$ such that $\Delta \xrightarrow{\text{EX}\varphi} \Delta_\varphi$ in $\mathcal{T}_0^\eta$, and hence, by the inductive hypothesis, Δ_φ has remained intact in $\mathcal{T}_m^\eta$. Therefore, Δ cannot be removed from $\mathcal{T}_m^\eta$ by an application of the rule STATEELIM^{BML}. $\qquad\square$

Theorem 13.1.25 (Soundness of the tableau for BML). If $\eta \in$ BML is satisfiable then $\mathcal{T}^\eta$ is open. ∎

This follows immediately from Lemma 13.1.23 and 13.1.24.

Completeness

Completeness of the tableau procedure means that if the input formula η is not satisfiable, then the final tableau $\mathcal{T}^\eta$ is closed, so the tableau procedure is guaranteed to establish the unsatisfiability. By contraposition, completeness means that if the final tableau is open, the input formula η is satisfiable.

A generic proof of completeness consists of proving that an open final tableau yields a Hintikka structure satisfying η, and then using the equivalence between satisfiability in Hintikka structure and in ITS. In some cases (e.g. BML, TLR) the construction of the Hintikka structure satisfying η from an open tableau for η is straightforward – the tableau itself can be used for that purpose. In other cases (e.g. LTL, CTL) the Hintikka structure satisfying η has to be pieced together from **fragments** extracted from the tableau.

Completeness of the Tableau for BML

Theorem 13.1.26. For any formula $\eta \in$ BML, if the final tableau $\mathcal{T}^\eta$ is open, then the formula is satisfiable. ∎

Proof. It suffices to show how from the open final tableau $\mathcal{T}^\eta$ one can construct a Hintikka structure satisfying η. That construction in the case of BML is straightforward: the final tableau $\mathcal{T}^\eta$ itself can be taken as such a Hintikka structure, with a labelling function assigning to each state its own label. The proof that $\mathcal{T}^\eta$ is a Hintikka structure for $ecl(\eta)$ is straightforward from the construction of the tableau and it is left as an exercise. $\qquad\square$

On the Complexity and Optimality

A closer look at the tableau procedure for BML, as described above, shows that it takes exponential time in the size of the input formula η. On the other hand, the satisfiability problem for BML is PSPACE-complete (see Section 11.4.2), so it is clear that the tableau, as described, very likely uses more space resources than necessary. However, it can be optimised to work in (nondeterministic) polynomial space by systematically guessing the 'right' offspring states of each successor prestate needed to satisfy a successor formula in the current state, and only keeping the necessary information in memory. For details on how this can be done see the presentation of Ladner's algorithm in Section 5.5.2.

13.1.7 A Generic Method for Model Checking

The tableau procedures for testing satisfiability can be smoothly modified to perform *local model checking*: given a finite rooted ITS $(\mathcal{T}, s)$ and a formula η, the model-checking tableau must decide whether $\mathcal{T}, s \models \eta$.

The idea of tableau-based model checking is simple: in a nutshell, the procedure simulates the construction of the pretableau in $\mathcal{T}$ by starting from s and advancing along the transitions in $\mathcal{T}$, while labelling the prestates and states of the tableau with the respective current states of $\mathcal{T}$. More precisely:

1. The states and prestates of the tableau are now labelled by pairs (r, Γ) where $r \in \mathcal{T}$ and $\Gamma \subseteq ecl(\eta)$, where in the case of states Γ is fully expanded.
2. The pretableau construction phase is similar to the one in the tableaux for satisfiability, but with modified construction rules, taking into account that the states and prestates they create are properly associated with states of $\mathcal{T}$.
3. The prestate and state elimination phases are essentially the same as in the tableaux for satisfiability.
4. When the final tableau is obtained, $\mathcal{T}, s \models \eta$ is declared true iff there is a state (s, Δ) in it such that $\eta \in \Delta$.

The soundness of the procedure follows from the following observations:

1. If a prestate in the pretableau is satisfied in some state of $\mathcal{T}$ then some offspring state of it is satisfied there, too.
2. A state (r, Γ) from the initial tableau is eliminated during the state elimination phase only if some formula from Γ is not true at r.
3. For every state (r, Γ) in the final tableau, $\mathcal{T}, r \models \Gamma$ holds.

13.1.8 Lean Full Expansions

A closer look at the construction of full expansions suggests a simple optimisation of that notion: if at least one component of a disjunctive formula φ in a set of formulae Γ already belongs to that set, usually there is no need to consider the extensions of Γ with other disjunctive components of φ in order to establish satisfiability of Γ. Indeed, one could argue that if any such extension leads to a satisfiable full expansion Δ of Γ by applying all other possible expansion steps, then same steps applied to Γ itself will produce a satisfiable full expansion, too, since it will be contained in Δ. This is *almost* the case, except when the formula is an eventuality; in that case, extra care must be taken to ensure realisation of that eventuality, whenever possible. This suggests a notion of **lean full expansions**, defined just like full expansions, but with the following modification of the clause (D-comp), now split into two cases, where the *principal disjunctive component* of an eventuality $\mathsf{EF}\psi$ is its first component (that is to be eventually satisfied) in the respective table of components.

(lean D-comp 1) For any disjunctive formula ψ in the current set Γ that has not been marked as 'used', if Γ does not contain any of its disjunctive components, then add one of its disjunctive components to Γ and mark ψ as 'used'.

(lean D-comp 2) For any eventuality ψ in the current set Γ that has not been marked as 'used', if Γ does not contain the principal disjunctive component of ψ, then add one of the disjunctive components of ψ to Γ and mark ψ as 'used'.

Recall that the preceding clause is applied nondeterministically, that is, all possibilities to add a missing disjunctive component are explored whenever applicable.

Clearly, every lean full expansion *is* a full expansion, but not every full expansion is lean. For example, $\{p \vee q, p\}$ is a full expansion of itself, but it also has another full expansion, viz. $\{p \vee q, p, q\}$. So, the effect of this modification is that possibly fewer, and smaller, full expansions are produced for a given set of formulae. The definition of *lean full expansions* is now obtained by modifying the set replacement operation (β) in the procedure FULLEXPANSION accordingly.

13.2 Tableaux for LTL

Here we will develop the generic tableau construction outlined in the previous section for the logic LTL. There are three major distinctions in the tableau method for LTL, compared to the one for BML:

1. In the case of LTL we are looking for a simpler, *linear model* satisfying the input formula.
2. However, this model must be infinite, while an open tableau for BML always produces a finite model.
3. LTL involves eventualities that present additional concern, because their satisfaction in a model (or, Hintikka structure) cannot be established locally, by assuring the existence of the necessary successors of every state, as it is the case for BML.

The tableau construction presented here takes amount of time and space exponential in the length of the formula, but we will discuss further how it can be optimised to work in polynomial space.

13.2.1 Preliminaries

This time we will choose to work with a small language, only containing $\top$, $\neg$ and $\wedge$ as Boolean connectives and X, G and U as temporal operators. We keep G in the language only in order to explicitly present the tableau rules for it. The other Boolean constants and connectives $\bot$, $\vee$, $\rightarrow$, as well as the additional temporal operators F and R will be assumed to be definable in a standard way. We leave it as a running exercise to the reader to extend

conjunctive		disjunctive		successor	
formula	components	formula	components	form.	comp.
$\neg\neg\varphi$	φ, φ	$\varphi \vee \psi$	φ, ψ	$X\varphi$	φ
$\varphi \wedge \psi$	φ, ψ	$\varphi \rightarrow \psi$	$\neg\varphi, \psi$	$\neg X\varphi$	$\neg\varphi$
$G\varphi$	$\varphi, XG\varphi$	$\neg G\varphi$	$\neg\varphi, X\neg G\varphi$		
$\neg(\varphi U\psi)$	$\neg\psi, \neg\varphi \vee \neg X(\varphi U\psi)$	$\varphi U\psi$	$\psi, \varphi \wedge X(\varphi U\psi)$		

Figure 13.2 Types and components of formulae in LTL.

the basic concepts and steps of the procedure outlined here to a language containing some, or all, of these connectives as primitives.

The conjunctive, disjunctive and successor formulae in LTL and their components are given in Figure 13.2. Recall that the eventualities in LTL are of the type $\varphi U\psi$ and $\neg G\varphi$.

Lemma 13.2.1.

(I) Every conjunctive formula φ of LTL is equivalent to the conjunction of its conjunctive components.

(II) Every disjunctive formula φ of LTL is equivalent to the disjunction of its disjunctive components. ∎

The proof is left as an exercise.

The notions of extended closure of an LTL-formula, fully expanded sets, full expansions and the procedure FULLEXPANSION computing the family of full expansions of a set of LTL-formulae obtained by saturation under the set-replacement operations, are defined as in Section 13.1. The local tableau for LTL is analogous to the one for BML, extending the propositional local tableau with the decomposition rules for the temporal operators of LTL:

Non-branching rules   **Branching rules**

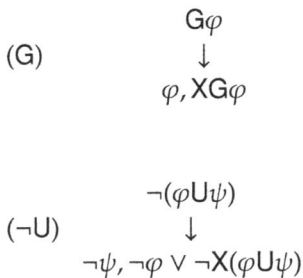

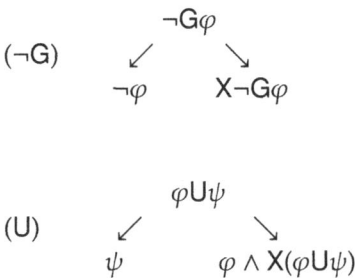

$$(G) \quad \begin{array}{c} G\varphi \\ \downarrow \\ \varphi, XG\varphi \end{array} \qquad (\neg G) \quad \begin{array}{c} \neg G\varphi \\ \swarrow \qquad \searrow \\ \neg\varphi \qquad X\neg G\varphi \end{array}$$

$$(\neg U) \quad \begin{array}{c} \neg(\varphi U\psi) \\ \downarrow \\ \neg\psi, \neg\varphi \vee \neg X(\varphi U\psi) \end{array} \qquad (U) \quad \begin{array}{c} \varphi U\psi \\ \swarrow \qquad \searrow \\ \psi \qquad \varphi \wedge X(\varphi U\psi) \end{array}$$

Proposition 13.2.2. For any finite set of LTL-formulae Γ:

$$\bigwedge \Gamma \equiv \bigvee \left\{ \bigwedge \Delta \mid \Delta \in \mathrm{FE}(\Gamma) \right\}.$$

The proof is similar to the proof of Proposition 13.1.12.

In this section we will present several running examples with two LTL formulae η_1, η_2 and with a set of formulae Γ, defined as follows.

η_1	$(p\mathsf{U}q) \wedge \mathsf{G}r$
η_2	$(p\mathsf{U}q) \wedge \mathsf{G}\neg q$
Γ	$\{p\mathsf{U}q,\ p \rightarrow \neg\mathsf{X}\mathsf{F}q\}$

Again, when a later example is related to these, this is indicated by a label at the beginning of the example.

Example 13.2.3 (Extended closure for η_1, η_2 and Γ).

1. The extended closure of η_1 is defined as follows:

$$ecl(\eta_1) = \{\eta_1, p\mathsf{U}q, \mathsf{G}r, p \wedge \mathsf{X}(p\mathsf{U}q), q, r, \mathsf{X}\mathsf{G}r, p, \mathsf{X}(p\mathsf{U}q)\}.$$

The procedure FULLEXPANSION produces the following two full expansions:
- $\Delta_1 = \{\eta_1, p\mathsf{U}q, \mathsf{G}r, q, r, \mathsf{X}\mathsf{G}r\}$.
- $\Delta_2 = \{\eta_1, p\mathsf{U}q, \mathsf{G}r, p \wedge \mathsf{X}(p\mathsf{U}q), p, \mathsf{X}(p\mathsf{U}q), r, \mathsf{X}\mathsf{G}r\}$.

2. The extended closure of η_2 is defined as follows:

$$ecl(\eta_2) = \{\eta_2, p\mathsf{U}q, \mathsf{G}\neg q, q, p \wedge \mathsf{X}(p\mathsf{U}q), \neg q, \mathsf{X}\mathsf{G}\neg q, p, \mathsf{X}(p\mathsf{U}q)\}.$$

The procedure FULLEXPANSION produces the following sets:
- $\Psi_1 = \{\eta_2, p\mathsf{U}q, \mathsf{G}\neg q, q, \neg q, \mathsf{X}\mathsf{G}\neg q\}$: patently inconsistent, removed.
- $\Psi_2 = \{\eta_2, p\mathsf{U}q, p \wedge \mathsf{X}(p\mathsf{U}q), p, \mathsf{X}(p\mathsf{U}q), \mathsf{G}\neg q, \neg q, \mathsf{X}\mathsf{G}\neg q\}$.

Eventually, only one full expansion is created.

3. Recall that $\varphi \rightarrow \psi$ is defined as an abbreviation of $\neg\varphi \vee \psi$, while $\mathsf{F}q$ is an abbreviation of $\top\mathsf{U}q$. For the sake of simplicity, we assume that the rules for $\rightarrow$ are primitive, which implies simpler formula components. The extended closure of Γ is defined as follows:

$$ecl(\Gamma) = \{p\mathsf{U}q, p \rightarrow \neg\mathsf{X}\mathsf{F}q, p \wedge \mathsf{X}(p\mathsf{U}q), q, p, \mathsf{X}(p\mathsf{U}q), \neg p, \neg\mathsf{X}\mathsf{F}q, \neg\mathsf{F}q, \neg q\}.$$

The procedure FULLEXPANSION produces the following sets:
- $\Gamma_1 = \Gamma \cup \{q, \neg p\}$.
- $\Gamma_2 = \Gamma \cup \{q, \neg\mathsf{X}\mathsf{F}q\}$.
- $\Gamma_3 = \Gamma \cup \{p \wedge \mathsf{X}(p\mathsf{U}q), p, \mathsf{X}(p\mathsf{U}q), \neg p\}$: patently inconsistent, removed.
- $\Gamma_4 = \Gamma \cup \{p \wedge \mathsf{X}(p\mathsf{U}q), p, \mathsf{X}(p\mathsf{U}q), \neg\mathsf{X}\mathsf{F}q\}$.

Remark 13.2.4. The procedure FULLEXPANSION may produce some 'nonminimal' full expansions. For instance, if $\Gamma = \{p\mathsf{U}q, p \wedge \mathsf{X}(p\mathsf{U}q)\}$ then

$$\mathrm{FE}(\Gamma) = \{\{p\mathsf{U}q, p \wedge \mathsf{X}(p\mathsf{U}q), p, \mathsf{X}(p\mathsf{U}q)\}, \{q, p\mathsf{U}q, p \wedge \mathsf{X}(p\mathsf{U}q), p, \mathsf{X}(p\mathsf{U}q)\}\}.$$

Although satisfiability of the latter implies satisfiability of the former, we may have to consider both alternatives in the tableau, for the sake of satisfying the eventuality $p\mathsf{U}q$.

13.2.2 Hintikka Traces

Since we are interested in satisfiability of LTL-formulae in linear models, we need to define the notion of *linear* Hintikka structure, further called *Hintikka trace*.

Definition 13.2.5. Given a closed set of formulae Γ, a **Hintikka trace (HT) for** Γ is a mapping $\mathcal{H} : \mathbb{N} \to \mathcal{P}(\Gamma)$ satisfying the following conditions for every $n \in \mathbb{N}$:

(HT1) $\mathcal{H}(n)$ is fully expanded.
(HT2) If $\varphi \in \mathcal{H}(n)$ is a successor formula, then $scomp(\varphi) \in \mathcal{H}(n+1)$.
(HT3) If $\varphi U \psi \in \mathcal{H}(n)$, then there exists $i \geq 0$ such that $\psi \in \mathcal{H}(n+i)$ and $\varphi \in \mathcal{H}(n+j)$
    for every j such that $0 \leq j < i$. ∇

Proposition 13.2.6. In every Hintikka trace $\mathcal{H}$:

(I) If $G\varphi \in \mathcal{H}(n)$, then $\varphi \in \mathcal{H}(n+i)$ for every $i \in \mathbb{N}$.
(II) If $\varphi U \psi \in \mathcal{H}(n)$, then $\psi \in \mathcal{H}(n)$ or ($\varphi \in \mathcal{H}(n)$ and $\varphi U \psi \in \mathcal{H}(n+1)$).
(III) If $\neg(\varphi U \psi) \in \mathcal{H}(n)$, then $\neg\psi \in \mathcal{H}(n)$ and ($\neg\varphi \in \mathcal{H}(n)$ or $\neg(\varphi U \psi) \in \mathcal{H}(n+1)$).
(IV) If $\neg(\varphi U \psi) \in \mathcal{H}(n)$, then: $\neg\psi \in \mathcal{H}(n+i)$ for every $i \in \mathbb{N}$ or there exists an $i \in \mathbb{N}$ such
    that $\neg\varphi \in \mathcal{H}(n+i)$ and $\neg\psi \in \mathcal{H}(n+j)$ for every $j \in \mathbb{N}$ such that $0 \leq j \leq i$.   ■

Proof. We leave the proofs of the first 3 claims as easy exercises, using conditions (HT1) and (HT2) from Definition 13.2.5. For the last claim, suppose $\neg(\varphi U \psi) \in \mathcal{H}(n)$ but $\neg\psi \notin \mathcal{H}(n+i)$ for some $i \in \mathbb{N}$. Then $\neg(\varphi U \psi) \notin \mathcal{H}(n+i)$, by contraposition of property (III). Let k be the first position for which $\neg(\varphi U \psi) \notin \mathcal{H}(n+k)$. Note that $k > 0$. Then, for all $j \in \mathbb{N}$ such that $0 \leq j \leq k-1$ we have that $\neg(\varphi U \psi) \in \mathcal{H}(n+j)$, and hence $\neg\psi \in \mathcal{H}(n+j)$, too. In particular, we have that $\neg(\varphi U \psi) \in \mathcal{H}(n+k-1)$, hence ($\neg\varphi \in \mathcal{H}(n+k-1)$ or $\neg(\varphi U \psi) \in \mathcal{H}(n+k)$) by property (III). Since the latter disjunct does not hold, we have that $\neg\varphi \in \mathcal{H}(n+k-1)$. Thus, we have that $\neg\varphi \in \mathcal{H}(n+k-1)$ and $\neg\psi \in \mathcal{H}(n+j)$ for every $j \in \mathbb{N}$ such that $0 \leq j \leq k-1$.   □

Definition 13.2.7. An LTL formula φ is **satisfiable in a Hintikka trace** $\mathcal{H}$ if $\varphi \in \mathcal{H}(n)$ for some $n \in \mathbb{N}$. ∇

Lemma 13.2.8. For any closed set of formulae Γ, every linear model $\sigma : \mathbb{N} \to \mathcal{P}(\text{PROP})$ generates a Hintikka trace $\mathcal{H} : \mathbb{N} \to \mathcal{P}(\Gamma)$ for Γ, where $\mathcal{H}(n) = \{\varphi \in \Gamma \mid \sigma, n \models \varphi\}$ for every $n \in \mathbb{N}$.   ■

The proof is by a straightforward verification of the conditions (HT1)–(HT3) in Definition 13.2.5, which is left as an exercise.

Typically, we will be interested in Hintikka traces for sets $ecl(\Gamma)$, where Γ is a set of formulae for which we want to find a model.

Theorem 13.2.9. An LTL formula η is satisfiable iff it is satisfiable in a Hintikka trace for $ecl(\eta)$.   ■

Proof. One direction is immediate by Lemma 13.2.8 for $\Gamma = ecl(\eta)$. For the converse, suppose $\eta \in \mathcal{H}(m)$ for some Hintikka trace $\mathcal{H} : \mathbb{N} \to \mathcal{P}(ecl(\eta))$ and $m \in \mathbb{N}$. Without restriction, we can assume that $m = 0$.

We define the linear model $\sigma : \mathbb{N} \to \mathcal{P}(\text{PROP})$ as $\sigma(n) := \text{PROP} \cap \mathcal{H}(n)$. We now show by induction on the main components that for every $\psi \in ecl(\eta)$ and every $n \in \mathbb{N}$ we have: if $\psi \in \mathcal{H}(n)$ then $\sigma, n \models \psi$.

Suppose $\psi \in \mathcal{H}(n)$ and assume that the claim holds for all main components of ψ and all states $n \in \mathbb{N}$. The argument essentially repeats the one in the proof of Theorem 13.1.17. The only differences are:

- $\psi = \mathsf{X}\psi_1$: the claim follows from condition (HT2) of the definition of Hintikka trace and the inductive hypothesis for ψ_1.
- $\psi = \psi_1 \mathsf{U} \psi_2$: the claim follows from condition (HT3) and the inductive hypotheses for ψ_1 and for ψ_2.
- When $\psi = \neg\psi_1$ and we do a nested induction on ψ_1:
    - The claim for $\psi_1 = \mathsf{X}\psi_1'$ follows from condition (HT2), and the inductive hypothesis for $\neg\psi_1'$.
    - The claim for $\psi_1 = \psi_1' \mathsf{U} \psi_2'$ follows from Proposition 13.2.6(III) and the inductive hypotheses for $\neg\psi_1'$ and for $\neg\psi_2'$.
    - The other cases are as in the proof of Theorem 13.1.17.

Finally, since $\eta \in \mathcal{H}(0)$ we have that $\sigma, 0 \models \eta$. $\qquad\qquad\square$

Corollary 13.2.10. A finite set of LTL formulae Γ is satisfiable iff it is satisfiable in a Hintikka trace for $ecl(\Gamma)$. ∎

13.2.3 Constructing Tableaux

The Pretableau Construction Phase

Given an input formula $\eta \in$ LTL we are now going to build a tableau for testing the satisfiability of η. The procedure consists of 3 phases, as described in Section 13.1.

The pretableau construction phase consists of alternating applications of two rules:

$\textsc{PrExp}^{\text{LTL}}$: producing all **offspring states** of a given prestate;
$\textsc{Next}^{\text{LTL}}$: producing the **successor prestate** of a given state.

The rule $\textsc{PrExp}^{\text{LTL}}$ involves the procedure $\textsc{FullExpansion}$, described in Section 13.1, for computing the family $\text{FE}(\Gamma)$ of full expansions of a given subset Γ of $ecl(\eta)$.

Rule $\textsc{PrExp}^{\text{LTL}}$: Given a prestate Γ to which the rule has not yet been applied, do the following:

1. Compute the family $\text{FE}(\Gamma) = \{\Delta_1, \dots \Delta_n\}$ and add these as (labels of) new states in the pretableau, called the **offspring states of** Γ.

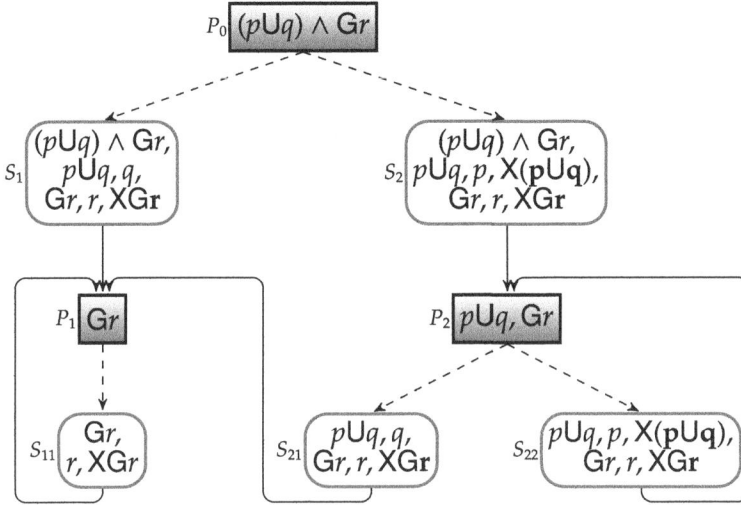

Figure 13.3 The LTL pretableau for η_1.

2. For each newly introduced state Δ, create an edge $\Gamma \dashrightarrow \Delta$.

3. If, however, the pretableau already contains a state with label Δ then do not create a new state with that label, but create an edge $\Gamma \dashrightarrow \Delta$ to that state.

We denote the set $\{ \Delta \mid \Gamma \dashrightarrow \Delta \}$ of offspring states of Γ by $\mathsf{states}(\Gamma)$.

Following the notation from Section 13.1, for any set of LTL-formulae Δ we denote:

$$\mathsf{X}(\Delta) := \{ \psi \mid \mathsf{X}\psi \in \Delta \} \cup \{ \neg\psi \mid \neg\mathsf{X}\psi \in \Delta \}.$$

Rule $\mathrm{NEXT}^{\mathrm{LTL}}$: Given a state with label Δ, to which the rule has not yet been applied, do the following:

1. Add a successor prestate Γ of Δ with (possibly empty) label $\mathsf{X}(\Delta)$.

2. Create an edge $\Delta \rightarrow \Gamma$.

3. If, however, the pretableau already contains a prestate with label Γ then do not create a new prestate with that label, but extend an arrow $\Delta \rightarrow \Gamma$ to that prestate.

The construction phase of building a pretableau for η begins with creating a single prestate $\{\eta\}$, followed by alternating applications of the rules PrExp and Next, respectively to the prestates and the states created at a previous stage of the construction. The construction phase ends when none of these rules can add any new states or prestates to the current graph. The resulting graph is the pretableau $\mathcal{P}^\eta$.

Example 13.2.11 (Pretableaux for η_1, η_2 and Γ). The pretableaux for η_1, η_2 and Γ are presented respectively in Figures 13.3, 13.4 and 13.5.

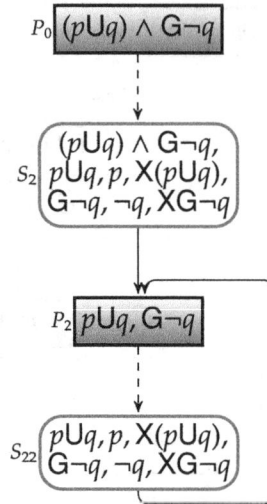

Figure 13.4 The LTL pretableau for η_2.

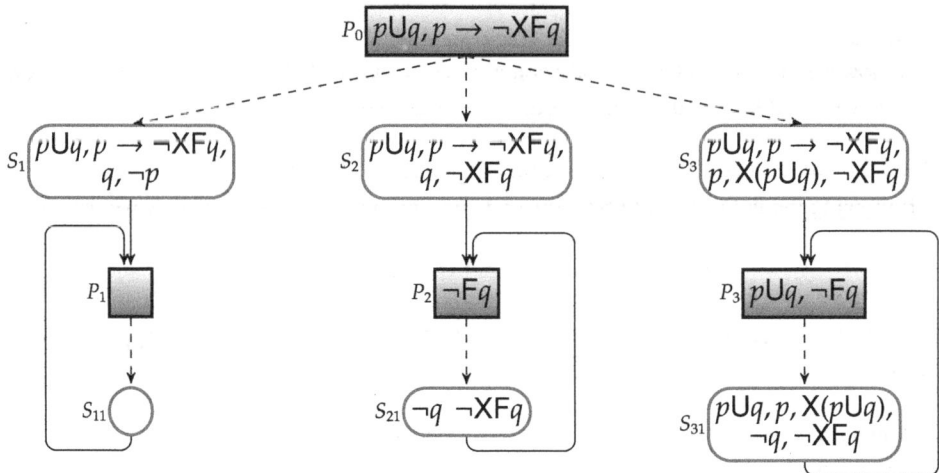

Figure 13.5 The LTL pretableau for Γ.

The Prestate Elimination Phase and Initial Tableau

In this phase, all prestates are removed from $\mathcal{P}^\eta$, together with their incoming and outgoing arrows, by applying the following **prestate elimination rule**:

Rule PRESTATEELIM^{LTL}: For every prestate Γ in $\mathcal{P}^\eta$, do the following:

1. Remove Γ from $\mathcal{P}^\eta$;
2. If there is a state Δ in $\mathcal{P}^\eta$ with $\Delta \to \Gamma$, then for every state $\Delta' \in \text{states}(\Gamma)$, create an edge $\Delta \to \Delta'$.

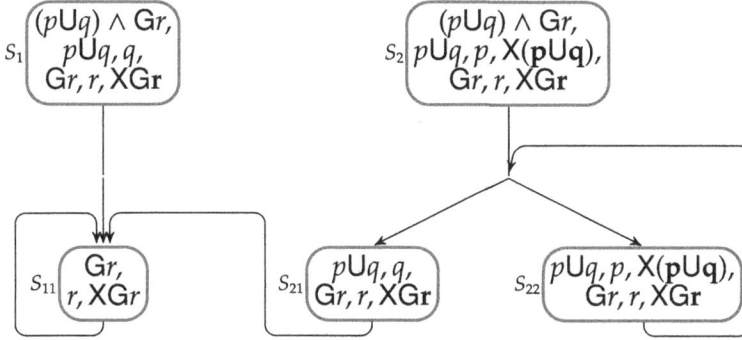

Figure 13.6 The LTL initial tableau for η_1.

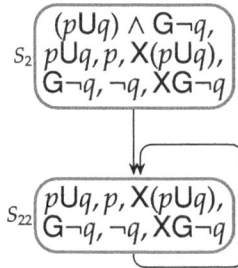

Figure 13.7 The LTL initial tableau for η_2.

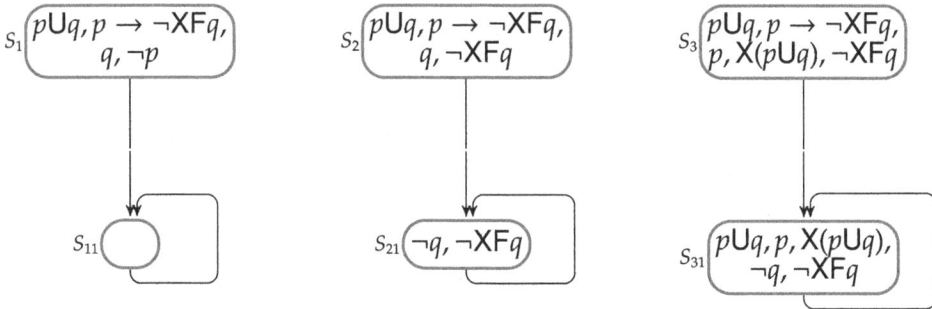

Figure 13.8 The LTL initial tableau for Γ.

The resulting graph is called the **initial tableau** for η, denoted $\mathcal{T}_0^\eta$. The offspring states of the input prestate $\{\eta\}$ are called **input states** of $\mathcal{T}_0^\eta$.

Example 13.2.12 (Initial tableaux for η_1, η_2 and Γ). The initial tableau for η_1, η_2 and Γ are presented respectively in Figures 13.6, 13.7 and 13.8. The initial states of the initial tableaux are those on top.

The State Elimination Phase

The purpose of the state elimination phase is to remove all 'bad' states from the tableau, the labels of which are not satisfiable in any Hintikka trace, and hence in any linear model for LTL. That will be done using the **state elimination rules** STATEELIM1^{LTL} and STATEE-LIM2^{LTL}, introduced later. The state elimination phase is carried out in a sequence of stages, starting at stage 0 with the initial tableau T_0^η, and eliminating at every stage n at most one state for the current tableau T_n^η, by applying one of the state elimination rules, to produce the new current tableau T_{n+1}^η.

One possible reason for existence of a 'bad' state in a current tableau is that it may lack a successor state. Such states can arise because some prestates may have no full expansions, and hence may yield no offspring states. Once such bad states are removed, some of their predecessor states may be left without successors, so they must be removed, too, etc., until stabilisation. Formally, the elimination of states with no successors is done by applying the following rule.

Rule STATEELIM1^{LTL}: If a state Δ has no successor states in the current tableau, then remove Δ from the tableau.

Another reason for a state to be 'bad', i.e. for its label not to be satisfiable in any Hintikka trace, is when that label contains an eventuality formula which is not 'realised' in any reachable (i.e. future) state. Such cases are handled by an additional state elimination rule. In order to formulate it, we have to formalise the notion of **eventuality realisation**. Hereafter, by a path in the current tableau T_n^η we mean a sequence of successor states.

Definition 13.2.13. An eventuality $\vartheta = \varphi \mathsf{U} \psi$ is **realised** at the state Δ in T_n^η if there exists a finite path $\Delta_0, \Delta_1, \ldots, \Delta_m$, where $\Delta_0 = \Delta$ and $m \geq 0$, in T_n^η, such that $\vartheta, \psi \in \Delta_m$ and $\vartheta, \varphi \in \Delta_i$ for every $i = 0, \ldots, m - 1$. We say that ϑ is realised on the path $\Delta_0, \Delta_1, \ldots, \Delta_m$ and call any such path a **witness of the realisation of the eventuality ϑ in Δ**.

If $\psi \in \Delta$, then we say that ϑ is **immediately realised** at the state Δ (on the singleton path Δ). ▽

Checking for realisation of an eventuality is a simple graph reachability problem, discussed in Chapter 3. It can be done more efficiently by following a **global** approach, that is, simultaneously for all eventualities, at all states in the current tableau by a standard marking procedure in time linear in the number of states in T_n^η and in the number of eventualities. This is essentially the labelling algorithm for model checking CTL formulae, presented in Section 7.3.2.

Now we can state the second state elimination rule.

Rule STATEELIM2^{LTL}: If an eventuality $\vartheta \in \Delta$ is not realised on any path starting from Δ in the current tableau, then remove Δ from the tableau.

The rules STATEELIM1^{LTL} and STATEELIM2^{LTL} are applied alternately, in any order, which may be determined by a specific strategy. This procedure continues until reaching a stage when no further elimination of states by an application of any of the rules is possible.

The Final Tableau

When the state elimination phase reaches a stabilisation stage the current tableau at that stage is the **final tableau for** η, denoted by $\mathcal{T}^\eta$, with a set of states denoted by S^η.

Definition 13.2.14. The final tableau $\mathcal{T}^\eta$ is **open** if $\eta \in \Delta$ for some $\Delta \in S^\eta$; otherwise, $\mathcal{T}^\eta$ is **closed**. ∇

The tableau procedure returns 'not satisfiable' if the final tableau is closed. Otherwise, it returns 'satisfiable' and, moreover, provides sufficient information for producing a finite Hintikka trace satisfying η, as described further in the completeness proof.

Example 13.2.15 (Final tableaux for η_1, η_2 and Γ).

1. From the initial tableau for η_1, no state gets eliminated by Rule STATEELIM1^{LTL}. There is only one eventuality, $p\mathsf{U}q$. We leave it to the reader to check that all states containing that eventuality realise it. Therefore, no state gets eliminated due to Rule STATEELIM2^{LTL}, either. Thus, the initial tableau is the final tableau. It is open and gives many possible Hintikka traces for the input formula.
2. In the initial tableau for η_2 there is only one eventuality, $p\mathsf{U}q$. It belongs to both states of the initial tableau but is not realised in any of them. Therefore, both states get eliminated due to Rule STATEELIM2^{LTL}. Thus, the final tableau is empty, therefore closed. The attempt to build a Hintikka trace for the input formula $(p\mathsf{U}q) \wedge \mathsf{G}\neg q$ has failed, hence it is declared not satisfiable.
3. From the initial tableau for Γ, no state gets eliminated by Rule STATEELIM1^{LTL}. There is only one eventuality, $p\mathsf{U}q$. The states S_1 and S_2 containing that eventuality realise it immediately. However, states S_3 and S_{31} containing that eventuality do not realise it, and therefore these states gets eliminated by Rule STATEELIM2^{LTL}. Thus, the final tableau is given in Figure 13.9. It is open, because each of the states S_1 and S_2 contain the input formula. It provides two Hintikka traces satisfying the input set Γ, one starting at S_1, and the other – at S_2. However, note that they yield the same linear model for Γ.

13.2.4 Soundness, Completeness and Optimality

Soundness

Recall that soundness of the tableau procedure means that if the input formula η is satisfiable, then the tableau $\mathcal{T}^\eta$ is open. We will establish the soundness of the tableau for LTL by proving that every state elimination rule is 'sound', in a sense that it never eliminates a state with a satisfiable label. The soundness of the overall procedure is then an immediate consequence.

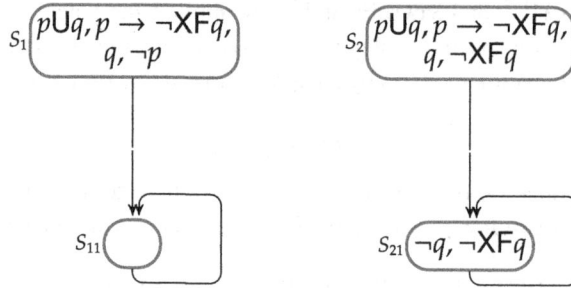

Figure 13.9 The LTL final tableau for Γ.

Lemma 13.2.16. Let Γ be a prestate in $\mathcal{P}^\eta$ such that $\sigma, i \models \Gamma$ for some linear LTL model σ and $i \in \mathbb{N}$. Then:

(I) $\sigma, i \models \Delta$ for at least one $\Delta \in \mathrm{FE}(\Gamma)$.
(II) Moreover, for any eventuality $\varphi U \psi \subset \Gamma$ such that $\sigma, i \models \psi$, the state Δ can be chosen to contain ψ. ∎

Proof. Claim (I) follows from Proposition 13.1.12.

For claim (II), let $\varphi U \psi \in \Gamma$ and $\sigma, i \models \psi$. We start the construction of the desired full expansion Δ of Γ by applying the rule to $\varphi U \psi$ to Γ. Now, it suffices to show that we can complete that construction by applying the set replacement operations, starting with the replacement $\Gamma \cup \{\varphi\}$ of Γ until saturation, by choosing at every step to replace the current set by an extension that is still satisfied at (σ, i). This claim is proved by induction on the number of applications of expansion steps. The base of the induction, for $\Gamma \cup \{\varphi\}$, holds by assumption. The inductive step is carried out by a straightforward consideration of all cases of set replacement operations. (In case of a set replacement operation applied to a disjunctive formula and offering a choice of two extensions, both satisfied at (σ, i), the procedure chooses any of them.) ☐

Note that the constructed full expansion Δ does not need to be minimal – indeed, this happens in the example $\Gamma = \{p U q, X(p U q)\}$ given earlier. For this reason we want to keep all full expansions in $\mathrm{FE}(\Gamma)$, not only the minimal ones.

Lemma 13.2.17. No satisfiable state $\Delta \in \mathcal{T}_n^\eta$ is removed by any application of the rules STATEELIM1^{LTL} and STATEELIM2^{LTL} during the state elimination phase. ∎

Proof. As in the proof of Lemma 13.1.24, it suffices to show that no satisfiable state $\Delta \in \mathcal{T}_0^\eta$ is removed by an application of STATEELIM1^{LTL} or STATEELIM2^{LTL} to $\mathcal{T}_n^\eta$ for any $n \in \mathbb{N}$. We will prove, by induction on n, a stronger claim, viz. that for every $n \in \mathbb{N}$, if $\Delta \in \mathcal{T}_n^\eta$ is satisfiable then:

1. There is a satisfiable state $\Theta \in \mathcal{T}_n^\eta$ such that $\Delta \to \Theta$ in $\mathcal{T}_n^\eta$.
2. For any eventuality $\varphi\mathsf{U}\psi \in \Delta$ there is a finite path of satisfiable states in $\mathcal{T}_n^\eta$ witnessing the realisation of that eventuality.
3. All satisfiable states in $\mathcal{T}_0^\eta$ are still present in $\mathcal{T}_n^\eta$.

Note that the inductive claim refers simultaneously to all satisfiable $\Delta \in \mathcal{T}_n^\eta$ and all eventualities in them. Let $n = 0$. Take any state $\Delta \in \mathcal{T}_0^\eta$ such that $\sigma, 0 \models \Delta$ for some linear model σ. Therefore, $\sigma, 1 \models \mathsf{X}(\Delta)$. (Recall that $\mathsf{X}(\Delta) = \{ \psi \mid \mathsf{X}\psi \in \Delta \} \cup \{ \neg\psi \mid \neg\mathsf{X}\psi \in \Delta \}$.) Then, by Lemma 13.2.16, at least one full expansion Θ of $\mathsf{X}(\Delta)$ is satisfied at $(\sigma, 1)$. By the construction of the initial tableau, there is a state (with label) Θ in $\mathcal{T}_0^\eta$ such that $\Delta \to \Theta$. Therefore, the state Δ cannot be removed from $\mathcal{T}_0^\eta$ by an application of the rule STATEELIM1^{LTL}.

Let $\varphi\mathsf{U}\psi \in \Delta$. Then there is $i \in \mathbb{N}$ such that $\sigma, i \models \psi$ and $\sigma, j \models \varphi$ for every $0 \leq j < i$. Moreover, we can choose a minimal such i, so all intermediate states in it would satisfy $\varphi\mathsf{U}\psi$, too – shown by induction on j. By iterating the preceding argument, we show that the trace $\sigma(0), \ldots, \sigma(i)$ can be 'simulated' by a path $\Delta(0), \ldots, \Delta(i)$ of states in $\mathcal{T}_0^\eta$, such that $\Delta(0) = \Delta$ and $\sigma, j \models \Delta(j)$ for $0 \leq j \leq i$, thus realising $\varphi\mathsf{U}\psi$ at Δ in $\mathcal{T}_0^\eta$. Indeed, we show by induction on j that each intermediate state $\Delta(j)$, for $0 \leq j < i$, contains both φ and $\varphi\mathsf{U}\psi$, using the fact that each $\Delta(j)$ is fully expanded and $\mathsf{X}(\varphi\mathsf{U}\psi)$ is a disjunctive component of $\varphi\mathsf{U}\psi$. To show that the last state $\Delta(i)$ can be chosen to contain ψ, we use Lemma 13.2.16. Thus, the state Δ cannot be removed from $\mathcal{T}_0^\eta$ by an application of the rule STATEELIM2^{LTL}. Consequently, all satisfiable states in $\mathcal{T}_0^\eta$ have remained in $\mathcal{T}_1^\eta$.

Now, assuming the claim holds for all $n < m$, take any satisfiable state $\Delta \in \mathcal{T}_m^\eta$. By the preceding argument (for $n = 0$), there is a satisfiable state Θ in $\mathcal{T}_0^\eta$ such that $\Delta \to \Theta$ in $\mathcal{T}_0^\eta$. By the inductive hypothesis, Θ has remained intact in $\mathcal{T}_m^\eta$. Therefore, Δ cannot be removed from $\mathcal{T}_m^\eta$ by an application of the rule STATEELIM1^{LTL}.

Likewise, for any $\varphi\mathsf{U}\psi \in \Delta$, the finite path of satisfiable states in $\mathcal{T}_0^\eta$ witnessing the realisation of that eventuality, produced by the argument for $n = 0$, will have remained intact in $\mathcal{T}_m^\eta$, and hence $\varphi\mathsf{U}\psi$ is realised at Δ in $\mathcal{T}_m^\eta$. Therefore, Δ cannot be removed from $\mathcal{T}_m^\eta$ by an application of the rule STATEELIM2^{LTL}, either. That completes the induction and the proof. $\qquad\square$

Theorem 13.2.18. If $\eta \in$ LTL is satisfiable then $\mathcal{T}^\eta$ is open. $\qquad\blacksquare$

Theorem 13.2.18 follows immediately from Lemma 13.2.16 and 13.2.17.

Completeness

To prove completeness of the tableaux for LTL it suffices to show how from the open final tableau $\mathcal{T}^\eta$ one can construct a Hintikka trace satisfying η, and then refer to Theorem 13.2.9. We can extract such a Hintikka trace from $\mathcal{T}^\eta$, by starting with any state Δ containing η and building up a path of successor states through $\mathcal{T}^\eta$, while ensuring that all eventualities appearing along that path eventually get realised on that path. Note, that *not* every path in T^η satisfies that requirement. Indeed, we have proved that every eventuality in a state Δ is realised along *some* path starting from Δ, but different eventualities may be realised along *different* paths.

So we have to guide the process of building a Hintikka trace. The idea is to maintain a queue of **pending eventualities** and build the Hintikka trace $\mathcal{H}(\eta)$ in a sequence of steps, each producing a finite **partial Hintikka trace** extending the previous one by appending a finite path realising the first pending eventuality from the current queue, while possibly adding new pending eventualities at the end of the queue. Thus, an infinite path is produced in the limit, as a concatenation of partial Hintikka traces, in which there are no unrealised eventualities. That is the required Hintikka trace.

The reason we can apply such a piecewise approach to the realisation of the eventualities is that if an eventuality belongs to a state in the final tableau T^η and is not realised on a given finite path in T^η starting at that state, then it gets propagated down that path, and thus its realisation can be deferred. More precisely:

Lemma 13.2.19. If $\Delta \in T^\eta$ and $\vartheta = \varphi\mathsf{U}\psi \in \Delta$ is not realised on a given path $\Delta_0, \ldots, \Delta_m$ in T^η, such that $\Delta_0 = \Delta$, then every state on that path contains φ, $\varphi\mathsf{U}\psi$ and $\mathsf{X}(\varphi\mathsf{U}\psi)$. ∎

The proof is by induction on i, using the fact that the states in the tableau are fully expanded sets. This is left as an exercise.

Thus, Lemma 13.2.19 allows the realisation of the eventuality ϑ at Δ to be deferred indefinitely, i.e. throughout any finite path, and then accomplished by appending to its last state Δ' another finite path realising ϑ at Δ', and hence at Δ. In order to formally organise the procedure of building the Hintikka trace, we do the following:

1. Fix a list of all states in T^η: $\Delta_0, \ldots, \Delta_{n-1}$, and a list of all eventualities occurring in T^η: $\vartheta_0, \ldots, \vartheta_{m-1}$.
2. For every state Δ_i and an eventuality $\vartheta_j \in \Delta_i$ select and fix a finite path in T^η, denoted $\pi(\Delta_i, \vartheta_j)$, witnessing the realisation of ϑ_j at Δ_i.

We are now ready to prove the completeness theorem.

Theorem 13.2.20 (Completeness of the tableau for LTL). For any formula $\eta \in$ LTL, if the final tableau T^η is open, then the formula is satisfiable. ∎

Proof. We construct a sequence of partial Hintikka traces

$$\mathcal{PHT}_0(\eta), \mathcal{PHT}_1(\eta), \ldots$$

as follows. We start with any state $\Delta \in T^\eta$ containing η. This state constitutes the singleton $\mathcal{PHT}_0(\eta)$, and we associate with it a list of **pending eventualities** Event_0 – these are all eventualities in Δ that are not immediately realised at Δ.

Thereafter the construction continues inductively as follows. Let $\mathcal{PHT}_n(\eta)$ be constructed, with a last state Δ_{i_n} and let Event_n be its list of pending eventualities, where ϑ_{j_n} is the first item, if any. We then take a copy of the path $\pi(\Delta_{i_n}, \vartheta_{j_n})$, witnessing the realisation of ϑ_{j_n} at Δ_{i_n}, and append it to $\mathcal{PHT}_n(\eta)$ by identifying its first state with the last state of $\mathcal{PHT}_n(\eta)$; if Event_n is empty, we simply extend $\mathcal{PHT}_n(\eta)$ with any successor state of Δ_{i_n}, to keep the path going. Thus, $\mathcal{PHT}_{n+1}(\eta)$ is produced. The new list of pending eventualities Event_{n+1} is produced by removing ϑ_{j_n} from the head of the list Event_n and appending to it a list of all eventualities in Δ_{i_n} that do not appear in Event_n and are not immediately realised at Δ_{i_n}.

This completes the inductive construction of the chain

$$\mathcal{PHT}_0(\eta), \mathcal{PHT}_1(\eta), \ldots,$$

and consequently, of $\mathcal{H}(\eta)$ as the union of that chain. It remains to show that $\mathcal{H}(\eta)$ defined as earlier is indeed a Hintikka trace satisfying η. This verification is now straightforward from the construction, and is left as an exercise. ☐

On the Complexity and Optimality

A closer look at the tableau procedure for LTL, as described previously, shows that in the worst case it takes time exponential in the size of the input formula η. On the other hand, as we know from Corollary 6.4.2, the satisfiability problem for LTL is in PSPACE, so it is clear that the tableau, as described, uses more space resources than necessary. It, however, can be optimised, by first noticing the following.

Corollary 13.2.21. The logic LTL has the small satisfiability witness property. ∎

Proof. The construction of $\mathcal{H}(\eta)$ in the proof of Theorem 13.2.20 can be made finite by propagating the list of pending eventualities to every next state in the partial Hintikka traces produced as earlier, and looping back from any state $\mathcal{H}_i(\eta)$ whose label Δ has appeared before, to a previous state $\mathcal{H}_j(\eta)$ with $j < i$, with the same label, and such that all eventualities listed in Event_j have been realised within the path $\mathcal{H}_j(\eta), \ldots, \mathcal{H}_i(\eta)$. Such a state is guaranteed to occur. Then the lengths of the prefix and the loop can be reduced within the bounds prescribed in the definition of small satisfiability witness in Section 6.3.2, thus essentially producing a 'short' ultimately periodic Hintikka trace, and thereby a small satisfiability witness for the input formula. We leave the details as an exercise. ☐

Now, the construction of a small satisfiability witness can be done in (nondeterministic) PSPACE by organising a depth-first expansion of the pretableau, and then testing for the suitability of the generated path by judicial memory use. More precisely, this can be done by 'guessing' the right 'short' Hintikka trace already in the pretableau construction phase, viz. by generating for every state constructed so far its unique successor prestate, and then selecting for it the 'right' offspring state, etc., and by checking on the fly that all occurring eventualities are satisfied, and remembering in the process only the polynomial amount of information needed for that, as detailed in Section 6.3.2. Again, we leave the details as an exercise.

13.2.5 Model-Checking Tableaux

In Section 13.1.7 we discussed how the generic tableau procedure for testing satisfiability can be modified to perform local model checking. Here we will illustrate the idea by developing a model-checking tableau-based method for LTL. We note again that this method is generally subefficient, as it works in EXPTIME, but can be optimised to PSPACE, like the satisfiability-testing tableau.

Recall the general, *universal* local model-checking problem for LTL: given a finite rooted ITS $(\mathcal{T}, s)$, where $\mathcal{T} = (S, R, L)$, and a formula $\eta \in$ LTL, decide whether $\mathcal{T}, s \models_\forall \eta$, meaning that every computation in $\mathcal{T}$ starting from s satisfies η. This problem is trivially reduced to the *existential* local model-checking problem: decide whether $\mathcal{T}, s \models_\exists \neg\eta$, meaning that *some* computation in $\mathcal{T}$ starting from s satisfies $\neg\eta$. The latter problem is closer in spirit to the satisfiability-testing problem, so we will construct a model-checking tableau for it. (See also the proof of Corollary 6.2.7.)

Given a finite rooted ITS $(\mathcal{T}, s)$, where $\mathcal{T} = (S, R, L)$, and a formula $\eta \in$ LTL, we denote for any $r \subset S$:

$$L[ecl(\eta), r] := (L(r) \cup \{ \neg p \mid p \in (\text{PROP} \cap ecl(\eta)) \setminus L(r) \}).$$

Following the idea in Section 13.1.7, we first construct a modified pretableau, in which the states and prestates are now labelled by pairs (r, Γ) where $r \in S$ and $\Gamma \subseteq ecl(\eta)$, where in the case of states Γ is fully expanded. The root prestate is $(s, \{\eta\} \cup L[ecl(\eta), s])$.

The pretableau construction phase is similar to the one in the tableaux for satisfiability, but employs modified rules PREXP^{LTL} and NEXT^{LTL}. The rule PREXP^{LTL} is modified as follows:

PREXP$^{\text{LTL}}(\mathcal{T})$: given a prestate (r, Γ) to which the rule has not yet been applied, do the following:

1. Compute the family FE(Γ) of all full expansions of Γ and add a new state in the pretableau with a label (r, Δ) for each $\Delta \in$ FE(Γ).
2. For each newly introduced state (r, Δ), create an edge $(r, \Gamma) \dashrightarrow (r, \Delta)$.
3. If, however, the pretableau already contains a state with label (r, Δ), then do not create a new state with that label but extend an arrow $(r, \Gamma) \dashrightarrow (r, \Delta)$ to that state.

We denote the set $\{ (r, \Delta) \mid (r, \Gamma) \dashrightarrow (r, \Delta) \}$ of **offspring states** of (r, Γ) by states(r, Γ).

The rule NEXT^{LTL} is now modified as follows:

Rule NEXT$^{\text{LTL}}(\mathcal{T})$: Given a state with label (r, Δ) to which the rule has not yet been applied, do the following:

if there are no R-successors of r in $\mathcal{T}$, remove the state (r, Δ) from the pretableau;
else:

1. For every $t \in S$ such that rRt, add a successor prestate of (r, Δ) with label $(t, X(\Delta) \cup L[ecl(\eta), t])$.
2. For each so introduced prestate (t, Γ), create an edge $(r, \Delta) \to (t, \Gamma)$.
3. If, however, the pretableau already contains a prestate with label (t, Γ) then do not create a new prestate with that label, but extend an arrow $(r, \Delta) \to (t, \Gamma)$ to that prestate.

Recall that the test for patent inconsistency of prestates is done at the beginning of the procedure computing their full expansions.

Because of the finiteness of $\mathcal{T}$ the pretableau construction phase is guaranteed to terminate, producing the pretableau $\mathcal{P}^{\mathcal{T}, s, \eta}$. The prestate and state elimination phases are essentially the same as in the tableau for satisfiability. When the final tableau $\mathcal{T}^{\mathcal{T}, s, \eta}$ is obtained, $\mathcal{T}, s \models_\exists \eta$ is declared true iff there is a state (s, Δ) in $\mathcal{T}^{\mathcal{T}, s, \eta}$ such that $\eta \in \Delta$.

The correctness of the procedure follows from the following theorem.

Theorem 13.2.22 (Correctness). For any formula η in LTL and a finite rooted ITS $(\mathcal{T}, s)$, the following hold:

(I) If a prestate (r, Γ) in the pretableau $\mathcal{P}^{\mathcal{T}, s, \eta}$ is such that $\mathcal{T}, r \models_\exists \Gamma$, then it has at least one offspring state (r, Δ) in the pretableau $\mathcal{P}^{\mathcal{T}, s, \eta}$ such that $\mathcal{T}, r \models_\exists \Delta$.

(II) A state (r, Δ) from the initial tableau $\mathcal{T}_0^{\mathcal{T}, s, \eta}$ is eliminated during the state elimination phase only if $\mathcal{T}, r \not\models_\exists \Delta$.

(III) For any state (r, Δ) from the initial tableau $\mathcal{T}_0^{\mathcal{T}, s, \eta}$ we have that $\mathcal{T}, r \models_\exists \Delta$ holds iff (r, Δ) is in the final tableau $\mathcal{T}^{\mathcal{T}, s, \eta}$, too. ■

Proof.

(I) Follows from Proposition 13.1.12.
(II) A slight modification of the proof of Lemma 13.2.17 as follows. Prove by induction on n that for every $n \in \mathbb{N}$, for every $\Delta \in \mathcal{T}_n^\eta$, and for every $r \in \mathcal{T}$, if $\mathcal{T}, r \models_\exists \Delta$ for some $r \in \mathcal{T}$ then:
  1. There is a state $(t, \Theta) \in \mathcal{T}_n^\eta$ such that $(r, \Delta) \to (t, \Theta)$ in $\mathcal{T}_n^\eta$ and $\mathcal{T}, t \models_\exists \Theta$ for some R-successor t of r.
  2. For any eventuality $\varphi U \psi \in \Delta$ there is a finite path $(r_0, \Delta_0), \ldots, (r_m, \Delta_m)$ in $\mathcal{T}_n^\eta$ such that $\Delta_0 = \Delta$ and witnessing the realisation of that eventuality and such that there is an R-path $r_0, \ldots, r_m$ in $\mathcal{T}$ such that $r_0 = r$ and $\mathcal{T}, r_i \models_\exists \Delta_i$ for all $0 \leq i \leq m$.
  3. All states $\Gamma \in \mathcal{T}_0^\eta$ such that $\mathcal{T}, t \models_\exists \Gamma$ for some $t \in \mathcal{T}$ are still present in $\mathcal{T}_n^\eta$.
  We leave the details to the reader.
(III) One direction follows from (II). For the other, suppose (r, Δ) is in the final tableau $\mathcal{T}^{\mathcal{T}, s, \eta}$. By a modification of the proof of Theorem 13.2.20 (the completeness for the satisfiability tableau) and using the arguments from the proof of claim (II), we can construct a path π in $\mathcal{T}$ starting from r and such that $\pi \models \Delta$. Again, we leave the details to the reader. □

13.3 Tableaux for TLR and CTL

We will adapt the tableau construction presented in the previous section for the logics TLR and CTL. We will present both cases simultaneously, by pointing out the specific differences wherever they occur. Naturally, the tableau construction for CTL subsumes the tableau for TLR, while the tableau for TLR subsumes the one for BML. The main differences between these are:

1. Unlike BML, the tableau for TLR has to test for realisation of eventualities, while unlike LTL, it has to test for satisfiability in a total ITS, so these will create some technical overhead compared to the constructions for BML and LTL.
2. On the other hand, again unlike the LTL case, the construction of a satisfying Hintikka structure from an open tableau for a TLR-formula will turn out straightforward, as in the case of BML.
3. Thus, the tableaux for LTL and TLR supplement each other in presenting important issues that apply to the tableau for the logic CTL. Furthermore, CTL involves two types of eventualities – existential and universal – which will be the main source of additional complications arising there.

Again, for simplicity of the exposition, here we will consider TLR and CTL over a language with one total transition relation; the extensions to the general case of a language with many transition relations is straightforward.

13.3.1 Preliminaries

Languages. In this section we will assume that the language of TLR contains $\top$, $\neg$, $\wedge$, EX, AX and EF as primitives connectives, whereas CTL will be assumed to extend TLR with EG, EU and AU. Accordingly, we will assume $\vee$, $\rightarrow$, AG, AF, ER, AR as definable. As we know, some of the primitive temporal connectives can still be eliminated as definable in terms of the others and the tableau construction can be seamlessly restricted. Nevertheless, we will offer an independent treatment for each of them.

Types and components of formulae. The conjunctive, disjunctive and successor formulae in CTL and their components are given in Figure 13.10.

Lemma 13.3.1.

(I) Every conjunctive formula φ of CTL is equivalent to the conjunction of its conjunctive components.

(II) Every disjunctive formula φ of CTL is equivalent to the disjunction of its disjunctive components. ∎

Eventualities. The only eventualities in TLR are of type $EF\varphi$, whereas there are two types of eventualities in CTL:

conjunctive		disjunctive	
formula	components	formula	components
$\neg\neg\varphi$	φ, φ	$\neg(\varphi \wedge \psi)$	$\neg\varphi, \neg\psi$
$\varphi \wedge \psi$	φ, ψ	$EF\varphi$	$\varphi, EXEF\varphi$
$\neg EF\varphi$	$\neg\varphi, \neg EXEF\varphi$	$\neg EG\varphi$	$\neg\varphi, \neg EXEG\varphi$
$EG\varphi$	$\varphi, EXEG\varphi$	$E(\varphi U\psi)$	$\psi, \varphi \wedge EXE(\varphi U\psi)$
$\neg E(\varphi U\psi)$	$\neg\psi, \neg\varphi \vee \neg EXE(\varphi U\psi)$	$A(\varphi U\psi)$	$\psi, \varphi \wedge AXA(\varphi U\psi)$
$\neg A(\varphi U\psi)$	$\neg\psi, \neg\varphi \vee \neg AXA(\varphi U\psi)$		

successor	
formula	component
$EX\varphi$ (existential)	φ
$AX\varphi$ (universal)	φ
$\neg AX\varphi$ (existential)	$\neg\varphi$
$\neg EX\varphi$ (universal)	$\neg\varphi$

Figure 13.10 Types and components of formulae in CTL.

- **existential eventualities**: $EF\varphi$ and $E(\varphi U\psi)$.
- **universal eventualities**: $\neg EG\varphi$ and $A(\varphi U\psi)$.

The notions of extended closure of a formula, fully expanded sets, full expansions and the procedure FULLEXPANSION computing the family of full expansions of a set of CTL-formulae (in particular, for TLR-formulae) obtained by saturation under the set-replacement operations are defined as in Section 13.1. The local tableau for CTL is analogous to the one for BML, extending the propositional local tableau with the decomposition rules for the temporal operators of CTL:

Proposition 13.3.2. For any finite set of CTL formulae Γ:

$$\bigwedge \Gamma \equiv \bigvee \left\{ \bigwedge \Delta \mid \Delta \in FE(\Gamma) \right\}. \qquad \blacksquare$$

The proof is similar to the proof of Proposition 13.1.12.

In this section we will present several running examples with the CTL formulae η_1, η_3 and the set of formulae Γ_2, defined as follows.

η_1	$p \wedge \neg AXq \wedge AX(\neg q \to p) \wedge EF(\neg p \wedge \neg q)$
Γ_2	$\{EF\neg p, A(pUq), \neg p \to EG\neg q\}$
η_3	$A(pUEX\neg q) \wedge (EGAXq \vee E((AXq)U(\neg p \wedge AXq)))$

Non-branching rules	**Branching rules**

$$\text{(EG)} \quad \begin{array}{c} \mathsf{EG}\varphi \\ \downarrow \\ \varphi, \mathsf{EXEG}\varphi \end{array} \qquad \text{(¬EG)} \quad \begin{array}{c} \neg\mathsf{EG}\varphi \\ \swarrow \qquad \searrow \\ \neg\varphi \qquad \mathsf{EX}\neg\mathsf{EG}\varphi \end{array}$$

$$\text{(¬EF)} \quad \begin{array}{c} \neg\mathsf{EF}\varphi \\ \downarrow \\ \neg\varphi, \neg\mathsf{EXEF}\varphi \end{array} \qquad \text{(EF)} \quad \begin{array}{c} \mathsf{EF}\varphi \\ \swarrow \qquad \searrow \\ \varphi \qquad \mathsf{EXEF}\varphi \end{array}$$

$$\text{(¬EU)} \quad \begin{array}{c} \neg\mathsf{E}(\varphi\mathsf{U}\psi) \\ \downarrow \\ \neg\psi, \neg\varphi \vee \neg\mathsf{EXE}(\varphi\mathsf{U}\psi) \end{array} \qquad \text{(EU)} \quad \begin{array}{c} \mathsf{E}(\varphi\mathsf{U}\psi) \\ \swarrow \qquad \searrow \\ \psi \qquad \varphi \wedge \mathsf{EXE}(\varphi\mathsf{U}\psi) \end{array}$$

$$\text{(¬AU)} \quad \begin{array}{c} \neg\mathsf{A}(\varphi\mathsf{U}\psi) \\ \downarrow \\ \neg\psi, \neg\varphi \vee \neg\mathsf{AXA}(\varphi\mathsf{U}\psi) \end{array} \qquad \text{(AU)} \quad \begin{array}{c} \mathsf{A}(\varphi\mathsf{U}\psi) \\ \swarrow \qquad \searrow \\ \psi \qquad \varphi \wedge \mathsf{AXA}(\varphi\mathsf{U}\psi) \end{array}$$

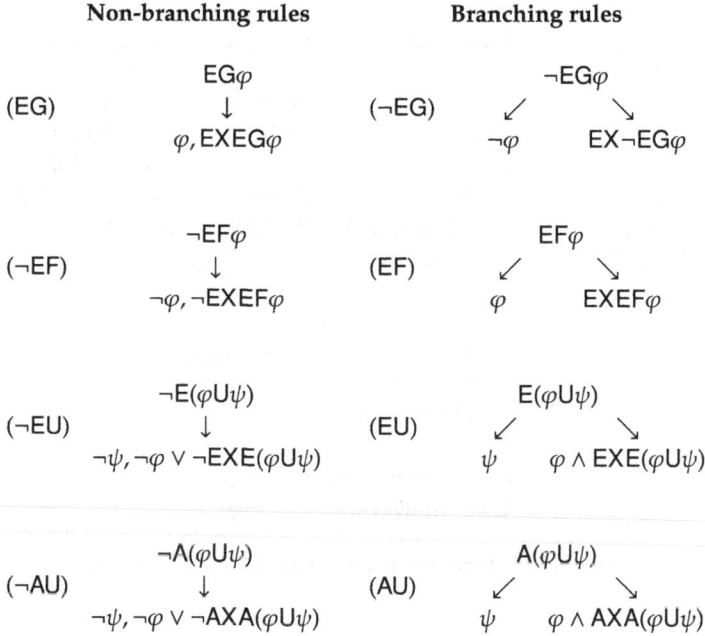

Figure 13.11 Local tableau rules for the temporal operators of CTL.

Every further example related to these running examples is indicated in the label at the beginning.

Example 13.3.3 (Extended closure for η_1, Γ_2 and η_3).

1. In order to reduce the number of formulae in the extended closure and in the initial states of the tableau, we replace the input formula η_1 by the set of its conjuncts:

$$\Gamma_1 := \{p, \neg\mathsf{AX}q, \mathsf{AX}(\neg q \rightarrow p), \mathsf{EF}(\neg p \wedge \neg q)\}.$$

   The extended closure of Γ_1 is provided as follows (assuming the optimised rules for $\rightarrow$, even though $\rightarrow$ is an abbreviation):

$$ecl(\Gamma_1) = \{p, \neg\mathsf{AX}q, \neg q, \mathsf{AX}(\neg q \rightarrow p), \neg q \rightarrow p, q,$$
$$\mathsf{EF}(\neg p \wedge \neg q), \neg p \wedge \neg q, \neg p, \mathsf{EXEF}(\neg p \wedge \neg q)\}.$$

   Hereafter, throughout this example we denote $\varphi := \mathsf{EF}(\neg p \wedge \neg q)$. It is easy to verify that Γ_1 has only one full expansion: $\Delta_1 = \Gamma_1 \cup \{\mathsf{EX}\varphi\}$.

2. Throughout this example we will use the following abbreviations:

$$\varphi := \mathsf{EF}\neg p; \ \psi := \mathsf{A}(p\mathsf{U}q); \ \chi := \mathsf{EG}\neg q.$$

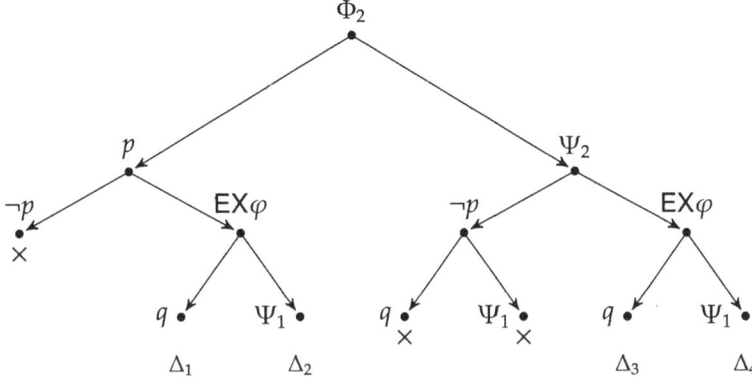

Figure 13.12 Compactified local tableau computing the full expansions of the set Γ_2.

The extended closure of Γ_2 is then given as follows:

$$ecl(\Gamma_2) = \Gamma_2 \cup \{\neg p, \mathsf{EX}\varphi, \ q, p \wedge \mathsf{AX}\psi, p, \mathsf{AX}\psi, \ \chi, \neg q, \mathsf{EX}\chi\}.$$

Some more notation: $\Psi_1 := \{p \wedge \mathsf{AX}\psi, p, \mathsf{AX}\psi\}$ and $\Psi_2 := \{\chi, \mathsf{EX}\chi, \neg q\}$. The procedure FULLEXPANSION computes the following full expansions of Γ_2, which can be seen from the sketch (with nonbranching steps compressed in singe nodes) of the execution of the local tableau with input set Γ_2 in Figure 13.12:

- $\Delta_1 = \Gamma_2 \cup \{\mathsf{EX}\varphi, p, q\}$; $\Delta_2 = \Gamma_2 \cup \Psi_1 \cup \{\mathsf{EX}\varphi, p\}$.
- $\Delta_3 = \Gamma_2 \cup \Psi_2 \cup \{\mathsf{EX}\varphi, q\}$; $\Delta_4 = \Gamma_2 \cup \Psi_1 \cup \Psi_2 \cup \{\mathsf{EX}\varphi\}$.

3. Throughout this example we will use the following abbreviations:

$$\varphi := \mathsf{A}(p\mathsf{U}\mathsf{EX}\neg q), \ \ \psi := \mathsf{EGAX}q, \ \ \chi := \mathsf{E}((\mathsf{AX}q)\mathsf{U}(\neg p \wedge \mathsf{AX}q)).$$

Thus, $\eta_3 = \varphi \wedge (\psi \vee \chi)$. Let us put $\Gamma := \{\eta_3, \varphi, \psi \vee \chi\}$. Now consider the extended closures

- $ecl(\varphi) = \{\varphi, \mathsf{EX}\neg q, \neg q, p \wedge \mathsf{AX}\varphi, p, \mathsf{AX}\varphi\}$,
- $ecl(\psi) = \{\psi, \mathsf{AX}q, q, \mathsf{EX}\psi\}$,
- $ecl(\chi) = \{\chi, \neg p \wedge \mathsf{AX}q, \neg p, \mathsf{AX}q, q, \mathsf{AX}q \wedge \mathsf{EX}\chi, \mathsf{EX}\chi\}$.

The extended closure of η_3 is

$$ecl(\eta_3) = \{\eta_3, \varphi, \psi \vee \chi, \psi, \chi\} \cup ecl(\varphi) \cup ecl(\psi) \cup ecl(\chi)$$

which is equal to

$$\Gamma \cup \{\psi, \chi\} \cup \{\mathsf{EX}\neg q, \neg q, p \wedge \mathsf{AX}\varphi, p, \mathsf{AX}\varphi, \ \mathsf{AX}q, q, \mathsf{EX}\psi, \neg p \wedge \mathsf{AX}q,$$
$$\neg p, \mathsf{AX}q \wedge \mathsf{EX}\chi, \mathsf{EX}\chi\}.$$

Some more notations:

- $\Gamma_1 = \{\neg p \wedge \mathsf{AX}q, \neg p, \mathsf{AX}q\}$; $\Gamma_2 = \{\mathsf{AX}q \wedge \mathsf{EX}\chi, \mathsf{AX}q, \mathsf{EX}\chi\}$.
- $\Gamma_3 = \{\mathsf{AX}q \wedge \mathsf{EX}\psi, \mathsf{AX}q, \mathsf{EX}\psi\}$; $\Gamma_4 = \{p \wedge \mathsf{AX}\varphi, p, \mathsf{AX}\varphi\}$.

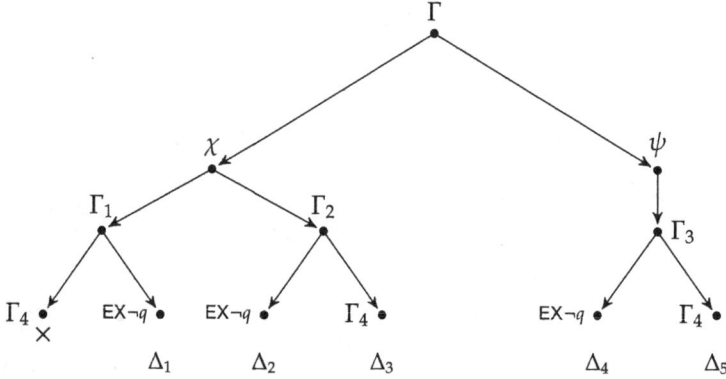

Figure 13.13 Compactified local tableau computing the full expansions of η_3.

The procedure FULLEXPANSION computes the following full expansions of η_3, which can be seen from the sketch (with nonbranching steps compressed in singe nodes) of the execution of the local tableau with input η_3 in Figure 13.13:

- $\Delta_1 = \Gamma \cup \Gamma_1 \cup \{\chi, \mathsf{EX}\neg q\}$; $\Delta_2 = \Gamma \cup \Gamma_2 \cup \{\chi, \mathsf{EX}\neg q\}$.
- $\Delta_3 = \Gamma \cup \Gamma_2 \cup \Gamma_4 \cup \{\chi\}$; $\Delta_4 = \Gamma \cup \Gamma_3 \cup \{\psi, \mathsf{EX}\neg q\}$.
- $\Delta_5 = \Gamma \cup \Gamma_3 \cup \Gamma_4 \cup \{\psi\}$.

13.3.2 Hintikka Structures

The definition and main properties of a Hintikka structure for CTL naturally extend those for BML and LTL in Sections 13.1.4 and 13.2.2.

Definition 13.3.4. Given a closed set of formulae Γ, a **Hintikka structure** (HS) for Γ is a tuple $\mathcal{H} = (S, R, H)$ such that (S, R) is a (total) transition system, and $H : S \to \mathcal{P}(\Gamma)$ is a labelling of the states in S with sets of formulae from Γ satisfying the following conditions for every $s \in S$:

(HS1) $H(s)$ is fully expanded.

(HS2) If $\varphi \in H(s)$ is an existential successor formula, then $scomp(\varphi) \in H(s')$ for some s' such that sRs'.

(HS3) If $\varphi \in H(s)$ is a universal successor formula, then $scomp(\varphi) \in H(s')$ for every s' such that sRs'.

(HS4) If $\mathsf{EF}\varphi \in H(s)$, then $\varphi \in H(s')$ for some s' such that sR^*s'.

(HS5) If $\mathsf{E}(\varphi\mathsf{U}\psi) \in H(s)$, then $\psi \in H(s')$ for some s' such that there is an R-path $s_0, s_1, \ldots s_n = s'$ where $s_0 = s$ and $\varphi \in H(s_i)$ for all $i = 0, \ldots, n-1$.

(HS6) If $\neg\mathsf{EG}\varphi \in H(s)$, then for every R-path $s_0, s_1, \ldots$ such that $s_0 = s$ there is some $n \in \mathbb{N}$ such that $\neg\varphi \in H(s_n)$.

(HS7) If $\mathsf{A}(\varphi\mathsf{U}\psi) \in H(s)$, then for every R-path $s_0, s_1, \ldots$ such that $s_0 = s$ there is some $n \in \mathbb{N}$ such that $\psi \in H(s_n)$ and $\varphi \in H(s_i)$ for all $i = 0, \ldots, n-1$. $\qquad\nabla$

Hintikka structures for TLR are obtained from the preceding definition by restricting the language to TLR and removing the clauses (HS5)–(HS7).

Lemma 13.3.5. In every Hintikka structure (S, R, H):

(HS8) If $\mathsf{EG}\varphi \in H(s)$, then $\varphi \in H(s_i)$ for every state s_i on some R-path $s_0, s_1, \ldots$ such that $s_0 = s$.

(HS9) If $\neg \mathsf{EF}\varphi \in H(s)$, then $\neg\varphi \in H(s_i)$ for every state s_i on every R-path $s_0, s_1, \ldots$ such that $s_0 = s$.

(HS10) If $\mathsf{E}(\varphi \mathsf{U} \psi) \in H(s)$ then $\psi \in H(s)$ or ($\varphi \in H(s)$ and $\mathsf{E}(\varphi \mathsf{U} \psi) \in H(s')$ for some s' such that sRs').

(HS11) If $\mathsf{A}(\varphi \mathsf{U} \psi) \in H(s)$ then $\psi \in H(s)$ or ($\varphi \in H(s)$ and $\mathsf{A}(\varphi \mathsf{U} \psi) \in H(s')$ for every s' such that sRs').

(HS12) If $\neg \mathsf{A}(\varphi \mathsf{U} \psi) \in H(s)$, then $\neg\psi \in H(s)$ and ($\neg\varphi \in H(s)$ or $\neg \mathsf{A}(\varphi \mathsf{U} \psi) \in H(s')$ for some s' such that sRs').

(HS13) If $\neg \mathsf{A}(\varphi \mathsf{U} \psi) \in H(s)$, then: there is an R-path $s_0, s_1, \ldots$, such that $s_0 = s$ and $\neg\psi \in H(s_i)$ for every $i \in \mathbb{N}$ or there exists an $i \in \mathbb{N}$ such that $\neg\varphi \in H(s_i)$ and $\neg\psi \in H(s_j)$ for every $j \in \mathbb{N}$ such that $0 \leq j \leq i$.

(HS14) If $\neg \mathsf{E}(\varphi \mathsf{U} \psi) \in H(s)$, then $\neg\psi \in H(s)$ and ($\neg\varphi \in H(s)$ or $\neg \mathsf{E}(\varphi \mathsf{U} \psi) \in H(s')$ for every s' such that sRs').

(HS15) If $\neg \mathsf{E}(\varphi \mathsf{U} \psi) \in H(s)$, then for every R-path $\sigma = s_0, s_1, \ldots$ with $s_0 = s$: $\neg\psi \in H(s_i)$ for every $i \in \mathbb{N}$ or there exists an $i \in \mathbb{N}$ such that $\neg\varphi \in H(s_i)$ and $\neg\psi \in H(s_j)$ for every $j \in \mathbb{N}$ such that $0 \leq j \leq i$. ∎

Proof. Claims (HS8)–(HS12) and (HS14) are quite straightforward, using the full expandedness (property (HS1)) of all states. The proofs of Claims (HS13) and (HS15) are very similar to the proof of the last claim of Proposition 13.2.6. □

Definition 13.3.6. A formula $\eta \in$ CTL is **satisfiable** in a Hintikka structure $\mathcal{H}$ for some closed set of formulae Γ containing η, with a labelling function H, if $\eta \in H(s)$ for some state s in $\mathcal{H}$; a set of CTL-formulae $\Delta \subseteq \Gamma$ is **satisfiable** in $\mathcal{H}$ if $\Delta \subseteq H(s)$ for some state s in $\mathcal{H}$. ▽

Lemma 13.3.7. For any set of CTL formulae Γ and for every total ITS $\mathcal{T} = (S, R, L)$ the structure $\mathcal{H}(\mathcal{T}) = (S, R, H)$, where $H(s) = \{\psi \in \Gamma \mid \mathcal{T}, s \models \psi\}$ for every $s \in S$, is a Hintikka structure for Γ. ∎

The proof is by a straightforward verification of (HS1)–(HS7) and is left as an exercise.

Theorem 13.3.8. A CTL formula η is satisfiable iff it is satisfiable in a Hintikka structure for $ecl(\eta)$. ∎

Proof. Analogous to the proof of Theorem 13.1.17. One direction is immediate by Lemma 13.3.7 for $\Gamma = ecl(\eta)$. For the converse, suppose $\eta \in H(s_0)$ for some state s_0 in some Hintikka structure $\mathcal{H} = (S, R, H)$. We define the ITS $\mathcal{T} = (S, R, L)$ where L is a state description in S defined as follows: $L(s) := \mathrm{PROP} \cap H(s)$.

We now show by a routine induction on $\varphi \in \mathrm{CTL}$ that for every $s \in S$, if $\varphi \in H(s)$ then $\mathcal{T}, s \models \varphi$. The proofs for all cases referring to the connectives in BML are as in the proof of Theorem 13.1.17. The remaining cases are:

- For $\varphi = \mathsf{EF}\psi$, $\varphi = \mathsf{E}(\psi\mathsf{U}\chi)$ and $\varphi = \mathsf{A}(\psi\mathsf{U}\chi)$ the claim follows respectively from clauses (HS4), (HS5) and (HS7) of Definition 13.3.4, and the inductive hypothesis.
- For $\varphi = \mathsf{EG}\psi$ the claim follows from property (HS8) in Lemma 13.3.5 and the inductive hypothesis.
- For $\varphi = \neg\psi$, the new cases in the nested induction on ψ are: $\psi = \mathsf{EG}\chi$, $\psi = \mathsf{EF}\chi$, $\psi = \mathsf{E}(\chi\mathsf{U}\chi)$ and $\psi = \mathsf{A}(\chi\mathsf{U}\chi)$. For each of these the claim follows from the inductive hypothesis and respectively from clause (HS6), and properties (HS9), (HS13) and (HS15) in Lemma 13.3.5.   □

Corollary 13.3.9 A finite set of CTL-formulae Γ is satisfiable iff it is satisfiable in a Hintikka structure for $ecl(\Gamma)$.   ■

13.3.3 Constructing Tableaux

The Pretableau Construction Phase

Given an input formula $\eta \in \mathrm{CTL}$ we are going to build a tableau for testing the satisfiability of η, following the construction outlined for BML in Section 13.1.5.

The pretableau construction phase is essentially the same, *mutatis mutandis*, for all logics considered here. It starts with an *initial prestate* containing the input formula $\{\eta\}$ or a set of input formulae Γ, and employs applications of two construction rules: PrExp, producing all full expansions of a given prestate, and Next, producing all successor prestates of a given state.

Rule PRExp^{CTL}: **Adding Offspring States of a Prestate** Given a prestate Γ to which the rule has not yet been applied, do the following:

1. Compute the family $\mathrm{FE}(\Gamma) = \{\Delta_1, \ldots \Delta_n\}$ of full expansions of Γ and add these as (labels of) new states in the pretableau, called *offspring states of* Γ.
2. For each newly introduced state Δ, create an edge $\Gamma \dashrightarrow \Delta$.
3. If, however, the pretableau already contains a state with label Δ then do not create a new state with that label, but extend an arrow $\Gamma \dashrightarrow \Delta$ to that state.

We denote the (finite) set $\{\Delta \mid \Gamma \dashrightarrow \Delta\}$ of offspring states of Γ by states(Γ).

The rule PrExp is the same for all tableau systems developed here. The only difference is in the specific set replacement operations employed by the procedure FULLEXPANSION, which correspond to the specific temporal operators of the given logic.

As before, we denote for any set of CTL formulae Γ:

$$X(\Gamma) := \{\psi \mid \mathsf{AX}\psi \in \Gamma\} \cup \{\neg\psi \mid \neg\mathsf{EX}\psi \in \Gamma\}.$$

Rule NEXT^{CTL}: **Adding Successor Prestates of a State** Given a state with label Δ, to which the rule has not yet been applied, for each successor formula $\varphi \in \Delta$ (i.e. $\varphi = \text{EX}\chi$ or $\varphi = \neg\text{AX}\chi$) do the following:

1. Add a successor prestate Γ of Δ with label $\text{X}(\Delta) \cup \{scomp(\varphi)\}$.
2. For each newly introduced prestate Γ, create an edge $\Delta \xrightarrow{\varphi} \Gamma$.
3. If Δ does not contain any successor formula, add one successor prestate Γ of Δ with label $\text{X}(\Delta)$ and create an edge $\Delta \xrightarrow{\top} \Gamma$. This is needed to ensure that every state has a successor.
4. If, however, the pretableau already contains a prestate Γ' with the label of Γ then do not create a new prestate with that label, but extend an arrow $\Delta \xrightarrow{\varphi} \Gamma'$ to that prestate.

Note that the rule Next is essentially the same for BML (except that adding at least one successor prestate is not required there), TLR and CTL, but it differs for LTL, where only one successor prestate is needed. Hereafter we will freely identify prestates or states with their labels, whenever this will not lead to confusion.

Building the Pretableau

The construction phase of building a pretableau for η begins with creating a single initial prestate $\{\eta\}$, followed by alternating applications of the rules PrExp^{CTL} and Next^{CTL} respectively to the prestates and the states created at a previous stage of the construction. This phase ends when none of these rules can add any new states or prestates to the current graph. The resulting graph is the pretableau $\mathcal{P}^\eta$.

Example 13.3.10 (Pretableaux for η_1, Γ_2 and η_3).

1. Recall that we replaced the input formula η_1 by the equally satisfiable set of its conjuncts:

$$\Gamma_1 := \{p, \neg\text{AX}q, \text{AX}(\neg q \to p), \text{EF}(\neg p \wedge \neg q)\}.$$

Γ_1 has only one full expansion: $\Delta_1 = \Gamma_1 \cup \{\text{EX}\varphi\}$, where $\varphi = \text{EF}(\neg p \wedge \neg q)$. The construction of the pretableau, given in Figure 13.14, goes as follows, where, for the sake of convenience, we add node labels for the states and prestates:
   1. The initial prestate is $P_0 = \Gamma_1$ (formally meaning, P_0 with label Γ_1).
   2. The only full expansion $\Delta_1 = \Gamma_1 \cup \{\text{EX}\varphi\}$ is the label of the only initial state S_0.
   3. S_0 has 2 successor prestates:

$$S_0 \xrightarrow{\neg\text{AX}q} P_{01} = \{\neg q, \neg q \to p\}, \text{ and } S_0 \xrightarrow{\text{EX}\varphi} P_{02} = \{\varphi, \neg q \to p\}.$$

   4. P_{01} has one offspring state $S_{01} = \{\neg q, \neg q \to p, p\}$, which has one successor prestate $S_{01} \xrightarrow{\top} P_{010} = \emptyset$, with the only offspring state $S_{010} = \emptyset$, the only successor prestate of which, along $\xrightarrow{\top}$, is again P_{010}.
   5. P_{02} has 2 offspring states:

$$S_{021} = \{\varphi, \text{EX}\varphi, \neg q \to p, q\} \text{ and } S_{022} = \{\varphi, \text{EX}\varphi, \neg q \to p, p\}.$$

   6. Both S_{021} and S_{022} have the same unique successor prestate along $\xrightarrow{\text{EX}\varphi}$: $P_{021} = \{\varphi\}$.

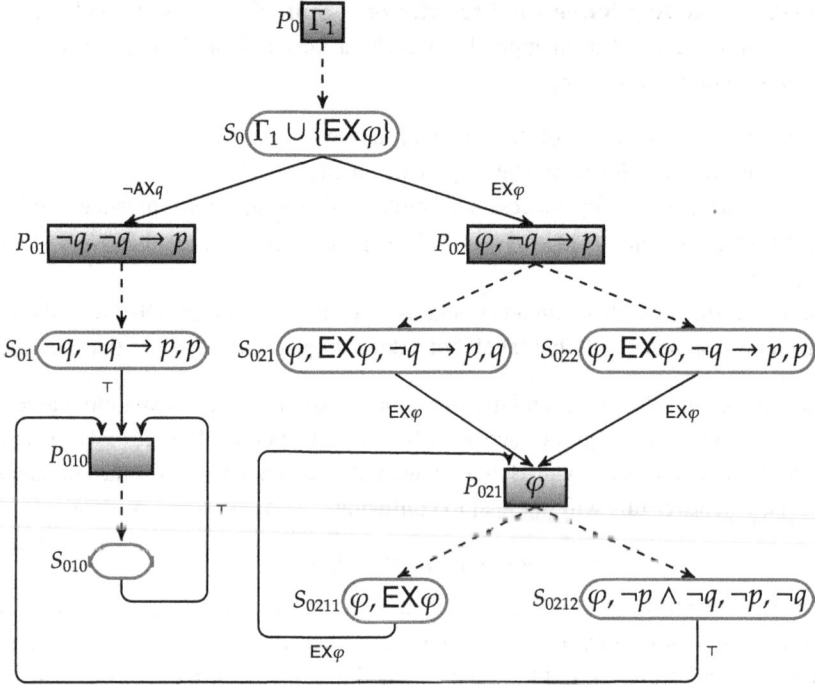

Figure 13.14 The CTL pretableau for η_1.

7. P_{021} has 2 offspring states:

$$S_{0211} = \{\varphi, \mathsf{EX}\varphi\} \text{ and } S_{0212} = \{\varphi, \neg p \wedge \neg q, \neg p, \neg q\}.$$

8. The pretableau now loops from each of these:

$$S_{0211} \xrightarrow{\mathsf{EX}\varphi} P_{021} \text{ and } S_{0212} \xrightarrow{\top} P_{010}.$$

2. Recall the following abbreviations related to Γ_2:
   - $\varphi := \mathsf{EF}\neg p;\ \psi := \mathsf{A}(p\mathsf{U}q);\ \chi := \mathsf{EG}\neg q.$
   - $\Psi_1 = \{p \wedge \mathsf{AX}\psi, p, \mathsf{AX}\psi\};\ \Psi_2 = \{\chi, \mathsf{EX}\chi, \neg q\}.$

   The full expansions of Γ_2, as computed in Figure 13.12:
   - $\Delta_1 = \Gamma_2 \cup \{\mathsf{EX}\varphi, p, q\};\ \Delta_2 = \Gamma_2 \cup \Psi_1 \cup \{\mathsf{EX}\varphi, p\}.$
   - $\Delta_3 = \Gamma_2 \cup \Psi_2 \cup \{\mathsf{EX}\varphi, q\};\ \Delta_4 = \Gamma_2 \cup \Psi_1 \cup \Psi_2 \cup \{\mathsf{EX}\varphi\}.$
   - $\Delta_5 = \Psi_1 \cup \Psi_2 \cup \{\psi, \chi\}.$

   The pretableau is given in Figure 13.15. We leave the verification of its construction as an exercise to the reader.

3. Recall the following abbreviations related to η_3.
   - $\varphi := \mathsf{A}(p\mathsf{U}\mathsf{EX}\neg q),\ \psi := \mathsf{EGAX}q,\ \chi := \mathsf{E}((\mathsf{AX}q)\mathsf{U}(\neg p \wedge \mathsf{AX}q)).$
   - $\Gamma = \{\eta_3, \varphi, \psi \vee \chi\}.$
   - $\Gamma_1 = \{\neg p \wedge \mathsf{AX}q, \neg p, \mathsf{AX}q\}.$

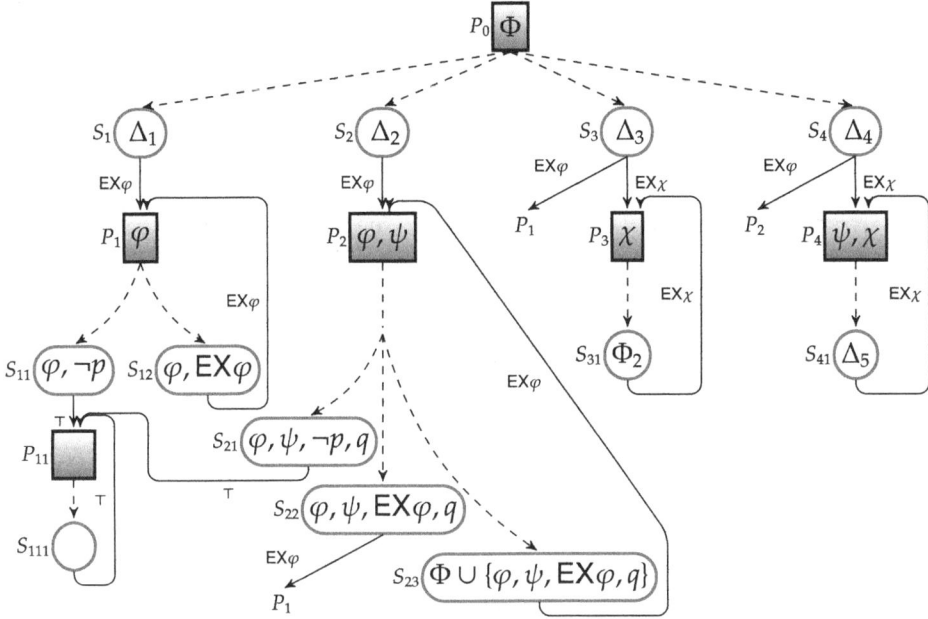

Figure 13.15 The CTL pretableau for Γ_2.

- $\Gamma_2 = \{\mathsf{AX}q \wedge \mathsf{EX}\chi, \mathsf{AX}q, \mathsf{EX}\chi\}$.
- $\Gamma_3 = \{\mathsf{AX}q \wedge \mathsf{EX}\psi, \mathsf{AX}q, \mathsf{EX}\psi\}$.
- $\Gamma_4 = \{p \wedge \mathsf{AX}\varphi, p, \mathsf{AX}\varphi\}$.

  The full expansions of η_3, as computed in Figure 13.13:
- $\Delta_1 = \Gamma \cup \Gamma_1 \cup \{\chi, \mathsf{EX}\neg q\}; \Delta_2 = \Gamma \cup \Gamma_2 \cup \{\chi, \mathsf{EX}\neg q\}$.
- $\Delta_3 = \Gamma \cup \Gamma_2 \cup \Gamma_4 \cup \{\chi\}; \Delta_4 = \Gamma \cup \Gamma_3 \cup \{\psi, \mathsf{EX}\neg q\}$.
- $\Delta_5 = \Gamma \cup \Gamma_3 \cup \Gamma_4 \cup \{\psi\}$.

The pretableau is given in Figure 13.16. We leave the verification of its construction as an exercise to the reader.

The Prestate Elimination Phase and Initial Tableau

In this phase, all prestates are removed from $\mathcal{P}^\eta$, together with their incoming and outgoing arrows, by applying the following **prestate elimination rule**:

Rule PRESTATEELIM^{CTL}: For every prestate Γ in $\mathcal{P}^\eta$, do the following:

1. Remove Γ from $\mathcal{P}^\eta$;
2. If there is a state Δ in $\mathcal{P}^\eta$ with $\Delta \xrightarrow{X} \Gamma$, then for every state $\Delta' \in \mathsf{states}(\Gamma)$, create an edge $\Delta \xrightarrow{X} \Delta'$.

The resulting graph is called the **initial tableau** for η, denoted $\mathcal{T}_0^\eta$. The offspring states of the input prestate $\{\eta\}$ are called **input states** of $\mathcal{T}_0^\eta$. The prestate elimination phase ends with the *initial tableau* $\mathcal{T}_0^\eta$.

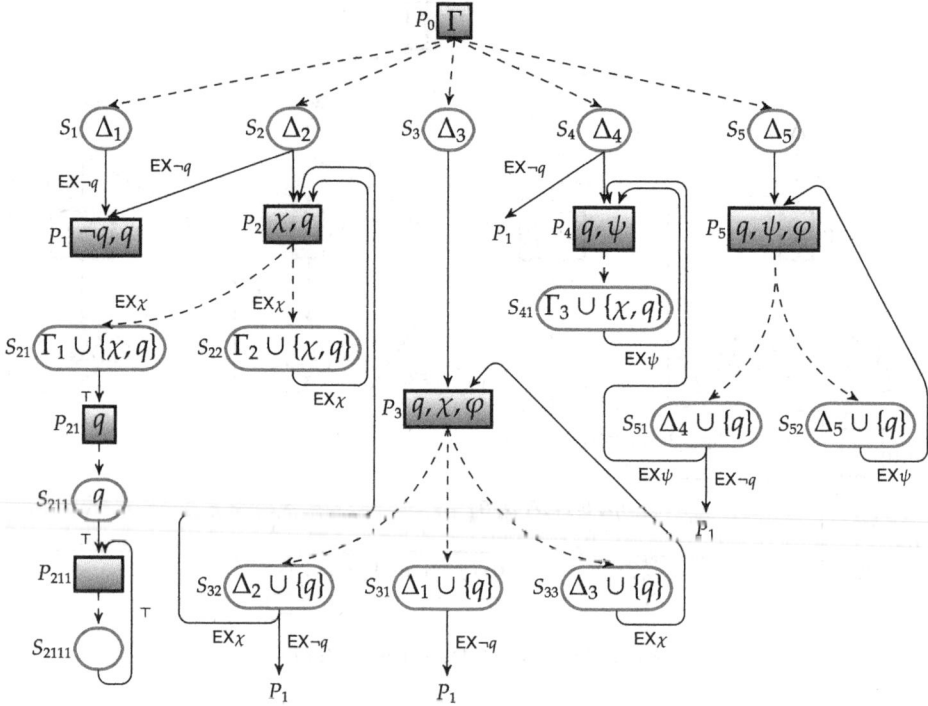

Figure 13.16 The CTL pretableau for η_3.

Example 13.3.11 (Initial tableaux for η_1, Γ_2 and η_3).

1. Recall the following notation related to η_1.
   $\Gamma_1 := \{p, \neg\mathsf{AX}q, \mathsf{AX}(\neg q \to p), \mathsf{EF}(\neg p \wedge \neg q)\}$; $\Delta_1 = \Gamma_1 \cup \{\mathsf{EX}\varphi\}$, where
   $\varphi = \mathsf{EF}(\neg p \wedge \neg q)$. The initial tableau is given in Figure 13.17.
2. Recall the following notations related to Γ_2:
   - $\varphi := \mathsf{EF}\neg p$; $\psi := \mathsf{A}(p\mathsf{U}q)$; $\chi := \mathsf{EG}\neg q$.
   - $\Psi_1 = \{p \wedge \mathsf{AX}\psi, p, \mathsf{AX}\psi\}$.
   - $\Psi_2 = \{\chi, \mathsf{EX}\chi, \neg q\}$.
   - $\Delta_1 = \Gamma_2 \cup \{\mathsf{EX}\varphi, p, q\}$.
   - $\Delta_2 = \Gamma_2 \cup \Psi_1 \cup \{\mathsf{EX}\varphi, p\}$.
   - $\Delta_3 = \Gamma_2 \cup \Psi_2 \cup \{\mathsf{EX}\varphi, q\}$.
   - $\Delta_4 = \Gamma_2 \cup \Psi_1 \cup \Psi_2 \cup \{\mathsf{EX}\varphi\}$.
   - $\Delta_5 = \Psi_1 \cup \Psi_2 \cup \{\psi, \chi\}$.
   The initial tableau is given in Figure 13.18.
3. Recall the following notations related to η_3.
   - $\varphi := \mathsf{A}(p\mathsf{U}\mathsf{EX}\neg q)$, $\psi := \mathsf{EG}\mathsf{AX}q$, $\chi := \mathsf{E}((\mathsf{AX}q)\mathsf{U}(\neg p \wedge \mathsf{AX}q))$.
   - $\Gamma = \{\eta_3, \varphi, \psi \vee \chi\}$.
   - $\Gamma_1 = \{\neg p \wedge \mathsf{AX}q, \neg p, \mathsf{AX}q\}$.

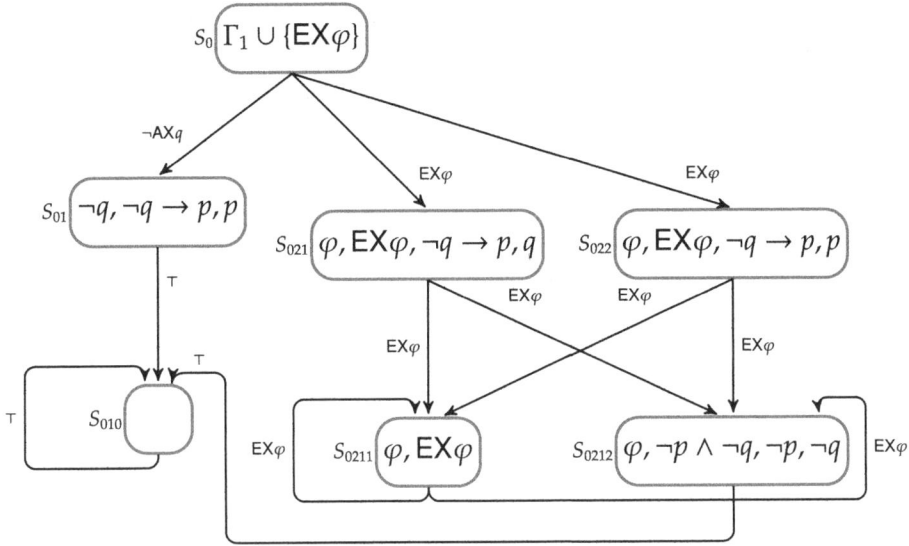

Figure 13.17 The CTL initial tableau for η_1.

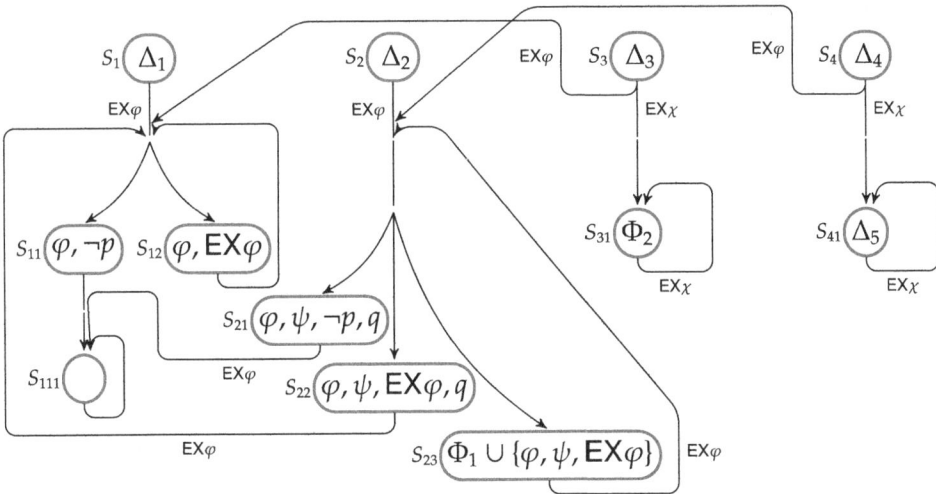

Figure 13.18 The CTL initial tableau for Γ_2.

- $\Gamma_2 = \{\mathsf{AX}q \wedge \mathsf{EX}\chi, \mathsf{AX}q, \mathsf{EX}\chi\}$.
- $\Gamma_3 = \{\mathsf{AX}q \wedge \mathsf{EX}\psi, \mathsf{AX}q, \mathsf{EX}\psi\}$.
- $\Gamma_4 = \{p \wedge \mathsf{AX}\varphi, p, \mathsf{AX}\varphi\}$.
- $\Delta_1 = \Gamma \cup \Gamma_1 \cup \{\chi, \mathsf{EX}\neg q\}$.
- $\Delta_2 = \Gamma \cup \Gamma_2 \cup \{\chi, \mathsf{EX}\neg q\}$.
- $\Delta_3 = \Gamma \cup \Gamma_2 \cup \Gamma_4 \cup \{\chi\}$.

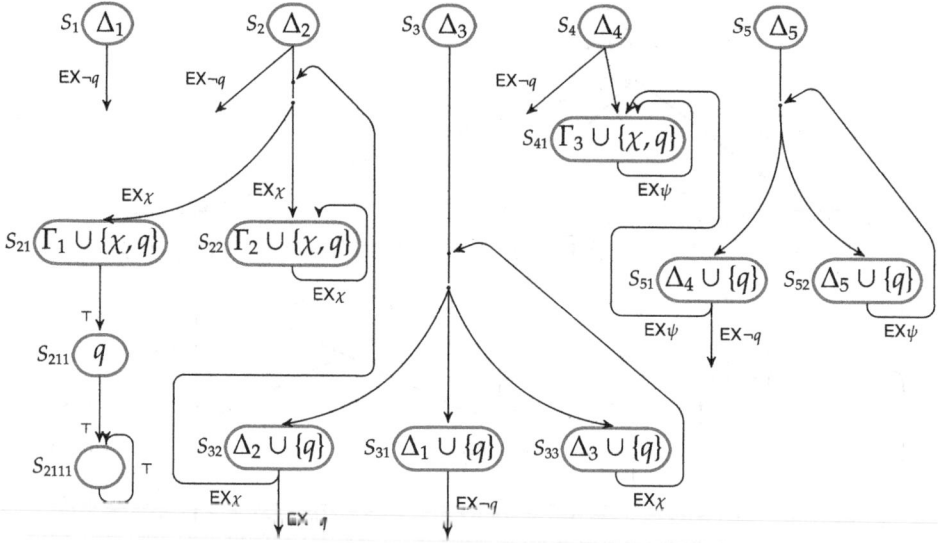

Figure 13.19 The CTL initial tableau for η_3.

- $\Delta_4 = \Gamma \cup \Gamma_3 \cup \{\psi, \text{EX}\neg q\}$.
- $\Delta_5 = \Gamma \cup \Gamma_3 \cup \Gamma_4 \cup \{\psi\}$.

The initial tableau is given in Figure 13.19.

The State Elimination Phase and Final Tableaux

The purpose of the state elimination phase is to remove all 'bad' states from the tableau, the labels of which are not satisfiable in any Hintikka structure, and hence in any ITS.

The only possible reason for the existence of such a 'bad' state in the case of BML was that it may lack a successor state needed to satisfy some successor formula in its label. Such states can arise because some prestates may have no full expansions, and hence may yield no offspring states. Once such a bad state is removed, their predecessor states may be left without a necessary successor, so they must be removed, too, etc., until stabilisation.

The same problem can occur in the cases of TLR and CTL. Formally, the elimination of states lacking all necessary successors is done by applying the following rule.

Rule STATEELIM1^{CTL}: If a state Γ contains in its label a formula $\text{EX}\psi$ and there are no outgoing arcs marked with $\text{EX}\psi$ from Γ to successor states in the current tableau, then remove that state (together with all incoming and outgoing arcs) from the tableau.

Another reason for a state to turn out 'bad' (i.e. for its label not to be satisfiable in any Hintikka structure), which also appeared in the tableau for LTL, is that its label may contain an eventuality formula which is not 'realised' in the tableau.

Since the logic TLR only contains existential eventualities, this problem for it is simpler, and is treated essentially like in the case of LTL. In the case of CTL, where there are universal eventualities, too, the problem is more complicated.

Both cases are handled by additional state elimination rules, corresponding to each type of eventualities. Before we state them, we have to precisely define the respective notions of realisation of eventualities.

Recall that a path in the current tableau (for TLR or CTL) is a sequence of successor states.

Definition 13.3.12 (Realisation of existential eventualities).

1. An eventuality $\chi = \mathsf{EF}\psi$ is **realised** at the state Δ in $\mathcal{T}_n^{\eta}$ if there exists a finite path $\Delta_0, \Delta_1, \ldots, \Delta_m$ in $\mathcal{T}_n^{\eta}$ such that $\Delta_0 = \Delta$, $\chi, \psi \in \Delta_m$ and $\chi \in \Delta_i$ for every $i = 0, \ldots, m - 1$.
2. An eventuality $\chi = \mathsf{E}(\varphi \mathsf{U} \psi)$ is **realised** at the state Δ in $\mathcal{T}_n^{\eta}$ if there exists a finite path $\Delta_0, \Delta_1, \ldots, \Delta_m$, where $\Delta_0 = \Delta$ and $m \geq 0$, in $\mathcal{T}_n^{\eta}$, such that $\chi, \psi \in \Delta_m$ and $\chi, \varphi \in \Delta_i$ for every $i = 0, \ldots, m - 1$.

In either case, we then say that χ is realised on the path $\Delta_0, \Delta_1, \ldots, \Delta_m$ and call any such path a **witness of the realisation of the eventuality** χ **in** Δ. If $\psi \in \Delta$ we say that χ is **immediately realised** at the state Δ (by the singleton path Δ). $\qquad \triangledown$

As in the case of LTL, testing for realisation of existential eventualities is a simple graph reachability problem, discussed in Chapter 3.

The realisation of universal eventualities is more subtle. In order to realise a universal eventuality $\mathsf{A}(\varphi \mathsf{U} \psi)$ at a state Δ in $\mathcal{T}_n^{\eta}$, it would be too much to insist that *every path* starting from Δ in $\mathsf{A}(\varphi \mathsf{U} \psi)$ must reach a ψ-state while passing through φ-states, because not all such paths are needed in a Hintikka structure that can be extracted from that tableau, but only those that belong to some '*branch*' of the tableau, regarded as a 'search tree'.

For instance, consider the formula $(\mathsf{EG}p \vee \mathsf{EG}\neg p) \wedge (\mathsf{AF}p \vee \mathsf{AF}\neg p)$. It is easily seen to be satisfiable, but a naive testing for realisation of universal eventualities in the tableau for it will produce a closed tableau.

Let us now define precisely the notion of a branch in the tableau for CTL. This refers to *logical* branching. These branches are not linear paths, but subgraphs, in the tableaux.

- A **branch in the pretableau** is a subgraph Br containing the input prestate, *one* offspring state of every prestate in Br and *all* successor prestates of every state in Br.
- A **branch in the initial tableau** is a subgraph consisting of all states obtained from some branch in the pretableau after the elimination of prestates.
- A **branch in the current tableau** is a subgraph consisting of the currently remaining states from some branch in the initial tableau.

Thus, for testing for realisation of a universal eventuality that belongs to a state Δ in $\mathcal{T}_n^{\eta}$ it suffices to select *one branch* in $\mathcal{T}_n^{\eta}$ and then test *all paths in that branch* that pass through Δ for realising that eventuality. More precisely:

Definition 13.3.13 (Realisation of universal eventualities). Consider a universal eventuality $\chi = A(\varphi U\psi) \in \Delta$ (respectively, $\chi = \neg EG\varphi \in \Delta$).

A branch Br in $\mathcal{T}_n^\eta$ is said to **realise** χ **at** Δ if every path in Br starting from Δ has a finite prefix $\Delta_0, \Delta_1, \ldots, \Delta_m$ such that $\Delta_0 = \Delta$ and consisting of states containing χ and realising that eventuality, i.e. $\chi, \psi \in \Delta_m$ and $\chi, \varphi \in \Delta_i$ for every $i = 0, \ldots, m-1$ (respectively, $\chi, \neg\varphi \in \Delta_m$ and $\chi \in \Delta_i$ for every $i = 0, \ldots, m-1$ for the case of $\chi = \neg EG\varphi$).

The subgraph of such a branch Br consisting of all states on the shortest finite prefixes realising χ along all paths in Br starting from Δ is called a **witness of the realisation of the eventuality** χ **at** Δ (on the branch Br).

We say that the universal eventuality χ is **realised at** Δ **in** $\mathcal{T}_n^\eta$ if there is at least one branch in $\mathcal{T}_n^\eta$ realising χ at Δ. ∇

Alternatively, realisation of universal eventualities can be defined by simultaneous recursion for all states of the tableau:

Definition 13.3.14 (Recursive realisation).

1. Let $\chi = A(\varphi U\psi) \in ecl(\eta)$. Then for any state $\Delta \in \mathcal{T}_n^\eta$, χ **is realised at** Δ if:
   (i) $\psi \in \Delta$, or
   (ii) $\varphi \in \Delta$ and, for every existential successor formula $\psi' \in \Delta$, there is a state $\Delta' \in \mathcal{T}_n^\eta$ such that $\Delta \xrightarrow{\psi'} \Delta'$ and χ is realised at Δ'.
2. Let $\chi = \neg EG\psi \in ecl(\eta)$. Then for any state $\Delta \in \mathcal{T}_n^\eta$, χ **is realised at** Δ if:
   (i) $\neg\psi \in \Delta$, or
   (ii) for every existential successor formula $\psi' \in \Delta$, there is a state $\Delta' \in \mathcal{T}_n^\eta$ such that $\Delta \xrightarrow{\psi'} \Delta'$ and χ is realised at Δ'. ∇

If $\psi \in \Delta$ in the case of $\chi = A(\varphi U\psi)$, or respectively, $\neg\psi \in \Delta$ in the case of $\chi = \neg EG\psi$, we say that χ is **immediately realised** at the state Δ (by the singleton path Δ).

This definition also yields a nondeterministic recursive procedure for identifying all states in the current tableau that realise a given universal eventuality.

Now we can formulate the second state elimination rule for both TLR and CTL tableaux.

Rule STATEELIM2^{CTL}: If a state $\Delta \in \mathcal{T}_n^\eta$ contains in its label an eventuality that is not realised at Δ in $\mathcal{T}_n^\eta$, then remove that state (together with all incoming and outgoing arcs) from the tableau.

Using the rules STATEELIM1^{CTL} and STATEELIM2^{CTL}, the state elimination phase is carried out in a sequence of stages, starting at stage 0 with the initial tableau $\mathcal{T}_0^\eta$, and eliminating at every stage n at most one state for the current tableau $\mathcal{T}_n^\eta$, by applying one of the state elimination rules, and producing the new current tableau $\mathcal{T}_{n+1}^\eta$. The rules STATEELIM1^{CTL} and STATEELIM2^{CTL} are applied alternately, in any order, which may be determined by a specific strategy. This procedure continues until at some stage no further elimination of states by an application of any of the rules is possible. The resulting graph $\mathcal{T}^\eta$ upon stabilisation of the state elimination phase is the **final tableau**. The final tableau $\mathcal{T}^\eta$ is **open** if it contains a state Δ such that $\eta \in \Delta$, otherwise it is **closed**.

Example 13.3.15 (Final tableaux for η_1, Γ_2 and η_3).

1. Recall the following notations related to η_1.
   - $\Gamma_1 := \{p, \neg \mathsf{AX}q, \mathsf{AX}(\neg q \to p), \mathsf{EF}(\neg p \wedge \neg q)\}$;
   - $\Delta_1 = \Gamma_1 \cup \{\mathsf{EX}\varphi\}$, where $\varphi = \mathsf{EF}(\neg p \wedge \neg q)$.

   Note that every state in the initial tableau has all necessary successors. Besides, the only eventuality in this tableau is φ and it is immediately realised at state S_{0212}, and therefore it is realised at all states where it occurs in the label, viz. S_0, S_{021}, S_{022}, S_{0211}, because S_{0212} is reachable by a required path from each of these states. Thus, the final tableau is the same as the initial tableau, given in Figure 13.17. It is open, because the initial state S_0 contains the input set of formulae. Furthermore, the final tableau itself constitutes a Hintikka structure satisfying Γ_1.

2. Recall the following notations related to Γ_2.
   - $\varphi := \mathsf{EF}\neg p$; $\psi := \mathsf{A}(p\mathsf{U}q)$; $\chi := \mathsf{EG}\neg q$.
   - $\Psi_1 = \{p \wedge \mathsf{AX}\psi, p, \mathsf{AX}\psi\}$.
   - $\Psi_2 = \{\chi, \mathsf{EX}\chi, \neg q\}$.
   - $\Delta_1 = \Gamma_2 \cup \{\mathsf{EX}\varphi, p, q\}$.
   - $\Delta_2 = \Gamma_2 \cup \Psi_1 \cup \{\mathsf{EX}\varphi, p\}$.
   - $\Delta_3 = \Gamma_2 \cup \Psi_2 \cup \{\mathsf{EX}\varphi, q\}$.
   - $\Delta_4 = \Gamma_2 \cup \Psi_1 \cup \Psi_2 \cup \{\mathsf{EX}\varphi\}$.
   - $\Delta_5 = \Psi_1 \cup \Psi_2 \cup \{\psi, \chi\}$.

   Let us now focus on the outcome of the state elimination phase.
   1. The state S_{41} is eliminated because it contains the eventuality χ but does not realise it: the formula $\neg p$ does not become true on the only path leading from S_{41}.
   2. Then the state S_4 is eliminated because it no longer has an $\mathsf{EX}\chi$-successor.
   3. All other states survive the elimination phase. In particular, note that in order to realise the universal eventuality ψ at state S_{23} it suffices to select at least one branch of the tableau leading from that state and realising ψ. Any branch passing from S_{23} to the state S_{21} can be selected as such.

   The final tableau is given in Figure 13.20. We leave it as an exercise to the reader to extract a Hintikka structure satisfying the input set Γ_2 from it, and then extend it to a model for that input set.

3. Recall the following notations related to η_3.
   - $\varphi := \mathsf{A}(p\mathsf{U}\mathsf{EX}\neg q)$, $\psi := \mathsf{EGAX}q$, $\chi := \mathsf{E}((\mathsf{AX}q)\mathsf{U}(\neg p \wedge \mathsf{AX}q))$.
   - $\Gamma = \{\eta_3, \varphi, \psi \vee \chi\}$.
   - $\Gamma_1 = \{\neg p \wedge \mathsf{AX}q, \neg p, \mathsf{AX}q\}$.
   - $\Gamma_2 = \{\mathsf{AX}q \wedge \mathsf{EX}\chi, \mathsf{AX}q, \mathsf{EX}\chi\}$.
   - $\Gamma_3 = \{\mathsf{AX}q \wedge \mathsf{EX}\psi, \mathsf{AX}q, \mathsf{EX}\psi\}$.
   - $\Gamma_4 = \{p \wedge \mathsf{AX}\varphi, p, \mathsf{AX}\varphi\}$.

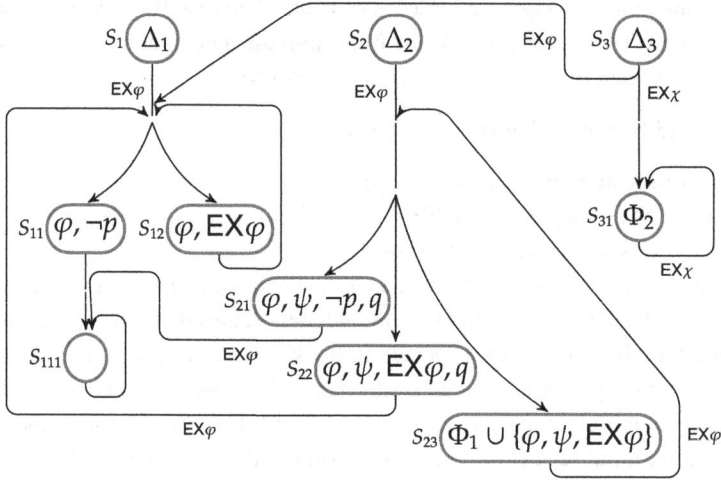

Figure 13.20 The CTL final tableau for Γ_3

- $\Delta_1 = \Gamma \cup \Gamma_1 \cup \{\chi, \mathsf{EX}\neg q\}$.
- $\Delta_2 = \Gamma \cup \Gamma_2 \cup \{\chi, \mathsf{EX}\neg q\}$.
- $\Delta_3 = \Gamma \cup \Gamma_2 \cup \Gamma_4 \cup \{\chi\}$.
- $\Delta_4 = \Gamma \cup \Gamma_3 \cup \{\psi, \mathsf{EX}\neg q\}$.
- $\Delta_5 = \Gamma \cup \Gamma_3 \cup \Gamma_4 \cup \{\psi\}$.

The state elimination phase:

1. First, the states S_1, S_2, S_{31}, S_{32}, S_4 and S_{51} are eliminated by Rule STATEELIM1^{CTL} because they have no successors corresponding to $\mathsf{EX}\neg q$.
2. Then states S_3 and S_{33} are eliminated by Rule STATEELIM2^{CTL} because they contain the existential eventuality χ but do not realise it. The eventuality χ is only immediately realised at states containing $\neg p \wedge \mathsf{AX} q$ in their label.
3. Likewise, the states S_5 and S_{52} are now eliminated by Rule STATEELIM2^{CTL} because they contain the universal eventuality φ but do not realise it on the only branch of the current tableau containing them. The eventuality φ is only immediately realised at states containing $\mathsf{EX}\neg q$ in their label.

We leave it to the reader to complete the elimination phase. At this stage, however, no state containing the input set of formulae Γ is left in the tableau. Therefore, the final tableau is closed. Hence, the input set Γ formula is declared unsatisfiable. Consequently, the input formula η_3 is found unsatisfiable, too.

13.3.4 Termination, Soundness and Completeness

Termination and Soundness

All phases of the tableau constructions for TLR and CTL terminate, for the same reasons as indicated in Section 13.1.6.

Recall, again, that soundness of the tableau procedure means that if the input formula η is satisfiable, then the tableau $\mathcal{T}^\eta$ is open. We will establish the soundness of the tableaux for TLR and CTL by following the same approach as in the previous cases, viz. proving that every state elimination rule is 'sound' in a sense that it never eliminates a state with a satisfiable label. The case of TLR is subsumed by the case of CTL.

Lemma 13.3.16. *Let η be a CTL formula and Γ be a prestate of $\mathcal{P}^\eta$ such that $\mathcal{T}, s \models \Gamma$ for some rooted ITS $(\mathcal{T}, s)$. Then:*

(I) $\mathcal{T}, s \models \Delta$ *for at least one* $\Delta \in \mathsf{states}(\Gamma)$.

(II) *Moreover, if* $\mathsf{EF}\psi, \mathsf{E}(\varphi\mathsf{U}\psi) \in \Gamma$, *or* $\mathsf{A}(\varphi\mathsf{U}\psi) \in \Gamma$ *and* $\mathcal{T}, s \models \psi$, *then* Δ *can be chosen to contain* ψ. *Respectively, if* $\neg\mathsf{EG}\psi \in \Gamma$ *and* $\mathcal{T}, s \models \neg\psi$, *then* Δ *can be chosen to contain* $\neg\psi$. ∎

The proof is obtained as an easy modification of the proof of Lemma 13.2.16.

Lemma 13.3.17. *No satisfiable state* $\Delta \in \mathcal{T}_0^\eta$ *is removed by any application of the rules* STATEELIM1^{CTL} *and* STATEELIM2^{CTL} *during the state elimination phase.* ∎

Proof. We follow the idea from the proofs of Lemma 13.1.24 and 13.2.17: to show that no satisfiable state $\Delta \in \mathcal{T}_0^\eta$ is removed by an application of Rule STATEELIM1^{CTL} or Rule STATEELIM2^{CTL} to $\mathcal{T}_n^\eta$ for any $n \in \mathbb{N}$. For that purpose, again, we prove by induction on n a stronger multiple claim, viz. that for every $n \in \mathbb{N}$, if $\Delta \in \mathcal{T}_n^\eta$ is satisfiable then:

1. For any existential successor formula $\varphi \in \Delta$ there is a satisfiable state $\Theta \in \mathcal{T}_n^\eta$ such that $\Delta \xrightarrow{\varphi} \Theta$ in $\mathcal{T}_n^\eta$.
2. For any existential eventuality $\mathsf{EF}\varphi \in \Delta$ or $\mathsf{E}(\varphi\mathsf{U}\psi) \in \Delta$ there is a finite path of satisfiable states in $\mathcal{T}_n^\eta$ realising that eventuality.
3. For any universal eventuality $\vartheta = \mathsf{A}(\varphi\mathsf{U}\psi) \in \Delta$ (respectively, $\vartheta = \neg\mathsf{EG}\varphi \in \Delta$) there is a branch Br in $\mathcal{T}_n^\eta$ containing a witness of the realisation of that eventuality and consisting of satisfiable states.
4. All satisfiable states in $\mathcal{T}_0^\eta$ are still present in $\mathcal{T}_n^\eta$.

Note that the inductive claim refers simultaneously to all satisfiable states $\Delta \in \mathcal{T}_n^\eta$, all successor formulae $\varphi \in \Delta$ and all existential and universal eventualities in Δ.

Let $n = 0$. Take any satisfiable $\Delta \in \mathcal{T}_0^\eta$ and let $\mathcal{T}, s \models \Delta$ for some rooted ITS $(\mathcal{T}, s)$. Claim 1 is exactly like in the proof of Lemma 13.1.24 for BML.

Now, to prove Claim 2, let us consider the case of an existential eventuality $\mathsf{E}(\varphi\mathsf{U}\psi) \in \Delta$, as the case of $\mathsf{EF}\varphi$ is simpler. The proof of this case is essentially the same as the proof for $\varphi\mathsf{U}\psi$ in Lemma 13.2.17 for LTL, and we leave it as an exercise.

The argument for Claim 3, i.e. the case of universal eventualities is a bit more involved. We will prove that for any satisfiable state Δ and a universal eventuality $\vartheta = \mathsf{A}(\varphi\mathsf{U}\psi) \in \Delta$ (respectively, $\vartheta = \neg\mathsf{EG}\psi \in \Delta$) there is a branch Br in the initial tableau containing a witness of the realisation of that eventuality consisting of satisfiable states.

We will consider the case $\vartheta = \mathsf{A}(\varphi \mathsf{U} \psi)$, the other case being analogous, but simpler. If $\psi \in \Delta$ then ϑ is immediately realised at Δ, and any branch Br that contains the state Δ (there is at least one such branch) can be selected. So, let us assume that $\psi \notin \Delta$, hence $\varphi, \mathsf{AXA}(\varphi \mathsf{U} \psi) \in \Delta$.

Let $\mathcal{T}, s \models \Delta$ for some rooted ITS $(\mathcal{T}, s)$. Then $\mathcal{T}, s \models \varphi$ and $\mathcal{T}, s \models \mathsf{AXA}(\varphi \mathsf{U} \psi)$, so every path in $\mathcal{T}$ starting at s has a finite prefix $s_0, s_1, \ldots, s_m$ such that $s_0 = s$ and ending with a state s_m, for $m > 0$, such that s_m satisfies ψ, and hence ϑ, while all intermediate states $s_0, s_1, \ldots, s_{m-1}$ satisfy φ and ϑ. We will call such a prefix of a path **fulfilling** ϑ, and the subsystem of $\mathcal{T}$ rooted at s and consisting of the states along all ϑ-fulfilling prefixes of paths starting at s – a **witness of the truth of** ϑ **at** s **in** $\mathcal{T}$. Hereafter we fix such a witness and denote it by $W(\mathcal{T}, s, \vartheta)$. Note that $W(\mathcal{T}, s, \vartheta)$ does not consist of s alone, but contains at least one nonsingleton path.

Now, we will construct a branch Br realising ϑ at Δ in $\mathcal{T}_0^\eta$ as follows. We start with any branch leading from an input state to Δ – by construction of the initial tableau there is at least one such branch. Then, we continue constructing Br from Δ by building a witness of the realisation of ϑ at Δ step by step, in accordance with $W(\mathcal{T}, s, \vartheta)$.

1. For every existential successor formula $\chi \in \Delta$ there is a successor r of s satisfying $scomp(\chi)$ in $\mathcal{T}$, and hence satisfying the successor prestate Γ_χ of Δ corresponding to χ. Then r satisfies at least one of the offspring states of Γ_χ, say Δ'_χ. Note that $r \in W(\mathcal{T}, s, \vartheta)$ and hence $\mathcal{T}, r \models \vartheta$. Furthermore, if $\mathcal{T}, r \models scomp(\chi)$ then Δ'_χ is chosen to contain ψ; such choice is guaranteed by Lemma 13.3.16.

2. Now, any family of successor states of Δ, one for every existential successor formula $\chi \in \Delta$ selected in such a way, provides an extension of the branch Br at Δ. If Δ does not contain any such formulae, then the required extension is provided by an offspring state of the only successor prestate Γ of Δ such that $\Delta \xrightarrow{\top} \Gamma$.

3. Thereafter the construction of Br repeats for every descendant of Δ along Br until reaching states containing ψ. Since the construction follows $W(\mathcal{T}, s, \vartheta)$, every path in Br starting from Δ is bound to reach such a state.

   From all such states onwards the branch is extended arbitrarily.

Once the branch Br realising ϑ at Δ in $\mathcal{T}_0^\eta$ is constructed, we show, as part of the inductive claim, that none of the satisfiable states in the witness of the realisation of ϑ at Δ on Br is eliminated from $\mathcal{T}_n^\eta$, and hence Br realises ϑ at Δ in $\mathcal{T}_n^\eta$ for every n.

This completes the inductive step for Claim 3. The inductive step for Claim 4 is now immediate.

Thus, in the long run, no satisfiable state gets eliminated in the state elimination phase.   □

Theorem 13.3.18 (Soundness of the tableaux for TLR and CTL).

(I) If $\eta \in$ CTL is satisfiable then $\mathcal{T}^\eta$ is open.

(II) If $\eta \in$ TLR is satisfiable then $\mathcal{T}^\eta$ is open.   ∎

Proof. The claim for CTL follows immediately from Lemma 13.3.16 and 13.3.17. The claim for TLR is proved by simply restricting the proofs of these lemmas to the language of TLR. $\qquad\square$

Completeness

To prove the completeness of both tableau procedures presented here it suffices to show how to construct a Hintikka structure $\mathcal{H}(\eta)$ satisfying the input formula η whenever the final tableau T^η is open. In the case of TLR the construction is straightforward; the case of CTL is complicated.

Theorem 13.3.19 (Completeness of the tableau for TLR). For any formula $\eta \in$ TLR, if the final tableau T^η is open, then the formula is satisfiable. $\qquad\blacksquare$

Proof. The final tableau T^η itself can be taken as such a Hintikka structure, with a labelling function assigning to each state its own label. The proof that T^η is indeed a Hintikka structure is straightforward from the construction of the tableau and left as an exercise. $\qquad\square$

Note that, although TLR involves existential eventualities like LTL, the complication arising in the completeness proof of the tableau for LTL does not arise here. The reason is that, in the case of TLR, all eventualities in a given state of the final tableau are realised (simultaneously) in the resulting ITS, whereas in the case of LTL they may not all be realised on an arbitrarily chosen path in that final tableau.

The latter complication is amplified in the case of CTL, because of the presence of universal eventualities, too. Indeed, selecting one open branch of an open tableau T^η to produce a Hintikka structure for CTL may work sometimes, e.g. if there is at most one universal eventuality in $ecl(\eta)$. In general, however, a more modular approach is needed, where eventualities are satisfied one by one, each of them at least once after every reappearance, as in the case of LTL. To that aim, the Hintikka structure $\mathcal{H}(\eta)$ is constructed from building blocks associated with pairs $\langle$ state, eventuality $\rangle$, extracted from T^η as follows.

First, we will define so called local fragments for all states in T^η.

Definition 13.3.20. A **local fragment** for a state $\Delta \in T^\eta$ consists of Δ together with all of its successor states in any fixed branch of T^η.

The state Δ is an **internal node** of the fragment, while all other states in the fragment are its **leaves**. $\qquad\nabla$

Then, we define realisation witness fragments for all states in T^η and eventualities in them.

Definition 13.3.21. For a universal eventuality $\vartheta = \mathsf{A}(\varphi \mathsf{U}\psi)$ (respectively, $\vartheta = \neg\mathsf{EG}\psi$) a **realisation witness fragment** is simply any witness of the realisation of ϑ in T^η, as per Definition 13.3.13.

The last states of every path in such a fragment, i.e. the states containing ψ (respectively, $\neg\psi$ in the case of $\vartheta = \neg\mathsf{EG}\psi$), are the **leaves** of that fragment, and all other states in it are its **interior nodes**. $\triangledown$

Definition 13.3.22. For an existential eventuality $\vartheta = \mathsf{EF}\psi$ or $\vartheta = \mathsf{E}(\varphi\mathsf{U}\psi)$, a **realisation witness fragment** is a path-witness of the realisation of ϑ in T^η, extended with local fragments for each of the intermediate states of the path.

All interior states in the path-witness are **interior nodes** of the fragment; all other nodes are the **leaves** of that fragment. $\triangledown$

Now, for every state Δ in T^η we fix a local fragment $\mathrm{LFR}(\Delta)$, and for every pair (Δ, ϑ) where Δ is a state in T^η and ϑ is an eventuality in Δ, we fix a realisation witness fragment $\mathrm{RWF}(\Delta, \vartheta)$. In each case, the state Δ is called the **root of the fragment**. Note that all these fragments may come from different branches of T^η.

Then we fix a list of all states in T^η: $\Delta_0, \ldots, \Delta_{n-1}$ and a list of all eventualities occurring in T^η: $\vartheta_0, \ldots, \vartheta_{m-1}$, and denote the fragment corresponding to (Δ_i, ϑ_j) (if there is one) by $\mathrm{FR}(i, j)$.

We will build the Hintikka structure $\mathcal{H}(\eta)$ in a sequence of steps, producing a chain by inclusion of **partial Hintikka structures** $\mathcal{H}_0(\eta), \mathcal{H}_1(\eta), \ldots$. Each of these will be a finite graph composed of fragments and consisting of interior nodes and leaves, where all unrealised eventualities will be listed in the leaves as 'pending realisation'. Each step will take care of the satisfaction of one eventuality at one of the current leaves, by grafting at that leaf a fragment realising that eventuality. In the process, new unrealised eventualities may occur and their realisation will be deferred to the new leaves. If no unrealised eventualities are listed at a leaf, a local fragment will be grafted at it in order to ensure totality of the transition relation. The union of the chain $\mathcal{H}_0(\eta), \mathcal{H}_1(\eta), \ldots$ will be the structure $\mathcal{H}(\eta)$, where there will be no leaves and no unrealised eventualities.

The crucial observation that makes this construction possible is that if an eventuality ϑ in the root of a given fragment is not realised within that fragment, then it is passed down to the leaves of the fragment. This enables the partial Hintikka structures $\mathcal{H}_n(\eta)$ not to falsify unrealised eventualities but to only defer their realisation by listing them at the leaves. More precisely:

Proposition 13.3.23. Let ϑ be an eventuality which belongs to a state $\Delta_i \in T^\eta$ but is not realised at Δ_i in the fragment $\mathrm{FR}(i, j)$. Then:

- If $\vartheta = \mathsf{E}(\varphi\mathsf{U}\psi)$ then there is a path in the fragment ending in a leaf, every state in which contains $\mathsf{EXE}(\varphi\mathsf{U}\psi)$.
- If $\vartheta = \neg\mathsf{AG}\varphi$ then there is a path in the fragment ending in a leaf, every state in which contains $\mathsf{EX}\neg\mathsf{AG}\varphi$.
- If $\vartheta = \mathsf{A}(\varphi\mathsf{U}\psi)$ then for every path in the fragment that does not realise ϑ every state on that path contains $\mathsf{AXA}(\varphi\mathsf{U}\psi)$; in particular, the leaves of all such paths contain $\mathsf{AXA}(\varphi\mathsf{U}\psi)$.

- If $\vartheta = \neg\mathsf{EG}\varphi$ is not realised at the state Δ_i in a fragment $FR(i, j)$ then for every path in the fragment that does not realise ϑ, every state on that path contains $\mathsf{AX}\neg\mathsf{EG}\varphi$; in particular, the leaves of all such paths contain $\mathsf{AX}\neg\mathsf{EG}\varphi$. ∎

We are now ready to prove the completeness theorem.

Theorem 13.3.24 (Completeness of the tableau for CTL). For any formula $\eta \in$ CTL, if the final tableau T^η is open, then the formula is satisfiable. ∎

Proof. We start the construction of $\mathcal{H}(\eta)$ with any state Δ containing η. This state is the label of the root Ψ_0 of the initial partial Hintikka structure $\mathcal{H}_0(\eta)$ having one leaf Ψ_0, and with a list of pending eventualities $\mathsf{Event}(\Psi_0)$ consisting of all eventualities in Δ that are not immediately realised at Δ. Thereafter the construction continues inductively as follows. Let $\mathcal{H}_n(\eta)$ be constructed and let $\mathsf{Leaves}(\mathcal{H}_n(\eta))$ be the list of all leaves in it. Let Ψ be the first leaf in that list, labelled with a state $\Delta_i \in T^\eta$, and let ϑ_j be the first eventuality in the list of pending eventualities $\mathsf{Event}(\Psi)$ at that leaf, if any. We then take a copy of the fragment $FR(i, j)$ and graft it to the leaf Ψ, by identifying that leaf with the root of the fragment (which has the same label Δ_i); if $\mathsf{Event}(\Psi)$ is empty, we graft a copy of the local fragment $LFR(\Delta_i)$ instead. Thus, $\mathcal{H}_{n+1}(\eta)$ is produced. The new list of leaves $\mathsf{Leaves}(\mathcal{H}_{n+1}(\eta))$ is obtained by removing Ψ from the list $\mathsf{Leaves}(\mathcal{H}_n(\eta))$ and then appending to it all leaves of the newly grafted fragment. Each of the new leaves inherits the list of pending eventualities of $\mathsf{Event}(\Psi)$ from which ϑ_j has been removed, to which the list of eventualities in their respective labels, that are not immediately realised, has been appended. Note that the graph $\mathcal{H}_{n+1}(\eta)$ is an extension of the graph $\mathcal{H}_n(\eta)$.

This completes the construction of the chain $\mathcal{H}_0(\eta), \mathcal{H}_1(\eta), \ldots$, and consequently, of $\mathcal{H}(\eta)$ as the union of that chain.

Now it remains to verify that $\mathcal{H}(\eta)$ defined as above is indeed a Hintikka structure satisfying η at its root Ψ_0. This verification is now straightforward from the construction, and is left as an exercise. □

Corollary 13.3.25. CTL has the small model property. ∎

Proof. The construction of $\mathcal{H}(\eta)$ can be made finite by identifying leaves with states introduced earlier with the same label and reusing identical fragments. That is, if a fragment $FR(i, j)$ is to be grafted to the leaf Ψ of the current partial HS $\mathcal{H}_n(\eta)$, and that fragment has already been grafted to another node Ψ' at an earlier stage, instead of grafting a new copy of $FR(i, j)$, the leaf Ψ is identified with Ψ' and all incoming arrows to Ψ are accordingly redirected to Ψ'.

A more careful inspection of the construction shows that the Hintikka structure $\mathcal{H}(\eta)$ has size $\mathcal{O}(2^{c|\eta|})$. We leave the details as an exercise. □

Corollary 13.3.26 (Tree model property for CTL). If η is a satisfiable CTL formula and $ecl(\eta)$ contains $n > 0$ formulae that are either existential eventuality formulae or existential successor formulae, then η has a tree model with branching factor bounded above by n. ∎

Proof. The preceding construction can be modified by defining the fragments as finite trees. Thus every partial Hintikka structure $\mathcal{H}_n(\eta)$ will be a finite tree, and eventually $\mathcal{H}(\eta)$ will be constructed as a tree, with a branching factor bounded above by n.   □

Unlike the case of LTL, the tableau method for TLR and CTL presented here has optimal worst-case complexity, viz. EXPTIME. Still it can be improved and its practical performance optimised in various ways; see some references in the bibliographic notes.

Just like in the cases of LTL and TLR, the tableau procedure for testing satisfiability in CTL can easily be modified to perform local model checking. It is however relatively inefficient, compared to the labelling algorithm for global model checking of CTL formulae presented in Chapter 7, so we will not discuss it further.

13.4 Exercises

Exercises on generic tableaux

Exercise 13.1. Define the extended closure of a BML-formula recursively on the logical structure of the formula.

Exercise 13.2. Show that the extended closure of a formula is always a finite set, with size linearly bounded by the length of the formula.

Exercise 13.3. Prove that for every BML formula η, if the final tableau $\mathcal{T}^\eta$ is nonempty then it is a Hintikka structure for $ecl(\eta)$.

Exercise 13.4. Show that the two versions of the state elimination rule STATEELIM^{BML} given in Section 13.1.5 are equivalent.

Exercise 13.5. Work out a formal procedure producing a model from an open final tableau for a given input formula η (set of formulae Γ). Then modify that procedure to produce a *minimal* model.

Exercise 13.6. Use tableaux to determine whether each of the following formulae of BML is valid. If it is not valid, construct a countermodel: an interpreted transition system and a state, at which the formula is false.

(a) $(\mathsf{EX}q \wedge \mathsf{AXEX}p) \to \mathsf{EXAX}p$ (d) $\mathsf{EX}(\mathsf{EX}q \wedge \mathsf{AX}p) \to \mathsf{EXAX}(p \vee q)$
(b) $\mathsf{EXAX}p \to \mathsf{AXEX}p$ (e) $\mathsf{EX}(\mathsf{EX}q \wedge \mathsf{AX}p) \to \mathsf{EXEX}(p \wedge q)$
(c) $\mathsf{EX}(\mathsf{EX}q \wedge \mathsf{AX}p) \to \mathsf{AXEX}p$ (f) $\mathsf{AX}(\mathsf{EX}q \wedge \mathsf{AX}p) \to \mathsf{AXEX}(p \wedge q)$

Exercise 13.7. Construct tableaux for the following input formulae or set of formulae and determine for each of them whether it is satisfiable. If so, use the final tableau to construct a model.

(a) $(\mathsf{EX}\neg p \to \mathsf{AX}q) \land \mathsf{AX}\neg q$

(b) $\mathsf{AX}(p \lor \mathsf{AX}q) \land \mathsf{EXAX}\neg q$

(c) $\{\mathsf{EX}\neg p \to \mathsf{AX}q, \mathsf{AX}\neg q, \mathsf{EX}p\}$

(d) $\{\mathsf{EX}\neg p \to \mathsf{AX}q, \mathsf{AX}\neg q, \neg\mathsf{AX}p\}$

(e) $(\mathsf{EX}p \to \mathsf{AXAX}\neg q) \land \mathsf{EX}(p \land \mathsf{EX}q)$

(f) $\{\mathsf{AX}\neg p \to \mathsf{EX}q, \mathsf{AX}\neg q, \mathsf{EX}\neg p\}$

(g) $\{\mathsf{AX}(p \lor \mathsf{AX}q), \mathsf{EXAX}\neg q, \mathsf{EX}\neg p\}$

(h) $\{\mathsf{EX}(\mathsf{EX}p \land \mathsf{AX}q), \mathsf{AX}(\mathsf{EX}\neg p \land \mathsf{EXAX}\neg q)\}$

Exercise 13.8. Using tableaux, check the validity of each of the following logical consequences. If not valid, construct a countermodel: a rooted ITS satisfying all formulae on the left but not the formula on the right.

(a) $\mathsf{EXAX}p, \mathsf{AXEX}q \models \mathsf{EXEX}(p \land q)$.

(b) $\mathsf{EX}p, \mathsf{AX}(p \to \mathsf{AX}q) \models \mathsf{EXAX}q$.

(c) $\mathsf{EX}p, \mathsf{AX}(p \to \mathsf{AX}q) \models \mathsf{EXEX}q$.

(d) $\mathsf{AX}p, \mathsf{EX}(\neg p \lor q), \mathsf{AX}(q \to \mathsf{EX}q) \models \mathsf{EXEX}q$.

(e) $\mathsf{AX}p, \mathsf{EX}(\neg p \lor q), \mathsf{AX}(q \to \mathsf{EX}q) \models \mathsf{EXAX}q$.

(f) $\mathsf{EX}p, \mathsf{AX}(\neg p \lor \mathsf{AX}q), \mathsf{AX}(\mathsf{EX}q \to p) \models \mathsf{EXAX}\neg q$.

(g) $\mathsf{AX}p, \mathsf{AX}(\neg q \to \mathsf{AX}\neg p), \mathsf{EXEX}p \models \mathsf{EX}(p \land q)$.

Exercise 13.9. Using tableaux, check the validity of each of the following logical equivalences. If not valid, construct a countermodel: a rooted ITS satisfying one but not the other formula.

(a) $\mathsf{EX}(p \lor q) \leftrightarrow (\mathsf{EX}p \lor \mathsf{EX}q)$.

(b) $\mathsf{AX}(p \lor q) \leftrightarrow (\mathsf{AX}p \lor \mathsf{AX}q)$.

(c) $\mathsf{EX}(p \land q) \leftrightarrow (\mathsf{EX}p \land \mathsf{EX}q)$.

(d) $\mathsf{AX}(p \land q) \leftrightarrow (\mathsf{AX}p \land \mathsf{AX}q)$.

(d) $\neg\mathsf{EX}(p \lor \mathsf{AX}q) \leftrightarrow \mathsf{AX}(p \to \mathsf{EX}\neg q)$.

(e) $\neg\mathsf{AX}(\mathsf{EX}p \to \mathsf{EX}q) \leftrightarrow (\mathsf{EXEX}p \land \mathsf{EXAX}\neg q)$.

(f) $\neg\mathsf{AX}(\mathsf{EX}p \to \mathsf{EX}q) \leftrightarrow \mathsf{EX}(\mathsf{EX}p \land \mathsf{AX}\neg q)$.

Exercise 13.10. Prove Lemma 13.1.2. Complete the details of the proofs of Proposition 13.1.12 and Theorem 13.1.17.

Exercises on tableaux for LTL

Exercise 13.11. Give an example of a satisfiable formula η such that not every path in $\mathcal{T}^\eta$ is a Hintikka trace.

Exercise 13.12. Using tableaux check the following LTL formulae for validity. If not valid, construct a linear model on which the formula is false.

(a) $\mathsf{F}^\infty p \to \mathsf{G}^\infty p$

(b) $\mathsf{G}^\infty p \to \mathsf{F}^\infty p$

(c) $\mathsf{G}p \land \mathsf{F}q \to p\mathsf{U}q$

(d) $\mathsf{G}(p \lor q) \to (\mathsf{G}p \lor \mathsf{G}q)$

(e) $\mathsf{X}(p \lor \mathsf{F}p) \to \mathsf{F}p$

(f) $\mathsf{F}p \to \mathsf{X}(p \lor \mathsf{F}p)$

(g) $p\mathsf{U}(q \land r) \to (p\mathsf{U}q \land p\mathsf{U}r)$

(h) $p\mathsf{U}(q \lor r) \to (p\mathsf{U}q \lor p\mathsf{U}r)$

(i) $(p\mathsf{U}q \lor p\mathsf{U}r) \to p\mathsf{U}(q \lor r)$

(j) $((\mathsf{G}p)\mathsf{U}q) \to \mathsf{G}(p\mathsf{U}q)$

(k) $\mathsf{G}(p\mathsf{U}q) \to ((\mathsf{G}p)\mathsf{U}q)$.

Exercise 13.13. Construct tableaux for the following LTL formulae or sets of formulae and determine for each of them whether it is satisfiable. If so, use the final tableau to construct a Hintikka trace satisfying the input and then provide a model for it.

(a) $G(p \leftrightarrow X \neg p)$

(b) $GF(pU(p \wedge \neg Xp))$

(c) $p \wedge ((p \rightarrow Xp)U \neg p)$

(d) $\{G(p \rightarrow Xp), \neg GFp\}$

(e) $\{G(p \rightarrow F \neg p), GFp\}$

(f) $\{G(p \rightarrow \neg Gp), FGp\}$

(g) $\{G(pUq), G(pU \neg q)\}$

(h) $\{G(p \rightarrow Xq), \neg FG(q \vee \neg p)\}$

(i) $\{GFp, GFq, G \neg (p \wedge q)\}$

(j) $\{GFp, FGq, \neg F(p \wedge q)\}$

(k) $\{G(pUq), G(pU \neg q), F \neg p\}$

(l) $\{q, (G(p \vee q))U(\neg pU \neg q)\}$

(m) $\{GF(pUq), GF(p \wedge \neg q), FG(Xq \rightarrow \neg p)\}$

(n) $(\bigwedge_{i=1}^{n} GFp_i) \wedge G \bigwedge_{i=1}^{n} (p_i \rightarrow \bigwedge_{j \neq i} \neg p_j)$.

Exercise 13.14. Using tableaux, check the validity of each of the following logical consequences in LTL. In case the formula is not valid, construct a countermodel.

(a) $Gp, Gq \models G(p \wedge q)$

(b) $p, G(p \rightarrow Xp) \models Gp$

(c) $p, G(p \rightarrow Fp) \models GFp$

(d) $p, G(p \rightarrow XFp) \models GFp$

(e) $pUq, pUr \models pU(q \wedge r)$

(f) $pUr, (p \rightarrow q)Ur \models qUr$

(g) $pUq, pU(q \rightarrow r) \models pUr$

(h) $(pUq)Ur \models pU(qUr)$

(i) $pU(qUr) \models (pUq)Ur$.

Exercise 13.15. Using tableau, check the validity of each of the following logical equivalences in LTL. If not valid, construct a falsifying model.

(a) $\neg Gp \leftrightarrow \neg p \vee X \neg Fp$

(b) $\neg Gp \leftrightarrow \neg p \vee XF \neg p$

(c) $\neg (pUq) \leftrightarrow (\neg p)Uq$

(d) $\neg (pUq) \leftrightarrow pU \neg q$

(e) $\neg (pUq) \leftrightarrow (\neg p)U \neg q$

(f) $\neg (pUq) \leftrightarrow (\neg q)U \neg p$

(g) $\neg (pUq) \leftrightarrow (Fq \rightarrow (\neg q)U \neg p)$

(h) $\neg (pUq) \leftrightarrow G \neg q \vee (\neg q)U(\neg p \wedge \neg q)$.

Exercise 13.16. Prove Lemma 13.2.1, Proposition 13.2.2, Lemma 13.2.8 and Lemma 13.2.19.

Exercise 13.17. Complete the proofs of Proposition 13.2.6, Proposition 13.2.6, the last step in the proof of Theorem 13.2.20, the proofs of Corollary 13.2.21, claims II and III in Theorem 13.2.22.

Exercises on tableaux for TLR and CTL

Exercise 13.18. Show that $ecl(\varphi)$ is finite for every $\varphi \in$ CTL.

Exercise 13.19. Define the notion of Hintikka structures for TLR.

Exercise 13.20. Develop an efficient algorithm for identifying all states in a current CTL tableau that realise a given universal eventuality, and determine its complexity. *Hint:* This is essentially the algorithm for testing nonemptiness of Büchi tree automata given in Chapter 14. See the proof of Theorem 14.6.6.

Exercise 13.21. Verify that the final tableau in Figure 13.17 in Example 13.3.15 constitutes a Hintikka structure satisfying Γ_1 and then extend it to an ITS which is a model for Γ_1.

Exercise 13.22. Verify the state elimination phase of Example 2 and the final tableau in Figure 13.20 in Example 13.3.15. Then extract from the final tableau a Hintikka structure satisfying Γ_2 and extend it to a model for Γ_2.

Exercise 13.23. Verify and complete the state elimination phase and determine the final tableau in Example 13.3.15 (third example).

Exercise 13.24. Complete the details of the proof of Theorem 13.3.19. In particular, prove that if the final tableau T^η for a TLR-formula η is nonempty then it is a Hintikka structure for $ecl(\eta)$.

Exercise 13.25. Complete the details at the end of the proof of Theorem 13.3.24, by showing that $\mathcal{H}(\eta)$ is indeed a Hintikka structure satisfying η at its root Ψ_0.

Exercise 13.26. Prove that, for any CTL formula η, if there are no universal eventualities in $ecl(\eta)$ and the final tableau T^η is open, then it defines a Hintikka structure satisfying η, just like in the case of TLR.

Exercise 13.27. Prove that, for any CTL formula η, if there is at most one universal eventuality and no existential eventualities in $ecl(\eta)$ and the final tableau T^η is open, then some open branch in it starting from an initial state defines a Hintikka structure satisfying η.

Is this still always true if $ecl(\eta)$ contains two universal, or one universal and one existential eventuality?

Exercise 13.28. Give an example of a satisfiable CTL-formula η for which no single branch of the open final tableau T^η defines a Hintikka structure satisfying η.

Exercise 13.29. Try to extend the tableau method for CTL to CTL^+ and to ECTL (see Sections 7.4.3 and 7.4.1) and analyse where the procedure no longer works as is.

Exercise 13.30. Using the tableau method check the following TLR formulae for validity. If not valid, construct a countermodel: a rooted ITS in which the formula is false.

(a) $\mathsf{AGEF}p \to \mathsf{EFAG}p$

(b) $\mathsf{EFAG}p \to \mathsf{AGEF}p$

(c) $\mathsf{AG}(p \to \mathsf{EX}p) \to (p \to \mathsf{AG}p)$

(d) $\mathsf{AG}(p \to \mathsf{AX}p) \to (p \to \mathsf{AG}p)$.

Exercise 13.31. Use the tableau method to check the following CTL formulae for validity. If they are not valid, construct a counter-model: a rooted ITS in which the formula is false.

(a) $\text{AGAF}p \to \text{AFAG}p$

(b) $\text{AFAG}p \to \text{AGAF}p$

(c) $\text{EGAF}p \to \text{AFEG}p$

(d) $\text{AFEG}p \to \text{EGAF}p$

(e) $\text{AX}(p \lor \text{AF}p) \to \text{AF}p$

(f) $\text{AX}(p \lor \text{EF}p) \to \text{AF}p$

(g) $\text{AF}p \to \text{AX}(p \lor \text{EF}p)$

(h) $\text{AG}p \land \text{AF}q \to \text{A}(p\text{U}q)$

(i) $\text{EG}p \land \text{AF}q \to \text{E}(p\text{U}q)$

(j) $\text{EG}p \land \text{EF}q \to \text{E}(p\text{U}q)$

(k) $\text{A}((\text{AG}p)\text{UEF}q) \to \text{AGA}(p\text{UEF}q)$

(l) $\text{AGA}(p\text{UEF}q) \to \text{A}((\text{AG}p)\text{UEF}q)$

(m) $\text{A}((\text{AG}p)\text{UAF}q) \to \text{AGA}(p\text{UAF}q)$

(n) $\text{AGA}(p\text{UAF}q) \to \text{A}((\text{AG}p)\text{UAF}q)$.

Exercise 13.32. Construct tableaux for the following CTL formulae or sets of formulae and determine for each of them whether it is satisfiable. If so, use the final tableau to construct a Hintikka structure satisfying the input and then provide a model for it.

(a) $\{\text{A}(p\text{U}q), \text{EX}\neg q, \text{EX}\neg p\}$

(b) $\{p, \text{AG}(p \to \text{EX}p), \text{E}(q\text{U}\neg p)\}$

(c) $\{p, \text{A}(p\text{U}q), \text{E}(\neg q\text{U}\neg p)\}$

(d) $\{\text{AG}(p \to \text{EX}p), \neg\text{EGEF}p\}$

(e) $\{\text{AG}(p \to \text{AF}\neg p), \text{AGEF}p\}$

(f) $\{\text{AG}(p \to \neg\text{AG}p), \text{EFEG}p\}$

(g) $\{\text{AG}(p \to \neg\text{AG}p), \text{EGAF}p\}$

(h) $\{\text{AG}(p \to \neg\text{EG}p), \text{AFEG}p\}$

(i) $\{\text{AG}(p \to \text{AX}q), \neg\text{AFEG}(q \lor \neg p)\}$

(j) $\{(\text{EX}q \to p), \text{A}(p\text{UEX}q), \text{E}(\neg q\text{U}\neg p)\}$

(k) $\{q, \text{A}(\text{AG}(p \lor q)\text{UA}(\neg p\text{U}\neg q))\}$

(l) $\{q, \text{A}(\text{AG}(p \lor q)\text{UE}(\neg p\text{U}\neg q))\}$

(m) $(\bigwedge_{i=1}^{n} \text{AGAF}p_i) \land \text{AG} \bigwedge_{i=1}^{n}(p_i \to \bigwedge_{j \neq i} \neg p_j)$ for any $n \geq 1$.

Exercise 13.33. Use tableaux to check the validity of each of the following logical consequences in CTL. If they are not valid, construct a countermodel.

(a) $p, \text{AG}(p \to \text{EX}p) \models \text{EG}p$

(b) $p, \text{AG}(p \to \text{EX}p) \models \text{AFEG}p$

(c) $p, \text{EG}(p \to \text{EX}p) \models \text{EGEX}p$

(d) $p, \text{EG}(p \to \text{AX}p) \models \text{EG}p$

(e) $\text{A}((\text{EG}p)\text{UAF}q) \models \text{EGA}(p\text{UAF}q)$

(f) $\text{EGA}(p\text{UAF}q) \models \text{A}((\text{EG}p)\text{UAF}q)$

(g) $\text{A}((\text{EG}p)\text{UEF}q) \models \text{EGA}(p\text{UEF}q)$

(h) $\text{EGA}(p\text{UEF}q) \models \text{A}((\text{EG}p)\text{UEF}q)$.

Exercise 13.34. Prove Lemma 13.3.1, Lemma 13.3.5, Lemma 13.3.7.

Exercise 13.35. Complete the proofs of Theorem 13.3.8, Lemma 13.3.16, Lemma 13.3.17, Corollary 13.3.25, Corollary 13.3.26.

13.5 Bibliographical Notes

The origins of the semantic tableau method for testing satisfiability of logical formulae go back to Gentzen's systems of Natural deduction and Sequent calculus, but the method was first explicitly developed by Beth (1955, 1970), Hintikka's (1955) method of model sets, and later by Smullyan (1968). It was adapted for modal logics by Kripke (1963) ('explicit tableau'), Zeman (1973), Hughes and Cresswell (1996) (called there the method of 'semantic diagrams') and especially in the works of Fitting on modal proof theory (see Fitting 1972, 1977, 1983). For a detailed survey and further references of tableaux for modal and temporal logics, see Goré (1999), and for a more recent account on modal tableaux, see

Fitting (2007). In particular, a standard tableau for the logic BML can be extracted from any of these. A very comprehensive reference on tableaux as logical deductive systems is the handbook D'Agostino et al. (1999).

The methodology presented here for developing tableau-based decision procedures for temporal logics goes back to works of Pratt (1979, 1980). The declarative and incremental types of tableau constructions for temporal logics are distinguished and discussed in Kesten et al. (1993).

Closure and extended closure, full expansions. The notion of closure of a formula goes back to Fischer and Ladner (1979), where they introduce for PDL what gradually became known as the **Fischer–Ladner closure**. Fully expanded sets and full expansions originate from 'downwards saturated sets' (Goré 1999) or 'atoms' (Kesten et al. 1993) and, eventually, from Hintikka's saturated sets in classical logic (see e.g. Smullyan 1968).

We note that in most of the publications the notion of closure (here, extended closure) of a formula is assumed closed under subformulae and negations (up to removing double negations), which usually makes it somewhat larger than necessary. This issue is partly addressed in Kesten et al. (1993), where the closure is not assumed closed under subformulae, but is still closed under negation. In this chapter, we follow a more size-optimal approach in defining closure, by not requiring that it is closed by subformulae, nor under negation, but only requiring that it contains the formulae that are really needed to evaluate the truth of the input formula.

Hintikka structures. The notion of Hintikka structure in the context of modal logics was probably first defined explicitly in Pratt (1979, 1980), deriving from Hintikka's model sets for propositional logic.

Tableaux for linear-time logics. The first construction of tableau for LTL, an optimised version of which is presented here, was given in Wolper (1983, 1985), where it is extended to tableau for ETL, too. For some variations and improvements of Wolper's tableau procedure for LTL (see Kesten et al. 1993) (for LTL+Past.) and Lichtenstein and Pnueli (2000). Manna and Pnueli (1995) devote the whole of Chapter 5 to a tableau method for satisfiability testing for LTL+Past. In Gough (1984), a tableau-based decision procedure for LTL+Past has been designed with a first phase to build a model graph, following with a second phase to prune nodes. The algorithm for LTL+Past described in Gough (1984) has been implemented and it is probably one of the first implementations for deciding LTL+Past.

A *one-pass tableau calculus* for LTL, which has a theoretically worse (double exponential time) worst-case complexity but is often practically very efficient, was developed by Schwendimann (1998a,b), and subsequently implemented by Widmann and Goré (see Widmann 2010).

For a report on the implemented version of the tableau for LTL presented here and its comparison with Widmann and Goré's implementation of Schwendimann's tableau, see Goranko et al. (2010).

Tableaux for branching-time logics and the modal μ-calculus. The first (top-down) tableau-based deductive systems and decision procedures for branching-time logic were developed, following the tableau-building method for PDL of Pratt (1979, 1980) in Ben-Ari et al. (1981) for the branching-time logic UB and in Clarke and Emerson (1981) and Emerson and Halpern (1982, 1985) for CTL (see also Emerson 1995). A one-pass tableau system has been developed for CTL in Abate et al. (2007).

Tableaux for full CTL* have been developed by Reynolds for the generalised bundled tree semantics in Reynolds (2007), and for the standard semantics in Reynolds (2009), with a full version presented in Reynolds (2011) and an improved tableaux for CTL* in Reynolds (2013).

An essentially tableau-based decision procedure for the modal μ-calculus was developed by Niwiński and Walukiewicz (1996). A more recent tableau system for $\mathcal{L}_\mu$ (though with a nonoptimal worst-case complexity) has been presented in Jungteerapanich (2009).

Tableaux for related logics. An optimal on-the-fly tableau-based decision procedure for PDL has been developed in Goré and Widmann (2009) and a cut-free tableau for PDL with converse can be found in Goré and Widmann (2010).

The incremental tableau technology presented here has been applied to produce an optimal (EXPTIME) tableau-based decision procedures for the alternating-time temporal logic ATL in Goranko and Shkatov (2009c) (cf. Chapter 9), further extended to ATL$^+$ in Cerrito et al. (2014) and to the full ATL* in David (2015). An implementation of the tableaux method for ATL is presented in David (2013) and its extension to ATL* in David (2015).

In a similar style, incremental tableau-based decision procedures have been developed for multiagent temporal-epistemic logics of linear time in Goranko and Shkatov (2009a) and Ajspur and Goranko (2013), and of branching time in Goranko and Shkatov (2009b).

14

The Automata-Based Approach

In this chapter we present the automata-based approach for a variety of temporal logics and classes of automata and compare the advantages and the drawbacks of the different constructions. We do not always aim at optimal complexity upper bounds but also take other criteria into account. This is not a chapter on automata theory but rather a chapter on automata for temporal logics. We focus our attention on reductions of decision problems for temporal logics into decision problems on automata instead of in-depth treatment of automata. References are provided, as usual, as bibliographical notes.

As already discussed in Section 1.1.3, the automata-based approach consists of reducing logical problems to automata-based decision problems in order to take advantage of known results and decision procedures from automata theory. The notion of models for logical formulae is substituted by the notion of words or trees accepted by automata (or any other type of structures accepted by automata). The correspondence between formulae and automata, which underlines the difference between a declarative statement (a formula) and an operational device (an automaton), allows to reduce many logical problems, viz.:

- satisfiability of a formula φ (i.e. existence of a model for φ) reduces to checking **non-emptiness** of an automaton $\mathcal{A}_\varphi$ (i.e. existence of a word/tree accepted by $\mathcal{A}_\varphi$) by using a map between models and, respectively, words or trees;
- validity of a formula φ (i.e. truth of φ is all models) reduces to checking **universality** of an automaton $\mathcal{A}_\varphi$ (i.e. checking whether $\mathcal{A}_\varphi$ accepts all words/trees);
- entailment of one formula φ by another formula ψ reduces to checking whether all what is accepted by the automaton $\mathcal{A}_\varphi$ is also accepted by the automaton $\mathcal{A}_\psi$ (the **inclusion problem**).

The idea in a nutshell: the automata considered here are not Turing-complete and have restricted computational power and decidable decision problems, so logical decision problems can be reduced to respective automata-based decision problems for which algorithms exist. This is all the magic around this approach to solve logical decision problems: design a reduction and then rely on automata-based decision procedures. Alternatively, this approach can be viewed as a means to solving logical decision problems by using a class of devices with limited computational power, i.e. automata. This is why it helps to better understand their computational power. The pioneering work along these lines was done by Büchi, who introduced the now called *Büchi automata* and proved them equivalent to formulae in monadic second-order logic (MSO) over $(\mathbb{N}, <)$ (see Chapter 8), by considering models of a formula built over the second-order variables $P_1, \ldots, P_N$ as ω-words over the alphabet $\mathcal{P}(\{P_1, \ldots, P_N\})$.

Here are some desirable properties of the automata-based approach.

- The reduction should be conceptually simple, as e.g. the translation from LTL formulae into alternating automata (see Section 14.3). The formula structure is reflected directly in the transition formulae of alternating automata. Nevertheless, showing correctness of the reduction requires some nontrivial work.

- The computational complexity of the automata-based target problem should be well characterised, see e.g. the translation from CTL formulae into nondeterministic Büchi tree automata. The nonemptiness problem for such automata has been shown to be in PTime, leading to an ExpTime upper bound for the CTL satisfiability problem, which is optimal (see Chapter 11.) In that way, one gets a complexity upper bound for solving the source logical problem.
- Last but not least, the reduction should preferably enable obtaining the optimal complexity for the source logical problem. For instance, CTL model checking can be shown to be in PTime by a reduction into hesitant alternating automata (HAA) and we know this is the optimal upper bound. Note that, in order to obtain the optimal bound in this case, it is necessary to consider that special class of automata with this approach.

In this chapter, we select several logics, mainly LTL and variants of it, as well as CTL, and we present several reductions from formulae to automata. To do so, we take advantage of notions from previous chapters but we also provide original reductions, emphasising the diversity of automata-based constructions. We present several methods for LTL-like logics but we also approach the treatment for CTL as a generalisation of some of the methods for LTL. We do not provide an exhaustive treatment but rather focus on interesting technical options. Finally, along the way, we deal with concepts that are, strictly speaking, not inherent to the reductions from formulae to automata, such as renaming techniques, alternation and computational complexity. See the bibliographical notes for further references on a much more exhaustive treatment of topics covered in this chapter.

Structure of the chapter. The content of this chapter can be summarised as follows.

- Section 14.1 provides a brief introduction to Büchi automata. It also introduces generalised Büchi automata, presents closure properties and shows the equivalence with the expressive power of ω-regular expressions.
- For each LTL formula φ, we show how to build a Büchi automaton that recognises exactly the models of $\text{Mod}(\varphi)$. Several variants are presented, which allows to make useful comparisons. This serves the purpose not only of illustrating the automata-based approach but also of providing different ways to synthesise automata from formulae. For the other temporal logics, we will not present such a variety of constructions but rather focus on original techniques or approaches.
- Exercise 14.19 is dedicated to a reduction from QLTL formulae into Büchi automata that leads to a nonelementary upper bound for QLTL satisfiability, see Section 14.8.
- For the linear-time logic ETL, we present a reduction into alternating Büchi word automata; this is the opportunity to illustrate the use of alternation (also presented for plain LTL), see Section 14.5.1. Similarly, Section 14.5.2 is dedicated to a translation from PSL formulae into alternating Büchi word automata.
- As far as branching-time logics are concerned, for each CTL formula φ, we show how to build a Büchi tree automaton that recognises the tree-like models with branching degree bounded by the size of φ, see Section 14.6.3. This is less precise than for LTL formulae,

since for CTL formulae we do not build automata that recognise exactly all their models. However, since any satisfiable CTL formula has a tree-like model of that form, the reduction preserves satisfiability and the Büchi tree automata accept exactly the tree-like models of the respective formulae. Section 14.6.2 deals with the simpler case of the basic temporal logic BML.

In summary, for CTL we present a reduction to nondeterministic Büchi tree automata, as well as a reduction to alternating Büchi tree automata, see Section 14.7.2. This is the opportunity to introduce tree automata and to show how CTL formulae can be naturally translated into Büchi tree automata in the presence of alternation.

Note that the current chapter does not deal with CTL* and the modal μ-calculus. There are automata-based techniques for these logics, too, but for them we prefer to present, instead, verification games in Chapter 15. In view of the close relationships between decision problems for automata and games, this allows us to avoid repetitions and to deter additional complex constructions herein.

14.1 Introduction to Nondeterministic Büchi Automata

14.1.1 Basic Concepts

Roughly speaking, a Büchi automaton is defined as a finite-state automaton except that infinite ω-words are accepted instead of finite words and the set of accepting states is used as an acceptance condition for ω-words. The formal definitions follow.

Definition 14.1.1. A **Büchi automaton** $\mathcal{A}$ is a tuple $\mathcal{A} = (\Sigma, Q, Q_0, \delta, F)$ such that:

- Σ is a finite **alphabet**.
- Q is a finite set of **states**.
- $Q_0 \subseteq Q$ is the set of **initial** states.
- the **transition relation** δ is a subset of $Q \times \Sigma \times Q$.
- $F \subseteq Q$ is a set of **accepting** states.

Given $q \in Q$ and $\mathrm{a} \in \Sigma$, we write $\delta(q, \mathrm{a})$ to denote the set of states q' such that $(q, \mathrm{a}, q') \in \delta$. The automaton $\mathcal{A}$ is said to be **deterministic** iff $\mathrm{card}(Q_0) = 1$ and $\mathrm{card}(\delta(q, \mathrm{a})) \leq 1$ for all $q \in Q$ and $\mathrm{a} \in \Sigma$. ∇

Definition 14.1.2. A **run** ρ of the Büchi automaton $\mathcal{A} = (\Sigma, Q, Q_0, \delta, F)$ is a sequence $q_0 \xrightarrow{\mathrm{a}_0} q_1 \xrightarrow{\mathrm{a}_1} q_2 \ldots$, where $q_0 \in Q_0$ and $(q_i, \mathrm{a}_i, q_{i+1}) \in \delta$ for every $i \geq 0$. The **label** of the run ρ is the word $w = \mathrm{a}_0 \mathrm{a}_1 \cdots \in \Sigma^\omega$.

Given a run ρ of $\mathcal{A}$, we define

$$\mathrm{inf}(\rho) := \{q \in Q \mid \text{ for all } i \in \mathbb{N} \text{ there exists } j > i \text{ such that } q = q_j\}.$$

The run ρ is **accepting** if some state of F is repeated infinitely often in ρ, that is, if $(\mathrm{inf}(\rho) \cap F) \neq \emptyset$. ∇

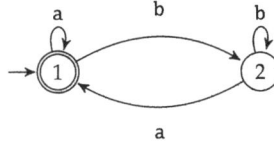

Figure 14.1 Büchi automaton $\mathcal{A}$ with $L(\mathcal{A}) = \{w \in \{a, b\}^\omega \mid$ the letter a occurs infinitely often$\}$.

Definition 14.1.3. The automaton $\mathcal{A}$ **accepts** the **language** $L(\mathcal{A})$ consisting of all of ω-words $w \in \Sigma^\omega$ for which there exists an accepting run of $\mathcal{A}$ with label w. This acceptance condition is called the **Büchi acceptance condition**. $\qquad\qquad\qquad\qquad\nabla$

A language $L \subseteq \Sigma^\omega$ is **Büchi-recognisable** whenever there is a Büchi automaton $\mathcal{A}$ such that $L(\mathcal{A}) = L$.

Example 14.1.4 (Büchi automaton). Consider the automaton in Figure 14.1, where the initial states are marked with an incoming arrow and the accepting states are doubly circled. One can verify that $\mathcal{A}$ accepts precisely those words over $\{a, b\}$ having infinitely many a's.

Given a Büchi automaton $\mathcal{A} = (\Sigma, Q, Q_0, \delta, F)$, we define its **size** $|\mathcal{A}|$ as follows:

$$|\mathcal{A}| := \mathrm{card}(\Sigma) + \mathrm{card}(Q) + \mathrm{card}(Q_0) + \mathrm{card}(\delta) + \mathrm{card}(F).$$

Note that the assumption $\mathrm{card}(Q_0) = 1$ does not restrict the class of accepted languages.

The most important decision problem for Büchi automata is the **nonemptiness problem**, defined as follows:

Input: a Büchi automaton $\mathcal{A}$,

Question: is $L(\mathcal{A}) \neq \emptyset$?

An algorithm for solving the nonemptiness problem for Büchi automata can be designed by performing simple reachability checks, as shown below. This is a mere consequence from results presented in Chapter 3.

Lemma 14.1.5. Let $\mathcal{A} = (\Sigma, Q, Q_0, \delta, F)$ be a Büchi automaton. $L(\mathcal{A}) \neq \emptyset$ iff there are $q_0 \in Q_0$ and $q_f \in F$ such that $q_0 R^* q_f$ and $q_f R^+ q_f$ in the directed graph (Q, R) with $R = \{(q, q') \in Q \times Q \mid q \xrightarrow{a} q' \in \delta\}$. $\qquad\qquad\blacksquare$

Theorem 14.1.6. The nonemptiness problem for the class of Büchi automata is NLogSpace-complete. $\qquad\qquad\qquad\qquad\qquad\qquad\qquad\qquad\qquad\qquad\blacksquare$

Indeed, NLogSpace-hardness can be shown by a reduction from the reachability problem for transition systems, see Chapter 3, while the NLogSpace upper bound is obtained with a proof similar to the proof of Theorem 3.2.3, see Chapter 3.

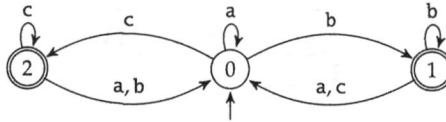

Figure 14.2 A generalised Büchi automaton $\mathcal{A}$.

14.1.2 Generalised Büchi Automata

Now we introduce a standard generalisation of the Büchi acceptance condition by considering conjunctions of classical Büchi conditions.

Definition 14.1.7. A **generalised Büchi automaton** (GBA) is a structure

$$\mathcal{A} = (\Sigma, Q, Q_0, \delta, \{F_1, \ldots, F_k\})$$

such that $F_1, \ldots, F_k \subseteq Q$ and Σ, Q, Q_0 and δ are defined as for Büchi automata. A run is defined exactly as for Büchi automata and a run ρ of $\mathcal{A}$ is declared **accepting** iff $\inf(\rho) \cap F_i \neq \emptyset$ for all $i \in [1, k]$. $\qquad \triangledown$

Example 14.1.8. Consider the generalised Büchi automaton

$$\mathcal{A} = (\{a, b, c\}, \{0, 1, 2\}, \{1\}, \delta, \{F_1, F_2\})$$

in Figure 14.2 with $F_1 = \{1\}$ and $F_2 = \{2\}$. As an exercise, show that it accepts those ω-words over $\{a, b, c\}$ having infinitely many b's and infinitely many c's.

Given a generalised Büchi automaton $\mathcal{A} = (\Sigma, Q, Q_0, \delta, \{F_1, \ldots, F_k\})$, we define its **size** $|\mathcal{A}|$ as follows:

$$|\mathcal{A}| := \mathrm{card}(\Sigma) + \mathrm{card}(Q) + \mathrm{card}(Q_0) + \mathrm{card}(\delta) + \sum_i \mathrm{card}(F_i).$$

Generalised Büchi automata will be useful extensions of Büchi automata to simplify some technicalities, but they turn out to be not more expressive than Büchi automata, as shown below.

Lemma 14.1.9. Let $\mathcal{A} = (\Sigma, Q, Q_0, \delta, \{F_1, \ldots, F_k\})$ be a generalised Büchi automaton. Then a (standard) Büchi automaton $\mathcal{A}^b = (\Sigma, Q^b, Q_0^b, \delta^b, F^b)$ such that $L(\mathcal{A}^b) = L(\mathcal{A})$ can be computed in logarithmic space in the size of $\mathcal{A}$. ∎

Proof. Let $\mathcal{A} = (\Sigma, Q, Q_0, \delta, \{F_1, \ldots, F_k\})$ be a generalised Büchi automaton. The idea of the proof consists of defining $\mathcal{A}^b$ from k copies of $\mathcal{A}$ and simulating the generalised accepting condition by passing from one copy to another:

1. $Q^b := Q \times [1, k]$,
2. $Q_0^b := Q_0 \times \{1\}$,
3. $F^b := F_1 \times \{1\}$,
4. $\delta^b((q, i), a)$ is defined as the union of the two following sets

- $\{(q', i) \mid q \overset{a}{\to} q' \in \delta, \ q \notin F_i\}$
  (stay in the same copy if no accepting state in F_i is reached),
- $\{(q', (i \bmod k) + 1) \mid q \overset{a}{\to} q' \in \delta, \ q \in F_i\}$
  (go to the next copy if an accepting state in F_i is reached).

Checking that $\mathcal{A}$ and $\mathcal{A}^b$ accept the same language is left as an exercise. The logarithmic space cost is due to the construction of $\mathcal{A}^b$ that requires only integer variables that count up to $\mathrm{card}(Q \times [1, k])$. In order to see why logarithmic space is sufficient, we assume that the generalised Büchi automata and the Büchi automata are encoded with a reasonably succinct encoding. We will provide high-level arguments, thus avoiding the tedious details. In the definition of $\mathcal{A}^b$, we need to build the sets Q^b, Q_0^b and F^b, and each of them is of cardinality bounded by $\mathrm{card}(Q) \cdot k$. Basically, to construct such sets we need an integer variable to count up to $\mathrm{card}(Q) \cdot k$, which requires space in $\mathcal{O}(\log(\mathrm{card}(Q)) + \log(k))$. For the construction of the relation δ^b, we need to enumerate all the elements in $Q \times [1, k] \times \Sigma \times Q \times [1, k]$ in order to determine the sets of states of the form $\delta^b((q, i), \mathsf{a})$. Such an enumeration requires space in $\mathcal{O}(\log(\mathrm{card}(Q)) + \log(k) + \log(\mathrm{card}(\Sigma)))$ and the satisfaction of the two conditions also requires at most space $\mathcal{O}(\log(\mathrm{card}(Q)) + \log(k) + \log(\mathrm{card}(\Sigma)))$. Consequently, the complete process of building $\mathcal{A}^b$ requires only logarithmic space in the size of $\mathcal{A}$. $\qquad\Box$

14.1.3 Closure Properties

In this section, we state several properties on Büchi automata that will turn out useful. Most of the proofs are omitted, but in Section 14.9 we provide bibliographical references where these missing proofs can be found.

First, we consider a construction of an automaton accepting the intersection of two languages. Given Büchi automata $\mathcal{A}^1 = (\Sigma, Q^1, Q_0^1, \delta^1, F^1)$ and $\mathcal{A}^2 = (\Sigma, Q^2, Q_0^2, \delta^2, F^2)$, we build a Büchi automaton $\mathcal{A} = (\Sigma, Q, Q_0, \delta, F)$ such that $\mathrm{L}(\mathcal{A}) = \mathrm{L}(\mathcal{A}^1) \cap \mathrm{L}(\mathcal{A}^2)$. As for finite-state automata, $\mathcal{A}$ is obtained as a synchronised product of $\mathcal{A}^1$ and $\mathcal{A}^2$, but now the states both in F^1 and in F^2 need to be visited infinitely often. The next definition presents such a product.

Definition 14.1.10. Let $\mathcal{A}^1$ and $\mathcal{A}^2$ be two Büchi automata. We build the (generalised) **product automaton** $\mathcal{A} := \mathcal{A}^1 \otimes \mathcal{A}^2$ with $\mathcal{A} = (\Sigma, Q, Q_0, \delta, F_1, F_2)$ as follows:

- $Q = Q^1 \times Q^2$.
- $Q_0 = Q_0^1 \times Q_0^2$.
- $F_1 = F^1 \times Q^2$ and $F_2 = Q^1 \times F^2$.
- $(q_1, q_2) \overset{a}{\to} (q_1', q_2') \overset{\text{def}}{\Leftrightarrow} q_1 \overset{a}{\to} q_1' \in \delta^1$ and $q_2 \overset{a}{\to} q_2' \in \delta^2$.

The proof of Lemma 14.1.11 is left as an exercise but its idea is similar to the proof of Lemma 14.1.9.

Lemma 14.1.11. Given two Büchi automata $\mathcal{A}^1$ and $\mathcal{A}^2$, $\mathrm{L}(\mathcal{A}^1 \otimes \mathcal{A}^2) = \mathrm{L}(\mathcal{A}^1) \cap \mathrm{L}(\mathcal{A}^2)$. $\qquad\blacksquare$

Theorem 14.1.12. The family of Büchi-recognisable sets is closed under intersection, union and complementation.   ∎

The proof for union is similar to the proof for standard finite-state automata, while the proof for intersection is a consequence of Lemma 14.1.11. However, the closure under complementation is much more difficult to show and the proof will be deferred to Section 15.2.3.

It is well known that every regular language can be accepted by a deterministic finite-state automaton. However, we will see further that this property does not hold for ω-regular languages and Büchi automata.

Homomorphisms

Definition 14.1.13. Let Σ and Σ' be finite nonempty alphabets. An **alphabet mapping** is a map $h : \Sigma \to \mathcal{P}(\Sigma')$.   ▽

Thus a letter $a \in \Sigma$ is rewritten as one of the letters from $h(a)$. The map h can naturally be extended to finite words, infinite words and languages, i.e. $h(L) = \{w' \subset (\Sigma')^\omega \mid w' \subset h(w),\ w \in L\}$. For instance, $h(a_1 \cdots a_n)$ is defined as the following set of words:

$$\{b_1 \cdots b_n \mid \text{for all } i \in [1, n],\ b_i \in h(a_i)\}.$$

Similarly, given a Büchi automaton $\mathcal{A} = (\Sigma, Q, Q_0, \delta, F)$, we write $h(\mathcal{A})$ to denote the Büchi automaton $(\Sigma', Q, Q_0, \delta', F)$ such that $q \xrightarrow{b} q' \in \delta' \overset{\text{def}}{\Leftrightarrow}$ there is $a \in \Sigma$ such that $q \xrightarrow{a} q' \in \delta$ and $b \in h(a)$.

Lemma 14.1.14. Let $h : \Sigma \to \mathcal{P}(\Sigma')$ be an alphabet mapping and $\mathcal{A}$ be a Büchi automaton over the alphabet Σ. Then $L(h(\mathcal{A})) = h(L(\mathcal{A}))$.   ∎

The proof is left as Exercise 14.7.

14.1.4 Equivalence with ω-Regular Expressions

In this section, we show that Büchi automata have the same expressiveness as the ω-regular expressions defined in Section 10.1.1. First we introduce a notation: given languages $L \subseteq \Sigma^*$ and $L' \subseteq \Sigma^\omega$, we denote $L \cdot L' := \{u \cdot u' \mid u \in L, u \in L'\}$.

Lemma 14.1.15. Let $\mathcal{A}_1$ and $\mathcal{A}_2$ be Büchi automata and $\mathcal{B}$ be a finite-state automata over the alphabet Σ. Then:

(I) There is a Büchi automaton that recognises the language $L(\mathcal{A}_1) \cup L(\mathcal{A}_2)$.
(II) There is a Büchi automaton that recognises the language $L(\mathcal{B}) \cdot L(\mathcal{A}_1)$.
(III) If $L(\mathcal{B})$ does not contain the empty word, then there is a Büchi automaton that recognises the language $L(\mathcal{B})^\omega$.   ∎

Proof. Property (I) is easily proved by using the nondeterminism in Büchi automata; actually, it is already a consequence of Theorem 14.1.12. For each of the properties (II) and

(III), we will provide the construction of the automaton $\mathcal{A}$ and we leave it to the reader to check that it, indeed, recognises the corresponding ω-language.

(II) Let $\mathcal{B} = (\Sigma, Q, Q_0, \delta, F)$ be a finite-state automaton and $\mathcal{A}_1$ be a Büchi automaton $(\Sigma, Q_1, Q_0^1, \delta_1, F_1)$. Without loss of generality we can assume that $\mathcal{B}$ and $\mathcal{A}_1$ do not share any state. We define the Büchi automaton $\mathcal{A} = (\Sigma, Q', Q_0', \delta', F')$ so that $L(\mathcal{A}) = L(\mathcal{B}) \cdot L(\mathcal{A}_1)$ as follows:

- $Q' := Q \cup Q_1$.
- $\delta' := \delta \cup \delta_1 \cup \{(q, \text{a}, q') \mid q' \in Q_0' \text{ and there is } q_f \in F \text{ such that } (q, \text{a}, q_f) \in \delta\}$.
- If $Q_0 \cap F = \emptyset$, then $Q_0' := Q_0$, otherwise $Q_0' := Q_0 \cup Q_0^1$.
- $F' := F_1$.

(III) Let $\mathcal{B} = (\Sigma, Q, Q_0, \delta, F)$ be a finite-state automaton such that ε is not accepted by $\mathcal{B}$. Without any loss of generality, we can assume that there is no transition leading to a state in Q_0. We define the Büchi automaton $\mathcal{A} = (\Sigma, Q', Q_0', \delta', F')$ so that $L(\mathcal{A}) = L(\mathcal{B})^\omega$ as follows:

- $Q' := Q$.
- $Q_0' := Q_0$ and $F' = Q_0$.
- $\delta' := \delta \cup \{(q, \text{a}, q_0) \mid q_0 \in Q_0 \text{ and there is } q_f \in F \text{ such that } (q, \text{a}, q_f) \in \delta\}$.

(This corresponds to adding a loop back to the initial states of $\mathcal{B}$.) $\qquad\square$

Let us recall some definitions regarding ω-regular expressions from Section 10.1.1. An ω-regular expression over the alphabet Σ is of the form $\bigcup_{i=1}^n E_i; F_i^\omega$ for some $n \geq 0$, regular expressions $E_1, \ldots, E_n$, and ε-free regular expressions $F_1, \ldots, F_n$. The language of infinite words over Σ defined by this expression is $\bigcup_{i=1}^n L(E_i)L(F_i)^\omega$, where $(\cdot)^\omega$ denotes infinite iteration. Note that in the case of $n = 0$, $L(E) = \emptyset$. Now a language L is ω-**regular** if there is some ω-regular expression E such that $L = L(E)$.

Theorem 14.1.16. Büchi automata and ω-regular expressions define the same class of ω-languages. $\qquad\blacksquare$

Proof. First, suppose that $E = \bigcup_{i=1}^n E_i; F_i^\omega$ is an ω-regular expression. By using the constructive proof for Lemma 14.1.15, one can build a Büchi automaton $\mathcal{A}$ so that $L(\mathcal{A}) = L(E)$. Since ω-regular languages are precisely definable by ω-regular expressions, we are done with the first part of the statement. Indeed, Lemma 14.1.15 guarantees that the class of ω-languages accepted by Büchi automata satisfies the following closure properties.

- If $X \subseteq \Sigma^*$ is regular, then X^ω is Büchi-recognisable.
- If $X \subseteq \Sigma^*$ is regular and Y is Büchi-recognisable, then XY^ω is Büchi-recognisable.
- Büchi-recognisable ω-languages are closed unions.

Second, suppose that $\mathcal{A} = (\Sigma, Q, Q_0, \delta, F)$ is a Büchi automaton such that $L = L(\mathcal{A})$. By Lemma 14.1.5, every ω-word $w \in L$ admits an accepting run beginning in an initial state, reaching an accepting state in F, and then looping back through it infinitely often. For all $q, q' \in Q$, let $X_{q,q'} = L(\mathcal{B}_{q,q'})$ where $\mathcal{B}_{q,q'}$ is the finite-state automaton recognising non-empty finite words such that $\mathcal{B}_{q,q'} = (\Sigma, Q, \{q\}, \delta, \{q'\})$, i.e. q is the initial state, q' is the unique accepting state. We write $E_{q,q'}$ to denote a regular expression such that $L(E_{q,q'}) = X_{q,q'}$ (we know that $E_{q,q'}$ can be computed effectively from $\mathcal{B}_{q,q'}$).

We get that

$$L(\mathcal{A}) = L\left(\bigcup_{q \in Q_0, q' \in F} E_{q,q'} E_{q',q'}^{\omega} \right).$$

So L is ω-regular.   □

Consequently, for any Büchi automaton $\mathcal{A}$ over the alphabet Σ, there are regular expressions $E_1, F_1, \ldots, E_N, F_N$ for some $N \geq 0$ such that

$$L(\mathcal{A}) = L\left(\bigcup_{i \in [1,N]} E_i \cdot (F_i)^{\omega} \right).$$

We leave it as Exercise 14.6 to show that the regular expression F_i can be assumed to be left-deletable in the sense of Definition 10.1.10. This is an important property that is needed in the translation from ω-regular expressions to PSL. It therefore provides the missing part in the proof that PSL can express all ω-regular properties.

Büchi-recognisable languages can also be characterised in several other ways, which may allow us to use the characterisation that is the most helpful when dealing with a speaking issue. For instance, any Büchi-recognisable language is equal to

- a Boolean combination of Büchi-recognisable languages obtained from deterministic Büchi languages only,
- a finite union of languages of the form $L(\mathcal{A})L(\mathcal{B})$ where $\mathcal{A}$ is a nondeterministic finite-state automaton and $\mathcal{B}$ is a deterministic Büchi automaton.

14.2 From LTL Formulae to Automata

In this section, we present several approaches for constructing automata that capture the sets of linear models of LTL formulae.

14.2.1 Finite-State Automata

We will define **finite-state automata** (recognising languages of finite words) accepting small satisfiability witnesses, as defined in Section 6.3.2. This will turn out to be partly satisfactory since a better solution consists of capturing exactly the linear models in $\mathrm{Mod}(\varphi)$ by a Büchi automaton (see Theorem 14.2.19 for instance).

In Section 6.3.2, we have seen that an LTL formula φ is satisfiable iff there is a small satisfiability witness for φ (see Definition 6.3.7), say $\Gamma_0, \ldots, \Gamma_i, \ldots, \Gamma_{i+l}$ with each $\Gamma_j \subseteq cl_{\mathrm{LTL}}(\varphi)$, $i \in [0, 2^{|\varphi|}]$ and $l \in [1, |\varphi|2^{|\varphi|}]$. Each Γ_j is a maximally consistent set and two consecutive sets Γ_j, Γ_{j+1} form a one-step consistent pair, which can be checked locally without taking the sets strictly before Γ_j and the sets strictly after Γ_{j+1} into account.

A small satisfiability witness is therefore a finite word over the alphabet $\mathcal{P}(cl_{\mathrm{LTL}}(\varphi))$ whose length is bounded by $(|\varphi| + 1)2^{|\varphi|}$. Hence the set of small satisfiability witnesses for φ is finite and therefore it is a regular language that can be recognised by a finite-state automaton $\mathcal{A}_\varphi$. Not every subset of $cl_{\mathrm{LTL}}(\varphi)$ is a letter appearing in such words; we only consider letters that are maximally consistent sets. We also discard words in which there are two consecutive letters Γ, Γ' where (Γ, Γ') is not one-step consistent. Moreover, we require that $\Gamma_0, \ldots, \Gamma_i, \ldots, \Gamma_{i+l}$ is accepted only if all the U-formulae in $\bigcup_{i \leq j < i+l} \Gamma_j$ are witnessed in $\Gamma_i, \ldots, \Gamma_{i+l-1}$. When the automaton reads the sequence of letters $\Gamma_i, \ldots, \Gamma_{i+l}$, in its states we encode the information (Δ, Δ') where Δ is the set of U-formulae requiring a witness in the loop and Δ' is the set of U-formulae that have already been witnessed in the loop. When the last letter Γ_{i+l} in a small satisfiability witness is read, we must have $\Delta \subseteq \Delta'$. Finally, when the finite-state automaton is in the prefix part, we only need to store the maximally consistent set Γ and the position $j \in [0, 2^{|\varphi|}]$ in the sequence. In the loop part, apart from $(\Gamma, j, \Delta, \Delta')$ we also need to store Γ_i to verify at the end that we indeed have a loop.

Let us now define $\mathcal{A}_\varphi = (\Sigma, Q, Q_0, \delta, F)$ formally:

- Σ is the set of maximally consistent sets with respect to $cl_{\mathrm{LTL}}(\varphi)$.
- $Q = (\Sigma \times [0, 2^{|\varphi|}]) \cup (\Sigma \times [1, |\varphi|2^{|\varphi|}] \times \Sigma \times \mathcal{P}(\Delta_\mathsf{U}) \times \mathcal{P}(\Delta_\mathsf{U}))$ with $\Delta_\mathsf{U} := \{\psi_1 \mathsf{U} \psi_2 \mid \psi_1 \mathsf{U} \psi_2 \in cl_{\mathrm{LTL}}(\varphi)\}$. The first type of elements takes care of the prefixes whereas the second type of elements takes care of loops.
- F is the set of states of the form $(\Gamma, j, \Gamma, \Delta, \Delta')$ with $\Delta \subseteq \Delta'$.
- $Q_0 = \Sigma \times \{0\}$.
- The transition relation δ is defined as follows. We distinguish three types of transitions: the ones related to sets in the prefix part of the small satisfiability witness, those that allow to jump from the prefix part to the loop part, and the ones related to sets in the loop. Then we define $q \xrightarrow{\mathsf{a}} q' \in \delta$ iff $\mathsf{a} = \Gamma$, (Γ, Γ') is one-step consistent, and:
  1. either $q = (\Gamma, j)$ and $q' = (\Gamma', j + 1)$ for some j,
  2. or $q = (\Gamma, j)$ for some j and $q' = (\Gamma', 1, \Gamma', \Gamma \cap \Delta_\mathsf{U}, \{\psi_1 \mathsf{U} \psi_2 \in \Delta_\mathsf{U} \mid \psi_2 \in \Gamma\})$,
  3. or $q = (\Gamma, j, \Gamma_f, \Delta_1, \Delta_2)$ and

$$q' = (\Gamma', j + 1, \Gamma_f, \Delta_1 \cup (\Gamma \cap \Delta_\mathsf{U}), \Delta_2 \cup \{\psi_1 \mathsf{U} \psi_2 \in \Delta_\mathsf{U} \mid \psi_2 \in \Gamma\}).$$

While firing the transition, we update the set of U-formulae that has been seen on the loop as well as the set of U-formulae $\psi_1 \mathsf{U} \psi_2$ for which ψ_2 has been realised.

Note that we encode the position in the sequence directly in the states. For instance, a maximally consistent set Γ_j with $j \leq i$ is encoded by a pair $(\Gamma_j, j) \in \mathcal{P}(cl_{\mathrm{LTL}}(\varphi)) \times [0, 2^{|\varphi|}]$. The finite-state automaton goes nondeterministically to the loop part of the small satisfiability witness. A maximally consistent set Γ_j with $j > i$ is encoded by a tuple $(\Gamma_j, j, \Gamma_f, \Delta, \Delta')$ where

- $\Gamma_j \subseteq cl_{LTL}(\varphi)$ and $j \in [1, |\varphi|2^{|\varphi|}]$,
- $\Gamma_f \subseteq cl_{LTL}(\varphi)$ (we remember which position the loop starts from),
- Δ is the set of U-formulae that occur in the loop part,
- Δ' is the set of U-formulae $\psi_1 U \psi_2$ for which ψ_2 is realised in the loop.

Accepting states are of the form $(\Gamma, j, \Gamma', \Delta, \Delta')$ where $\Gamma = \Gamma'$ (i.e. a loop is built) and $\Delta \subseteq \Delta'$ (reflecting condition (SSW4) in Definition 6.3.7).

Example 14.2.1. Let $\varphi = FGp \wedge FGq$. In the following, we present a list of states from $\mathcal{A}_\varphi$ corresponding to an accepting run. Letters are omitted since they are maximally consistent sets uniquely determined by the states. The first five states correspond to the prefix of the ultimately periodic model associated to the accepting run, whereas the last two states correspond to the loop. Presently, no U-formula needs a witness in the loop; that is why the last two elements of the state $(\Gamma, 1, \Gamma, \emptyset, \emptyset)$ can be empty. Finally, note that $(\Gamma, 1, \Gamma, \emptyset, \emptyset)$ is an accepting state in F.

1. $(\Gamma_0 \cup \{\neg Gp, \neg Gq, \neg p, \neg q\}, 0)$ with $\Gamma_0 = \{FGp \wedge FGq, FGp, FGq\}$,
2. $(\Gamma_0 \cup \{\neg Gp, \neg Gq, \neg p, \neg q\}, 1)$,
3. $(\Gamma_0 \cup \{\neg Gp, \neg Gq, \neg p, \neg q\}, 2)$,
4. $(\Gamma_0 \cup \{\neg Gp, Gq, \neg p, q\}, 3)$,
5. $(\Gamma_0 \cup \{Gp, Gq, p, q\}, 4)$ with $\Gamma = \Gamma_0 \cup \{Gp, Gq, p, q\}$,
6. $(\Gamma, 1, \Gamma, \emptyset, \emptyset)$,
7. $(\Gamma, 2, \Gamma, \emptyset, \emptyset)$.

By observing that each accepting run of $\mathcal{A}_\varphi$ corresponds to a correct guess in Algorithm 4, and conversely each correct guess leads to an accepting run of $\mathcal{A}_\varphi$, one obtains the following completeness result.

Lemma 14.2.2. $L(\mathcal{A}_\varphi)$ is the set of small satisfiability witnesses for φ. ∎

A detailed proof of Lemma 14.2.2 is left as an exercise.
From Theorem 6.3.8, we obtain the following result.

Theorem 14.2.3. For every LTL formula φ, one can build a finite-state automaton $\mathcal{A}_\varphi$ of size in $2^{O(|\varphi|)}$ such that φ is satisfiable iff $L(\mathcal{A}_\varphi) \neq \emptyset$. ∎

Note that the proof of Corollary 6.4.2 actually contains a nondeterministic polynomial-space algorithm to test the nonemptiness of the finite-state automaton $\mathcal{A}_\varphi$ defined earlier. Now we evaluate the advantages of using such a translation into finite-state automata.

Advantages: Nonemptiness of $\mathcal{A}_\varphi$ can be checked on the fly in polynomial space; so it meets the optimal worst-case complexity upper bound. The nondeterministic polynomial-space algorithm is precisely Algorithm 4 from Chapter 6.
Drawbacks: The automaton $\mathcal{A}_\varphi$ recognises small satisfiability witnesses that would enable building LTL models, but $\mathcal{A}_\varphi$ captures only a subset of the LTL models for φ, namely the ultimately periodic models with prefix lengths and loop lengths exponentially

bounded. Nevertheless, this is sufficient for testing satisfiability. Here, the automata-based approach remains a means to express the existence of finite words of bounded lengths that witness satisfiability, without having automata that recognise all the linear models of formulae.

14.2.2 An Approach Using Closure Properties

In this section, we present a modular approach to building a Büchi automaton accepting $\text{Mod}(\varphi)$. This is done by induction on the structure of φ, by using the fact that Büchi-recognisable languages are effectively closed under Boolean operations. This will turn out to be partly satisfactory because complementation of Büchi automata causes an exponential blow-up (see Theorem 15.2.16) and repeating complementation operations leads to non-elementary bounds in the worst-case.

Recall that the automata-based approach for LTL consists of representing the set of models in $\text{Mod}(\varphi)$ by an ω-regular language that can be effectively defined with the help of a Büchi automaton. That way satisfiability of φ, which is equivalent to the nonemptiness of $\text{Mod}(\varphi)$, becomes equivalent to the nonemptiness of a Büchi automaton – an easy problem to solve once the automaton is built.

Given an LTL formula φ built over atomic propositions in $\text{PROP}(\varphi)$ and a Büchi automaton $\mathcal{A}$ over the alphabet $\Sigma = \mathcal{P}(\Pi)$ for some $\Pi \supseteq \text{PROP}(\varphi)$, we write $\varphi \approx_\Sigma \mathcal{A}$ whenever $\text{Mod}_\Pi(\varphi) = \text{L}(\mathcal{A})$. We recall that $\text{Mod}_\Pi(\varphi)$ is the set of linear models for the formula φ over the set of atomic propositions Π. When $\Pi = \text{PROP}(\varphi)$, we write $\varphi \approx \mathcal{A}$ instead of $\varphi \approx_\Sigma \mathcal{A}$.

Theorem 14.2.4. Given an LTL formula φ, a Büchi automaton $\mathcal{A}_\varphi$ can be effectively built such that $\varphi \approx \mathcal{A}_\varphi$. ∎

Theorem 14.2.4 admits several proofs depending on the way the automaton $\mathcal{A}_\varphi$ is built. In the recursive construction, the cases for Boolean connectives are dealt with by using that Büchi-recognisable sets are effectively closed under union, intersection and complementation (see Theorem 14.1.12 and Section 15.2.3). The cases for the temporal operators X, F and U require a separate treatment and the case for U represents the most complex situation. The next few lemmas deal with respective cases in the induction step.

Lemma 14.2.5. Let φ_1 and φ_2 be LTL formulae, Π be a finite set of atomic propositions such that $\text{PROP}(\varphi_1) \cup \text{PROP}(\varphi_2) \subseteq \Pi$ and $\mathcal{A}_1, \mathcal{A}_2$ be Büchi automata such that $\varphi_1 \approx_\Sigma \mathcal{A}_1$ and $\varphi_2 \approx_\Sigma \mathcal{A}_2$ with $\Sigma = \mathcal{P}(\Pi)$. Let $\mathcal{B}$ be a Büchi automaton over Σ.

(I) If $\text{L}(\mathcal{B}) = \text{L}(\mathcal{A}_1) \cup \text{L}(\mathcal{A}_2)$, then $\varphi_1 \vee \varphi_2 \approx_\Sigma \mathcal{B}$.

(II) If $\text{L}(\mathcal{B}) = \text{L}(\mathcal{A}_1) \cap \text{L}(\mathcal{A}_2)$, then $\varphi_1 \wedge \varphi_2 \approx_\Sigma \mathcal{B}$.

(III) If $\text{L}(\mathcal{B}) = \Sigma^\omega \setminus \text{L}(\mathcal{A}_1)$, then $\neg\varphi_1 \approx_\Sigma \mathcal{B}$. ∎

The proof of Lemma 14.2.5 is by an easy verification. The next lemma makes similar statements for the temporal operators X and F.

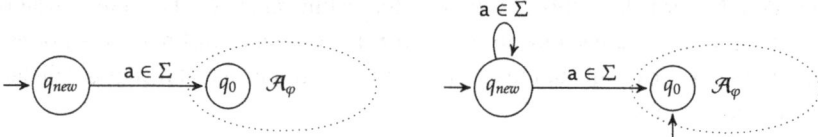

Figure 14.3 Büchi automata $\mathcal{A}_{X\varphi}$ (left) and $\mathcal{A}_{F\varphi}$ (right).

Lemma 14.2.6. Let φ be an LTL formula, Π be a finite set of atomic propositions such that $\text{PROP}(\varphi) \subseteq \Pi$, and $\mathcal{A} = (\Sigma, Q, Q_0, \delta, F)$ be a Büchi automaton such that $\varphi \approx_\Sigma \mathcal{A}$ with $\Sigma = \mathcal{P}(\Pi)$.

(I) Let $\mathcal{A}' := (\Sigma, Q \uplus \{q_{new}\}, \{q_{new}\}, \delta', F)$ be the Büchi automaton obtained from $\mathcal{A}$ by adding a new state q_{new} with

$$\delta' := \delta \uplus \{q_{new} \xrightarrow{a} q_0 : a \in \Sigma, \ q_0 \in Q_0\}$$

(see Figure 14.3 for a graphical representation). Then $X\varphi \approx_\Sigma \mathcal{A}'$.

(II) Let $\mathcal{A}' := (\Sigma, Q \uplus \{q_{new}\}, Q_0 \uplus \{q_{new}\}, \delta', F)$ be the Büchi automaton obtained from $\mathcal{A}$ by adding a new state q_{new} with

$$\delta' := \delta \uplus \{q_{new} \xrightarrow{a} q_0, q_{new} \xrightarrow{a} q_{new} \mid a \in \Sigma, \ q_0 \in Q_0\}$$

(see Figure 14.3 for a graphical representation). Then $F\varphi \approx_\Sigma \mathcal{A}'$.   ■

The proof of Lemma 14.2.6 is left as Exercise 14.20. Now we get to the case of the temporal operator U.

Lemma 14.2.7. Let φ_1 and φ_2 be LTL formulae, Π be a finite set of atomic propositions such that $\text{PROP}(\varphi_1) \cup \text{PROP}(\varphi_2) \subseteq \Pi$ and $\mathcal{A}_1, \mathcal{A}_2$ be Büchi automata such that $\varphi_1 \approx_\Sigma \mathcal{A}_1$ and $\varphi_2 \approx_\Sigma \mathcal{A}_2$ with $\Sigma = \mathcal{P}(\Pi)$. Then there exists a Büchi automaton $\mathcal{B}$ over the alphabet Σ such that $\varphi_1 U\varphi_2 \approx_\Sigma \mathcal{B}$ and the size of $\mathcal{B}$ is at most exponential in the respective sizes of $\mathcal{A}_1$ and $\mathcal{A}_2$.   ■

Proof. Let φ_1 and φ_2 be two formulae such that $\text{PROP}(\varphi_1) \cup \text{PROP}(\varphi_2) \subseteq \Pi$. For every $i \in \{1, 2\}$, we assume that we have a Büchi automaton $\mathcal{A}_i = (\Sigma, Q^i, Q_0^i, \delta^i, F^i)$ such that $\varphi_i \approx_\Sigma \mathcal{A}_i$ with $\Sigma = \mathcal{P}(\Pi)$. In what follows, we explain how to construct a Büchi automaton $\mathcal{B}$ such that $\varphi_1 U\varphi_2 \approx_\Sigma \mathcal{B}$. The construction of $\mathcal{B}$ from $\mathcal{A}_1$ and $\mathcal{A}_2$ is based on the following idea. Recall that $w, 0 \models \varphi_1 U\varphi_2$ iff there is $j \geq 0$ such that $w, 0 \models \varphi_1$ and $\cdots$ and $w, j-1 \models \varphi_1$, and $w, j \models \varphi_2$. This means that $w[0, +\infty) \in L(\mathcal{A}_1), \ldots, w[j-1, +\infty) \in L(\mathcal{A}_1)$ and $w[j, +\infty) \in L(\mathcal{A}_2)$. Recall that $w[i, +\infty)$ is the infinite **suffix** $w(i)w(i+1)w(i+2)\ldots$. An accepting run of $\mathcal{B}$ for the linear model w simulates the launch of a copy of $\mathcal{A}_1$ at each position in $[0, j-1]$ and a copy of $\mathcal{A}_2$ is started at the position j. Note that in order to keep track of at most j copies of $\mathcal{A}_1$, it is sufficient to store a set of states of cardinality at most $\max(\text{card}(Q^1), j)$. Indeed, if at a given position two copies have the same state, then these two copies can be identified. However, it is necessary to check that the accepting conditions are verified for each copy. This is done in the following detailed definition.

- The set of states of $\mathcal{B} = (\Sigma, Q, Q_0, \delta, F)$ is the following:

$$\{X \subseteq Q^1 \mid X \cap Q_0^1 \neq \emptyset\} \cup \mathcal{P}(Q^1) \times \mathcal{P}(Q^1) \times Q^2.$$

The first set in the union refers to states in $\mathcal{A}_1$ in which at least one state is initial (before reaching a position j satisfying φ_2). The second set of the union is made of two subsets of Q^1 and of a state in $\mathcal{A}_2$. Because each run of the form

$$q_0^k \xrightarrow{w(k+0)} q_1^k \xrightarrow{w(k+1)} q_2^k \xrightarrow{w(k+2)} \cdots$$

visits an accepting state of $\mathcal{A}_1$ infinitely often, we split the subsets of Q^1 into two parts in order to guarantee that the accepting states are visited infinitely often, as is done also in the proof of the forthcoming Theorem 14.3.12. Sets of states and states are updated by firing the transitions from $\mathcal{A}_1$ and $\mathcal{A}_2$ synchronously (see further).
- The initial states of $\mathcal{B}$ are in $Q_0 = \{\{q\} \mid q \in Q_0^1\} \cup (\{\emptyset\} \times \{\emptyset\} \times Q^2)$.
- The accepting states are in $F = \{\emptyset\} \times \mathcal{P}(Q^1) \times F^2$.
- The transitions in $\mathcal{B}$ are defined as follows:
  - $X \xrightarrow{a} X' \in \delta$ for $X, X' \subseteq Q^1$ iff $X' = \{q_0\} \cup Y$ for some $q_0 \in Q_0^1$ for $X \xrightarrow{a} Y$ in δ^1.
    This notation is just a shortcut to state the existence of a map $\mathfrak{f} : X \to Q^1$ such that $\mathrm{ran}(\mathfrak{f}) = Y$ ($\mathrm{ran}(\mathfrak{f})$ is the range of $\mathfrak{f}$) and for $q \in X$, $q \xrightarrow{a} \mathfrak{f}(q) \in \delta^1$.
  - $X \xrightarrow{a} (Y \setminus F^1, Y \cap F^1, q_0) \in \delta$ with $X, Y \subseteq Q^1$, $q_0 \in Q_0^2$ and $X \xrightarrow{a} Y$ in δ^1.
  - $(Y, Y', q) \xrightarrow{a} (Z, Z', q') \in \delta \overset{\mathrm{def}}{\Leftrightarrow} q \xrightarrow{a} q' \in \delta^2$ and
    - if $Y = Z = \emptyset$ and $q \notin F^2$, then $Y' \xrightarrow{a} Z'$ in δ^1 (we are waiting for hitting a state in F^2),
    - if $q \in F^2$ and $Y = \emptyset$ (i.e. $(Y, Y', q) \in F$) then $Z = Z \setminus F^1$, $Z' = Z' \cap F^1$ with $Y' \xrightarrow{a} (Z \uplus Z')$ in δ^1,
    - if $Y \neq \emptyset$, then $Z = X \setminus F^1$, $Z' = X' \cup (X \cap F^1)$ with $Y \xrightarrow{a} X$, $Y' \xrightarrow{a} X'$.

Assuming that $w, 0 \models \varphi_1 \mathsf{U} \varphi_2$, the following runs can be exhibited.

- By definition of $\mathcal{A}_1$, if $j > 0$ then there is an accepting run of the form

$$q_0^0 \xrightarrow{w(0)} q_1^0 \xrightarrow{w(1)} q_2^0 \xrightarrow{w(2)} \cdots .$$

- More generally, for all $k \in [0, j-1]$, there is an accepting run (in $\mathcal{A}_1$) of the form

$$q_0^k \xrightarrow{w(k+0)} q_1^k \xrightarrow{w(k+1)} q_2^k \xrightarrow{w(k+2)} \cdots .$$

- Similarly, by definition of $\mathcal{A}_2$, there is an accepting run of the form

$$q_0^j \xrightarrow{w(j+0)} q_1^j \xrightarrow{w(j+1)} q_2^j \xrightarrow{w(j+2)} \cdots .$$

$$q_0^0 \xrightarrow{w(0)} q_1^0 \xrightarrow{w(1)} q_2^0 \xrightarrow{w(2)} q_3^0 \xrightarrow{w(3)} \mathbf{q_4^0} \xrightarrow{w(4)} q_5^0 \xrightarrow{w(5)} q_6^0 \xrightarrow{w(6)} q_7^0 \xrightarrow{w(7)} q_8^0 \text{- ->}$$

$$q_0^1 \xrightarrow{w(1)} q_1^1 \xrightarrow{w(2)} q_2^1 \xrightarrow{w(3)} q_3^1 \xrightarrow{w(4)} q_4^1 \xrightarrow{w(5)} q_5^1 \xrightarrow{w(6)} q_6^1 \xrightarrow{w(7)} q_7^1 \text{- ->}$$

$$q_0^2 \xrightarrow{w(2)} q_1^2 \xrightarrow{w(3)} q_2^2 \xrightarrow{w(4)} \mathbf{q_3^2} \xrightarrow{w(5)} q_4^2 \xrightarrow{w(6)} q_5^2 \xrightarrow{w(7)} q_6^2 \text{- ->}$$

$$q_0^3 \xrightarrow{w(3)} q_1^3 \xrightarrow{w(4)} q_2^3 \xrightarrow{w(5)} \mathbf{q_3^3} \xrightarrow{w(6)} q_4^3 \xrightarrow{w(7)} q_5^3 \text{- ->}$$

$$\{q_0^0\} \quad \{q_1^1, q_0^0\} \quad \{q_2^2, q_1^1, q_0^2\} \quad q_3^0, q_2^1, q_1^2 \parallel q_0^3 \quad q_2^2 \mid \mathbf{q_4^0}\mathbf{q_3^2} \mid q_1^3 \quad \mid q_5^0, q_4^1, \mathbf{q_3^2} \mid q_2^3 \quad \mid \underline{q_6^0, q_5^1, q_4^2 \mid \mathbf{q_3^3}} \quad q_7^0, q_6^1, q_5^2 \parallel q_4^3 \quad q_8^0, q_6^2 \mid \mathbf{q_7^1} \mid q_4^3 \text{- ->}$$

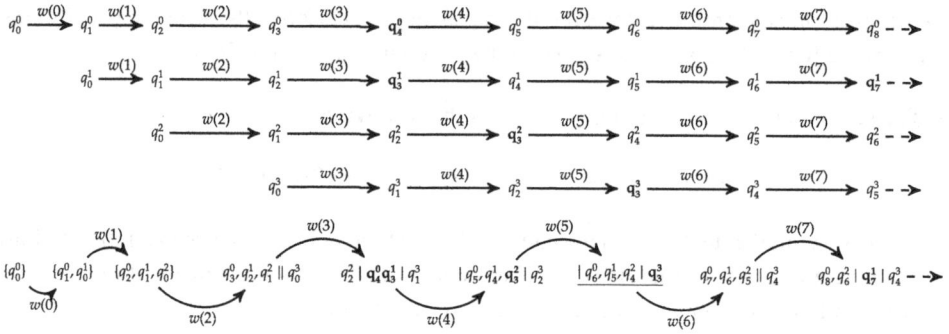

Figure 14.4 Accepting runs for $\mathcal{A}_1$, $\mathcal{A}_2$ and the corresponding accepting run for $\mathcal{B}$.

The automaton for $\varphi_1 \mathsf{U}\varphi_2$ uses a **subset construction** similar to the proof of the forthcoming Theorem 14.3.12 by considering a run of the following form (apart from the bookkeeping mechanism for the acceptance conditions; see Figure 14.7 for details):

$$\emptyset \cup \{q_0^0\} \xrightarrow{w(0)} \{q_1^0\} \cup \{q_0^1\} \xrightarrow{w(1)} \{q_1^1, q_2^0\} \cup \{q_0^2\} \xrightarrow{w(2)} \cdots \{q_1^{j-2}, q_2^{j-3}, \ldots, q_{j-1}^0\} \cup \{q_0^{j-1}\} \xrightarrow{w(j-1)}$$

$$(\{q_1^{j-1}, q_2^{j-2}, \ldots, q_j^0\}, q_0^j) \xrightarrow{w(j)} (\{q_2^{j-1}, q_3^{j-2}, \ldots, q_{j+1}^0\}, q_1^j) \xrightarrow{w(j+1)}$$

$$\times (\{q_3^{j-1}, q_4^{j-2}, \ldots, q_{j+2}^0\}, q_2^j) \cdots .$$

In Figure 14.4, we present three accepting runs of $\mathcal{A}_1$ and one accepting run of $\mathcal{A}_2$ witnessing the satisfaction of $\varphi_1 \mathsf{U}\varphi_2$ on w with $j = 3$. In order to illustrate the construction of $\mathcal{B}$, below those runs we also present the corresponding accepting run of $\mathcal{B}$. Accepting states of the Büchi automata $\mathcal{A}_1$ and $\mathcal{A}_2$ are represented in boldface, whereas those of $\mathcal{B}$ are underlined. Moreover, the states of $\mathcal{B}$ belonging to $\mathcal{P}(Q^1) \times \mathcal{P}(Q^1) \times Q^2$ are represented by three elements separated by '|'. $\square$

Remark 14.2.8. The construction would be similar if we defined $\mathcal{B}$ as an alternating Büchi automaton (notion to be defined in Section 14.3) and then eliminate nondeterminism (at the cost of an exponential blow-up, see Section 14.3).

In the forthcoming proof of Theorem 14.2.4, the induction step may require assumptions of the form $\varphi_1 \approx \mathcal{A}_1$, $\varphi_2 \approx \mathcal{A}_2$ but with $\mathrm{PROP}(\varphi_1) \neq \mathrm{PROP}(\varphi_2)$, whence Lemma 14.2.5 and Lemma 14.2.7 do not apply, strictly speaking. In that case, before performing the construction of a Büchi automaton from $\mathcal{A}_1$ and $\mathcal{A}_2$ in the induction step involving φ_1 and φ_2, we first need to perform an operation that consists of adding dummy atomic propositions in $\mathcal{A}_1$ and $\mathcal{A}_2$. This is the purpose of Lemma 14.2.9.

Lemma 14.2.9. Let $\Pi \subseteq \Pi'$ be finite sets of atomic propositions and $\mathcal{A} = (\Sigma, Q, Q_0, \delta, F)$ be a Büchi automaton over the alphabet Σ with $\Sigma = \mathcal{P}(\Pi)$. Let $\mathcal{A}' = (\Sigma', Q, Q_0, \delta', F)$ be the variant Büchi automaton over the alphabet $\Sigma' = \mathcal{P}(\Pi') \supseteq \Sigma$ such that for all $\mathsf{a} \in \Sigma'$,

$q \xrightarrow{a} q' \in \delta' \overset{\text{def}}{\Leftrightarrow} q \xrightarrow{a \cap \Pi} q' \in \delta$. Then $\mathrm{L}(\mathcal{A})$ is equal to the following set:

$$\{w' \in \Sigma^\omega \mid \text{there exists } w \in \mathrm{L}(\mathcal{A}') \text{ such that for all } j, \ w'(j) = w(j) \cap \Pi\}. \qquad \blacksquare$$

In the preceding lemma the automaton $\mathcal{A}$ behaves as $\mathcal{A}'$ where the atomic propositions from $\Pi' \setminus \Pi$ are ignored. The Büchi automaton $\mathcal{A}'$ can be also viewed as the automaton $\mathcal{A}$ in which additional atomic propositions are added (those in $\Pi' \setminus \Pi$) but what matters to fire a transition is the restriction of the letter to atomic propositions in Π. The proof of Lemma 14.2.9 is left as Exercise 14.20.

Proof (Theorem 14.2.4). The proof is by structural induction using the previous Lemmas 14.2.5–14.2.9. A notable feature is that the Büchi automaton $\mathcal{A}_\varphi$ can be built recursively over the structure of φ. For the base case, we assume that φ is an atomic proposition p. We have $p \approx \mathcal{A}_p$ with $\mathcal{A}_p = (\{\emptyset, \{p\}\}, \{q_0, q_f\}, \{q_0\}, \{q_0 \xrightarrow{\{p\}} q_f, q_f \xrightarrow{\{p\} \text{ or } \emptyset} q_f\}, \{q_f\})$:

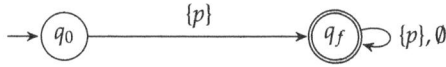

Now we do the induction steps depending on the outermost connective for φ.

$\varphi = \varphi_1 \vee \varphi_2$ **or** $\varphi = \varphi_1 \wedge \varphi_2$: By inductive hypothesis, for every $i \in \{1, 2\}$ there exists $\mathcal{A}_i$ such that $\varphi_i \approx \mathcal{A}_i$. By Lemma 14.2.9, let $\mathcal{A}'_i$ be the variant of $\mathcal{A}_i$ over the alphabet $\mathcal{P}(\mathrm{PROP}(\varphi))$ such that $\mathrm{L}(\mathcal{A}_i)$, is equal to

$$\{w' \in (\mathcal{P}(\mathrm{PROP}(\varphi_i)))^\omega \mid \text{there is } w \in \mathrm{L}(\mathcal{A}'_i) \text{ s.t. for all } j, \ w'(j) = w(j) \cap \mathrm{PROP}(\varphi_i)\}.$$

By Theorem 14.1.12 one can effectively build a Büchi automaton $\mathcal{B}$ such that $\mathrm{L}(\mathcal{B}) = \mathrm{L}(\mathcal{A}'_1) \cap \mathrm{L}(\mathcal{A}'_2)$ and a Büchi automaton $\mathcal{B}'$ such that $\mathrm{L}(\mathcal{B}) = \mathrm{L}(\mathcal{A}'_1) \cup \mathrm{L}(\mathcal{A}'_2)$. Then, by Lemma 14.2.5(II), $\varphi \approx \mathcal{B}$ or by Lemma 14.2.5(I), $\varphi \approx \mathcal{B}'$.

$\varphi = \neg\varphi_1$: By the inductive hypothesis there exists $\mathcal{A}_1$ such that $\varphi_1 \approx \mathcal{A}_1$. By Theorem 14.1.12, one can effectively build a Büchi automaton $\mathcal{B}$ such that $\mathrm{L}(\mathcal{B}) = (\mathcal{P}(\mathrm{PROP}(\varphi_1)))^\omega \setminus \mathrm{L}(\mathcal{A}'_1)$. By Lemma 14.2.5(III), $\varphi \approx \mathcal{B}$.

$\varphi = \mathsf{X}\varphi_1$ **or** $\varphi = \mathsf{F}\varphi_1$: By inductive hypothesis, there exists $\mathcal{A}_1$ such that $\varphi_1 \approx \mathcal{A}_1$. By Lemma 14.2.6(I)–(II), one can effectively build a Büchi automaton $\mathcal{B}$ such that $\varphi \approx \mathcal{B}$.

$\varphi = \varphi_1 \mathsf{U}\varphi_2$: By inductive hypothesis, for every $i \in \{1, 2\}$, there exists $\mathcal{A}_i$ such that $\varphi_i \approx \mathcal{A}_i$. By Lemma 14.2.9, let $\mathcal{A}'_i$ be the variant of $\mathcal{A}_i$ over the alphabet $\mathcal{P}(\mathrm{PROP}(\varphi))$ such that $\mathrm{L}(\mathcal{A}_i)$ is equal to

$$\{w' \in (\mathcal{P}(\mathrm{PROP}(\varphi_i)))^\omega \mid \text{there is } w \in \mathrm{L}(\mathcal{A}'_i), \text{ s.t. for all } j, \ w'(j) = w(j) \cap \mathrm{PROP}(\varphi_i)\}.$$

By Lemma 14.2.7, one can effectively build a Büchi automaton $\mathcal{B}$ such that $\varphi \approx \mathcal{B}$. $\qquad \square$

In the construction of $\mathcal{A}_\varphi$ in the proof of Theorem 14.2.4 each connective introduces an exponential blow-up in the worst-case. Actually, only the temporal operator U and negation $\neg$ meet this exponential bound, apart from the fact that the alphabet can be of exponential size. A crude complexity analysis of the construction of $\mathcal{A}_\varphi$ implies that the size of $\mathcal{A}_\varphi$ is nonelementary in the size of φ.

Let us summarise the advantages and drawbacks of building $\mathcal{A}_\varphi$ inductively from φ such that $\varphi \approx \mathcal{A}_\varphi$:

Advantage I: The construction of $\mathcal{A}_\varphi$ is modular and uses standard constructions on Büchi automata.

Advantage II: $\mathcal{A}_\varphi$ accepts exactly the linear models from $\mathrm{Mod}(\varphi)$.

Disadvantage: In the worst-case, the size of $\mathcal{A}_\varphi$ is nonelementary in the size of φ. Its number of states can be written as a tower of exponentials of the form

$$2^{2^{\cdot^{\cdot^{\cdot^{2^{p(|\varphi|)}}}}}}$$

whose height is linear in the size of φ and $p(.)$ is some fixed polynomial.

14.2.3 An Elementary Modular Approach

In this section, we propose another modular approach that builds a Büchi automaton accepting $\mathrm{Mod}(\varphi)$ by induction on the structure of φ by essentially using the renaming technique (see Section 5.2.1). It has the advantage of building automata of exponential size in the worst-case and to be fully modular, even though it is not based on closure properties for ω-regular languages. Thus the construction presented here will have the advantages of the one in Section 14.2.2 but not its drawback, viz. the nonelementary blowup in size.

Outline. Given an LTL formula φ built over the atomic propositions in $\mathrm{PROP}(\varphi) = \{p_1, \ldots, p_M\}$, we aim at building in a modular way a Büchi automaton $\mathcal{A}$ over the alphabet $\Sigma \times \{0, 1\}$ with $\Sigma = \mathcal{P}(\mathrm{PROP}(\varphi))$ satisfying the following properties.

(T1) For every LTL model $\sigma : \mathbb{N} \to \Sigma$, there is a unique ω-word $\sigma' \in (\Sigma \times \{0, 1\})^\omega$ accepted by $\mathcal{A}$ such that the Σ-projection of σ' is equal to σ and:
(†) for all $i \geq 0$, we have $\sigma, i \models \varphi$ iff at position i, the $\{0, 1\}$-projection of σ' is equal to 1.
Note that there cannot be two different σ' satisfying (†) for a fixed model σ.

(T2) $\mathcal{A}$ is defined as a generalised Büchi automaton obtained by intersecting Büchi automata, each of them having a similar structure (at most 3 states) and being explicitly related to a single subformula of φ.

(T3) The size of $\mathcal{A}$ is at most exponential in the size of φ.

When $\mathcal{A}$ satisfies the condition (T1), we say that $\mathcal{A}$ is a **transducer** for φ. Conditions (T2) and (T3) provide quantitative requirements about the construction of $\mathcal{A}$. In automata theory, a (synchronous) transducer is an operational model that takes an input word and returns an output word, which can actually be encoded by a standard automaton over a product alphabet $\Sigma_i \times \Sigma_o$ where Σ_i is the input alphabet and Σ_o is the output alphabet. In the sequel, 'transducer' is simply a fancy name for a Büchi automaton over a product alphabet with output alphabet $\{0, 1\}$ and input alphabet $\mathcal{P}(\mathrm{PROP}(\varphi))$. The reference to transducers only helps to understand what is expected from $\mathcal{A}$ but in the sequel no previous knowledge on transducers is needed or expected. In particular, this means that if

$$\begin{pmatrix} a_0 \\ b_0 \end{pmatrix}\begin{pmatrix} a_1 \\ b_1 \end{pmatrix}\begin{pmatrix} a_2 \\ b_2 \end{pmatrix}\begin{pmatrix} a_3 \\ b_3 \end{pmatrix} \cdots \in \mathrm{L}(\mathcal{A})$$

then for all $i \geq 0$, we have $a_0 a_1 a_2 \cdots, i \models \varphi$ iff $b_i = 1$. This is just a reformulation of (†).

More specifically, $\mathcal{A}$ takes as input LTL models (on a given finite set of atomic propositions) and outputs the truth value of φ on each position. $\mathcal{A}$ is constructed by composing Büchi automata with simple structures; each such automaton is related to a subformula of φ. Moreover, two subformulae with identical outermost connectives produce Büchi automata that are identical modulo the renaming of letters of the alphabet (this will become clear in the sequel). Note that $\mathrm{Mod}(\varphi)$ is then defined as the Σ-projection of ω-words in $\mathrm{L}(\mathcal{A})$ starting by a letter in $\Sigma \times \{1\}$, which can be viewed as a form of completeness of the construction. Obviously, if φ holds true at the first position, then φ is satisfiable in the model.

Renaming, or how to use new atomic propositions. Let φ be an LTL formula built over the atomic propositions $p_1, \ldots, p_M$ and $\psi_1, \ldots, \psi_N$ be the subformulae of φ ordered by increasing size. In case of conflict, we make an arbitrary choice for the formulae of identical sizes. Consequently, the first M subformulae $\psi_1, \ldots, \psi_M$ are atomic propositions, $\psi_N = \varphi$, and if ψ_a is a strict subformula of ψ_b, then $a < b$.

Now we introduce new atomic propositions $p_{M+1}, \ldots, p_N$; to each nonatomic subformula ψ_i of φ, we associate a new atomic proposition p_i that holds true exactly when the subformula ψ_i holds true. It is not necessary to introduce new atomic propositions for the elements in $\mathrm{PROP}(\varphi)$ since these are already the atomic propositions $p_1, \ldots, p_M$.

Next we define three alphabets $\Sigma \subset \Sigma_{\mathrm{trans}} \subseteq \Sigma_{\mathrm{renam}}$ that will be used throughout this section:

- $\Sigma = \mathcal{P}(\{p_1, \ldots, p_M\})$ (linear models in $\mathrm{Mod}(\varphi)$ are built over Σ),
- $\Sigma_{\mathrm{trans}} = \mathcal{P}(\{p_1, \ldots, p_M, p_N\})$,
- $\Sigma_{\mathrm{renam}} = \mathcal{P}(\{p_1, \ldots, p_N\})$.

Then we transform φ into a formula φ_{Ren} by using successive renamings (cf. Section 6.7.2). To do so, for all $i \in [M+1, N]$, we define the formula φ_{Ren}^i as follows.

- If $\psi_i = \neg\psi_{i_1}$ then $\varphi_{\mathrm{Ren}}^i := \mathsf{G}(p_i \leftrightarrow \neg p_{i_1})$.
- If $\psi_i = \mathsf{X}\psi_{i_1}$ then $\varphi_{\mathrm{Ren}}^i := \mathsf{G}(p_i \leftrightarrow \mathsf{X}p_{i_1})$.
- If $\psi_i = \psi_{i_1} \mathsf{O} \psi_{i_2}$ ($\mathsf{O} \in \{\wedge, \mathsf{U}\}$) then $\varphi_{\mathrm{Ren}}^i := \mathsf{G}(p_i \leftrightarrow (p_{i_1} \mathsf{O} p_{i_2}))$.

For instance, $\mathsf{G}(p_i \leftrightarrow (p_{i_1} \mathsf{O} p_{i_2}))$ simply refers to the validity of the formula $\mathsf{G}(\psi_i \leftrightarrow (\psi_{i_1} \mathsf{O} \psi_{i_2}))$. Now let

$$\varphi_{\mathrm{Ren}} := \bigwedge_{i \in [M+1, N]} \varphi_{\mathrm{Ren}}^i.$$

Lemma 14.2.10. $\mathrm{Mod}(\varphi) = \mathrm{Mod}(\exists\, p_{M+1} \cdots p_N\, (\varphi_{\mathrm{Ren}} \wedge p_N))$. ∎

The proof of this lemma is left as Exercise 14.20 and it is based on performing successive renamings, see also Section 6.7.2. Furthermore, we can show a more general property.

Lemma 14.2.11. For every LTL model $\sigma : \mathbb{N} \to \Sigma$, there is a unique LTL model $\sigma' : \mathbb{N} \to \Sigma_{\mathrm{renam}}$ such that

(I) $\sigma \approx_{\{p_1,\dots,p_M\}} \sigma'$, i.e. σ and σ' agree on the atomic propositions $p_1, \dots, p_M$,

(II) $\sigma', 0 \models \varphi_{\mathrm{Ren}}$,

(III) for all $i \geq 0$ and all $j \in [M + 1, N]$, we have $\sigma, i \models \psi_j$ iff $\sigma', i \models p_j$ (ψ_j and p_j hold true exactly at the same positions but on different linear models). ∎

The proof of Lemma 14.2.11 is left as Exercise 14.20.

On the role of the formula φ_{Ren}. The sets Σ_{trans} and $\Sigma \times \{0, 1\}$ are both of cardinality 2^{M+1} and we write $h_0 : \Sigma_{\mathrm{trans}} \to \Sigma \times \{0, 1\}$ to denote the bijection such that $h_0(\mathsf{a}) := \begin{pmatrix} \mathsf{b} \\ i \end{pmatrix}$ where $\mathsf{b} := \mathsf{a} \cap \{p_1, \dots, p_M\}$ and $i = 1 \stackrel{\mathrm{def}}{\Leftrightarrow} p_N \in \mathsf{a}$. Hence the value $i \in \{0, 1\}$ simply witnesses the presence of p_N in a. Given a Büchi automaton $\mathcal{A} = (\Sigma_{\mathrm{trans}}, Q, Q_0, \delta, F)$, we write $h_0(\mathcal{A}) = (\Sigma \times \{0, 1\}, Q, Q_0, \delta', F)$ to denote the Büchi automaton (over the alphabet $\Sigma \times \{0, 1\}$) such that for all $q, q' \in Q$ and all $\mathsf{b} \in \Sigma \times \{0, 1\}, q \stackrel{\mathsf{b}}{\to} q' \in \delta' \stackrel{\mathrm{def}}{\Leftrightarrow} q \stackrel{h_0^{-1}(\mathsf{b})}{\longrightarrow} q' \in \delta$.

Lemma 14.2.12. Given a Büchi automaton $\mathcal{A}$ over Σ_{trans}, if

$$\mathrm{L}(\mathcal{A}) = \mathrm{Mod}(\exists\, p_{M+1} \cdots p_{N-1}\, \varphi_{\mathrm{Ren}}),$$

then $h_0(\mathcal{A})$ is a transducer for φ. ∎

Proof. We have to check that $h_0(\mathcal{A})$ verifies condition (T1). The free atomic propositions in $\exists\, p_{M+1} \cdots p_{N-1}\, \varphi_{\mathrm{Ren}}$ are precisely $p_1, \dots, p_M, p_N$ and the linear models in $\mathrm{Mod}(\exists\, p_{M+1} \cdots p_{N-1}\, \varphi_{\mathrm{Ren}})$ are over the alphabet Σ_{trans}. Consequently, $h_0(\mathcal{A})$ is clearly a Büchi automaton over the alphabet $\Sigma \times \{0, 1\}$ by definition of h_0.

Let $\sigma : \mathbb{N} \to \Sigma$ be an LTL model. There is a unique $\sigma' : \mathbb{N} \to \Sigma_{\mathrm{renam}}$ satisfying conditions (I)–(III) from the statement of Lemma 14.2.11. In particular, this means that for all positions $i \geq 0$, we have $\sigma, i \models \varphi$ iff $\sigma', i \models p_N$. Let σ'' be the restriction of σ' to Σ_{trans}, i.e. for all $i \geq 0$, we have $\sigma''(i) := \sigma'(i) \cap \{p_1, \dots, p_M, p_N\}$. Still, for all positions $i \geq 0$, we have $\sigma, i \models \varphi$ iff $\sigma'', i \models p_N$.

Let $\sigma''' : \mathbb{N} \to \Sigma \times \{0, 1\}$ be such that for all $i \geq 0$, we have $\sigma'''(i) = h_0(\sigma''(i))$. For all $i \geq 0$, we have that $\sigma, i \models \varphi$ iff the second component of $\sigma'''(i)$ is equal to 1. Since $\sigma'' \in \mathrm{L}(\mathcal{A})$, we obtain that $\sigma''' \in \mathrm{L}(h_0(\mathcal{A}))$ (by definition of h_0), which completes the proof. ∎

It remains to show how the Büchi automaton $\mathcal{A}$ from Lemma 14.2.12 can be built. This is the place where the simple structure of the formula φ_{Ren} really comes into play.

$(p_2 \in \mathsf{a}$ and $p_3 \in \mathsf{a})$ iff $p_1 \in \mathsf{a}$ $\qquad\qquad\qquad$ $p_2 \notin \mathsf{a}$ iff $p_1 \in \mathsf{a}$

$$\rightarrow \overset{\curvearrowright}{\textcircled{q}} \qquad\qquad\qquad\qquad \rightarrow \overset{\curvearrowright}{\textcircled{q}}$$

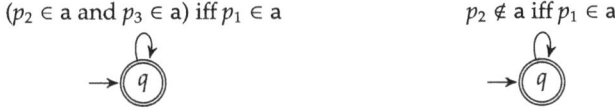

Figure 14.5 Büchi automata for $\mathsf{G}(p_1 \leftrightarrow (p_2 \wedge p_3))$ (left) and $\mathsf{G}(p_1 \leftrightarrow \neg p_2)$ (right).

Let h be the map $\Sigma_{\mathrm{renam}} \rightarrow \Sigma_{\mathrm{trans}}$ such that $h(\mathsf{a}) := \mathsf{a} \cap \{p_1, \ldots, p_M, p_N\}$. So the map h can be understood as a means to 'forget' about the atomic propositions $p_{M+1}, \ldots, p_{N-1}$. Given a Büchi automaton $\mathcal{A} = (\Sigma_{\mathrm{renam}}, Q, Q_0, \delta, F)$, we write $h(\mathcal{A}) = (\Sigma_{\mathrm{trans}}, Q, Q_0, \delta', F)$ to denote the Büchi automaton (over the alphabet Σ_{trans}) such that for all $q, q' \in Q$ and all $\mathsf{b} \in \Sigma_{\mathrm{trans}}$, $q \overset{\mathsf{b}}{\rightarrow} q' \in \delta' \overset{\mathrm{def}}{\Leftrightarrow}$ there is $\mathsf{b}' \in \Sigma_{\mathrm{renam}}$ such that $h(\mathsf{b}') = \mathsf{b}$ and $q \overset{\mathsf{b}'}{\rightarrow} q' \in \delta$.

Lemma 14.2.13. Let $\mathcal{A}_{\varphi_{\mathrm{Ren}}}$ be a Büchi automaton over the alphabet Σ_{renam}. If $\mathrm{L}(\mathcal{A}_{\varphi_{\mathrm{Ren}}}) = \mathrm{Mod}(\varphi_{\mathrm{Ren}})$, then $\mathrm{L}(h(\mathcal{A}_{\varphi_{\mathrm{Ren}}})) = \mathrm{Mod}(\exists \, p_{M+1} \cdots p_{N-1} \, \varphi_{\mathrm{Ren}})$. ∎

Proof. Let $\sigma \in \mathrm{L}(h(\mathcal{A}_{\varphi_{\mathrm{Ren}}}))$ with $h : \Sigma_{\mathrm{renam}} \rightarrow \Sigma_{\mathrm{trans}}$. This means that there exists $\sigma' \in \mathrm{L}(\mathcal{A}_{\varphi_{\mathrm{Ren}}})$ such that for all $i \geq 0$, we have $h(\sigma'(i)) = \sigma(i)$. By definition of $\mathcal{A}_{\varphi_{\mathrm{Ren}}}$, we get that $\sigma', 0 \models \varphi_{\mathrm{Ren}}$ and therefore $\sigma', 0 \models \exists \, p_{M+1} \cdots p_{N-1} \varphi_{\mathrm{Ren}}$. Hence we get $\sigma, 0 \models \exists \, p_{M+1} \cdots p_{N-1} \varphi_{\mathrm{Ren}}$, i.e. $\sigma \in \mathrm{Mod}(\exists \, p_{M+1} \cdots p_{N-1} \, \varphi_{\mathrm{Ren}})$. The proof for the other direction is analogous. □

Since $\mathcal{A}_{\varphi_{\mathrm{Ren}}}$ and $h(\mathcal{A}_{\varphi_{\mathrm{Ren}}})$ share the same set of states and the same set of transitions (modulo the renaming of letters), testing $h(\mathcal{A}_{\varphi_{\mathrm{Ren}}})$ for nonemptiness is not more complex than testing $\mathcal{A}_{\varphi_{\mathrm{Ren}}}$. Consequently, in order to get a transducer for φ, it is sufficient to adequately define $\mathcal{A}_{\varphi_{\mathrm{Ren}}}$ and we pose $T(\mathcal{A}) := h_0(h(\mathcal{A}))$ when $\mathcal{A}$ is a Büchi automaton over Σ_{renam} as should be $\mathcal{A}_{\varphi_{\mathrm{Ren}}}$. It remains to define $\mathcal{A}_{\varphi_{\mathrm{Ren}}}$ as a product of simple Büchi automata.

Automata. The formula φ_{Ren} is a conjunction of simple formulae of the form $\mathsf{G}(p_1 \leftrightarrow \psi(p_2, p_3))$ where $\psi(p_2, p_3)$ contains exactly one logical connective and only the atomic propositions p_2 and p_3 can occur in it. For each of these simple formulae, we construct a Büchi automaton that recognises its models.

- Let $\varphi_\wedge = \mathsf{G}(p_1 \leftrightarrow (p_2 \wedge p_3))$ be the simple LTL formula stating that throughout the run, p_1 is equivalent to the conjunction $(p_2 \wedge p_3)$. Given a finite set of atomic propositions $\Pi \supseteq \{p_1, p_2, p_3\}$, Figure 14.5 contains a simple Büchi automaton accepting linear models of $\varphi_\wedge$ over the alphabet $\Sigma = \mathcal{P}(\Pi)$. A transition labelled by '$(p_2 \in \mathsf{a}$ and $p_3 \in \mathsf{a})$ iff $p_1 \in \mathsf{a}$' represents a finite set of transitions labelled by a letter satisfying the equivalence in the obvious way $(\{p_2, p_3\} \subseteq \mathsf{a}$ iff $p_1 \in \mathsf{a})$; recall that a letter a is any subset of Π. We use a similar convention for the next automata.
- Similarly, $\varphi_\neg = \mathsf{G}(p_1 \leftrightarrow \neg p_2)$ is the formula stating that throughout the run, p_1 is equivalent to the negation of p_2. Figure 14.5 presents a Büchi automaton accepting linear models of $\varphi_\neg$ over the alphabet $\Sigma = \mathcal{P}(\Pi)$.

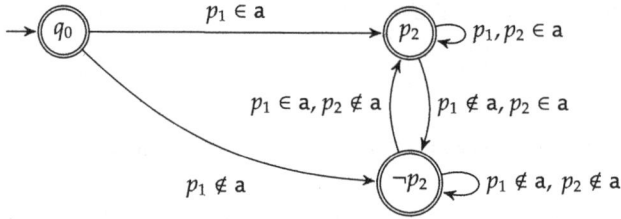

Figure 14.6 Büchi automaton for $G(p_1 \leftrightarrow Xp_2)$.

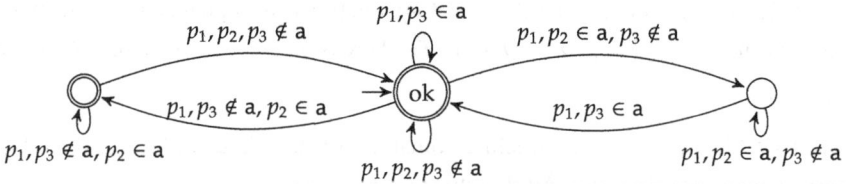

Figure 14.7 Büchi automaton for $G(p_1 \leftrightarrow (p_2 \cup p_3))$.

- Likewise, Figure 14.6 presents a Büchi automaton accepting linear models of $\varphi_X = G(p_1 \leftrightarrow Xp_2)$ over $\Sigma = \mathcal{P}(\Pi)$.
- Figure 14.7 presents a Büchi automaton accepting linear models of $\varphi_U = G(p_1 \leftrightarrow (p_2 \cup p_3))$ over $\Sigma = \mathcal{P}(\Pi)$.

We leave the proofs that the Büchi automata presented in Figures 14.5–14.7 recognise the models of the respective simple formulae to Exercise 14.10.

Modular construction of $\mathcal{A}_\varphi$. So it remains to define a transducer $\mathcal{A}_\varphi$ using:

1. the formula $\exists p_{M+1} \cdots p_{N-1} \, \varphi_{\text{Ren}}$,
2. Lemma 14.2.13 to eliminate second-order quantification and,
3. simple Büchi automata for the subformulae $\varphi_{\text{Ren}}^{M+1}, \ldots, \varphi_{\text{Ren}}^{N}, p_N$, as well as synchronisation.

For each $i \in [M+1, N]$, let $\mathcal{A}_i = (\Sigma_{\text{renam}}, Q^i, Q_0^i, \delta^i, F^i)$ be a Büchi automaton accepting the models of φ_{Ren}^i over the alphabet Σ_{renam}. It is easy to design the Büchi automata $\mathcal{A}_i$; see Figures 14.5–14.7. Observe that if the outermost connective of ψ_i is Boolean, then $\mathcal{A}_i$ has a unique state, otherwise $\mathcal{A}_i$ has three states. Let $\mathcal{A} = (\Sigma_{\text{trans}}, Q, Q_0, \delta, \{F_{M+1}', \ldots, F_N'\})$ be a generalised Büchi automaton defined as the product of the Büchi automata $\mathcal{A}_{M+1}, \ldots, \mathcal{A}_N$, following constructions provided in Section 14.1. This enables us to guarantee that $L(\mathcal{A}) = L(\mathcal{A}_{M+1}) \cap \cdots \cap L(\mathcal{A}_N)$.

Theorem 14.2.14. $L(\mathcal{A}) = \text{Mod}(\varphi_{\text{Ren}})$. ∎

The preceding equality is simply due to the definition of φ_{Ren}. Indeed, for all $i \in [M+1, N]$, we have $L(\mathcal{A}_i) = \text{Mod}_{\{p_1, \ldots, p_N\}}(\varphi_{\text{Ren}}^i)$. Since $\varphi_{\text{Ren}} = \bigwedge_{i \in [M+1, N]} \varphi_{\text{Ren}}^i$ and

$PROP(\varphi_{Ren}) = \{p_1, \ldots, p_N\}$, we get that $L(\mathcal{A}_{M+1}) \cap \cdots \cap L(\mathcal{A}_N) = Mod(\varphi_{Ren})$, which is exactly the statement of the preceding theorem.

More precisely, the product automaton $\mathcal{A}$ is defined as a slight variant of the usual product construction presented in Section 14.1:

- $Q = Q^{M+1} \times \cdots \times Q^N$ and $Q_0 = Q_0^{M+1} \times \cdots \times Q_0^N$.
- For every $i \in [M+1, N]$, $F^i = Q^{M+1} \times \cdots \times Q^{i-1} \times F^i \times Q^{i+1} \times \cdots \times Q^N$. (This guarantees that some element in F^i is visited infinitely often.)
- $(q_{M+1}, \ldots, q_N) \overset{a}{\to} (q'_{M+1}, \ldots, q'_N) \in \delta \overset{\text{def}}{\Leftrightarrow}$ for all $i \in [M+1, N]$, $q_i \overset{a}{\to} q'_i \in \delta_i$.
  (Strong synchronisation, i.e. all the Büchi automata make a step forwards synchronously.)

However, observe that whenever ψ_i is not an U-formula, $F^{i'} = Q$ since $F^i = Q^i$ and therefore it can be eliminated from the set of sets of accepting states. Hence the set of sets of accepting states can be restricted to the sets $F^{i'}$ such that ψ_i is an U-formula. So, $card(Q) \leq 3^{n_T}$ where n_T denotes the number of subformulae with outermost connective a temporal connective ($n_T \leq (N - M)$). Indeed, for all $i \in [M+1, N]$, if the outermost connective of ψ_i is Boolean, then $\mathcal{A}_i$ has a single state, otherwise (recall that ψ_i is either an X-formula or an U-formula) $\mathcal{A}_i$ has three states.

By Lemma 14.2.12 and Lemma 14.2.13, we get the following result.

Theorem 14.2.15. $T(\mathcal{A})$ is a transducer for φ.   ∎

Satisfiability of φ can now be checked on the fly in polynomial space by using a variant of $T(\mathcal{A})$. Indeed, the linear models of φ correspond to the ω-words of $T(\mathcal{A})$ starting by a letter whose second component is 1 (simply meaning that φ holds true at the first position).

We summarise the advantages and drawbacks of building $T(\mathcal{A})$ inductively from φ:

Advantages: The construction of $T(\mathcal{A})$ is modular; each logical connective has its own (minimal) temporal transducer template. It is worth noting that in order to build $T(\mathcal{A})$, there is no need to define intermediate formulae in QLTL (but it helps to understand the correctness of the construction) since it is sufficient to build the synchronised product of the automata $\mathcal{A}_{M+1}, \ldots, \mathcal{A}_N$. Each automaton $\mathcal{A}_i$ is very simple (at most equipped with three states) and it takes care of a specific subformula of φ.

Drawbacks: The number of states for $T(\mathcal{A})$ is bounded by 3^{n_T}. This is indeed a drawback since we shall see that this bound can be slightly improved.

14.2.4 A Global Construction

This section presents a translation in which accepting runs are exactly Hintikka traces. This provides a natural reduction for which nonemptiness of the Büchi automata can be tested on the fly in nondeterministic polynomial space. We introduce a notion of **maximal traces** for LTL formulae that is very similar to, but (being built from maximal consistent sets) not exactly the same as, the notion of Hintikka traces defined in Definition 13.2.5. It is strongly related to the definition of small satisfiability witnesses for satisfiable LTL formulae in Section 6.3.2.

Definition 14.2.16. A **maximal trace** for φ is a mapping $\mathcal{H} : \mathbb{N} \to \mathcal{P}(cl_{\text{LTL}}(\varphi))$ satisfying the following conditions for every $n \in \mathbb{N}$:

(H1) $\mathcal{H}(n)$ is maximally consistent with respect to $cl_{\text{LTL}}(\varphi)$.
(H2) $(\mathcal{H}(n), \mathcal{H}(n+1))$ is one-step consistent (in the sense of Definition 6.3.5).
(H3) If $\psi_1 \cup \psi_2 \in \mathcal{H}(n)$, then there exists $i \geq 0$ such that $\psi_2 \in \mathcal{H}(n+i)$ and $\psi_1 \in \mathcal{H}(n+j)$ for every $j \in [0, i-1]$.

A maximal trace $\mathcal{H}$ **satisfies** φ iff $\varphi \in \mathcal{H}(0)$. $\qquad\qquad\qquad\qquad\qquad \nabla$

The next lemma is a variant of Theorem 6.3.8 about small satisfiability witnesses for LTL formulae and of Theorem 13.1.17 about Hintikka traces for LTL formulae.

Lemma 14.2.17. An LTL formula φ is satisfiable iff there exists a maximal trace $\mathcal{H}$ that satisfies φ. ∎

Proof. Suppose that φ is LTL satisfiable, i.e. there is a linear model σ such that $\sigma, 0 \models \varphi$. Hence $\mathcal{H} = cl_{\text{LTL}}(\varphi, \sigma, 0), cl_{\text{LTL}}(\varphi, \sigma, 1), cl_{\text{LTL}}(\varphi, \sigma, 2), \ldots$. is a maximal trace (see Section 6.3.2 for the definition of $cl_{\text{LTL}}(\varphi, \sigma, i)$).

Conversely, if $\mathcal{H}$ is a maximal trace satisfying φ, then we define the LTL model σ such that for all $j \geq 0$, we have $\sigma(j) := \mathcal{H}(j) \cap \text{PROP}(\varphi)$. By structural induction, one can show that $\sigma, 0 \models \varphi$, as done in the respective proofs of Theorem 6.3.8 and Theorem 13.1.17. $\qquad\qquad\qquad\qquad \square$

Now we show how to construct $\mathcal{A}$ in Section 14.2.3 from the formula φ such that $\mathrm{L}(\mathcal{A}) = \text{Mod}(\varphi_{\text{Ren}})$ relates to maximal traces. First, recall that given an LTL formula φ, the sets $cl_{\text{LTL}}(\varphi)$ (see Section 6.3.1) and $sub(\varphi)$ are related, since by Lemma 4.1.3, for every $\psi \in sub(\varphi), \{\psi, \sim\psi\} \subseteq cl_{\text{LTL}}(\varphi)$, where (see Chapter 4)

$$\sim\psi = \begin{cases} \psi', & \text{if } \psi = \neg\psi' \\ \neg\psi, & \text{otherwise.} \end{cases}$$

So, if φ is built over the atomic propositions $p_1, \ldots, p_M$ and with subformulae $\psi_1, \ldots, \psi_N$ ordered by increasing size and with associated (possibly new) variables $\{p_1, \ldots, p_N\}$, any set $X \subseteq \{p_1, \ldots, p_N\}$ can be viewed as a subset of $cl_{\text{LTL}}(\varphi)$. Indeed, let $h : \mathcal{P}(\{p_1, \ldots, p_N\}) \to \mathcal{P}(cl_{\text{LTL}}(\varphi))$ be the map such that for all $X \subseteq \{p_1, \ldots, p_N\}$, $h(X)$ is defined as the smallest set satisfying the following conditions for every $i \in [1, N]$,

- $p_i \in X$ implies $\psi_i \in h(X)$.
- $p_i \notin X$ implies $\sim\psi_i \in h(X)$.

The map h allows us to view the subsets of $\{p_1, \ldots, p_N\}$ as subsets of $cl_{\text{LTL}}(\varphi)$.

We can now provide a simple characterisation for the sets of maximal traces.

Lemma 14.2.18. Let φ be an LTL formula and φ_{Ren} be the formula defined from φ in Section 14.2.3. If $\mathcal{A}$ is a Büchi automaton over the alphabet $\mathcal{P}(\{p_1, \ldots, p_N\})$ such that $\mathrm{L}(\mathcal{A}) = \mathrm{Mod}(\varphi_{\mathrm{Ren}})$, then $\mathrm{L}(h(\mathcal{A}))$ is the set of maximal traces for $cl_{\mathrm{LTL}}(\varphi)$. ∎

Assuming that $\mathcal{A}$ is equal to $(\mathcal{P}(\{p_1, \ldots, p_N\}), Q, Q_0, \delta, F)$, the automaton $h(\mathcal{A})$ is defined as $(\mathcal{P}(cl_{\mathrm{LTL}}(\varphi)), Q, Q_0, \delta', F)$ where for all $q, q' \in Q$ and for all $\mathsf{b} \in \mathcal{P}(cl_{\mathrm{LTL}}(\varphi))$:

$q \xrightarrow{\mathsf{b}} q' \in \delta' \stackrel{\text{def}}{\Leftrightarrow}$ there is $\mathsf{b}' \in \mathcal{P}(\{p_1, \ldots, p_N\})$ such that $h(\mathsf{b}') = \mathsf{b}$ and $q \xrightarrow{\mathsf{b}'} q' \in \delta$.

The proof of the lemma is left as Exercise 14.20.

However, it is worth noting that in the construction of $\mathcal{A}$, the small Büchi automata related to formulae with outermost Boolean connectives ($\wedge$ and $\neg$) take care of the condition (H1), while the small Büchi automata related to formulae with outermost temporal connectives (X and U) take care of condition (H2). Condition (H3) is taken care of by the acceptance conditions.

A large part of Section 14.2.3 is dedicated to defining the Büchi automaton $\mathcal{A}$ such that $\mathrm{L}(\mathcal{A}) = \mathrm{Mod}(\varphi_{\mathrm{Ren}})$. However, what we really need is to define an automaton whose accepting runs correspond to maximal traces. The automaton $h(\mathcal{A})$ is probably not that easy to manipulate (because of the way $\mathcal{A}$ is defined in Section 14.2.3). In what follows we provide a definition that is more explicitly related to the definition of maximal traces. The simple idea in the construction is to directly design an automaton, say $\mathcal{A}_\varphi$, whose accepting runs are the maximal traces satisfying φ. Moreover, we improve the bound from Section 14.2.3 since the number of states for $\mathcal{A}_\varphi$ will be in $2^{\mathcal{O}(|\varphi|)}$. We build a Büchi automaton $\mathcal{A}_\varphi$ over the alphabet $\mathcal{P}(\{p_1, \ldots, p_M\}) = \mathcal{P}(\mathrm{PROP}(\varphi))$ such that:

- $\mathrm{Mod}(\varphi) = \mathrm{L}(\mathcal{A}_\varphi)$.
- If $\Gamma_0 \xrightarrow{a_0} \Gamma_1 \xrightarrow{a_1} \Gamma_2 \xrightarrow{a_2} \Gamma_3 \ldots$ is an accepting run of $\mathcal{A}_\varphi$, then $\Gamma_0 \Gamma_1 \cdots$ is a maximal trace satisfying φ. Consequently, the states of $\mathcal{A}_\varphi$ are maximally consistent subsets of $cl_{\mathrm{LTL}}(\varphi)$.
- If $\mathcal{H}$ is a Hintikka trace satisfying φ, then

$$\mathcal{H}(0) \xrightarrow{\mathcal{H}(0) \cap \mathrm{PROP}} \mathcal{H}(1) \xrightarrow{\mathcal{H}(1) \cap \mathrm{PROP}} \mathcal{H}(2) \xrightarrow{\mathcal{H}(2) \cap \mathrm{PROP}} \mathcal{H}(3) \ldots$$

is an accepting run of $\mathcal{A}_\varphi$. In particular, the generalised Büchi acceptance condition is taken care of by condition (H3).

Given an LTL formula φ, let us build the generalised Büchi automaton

$$\mathcal{A}_\varphi = (\Sigma, Q, Q_0, \delta, \{F_1, \ldots, F_k\})$$

where:

- $\Sigma = \mathcal{P}(\mathrm{PROP}(\varphi))$.
- Q is the set of maximally consistent subsets of $cl_{\mathrm{LTL}}(\varphi)$.
- $Q_0 = \{\Gamma \in Q : \varphi \in \Gamma\}$.
- $\Gamma \xrightarrow{a} \Gamma' \in \delta \stackrel{\text{def}}{\Leftrightarrow} (\Gamma, \Gamma')$ is one-step consistent, $(\Gamma \cap \mathrm{PROP}(\varphi)) \subseteq a$ and $\{p : \neg p \in \Gamma\} \cap a = \emptyset$.

- If the temporal operator U does not occur in φ, then $F_1 = Q$ and $k = 1$. Otherwise, suppose that $\{\psi_1 U \psi_1', \ldots, \psi_k U \psi_k'\}$ is the set of U-formulae in $cl_{\mathrm{LTL}}(\varphi)$. Then, for every $i \in [1, k]$, $F_i = \{\Gamma \in Q : \psi_i U \psi_i' \notin \Gamma \text{ or } \psi_i' \in \Gamma\}$.

Note that here we assume that the logical connectives appearing in φ are among $\neg$, $\wedge$, X, U. Observe that $\mathrm{card}(Q) \leq 2^{|\varphi|}$ and $\mathcal{A}_\varphi$ can be built in exponential time in $|\varphi|$.

Theorem 14.2.19. $\mathrm{Mod}(\varphi) = \mathrm{L}(\mathcal{A}_\varphi)$. ∎

Proof. Let σ be a linear model in $\mathrm{Mod}(\varphi)$. Then $\mathcal{H} : \mathbb{N} \to \mathcal{P}(cl_{\mathrm{LTL}}(\varphi))$, where $\mathcal{H}(n) := cl_{\mathrm{LTL}}(\varphi, \sigma, n)$ for $n \geq 0$, is a maximal trace satisfying φ. Clearly, $\rho = \mathcal{H}(0) \xrightarrow{\sigma(0)} \mathcal{H}(1) \xrightarrow{\sigma(1)} \mathcal{H}(2) \xrightarrow{\sigma(2)} \mathcal{H}(3) \cdots$ is an infinite run for $\mathcal{A}_\varphi$. One can also easily establish that $(\star)$ ρ is accepting.

Conversely, let $\Gamma_0 \xrightarrow{a_0} \Gamma_1 \xrightarrow{a_1} \Gamma_2 \xrightarrow{a_2} \Gamma_3 \ldots$ be an accepting run of $\mathcal{A}_\varphi$. One can show that $\Gamma_0 \Gamma_1 \cdots$ is a maximal trace satisfying φ, which will guarantee that $a_0 a_1 \cdots$ is a model for φ (see the proof of Theorem 13.2.9). Only the satisfaction of condition (H3) needs a more careful analysis. Let $\psi_1 U \psi_2 \in \mathcal{H}(n)$. For a *reductio ad absurdum*, we distinguish two cases:

Case 1: Suppose that $\psi_2 \notin \mathcal{H}(n')$ for every $n' \geq n$. Since $(\mathcal{H}(n), \mathcal{H}(n+1))$ is one-step consistent, either $\psi_2 \in \mathcal{H}(n)$ or $\psi_1 \in \mathcal{H}(n)$ and $\psi_1 U \psi_2 \in \mathcal{H}(n+1)$. As $\psi_2 \notin \mathcal{H}(n)$, we get $\psi_1 \in \mathcal{H}(n)$ and $\psi_1 U \psi_2 \in \mathcal{H}(n+1)$. By a simple induction we can show that for all $n' \geq n$, $\psi_1 \in \mathcal{H}(n')$ and $\psi_1 U \psi_2 \in \mathcal{H}(n')$. Consequently, for every $n' \geq n$, $\Gamma_{n'} \notin \{\Gamma \in Q : \psi_1 U \psi_2 \notin \Gamma \text{ or } \psi_2 \in \Gamma\}$, whence $\mathcal{A}_\varphi$ cannot accept the run $\Gamma_0 \xrightarrow{a_0} \Gamma_1 \xrightarrow{a_1} \Gamma_2 \xrightarrow{a_2} \Gamma_3 \ldots$. Indeed, on that run no state from $\{\Gamma \in Q : \psi_1 U \psi_2 \notin \Gamma \text{ or } \psi_2 \in \Gamma\}$ is visited infinitely often, which leads to a contradiction.

Case 2: Suppose that there is a minimal $n'' \geq n$ such that $\psi_2 \in \mathcal{H}(n'')$ and there exists $n' \in [n, n'' - 2]$ such that for all $j \in [n, n']$, we have $\psi_1 \in \mathcal{H}(j)$ and $\psi_1 \notin \mathcal{H}(n'' - 1)$. As earlier, we can show by a simple induction that $\psi_1 \in \mathcal{H}(j)$ and $\psi_1 U \psi_2 \in \mathcal{H}(j)$ for all $j \in [n, n'' - 1]$, which leads to a contradiction too. □

We summarise the advantages and drawbacks of building $\mathcal{A}_\varphi$ as earlier:

Advantage I: In the worst-case, the size of $\mathcal{A}_\varphi$ is exponential in the size of φ and non-emptiness of $\mathcal{A}_\varphi$ can be checked on the fly in polynomial space. The number of states is bounded by $2^{|\varphi|}$.

Advantage II: $\mathcal{A}_\varphi$ accepts exactly the set of linear models from the set $\mathrm{Mod}(\varphi)$.

Disadvantage: The construction of $\mathcal{A}_\varphi$ is global and not modular unlike some of the previous constructions.

14.2.5 PSPACE *Upper Bounds*

It is time to collect the different results and to re-establish the PSPACE upper bound, already obtained in Chapter 6.

Corollary 14.2.20. SAT(LTL) is in PSPACE. ∎

Proof. Given an LTL formula, we have proved that φ is satisfiable iff $L(\mathcal{A}_\varphi) \neq \emptyset$ where $\mathcal{A}_\varphi$ is a generalised Büchi automaton. More precisely, $L(\mathcal{A}_\varphi) = \text{Mod}(\varphi)$. By Lemma 14.1.9, from a generalised Büchi automaton it is possible to build a standard Büchi automaton (in logarithmic space) that accepts the same language. Since $\mathcal{A}_\varphi$ can be built in polynomial space in the size of φ, it is possible to compute a Büchi automaton $\mathcal{A}'_\varphi$ in polynomial space such that φ is satisfiable iff $L(\mathcal{A}'_\varphi) \neq \emptyset$. $\mathcal{A}_\varphi$ can be built in polynomial space since the following conditions are satisfied:

1. Each state of $\mathcal{A}_\varphi$ can be built in polynomial space.
2. Checking whether a state is initial or belongs to a set of accepting states can be checked in polynomial space.
3. There is a linear amount of sets of accepting states.
4. The transition relation can be checked in polynomial space.

Additionally, the nonemptiness problem for Büchi automata is NLOGSPACE-complete (see Theorem 14.1.6) and composing a polynomial-space reduction with a nondeterministic logarithmic space test can be done in nondeterministic polynomial space. By Savitch's Theorem, NPSPACE = PSPACE and therefore checking whether φ is satisfiable can be done in polynomial space in the size of φ. $\qquad \square$

An alternative proof that does not use structural properties of complexity classes is to test the nonemptiness of $L(\mathcal{A}_\varphi)$ on the fly which can be done by using a polynomial amount of space with a nondeterministic algorithm.

We now consider an instance of the existential model-checking problem for LTL: we wish to check whether $\mathcal{T}, s \models_\exists \varphi$ with $\mathcal{T} = (S, R, L)$.

Definition 14.2.21. Let Π be a finite set of atomic propositions, Σ be the alphabet $\mathcal{P}(\Pi)$, $\mathcal{T} = (S, R, L)$ be a finite interpreted transition system built over the atomic propositions in Π, $s \in S$, and $\mathcal{A} = (\Sigma, Q, Q_0, \delta, F)$ be a Büchi automaton over the alphabet Σ. The **synchronised product**

$$\mathcal{T} \parallel \mathcal{A}_\varphi := (\{\mathsf{a}_0\}, S \times Q, \{s\} \times Q_0, \delta', S \times Q)$$

is a Büchi automaton over a unary alphabet (namely $\{\mathsf{a}_0\}$) such that the transition relation δ' is defined as follows: for all $(s', q'), (s'', q'')$, we have $(s', q') \xrightarrow{\mathsf{a}_0} (s'', q'') \overset{\text{def}}{\Leftrightarrow} (s, s') \in R$ and $q' \in \delta(q, L(s))$. $\qquad \triangledown$

The alphabet in the synchronised product is unary and, in fact, plays no role in the main property stated as follows. Synchronisation is performed between the valuation of a state of the interpreted transition system and the valuation of the state of the Büchi automaton $\mathcal{A}$. Our intention is to build a synchronised product $\mathcal{T} \parallel \mathcal{A}_\varphi$ where $\mathcal{A}_\varphi$ is a Büchi automaton accepting the models for φ and synchronisation is performed to guarantee that propositional valuations in $\mathcal{T}$ coincide with letters in $\mathcal{A}_\varphi$.

Lemma 14.2.22. Let φ be an LTL formula, $\mathcal{T}$ be a finite interpreted transition system built over the same set of atomic propositions and s be a state of $\mathcal{T}$. Then $L(\mathcal{T} \parallel \mathcal{A}_\varphi) \neq \emptyset$ iff $\mathcal{T}, s \models_\exists \varphi$, where $L(\mathcal{A}_\varphi) = \text{Mod}(\varphi)$. ∎

The proof of Lemma 14.2.22 is left as Exercise 14.13.

Corollary 14.2.23. The size of $\mathcal{T} \parallel \mathcal{A}_\varphi$ is in $2^{\mathcal{O}(|\varphi|)} \cdot |\mathcal{T}|$ and, by building it on the fly, $\mathcal{T}, s \models_\exists \varphi$ can be checked in space in $\mathcal{O}(|\varphi| + \log(|\mathcal{T}|))$ with a nondeterministic algorithm. ∎

This is precisely the algorithm given in Chapter 6 for guessing small model-checking witnesses.

Theorem 14.2.24. $\text{MC}^\exists(\text{LTL})$ and $\text{MC}^\forall(\text{LTL})$ are in PSPACE. ∎

The upper bound for $\text{MC}^\forall(\text{LTL})$ is a direct consequence of the upper bound for $\text{MC}^\exists(\text{LTL})$. Indeed, $\mathcal{T}, s \models_\forall \psi$ iff $\mathcal{T}, s \not\models_\exists \neg\psi$. Since $\text{MC}^\exists(\text{LTL})$ is in PSPACE and PSPACE = co-PSPACE, we get that $\mathcal{T}, s \models_\forall \varphi$ can be checked in polynomial space in the sum of the respective sizes of the formula φ and the interpreted transition system $\mathcal{T}$.

14.3 Introduction to Alternating Automata on Words

One way to classify automata on infinite words (or trees) is by the mode of branching of transitions. In a nondeterministic automaton, when the automaton is in a state q and reads a letter a, the transition function associates a set X of possible states to continue successfully the run. Universal mode, which is the dual of the existential mode used in nondeterministic automata, requires that all the runs from a location in X should lead to acceptance. In alternating automata, both existential and universal modes are allowed and the transitions are defined via positive Boolean formulae on the set of states. A positive Boolean formula is built from atomic formulae with disjunction $\vee$ and conjunction $\wedge$ (no negation used). For example, the transition formula $q_1 \vee q_2$ specifies that at the next stage there is run starting with q_1 or there is run starting with q_2 (standard existential mode, also known as nondeterminism). By contrast, $q_1 \wedge q_2$ specifies that at the next stage there are at least two runs, one starting at the state q_1 and another one starting at the state q_2. Runs, as words for nondeterministic automata, are replaced by trees for alternating automata because of the universal mode.

Alternating automata usually provide conciseness and simpler translations from temporal formulae, sometimes at the cost of proving more properties at the level of automata. Optimal worst-case complexity results about temporal logics can be obtained in this way too. The forthcoming sections are not intended as a comprehensive treatment of alternating automata, but should provide enough information to show correctness of the reductions.

14.3.1 Alternation Defined Formally

Given a finite set X, we write $\mathbb{B}^+(X)$ to denote the set of **positive Boolean formulae** built over the elements of X. Elements of $\mathbb{B}^+(X)$ respect the following grammar:

$$\mathcal{F} ::= \bot \mid \top \mid x \mid (\mathcal{F} \vee \mathcal{F}) \mid (\mathcal{F} \wedge \mathcal{F})$$

where $x \in X$. For example, $(q \vee q') \wedge q'' \in \mathbb{B}^+(\{q, q', q''\})$. Every subset $Y \subseteq X$ can be viewed as a propositional valuation such that $x \in Y$ iff x is interpreted as true. So, we write $Y \models \mathcal{F}$ with $\mathcal{F} \in \mathbb{B}^+(X)$ to denote that $\mathcal{F}$ holds true under the propositional valuation induced by the subset Y. Thus $Y \models x$ iff $x \in Y$ and $Y \models \mathcal{F} \vee \mathcal{F}'$ iff $(Y \models \mathcal{F}$ or $Y \models \mathcal{F}')$.

Lemma 14.3.1. Let $Y, Y' \subseteq X$ and $\mathcal{F}, \mathcal{F}' \in \mathbb{B}^+(X)$.

(I) If $Y \subseteq Y'$ and $Y \models \mathcal{F}$, then $Y' \models \mathcal{F}$.
(II) If $Y \models \mathcal{F}$ and $Y' \models \mathcal{F}'$, then $Y \cup Y' \models \mathcal{F} \wedge \mathcal{F}'$. ∎

The proof of this lemma is a direct consequence of the semantics on positive Boolean formulae $\mathbb{B}^+(X)$.

In a nondeterministic Büchi automaton, the transition relation $\delta \subseteq Q \times \Sigma \times Q$ can be viewed as a transition function with profile $Q \times \Sigma \to \mathcal{P}(Q)$. More generally, in alternating automata, the transition function is of the form $Q \times \Sigma \to \mathbb{B}^+(Q)$. In Definition 14.3.2 below, we first define alternating automata without specifying the acceptance condition. Then we introduce the important types of alternating automata by only specifying the different acceptance conditions.

Definition 14.3.2 (Alternating automaton on ω-words). An **alternating automaton** is a structure $\mathcal{A} = (\Sigma, Q, q_0, \delta, Acc)$ such that:

- Σ is a finite alphabet,
- Q is the finite set of states,
- $q_0 \in Q$ is the initial state,
- Acc is an acceptance condition defined as a subset of Q^ω. Depending on the type of alternating automata, we specify subsequently how Acc is finitely represented.
- $\delta : Q \times \Sigma \to \mathbb{B}^+(Q)$ is the transition function. ▽

Alternating automata are a simplified version of alternating Turing machines, as defined in Definition 11.1.11.

Definition 14.3.3 (Types of alternating automata). An alternating automaton $\mathcal{A}$ is:

1. **deterministic** iff the image of transition function δ is restricted to single states.
2. **nondeterministic** iff the image of transition function δ is restricted to disjunctions of single states or to $\bot$.
3. **universal** iff the image of transition function δ is restricted to conjunctions of single states or to $\top$. ▽

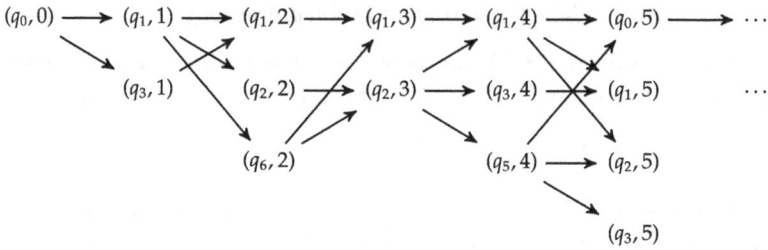

Figure 14.8 An example of a DAG-like run.

Runs in alternating automata are defined subsequently as directed acyclic graphs, which is a compact way to represent tree-like structures, by sharing identical subtrees.

Definition 14.3.4 (Runs for alternating automata). Let $\mathcal{A} = (\Sigma, Q, q_0, \delta, Acc)$ be an alternating automaton. A **run** of $\mathcal{A}$ on the ω-word $a_0 a_1 a_2 \ldots \in \Sigma^\omega$ is a (possibly infinite) directed acyclic graph (DAG) ρ, for which nodes are labelled by elements from Q:

(R1) $\rho = (V, E)$ where $V \subseteq Q \times \mathbb{N}$ and $(q_0, 0) \in V$.
(R2) $E \subseteq \bigcup_{l \geq 0} (Q \times \{l\}) \times (Q \times \{l + 1\})$.
(R3) For every $(q, l) \in V \setminus \{(q_0, 0)\}$, there is $q' \in Q$ such that $((q', l - 1), (q, l)) \in E$.
(R4) For every $(q, l) \in V$ we have $\{q' \mid ((q, l), (q', l + 1)) \in E\} \models \delta(q, a_l)$.

A node (q, l) is said to be of **level** l. A run ρ is **accepting** whenever every infinite path through that run defines an ω-word in Q^ω that belongs to Acc. Otherwise said, each path in ρ has to satisfy the acceptance condition Acc. ∇

According to this definition, $(q_0, 0)$ has no predecessor and it is the unique node of level 0.

Example 14.3.5. Let $\mathcal{A} = (\Sigma, Q, q, \delta, F)$ be an alternating automaton with a singleton alphabet $\Sigma = \{a\}$ and $Q = \{q_0, \ldots, q_7\}$ such that δ is defined as follows.

$$\delta(q_0, a) = q_1 \wedge q_3 \qquad\qquad \delta(q_1, a) = (q_1 \wedge q_2 \wedge q_6) \vee q_0 \vee q_1$$
$$\delta(q_2, a) = q_2 \vee (q_1 \wedge q_3 \wedge q_5) \qquad\qquad \delta(q_3, a) = q_1$$
$$\delta(q_4, a) = \bot \qquad\qquad \delta(q_5, a) = (q_0 \wedge q_2 \wedge q_3)$$
$$\delta(q_6, a) = q_1 \wedge q_2 \qquad\qquad \delta(q_7, a) = \top.$$

A run of $\mathcal{A}$ is presented in Figure 14.8.

The language $L(\mathcal{A})$ is defined as the set of ω-words in Σ^ω having an accepting run.

Definition 14.3.6 (Acceptance conditions). Let $\mathcal{A} = (\Sigma, Q, q_0, \delta, Acc)$ be an alternating automaton. Then we have:

1. $\mathcal{A}$ is an **alternating Büchi automaton** iff there is $F \subseteq Q$ such that for every ω-word $w \in Q^\omega$, we have $w \in Acc$ iff $\inf(w) \cap F \neq \emptyset$. This is the standard Büchi acceptance condition and in this case $\mathcal{A}$ is denoted by $(\Sigma, Q, q_0, \delta, F)$.

2. Dually, $\mathcal{A}$ is an **alternating co-Büchi automaton** iff there is $F \subseteq Q$ such that for every ω-word $w \in Q^\omega$, we have $w \in Acc$ iff $\inf(w) \cap F = \emptyset$. This is the standard co-Büchi acceptance condition and in this case $\mathcal{A}$ is denoted again by $(\Sigma, Q, q_0, \delta, F)$. Note that the structure $(\Sigma, Q, q_0, \delta, F)$ cannot be interpreted on its own, since one needs to specify whether F is interpreted as a Büchi acceptance condition or as a co-Büchi acceptance condition.

3. $\mathcal{A}$ is an **alternating generalised Büchi automaton** iff there are $F_1, \ldots, F_K \subseteq Q$ such that for every ω-word $w \in Q^\omega$, $w \in Acc$ iff $\inf(w) \cap F_i \neq \emptyset$ for all $i \in [1, K]$.

4. $\mathcal{A}$ is an **alternating parity automaton** iff there is a map $\mathfrak{f} : Q \to [0, k]$ for some natural number k such that for every ω-word $w \in Q^\omega$, we have $w \in Acc$ iff the greatest number in $\{\mathfrak{f}(q) : q \in \inf(\rho)\}$ is even. $\mathcal{A}$ is then denoted by $(\Sigma, Q, q_0, \delta, \mathfrak{f})$. $\quad\triangledown$

These acceptance conditions are standard and one can define similar classes of nondeterministic automata accepting languages of ω-words. Moreover, parity acceptance conditions capture all the conditions from Definition 14.3.6, as shown by the next lemma, the proof of which is left as Exercise 14.23.

Lemma 14.3.7. Alternating Büchi (resp. co-Büchi) automata are particular cases of alternating parity automata. $\quad\blacksquare$

A nondeterministic Büchi automaton can be viewed as an alternating Büchi automaton by replacing each set $\delta(q, \mathsf{a})$ by the positive formula $\bigvee_{q' \in \delta(q,\mathsf{a})} q'$ (recall that the empty disjunction is understood as $\perp$). For that we need to solve a minor technical issue. A nondeterministic Büchi automaton has a set of initial states, whereas an alternating Büchi automaton has a single initial state. To resolve this difference, we introduce a new initial state q_0^{new} such that the positive Boolean formula $\delta'(q_0^{new}, \mathsf{a})$ in the alternating Büchi automaton is equal to $\bigvee_{q_0 \in Q_0} \bigvee_{q' \in \delta(q_0,\mathsf{a})} q'$. Alternatively, we could have defined Büchi automata with sets of initial states that are singletons only, but it is more convenient to deal with arbitrary finite sets.

Example 14.3.8. Given the alphabet $\Sigma = \{\emptyset, \{p\}, \{q\}, \{p, q\}\}$ (set of valuations over the atomic propositions p and q), we will build a simple alternating Büchi automaton $\mathcal{A}$ that accepts the ω-words in Σ^ω such that:

1. a letter without p occurs only finitely often and
2. a letter without q occurs only finitely often,

which can be expressed by the LTL formula $\mathsf{FG}p \wedge \mathsf{FG}q$.

Let $\mathcal{A} = (\Sigma, Q, q_0, \delta, F)$ with $Q = \{\mathsf{FG}p \wedge \mathsf{FG}q, \mathsf{FG}p, \mathsf{FG}q, \mathsf{G}p, \mathsf{G}p\}$. Each state is an LTL formula that is intended to say that from that point, the ω-word satisfies the state/formula. We know that we can encode such a simple property by nondeterministic

Büchi automata, but let us do it here for the sake of illustration. Conjunctions in LTL formulae (as in $FGp \wedge FGq$) are taking care directly by conjunctions in transition formulae. A similar correspondence applies with disjunctions. The transition function is defined such that the first item can be read as follows: $FGp \wedge FGq$ holds true at a position labelled by $\emptyset$ iff FGp and FGq hold true at the next position. Similarly, FGp holds true at a position labelled by $\{p\}$ iff either Gp holds true at the current position or FGp holds true at the next position. A similar reading can be done for the other clauses in the definition of δ. Observe that obligations at the current position induce obligations at the next position but the tree-like structure of runs allow to specify more than one obligation. By the way, decomposition of positive Boolean formulae from transition functions is strongly related to local tableau steps, see e.g. Chapter 13. Similarly, successor rules in tableaux also correspond to transition functions:

- $\delta(FGp \wedge FGq, \emptyset) = (FGp) \wedge (FGq)$.
- $\delta(FGp \wedge FGq, \{p\}) = (Gp \vee FGp) \wedge (FGq)$.
- $\delta(FGp \wedge FGq, \{q\}) = (FGp) \wedge (Gq \vee FGq)$.
- $\delta(FGp \wedge FGq, \{p, q\}) = ((Gp \vee FGp) \wedge (Gq \vee FGq))$.
- $\delta(FGp, a) = FGp$ with $p \notin a$.
- $\delta(FGp, a) = (Gp) \vee (FGp)$ with $p \in a$.
- $\delta(FGq, a) = FGq$ with $q \notin a$.
- $\delta(FGq, a) = (Gq) \vee (FGq)$ with $q \in a$.
- $\delta(Gp, a) = \perp$ with $p \notin a$; $\delta(Gp, a) = Gp$ with $p \in a$.
- $\delta(Gq, a) = \perp$ with $q \notin a$; $\delta(Gq, a) = Gq$ with $q \in a$.

Here is an accepting run for the ω-word $w_0 = \emptyset^3 \cdot \{q\} \cdot \{p, q\}^{\omega}$:

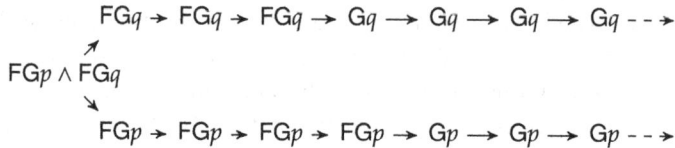

$$FGq \rightarrow FGq \rightarrow FGq \rightarrow Gq \rightarrow Gq \rightarrow Gq \rightarrow Gq \dashrightarrow$$
$$\nearrow$$
$$FGp \wedge FGq$$
$$\searrow$$
$$FGp \rightarrow FGp \rightarrow FGp \rightarrow FGp \rightarrow Gp \rightarrow Gp \rightarrow Gp \dashrightarrow$$

We omit the representation of levels since these can easily be deduced.

14.3.2 Complementing Alternating Automata

Nondeterministic Büchi automata are known to be difficult to complement. By contrast, alternating automata are easier to complement by considering dual transition formulae (see the following definition) and by complementing the acceptance condition in runs. For instance, the complement of a Büchi acceptance condition is a co-Büchi acceptance condition.

Definition 14.3.9 (Dual transition function). Given a transition function $\delta : Q \times \Sigma \rightarrow \mathbb{B}^+(Q)$, we write $\bar{\delta}$ to denote its **dual transition function** defined as follows: $\bar{\delta}(q, a) := \overline{\delta(q, a)}$ where the **dual** of a positive Boolean formula satisfies the clauses

- $\overline{q} := q$ for $q \in Q$,
- $\overline{\top} := \bot$ and $\overline{\bot} = \top$,
- $\overline{\mathcal{F} \wedge \mathcal{F}'} := \overline{\mathcal{F}} \vee \overline{\mathcal{F}'}$,
- $\overline{\mathcal{F} \vee \mathcal{F}'} := \overline{\mathcal{F}} \wedge \overline{\mathcal{F}'}$. $\hspace{3cm} \triangledown$

As mentioned, one can complement an alternating automaton by dualising its transition function and the acceptance condition. Formally, given an alternating automaton $\mathcal{A} = (\Sigma, Q, q_0, \delta, Acc)$, its dual is defined as the alternating automaton $\overline{\mathcal{A}} = (\Sigma, Q, q_0, \overline{\delta}, \Sigma^\omega \setminus Acc)$. Note that $\mathcal{A}$ and $\overline{\mathcal{A}}$ have the same set of states and the same alphabet, while $\overline{\delta}$ is the dual of δ.

Theorem 14.3.10. Let $\mathcal{A}$ be an alternating Büchi automaton over the alphabet Σ and let $\overline{\mathcal{A}}$ be its dual alternating co-Büchi automaton. Then we have $L(\overline{\mathcal{A}}) = \Sigma^\omega \setminus L(\mathcal{A})$. $\hspace{1cm}$ ∎

The proof of this theorem uses a game-based approach for alternating automata. A sketch is presented below, and Exercise 14.27 is dedicated to prove other bits of it. The proof would be analogous for alternating automata in full generality.

Proof. (Sketch) Let $\mathcal{A} = (\Sigma, Q, q_0, \delta, F)$ be an alternating automaton with Büchi acceptance condition and $\overline{\mathcal{A}} = (\Sigma, Q, q_0, \overline{\delta}, F)$ be its dual with co-Büchi acceptance condition.

To begin with, for each word $w \in \Sigma^\omega$, given $\mathcal{A}$ we define a 2-player Büchi game $\mathcal{G}_{\mathcal{A},w}$ such that player A has a (memoryless) winning strategy iff w is accepted by $\mathcal{A}$. Then, it can be shown that for a dual co-Büchi game $\mathcal{G}_{\overline{\mathcal{A}},w}$, player A does not have a winning strategy in $\mathcal{G}_{\mathcal{A},w}$ iff player P has a (memoryless) winning strategy in $\mathcal{G}_{\overline{\mathcal{A}},w}$, which is then equivalent to w not being accepted by $\mathcal{A}$.

The game. Let $w = \mathsf{a}_0 \mathsf{a}_1 \mathsf{a}_2 \cdots \in \Sigma^\omega$ be an ω-word. We associate a **game arena** (V, Own, E) for the two players Automaton A and Pathfinder P (see Section 2.2.3 for definitions on 2-player games):

- The (infinite) set of nodes V is equal to $V_A \uplus V_P$ with

$$V_A = (Q \times \mathbb{N}) \quad V_P = (Q \times \mathcal{P}(Q) \times \mathbb{N}).$$

- The binary relation $V \times V \subseteq E$ is the least set such that
  - $((q, l), ((q, l), X, l+1)) \in E$ iff $X \models \delta(q, \mathsf{a}_l)$,
  - $(((q, l), X, l+1), (q', l+1)) \in E$ iff $q' \in X$.
- For every $v \in V$, $Own(v) = A$ iff $v \in V_A$ (*Own* is of the form $V \to \{A, P\}$).

In order to define the winning condition of the game, let us consider the set $\mathfrak{F} = \{(q, l) \in V_A \mid q \in F\}$.

A **play** λ is a maximal path in $\mathcal{G}_{\mathcal{A},w}$ with $\lambda(0) = (q_0, 0)$ (alternation of nodes from V_A and V_P).

Given the preceding game arena, it is possible to define different games depending on the winning conditions for the player A and for the player P, respectively. For instance, in the Büchi game $\mathcal{G}_{\mathcal{A},w}$, player A (resp. P) **wins** the play if:

- either λ has length n and $\lambda(n-1) \in V_P$ [resp. $\lambda(n-1) \in V_A$],
- or λ is infinite and some state in $\mathfrak{F}$ occurs infinitely often (resp. and all the states in $\mathcal{F}$ occurs finitely) in λ.

Naturally, this leads to the definition of the game

$$\mathcal{G}^B_{\mathcal{A},w} = (V, Own, E, (q_0, 0), Win_B),$$

where Win_B is the winning condition defined from the preceding characterisation. Similarly, in the co-Büchi game for $\mathcal{G}^{coB}_{\mathcal{A},w}$, player A (resp. P) **wins** the play if

- either λ has length n and $\lambda(n-1) \in V_P$ [resp. $\lambda(n-1) \in V_A$],
- or λ is infinite and all the states in $\mathfrak{F}$ occurs finitely [resp. some state in $\mathfrak{F}$ occurs infinitely often] in λ.

Naturally, this leads to the definition of the game

$$\mathcal{G}^{coB}_{\mathcal{A},w} = (V, Own, E, (q_0, 0), Win_{coB}).$$

Observe that between the Büchi game and the co-Büchi game, winning conditions for infinite plays are complemented.

As usual, a **memoryless strategy** for player A is a partial function $\mathfrak{str}_A : V_A \to V_P$. A play λ is played according to $\mathfrak{str}_A$ iff for every k, $\lambda(2k+1) = \mathfrak{str}_A(\lambda(2k))$. Similar definitions apply to Player P. A memoryless strategy $\mathfrak{str}_A$ is **winning** for Player A iff A wins in any play where she plays according to $\mathfrak{str}_A$, and likewise for Player P.

In order to show that $L(\overline{\mathcal{A}}) = \Sigma^\omega \setminus L(\mathcal{A})$, one can prove (I)–(III):

(I) A has a memoryless winning strategy in $\mathcal{G}^B_{\mathcal{A},w}$ iff $w \in L(\mathcal{A})$.

(II) In $\mathcal{G}^B_{\mathcal{A},w}$, either A or P has a memoryless winning strategy (direct consequence of determinacy of such games).

(III) A has a memoryless winning strategy in the Büchi game for $\mathcal{G}^B_{\mathcal{A},w}$ iff P has a memoryless winning strategy in the co-Büchi game for $\mathcal{G}^{coB}_{\overline{\mathcal{A}},w}$. $\qquad\qquad\square$

We have seen that for complementing an alternating Büchi automaton $\mathcal{A}$, it is sufficient to consider the dual alternating co-Büchi automaton $\overline{\mathcal{A}}$. However, it would be more elegant, and certainly easier for proofs, if the two automata had the same acceptance conditions, since dualising a transition function is easy.

Parity acceptance conditions generalise both Büchi acceptance conditions as well as co-Büchi acceptance conditions (see Lemma 14.3.7) and the complement of such a condition remains a parity acceptance condition, which is also easy to define – this can be done in linear time.

Theorem 14.3.11. Let $\mathcal{A} = (\Sigma, Q, q_0, \delta, \mathfrak{f})$ be an alternating parity automaton and $\overline{\mathcal{A}}$ be its dual alternating parity automaton $(\Sigma, Q, q_0, \overline{\delta}, \mathfrak{f}+1)$. Then we have $L(\overline{\mathcal{A}}) = \Sigma^\omega \setminus L(\mathcal{A})$. $\qquad\blacksquare$

The proof is similar to the proof of Theorem 14.3.10, except that we have to observe that the parity map $\mathfrak{f} + 1$ changes the oddity of all states in Q. A bit later in this section we will introduce the class of weak alternating Büchi automata, for which acceptance conditions are closed under complementation as parity acceptance condition.

First, let us explain why alternating Büchi automata are not strictly more expressive than nondeterministic Büchi automata. Their main assets do not rest in higher expressive power but on the fact that temporal formulae can be easily translated into alternating automata because of the presence of the universal and existential modes, partly mimicking Boolean operators at the logical level.

Theorem 14.3.12. Given an alternating Büchi automaton $\mathcal{A}$, there is a nondeterministic Büchi automaton $\mathcal{A}'$ with exponentially many states in the size of $\mathcal{A}$ such that $L(\mathcal{A}) = L(\mathcal{A}')$. ∎

Proof. The idea of the proof for building $\mathcal{A}'$ is to guess the set of states at each level of an accepting run of $\mathcal{A}$. States of $\mathcal{A}'$ record the states of an accepting run of $\mathcal{A}$. For instance, for the run in Figure 14.8, the corresponding run in the nondeterministic Büchi automaton $\mathcal{A}'$ is the following:

$$\{q_0\} \to \{q_1, q_3\} \to \{q_1, q_2, q_7\} \to \{q_1, q_2\} \to \{q_1, q_3, q_5\} \to \{q_0, q_1, q_2, q_3\} \cdots .$$

Hence if the set of states of $\mathcal{A}$ is Q, then the set of states of $\mathcal{A}'$ is equal to $\mathcal{P}(Q)$. Indeed, if $\rho = (V, E)$ is an accepting run of $\mathcal{A}$, the state of the corresponding run ρ' in $\mathcal{A}'$ at the position l is $\{q \mid (q, l) \in V\}$. However, we also need to encode the Büchi acceptance condition on infinite paths of runs for $\mathcal{A}$ as a Büchi acceptance condition in $\mathcal{A}'$. To do so, $\mathcal{A}'$ has to remember which accepting states have been visited to ensure that every infinite branch visits infinitely many accepting states. But when considering states in $\mathcal{P}(Q)$, the satisfaction of the acceptance condition from $\mathcal{A}$ may be lost and we need to introduce a rigorous bookkeeping mechanism. In order to simulate this, $\{q \mid (q, l) \in V\}$ is divided into two disjoint parts (X, X') (with the intended invariant $X \uplus X' = \{q \mid (q, l) \in V\}$) that are updated synchronously with respect to δ, except that we require the following rules, where X contains the set of states waiting to hit an accepting state.

1. Whenever a state from X produces an accepting state at the next step, the new state is inserted into the next value for X' (instead of being inserted into the next value for X). In that way, the path passing through the set/state has visited an accepting state.
2. When X is the empty set (i.e. all the paths have visited at least once an accepting state), the next value of X' is transferred to the next value of X.

This simple mechanism is sufficient to simulate the acceptance condition in DAG-like accepting runs for $\mathcal{A}$.

Hence states of $\mathcal{A}'$ are in $\mathcal{P}(Q) \times \mathcal{P}(Q)$. Now we provide the formal definition for $\mathcal{A}'$ that implements what is discussed earlier. Let $\mathcal{A} = (\Sigma, Q, q_0, \delta, F)$ be an alternating Büchi automaton. We build the nondeterministic Büchi automaton $\mathcal{A}' = (\Sigma, Q', Q'_0, \delta', F')$ as follows:

- $Q' := \mathcal{P}(Q) \times \mathcal{P}(Q)$,
- $Q_0' := \{(\{q_0\}, \emptyset)\}$ and $F' := \emptyset \times \mathcal{P}(Q)$,
- the transition function distinguishes two cases for $\delta'((X, Y), \mathsf{a})$:

  (**final**) When $X = \emptyset$, the second part is transferred to the first part:

  $$\delta'((\emptyset, Y), \mathsf{a}) := \big\{(Z \setminus F, Z \cap F) \mid Z \subseteq Q, \text{for every } q \in Y, \text{ we have } Z \models \delta(q, \mathsf{a})\big\}$$

  (**nonfinal**) When $X \neq \emptyset$, if a state in X produces an accepting state, then it is inserted in the second part,

  $$\delta'((X, Y), \mathsf{a}) := \big\{(Z \setminus F, Z' \cup (Z \cap F)) \mid Z, Z' \subseteq Q, \text{for every } q \in X$$
  $$\text{we have } Z \models \delta(q, \mathsf{a}) \text{ and for } q \in Y,$$
  $$\text{we have } Z' \models \delta(q, \mathsf{a})\big\}.$$

We leave it as Exercise 14.26 to show that $L(\mathcal{A}) = L(\mathcal{A}')$. $\square$

Consequently, alternating Büchi automata and nondeterministic Büchi automata define the same class of languages over ω-words but their conciseness differs.

14.3.3 Weak Automata

Alternating Büchi automata are too general for LTL formulae so we are looking for special subclasses of alternating Büchi automata that match LTL in expressiveness. This is why we introduce the class of *weak alternating Büchi automata* as well as the class of *very weak alternating Büchi automata*; this latter class defines exactly the set of models definable by LTL formulae (see Theorem 14.4.7). Moreover, we have seen in Theorem 14.3.10 that alternating automata can easily be complemented by dualising the transition function and by complementing the acceptance condition. We will demonstrate how complementation can easily be performed with weak alternating Büchi automata.

In **weak alternating automata** defined here, the set of states is partitioned into partially ordered sets and each set is classified as accepting or rejecting. Each run of the automaton eventually gets trapped in some set of the partition. The class of weak alternating automata is particularly interesting since it is as expressive as nondeterministic Büchi automata.

Definition 14.3.13. A **weak alternating Büchi automaton** $\mathcal{A}$ is a structure

$$(\Sigma, Q, q_0, \delta, F, (\{Q_1, \ldots, Q_K\}, \leq))$$

such that:

- $(\Sigma, Q, q_0, \delta, F)$ is defined as an alternating Büchi automaton,
- $\{Q_1, \ldots, Q_K\}$ is a partition of Q equipped with a partial ordering $\leq$,
- for every $i \in [1, K]$, either $Q_i \subseteq F$ or $Q_i \cap F = \emptyset$,
- for all $q \in Q_i$ and $q' \in Q_j$ such that q' occurs in $\delta(q, \mathsf{a})$ for some letter a, we have $Q_j \leq Q_i$.

A **very weak alternating Büchi automaton** is a weak alternating Büchi automaton in which every element of the partition is a singleton. ▽

The terms 'weak' and 'very weak' are far from ideal but since these are standard expressions, we stick to them.

The automaton $\mathcal{A}$ defined in Example 14.3.8 can be shown to be a very weak alternating Büchi automaton with any partial ordering satisfying the conditions

$$\mathsf{G}p < \mathsf{FG}p, \quad \mathsf{G}q < \mathsf{FG}q, \quad \mathsf{FG}p, \mathsf{FG}q < \mathsf{FG}p \wedge \mathsf{FG}q$$

and $F = \{\mathsf{G}p, \mathsf{G}q\}$. There is no need to specify the partition since each element of the partition is a singleton and can therefore be identified with a state.

In a weak alternating Büchi automaton, each set Q_i is accepting ($Q_i \subseteq F$) or rejecting ($Q_i \cap F = \emptyset$). Since transitions from a state in Q_i lead to states in Q_i or in a lower subset, in an accepting run of a weak alternating Büchi automaton, every infinite path ultimately remains in a fixed Q_i.

Lemma 14.3.14. Languages defined by weak alternating Büchi automata are closed under union, intersection and complementation. ∎

Proof. The proof for union and intersection is by an easy verification using conjunction and disjunction in transition formulae, respectively. As for complementation, observe that if $\mathcal{A} = (\Sigma, Q, q_0, \delta, F)$ is a weak alternating Büchi automaton, then the alternating co-Büchi automaton $\overline{\mathcal{A}} = (\Sigma, Q, q_0, \overline{\delta}, F)$ recognises the complementary language (see Theorem 14.3.10). By weakness of $\mathcal{A}$, there is an ordered partition $(\{Q_1, \ldots, Q_K\}, \leq)$ of Q and $J \leq K$ such that $F = Q_1 \cup \cdots \cup Q_J$, and for all $q \in Q_i$ and all $q' \in Q_j$ such that q' occurs in $\delta(q, \mathtt{a})$ for some letter $\mathtt{a}$, we have $Q_j \leq Q_i$. It is not difficult to show that for all $q \in Q_i$ and all $q' \in Q_j$ such that q' occurs in $\overline{\delta}(q, \mathtt{a})$, we have $Q_j \leq Q_i$. Moreover, in an accepting run of $\overline{\mathcal{A}}$, for all infinite paths π, the states in F occur only finitely many times. By the weakness condition, this means that there is $j \in [J+1, K]$ such that from some level all the states in π belong to Q_j, which is equivalent to the property that for all infinite paths π, some state in $Q_{J+1} \cup \cdots \cup Q_K$ ($= Q \setminus F$) occurs infinitely often. Hence the alternating co-Büchi automaton $\overline{\mathcal{A}}$ accepts the same language as the weak alternating Büchi automaton $(\Sigma, Q, q_0, \overline{\delta}, Q \setminus F)$. □

14.3.4 Back to Alternating Büchi Automata

Next we state an interesting result, that allows us to obtain more important properties of alternating Büchi automata. We will not provide a proof here, but refer to a reference in the bibliographic notes instead.

Proposition 14.3.15. For every alternating co-Büchi automaton $\mathcal{A}$, there is a weak alternating Büchi automaton $\mathcal{A}'$ such that $\mathrm{L}(\mathcal{A}) = \mathrm{L}(\mathcal{A}')$ and the size of $\mathcal{A}'$ is only quadratic in the size of $\mathcal{A}$. ∎

Theorem 14.3.16. The nonemptiness problem for alternating Büchi automata is PSPACE-complete. ∎

For the PSPACE upper bound, it is sufficient to observe that given an alternating Büchi automaton $\mathcal{A}$, nonemptiness of $L(\mathcal{A}')$ for the nondeterministic Büchi automaton $\mathcal{A}'$ constructed in the proof of Theorem 14.3.12 can be tested on the fly in polynomial space in the size of $\mathcal{A}$. Indeed, one needs to store several subsets of states from the original automaton. PSPACE-hardness is left as Exercise 14.24.

We are now in the position to show that alternating Büchi automata are easy to complement, even if we preserve the type of acceptance condition (unlike the complementation used in Theorem 14.3.10).

Proposition 14.3.17. Let $\mathcal{A}$ be an alternating Büchi automaton. There is an alternating Büchi automaton $\mathcal{A}'$ such that $L(\mathcal{A}') = \Sigma^{\omega} \setminus L(\mathcal{A})$ and the number of states of $\mathcal{A}'$ is quadratic in that of $\mathcal{A}$. ∎

The proof can be decomposed into the following steps:

1. Given $\mathcal{A}$, produce an alternating co-Büchi automaton $\mathcal{B}$ such that $L(\mathcal{B}) = \Sigma^{\omega} \setminus L(\mathcal{A})$ (by dualisation), see Theorem 14.3.10.
2. Apply Proposition 14.3.15.

Remark 14.3.18. In Proposition 14.3.17, $\mathcal{A}'$ is an alternating Büchi automaton and not an alternating co-Büchi automaton as in Theorem 14.3.10.

Theorem 14.3.19. Weak alternating Büchi automata, alternating Büchi automata and nondeterministic Büchi automata accept the same class of languages. ∎

Proof. We have already seen that nondeterministic Büchi automata can be viewed as alternating Büchi automata. Similarly, by Theorem 14.3.12, every alternating Büchi automaton can be translated into a nondeterministic Büchi automaton accepting the same language. Since weak alternating Büchi automata are syntactic restrictions of alternating Büchi automata, it remains to show that every alternating Büchi automaton can be translated into a weak alternating Büchi automaton accepting the same language. Let $\mathcal{A}$ be an alternating Büchi automaton.

- By Theorem 14.3.10, there is an alternating co-Büchi automaton $\mathcal{A}_1$ such that $\Sigma^{\omega} \setminus L(\mathcal{A}) = L(\mathcal{A}_1)$.
- By Proposition 14.3.15, there is a weak alternating Büchi automaton $\mathcal{A}_2$ such that $L(\mathcal{A}_2) = L(\mathcal{A}_1)$.
- By Lemma 14.3.14, there is a weak alternating Büchi automaton $\mathcal{A}_3$ such that $\Sigma^{\omega} \setminus L(\mathcal{A}_2) = L(\mathcal{A}_3)$, i.e. $L(\mathcal{A}_3) = L(\mathcal{A})$. □

By contrast, very weak alternating Büchi automata will be shown to be strictly less expressive than weak alternating Büchi automata since they only capture languages definable in first-order logic, hence definable by LTL formulae (see Theorem 14.4.7).

14.4 From LTL Formulae to Alternating Büchi Automata

In this section, we design a translation from LTL formulae into alternating Büchi automata that not only accept exactly the linear models of the respective formulae but also have a simple structure, since they are very weak (in terms of Definition 14.3.13). Unlike the translation into nondeterministic Büchi automata (see Section 14.2), this translation will produce automata with a number of states linear in the size of the input LTL formulae and the transition formulae will reflect the formula structure quite well. However, strictly speaking, the reduction cannot be performed in polynomial-time since the cardinality of the alphabet is exponential in the number of atomic propositions. This exponential blow-up disappears when dealing with model checking, since we can restrict attention only to valuations appearing in the interpreted transition system given as input. Moreover, the design of automata reflects the structure of formulae: the translation is simple but there is a price to pay. The correctness proof is a bit more involved because it takes advantage of properties of runs for alternating automata.

14.4.1 The Translation

Let φ be an LTL formula. Without any loss of generality, we can assume that φ is in a negation normal form, i.e. may contain $\wedge$, $\vee$, X, U and the **release operator** R, and negations occurring only in front of atomic propositions. We know (see Section 6.1.1), that every LTL formula has an equivalent formula in such a form that can be computed in polynomial time. We make this assumption herein in order to simplify the technical details. We build an alternating Büchi automaton $\mathcal{A}_\varphi = (\Sigma, Q, q_0, \delta, F)$ as follows.

- $Q := \{\mathsf{q}_\psi : \psi \in sub(\varphi)\}$ where $sub(\varphi)$ is the set of subformulae of φ. For instance $\mathsf{q}_p \vee \mathsf{q}_{q \wedge \mathsf{X}q}$ is a disjunctive transition formula containing exactly the states q_p and $\mathsf{q}_{q \wedge \mathsf{X}q}$. Intuitively, from a state q_ψ, the current suffix has the obligation to satisfy the formula ψ.
- $q_0 := \mathsf{q}_\varphi$.
- $\Sigma := \mathcal{P}(\mathrm{PROP}(\varphi))$.
- F is equal to the set of states from Q that are not indexed by an U-formula (formulae whose outermost connective is U), if any.
- Now we will define the transition function δ. Boolean connectives in a state q_ψ are taken care by Boolean connectives in transition formulae that have operational interpretations. For instance, $\delta(\mathsf{q}_{\mathsf{X}\psi_1 \wedge (\mathsf{X}\psi_2 \vee \mathsf{X}\psi_3)}, \mathsf{a})$ will be defined as $\mathsf{q}_{\psi_1} \wedge (\mathsf{q}_{\psi_2} \vee \mathsf{q}_{\psi_3})$. Naturally, universal mode of alternating automata is exactly what is needed to deal with conjunctions in the formula.

$$\delta(\mathsf{q}_p, \mathsf{a}) := \top \quad \text{if } p \in \mathsf{a} \qquad\qquad \delta(\mathsf{q}_{\psi_1 \wedge \psi_2}, \mathsf{a}) := \delta(\mathsf{q}_{\psi_1}, \mathsf{a}) \wedge \delta(\mathsf{q}_{\psi_2}, \mathsf{a})$$
$$\delta(\mathsf{q}_p, \mathsf{a}) := \bot \quad \text{if } p \notin \mathsf{a} \qquad\qquad \delta(\mathsf{q}_{\psi_1 \vee \psi_2}, \mathsf{a}) := \delta(\mathsf{q}_{\psi_1}, \mathsf{a}) \vee \delta(\mathsf{q}_{\psi_2}, \mathsf{a})$$
$$\delta(\mathsf{q}_{\neg p}, \mathsf{a}) := \top \quad \text{if } p \notin \mathsf{a} \qquad\qquad \delta(\mathsf{q}_{\psi \mathsf{U} \chi}, \mathsf{a}) := \delta(\mathsf{q}_\chi, \mathsf{a}) \vee (\delta(\mathsf{q}_\psi, \mathsf{a}) \wedge \mathsf{q}_{\psi \mathsf{U} \chi})$$
$$\delta(\mathsf{q}_{\neg p}, \mathsf{a}) := \bot \quad \text{if } p \in \mathsf{a} \qquad\qquad \delta(\mathsf{q}_{\psi \mathsf{R} \chi}, \mathsf{a}) := \delta(\mathsf{q}_\chi, \mathsf{a}) \wedge (\delta(\mathsf{q}_\psi, \mathsf{a}) \vee \mathsf{q}_{\psi \mathsf{R} \chi})$$
$$\delta(\mathsf{q}_{\mathsf{X}\psi}, \mathsf{a}) := \mathsf{q}_\psi.$$

It is easy to verify that the range of δ remains in $\mathbb{B}^+(Q)$. The definition of δ is well founded since the definition of $\delta(q_\psi, a)$ requires only the definition of $\delta(q_{\psi'}, a)$ with $\psi' <^+_{sub} \psi$ where $<^+_{sub}$ is the transitive closure of the subformula relation. With the preceding definition, for the abbreviations F and G, we get that

$$\delta(q_{F\psi}, a) := \delta(q_\psi, a) \vee q_{F\psi}$$

and

$$\delta(q_{G\psi}, a) := \delta(q_\psi, a) \wedge q_{G\psi}.$$

Furthermore, note that the definition of $\delta(q_{\psi U \chi}, a)$ reflects the validity

$$(\psi U \chi) \leftrightarrow (\chi \vee (\psi \wedge X((\psi U \chi)))).$$

Likewise, the definition of $\delta(q_{\psi R \chi}, a)$ corresponds to the validity

$$(\psi R \chi) \leftrightarrow (\chi \wedge (\psi \vee X((\psi R \chi)))).$$

By way of example, let φ be FGp and let us define $\mathcal{A}_\varphi$. The alphabet Σ is $\{\emptyset, \{p\}\}$. The set F is $\{q_{Gp}, q_p\}$. Finally, the transition function δ is represented by the table:

q	$\delta(q, \emptyset)$	$\delta(q, \{p\})$
q_{FGp}	q_{FGp}	$q_{Gp} \vee q_{FGp}$
q_{Gp}	$\bot$	q_{Gp}
q_p	$\bot$	$\top$

Clearly, each $\mathcal{A}_\varphi$ constructed as previously is an alternating Büchi automaton. Moreover, as stated in the next lemma, one can show that it is very weak, where the transitive closure of the main component relation induces the partial ordering $\leq$ for the singleton sets of the partition. The proof is left as Exercise 14.25.

Lemma 14.4.1. Let φ be an LTL formula. Then, $\mathcal{A}_\varphi$ is a very weak alternating Büchi automaton where the partial ordering $\leq$ on singletons of the form $\{q_\psi\}$ is defined by $\{q_\psi\} \leq \{q_{\psi'}\}$ iff $\psi <^+_{sub} \psi'$. ∎

Example 14.4.2. Let us consider the LTL formula $G(q \to Fp)$ where its negation normal form is $\varphi = G(\neg q \vee Fp)$, as well as the alternating Büchi automaton $\mathcal{A}_\varphi = (\Sigma, Q, q_0, \delta, F)$. The transition formula $\delta(q_\varphi, \emptyset)$ is computed as follows:

$$\begin{aligned}
\delta(q_\varphi, \emptyset) &= \delta(q_{\neg q \vee Fp}, \emptyset) \wedge q_\varphi \\
&= (\delta(q_{\neg q}, \emptyset) \vee \delta(q_{Fp}, \emptyset)) \wedge q_\varphi \\
&= (\top \vee (\delta(q_p, \emptyset) \vee q_{Fp})) \wedge q_\varphi \\
&\equiv q_\varphi.
\end{aligned}$$

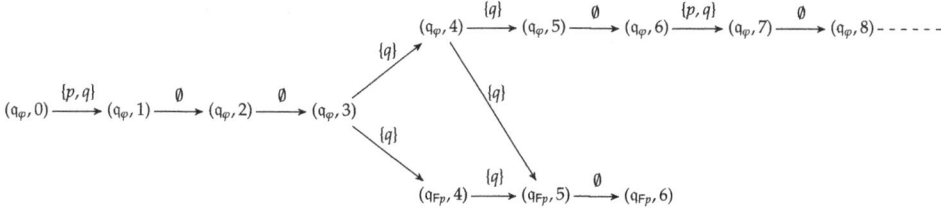

Figure 14.9 Accepting run on σ in $\mathcal{A}_{G(\neg q \vee Fp)}$.

Similarly, $\delta(q_\varphi, \{q\})$ is computed as follows:

$$
\begin{aligned}
\delta(q_\varphi, \{q\}) &= \delta(q_{\neg q \vee Fp}, \{q\}) \wedge q_\varphi \\
&= (\delta(q_{\neg q}, \{q\}) \vee \delta(q_{Fp}, \{q\})) \wedge q_\varphi \\
&= (\bot \vee (\delta(q_p, \{q\}) \vee q_{Fp})) \wedge q_\varphi \\
&= (\bot \vee (\bot \vee q_{Fp})) \wedge q_\varphi \\
&\equiv q_{Fp} \wedge q_\varphi.
\end{aligned}
$$

Finally, $\delta(q_\varphi, \{p\})$ is computed as follows:

$$
\begin{aligned}
\delta(q_\varphi, \{p\}) &= \delta(q_{\neg q \vee Fp}, \{p\}) \wedge q_\varphi \\
&= (\delta(q_{\neg q}, \{p\}) \vee \delta(q_{Fq}, \{p\})) \wedge q_\varphi \\
&= (\top \vee (\delta(q_p, \{p\}) \vee q_{Fp})) \wedge q_\varphi \\
&= (\top \vee (\top \vee q_{Fp})) \wedge q_\varphi \\
&\equiv q_\varphi.
\end{aligned}
$$

In Figure 14.9, we present an accepting run on the model

$$
\sigma = \{p, q\} \cdot \emptyset \cdot \emptyset \cdot \{q\} \cdot \{q\} \cdot \emptyset \cdot \{p, q\} \cdot \emptyset^\omega
$$

in $\mathcal{A}_\varphi$. To ease the correspondence between the ω-word and the run, we label edges by letters. Note that the run has a unique infinite path.

Before proving the correctness of the reduction, we need the following.

Lemma 14.4.3. Let φ be an LTL formula, $\Pi = \text{PROP}(\varphi)$ and Π' be a finite set of atomic propositions including Π. Let $\mathcal{B}_\varphi$ be the alternating Büchi automaton defined as for $\mathcal{A}_\varphi$ except that the letters belong to $\mathcal{P}(\Pi')$ (instead of $\mathcal{P}(\Pi)$). If $L(\mathcal{A}_\varphi) = \text{Mod}_\Pi(\varphi)$, then $L(\mathcal{B}_\varphi) = \text{Mod}_{\Pi'}(\varphi)$. ∎

The proof of this lemma is an easy verification (Exercise 14.25).

Now we need to present simple constructions on (accepting) runs that will be useful in the proof of Theorem 14.4.6. Let $\rho = (V, E)$ be a run for the alternating automaton $\mathcal{A}$. We write $\rho^{+1} = (V^{+1}, E^{+1})$ to denote the isomorphic DAG obtained from ρ by mapping each vertex (q, l) to $(q, l+1)$. Strictly speaking, ρ^{+1} is not a run of $\mathcal{A}$. Moreover, we write $\rho[(q_0, 0) \leftarrow (q, 0)]$ to denote the DAG obtained from ρ by replacing $(q_0, 0)$ with $(q, 0)$.

In the sequel, the DAG $\rho[(q_0, 0) \leftarrow (q, 0)]$ will most of the time be an accepting run too, possibly for another alternating automaton in which q is indeed an initial state.

The proof of Theorem 14.4.6 makes use of the fact that accepting runs can be restricted to the ones in which condition (R4) is replaced by the more restrictive condition (R4′):

(R4′) For every $(q, l) \in V$ we have $\{q' \mid ((q, l), (q', l + 1)) \in E\} \models \delta(q, a_l)$ *and* for no strict subset Y of $\{q' \mid ((q, l), (q', l + 1)) \in E\} \subseteq Q$, we have $Y \models \delta(q, a_l)$.

An accepting run on $a_0 a_1 \cdots$ in an alternating Büchi automaton $\mathcal{A}$ is said to be **minimal** if it satisfies the condition (R4′). The following lemma states that when restricting accepting runs to minimal ones does not modify the language of accepted ω-words.

Lemma 14.4.4. Let $\mathcal{A} = (\Sigma, Q, q_0, \delta, Acc)$ be an alternating automaton. For every ω-word $u \in \Sigma^\omega$, there is an accepting run on u in $\mathcal{A}$ iff there is a minimal accepting run on u in $\mathcal{A}$. ∎

Proof. Let $\rho = (V, E)$ be an accepting run on u. By induction on the levels, we will build a minimal accepting run $\rho' = (V', E')$ on u such that $V' \subseteq V$, $E' \subseteq E$ and therefore the infinite paths in ρ' are also infinite paths in ρ. Hence the satisfaction of the acceptance condition will be a consequence of the fact that ρ' is a subgraph of ρ. First, $(q_0, 0) \in V'$ and $E' = \emptyset$. Now suppose that all the vertices of level l have been defined, say they are elements of the set V'_l and they belong to V too (actually, to the set of nodes from V of level l). We define the vertices of level $l + 1$ in V'_{l+1} and the new edges in E'. For every (q, l) in V'_l, we know that $\{q' \mid ((q, l), (q', l + 1)) \in E\} \models \delta(q, a_l)$. Let $Y_{(q,l)}$ be a subset of $\{q' \mid ((q, l), (q', l + 1)) \in E\}$ such that $Y_{(q,l)} \vdash \delta(q, a_l)$ and for no strict subset Y of $Y_{(q,l)}$, we have $Y \models \delta(q, a_l)$. We put

$$V'_{l+1} := \bigcup_{(q,l) \in V'_l} Y_{(q,l)}$$

and extend E' in such a way that for every (q, l) in V'_l and for every $(q', l + 1)$ in $Y_{(q,l)}$, $(q, l) \rightarrow (q', l + 1)$ is in E'. It is easy to see that the limit structure ρ' obtained in such a way is a subgraph of ρ and ρ' is a minimal accepting run on u. □

An obvious consequence of Lemma 14.4.4 is that for showing the correctness of the construction $\mathcal{A}_\varphi$, it is sufficient to restrict ourselves to minimal accepting runs. Such runs have useful features, stated as follows.

Lemma 14.4.5. Let φ be a formula in negation normal form and $\mathcal{A}_\varphi = (\Sigma, Q, q_0, \delta, F)$ be its corresponding alternating Büchi automaton.

(I) For every linear model $\sigma \in \Sigma^\omega$, there is an accepting run on σ in $\mathcal{A}_\varphi$ iff there is a minimal accepting run on σ in $\mathcal{A}_\varphi$.

(II) Let $\rho = (V, E)$ be a minimal accepting run on σ and $(q_\psi, l) \in V$. Then, for every $(q_\psi, l) \rightarrow (q_{\psi'}, l + 1) \in E$,

- if ψ is neither an U-formula nor a R-formula, then $\psi' <^+_{sub} \psi$,
- otherwise, $\psi' <^+_{sub} \psi$ or $\psi' = \psi$.

(III) Let $\rho = (V, E)$ be a minimal accepting run. Let $(q_{\psi_0}, 0) \to (q_{\psi_1}, 1) \to \cdots$ be an infinite path in ρ. There is $N \geq 0$ such that $q_{\psi_N} = q_{\psi_{N+1}} = q_{\psi_{N+2}} = \cdots$ and ψ_N is an R-formula. ∎

Proof. (I) This is an immediate application of Lemma 14.4.4.

(II) This is an immediate consequence of the fact that the states in $\delta(q_\psi, a)$ are of the form $q_{\psi'}$ such that if ψ is neither an U-formula nor a R-formula, then $\psi' <^+_{sub} \psi$, otherwise, $\psi' <^+_{sub} \psi$ or $\psi' = \psi$.

(III) When ψ is neither an U-formula nor a R-formula, $\delta(q_\psi, a)$ does not contain q_ψ and therefore there is no edge of the form $(q_\psi, l) \to (q_\psi, l+1)$ in any minimal run. Since the relation $<^+_{sub}$ is well founded, this leads to (III). □

Let us show that the language accepted by the alternating automaton $\mathcal{A}_\varphi$ corresponds to the set of models satisfying φ, which is essentially a correctness and completeness claim.

Theorem 14.4.6. $L(\mathcal{A}_\varphi) = \text{Mod}_\Pi(\varphi)$ where $\Pi = \text{PROP}(\varphi)$. ∎

Proof. The proof is by structural induction. First, let us do the base case, when $\varphi := p$. Let σ be a linear model in $\{\emptyset, \{p\}\}^\omega$. Obviously, $\sigma, 0 \models p$ iff $p \in \sigma(0)$. By construction of $\mathcal{A}_p$, if there is a run ρ of $\mathcal{A}_p$ on the linear model σ, then $p \in \sigma(0)$ and ρ is accepting. Similarly, if there is no accepting run on σ, then $p \notin \sigma(0)$. Hence a linear model is in $L(\mathcal{A}_\varphi)$ iff it belongs to $\text{Mod}_{\{\emptyset,\{p\}\}}(\varphi)$. A similar reasoning can be performed with $\varphi := \neg p$.

Now we deal with the induction step.

$\varphi = X\varphi_1$: By definition, $\mathcal{A}_\varphi$ is equal to $\mathcal{A}_{\varphi_1}$ except that it has an additional state, namely q_φ, that is also the initial state of $\mathcal{A}_\varphi$. Moreover, the transition function δ for $\mathcal{A}_\varphi$ extends the transition function for $\mathcal{A}_{\varphi_1}$ with $\delta(q_\varphi, a) = q_{\varphi_1}$ for every letter $a \subseteq \text{PROP}(\varphi) = \text{PROP}(\varphi_1)$. For every linear model $\sigma \in \mathcal{P}(\text{PROP}(\varphi_1))^\omega$, we have $\sigma, 0 \models \varphi$ iff $\sigma, 1 \models \varphi_1$ iff (by inductive hypothesis) there is an accepting run ρ_1 of $\mathcal{A}_{\varphi_1}$ on $\sigma[1, +\infty)$ (i.e. σ with the first letter removed) iff ρ is an accepting run of $\mathcal{A}_\varphi$ on σ where $\rho = (\{(q_\varphi, 0)\} \cup V_1^{+1}, \{(q_\varphi, 0) \to (q_{\varphi_1}, 1)\} \cup E_1^{+1})$ and $\rho_1 = (V_1, E_1)$. Roughly speaking, ρ is obtained from ρ_1 by adding an edge from $(q_\varphi, 0)$ to $(q_{\varphi_1}, 1)$. It is easy to check that ρ is an accepting run of $\mathcal{A}_\varphi$ as shown.

- Satisfaction of conditions (R1)-(R3) is by easy verification, since ρ_1 is already a run of $\mathcal{A}_{\varphi_1}$ on $\sigma[1, +\infty)$.
- Satisfaction of condition (R4) is also by easy verification but, additionally, we have to check that $\{q' \mid ((q_\varphi, 0), (q', 1)) \in E\} \models \delta(q_\varphi, \sigma(0))$. However, that is immediate since

$$\{q' : ((q_\varphi, 0), (q', 1)) \in E\} = \{q_{\varphi_1}\}$$

and $\delta(q_\varphi, \sigma(0)) = q_{\varphi_1}$.

- It remains to check that every infinite path in ρ is accepting. This is a simple consequence of the fact that every accepting state of $\mathcal{A}_\varphi$ is an accepting state of $\mathcal{A}_{\varphi_1}$ and there is a bijection between the infinite paths of ρ and the infinite paths of ρ_1.

In the forthcoming remaining cases, we will leave it to the reader to check that the constructed DAGs are indeed accepting runs.

Conversely, if $\rho = (V, E)$ is an accepting run of $\mathcal{A}_\varphi$ on σ, then by definition of δ, $(\mathsf{q}_\varphi, 0) \to (\mathsf{q}_{\varphi_1}, 1)$ in E. The DAG restricted to the descendants of $(\mathsf{q}_{\varphi_1}, 1)$ is obviously an accepting run of $\mathcal{A}_{\varphi_1}$ on $\sigma[1, +\infty)$, whence $\sigma, 0 \models \varphi$ by the inductive hypothesis.

$\varphi = \varphi_1 \wedge \varphi_2$: Given $i \in \{1, 2\}$, let $\mathcal{B}_i = (\Sigma, Q_i, \mathsf{q}_{\varphi_i}, \delta_i, F_i)$ be the very weak alternating Büchi automaton obtained from $\mathcal{A}_{\varphi_i}$ such that $L(\mathcal{B}_i) = \mathrm{Mod}_\Pi(\varphi_i)$ with $\Pi = \mathrm{PROP}(\varphi)$ and $\Sigma = \mathcal{P}(\Pi)$ (see Lemma 14.4.3). We need this preliminary step, since φ_1 and φ_2 do not necessarily contain the same set of atomic propositions.

For every linear model $\sigma \in \Sigma^\omega$, we have $\sigma, 0 \models \varphi$ iff $\sigma, 0 \models \varphi_1$ and $\sigma, 0 \models \varphi_2$ iff there is an accepting run ρ_1 on σ in $\mathcal{B}_1$ and there is an accepting run ρ_2 on σ in $\mathcal{B}_2$ (by the inductive hypothesis and by Lemma 14.4.3). Given a run $\rho_1 = (V_1, E_1)$ on σ in $\mathcal{B}_1$ and a run $\rho_2 = (V_2, E_2)$ on σ in $\mathcal{B}_2$, we build a DAG $\rho = (V, E)$ as follows:

- $V := (V_1 \cup V_2 \cup \{(\mathsf{q}_\varphi, 0)\}) \setminus \{(\mathsf{q}_{\varphi_1}, 0), (\mathsf{q}_{\varphi_2}, 0)\}$.

  (Remove the root nodes and add the new root node $(\mathsf{q}_\varphi, 0)$.)

- $E := (E_1 \cup E_2 \cup \{(\mathsf{q}_\varphi, 0) \to (\mathsf{q}_{\varphi'}, 1) : (\mathsf{q}_{\varphi_i}, 0) \to (\mathsf{q}_{\varphi'}, 1) \in E_i, i \in [1, 2]\}) \setminus \{(\mathsf{q}_{\varphi_i}, 0) \to (\mathsf{q}_{\varphi'}, 1) : i \in [1, 2]\}$.

Roughly speaking, ρ is obtained from ρ_1 and ρ_2 by substituting $(\mathsf{q}_{\varphi_1}, 0)$ by $(\mathsf{q}_\varphi, 0)$, $(\mathsf{q}_{\varphi_2}, 0)$ by $(\mathsf{q}_\varphi, 0)$ and by taking the union. In the sequel, we write $\rho_1 \wedge \rho_2$ to denote ρ. By definition of δ, ρ is a run on σ in $\mathcal{A}_\varphi$. If we assume that

(Sharing) for every $(\mathsf{q}_\psi, l) \in V_1 \cap V_2$, for every $(\mathsf{q}_{\psi'}, l+1) \in V_1 \cup V_2$, $(\mathsf{q}_\psi, l) \to (\mathsf{q}_{\psi'}, l+1)$ in E_1 iff $(\mathsf{q}_\psi, l) \to (\mathsf{q}_{\psi'}, l+1)$ in E_2,

and if ρ_1 and ρ_2 are accepting runs then ρ is an accepting run, too. Indeed, any infinite path in ρ is necessarily an infinite path of ρ_2 or an infinite path of ρ_1. Moreover, the set of accepting states of $\mathcal{A}_\varphi$ is the union of the accepting states of $\mathcal{B}_1$ and $\mathcal{B}_2$ plus q_φ. When ρ_1 is an accepting run on σ in $\mathcal{B}_1$ and ρ_2 is an accepting run on σ in $\mathcal{B}_2$, we can assume without any loss of generality that they satisfy the condition **Sharing**. Consequently, if $\sigma, 0 \models \varphi$, then ρ is an accepting run of $\mathcal{A}_\varphi$ on σ.

Conversely, let $\rho = (V, E)$ be a minimal accepting run on σ in $\mathcal{A}_\varphi$. Assuming that ρ satisfies the minimality condition (R4') it is easy to find ρ_1 and ρ_2 such that:

- ρ_1 is an accepting run on σ in $\mathcal{B}_1$ and ρ_2 is an accepting run on σ in $\mathcal{B}_2$,
- ρ_1 and ρ_2 satisfy the condition **Sharing**,
- ρ can be decomposed as ρ_1 and ρ_2 according to the preceding definition, i.e. $\rho = \rho_1 \wedge \rho_2$ (minimality simplifies the proof of existence of such a decomposition).

By inductive hypothesis $\sigma, 0 \models \varphi_1$ and $\sigma, 0 \models \varphi_2$, which leads to $\sigma \in \mathrm{Mod}_\Pi(\varphi)$.

$\varphi = \varphi_1 \vee \varphi_2$: Without any loss of generality, we can assume that $\mathrm{PROP}(\varphi_1) = \mathrm{PROP}(\varphi_2) = \mathrm{PROP}(\varphi)$, otherwise we consider a preliminary phase as done for the case $\varphi = \varphi_1 \wedge \varphi_2$.

For every linear model $\sigma \in \Sigma^\omega$, we have $\sigma, 0 \models \varphi$ iff $\sigma, 0 \models \varphi_1$ or $\sigma, 0 \models \varphi_2$ iff there is an accepting run ρ_1 on σ in $\mathcal{A}_{\varphi_1}$ or there is an accepting run ρ_2 on σ in $\mathcal{A}_{\varphi_2}$ (by inductive hypothesis). Note that the minimal accepting runs of $\mathcal{A}_\varphi$ are the minimal accepting runs of $\mathcal{A}_{\varphi_1}$ or the minimal accepting runs of $\mathcal{A}_{\varphi_2}$ except that the root node is replaced by $(\mathsf{q}_\varphi, 0)$. Consequently, we have $\sigma, 0 \models \varphi$ iff there is an accepting run of $\mathcal{A}_\varphi$ on σ.

$\varphi = \varphi_1 \mathsf{U} \varphi_2$: First, let us assume that $\sigma, 0 \models \varphi$. By definition of the satisfaction relation, there is $n \in \mathbb{N}$ such that $\sigma, n \models \varphi_2$ and for every $i \in [0, n-1]$, we have $\sigma, i \models \varphi_1$. By induction on n, let us show that there is an accepting run on σ in $\mathcal{A}_\varphi$.

$n = 0$: This means that $\sigma, 0 \models \varphi_2$ and by the first inductive hypothesis, there is an accepting run $\rho_2 = (V_2, E_2)$ on σ in $\mathcal{A}_{\varphi_2}$. Let ρ be $\rho_2[(\mathsf{q}_{\varphi_2}, 0) \leftarrow (\mathsf{q}_\varphi, 0)]$. Roughly speaking, ρ is obtained from ρ_2 by substituting $(\mathsf{q}_{\varphi_2}, 0)$ by $(\mathsf{q}_\varphi, 0)$. By definition of δ, ρ is a run on σ in $\mathcal{A}_\varphi$ and it is accepting because there is a bijection between the infinite paths of ρ and the infinite paths of ρ_2, and every accepting state of $\mathcal{A}_{\varphi_2}$ is an accepting state of $\mathcal{A}_\varphi$.

$n > 0$: By definition of the satisfaction relation $\models$, we have $\sigma, 0 \models \varphi_1$ and $\sigma, 1 \models \varphi$. By the first induction hypothesis, there is an accepting run $\rho_1 = (V_1, E_1)$ on σ in $\mathcal{A}_{\varphi_1}$. By the second inductive hypothesis, there is an accepting run $\rho_2 = (V_2, E_2)$ on $\sigma[1, +\infty)$ in $\mathcal{A}_\varphi$. Let $\rho = (V, E)$ be the DAG defined as follows. Roughly speaking ρ is obtained from ρ_1 and ρ_2 by replacing $(\mathsf{q}_{\varphi_1}, 0)$ by $(\mathsf{q}_\varphi, 0)$, by shifting ρ_2 by $+1$ and then by adding an edge from $(\mathsf{q}_\varphi, 0)$ to $(\mathsf{q}_{\varphi_2}, 1)$ (obtained by shifting $(\mathsf{q}_\varphi, 0)$ from ρ_2).

- $V = (V_1 \cup V_2^{+1} \cup \{(\mathsf{q}_\varphi, 0)\}) \setminus \{(\mathsf{q}_{\varphi_1}, 0)\}$.
- $E = (E_1 \cup E_2^{+1} \cup \{(\mathsf{q}_\varphi, 0) \to (\mathsf{q}_\varphi, 1)\} \cup \{(\mathsf{q}_\varphi, 0) \to (\mathsf{q}_\psi, 1) : (\mathsf{q}_{\varphi_1}, 0) \to (\mathsf{q}_\psi, 1) \in E_1\}) \setminus \{(\mathsf{q}_{\varphi_1}, 0) \to (\mathsf{q}_\psi, 1) : (\mathsf{q}_{\varphi_1}, 0) \to (\mathsf{q}_\psi, 1) \in E_1\}$.

By definition of δ, ρ is a run on σ in $\mathcal{A}_\varphi$. This is also an accepting run since there is a bijection between the infinite paths of ρ and the union of the infinite paths of ρ_1 and ρ_2. Moreover, every accepting state of $\mathcal{A}_{\varphi_1}$ is also an accepting state in $\mathcal{A}_\varphi$.

Now suppose $\rho = (V, E)$ is a minimal accepting run on σ in $\mathcal{A}_\varphi$. By satisfaction of the condition (R4$'$) and by acceptance, there is no infinite path that contains only the state q_φ. Let N be the unique natural number such that $\{(\mathsf{q}_\varphi, 0), \ldots, (\mathsf{q}_\varphi, N)\} \subseteq V$ and $(\mathsf{q}_\varphi, N+1) \notin V$. Such a value N exists because ρ is minimal. We consider the two possible cases:

$N = 0$: Let ρ_2 be the DAG obtained from ρ by replacing $(\mathsf{q}_\varphi, 0)$ by $(\mathsf{q}_{\varphi_2}, 0)$. By satisfaction of (R4$'$), no state (q_ψ, l) occurs in ρ_2 with $\psi \in sub(\varphi_1) \setminus sub(\varphi_2)$. Consequently, ρ_2 is an accepting run on σ in $\mathcal{A}_{\varphi_2}$. By inductive hypothesis, $\sigma, 0 \models \varphi_2$ and therefore $\sigma, 0 \models \varphi$.

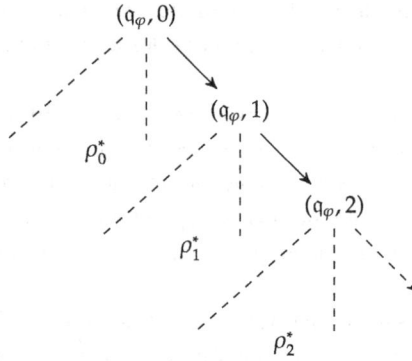

Figure 14.10 Construction of the accepting run ρ for the operator R.

$N > 0$: By definition of δ:
- the generated subgraph ρ_1' obtained from $(q_\varphi, 1)$ in ρ is isomorphic to an accepting run ρ_1 on $\sigma[1, +\infty)$ in $\mathcal{A}_\varphi$ with $\rho_1^{+1} = \rho_1'$,
- there is an accepting run ρ_2 on σ in $\mathcal{A}_{\varphi_1}$ obtained from ρ by replacing $(q_\varphi, 0)$ by $(q_{\varphi_1}, 0)$ and by deleting the generated subgraph ρ_1'.

By the first inductive hypothesis, we have $\sigma, 0 \models \varphi_1$ whereas by the second inductive hypothesis, we have $\sigma, 1 \models \varphi$. Consequently, $\sigma, 0 \models \varphi$.

$\varphi = \varphi_1 R \varphi_2$: If $\sigma, 0 \models \varphi$, then either for all $i \in \mathbb{N}$, we have $\sigma, i \models \varphi_2$ or there is $n \in \mathbb{N}$ such that $\sigma, n \models \varphi_1 \wedge \varphi_2$ and for every $k \in [0, n-1]$, we have $\sigma, k \models \varphi_2$.

In the first case, for all $i \in \mathbb{N}$, there is an accepting run $\rho_i = (V_i, E_i)$ on $\sigma[\iota, +\infty)$ in $\mathcal{A}_{\varphi_2}$. Let ρ_i^* be the DAG obtained from ρ_i by replacing $(q_{\varphi_2}, 0)$ by $(q_\varphi, 0)$ and then by substituting each node (q_ψ, l) by $(q_\psi, l+i)$. Let ρ be the DAG defined as the union of all the DAGs ρ_i^* augmented with the infinite path $(q_\varphi, 0) \to (q_\varphi, 1) \to (q_\varphi, 2) \cdots$. By definition of δ, ρ is a run on σ in $\mathcal{A}_\varphi$. It is accepting, since every accepting state of $\mathcal{A}_{\varphi_2}$ is also an accepting state of $\mathcal{A}_{\varphi_1}$. The construction of ρ is illustrated in Figure 14.10.

In the second case, the proof is by induction on n.

$n = 0$: So $\sigma, 0 \models \varphi_1 \wedge \varphi_2$. Without loss of generality we can assume that $\text{PROP}(\varphi_1) = \text{PROP}(\varphi_2) = \text{PROP}(\varphi)$, otherwise we consider a preliminary step, as done for the case $\varphi = \varphi_1 \wedge \varphi_2$. By the inductive hypothesis, there is an accepting run ρ_1 on σ in $\mathcal{A}_{\varphi_1}$ and there is an accepting run ρ_2 on σ in $\mathcal{A}_{\varphi_2}$. Moreover, without loss of generality we can assume that ρ_1 and ρ_2 satisfy the condition **Sharing**. Let ρ be the DAG defined as $\rho_1 \wedge \rho_2$ for the case for conjunctions except that the root node is $(q_{\varphi_1 R \varphi_2}, 0)$. One can show that ρ is an accepting run on σ in $\mathcal{A}_\varphi$. Indeed, it is a run since $Y \models \delta(q_{\varphi_1}, \sigma(0)) \wedge \delta(q_{\varphi_2}, \sigma(0))$ implies $Y \models \delta(q_{\varphi_1 R \varphi_2}, \sigma(0))$. ρ is accepting, due to the satisfaction of the condition **Sharing**.

$n > 0$: By definition of the satisfaction relation $\models$, we have $\sigma, 0 \models \varphi_2$ and $\sigma, 1 \models \varphi$. By the first induction hypothesis, there is an accepting run $\rho_1 = (V_1, E_1)$ on σ in

$\mathcal{A}_{\varphi_2}$. By the second inductive hypothesis, there is an accepting run $\rho_2 = (V_2, E_2)$ on $\sigma[1, +\infty)$ in $\mathcal{A}_\varphi$. Let $\rho = (V, E)$ be the DAG defined as follows. Roughly speaking, ρ is obtained from ρ_1 and ρ_2 by replacing $(\mathsf{q}_{\varphi_2}, 0)$ by $(\mathsf{q}_\varphi, 0)$, by shifting ρ_2 by +1 and then by adding an edge from $(\mathsf{q}_\varphi, 0)$ to $(\mathsf{q}_\varphi, 1)$ (obtained by shifting $(\mathsf{q}_\varphi, 0)$ from ρ_2).

- $V = (V_1 \cup V_2^{+1} \cup \{(\mathsf{q}_\varphi, 0)\}) \setminus \{(\mathsf{q}_{\varphi_1}, 0)\}$.
- $E = (E_1 \cup E_2^+ \cup \{(\mathsf{q}_\varphi, 0) \to (\mathsf{q}_\varphi, 1)\} \cup \{(\mathsf{q}_\varphi, 0) \to (\mathsf{q}_\psi, 1) : (\mathsf{q}_{\varphi_2}, 0) \to (\mathsf{q}_\psi, 1) \in E_1\}) \setminus \{(\mathsf{q}_{\varphi_2}, 0) \to (\mathsf{q}_\psi, 1) : (\mathsf{q}_{\varphi_2}, 0) \to (\mathsf{q}_\psi, 1) \in E_1\}$.

By definition of δ, ρ is a run on σ in $\mathcal{A}_\varphi$. This is also an accepting run since there is a bijection between the infinite paths of ρ and the union of the infinite paths of ρ_1 and ρ_2. Moreover, every accepting state of $\mathcal{A}_{\varphi_2}$ is also an accepting state in $\mathcal{A}_\varphi$. Note that the preceding argument is similar to a case for Until formulae.

Conversely, if ρ is an accepting run on σ in $\mathcal{A}_\varphi$, then one can show that $\sigma, 0 \models \varphi$. The proof is left to the reader but it does not use any essentially new ingredients. □

In summary, we have seen that the following claims are equivalent:

1. $\sigma, 0 \models \varphi$,
2. $\sigma \in L(\mathcal{A}_\varphi)$ (Theorem 14.4.6),
3. There is a minimal accepting run ρ on σ in $\mathcal{A}_\varphi$ (Lemma 14.4.4),
4. There is a minimal accepting run ρ on σ in $\mathcal{A}_\varphi$ such that every infinite path in ρ eventually gets trapped in a state of the form $\mathsf{q}_{\psi_1 R \psi_2}$ (Lemma 14.4.5(III)),
5. $\sigma \in L(\mathcal{A}'_\varphi)$ where $\mathcal{A}'_\varphi$ is defined as $\mathcal{A}_\varphi$, except that the accepting states are restricted to R-formulae.

There is another consequence that is worth being drawn attention to. Suppose that φ is an LTL formula in negation normal form and φ^- is the negation normal form of $\neg\varphi$ obtained from φ by replacing $\vee$ [resp. $\wedge$, U, R, p, $\neg p$] by $\wedge$ [resp. $\vee$, R, U, $\neg p$, p]. From the proof of Lemma 14.3.14, we know that $(\Sigma, Q, q_0, \overline{\delta}, Q \setminus F)$ accepts the linear models of φ^- where $\mathcal{A}'_\varphi = (\Sigma, Q, q_0, \delta, F)$. However, with arguments similar to the ones presented here, $\mathcal{B} = (\Sigma, Q, q_0, \overline{\delta}, F')$ where F' is the set of U-formulae of Q, also accepts the linear models of φ^-. Now it is worth noting that $\mathcal{B}$ and $\mathcal{A}'_{\varphi^-}$ are isomorphic structures (we already knew that they accept the same languages). Indeed, every state q_ψ in $\mathcal{B}$ maps to q_{ψ^-} where ψ^- is obtained from ψ by replacing $\vee$ [resp. $\wedge$, U, R, p, $\neg p$] by $\wedge$ [resp. $\vee$, R, U, $\neg p$, p].

14.4.2 LTL versus Very Weak Alternating Automata

We have shown that every LTL formula can be translated into a very weak alternating Büchi automaton accepting its set of linear models. A translation in the other direction is also possible as shown below, which implies that this class of alternating automata is strictly weaker than the class of alternating Büchi automata. Indeed:

- LTL is strictly less expressive than ETL or the linear modal μ-calculus LT_μ (Corollary 10.3.4);
- for every formula φ of ETL there is an ω-regular expression E_φ such that $L(E_\varphi) = \text{Mod}(\varphi)$ (Theorem 10.1.6);
- (alternating) Büchi automata and ω-regular expressions define the same class of ω-languages (Theorem 14.1.16).

Theorem 14.4.7. Let $\Sigma = \mathcal{P}(\Pi)$ be a finite alphabet for some finite $\Pi \subseteq \text{PROP}$. For every very weak alternating Büchi automaton $\mathcal{A}$ over the alphabet Σ there is an LTL formula φ built over atomic propositions in Π such that $\text{Mod}_\Pi(\varphi) = L(\mathcal{A})$. ∎

Proof. First, we introduce a variant of alternating Büchi automata in which initial states are replaced by initial positive Boolean formulae. These are of the form $\mathcal{A} = (\Sigma, Q, I, \delta, F)$ with $I \in \mathcal{B}^+(Q)$. Runs $\rho = (V, E)$ are still labelled DAGs except that they may have more than one root: $\text{card}(\{q \in Q \mid (q, 0) \in V\}) \geq 1$. Moreover, we require that $\{q \in Q \mid (q, 0) \in V\} \models I$. Given a (very weak) alternating Büchi automaton $\mathcal{A}$, we write $\mathcal{A}(I')$ to denote the variant automaton obtained from $\mathcal{A}$ by considering the initial condition I'.

Let $\mathcal{A} = (\Sigma, Q, I, \delta, F)$ be a very weak alternating Büchi automaton with initial positive Boolean formula I. For each transition formula $\mathcal{F} \in \mathcal{B}^+(Q)$, we construct an LTL formula $\chi(\mathcal{F})$ such that $\text{Mod}_\Pi(\chi(\mathcal{F})) = L(\mathcal{A}(\mathcal{F}))$ where $\mathcal{A}(\mathcal{F})$ is a very weak alternating Büchi automaton with initial positive Boolean formula $\mathcal{F}$. The construction is by structural induction. Consequently, φ is defined as $\chi(I)$. Let $\mathcal{F} \in \mathcal{B}^+(Q)$. If, for all the states q occurring in $\mathcal{F}$, the formula $\chi(q)$ is already built, then $\chi(\mathcal{F})$ is obtained from $\mathcal{F}$ by replacing each state q by $\chi(q)$, as LTL formulae are closed under disjunctions and conjunctions; besides, $\chi(\bot) :=\bot$ and $\chi(\top) := \top$.

Let $q \in Q$ and $\delta(q)$ be the set of states q' such that q' occurs in $\delta(q, a)$ for some letter a. Since $\mathcal{A}$ is a very weak alternating automaton, by inductive hypothesis, we can assume that for all $q' \in (\delta(q, a) \setminus \{q\})$, $\chi(q')$ is already known and therefore $\chi(\mathcal{F})$ is known for each $\mathcal{F} \in \mathcal{B}^+(\delta(q) \setminus \{q\})$.

For each letter $a \in \Sigma$, $\delta(q, a)$ is propositionally equivalent to a positive Boolean formula of the form $(q \wedge \mathcal{F}_{1,a}) \vee \mathcal{F}_{2,a}$ where $\mathcal{F}_{1,a}, \mathcal{F}_{2,a} \in \mathcal{B}^+(\delta(q) \setminus \{q\})$. For instance, it is sufficient to rewrite $\delta(q, a)$ in disjunctive normal form and to adequately gather the disjuncts in which q occurs.

Given a letter $a \in \Sigma$, with a mild abuse of notation we write a to denote the Boolean formula

$$\left(\bigwedge_{p \in a} p \right) \wedge \left(\bigwedge_{p \in (\Pi \setminus a)} \neg p \right).$$

Moreover, let us define the formulae φ_q^1 and φ_q^2 as follows:

$$\varphi_q^1 = \bigvee_{a \in \Sigma} (a \wedge X \chi(\mathcal{F}_{1,a})) \qquad \varphi_q^2 = \bigvee_{a \in \Sigma} (a \wedge X \chi(\mathcal{F}_{2,a})).$$

If $q \in F$, then $\chi(q) := (\varphi_q^1 U \varphi_q^2) \vee G\varphi_q^1$, otherwise $\chi(q) := \varphi_q^1 U \varphi_q^2$.

In order to show that for all $\mathcal{F} \in \mathcal{B}^+(Q)$, we have $\text{Mod}_\Pi(\chi(\mathcal{F})) = L(\mathcal{A}(\mathcal{F}))$, it is sufficient to establish that $\text{Mod}_\Pi(\chi(q)) = L(\mathcal{A}(q))$ for all $q \in Q$.

Let $q \in Q$ and $\sigma \in \text{Mod}_\Pi(\chi(q))$. If $q \notin F$, then there is $k \in \mathbb{N}$ such that $\sigma, k \models \varphi_q^2$ and for all $i \in [0, k-1]$, we have $\sigma, i \models \varphi_q^1$. Hence for all $i \in [0, k-1]$, $\sigma[i + 1, +\infty) \in \text{Mod}_\Pi(\chi(\mathcal{F}_{1,\sigma(i)}))$ and $\sigma[k + 1, +\infty) \in \text{Mod}_\Pi(\chi(\mathcal{F}_{2,\sigma(k)}))$. By the inductive hypothesis, we know that $\text{Mod}_\Pi(\chi(\mathcal{F}_{1,\sigma(i)})) = L(\mathcal{A}(\mathcal{F}_{1,\sigma(i)}))$ and $\text{Mod}_\Pi(\chi(\mathcal{F}_{2,\sigma(k)})) = L(\mathcal{A}(\mathcal{F}_{2,\sigma(k)}))$. Since $\delta(q, a)$ is equivalent to $(q \wedge \mathcal{F}_{1,a}) \vee \mathcal{F}_{2,a}$, this guarantees that $\sigma \in L(\mathcal{A}(q))$. Indeed, an accepting run of $\mathcal{A}(q)$ is of the form described, where the weak alternating Büchi automata refer to accepting runs of these automata from the appropriate suffixes.

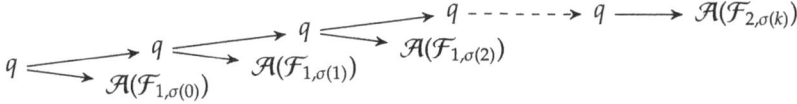

If $q \in F$, then the proof is analogous apart from the satisfaction of the formula $G\varphi_q^1$. In that case, we obtain an accepting run with an infinite path labelled by q.

The proof of the other direction is analogous and is omitted herein. $\qquad \square$

14.5 Extensions of LTL

14.5.1 Translating ETL Formulae

This section presents a translation from ETL formulae to alternating Büchi automata that accept their models. We provide a direct reduction from ETL formulae into alternating Büchi automata, such that the number of states remains linear in the size of formulae. Even though the alphabet is of exponential size, we can establish a PSPACE complexity upper bound for SAT(ETL) by on the fly guessing of the equivalent nondeterministic Büchi automaton obtained from an alternating Büchi automaton. To do so, we make use of Theorem 14.3.12.

In the rest of this section, without any loss of generality, we can assume that whenever an ETL subformula $\mathcal{A}(\psi_1, \ldots, \psi_T)$ is considered for a finite-state $\mathcal{A} = (\Sigma, Q, Q_0, \delta, F)$, the set Q_0 is a singleton set $\{q_0\}$. Indeed, it is always possible to add ε-transitions in order to have a single initial state and then to remove such ε-transitions. We recall that ε-transitions are *silent* transitions that do not read any letter and usually they can be eliminated, thanks to nondeterminism.

Theorem 14.5.1. For every ETL formula φ there is an alternating Büchi automaton $\mathcal{A}_\varphi$ such that $L(\mathcal{A}_\varphi) = \text{Mod}_\Pi(\varphi)$, where $\Pi = \text{PROP}(\varphi)$ and the number of states in $\mathcal{A}_\varphi$ is linear in the size of φ. $\qquad \blacksquare$

Proof. Let φ be an ETL formula. Without any loss of generality, negation in φ occurs only in front of atomic propositions and in front of automata-based formulae. Double negations have also been eliminated. We build an alternating Büchi automaton $\mathcal{A}_\varphi = (\Sigma_\varphi, Q_\varphi, q_{0,\varphi}, \delta_\varphi, F_\varphi)$ as follows.

- $Q_\varphi := \{q_\psi \mid \psi \in \Gamma\}$ where Γ is the least set closed under subformulae and allowing to apply the rules
  - if $q_{\mathcal{A}(\psi_1,...,\psi_T)} \in Q_\varphi$ with $\mathcal{A} = (\Sigma, Q, q_0, \delta, F)$, then for every state $q \in Q$, $q_{\mathcal{A}_q(\psi_1,...,\psi_T)} \in Q_\varphi$ where $\mathcal{A}_q = (\Sigma, Q, q, \delta, F)$,
  - if $q_{\neg\mathcal{A}(\psi_1,...,\psi_T)} \in Q_\varphi$ with $\mathcal{A} = (\Sigma, Q, q_0, \delta, F)$, then for every state $q \in Q$, $q_{\neg\mathcal{A}_q(\psi_1,...,\psi_T)} \in Q_\varphi$,
  - if $q_\psi \in Q_\varphi$, then $q_{\overline{\psi}} \in Q_\varphi$ where $\overline{\psi}$ is the negation normal form of $\neg\psi$ obtained by pushing negations inwards as deep as possible. Note that $\overline{\overline{\psi}} = \psi$.
- $q_{0,\varphi} := q_\varphi$.
- $\Sigma_\varphi := \mathcal{P}(\mathrm{PROP}(\varphi))$.
- $F_\varphi := \{q_{\neg\mathcal{A}_q(\psi_1,...,\psi_l)} \mid q_{\neg\mathcal{A}_q(\psi_1,...,\psi_T)} \in Q_\varphi\}$.
- Let us define the transition function δ_φ. Boolean connectives in a state q_ψ are taken care of by the Boolean connectives in transition formulae that have operational interpretations.
  - $\delta_\varphi(q_p, \mathsf{a}) := \top$ if $p \in \mathsf{a}$ and $\delta_\varphi(q_p, \mathsf{a}) := \bot$ if $p \notin \mathsf{a}$,
  - $\delta_\varphi(q_{\neg p}, \mathsf{a}) := \top$ if $p \notin \mathsf{a}$ and $\delta_\varphi(q_{\neg p}, \mathsf{a}) := \bot$ if $p \in \mathsf{a}$,
  - $\delta_\varphi(q_{\psi_1 \wedge \psi_2}, \mathsf{a}) := \delta_\varphi(q_{\psi_1}, \mathsf{a}) \wedge \delta_\varphi(q_{\psi_2}, \mathsf{a})$,
  - $\delta_\varphi(q_{\psi_1 \vee \psi_2}, \mathsf{a}) := \delta_\varphi(q_{\psi_1}, \mathsf{a}) \vee \delta_\varphi(q_{\psi_2}, \mathsf{a})$,
  - $\delta_\varphi(q_{\mathcal{A}_q(\psi_1,...,\psi_T)}, \mathsf{a}) = \top$ if $\mathcal{A} = (\Sigma, Q, q_0, \delta, F)$ and $q \in F$.
  - $\delta_\varphi(q_{\mathcal{A}_q(\psi_1,...,\psi_l)}, \mathsf{a})$ is equal to the transition formula when $q \notin F$:

$$\bigvee_{q \xrightarrow{\mathsf{a}_i} q' \in \delta} \delta_\varphi(q_{\psi_i}, \mathsf{a}) \wedge q_{\mathcal{A}_{q'}(\psi_1,...,\psi_T)}.$$

  - $\delta_\varphi(q_{\neg\mathcal{A}_q(\psi_1,...,\psi_T)}, \mathsf{a}) = \bot$ if $\mathcal{A} = (\Sigma, Q, q_0, \delta, F)$ and $q \in F$.
  - $\delta_\varphi(q_{\neg\mathcal{A}_q(\psi_1,...,\psi_T)}, \mathsf{a})$ is equal to the transition formula when $q \notin F$:

$$\bigwedge_{q \xrightarrow{\mathsf{a}_i} q' \in \delta} \delta_\varphi(q_{\overline{\psi_i}}, \mathsf{a}) \vee q_{\neg\mathcal{A}_{q'}(\psi_1,...,\psi_T)}.$$

It is easy to verify that the range of δ_φ remains in $\mathbb{B}^+(Q_\varphi)$ and the definition of δ_φ is well founded. Clearly, $\mathcal{A}_\varphi$ is an alternating Büchi automaton.

Before going any further, we explain why the construction for $\mathcal{A}_\varphi$ generalises the definitions from Section 14.4. Let us see how the operators Until and Release are dealt with in the preceding definition. For instance, an LTL formula of the form $\varphi_1 \mathsf{U} \varphi_2$ (assuming that φ_1 and φ_2 are in negation normal form) can be written in ETL as $\mathcal{A}^{\mathsf{U}}(\varphi_1, \varphi_2)$, where $\mathcal{A}^{\mathsf{U}}$ is the finite-state automaton with $L(\mathcal{A}^{\mathsf{U}}) = \mathsf{a}_1^* \cdot \mathsf{a}_2$:

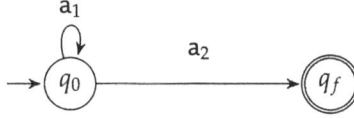

By definition, $\delta_\varphi(q_{\mathcal{A}^U(\varphi_1,\varphi_2)}, a)$ is equal to

$$(\delta_\varphi(q_{\varphi_1}, a) \wedge q_{\mathcal{A}^U_{q_0}(\varphi_1,\varphi_2)}) \vee (\delta_\varphi(q_{\varphi_2}, a) \wedge q_{\mathcal{A}^U_{q_f}(\varphi_1,\varphi_2)}).$$

Considering that $q_{\mathcal{A}^U_{q_0}(\varphi_1,\varphi_2)}$ is equal to $q_{\mathcal{A}^U(\varphi_1,\varphi_2)}$ (and therefore equivalent to $q_{\varphi_1 U \varphi_2}$) and $q_{\mathcal{A}^U_{q_f}(\varphi_1,\varphi_2)}$ is equivalent to true, we get that the transition formula $\delta_\varphi(q_{\mathcal{A}^U(\varphi_1,\varphi_2)}, a)$ is equivalent to

$$(\delta_\varphi(q_{\varphi_1}, a) \wedge q_{\mathcal{A}^U(\varphi_1,\varphi_2)}) \vee \delta_\varphi(q_{\varphi_2}, a)$$

which is precisely the definition for $\delta_\varphi(q_{\varphi_1 U \varphi_2}, a)$ in the construction done in Section 14.4.

Similarly, $\varphi_1 R \varphi_2$ can be written in ETL as $\neg \mathcal{A}^U(\overline{\varphi_1}, \overline{\varphi_2})$, where $\mathcal{A}^U$ is the finite-state automaton. By definition, $\delta_\varphi(q_{\neg \mathcal{A}^U(\overline{\varphi_1},\overline{\varphi_2})}, a)$ is equal to

$$(\delta_\varphi(q_{\overline{\overline{\varphi_1}}}, a) \vee q_{\neg \mathcal{A}^U_{q_0}(\overline{\varphi_1},\overline{\varphi_2})}) \wedge (\delta_\varphi(q_{\overline{\overline{\varphi_2}}}, a) \vee q_{\neg \mathcal{A}^U_{q_f}(\overline{\varphi_1},\overline{\varphi_2})}).$$

Considering that $\overline{\overline{\varphi_i}} = \varphi_i$, $q_{\neg \mathcal{A}^U_{q_0}(\overline{\varphi_1},\overline{\varphi_2})}$ is equal to $q_{\neg \mathcal{A}^U(\overline{\varphi_1},\overline{\varphi_2})}$ (and therefore equivalent to $q_{\varphi_1 R \varphi_2}$) and $q_{\neg \mathcal{A}^U_{q_1}(\overline{\varphi_1},\overline{\varphi_2})}$ is equivalent to $\bot$, we get that $\delta_\varphi(q_{\neg \mathcal{A}^U(\overline{\varphi_1},\overline{\varphi_2})}, a)$ is equivalent to

$$(\delta_\varphi(q_{\varphi_1}, a) \vee q_{\neg \mathcal{A}^U(\overline{\varphi_1},\overline{\varphi_2})}) \wedge \delta_\varphi(q_{\varphi_2}, a)$$

which is precisely the definition for $\delta_\varphi(q_{\varphi_1 R \varphi_2}, a)$ in the construction in Section 14.4.

It remains to show that $L(\mathcal{A}_\varphi) = \text{Mod}_\Pi(\varphi)$ where $\Pi = \text{PROP}(\varphi)$, which can be done by structural induction. The case with atomic propositions and the induction steps with Boolean connectives can be shown following techniques from Section 14.4. For example, we consider the case $\varphi = \mathcal{A}_q(\psi_1, \ldots, \psi_T)$ when q is not an accepting state. Let $\mathcal{A}_\varphi$ be the alternating Büchi automaton defined with the preceding construction. By the inductive hypothesis, there is $\mathcal{A}_{\psi_i}$ such that $L(\mathcal{A}_{\psi_i}) = \text{Mod}_\Pi(\psi_i)$ with $\Pi = \text{PROP}(\varphi)$. Note that $\mathcal{A}_{\psi_i}$ can be defined as the restriction of $\mathcal{A}_\varphi$ to the states q_ψ with q_ψ in Q_{ψ_i}. Let σ be a model such that $\sigma, 0 \models \mathcal{A}_q(\psi_1, \ldots, \psi_T)$ with $\mathcal{A} = (\Sigma, Q, q_0, \delta, F)$. By definition of the satisfaction relation $\models$, there is an accepting run $q_0 \xrightarrow{a_{i_0}} q_1 \xrightarrow{a_{i_1}} q_2 \cdots \xrightarrow{a_{i_{m-1}}} q_m$ of $\mathcal{A}$ such that for every $j \in [0, m-1]$, we have $\sigma, j \models \psi_{i_j}$. By the inductive hypothesis $\sigma[j, +\infty), 0 \models \psi_{i_j}$ iff $\sigma[j, +\infty) \in L(\mathcal{A}_{\psi_{i_j}})$ iff there is an accepting run ρ_j on $\sigma[j, +\infty)$. By adequately appending the runs $\rho_0, \ldots, \rho_{m-1}$ it is possible to build an accepting run ρ on σ (in $\mathcal{A}_\varphi$). In what follows, we present an illustration of this construction. Note that in order to obtain a DAG, sub-run sharing is needed but for the sake of clarity this is not represented in the picture.

$$q_{\mathcal{A}_{q_0}(\psi_1,\ldots,\psi_T)}$$

$$q_{\mathcal{A}_{q_1}(\psi_1,\ldots,\psi_T)} \qquad \rho_0$$

$$q_{\mathcal{A}_{q_2}(\psi_1,\ldots,\psi_T)} \qquad \rho_1$$

$$\rho_2$$

$$q_{\mathcal{A}_{q_{m-1}}(\psi_1,\ldots,\psi_T)}$$

$$q_{\mathcal{A}_{q_m}(\psi_1,\ldots,\psi_T)} \qquad \rho_{m-1}$$

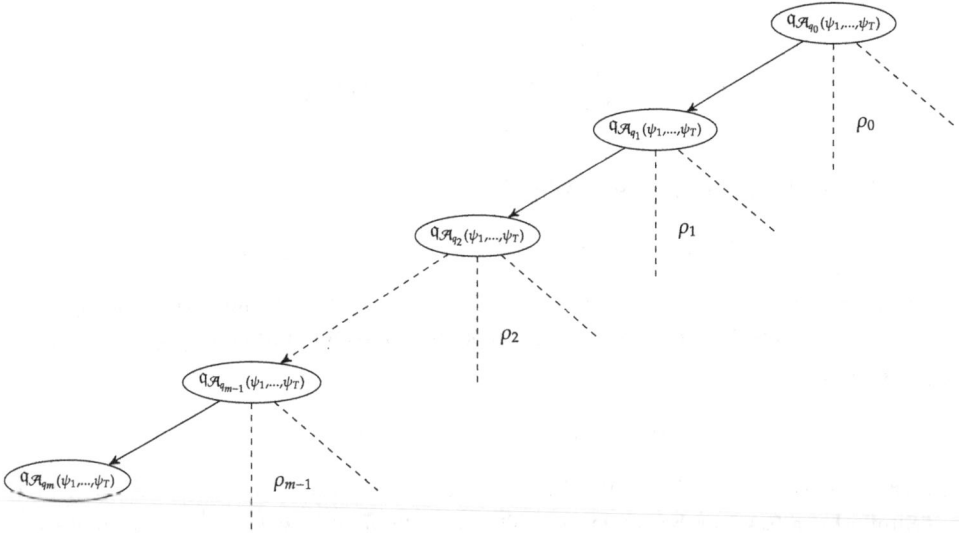

Conversely, suppose that $\sigma \in \mathrm{L}(\mathcal{A}_\varphi)$. Assuming that there is a minimal run and considering that accepting states in $\mathcal{A}_\varphi$ are not of the form $q_{\mathcal{A}_q(\psi_1,\ldots,\psi_T)}$, there is a path in ρ of the form

$$q_{\mathcal{A}_{q_0}(\psi_1,\ldots,\psi_T)} \to q_{\mathcal{A}_{q_1}(\psi_1,\ldots,\psi_T)} \to \cdots \to q_{\mathcal{A}_{q_m}(\psi_1,\ldots,\psi_T)}$$

with $q_m \in F$. This induces an accepting run $q_0 \xrightarrow{a_{i_0}} q_1 \xrightarrow{a_{i_1}} q_2 \cdots \xrightarrow{a_{i_{m-1}}} q_m$ of $\mathcal{A}$ which guarantees that $\sigma, 0 \models \varphi$ by the inductive hypothesis. $\qquad\square$

So far, we have seen that for every ETL formula φ, one can build an alternating Büchi automaton $\mathcal{A}_\varphi$ such that $\mathrm{L}(\mathcal{A}_\varphi) = \mathrm{Mod}_\Pi(\varphi)$ where $\Pi = \mathrm{PROP}(\varphi)$, its number of states is quadratic in the size of φ and the cardinality of its alphabet is exponential in the size of φ. The nonemptiness problem for alternating Büchi automata can be solved in polynomial space, whence SAT(ETL) can be solved in exponential space. However, it can be shown that the problem can be solved in polynomial space by simulating the corresponding nondeterministic Büchi automaton on the fly. This is obviously the best we can hope for, since SAT(LTL) is already PSpace-complete and there is an obvious logarithmic-space reduction from SAT(LTL) to SAT(ETL).

Theorem 14.5.2. SAT(ETL) is in PSpace. ∎

Proof. Let φ be an ETL formula. We have seen how to build an alternating Büchi automaton $\mathcal{A}_\varphi = (\Sigma_\varphi, Q_\varphi, q_{0,\varphi}, \delta_\varphi, F_\varphi)$ such that $\mathrm{L}(\mathcal{A}_\varphi) = \mathrm{Mod}_\Pi(\varphi)$ with $\Pi = \mathrm{PROP}(\varphi)$. Instead of building $\mathcal{A}_\varphi$, we guess an accepting run for the equivalent nondeterministic Büchi automaton $\mathcal{B}$ defined on the fly as done in Theorem 14.3.12. The Büchi automaton $\mathcal{B}$ is of the form $(\Sigma_\varphi, Q', Q'_0, \delta', F')$ with $Q' = \mathcal{P}(Q_\varphi) \times \mathcal{P}(Q_\varphi)$ such that F', Q' and δ' can be decided in polynomial-space in the size of φ. Consequently, in order to check nonemptiness of $\mathrm{L}(\mathcal{B})$ (which is equivalent to checking the satisfiability status of the ETL formula φ) it is sufficient to guess a witness run on the fly that is of length at most exponential in the size of φ. Each step requires polynomial space and counting until an exponential value does so, too. Consequently, the ETL satisfiability problem is in NPSPACE; by Savitch's Theorem, the problem is therefore in PSPACE. □

Using arguments from Section 14.2.5, and more specifically an adaptation of Lemma 14.2.22, we can get the following corollary.

Theorem 14.5.3. $MC^{\exists}(ETL)$ is in PSPACE. ∎

Note that given an ETL formula φ, we can build an equivalent nondeterministic Büchi automaton $\mathcal{A}_\varphi$ such that

1. each state of $\mathcal{A}_\varphi$ can be built in polynomial space (in the size of φ),
2. checking whether a state is initial or accepting can be done in polynomial space,
3. the transition relation can be checked in polynomial space.

14.5.2 A Direct Translation for PSL Formulae

This section is dedicated to translating PSL formulae into alternating Büchi automata that accept their models. We provide a direct reduction from PSL formulae into alternating Büchi automata, such that the number of states is at most exponential in the size of formulae.

Let E be a semi-extended regular expression (SERE) built over Boolean expressions with atomic propositions in Π. Operators in such expressions include union, composition, Kleene star operator and intersection (see Section 6.7.3). We write $L(E)$ to denote the set of finite parts of a computation $\rho : [n] \to \mathcal{P}(\Pi)$ such that $\rho \models E$ where $[n]$ is the subset of $\mathbb{N}$ equal to $\{0, \ldots, n-1\}$.

Proposition 14.5.4. Given a semi-extended regular expression E built over Boolean expressions with atomic propositions in Π, there is a finite-state automaton $\mathcal{A}$ such that $L(\mathcal{A}) = L(E)$ and $\mathcal{A}$ has a number of states exponential in the size of E. ∎

If we discard the intersection operator in SEREs (leading to standard regular expressions), we know that such an automaton exists and it can have at most a number of states that is polynomial in the size of E. Products of finite-state automata need to be considered when the intersection operator is allowed, which explains the potential exponential amount of states in $\mathcal{A}$.

Lemma 14.5.5. Let E be a semi-extended regular expression built over Boolean expressions with atomic propositions in Π. There is a Büchi automaton $\mathcal{A}$ such that $L(\mathcal{A}) = \mathrm{Mod}_\Pi(\mathrm{Cl}(E))$ and $\mathcal{A}$ has a number of states at most exponential in the size of E. ∎

Recall that $\mathrm{Cl}(E)$ is defined in Section 6.7.3.

Proof. Let $\mathcal{A}^\star = (\Sigma, Q, q_0, \delta, F)$ be the finite-state automaton for E from Proposition 14.5.4. If $L(\mathcal{A}^\star)$ is empty, then we pick a fixed Büchi automaton with empty language. If $\varepsilon \in L(E)$, then we pick a fixed Büchi automaton with universal language. Otherwise, observe that $\sigma \models \mathrm{Cl}(E)$ iff one of the following conditions holds:

1. a (finite) prefix of σ belongs to $L(E)$ or
2. for all $j \geq 0$, there is σ' such that $\sigma[0, j]\sigma'$ has a (finite) prefix that belongs to $L(E)$.

Given $\mathcal{A}^\star$, it is quite simple to design a Büchi automaton $\mathcal{A}_1$ such that $L(\mathcal{A}_1) = \{\sigma \in \Sigma^\omega \mid \exists\, i \geq 0$ such that $\sigma[0, i] \in L(E)\}$. Indeed, first we can assume that no accepting state in $\mathcal{A}^\star$ has an outgoing transition and then we can construct $\mathcal{A}_1$ from $\mathcal{A}^\star$ by just adding self-loops to each accepting state for every letter in Σ.

Secondly, let $Q' \subseteq Q$ be all the states in Q that are reachable from q_0 and productive. This simply means that the set Q' contains the states that can be reached from q_0 and that can reach at least one accepting state in F. Let $\mathcal{A}_2 = (\Sigma, Q', q_0, \delta', Q')$ be the restriction of $\mathcal{A}^\star$ to the states in Q'. One can show that $L(\mathcal{A}_1) \cup L(\mathcal{A}_2) = \mathrm{Mod}_\Pi(\mathrm{Cl}(E))$, which is left as an exercise. It is then quite easy to design a Büchi automaton $\mathcal{A}$ such that $L(\mathcal{A}) = L(\mathcal{A}_1) \cup L(\mathcal{A}_2)$. Note also that $\mathcal{A}$ is built from simple transformations on $\mathcal{A}^\star$ and therefore the number of states in $\mathcal{A}$ can be shown to be at most exponential in the size of E. $\qquad\square$

Theorem 14.5.6. For every PSL formula φ, there is an alternating Büchi automaton $\mathcal{A}_\varphi$ such that $L(\mathcal{A}_\varphi) = \mathrm{Mod}_\Pi(\varphi)$ where $\Pi = \mathrm{PROP}(\varphi)$ and the number of states in $\mathcal{A}_\varphi$ is exponential in the size of φ. $\qquad\blacksquare$

Proof. Let φ be a PSL formula. Without any loss of generality, negation in φ occurs only in front of atomic propositions and in front of subformulae of the form either $E \diamond\!\!\rightarrow \psi$ or $\mathrm{Cl}(E)$. So, Boolean connectives include $\wedge$, $\vee$ and $\neg$. Moreover, we assume that all the atomic propositions occurring in SEREs are among Π and $\varepsilon \notin L(E)$ (otherwise, the formulae $E \diamond\!\!\rightarrow \psi$ and $\mathrm{Cl}(E)$ can be simplified to equivalent formulae without the occurrence of E).

We extend the notion of subformulae so that $\mathrm{Cl}(E)$ is understood as an atomic formula and if $E \diamond\!\!\rightarrow \psi$ belongs to $sub(\varphi)$, then $\psi \in sub(\varphi)$ too. Moreover, for each $E \diamond\!\!\rightarrow \psi \in sub(\varphi)$ so that $L(\mathcal{A}_E) = L(E)$ where $\mathcal{A}_E$ is defined from Proposition 14.5.4, we consider the expression $(E \diamond\!\!\rightarrow \psi, q)$ for each state q of $\mathcal{A}_E$. Similarly, for each $\mathrm{Cl}(E) \in sub(\varphi)$ so that $L(\mathcal{B}_E) = \mathrm{Mod}_\Pi(\mathrm{Cl}(E))$ where $\mathcal{B}_E$ is defined from Lemma 14.5.5, we consider the expression $(\mathrm{Cl}(E), q)$ for each state q of $\mathcal{B}_E$. Observe that $L(\mathcal{B}_E)$ is the union of a reachability language $L(\mathcal{A}_1)$ and a safety language $L(\mathcal{A}_2)$. Consequently, $\mathcal{B}_E$ can be constructed so that $\mathcal{B}_E$ never hits a non-accepting state going through an accepting state. This is a useful property for the correctness of the construction. Let F be the set of accepting states in $\mathcal{B}_E$.

We build an alternating Büchi automaton $\mathcal{A}_\varphi = (\Sigma_\varphi, Q_\varphi, q_{0,\varphi}, \delta_\varphi, F_\varphi)$ as follows.

- Q_φ is equal to $\{q_\psi \mid \psi \in sub(\varphi)\}$ augmented with subformulae according to the following rules:
  - If $q_{E \diamond\!\!\rightarrow \psi} \in Q_\varphi$, then for every state q of $\mathcal{A}_E$, $(E \diamond\!\!\rightarrow \psi, q) \in Q_\varphi$.
  - If $q_{\mathrm{Cl}(E)} \in Q_\varphi$, then for every state q of $\mathcal{B}_E$, $(\mathrm{Cl}(E), q) \in Q_\varphi$.

- If $q_{\neg(E \Diamond\!\!\!\rightarrow \psi)} \in Q_\varphi$, then for every state q of $\mathcal{A}_E$, $\neg(E \Diamond\!\!\!\rightarrow \psi, q) \in Q_\varphi$.
  (Note that $\neg(E \Diamond\!\!\!\rightarrow \psi, q)$ is, strictly speaking, not a PSL formula.)
- If $q_{\neg\text{Cl}(E)} \in Q_\varphi$, then for every state q of $\mathcal{B}_E$, $\neg(\text{Cl}(E), q) \in Q_\varphi$.
- if $q_\psi \in Q_\varphi$, then $q_{\overline{\psi}} \in Q_\varphi$ where $\overline{\psi}$ is the negation normal form of $\neg\psi$ by pushing negations inwards as deep as possible. Note that $\overline{\overline{\psi}} = \psi$.
- $q_{0,\varphi} := q_\varphi$.
- $\Sigma_\varphi := \mathcal{P}(\Pi)$.
- $F_\varphi := \{\neg(E \Diamond\!\!\!\rightarrow \psi, q) \mid \neg(E \Diamond\!\!\!\rightarrow \psi, q) \in Q_\varphi\} \cup \{(\text{Cl}(E), q) \mid (\text{Cl}(E), q) \in Q_\varphi, q \in F\} \cup \{(\neg\text{Cl}(E), q) \mid \neg(\text{Cl}(E), q) \in Q_\varphi, q \notin F\}$.
- Let us define the transition function δ_φ. Boolean connectives in a state q_ψ are taken care of by Boolean connectives in transition formulae that have operational interpretations.
  - $\delta_\varphi(q_p, a) := \top$ if $p \in a$ and $\delta_\varphi(q_p, a) := \bot$ if $p \notin a$,
  - $\delta_\varphi(q_{\neg p}, a) := \top$ if $p \notin a$ and $\delta_\varphi(q_{\neg p}, a) := \bot$ if $p \in a$,
  - $\delta_\varphi(q_{\psi_1 \wedge \psi_2}, a) := \delta_\varphi(q_{\psi_1}, a) \wedge \delta_\varphi(q_{\psi_2}, a)$,
  - $\delta_\varphi(q_{\psi_1 \vee \psi_2}, a) := \delta_\varphi(q_{\psi_1}, a) \vee \delta_\varphi(q_{\psi_2}, a)$,
  - $\delta_\varphi((E \Diamond\!\!\!\rightarrow \psi, q), a) :=$

$$\bigvee_{q \xrightarrow{a} q' \text{ in } \mathcal{A}_E} (E \Diamond\!\!\!\rightarrow \psi, q') \vee \bigvee_{q \xrightarrow{a} q' \text{ in } \mathcal{A}_E, \, q' \in F_E} \delta_\varphi(q_\psi, a)$$

  where F_E is the set of accepting states of $\mathcal{A}_E$,
  - $\delta_\varphi(q_{E \Diamond\!\!\!\rightarrow \psi}, a) :=$

$$\bigvee_{q'_0 \xrightarrow{a} q' \text{ in } \mathcal{A}_E} (E \Diamond\!\!\!\rightarrow \psi, q') \vee \bigvee_{q'_0 \xrightarrow{a} q' \text{ in } \mathcal{A}_E, \, q' \in F_E} \delta_\varphi(q_\psi, a)$$

  where q'_0 is the initial state of $\mathcal{A}_E$,
  - $\delta_\varphi(\neg(E \Diamond\!\!\!\rightarrow \psi, q), a) :=$

$$\bigwedge_{q \xrightarrow{a} q' \text{ in } \mathcal{A}_E} \neg(E \Diamond\!\!\!\rightarrow \psi, q') \wedge \bigwedge_{q \xrightarrow{a} q' \text{ in } \mathcal{A}_E, \, q' \in F_E} \delta_\varphi(q_{\overline{\psi}}, a)$$

  where F_E is the set of accepting states of $\mathcal{A}_E$,
  - $\delta_\varphi(q_{\neg(E \Diamond\!\!\!\rightarrow \psi)}, a) :=$

$$\bigwedge_{q'_0 \xrightarrow{a} q' \text{ in } \mathcal{A}_E} \neg(E \Diamond\!\!\!\rightarrow \psi, q') \wedge \bigwedge_{q'_0 \xrightarrow{a} q' \text{ in } \mathcal{A}_E, \, q' \in F_E} \delta_\varphi(q_{\overline{\psi}}, a)$$

  - $\delta_\varphi(q_{\text{Cl}(E)}, a) := \bigvee_{q'_0 \xrightarrow{a} q' \text{ in } \mathcal{B}_E} (\text{Cl}(E), q')$ where q'_0 is the initial state of $\mathcal{B}_E$,
  - $\delta_\varphi((\text{Cl}(E), q), a) := \bigvee_{q \xrightarrow{a} q' \text{ in } \mathcal{B}_E} (\text{Cl}(E), q')$,
  - $\delta_\varphi(q_{\neg\text{Cl}(E)}, a) := \bigwedge_{q'_0 \xrightarrow{a} q' \text{ in } \mathcal{B}_E} \neg(\text{Cl}(E), q')$ where q'_0 is the initial state of $\mathcal{B}_E$,
  - $\delta_\varphi(\neg(\text{Cl}(E), q), a) := \bigwedge_{q \xrightarrow{a} q' \text{ in } \mathcal{B}_E} \neg(\text{Cl}(E), q')$.

Observe that the range of δ_φ remains in $\mathbb{B}^+(Q_\varphi)$ and the definition of δ_φ is well founded. So, $\mathcal{A}_\varphi$ is indeed an alternating Büchi automaton. It remains to show that $L(\mathcal{A}_\varphi) = \text{Mod}_\Pi(\varphi)$, which can be done by structural induction. Again, the case with atomic propositions and the induction step with Boolean connectives can be shown following previous reasoning. The other cases in the induction step are left as Exercise 14.26. $\square$

Theorem 14.5.7. SAT(PSL) is in ExpSpace.   ■

Using arguments from Section 14.2.5, and more specifically an adaptation of Lemma 14.2.22, we can get the following corollary.

Theorem 14.5.8. $MC^\exists$(PSL) is in ExpSpace.   ■

14.6 Tree Automata for Branching-Time Logics

In this section, we show how to translate a CTL formula φ into a Büchi tree automaton $\mathcal{A}_\varphi$ such that φ is satisfiable iff $L(\mathcal{A}_\varphi)$ is nonempty. The Büchi tree automaton $\mathcal{A}_\varphi$ does not accept exactly the CTL models for φ but rather a symbolic representation of tree-like models with branching factor bounded by the size of φ. In Chapter 13 on tableaux-based proof systems, Hintikka structures have played the role of symbolic models; each logic came with an adequate notion of Hintikka structures. In this section, symbolic models are defined as a variant of Hintikka structures defined as infinite Σ, k-trees where Σ contains the set of fully expanded sets with respect to φ and $k = |\varphi|$. Even though symbolic models are Σ, k-trees, we also have to deal with the case when a state of the model has less than k successors. To do so, we introduce a dummy value $\circledast$ in Σ that means that its subtrees rooted at positions of the tree labelled by $\circledast$ should be disregarded (which is encoded by the fact that all descendants are labelled by $\circledast$ too). Section 14.6.2 illustrates the main ideas on the logic BML whereas Section 14.6.3 deals with the translation for CTL.

14.6.1 Introduction to Büchi Tree Automata

Section 14.2 is dedicated to translations from LTL formulae to Büchi automata that accept the models of the formulae. We have seen that several types of transformations can be defined, an exponential blow-up being unavoidable if alternation is excluded from automata. It is fortunate that LTL models are ω-words and Büchi automata accept ω-words too. By contrast, models for branching-time temporal logics are interpreted over transition systems (see e.g. Chapter 7). Extending the automata-based approach to such temporal logics might mean that we have to introduce a class of automata that accept such models. Actually, it is possible to slightly deviate from this idea by only considering tree-like models since branching-time temporal logics introduced in Chapter 7 have the tree model property. For example, we know from Theorem 7.2.6 that for every CTL formula φ, φ is satisfiable iff φ is satisfiable in an infinite tree-like model with branching factor bounded by the size of φ. Automata accepting (either finite or infinite) trees have been quite well studied and enjoy almost all nice properties of automata accepting ω-words. In this section, we introduce the class of Büchi tree automata. However, note that forthcoming translations from CTL formulae to Büchi tree automata do not produce automata that accept all models of the formulae but rather tree-like models only. Actually, the Büchi tree automata accept Hintikka structures for CTL (cf. Definition 13.3.4) with tree-like shapes.

We recall that, given $k \geq 1$ and a finite alphabet Σ, an infinite Σ, k-**tree** Tr is a mapping $[1, k]^* \rightarrow \Sigma$. Let us introduce a bit more terminology. Given $u, v \in [1, k]^*$,

- if $u = \varepsilon$, then u is the **root** of Tr,
- if $v = u \cdot i$ for some $i \in [1, k]$, then u is a **predecessor** of v and v is a **successor** of u,
- if there is $v' \in [1, k]^*$ such that $u \cdot v' = v$, then u precedes v, written $u \preceq v$,
- $u \prec v$ whenever $u \preceq v$ and $u \neq v$.

A **branch** Br starting at a node u is a maximal (infinite) sequence starting at u such that for two consecutive nodes, one is the predecessor of the other. This means that there is a sequence $u_0, u_1, \ldots$ such that $u_0 = u$ and for every $i \in \mathbb{N}$, u_i is a predecessor of u_{i+1}.

A **Büchi tree automaton** $\mathcal{A}$ for Σ, k-trees is a tuple $\mathcal{A} = (\Sigma, Q, Q_0, \delta, F)$ such that:

- Q is a finite nonempty set of **states**,
- $Q_0 \subseteq Q$ is the set of **initial** states,
- the **transition relation** δ is a subset of $Q \times \Sigma \times Q^k$,
- $F \subseteq Q$ is a set of **accepting** states.

When the automaton $\mathcal{A}$ is in state q and it is reading the node u of a Σ, k-tree Tr, it chooses a transition $(q, \text{Tr}(u), q_1, \ldots, q_k)$ in δ, makes k copies of itself and then moves to the nodes $u \cdot i$ with state q_i, for every $i \in [1, k]$.

Definition 14.6.1. A **run** ρ of the Büchi tree automaton $\mathcal{A} = (\Sigma, Q, Q_0, \delta, F)$ on a Σ, k-tree Tr is a Q, k-tree such that $\rho(\varepsilon) \in Q_0$ and for every $u \in [1, k]^*$, $(\rho(u), \text{Tr}(u), \rho(u \cdot 1), \ldots, \rho(u \cdot k)) \in \delta$. A run ρ is **accepting** iff for every branch in Tr there is a state in F that occurs infinitely often. $\qquad \nabla$

As usual, other types of acceptance conditions (Muller, parity, etc.) would lead to different classes of automata and in the branching case to different classes of accepted languages, see the bibliographical references in Section 14.9.

The automaton $\mathcal{A}$ **accepts** the **language** $\text{L}(\mathcal{A})$ made of the infinite Σ, k-trees Tr for which there exists an accepting run of $\mathcal{A}$ on Tr.

Example 14.6.2. Let $\Sigma = \{\text{a}, \text{b}\}$, $k = 2$ and L be the set of infinite Σ, k-trees such that on every branch, the letter a occurs infinite often. Let $\mathcal{A} = (\Sigma, \{q_1, q_2\}, \{q_1\}, \delta, \{q_1\})$ be the automaton such that

$$\delta = \{(q_1, \text{a}, q_1, q_1), (q_2, \text{a}, q_1, q_1), (q_1, \text{b}, q_2, q_2), (q_2, \text{b}, q_2, q_2)\} .$$

One can check that $\text{L}(\mathcal{A})$ is equal to the language L. By way of example, we present a Σ, 2-tree and its accepting run in $\mathcal{A}$.

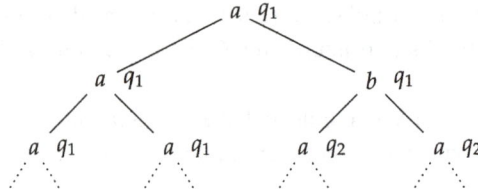

Lemma 14.6.3. Given $k \geq 1$ and an alphabet Σ, the class of languages of Σ, k-trees accepted by Büchi tree automata is closed under union and intersection. ∎

The proof is left as Exercise 14.29. Note that Büchi tree automata are not closed under complementation unlike Büchi word automata. This is an interesting difference when passing from infinite words to infinite trees. By contrast, Muller and Rabin tree automata are closed under complementation, see the bibliographical references in Section 14.9.

From now on we focus on showing that checking whether $L(\mathcal{A}) \neq \emptyset$ can be solved in polynomial time. To do so, we establish preliminary results and introduce a few notions. A **finite tree** rooted at $u \in [1, k]^*$ is a finite subset $X \subseteq [1, k]^*$ such that

1. $u \in X$,
2. for every $v \in X$, we have $u \preceq v$,
3. if $v \cdot i \in (X \setminus \{u\})$ then $v \in X$ and for every $i' \in [1, k]$, we have $v \cdot i' \in X$.

A **leaf** of X is a node v of X such that there is no v' such that $v \prec v'$ and $v' \in X$. In the following, we present a finite tree rooted at ε whose leaves are framed in boxes.

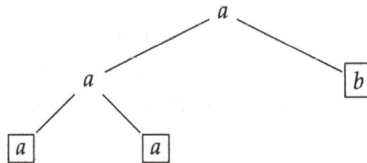

Lemma 14.6.4 roughly states that an accepting run can be viewed as an infinite tree that can be tiled by finite trees whose leaves are made of accepting states only.

Lemma 14.6.4. Let $\rho : [1, k]^* \to Q$ be a run of the Büchi tree automaton $\mathcal{A} = (\Sigma, Q, Q_0, \delta, F)$ on some Σ, k-tree Tr. The following properties are equivalent:

(I) ρ is accepting.
(II) For every $u \in [1, k]^*$, there is a finite tree X rooted at u such that $\mathrm{card}(X) \geq 2$ and for every leaf v of X, we have $\rho(v) \in F$. ∎

Proof. First, suppose that ρ is accepting. For every branch starting at ε, there is a state in F occurring infinitely often. Let $u \in [1, k]^*$ and Z_u be the set defined as

$$Z_u = \{v : u \prec v, \ \rho(v) \in F, \ \text{if } u \prec v' \preceq v \text{ and } \rho(v') \in F \text{ then } v' = v\}.$$

Since ρ is accepting, every branch starting at u hits a node in Z_u. By König's Lemma, the set $X_u := \{v' : u \preceq v' \preceq v, \ v \in Z_u\}$ is finite. It is then easy to show that card$(X_u) \geq 2$ and X_u is precisely a finite tree rooted at u such that for every leaf v of X_u, we have $\rho(v) \in F$.

Now suppose that Lemma 14.6.4(II) holds true. Let u belong to a branch Br. By assumption, there is a finite tree X rooted at u such that card$(X) \geq 2$ and for every leaf v of X, we have $\rho(v) \in F$. Since X is finite, there is a leaf $v \in X$ such that $v \in$ Br. This implies that $u \prec v$ and $\rho(v) \in F$. Hence by repeating this reasoning on v, we can find $v' \in$ Br such that $v \prec v'$ and $\rho(v') \in F$. By induction, one get that there is a state in F that occurs infinitely often on Br since F is a finite set. $\qquad\qquad\square$

A **finite** Σ, k-**tree** Tr is a map Tr $: X \to \Sigma$ such that X is a finite tree rooted at ε. Such finite structures are the counterparts of infinite Σ, k-trees, just like finite words are the counterparts of infinite ω-words. As Büchi automata (on infinite words) and finite-state automata are identical objects but interpreted differently, Büchi tree automata can also be understood as devices to accept finite Σ, k-trees. More precisely, a **finite tree pseudo-automaton** is a structure $\mathcal{A} = (\Sigma, Q, Q_0, \delta, F)$ defined as a Büchi tree automaton except that runs and the acceptance condition are defined differently. Actually, we introduce the prefix 'pseudo' because we use a variant of (standard) finite tree automata in which no constraint is required for letters at the leaves of the accepted finite Σ, k-trees, which is sufficient for our future needs.

A run ρ of $\mathcal{A}$ on a finite Σ, k-tree Tr $: X \to \Sigma$ is a finite Q, k-tree of the form $\rho : X \to Q$ such that $\rho(\varepsilon) \in Q_0$ and for every $u \in X$ such that $u \cdot 1, \ldots, u \cdot k \in X$, we have $(\rho(u), \text{Tr}(u), \rho(u \cdot 1), \ldots, \rho(u \cdot k)) \in \delta$. The run ρ is **accepting** iff for every leaf u of X, we have $\rho(u) \in F$. Moreover, the automaton $\mathcal{A}$ **accepts** the **language** $\text{L}(\mathcal{A})$ made of finite Σ, k-trees Tr for which there exists an accepting run of $\mathcal{A}$ on Tr. Even though finite tree pseudo-automata are interesting for their own sake, in this section they are mainly instrumental to explain why the nonemptiness problem for Büchi tree automata can be decided in polynomial time. Actually, we make use of the following complexity result.

Lemma 14.6.5. The nonemptiness problem for finite tree pseudo-automata is decidable in polynomial time. $\qquad\qquad\blacksquare$

Proof. Let $\mathcal{A} = (\Sigma, Q, Q_0, \delta, F)$ be a finite tree pseudo-automaton. Nonemptiness of $\text{L}(\mathcal{A})$ can be checked by the computation of a least fixpoint set X such that $X \cap Q_0 \neq \emptyset$ iff $\text{L}(\mathcal{A}) \neq \emptyset$. Initially $X := F$ and $X_{\text{prev}} := \emptyset$. Then, perform the steps (1)–(3) until $X = X_{\text{prev}}$:

1. Let Y be the set of all states q in $Q \setminus X$ such that $\delta \cap \{q\} \times \Sigma \times X^k \neq \emptyset$;
2. $X_{\text{prev}} := X$;
3. $X := X \cup Y$.

Finally, the algorithm returns the Boolean value $(X \cap Q_0 \neq \emptyset)$. The number of times the sequence of instructions (1)-(3) is performed is bounded by card(Q). Moreover, Step 1 can be easily performed in linear time in the size of $\mathcal{A}$. Hence the algorithm runs in quadratic time. As far as correctness is concerned, given an accepting run ρ on a finite Σ, k-tree, we can conclude that $X \cap Q_0 \neq \emptyset$. Similarly, assuming that $X \cap Q_0 \neq \emptyset$, we can build an accepting run by analysing how a state from Q_0 has been inserted in X.   □

Let $\mathcal{A} = (\Sigma, Q, Q_0, \delta, F)$ be a Büchi tree automaton. Given $q \in Q$, we write $\mathcal{A}_q^{fin}$ to denote the following finite tree pseudo-automaton defined from $\mathcal{A}$:

- If $q \notin F$, then $\mathcal{A}_q^{fin} := (\Sigma, Q, \{q\}, \delta, F)$.
- Otherwise, $\mathcal{A}_q^{fin} := (\Sigma, Q \uplus \{q_{new}\}, \{q_{new}\}, \delta', F)$ where δ' is the smallest extension of δ such that for all $a \in \Sigma$ and for all $q_1, \ldots, q_k \in Q$, we have $(q_{new}, a, q_1, \ldots, q_k) \in \delta'$ iff $(q, a, q_1, \ldots, q_k) \in \delta$. Note that $L(\mathcal{A}_q^{fin})$ does not contain trees with a unique node.

Given a finite tree X rooted at $u \in [1, k]^*$ and a run ρ on some infinite Σ, k-tree Tr, we write ρ_X^{fin} to denote $\rho_X^{fin} : Z \to Q$ such that $Z := \{v \mid u \cdot v \in X\}$ and $\rho_X^{fin}(v) := \rho(u \cdot v)$ for every $v \in Z$. Now condition (II) in Lemma 14.6.4 can be reformulated as follows: for every $u \in [1, k]^*$, there is an accepting run ρ' of $\mathcal{A}_{\rho(u)}^{fin} : X \to Q$ such that for every $v \in Z$, we have $\rho'(v) = \rho(u \cdot v)$ and $Z := \{v \mid u \cdot v \in X\}$.

Theorem 14.6.6. The nonemptiness problem for Büchi tree automata is decidable in polynomial time.   ■

Proof. Let $\mathcal{A} = (\Sigma, Q, Q_0, \delta, F)$ be a Büchi tree automaton. The algorithm consists of computing the maximal subset $X \subseteq Q$ such that for every $q \in X$, $L(\mathcal{B}_q^{fin}) \neq \emptyset$ with $\mathcal{B} = (\Sigma, X, Q_0 \cap X, \delta \cap X \times \Sigma \times (X)^k, F \cap X)$, and checks that $Q_0 \cap X$ is nonempty. To do so, we perform the computation of a greatest fixpoint set X. Initially $X := Q$, $X_{prev} := \emptyset$ and $\mathcal{B} := \mathcal{A}$. Then, perform the steps (1)–(3) until $X = X_{prev}$:

1. Let Y be the set of all states q in X such that $L(\mathcal{B}_q^{fin}) \neq \emptyset$;
2. $X_{prev} := X$; $X := Y$;
3. $\mathcal{B} := (\Sigma, X, Q_0 \cap X, \delta \cap X \times \Sigma \times (X)^k, F \cap X)$.

Finally, the algorithm returns the Boolean value $(X \cap Q_0 \neq \emptyset)$. The number of times the sequence of instructions (1)-(3) is performed is bounded by $\mathrm{card}(Q)$. Moreover, Step 1 can easily be performed in cubic time in the size of $\mathcal{A}$ thanks to Lemma 14.6.5. Hence the algorithm runs in polynomial time.

It remains to establish the correctness of the algorithm. By Lemma 14.6.4, every state in $Q \setminus X$ cannot participate to any accepting run. Consequently, if the preceding algorithm disregards all the initial states in Q_0, then $L(\mathcal{A})$ is necessarily empty. Conversely, suppose that there is some initial state q_0 in Q_0 that belongs to X after running the algorithm. This means that for every $q \in X$, $L(\mathcal{B}_q^{fin}) \neq \emptyset$. Let us build an accepting run ρ of $\mathcal{A}$ by using this information for an infinite number of steps. First, $\rho(\varepsilon) := q_0$ and $X_0 := \{\varepsilon\}$. At each step i, the map ρ is defined for a finite tree X_i rooted at ε. Let us define X_{i+1} with $X_i \subset X_{i+1}$ as follows. For every leaf u of X_i, $L(\mathcal{B}_{\rho(u)}^{fin})$ is nonempty and therefore there is an accepting run $\rho^\star : Y \to X$ of $\mathcal{B}_{\rho(u)}^{fin}$. The set X_{i+1} includes X_i and it is augmented with $\{u \cdot v \mid v \in Y\}$ and $\rho(u \cdot v) := \rho^\star(v)$ for every $v \in Y$. We do this for every leaf of X_i, which completes the step $i + 1$. By Lemma 14.6.5, the run ρ obtained after ω steps is accepting.   □

14.6.2 Translating BML Formulae

Let φ be a BML formula. We write $ecl(\varphi)$ to denote its extended closure according to Definition 13.1.3 where the definition of types and components are taken from Figure 13.1. We recall that a subset $X \subseteq ecl(\varphi)$ is fully expanded whenever X is not patently inconsistent (see Definition 13.1.7) and for every conjunctive [resp. disjunctive] formula in X, all its conjunctive [resp. disjunctive] components are in X (see Definition 13.1.8). We write $\text{FE}^{\circledast}(\varphi)$ to denote the set of fully expanded subsets of $ecl(\varphi)$ augmented with the dummy value $\circledast$. Note that $\text{card}(\text{FE}^{\circledast}(\varphi))$ is in $\mathcal{O}(2^{|\varphi|})$ and checking whether $X \subseteq ecl(\varphi)$ belongs to $\text{FE}^{\circledast}(\varphi)$ can be done in polynomial time in the size of φ.

Definition 14.6.7. A **Hintikka tree** for φ is a $\text{FE}^{\circledast}(\varphi)$, k-tree Tr such that

(1) $\Sigma = \text{FE}^{\circledast}(\varphi)$ and $k = |\varphi|$,
(2) $\varphi \in \text{Tr}(\varepsilon)$,
(3) for every $u \in [1, k]^*$, if $\text{Tr}(u) = \circledast$ then $\text{Tr}(u \cdot 1) = \cdots = \text{Tr}(u \cdot k) = \circledast$,
(4) for every $u \in [1, k]^*$ such that $\text{Tr}(u) \neq \circledast$,
    1. for every $i \in [1, k]$ such that $\text{Tr}(u \cdot i) \neq \circledast$, for every universal successor formula $\psi \in \text{Tr}(u)$, we have $scomp(\psi) \in \text{Tr}(u \cdot i)$ ($scomp(\psi)$ is the successor component of ψ, see Section 13.1),
    2. for every existential formula $\psi \in \text{Tr}(u)$, there is $i \in [1, k]$ such that $\text{Tr}(u \cdot i) \neq \circledast$ and $scomp(\psi) \in \text{Tr}(u \cdot i)$. ∇

A Hintikka tree for φ can be viewed as a tree unfolding of a Hintikka structure for $ecl(\varphi)$, following Definition 13.1.14, such that each state has at most $|\varphi|$ successors (which is sufficient to satisfy existential successor formulae from φ). If less than $|\varphi|$ successors are needed, dummy branches are introduced thanks to the value $\circledast$. Hence we can establish the following result.

Lemma 14.6.8. For every BML formula φ, there is a Hintikka tree for φ iff φ is satisfiable. ∎

Proof. First, suppose that Tr is a Hintikka tree for φ. As in the proof of Theorem 13.1.17, we define the interpreted transition system $\mathcal{T} = (S, R, L)$ where

- $S := \{u \in [1, k]^* : \text{Tr}(u) \neq \circledast\}$,
- uRv iff v is a successor of u in the tree Tr, for all $u, v \in S$,
- for every $u \in S$, $L(u) := \text{PROP} \cap \text{Tr}(u)$.

As in the proof of Theorem 13.1.17, we can show by induction on the main components of $\psi \in ecl(\varphi)$ that for every $u \in S$:

$$\text{if } \psi \in \text{Tr}(u) \text{ then } \mathcal{T}, u \models \psi.$$

Hence $\mathcal{T}, \varepsilon \models \varphi$ and therefore φ is satisfiable.

For the other direction, suppose that φ is satisfiable. So there is a rooted tree-like interpreted transition system $(\mathcal{T}, \varepsilon)$ with branching factor bounded by $k = |\varphi|$ such that

$\mathcal{T}, r \models \varphi$, see Theorem 7.2.6. Let $\mathcal{T} = (S, R, L)$. Let us build an $\mathrm{FE}^{\circledast}(\varphi)$, $|\varphi|$-tree $\mathtt{Tr}$ from $(\mathcal{T}, \varepsilon)$. Since $(\mathcal{T}, r)$ may be an incomplete infinite k-tree, for every $u \in [1, k]^*$, if u does not belong to S, then $\mathtt{Tr}(u) := \circledast$. Otherwise, $\mathtt{Tr}(u) := \{\psi \in ecl(\varphi) : \mathcal{T}, u \models \psi\}$. It is easy to check that indeed $\mathtt{Tr}$ is a Hintikka tree for φ.   □

In order to build a Büchi tree automaton $\mathcal{A}_\varphi$ such that φ is satisfiable iff $\mathrm{L}(\mathcal{A}_\varphi)$ is nonempty, it remains to define $\mathcal{A}_\varphi$ so that it accepts exactly the Hintikka trees for φ. Let $\mathcal{A}_\varphi = (\Sigma, Q, Q_0, \delta, F)$ be defined as follows:

- $\Sigma := \mathrm{FE}^{\circledast}(\varphi)$, $Q := \mathrm{FE}^{\circledast}(\varphi)$,
- $Q_0 := \{X \in Q : \varphi \in X\}$, $F := Q$,
- $(X, Y, X_1, \ldots, X_k) \in \delta \overset{\text{def}}{\Leftrightarrow}$
  - $X = Y$,
  - if $X = \circledast$, then $X_1 = \cdots = X_k = \circledast$,
  - if $X \neq \circledast$ then for every universal successor formula $\psi \in X$ and for every $i \in [1, k]$ such that $X_i \neq \circledast$, $scomp(\psi) \in X_i$,
  - if $X \neq \circledast$ then for every existential successor formula $\psi \in X$, there is $i \in [1, k]$ such that $X_i \neq \circledast$ and $scomp(\psi) \in X_i$.

The definition of $\mathcal{A}_\varphi$ faithfully mimics the definition for Hintikka trees from Definition 14.6.7. Hence the following property becomes easy to show.

Theorem 14.6.9. $\mathrm{L}(\mathcal{A}_\varphi)$ is equal to the set of Hintikka trees for φ.   ■

Consequently, $\mathrm{L}(\mathcal{A}_\varphi) \neq \emptyset$ iff φ is satisfiable by Lemma 14.6.8. Note that building $\mathcal{A}_\varphi$ requires exponential time in the size of φ and checking its nonemptiness can be done in exponential time in the size of φ by Theorem 14.6.6. Hence the satisfiability problem for BML can be checked in exponential time. Of course, this is not optimal for BML since the satisfiability problem for BML is PSPACE-complete, see Theorem 11.3.2. When dealing with CTL in Section 14.6.3 by slightly adapting the developments from the current section, we exhibit an exponential-time decision procedure for the CTL satisfiability problem, which is optimal this time. However, it would be possible to regain the PSPACE upper bound for BML by working on the very properties of $\mathcal{A}_\varphi$ since $\mathcal{A}_\varphi$ is not just any tree automaton and it has certain structural properties.

14.6.3 Extending the Translation for CTL

We adapt the automated-based approach presented in Section 14.6.2 for the logic CTL. The automaton construction for CTL subsumes the automaton construction for BML but there is an essential difference: unlike BML, branches of Hintikka trees for CTL formulae have to satisfy acceptance conditions corresponding to realisation of eventualities. However, the extra work for passing from BML to CTL is relatively modest. Another minor difference is related to the fact that models of CTL are *total* interpreted transition systems whereas no totality assumption is made for BML (as a consequence, the dummy value ⊛ can be removed).

In the following, we assume that the only temporal operators in CTL are AU, EU, AX and EX and the CTL models are *total* interpreted transition systems. Moreover, the path quantifiers A and E are relative to infinite R-paths.

Let φ be a formula in CTL. We write $ecl(\varphi)$ to denote its extended closure where the definition for types and components is taken from Figure 13.10. A subset $X \subseteq ecl(\varphi)$ is fully expanded whenever X is not patently inconsistent and for every conjunctive [resp. disjunctive] formula in X, all its conjunctive [resp. disjunctive] components are in X. We write FE(φ) to denote the set of fully expanded subsets of $ecl(\varphi)$. As for BML, card(FE(φ)) is in $\mathcal{O}(2^{|\varphi|})$ and checking whether $X \subseteq ecl(\varphi)$ belongs to FE(φ) can be checked in polynomial time in the size of φ.

Definition 14.6.10. A **Hintikka tree** for φ is a Σ, k-tree Tr such that the following conditions are satisfied for every $u \in [1, k]^*$:

(1) $\Sigma = \text{FE}(\varphi)$ and $k = |\varphi|$,
(2) $\varphi \in \text{Tr}(\varepsilon)$,
(3) for every $u \in [1, k]^*$,
  1. for every $i \in [1, k]$, for every universal successor formula $\psi \in \text{Tr}(u)$, we have $scomp(\psi) \in \text{Tr}(u \cdot i)$,
  2. for every existential formula $\psi \in \text{Tr}(u)$, there is $i \in [1, k]$ such that $scomp(\psi) \in \text{Tr}(u \cdot i)$,
(4) if $\text{E}(\psi_1 \text{U} \psi_2) \in \text{Tr}(u)$, then $\psi_2 \in \text{Tr}(v)$ for some $u \preceq v$ and for every $u \preceq v' \prec v$, we have $\psi_1 \in \text{Tr}(v')$,
(5) if $\text{A}(\psi_1 \text{U} \psi_2) \in \text{Tr}(u)$, for every branch Br from u, there is v on Br such that $\psi_2 \in \text{Tr}(v)$ and for every $u \preceq v' \prec v$, we have $\psi_1 \in \text{Tr}(v')$. ∇

Conditions (4) and (5) guarantee the satisfaction of eventualities. At first glance, it is surprising that there are no conditions for negated formulae of the form $\neg\text{E}(\psi_1 \text{U} \psi_2)$ and $\neg\text{A}(\psi_1 \text{U} \psi_2)$ but they are already taken care of by the other conditions. Indeed, following the proof of Lemma 13.3.5, we can establish the following properties whenever Tr is a Hintikka tree for φ:

(5′) if $\neg\text{E}(\psi_1 \text{U} \psi_2) \in \text{Tr}(u)$, then for every branch Br starting at u, $\neg\psi_2 \in \text{Tr}(v)$ for every v on Br or there is v on Br such that $\neg\psi_1 \in \text{Tr}(v)$ and for every $u \preceq v' \preceq v$, we have $\neg\psi_2 \in \text{Tr}(v')$.
(6′) if $\neg\text{A}(\psi_1 \text{U} \psi_2) \in \text{Tr}(u)$, then there is a branch Br starting at u such that $\neg\psi_2 \in \text{Tr}(v)$ for every v on Br or there is v on Br such that $\neg\psi_1 \in \text{Tr}(v)$ and for every $u \preceq v' \preceq v$, we have $\neg\psi_2 \in \text{Tr}(v')$.

Here is the counterpart of Lemma 14.6.8 that can be proved similarly, using the proof for Theorem 13.3.8.

Lemma 14.6.11. For every CTL formula φ, there is a Hintikka tree for φ iff φ is satisfiable.   ∎

Again, in order to build a Büchi tree automaton $\mathcal{A}_\varphi$ such that φ is satisfiable iff $\mathrm{L}(\mathcal{A}_\varphi)$ is nonempty, it is sufficient to define $\mathcal{A}_\varphi$ so that it accepts exactly the Hintikka trees for φ. To do so, we introduce the class of **generalised Büchi tree automata** of the form $(\Sigma, Q, Q_0, \delta, F_1, \ldots, F_N)$ where $F_1, \ldots, F_N$ are sets of accepting states. Runs are defined as for Büchi tree automata but a run ρ is **accepting** iff for every branch Br in Tr and for every set of accepting states F_i, there is a state in F_i that occurs infinitely often on Br. As for Büchi word automata, we can show that generalised Büchi tree automata do not add any expressive power. Neither are they more succinct than the nongeneralised variant, but they facilitate the following definitions. This is witnessed by Lemma 14.6.12 whose proof is left as Exercise 14.29.

Lemma 14.6.12. For every generalised Büchi tree automaton $\mathcal{A}$, one can build a Büchi tree automaton $\mathcal{A}'$ such that $\mathrm{L}(\mathcal{A}) = \mathrm{L}(\mathcal{A}')$ and $\mathcal{A}'$ can be built in logarithmic space in the size of $\mathcal{A}$.   ∎

Let $\mathcal{A}_\psi = (\Sigma, Q, Q_0, \delta, F_{\chi_1}, \ldots, F_{\chi_N})$ be defined as follows:

- $\Sigma := \mathrm{FE}(\varphi)$; $Q := \mathrm{FE}(\varphi)$; $Q_0 := \{X \in Q \mid \varphi \in X\}$,
- $(X, Y, X_1, \ldots, X_k) \in \delta \overset{\text{def}}{\Leftrightarrow}$,
  - $X = Y$,
  - for every universal successor formula $\psi \in X$ and for every $l \in [1, k]$, $scomp(\psi) \in X_l$,
  - for every existential successor formula $\psi \in X$, there is $i \in [1, k]$ such that $scomp(\psi) \in X_i$,
- for every formula χ of the form either $\mathrm{E}(\psi_1 \mathsf{U} \psi_2)$ or $\mathrm{A}(\psi_1 \mathsf{U} \psi_2)$, we consider the set of accepting states F_χ so that $F_\chi := \{X \in Q \mid \psi_2 \in X \text{ or } \chi \notin X\}$.

Again, the definition of $\mathcal{A}_\varphi$ faithfully mimics the definition for Hintikka trees from Definition 14.6.10. Conditions (5)–(6) are taken care of by the Büchi acceptance conditions induced by the sets of the form F_χ. Hence the following is easy to show.

Lemma 14.6.13. $\mathrm{L}(\mathcal{A}_\varphi)$ is equal to the set of Hintikka trees for φ.   ∎

Consequently, $\mathrm{L}(\mathcal{A}_\varphi) \neq \emptyset$ iff φ is satisfiable by Lemma 14.6.11. Again, building $\mathcal{A}_\varphi$ requires exponential time in the size of φ and checking its nonemptiness can be done in exponential time in the size of φ by Theorem 14.6.6 and by Lemma 14.6.12. Hence the satisfiability problem for CTL can be checked in exponential time.

14.7 Alternating Tree Automata and CTL

14.7.1 Alternating Büchi Automata on Trees

Here we define the class of alternating Büchi tree automata that combine features from alternating Büchi word automata (Section 14.3) and from Büchi tree automata (Section 14.6.1). Like the other classes of alternating automata, both existential and universal modes are possible and the transition function is defined with the help of positive Boolean formulae. However, the atomic formulae of such Boolean formulae are not reduced to states but rather to states enriched with *directions*. When defining an alternating Büchi tree automaton accepting a set of Σ, k-trees, the directions are elements of $[1, k]$. In that way, firing a transition amounts to launching several copies of the automaton that move to the children nodes but more than one copy could be attached to a single child. This is why runs of alternating Büchi tree automata are trees but not necessarily of branching factor k as in Büchi tree automata (for which there is exactly one copy per child in a run).

In the following, we introduce this standard class of automata in order to design a simple translation from CTL formulae to alternating Büchi tree automata that recognise Hintikka trees.

Definition 14.7.1. An **alternating Büchi tree automaton** $\mathcal{A}$ for Σ, k-trees is a tuple $\mathcal{A} = (\Sigma, Q, q_0, \delta, F)$ such that:

- Q is a finite nonempty set of **states**,
- $q_0 \in Q$ is the **initial** state,
- $\delta : Q \times \Sigma \to \mathbb{B}^+([1, k] \times Q)$ is the **transition function**. As usual, $\mathbb{B}^+([1, k] \times Q)$ denotes the set of positive Boolean formulae built over $[1, k] \times Q$.
- $F \subseteq Q$ is a set of **accepting** states. $\qquad\qquad\qquad\qquad\qquad\qquad\qquad\qquad\qquad \triangledown$

For example, assuming that $\delta(q, \mathrm{a}) = (1, q_1) \wedge (1, q_2) \wedge (2, q_3) \wedge (2, q_4)$, when the automaton $\mathcal{A}$ is in state q and it is reading the node u of a Σ, k-tree $\mathtt{Tr}$ with $\mathtt{Tr}(u) = \mathrm{a}$, it has to satisfy the positive Boolean formula $\delta(q, \mathrm{a})$ by making several copies of itself: one copy moves to the child $u \cdot 1$ with state q_1, another one with state q_2, similarly one copy moves to the child $u \cdot 2$ with state q_3 and another one with state q_4.

Definition 14.7.2 (Runs for alternating Büchi tree automata). Let $A = (\Sigma, Q, q_0, \delta, F)$ be an alternating Büchi tree automaton. A **run** ρ on a Σ, k-tree $\mathtt{Tr}$ is a (possibly infinite) tree for which nodes are labelled by elements from $Q \times [1, k]^*$:

(AR1) $\rho = (V, E)$ where $V \subseteq Q \times [1, k]^*$ and $(q_0, \varepsilon) \in V$ is the root.
(AR2) $E \subseteq \bigcup_{u \in [1,k]^*} \bigcup_{i \in [1,k]} (Q \times \{u\}) \times (Q \times \{u \cdot i\})$.
(AR3) For every $(q, u \cdot i) \in V \setminus \{(q_0, \varepsilon)\}$, there is $q' \in Q$ such that $((q', u), (q, u \cdot i)) \in E$.
(AR4) For every $(q, u) \in V$ we have $\{(i, q') \mid ((q, u), (q', u \cdot i)) \in E\} \models \delta(q, \mathtt{Tr}(u))$.

A node $(q, u) \in V$ such that the length of u is l is said to be of **level** l. A run ρ is **accepting** whenever every infinite path through that run visits F infinitely often. $\qquad\qquad \triangledown$

As presented in Section 14.3 for ω-words, other types of acceptance conditions can be defined for alternating tree automata. The automaton $\mathcal{A}$ **accepts** the **language** $\mathrm{L}(\mathcal{A})$ made of the infinite Σ, k-trees $\mathtt{Tr}$ for which there exists an accepting run of $\mathcal{A}$ on $\mathtt{Tr}$.

Proposition 14.7.3. Given an alternating Büchi tree automaton $\mathcal{A}$, there is a nondeterministic Büchi tree automaton $\mathcal{A}'$ with exponentially many states in the size of $\mathcal{A}$ such that $\mathrm{L}(\mathcal{A}) = \mathrm{L}(\mathcal{A}')$. $\qquad\qquad\qquad\qquad\qquad\qquad\qquad\qquad\qquad\qquad\qquad\qquad\qquad\qquad\qquad \blacksquare$

The proof is similar to the proof of Theorem 14.3.12 and it is left as Exercise 14.30.

Proposition 14.7.4. The nonemptiness problem for alternating Büchi tree automata is decidable in exponential time.   ∎

Given an alternating Büchi tree automaton $\mathcal{A}$, by Proposition 14.7.3, there is a nondeterministic Büchi tree automaton $\mathcal{A}'$ such that $L(\mathcal{A}) = L(\mathcal{A}')$ and $\mathcal{A}'$ can be built in exponential time in the length of $\mathcal{A}$. By Theorem 14.6.6, nonemptiness of $L(\mathcal{A}')$ can be checked in polynomial time in the size of $\mathcal{A}'$, whence in exponential time in $|\mathcal{A}|$. Note that the problem is also known to be ExpTime-hard. Indeed, ExpTime-hardness is inherited from the ExpTime-hardness of the nonemptiness problem for alternating tree automata accepting finite trees, since the universality problem for such alternating tree automata is known to be ExpTime-hard.

Definition 14.3.13 has a counterpart for trees. In weak alternating Büchi tree automata, the set of states is partitioned into partially ordered sets and each set is classified as accepting or rejecting. By default, we assume that the following definitions are for automata for Σ, k-trees.

Definition 14.7.5. A **weak alternating Büchi tree automaton** $\mathcal{A}$ is a structure

$$(\Sigma, Q, q_0, \delta, F, (\{Q_1, \ldots, Q_K\}, \leq))$$

such that:

- $(\Sigma, Q, q_0, \delta, F)$ is an alternating Büchi tree automaton,
- $\{Q_1, \ldots, Q_K\}$ is a partition of Q equipped with a partial ordering $\leq$,
- for every $i \in [1, K]$, either $Q_i \subseteq F$ or $Q_i \cap F = \emptyset$,
- for all $q \in Q_i$ and $q' \in Q_j$ such that q' occurs in $\delta(q, \mathsf{a})$ for some letter a, we have $Q_j \leq Q_i$.

A **very weak** alternating Büchi automaton is a weak alternating Büchi tree automaton in which every element of the partition is a singleton.   ▽

Lemma 14.7.6. The class of languages defined by weak alternating Büchi tree automata is closed under unions, intersections and complementations.   ∎

Proof. The proof is similar to the proof of Lemma 14.3.14. The proof for unions and intersections is by an easy verification using conjunction and disjunction in transition formulae, respectively. As far as complementations are concerned, observe that if $\mathcal{A} = (\Sigma, Q, q_0, \delta, F)$ is a weak alternating Büchi tree automaton, then the alternating co-Büchi tree automaton $\overline{\mathcal{A}} = (\Sigma, Q, q_0, \overline{\delta}, F)$ recognises the complement language by generalising Theorem 14.3.10. By the weakness of $\mathcal{A}$, there is an ordered partition $(\{Q_1, \ldots, Q_K\}, \leq)$ of Q and $J \leq K$ such that $F = Q_1 \cup \cdots \cup Q_J$, and for all $q \in Q_i$ and all $q' \in Q_j$ such that q' occurs in $\delta(q, \mathsf{a})$ for some letter a, we have $Q_j \leq Q_i$. It is not difficult to show that for all $q \in Q_i$ and all $q' \in Q_j$ such that q' occurs in $\overline{\delta}(q, \mathsf{a})$, we have $Q_j \leq Q_i$. Moreover, in an accepting run of $\overline{\mathcal{A}}$, for all infinite paths π, the states in F occur only finitely many times. By weakness, this means that there is $j \in [J + 1, K]$ such that from some level, all the states in π belong to Q_j, which is equivalent to the property that for all infinite paths π, some state in $Q_{J+1} \cup \cdots \cup Q_K$ $(= Q \setminus F)$ occurs infinitely often. Hence the alternating co-Büchi tree automaton $\overline{\mathcal{A}}$ accepts the same language as the weak alternating Büchi tree automaton $(\Sigma, Q, q_0, \overline{\delta}, Q \setminus F)$. $\square$

14.7.2 Translating CTL Formulae

In this section, we show how to translate a CTL formula φ into an alternating Büchi tree automaton $\mathcal{A}_\varphi$ such that φ is satisfiable iff $L(\mathcal{A}_\varphi)$ is nonempty. The alternating Büchi tree automaton $\mathcal{A}_\varphi$ does not accept exactly the CTL models for φ but rather a symbolic representation of tree-like models with branching factor bounded by the size of φ (see Theorem 7.2.6). By contrast to what is done in Section 14.6.3, the number of states in $\mathcal{A}_\varphi$ is polynomial in $|\varphi|$.

Let φ be a CTL formula. Without any loss of generality, we can assume that φ is in negation normal form, i.e. contains $\wedge$, $\vee$, EX, AX, EU, ER, AX, AU, AR and negations occurring only in front of atomic propositions. Clearly, every CTL formula is equivalent to a formula in such a form. For instance $E(\psi_1 R \psi_2)$ is logically equivalent to $\neg A(\neg \psi_1 U \neg \psi_2)$, i.e. $E(\cdot R \cdot)$ and $A(\cdot U \cdot)$ are dual operators. We build an alternating Büchi tree automaton $\mathcal{A}_\varphi = (\Sigma, Q, q_0, \delta, F)$ accepting Σ, k-trees as follows:

- Q is equal to $\{q_\psi \mid \psi \in sub(\varphi)\}$, where $sub(\varphi)$ is the set of subformulae of φ.
- $q_0 := q_\varphi$.
- $\Sigma := \mathcal{P}(\mathrm{PROP}(\varphi))$.
- F is equal to the set of formulae that are neither of the form $q_{A\psi U \chi}$ nor of the form $q_{E\psi U \chi}$.
- Let us define the transition function δ.

$$\begin{aligned}
\delta(q_p, a) &:= \top \text{ if } p \in a \\
\delta(q_p, a) &:= \bot \text{ if } p \notin a \\
\delta(q_{\neg p}, a) &:= \top \text{ if } p \notin a \\
\delta(q_{\neg p}, a) &:= \bot \text{ if } p \in a \\
\delta(q_{\psi_1 \wedge \psi_2}, a) &:= \delta(q_{\psi_1}, a) \wedge \delta(q_{\psi_2}, a) \\
\delta(q_{\psi_1 \vee \psi_2}, a) &:= \delta(q_{\psi_1}, a) \vee \delta(q_{\psi_2}, a)
\end{aligned}$$

Now we define the transition function for the states related to temporal operators.

$$\begin{aligned}
\delta(q_{EX\psi}, a) &:= (1, q_\psi) \vee \cdots \vee (k, q_\psi) \\
\delta(q_{AX\psi}, a) &:= (1, q_\psi) \wedge \cdots \wedge (k, q_\psi) \\
\delta(q_{E\psi U \chi}, a) &:= \delta(q_\chi, a) \vee (\delta(q_\psi, a) \wedge ((1, q_{E\psi U \chi}) \vee \cdots \vee (k, q_{E\psi U \chi}))) \\
\delta(q_{A\psi U \chi}, a) &:= \delta(q_\chi, a) \vee (\delta(q_\psi, a) \wedge ((1, q_{A\psi U \chi}) \wedge \cdots \wedge (k, q_{A\psi U \chi}))) \\
\delta(q_{A\psi R \chi}, a) &:= \delta(q_\chi, a) \wedge (\delta(q_\psi, a) \vee ((1, q_{A\psi R \chi}) \wedge \cdots \wedge (k, q_{A\psi R \chi}))) \\
\delta(q_{E\psi R \chi}, a) &:= \delta(q_\chi, a) \wedge (\delta(q_\psi, a) \vee ((1, q_{E\psi R \chi}) \vee \cdots \vee (k, q_{E\psi R \chi}))).
\end{aligned}$$

It is easy to verify that the range of δ remains in $\mathbb{B}^+([1,k] \times Q)$. The definition of δ is well founded since the definition of $\delta(q_\psi, a)$ requires only the definition of $\delta(q_{\psi'}, a)$ with $\psi' <_{sub}^+ \psi$ where $<_{sub}^+$ is the transitive closure of the subformula relation. Furthermore, note that the definition of $\delta(q_{\mathsf{E}\psi\mathsf{U}\chi}, \mathsf{a})$ reflects the fact that $\mathsf{E}\psi\mathsf{U}\chi \leftrightarrow (\chi \vee (\psi \wedge \mathsf{EX}(\mathsf{E}\psi\mathsf{U}\chi)))$ is valid; similar observations can be made for ER, AR and AU.

Clearly, each structure $\mathcal{A}_\varphi$ is a well-defined alternating Büchi tree automaton. Moreover, one can show that it is a very weak one, where the transitive closure of the main component relation induces the partial ordering $\leq$ for the singleton sets of the partition. For the sake of conciseness, we write $\diamond q$ instead of $(1, q) \vee \cdots \vee (k, q)$ and $\square q$ instead of $(1, q) \wedge \cdots \wedge (k, q)$. Actually, **amorphous automata** (see the reference in the bibliographical notes) have been introduced to accept trees whose branching factor can vary from node to node and $\diamond q$ would be equivalent to $(1, q) \vee \cdots \vee (k, q)$ but this time k is the branching factor of the current node.

Lemma 14.7.7. Let φ be a CTL formula in negation normal form. Then, $\mathcal{A}_\varphi$ is a very weak alternating Büchi tree automaton where the partial ordering $\leq$ on singletons of the form $\{q_\psi\}$ is defined by $\{q_\psi\} \leq \{q_{\psi'}\}$ iff $\psi \in sub(\psi')$. ∎

The proof is left as Exercise 14.29. For the proof of correctness of the reduction, we need the following lemma.

Lemma 14.7.8. Let φ be a CTL formula, $\Pi = \mathrm{PROP}(\varphi)$ and Π' be a finite set of atomic propositions including Π. Let $\mathcal{B}_\varphi$ be the alternating Büchi tree automaton defined as for $\mathcal{A}_\varphi$ except that the letters belong to $\mathcal{P}(\Pi')$ (instead of $\mathcal{P}(\Pi)$). If $\mathrm{L}(\mathcal{A}_\varphi)$ is equal to the class of $\mathcal{P}(\Pi)$, k-trees satisfying φ, then $\mathrm{L}(\mathcal{B}_\varphi)$ is equal to the class of $\mathcal{P}(\Pi')$, k-trees satisfying φ. ∎

The proof of this lemma is by an easy verification. For the proof of the later Theorem 14.7.12, we will use the fact that accepting runs can be restricted to the ones in which condition (AR4) is replaced by the more restrictive condition (AR4′):

(AR4′) For every $(q, u) \in V$ we have $\{(i, q') \mid ((q, u), (q', u \cdot i)) \in E\} \models \delta(q, \mathrm{Tr}(u))$ *and* for no strict subset Y of $\{(i, q') \mid ((q, u), (q', u \cdot i)) \in E\}$, we have $Y \models \delta(q, \mathrm{Tr}(u))$.

An accepting run on Tr in an alternating Büchi tree automaton $\mathcal{A}$ satisfying the condition (AR4′) is said to be **minimal**. Lemma 14.7.9 states that restricting accepting runs to minimal ones does not change the language of accepted Σ, k-trees.

Lemma 14.7.9. Let $\mathcal{A} = (\Sigma, Q, q_0, \delta, F)$ be an alternating Büchi tree automaton. For every Σ, k-tree Tr, there is an accepting run on Tr in $\mathcal{A}$ iff there is a minimal accepting run on Tr in $\mathcal{A}$. ∎

Proof. Let $\rho = (V, E)$ be an accepting run on an infinite Σ, k-tree Tr. By induction on the levels, we will build a minimal accepting run $\rho' = (V', E')$ on u such that $V' \subseteq V, E' \subseteq E$ and therefore the infinite paths in ρ' are also infinite paths in ρ. Hence the satisfaction of the acceptance condition will be a consequence of the fact that ρ' is a subgraph of ρ. First, $(q_0, \varepsilon) \in V'$ and $E' = \emptyset$. Suppose that all the vertices of level l have been defined, say they are elements of the set V'_l and they belong to V too. Let us define the vertices of level $l + 1$

in V'_{l+1} and the new edges in E'. For every (q, u) in V'_l, we know that $\{(i, q') \mid ((q, u), (q', u \cdot i)) \in E\} \models \delta(q, \text{Tr}(u))$. Let $Y_{(q,u)}$ be a subset of $\{(i, q') \mid ((q, u), (q', u \cdot i)) \in E\}$ such that $Y_{(q,u)} \models \delta(q, \text{Tr}(u))$ and for no strict subset Y of $Y_{(q,u)}$, we have $Y \models \delta(q, \text{Tr}(u))$. Moreover, $Z_{(q,u)} := \{(q', u \cdot i) \mid (q', i) \in Y_{(q,u)}\}$. We pose

$$V'_{l+1} := \bigcup_{(q,u) \in V'_l} Z_{(q,u)}$$

and we extend E' in such a way that for every (q, u) in V'_l and for every $(q', u \cdot i)$ in $Z_{(q,u)}$, $(q, u) \to (q', u \cdot i)$ is in E'. It is easy to see that the limit structure ρ' obtained in such a way is a subgraph of ρ and ρ' is a minimal accepting run on the tree Tr. $\square$

Consequently, for showing the correctness of the construction $\mathcal{A}_\varphi$ it is sufficient to restrict ourselves to minimal accepting runs. Such runs have some useful properties stated as follows.

Lemma 14.7.10. Let φ be a CTL formula in negation normal form and $\mathcal{A}_\varphi = (\Sigma, Q, q_0, \delta, F)$ be its corresponding alternating Büchi tree automaton.

(I) For every Σ, k-tree Tr, there is an accepting run on Tr in $\mathcal{A}_\varphi$ iff there is a minimal accepting run on Tr in $\mathcal{A}_\varphi$.

(II) Let $\rho = (V, E)$ be a minimal accepting run on Tr and $(q_\psi, u) \in V$. Then, for every $(q_\psi, u) \to (q_{\psi'}, u \cdot i) \in E$,
  - if ψ is neither an U-formula nor a R-formula (possibly prefixed by E or A), then $\psi' <^+_{sub} \psi$,
  - otherwise, $\psi' <^+_{sub} \psi$ or $\psi' = \psi$.

(III) Let $\rho = (V, E)$ be a minimal accepting run. Let $(q_{\psi_0}, u_0) \to (q_{\psi_1}, u_1) \to \cdots$ be an infinite path in ρ. There is $N \geq 0$ such that $q_{\psi_N} = q_{\psi_{N+1}} = q_{\psi_{N+2}} = \cdots$ and ψ_N is either a $\mathcal{Q}$U-formula or a $\mathcal{Q}$R-formula with $\mathcal{Q} \in \{\text{E}, \text{A}\}$. ∎

The proof is similar to the proof of Lemma 14.4.5.

Theorem 14.7.11. $\text{L}(\mathcal{A}_\varphi)$ accepts exactly the Σ, k-trees satisfying φ. ∎

Proof. The proof is by structural induction, like the proof of Theorem 14.4.6.

First, let us present simple constructions on (accepting) runs that will be useful in the proof. Let $\rho = (V, E)$ be a run of an alternating Büchi tree automaton $\mathcal{A}$. We write $\rho^{+u} = (V^{+u}, E^{+u})$ for some $u \in [1, k]^*$ to denote the isomorphic tree obtained from ρ by mapping each vertex (q, v) to $(q, u \cdot v)$. Strictly speaking, ρ^{+u} is not a run of $\mathcal{A}$. Moreover, we write $\rho[(q_0, \varepsilon) \leftarrow (q, \varepsilon)]$ to denote the tree obtained from ρ by replacing (q_0, ε) by (q, ε). In the sequel the tree $\rho[(q_0, \varepsilon) \leftarrow (q, \varepsilon)]$ will be an accepting run most of the time, too, possibly for another automaton (in that case, q should be an initial state).

First, let us do the base case, when $\varphi = p$. Let Tr be a Σ, k-tree. Obviously, $\text{Tr}, \varepsilon \models p$ iff $p \in \text{Tr}(\varepsilon)$. By construction of $\mathcal{A}_p$, if there is a run ρ of $\mathcal{A}_p$ on the Σ, k-tree Tr, then $p \in \text{Tr}(\varepsilon)$ and ρ is accepting. Similarly, if there is no accepting run on Tr, then $p \notin \text{Tr}(\varepsilon)$.

Hence a Σ, k-tree Tr is in $L(\mathcal{A}_\varphi)$ iff it satisfies φ. A similar reasoning can be performed with $\varphi = \neg p$.

Now we deal with the induction step.

$\varphi = \text{EX}\varphi_1$: By definition, $\mathcal{A}_\varphi$ is equal to $\mathcal{A}_{\varphi_1}$ except that it has an additional state, namely q_φ, that is also the initial state of $\mathcal{A}_\varphi$. Moreover, the transition function δ for $\mathcal{A}_\varphi$ extends the transition function for $\mathcal{A}_{\varphi_1}$ with

$$\delta(q_\varphi, a) := (1, q_{\varphi_1}) \vee \cdots \vee (k, q_{\varphi_1}),$$

for every letter $a \subseteq \text{PROP}(\varphi) = \text{PROP}(\varphi_1)$. For every Σ, k-tree Tr, we have $\text{Tr}, \varepsilon \models \varphi$ iff there is $i \in [1, k]$ such that $\text{Tr}, i \models \varphi_1$. Let $\text{Tr}_{|i}$ be the Σ, k-tree such that for every $u \in [1, k]^*$, we have $\text{Tr}_{|i}(u) = \text{Tr}(i \cdot u)$. By the inductive hypothesis, $\text{Tr}, i \models \varphi_1$ iff there is an accepting run ρ_1 of $\mathcal{A}_{\varphi_1}$ on $\text{Tr}_{|i}$, which is equivalent to the fact that ρ is an accepting run of $\mathcal{A}_\varphi$ on Tr where $\rho = (\{(q_\varphi, \varepsilon)\} \cup V_1^{+i}, \{(q_\varphi, \varepsilon) \to (q_{\varphi_1}, i)\} \cup E_1^{+i})$ and $\rho_1 = (V_1, E_1)$. We write (V_1^{+i}, E_1^{+i}) to denote the unique structure isomorphic to (V_1, E_1) (that is almost a run) such that $V_1^{+i} = \{(q, i \cdot u) \mid (q, u) \in V_1\}$. Roughly speaking, ρ is obtained from ρ_1 by making one copy of ρ_1 and by adding the edge $(q_\varphi, \varepsilon) \to (q_{\varphi_1}, i)$. It is easy to check that ρ is an accepting run of $\mathcal{A}_\varphi$, as shown:

- Satisfaction of conditions (AR1)–(AR3) is by an easy verification since ρ_1 is already a run of $\mathcal{A}_{\varphi_1}$ on $\text{Tr}_{|i}$.
- Satisfaction of condition (AR4) is also by an easy verification but additionally we have to check that $\{(j, q_\psi) \mid ((q_\varphi, \varepsilon), (q_\psi, j)) \in E\} \models \delta(q_\varphi, \text{Tr}(\varepsilon))$. However, that is immediate since

$$\{(j, q_\psi) \mid ((q_\varphi, \varepsilon), (q_\psi, j)) \in E\} = \{(i, q_{\varphi_1})\}$$

and $\delta(q_\varphi, \text{Tr}(\varepsilon)) = (1, q_{\varphi_1}) \vee \cdots \vee (k, q_{\varphi_1})$.
- It remains to check that every infinite path in ρ is accepting. This is a simple consequence of the fact that every accepting state of $\mathcal{A}_\varphi$ is an accepting state of $\mathcal{A}_{\varphi_1}$ and every infinite path of ρ has an infinite suffix that is an infinite path of ρ_1.

In the forthcoming remaining cases, we will leave it to the reader to check that the constructed trees are indeed accepting runs. Conversely, if $\rho = (V, E)$ is an accepting run of $\mathcal{A}_\varphi$ on Tr, then by definition of δ, there is $i \in [1, k]$ such that $(q_\varphi, \varepsilon) \to (q_{\varphi_1}, i)$ in E. The tree restricted to the descendants of (q_{φ_1}, i) is obviously an accepting run of $\mathcal{A}_{\varphi_1}$ on $\text{Tr}_{|i}$, whence $\text{Tr}, \varepsilon \models \varphi$ by the inductive hypothesis.

Here, we omit the case $\varphi = \text{AX}\varphi_1$, which is very similar to $\varphi = \text{EX}\varphi_1$.

$\varphi = \varphi_1 \wedge \varphi_2$: Given $i \in \{1, 2\}$, let $\mathcal{B}_i = (\Sigma, Q_i, q_{\varphi_i}, \delta_i, F_i)$ be the alternating Büchi tree automaton obtained from $\mathcal{A}_{\varphi_i}$, such that $L(\mathcal{B}_i)$ is the set of Σ, k-trees satisfying φ_i with $\Pi = \text{PROP}(\varphi)$ and $\Sigma = \mathcal{P}(\Pi)$ (see Lemma 14.7.8). We need this preliminary step since φ_1 and φ_2 do not necessarily contain the same atomic propositions.

For every Σ, k-tree Tr, we have $\text{Tr}, \varepsilon \models \varphi$ iff $\text{Tr}, \varepsilon \models \varphi_1$ and $\text{Tr}, \varepsilon \models \varphi_2$ iff there is an accepting run ρ_1 on Tr in $\mathcal{B}_1$ and there is an accepting run ρ_2 on Tr in $\mathcal{B}_2$ (by the inductive hypothesis and by Lemma 14.7.8).

Given a run $\rho_1 = (V_1, E_1)$ on Tr in $\mathcal{B}_1$ and a run $\rho_2 = (V_2, E_2)$ on Tr in $\mathcal{B}_2$, we build a tree $\rho = (V, E)$ as follows:

- $V := (V_1 \cup V_2 \cup \{(\mathsf{q}_\varphi, \varepsilon)\}) \setminus \{(\mathsf{q}_{\varphi_1}, \varepsilon), (\mathsf{q}_{\varphi_2}, \varepsilon)\}$
  (Remove the root nodes and add the new root node $(\mathsf{q}_\varphi, \varepsilon)$.)
- $E := (E_1 \cup E_2 \cup \{(\mathsf{q}_\varphi, \varepsilon) \to (\mathsf{q}_{\varphi'}, j) : (\mathsf{q}_{\varphi_i}, \varepsilon) \to (\mathsf{q}_{\varphi'}, j) \in E_i, i \in [1, 2]\}) \setminus$
  $\{(\mathsf{q}_{\varphi_i}, \varepsilon) \to (\mathsf{q}_{\varphi'}, j) : i \in [1, 2]\}$.

Roughly speaking, ρ is obtained from ρ_1 and ρ_2 by substituting $(\mathsf{q}_{\varphi_1}, \varepsilon)$ by $(\mathsf{q}_\varphi, \varepsilon)$, $(\mathsf{q}_{\varphi_2}, \varepsilon)$ by $(\mathsf{q}_\varphi, \varepsilon)$ and by taking the union. In the sequel, we write $\rho_1 \wedge \rho_2$ to denote ρ. The run ρ is accepting since every infinite path in ρ is necessarily an infinite path of ρ_2 or an infinite path of ρ_1. Moreover, the set of accepting states of $\mathcal{A}_\varphi$ is the union of the accepting states of $\mathcal{B}_1$ and $\mathcal{B}_2$ plus q_φ. Consequently, if $\text{Tr}, \varepsilon \models \varphi$, then ρ is an accepting run of $\mathcal{A}_\varphi$ on Tr.

Conversely, let $\rho = (V, E)$ be a minimal accepting run on Tr in $\mathcal{A}_\varphi$. Assuming that ρ satisfies the minimality condition (AR4'), one can easily find ρ_1 and ρ_2 such that:

- ρ_1 is an accepting run on Tr in $\mathcal{B}_1$ and ρ_2 is an accepting run on Tr in $\mathcal{B}_2$,
- ρ_1 and ρ_2 satisfy the condition (sharing) (see the proof of Theorem 14.4.6),
- ρ can be decomposed as ρ_1 and ρ_2 according to the preceding definition, i.e. $\rho = \rho_1 \wedge \rho_2$ (minimality simplifies the proof of existence of such a decomposition).

By the inductive hypothesis, $\text{Tr}, \varepsilon \models \varphi_1$ and $\text{Tr}, \varepsilon \models \varphi_2$, so $\text{Tr}, \varepsilon \models \varphi$. We omit the case $\varphi = \varphi_1 \vee \varphi_2$, which is by an easy verification.

$\varphi = \mathsf{E}\varphi_1 \mathsf{U}\varphi_2$: First, let us assume that $\text{Tr}, \varepsilon \models \varphi$. By definition of the satisfaction relation, there is some $u \in [1, k]^*$ such that $\text{Tr}, u \models \varphi_2$ and for every strict prefix $v \prec u$, we have $\text{Tr}, v \models \varphi_1$. By induction on the length $|u|$, let us show that there is an accepting run on Tr in $\mathcal{A}_\varphi$.

$|u| = 0$: This means that $\text{Tr}, \varepsilon \models \varphi_2$ and by the first inductive hypothesis, there is an accepting run $\rho_2 = (V_2, E_2)$ on Tr in $\mathcal{A}_{\varphi_2}$. Let ρ be $\rho_2[(\mathsf{q}_{\varphi_2}, \varepsilon) \leftarrow (\mathsf{q}_\varphi, \varepsilon)]$. Roughly speaking, ρ is obtained from ρ_2 by substituting $(\mathsf{q}_{\varphi_2}, \varepsilon)$ by $(\mathsf{q}_\varphi, \varepsilon)$. By definition of δ, ρ is a run on Tr in $\mathcal{A}_\varphi$ and it is accepting because there is a bijection between the infinite paths of ρ and the infinite paths of ρ_2, and every accepting state of $\mathcal{A}_{\varphi_2}$ is an accepting state of $\mathcal{A}_\varphi$.

$|u| = n > 0$: Let $u = i_1 \cdots i_n$. By definition of the satisfaction relation $\models$, we have $\text{Tr}, \varepsilon \models \varphi_1$ and $\text{Tr}, i_1 \models \varphi$. By the first induction hypothesis, there is an accepting run $\rho_1 = (V_1, E_1)$ on Tr in $\mathcal{A}_{\varphi_1}$. By the second inductive hypothesis, there is an accepting run $\rho_2 = (V_2, E_2)$ on $\text{Tr}_{|i_1}$ in $\mathcal{A}_\varphi$. Let $\rho = (V, E)$ be the tree defined as follows. Roughly speaking ρ is obtained from ρ_1 and ρ_2 by replacing $(\mathsf{q}_{\varphi_1}, \varepsilon)$ by $(\mathsf{q}_\varphi, \varepsilon)$ in ρ_1, by shifting ρ_2 by i_1 and then by adding an edge from $(\mathsf{q}_\varphi, \varepsilon)$ to $(\mathsf{q}_\varphi, i_1)$ (obtained by shifting $(\mathsf{q}_\varphi, \varepsilon)$ from ρ_2).

- $V = (V_1 \cup V_2^{+i_1} \cup \{(\mathsf{q}_\varphi, \varepsilon)\}) \setminus \{(\mathsf{q}_{\varphi_1}, \varepsilon)\}$.
- $E = (E_1 \cup E_2^{+i_1} \cup \{(\mathsf{q}_\varphi, \varepsilon) \to (\mathsf{q}_\varphi, i_1)\} \cup \{(\mathsf{q}_\varphi, \varepsilon) \to (\mathsf{q}_\psi, i) \mid (\mathsf{q}_{\varphi_1}, \varepsilon) \to$
  $(\mathsf{q}_\psi, i) \in E_1\}) \setminus \{(\mathsf{q}_{\varphi_1}, \varepsilon) \to (\mathsf{q}_\psi, i) \mid (\mathsf{q}_{\varphi_1}, \varepsilon) \to (\mathsf{q}_\psi, i) \in E_1\}$.

By definition of δ, ρ is a run on Tr in $\mathcal{A}_\varphi$. This is also an accepting run since there is a bijection between the infinite paths of ρ and the union of the infinite paths of ρ_1 and ρ_2. Moreover, every accepting state of $\mathcal{A}_{\varphi_1}$ is also an accepting state in $\mathcal{A}_\varphi$.

Now suppose that $\rho = (V, E)$ is a minimal accepting run on Tr in $\mathcal{A}_\varphi$. By satisfaction of the condition (AR4$'$) and by acceptance, there is no infinite path that contains only the state q_φ. Let N be the maximal natural number such that for every $(q, u) \in V$, we have that $|u| \geq N + 1$ implies $q \neq \mathsf{q}_\varphi$. Such a value N exists since ρ is minimal.

$N = 0$: Let ρ_2 be the tree obtained from ρ by replacing $(\mathsf{q}_\varphi, \varepsilon)$ by $(\mathsf{q}_{\varphi_2}, \varepsilon)$. By satisfaction of (AR4$'$), no state (q_ψ, v) occurs in ρ_2 with $\psi \in sub(\varphi_1) \setminus sub(\varphi_2)$. Consequently, ρ_2 is an accepting run on Tr in $\mathcal{A}_{\psi_2}$. By the inductive hypothesis, Tr, $\varepsilon \vdash \varphi_2$ and therefore Tr, $\varepsilon \vdash \varphi$.

$N > 0$: By definition of δ:

- since $\delta(\mathsf{q}_{\mathsf{E}\psi\mathsf{U}\chi}, \mathsf{a}) := \delta(\mathsf{q}_\chi, \mathsf{a}) \vee (\delta(\mathsf{q}_\psi, \mathsf{a}) \wedge ((1, \mathsf{q}_{\mathsf{E}\psi\mathsf{U}\chi}) \vee \cdots \vee (k, \mathsf{q}_{\mathsf{E}\psi\mathsf{U}\chi})))$, there is $i_1 \in [1, k]$ such that $(\mathsf{q}_\varphi, i_1) \in V$ and $(\mathsf{q}_\varphi, \varepsilon) \to (\mathsf{q}_\varphi, i_1)$ is in E.
- the generated subtree ρ_1' obtained from $(\mathsf{q}_\varphi, i_1)$ in ρ is isomorphic to an accepting run ρ_1 on Tr$_{|i_1}$ in $\mathcal{A}_\varphi$ with $\rho_1^{+i_1} = \rho_1'$,
- there is an accepting run ρ_2 on Tr in $\mathcal{A}_{\varphi_1}$ obtained from ρ by replacing $(\mathsf{q}_\varphi, \varepsilon)$ by $(\mathsf{q}_{\varphi_1}, \varepsilon)$ and by deleting the generated subtree ρ_1'.

By the first inductive hypothesis, we have Tr, $\varepsilon \models \varphi_1$ whereas by the second inductive hypothesis, we have Tr, $i_1 \models \varphi$. Consequently, Tr, $\varepsilon \models \varphi$.

The cases $\varphi = \mathsf{A}\varphi_1\mathsf{R}\varphi_2$, $\varphi = \mathsf{E}\varphi_1\mathsf{R}\varphi_2$ and $\varphi = \mathsf{A}\varphi_1\mathsf{U}\varphi_2$ are left as Exercise 14.31.   □

Theorem 14.7.12. *The formula φ is CTL satisfiable iff* $L(\mathcal{A}_\varphi)$ *is nonempty.*   ∎

Note that from the definition for $\mathcal{A}_\varphi$, it is easy to define the alternating Büchi tree automaton $\mathcal{B}_\varphi$ that accepts exactly the Σ, 1-trees satisfying φ. Such Σ, 1-trees are precisely LTL models and for such a class of structures, φ is equivalent to the LTL formulae in which E and A are erased. Interestingly, $\mathcal{B}_\varphi$ is precisely equal to the alternating Büchi word automaton defined in Section 14.4. Hence the reduction from CTL formulae into alternating Büchi tree automata presented in this section can be viewed as a generalisation of the reduction from LTL formulae to alternating Büchi word automata.

Theorem 14.4.7 relating LTL and weak alternating Büchi automata can also be generalised to CTL and weak alternating Büchi tree automata. Indeed, in this section we have shown that every CTL formula can be translated into a very weak alternating Büchi tree automaton. A translation in the other direction is also possible, as stated below.

Proposition 14.7.13. Let $\Sigma = \mathcal{P}(\Pi)$ be a finite alphabet for some finite $\Pi \subseteq$ PROP. For every very weak alternating Büchi tree automaton $\mathcal{A}$ for Σ, k-trees, there is a CTL formula φ built over the atomic propositions in Π such that $L(\mathcal{A})$ is equal to the set of Σ, k-trees satisfying φ. ■

The proof is similar to the proof of Theorem 14.4.7.

14.8 Exercises

Exercises on Büchi automata

Exercise 14.1. Construct Büchi automata over the alphabet $\Sigma = \{a, b\}$ that accept the set of infinite words

(a) with at least one occurrence of a,
(b) with exactly one occurrence of a,
(c) in which the letters a and b are repeated infinitely often,
(d) with a finite and even number of a.

Exercise 14.2. Show that the Büchi automaton in Figure 14.1 accepts those words over $\{a, b\}$ having infinitely many a's.

Exercise 14.3. An ultimately periodic word over the alphabet Σ is a word of the form $u \cdot (v)^\omega$ where u and v are finite words over Σ and v is nonempty. Show that any nonempty language $L(\mathcal{A})$, for some Büchi automaton $\mathcal{A}$, has an ultimately periodic word.

Exercise 14.4. As in Exercise 11.12, for $n \geq 0$, let us consider the following LTL models restricted to the atomic proposition p:

$$\sigma_1^n := (\{p\} \cdot \emptyset)^n \cdot \{p\}^\omega$$
$$\sigma_2^n := \emptyset \cdot (\{p\} \cdot \emptyset)^n \cdot \{p\}^\omega$$
$$\sigma_3^n := (\{p\} \cdot \emptyset)^\omega.$$
$$\sigma_4^n := (\emptyset \cdot \{p\})^n \cdot \emptyset^\omega$$
$$\sigma_5^n := \{p\} \cdot (\emptyset \cdot \{p\})^n \cdot \emptyset^\omega$$
$$\sigma_6^n := (\emptyset \cdot \{p\})^\omega.$$

(a) For all $j \in [1, 6]$ and for all $n \geq 0$, show that there exist Büchi automata $\mathcal{A}_j^{\geq n}$ and $\mathcal{A}_j^{=n}$ such that:
    (a) $\mathcal{A}_j^{\geq n}$ and $\mathcal{A}_j^{=n}$ have $\mathcal{O}(n)$ states and can be built uniformly in space $\mathcal{O}(\log(n))$.
    (b) $L(\mathcal{A}_j^{\geq n})$ is the set of models $\sigma : \mathbb{N} \to \{\emptyset, \{p\}\}$ such that $\sigma \approx \sigma_j^m$ for some $m \geq n$. (Stuttering equivalence $\approx$ is introduced in Definition 6.6.4.)
    (c) $L(\mathcal{A}_j^{=n})$ is the set of models $\sigma : \mathbb{N} \to \{\emptyset, \{p\}\}$ such that $\sigma \approx \sigma_j^n$.
(b) Show that the model-checking problem for $\text{LTL}_1(U)$ is in PTime.

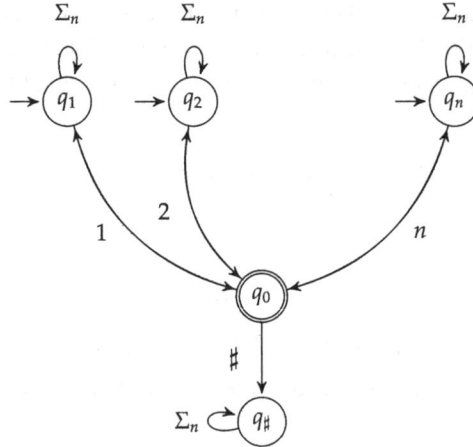

Figure 14.11 Büchi automaton $\mathcal{A}_n$.

Exercise 14.5.

(a) Let Σ_n be the alphabet $\{1, \ldots, n, \sharp\}$ and $\mathcal{A}_n$ be the Büchi automaton presented in Figure 14.11. Show that any ω-word in

$$(\Sigma_n^* \mathsf{a}_1 \mathsf{a}_2 \Sigma_n^* \mathsf{a}_2 \mathsf{a}_3 \cdots \mathsf{a}_{k-1} \mathsf{a}_k \Sigma_n^* \mathsf{a}_k \mathsf{a}_1)^\omega$$

with $\mathsf{a}_1 \cdots \mathsf{a}_k \in [1, n]^*$ belongs to $L(\mathcal{A}_n)$.

(b) Let $\mathfrak{f} : [1, n] \to [1, n]$ be a bijection. Show that the ω-word $(\mathfrak{f}(1) \cdots \mathfrak{f}(n) \sharp)^\omega$ does not belong to $L(\mathcal{A}_n)$.

(c) Let $\mathcal{B}$ be a Büchi automaton such that $L(\mathcal{B}) = \Sigma_n^\omega \setminus L(\mathcal{A})$. Let $\mathfrak{f}_1$ and $\mathfrak{f}_2$ be two distinct bijections, $u_1 = (\mathfrak{f}_1(1) \cdots \mathfrak{f}_1(n) \sharp)^\omega$ and $u_2 = (\mathfrak{f}_2(1) \cdots \mathfrak{f}_2(n) \sharp)^\omega$. Suppose $\rho_1 = q_0^1 \xrightarrow{u_1(0)} q_1^1 \xrightarrow{u_1(1)} \cdots$ is an accepting run of $\mathcal{B}$ and $\rho_2 = q_0^2 \xrightarrow{u_2(0)} q_1^2 \xrightarrow{u_2(1)} \cdots$ is an accepting run of $\mathcal{B}$. We write M_1 [resp. M_2] to denote the set of states occurring infinitely often in ρ_1 [resp. ρ_2]. Show that $M_1 \cap M_2 = \emptyset$.

(d) Show that $\mathcal{B}$ contains at least $n!$ many states and conclude.

Exercise 14.6. Show that every ω-regular language can be described by an ω-regular expression of the form $\bigcup_{i=1}^n E_i F_i^\omega$ for some $n \geq 0$, such that all F_i are left-deletable in the sense of Definition 10.1.10.

Hint: Recall that left-deletability of F means that the left quotient of the language of F with itself is contained in itself again. Then recall the proof of Theorem 14.1.16 which provides an effective translation from Büchi automata to ω-regular expressions of this form and check that the F_i describe the languages of a finite automaton with a single accepting state that is initial as well. Conclude from this that its language must be left-deletable.

Exercise 14.7. Prove Lemma 14.1.11, Lemma 14.1.14, Lemma 14.2.2 and complete the proof of Lemma 14.1.9.

Exercises on LTL and Büchi automata

Exercise 14.8. Repeat Exercises 13.12, 13.13, 13.14 and 13.15 using Büchi automata instead of tableaux this time.

Exercise 14.9. For a fixed $n \geq 0$, let LTL_n^- be a fragment of LTL defined as follows:

$$\varphi ::= p_1 \mid \cdots \mid p_n \mid \varphi_1 \vee \varphi_2 \mid \varphi_1 \wedge \varphi_2 \mid \mathsf{X}\varphi_1 \mid \mathsf{F}\varphi_1.$$

For each formula $\varphi \in \text{LTL}_n^-$, determine the size of $\mathcal{A}_\varphi$ such that $\varphi \approx \mathcal{A}_\varphi$ by using the construction from Section 14.2.2.

Exercise 14.10.

(a) Show that the Büchi automaton over the alphabet Σ in Figure 14.5 (left) accepts the models of the formula $\mathsf{G}(p_1 \leftrightarrow (p_2 \wedge p_3))$.
(b) Show that the Büchi automaton over the alphabet Σ in Figure 14.5 (right) accepts the models of the formula $\mathsf{G}(p_1 \leftrightarrow \neg p_2)$.
(c) Show that the Büchi automaton over the alphabet Σ in Figure 14.6 accepts the models of the formula $\mathsf{G}(p_1 \leftrightarrow \mathsf{X}p_2)$.
(d) Show that the Büchi automaton over the alphabet Σ in Figure 14.7 accepts the models of the formula $\mathsf{G}(p_1 \leftrightarrow (p_2 \mathsf{U}p_3))$.

Exercise 14.11. Show that the automaton $\mathcal{A}_\varphi$ defined in Section 14.2.4 can be built in exponential time.

Exercise 14.12. Prove the statement $(\star)$ in the proof of Theorem 14.2.19.

Exercise 14.13. Prove Lemma 14.2.22.

Exercise 14.14. Formally define a Büchi automaton $\mathcal{B}$ accepting the models in $\text{Mod}(\varphi)$ from the transducer $T(\mathcal{A})$ defined in Section 14.2.3. Explain how the nonemptiness of $\text{L}(\mathcal{A})$ can be checked in nondeterministic polynomial space.

Exercise 14.15. Let $\mathcal{A} = (\Sigma, Q, q_0, \delta, F)$ be a weak alternating Büchi automaton with ordered partition $(\{Q_1, \ldots, Q_K\}, \leq)$. This means that for all $q \in Q_i$ and all $q' \in Q_j$ such that q' occurs in $\delta(q, \mathsf{a})$ for some letter a, we have $Q_j \leq Q_i$. Show that for all $q \in Q_i$ and all $q' \in Q_j$ such that q' occurs in $\overline{\delta}(q, \mathsf{a})$, we have $Q_j \leq Q_i$ where $\overline{\delta}$ is the dual of δ (see Definition 14.3.9).

Exercise 14.16. Construct Büchi automata recognising the models of the following formulae: $\mathsf{GF}p \wedge \mathsf{GF}q$, $\mathsf{G}(\mathsf{F}p \rightarrow \mathsf{F}q)$ and $\mathsf{G}p \wedge \mathsf{G}(p \rightarrow q) \wedge \mathsf{F}(\neg q)$.

Exercise 14.17. We write LTL+O to denote the extension of LTL by adding a single operator O of arity $n \geq 1$ with semantics defined as follows. Let *tr* be the mapping from the set of LTL+O formulae into the set of LTL formulae such that t is homomorphic for $\neg$, $\wedge$, X and U, and

- $tr(\mathsf{O}(\varphi_1, \ldots, \varphi_n)) := \varphi_{\mathsf{O}}[tr(\varphi_1)/p_1, \ldots, tr(\varphi_n)/p_n]$, where $\varphi_{\mathsf{O}}[tr(\varphi_1)/p_1, \ldots, tr(\varphi_n)/p_n]$ is the formula obtained from the LTL formula φ_{O} built over $p_1, \ldots, p_n$, by simultaneously replacing every occurrence of p_i by $tr(\varphi_i)$,
- $tr(p) := p$ for the propositional variable p.

By definition, $w, i \models \varphi$ in LTL+O iff $w, i \models tr(\varphi)$ in LTL. By way of example, the 'weak until' operator is usually defined by $\varphi \mathsf{W} \psi := (\mathsf{G}\varphi) \vee \varphi \mathsf{U} \psi$ and the formula φ_{W} takes the value $(\mathsf{G}p_1) \vee p_1 \mathsf{U} p_2$.

(a) Characterise the complexity of the model-checking and satisfiability problems for LTL+O when the size of a formula is defined from its DAG size (which is, by default, the size measure in this book).
(b) Propose an automata-based decision procedure for deciding the satisfiability problem for LTL+O without using an explicit translation into LTL.

Exercise 14.18. In this problem, we show how the reduction from LTL formulae to Büchi automata from Section 14.2.4 can be extended to LTL+Past.

The pair of expanded sets (Γ_1, Γ_2) is **one-step consistent** iff the following conditions are satisfied:

(a) $\mathsf{X}\psi \in \Gamma_1$ implies $\psi \in \Gamma_2$.
(b) $\neg\mathsf{X}\psi \in \Gamma_1$ implies $\sim\psi \in \Gamma_2$.
(c) $\mathsf{Y}\psi \in \Gamma_2$ implies $\psi \in \Gamma_1$.
(d) $\neg\mathsf{Y}\psi \in \Gamma_2$ implies $\sim\psi \in \Gamma_1$.
(e) $\psi_1 \mathsf{U} \psi_2 \in \Gamma_1$ implies $\psi_2 \in \Gamma_1$ or ($\psi_1 \in \Gamma_1$ and $\psi_1 \mathsf{U} \psi_2 \in \Gamma_2$).
(f) $\psi_1 \mathsf{S} \psi_2 \in \Gamma_2$ implies $\psi_2 \in \Gamma_2$ or ($\psi_1 \in \Gamma_2$ and $\psi_1 \mathsf{S} \psi_2 \in \Gamma_1$).
(g) $\neg(\psi_1 \mathsf{U} \psi_2) \in \Gamma_1$ implies $\sim\psi_2 \in \Gamma_1$ and ($\sim\psi_1 \in \Gamma_1$ or $\neg(\psi_1 \mathsf{U} \psi_2) \in \Gamma_2$).
(h) $\neg(\psi_1 \mathsf{S} \psi_2) \in \Gamma_2$ implies $\sim\psi_2 \in \Gamma_2$ and ($\sim\psi_1 \in \Gamma_2$ or $\neg(\psi_1 \mathsf{S} \psi_2) \in \Gamma_1$).

We also extend the notion of maximal trace (see Definition 14.2.16) to LTL+Past formulae. A **maximal trace** for φ is a mapping $\mathcal{H} : \mathbb{N} \to \mathcal{P}(cl_{\text{LTL+Past}}(\varphi))$ satisfying the following conditions for every $n \in \mathbb{N}$:

(H1) $\mathcal{H}(n)$ is maximallly consistent with respect to the closure set of φ.
(H2) $(\mathcal{H}(n), \mathcal{H}(n+1))$ is one-step consistent (see earlier).
(H3) If $\psi_1 \mathsf{U} \psi_2 \in \mathcal{H}(n)$, then there exists $i \geq 0$ such that $\psi_2 \in \mathcal{H}(n+i)$ and $\psi_1 \in \mathcal{H}(n+j)$ for every $j \in [0, i-1]$.
(H4) If $\psi_1 \mathsf{S} \psi_2 \in \mathcal{H}(n)$, then there exists $i \in [0, n]$ such that $\psi_2 \in \mathcal{H}(n-i)$ and $\psi_1 \in \mathcal{H}(n-j)$ for every $j \in [0, i-1]$.
(H5) No formula of the form $\mathsf{Y}\psi$ belongs to $\mathcal{H}(0)$.

A maximal trace $\mathcal{H}$ **satisfies** $\varphi \overset{\text{def}}{\Leftrightarrow} \varphi \in \mathcal{H}(0)$.

(a) Show that if the LTL+Past formula φ is satisfiable, then there is a maximal trace for φ.
(b) Show that if there is a maximal trace for φ, then φ is satisfiable.
(c) Given the LTL+Past formula φ, design a Büchi automaton $\mathcal{A}_\varphi$ such that $\text{Mod}(\varphi) = L(\mathcal{A}_\varphi)$.
(d) Adapt Theorem 6.3.8 to LTL+Past and prove the new statement for LTL+Past.
(e) Prove that SAT(LTL+Past) can be solved in polynomial space.

Exercise 14.19. In this problem, we show how SAT(QLTL) can be solved with non-elementary complexity: the satisfiability status of a formula $\varphi \in$ QLTL can be checked in time expressed as a tower of exponentials

$$2^{2^{\cdot^{\cdot^{\cdot^{2^{p(|\varphi|)}}}}}}$$

whose height is bounded by the size of φ and $p(\cdot)$ is a polynomial.

First, recall a result from Section 14.2.2. Let φ_1 and φ_2 be LTL formulae, Π be a finite set of atomic propositions such that $\text{PROP}(\varphi_1) \cup \text{PROP}(\varphi_2) \subseteq \Pi$ and $\Sigma = \mathcal{P}(\Pi)$. Assuming that $\mathcal{A}_1$, $\mathcal{A}_2$ are Büchi automata such that $\varphi_i \approx_\Sigma \mathcal{A}_i$ and $\mathcal{A}_i$ has n_i states for $i = 1, 2$, we have seen that we can build a Büchi automaton

(a) $\mathcal{A}_\vee$ such that $\varphi_1 \vee \varphi_2 \approx_\Sigma \mathcal{A}_\vee$ and $\mathcal{A}_\vee$ has $\mathcal{O}(n_1 + n_2)$ states,
(b) $\mathcal{A}_\wedge$ such that $\varphi_1 \wedge \varphi_2 \approx_\Sigma \mathcal{A}_\wedge$ and $\mathcal{A}_\wedge$ has $\mathcal{O}(n_1 \cdot n_2)$ states,
(c) $\mathcal{A}_\neg$ such that $\neg\varphi_1 \approx_\Sigma \mathcal{A}_\neg$ and $\mathcal{A}_\neg$ has $2^{\mathcal{O}(n_1 \cdot \log(n_1))}$ states,
(d) $\mathcal{A}_\mathsf{U}$ such that $\varphi_1 \mathsf{U} \varphi_2 \approx_\Sigma \mathcal{A}_\mathsf{U}$ and $\mathcal{A}_\mathsf{U}$ has $2^{2n_1} \cdot (n_2 + 1)$ states.

More can be found in Section 14.1.3 and in Section 15.2.3.

(a) Let φ be an QLTL formula, p be a propositional variable and $\mathcal{A} = (\Sigma, Q, Q_0, \delta, F)$ be a Büchi automaton such that $\varphi \approx_\Sigma \mathcal{A}$ where $\Sigma = \mathcal{P}(\Pi)$ and $\text{PROP}(\varphi) \subseteq \Pi$. Let $\mathcal{A}' = (\Sigma', Q, Q_0, \delta', F)$ be the Büchi automaton such that:
   • $\Sigma' = \mathcal{P}(\Pi \setminus \{p\})$,
   • for all $q, q' \in Q, q \xrightarrow{Y} q' \in \delta' \overset{\text{def}}{\Leftrightarrow}$ there is $X \in \Sigma$ such that $Y = X \setminus \{p\}$ and $q \xrightarrow{X} q' \in \delta$.
   Show that $(\exists\, p\, \varphi) \approx_{\Sigma'} \mathcal{A}'$.
(b) Show that the satisfiability status of a formula $\varphi \in$ QLTL can be checked in time expressed as a tower of exponentials

$$2^{2^{\cdot^{\cdot^{\cdot^{2^{p'(|\varphi|)}}}}}}$$

whose height is bounded by the size of φ and $p'(\cdot)$ is a fixed polynomial.

Exercise 14.20. Prove Lemma 14.2.10, Lemma 14.2.6, Lemma 14.2.9, Lemma 14.2.11 and Lemma 14.2.18.

Exercise 14.21. Show that the set of minimal models (in the sense of Exercise 6.20) for any LTL formula is Büchi recognisable.

Exercises on alternating automata on ω-words

Exercise 14.22. Repeat Exercises 13.12, 13.13, 13.14 and 13.15 using alternating Büchi automata instead of tableaux.

Exercise 14.23. Show that alternating Büchi (resp. co-Büchi) automata are alternating parity automata and that generalised Büchi automata can be transformed into alternating parity automata.

Exercise 14.24. Show that the nonemptiness problem for alternating Büchi automata is PSPACE-hard.

Exercise 14.25. Prove Lemma 14.3.1, Lemma 14.4.3 and Lemma 14.4.1.

Exercise 14.26. Complete the proofs of Theorem 14.3.12, Theorem 14.4.6 and Theorem 14.5.6.

Exercise 14.27. This exercise is dedicated to proving Theorem 14.3.10. Let $\mathcal{A} = (\Sigma, Q, q_0, \delta, F)$ be an alternating automaton with Büchi acceptance condition and $\overline{\mathcal{A}} = (\Sigma, Q, q_0, \overline{\delta}, F)$ be its dual with co-Büchi acceptance condition.

(a) Let $a \in \Sigma$ and $q \in Q$. By structural induction, show that for any $X \subseteq Q$, the following conditions are equivalent:
   ($\star$) $X \models \delta(q, a)$,
   ($\star\star$) for every set of states $X' \subseteq Q$ such that $X' \models \overline{\delta(q, a)}$ implies $X \cap X' \neq \emptyset$.
   Conclude that
   (**P***) for any set of states X, we have $X \models \delta(q, a)$ iff for every set of states $X' \subseteq Q$ such that $X' \models \overline{\delta(q, a)}$, we have $X \cap X' \neq \emptyset$.
(b) Using Property (P*), show that if A has a memoryless winning strategy in the Büchi game for $\mathcal{G}^B_{\mathcal{A},w}$ then P has a memoryless winning strategy in the co-Büchi game for $\mathcal{G}^{coB}_{\overline{\mathcal{A}},w}$.
(c) Using Property (P*), show that if P has a memoryless winning strategy in the co-Büchi game for $\mathcal{G}^{coB}_{\overline{\mathcal{A}},w}$ then A has a memoryless winning strategy in the Büchi game for $\mathcal{G}^B_{\mathcal{A},w}$.

Exercises on Büchi tree automata

Exercise 14.28. Repeat Exercises 13.30, 13.31, 13.32 using Büchi tree automata rather than tableaux.

Exercise 14.29. Prove Lemma 14.6.3, Lemma 14.6.12 and Lemma 14.7.7.

Exercise 14.30. Prove Proposition 14.7.3 by adapting the proof of Theorem 14.3.12.

Exercise 14.31. Complete the remaining cases in Theorem 14.7.11 with $\varphi = A\varphi_1 R\varphi_2$, $\varphi = E\varphi_1 R\varphi_2$ and $\varphi = A\varphi_1 U\varphi_2$.

14.9 Bibliographical Notes

In these bibliographical notes we focus on references to material presented in this chapter, but much more could be said, so we have also provided references to chapters or books that cover more specialised topics.

A classical general reference to automata on infinite objects is Thomas (1990). We also invite the reader to consult D'Souza and Shankar (2012) for a presentation of modern applications of automata theory, including those related to temporal logics.

Automata recognising infinite words. Büchi (1962) has initiated the study of finite-state automata working on ω-words. The connection between monadic second-order logic MSO and the now called Büchi automata (see e.g. Büchi 1962; proofs can also be found in Straubing 1994; Perrin and Pin 2004) has been useful to show the decidability of MSO. This pioneering work illustrates best the automata-based approach for which logical problems are reduced to decision problems on automata. Besides, it also contains results on Büchi automata that are also interesting on their own; for instance that the set of languages accepted by Büchi automata has been shown to be closed under complementation. The nonemptiness problem for nondeterministic Büchi automata was shown to be in PTIME in Emerson and Lei (1987) and in space $\mathcal{O}((\log(n))^2)$ in Vardi and Wolper (1994). Historical notes about automata for infinite words can be found in Perrin and Pin (2004, Chapter 1, Section 13), whereas a self-contained introduction to Büchi automata can be found in Mukund (2012).

The complementation problem for nondeterministic automata is central to the automata-theoretic approach to formal verification. In Sistla et al. (1987) an algorithm for the complementation of Büchi automata is provided that yields the PSPACE upper bound for ETL. The automata built there are of size $\mathcal{O}(16^{n^2})$. Safra (1988) introduced a determinisation construction, based on the now called Safra trees, which also provides a $2^{\mathcal{O}(n\log(n))}$ complementation construction (see also Chapter 15), matching a lower bound found by Michel (1988). See more references about complementation in Fogarty et al. (2011).

There are other useful and important acceptance conditions besides Büchi's, defining different classes of automata. For instance, a few years after Büchi initiated the study of finite-state automata working on ω-words, Muller (1963) independently proposed an alternative definition of finite-state automata in which the accepting condition is defined as a *set* of sets of accepting states, thus defining the now called *Muller automata*.

From LTL formulae to Büchi automata. The reductions of LTL model-checking and satisfiability-testing problems to nonemptiness of Büchi automata with optimal upper bounds have been introduced in Vardi and Wolper (1986a, 1994). The PSPACE upper bound for the satisfiability problem for LTL and ETL respectively is established in Sistla and

Clarke (1982, 1985). There are many versions and refinements of the original translation from Vardi and Wolper (1994), some of them are more amenable to implementation and lead to more efficient algorithms than others. See, for instance, one of them in Demri and Gastin (2012), which produces automata that can be used for teaching purposes.

Transducers and temporal logics. The translation from LTL formulae to transducers presented in Section 14.2.3 goes back to the less known work by Michel (1984) (in French) and Michel and Stefani (1988). More recently, Cristau (2009) developed a similar proof method for linear-time temporal logics over linear orders. As far as we know, the relationship between transducers and the more standard automata-based approach for LTL presented in Section 14.2.4 has not been published so far elsewhere but heavily relies on Michel (1984) and Cristau (2009).

CTL. The translation of CTL into Büchi tree automata can be obtained as an adjustment of results from Vardi and Wolper (1986a) for PDL (see also Vardi and Wilke 2007). Proposition 14.7.13 is stated in Vardi and Wilke (2007, Theorem 5.11).

Alternating automata. An early work on alternating Turing machines that already contains results presented in Chandra et al. (1981) can be found in Kozen (1976), where 'alternation' is called 'parallel computation'. Alternating tree automata (for infinite trees) were introduced in Muller and Schupp (1987). The main result there states that the dual of an alternating automaton accepts the complemented language (for any acceptance condition that is definable in the Borel hierarchy). This is shown by using game theory and Martin's determinacy theorem. Alternating automata for finite trees were introduced in Slutzki (1987). Even though alternating automata on ω-words are advocated in Muller et al. (1986), the first work on translating temporal logics into *alternating* automata can be found in Muller et al. (1988). The proof of Theorem 14.3.12 is due to Miyano and Hayashi (1984) and then is extended to trees in Proposition 14.7.3 (see also Miyano and Hayashi 1984).

Weak alternating automata were introduced in Muller et al. (1986) (see also Kupferman and Vardi 2001). The proof of Proposition 14.3.15 can be obtained from the proof of Kupferman and Vardi (2001, Theorem 4.1). Theorem 14.3.16 is due to Chandra et al. (1981), while Proposition 14.3.17 is due to Kupferman and Vardi (2001). The translation from LTL formulae into alternating automata can be found in Vardi (1997).

Vardi (2007) contains further historical notes about automata-based techniques for temporal logics.

Games and alternating automata. The use of games as an alternative to automata is advocated in Gurevich and Harrington (1982). Chapter 15 is dedicated to verification games and more references relating them to automata are provided there.

In the proof sketch of Theorem 14.3.10, Property (I) is the counterpart of Löding and Thomas (2000, Lemma 1) for alternating Büchi automata and its proof is a very slight variant of the proof of Klaedtke (2002, Lemma 4.13). It simply expresses that accepting runs in alternating Büchi automata can be viewed as winning memoryless strategies in games with Büchi acceptance conditions. Property (II) is a direct consequence of determinacy of such games, see the proof of Löding and Thomas (2000, Lemma 2) (standard results go beyong Büchi acceptance conditions). The proof of Property (III) is a variant of the proof of Löding and Thomas (2000, Lemma 2) (see also Klaedtke (2002, Lemma 4.13) where the earlier mentioned property (P^*) (see Exercise 14.27) is used instead of Löding and Thomas (2000, Remark 1).

Alternating automata and LTL formulae. The translation from LTL formulae to alternating Büchi automata, plus the translation from very weak alternating Büchi automata to LTL formulae can be found in Rohde (1997) and Vardi and Wilke (2007). In the PhD thesis (Rohde 1997), very weak alternating automata are introduced for recognising transfinite words. A more sophisticated translation into very weak alternating automata can be found in Gastin and Oddoux (2001).

In Diekert and Gastin (2008) a self-contained presentation of several formalisms equivalent to LTL are presented, for instance *counter free Büchi automata* defining exactly the models of LTL formulae. Also, it is shown there that checking whether a Büchi automaton defines a first-order language is PSPACE-complete. Correspondence with very weak alternating Büchi automata is also provided there via aperiodicity.

A neat treatment of alternating automata and logics over infinite words can be found in Löding and Thomas (2000).

ETL and alternating automata. Piterman's MSc thesis (Piterman 2000) contains a wealth of results relating variants of ETL and alternating automata. For instance, in ETL, the automata-based operators are defined with (one-way) finite-state automata, whereas in Piterman (2000), richer classes of automata are considered (two-way, alternating, etc.).

About PSL. An automata-based construction for PSL formulae is designed in Bustan et al. (2005) in order to define verification algorithms. Automata constructions are also defined in Lange (2007) where a systematic analysis of the computational complexity of PSL fragments is performed.

Tree automata. A general reference on tree automata and techniques is Comon-Lundh et al. (n.d.). The nonemptiness problem for Büchi tree automata on binary infinite trees is shown to be in PTIME in Rabin (1970), whereas the PTIME upper bound is shown for k-ary infinite trees in Vardi and Wolper (1986b). The proof of Theorem 14.6.6 is due to Vardi and Wolper (1986b). The reductions in Section 14.6.2 and Section 14.6.3 are due to Vardi and Wolper (1986a). For a proof that Büchi tree automata are not closed under complementation, see e.g. Thomas (1990), whereas Muller and Rabin tree automata are closed under complementation (see e.g. Thomas 1990).

It is shown in Kupferman et al. (2006) that the language L is accepted by a nondeterministic Büchi automaton but not by a deterministic Büchi automaton iff LΔ (set of trees such that all branches belong to L) is accepted by a Rabin tree automaton but not by a Büchi tree automaton. The EXPTIME upper bound for CTL satisfiability is established in Emerson and Halpern (1985) and Fischer and Ladner (1979).

Details on amorphous automata can be found in Vardi and Wilke (2007). Reductions from alternating tree automata to nondeterministic tree automata can be found in Muller and Schupp (1995).

Other automata constructions. Further details on automata-based constructions for temporal logics can be found in Emerson and Jutla (2000), in Kupferman et al. (2000) for CTL*, in Vardi (1988) and Vardi and Wilke (2007) for the linear μ-calculus and in Vardi and Wilke (2007) for the modal μ-calculus.

15

The Game-Theoretic Framework

In this chapter we will develop a game-theoretic approach to the main decision problems for temporal logics. We will present model-checking games and satisfiability-checking games and use them to characterise the model checking and the satisfiability-checking problem for temporal logics. These games are defined by means of an arena on which two players perform plays. The characterisations then relate the model-checking problem, i.e. the question of whether a given state of an interpreted transition system satisfies a temporal formula, to the existence of a winning strategy for the proponent player in the respective model-checking game. Likewise, the satisfiability problem, asking the question of whether a given temporal formula is satisfiable, corresponds to the question of whether the proponent player has a winning strategy in the respective satisfiability game.

These game-theoretic characterisations are of particular interest in the context of program verification. Consider the model-checking problem which is used to prove whether some (abstracted) system is correct with respect to a property formulated as a temporal formula. If model checking returns true, i.e. the property is satisfied and the system is therefore verified, then one can continue the system development process and consider another property for instance. However, if the property is not satisfied, i.e. model checking has returned false, then typically the system needs to be redesigned so that the error causing the non-satisfaction of the formula is rectified. In order to do this successfully, it is important to know *why* the property is not satisfied. Game-theoretic characterisations are designed to yield such explanations: the certificate for nonsatisfaction of a property is a winning strategy for the opponent player, called here Refuter and denoted by **R**. Failure certificates are also important in satisfiability problems, for instance in checking whether a program specification made up of several parts is realisable.

While satisfiability of a temporal formula of BML seems easy to certify by giving a model, it is usually more difficult for logics like CTL and LTL, and much more so for complex logics like CTL* and $\mathcal{L}_\mu$. Again, winning strategies in satisfiability games yield certificates that can be used for building such satisfying models.

Before we actually consider temporal logics and their associated games, we introduce the game-theoretic framework abstractly and present the basic concepts like players, plays, winning conditions, winning strategies, etc. Then we consider a particular type of game, called *parity game*, which is appealing because of its simplicity and its algorithmic properties. The decision problem underlying the game-theoretic framework is that of *solving* a game, which is a synonym for deciding the existence of winning strategies and computing them. Given the link to model checking and satisfiability checking described earlier, game solving provides another route to decision problems of temporal logics. One of the major landmarks on this route is the Main Reduction Theorem, presented in this chapter. It states that all games with *regular* winning conditions can be reduced to parity games. We then present algorithms for solving parity games which, by the constructive content of this theorem, translate to algorithms for model checking and satisfiability checking temporal logics.

The price to pay for this powerful and neat framework lies in the combinatorics involved in the proof of the Main Reduction Theorem: it uses some heavy automata-theoretic machinery, namely the determinisation of parity automata, and the respective automata-theoretic constructions are given as well. The reader who is only interested in obtaining game-theoretic characterisations but not necessarily algorithms for temporal logics may skip Section 15.2. Still, some of the games, like the CTL* model-checking games, do not rely on very difficult automata constructions and others like the $\mathcal{L}_\mu$ model-checking games do not need them at all.

Structure of the chapter. This chapter is divided into four sections. Section 15.1 defines and studies the abstract games that arise as model checking or satisfiability checking games for temporal logics. It ends with the Main Reduction Theorem which shows how to reduce such games to parity games. Section 15.2 provides the necessary (and useful) automata-theoretic constructions for such reductions. These constructions, when considered on their own, have nothing to do with games and therefore do not add anything to the understanding of how to design such games for temporal logics; they are only needed in order to solve such games algorithmically. Yet, this section is not part of Chapter 14 on automata because its content is predominantly used in decision procedures for the intuitively more complex temporal logics like $\mathcal{L}_\mu$ and CTL* which are only being presented here, in this chapter. The complementation procedure for Büchi automata that is included in Section 15.2 is the only one actually used in Chapter 14.

The last two sections contain the actual definition of games for temporal logics. Section 15.3 does that for model-checking problems. Model-checking games have in fact been presented in earlier chapters, for instance for $\mathcal{L}_\mu$ in Section 8.4. Here we focus on two aspects. First, we consider algorithmic aspects, namely why these model-checking games are in fact parity games which most of all yield an algorithm for $\mathcal{L}_\mu$ model checking. The second focus of that section is the model-checking problem for CTL*. Unlike CTL, which is directly translated into $\mathcal{L}_\mu$, the translation from CTL* into $\mathcal{L}_\mu$ is far more complex and therefore model-checking games for CTL* cannot simply be read off the ones for $\mathcal{L}_\mu$. This is why Section 15.3 explicitly presents model-checking games for CTL* and introduces an important machinery that is used to deal with least fixpoint constructs (cf. 'eventualities' in tableau-based procedures, Chapter 13). Finally, Section 15.4 presents satisfiability-checking games for $\mathcal{L}_\mu$ and CTL* only, as the simpler temporal logics have already been dealt with in the previous chapters, using tableaux and automata. These games are also linked to the model-checking games of the section before.

15.1 Parity Games

15.1.1 Some Cases of Regular Games

Parity games are a particular kind of 2-player games on graphs that enjoy nice properties, in particular memoryless determinacy and a rich algorithmic theory. They will turn out a perfect tool for game-theoretic characterisations of temporal logic decision problems.

In a parity game, each node is given a *priority*, which is simply a natural number. The winner of a play, i.e. an infinite sequence of nodes, is determined by the highest priority that occurs infinitely often in this play. We will represent the winning condition in a parity game implicitly, in terms of the priority function, rather than explicitly as a set of plays, as explained in the following definition. We invite the reader to recall the basic concepts of games from Section 2.2.3.

Definition 15.1.1. A **parity game** is a tuple $\mathcal{G} = (V, Own, E, v_I, \Omega)$, where (V, Own, E) is a game arena, v_I is a designated starting node and $\Omega : V \to \mathbb{N}$ is called the **priority function**.

Let Π be the set of all plays in this arena, regardless of whether they are starting in v_I. The priority function Ω uniquely determines the winning condition for Player 0:

$$Win_\Omega^{\text{parity}} := \{\lambda \in \Pi \mid \lambda = v_0, v_1, \ldots, \text{ such that } \max \inf(\lambda) \text{ is even}\}.$$

Sometimes we will consider parity games (V, Own, E, Ω) without particular starting nodes, for instance when we are interested in the winner from any node in the game or when we prove general results about parity games that do not depend on a particular starting node.

The **index** of the parity game $\mathcal{G}$ is the number of different priorities it uses, i.e. $\text{card}(\{\Omega(v) \mid v \in V\})$. ∇

Hence, in a play of a parity game Player 0 wants to visit infinitely often an even priority such that no greater odd priority is visited infinitely often in the play. Player 1 attempts the same for odd priorities. The players' names can be used to recall the definition of the winning condition: player i attempts to maximise priorities which are i modulo 2.

Also, recall the following graphical convention: the nodes in a game arena that are owned by Player 0 are drawn as circles, while the nodes owned by Player 1 are drawn as square boxes. Besides, the starting node, if any is specified, is marked with an incoming arrow.

Lastly, recall again from Definition 2.2.9 that a **strategy** for Player $\mathbf{P}$ in a given game arena is a (partial) function $\mathfrak{str} : V^* V_\mathbf{P} \to V$ which assigns to every history $v_0, \ldots, v_n$ owned by player $\mathbf{P}$ a node $w \in V$ with $(v_n, w) \in E$. Then, a play $\lambda = v_0, v_1, \ldots$ **conforms** to a strategy $\mathfrak{str}$ for player $\mathbf{P}$ if for every $i \in \mathbb{N}$ with $v_i \in V_\mathbf{P}$ we have $v_{i+1} = \mathfrak{str}(v_0, \ldots, v_i)$.

Now, given a (not necessarily parity) game $\mathcal{G}$, i.e. game arena plus a winning condition, a **winning strategy** for player $\mathbf{P}$ is a strategy for him[1] such that every play that conforms to this strategy is winning for him in $\mathcal{G}$. A strategy for player $\mathbf{P}$ in a game with node set V is called **memoryless**, or **positional**, if it only takes into account the current position in the game, rather than the entire history of the play, i.e. for all histories η, η' and all $v \in V_\mathbf{P}$ it holds that $\mathfrak{str}(\eta, v) = \mathfrak{str}(\eta', v)$. Thus, we can also define a memoryless strategy for player $\mathbf{P}$ as a function of type $V_\mathbf{P} \to V$.

Most of the concrete strategies that we will consider in examples here will be memoryless, for a good reason to be established later, viz. **memoryless determinacy**: memoryless strategies suffice to win any parity game for the player who has a winning strategy in it.

Example 15.1.2. The following depicts a parity game with nodes $\{a, \ldots, f\}$ and no specified starting node. The labels alongside the nodes are their priorities.

---

[1] Both players will be randomly referred to as 'he/him' or 'she/her'. This is only done out of necessity imposed by the language, but without assuming that they have any specific gender.

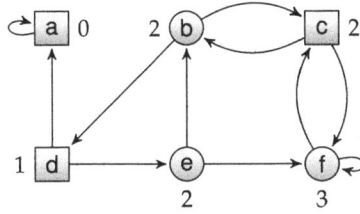

It is not hard to see that, in order to win, Player 0 needs to force a play into one of three cycles: (i) the self-loop on a, (ii) the cycle between b and c and (iii) the cycle between d, e and b. Conversely, any play that stays in cycles (ii) and (iii) will also be winning for her. However, she cannot force a play to stay in cycle (ii) because it contains a node controlled by Player 1 who can diverge into the cycle on the two nodes on the right which is winning for her. The situation is different for cycle (iii) which also contains a node owned by Player 1, but here he can only escape into cycle (i), which is not beneficial to him.

Thus, Player 0 wins this parity game starting in any of the nodes a, b, d and e, while Player 1 has a winning strategy if the game is started in c or f.

With every parity game we can naturally associate a *dual* one, obtained by swapping the players and complementing the winning condition. In essence, that dual game formalises the other player's view on the original game.

Definition 15.1.3. Let $\mathcal{G} = (V, Own, E, v_I, Win)$ be a game. The **dual game** to $\mathcal{G}$ is the game $\overline{\mathcal{G}} = (V, \overline{Own}, E, v_I, \overline{Win})$ where $\overline{Own}(v) = 1 - Own(v)$ for any $v \in V$ and $\overline{Win} = \Pi \setminus Win$ assuming that Π is the set of all plays in $\mathcal{G}$. ∇

Hereafter, for any $\mathbf{P} \in \{0, 1\}$ we denote $\overline{\mathbf{P}} := 1 - \mathbf{P}$. The following lemma explains the term 'dual games'. Its proof is left as Exercise 15.7.

Lemma 15.1.4. Let $\mathcal{G}$ be a game and $\overline{\mathcal{G}}$ be its dual game. For any $\mathbf{P} \in \{0, 1\}$ we have that Player $\mathbf{P}$ has a winning strategy for $\mathcal{G}$ iff Player $\overline{\mathbf{P}}$ has a winning strategy for $\overline{\mathcal{G}}$.   ∎

Next, we observe that the class of parity games is closed under duality, in the sense that the dual game to a parity game can be defined as a parity game again. Its proof simply uses the fact that raising all priorities in a game by 1 turns even ones into odd ones, and vice versa. The details are left as Exercise 15.7.

Lemma 15.1.5. Let $\mathcal{G} = (V, Own, E, v_I, \Omega)$ be a parity game. For any $\mathbf{P} \in \{0, 1\}$ we have that Player $\mathbf{P}$ has a winning strategy for $\mathcal{G}$ iff Player $\overline{\mathbf{P}}$ has a winning strategy for the parity game $(V, \overline{Own}, E, v_I, \Omega')$ where $\overline{Own}(v) = 1 - Own(v)$ and $\Omega'(v) = 1 + \Omega(v)$ for any $v \in V$.   ∎

An important consequence of this lemma is the fact that – considering aspects like algorithmic solving, existence of memoryless strategies, etc. – parity games are symmetric. Suppose we have an algorithm which determines whether Player 0 has a winning strategy in a given parity game. By dualising the game, this algorithm can also be used to determine whether Player 1 has a winning strategy in the game.

Further we will consider 4 classes of games with simpler winning conditions: reachability, safety, Büchi and co-Büchi games. Each of these classes of games can be seen as parity games with a restricted number of priorities. Furthermore, they will be respectively paired as duals to each other.

We will start with the simple concept of a *reachability game*. Intuitively, in such a game, Player 0 only needs to visit a certain set of nodes once in order to win. Clearly, this can be modelled with an explicit winning condition as the set of all plays which contain one of these nodes. As with parity games, we represent the winning condition implicitly by only giving that set of nodes.

Definition 15.1.6. A **reachability game** is a tuple $\mathcal{G} = (V, Own, E, F)$ where (V, Own, E, v_I) is an arena, $v_I \in V$ and $F \subseteq V$ is a set of designated target nodes. Player 0 wins a play $\lambda = v_0, v_1, \ldots$ in $\mathcal{G}$ if there is some $i \in \mathbb{N}$ with $v_i \in F$. ▽

Note that reachability games are not closed under duals. Clearly, the game from the perspective of Player 1 is a different one: he must try *not* to reach the set F which cannot be expressed in terms of reaching $V \setminus F$ in the same game, nor any other set of states. Indeed, the dual of a reachability game is a *safety* game.

Definition 15.1.7. A **safety game** is a tuple $\mathcal{G} = (V, Own, E, v_I, F)$ where (V, Own, E) is an arena, $v_I \in V$ and $F \subseteq V$ is a set of designated nodes. Player 0 wins a play $\lambda = v_0, v_1, \ldots$ in $\mathcal{G}$ if, for all $i \in \mathbb{N}$, we have $v_i \in F$. ▽

Example 15.1.8. Consider the following two-node reachability game shown on the left in which Player 0 is supposed to reach node b. Clearly, she can do so from node a by taking the edge from a to b.

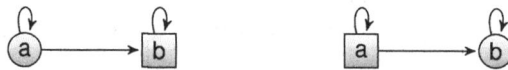

The game on the right is obtained by swapping the players' roles and objectives. It is now a safety game in which Player 0 is supposed to stay away from node b. Now Player 1 can use the same strategy of moving to the right in order to win this game.

The following lemma states that the concepts of reachability and safety game are in fact dual to each other. Its proof is left as Exercise 15.7.

Lemma 15.1.9. For any $\mathbf{P} \in \{0, 1\}$, Player $\mathbf{P}$ wins the reachability game $\mathcal{G} = (V, Own, E, v_I, F)$ iff Player $\overline{\mathbf{P}}$ wins the safety game $\overline{\mathcal{G}} = (V, \overline{Own}, E, v_I, V \setminus F)$. ∎

As mentioned, these classes of games can actually be seen as special parity games. The reaching of a particular set of nodes can in general not be expressed by the visitation of infinitely many nodes with certain priorities on the same arena, but with a little addition to this arena, it can.

Lemma 15.1.10. Let $\mathcal{G} = (V, \mathit{Own}, E, v_I, F)$ be a reachability game. Then we define a parity game $\mathcal{G}' = (V', \mathit{Own}', E', v_I, \Omega)$ where:

- $V' = V \cup \{v_{\mathsf{end}}\}$ for some $v_{\mathsf{end}} \notin V$,
- Own' extends Own by $\mathit{Own}'(v_{\mathsf{end}}) = 0$,
- $E' = (E \setminus \{(u, v) \mid u \in F\}) \cup \{(v_{\mathsf{end}}, v_{\mathsf{end}})\} \cup \{(u, v_{\mathsf{end}}) \mid u \in F\}$ and
- the priority function given as

$$\Omega(v) = \begin{cases} 2, & \text{if } v = v_{\mathsf{end}}, \\ 1, & \text{otherwise.} \end{cases}$$

Then for every $\mathbf{P} \in \{0, 1\}$, Player $\mathbf{P}$ wins the reachability game $\mathcal{G}$ iff Player $\mathbf{P}$ wins the parity game $\mathcal{G}'$. ∎

Proof. First we consider the case of Player 0. Suppose she has a winning strategy $\mathfrak{str}$ for $\mathcal{G}$. We will construct a strategy $\mathfrak{str}'$ for her in $\mathcal{G}'$ as

$$\mathfrak{str}'(v_0 \ldots v_n) = \begin{cases} v_{\mathsf{end}}, & \text{if } v_n \in F \cup \{v_{\mathsf{end}}\}, \\ \mathfrak{str}(v_0 \ldots v_n), & \text{otherwise.} \end{cases}$$

It should be clear that this is winning for Player 0 in $\mathcal{G}'$ because following $\mathfrak{str}$ guarantees visiting F eventually. From then on, $\mathfrak{str}'$ ensures that only nodes with priority 2 are being visited. Hence, the greatest priority seen infinitely often is even.

For the converse direction we note that any winning strategy in $\mathcal{G}'$ must ensure a visit to v_{end} because it is the only node with an even priority in the game. As this node is only reachable from nodes in F, this strategy also ensures visits to F, and it is therefore also a winning strategy for Player 0 in the reachability game $\mathcal{G}$.

The case for Player 1 is analogous. □

We remark that it is equally possible to see safety games as reachability games. This is a consequence of Lemma 15.1.5, Lemma 15.1.9 and Lemma 15.1.10. Carrying out the reduction in detail is left as Exercise 15.8.

Definition 15.1.11. A parity game $\mathcal{G} = (V, \mathit{Own}, E, v_I, \Omega)$ is called a **Büchi game** if $\Omega : V \to \{1, 2\}$. It is called a **co-Büchi game** if $\Omega : V \to \{0, 1\}$. ▽

Büchi and co-Büchi games are parity games by definition. Note that reachability and safety games are special cases of both Büchi and co-Büchi games. For instance, a reachability game is just a Büchi game with the special requirement that no edge leads from a node with priority 2 to a node with priority 1. In the presence of this requirement, one could also prioritise the nodes in a reachability game using the priorities 0 and 1 which makes it a co-Büchi game. Analogously, one can see that safety games are also special cases of Büchi and co-Büchi games. Thus, these four types of games form a hierarchy.

We also remark that Büchi and co-Büchi games are dual to each other. Using the dual-isation construction given in Lemma 15.1.4 one can easily see that the dual to a co-Büchi game is a Büchi game because lifting the priorities 0 and 1 by 1 obviously yields priorities 1 and 2. Applying this construction to a Büchi game results in a game with priorities 2 and 3. Note that the winner in a parity game is not determined by the absolute values of the priorities but only by their parities and the standard linear order on them. Subtracting (if possible) 2 from all priorities in a parity game preserves their parities and the order among them, and it therefore also preserves winning strategies, see Exercise 15.9. Thus, such a game can easily be turned into a co-Büchi game by shifting the priorities down to 0 and 1 again.

Suppose we have a co-Büchi game, i.e. a parity game in which the only priorities are 0 and 1. Suppose furthermore that no edge leads from a priority-0 node to a priority-1 node. In that case we could reassign the priorities by changing all 0's to 2's, and the game would be a Büchi game that is equivalent to the original co-Büchi game because every play in which the maximal priority occurring infinitely often is 2 corresponds to a play in the original game in which the maximal priority occurring infinitely often is 0. This is because after reaching 2 one cannot reach 1 anymore. This observation leads to the definition of a restricted class of games which can be seen as both Büchi or co-Büchi games.

Definition 15.1.12. Let $\mathcal{G} = (V, Own, E, v_I, \Omega)$ be a parity game, and $C_1, \ldots, C_m$ be the set of its strongly connected components (SCC) when seen as a directed graph. $\mathcal{G}$ is called **weak**, if, for all $i = 1, \ldots, m$ and all $v, w \in C_i$, we have $\Omega(v) = \Omega(w)$. $\vee$

Thus, in a weak parity game, or simply just weak game, all nodes of the same strongly connected component have the same priority. This is a strong restriction which makes these games very easy to solve in comparison to arbitrary parity games. In particular, the index of these parity games is irrelevant for solving them. It should be clear that weakness is indeed a restriction because there are games that are not weak, for instance the one of Example 15.1.2. It contains an SCC – all nodes apart from a – which itself contains two cycles that are winning for different players. This is clearly impossible in weak games. Hence, the priorities of this game cannot even be re-assigned to make it weak. On the other hand, suppose the edge from c to b was missing. Recall that Player 1 would not use it in his winning strategy anyway. The resulting game would still not be weak because its SCCs – now there are three of them – still contain nodes of different priorities. If, moreover, the priority of c was 3 and of d was 2, then it would be weak; and this reassignment of priorities would even preserve winning regions and strategies.

15.1.2 Attractors for Reachability Games

In this section we will introduce a concept that can be used to solve reachability games and, later on, will play an important role in solving parity games.

Definition 15.1.13. Let $\mathcal{A} = (V, Own, E)$ be a game arena, let $U \subseteq V$ be a set of nodes, and let $\mathbf{P} \in \{0, 1\}$. The **P-attractor** of U is defined as $Attr_{\mathbf{P}}(U) := \bigcup_{i=0}^{n} Attr_{\mathbf{P}}^{n}(U)$ where

$$Attr_{\mathbf{P}}^{0}(U) := U$$

$$Attr_{\mathbf{P}}^{i+1}(U) := Attr_{\mathbf{P}}^{i}(U)$$
$$\cup \{v \in V_{\mathbf{P}} \mid \text{there is } u \in Attr_{p}^{i}(U) \text{ such that } (v, u) \in E\}$$
$$\cup \{v \in V_{\overline{\mathbf{P}}} \mid \text{for all } u \in V : (v, u) \in E \text{ implies } u \in Attr_{\mathbf{P}}^{i}(U)\}.$$

Sometimes we will just call it the **attractor** of U if the player $\mathbf{P}$ is clear from the context.

∇

Intuitively, the $\mathbf{P}$-attractor of U in a game (arena) is the set of all nodes from which $\mathbf{P}$ can force the game into the set U in a finite number of steps. More precisely, the sets $Attr_{\mathbf{P}}^{i}(U)$ consist of all nodes from which player $\mathbf{P}$ has a strategy to visit a node in U in at most i many steps. This is clearly true for $i = 0$. For $i > 0$ note that $Attr_{\mathbf{P}}^{i+1}(U)$ contains all nodes which are owned by Player $\mathbf{P}$ and have a successor in $Attr_{\mathbf{P}}^{i}(U)$. Thus, Player $\mathbf{P}$ can use that edge in such a node to move into the area from which he can enforce a visit into U in at most i many steps. It also contains all nodes that belong to her opponent such that all their successor nodes are already in $Attr_{\mathbf{P}}^{i}(U)$. Thus, the opponent has no choice but to move into this region in one step which means that Player $\mathbf{P}$ can enforce this visit by letting the opponent make the first step.

Example 15.1.14. Consider the following game.

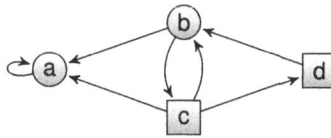

We are interested in the attractor of the set of nodes $\{a\}$ for Player 0. Clearly, we have $Attr_{0}^{0}(\{a\}) = \{a\}$. Then Player 0 can force a visit to a in one step from b and a itself, thus $Attr_{0}^{1}(\{a\}) = \{a, b\}$. Note that c does not belong to $Attr_{0}^{1}(\{a\})$ because it is controlled by Player 1 who can move to a node outside of $Attr_{0}^{0}(\{a\})$. Then d belongs to $Attr_{0}^{2}(\{a\})$ because all its outgoing edges – of which there is only one – end in $Attr_{0}^{1}(\{a\})$. Thus, we have $Attr_{0}^{2}(\{a\}) = \{a, b, d\}$, and therefore we have c $\in Attr_{0}^{3}(\{a\})$, because all its successors in the game graph belong to $Attr_{0}^{2}(\{a\})$. So, the attractor of $\{a\}$ for Player 0 in this game consists of all nodes, meaning that she can enforce a visit to node a from any other node in this game. Her 'attractor strategy' (see definition further) requires her to choose the edge to a from b and nothing else.

It is not too difficult to turn the definition of an attractor into an algorithm that computes the attractor for some player and a given set of nodes. One can use a form of breadth-first search starting from U and successively adding nodes that satisfy the condition in the

---

Algorithm 10 Computing the attractor of a region in a game arena.

```
 1: procedure COMPUTEATTR(P,(V, Own, E), U)                              ▷ U ⊆ V
 2:     A ← U
 3:     W ← E ∩ {(v, u) | u ∈ U}
 4:     str ← []
 5:     while W ≠ ∅ do
 6:         remove some (v, w) from W
 7:         if v ∈ V_P then
 8:             A ← A ∪ {v}
 9:             str ← str[v ↦ w]
10:             E ← E \ {(v, u) | u ∈ V}
11:             W ← W ∪ {(u, v) | u ∈ V, (u, v) ∈ E}
12:         else
13:             E ← E \ {(v, w)}
14:             if E(v) = ∅ then
15:                 A ← A ∪ {v}
16:                 W ← W ∪ {(u, v) | u ∈ V, (u, v) ∈ E}
17:             end if
18:         end if
19:     end while
20:     return (A, str)
21: end procedure
```

---

definition of an attractor. This may not lead to an optimal algorithm because, once a node v has been found to belong to the **P**-attractor, one needs to inspect its predecessors. Those that are owned by **P** also belong to them and can equally be marked. However, those that belong to the opponent are more difficult to process because they can only be marked once *all* their successors belong to the **P**-attractor. A naïve approach would be to re-schedule them for later consideration. However, this would result in a nonoptimal running time.

Instead we can focus the attractor computation on the set of edges in the arena. This is what Algorithm 10 does. It maintains a set A in which it collects the nodes that belong to the **P**-attractor of U and a (partial) function str which is used to compute a memoryless strategy for Player **P** which enforces the visit to the target set U – the so-called **attractor strategy**. It also maintains a worklist W of edges which are still to be inspected.

Theorem 15.1.15. Given a game arena (V, Own, E), a player $\mathbf{P} \in \{0, 1\}$ and a set of nodes $U \subseteq V$, Algorithm 10 computes $Attr_{\mathbf{P}}(U)$ and a corresponding attractor strategy in time $\mathcal{O}(\mathrm{card}(E))$.   ∎

Proof. The claim about the running time is easily verified. Note that each edge of the game arena is processed at most twice: it can be added to the worklist, and then it gets removed from the worklist and the game arena. The rest only consists of maintaining the information about which nodes belong to the attractor and what is the attractor strategy. This can be done in constant time.

Soundness – every node returned by the algorithm lies in the attractor – and completeness – every node in the attractor is found by the algorithm – of the computation is also not hard to verify. By induction on i it is possible to show that every node in $Attr_{\mathbf{P}}^{i}(U)$ will be added to the set A eventually. Thus, the algorithm is complete. Soundness can be shown by inspecting the circumstances under which a node gets added to the set A. Either it belongs to U, in which case it is clearly in the attractor, or it is owned by Player $\mathbf{P}$ and gets added in line 9, in which case it again belongs to the attractor. Finally, it can get added in line 16 when it belongs to Player $\mathbf{P}$'s opponent and has no successors at this point in the run. This is only possible if all outgoing edges have been removed, and only those edges are removed which point to a node that is in the attractor already. Thus, the node that is added in line 16 also belongs to the attractor. $\qquad\Box$

We conclude this section with two observations about attractors in parity games.

Lemma 15.1.16. Let $\mathcal{G} = (V, Own, E, \Omega)$ be a parity game, $\mathbf{P} \in \{0, 1\}$ and let $W \subseteq V$ be a set of nodes such that Player $\mathbf{P}$ has a winning strategy for the game starting in any $v \in W$. Then he also has a winning strategy for the game starting in any $v \in Attr_{\mathbf{P}}(W)$. $\qquad\blacksquare$

Proof. Suppose $\mathfrak{str}_{\mathsf{par}}$ is the strategy that allows him to win the parity game from any node in W, and $\mathfrak{str}_{\mathsf{attr}}$ is the strategy that allows him to enforce a visit to W from any node in $Attr_{\mathbf{P}}(W)$. W.l.o.g. we can assume $\mathfrak{str}_{\mathsf{attr}}$ to be memoryless. Consider the strategy $\mathfrak{str}$ which acts like $\mathfrak{str}_{\mathsf{par}}$ whenever that is defined. On all other sequences $v_0, \ldots, v_n$ with $v_n \in Attr_{\mathbf{P}}(W)$ it maps to $\mathfrak{str}_{\mathsf{attr}}(v_n)$. Thus, it enforces Player $\mathbf{P}$ to play according to $\mathfrak{str}_{\mathsf{par}}$ if possible, and in the attractor region play in order to reach W. This is a winning strategy for Player $\mathbf{P}$ because any play that conforms to this strategy has a suffix which is a play conforming to $\mathfrak{str}_{\mathsf{par}}$. Note that the maximal priority occurring infinitely often in this play and in its suffix are the same because a sequence can differ from its suffixes by finitely many elements only. $\qquad\Box$

Lemma 15.1.17. Let $\mathcal{A} = (V, Own, E)$ be a game arena, $W \subseteq V$ and $\mathbf{P} \in \{0, 1\}$. Let $V' = V \setminus Attr_{\mathbf{P}}(W)$. If $V' \neq \emptyset$ then $\mathcal{A}' = (V', Own, E \cap V' \times V')$ is a game arena as well. $\qquad\blacksquare$

Proof. This claim is verified by recalling the weak requirement for being an arena: the lemma simply states that removing the attractor of some region does not leave any dead-ends, i.e. nodes without successors. Suppose $\mathcal{A}'$ did contain such a node v, whereas in $\mathcal{A}$ it was no dead-end. Then all its successors must have been removed, but only elements of $Attr_{\mathbf{P}}(W)$ are being removed. Thus, all its successors belong to $Attr_{\mathbf{P}}(W)$ in which case it must belong to the attractor, too. $\qquad\Box$

Further we will consider games that result from the removal of an attractor region. Suppose $\mathcal{G}$ is a game, and A is some player's attractor for some set of states in this game. We will simply write $\mathcal{G} \setminus A$ for the game that is obtained from $\mathcal{G}$ by removing all nodes in A as well as all edges leading into or out of A.

15.1.3 Weak Parity Games

Theorem 15.1.18. Weak parity games with n nodes and e edges can be solved in time $\mathcal{O}(n \cdot e)$. ∎

Proof. According to Lemma 3.2.6, the SCC decomposition of a directed graph with e edges can be done in time $\mathcal{O}(e)$ (assuming that there are no more nodes than edges). Now consider any terminal SCC in their topological order, i.e. one which does not have any edge that lead out of this SCC. Recall that, since the game is weak, all nodes in this SCC have the same priority, in particular the same parity. Thus, we can call these SCCs even or odd, depending on the common parity of their nodes' priorities.

Reaching any node in an even terminal SCC is winning for Player 0 because any play that does so will eventually only visit even priorities. Thus, the greatest that is seen infinitely often must be even. The same holds for Player 1 and odd priorities. Thus, we can compute the 0-attractor of the set of all even terminal SCCs which is part of Player 0's winning region. Equally, we can compute the 1-attractor of the set of all odd terminal SCCSs which is winning for Player 1. Computing and removing attractors can be done in time $\mathcal{O}(e)$. The result is a smaller parity game which is clearly still weak. This can be solved recursively. The number of recursive steps is bounded by n because in each step at least one node must be removed and every finite graph has a terminal SCC. □

Note that the SCC decomposition computed at the beginning cannot be reused because removing attractors might remove edges from SCCs because of which they may not be strongly connected anymore. On the other hand, the SCC decomposition in the next recursive call will always be a refinement of the previous one. Thus, it is possible to decompose each old SCC separately which may be more efficient in practice.

15.1.4 Memoryless Determinacy

In this section we will prove two important results about parity games: first, they are determined, i.e. in each game exactly one player has a winning strategy. Secondly, if a player has a winning strategy then she has a memoryless winning strategy. It is possible to prove both results together, and this can even be done in a way that an algorithm for solving parity games can be extracted from this proof. On the slight downside, this proof cannot cope with the format we have introduced, namely that a game has a designated starting node. The proof uses induction on the number of priorities and number of nodes. Thus, the hypothesis must be strengthened in order to allow the game to be started in any node of the game. We will distinguish these two slightly different approaches to game solving by calling them global and local, respectively.

Definition 15.1.19. We will refer to the problem of solving a parity game $\mathcal{G} = (V, Own, E, v_I, \Omega)$ with a designated starting node as the **local parity game problem**. Thus, a solution for it is a computation of the winner plus possibly a winning strategy for that player when starting in v_I. Respectively, the **global parity game problem** asks for the winners and their corresponding winning strategies for all nodes in the game taken as starting nodes. In that case, we consider a parity game to be just a tuple (V, Own, E, Ω), i.e. without a designated starting node. ▽

It is not difficult to see that there is no essential difference between global and local solving. Clearly, any algorithm that solves parity games globally can also be used to solve the local parity game problem by simple disregarding its output for all but the designated starting node. On the other hand, any local algorithm can be used n times on a parity game with n nodes in order to solve it globally. This is clear as far as only the decision problem of solving the game is concerned. The computation problem which also asks for a winning strategy may raise further question regarding the well-definedness of the global solving problem. Suppose that a player wins from more than one node. Then there may be two winning strategies, depending on which node the game is started in. We will show that in such cases there is also a *global winning strategy*, i.e. a single strategy which is winning for all the nodes that this player can win from. We will prove this in a slightly more restricted form, namely for memoryless strategies only. This is not an essential restriction because, as we will see soon, one can always restrict attention to memoryless winning strategies in parity games.

Lemma 15.1.20. Let $\mathcal{G} = (V, Own, E, \Omega)$ be a parity game and $v_1, \ldots, v_k$ be nodes in this game such that, for each $\mathbf{P} \in \{0, 1\}$, Player $\mathbf{P}$ wins the game starting in v_i with some memoryless strategy $\mathfrak{str}_i$ for $i = 1, \ldots, k$. Then there is also a memoryless strategy $\mathfrak{str}$ which is winning for Player $\mathbf{P}$ for all nodes $v_1, \ldots, v_k$. ■

Proof. For $i = 1, \ldots, k$ we define $R_i \subseteq V$ to be the set of all nodes which can be reached in a play starting in v_i that conforms to strategy $\mathfrak{str}_i$. It is the least set that contains v_i and satisfies the following two conditions.

- For all $v \in V_\mathbf{P} \cap R_i$ we have $\mathfrak{str}_i(v) \in R_i$.
- For all $v \in V_{\overline{\mathbf{P}}} \cap R_i$ we have $E(v) \subseteq R_i$.

It is easy to see that Player $\mathbf{P}$ wins the parity game starting in any node $v \in R_i$ with strategy $\mathfrak{str}_i$ because no winning strategy can take a player out of their winning region. Note that $R_1, \ldots, R_k$ can be arbitrary subsets of V that need not be disjoint. We define a partial memoryless strategy $\mathfrak{str}$ for player $\mathbf{P}$ as $\mathfrak{str}(v) := \mathfrak{str}_i(v)$ where i is least such that $v \in R_i$. It remains to be seen that it is winning for Player $\mathbf{P}$ on all $v_1, \ldots, v_k$. We will show that it is in fact winning for player $\mathbf{P}$ on $R := \bigcup_{i=1}^k R_i$ which is clearly stronger. Note that $\mathfrak{str}$ is not defined on nodes outside of R. This is not a problem though, because we have $v_i \in R$ for all $i = 1, \ldots, n$, and we are only interested in a strategy that is winning for Player $\mathbf{P}$ on all these v_i.

Let $v \in R$ and $\mathfrak{str}'$ be an arbitrary strategy for Player $\overline{\mathbf{P}}$. We will show that $\mathfrak{str}$ wins against this arbitrary strategy. Consider the unique play $\lambda_0 = u_0, u_1, \ldots$ that results from the interaction between $\mathfrak{str}$ and $\mathfrak{str}'$. For each $j \geq 0$ let i_j be such that $\mathfrak{str}$ lets Player $\mathbf{P}$ make a choice according to strategy i_j in node u_j if $u_j \in V_{\mathbf{P}}$. Note that we have $i_0 \geq i_1 \geq i_2 \geq \ldots$ because $\mathfrak{str}$ starts with some strategy $\mathfrak{str}_{i_0}$ such that i_0 is least with $u_0 \in R_{i_0}$. It then proceeds like that strategy unless it reaches some node which belongs to some R_{i_1} with $i_1 < i_0$ in which case it follows strategy $\mathfrak{str}_{i_1}$. Since only finitely many strategies are considered, there must be some $m \in \{1, \ldots, k\}$ and some $n \in \mathbb{N}$ such that $u_j \in R_{i_m}$ for all $j \geq n$. Thus, the play $\lambda_n = u_n, u_{n+1}, \ldots$ conforms to strategy $\mathfrak{str}_m$ and therefore the greatest priority occurring infinitely often in it is even if $\mathbf{P} = 0$, respectively odd if $\mathbf{P} = 1$. Since λ_n is a suffix of λ_0 and therefore, λ_0 contains only finitely many more nodes than λ_n, the winner of λ_0 must be the same as that of λ_n, namely player $\mathbf{P}$. Thus, $\mathfrak{str}$ is indeed winning for Player $\mathbf{P}$. $\quad\square$

The important consequence of this lemma to remember is that we can restrict our attention to two strategies in a finite parity game: one for each player, regardless of the starting node. We invite the reader to ponder over the case of parity games of infinite size using the Axiom of Choice. We will mostly be concerned with games of finite size. The next theorem states memoryless determinacy in the context of global game solving.

Theorem 15.1.21. Let $\mathcal{G} = (V, \mathit{Own}, E, \Omega)$ be a parity game. Then there are two sets $W_0, W_1 \subseteq V$ and two memoryless strategies $\mathfrak{str}_0, \mathfrak{str}_1$ such that

- $W_0 \cap W_1 = \emptyset$ and $W_0 \cup W_1 = V$; and
- for each $\mathbf{P} \in \{0, 1\}$, the strategy $\mathfrak{str}_{\mathbf{P}}$ is winning for Player $\mathbf{P}$ in the game $\mathcal{G}$ started in any node $v \in W_{\mathbf{P}}$. $\quad\blacksquare$

Proof. We will prove this by induction on the number of priorities occurring in $\mathcal{G}$. The base case is quite trivial. Suppose there is only one priority occurring in $\mathcal{G}$. If it is even then let $W_0 = V$ and $W_1 = \emptyset$, otherwise swap them around. Let $\mathfrak{str}_0, \mathfrak{str}_1$ be arbitrary memoryless strategies. Clearly, Player 0 wins with an arbitrary strategy from any node in a parity game in which no other priority but an even one occurs; the same goes for Player 1 and odd priorities.

Now, suppose that the number of priorities in $\mathcal{G}$ is $k > 1$, and let n be the highest among them. We need to consider two cases depending on whether n is even or odd. These are entirely dual, though. Thus, we will only consider the case of n being even, while the other is dealt with by swapping the players, the parities, etc. Define W_1 to be the set of all nodes on which Player 1 has a memoryless strategy. According to Lemma 15.1.20 there is a memoryless strategy $\mathfrak{str}_1$ with which Player 1 wins from all nodes in W_1. According to Lemma 15.1.16 we have $\mathit{Attr}_1(W_1) \subseteq W_1$. On the other hand, we clearly have $W_1 \subseteq \mathit{Attr}_1(W_1)$, and according to Lemma 15.1.17, the game $\mathcal{G}'$ which is obtained from $\mathcal{G}$ by removing W_1 is still a parity game. We will show that Player 0 has a memoryless winning strategy $\mathfrak{str}_0$ for all nodes in $W_0 := V \setminus W_1$. There are two cases to consider.

(1) Suppose that $\mathcal{G} \setminus W_1$ does not contain any node with priority n, i.e. all nodes with the highest priority in $\mathcal{G}$ fall into W_1. Then $\mathcal{G} \setminus W_1$ is a parity game whose highest priority is less than n. The induction hypothesis yields a partitioning into winning regions W_0' and W_1' for the two players, as well as memoryless winning strategies $\mathfrak{str}_0'$ and $\mathfrak{str}_1'$. Now we must have $W_1' = \emptyset$, for if Player 1 had a memoryless winning strategy for the game $\mathcal{G} \setminus W_1$ starting in some node v then this would also be a memoryless winning strategy for him/her in the game $\mathcal{G}$. Thus, v would belong to W_1 by assumption and would therefore not be in $\mathcal{G} \setminus W_1$. If W_1' is empty then $\mathfrak{str}_1'$ is vacuous, and we can simply choose W_0 and $\mathfrak{str}_0$ as W_0' and $\mathfrak{str}_0'$.

(2) Let $N := \{v \in V \setminus W_1 \mid \Omega(v) = n\}$. In this case we assume that $N \neq \emptyset$. Let $A := Attr_0(N)$, and $\mathfrak{str}_0''$ be a corresponding strategy for Player 0 to move into N from anywhere in A. Since it is an attractor strategy it can be assumed to be memoryless. Now consider the game $\mathcal{G}' := (\mathcal{G} \setminus W_1) \setminus A$. Again, this is a parity game in which the highest priority is less than n, and by the induction hypothesis it can be partitioned into winning regions W_0' and W_1' for the two players with corresponding memoryless winning strategies $\mathfrak{str}_0'$ and $\mathfrak{str}_1'$.

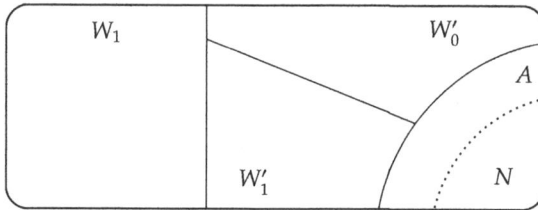

Again, W_1' would also be a winning region for Player 1 in the larger game $\mathcal{G}$ because Player 0 cannot force a play into A or W_0' from W_1'. Thus, by assumption, W_1' is empty because any node in it would have been included in W_1 already.

Note there there is no edge from a player-1-node in A into W_1, and for every player-0-node in A there must be an edge that does not lead into W_1. This gives Player 0 a memoryless winning strategy on W_0' and A: when in W_0', play according to the memoryless strategy $\mathfrak{str}_0'$; when in A, play according to the attractor strategy $\mathfrak{str}_0''$. Thus, let $W_0 := W_0' \cup A$ and $\mathfrak{str}_0 := \mathfrak{str}_0' \cup \mathfrak{str}_0''$. It remains to be seen that $\mathfrak{str}_0$ is indeed a memoryless winning strategy on W_0. Clearly, it is memoryless because it is obtained as the union of two memoryless strategies on two disjoint parts of the game $\mathcal{G} \setminus W_1$. Consider any play that conforms to $\mathfrak{str}_0$. It will either be trapped in W_0', in which case it has a suffix that conforms to Player 0's winning strategy $\mathfrak{str}_0'$, or it visits A infinitely often, in which case it visits N infinitely often, too. In both cases the highest priority occurring infinitely often in this play is even, and therefore it is winning for Player 0. $\qquad\square$

15.1.5 An Algorithm for Parity Games

Theorem 15.1.21 claims the existence of winning regions and memoryless winning strategies in parity games but its proof cannot directly be used as an algorithm for computing

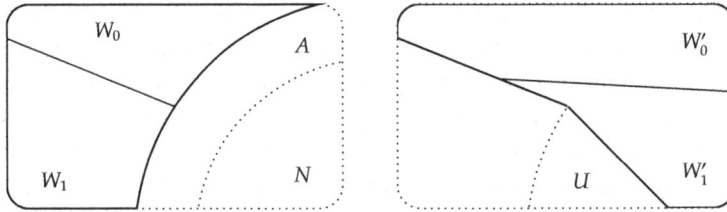

Figure 15.1 Recursive solving of parity games.

them. This is because it is not constructive: it assumes that Player 1's winning region W_1 is given and only shows that the rest is a winning region for Player 0. An algorithm for computing winning regions and strategies would have to construct W_0 and W_1 and could not rely on the assumption that W_1 was given already. Nevertheless, it is possible to design an algorithm for solving parity games that uses the same principles as used in the proof of Theorem 15.1.21. The computation of W_1 can be achieved by using two recursive calls as opposed to the one use of the induction hypothesis in each case of the aforementioned proof.

Here, the recursion uses both the number of priorities and the number of nodes as a decreasing parameter in order to guarantee termination. Clearly, an empty game can easily be partitioned into the (empty) winning regions using (empty) winning strategies. Also, if there is a single priority for all nodes in the game then the parity of that priority determines the winner for the entire game, and an arbitrary memoryless strategy is winning for her.

So suppose that a game $\mathcal{G}$ has nodes of at least two different priorities. Let n be the maximal among them. Again, we assume n to be even, while the case of an odd n is handled in the same way, the roles of the players just have to be swapped. First let N be the set of all nodes of priority n, and let A be the 0-attractor of that set with an attractor strategy $\mathfrak{str}_A$. Consider the game $\mathcal{G} \setminus A$. According to Lemma 15.1.17 it is still a parity game, and clearly its maximal priority is strictly less than n because $N \subseteq A$. We can solve this game recursively and obtain a partitioning of its set of nodes into winning regions W_0 and W_1 with suitable memoryless strategies $\mathfrak{str}_0$ and $\mathfrak{str}_1$ for the two players. The situation is depicted on the left side of Figure 15.1.

If W_1 is empty then Player 0 can win on $W_0 \cup A$ which is the entire node set of $\mathcal{G}$: on W_0 she uses the strategy $\mathfrak{str}_0$, and on A she uses the attractor strategy $\mathfrak{str}_A$. Note that the latter can only guarantee a single visit to N, and in N she either moves into W_0 or into A again. In any case, this can only cause plays which are won by Player 0 either because $\mathfrak{str}_0$ is a winning strategy or a node in N is visited infinitely often which must be with the largest priority in this play.

However, if $W_1 \neq \emptyset$ then using the attractor strategy $\mathfrak{str}_A$ may be fatal for Player 0 because it does not guarantee anything good to happen once N has been reached. It could be the case that all successors of nodes in N lie in W_1. We therefore need to check whether

Player 1's winning strategy $\mathfrak{str}_1$ for the game $\mathcal{G} \setminus A$, which takes him/her into W_1, is winning on further nodes in the larger game $\mathcal{G}$. We therefore compute the 1-attractor of W_1 in $\mathcal{G}$ and call it U, together with the corresponding attractor strategy $\mathfrak{str}_U$. Note that the attractor can intersect with A but not with W_0. Again, $\mathcal{G} \setminus U$ is a parity game according to Lemma 15.1.17. It may contain the highest priority n, but it is certainly smaller than $\mathcal{G}$ because of $\emptyset \neq W_1 \subseteq U$. Thus, we can solve this recursively, as well, and obtain winning regions W_0' and W_1' as well as memoryless winning strategies $\mathfrak{str}_0'$ and $\mathfrak{str}_1'$ for the two players. The situation is depicted on the right side of Figure 15.1.

Finally, we need to convince ourselves that we have solved the entire game $\mathcal{G}$. Clearly, Player 1 wins in U by playing his attractor strategy into W_1 and then using his memoryless strategy $\mathfrak{str}_1$ there. It is winning on W_1 in $\mathcal{G} \setminus A$, but he cannot be forced into A. Thus, it is winning on W_1 in $\mathcal{G}$, as well. The combination of this strategy with the attractor strategy $\mathfrak{str}_U$ is therefore winning on U. On the other hand, Player 1 wins on W_1' in $\mathcal{G} \setminus U$ with strategy $\mathfrak{str}_1'$. This must be winning in $\mathcal{G}$, as well, and therefore the combination of $\mathfrak{str}_1$, $\mathfrak{str}_U$ and $\mathfrak{str}_1'$ is a memoryless winning strategy for Player 1 on $U \cup W_1'$.

On the other hand, Player 0 has a memoryless strategy on the remaining part of the game, viz. W_0'. Note that it contains W_0 because adding parts of the 0-attractor A cannot make Player 1 the winner of a node from W_0 in the game $\mathcal{G} \setminus A$. The computed strategy $\mathfrak{str}_0'$ thus suffices as a winning strategy in the entire game $\mathcal{G}$.

This procedure can straightforwardly be implemented as a recursive algorithm for solving parity games. Its pseudo-code is given as Algorithm 11.

Theorem 15.1.22. Algorithm 11 solves parity games with n nodes and m edges in time $\mathcal{O}(m \cdot 2^n)$. ∎

Proof. Its correctness and termination has been argued. We therefore only consider its worst-case runtime. We note that the effort spent in every recursive call – i.e. attractor computations as well as merging memoryless winning strategies and winning regions – requires no more than time $\mathcal{O}(m)$. Starting with a parity game of n nodes, the two recursive descends use parity games of smaller size. Thus, there can be at most $2^{n+1} - 1$ many recursive calls altogether which results in an overall runtime of $\mathcal{O}(m \cdot 2^n)$. □

We remark that in practice, the runtime also depends on the number k of different priorities present in the game. Note that the recursive descend stops as soon as either n equals 0 or k equals 1. Since there cannot be more priorities than nodes, we always have $n \geq k$. This is why not every branch of the recursion tree must have length n.

The complexity result given in Theorem 15.1.22 is not optimal. It is possible to solve parity games in time that is polynomial in the number of nodes but exponential in the number of priorities in the game. We will achieve this by examining the connection between parity games and model checking the modal μ-calculus in Section 15.3.1.

Algorithm 11 Solving parity games recursively.

1: **procedure** SOLVE($\mathcal{G} = (V, Own, E, v_I, \Omega)$)
2:      **if** $V = \emptyset$ **then**
3:          **return** $(\emptyset, \emptyset, [], [])$
4:      **end if**
5:      $n \leftarrow \max\{\Omega(v) \mid v \in V\}$
6:      **if** $n = 0$ **then**
7:          **let** $\mathfrak{str}$ be an arbitrary memoryless strategy for Player 0
8:          **return** $(V, \emptyset, \mathfrak{str}, [])$
9:      **else**   ▷ assume n to be even, otherwise swap players
10:          $N \leftarrow \{v \in V \mid \Omega(v) = n\}$
11:          $(A, \mathfrak{str}_A) \leftarrow$ COMPUTEATTR$(0, (V, Own, E), N)$
12:          $(W_0, W_1, \mathfrak{str}_0, \mathfrak{str}_1) \leftarrow$ SOLVE$(\mathcal{G} \setminus A)$
13:          **if** $W_1 = \emptyset$ **then**
14:              **return** $(W_0 \cup A, \emptyset, \mathfrak{str}_0 \cup \mathfrak{str}_A, [])$
15:          **end if**
16:          $(U, \mathfrak{str}_U) \leftarrow Attr_1(W_1)$
17:          $(W'_0, W'_1, \mathfrak{str}'_0, \mathfrak{str}'_1) \leftarrow$ SOLVE$(\mathcal{G} \setminus U)$
18:          **return** $(W'_0, W'_1 \cup U, \mathfrak{str}'_0, \mathfrak{str}_1 \cup \mathfrak{str}'_1 \cup \mathfrak{str}_U)$
19:      **end if**
20: **end procedure**

15.1.6 One-Player Games

At the end of this section we consider a special case, so-called 1-player games. We restrict our attention to parity games.

Definition 15.1.23. A parity game $\mathcal{G} = (V, Own, E, v_I, \Omega)$ is called a **1-player parity game**, or simply **1-player game**, if $Own(v) = Own(w)$ for all $v, w \in V$. ∇

The fact that one player never has a move in a game makes it very easy to solve.

Theorem 15.1.24. 1-player games can be solved in NLOGSPACE.   ∎

Proof. Suppose $\mathcal{G} = (V, Own, E, v_I, \Omega)$ is a 1-player game with $Own(v) = 0$ for every $v \in V$. It should be clear that Player 0 has a winning strategy for $\mathcal{G}$ iff there is a node v that is reachable from v_I and such that:

- $\Omega(v)$ is even,
- and v is reachable from v on a path of length ≥ 1 on which no node has a priority that is larger than $\Omega(v)$.

If this is the case, then Player 0's winning strategy consists of moving to that node v and from v back to itself. The greatest priority seen infinitely often in this play is the one of v, which is even. Conversely, if Player 0 has a winning strategy then this induces a single play, because Player 1 has nothing to choose. Since there are only finitely many different nodes, this play must contain one node that is seen infinitely often and whose priority is even and maximal in this play.

Finally, reachability can be checked in NLOGSPACE as shown in Theorem 3.2.2. □

15.1.7 The Main Reduction Theorem

In this section we will prove an important result that we will use later, when we give game-theoretic characterisations of the model checking and satisfiability-checking problems for various temporal logics. Intuitively, it says that we only need to consider parity games, even though there are other classes of games with winning conditions which are not parity conditions. However, for as long as the winning condition is **regular**, in the sense of Definition 2.2.16, it can be reduced to a parity game. This reduction comes at a price, though.

It is possible to relax the definition. For instance, it is known from Büchi's Theorem that the class of ω-regular languages is closed under complements. Thus, instead of requiring that the winning condition for Player 0 is ω-regular, one can equally do so for Player 1. This may come in handy when one considers the way that these languages should be represented. We will use nondeterministic Büchi automata (NBA) as the standard representation tool for the winning conditions in regular games. Sometimes, it is easier to come up with an NBA for the complement of some language than for the language itself. Thus, it may be easier to see a game as being regular from Player 1's point of view. We will also consider special cases, for instance when the winning condition can be recognised by a co-Büchi automaton or a weak parity automaton. Note that the co-Büchi recognisable languages are properly included in the regular languages. (Recall that parity and co-Büchi acceptance conditions are provided in Definition 14.3.6 whereas weak parity automata are introduced in Definition 14.3.13. Also note that in this chapter we use a slightly different presentation of co-Büchi automata with an acceptance component F such that nodes in $Q \setminus F$ (rather than F itself as used in the previous chapter) must not be seen infinitely often. This is not an essential difference, though.)

Furthermore, it is also known that the class of ω-regular languages is closed under (inverse) homomorphisms. This will allow us to consider winning conditions that are formulated more abstractly and not precisely in terms of the occurrences of single nodes. The parity winning condition is an example of that. It can be given as an ω-regular language over the alphabet of priorities which is the image of a homomorphism from the set of nodes in the game. We will use specialised symbolic representations of game rules that we consider to be the alphabet underlying the formal languages of winning conditions.

We will define model checking and satisfiability-checking games in a rule-based way. These rules explain which edges are present in a game. We therefore consider the taking of such an edge in a play as the application of a rule, as well.

Definition 15.1.25. Let $\mathcal{G} = (V, \mathit{Own}, E, v_I, \mathit{Win})$ be a game. Let R be a finite set of **'symbolic rules'**. Intuitively, R is just a set of names which is used to represent moves from one node to another in $\mathcal{G}$. A **symbolic representation of the game rules** is a function $\mathfrak{f} : E \to R$ which associated every edge in the game with a symbolic rule name.

The symbolic representation of a play $\lambda = v_0, v_1, \ldots$ is the sequence $\mathfrak{f}(\lambda) = \mathfrak{f}(v_0, v_1), \mathfrak{f}(v_1, v_2), \ldots$ Let $\mathfrak{f}(Win)$ denote the set of all symbolically represented winning plays for Player 0.

We will only consider symbolic representations that are 'faithful', in the sense that $\lambda \in Win$ iff $\lambda' \in Win$ whenever $\mathfrak{f}(\lambda) = \mathfrak{f}(\lambda')$.

We say that the winning condition is **regular** or **Büchi-recognisable**, respectively **co-Büchi-recognisable** under $\mathfrak{f}$, if there is a nondeterministic Büchi, respectively co-Büchi, automaton $\mathcal{A}$ over the alphabet R such that $L(\mathcal{A}) = \mathfrak{f}(Win)$. We will often assume that $\mathfrak{f}$ is clear from the context and simply say that the winning condition is regular for instance.

$\triangledown$

Note that this definition generalises the case in which the winning condition can be recognised by a finite automaton directly, when $R = E$ and $\mathfrak{f}$ is the identity function. Using proper symbolic encodings where R is much smaller than E can result in smaller automata and better complexity bounds.

The key idea for the reduction from abstract games to parity games is simple: suppose the winning condition for some abstract game $\mathcal{G}$ can be recognised by a finite automaton $\mathcal{A}$ with some acceptance condition, like the Büchi condition. We consider a second game which is obtained as the product of $\mathcal{G}$ and $\mathcal{A}$. Intuitively, we let the players 0 and 1 play the original game and at the same time we follow the plays that they produce with the automaton $\mathcal{A}$. Now its acceptance condition should become the new winning condition because with this condition it signals whether a resulting play was won by Player 0. This idea has a slight flaw, though, as shown in the following example.

Example 15.1.26. Consider the game $\mathcal{G}$ with its arena and a symbolic encoding of the game moves into the set $R = \{a, b, c\}$ depicted on the left as follows.

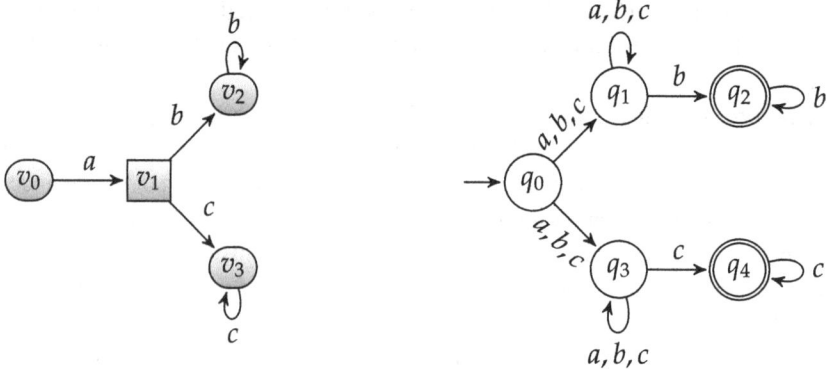

The starting node of $\mathcal{G}$ is v_0. Suppose that the winning condition of Player 0 is $R^+ b^\omega \cup R^+ c^\omega$, which is recognised by the Büchi automaton on the right. It should be clear that Player 0 wins $\mathcal{G}$. The product game $\mathcal{G}'$ is

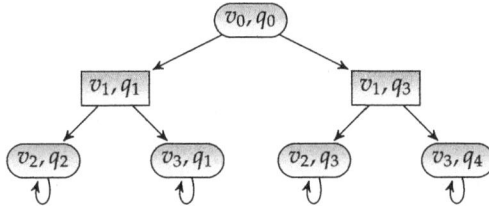

with its winning condition inherited from the NBA's acceptance condition: Player 0 wins a play if it gets trapped in a state whose automaton state component is accepting, i.e. either node (v_2, q_2) or node (v_3, q_4). It should be clear that player 1 wins $\mathcal{G}'$.

The problem which causes this simple reduction to fail is nondeterminism. At any moment in a game the choices of Player 1 may determine which play is actually going to be constructed in the limit. Suppose that all of them are being accepted by a nondeterministic automaton. Then Player 0 should win. However, this automaton may have different accepting runs for these plays and it may be necessary to choose some branching in the automaton at a moment *before* some branching in the game occurs. This will cause winning plays for Player 1 in the product game that he can enforce and which simply correspond to the product of a play in the original game and some nonaccepting run on it. This is of course not a sufficient condition for concluding that Player 1 can enforce a winning play for him in the original game, since there may be different accepting runs on this play as well.

The solution to this problem is *automata determinisation*, as a deterministic automaton has exactly one run per input word. This eliminated spurious choices made by Player 0 in the product game which only corresponds to branching in the automaton. We leave it as Exercise 15.12 to consider the preceding example with a deterministic automaton for this acceptance condition.

Theorem 15.1.27 (Main Reduction Theorem). Let $\mathcal{G}$ be a game with n nodes such that its winning condition is recognised by a deterministic parity automaton with m states and index k. Then there is a parity game $\mathcal{G}'$ with at most $n \cdot m$ nodes and index k that is won by Player 0 iff $\mathcal{G}$ is won by Player 0. ∎

Proof. Let $\mathcal{G} = (V, Own, E, v_I, Win)$ be a game, $\mathfrak{f}$ a symbolic rule representation over some set of names R and $\mathcal{A} = (Q, R, q_I, \delta, \Omega)$ a deterministic parity automaton recognising $\mathfrak{f}(Win)$. Consider the parity game $\mathcal{G}' = (V \times Q, Own', E', (v_I, q_I), \Omega')$ such that for all $v, w \in V, q, q' \in Q$ we have

- $Own'(v, q) = Own(v)$,
- $((v, q), (w, q')) \in E'$ iff $(v, w) \in E$ and $q' = \delta(q, \mathfrak{f}(v, w))$,
- $\Omega'(v, q) = \Omega(q)$.

Clearly, $\mathcal{G}'$ is a parity game of size at most $\text{card}(V) \cdot \text{card}(Q)$. It remains to be seen that this construction preserves Player 0 as the winner of these games.

Suppose Player 0 has a winning strategy $\mathfrak{str}$ for $\mathcal{G}$. This induces a strategy $\mathfrak{str}'$ in $\mathcal{G}'$ as $\mathfrak{str}'((v_0, q_0), \ldots, (v_n, q_n)) = (w, \delta(q_n, \mathfrak{f}(v_n, w)))$ where $w = \mathfrak{str}(v_0, \ldots, v_n)$ and $q_0 = q_I$. Thus, in the first component she simply moves according to her strategy in $\mathcal{G}$, and this also determines what happens in the second component because $\mathcal{A}$ is deterministic. Now suppose that $(v_0, q_0), (v_1, q_1), \ldots$ conforms to $\mathfrak{str}'$. Then $\lambda = v_0, v_1, \ldots$ is a play that conforms to $\mathfrak{str}$ in $\mathcal{G}$ and it is therefore winning for Player 0. Thus, we have $\mathfrak{f}(\lambda) \in \mathfrak{f}(Win)$. Note that $q_0, q_1, \ldots$ is $\mathcal{A}'s$ unique run on $\mathfrak{f}(\lambda)$. It must be accepting, for, otherwise we would not have $L(\mathcal{A}) = \mathfrak{f}(Win)$. Then the greatest priority occurring infinitely often in the sequence $q_0, q_1, \ldots$ is even, and so is the greatest priority occurring infinitely often in λ. Thus, it is won by Player 0 which confirms that she has a winning strategy for the product game.

Now suppose that Player 0 has a winning strategy $\mathfrak{str}'$ for $\mathcal{G}'$. This induces a strategy $\mathfrak{str}$ in $\mathcal{G}$ as follows. In order to determine $\mathfrak{str}(v_0, \ldots, v_n)$, let $(w, q) = \mathfrak{str}'((v_0, q_0), \ldots, (v_n, q_n))$ where, for $i = 1, \ldots, n$ we have $q_i = \delta(q_{i-1}, \mathfrak{f}(v_{i-1}, v_i))$. Define $\mathfrak{str}(v_0, \ldots, v_n)$ to be w. Thus, this strategy consults the unique extension of its history in the product game, uses the strategy there and forgets the automaton component. In subsequent moves, this automaton component is uniquely recovered anyway when the next move is determined. Now suppose that $\lambda = v_0, v_1, \ldots$ is a play that conforms to $\mathfrak{str}$. Then it has a unique extension $(v_0, q_0), (v_1, q_1), \ldots$ which conforms to $\mathfrak{str}'$. Thus, it is winning for Player 0 there which means that its projection onto $q_0, q_1, \ldots$ is an accepting run. Since it is the unique run on λ we must have $\lambda \in L(\mathcal{A})$ which, by assumption, yields that λ is winning according to *Win*. $\qquad\square$

This result can clearly be specialised to smaller classes of games.

Corollary 15.1.28. Let $\mathcal{G}$ be a game with n nodes such that its winning condition is recognised by a deterministic co-Büchi automaton with m states. There is a co-Büchi game $\mathcal{G}'$ with at most $n \cdot m$ nodes that is won by Player 0 iff $\mathcal{G}$ is won by Player 0. $\qquad\blacksquare$

We remark that determinism in this context should be understood as having a unique run on every input word. This implies that there is *at least one* run for any input word. Thus, these automata may not reject by having no transition with which to respond to some input symbol. A product construction with such automata would result in possibly ill-formed games in which nodes have no successors.

Finally, we have a closer look at a consequence arising from the fact that parity games can always be won with memoryless strategies. Recall the concept of a finite-memory strategy, c.f. Definition 2.2.15.

Corollary 15.1.29. Let $\mathcal{G}$ be a game with n nodes such that its winning condition is recognised by a deterministic parity automaton with m states. If Player 0 has a winning strategy for $\mathcal{G}$ then she has an m-bounded winning strategy. $\qquad\blacksquare$

Proof. Suppose Player 0 has a winning strategy for $\mathcal{G}$. According to Theorem 15.1.27 she has a winning strategy for the parity game $\mathcal{G}'$ that is obtained as the product of $\mathcal{G}$ and the deterministic parity automaton for the winning condition. According to Theorem 15.1.21 she also has a memoryless strategy $\mathfrak{str}'$ for $\mathcal{G}'$. It is easy to check that the translation back into a winning strategy $\mathfrak{str}$ for $\mathcal{G}$ in the proof of Theorem 15.1.27 yields a strategy that uses no more than memory m because there are at most m different positions of the form (v, q) for every node v of the game $\mathcal{G}$. $\qquad\square$

15.2 Constructions for Automata on Infinite Words

In this section we present the construction that turns nondeterministic Büchi automata into deterministic parity automata, which is necessary in order to facilitate reductions from arbitrary regular games to parity games using the Main Reduction Theorem. We will also consider a few other constructions, for example the conceptually simpler determinisation of co-Büchi automata. This will come in handy for games whose winning conditions can be defined using co-Büchi automata. Moreover, we provide some methods that can be used in order to simplify the construction of automata for the respective winning conditions.

15.2.1 Co-Büchi Determinisation

For the remainder of this section we fix a finite automaton $\mathcal{A} = (\Sigma, Q, q_I, \delta, F)$ which accepts with the co-Büchi conditions, i.e. a word belongs to its language iff there is a run which eventually only sees accepting states from F. We will show how to construct an equivalent deterministic co-Büchi automaton $\mathcal{D}$. This uses a refined powerset construction, known as the Miyano–Hayashi, or *breakpoint construction*. It is, in fact, not new here; it is exactly the same construction as the one used to translate an alternating into a nondeterministic Büchi automaton, see Theorem 14.3.12.

First, here is an intuitive description. States in $\mathcal{D}$ are pairs of sets of states in Q. One component is used to follow *all* runs of $\mathcal{A}$ on an input word. The second component is used to trace the accepting states therein. The automaton basically operates in two modes: when there are accepting states that are being traced, then it only traces them and ignores other accepting states that may come in from nonaccepting ones in the powerset construction. When these traces have died out, i.e. there are no more runs through accepting states only that can be traced, it looks at all runs again and waits for new accepting states to be traced.

Now, here are the details. We define $\mathcal{D} = (\Sigma, 3^Q, (S_I, T_I), \delta', F')$ with its components explained as follows.

- The state set is the set of all functions from Q to a set of three possible values. We define such functions by using pairs of sets (S, T) where $T \subseteq S \subseteq Q$ as follows: for every state $q \in Q$ there are three possibilities: either it belongs to T and S, or it belongs to S but not to T, or it belongs to neither of S and T. The three possible values reflect these three cases. Hereafter we consider the states of $\mathcal{D}$ as represented by such pairs (S, T).
- The initial state is the pair (S_I, T_I) where $S_I = \{q_I\}$, and $T_I = S_I$ if $q_I \in F$ and $T_I = \emptyset$ otherwise.

- The transition function resembles the two modes mentioned earlier. For all $a \in \Sigma$ and $S \subseteq Q$ we have

$$\delta'((S, \emptyset), a) = \left(\bigcup_{q \in S} \delta(q, a), F \cap \bigcup_{q \in S} \delta(q, a) \right).$$

Moreover, if $\emptyset \neq T \subseteq S \subseteq Q$ then we have

$$\delta'((S, T), a) = \left(\bigcup_{q \in S} \delta(q, a), F \cap \bigcup_{q \in T} \delta(q, a) \right).$$

Notice that, unlike the previous case, in the second component we only continue a step of the powerset construction on T restricted to accepting states.

- The accepting states are $F' = \{(S, T) \mid T \neq \emptyset\}$.

Theorem 15.2.1. For every nondeterministic co-Büchi automaton with n states there is an equivalent deterministic co-Büchi automaton with at most 3^n states. ∎

Proof. Let $\mathcal{A}$ be the initially fixed co-Büchi automaton and let $n = \mathrm{card}(Q)$. It should be clear that the corresponding $\mathcal{D}$ defined previously is a deterministic automaton with at most 3^n states. It remains to be seen that it is equivalent to $\mathcal{A}$ when taken as a co-Büchi automaton.

For the direction $\mathrm{L}(\mathcal{A}) \subseteq \mathrm{L}(\mathcal{D})$ suppose that $\rho = q_0, q_1, \ldots$ is an accepting run of $\mathcal{A}$ on some word $w \in \Sigma^\omega$. Then there is some $k \in \mathbb{N}$ such that $q_j \in F$ for all $j \geq k$. On the other hand, consider the unique run $\rho' = (S_0, T_0), (S_1, T_1), \ldots$ of the deterministic automaton $\mathcal{D}$ on w. We must have $q_j \in S_j$ for every $j \in \mathbb{N}$. Suppose that this run was not accepting. Then we would have $T_j = \emptyset$ for infinitely many j, in particular for some j with $j \geq k$. Then $q_{k+1} \in T_{k+1}$ because $q_{k+1} \in S_{k+1}$ and whenever $T_j = \emptyset$ then $T_{j+1} = S_{j+1} \cap F$. Therefore, we must have $q_j \in T_j$ for every $j > k$ because each such q_j is a successor of q_{j-1} for the correspondingly read input symbol, and it belongs to F. This contradicts the assumption that $T_j = \emptyset$ for infinitely many j.

For the direction $\mathrm{L}(\mathcal{A}) \supseteq \mathrm{L}(\mathcal{D})$ suppose that $\rho' = (S_0, T_0), (S_1, T_1), \ldots$ is an accepting run of $\mathcal{D}$ on some $w \in \Sigma^\omega$. Then there is some $k \in \mathbb{N}$ such that $T_j \neq \emptyset$ for all $j \geq k$. Starting with some $q_k \in T_k$ it is easy to construct an infinite sequence $q_k, q_{k+1}, \ldots$ such that $q_{k+j} \in T_{k+j}$ and $q_{k+j+1} \in \delta(q_{k+j}, w(k + j))$ for every $j \in \mathbb{N}$. Note that this sequence only contains final states. It is not hard to extend this sequence to a run on w: since $T_k \subseteq S_k$ we also have $q_k \in S_k$. Now, for every $j > 1$ we have $q_j \in S_j$ only if there is some $q_{j-1} \in S_{j-1}$ with $q_j \in \delta(q_{j-1}, w(j - 1))$. This makes it possible to extend this sequence backwards to a run $q_0, q_1, \ldots$ of $\mathcal{A}$ on w. Note that $S_0 = \{q_I\}$, thus $q_0 = q_I$, and so we have $w \in \mathrm{L}(\mathcal{A})$. □

Recall that a weak parity automaton is also a co-Büchi automaton. A close inspection into the determinisation construction for the latter shows that the property of being weak is not necessarily preserved. Hence, there is no obvious way to restrict this construction to weak parity automata.

Corollary 15.2.2. For every nondeterministic weak parity automaton with n states there is an equivalent deterministic co-Büchi automaton with at most 3^n states. ∎

Sometimes the winning condition for either of the players can be decomposed into parts that may be easier to handle separately. Also it is generally advisable to avoid costly constructions like determinisation of large automata, for instance by decomposing an automaton, determinising its parts and then recomposing these to a deterministic automaton for the language of the original automaton. This may not always be possible but in the case of co-Büchi recognisable languages and a decomposition into a finite union this is possible, and helpful in handling, e.g. model-checking games for CTL* later on.

Theorem 15.2.3. Let $k \in \mathbb{N}$ and, for $i = 0, \ldots, k - 1$, let $\mathcal{A}_i$ be a deterministic co-Büchi automaton with n_i states respectively. Then there is a deterministic co-Büchi automaton with $k \cdot n_0 \cdots n_{k-1}$ many states that recognises $\bigcup_{i=0}^{k-1} \mathrm{L}(\mathcal{A}_i)$. ∎

Proof. For $i = 0, \ldots, k - 1$ let $\mathcal{A}_i = (\Sigma, Q_i, q_{0,i}, \delta_i, F_i)$. We construct a deterministic co-Büchi $\mathcal{A}$ as follows. $\mathcal{A} = (\Sigma, Q, (q_{0,0}, \ldots, q_{0,k-1}, 0), \delta, F)$ where

- $Q = Q_0 \times \ldots \times Q_{k-1} \times \{0, \ldots, k - 1\}$,
- $F = \bigcup_{i=0}^{k-1} Q_0 \times \ldots \times Q_{i-1} \times F_i \times Q_{i+1} \times \ldots \times Q_{k-1} \times \{i\}$,
- the transition relation δ is defined as

$$\delta\big((q_0, \ldots, q_{k-1}, j), \mathsf{a}\big) := (\delta_0(q_0, \mathsf{a}), \ldots, \delta_{k-1}(q_{k-1}, \mathsf{a}), j')$$

where $j' = j$ if $q_j \in F_j$ and $j' = (j + 1) \mod k$, otherwise.

The estimation on $\mathcal{A}$'s size is easy to check. In order to see correctness of this construction, note that $\mathcal{A}$ simulates all $\mathcal{A}_i$ on an input word. In its last component it signals which of them it currently checks for the visitation of accepting states. If that component leaves its acceptance set then it checks the next one in turn. Thus, a word is accepted by one of the $\mathcal{A}_i$'s iff $\mathcal{A}$ eventually stays in states in which the ith component is an accepting state of $\mathcal{A}_i$ and the signal is i, as well, for some $i \in \{0, \ldots, k - 1\}$. A detailed proof is left as Exercise 15.13. □

15.2.2 Büchi Determinisation

Finally, we provide a construction that turns a nondeterministic Büchi automaton into an equivalent deterministic parity automaton. This is different from the previous construction in the sense that the deterministic target uses an unbounded number of priorities, unlike the determinisation of co-Büchi automata which results in deterministic automata with two priorities only. In particular, Büchi automata cannot be determinised as such; there are ω-regular languages that cannot be recognised by a deterministic Büchi automaton, for instance $(\mathsf{b}^*\mathsf{a})^*\mathsf{b}^\omega$ or – using temporal logic notation – FGb. Even worse so, determinising Büchi automata is also conceptually more difficult than determinising co-Büchi automata. The construction presented here – as well as all known ones – uses macro-states with more structure than simply pairs of state sets, as in the co-Büchi determinisation. For presentation purposes we fix an NBA $\mathcal{A} = (\Sigma, Q, q_I, \delta, F)$ and let $n := \text{card}(Q)$. As usual, we use $[n]$ to denote $\{0, \dots, n-1\}$.

Definition 15.2.4. We consider finite trees of the form $T \subseteq [n]^*$ that are

- prefix-closed: if $xi \in T$ then $x \in T$ for all $x \in [n]^*$ and all $i \in [n]$,
- left-sibling closed: if $xi \in T$ and $j < i$ then $xj \in T$ for all $x \in [n]^*$ and all $i, j \in [n]$.

A **history tree** for $\mathcal{A}$ is a finite tree whose nodes are labelled with nonempty subsets of Q, such that the following properties are satisfied. We write $T(x)$ for the label of the node x in the tree T.

- The labels of siblings are disjoint: for all $x \in [n]^*$ and all $i \neq j$ in $[n]$ we have $T(xi) \cap T(xj) = \emptyset$.
- The labels of parent nodes are a proper superset of the union of all their children's labels: for all $x \in [n]^*$ we have $\bigcup \{T(xi) \mid xi \in T\} \subsetneq T(x)$. $\triangledown$

The **initial history tree** consists of its root node only, and that is labelled with $\{q_I\}$. Given a history tree, for every $\text{a} \in \Sigma$ we explain how to obtain its a-successor. This mechanism is very reminiscent of a deterministic automaton with a starting state and a unique a-successor for every state. In fact, history trees will be used as states of an automaton. At first, this will not be a parity automaton, though, but a deterministic automaton with an abstract acceptance condition which can be turned into a parity condition by keeping further information in its states. But first we focus on the construction of the deterministic device and its correctness.

Definition 15.2.5. Let T be a history tree and $\text{a} \in \Sigma$. The a-**successor** of T is the history tree T' that is obtained from T in six consecutive steps. First, let T' consist of all the nodes in T. The labels, as well as the tree structure, will gradually be changed as follows.

1. **Powerset construction.** The new label $T'(x)$ of a node $x \in T$ is the set of all a-successors of states in $T(x)$: $T'(x) := \bigcup \{\delta(q, \text{a}) \mid q \in T(x)\}$.
2. **Spawning off final states.** Add a new child xi to every node such that $xi \notin T'$ but $xj \in T'$ for every $j < i$. Thus, the new children are always rightmost siblings. Their label is obtained as the set of accepting states in their parent's label: $T'(xi) := F \cap T'(x)$, if xi is a newly created node.
3. **Horizontal clean-up.** Remove any state from the label of a node and the labels of all its descendants if it also appears in the label of a left sibling: $T'(xi) := T'(xi) \setminus \{q \mid$ there is $j < i$ such that $q \in T'(xj)\}$.
4. **Deletion of empty nodes.** Note that the second and third step can create empty labels; either by spawning off a new child for a node that does not contain accepting states, or by removing states from nodes that occur in a sibling further to the left. This violates the definition of being a history tree. Let $T' := T' \setminus \{x \mid T'(x) = \emptyset\}$.

   It is not hard to see that the previous steps preserve the history-tree invariant of labels always being a subset of the label on the parent node. Hence, if a node has an empty label then so have all its descendants which means that the removal of nodes with empty labels still results in a (history) tree.

5. **Vertical clean-up.** Remove all the descendants of every node whose label equals the union of its children's labels. Let $T' := T' \setminus \{x \mid T'(x) \subseteq \bigcup\{T'(xi) \mid i \in [n+1]\}\}$. Note that $[n+1]$ is needed here because the second step may have created an additional rightmost child for a node.

6. **Left shift.** At this point T' satisfies the two properties on the occurrences of states in the labels of a history tree, but it may not be a history tree itself because it may not be left-sibling closed due to deletions in step 4. This is repaired in this last step which moves a node xi to $x(i-1)$ if $xi \in T'$ but $x(i-1) \notin T'$ for as long as such a node exists. Clearly, the subtree under xi is moved with the node.

We are particularly interested in those nodes whose descendants are being deleted in step 5 of this procedure. We call them **successful** in the transition from T to T'. $\qquad\qquad\qquad \triangledown$

In order to explain why successful nodes are particularly interesting, we need to understand what happens in a sequence $T_0, T_1, \ldots$ of history trees on a word $w = a_0 a_1 \ldots \in \Sigma^\omega$ such that T_0 is the initial history tree and T_{i+1} is the a_i-successor of T_i for every $i \in \mathbb{N}$. First note that the labels of the root nodes of the trees in this sequence are obtained simply by ordinary power set construction. Thus, it contains every possible run of $\mathcal{A}$ on w. However, the single runs are not easily visible because the origin of a state from the previous tree is not made explicit, and even if it was, it would still not be obvious to decide whether some run of these is accepting. An accepting run however needs to visit some accepting state at some point, and from then on visit it over and over again. This is why accepting states are always spawned off in every transition.

Another important property is the following: if a state occurs in the label of some node $i_1 \ldots i_k$ then it also occurs in the labels of all nodes $i_1 \ldots i_h$ with $0 \le h < k$, i.e. in all its ancestors. Thus, children of a node trace a subset of the runs that the parent node traces.

Now consider a successful node x in some tree T_i of the sequence mentioned earlier. Its descendants were deleted because their labels were equal to the labels of all their children. However, all these children were created with labels consisting of accepting states only. Thus, each run on w that hits a state in $T_i(x)$ must have visited an accepting state beforehand. Suppose, furthermore, that x is successful over and over again. Then, between each two moments of x being successful, take any state in $T(x)$ and consider the runs on w that hit that state at that moment. All of them can be traced back to accepting states at some point after the previous moment that x was successful. Now, König's Lemma can be used to show that there must be an accepting run of $\mathcal{A}$ on w.

This informal description is based on some nontrivial assumption: we have considered a tree node x in two different history trees T_i and T_j, $j > i$ of the sequence $T_0, T_1, \ldots$ but x was actually meant to be the same node in T_i and T_j. Note that the tree structures can change in history transitions, mainly because tree nodes get shifted to the left. Thus, T_i and T_j may both contain a node x but the x in T_i may have got shifted to a position further left, and x in T_j may therefore have been newly created in between. In that case we cannot argue about tracing back runs from $T_j(x)$ to $T_i(x)$. Thus, we need another definition that makes the vague notion of 'being the same node' precise.

Definition 15.2.6. Let T be a history tree and T' be its a-successor for some a $\in \Sigma$. A node $x \in T \cap T'$ that did not get shifted in step 6 of the preceding construction is called **stable** in the transition from T to T'. $\triangledown$

It is not hard to see that a node can only be stable in a transition if its left siblings and all its ancestors are also stable in that transition.

With these two notions at hand, we can now prove the main lemmas for the soundness and completeness of the NBA determinisation procedure.

Lemma 15.2.7. Let $w = a_0 a_1 \ldots \in \Sigma^\omega$ and $T_0, T_1, \ldots$ be the corresponding sequence of history trees for $\mathcal{A}$ on w. If $w \in L(\mathcal{A})$ then there is an x that is stable in the transitions from T_i to T_{i+1} for all but finitely many i, and successful in the transitions from T_i to T_{i+1} for infinitely many i.   ∎

Proof. Suppose there is an accepting run $\rho = q_0, q_1, \ldots$ with $q_0 = q_I$ of $\mathcal{A}$ on w. We say that a tree node x of T_i hits ρ if $q_i \in T_i(x)$. Note that the root ε hits ρ in every transition and the root is eventually always stable assuming, w.l.o.g., that $\mathcal{A}$ never gets stuck. Thus, the set of nodes that are eventually always stable and eventually always hit ρ is not empty. Let x be the leftmost and furthest down among them, i.e. the minimal one with respect to the total order $\prec$ defined by $x \prec x'$ iff there are $y, z, z' \in [n]^*$ and $j, j' \in [n]$ with $j < j'$ such that $x = yjz$ and $x' = yj'z'$, or there is $z \in [n]^+$ with $x' = xz$. It remains to be shown that x is successful in infinitely many transitions.

Since ρ is accepting there are infinitely many $i_0 < i_1 < i_2 < \ldots$ such that $q_{i_j} \in F$ for all $j \in \mathbb{N}$. Hence, in the transitions from T_{i_j-1} to T_{i_j}, node x gets a new rightmost child, say xh, that contains at least q_{i_j}. Consider the appearances of $q_{i_j}, q_{i_j+1}, q_{i_j+2}, \ldots$ in nodes of $T_{i_j}, T_{i_j+1}, T_{i_j+2}, \ldots$. Because of horizontal clean-ups and left-shifts, xh needs not be the leftmost child of x that hits ρ in all these moments. Since there are only finitely many nodes to the left of xh, the nodes that hit the run ρ can only move further to the left finitely many times. In particular, if there is some child xh' of x that eventually always hits ρ then x cannot have been the leftmost node furthest down that eventually always hits ρ. Thus, all its children must disappear eventually. There are only two possibilities for this to happen. First, x itself may get removed in step 4 of the construction because of the horizontal clean-up in step 3. But then ρ eventually always gets hit by some left sibling of x contradicting the assumption that x itself is leftmost among them. The other possibility is the vertical clean-up in step 5. This, however, makes x successful in some T_{i_j+k} for some $k \geq 0$ and all $j \in \mathbb{N}$, i.e. always eventually successful.   □

For the opposite direction we introduce some notation. Given a fixed word $w = a_0 a_1 \ldots$, let $i, j \in \mathbb{N}$ with $i \leq j$. We write $q \xrightarrow{i,j} q'$ if there is a (partial) run of $\mathcal{A}$ of length $j - i + 1$ measured as number of transitions taken, that starts in q, reads $a_i \ldots a_j$ and ends in q'. We write $q \xrightarrow{i,j}_F q'$ if there is such a partial run that visits the set F of accepting states of $\mathcal{A}$.

Note that partial runs are composable, in particular if we have $q \xrightarrow{i,j}_F q'$ and $q' \xrightarrow{j+1,h}_F q''$ then we also have $q \xrightarrow{i,h}_F q''$.

Lemma 15.2.8. Let $w = a_0 a_1 \dots \in \Sigma^\omega$ and $T_0, T_1, \dots$ be the corresponding sequence of history trees for $\mathcal{A}$ on w. If there is an x that is stable in the transitions from T_i to T_{i+1} for all but finitely many i and successful in the transitions from T_i to T_{i+1} for infinitely many i, then $w \in L(\mathcal{A})$. ∎

Proof. Suppose that x is eventually always stable and always eventually successful, i.e. let $i_0 < i_1 < i_2 < \dots$ be such that x is stable in all transitions from T_{i_0+j} to T_{i_0+j+1} for all $j \in \mathbb{N}$, and successful in the transition from T_{i_j-1} to T_{i_j} for all $j \in \mathbb{N}$. First we note that for every $j \in \mathbb{N}$ and every $q' \in T_{i_{j+1}}(x)$ there is a $q \in T_{i_j}(x)$ such that $q \xrightarrow{i_j, i_{j+1}-1} q'$. This is simply because x is stable in all transitions of this phase from T_{i_j} to $T_{i_{j+1}}$, and the labels of node x in all these transitions have evolved according to the usual powerset construction. In particular, every state belongs to a label because there is some predecessor state for the corresponding alphabet letter in the label of the same node in the previous history tree. Thus we get the following for every $j \in \mathbb{N}$: for every $q' \in T_{i_{j+1}}$ there is a $q \in T_{i_j}$ such that $q \xrightarrow{i_j, i_{j+1}-1} q'$. This would be enough to construct a run of $\mathcal{A}$ on w but it is not enough to show that it is accepting.

Recall that x is successful in every transition from T_{i_j-1} to T_{i_j} for every $j \in \mathbb{N}$. Take any $j \in \mathbb{N}$. Then x cannot have any children in T_{i_j}. On the other hand, if x is also successful in $T_{i_{j+1}}$ then all states in $T_{i_{j+1}}(x)$ must have – at least temporarily before step 5 of the construction – occurred in the label of some child x_h which then got deleted in step 5. Now, all these children must have been created at some moment between i_j and i_{j+1} because in T_{i_j} they were not present. New children only get created in step 2 of the construction, i.e. their label must have contained states from F only. Thus, we even get the following stronger result for every $j \in \mathbb{N}$: for every $q' \in T_{i_{j+1}}$ there is a $q \in T_{i_j}$ such that $q \xrightarrow{i_j, i_{j+1}-1}_F q'$.

Now consider the layered directed acyclic graph with nodes of the form (q, j) such that $q \in T_{i_j}(x)$ and edges from a (q, j) to a $(q', j+1)$ if $q \xrightarrow{i_j, i_{j+1}-1}_F q'$. This is finitely branching because there are only finitely many different states q. It also contains branches of arbitrary length because every (q', j) can be traced back to some $(q, 0)$ in this graph. By Kőnig's Lemma there are $q_{i_j} \in T_{i_j}(x)$ for every $j \in \mathbb{N}$ such that

$$q_{i_0} \xrightarrow{i_0, i_1-1}_F q_{i_1} \xrightarrow{i_1, i_2-1}_F q_{i_2} \xrightarrow{i_2, i_3-1}_F \dots$$

Finally, since $q_{i_0} \in T_{i_0}(x)$ and whenever a state occurs in the label of some node it also occurs in the label of all its ancestors, we also have $q_{i_0} \in T_{i_0}(\varepsilon)$. The root ε is stable in all transitions, thus we also have $q_I \xrightarrow{0, i_0-1} q_{i_0}$ which, together with the infinite path, shows that there is a run of $\mathcal{A}$ on w that visits infinitely many accepting states. Hence, we have $w \in L(\mathcal{A})$. □

As mentioned earlier, this technology can be used to devise a deterministic automaton that is equivalent to $\mathcal{A}$. It is not too hard to see that its size is bounded. The exact estimation is left as Exercise 15.16.

Lemma 15.2.9. There are at most $2^{\mathcal{O}(n \cdot \log n)}$ many different history trees for a Büchi automaton with n states. ∎

The history-tree construction therefore yields a deterministic device with an abstract acceptance mechanism on the infinite occurrences of certain transitions. This can easily be modelled as a finite automaton with a Rabin condition on transitions. A Rabin condition is a disjunction of conjunctions, each of them prescribing which event needs to be seen infinitely often and which must not be seen infinitely often. Recall that acceptance is characterised in the previous lemmas by the existence of a node that is infinitely often successful and not infinitely often unstable. As a last step we describe how a parity condition can be used to capture this. This requires a blow-up of the state space, though.

First we consider extended history trees that contain, in each node and in addition to the usual label of a set of states from $\mathcal{A}$, two binary flags called the *stable*-flag and the *successful*-flag. The values of these flags can be *true* or *false*, and they are being used to record whether the corresponding node was stable, respectively successful, in the transition that led to this history tree. We simply write $ust_T(x)$ to state that the stable-flag of x is unset in T and $suc_T(x)$ to indicate that its successful-flag is set in T. Note that $suc_T(x)$ implies that $ust_T(x)$ does not hold.

The second cause for a blow-up is more fundamental.

Definition 15.2.10. A **latest introduction record** (LIR) for a history tree T is a list $x_1, \ldots, x_m$ of all the nodes in T such that for every i, j we have the following. If

- $x_j = x_i h$ for some $h \in [n]$, or
- $x_i = yh$ and $x_j = yh'$ for some $y \in [n]^*$ and $h, h' \in [n]$ with $h < h'$

then $i < j$, i.e. parent nodes and left siblings occur earlier in the list.   ▽

Theorem 15.2.11. For every nondeterministic Büchi automaton $\mathcal{A}$ with n states there is a deterministic parity automaton $\mathcal{B}$ with at most $2^{\mathcal{O}(n \log n)}$ many states and $\mathcal{O}(n)$ many priorities such that $L(\mathcal{B}) = L(\mathcal{A})$. ∎

Proof. The states of $\mathcal{B}$ – henceforth referred to as *macro-states* in order not to confuse them with the states of $\mathcal{A}$ – are pairs of extended history trees for $\mathcal{A}$ and corresponding LIRs. The initial macro-state is the initial history tree, extended with both flags in its only node set to *false*, and the LIR that contains the root node only.

The transition function maps a state (T, L) under an alphabet symbol a to the pair (T', L'), obtained as follows. T' is the unique a-successor of the history tree T in which any node x gets their stable-flag and successful-flag set iff x is stable, respectively successful in the transition from T to T'. The LIR gets updated accordingly: L' is obtained from L by removing those nodes that have died in the transition from T to T' and then adding those nodes that have been newly created to the end of this list such that the LIR property from Definition 15.2.10 is satisfied.

The acceptance condition Ω of $\mathcal{B}$ uses the LIR and the flags of the nodes occurring in them. Take some macro-state (T, L) with the LIR $L = (x_1, \ldots, x_k)$, and let $m = \min\{i \mid ust_T(x_i) \text{ or } suc_T(x_i)\}$ be the index of the earliest node in this LIR that is either unstable or successful in the corresponding history tree. Recall that both are impossible. We assume the convention that the minimum over the empty set – in case no node is unstable or successful – is n, which is an upper bound on k. Then we define

$$\Omega(T, L) = 2 \cdot (n - m) + \begin{cases} 1, & \text{if } ust_T(x_m), \\ 0, & \text{otherwise.} \end{cases}$$

Thus, the priority of a macro-state is mainly determined by the position of the earliest node that is unstable or successful. If it is unstable then the priority is odd, if it is successful it is even. If no such node exists, the priority is 0.

We leave it as Exercise 15.17 to check that the estimations on the size and index of $\mathcal{B}$ are correct. Instead, we now focus on correctness. It remains to be seen that the highest priority occurring infinitely often in a run of $\mathcal{B}$ on some word w is even iff $w \in L(\mathcal{A})$. According to Lemma 15.2.7 and 15.2.8, the latter is equivalent to some node in the (extended) history trees of this run being eventually always stable and infinitely often successful.

Suppose that the highest priority seen on this run is even and of the form $2(n - m)$ for some m. Then, after some finite prefix, no higher priority than $2(n - m)$ will be seen. Thus, the first m nodes in the LIRs occurring after this prefix must all be stable from then on. This also means that the first m positions in these LIRs are always the same from then on. If then $2(n - m)$ is indeed seen over and over again, the mth node in these LIRs must be successful.

Suppose, on the other hand, that there is an eventually always stable and always eventually successful node in the sequence of history trees in such a run. Let x be the one with these properties that gets introduced at the earliest. Eventually x will have found a fixed position in the LIRs and not move further to their beginnings as the run proceeds. Let m be that position. Since x is successful infinitely often, the even priority $2(n - m)$ will occur infinitely often. It remains to be seen that no larger odd priority can occur infinitely often. This would only be possible if there was a node y at a position before x in the LIR that is unstable. But being unstable means that it moves further left in the history trees and this can only happen finitely often for a fixed node. Infinite occurrences of instability require the new nodes to be introduced over and over again but these get inserted after x in the LIRs eventually. Thus, there can be at most finitely many occurrences of greater odd priorities.

$\square$

An easy consequence of the fact that nondeterministic Büchi automata can be translated into deterministic parity automata is a characterisation of ω-regular languages using ω-regular expressions in which the infinite-repetition operator is only applied to left-deletable regular expressions (cf. Definition 10.1.10). Left-deletability means that the left quotient of the language with itself is again contained in itself. Intuitively, a left-deletable regular language can be defined by a deterministic automaton for which all accepting states are also initial. Note that this does, indeed, require determinism: take $(\mathtt{ba} + \mathtt{baa})^*$, for instance. It is easy to construct an NFA for this language that has a single initial and accepting state. However, this language is not left-deletable (cf. Example 10.1.11).

Theorem 15.2.12. Let L be an ω-regular language. Then $L = L(E)$ for some ω-regular expression E of the form $\bigcup_{i=1}^{n} E_i F_i^{\omega}$ such that each F_i is left-deletable. ∎

Proof. Suppose that L is defined by some nondeterministic Büchi automaton $\mathcal{A}$. According to Theorem 15.2.11 there is an equivalent deterministic parity automaton $\mathcal{B} = (\Sigma, Q, q_I, \delta, \Omega)$. We then have

$$L(\mathcal{B}) = \bigcup_{\substack{q \in Q \\ \Omega(q) \text{ even}}} L(\mathcal{A}_{q_I, q})\big(L(\mathcal{A}_q^{\leq \Omega(q)})\big)^{\omega}$$

where $\mathcal{A}_q$ is the DFA $(\Sigma, Q, q_I, \delta, \{q\})$ and $\mathcal{A}_q^{\leq k}$ is the DFA $(\Sigma, Q^{\leq k}, q, \delta^{\leq k}, \{q\})$ with $Q^{\leq k} = \{q \in Q \mid \Omega(q) \leq k\}$ and $\delta^{\leq k}$ is the restriction of δ to the states in $Q^{\leq k}$. Thus, $\mathcal{A}_q$ is obtained by turning the DPA $\mathcal{A}$ into a DFA with q as the single accepting state; $\mathcal{A}_q^{\leq \Omega(q)}$ is obtained by making q the single initial and accepting state and deleting all states with greater priorities. It should be clear that the preceding equation holds since a word is accepted by $\mathcal{B}$ iff there is a (unique) run on it that must eventually visit a state with an even priority and from then on revisit it infinitely often and never see a state with a greater priority.

It should be clear that each $\mathcal{A}_q$ can be described by a regular expression. What remains to be seen is that each $L(\mathcal{A}_q^{\leq \Omega(q)})$ is left-deletable. Recall that $\mathcal{A}_q^{\leq \Omega(q)}$ has a unique initial and accepting states. Let $\mathcal{A}'$ be a DFA with this property and suppose that there is a word $uv \in L(\mathcal{A}')$ such that $u \in L(\mathcal{A}')$. Then there is a run $q_0, \ldots, q_{|u|}, \ldots, q_{|uv|}$ of $\mathcal{A}'$ on uv and, since there is only a single accepting state which is also initial, we have that $q_0 = q_{|uv|}$ is that state. On the other hand, there must be an accepting run on u but u is a prefix of uv and $\mathcal{A}'$ is deterministic. Hence, this unique run is $q_0, \ldots, q_{|u|}$ and with the same argument we get that $q_0 = q_{|u|}$ being accepting, too. Thus, $q_{|u|}, \ldots, q_{|uv|}$ is in fact a run on v that starts in an initial state and ends in an accepting one so we also have $v \in L(\mathcal{A}')$. Hence, the languages of deterministic finite automata with a single initial and accepting state are always left-deletable, and we can therefore describe the language of $\mathcal{B}$ and consequently of $\mathcal{A}$ as well by an ω-regular expression of the required kind. □

15.2.3 Complementations

Complementation constructions for automata recognising winning plays are also quite useful. With such constructions at hand we can choose to recognise the complement of a set of plays, and this will be particularly useful for winning conditions that are inherently nondeterministic, by specifying the existence of something that happens along a play. Complementation for nondeterministic automata is usually complicated and hard, but we are in the lucky situation of having already shown how to do determinisation of such automata. This can be used with a little bit more overhead to obtain a complementation construction as well. Note that such a construction is also needed for the machinery in Chapter 14, in particular for the translation from QLTL to nondeterministic Büchi automata (see Exercise 14.19).

Complementing deterministic automata is typically very easy. The complement of a language recognised by a deterministic automaton is recognised by the same automaton with the dual acceptance condition. This must apply to a run on a word iff the original one does not apply. We need two complementation results in particular – for parity and for co-Büchi automata. The first one is easy because the parity condition is closed under duals, i.e. the complement of a parity condition can easily be expressed as a parity condition again.

Lemma 15.2.13. For every DPA $\mathcal{A}$ of size n and index k over some alphabet Σ there is a DPA $\overline{\mathcal{A}}$ of size at most $n + 1$ and index at most $k + 1$ that recognises $\Sigma^\omega \setminus \mathrm{L}(\mathcal{A})$. ∎

The proof details are left as Exercise 15.20.

Next, we consider deterministic co-Büchi automata. The co-Büchi condition is not closed under duals; the complement of 'eventually only accepting states' is 'infinitely often nonaccepting states', i.e. a Büchi condition. There is no need to obtain complement co-Büchi automata for our purposes, as Büchi automata suffice.

Lemma 15.2.14. For every deterministic co-Büchi automaton $\mathcal{A}$ of size n over some alphabet Σ there is a DPA $\overline{\mathcal{A}}$ of size at most $n + 1$ and index at most $k + 1$ that recognises $\Sigma^\omega \setminus \mathrm{L}(\mathcal{A})$. ∎

This lemma is, in fact, just a special case of Lemma 15.2.13. Recall that Büchi- and co-Büchi conditions are special parity conditions.

The following lemma provides the final missing part in a possible complementation construction for nondeterministic Büchi automata.

Lemma 15.2.15. For every NPA $\mathcal{A}$ of size n and index k there is an NBA $\mathcal{A}'$ of size at most $n \cdot k$ such that $\mathrm{L}(\mathcal{A}') = \mathrm{L}(\mathcal{A})$. ∎

Proof. The crucial insight into this translation is the fact that the NPA $\mathcal{A}$ recognises a given word iff there is a run and an even priority $\mathfrak{p}$ such that at some point in this run no priority larger than $\mathfrak{p}$ is seen anymore, and $\mathfrak{p}$ is seen infinitely often. This is obviously just a disjunction of conditions that are definable as Büchi acceptance conditions, and an NBA can simply simulate an NPA in order to guess the accepting run.

Let $\mathcal{A} = (\Sigma, Q, q_I, \delta, \Omega)$ and let $\Omega(Q) := \{\Omega(q) \mid q \in Q\}$. We construct $\mathcal{A}'$ as $(\Sigma, Q \times \Omega(Q), (q_I, \max \Omega(Q)), \delta', F)$ with

$$\delta'\big((q, \mathfrak{p}), \mathtt{a}\big) := \{(q', \mathfrak{p}') \mid q' \in \delta(q, a), \Omega(q') \leq \mathfrak{p}', \mathfrak{p}' \leq \mathfrak{p}\}.$$

Thus, $\mathcal{A}'$ simulates in its first state component $\mathcal{A}$, and in its second component it maintains a number that is used to prevent transitions to states with higher priorities. Together with the easily seen invariant that the second component never increases, we get that it provides an upper bound on the priorities that can still be seen in the rest of any run. With this mechanism, $\mathcal{A}'$ can guess the moment at which $\mathcal{A}$ does not see any priorities anymore that are larger than the one that determines acceptance. Now all we need to ensure is that it accepts iff that determining one – in the sense that it is the largest which occurs infinitely often – is even. To this end, we define

$$F := \{(q, \mathfrak{p}) \mid \Omega(q) = \mathfrak{p} \text{ and } \mathfrak{p} \text{ is even}\}.$$

For the correctness of this construction suppose that $w = \mathsf{a}_1 \mathsf{a}_2 \ldots \in \mathrm{L}(\mathcal{A})$, i.e. there is an accepting run $q_0, \mathsf{a}_1 q_1, \mathsf{a}_2 q_2, \ldots$ with $q_0 = q_I$ of $\mathcal{A}$ on w. Let $\mathfrak{p}$ be the necessarily even priority that is largest among $\{\Omega(q) \mid \text{there are infinitely many } i \text{ with } q = q_i\}$. It is not hard to see that

$$(q_0, \max \Omega(Q)), \mathsf{a}_1, (q_1, \mathfrak{p}), \mathsf{a}_2, (q_2, \mathfrak{p}), \ldots$$

for instance is an accepting run of $\mathcal{A}'$ on w. The other direction is shown in the same way. $\qquad\square$

Putting this together with some previous results we obtain the following.

Theorem 15.2.16. For every NBA $\mathcal{A}$ of size n over some alphabet Σ there is an NBA $\overline{\mathcal{A}}$ of size at most $2^{\mathcal{O}(n \log n)}$ that recognises $\Sigma^{\omega} \setminus \mathrm{L}(\mathcal{A})$. $\qquad\blacksquare$

Proof. Let $\mathcal{A}$ be such an NBA. According to Theorem 15.2.11 there is an equivalent DPA $\mathcal{B}$ of size $2^{\mathcal{O}(n \log n)}$ and index $\mathcal{O}(n)$, and according to Lemma 15.2.13 there is also a DPA $\overline{\mathcal{B}}$ of asymptotically the same size and index that recognises $\Sigma^{\omega} \setminus \mathrm{L}(\mathcal{A})$. Since every DPA is also an NPA we can use Lemma 15.2.15 and obtain an NBA of size $\mathcal{O}(n) \cdot 2^{\mathcal{O}(n \log n)} = 2^{\mathcal{O}(n \log n)}$ for this language. $\qquad\square$

15.2.4 Other Useful Constructions

Besides the transformation of nondeterministic automata (that will be used to easily recognise winning plays in games) into deterministic automata, which makes the Main Reduction Theorem applicable, we need a few more automata-theoretic constructions which will allow the definitions of winning plays to be decomposed and to construct deterministic automata modularly. We present them here without further explanation – it will become clear later in this chapter when they will actually be used.

For the next lemma recall that a safety condition is of the form 'stay in F forever' for some state set F. In an automaton that should only accept runs which obey this condition, this can easily be modelled as a parity condition of index 1, viz. all states in F receive priority 0, and all other states are removed. Thus, a safety automaton is a parity automaton in which all states have priority 0. It is particularly easy to form the intersection of a genuine parity and a safety condition. Again, the details are left as Exercise 15.22.

Lemma 15.2.17. Given a DPA $\mathcal{A}$ of size n and index k, as well as a deterministic safety automaton $\mathcal{B}$ of size m, there is a DPA $\mathcal{C}$ of size nm and index k such that $\mathrm{L}(\mathcal{C}) = \mathrm{L}(\mathcal{A}) \cap \mathrm{L}(\mathcal{B})$. $\qquad\blacksquare$

Intersection of a DPA with a DBA is a little more complicated, but also possible.

Lemma 15.2.18. Given a DPA $\mathcal{A}$ of size n and index k, as well as a DBA $\mathcal{B}$ of size m. There is a DPA $\mathcal{C}$ of size $2nmk$ and index at most $k+1$ such that $L(\mathcal{C}) = L(\mathcal{A}) \cap L(\mathcal{B})$.
∎

Proof. Let $\mathcal{A} = (\Sigma, Q^{\mathcal{A}}, q_I^{\mathcal{A}}, \delta^{\mathcal{A}}, \Omega)$ and $\mathcal{B} = (\Sigma, Q^{\mathcal{B}}, q_I^{\mathcal{B}}, \delta^{\mathcal{B}}, F)$. The DPA for their intersection simulates both of them at the same time in a product construction. Recall that it has to accept iff the highest priority seen infinitely often with regards to Ω is even, and there are infinitely many states visited in F. Clearly, the moments that witness the acceptance conditions of the two components need not coincide. This is why we use a third component in the states that remembers the largest priority seen with regards to Ω since the last visit to F, and another bit in order to know when we have to reset this counter.

Let $\mathcal{C} = (\Sigma, Q^{\mathcal{A}} \times Q^{\mathcal{B}} \times P \times \{0, 1\}, (q_I^{\mathcal{A}}, q_I^{\mathcal{B}}, \min P, 0), \delta, \Omega')$ where $P := \{\Omega(q) \mid q \in Q^{\mathcal{A}}\}$. The transition function – recall that $\mathcal{C}$ is supposed to be deterministic like $\mathcal{A}$ and $\mathcal{B}$ – is defined via

$$\delta((q, q', \mathfrak{p}, b), \mathsf{a}) := \begin{cases} (\delta^{\mathcal{A}}(q, \mathsf{a}), \delta^{\mathcal{B}}(q', \mathsf{a}), \max\{\mathfrak{p}, \Omega(q)\}, b'), & \text{if } b = 0 \\ (\delta^{\mathcal{A}}(q, \mathsf{a}), \delta^{\mathcal{B}}(q', \mathsf{a}), \Omega(q), b'), & \text{otherwise} \end{cases}$$

where $b' = 1$ iff $q' \in F$. At last, we set $\Omega'(q, q', \mathfrak{p}, b) := \mathfrak{p}$.

The estimations on the size and index of $\mathcal{C}$ are easily verified. We leave it as Exercise 15.23 to formally prove the correctness of this construction. □

15.3 Model Checking

15.3.1 The Full Modal Mu-Calculus

We recall the local model-checking games for the modal μ-calculus $\mathcal{L}_\mu$ from Section 8.4. Given a rooted transition system $\mathcal{T} = (S, \{\xrightarrow{a}\}_{a \in Act}, L, s_0)$ and an $\mathcal{L}_\mu$ formula φ, the model-checking game is defined as some $(\mathcal{C}, \mathcal{C}_\mathbf{V}, \mathcal{C}_\mathbf{R}, C_0, R)$ where the set of configurations C is the product of the state set of $\mathcal{T}$ and the subformulae of φ. It is partitioned into nodes owned by the players $\mathbf{V}$ and $\mathbf{R}$, has a designated starting configuration and has rules and a winning condition. The rules only explain which configuration is a possible successor of another configuration. This can be seen as a definition of an edge relation in a game arena.

We will use this already defined game in order to introduce a new rule-based notion for games. The rules for the model-checking game on the transition system $\mathcal{T}$ as earlier and a closed $\mathcal{L}_\mu$ formula φ are shown in Figure 15.2. These rules are to be read from top to bottom. The annotation on the left is simply a name for that rule. The game configuration on the top of the line describes the kind of situation in which the rule is applicable. Recall that the configurations of the $\mathcal{L}_\mu$ model-checking games are pairs consisting of a state and a subformula of the input formula φ. We write such a pair as $s \vdash \psi$. This should indicate that $\mathbf{V}$ is playing the game in order to prove that $\mathcal{T}, s \models \psi$ (under some suitable interpretation of free variables in ψ) holds. The annotation on the right side of a rule explains which player makes what kind of choice in such a situation. For instance, in rule ($\wedge$) when the current

$$(\wedge)\ \frac{s \vdash \psi_1 \wedge \psi_2}{s \vdash \psi_i}\ \mathbf{R} : i \in \{1,2\} \qquad\qquad (\vee)\ \frac{s \vdash \psi_1 \vee \psi_2}{s \vdash \psi_i}\ \mathbf{V} : i \in \{1,2\}$$

$$(\Diamond)\ \frac{s \vdash \langle a \rangle \psi}{t \vdash \psi}\ \mathbf{V} : t \text{ with } s \xrightarrow{a} t \qquad\qquad (\Box)\ \frac{s \vdash [a]\psi}{t \vdash \psi}\ \mathbf{R} : t \text{ with } s \xrightarrow{a} t$$

$$(\mathrm{FP})\ \frac{s \vdash \tau X.\psi}{s \vdash X} \qquad\qquad (\mathrm{Var})\ \frac{s \vdash X}{s \vdash fp_\varphi(X)}$$

Figure 15.2 The rules for the model-checking games for $\mathcal{L}_\mu$.

formula is a conjunction, Player 1 chooses one of the conjuncts that the play continues with. If the current configuration features a formula of the form $\langle a \rangle \psi$ then $\mathbf{V}$ chooses some state t such that $s \xrightarrow{a} t$. The next configuration to continue with is given below the line. Intuitively, it denotes the result of the application of this rule.

Note that the rules contain variables for formulae and states. Thus, applying a rule requires a current game configuration to be matched against the top configurations of the available rules, and the next configuration is obtained as the bottom one in that rule with the same instantiations of these meta-variables.

Sometimes applying a rule will result in a unique successor configuration. Here this is the case for the rules (FP) and (Var) which realise the unfolding of fixpoint constructs. In such cases we do not attribute these transformations as choices to one of the players. Thus, no player is mentioned in these rules. In the framework of the 2-player games we consider here, every node must be owned by one of the players, though. Note that such nodes can be assigned arbitrarily; it does not matter for the result of the game whether $\mathbf{V}$ or $\mathbf{R}$ makes the move to the unique successor configuration.

The winning conditions of the model-checking games for $\mathcal{L}_\mu$ explain in which cases $\mathbf{V}$ and $\mathbf{R}$ win a finite or infinite play. First of all, it is easy to turn such games with finite plays into games which only feature infinite plays such that winning is preserved. Furthermore, we need to see that the winning condition on infinite plays in the model-checking games, which regard the infinite occurrences of fixpoint variables, can indeed be seen as a parity winning condition.

Theorem 15.3.1. For every transition system $\mathcal{T}$ with root s and every $\mathcal{L}_\mu$ formula φ there is a parity game of size $\mathcal{O}(|\mathcal{T}| \cdot |\varphi|)$ and with at most $ad(\varphi) + 1$ many priorities which is won by Player 0 iff $\mathcal{T}, s \models \varphi$. ∎

Proof. Let $(\mathcal{C}, \mathcal{C}_\mathbf{V}, \mathcal{C}_\mathbf{R}, C_0, R)$ be the graph of the model-checking game for $\mathcal{T}$ and φ with $C_0 = s \vdash \varphi$. Consider the parity game $\mathcal{G} = (V, Own, E, v_I, \Omega)$ where $V := \mathcal{C} \cup \{0, 1\}$ for some nodes 0, 1 not occurring in $\mathcal{C}$. Define v_I as C_0. The owner function is given as

$$Own(v) := \begin{cases} 0, & \text{if } v \in \mathcal{C}_\mathbf{V} \cup \{0\} \\ 1, & \text{otherwise.} \end{cases}$$

The edge relation is defined by vEw if

- (v, w) is an instance of some game rule in R, or
- v is some configuration in which **V** wins a finite play and $w = 0$, or
- v is some configuration in which **R** wins a finite play and $w = 1$, or
- $v = w = 0$, or $v = w = 1$.

Thus, the parity game graph is the same as the model-checking game graph. It contains two additional nodes as immediate successors of those configurations which do not have successors in the model-checking game. These nodes have loops to themselves. This guarantees that the parity game is total.

Finally, we need to define the priority function. We set $\Omega(v) = v$ for $v \in \{0, 1\}$. This models the winning of finite plays through infinite plays. Furthermore, recall that the other nodes are of the form (s, ψ) for some state s and some subformula ψ. Whenever ψ is not a variable, we set $\Omega(s, \psi) = 0$. This leaves the case of nodes of the form (s, X) to be defined. We recall the dependency relation $\succeq_\varphi$ between variables occurring in φ, c.f. Definition 8.2.10. Choose Ω on these nodes to be the least natural number obeying two conditions.

- For any s and X, $\Omega(s, X)$ must be even if X is a variable of type ν and odd otherwise.
- Ω must be monotone with respect to $\succeq_\varphi$, i.e. for all variables X, Y and all states s, r we must have $\Omega(s, X) \geq \Omega(r, Y)$ if $X \succeq_\varphi Y$.

Correctness of this construction is easily established: any winning strategy for Player 0 in the parity game is also a winning strategy for **V** in the model-checking games. The other direction almost holds, but formally a winning strategy in the model-checking games must be extended by moves into the nodes 0 and 1. Since these moves are deterministic, this is easily done. The correspondence between winning strategies holds because of the similarity between the winning conditions in the two kinds of games. Suppose a play in the model-checking games is won by some player in the finite case. This play, extended ad infinitum through one of the nodes 0 or 1 – which can be done in a unique way – is won by the corresponding player in the parity game (Player 0 instead of **V**, Player 1 instead of **R**). Now consider an infinite play. If the outermost variable occurring infinitely often is of type μ, for instance, then this results in infinitely many odd priorities being seen in the same play in the parity game. Furthermore, the monotonicity constraint on Ω guarantees that no larger even priority occurs infinitely often because this would correspond to an outer variable of type ν which also occurs infinitely often in the model-checking play.

Note that the number of priorities in the parity game can be larger by at most one than the alternation depth of the formula. Consider for example $\nu X.\mu Y.(p \wedge \Diamond X) \vee \Diamond Y$ which has alternation depth 2. The parity game will contain nodes with priorities 0, 1 and 2, though.

The correspondence between parity games and the model-checking problem is completed by Theorem 8.4.10 and 8.4.13 which prove soundness and completeness of the model-checking games. $\qquad\square$

The essence of Theorem 15.3.1 is the fact that the local model-checking game for a transition system and a $\mathcal{L}_\mu$ formula is indeed a parity game. Thus, model checking for $\mathcal{L}_\mu$ can be reduced (in linear time) to the problem of solving a parity game. Indeed, a slightly stronger result holds: model checking a transition system of size n and a $\mathcal{L}_\mu$-formula of size m and alternation depth k can be reduced to solving a parity game of size $\mathcal{O}(n \cdot m)$ and index $k + 1$.

This raises the question of whether solving parity games can also be reduced to model checking the modal μ-calculus. The answer to this question is, trivially, 'yes': it is possible to solve parity games in exponential time, and the model-checking problem for $\mathcal{L}_\mu$ has both positive and negative instances. Thus, one can easily construct such a reduction that works in exponential time. We are, of course, interested in reductions that truly transform the problem rather than solve it directly. The real question is therefore whether there is a polynomial-time, or even linear-time reduction. The answer to this question is positive, too. In fact, an even stronger result holds: it is possible to *define* the winning regions in a parity game by formulae of $\mathcal{L}_\mu$ (up to a fixed index of the game). This is stronger because it does not just mean that from a parity game we construct an interpreted transition system and a $\mathcal{L}_\mu$ formula, but we take the parity game as an interpreted transition system, and a fixed (up to the index) formula can be used to solve parity games using $\mathcal{L}_\mu$ model checking. We start by introducing these formulae and the view of a parity game as such a transition system (see also Section 10.3.5).

Definition 15.3.2. Let $k \geq 1$ and $\mathcal{G} = (V, Own, E, v_I, \Omega)$ be a parity game of index at most k. The rooted mono-transition system associated with this parity game is (V, E, L, v_I) over the set $\{\text{prio}_j \mid j = 0, \ldots, k-1\} \cup \{\text{own}_0, \text{own}_1\}$ of atomic propositions where

- $\text{own}_i \in L(v)$ iff $Own(v) = 1$ for every $i \in \{0, 1\}$ and
- $\text{prio}_j \in L(v)$ iff $\Omega(v) = j$.   ▽

Thus, the graph structure of the transition system is the same as that of the parity game, and the owner and priority information about a node is encoded in a straightforward way in the node's label. Note that each node is labelled with exactly two propositions: a own_i and a prio_j. We will not distinguish formally between a parity game and its associated transition system but will assume that it is clear from the context which view is taken onto such a graph.

Walukiewicz formulae are $\mathcal{L}_\mu$ formulae that are interpreted over the transition system associated with a parity game.

Definition 15.3.3. Let $k \geq 1$. The kth **Walukiewicz formula** is

$$\Xi_k := \tau X_{k-1} \ldots \mu X_1.\nu X_0.\left(\left(\text{own}_0 \wedge \Diamond\Big(\bigvee_{j=0}^{k-1} \text{prio}_j \wedge X_j\Big)\right) \vee \right.$$
$$\left.\left(\text{own}_1 \wedge \Box\Big(\bigwedge_{j=0}^{k-1} \text{prio}_j \to X_j\Big)\right)\right)$$

where $\tau = \mu$ if $k - 1$ is odd, and $\tau = \nu$ otherwise.   ▽

Note that the fixpoint type of a variable X_j in a Walukiewicz formula is determined by the parity of j: μ for odd ones and ν for even ones. We also remark that the disjunction behind the diamond operator is equivalent to the conjunction behind the box operator on the class of transition systems considered here where each node is labelled with exactly one proposition of the form prio_j. Using disjunctions behind the diamond operator and conjunctions behind the box operator has the advantage of the modal operators commuting with the Boolean operators in their argument. This could be used to rewrite the formula in order to evaluate it more efficiently.

Evaluating the Walukiewicz formulae is exactly the way in which solving parity games reduces to model checking for the μ-calculus.

Theorem 15.3.4. Let $k \geq 1$ and $\mathcal{G}$ be a parity game of index k with starting node v_I. Then Player 0 wins $\mathcal{G}$ from v_I iff $\mathcal{G}, v_I \models \Xi_k$. ∎

Proof. Let $k \geq 1$ be fixed and define, for $j = 0, \ldots, k-1$, a formula $\Psi_{j,k}$ as follows.

$$\Psi_k := \left(\mathsf{own}_0 \wedge \Diamond (\bigvee_{j=0}^{k-1} \mathsf{prio}_j \wedge X_j) \right) \vee \left(\mathsf{own}_1 \wedge \Box (\bigwedge_{j=0}^{k-1} \mathsf{prio}_j \rightarrow X_j) \right)$$

$$\Psi_{0,k} := \nu X_0 . \Psi_k$$
$$\Psi_{2i+1,k} := \mu X_{2i+1} . \Psi_{2i,k}$$
$$\Psi_{2i+2,k} := \nu X_{2i+2} . \Psi_{2i+1,k}$$

where $i = 0, \ldots, \lfloor (k-1)/2 \rfloor - 1$. Thus, in particular, we have $\Psi_{k-1,k} = \Xi_k$.

Clearly, for $j < k-1$, $\Psi_{j,k}$ contains $X_{j+1}, \ldots, X_{k-1}$ as free variables. Thus, its meaning is only well defined under an environment ρ interpreting these variables.

Consider Ψ_k. It describes what happens in one step of a parity game from Player 0's perspective: either Player 0 makes a choice in one of her nodes and the play proceeds with *some* successor – hence the diamond operator – or Player 1 makes a choice in one of his node and the play proceeds with *any* successor – hence the box operator. Note how this formula requires these successors to belong to the current interpretation of the variable X_j where j is the successor's priority.

Now $\Psi_{0,k}$ defines – under some interpretation ρ of the variables $X_1, \ldots, X_{k-1}$ – the largest set of nodes X_0 such that Player 0 has a strategy to force the game onto nodes with priority 0 that belong to X_0 as well, or onto some node w that belongs to $\rho(X_{\Omega(w)})$. Thus, it describes the set of all nodes from which Player 0 can enforce a play that visits – after one step – only nodes of priority 0 or some node w in $\rho(X_{\Omega(w)})$ when $\Omega(w) \geq 1$.

Note that this strategy does not consider the priority of the node that the game is started in: formula Ψ_k only contains the atomic propositions for the priorities under the scope of a modality. This is not a problem since the parity winning condition is invariant under changing finitely many priorities in a play.

Next consider $\Psi_{1,k} = \mu X_1 . \Psi_{0,k}$. Thus, it defines – under some interpretation ρ of the variables $X_2, \ldots, X_{k-1}$ – the least set X_1 such that Player 0 can enforce a play which either stays on nodes of priority 0 only, or enters a node of priority 1, or enters some node w in $\rho(X_{\Omega(w)})$ when $\Omega(w) \geq 2$. Note the crucial difference to $\Psi_{0,k}$ which was defined a greatest set, or, in other words, a set of nodes onto which Player 0 can stay forever. Here, $\Psi_{1,k}$ defines a least set or, in other words, a set which can only be visited finitely often. Thus, $\Psi_{1,k}$ defines the set of all nodes from which Player 0 can enforce a play which finitely often visits a node of priority 1, until it either visits nodes of priority 0 only or enters some node w in $\rho(X_{\Omega(w)})$ when $\Omega(w) \geq 2$.

Now, consider $\Psi_{2,k}$, again under a given interpretation ρ of its free variables. This defines again a greatest set, namely the set of all nodes from which Player 0 can enforce a play which either visits nodes of priority 2 infinitely often, or it visits nodes of priority 1 only finitely often, followed by node of priority 0 only, or it reaches a node w in $\rho(X_{\Omega(w)})$ when $\Omega(w) \geq 3$.

This scheme can be iterated for $i = 2, \ldots, k-1$ to show that under some ρ, $\Psi_{i,k}$ defines the set of all nodes from which Player 0 has a strategy to enforce a play that either visits a node w in $\rho(X_{\Omega(w)})$ when $i < \Omega(w) < k$, or among the remaining priorities $0, \ldots, i$ the greatest that occurs infinitely often is even. It should be clear that this generalises the special case of parity winning conditions, namely, for $i = k - 1$ this formula defines the set of all nodes from which Player 0 wins the underlying parity game.   □

This characterisation of winning regions in parity games as $\mathcal{L}_{\mu}$-definable sets of nodes in a transition system can be used to obtain an algorithm for solving parity games that has a better asymptotic complexity than the recursive algorithm that is derived from the proof of memoryless determinacy in Theorem 15.1.22.

Corollary 15.3.5. Parity games with n nodes, e edges and index k can be solved in time $\mathcal{O}(e \cdot n^{k+2})$.   ■

Proof. By Theorem 15.3.4 we can reduce the solving of a parity game with n nodes, e edges and index k to the evaluation of a $\mathcal{L}_{\mu}$ formula of size $\mathcal{O}(k)$ and alternation depth k on a transition system with n nodes and e edges. Theorem 8.3.5 says that the latter can be done in time $\mathcal{O}(e \cdot k \cdot n^{k+1})$, and bearing in mind that we can always assume $k \leq n$ because no parity game can have more priorities than nodes, we obtain the stated result.   □

15.3.2 The Alternation-Free Mu-Calculus

The results of the previous section use that fact that the index of a parity game that captures the model-checking problem for a transition system and a $\mathcal{L}_{\mu}$ formula can be chosen to only depend on the alternation depth of the formula: the priorities are being assigned in order such that they respect the dependency ordering of the variables, and they need to be chosen as even or odd depending on the fixpoint type of a variable. Thus, the model-checking parity games for alternation-free formulae, for instance, can be constructed in a way that only uses the priorities 0 and 1, i.e. they result in co-Büchi games. On the other hand, alternation-freeness means that there is no dependency between fixpoint variables of different types, and the model-checking game rules closely follow the syntactic structure of the formula. Thus, no play in the model-checking game for an alternation-free formula can visit both priorities 0 and 1 infinitely often. Hence, it would be equally possible to assign the priority 2 instead of 0, and the result would be an equivalent Büchi game. Recall that weak parity games have been introduced as a subclass of both Büchi and co-Büchi games.

We motivated the study of weak parity games because of their connection to the model-checking problem for alternation-free formulae. This is formalised in the next theorem which is basically just a special case of Theorem 15.3.1. We leave the proof as Exercise 15.24.

Theorem 15.3.6. For every transition system $\mathcal{T}$ with root s and every alternation-free $\mathcal{L}_\mu$-formula φ there is a weak parity game of size $\mathcal{O}(|\mathcal{T}| \cdot |\varphi|)$ which is won by Player 0 iff $\mathcal{T}, s \models \varphi$. ∎

Note that simple temporal logics like CTL can be embedded into the alternation-free fragment of $\mathcal{L}_\mu$. Combining such a translation with the construction of model-checking games for the alternation-free μ-calculus as a weak parity game yields a simple game-theoretic characterisation of the model-checking problem for such simple temporal logics.

Corollary 15.3.7. There is a linear-time reduction from model checking the alternation-free μ-calculus or CTL to the problem of solving a weak parity game. ∎

15.3.3 The Full Branching-Time Logic CTL*

For the remainder of this section we fix a total rooted transition system $\mathcal{T} = (S, \rightarrow, L, s_0)$ and a CTL* formula ϑ in negation normal form. Recall that we can always assume such a CTL* formula to be decomposed into blocks which consist of a path quantifier, E or A, followed by a linear-time formula over propositional literals or smaller blocks. This block structure will play a crucial role in the definition of the model-checking games for CTL*. We begin by defining its arena; the winning conditions require a few more technical constructions because plays in these model-checking games – unlike those for $\mathcal{L}_\mu$– do not just feature sequences of subformulae but sequences of sets of subformulae. Here we use **V** and **R** as the players instead of players 0 and 1 which we have used for parity games. This distinction is, of course, not crucial; it simply helps to separate the model-checking games which we define as abstract 2-player games from the parity games which we use in order to solve such abstract games by reduction when their winning conditions cannot immediately be defined as a parity condition. Note that the model-checking games for $\mathcal{L}_\mu$ can immediately be seen as parity games. Here this is no longer the case.

The Game Rules and Winning Conditions

Like the $\mathcal{L}_\mu$ model checking, the CTL* model-checking games operate on a limited space of formulae made up from the input formula, viz. its **Fischer–Ladner closure**, defined as follows.

Definition 15.3.8. Let φ be a CTL* formula in negation normal form. Then $\mathit{fl}(\varphi)$ is the smallest set that contains φ and satisfies the following.

- If $\psi_1 \vee \psi_2 \in \mathit{fl}(\varphi)$ or $\psi_1 \wedge \psi_2 \in \mathit{fl}(\varphi)$ then $\{\psi_1, \psi_2\} \subseteq \mathit{fl}(\varphi)$.
- If $\mathsf{Q}\psi \in \mathit{fl}(\varphi)$ for some $\mathsf{Q} \in \{\mathsf{E}, \mathsf{A}, \mathsf{X}\}$ then $\psi \in \mathit{fl}(\varphi)$.
- If $\psi_1 \mathsf{U} \psi_2 \in \mathit{fl}(\varphi)$ then $\{\psi_1, \psi_2, \mathsf{X}(\psi_1 \mathsf{U} \psi_2)\} \subseteq \mathit{fl}(\varphi)$.
- If $\psi_1 \mathsf{R} \psi_2 \in \mathit{fl}(\varphi)$ then $\{\psi_1, \psi_2, \mathsf{X}(\psi_1 \mathsf{R} \psi_2)\} \subseteq \mathit{fl}(\varphi)$. $\triangledown$

It should be clear from the definition that the Fischer–Ladner closure of every CTL* formula φ is finite and that its size is linear in $|\varphi|$. The Fischer–Ladner closure is just a collection of all those formulae that may occur in the model-checking game with no particular semantical meaning at this point. Note that it freely mixes state and path formulae, whereas the games, to be introduced later, use them in a more structured way.

Now, we can formally define the model-checking games for CTL*.

Definition 15.3.9. The **model-checking game** for the interpreted transition system $\mathcal{T} = (S, \rightarrow, L, s_0)$ and a CTL* formula ϑ in negation normal form is defined as follows.

- Its configurations are of the form $s \vdash \mathsf{E}(\Gamma)$ or $s \vdash \mathsf{A}(\Delta)$ where $s \in S$ and $\Gamma, \Delta \subseteq \mathit{fl}(\vartheta)$. We will omit as many parentheses as possible for these sets and simply write $\mathsf{E}\psi$ instead of $\mathsf{E}(\{\psi\})$ as well as $\mathsf{A}(\psi, \Delta)$ instead of $\mathsf{A}(\{\psi\} \cup \Delta)$ for instance.
- The game starts in the initial configuration $s_0 \vdash \mathsf{A}(\vartheta)$. The A is only put here in order to ensure that the formula component of every configuration starts with a path quantifier.
- The game rules are presented in Figure 15.3. Note that ℓ is a literal over atomic propositions in rules (ALit) and (ELit), and Q stands for either E or A in rules (AQ) and (EQ). Here we use a new notation to state that a player has two choices: we write both alternatives side by side below the line. In rules (AX) and (EX) we simply write $\mathbf{V} : s \rightarrow t$ to state that $\mathbf{V}$ chooses a transition from the given state s to some successor state t, likewise for $\mathbf{R}$. $\triangledown$

Note that the applicability of the rules is determined by the occurrence of a formula of a particular kind in a set. It is therefore possible that two or more rules are applicable to a given configuration. The order in which they are applied does not affect soundness and completeness of these games and it is therefore irrelevant. It only becomes relevant in the formalisation of these model-checking games as abstract 2-player games, in order to reduce the model-checking problem to the problem of solving parity games. In order to make this reduction well defined, one can introduce an arbitrary total order on the model-checking game rules which gives certain rules a precedence over others such that the question of which player owns which configuration becomes well defined.

The four rules for the Boolean connectives – conjunctions and disjunctions, each inside an existentially or universally quantified block – indicate that a formula set under an E-quantifier is to be interpreted as a conjunction, and any one under an A-quantifier is to be interpreted as a disjunction. Thus, a configuration of the form $s \vdash \mathsf{E}\Gamma$ can be understood as $\mathbf{V}$'s attempt to construct a path starting in s on which *all* formulae in Γ hold. Likewise,

$$(\text{E}\wedge)\ \frac{s\vdash \mathsf{E}(\varphi\wedge\psi,\Gamma)}{s\vdash \mathsf{E}(\varphi,\psi,\Gamma)} \qquad\qquad (\text{EU})\ \frac{s\vdash \mathsf{E}(\varphi\mathsf{U}\psi,\Gamma)}{s\vdash \mathsf{E}(\psi,\Gamma)\quad s\vdash \mathsf{E}(\varphi,\mathsf{X}(\varphi\mathsf{U}\psi),\Gamma)}\ \mathbf{V}$$

$$(\text{A}\vee)\ \frac{s\vdash \mathsf{A}(\varphi\vee\psi,\Delta)}{s\vdash \mathsf{A}(\varphi,\psi,\Delta)} \qquad\qquad (\text{AU})\ \frac{s\vdash \mathsf{A}(\varphi\mathsf{U}\psi,\Delta)}{s\vdash \mathsf{A}(\psi,\varphi,\Delta)\quad s\vdash \mathsf{A}(\psi,\mathsf{X}(\varphi\mathsf{U}\psi),\Delta)}\ \mathbf{R}$$

$$(\text{ALit})\ \frac{s\vdash \mathsf{A}(\ell,\Delta)}{s\vdash \mathsf{A}\Delta}\ \text{if } s\not\models\ell \qquad (\text{ER})\ \frac{s\vdash \mathsf{E}(\varphi\mathsf{R}\psi,\Gamma)}{s\vdash \mathsf{E}(\psi,\varphi,\Gamma)\quad s\vdash \mathsf{E}(\psi,\mathsf{X}(\varphi\mathsf{R}\psi),\Gamma)}\ \mathbf{V}$$

$$(\text{ELit})\ \frac{s\vdash \mathsf{E}(\ell,\Gamma)}{s\vdash \mathsf{E}\Gamma}\ \text{if } s\models\ell \qquad (\text{AR})\ \frac{s\vdash \mathsf{A}(\varphi\mathsf{R}\psi,\Delta)}{s\vdash \mathsf{A}(\psi,\Delta)\quad s\vdash \mathsf{A}(\varphi,\mathsf{X}(\varphi\mathsf{R}\psi),\Delta)}\ \mathbf{R}$$

$$(\text{E}\vee)\ \frac{s\vdash \mathsf{E}(\varphi\vee\psi,\Gamma)}{s\vdash \mathsf{E}(\varphi,\Gamma)\quad s\vdash \mathsf{E}(\psi,\Gamma)}\ \mathbf{V} \qquad (\text{A}\wedge)\ \frac{s\vdash \mathsf{A}(\varphi\wedge\psi,\Delta)}{s\vdash \mathsf{A}(\varphi,\Delta)\quad s\vdash \mathsf{A}(\psi,\Delta)}\ \mathbf{R}$$

$$(\text{AQ})\ \frac{s\vdash \mathsf{A}(\mathsf{Q}\psi,\Delta)}{s\vdash \mathsf{A}\Delta\quad s\vdash \mathsf{Q}\psi}\ \mathbf{V} \qquad\qquad (\text{EQ})\ \frac{s\vdash \mathsf{E}(\mathsf{Q}\psi,\Gamma)}{s\vdash \mathsf{E}\Gamma\quad s\vdash \mathsf{Q}\psi}\ \mathbf{R}$$

$$(\text{AX})\ \frac{s\vdash \mathsf{A}(\mathsf{X}\varphi_1,\dots,\mathsf{X}\varphi_k)}{t\vdash \mathsf{A}(\varphi_1,\dots,\varphi_k)}\ \mathbf{R}:s\to t \qquad (\text{EX})\ \frac{s\vdash \mathsf{E}(\mathsf{X}\varphi_1,\dots,\mathsf{X}\varphi_k)}{t\vdash \mathsf{E}(\varphi_1,\dots,\varphi_k)}\ \mathbf{V}:s\to t$$

Figure 15.3 The rules for the CTL* model-checking games.

a formula of the form $s\vdash \mathsf{A}\Delta$ should be understood as **R**'s obligation to construct a path starting in s in which *none* of the formulae in Δ hold. Phrased positively, all paths starting in s should satisfy *some* formula in Δ.

The reason for this preservation of subformulae for certain Boolean connectives is the following. Suppose we have $s\models \mathsf{E}(\varphi\vee\psi)$. Then we must have $s\models \mathsf{E}\varphi$ or $s\models \mathsf{E}\psi$ (and vice versa). On the other hand, we have $\mathsf{E}(\varphi\wedge\psi)\not\equiv \mathsf{E}\varphi\wedge \mathsf{E}\psi$. This leaves two options for the design of model-checking games for CTL*.

1. The players choose entire paths. For instance, a formula of the form $\mathsf{E}\varphi$ could be dealt with by letting **V** choose a path and then continue the game on that path in order to verify or refute φ on it. This has an obvious disadvantage: even a finite system may contain infinitely many paths. Thus, it is not clear whether such a game could be used in order to achieve decidability and optimal complexity results without using any external combinatorial argument which allows us to restrict the search space to be finite.

2. The players choose states. Because of the inequivalence stated previously (and similar ones), it is necessary to preserve choices. For instance, it may be the case that all paths starting in s satisfy φ or ψ but different paths may satisfy different formulae. Thus, if a path starting in s is constructed in a state-by-state manner then it may be necessary to postpone the decision about which or φ or ψ is indeed satisfied to a later moment. This is realised by the formula sets in the configurations chosen here.

Next we consider the winning conditions for these games. There are finite plays and infinite plays. As with the model-checking games for $\mathcal{L}_\mu$, finite plays result from reaching a configuration in which the truth value of a formula (set) in some state is immediate.

Definition 15.3.10 (Winning conditions on finite plays). Let $\mathcal{T}$ be fixed as earlier, and ℓ be an arbitrary propositional literal. **V** wins a play that reaches a configuration of the form

- $s \vdash \mathsf{E}\emptyset$, or
- $s \vdash \mathsf{A}(\ell, \Delta)$ such that $\mathcal{T}, s \models \ell$.

R wins a play that reaches a configuration of the form

- $s \vdash \mathsf{A}\emptyset$, or
- $s \vdash \mathsf{E}(\ell, \Gamma)$ such that $\mathcal{T}, s \not\models \ell$.

We will call such configurations **final**. $\triangledown$

Note that a final configuration of the form $s \vdash \mathcal{O}\emptyset$ can be created by the rules (ALit), (ELit), (AQ) and (EQ). Moreover, in a configuration that has a propositional literal in its formula set, the truth value of that literal in the current ITS state determines whether the configuration is final or rule (ALit) or (ELit) needs to be applied.

As with the model-checking games for $\mathcal{L}_\mu$, the winning conditions for final plays cover cases in which a configuration is obviously true or obviously false under some suitable interpretation. This is caused by formulae which cannot be decomposed further by the game rules. On the other hand, the winning conditions for infinite plays determine logical truth or falsity in a different way: they are supposed to detect whether some least or greatest fixpoint construct has been unfolded infinitely often in order to determine its truth value. As a rule of thumb, least fixpoint constructs can only be unfolded finitely often in order to be true, greatest fixpoint constructs can only be unfolded finitely often in order to be false. Thus, in the $\mathcal{L}_\mu$ model-checking games, this, together with the possibility to nest such constructs, immediately leads to the parity winning conditions. Here, the situation is slightly different.

Example 15.3.11. Consider the interpreted transition system $\mathcal{T} = (\{s\}, \rightarrow, L)$ with $s \rightarrow s$ and $L(s) = \{q\}$. The model-checking game on this ITS and the formula $\mathsf{EGF}q$ is shown in Figure 15.4.

Recall that the temporal operators G and F can be seen as special cases of R and U, and it is therefore possible to specialise the corresponding game rules for them. The formal details are left as an exercise. Here we present the game arenas representing the corresponding model-checking games after fixing a suitable precedence order for the application of the rules. We also start the game in the configuration $s \vdash \mathsf{EGF}q$ rather than putting an additional universal path quantifier in front of the formula (which would be redundant here).

We try to stick to the convention of depicting nodes as circles and boxes. However, the nodes contents may become very long. This is why **R**'s nodes (i.e. Player 1 in the model-checking games) will be shown as rectangles, whereas player **V**'s circle nodes may become

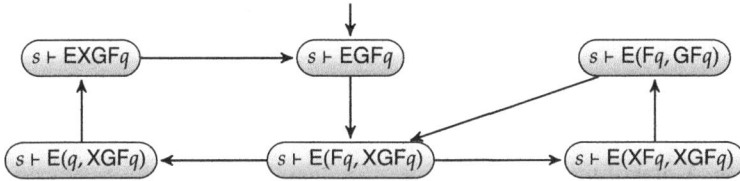

Figure 15.4 The model-checking game for T and EGFq in Example 15.3.11.

stretched. Those nodes in which a deterministic rule with a unique result is applied will be shown as either, i.e. we simply assign them to any player.

Note that we have $T, s \models$ EGFq. Thus, **V** should win the model-checking game. Intuitively, one of the two cycles should be good for **V**, i.e. some infinite play must be winning for her.

Consider the linear-time temporal formulae that are being seen along the left cycle. **V** is obliged to construct a path on which GFq holds which, by rule (ER), gets turned into the obligation to construct a path on which both Fq and XGFq holds. (Recall that formula sets under an existential quantifier are interpreted conjunctively.) For the left cycle, **V** has chosen to prove Fq by proving q using rule (EU). Since q holds in s, it is discarded with rule (ELit). Then all formulae start with a X-operator, and **V** is supposed to select the next state on the path to be constructed. Since s is its only successor, we get back to the starting configuration. Note that it is the G-operator which causes the cycle, and it is defined as a greatest fixpoint. Thus, the infinite continuation of this should be a play that is won by **V** because it results from the infinite unfolding of a greatest fixpoint construct.

The play which cycles around on the right side also features a greatest fixpoint construct that is being unfolded infinitely often. However, it also features a least fixpoint construct, namely Fq. In this play, **V** never proves Fq. Instead, she keeps deferring it with rule (EU) ad infinitum.

This phenomenon arises with the use of formula sets: an infinite play can have more than one temporal construct which gets unfolded infinitely often along the way. The question is: who should be the winner of such a play? Recall that a formula set inside an E-quantifier is interpreted as a conjunction. Now this conjunction has two temporal formulae that are unfolded infinitely often. Since one of them is a greatest fixpoint construct it is true along the corresponding path in the ITS. Since the other is a least fixpoint construct, it is false. A conjunction in which one element is false should clearly also be false, and thus, **R** should win the play that cycles around on the right.

Finally, consider a play that takes the route to the left and the route to the right both infinitely often. This should be won by **V** again because every move to the left corresponds to proving that q holds. In such plays, **V** has constructed a path on which q holds infinitely often. This is of course just what the formula expresses as a CTL* property. Note that it is the greatest fixpoint construct G which spawns off the least fixpoint construct F infinitely often in such plays. The latter only gets unfolded finitely often each time.

In the following we will make these vague notions of 'spawning off' and being unfolded (in)finitely often precise.

Definition 15.3.12. Let $s_0 \vdash Q_0\Phi_0, s_1 \vdash Q_1\Phi_1, \ldots$ be an infinite play of a CTL* model-checking game. It is called an **E-play** if there is some $n \in \mathbb{N}$ such that $Q_i = \mathsf{E}$ for all $i \geq n$. It is called an **A-play** if there is some $n \in \mathbb{N}$ such that $Q_i = \mathsf{A}$ for all $i \geq n$. $\qquad\nabla$

Lemma 15.3.13. Every play is either an E- or an A-play. $\qquad\blacksquare$

Proof. We simply need to show that no play can contain infinitely many applications of rules (EQ) or (AQ) in which the two players select to start a new block. Note that the rules do not create new formulae but the formulae in a successor configuration always belong to the Fischer–Ladner closure of the formulae in the preceding one. Thus, whenever such a choice with these rules is made for some formula $Q\psi \in \mathit{fl}(\vartheta)$ then the remainder of the play can only feature formulae in $\mathit{fl}(\psi)$. Since $Q\psi \notin \mathit{fl}(\psi)$ the number of available formulae has decreased strictly which means that these rules can only be applied finitely many times. Hence, the outermost path quantifier can only change finitely many times in a play. $\qquad\square$

Now, we introduce a **connection relation** on formulae of successive configurations in a play.

Definition 15.3.14. Suppose that $s \vdash Q\Phi$ is a configuration to which some rule r applies which results in the configuration $t \vdash Q'\Phi'$. We say that some $\varphi \in \Phi$ is **connected** to $\psi \in \Phi'$, if

- the rule replaces φ by ψ (and possibly other formulae) inside the outer path quantifier (cf. the conjunctions and disjunctions in (E∧), (A∧), (E∨) or (A∨), as well as the U-formulae and R-formulae in rules (EU), (AU), (ER) or (AR)), or
- the rule replaces φ by ψ which becomes the new outer path quantifier (cf. formula $Q\psi$ in (AQ) or (EQ)), or
- $\varphi = \mathsf{X}\psi$, and r is (EX) or (AX), or
- $\varphi = \psi$ and r operates on a formula that is different to φ.

We write $\varphi \rightsquigarrow \psi$ to state that φ is connected to ψ in the context of two configurations that they belong to. $\qquad\nabla$

Not every formula in some configuration must be connected to some formula in the successor configuration in a play. Take for instance **R**'s choice with rule (EQ) to discard a formula of the form $Q\psi$. It cannot be connected to any formula in the successor. On the other hand, for every formula ψ in a configuration that is not initial in a play there must be some φ in the preceding configuration such that φ is connected to ψ. Intuitively, φ is the reason for ψ to be there and no formula appears in a configuration without a reason. This gives us the first simple combinatorial result about infinite plays, but first we use this connection relation to define the concept of a *thread*.

Definition 15.3.15. Let $s_0 \vdash Q_0 \Phi_0, s_1 \vdash Q_1 \Phi_1, \ldots$ be an infinite play in the model-checking game for $\mathcal{T}$, s_0 and ϑ. A **thread** is an infinite sequence $\varphi_0, \varphi_1, \ldots$ such that for all $i \in \mathbb{N}$: $\varphi_i \in \Phi_i$ and $\varphi_i \rightsquigarrow \varphi_{i+1}$.

Such a thread is called μ-**thread** if there is some formula φ of the form $\psi_1 \mathsf{U} \psi_2$ such that $\varphi = \varphi_i$ for infinitely many i. If there is some φ of the form $\psi_1 \mathsf{R} \psi_2$ then the thread is called a ν-**thread**. $\qquad \triangledown$

Lemma 15.3.16. Every infinite play has a thread. $\qquad \blacksquare$

Proof. Since every formula in a configuration is connected backwards to some formula in the preceding configuration, the sequence of formula sets forms a tree with $\rightsquigarrow$ as edges such that there are paths of arbitrary length in this tree. The size of each configuration is bounded, hence the tree is finitely branching, and by Kőnig's Lemma it has an infinite path. This is a thread in this play. $\qquad \square$

Lemma 15.3.17. Every thread is either a μ-thread or a ν-thread. $\qquad \blacksquare$

Proof. A key ingredient to this result is the observation that the connection relation generally follows the strict subformula relation with two exceptions: a formula can be connected to itself, and a formula of the form $\varphi \mathsf{U} \psi$ can be connected to $\mathsf{X}(\varphi \mathsf{U} \psi)$, likewise for $\varphi \mathsf{R} \psi$. As a consequence, we immediately obtain that no thread can be a μ-thread and a ν-thread for otherwise there would be some formulae $\varphi \mathsf{U} \psi$ and $\varphi \mathsf{R} \psi'$ that would both have to be subformulae of each other.

It remains to be seen that a thread must be either of these. First we observe that the formulae in a thread must change infinitely often. Suppose this was not the case. Then from some point on, the rules that are bcing played in this play do not operate on the formula in the thread anymore. A close inspection of the game rules reveals however, that the rules remove temporal or Boolean operators apart from rules (EU), (AU), (ER) and (AR) which can create an X-operator. However, they remove temporal operators that are not under the scope of an X-operator. This means that applying any sequence of rule applications to some configuration will result in a configuration to which only rules (EX) or (AX) can be applied. These rules reduce all formulae in the current configuration, in particular the one in the thread. Thus, any thread must contain infinitely parts in which we have connections of the form $\mathsf{X}(\varphi \mathsf{U} \psi) \rightsquigarrow \varphi \mathsf{U} \psi$, or $\mathsf{X}(\varphi \mathsf{R} \psi) \rightsquigarrow \varphi \mathsf{R} \psi$ respectively. Since formulae are not infinitely large, it must also contain infinitely many parts in which they are connected in the other way. Since there are only finitely many formulae of that form, every thread must be either a μ-thread or a ν-thread. $\qquad \square$

An even closer inspection of the game rules reveals that for every thread there is some $\chi = \varphi \mathsf{U} \psi$ or $\chi = \varphi \mathsf{R} \psi$ such that eventually all formulae in this thread are either χ or $\mathsf{X}\chi$. Nevertheless, Lemma 15.3.16 and 15.3.17 are almost sufficient to base the winning conditions for infinite plays on.

Definition 15.3.18 (Winning conditions for infinite plays). **V** wins an infinite play λ in the model-checking game for CTL* if

- λ is an E-play and contains no μ-thread, or
- λ is an A-play and contains a ν-thread.

Likewise, **R** wins an infinite play λ if

- λ is an E-play and contains a μ-thread, or
- λ is an A-play and contains no ν-thread. ∇

   It is important to note that every play has been assigned a unique winner with these winning conditions. Lemma 15.3.16 and 15.3.17 provide half the proof of this result. Checking the details is left as Exercise 15.27.

Lemma 15.3.19. A play in a CTL* model-checking game is won by **V** iff it is not won by **R**.   ∎

   We will write $\mathcal{G}^T(s, \vartheta)$ for the CTL* model-checking game in T and ϑ that starts in the configuration $s \vdash A\vartheta$ and proceeds according to the rules in Figure 15.3 and the winning conditions in Definition 15.3.10 and 15.3.18.

Soundness and Completeness

The aim of this section is to prove that the model-checking games for CTL* do indeed characterise the model-checking problem for CTL*, in the sense that solving the games is equivalent to solving the model-checking problem. This entails two proof obligations: **soundness** means that the games do not characterise anything wrong w.r.t. the satisfaction relation, i.e. whenever **V** has a winning strategy then the underlying formula holds in the underlying ITS. **Completeness** is the opposite direction, i.e. whenever satisfaction holds then this should also be captured by the game-theoretic characterisation in the sense that **V** has a winning strategy then.

   We need some technical ingredients for this. Again, we fix some ITS $T = (S, \rightarrow, L)$ and some CTL* formula ϑ and consider everything with respect to the game played on this ITS and this formula.

Definition 15.3.20. Let π be a path in T. A configuration of the form $s \vdash E\Gamma$ is said to be **witnessed by** π if $\pi(0) = s$ and $T, \pi \models \bigwedge \Gamma$. It is called **true**, if there is some path π that witnesses this configuration. In other words, $s \vdash E\Gamma$ is called true if $T, s \models E \bigwedge \Gamma$ holds. Such a configuration is called **false** if it is not witnessed by any path starting in s, i.e. if $T, s \not\models E \bigwedge \Gamma$ holds.

   A configuration of the form $s \vdash A\Delta$ is said to be **refuted by** π if $\pi(0) = s$ and $T, \pi \not\models \bigvee \Delta$. It is called **false** if it is refuted by some path. In other words, $s \vdash A\Delta$ is false if $T, s \not\models A \bigvee \Delta$. Such a configuration is called **true** if it is not refuted by any path, i.e. if $T, s \models A \bigvee \Delta$. ∇

   The next lemma shows how the game rules affect truth of a configuration.

Lemma 15.3.21. Let C be a configuration of the model-checking game for $\mathcal{T}$ and ϑ that is true. In case that C is of the form $s \vdash E\Gamma$, suppose that it is witnessed by some path π in $\mathcal{T}$. Then:

a) The rules (EU), (ER) and (E$\vee$) can be applied to C to yield a successor that is also witnessed by π and, hence, is also true.

b) Any successor obtained by applying (E$\wedge$) or (ELit) is also witnessed by π and therefore also true.

c) Rule (EX) can be applied to yield a successor which is witnessed by $\pi[1, +\infty)$ and true.

d) Every successor obtained by applying rule (AU), (AR), (A$\wedge$), (A$\vee$), (ALit), (EQ) or (AX) to C is true.

e) Rule (AQ) can be applied to yield a successor that is true.

Proof. Consider rule (ER) from statement (a). We have

$$\varphi R\psi \wedge \Gamma \equiv (\psi \wedge (\varphi \vee X(\varphi R\psi))) \wedge \Gamma \equiv (\psi \wedge \varphi \wedge \Gamma) \vee (\psi \wedge X(\varphi R\psi) \wedge \Gamma)$$

and therefore $\mathcal{T}, \pi \models \varphi R\psi \wedge \Gamma$ iff $\mathcal{T}, \pi \models \psi \wedge \varphi \wedge \Gamma$ or $\mathcal{T}, \pi \models \psi \wedge X(\varphi R\psi) \wedge \Gamma$ for any $\mathcal{T}$ and π. This shows that player **V** can make a choice with rule (ER) that preserves the witness for the configuration that it is applied to.

Next consider rule (AQ) from statement (e). Assume we have $\mathcal{T}, s \models A(Q\psi \vee \Delta)$. Note that $Q\psi$ is a state formula, thus we have $A(Q\psi \vee \Delta) \equiv Q\psi \vee A\Delta$ and therefore $\mathcal{T}, s \models Q\psi$ or $\mathcal{T}, s \models A\Delta$. This shows that one way to apply rule (AQ) must lead to a true configuration.

The remaining cases are similar and are left as Exercise 15.27. □

This lemma suggests a strategy for **V**, namely to preserve truth, possibly helped by a witnessing path. Note that Lemma 15.3.21 shows in particular that **V** *can* preserve truth with her choices whereas **R** *must* preserve truth with his choices.

Definition 15.3.22 (Strategy for V). Let $\mathfrak{str}_0$ be the following strategy for **V** in the model-checking game on $\mathcal{T}$ and ϑ:

- In a false configuration **V** makes arbitrary choices.
- If the game reaches a true configuration of the form $s \vdash E\Gamma$ then this must be witnessed by some path. Then **V** makes a choice that preserves truth and the witness path. If that choice is being made with rule (EU) and both choices would preserve the witness then **V** chooses the left one (i.e. **V** unfolds $\varphi U\psi$ to ψ rather than φ, $X(\varphi U\psi)$).
- If the game reaches a true configuration of the form $s \vdash A\Delta$ then **V** makes a choice that preserves truth. ∇

Lemma 15.3.21 shows that **V** can indeed play like this, i.e. this strategy is well defined. Furthermore, it shows that **R** must preserve truth with his moves. Thus, any play that is started in a true configuration and conforms to $\mathfrak{str}_0$ will only contain true configurations.

We will show that $\mathfrak{str}_0$ is a winning strategy whenever started in a true configuration. This yields completeness of the model-checking games. The following lemmas separate the proof into some cases.

Lemma 15.3.23. Any E-play that starts in a true configuration and conforms to $\mathfrak{str}_0$ is won by **V**. ∎

Proof. Suppose λ is an E-play that starts in a true configuration and conforms to $\mathfrak{str}_0$. By the preceding comment, we know that it only visits true configurations. Strategy $\mathfrak{str}_0$ guarantees even more: there must be some path π such that eventually all configurations in λ are being witnessed respectively by π or its suffixes. This is because an E-play eventually only contains existentially path quantified configurations, and in such configurations strategy $\mathfrak{str}_0$ makes **V** preserve the witnessing path as well. To be precise, there is some $n_0 \in \mathbb{N}$ such that C_{n_0} and all the following configurations are being witnessed by π until rule (EX) is being applied. The next configurations are being witnessed by $\pi[1, +\infty)$ until rule (EX) is being applied for the next time, after which configurations are being witnessed by $\pi[2, +\infty)$, etc. Thus, the play looks like

$$\overset{(\text{EX})}{\ldots, s_{n_0} \vdash \mathsf{E}\Gamma_{n_0},} \quad \overset{(\text{EX})}{s_{n_0} \vdash \mathsf{E}\Gamma_{n+1}, \quad \ldots,} \quad \overset{(\text{EX})}{s_{n_1} \vdash \mathsf{E}\Gamma_{n_1}, \quad \ldots, \quad s_{n_2} \vdash \mathsf{E}\Gamma_{n_2}, \quad \ldots}$$

with $\pi = s_{n_0}, s_{n_1}, s_{n_2}, \ldots$.

Now, suppose for the sake of contradiction, that λ is being won by **R**. Then it must contain a μ-thread with some $\varphi \mathsf{U} \psi$ which occurs infinitely often on this thread. W l o g. we can assume that n_0 is chosen large enough such that $\varphi \mathsf{U} \psi \in \Gamma_{n_i}$ for every $i \in \mathbb{N}$. By the preservation of truth and the witnessing by suffixes of π we have $\mathcal{T}, \pi[i, +\infty) \models \varphi \mathsf{U} \psi$ for every $i \in \mathbb{N}$. For every $i \in \mathbb{N}$ define

$$f(i) := \min\{j \mid \pi[i, +\infty) \models \varphi \mathsf{U}^j \psi\}$$

where $\varphi \mathsf{U}^0 \psi := \bot$ and $\varphi \mathsf{U}^{j+1} \psi := \psi \vee (\varphi \wedge \mathsf{X}(\varphi \mathsf{U}^j \psi))$.

Intuitively, $f(i)$ states how many times $\varphi \mathsf{U} \psi$ has to be unfolded on $\pi[i, +\infty)$ in order to see it being satisfied. Note that $f(i)$ is well defined because $\varphi \mathsf{U} \psi$ is equivalent to the infinite disjunction of $\varphi \mathsf{U}^j \psi$ over all $j \in \mathbb{N}$. Furthermore, we must have $f(i) > f(i+1)$: recall that $\varphi \mathsf{U} \psi$ in Γ_{n_i} is connected (transitively) to itself in $\Gamma_{n_{i+1}}$. A close inspection of the game rules shows that this can only happen if it gets unfolded with rule (EU) which produces φ and $\mathsf{X}(\varphi \mathsf{U} \psi)$ in a configuration C in between. Since it is witnessed by $\pi[i, +\infty)$ we have $\pi[i, +\infty) \models \varphi \wedge \mathsf{X}(\varphi \mathsf{U} \psi)$. Furthermore, we have $\pi[i, +\infty) \not\models \psi$ for otherwise strategy $\mathfrak{str}_0$ would have required **V** to choose the other alternative with rule (EU). Thus, we have $f(i) > 1$ and whenever $\varphi \mathsf{U}^j \psi$ holds in $\pi[i, +\infty)$ for some $j \geq 1$ then we have $\pi[(i+1), +\infty) \models \varphi \mathsf{U}^{j-1} \psi$.

This shows a contradiction: if the play did have a μ-thread then it has an U-formula which gets unfolded infinitely often along that path. The annotations with the number of necessary unfoldings start with a finite number and decrease strictly with every unfolding. Thus, there must be some j with $f(j) = 0$ eventually, meaning $\pi[j, +\infty) \models \varphi \mathsf{U}^0 \psi$, which is impossible. We conclude that the play cannot have a μ-thread and is therefore won by **V**. $\qquad\square$

Lemma 15.3.24. Any A-play that starts in a true configuration and conforms to $\mathfrak{str}_0$ is won by **V**. $\qquad\blacksquare$

Proof. Again, strategy $\mathfrak{str}_0$ guarantees that all configurations of such a play $\lambda = C_0, C_1, \dots$ with $C_i = s_i \vdash Q_i \Delta_i$ for all $i \in \mathbb{N}$, must be true. Since it is an A-play there must be some n_0 such that $Q_i = A$ for all $i \geq n_0$. Since Q_{n_0} is true we have $\mathcal{T}, \pi \models \bigvee \Delta_{n_0}$ for any path π starting in s_{n_0}, in particular the path $\pi = s_{n_0}, s_{n_1}, s_{n_2}, \dots$ where s_{n_i} is the state reached after i applications of rule (AX) in this play.

We will construct a ν-thread starting in C_{n_0}. It should be clear that it can be extended backwards to C_0 to become a ν-thread in λ. We start with some $\varphi_0 \in \Delta_{n_0}$ such that $\mathcal{T}, \pi \models \varphi_0$. Such a formula must exist, for otherwise C_{n_0} would not be true. We follow the connection relation from this formula and show that we must eventually reach a formula of the form $\varphi R \psi$ and follow its unfoldings ad infinitum given that λ is assumed to be an infinite play. The thread is constructed by iterative case distinction. Suppose $\varphi_{n_0} \rightsquigarrow \dots \rightsquigarrow \varphi_{n_i+j}$ has been constructed already such that $\mathcal{T}, \pi[i, +\infty) \models \varphi_{n_i+j}$ for some $i, j \in \mathbb{N}$. We extend this with some formula from Δ_{n_i+j+1} depending on the next rule that is being applied in configuration C_{n_0+i}. If this rule does not operate on φ_{n_i+j} then let $\varphi_{n_i+j+1} = \varphi_{n_i+j}$. Note that we have $\varphi_{n_i+j} \rightsquigarrow \varphi_{n_i+j+1}$ because the only rules that could discard φ_{n_i+j} would be (ALit) or (AQ). However, the former never discards a formula that is true in the current state, and the latter cannot be applicable in this case anymore because we assumed to be in the suffix of the play in which the path quantifier does not get changed any further with this rule.

If $\varphi_{n_i+j} = \psi_1 \vee \psi_2$ and rule (A$\vee$) is being played then we must have $\mathcal{T}, \pi[i, +\infty) \models \psi_h$ for some $h \in \{1, 2\}$. Take φ_{n_i+j+1} to be that ψ_h. Likewise, if $\varphi_{n_i+j} = \psi_1 \wedge \psi_2$ then both conjuncts are being fulfilled on the current path, so no matter which one is present after an application of rule (A$\wedge$), it can be used to extend the sequence of connected formulae. If $\varphi_{n_i+j} = X\psi$ and rule (AX) is being applied then take $\varphi_{n_{i+1}} = \psi$ to be the next formula in this sequence. Note that the invariant of these formulae being satisfied by a corresponding suffix of π still holds, because then we have $\mathcal{T}, \pi[(i+1), +\infty) \models \psi$.

If $\varphi_{n_i+j} = \psi_1 U \psi_2$ and rule (AU) is being used next, then there are two cases depending on which alternative is being chosen with this rule. If it is the left one then we can take φ_{n_i+j+1} to be ψ_1 or ψ_2 because either of them must be satisfied by $\pi[i, +\infty)$. If $\varphi = \psi_1 R \psi_2$ and the left alternative of rule (AR) was chosen then we use ψ_2 which must be true on this path. Similarly, if the right alternative was chosen and ψ_2, respectively ψ_1, is satisfied by $\pi[i, +\infty)$ then we can use this one.

Note that the cases considered up to now all have connected φ_{n_i+j} to a formula that is strictly smaller than itself. The two remaining cases are those of the right alternatives with rules (AU) and (AR) when $\pi[i, +\infty)$ only satisfies $X(\psi_1 U \psi_2)$, or $X(\psi_1 R \psi_2)$, respectively. Consider the former case. If we had $\mathcal{T}, \pi[i, +\infty) \models \psi_1 U \psi_2$ then there must be some k such that $\pi[(i+k), +\infty) \models \psi_2$. Thus, if we continue the iterative construction of this thread through this U-formula we will eventually reach a configuration $C_{n_{i+k}+j'}$ for some j' which contains ψ_2 such that $\mathcal{T}, \pi[(i+k), +\infty) \models \psi_2$.

Putting all this together, we obtain a thread

$$\varphi_{n_0} \rightsquigarrow \varphi_{n_0+1} \rightsquigarrow \ldots \rightsquigarrow \varphi_{n_1} \rightsquigarrow \ldots$$

such that for all i, j we have that $\pi[i, +\infty) \models \varphi_{n_i+j}$ and either

- φ_{n_i+j} is of the form $\psi_1 R \psi_2$, or
- there are i', j' with $i' > i$ or $i' = i$ and $j' > j$, and $\varphi_{n_{i'}+j'}$ is strictly smaller than φ_{n_i+j}.

Thus, this thread will either contain infinitely many R-formulae or it will eventually end up in a propositional literal. The latter case would contradict the assumption that λ is infinite, because a universally path quantified configuration which contains a proposition literal that is satisfied in the current state is final and the play would end there. $\qquad\square$

We are now just a small step away from showing completeness of the CTL* model checking games.

Theorem 15.3.25 (Completeness). Let $\mathcal{T}$ be an ITS with some state s_0 and $\vartheta \in$ CTL*. If $\mathcal{T}, s_0 \models \vartheta$ then **V** wins the model-checking game $\mathcal{G}^{\mathcal{T}}(s_0, \vartheta)$. $\qquad\blacksquare$

Proof. Suppose $\mathcal{T}, s_0 \models \vartheta$. Then the starting configuration $s_0 \vdash A\vartheta$ of the model-checking game on $\mathcal{T}$ and ϑ is true. Consider **V**'s strategy $\mathfrak{str}_0$ as defined in Definition 15.3.22. It remains to be seen that it is indeed a winning strategy. Consider an arbitrary play $\lambda = C_0, C_1, \ldots$ that conforms to this strategy. Since $\mathfrak{str}_0$ guarantees the preservation of truth, this play cannot be winning for **R** because he only wins a finite play when it reaches a configuration that is false. According to Lemma 15.3.19, **V** must win this play.

So, suppose that the play is infinite. According to Lemma 15.3.13 it must either by an E- or an A-play. Lemmas 15.3.23 and 15.3.24 show that it is won by **V**, too. $\qquad\square$

Soundness can be proved in a very analogous way. Define a strategy $\mathfrak{str}_1$ for **R** which preserves falsity and the paths that refute universally path quantified configurations. Note the symmetry in the game rules and winning conditions. Here is it important that **R** chooses the left alternative in rule (AR) whenever possible, just like strategy $\mathfrak{str}_0$ demanded **V** to choose the left alternative in rule (EU) whenever possible. This strategy turns out to be a winning strategy. Again, **V** cannot win a finite play against this strategy because she only wins finite plays in true configurations. Preservation of refuting paths means that an A-play will eventually follow a predetermined path on which all formulae in configurations occurring in this play are false. Then this play cannot have a ν-thread because if a R-formula is not satisfied along some path then there must be some finite approximant that is not satisfied, and the indices of these approximants must decrease along the thread. It is also possible to construct a μ-thread in some E-play in which all configurations are false. Thus, we have obtained the following.

Theorem 15.3.26 (Soundness). Let $\mathcal{T}$ be an ITS with some state s_0 and $\vartheta \in \text{CTL}^*$. If $\mathcal{T}, s_0 \not\models \vartheta$ then **R** wins the model-checking game $\mathcal{G}^{\mathcal{T}}(s_0, \vartheta)$. ∎

Putting Theorem 15.3.25 and 15.3.26 together, we obtain that the model-checking games for CTL* exactly characterise its model-checking problem.

Corollary 15.3.27. Let $\mathcal{T}$ be an ITS with some state s_0 and $\vartheta \in \text{CTL}^*$. We have $\mathcal{T}, s_0 \models \vartheta$ iff **V** wins the model-checking game $\mathcal{G}^{\mathcal{T}}(s_0, \vartheta)$. ∎

A Game-Based Decision Procedure for CTL* Model Checking

Corollary 15.3.27 gives a game-theoretic characterisation of the model-checking problem for CTL*. This does not immediately show how to solve such games – and, hence, the model-checking problem – algorithmically. Note that the winning condition is not given as a parity condition. The key contribution of this section is to show that the winning condition of the CTL* model-checking games are regular and, moreover, can be defined by a weak parity automaton. Then we can use the reduction technique developed in Section 15.1.7 in order to reduce the CTL* model-checking games to parity games.

A naïve approach considers the winning condition for **V** as a formal language over the alphabet of all possible configurations. This is suboptimal; recall that the number of different configurations is exponential in the size of the input formula. It is possible to abstract them using a symbolic encoding of the rule applications. This reduces the alphabet to one of size linear in the input formula. The price to pay for this reduction is the fact that small automata cannot recognise the language of all plays in a certain game anymore. This is no problem, though. Recall that the reduction to parity games forms a product of the model-checking game with a deterministic automaton for the winning condition. Thus, these automata are only run on plays anyway, and there is no need to make them recognise exactly those plays that are being won by **V**. Instead it suffices to make them recognise any sequence of alphabet symbols that is a winning for **V** *if* it encodes a play. In terms of formal languages, this abstraction overapproximates the language of all plays won by **V**.

As before, hereafter we fix an ITS $\mathcal{T} = (S, \rightarrow, L)$ and a CTL* formula ϑ.

Definition 15.3.28. We define the **alphabet of symbolic rule applications** in a model-checking game for ϑ as

$$\Sigma_\vartheta := \{\text{EAnd}(\varphi, \psi), \text{AAnd}_d(\varphi, \psi) \mid \varphi \wedge \psi \in \textit{fi}(\vartheta), d \in \{\text{lft}, \text{rgh}\}\}$$
$$\cup \{\text{AOr}(\varphi, \psi), \text{EOr}_d(\varphi, \psi) \mid \varphi \vee \psi \in \textit{fi}(\vartheta), d \in \{\text{lft}, \text{rgh}\}\}$$
$$\cup \{\text{EU}_d(\varphi, \psi), \text{AU}_d(\varphi, \psi) \mid \varphi \text{U} \psi \in \textit{fi}(\vartheta), d \in \{\text{lft}, \text{rgh}\}\}$$
$$\cup \{\text{ER}_d(\varphi, \psi), \text{AR}_d(\varphi, \psi) \mid \varphi \text{R} \psi \in \textit{fi}(\vartheta), d \in \{\text{lft}, \text{rgh}\}\}$$
$$\cup \{\text{ELit}(\ell), \text{ALit}(\ell) \mid \ell \text{ literal in } \textit{fi}(\vartheta)\}$$
$$\cup \{\text{EQ}_d(\text{Q}\varphi), \text{AQ}_d(\text{Q}\varphi) \mid \text{Q} \in \{\text{E}, \text{A}\}, \text{Q}\varphi \in \textit{fi}(\vartheta), d \in \{\text{lft}, \text{rgh}\}\}$$
$$\cup \{\text{EX}, \text{AX}, \text{Win}_\text{V}, \text{Win}_\text{R}\}. \qquad \nabla$$

Note that an alphabet symbol uniquely identifies a rule that is being used, together with the formula on which it operates and – if applicable – the alternative that has been chosen by the corresponding player. For instance, symbol $\mathsf{AR}_{\mathsf{rgh}}(\varphi \mathsf{R} \psi)$ identifies an application of rule (AR) on $\varphi \mathsf{R} \psi$ in which $\mathbf{R}$ has chosen the right alternative. The latter is indicated by the subscript rgh. Likewise, $\mathsf{EOr}_{\mathsf{lft}}(\varphi \vee \psi)$ is used to mark a transition from some configuration $s \vdash \mathsf{E}(\varphi \vee \psi, \Gamma)$ to $s \vdash \mathsf{E}(\varphi, \Gamma)$ as the left alternative of rule (E∨). Note that rules (EX) and (AX) operate on all formulae in the present configuration. That is why we do not need to mark the symbolic representation of these rules with a principal formula. Finally, the symbols $\mathsf{Win}_\mathbf{P}$ for $\mathbf{P} \in \{\mathbf{V}, \mathbf{R}\}$ are used to symbolically encode finite plays; they should indicate that a final position in which Player $\mathbf{P}$ wins has been reached.

It should be clear that any play $\lambda = C_0, C_1, \ldots$ can be represented symbolically as a word over the alphabet Σ_ϑ in which the ith letter symbolically encodes the rule application that resulted in the transition from C_i to C_{i+1}. We will not distinguish formally between a play and its symbolic encoding as a word over Σ_ϑ. We assume that finite plays are encoded as infinite words ending on $(\mathsf{Win}_\mathbf{P})^\omega$ for some $\mathbf{P} \in \{\mathbf{V}, \mathbf{R}\}$.

Next, we show that all types of winning plays for $\mathbf{V}$ can be accepted by weak parity automata.

Lemma 15.3.29. There is a deterministic weak parity automaton $\mathcal{D}^{\mathsf{fin}}$ of constant size that accepts a finite play of the model-checking game on ϑ iff it is won by $\mathbf{V}$. ∎

Proof. The convention we adopted for encoding finite plays symbolically makes the definition of this automaton very simple. It accepts a word over Σ_ϑ if it contains the symbol $\mathsf{Win}_\mathbf{V}$. This can obviously be achieved with a deterministic weak parity automaton that has two states only. □

Note how we make use of the fact that these automata are only supposed to work on the symbolic encoding of a play but not on an arbitrary sequence of symbolic rule applications of which there are more. Thus, $\mathcal{D}^{\mathsf{fin}}$ will also accept other sequences that do not correspond to encodings of finite plays. This is irrelevant, though, because of the way that it will be used later on. $\mathcal{D}^{\mathsf{fin}}$ is not supposed, either, to check whether the given sequence of symbols does indeed encode a finite play that is won by $\mathbf{V}$. This would of course be impossible without access to the actual configurations but the automata constructed here do not see these configurations anymore.

Lemma 15.3.30. There is a nondeterministic weak parity automaton $\mathcal{A}_\vartheta^\mathsf{A}$ of size $\mathcal{O}(|\vartheta|^2)$ that accepts an A-play of the model-checking game for ϑ iff it is won by player $\mathbf{V}$. ∎

Proof. Recall that an A-play is won by $\mathbf{V}$ only if it contains a ν-thread. We will construct $\mathcal{A}_\vartheta^\mathsf{A}$ to guess a thread and verify that it is a ν-thread. Let $\mathsf{A}\chi_1, \ldots, \mathsf{A}\chi_m$ be all universally path quantified formulae in $fi(\vartheta)$ and $\varphi_1 \mathsf{R} \psi_1, \ldots, \varphi_k \mathsf{R} \psi_k$ be all R-formulae in $fi(\vartheta)$. The overall structure of $\mathcal{A}_\vartheta^\mathsf{A}$ is as follows with its components being explained later. The dashed edges may or may not exist depending on the exact structure of the components that they leave.

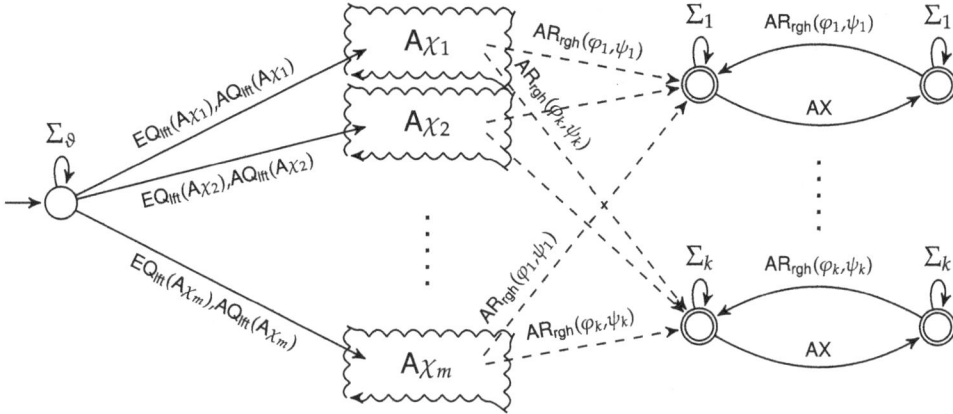

where, for $i = 1, \ldots, k$, Σ_i consists of all letters of the form $\mathsf{AOr}(\varphi', \psi')$, $\mathsf{AAnd}_d(\varphi', \psi')$, $\mathsf{AR}_d(\varphi', \psi')$, $\mathsf{AU}_d(\varphi', \psi')$ and $\mathsf{ALit}(\ell)$ such that $\varphi' \neq \varphi_i$ and $\psi' \neq \psi_i$.

$\mathcal{A}_\vartheta^\mathsf{A}$ intuitively works as follows. In its initial state it reads any finite prefix of an A-play. At some point it guesses that it sees a last application of rule (AQ) which enters the part of the play in which all successive configurations are universally path quantified. Then it starts guessing a thread by following particular subformulae. Note that after an application of rule (AQ) on a formula of the form $\mathsf{A}\chi_i$, any thread will go through χ_i. In the components marked $\mathsf{A}\chi_i$, which are described in detail in the following, it follows a thread until it guesses at some point that an occurring $\varphi_i \mathsf{R} \psi_i$ will be unfolded infinitely often. Then it changes to the corresponding right-most component in which it only verifies that this does happen, indeed. The two states are used in order to distinguish whether the thread currently contains $\varphi_i \mathsf{R} \psi_i$ or $\mathsf{X}(\varphi_i \mathsf{R} \psi_i)$.

The component $\mathsf{A}\chi_i$ has one state for every formula in $fi(\chi_i)$. Its transitions only accept the letters $\mathsf{AOr}(\varphi, \psi)$, $\mathsf{AAnd}_d(\varphi, \psi)$, $\mathsf{AR}_d(\varphi, \psi)$, $\mathsf{AU}_d(\varphi, \psi)$, $\mathsf{ALit}(\ell)$ and $\mathsf{AQ}_{\mathsf{rgh}}(\mathsf{Q}\varphi)$ for some φ, ψ and d. The other rules cannot be seen, unless the play is not in its final universally path quantified part. The transitions follow the connection relation.

- In state $\varphi \vee \psi$ there are transitions with letter $\mathsf{AOr}(\varphi, \psi)$ to both φ and ψ.
- In state $\varphi \wedge \psi$ there is a transition to φ with letter $\mathsf{AAnd}_{\mathsf{lft}}(\varphi, \psi)$ and a transition to ψ with letter $\mathsf{AAnd}_{\mathsf{rgh}}(\varphi, \psi)$.
- In state $\varphi \mathsf{U} \psi$ there are transitions to both φ and ψ with letter $\mathsf{AU}_{\mathsf{lft}}(\varphi, \psi)$ and transitions to both ψ and $\mathsf{X}(\varphi \mathsf{R} \psi)$ with letter $\mathsf{AU}_{\mathsf{rgh}}(\varphi, \psi)$.
- In state $\varphi_i \mathsf{R} \psi_i$ there is a transition to ψ_i with letter $\mathsf{AR}_{\mathsf{lft}}(\varphi_i, \psi_i)$ and there are transitions to both φ_i and $\mathsf{X}(\varphi_i \mathsf{R} \psi_i)$ with letter $\mathsf{AR}_{\mathsf{rgh}}(\varphi_i, \psi_i)$. Additionally, there is a transition to the ith component depicted on the right in $\mathcal{A}_\vartheta^\mathsf{A}$'s transition graph shown earlier. Note that this creates proper nondeterminism.
- In state $\mathsf{X}\varphi$ there is a transition to φ with letter AX.

Additionally, any state has a transition to itself with any of the letters allowed in this component, which have not been mentioned in these five cases.

The size estimation follows from the fact that the size of each $A\chi_i$-component is bounded by $\mathrm{card}(\mathit{fi}(\vartheta))$ and there can be at most $|\vartheta|$ many of them. It should also be clear that $\mathcal{A}_\vartheta^A$ is indeed a weak parity automaton. Here we use the conventional notation of accepting states in order to denote states with an even priority. The others are supposed to have an odd priority. Note that its strongly connected components are either all prioritised oddly (the leftmost and the ones in the middle), or evenly (the rightmost).

Correctness of this construction is easy to prove in detail given the intuitive description of $\mathcal{A}_\vartheta^A$'s functionality. It is easy to contruct an accepting run on an A-play with a μ-thread by following the thread once it has entered the final part in which the outer path quantifier does not change anymore. Conversely, given an A-play without a μ-thread we observe that $\mathcal{A}_\vartheta^A$ must get stuck eventually if it manages to reach one of its rightmost components in which it follows a single R-formula and its unfoldings infinitely often.   □

Lemma 15.3.31. There is a deterministic co-Büchi automaton $\mathcal{A}_\vartheta^F$ of size $2^{\mathcal{O}(|\vartheta|)}$ that accepts an E-play of the model-checking game for ϑ iff it is won by player **V**.   ∎

Proof. We describe $\mathcal{A}_\vartheta^E$'s behaviour intuitively. It uses as its state set $\{A, E\} \times 2^{\mathit{fi}(\vartheta)} \times 2^{\mathcal{U}}$ where $\mathcal{U}$ is the set of all formulae of the form $\varphi \mathsf{U} \psi$ in $\mathit{fi}(\varphi)$. It starts in the state $(A, \{\vartheta\}, \emptyset)$. In its left and middle component it simply constructs the underlying configuration. For instance, if the next letter to be read is $\mathsf{AAnd}_{\mathrm{rgh}}(\varphi, \psi)$ then it replaces $\varphi \wedge \psi$ by ψ in this middle component. If the next letter to be read is $\mathsf{AQ}_{\mathrm{lft}}(\mathsf{E}\varphi)$ then it changes into $(E, \{\varphi\}, \emptyset)$.

Its right component is used to trace all U-formulae occurring in a configuration. After every letter of the form $\mathsf{EQ}_{\mathrm{lft}}(\mathsf{Q}\varphi)$ this right component is reset to $\emptyset$. If the right component is $\emptyset$ then its next transition replaces it by $\Phi \cap \mathcal{U}$ where Φ is the value of the middle component in the state that is being reached. Whenever it reads letter $\mathsf{AU}_{\mathrm{lft}}(\varphi, \psi)$ then it deletes $\varphi \mathsf{U} \psi$ from its right component.

It should be clear that $\mathcal{A}_\vartheta^E$ is indeed a deterministic automaton of size at most $2^{2\mathrm{card}(\mathit{fi}(\vartheta))+1}$. We have yet to define the acceptance condition. States of the form $(E, \Phi, \emptyset)$ receive an even priority, i.e. are accepting in the sense of a Büchi automaton, others receive an odd priority.

Now suppose that λ is an E-play. Consider the unique run of $\mathcal{A}_\vartheta^E$ on it. Clearly, it will eventually see states of the form (E, Φ, Φ') only. Suppose that λ contains a μ-thread with some $\varphi \mathsf{U} \psi$ occurring infinitely often. Then this formula will eventually be added to the right component and stay there because eventually player **V** will not use the left alternative with rule (EU) anymore. Thus, the run would not be accepting.

On the other hand, suppose that λ contains no μ-thread. Then any $\varphi \mathsf{U} \psi$ that is present in an existentially path quantified configuration on this path and the right state component in the corresponding position in the automaton's run will eventually be unfolded with the left alternative of rule (EU). Thus, the symbolic encoding of the play must eventually contain the letter $\mathsf{EU}_{\mathrm{lft}}(\varphi, \psi)$ which will remove this U-formula from the right state component which therefore has to become empty eventually. Either it stays empty forever, or it becomes empty again and again. Thus, the run is accepting. □

Theorem 15.3.32. Let $\mathcal{T}$ be an ITS with n states, s be a state in $\mathcal{T}$ and ϑ be a CTL* formula. There is a co-Büchi game of size at most $n \cdot 2^{\mathcal{O}(|\vartheta|)}$ that is won by Player 0 iff $\mathcal{T}, s \models \vartheta$. ■

Proof. According to Corollary 15.3.27 we have $\mathcal{T}, s \models \vartheta$ iff player **V** wins the model-checking game $\mathcal{G}^{\mathcal{T}}(s, \vartheta)$. Note that the size of the game is bounded by $n \cdot 2^{|\vartheta|+1}$.

The set of plays *Win* won by player **V** in this games can be partitioned disjointly into $Win = Win^{\text{fin}} \cup Win^{\text{A}} \cup Win^{\text{E}}$ holding respectively the sets of finite plays, A-plays and E-play won by her. According to Lemma 15.3.29 and 15.3.31, Win^{fin} and Win^{E} can be recognised respectively by a deterministic weak parity automaton of size 2 and a deterministic co-Büchi automaton of size $2^{\mathcal{O}(|\vartheta|)}$.

Win^{A} can be recognised by a nondeterministic weak parity automaton of size $\mathcal{O}(|\vartheta|)$. Hence, by Corollary 15.2.2 there is an equivalent deterministic co-Büchi automaton of size at most $3^{\mathcal{O}(|\vartheta|)}$, equivalently, $2^{\mathcal{O}(|\vartheta|)}$. According to Theorem 15.2.3 there is a deterministic co-Büchi automaton of size $2^{\mathcal{O}(|\vartheta|)}$ that recognises *Win* (when restricted to sequences encoding proper plays).

Finally, Corollary 15.1.28 – the main reduction theorem for co-Büchi games – says that the model-checking game can be paired with this deterministic co-Büchi automaton in order to yield a co-Büchi game that is won by Player 0 iff the underlying model-checking game is won by player **V**. The size of this co-Büchi game is the product of the sizes of the model-checking game and the deterministic co-Büchi automaton, i.e. $n \cdot 2^{|\vartheta|+1} \cdot 2^{\mathcal{O}(|\vartheta|)} = n \cdot 2^{\mathcal{O}(|\vartheta|)}$. □

Since solving co-Büchi games requires at least linear time, this is not an optimal result. Note that model checking CTL* is PSPACE-complete, while this reduction to co-Büchi games only yields an EXPTIME upper bound. The PSPACE upper bound is usually obtained by reducing CTL* model checking to LTL model checking. This also works in the game-theoretic framework.

Theorem 15.3.33. The model-checking problem for LTL can be solved in PSPACE. ■

Proof. Let $\mathcal{T}$ be an ITS with n states and ϑ be an LTL formula. Recall that ϑ, regarded as an LTL formula with the implicit universal path quantification, is equivalent to the CTL* formula $A\vartheta$, where there are no other path quantifiers in ϑ.

We consider the special case of playing the CTL* model-checking game on $A\vartheta$. We can assume that the game starts in a position $s \vdash A\vartheta$ rather than $s \vdash AA\vartheta$, because the latter has the former as the unique successor.

Rules $(E\wedge)$, $(E\vee)$, (EU), (ER), (EQ), (AQ), $(ELit)$ and (EX) can never be used in the game on such a formula. The remaining rules, however, are either deterministic or incorporate choices made by player **R**. Thus, the LTL model-checking game is a 1-player game of size $n \cdot 2^{|\vartheta|}$. Moreover, every play in this game is an A-play which also simplifies the winning conditions: a deterministic co-Büchi automaton for the winning condition is obtained from the union construction in Theorem 15.2.3 using the simple automaton $\mathcal{A}_\vartheta^{\text{fin}}$ recognising finite plays won by player **V** from Lemma 15.3.29 with a deterministic variant of $\mathcal{A}_\vartheta^{\text{A}}$ from Lemma 15.3.30. The reduction in Theorem 15.3.32 yields a 1-player parity game of size linear in n and exponential in $|\vartheta|$. According to Theorem 15.1.24 it can be solved in nondeterministic polynomial-space which – according to Savitch's Theorem – equals PSPACE.   □

15.4 Satisfiability Checking

Now we turn to the other fundamental logical decision problem: satisfiability checking. Again, we are interested in giving it a game-theoretic characterisation in the sense of games between two players. We keep the names **V** and **R**, even though – strictly speaking – their role is not to verify and to refute. Instead, the task of player **V** now is to show that the input formula has a model, whereas player **R** wants to show that it is unsatisfiable. Note that these tasks are not as symmetric, like in the model-checking games, anymore: player **V** can fulfil her task by providing a witnessing model, whereas player **R** cannot prove unsatisfiability with some witness in an equally obvious manner.

Still, it is possible to characterise satisfiability problems for temporal logics game-theoretically. This lack of symmetry will show up in the game rules and winning conditions, which will not be as symmetric as they are for model-checking games anymore. Symmetry prevails on the level of existence of winning strategies: the games are equally determined, and this symmetry provides an interesting and useful characterisation of unsatisfiability in the form of a winning strategy. Thus, the game-theoretic framework turns the universal property of being unsatisfiable into an existential property of player **R** having a winning strategy. This existential characterisation is important and useful in order to provide a reason for why a formula is not satisfiable.

The symmetry break in the game rules can easily be explained on the level of propositional logic. In the model-checking games for the modal μ-calculus, for instance, a disjunction leads to a choice by **V** because a disjunction is satisfied iff one of its disjuncts is satisfied. A conjunction, on the other hand, is unsatisfied iff one of its conjuncts is unsatisfied which makes it a choice for player **R**. Satisfiability, on the other hand, is not such a modular property. A conjunction can be unsatisfiable even though both conjuncts may be satisfiable. Thus, we cannot expect the rules to separate conjunctions. Instead, we must keep them together in order to decompose formulae with the aim of testing the satisfiability. Luckily, this is not entirely new now, because it is exactly what happens in the CTL* model-checking games inside an E-block. In order to define satisfiability games for temporal logics, we will be able to reuse much of the machinery that has been developed for the CTL* model-checking games.

$$(\wedge) \ \frac{\varphi \wedge \psi, \Gamma}{\varphi, \psi, \Gamma} \qquad (\texttt{Mod}) \ \frac{\langle a_1 \rangle \varphi_1, \ldots, \langle a_n \rangle \varphi_n, [b_1] \psi_1, \ldots, [b_m] \psi_m, \ell_1, \ldots, \ell_k}{\varphi_1, \{\psi_j \mid b_j = a_1\} \qquad \ldots \qquad \varphi_n, \{\psi_j \mid b_j = a_n\}} \ \mathbf{R}$$

$$(\vee) \ \frac{\varphi \vee \psi, \Gamma}{\varphi, \Gamma \qquad \psi, \Gamma} \ \mathbf{V} \qquad (\texttt{FP}) \ \frac{\tau X.\varphi, \Gamma}{X, \Gamma} \qquad (\texttt{Var}) \ \frac{X, \Gamma}{\varphi, \Gamma} \ \text{if } fp_{\vartheta}(X) = \tau X.\varphi$$

Figure 15.5 The rules for the $\mathcal{L}_\mu$ satisfiability games.

We start again with the full modal μ-calculus. Simpler logics like its alternation-free fragment or CTL do not necessarily lead to much simpler games. Note that satisfiability solving is EXPTIME-hard for all of them (cf. Theorem 11.4.6). We then consider CTL*. The 2EXPTIME-hardness of its satisfiability problem suggests that we need to work on more complicated structures than formula sets for this logic.

15.4.1 Mu-Calculi

For the remainder of this section we fix a closed and guarded $\mathcal{L}_\mu$ formula ϑ in negation normal form and explain the satisfiability-checking game $\mathcal{G}(\vartheta)$ for this fixed formula. Guardedness is a crucial prerequisite for the correctness of these games. Recall that every $\mathcal{L}_\mu$ formula can equivalently be transformed into one in guarded form (Theorem 8.3.23).

The Satisfiability-Checking Game for $\mathcal{L}_\mu$

The configurations of the satisfiability game $\mathcal{G}(\vartheta)$ are subsets of $fi(\vartheta)$ (cf. Definition 8.3.15). We avoid using brackets as much as possible and write, for instance, φ, Γ in order to denote the unique set Γ' such that $\varphi \in \Gamma'$ and $\Gamma = \Gamma' \setminus \{\varphi\}$.

The rules for the $\mathcal{L}_\mu$ satisfiability game $\mathcal{G}(\vartheta)$ are presented in Figure 15.5. In rule (Mod), the ℓ_i's are supposed to be propositional literals over the underlying atomic propositions. Note that there is only one rule per player that provides a genuine choice: player $\mathbf{V}$ chooses disjuncts and player $\mathbf{R}$ selects which modalities are being followed.

As in the CTL* model-checking games, there are finite and infinite plays.

Definition 15.4.1 (Winning conditions for finite plays). Player $\mathbf{V}$ wins a play $C_0, C_1, \ldots$ of $\mathcal{G}(\vartheta)$ if there is some $n \in \mathbb{N}$ such that C_n is of the form $\ell_1, \ldots, \ell_k$ and there are no i, j with $\ell_i = \overline{\ell_j}$.

Player $\mathbf{R}$ wins such a play if there is some $n \in \mathbb{N}$ and some atomic proposition p such that $\{p, \neg p\} \subseteq C_n$. $\qquad \nabla$

The winning conditions for infinite plays are supposed to capture the (absence of) infinite unfoldings of least fixpoint constructs. We recall the connection relation $\rightsquigarrow$ between formulae of two successive configurations: in an application of rule $(\wedge)$, $\varphi \wedge \psi$ is connected to both φ and ψ in the successor, and all other formulae there are connected to itself, etc. The definition of a thread is slightly different, though.

Definition 15.4.2. Let $\Gamma_0, \Gamma_1, \ldots$ be an infinite play of $\mathcal{G}(\vartheta)$. A **thread** is an infinite sequence $\varphi_0, \varphi_1, \ldots$ such that for all $i \in \mathbb{N}$, φ_i in Γ_i is connected to φ_{i+1} in Γ_{i+1}.

Such a thread is called a μ-**thread** if the outermost (with respect to $\succeq_\vartheta$) variable that occurs infinitely often in it is of fixpoint type μ. If this variable is of fixpoint type ν then the thread is called a ν-**thread**. $\triangledown$

The proof of the following lemma is along the lines of the proofs of Lemma 15.3.16 and 15.3.17. The details are left as Exercise 15.27.

Lemma 15.4.3.

a) Every infinite play of $\mathcal{G}(\vartheta)$ has a thread.
b) Every thread in a play of $\mathcal{G}(\vartheta)$ is either a μ-thread or a ν-thread, but not both.   ■

The notion of a thread is used to define the winning conditions for infinite plays. The previous lemma implies that these winning conditions cover all possible cases.

Definition 15.4.4 (Winning conditions for infinite plays). Player **V** wins an infinite play $C_0, C_1, \ldots$ of $\mathcal{G}(\vartheta)$ if it contains no μ-thread. Player **R** wins such a play if it contains a μ-thread. $\triangledown$

Correctness Proofs

Our main aim now is to show that these games are sound and complete with respect to $\mathcal{L}_\mu$ satisfiability. We will use the $\mathcal{L}_\mu$ model-checking games in order to prove their correctness.

Theorem 15.4.5 (Completeness). Let ϑ be a closed and guarded $\mathcal{L}_\mu$ formula. If ϑ is satisfiable then player **V** has a winning strategy for the game $\mathcal{G}(\vartheta)$.   ■

Proof. Suppose that ϑ has a model $\mathcal{T} = (S, \{\xrightarrow{a}\}_{a \in Act}, L, s_0)$. According to Theorem 8.4.10, player **V** has a positional winning strategy $\mathfrak{str}$ for the model-checking game $\mathcal{G}^{\mathcal{T}}(s_0, \vartheta)$. We will use $\mathfrak{str}$ in order to define a strategy $\mathfrak{str}'$ for **V** in the satisfiability game $\mathcal{G}(\vartheta)$.

Her strategy requires her to keep track of a state in $\mathcal{T}$ for every configuration in the satisfiability game. Intuitively, we see this as annotating such a configuration Γ with a state s and write this as $s \vdash \Gamma$. This annotation will help player **V** to make her choices in the satisfiability game.

V begins by annotating the starting configuration with the state s_0, i.e. in $s_0 \vdash \vartheta$. Depending on the next rule of the satisfiability game to be applied, **V** annotates successor configurations as follows. If the rule is $(\wedge)$, $(\texttt{FP})$ or $(\texttt{Var})$, **V** uses the current state. Moreover, this – and the following – preserves an important invariant: if the satisfiability game reaches an annotated configuration $s \vdash \Gamma$ then for every $\varphi \in \Gamma$ there is a play in the model-checking game $\mathcal{G}^{\mathcal{T}}(s_0, \vartheta)$ that conforms to $\mathfrak{str}$ and that contains the configuration $s \vdash \varphi$. This ensures that we can appeal to $\mathfrak{str}$ in order to define the satisfiability game strategy $\mathfrak{str}'$. It is easy to see that this invariant holds at the beginning and is preserved by the three deterministic rules mentioned previously. As we will see, it can be also preserved by the two remaining rules.

Consider the case of rule ($\vee$). Thus, the satisfiability game has been played as $C_0, \ldots, C_n$ with $C_n = \varphi \vee \psi, \Gamma$ for some φ, ψ, Γ. Player **V**'s view on it is that of an annotated configuration $s \vdash \varphi_1 \vee \varphi_2, \Gamma$. According to the invariant, the strategy $\mathfrak{str}$ in the model-checking game is defined on the position $s \vdash \varphi_1 \vee \varphi_2$. Since this configuration requires player **V** to make a choice, we have $\mathfrak{str}(s \vdash \varphi_1 \vee \varphi_2) = s \vdash \varphi_i$ for some $i \in \{1, 2\}$. We define $\mathfrak{str}'(C_0, \ldots, C_n) := \varphi_i, \Gamma$. Thus, player **V** chooses disjuncts in the satisfiability games according to her choices for disjuncts in the model-checking game, using the annotation that yields satisfaction of a disjunct in a particular state of an ITS chosen at the beginning. Note that strategy $\mathfrak{str}'$ need not be positional.

Finally, consider the case of rule (Mod) which requires player **R** to make a choice. Assume that the current play in the satisfiability game has reached the annotated configuration

$$s \vdash \langle a_1 \rangle \varphi_1, \ldots, \langle a_n \rangle \varphi_n, [b_1] \psi_1, \ldots, [b_m] \psi_m, \ell_1, \ldots, \ell_k.$$

According to the invariant stated earlier, for every formula χ in this configuration there is a play of the model-checking game that conforms to $\mathfrak{str}$ and contains the configuration $s \vdash \chi$. An immediate consequence of this is the fact that we cannot have $\ell_i = \overline{\ell_j}$ for any $1 \le i, j \le k$ because then there would be some atomic proposition p such that strategy $\mathfrak{str}$ would take player **V** to both $s \vdash p$ and $s \vdash \neg p$. Surely, **V** can only win in one of these two configurations. Hence, if $\mathfrak{str}$ is a winning strategy then the satisfiability play continues with a choice by player **R** with rule (Mod). Since we need to construct a strategy for player **V**, we need to be able to respond to all possible choices by player **R**. In other words, we need to find annotations for every possible successor configuration that preserve the aforementioned invariant.

Note that there are exactly n successor configurations: one for each $\Diamond$-formula in the current configuration. Moreover, player **V** makes choices in configurations of the form $s \vdash \langle a_i \rangle \varphi_i$ of the model-checking game. For every $i = 1, \ldots, n$ let t_i be the uniquely defined state of $\mathcal{T}$ such that $\mathfrak{str}(s \vdash \langle a_i \rangle \varphi_i) = t_i \vdash \varphi_i$. Player **V** now annotates the ith successor configuration $\varphi_i, \{\psi_j \mid b_j = a_i\}$ with t_i. It remains to be seen that the invariant is not broken, i.e. that strategy $\mathfrak{str}$ can also be used to follow the ψ_j's. Take some ψ_j such that $b_j = a_i$. Recall that, by the invariant, there is a play in the model-checking game $\mathcal{G}^{\mathcal{T}}(s_0, \vartheta)$ that conforms to $\mathfrak{str}$ and reaches the configuration $s \vdash [b_j] \psi_j$. Since it requires player **R** to make a choice, all possible successors are also configurations in a play that conforms to $\mathfrak{str}$. If we have $\mathfrak{str}(s \vdash \langle a_i \rangle \varphi_i) = t_i \vdash \varphi_i$ we must have $s \xrightarrow{a_i} t_i$. Thus, if $a_i = b_j$ we also have $s \xrightarrow{b_j} t_i$ and $t_i \vdash \psi_j$ as a valid successor to $s \vdash [b_j] \psi_j$ in the model-checking game, which shows that the invariant is indeed preserved.

It remains to be seen that this strategy $\mathfrak{str}'$ is indeed a winning strategy for player **V** in the satisfiability game $\mathcal{G}(\vartheta)$. We have already seen that no finite play that conforms to $\mathfrak{str}'$ can be won by player **R**. So, suppose there was an infinite play $\lambda = C_0, C_1, \ldots$ that conforms to $\mathfrak{str}'$ but is won by player **R**. Then it would have to contain a μ-thread. Let $\varphi_0, \varphi_1, \ldots$ be that μ-thread and $s_0, s_1, \ldots$ be the sequence of annotations that player **V** has used in this play in order to help her transfer the choices with the model-checking game strategy $\mathfrak{str}$ to choices with the satisfiability game strategy $\mathfrak{str}'$. The sequence $s_0 \vdash \varphi_0, s_1 \vdash \varphi_1, \ldots$ can contain subwords of repeated pairs of states and formulae. This happens whenever a rule is applied to some formula which is not the one on the thread. Let $\lambda = s_{i_0} \vdash \varphi_{i_0}, s_{i_1} \vdash \varphi_{i_1}, \ldots$ be the maximal subsequence such that adjacent pairs in this subsequence are unequal. The last observation we need to make is the following: λ is a play of the model-checking game $\mathcal{G}^T(s_0, \vartheta)$ that conforms to strategy $\mathfrak{str}$.

- It is not hard to see that λ is a play of the model-checking game, because the satisfiability game rules can be seen as extensions of the model-checking game rules with side formulae. The transformations on formulae that are being realised by the satisfiability game rules are the same as those in the model-checking game rules. Moreover, the connection relation underlying the notion of a thread only connects formulae in the way that the model-checking game rules transform them, or connects formulae to themselves whenever the satisfiability game rules operate on other formulae. Connections of the latter form are being deleted in λ'. Thus, λ' is indeed a play of the model-checking game $\mathcal{G}^T(s_0, \vartheta)$.
- The play λ' conforms to $\mathfrak{str}$ simply because the annotations have been chosen with respect to $\mathfrak{str}$.

Thus, if λ contains a μ-thread then it gives rise to a model-checking play λ' that conforms to $\mathfrak{str}$ and in which the outermost variable occurring infinitely often is of type μ. This contradicts the assumption that $\mathfrak{str}$ is a winning strategy. We conclude by Lemma 15.4.3 that λ must, indeed, be won by player **V** which makes $\mathfrak{str}'$ a winning strategy. $\qquad\square$

The soundness proof makes use of a construction that turns a strategy for player **V** into a tree-shaped ITS. Let $\mathfrak{str}$ be such a strategy. We construct the ITS $\mathcal{T}_{\mathfrak{str}}$ as follows. Its states are sequences of configurations from $\mathcal{G}(\vartheta)$. Intuitively, we regard the tree of all plays that conform to $\mathfrak{str}$ as an ITS by dividing its sequences of configurations at those moments in which rule (Mod) is being played. Formally, we start its construction with a state s_0 which holds the single configuration ϑ. Any rule, apart from (Mod), that is being played next extends the sequence of configurations in the current state. These rules are deterministic, apart from ($\vee$) for which the strategy $\mathfrak{str}$ yields the successor configuration that is to be continued with. When rule (Mod) is to be applied then we finish the construction of the current state s, and for every possible successor configuration C_i we open a new state s_i. This is only well defined when ϑ is guarded, for otherwise there could be states whose construction is never being finished. Guardedness ensures that on every infinite path in the satisfiability game, rule (Mod) is being played infinitely often.

Finally, the labelling of the states is obtained as follows. Suppose the sequence $C_0, \ldots, C_n$ is a state s in $\mathcal{T}_{\mathfrak{str}}$. Then C_n is a configuration in which (Mod) is applied. Let $L(s) := \{p \mid p \in C_n\}$. Thus, a state's label is obtained as the set of all positive literals occurring in the last configuration that contributes to the creation of that state. Recall that configurations of the satisfiability games consist of formula sets only. We will, therefore, also denote a configuration by a letter, e.g. like Γ, Γ' which is usually used for formula sets. We write $[\Gamma_1; \ldots; \Gamma_m]$ to denote the sequence obtained from the configurations $\Gamma_1, \ldots, \Gamma_m$.

Example 15.4.6. Take the formula $\varphi := \nu X.\langle a \rangle p \wedge \langle b \rangle \neg p \wedge \Box(q \wedge X)$. It says that a model must have an a-successor labelled with p and a b-successor not labelled with p.

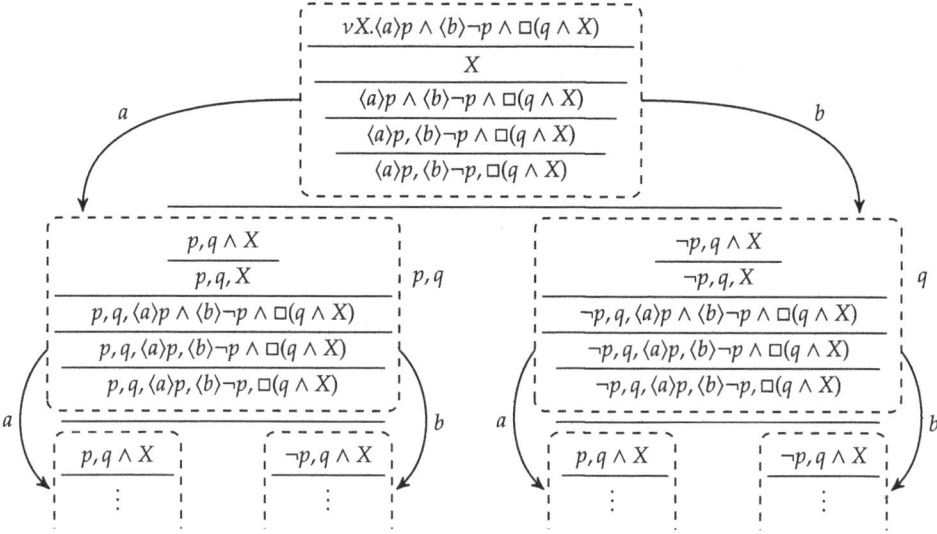

Figure 15.6 Turning a winning strategy for **V** into a model for the input formula.

Furthermore, every successor must be labelled with q and needs to satisfy this property recursively. The first parts of the game $\mathcal{G}(\varphi)$ are shown in Figure 15.6. The game contains several plays which player **R** would choose with rule (Mod). In order to avoid too much clutter, we do not write down the names of the game rules that are being played; they can easily be inferred. Since the input formula contains no disjunctions, player **V** makes no choices and the tree of all plays represents her strategy $\mathfrak{str}$ (which does not require her to do anything).

Figure 15.6 also shows how this strategy $\mathfrak{str}$ induces an ITS $\mathcal{T}_{\mathfrak{str}}$. The sequences of configurations that are not interrupted by applications of rule (Mod), for instance like $[\{p, q \wedge X\}; \ldots; \{p, q, \langle a\rangle p, \langle b\rangle\neg p, \Box(q \wedge X)\}]$ are grouped together using dashed boxes. They form the ITS's states. Transitions are also induced by rule (Mod): there is a transition for every $\langle\cdot\rangle$-formula in the current transition and therefore for each of **R**'s possible choices.

Theorem 15.4.7 (Soundness). Let ϑ be a closed and guarded $\mathcal{L}_\mu$ formula. If player **V** has a winning strategy for $\mathcal{G}(\vartheta)$ then ϑ is satisfiable. ∎

Proof. If we assume that ϑ is guarded and player **V** has a strategy $\mathfrak{str}$ for the game $\mathcal{G}(\varphi)$, then the ITS $\mathcal{T}_{\mathfrak{str}}$ is well defined. We will use player **V**'s winning strategy $\mathfrak{str}$ in the satisfiability game $\mathcal{G}(\vartheta)$ in order to define a strategy $\mathfrak{str}'$ for player **V** in the model-checking game $\mathcal{G}^{\mathcal{T}_{\mathfrak{str}}}(s_0, \vartheta)$ where s_0 is a finite sequence of configurations of the form $[\vartheta; \ldots]$.

We observe that the application of model-checking game rules can be traced in the states of $\mathcal{T}_{\mathfrak{str}}$ as follows.

For the rule ($\wedge$) we have a configuration of the form $[\Gamma_1; \ldots; \Gamma_m] \vdash \varphi \wedge \psi$. Then there is some i with $1 \leq i < m$ such that $\varphi \wedge \psi \in \Gamma_i$ and $\varphi \in \Gamma_{i+1}$ and $\psi \in \Gamma_{i+1}$. Similarly, the unfolding of fixpoint formulae with rules (FP) and (Var) can be traced in the sequences of satisfiability game configurations in the current state.

Now consider $(\vee)$ and suppose that the model-checking game has reached a configuration $[\Gamma_1; \ldots; \Gamma_m] \vdash \varphi_1 \vee \varphi_2$. By assumption, there is some i with $1 \leq i < m$ and $\varphi_1 \vee \varphi_2 \in \Gamma_i$ such that the satisfiability game rule $(\vee)$ is being applied in Γ_i to yield Γ_{i+1}. This means that $\mathfrak{str}(\ldots, \Gamma_1, \ldots, \Gamma_i) = \Gamma_{i+1}$. Let $j \in \{1, 2\}$ be chosen such that $\varphi_j \in \Gamma_{i+1}$. Intuitively, it names the disjunct that is chosen by player **V** in the satisfiability game at that moment. We construct $\mathfrak{str}'$ such that it preserves the invariant of the formulae being traceable in the states: simply set

$$\mathfrak{str}'([\Gamma_1; \ldots; \Gamma_m] \vdash \varphi_1 \vee \varphi_2) := [\Gamma_1; \ldots; \Gamma_m] \vdash \varphi_j.$$

Next, consider $(\Diamond)$ and suppose that the model-checking game has reached a configuration $[\Gamma_1; \ldots; \Gamma_m] \vdash \langle a \rangle \varphi$. By the invariant we have $\langle a \rangle \varphi \in \Gamma_i$ for some $i \leq m$. Now, note that the satisfiability game rules only change modal formulae with rule (Mod) which leads to a new state in $\mathcal{T}_{\mathfrak{str}}$. All other rules preserve such formulae. Thus, we also have $\langle a \rangle \varphi \in \Gamma_m$. Then the state $[\Gamma_1; \ldots; \Gamma_m]$ has several successors in $\mathcal{T}_{\mathfrak{str}}$, namely one for each $\Diamond$-formula in Γ_m and in particular an a-successor $[\Gamma'_1; \ldots; \Gamma'_{m'}]$ such that $\varphi \in \Gamma'_1$. Let strategy $\mathfrak{str}'$ choose this successor, i.e.

$$\mathfrak{str}'([\Gamma_1; \ldots; \Gamma_m] \vdash \langle a \rangle \varphi) := [\Gamma'_1; \ldots; \Gamma'_{m'}] \vdash \varphi$$

such that $[\Gamma_1; \ldots; \Gamma_m] \xrightarrow{a} [\Gamma'_1; \ldots; \Gamma'_{m'}]$ and $\varphi \in \Gamma'_1$.

The case of rule $(\Box)$ is similar. Note that player **R** makes a choice here. Hence, we need to show that the invariant is preserved, in the sense that every successor to some $[\Gamma_1; \ldots; \Gamma_m] \vdash [a]\varphi$ is of the form $[\Gamma'_1; \ldots; \Gamma'_{m'}] \vdash \varphi$ such that $\varphi \in \Gamma'_1$. This is shown as in the previous case.

This defines a strategy $\mathfrak{str}'$ for player **V** in the model-checking game $\mathcal{G}^{\mathcal{T}_{\mathfrak{str}}}(s_0, \vartheta)$. It remains to be seen that it is indeed a winning strategy. Let $\lambda = s_0 \vdash \varphi_0, s_1 \vdash \varphi_1, \ldots$ be a play that conforms to $\mathfrak{str}'$. Remember that the states $s_0, s_1, \ldots$ are sequences of configurations of the satisfiability game $\mathcal{G}(\vartheta)$ such that their concatenation is a play which conforms to player **V**'s winning strategy $\mathfrak{str}$. Moreover, by the earlier invariant and a close inspection of the similarity between the model checking and satisfiability-checking game rules, we see again that the sequence of formulae $\varphi_0, \varphi_1, \ldots$ can be extended to a thread in this play. This is done by repeating single occurrences suitably many times, thus reversing the collapsing of sequences of satisfiability configurations into a single state in $\mathcal{T}_{\mathfrak{str}}$. As an immediate consequence, we find that λ cannot be an infinite play that is won by player **R**, because this would give rise to a μ-thread in a play conforming to $\mathfrak{str}$. So, suppose that it was a finite play. Then it would end in a configuration $s \vdash \ell$ such that s is of the form $[\Gamma_1; \ldots; \Gamma_m]$ and we have $\mathcal{T}_{\mathfrak{str}}, s \not\models \ell$. Now, recall that a state's label in $\mathcal{T}_{\mathfrak{str}}$ was chosen as the propositional part of the last satisfiability configuration that contributes to it. Thus, suppose that $\ell = p$ for some atomic proposition p; the case of a negative literal is analogous. Because of $\mathcal{T}_{\mathfrak{str}}, s \not\models p$ we have $p \notin L(s)$ which means $p \notin \Gamma_m$. This, however, contradicts the invariant stating that the formulae of a model-checking configuration can be found in the satisfiability configurations contributing to its state. Note that literals are being preserved until the next application of rule (Mod) which is why it suffices to consider Γ_m for an occurrence of p in it.

Now we refer to Lemma 8.4.3, stating that every play of the $\mathcal{L}_\mu$ model-checking game has a unique winner. That lets us conclude that player **V** is the winner of every play conforming to $\mathfrak{str}'$. This makes $\mathfrak{str}'$ a winning strategy for player **V** in the model-checking game $\mathcal{G}^{\mathcal{T}_{\mathfrak{str}}}(s_0, \vartheta)$ which, by Theorem 8.4.13 means $\mathcal{T}_{\mathfrak{str}}, s_0 \models \vartheta$. Hence, ϑ is indeed satisfiable.

$\square$

A Game-Based Decision Procedure for $\mathcal{L}_\mu$

Theorem 15.4.5 and 15.4.7 yield a sound and complete game-theoretic characterisation of the satisfiability problem for (guarded) formulae of the modal μ-calculus. However, it is not immediately clear whether this characterisation can also be used to obtain a decision procedure for its satisfiability problem. We will show that this is indeed true: as with the CTL* model-checking games, the winning conditions that are concerned with the presence or absence of certain threads can be formulated as an ω-regular language of plays. Again, we will use a symbolic encoding of the game rules in order to keep automata recognising winning plays small. There is one crucial difference to the automata used to reduce the CTL* model-checking games to parity games, though. A μ-thread in the $\mathcal{L}_\mu$ satisfiability games is not co-Büchi recognisable anymore. Note that a μ-thread in a CTL* model-checking game eventually enters an U-formula and basically resides on it forever. A thread in a $\mathcal{L}_\mu$ satisfiability game can change formulae all the time and, most of all, can see as many variables infinitely often as there are in the input formula.

As before, let ϑ be fixed.

Definition 15.4.8. The **alphabet of symbolic rule applications** for the satisfiability game $\mathcal{G}(\vartheta)$ is

$$\Sigma_\vartheta := \{\mathsf{And}(\varphi, \psi) \mid \varphi \wedge \psi \in \mathit{fi}(\vartheta)\}$$
$$\cup \{\mathsf{Or}_d(\varphi, \psi) \mid \varphi \vee \psi \in \mathit{fi}(\vartheta), d \in \{\mathsf{lft}, \mathsf{rgh}\}\}$$
$$\cup \{\mathsf{Unf}(X) \mid \tau X.\varphi \in \mathit{fi}(\vartheta)\}$$
$$\cup \{\mathsf{Mod}(\langle a \rangle \varphi) \mid \langle a \rangle \varphi \in \mathit{fi}(\vartheta)\}. \qquad \triangledown$$

Again, an alphabet symbol uniquely identifies which rule is to be applied and what is the next configuration. Every play of $\mathcal{G}(\vartheta)$ is uniquely represented by a word in Σ_ϑ^+ or Σ_ϑ^ω. In order not to have to deal with technical distinctions between finite and infinite plays we introduce the convention that only infinite words represent plays, and finite plays are being represented by extending them in an arbitrary way ad infinitum. The next two lemmas will be used to show that winning plays for player **R** (and therefore for **V** as their complement too) are (ω-)regular.

Alternatively, we could try to characterise **V** winning plays directly. However, it is not obviously possible to give an automaton that accepts her infinite winning plays. The reason is the fact that such an automaton would have to check all threads in a given play for not being μ-threads. It should be clear that nondeterminism is of no use for this. The infinite winning plays of **R** are defined by the existence of some μ-thread though for which nondeterministic automata are indeed of use.

Lemma 15.4.9. There is a nondeterministic parity automaton $\mathcal{A}_\vartheta^{\mathsf{inf}}$ of size $\mathcal{O}(|\vartheta|)$ and index at most $ad(\vartheta) + 1$ that accepts an infinite play of $\mathcal{G}(\vartheta)$ iff it is won by player **R**.   ∎

Proof. First we create a priority scheme $\Omega : \mathrm{VAR} \cap fi(\vartheta) \to \mathbb{N}$ that satisfies the following.

- If X is μ-bound in ϑ then $\Omega(X)$ is even, otherwise it is odd.
- For all $X, Y \in fi(\vartheta) \cap \mathrm{VAR}$: if $X \succ_\vartheta Y$ and X and Y are of different fixpoint types then $\Omega(X) > \Omega(Y)$.

It should be clear that such a function Ω exists, and that it can be chosen such that its maximal value is $ad(\vartheta) + 1$ by considering the syntax tree of ϑ and assigning priorities increasingly in a bottom-up fashion. Larger priorities only need to be assigned whenever an outer variable is reached that has a different fixpoint type to those that depend on it. We extend Ω to the whole of $fi(\vartheta)$ by setting $\Omega(\psi) = 0$ for every $\psi \in fi(\vartheta) \setminus \mathrm{VAR}$.

$\mathcal{A}_\vartheta^{\mathsf{inf}}$'s way to work is also easily described. It guesses a thread through the play in its input. In order to do so, it remembers in its state set the current formula in the thread. If the next rule application modifies this formula, then it updates its state, otherwise it remains in that state. The parity acceptance condition Ω ensures that the greatest priority seen infinitely often is even in a run iff the thread that is represented by this run visits a μ-bound variable infinitely often and no outer ν-bound variables infinitely often as well.

Formally, we define $\mathcal{A}_\vartheta^{\mathsf{inf}} = (\Sigma_\vartheta, fi(\vartheta), \vartheta, \delta, \Omega)$, where

$$\delta(\varphi \wedge \psi, \mathsf{And}(\varphi, \psi)) := \{\varphi, \psi\}$$
$$\delta(\varphi \vee \psi, \mathsf{Or}_{\mathsf{lft}}(\varphi, \psi)) := \{\varphi\}$$
$$\delta(\varphi \vee \psi, \mathsf{Or}_{\mathsf{rgh}}(\varphi, \psi)) := \{\psi\}$$
$$\delta(\tau X.\varphi, \mathsf{Unf}(X)) := \{X\}$$
$$\delta(X, \mathsf{Unf}(X)) := \{\varphi\} \quad \text{if } fp_\vartheta X = \tau X.\varphi$$
$$\delta(\langle a \rangle \varphi, \mathsf{Mod}(\langle a' \rangle \varphi')) := \begin{cases} \{\varphi\}, & \text{if } a' = a \text{ and } \varphi' = \varphi \\ \emptyset, & \text{otherwise} \end{cases}$$
$$\delta([b]\psi, \mathsf{Mod}(\langle a \rangle \varphi)) := \begin{cases} \{\psi\}, & \text{if } b = a \\ \emptyset, & \text{otherwise} \end{cases}$$
$$\delta(\psi, r) := \{\psi\} \quad \text{in all other cases.}$$

It is clear that $\mathcal{A}_\vartheta^{\mathsf{inf}}$ is of the prescribed size. Furthermore, it is easily checked that a μ-thread in a symbolically encoded play leads to an accepting run on that play. Conversely, every accepting run must never get stuck and exhibits a thread in the input play because the transitions follow the connection relation. This thread must be a μ-thread because only μ-variables have even priorities in Ω.   □

Lemma 15.4.10. There is a deterministic reachability automaton $\mathcal{A}_\vartheta^{\text{fin}}$ of size $2^{|\vartheta|}$ that accepts a finite play of $\mathcal{G}(\vartheta)$ iff it is won by player **R**. ∎

Proof. $\mathcal{A}_\vartheta^{\text{fin}}$'s way to work is easily described: in its state set it reconstructs from the symbolic rule representations the current configuration. It accepts as soon as this configuration makes **R** win the play.

Formally, $\mathcal{A}_\vartheta^{\text{fin}} = (\Sigma_\vartheta, 2^{fi(\vartheta)}, \{\vartheta\}, \delta, F)$ with

- $\delta(\Gamma, r)$ being the configuration that is obtained from applying rule r to the configuration Γ;
- $F := \{\Gamma \mid \Gamma \text{ consists of literals only and contains two complementary literals}\}$.

It is easy to see that $\mathcal{A}_\vartheta^{\text{fin}}$ is of the stated size and correct with respect to its specification. □

Now we can use results about combining automata and about transforming games with abstract ω-regular winning conditions into parity games in order to achieve a reduction from the $\mathcal{L}_\mu$ satisfiability games to parity games and, hence, a decidability result.

Theorem 15.4.11. For every closed and guarded $\vartheta \in \mathcal{L}_\mu$ of size n and alternation depth k there is a parity game of size $2^{\mathcal{O}(nk \cdot \log n)}$ and index $\mathcal{O}(nk)$, in which Player 0 has a winning strategy iff ϑ is satisfiable. ∎

Proof. According to Theorem 15.4.5 and 15.4.7 satisfiability of ϑ is equivalent to player **V** winning the game $\mathcal{G}(\vartheta)$.

First we show that the winning conditions of $\mathcal{G}(\vartheta)$ can be recognised by a deterministic parity automaton. Let $n := |\vartheta|$ and $k := ad(\vartheta)$. Take the NPA $\mathcal{A}_\vartheta^{\text{inf}}$ recognising **R**'s infinite winning plays according to Lemma 15.4.9. It can be transformed into an equivalent NBA $\mathcal{B}_\vartheta^{\text{inf}}$ of size $\mathcal{O}(nk)$ according to Lemma 15.2.15. The result can be determinised and complemented into a DPA $\mathcal{D}_\vartheta^{\text{inf}}$ of size $2^{\mathcal{O}(nk \log n)}$ – given that we can assume $k \leq n$ – and index $\mathcal{O}(nk)$. Note that it recognises all plays which are not infinite and winning for **R**, i.e. all plays that are either finite or not winning for **R**.

Now take the deterministic reachability automaton $\mathcal{A}_\vartheta^{\text{fin}}$ recognising **R**'s finite winning plays according to Lemma 15.4.10. Again, it can be complemented at no additional blow-up to yield a deterministic safety automaton $\mathcal{D}_\vartheta^{\text{fin}}$ of size 2^n that recognises all plays which are not won by **R** in finitely many steps. By Lemma 15.2.17 the two can be combined into a DPA $\mathcal{D}_\vartheta$ of size $2^n \cdot 2^{\mathcal{O}(nk \log n)} = 2^{\mathcal{O}(nk \log n)}$ and index $\mathcal{O}(nk)$ that recognises the intersection of their two languages, i.e. the set of all plays that are not won by **R** and therefore those that are won by **V**. Now we can apply the Main Reduction Theorem (Theorem 15.1.27) and obtain a parity game of size $2^n \cdot 2^{\mathcal{O}(nk \log n)} = 2^{\mathcal{O}(nk \log n)}$ and index $\mathcal{O}(nk)$ that is equivalent to the satisfiability game $\mathcal{G}(\vartheta)$. □

This yields an upper bound that matches the lower ExpTime-bound for satisfiability in $\mathcal{L}_\mu$ inherited from TLR (cf. Theorem 11.4.6), which is a fragment of CTL, and CTL can be translated into $\mathcal{L}_\mu$ at a linear blow-up only.

Theorem 15.4.12. The satisfiability problem for guarded formulae of $\mathcal{L}_\mu$ is in ExpTime. ■

Proof. This upper bound follows from the reduction of $\mathcal{L}_\mu$ satisfiability to the problem of solving a parity game of size $2^{\mathcal{O}(nk \log n)}$ and index $\mathcal{O}(nk)$ for guarded formulae of size n and alternation depth k (Theorem 15.4.11). Note that the out-degree of the graphs underlying these satisfiability games – and thus also the resulting parity games – is bounded by the number of different $\langle \cdot \rangle$-formulae in the input formula, and therefore also by its size n. Thus, the number of edges is at most $n \cdot 2^n$. According to Corollary 15.3.5 such games can be solved in time $\mathcal{O}(n \cdot 2^n \cdot (2^{\mathcal{O}(nk \log n)})^{\mathcal{O}(nk)}) = 2^{\mathcal{O}(n^2 k^2 \log n)}$, i.e. in ExpTime. □

Recall that there is a linear translation from CTL to (the alternation-free) modal μ-calculus (Theorem 8.1.14). It is easily verified that this translation produces guarded formulae. Hence, we immediately get an upper bound on the satisfiability problem for CTL as well.

Corollary 15.4.13. The satisfiability problem for CTL is in ExpTime. ■

Two Special Cases

We consider the special case of satisfiability for a formula of the linear-time μ-calculus LT_μ. Remember that it is obtained semantically from $\mathcal{L}_\mu$ by interpreting it over computation paths only. Then the two modal operators coincide and are therefore being replaced by a single next-time operator $\bigcirc$ just like the one in other linear-time formalisms like LTL.

A decision procedure for LT_μ can be obtained by considering the game-based procedure for $\mathcal{L}_\mu$ and then by specialising it to the case when there is only one modal operator. It is not hard to see that this should only affect the one rule in the $\mathcal{L}_\mu$ satisfiability games that deals with modal operators. Recall the game rules in Figure 15.5. Now there is only one modal operator $\bigcirc$, and applying the rules for fixpoints and Boolean operators successively will result in a configuration in which every formula is either a literal or preceded by a $\bigcirc$-operator. Since we ask whether there is an ITS consisting of a single computation path only that is a model for the input formula, such a configuration is satisfiable iff the literal part can be realised in a state, and all the $\bigcirc$-preceded formulae can be satisfied by the unique successor on this computation path.

Hence, the satisfiability game rules for LT_μ are obtained from the ones for $\mathcal{L}_\mu$ by replacing rule (Mod) by the following.

$$(\bigcirc) \quad \frac{\bigcirc \varphi_1, \ldots, \bigcirc \varphi_n, \ell_1, \ldots, \ell_k}{\varphi_1, \ldots, \varphi_n}$$

where the ℓ_i are literals. Note that – unlike the case of the $\mathcal{L}_\mu$ rule (Mod) – there is no choice involved in rule $(\bigcirc)$ anymore. This makes the satisfiability games for LT_μ computationally simpler than those for $\mathcal{L}_\mu$ because rule (Mod) was the only one in which player **R** made a choice. Hence, the LT_μ satisfiability games are in fact 1-player games.

Theorem 15.4.14. The satisfiability problem for guarded formulae of LT_μ is in PSPACE. ∎

Proof. Just like the satisfiability games for $\mathcal{L}_\mu$ can be reduced to parity games of exponential size and linear index via the Main Reduction Theorem, we can do the same for the LT_μ satisfiability games and obtain, for a guarded formula of size n and alternation depth k, a parity game of size $2^{\mathcal{O}(nk \log n)}$ and index $\mathcal{O}(nk)$. However, this time the parity game is in fact a 1-player game. So we can use Theorem 15.1.24 and obtain a nondeterministic decision procedure for LT_μ that runs in space that is logarithmic in a function that is exponential in n, i.e. in nondeterministic polynomial space. According to Savitch's Theorem, it can also be decided in PSPACE. □

Note that, even though LT_μ is presented as a separate logic with its own syntax, it can also be regarded as $\mathcal{L}_\mu$ interpreted over a particular class of structures only: computation paths as transition systems. Notice how this speciality of the underlying class of models translates into the design of a decision procedure for LT_μ, namely by replacing rule (Mod) with (◯) which ensures that in any considered state, exactly one successor state exists.

Another special case that we consider here concerns **deterministic models**, i.e. those in which every state has at most one a-successor for every action a. This is needed for the satisfiability-preserving translation from ATL to $\mathcal{L}_\mu$ (see Section 9.3.3).

Theorem 15.4.15. The problem of deciding whether a given $\mathcal{L}_\mu$ formula is satisfiable in a deterministic model is in ExpTime. ∎

The proof is left as Exercise 15.29.

15.4.2 The Full Branching-Time Logic CTL*

Satisfiability Games for CTL*

Lastly, we provide a game-theoretic characterisation of the satisfiability problem for CTL*. As with the other games, the design starts with the format of a configuration. So far, we have seen games which feature a single formula in it, e.g. model checking $\mathcal{L}_\mu$ for instance, or sets of formulae. The purpose of using formula sets has been similar for different games: the underlying semantic problem does not allow games to modularly decompose formulae. For instance, it is not the case that a conjunction is satisfiable iff both conjuncts are. That is why the corresponding rule for conjunctions in satisfiability games for $\mathcal{L}_\mu$ puts both its conjuncts into the current set. In CTL* we have the general inequivalence $\mathsf{A}(\varphi \vee \psi) \not\equiv \mathsf{A}\varphi \vee \mathsf{A}\psi$. Thus, in model-checking games for CTL* we keep disjunctions inside a universal path quantifier (and conjunctions inside an existential path quantifier).

It should be clear that satisfiability games for CTL* have to obey both phenomaena: we need to work with formula sets in order to preserve (un)satisfiability. Moreover, if these are state formulae beginning with a path quantifier then we have to maintain sets of formulae in them as well. A configuration for the CTL* satisfiability game $\mathcal{G}(\vartheta)$ on a CTL* state formula ϑ in negation normal form is a special set of sets of formulae, of the form

$$\mathsf{E}\Gamma_1, \ldots, \mathsf{E}\Gamma_n, \mathsf{A}\Delta_1, \ldots \mathsf{A}\Delta_m, \Lambda$$

where $\Delta_i, \Gamma_j \subseteq \mathit{fi}(\vartheta)$ for $i = 1, \ldots, n$ and $j = 1, \ldots, m$, or Λ is a set of literals of the form p or $\neg p$. This includes the special cases of $\Lambda = \emptyset$, $m = 0$ and $n = 0$. An empty configuration is therefore theoretically possible, but it cannot be reached from the initial configuration $\mathsf{A}\vartheta$ by the game rules presented later. Note that we will avoid using brackets and write $\mathsf{A}\vartheta$ instead of $\mathsf{A}\{\vartheta\}$. We also use the same conventions as were being introduced for other games operating on formula sets and write e.g. $\mathsf{E}(\varphi \wedge \psi, \Gamma)$ for the E-prefixed set that contains $\varphi \wedge \psi$ and has Γ as its rest.

The game is played between players **V** and **R** as before. Intuitively, in a configuration of the preceding form, player **V** tries to show that there is a model for the formula

$$\left(\bigwedge_{i=1}^{n} \mathsf{E} \bigwedge \Gamma_i \right) \wedge \left(\bigwedge_{i=1}^{m} \mathsf{A} \bigvee \Delta_i \right) \wedge \bigwedge \Lambda.$$

Thus, formula sets under an existential path quantifier are interpreted conjunctively and denoted Γ, Γ_1, etc.; formula sets under a universal path quantifier are interpreted disjunctively and denoted Δ, Δ_1, etc. The entire configuration represents again a conjunction. As a consequence of this interpretation we can identify configurations which are obviously (un)satisfiable and declare them as already final winning positions for the two players. Again, we will explain the satisfiability games in reference to a fixed formula ϑ in negation normal form.

Definition 15.4.16 (Winning conditions for finite plays). Player **V** wins a play $C_0, C_1, \ldots$ of $\mathcal{G}(\vartheta)$ if there is some $n \in \mathbb{N}$ such that C_n is of the form $\ell_1, \ldots, \ell_k$, all being literals over the atomic propositions, and there are no i, j such that $\ell_i = \overline{\ell_j}$.

Player **R** wins such a play if there is an $n \in \mathbb{N}$ such that either

- there is some atomic proposition p with $\{p, \neg p\} \subseteq C_n$, or
- $\mathsf{A}\emptyset \in C_n$. $\triangledown$

Next we define the game rules. There are more rules here, due to the more complex nature of a configuration in such games compared to the games that were considered before. Roughly speaking, we need one rule for every logical operator in *any* position in a configuration. In particular, it should be clear that, for instance, conjunctions need to be dealt with differently in a set of the form Γ (interpreted conjunctively) as one of the form Δ (interpreted disjunctively). The collection of all rules is presented in Figure 15.7. In these rules, ℓ stands for a literal over atomic propositions; Λ for a set of such literals; $\mathsf{Q}\varphi$ stands for a path-quantified formula, i.e. either $\mathsf{E}\varphi$ or $\mathsf{A}\varphi$; and $\mathsf{X}\Gamma$, resp. $\mathsf{X}\Delta$, stands for the set of formulae obtained by prefixing every formula in Γ, resp. Δ, with a X-operator. In rules (X) and (X$^-$) we assume Λ not to contain a proposition and its negation, for otherwise the configuration would be final and winning for player **R** already. In rule (X), we have $n \geq 1$. The case of $n = 0$ is special and handled by rule (X$^-$). Intuitively, a tree model is being constructed

$$(E\wedge)\ \frac{E(\varphi \wedge \psi, \Gamma), \Phi}{E(\varphi, \psi, \Gamma), \Phi} \qquad\qquad (EU)\ \frac{E(\varphi U\psi, \Gamma), \Phi}{E(\psi, \Gamma), \Phi \qquad E(\varphi, X(\varphi U\psi), \Gamma), \Phi}\ V$$

$$(A\vee)\ \frac{A(\varphi \vee \psi, \Delta), \Phi}{A(\varphi, \psi, \Delta), \Phi} \qquad\qquad (AU)\ \frac{A(\varphi U\psi, \Delta), \Phi}{A(\psi, \varphi, \Delta), A(\psi, X(\varphi U\psi), \Delta), \Phi}$$

$$(ELit)\ \frac{E(\ell, \Gamma), \Phi}{E\Gamma, \Phi, \ell} \qquad\qquad (ER)\ \frac{E(\varphi R\psi, \Gamma), \Phi}{E(\psi, \varphi, \Gamma), \Phi \qquad E(\psi, X(\varphi R\psi), \Gamma), \Phi}\ V$$

$$(EQ)\ \frac{E(Q\varphi, \Gamma), \Phi}{E\Gamma, Q\varphi, \Phi} \qquad\qquad (AR)\ \frac{A(\varphi R\psi, \Delta), \Phi}{A(\psi, \Delta), A(\varphi, X(\varphi R\psi), \Delta), \Phi}$$

$$(E\vee)\ \frac{E(\varphi \vee \psi, \Gamma), \Phi}{E(\varphi, \Gamma), \Phi \qquad E(\psi, \Gamma), \Phi}\ V \qquad\qquad (A\wedge)\ \frac{A(\varphi \wedge \psi, \Delta), \Phi}{A(\varphi, \Delta), A(\psi, \Delta), \Phi}$$

$$(ALit)\ \frac{A(\ell, \Delta), \Phi}{A\Delta, \Phi \qquad \Phi, \ell}\ V \qquad\qquad (AQ)\ \frac{A(Q\varphi, \Delta), \Phi}{A\Delta, \Phi \qquad Q\varphi, \Phi}\ V$$

$$(X)\ \frac{EX\Gamma_1, \dots, EX\Gamma_n, AX\Delta_1, \dots, AX\Delta_m, \Lambda}{E\Gamma_1, A\Delta_1, \dots, A\Delta_m \quad \dots \quad E\Gamma_n, A\Delta_1, \dots, A\Delta_m}\ R$$

$$(X^-)\ \frac{AX\Delta_1, \dots, AX\Delta_m, \Lambda}{A\Delta_1, \dots, A\Delta_m} \qquad\qquad (Ett)\ \frac{E\emptyset, \Phi}{\Phi}$$

Figure 15.7 The rules for the CTL* satisfiability games.

by playing the rules, and paths in this tree are only created for formulae requiring this, i.e. formulae starting with an existential path quantifier. If there are no such formulae, we still need to continue with the construction because CTL* models are supposed to be total and not contain dead ends.

The winning conditions for infinite plays need to capture the infinite unfolding of the temporal fixpoint constructs U and R. Recall that – as a rule of thumb – an infinite unfolding of a U-formula should be winning for player **R**, that of a R-formula should be winning for player **V**. However, as seen in the model-checking games for CTL* and the satisfiability games for $\mathcal{L}_\mu$ (with explicit least and greatest fixpoint operators), the fact that these formulae occur inside sets makes the definition of a winner complicated. Here it is even more complicated, because the unfoldings occur within a set, which occurs in a set, as well. We start by introducing some technical conventions in order to make these phenomena explicit.

Definition 15.4.17. A **block** in a configuration is a literal or a formula set of the form $E\Gamma$ or $A\Delta$.

The satisfiability game $\mathcal{G}(\vartheta)$ naturally induces a **connection relation** $\rightsquigarrow$ between blocks B, B' of successive configurations C_i, C_{i+1} in a play $C_0, C_1, \dots$. We have $B, C_i \rightsquigarrow B', C_{i+1}$ if the rule that was played between C_i and C_{i+1}

- did not operate on B and $B' = B$, or
- transformed B into B'.   ▽

The connections resulting from applications of rules (E∧), (A∨) and (X⁻) are obvious and can be read off the game rules right away. Rules (E∨), (EU), (AU), (ER), (AR), (ALit), (AQ) and (X) connect a block in the upper configuration to the corresponding block in the lower configuration depending on which one was chosen by the respective player. For instance, if player **V** chose $E(\psi, \Gamma)$, Φ in rule (E∨), then we have $E(\varphi \vee \psi, \Gamma) \rightsquigarrow E(\psi, \Gamma)$. Here we left out the context of the two corresponding configurations that the two blocks belong to.

The connections created by rule (ALit) and (AQ) may be less clear; we have, concerning the former, $A(\ell, \Delta) \rightsquigarrow \ell$ if player **V** chose the right alternative. Otherwise we have $A(\ell, \Delta) \rightsquigarrow A\Delta$.

Rule (A∧) creates two connections: we have $A(\varphi \wedge \psi, \Delta) \rightsquigarrow A(\varphi, \Delta)$ and $A(\varphi \wedge \psi, \Delta) \rightsquigarrow A(\psi, \Delta)$. The same holds for rule (ELit) and (EQ). In the latter, we have $E(Q\varphi, \Gamma) \rightsquigarrow E\Gamma$ and $E(Q\varphi, \Gamma) \rightsquigarrow Q\varphi$.

Definition 15.4.18. Let $C_0, C_1, \ldots$ be an infinite play of $\mathcal{G}(\vartheta)$. A **trace** is an infinite sequence of blocks $B_0, B_1, \ldots$ such that for all $i \in \mathbb{N}$ we have $B_i, C_i \rightsquigarrow B_{i+1}, C_{i+1}$.

A trace $Q_0\Delta_0, Q_1\Delta_1, \ldots$ is called **E-trace** if there is some $n \in \mathbb{N}$ such that for all $i \geq n$ we have $Q_i = E$. An **A-trace** is defined likewise.   ▽

It should be clear that no infinite trace can be both an E-trace and an A-trace. What is less obvious is the fact that every infinite trace is of either of these two types. The proof is left as Exercise 15.28.

Lemma 15.4.19. Every infinite trace of an infinite play is either an E- or an A-trace.   ∎

The following will be necessary to show that the winning conditions cover all possible plays.

Lemma 15.4.20. Every infinite play has a trace.   ∎

Proof. This follows immediately from Kőnig's Lemma because every block in a configuration that is not the first in a play is connected to a block in the preceding configuration. Also, the number of possible blocks in every configuration is bounded exponentially by the size of the input formula. Thus, the connection relation forms a finitely branching DAG with paths of arbitrary lengths, and so it must contain an infinite path which is a trace.   □

The distinction between E- and A-traces is important because they ultimately contain formula sets of different kind: E-traces eventually only contain conjunctively interpreted blocks, A-traces eventually only contain disjunctively interpreted blocks. Recall that, for instance, a least fixpoint construct that is unfolded infinitely often can be seen as being false. Thus, it matters whether this happens in an E-trace or in an A-trace. Before we explain how it matters in detail, namely in the form of winning conditions for infinite plays, we need to recall the notion of thread, which is slightly more involved now than it was in the previous games.

Definition 15.4.21. The satisfiability game $\mathcal{G}(\vartheta)$ also induces a connection relation on formulae inside blocks in a configuration. We use the same symbol $\rightsquigarrow$ as we used for the connection between blocks. We have $\varphi, B \rightsquigarrow \varphi', B'$ for some $\varphi \in B$ and $\varphi' \in B'$ if we have $B \rightsquigarrow B'$, i.e. the containing blocks are connected by the application of some game rule which

- did not transform φ, and we have $\varphi' = \varphi$, or
- transformed φ into φ'.

A **thread** in an infinite trace $B_0, B_1, \ldots$ is an infinite sequence $\varphi_0, \varphi_1, \ldots$ such that $\varphi_i, B_i \rightsquigarrow \varphi_{i+1}, B_{i+1}$ for all $i \in \mathbb{N}$. Such a thread is called a μ**-thread** if there is some ψ of the form $\psi_1 U \psi_2$ and some $n \in \mathbb{N}$ such that $\varphi_i = \psi$ or $\varphi_i = X\psi$ for all $i \geq n$. A thread is called ν**-thread** if the same is true for some formula ψ of the form $\psi_1 R \psi_2$. $\triangledown$

Threads inside traces in a play of a satisfiability game are the same as threads in a play of a CTL* model-checking game. Note that those plays do not possess traces. In fact, the entire play can be seen as a single trace because every configuration there consists of a quantifier-prefixed set of formulae. The close resemblance between threads in model-checking and satisfiability-checking games for CTL* makes it easy to carry over results from the previous ones. We therefore omit the proof of the following lemma. It is very similar to the corresponding result about traces.

Lemma 15.4.22.

a) Every trace has at least one thread.
b) Every thread is either a μ-thread or a ν-thread, but not both. ∎

With threads at hand we can now distinguish two kinds of traces which will allow us to define winning conditions for infinite plays.

Definition 15.4.23 (Winning conditions for infinite plays). A trace is called **good** if

- it is an A-trace and contains a ν-thread, or
- it is an E-trace and contains no μ-thread.

Otherwise, the trace is called **bad**.

Player **V** wins an infinite play of the satisfiability game $\mathcal{G}(\vartheta)$ if all its traces are good. Player **R** wins it if it contains a bad trace. $\triangledown$

It is not hard to see with the help of Lemmas 15.4.19, 15.4.20 and 15.4.22 that every play has a unique winner. Intuitively, a bad trace demands the existence of a path in a model which cannot be satisfied. Recall that an E-trace is eventually interpreted as a sequence of conjunctions, and a μ-thread in this can be seen as a formula that is false. Likewise, an A-trace is a sequence of disjunctions in the end, and if it does not contain a ν-thread which

$$A\big(G(\neg p \vee \mathsf{EX}\mathsf{F}p)\big), A\big(\mathsf{F}\mathsf{G}\neg p\big), p$$

$$A\big(\neg p \vee \mathsf{EX}\mathsf{F}p\big), A\big(\mathsf{X}\mathsf{G}(\neg p \vee \mathsf{EX}\mathsf{F}p)\big), A\big(\mathsf{G}\neg p, \mathsf{X}\mathsf{F}\mathsf{G}\neg p\big), p$$

$$A\big(\neg p, \mathsf{EX}\mathsf{F}p\big), A\big(\mathsf{X}\mathsf{G}(\neg p \vee \mathsf{EX}\mathsf{F}p)\big), A\big(\neg p, \mathsf{X}\mathsf{F}\mathsf{G}\neg p\big), A\big(\mathsf{X}\mathsf{G}\neg p, \mathsf{X}\mathsf{F}\mathsf{G}\neg p\big), p$$

$$E\big(\mathsf{X}\mathsf{F}p\big), A\big(\mathsf{X}\mathsf{G}(\neg p \vee \mathsf{EX}\mathsf{F}p)\big), A\big(\mathsf{X}\mathsf{F}\mathsf{G}\neg p\big), A\big(\mathsf{X}\mathsf{G}\neg p, \mathsf{X}\mathsf{F}\mathsf{G}\neg p\big), p$$

$$E\big(\mathsf{F}p\big), A\big(G(\neg p \vee \mathsf{EX}\mathsf{F}p)\big), A\big(\mathsf{F}\mathsf{G}\neg p\big), A\big(\mathsf{G}\neg p, \mathsf{X}\mathsf{F}\mathsf{G}\neg p\big)$$

$$E\big(\mathsf{X}\mathsf{F}p\big), A\big(\neg p, \mathsf{EX}\mathsf{F}p\big), A\big(\mathsf{X}\mathsf{G}(\neg p \vee \mathsf{EX}\mathsf{F}p)\big), A\big(\neg p, \mathsf{X}\mathsf{F}\mathsf{G}\neg p\big), A\big(\mathsf{X}\mathsf{G}\neg p, \mathsf{X}\mathsf{F}\mathsf{G}\neg p\big)$$

$$E\big(\mathsf{X}\mathsf{F}p\big), A\big(\mathsf{X}\mathsf{G}(\neg p \vee \mathsf{EX}\mathsf{F}p)\big), A\big(\mathsf{X}\mathsf{G}\neg p, \mathsf{X}\mathsf{F}\mathsf{G}\neg p\big), \neg p$$

$$E\big(\mathsf{F}p\big), A\big(G(\neg p \vee \mathsf{EX}\mathsf{F}p)\big), A\big(\mathsf{G}\neg p, \mathsf{F}\mathsf{G}\neg p\big)$$

$$Ep, A\big(\neg p, \mathsf{EX}\mathsf{F}p\big), A\big(\mathsf{X}\mathsf{G}(\neg p \vee \mathsf{EX}\mathsf{F}p)\big), A\big(\neg p, \mathsf{X}\mathsf{F}\mathsf{G}\neg p\big), A\big(\mathsf{X}\mathsf{G}\neg p, \mathsf{X}\mathsf{F}\mathsf{G}\neg p\big)$$

$$E\big(\mathsf{X}\mathsf{F}p\big), A\big(\mathsf{X}\mathsf{G}(\neg p \vee \mathsf{EX}\mathsf{F}p)\big), A\big(\mathsf{X}\mathsf{F}\mathsf{G}\neg p\big), A\big(\mathsf{X}\mathsf{G}\neg p, \mathsf{X}\mathsf{F}\mathsf{G}\neg p\big), p$$

$$\vdots$$

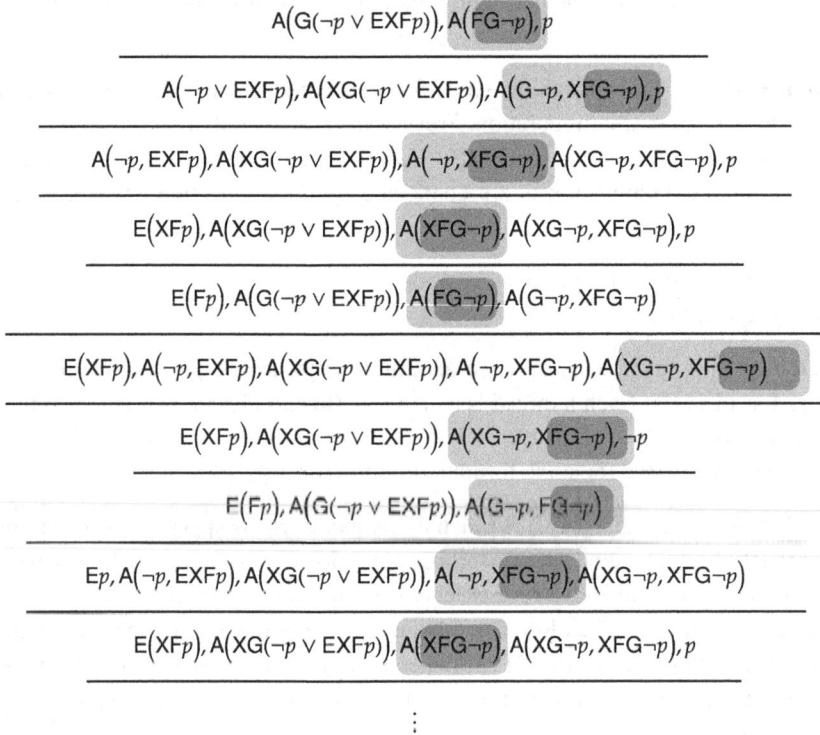

Figure 15.8 A play in the satisfiability game for the CTL* formula of Example 15.4.24.

corresponds to a true formula, then the entire disjunction is false. Configurations on the top-level are conjunctions, and that is why one bad trace is enough to make player **V** lose the play.

We present an example in order to show how the notions on good and bad traces are linked to the existence of models. The soundness proof will use the same principle than that used in Theorem 15.4.7: from a winning strategy for player **V** we extract a model by compressing the tree of all plays conforming to this strategy. The use of rules (X) and (X$^-$) form the branching in this model.

Example 15.4.24. Consider $\vartheta := p \wedge \mathsf{AG}(p \to \mathsf{EX}\mathsf{F}p) \wedge \mathsf{AF}\mathsf{G}\neg p$. It is unsatisfiable, because it expresses the negation of the following valid limit closure property: if p holds now, and whenever p holds somewhere then it holds again somewhere later, then there must be a path on which it holds infinitely often. We present a play of the satisfiability game on ϑ in Figure 15.8. In order to save space, we start with a configuration that is clearly equivalent to ϑ, and we often execute more than one rule in one step when they operate on different blocks inside of a configuration. We also use specialised versions of the unfolding rules, like the following two, and leave it as Exercise 15.30 to explain why these are suitable for the specialised G- and F-operator.

$$(\mathtt{AF}) \ \frac{\mathsf{A}(\mathsf{F}\varphi, \Delta), \Phi}{\mathsf{A}(\varphi, \mathsf{XF}\varphi, \Delta), \Phi} \qquad (\mathtt{AG}) \ \frac{\mathsf{A}(\mathsf{G}\varphi, \Delta), \Phi}{\mathsf{A}(\varphi, \Delta), \Phi \quad \mathsf{A}(\mathsf{XG}\varphi, \Delta), \Phi} \ \mathbf{R}.$$

In the first step in Figure 15.8 we use rules (AR) and (AU) to unfold the topmost temporal operators G and F under the universal path quantifiers. In the second step we use rules (A∨) and (AG). Then all formulae inside the blocks are either literals, or path quantified, or preceded by a X-operator. It should be clear that **V** cannot promote the literals $\neg p$ with rule (ALit) because of the proposition p outside. **V** therefore must discard them with this rule which means that she has to promote the EXFp to its own block with rule (AQ) for otherwise she would have created A∅ and lost immediately. The result is shown as the 4th configuration to which rule (X) applies.

Intuitively, this starts the construction of the next state in a possible model. The temporal operators are unfolded and the Boolean connectives are resolved. Player **V** has the choice with rules (ELit) to either promote p from the existential block or to discard it. Suppose she did the latter. Then she can promote $\neg p$ with rule (ALit) twice and rule (X) becomes applicable again.

The resulting configuration – resembling the start of a third state on a path of a possible model – is simpler but not dissimilar to the configuration after the first application of rule (X). Again, **V** would have the choice to either promote or dismiss $\neg p$. With this **V** determines whether these states satisfy p. If **V** chooses to always promote $\neg p$ then she would also have to never choose p when unfolding Fp in the existential block. This would create a bad E-trace because it would contain a μ-thread. Suppose therefore that **V** chooses to dismiss $\neg p$. Then she can promote p from the E-block which becomes empty and gets discarded with rule (Ett). Clearly, this kills the possible bad E-trace through it. This features a repetition on a configuration that was visited before.

Altogether, the game on this ϑ works as follows: **V** chooses at each stage after applications of rule (X), which create a single configuration only, whether to have p in the literal part of the configurations. If **V** eventually chooses not to have p ever again, then the resulting play has a bad E-trace. It remains to be seen what happens when she chooses to have p infinitely often in the only infinite play. The result is essentially given by the repeating configurations in Figure 15.8. The lightly shadowed blocks form an A-trace in this play. The darkly shadowed formulae in this trace form a thread which is easily seen to be a μ-thread. Since there are blocks on this trace that contain a single formula only, this is also the only thread in this trace, which means that it is bad A-trace.

Thus, **R** is the winner of this play. In fact, he has a simple winning strategy by not doing anything. Player **V**'s choices will either lead to **R**'s winning immediately when **V** makes foolish choices about promoting literals, or **V** creates a bad E- or A-trace.

Correctness Proofs

Now, we prove that these games are sound and complete with respect to CTL* satisfiability. The model-checking games will come in handy for this.

Theorem 15.4.25 (Completeness). For every state formula ϑ of CTL*, if ϑ is satisfiable then player **V** wins the game $\mathcal{G}(\vartheta)$. ∎

Proof. Suppose there is a total ITS $\mathcal{T} = (S, \to, L)$ with a state s_0 such that $\mathcal{T}, s_0 \models \vartheta$. Since ϑ is assumed to be a state formula we have $\vartheta \equiv \mathsf{A}\vartheta$. We need to describe a strategy $\mathfrak{str}$ for player **V** in the game $\mathcal{G}(\vartheta)$ and show that it is indeed a winning strategy. It uses two aspects. First of all, she keeps an annotation in the form of a state with every configuration that is being reached. The initial configuration gets annotated with the state s_0. We write this as $s_0 \vdash \mathsf{A}\vartheta$. Second, **V** makes use of a strategy $\mathfrak{str}_{\mathrm{mc}}$ which she has for the model-checking game $\mathcal{G}^{\mathcal{T}}(s_0, \vartheta)$ according to Theorem 15.3.25: whenever the satisfiability game reaches a configuration

$$s \vdash \mathsf{E}\Gamma_1, \ldots, \mathsf{E}\Gamma_n, \mathsf{A}\Delta_1, \ldots, \mathsf{A}\Delta_m, \Lambda$$

which requires **V** to make a choice with some rule on a block $\mathsf{Q}\Delta$ in this configuration, she chooses $\mathfrak{str}_{\mathrm{mc}}(s \vdash \mathsf{Q}\Delta)$. A close inspection of the similarities between the CTL* model-checking and satisfiability-checking game rules reveals that this is possible. Intuitively, **V**'s state annotation lets her keep track of the satisfiability game in the model-checking game, and whenever **V** has to make a choice in the former she lifts her choice in the latter by ignoring the blocks which are also around in the satisfiability configuration. Note that a block in the satisfiability game is the same as the formula part in a model-checking configuration.

Moreover, when player **R** makes a choice with any rule other than (X) or (X⁻), or a deterministic rule is being played, **V** simply preserves the state annotation. In rule (X) **V** first lets **R** choose the successor configuration, determined by a single block of the form $\mathsf{E}\Gamma$ in the current one. Suppose its annotation is s. Then **V** annotates the successor with the state that is given to her by $\mathfrak{str}_{\mathrm{mc}}(s \vdash \mathsf{E}\Gamma)$. Recall that in such a configuration in the model-checking game, **V** needs to choose some state t with $s \to t$, and the play continues with $t \vdash \mathsf{E}\Gamma$.

In order to check that this $\mathfrak{str}$ is indeed a winning strategy for player **V**, we need one last observation: every trace in a play of $\mathcal{G}(\vartheta)$ that conforms to $\mathfrak{str}$ corresponds to a play conforming to $\mathfrak{str}_{\mathrm{mc}}$ in $\mathcal{G}^{\mathcal{T}}(s_0, \vartheta)$. The correspondence is given as follows. Let $\mathsf{A}\vartheta, \mathsf{Q}_1\Delta_1, \mathsf{Q}_2\Delta_2, \ldots$ be such a trace. We can add the annotations that **V** has used in order to make her choices, resulting in

$$s_0 \vdash \mathsf{A}\vartheta, \quad s_1 \vdash \mathsf{Q}_1\Delta_1, \quad s_2 \vdash \mathsf{Q}_2\Delta_2, \ldots$$

This sequence may contain repetitions of the same state-block pairs because in the satisfiability game some rules may have operated on blocks which are not contained in this trace, and those rules have left these blocks untouched. Collapsing all repetitions to a single occurrence of a state-block pair creates the proposed play in the model-checking game.

Now it is easy to see that $\mathfrak{str}$ is indeed a winning strategy. Suppose it was not, i.e. suppose player **R** could enforce a play that is winning for him. Then this play would contain a bad trace, and this bad trace can be seen as a play in $\mathcal{G}^{\mathcal{T}}(s_0, \vartheta)$. Now recall that a bad trace is either an E-trace with a μ-thread, or a A-trace with no ν-thread. In both cases, the model-checking play corresponding to a bad trace is won by player $\mathbf{R}$. Since it was conforming to $\mathfrak{str}_{mc}$ this could not have been a winning strategy which contradicts our assumption. □

The proof of soundness is not short, yet it only uses techniques that have been seen before in this chapter. It is therefore left as Exercise 15.40.

Theorem 15.4.26 (Soundness). For every state formula ϑ of CTL*, if player $\mathbf{V}$ wins the game $\mathcal{G}(\vartheta)$ then ϑ is satisfiable. ∎

A Game-Based Decision Procedure for CTL*

What remains is to see how a decision procedure for CTL* satisfiability can be derived from its game-theoretic characterisation in Theorem 15.4.25 and 15.4.26. As for the $\mathcal{L}_\mu$ satisfiability games, all we need to do is to show that the winning conditions can be defined as an ω-regular language over some suitable alphabet of rule applications. Again, we use a symbolic representation to keep the alphabet small. Here, the information that needs to be put into an alphabet symbol representing a rule application is not only a unique identifier for the rule and the formula that it operators on, but also the block that it operates on. Consider for instance the configuration $\mathsf{E}(p \vee q, r), \mathsf{E}(p \vee q, \mathsf{X}r \vee \mathsf{XX}r)$. Clearly, we need to apply rule $(\mathsf{E}\vee)$ in this case, but the next configuration is not uniquely identified by the information that it operates on $p \vee q$ because this subformula occurs in two different blocks. Thus, we use the set

$$
\begin{aligned}
\Sigma_\vartheta := \; & \{\mathsf{EAnd}(\varphi, \psi, \Gamma), \mid \varphi, \psi \in \mathit{fi}(\vartheta), \Gamma \subseteq \mathit{fi}(\vartheta)\} \\
& \cup \{\mathsf{AOr}(\varphi, \psi, \Delta), \mathsf{AAnd}(\varphi, \psi, \Delta) \mid \varphi, \psi \in \mathit{fi}(\vartheta), \Delta \subseteq \mathit{fi}(\vartheta)\} \\
& \cup \{\mathsf{EOr}_d(\varphi, \psi, \Gamma) \mid \varphi, \psi \in \mathit{fi}(\vartheta), \Gamma \subseteq \mathit{fi}(\vartheta), d \in \{\mathsf{lft}, \mathsf{rgh}\}\} \\
& \cup \{\mathsf{EU}_d(\varphi, \psi, \Gamma), \mathsf{ER}_d(\varphi, \psi, \Gamma) \mid \varphi, \psi \in \mathit{fi}(\vartheta), \Gamma \subseteq \mathit{fi}(\vartheta), d \in \{\mathsf{lft}, \mathsf{rgh}\}\} \\
& \cup \{\mathsf{AU}_d(\varphi, \psi, \Delta), \mathsf{AR}_d(\varphi, \psi, \Delta) \mid \varphi, \psi \in \mathit{fi}(\vartheta), \Delta \subseteq \mathit{fi}(\vartheta), d \in \{\mathsf{lft}, \mathsf{rgh}\}\} \\
& \cup \{\mathsf{ELit}(\ell, \Gamma) \mid \ell \in \mathit{Lit}(\vartheta), \Gamma \subseteq \mathit{fi}(\vartheta)\} \\
& \cup \{\mathsf{ALit}_d(\ell, \Delta) \mid \ell \in \mathit{Lit}(\vartheta), \Delta \subseteq \mathit{fi}(\vartheta), d \in \{\mathsf{lft}, \mathsf{rgh}\}\} \\
& \cup \{\mathsf{EQ}(\mathsf{Q}\varphi, \Gamma) \mid \mathsf{Q}\varphi \in \mathit{fi}(\vartheta), \Gamma \subseteq \mathit{fi}(\vartheta)\} \\
& \cup \{\mathsf{AQ}_d(\mathsf{Q}\varphi, \Delta) \mid \mathsf{Q}\varphi \in \mathit{fi}(\vartheta), \Delta \subseteq \mathit{fi}(\vartheta), d \in \{\mathsf{lft}, \mathsf{rgh}\}\} \\
& \cup \{\mathsf{X}(\Gamma) \mid \Gamma \subseteq \mathit{fi}(\vartheta)\} \cup \{\mathsf{X}^-, \mathsf{Att}\}
\end{aligned}
$$

where $\mathit{Lit}(\vartheta)$ denotes the set of all literals in $\mathit{fi}(\vartheta)$. It is easily verified that the size of Σ_ϑ is exponential in $|\vartheta|$. Again, every play of $\mathcal{G}(\vartheta)$ uniquely corresponds to a sequence of symbols in Σ_ϑ but the converse is not true. However, this is no problem, since a decision procedure for CTL* is obtained by a reduction to solving parity games that are formed as the product of the graph of game configurations with a deterministic automaton verifying the winning condition. In essence, no automaton to be defined later will ever be used on a sequence that does not correspond to a play. We will define automata that verify certain aspects of the winning conditions separately and then put them together using automata-theoretic constructions in order to realise this reduction.

Lemma 15.4.27. For every state formula ϑ of CTL*, there is a deterministic safety automaton $\mathcal{A}_\vartheta^{\text{fin}}$ of size $2^{2^{\mathcal{O}(|\vartheta|)}}$ that accepts a play of $\mathcal{G}(\vartheta)$ iff it is not won by player **R** with his winning condition for finite plays.   ∎

We leave the details of the construction as Exercise 15.42. It should be clear that such an automaton can deterministically keep track of the current configuration in its state set and update it in every transition with the information that is given in the alphabet symbol encoding the next rule application. The automaton rejects by getting stuck as soon as a suitable configuration has been reached.

Lemma 15.4.28. For every state formula ϑ of CTL*, there is a deterministic Büchi automaton $\mathcal{A}_\vartheta^{\text{E}}$ of size $2^{2^{\mathcal{O}(|\vartheta|)}}$ that accepts a play of $\mathcal{G}(\vartheta)$ iff it does not contain a bad E-trace.   ∎

Proof. It is not hard to construct a nondeterministic co-Büchi automaton which accepts a play of $\mathcal{G}(\vartheta)$ iff it contains a bad E-trace. It needs to keep track of a trace and a thread in the current place, thus it needs to store a block and a formula of that block in its state space. The alphabet symbols carry enough information such that this nondeterministic co-Büchi automaton can update its state accordingly and keep track of such a thread. Its size is therefore bounded by $n \cdot 2^n$ for $n := |\vartheta|$. It should be clear that a co-Büchi acceptance condition suffices to check whether the guessed thread eventually stays on an U-formula or its unfolding.

According to Theorem 15.2.1 there is also a deterministic co-Büchi automaton that accepts the same language and is of size at most 3^{n2^n}, hence $2^{2^{\mathcal{O}(n)}}$. According to Lemma 15.2.14 there is also a deterministic Büchi automaton of the same (asymptotic) size for the complement language, i.e. recognising the set of all plays that do not contain a bad E-trace.   □

Lemma 15.4.29. For every state formula ϑ of CTL*, there is a deterministic parity automaton $\mathcal{A}_\vartheta^{\text{A}}$ of size $2^{2^{\mathcal{O}(n)}}$ and index $2^{\mathcal{O}(n)}$ that accepts a play of $\mathcal{G}(\vartheta)$ iff it does not contain a bad A-trace.   ∎

Proof. We start the construction with a nondeterministic co-Büchi automaton $\mathcal{B}_\vartheta^{\text{Amark}}$ that recognises an auxiliary property, namely 'this A-trace has a ν-thread'. In order to do so, we extend its alphabet to $\Sigma_\vartheta^{\text{mark}} := \Sigma_\vartheta \times \{\text{E}, \text{A}\} \times \mathcal{P}(\text{fi}(\vartheta))$ so that a word over this alphabet does not only encode a play of the satisfiability game $\mathcal{G}(\vartheta)$ but also marks a trace in this play. Note that $\mathcal{B}_\vartheta^{\text{Amark}}$ does not check whether the additional components in the input really form a trace or are just arbitrary sequences of path quantifiers and formula sets. It is only required to accept and reject correctly when they do indeed form a trace in the input word encoding a play. Then it should be clear that $\mathcal{B}_\vartheta^{\text{Amark}}$ only needs at most $n := |\vartheta|$ many states.

It operates in the same way as the nondeterministic weak parity (and therefore also co-Büchi) automaton recognising A-plays in the CTL* model-checking games, as constructed in the proof of Lemma 15.3.30.

Using Theorem 15.2.1 and Lemma 15.2.14 we obtain a deterministic Büchi automaton $\mathcal{A}_\vartheta^{\mathsf{Amark}}$ of size $2^{\mathcal{O}(n)}$ for the complement of this property. It can easily be paired with a deterministic safety automaton of size at most 2^{n+1} over the same alphabet $\Sigma_\vartheta^{\mathsf{Amark}}$ that checks whether the additional markings in the extended alphabet do indeed form an A-trace. A simple product construction between the two yields a deterministic Büchi automaton of size $2^{\mathcal{O}(n)}$ which accepts a word over the extended alphabet iff the additional markings form an A-trace that has no ν-thread. Next, we project its alphabet down to Σ_ϑ and obtain a nondeterministic Büchi automaton that recognises the set of all plays that contain an A-trace with no ν-thread. This does not increase the automaton's size which is still $2^{\mathcal{O}(n)}$.

Finally, using Theorem 15.2.11 and Lemma 15.2.13 we obtain a DPA for the complement of this language which is the set of all plays that do not contain a bad A-trace. Its size is $2^{\mathcal{O}(2^{\mathcal{O}(n)} \cdot \log 2^{\mathcal{O}(n)})} = 2^{2^{\mathcal{O}(n)}}$ and its index is $\mathcal{O}(2^{\mathcal{O}(n)}) = 2^{\mathcal{O}(n)}$. $\qquad\square$

Corollary 15.4.30. For every state formula ϑ of CTL*, there is a DPA $\mathcal{A}_\vartheta^{\mathsf{E}}$ of size $2^{2^{\mathcal{O}(n)}}$ and index $2^{\mathcal{O}(n)}$ with $n = |\vartheta|$ that accepts a play of $\mathcal{G}(\vartheta)$ iff it is won by player **V**. $\qquad\blacksquare$

Proof. Clearly, a play is won by **V** iff it is not won by **R**, i.e. if it

1. is not won by **R** with his winning condition for finite plays,
2. does not contain a bad E-trace and
3. does not contain a bad A-trace.

Thus, the plays that are winning for player **V** are exactly those that are in the intersection of the deterministic safety automaton from Lemma 15.4.27, the DBA from Lemma 15.4.28 and the DPA from Lemma 15.4.29, all of which are of size $2^{2^{\mathcal{O}(n)}}$. The latter has index of order $2^{\mathcal{O}(n)}$. According to Lemma 15.2.17 the intersection of the languages of a deterministic safety automaton and a DPA can easily be formed in a product construction that increases the index by at most 1. Then we can form the product of the resulting automaton with the DBA, using Lemma 15.2.18, and obtain a single DPA of the required size and index that recognises plays that are won by **V**. $\qquad\square$

This allows us to form a reduction from the satisfiability problem for CTL* to the problem of solving a parity game.

Theorem 15.4.31. For every CTL* state formula ϑ of size n there is a parity game of size $2^{2^{\mathcal{O}(n)}}$ and index $2^{\mathcal{O}(n)}$ that is won by Player 0 iff ϑ is satisfiable. $\qquad\blacksquare$

Proof. This follows from the characterisation of CTL* satisfiability by games of doubly exponential size (Theorem 15.4.25 and 15.4.26) whose winning conditions can be recognised by a deterministic parity automaton of doubly exponential size and exponential index (Corollary 15.4.30) and the Main Reduction Theorem (Theorem 15.1.27). $\qquad\square$

Corollary 15.4.32. The satisfiability problem for CTL* is in 2ExpTime. $\qquad\blacksquare$

Proof. This upper bound follows from the doubly exponential reduction to the parity game solving problem in Theorem 15.4.31 and the fact that these parity games have $2^{2^{\mathcal{O}(n)}}$ nodes, index $2^{\mathcal{O}(n)}$ and at most $2^{2^{\mathcal{O}(n)}} \cdot 2^n$ many edges because the branching-degree of the satisfiability games is bounded by the maximal number of E-blocks that can occur in a configuration. Hence, such games can be solved in time

$$\mathcal{O}\left(2^{2^{\mathcal{O}(n)}} \cdot 2^n \cdot (2^{2^{\mathcal{O}(n)}})^{2^{\mathcal{O}(n)}}\right) = 2^{2^{\mathcal{O}(n)}}. \qquad \square$$

Note that this matches the lower bound that was proved for the fragment CTL^+ of CTL^* (Theorem 11.3.4).

15.4.3 Small Model Properties

Note how that satisfiability game framework reduces the question of whether a formula of $\mathcal{L}_\mu$, CTL^* and all other logics subsumed by them, is satisfiable to the problem of deciding whether a particular node in a finite parity game is won by Player 0. It is natural to ask about the possibility to obtain a model in the positive case. The game-based framework is indeed strong enough not only to decide the decision problem of satisfiability but also to solve the underlying computation problem of obtaining models for satisfiable formulae.

Since a model of a formula witnesses its satisfiability, it is reasonable to check whether something witnessing the fact that player 0 wins a node in a parity game could correspond to such models. This is indeed the case; note that winning strategies play that corresponding role on the side of the parity games.

Theorem 15.4.33. Every satisfiable guarded $\mathcal{L}_\mu$-formula of size n and alternation depth k has a model of size at most $2^{\mathcal{O}(nk \log n)}$. ∎

Proof. Let $\varphi \in \mathcal{L}_\mu$ be guarded and satisfiable. According to the completeness Theorem 15.4.5 for the $\mathcal{L}_\mu$ satisfiability games, player **V** was a winning strategy for the game $\mathcal{G}(\varphi)$. According to the Main Reduction Theorem 15.1.27, Player 0 has a winning strategy for the parity game $\mathcal{G}'$ that is obtained as the product of $\mathcal{G}(\varphi)$ and a deterministic parity automaton recognising winning plays for **V**. The proof of Theorem 15.4.12 estimates the size of $\mathcal{G}'$ to be of order $2^{\mathcal{O}(nk \log n)}$. According to Theorem 15.1.21, Player 0 has a memoryless winning strategy for $\mathcal{G}'$. This directly translates back into a winning strategy $\mathfrak{str}'$ for player **V** in $\mathcal{G}(\varphi)$ along the lines of the proof of Theorem 15.1.27. Note that $\mathfrak{str}'$ need not be memoryless. However, it is a finite-memory strategy in the sense that the history of a configuration C of $\mathcal{G}(\varphi)$ is encoded entirely in the state of the deterministic parity automata that is run alongside plays of $\mathcal{G}(\varphi)$. Hence, in order to perform a choice in $\mathcal{G}(\varphi)$, player **V** only needs to store one of $2^{\mathcal{O}(nk \log n)}$ many states of this DPA and consult a memoryless winning strategy in the corresponding parity game. Thus, **V** has a winning strategy for $\mathcal{G}(\varphi)$ that needs a memory of size at most $2^{\mathcal{O}(nk \log n)}$, and this strategy $\mathfrak{str}$ can be used to obtain the a priori infinite ITS $\mathcal{T}_{\mathfrak{str}}$ that is a model of φ according to Theorem 15.4.7. However, since each of player **V**'s choices in $\mathcal{G}(\varphi)$ with $\mathfrak{str}$ is made with reference to a memory of at most $2^{\mathcal{O}(nk \log n)}$ many elements, $\mathcal{T}_{\mathfrak{str}}$ can be finitely represented as a graph with at most $2^n \cdot 2^{\mathcal{O}(nk \log n)} = 2^{\mathcal{O}(nk \log n)}$ nodes. The factor 2^n represents the number of different configurations in $\mathcal{G}(\varphi)$. $\qquad\square$

The same principles can be used to obtain a small model theorem for CTL*. The proof details are left as Exercise 15.43.

Theorem 15.4.34. Every satisfiable CTL*-formula of size n has a model of size at most $2^{2^{\mathcal{O}(n)}}$. $\qquad\blacksquare$

According to Theorem 10.2.9, ATL* can be embedded into $\mathcal{L}_\mu$, as well, so we also get decidability and the small model property for this alternating-time temporal logic as well.

Corollary 15.4.35. Satisfiability in ATL* is decidable, and ATL* has the small model property. $\qquad\blacksquare$

The exact bounds on small models for ATL*, as well as the complexity of its satisfiability problem, can easily be derived from the estimation on the blow-up in formulae when translating ATL* into $\mathcal{L}_\mu$ (cf. Exercise 10.15). We remark that these bounds are not optimal, see the bibliographic notes in Section 9.5 for details.

15.5 Exercises

Exercises on abstract 2-player games

Exercise 15.1. Show that there is no game $\mathcal{G}$ on a game arena, for which both players 0 and 1 have a winning strategy.

Exercise 15.2. Show that there is no memoryless winning strategy for Player 0 in the game $\mathcal{G}_2$ defined in Example 2.2.8.

Hint: Suppose there was a memoryless strategy $\mathfrak{str}$. Then it is in fact a function of type $\{a, b\} \to \{1, 2\}$. There are only four functions of this kind, and so it suffices to show that none of these is a winning strategy.

Exercise 15.3. Let $\mathcal{G} = (V, Own, E, v_I, Win)$ be a game with Π being the set of all plays in this game. Define $\Pi_\mathbf{P} := \{\lambda \in \Pi \mid Win(\lambda) = \mathbf{P}\}$ to be the set of all plays which are being won by player $\mathbf{P}$. Show that Π_0 is a regular language over the alphabet V iff Π_1 is a regular language. (*NB:* This is not just an immediate consequence of the complementation closure for regular languages.)

Exercise 15.4. Consider the game $\mathcal{G}$ from Example 2.2.5.

(a) Draw the game arena that has as nodes all sequences of length at most 3 of nodes from $\mathcal{G}$ that can occur consecutively in a play of $\mathcal{G}$. The edges in this game realise a 'sliding window' of size 3, i.e. there is an edge from a1 to a1b and one from a1b to 1b1 for example.

(b) Now we consider a suitable translation of the winning condition Win_{count} from Example 2.2.8 for this game.

$$Win'_{count}(\lambda) = \begin{cases} 0, & \text{if } \max(\inf(\lambda) \cap (V^{\leq 2}\{1, 2\}) = |\inf(\lambda) \cap V^{\leq 2}\{a, b\}| \\ 1, & \text{otherwise} \end{cases}$$

where $V^{\leq 2}$ denotes all sequences of length at most 2 of nodes in $\mathcal{G}$. Hence, it expresses the same as Win_{count} when considering the *last* old node in the new sequences of nodes only.

Show that Player 0 has a memoryless strategy for the game with this winning condition.

Exercises on parity games

Exercise 15.5. Consider the class of so-called reachability games which are of the form (V, Own, E, v_I, Win) such that there is a particular node $v_0 \in V$ with $Win(\lambda) = 0$ iff v_0 is contained in λ. Thus, Player 0 wins any play that passes through v_0.

(a) Show that solving reachability games is PTIME-hard by a reduction from the $(\log n \times n)$-tiling game problem, see Proposition 11.1.21.
(b) Give an algorithm for solving reachability games that runs in time $\mathcal{O}(card(E))$. *Hint:* Consider marking nodes from which Player 0 has a winning strategy and extending the marking along the edges of the game arena.

Exercise 15.6.

(a) Show that parity games can always be normalised so that:
    • the lowest priority occurring in the game is 0 or 1 and
    • if there are two nodes with priorities $\mathfrak{p}_1$ and $\mathfrak{p}_2$ such that $\mathfrak{p}_1 + 1 < \mathfrak{p}_2$ then there is a node with priority $\mathfrak{p}_1 + 1$.
(b) Show that parity games can always be normalised so that each node has a unique priority.

Exercise 15.7. Prove Lemma 15.1.4, Lemma 15.1.5 and Lemma 15.1.9.

Exercise 15.8. Give a reduction from safety games to parity games analogously to the reduction from reachability games to parity games in Lemma 15.1.10.

Exercise 15.9. Let $\mathcal{G} = (V, Own, E, v_I, \Omega)$ be a parity game such that $\Omega(v) \geq 2$ for all $v \in V$. Consider the parity game $\mathcal{G}' = (V, Own, E, v_I, \Omega')$ where $\Omega'(v) = \Omega(v) - 2$ for any $v \in V$. Show that player $\mathbf{P}$ for any $\mathbf{P} \in \{0, 1\}$ has a winning strategy for $\mathcal{G}$ iff she has a winning strategy for $\mathcal{G}'$.

Exercise 15.10. Construct an NBA over the alphabet $\{0, \ldots, k-1\}$ which accepts the languages of all words that are winning for Player 0 and Player 1 respectively when interpreted as the priorities in a play of a parity game.

Exercise 15.11. Show that the priorities in a weak parity game can be changed so that it becomes a Büchi game or a co-Büchi game on the same arena, such that the players winning regions and strategies are preserved.

Exercise 15.12. Consider the abstract game $\mathcal{G}$ in Example 15.1.26 with the winning condition intuitively described as 'eventually only b or eventually only c'.

(a) Give a deterministic parity automaton for the language of symbolically encoded winning plays for Player 0.
   Hint: It is possible to construct a co-Büchi automaton.
(b) Construct the product of the game $\mathcal{G}$ with the automaton from (a). Show that it is won by Player 0.

Exercise 15.13. Prove in detail the correctness of the construction in Theorem 15.2.3.

Exercise 15.14. Formulate the algorithm for solving weak parity games that is sketched in the proof of Theorem 15.1.18.

Exercises on automata constructions

Exercise 15.15. Construct the deterministic co-Büchi automaton for the following nondeterministic one according to Theorem 15.2.1.

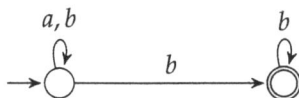

Exercise 15.16. Prove the upper bound on the number of possible history trees for a nondeterministic Büchi automaton as given in Lemma 15.2.9.
   Hint: The number of different trees with m nodes can be estimated as at most 4^m.

Exercise 15.17. Check that the estimations on the size and index, i.e. number of possibly different priorities, of the deterministic parity automaton constructed in the proof of Theorem 15.2.11 are correct.

Exercise 15.18. Consider the automaton in Exercise 15.15 as a nondeterministic Büchi automaton. Construct runs of the DPA according to Theorem 15.2.11 for this NBA on the words $(bba)^\omega$ and bab^ω.

Exercise 15.19. Consider the following NBA.

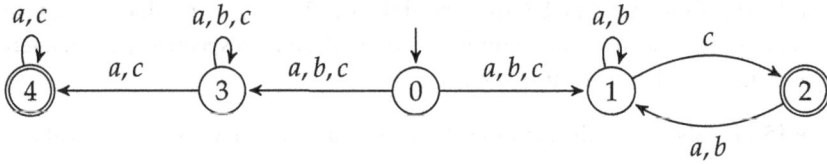

Construct the runs of the DPA according to Theorem 15.2.11 on the following words: $(abc)^\omega$, $bc(ab)^\omega$ and cba^ω.

Exercise 15.20. Prove Lemma 15.2.13 and 15.2.14.

Hint: The possible increase in the state space, and therefore also the index, by 1 is necessary because a DPA $\mathcal{A}$ needs to be made total before it can be complemented by simply changing the states' priorities. This may require the addition of a new sink state with an odd priority such that for every word there is not just at most, but exactly one, run of $\mathcal{A}$.

Exercise 15.21. Prove Lemma 15.2.15.

Hint: Intuitively, the NBA can work as follows. It starts to simulate the NPA for a while, ignoring priorities. At some point it guesses an even priority which will be the largest seen at all and verifies with its Büchi condition that it is indeed seen infinitely often. This requires the change into a different component of the NBA. In order to ensure that no larger priority is seen at all, all states which such priorities are missing in this component. Check whether Lemma 14.1.15 can be used for this.

Exercise 15.22. Prove Lemma 15.2.17. *Hint:* Consider a typical product construction.

Exercise 15.23. Show that the product construction between a DPA and a DBA, as presented in the proof of Lemma 15.2.18, yields a correct DPA, i.e. its language is in fact that intersection of the languages of the input DPA and the DBA.

Exercises on model-checking games

Exercise 15.24. Prove Theorem 15.3.6.

Hint: Analyse the construction of the model-checking games which is being used in the proof of Theorem 15.3.1. Note that the SCC decomposition of the game is induced by the structure of fixpoint subformulae. Also note that the assigning of priority 0 to every node that does not contain a variable, as it is being done in the construction in the proof of Theorem 15.3.1 is not strictly necessary. It is possible to assign larger priorities to these nodes as well for as long as they are at most as large as those that are being visited infinitely often in a corresponding play.

Exercise 15.25. Show how to construct weak parity games of linear size that capture the model-checking problem for CTL.

Exercise 15.26. Extend the model-checking games for CTL* by rules and winning conditions for the temporal operators G and F. *Hint:* Express them using R and U, and then consider what the rules for these would do on them and what the rules for literals would do afterwards.

Exercise 15.27. Prove Lemma 15.3.19 and Lemma 15.4.3, and carry out the missing cases in the proof of Lemma 15.3.21.

Exercise 15.28. Prove Lemma 15.4.19. *Hint:* Consider the cases in which a game rule connects two blocks with different path quantifiers and reason using an argument on the size of blocks on a trace.

Exercises on satisfiability games

Exercise 15.29. Prove Theorem 15.4.15. *Hint:* Consider changing (Mod) such that the constructed models become deterministic.

Exercise 15.30. Show that the specialised rules (AG) and (AF) (cf. Example 15.4.24) for G- and F-operators have the same effect as the rules (AR) and (AU) when applied to the R- and U-formulae defining those as abbreviations.

Give suitable specialised rules for G- and F-formulae inside of existential blocks.

Exercise 15.31. Use satisfiability-checking games for $\mathcal{L}_\mu$ to show that each of the following $\mathcal{L}_\mu$ formulae is valid cf. Exercises 8.7 and 8.8).

(a) $(\mu X.\langle a\rangle\top \wedge (p \vee [a]X)) \rightarrow \nu X.\langle a\rangle\top \wedge (p \vee [a]X)$
(b) $\mu X.\mu Y.p \vee \langle a\rangle X \vee \langle b\rangle Y \equiv \mu X.p \vee \langle a\rangle X \vee \langle b\rangle Y \equiv \mu Y.\mu X.p \vee \langle a\rangle X \vee \langle b\rangle Y$
(c) $(\mu X.\nu Y.[a]X \vee [b]Y) \rightarrow \nu Y.\mu X.[a]X \vee [b]Y$

Exercise 15.32. Using satisfiability-checking games for $\mathcal{L}_\mu$ determine whether each of the following $\mathcal{L}_\mu$ formulae is satisfiable. In case it is, extract a satisfying model from a winning strategy for player **V**.

(a) $\Diamond\neg p \wedge \nu Z.p \wedge \Box Z$
(b) $\Diamond\Diamond\neg p \wedge \nu Z.p \wedge \Box Z$
(c) $\Diamond\Box\neg p \wedge \neg p \wedge \mu Z.p \vee \Box Z$
(d) $\Diamond\neg p \wedge \neg q \wedge \nu Z.q \vee (p \wedge \Box Z)$
(e) $\neg q \wedge \Box(\neg q \wedge \neg p) \wedge \mu Z.q \vee (p \wedge \Diamond Z)$
(f) $\neg q \wedge \Box\neg q \wedge \mu Z.q \vee (p \wedge \Diamond Z)$

Exercise 15.33. Using satisfiability-checking games for $\mathcal{L}_\mu$ determine whether each of the following $\mathcal{L}_\mu$ formulae is valid. In case it is not, extract a falsifying model from a winning strategy for player **V**.

(a) $\nu Y.(\mu Z.P \vee \Diamond Z) \wedge \Diamond Y \rightarrow \nu Y.\mu Z.(P \vee \Diamond Z) \wedge \Diamond Y$
(b) $\nu Y.\mu Z.(P \vee \Diamond Z) \wedge \Diamond Y \rightarrow \nu Y.(\mu Z.P \vee \Diamond Z) \wedge \Diamond Y$

Exercise 15.34. Consider the CTL formulae listed in Exercise 13.31. For each of them:

(a) Translate the formula to the alternation-free $\mathcal{L}_\mu$.
(b) Then use satisfiability-checking games for $\mathcal{L}_\mu$ to determine whether the resulting translation is valid. In case it is not, extract a falsifying model from a winning strategy for player **V**.

(c) Now, determine, using the CTL* satisfiability games, whether the original formula is valid. In case it is not, extract a falsifying model from a winning strategy for player **V**.

(d) Compare the results and the obtained models (if applicable) from the previous two items.

(e) Compare these results and the obtained models (if applicable) also with the results from the execution of the tableaux method presented in Chapter 13.

Exercise 15.35. Consider the sets of CTL formulae listed in Exercise 13.32. For each of them:

(a) Translate the conjunction of the formulae to the alternation-free $\mathcal{L}_\mu$.

(b) Then use satisfiability-checking games for $\mathcal{L}_\mu$ to determine whether the resulting translation is satisfiable. In case it is, extract a satisfying model from a winning strategy for player **V**.

(c) Determine, using the CTL* satisfiability games, whether the original set of formulae is satisfiable. In case it is, extract a satisfying model from a winning strategy for player **V**.

(d) Compare the results and the obtained models (if applicable) from the previous two items.

(e) Compare these results and the obtained models (if applicable) also with the results from the execution of the tableaux method presented in Chapter 13.

Exercise 15.36. Consider the logical consequences in CTL listed in Exercise 13.33. For each of them:

(a) Translate it to the alternation-free $\mathcal{L}_\mu$.

(b) Then use satisfiability-checking games for $\mathcal{L}_\mu$ to determine whether the resulting logical consequence is valid. In case it is not, extract a model from a winning strategy for player **V**.

(c) Determine, using the CTL* satisfiability games, whether the original logical consequence is valid. In case it is not, extract a falsifying model from a winning strategy for player **V**.

(d) Compare the results and the obtained models (if applicable) from the previous two items.

(e) Compare these results and the obtained models (if applicable) also with the results from the execution of the tableaux method presented in Chapter 13.

Exercise 15.37. Determine, using CTL* satisfiability games, whether each of the following CTL* formulae is satisfiable. In case it is, extract a satisfying model from a winning strategy for player **V**.

(a) $\mathsf{EFG}p \wedge \mathsf{AFG}\neg p$

(b) $\mathsf{EFG}p \wedge \mathsf{AGAF}\neg p$

(c) $\mathsf{EGF}p \wedge \mathsf{AGF}\neg p$

(d) $\mathsf{EGF}p \wedge \mathsf{AFAG}\neg p$

(e) $\mathsf{EGEF}p \wedge \neg\mathsf{EGF}p$

(f) $\mathsf{AFG}p \wedge \neg\mathsf{AFAG}p$

(g) $\mathsf{AGF}p \wedge \neg\mathsf{AGAF}p$

(h) $p \wedge \mathsf{AG}(p \rightarrow \mathsf{E}(q\mathsf{U}p)) \wedge \mathsf{AF}(\neg q\mathsf{R}\neg p)$

Exercise 15.38. Determine, using CTL* satisfiability games, whether each of the following CTL* formulae is valid. In case it is not, extract a falsifying model from a winning strategy for player **V**.

(a) $\mathsf{AFEG}p \to \mathsf{AFG}p$

(b) $\mathsf{AGEF}p \to \mathsf{EGF}p$

(c) $\mathsf{AGEF}p \to \mathsf{AGF}p$

(d) $\mathsf{EFEG}p \to \mathsf{EFG}p$

(e) $\mathsf{A}(\mathsf{G}p \to \mathsf{AG}p)$

(f) $\mathsf{AG}(p \to \mathsf{EXF}p) \to (p \to \mathsf{EGF}p)$

(g) $\mathsf{AG}(p \to \mathsf{AXF}p) \to (p \to \mathsf{AGF}p)$

(h) $p \land \mathsf{AG}(p \to \mathsf{E}(q\mathsf{U}p)) \to \mathsf{EG}(q\mathsf{U}p)$

(i) $\neg(\mathsf{A}(p\mathsf{U}q)) \to \mathsf{E}(\mathsf{G}\neg q \lor ((\neg q)\mathsf{U}(\neg q \land \neg p)))$

(j) $\mathsf{E}(\mathsf{G}\neg q \lor ((\neg q)\mathsf{U}(\neg q \land \neg p))) \to \neg(\mathsf{A}(p\mathsf{U}q))$

Exercise 15.39. Using CTL* satisfiability games verify each of the equivalences between CTL^2 formulae and their translations into CTL listed in Figure 7.8.

Exercise 15.40. Prove Theorem 15.4.26.

Hint: First, construct a tree model from a winning strategy for player **V** by collapsing the tree of all conforming plays, like it is done in the proof of Theorem 15.4.7. Then show that this is a model of the input formula by using the model-checking games for CTL* and the correspondence between plays in those games and traces in the satisfiability games as defined in the proof of Theorem 15.4.25.

Exercise 15.41. Compute the exact size of the alphabet Σ_ϑ of symbolic rule applications in the CTL* satisfiability game $\mathcal{G}(\vartheta)$.

Exercise 15.42. Construct the deterministic safety automaton of Lemma 15.4.27 explicitly.

Exercises on small model properties

Exercise 15.43. Prove Theorem 15.4.34 using the same lines of reasoning that lead to the small model property of $\mathcal{L}_\mu$ (Theorem 15.4.33).

Exercise 15.44. Construct a family $(\varphi_n)_{n\geq 1}$ of satisfiable LT$_\mu$ formulae such that $|\varphi_n| = \mathcal{O}(n)$ but every model of φ_n has size $\Omega(2^n)$.

Hint: Formalise a binary counter with n bits as atomic propositions such that every model of φ_n must be a computation path representing the sequence $0, ..., 2^n - 1$.

Is this construction already possible with LTL instead of LT$_\mu$?

Exercise 15.45. Construct a family $(\varphi_n)_{n\geq 1}$ of satisfiable CTL* formulae such that $|\varphi_n| = \mathcal{O}(n)$ but every model of φ_n has size $\Omega(2^{2^n})$.

Hint: Consider the proof of 2ExpTime-hardness of CTL$^+$ in Theorem 11.3.4.

15.6 Bibliographical Notes

Origins. The use of games in logic goes back to the Antiquity, when debate with argumentation was regarded by Zeno of Elea, Socrates and the philosophers in the Megarian and Stoic schools as a kind of a game – a view reflected in the word *dialectics* coined then, which was used as synonym for logic until the late medieval times. The idea of dialogue-based logical games was revived in the late 19th century by Charles S. Peirce (who perhaps gave the first explicit game-theoretic semantics of the first-order quantifiers) and developed further mid- to late 20th century, starting with works of Skolem, Lorenzen, Lorenz, Novikov, Henkin, Hintikka, Hodges, Väänänen and others, into formal *game-theoretic semantics* for classical logic, as well as various nonclassical logics. Game-theoretic semantics defines the notion of truth of a logical formula in terms of existence of a winning strategy of the Proponent player in the respective *evaluation game*. The idea of evaluation games, underlying the game-based approach to model checking, is especially important for logical languages where traditional compositional semantics is not readily available, e.g. infinitary logics. See further historical notes and details on the use of games in logic in Hodges (2013) and the recent van Benthem (2014) for a broad modern exposition on the interaction between logic and games.

The mathematical foundations of model-checking games are rooted in the works on solving finite and infinite games by Zermelo, Borel, von Neumann, Gale and Stewart, Büchi and Landweber, Davis, Martin, Gurevich and Harrington and McNaughton (see Gurevich and Harrington 1982; McNaughton 1993).

The explicit use of model-checking games in modal and temporal logics begins in the early 1990s, in works of Stirling (1995) and Niwiński and Walukiewicz (1996) and soon expands into an active and fruitful research area, also closely related to the automata-theoretic approach. See Grädel et al. (2002) for a comprehensive coverage of the area, from a mathematical, logical and computer science perspective.

Parity games. Parity games have emerged from the study of infinite games played on finite directed graphs in which the nodes are coloured and the winning conditions make assertions about occurrences of colours (McNaughton 1993). There is an interesting example of the tight connection between automata and game theory which is not exploited any further here: the main question of determinacy of such games has led to an elegant proof by Gurevich and Harrington (1982) of a fundamental result in the theory of tree automata, namely Rabin's Theorem (Rabin 1969) stating that the class of regular tree languages is closed under complementation.

The parity condition as a means to define the winner in plays of an infinite game on a finite game graph has been invented by Mostowski (1984) and Emerson and Jutla (1991) in the context of an acceptance condition for finite automata. Weaker conditions have been considered in different forms by Muller et al. (1986) in terms of a restricted graph structure of the underlying automaton, and by Löding and Thomas (2000) using occurrences of priorities, rather than infinite occurrences.

Solving parity games. The intrinsically difficult question of the exact complexity of solving parity games has led to numerous attempts to provide upper bounds and therefore to many different algorithms. It was noted early that solving parity games is in NP and, by determinacy also in coNP, i.e. in NP ∩coNP (Emerson et al. 2001), which is a very sparse complexity class since not many problems are known to belong to it without already belonging to PTIME. Most of all, solving parity games is unlikely to be NP-complete because this would entail NP =coNP.

Jurdziński showed that the problem is even closer to P, namely it belongs to UP (Jurdziński 1998), the class of problem that can be recognised by a nondeterministic polynomial-time Turing machine with a unique accepting run. By determinacy, it is even in UP ∩coUP. It also belongs to the complexity class PLS, which stands for 'polynomial local search'. This follows easily from strategy improvement algorithms, see later, but has also been shown using a formalisation of the determinacy proof in bounded arithmetic by Beckmann and Moller (2008).

The determinacy proof and the simple recursive algorithm extracted from it that are presented in this chapter are due to Zielonka (1998). Schewe's Big-Step algorithm (Schewe 2007) is a modification thereof which leads to better complexity bounds.

It is just as possible to extract algorithms from Emerson, Jutla and Sistla's proof of containment in NP (Emerson et al. 2001), which characterises the existence of a memoryless winning strategy by a polynomial-time checkable witness in the form of so-called progress measures. Jurdziński (2000) has shown how to compute them deterministically, resulting in the Small Progress Measures algorithm. Lange (2005) has suggested to let SAT solvers search for such witnessing progress measures, and Heljanko et al. (2012) have extended this to specialised solvers for difference logic.

There are several deterministic algorithms that use strategy improvement, i.e. starting from a given strategy they successively improve it until either a winning strategy is found or one can be sure that none exists. It originates from other games, namely payoff and stochastic games (Puri 1995; Ludwig 1995), to which parity games can be reduced (Jurdziński 1998). Thus, algorithms for those games are in principle also applicable to parity games, and Vöge and Jurdziński (2000) have used this to devise the first strategy improvement algorithm for them, followed by Schewe (2008b) and Friedmann and Lange (2012). Vorobjov et al. have considered randomised versions (Petersson and Vorobyov 2001; Björklund et al. 2003; Björklund and Vorobyov 2005).

While it was in principle not impossible that one of these algorithms was, in fact, a polynomial-time algorithm whose running time was just badly estimated, Friedmann has shown that this is not the case for practically all of them (Friedmann 2009, 2010, 2011b,a, 2013). It is possible, though, to solve parity games in genuinely sub-exponential time as shown by Jurdziński et al. (2008).

Friedmann and Lange (2009) have created PGSOLVER, which provides tool support for parity game solving. It achieves practical efficiency through heuristics and preprocessing which is not dealt with here. The game-based approach to decision procedures for temporal logics is also implemented in a tool called MLSOLVER which realises corresponding reductions to parity games and uses PGSOLVER as a backend (Friedmann and Lange 2010).

Theorem 15.1.24, stating that solving 1-player games is in NLOGSPACE, makes implicit use of a result by Immerman (1988) and Szelepcsényi (1988) about the closure of

NLogSpace under complement. This way, we can present the theorem regardless of which player is the only one to make choices in the game.

Parity games and the μ-calculus. The game-theoretic approach to temporal logics has become very prominent in connection with the modal μ-calculus, mainly because its formulae can easily get very difficult to understand and a game-theoretic semantics can help explain the properties expressed by such formulae. Emerson and Jutla (1991) described a connection between $\mathcal{L}_\mu$ and games for the purpose of obtaining decision procedures using the automata-theoretic framework. This connection has been elaborated in subsequent years forming the now well-known equivalence between $\mathcal{L}_\mu$ model checking and parity game solving (Stirling 1995; Emerson et al. 2001; Niwiński 2002). The definability of winning regions in parity games by formulae of $\mathcal{L}_\mu$ is due to Walukiewicz (1996).

The game-theoretic framework is not restricted to the temporal logics presented in this book. For instance, Grädel (2002) gives a survey of model-checking games for richer formalisms like first-order logic and fixpoint extensions thereof. Lange (2002b) has also defined model-checking games for richer modal fixpoint logics beyond the expressive power of MSO.

Games for temporal logics. The game-theoretic procedure for model checking CTL* presented in this chapter originates from Lange and Stirling's **focus games**. Recall that the Boolean operators in such logics cannot fully be decomposed into players' choices as it is done in the $\mathcal{L}_\mu$ model-checking games, because they conjoin genuine path formulae. Configurations in these games become sets of formulae, and then some machinery like the μ- and ν-threads of this chapter is needed in order to define a correct game-theoretic semantics. Focus games use a device called *focus* as an attempt to track infinite unfoldings of fixpoint formulae. They are used to give game-theoretic characterisations of CTL*'s model-checking problem (Lange and Stirling 2002) and the satisfiability problems for LTL, CTL (Lange and Stirling 2001) and the related propositional dynamic logic (Lange 2002a). A similar approach has been taken by Bhat et al. (1995) for model checking CTL*, which also invents its own machinery for tracking unfulfilled eventualities.

The approach presented here is more modular in that it separates the game with an abstract winning condition on the existence of threads from the algorithm for solving games, i.e. the decision procedure. Focus games in their early presentation have not made that distinction and have therefore also not been successfully used to give game-theoretic characterisations of satisfiability problems for logics that require far more complex conditions on threads, and therefore combinatorially more involved results, like $\mathcal{L}_\mu$ and CTL*. Instead, their correctness proofs need to mimic determinisation constructions. This becomes particularly visible through Dax and Lange's (2004) foci games, which essentially incorporate a powerset-like determinisation construction in order to get rid of the focus while still being able to detect unfulfilled eventualities.

The decision procedures for these logics as presented here supersede, on one hand, the focus games approach that was started for simpler temporal logics, and, on the other hand, repeat steps that have been taken before in obtaining decision procedures for such logics, now using slightly more modern machinery. For instance, Niwiński and Walukiewicz (1996) gave a game-based decision procedure for $\mathcal{L}_\mu$ (but called it tableaux). They were lacking, at that time, the determinisation of Büchi automata into parity automata which required them to use determinacy of certain games instead. This is also very much related to the approach via tree automata by Emerson and Jutla (2000). Essentially, tree automata complementation, NBA determinisation and the determinacy result used in Niwiński and Walukiewicz's tableaux are combinatorial prices to pay for finding unfulfilled least fixpoint unfoldings.

The procedure presented here for $\mathcal{L}_\mu$ is only optimal for guarded formulae. Friedmann and Lange (2013) have shown how guarded transformation can be avoided and a game-based decision procedure along the same lines as those used here can still be achieved. The decision procedure for CTL* presented here uses the same principles as those by Friedmann et al. (2013), who also specialise this approach to the fragments CTL+ and CTL and show where the simpler syntax leads to savings in the combinatorial price to pay, i.e. they analyse more precisely what kind of determinisation of ω-automata is really needed for what kind of temporal formulae.

Automata-theoretic constructions. This chapter presents two determinisation constructions. The first and simpler one for co-Büchi and weak parity automata is the so-called Miyano–Hayashi construction (Miyano and Hayashi 1984), which was originally invented to translate alternating into nondeterministic Büchi automata. The second and more complex construction to determinise Büchi automata goes back to Safra (1988, 1989), who first solved that problem. His construction produces Rabin automata which are not as nice in the context that determinisation is used here, because they would result in reductions to Rabin games which – as opposed to parity games – are not self-dual and do not admit memoryless winning strategies for both players. Piterman (2006) has managed to refine Safra's construction so that it produces parity automata directly. Subsequent work by Schewe (2009) and Kähler and Wilke (2008) is based on the same principles. The construction shown in this chapter follows the presentation by Schewe. Based on this determinisation procedure we obtain, with just a little bit more effort, a complementation procedure for Büchi automata. While all known determinisation procedures are very similar and more or less variations on Safra's approach, many different procedures for complemeting Büchi automata have been invented (that do not necessarily use, nor yield, determinisation) (cf. Büchi 1962; Pécuchet 1986; Sistla et al. 1987; Klarlund 1991; Thomas 1999; Kupferman and Vardi 2001).

References

Abadir, M.S., Albin, K., Havlicek, J., Krishnamurthy, N., and Martin, A.K. 2003. Formal Verification Successes at Motorola. *Formal Methods in System Design*, **22**(2), 117–123.

Abate, P., Goré, R., and Widmann, F. 2007. One-Pass Tableaux for Computation Tree Logic. Pages 32–46 of: *LPAR'07*. Lecture Notes in Computer Science, vol. 4790. Springer.

Abdou, J., and Keiding, H. 1991. *Effectivity Functions in Social Choice Theory*. Kluwer.

Abrahamson, K. 1979. Modal Logic of Concurrent Nondeterministic Programs. Pages 21–33 of: *International Symposium on Semantics of Concurrent Computation, Evian, France*. Lecture Notes in Computer Science, vol. 70. Springer.

Abrahamson, K. 1980. *Decidability and Expressiveness of Logics of Programs*. Ph.D. thesis, University of Washington.

Accellera Organization, Inc. 2004. *Formal Semantics of Accellera Property Specification Language*. In Appendix B of http://www.eda.org/vfv/docs/PSL-v1.1.pdf.

Aceto, L., Ingolfsdottir, A., and Srba, J. 2012a. The Algorithmics of Bisimilarity. *In:* Sangiorgi and Rutten (2012).

Aceto, L., Ingólfsdóttir, A., Levy, P. B., and Sack, J. 2012b. Characteristic Formulae for Fixed-Point Semantics: A General Framework. *Mathematical Structures in Computer Science*, **22**(2), 125–173.

Adler, I. M., and Immerman, N. 2001. An n! Lower Bound on Formula Size. Pages 197–208 of: *LICS'01*. IEEE.

Ågotnes, T., Goranko, V., and Jamroga, W. 2007. Alternating-Time Temporal Logics with Irrevocable Strategies. Pages 15–24 of: *Proceedings of TARK XI*.

Ågotnes, T., Goranko, V., and Jamroga, W. 2008. *Strategic Commitment and Release in Logics for Multi-Agent Systems (Extended abstract)*. Tech. rept. IfI-08-01. Clausthal University of Technology.

Aho, A., Hopcroft, J., and Ullman, J. 1974. *The Design and Analysis of Computer Algorithms*. Addison-Wesley.

Aho, A., Hopcroft, J., and Ullman, J. 1983. *Data Structures and Algorithms*. Addison-Wesley.

Ajspur, M., and Goranko, V. 2013. Tableaux-Based Decision Method for Single-Agent Linear Time Synchronous Temporal Epistemic Logics with Interacting Time and Knowledge. Pages 80–96 of: *ICLA 2013*.

Alberucci, L., and Facchini, A. 2009. The Modal μ-Calculus over Restricted Classes of Transition Systems. *The Journal of Symbolic Logic*, **74**(4), 1367–1400.

Alpern, B., and Schneider, F. 1987. Recognizing Safety and Liveness. *Distributed Computing*, **2**(3), 117–126.

Alur, R., Henzinger, Th., and Kupferman, O. 1997 (October). Alternating-Time Temporal Logic. Pages 100–109 of: *FOCS'97*.

Alur, R., Henzinger, T. A., Kupferman, O., and Vardi, M. 1998a. Alternating Refinement Relations. Pages 163–178 of: *CONCUR'98*. Lecture Notes in Computer Science, vol. 1466. Springer.

Alur, R., Henzinger, T.A., and Kupferman, O. 1998b. Alternating-Time Temporal Logic. Pages 23–60 of: *COMPOS'97*. Lecture Notes in Computer Science, vol. 1536. Springer.

Alur, R., Henzinger, T.A., Mang, F. Y. C., Qadeer, S., Rajamani, S.K., and Tasiran, S. 1998c. MOCHA: Modularity in Model-Checking. Pages 521–525 of: *CAV'98*. Lecture Notes in Computer Science, vol. 1427. Springer.

Alur, R., Henzinger, Th., and Kupferman, O. 2002. Alternating-Time Temporal Logic. *Journal of the Association for Computing Machinery*, **49**(5), 672–713.

Alur, R., Etessami, K., and Madhusudan, P. 2004. A Temporal Logic of Nested Calls and Returns. Pages 467–481 of: *TACAS'04*. Lecture Notes in Computer Science, vol. 2988. Springer.

Andersen, H.R. 1994a. Model Checking and Boolean Graphs. *Theoretical Computer Science*, **126**(1), 3–30.

Andersen, H.R. 1994b. *A Polyadic Modal μ-Calculus*. Tech. rept. ID-TR: 1994-195. Dept. of Computer Science, Technical University of Denmark, Copenhagen.

Andréka, H., Németi, I., and van Benthem, J. 1998. Modal Languages and Bounded Fragments of Predicate Logic. *Journal of Philosophical Logic*, **27**(3), 217–274.

Arenas, M., Barceló, P., and Libkin, L. 2011. Regular Languages of Nested Words: Fixed Points, Automata, and Synchronization. *Theory of Computing Systems*, **49**(3), 639–670.

Armoni, R., Fix, L., Flaisher, A., Gerth, R., Ginsburg, B., Kanza, T., Landver, A., Mador-Haim, S., Singerman, E., Tiemeyer, A., Vardi, M.Y., and Zbar, Y. 2002. The ForSpec Temporal Logic: A New Temporal Property Specification Language. Pages 296–311 of: *TACAS'02*. Lecture Notes in Computer Science, vol. 2280. Springer.

Arnold, A. 1994. *Finite Transition Systems: Semantics of Communicating Systems*. Prentice Hall.

Arnold, A. 1999. The Modal μ-Calculus Alternation Hierarchy Is Strict on Binary Trees. *RAIRO – Theoretical Informatics and Applications*, **33**, 329–339.

Arnold, A., and Nivat, M. 1980. The Metric Space of Infinite Trees. Algebraic And Topological Properties. *Fundamenta Informaticae*, **3**(4), 181–205.

Arnold, A., and Nivat, M. 1982. Comportements de processus. Pages 35–68 of: *AFCET*.

Arnold, A., and Niwiński, D. 2001. *Rudiments of μ-calculus*. Elsevier.

Arora, S., and Barak, B. 2009. *Computational Complexity – A Modern Approach*. Cambridge University Press.

Auffray, Y., and Enjalbert, P. 1989. Modal Theorem Proving An Equational Viewpoint. Pages 441–445 of: *IJCAI'89*.

Baader, F., Calvanese, D., McGuinness, D., Nardi, D., and Patel-Schneider, P. (eds). 2003. *The Description Logic Handbook: Theory, Implementation and Applications*. Cambridge University Press.

Baier, C., and Katoen, J.P. 2008. *Principles of Model Checking*. MIT Press.

Banach, S. 1922. Sur les opérations dans les ensembles abstraits et leur application aux équations integrales. *Fundamenta Mathematicae*, **3**, 133–181.

Banieqbal, B., and Barringer, H. 1989. Temporal Logic with Fixed Points. Pages 62–74 of: *Temporal Logic in Specification, Altrincham, UK, April 8-10, 1987, Proceedings*. Lecture Notes in Computer Science, vol. 398. Springer.

Barringer, H., Kuiper, R., and Pnueli, A. 1986. A Really Abstract Concurrent Model and Its Temporal Logic. Pages 173–183 of: *POPL'86*. ACM.

Bauland, M., Schneider, Th., Schnoor, H., Schnoor, I., and Vollmer, H. 2009. The Complexity of Generalized Satisfiability for Linear Temporal Logic. *Logical Methods in Computer Science*, **5**(1).

Bauland, M., Mundhenk, M., Schneider, Th., Schnoor, H., Schnoor, I., and Vollmer, H. 2011. The Tractability of Model Checking for LTL: The Good, the Bad, and the Ugly Fragments. *ACM Transactions on Computational Logic*, **12**(2), 13.

Beckmann, A., and Moller, F. 2008. On the complexity of parity games. Pages 237–248 of: *Visions of Computer Science – BCS International Academic Conference, Imperial College, London, UK, 22–24 September 2008*.

Beer, I., Ben-David, S., Eisner, C., Fisman, D., Gringauze, A., and Rodeh, Y. 2001. The Temporal Logic Sugar. Pages 363–367 of: *CAV'01*. Lecture Notes in Computer Science, vol. 2102. Springer.

Bekić, H. 1984. *Programming Languages and Their Definition, Selected Papers*. Lecture Notes in Computer Science, vol. 177. Springer.

Ben-Ari, M., Pnueli, A., and Manna, Z. 1981. The Temporal Logic of Branching Time. Pages 164–176 of: *POPL'81*. ACM.

Ben-Ari, M., Pnueli, A., and Manna, Z. 1983. The Temporal Logic of Branching Time. *Acta Informatica*, **20**, 207–226.

Bérard, B., Bidoit, M., Finkel, A., Laroussinie, F., Petit, A., Petrucci, L., and Schnoebelen, Ph. 2001. *Systems and Software Verification, Model-Checking Techniques and Tools*. Springer.

Bergstra, J.A., and Klop, J.W. 1985. Algebra of Communicating Processes with Abstraction. *Theoretical Computer Science*, **37**, 77–121.

Beth, E.W. 1955. Semantic Entailment and Formal Derivability. *Nieuwe Reeks*, **18**(13), 309–342.

Beth, E.W. 1970. *Formal Methods: An Introduction to Symbolic Logic and to the Study of Effective Operations in Arithmetic and Logic*. D. Reidel.

Bhat, G., and Cleaveland, R. 1996a. Efficient Local Model-Checking for Fragments of the Modal μ-Calculus. Pages 107–126 of: *TACAS'96*. Lecture Notes in Computer Science, vol. 1055. Springer.

Bhat, G., and Cleaveland, R. 1996b. Efficient Model Checking via the Equational mu-Calculus. Pages 304–312 of: *LICS'96*. IEEE.

Bhat, G., Cleaveland, R., and Grumberg, O. 1995. Efficient On-the-Fly Model Checking for CTL*. Pages 388–397 of: *LICS'95*. IEEE.

Björklund, H., and Vorobyov, S. 2005. Combinatorial Structure and Randomized Subexponential Algorithms for Infinite Games. *Theoretical Computer Science*, **349**(3), 347–360.

Björklund, H., Sandberg, S., and Vorobyov, S. G. 2003. A Discrete Subexponential Algorithm for Parity Games. Pages 663–674 of: *STACS'03*. Lecture Notes in Computer Science, vol. 2607. Springer.

Blackburn, P., de Rijke, M., and Venema, Y. 2001. *Modal Logic*. Cambridge University Press.

Blackburn, P., van Benthem, J., and Wolter, F. (eds). 2007. *Handbook of Modal Logic*. Elsevier.

Boy de la Tour, Th. 1992. An Optimality Result for Clause Form Translation. *Journal of Symbolic Computation*, **14**, 283–301.

Bozzelli, L. 2008. The Complexity of CTL* + Linear Past. Pages 186–200 of: *FOSSACS'08*. Lecture Notes in Computer Science, vol. 4962. Springer.

Bradfield, J.C. 1996. The Modal μ-calculus Alternation Hierarchy Is Strict. Pages 233–246 of: *CONCUR'96*. Lecture Notes in Computer Science, vol. 1119. Springer.

Bradfield, J.C. 1998. Simplifying the Modal Mu-Calculus Alternation Hierarchy. Pages 39–49 of: *STACS'98*. Lecture Notes in Computer Science, vol. 1373. Springer.

Bradfield, J.C. 1999. Fixpoint Alternation: Arithmetic, Transition Systems, and the Binary Tree. *RAIRO – Theoretical Informatics and Applications*, **33**(4/5), 341–356.

Bradfield, J.C., and Stirling, C. 2007. Modal μ-Calculi. *In:* Blackburn et al. (2007).

Brihaye, Th., Laroussinie, F., Markey, N., and Oreiby, Gh. 2007. Timed Concurrent Game Structures. Pages 445–459 of: *CONCUR'07*. Lecture Notes in Computer Science, vol. 4703. Springer.

Brihaye, Th., Lopes, A. Da Costa, Laroussinie, F., and Markey, N. 2009. ATL with Strategy Contexts and Bounded Memory. Pages 92–106 of: *LFCS'09*. Lecture Notes in Computer Science, vol. 5407. Springer.

Browne, A., Clarke, E.M., Jha, S., Long, D.E., and Marrero, W. 1997. An Improved Algorithm for the Evaluation of Fixpoint Expressions. *Theoretical Computer Science*, **178**(1–2), 237–255.

Browne, M., Clarke, E., and Grümberg, O. 1988. Characterizing Finite Kripke Structures in Propositional Temporal Logic. *Theoretical Computer Science*, **59**, 115–131.

Bruse, F., Friedmann, O., and Lange, M. 2015. On Guarded Transformation in the μ-Calculus. *Logic Journal of the IGPL* **23**(2), 194–216.

Büchi, J.R. 1962. On a Decision Method in Restricted Second Order Arithmetic. Pages 1–12 of: *Congress on Logic, Method, and Philosophy of Science*. Stanford University Press.

Bull, R. 1969. On Modal Logic with Propositional Quantifiers. *The Journal of Symbolic Logic*, **34**(2), 257–263.

Bull, R., and Segerberg, K. 1984. Basic Modal Logic. Pages 1–88 of: Gabbay, D.M., and Guenthner, F. (eds), *Handbook of Philosophical Logic, Volume II*. Reidel.

Bulling, N., Dix, J., and Jamroga, W. 2010. Model Checking Logics of Strategic Ability: Complexity. Pages 125–159 of: *Specification and Verification of Multi-Agent Systems*. Springer.

Bulling, N., and Jamroga, W. 2014. Comparing Variants of Strategic Ability: How Uncertainty and Memory Influence General Properties of Games. *Autonomous Agents and Multi-Agent Systems*, **28**(3), 474–518.

Burgess, J. 1984. Basic Tense Logic. *In:* Gabbay and Guenthner (1984).

Bustan, D., and Havlicek, J. 2006. Some Complexity Results for SystemVerilog Assertions. Pages 205–218 of: *CAV'06*. Lecture Notes in Computer Science, vol. 4144. Springer.

Bustan, D., Fisman, D., and Havlicek, D. 2005. *Automata Constructions for PSL*. Tech. rept. MCS05-04. The Weizmann Institute of Science.

Cerrito, S., David, A., and Goranko, V. 2014. Optimal Tableaux-Based Decision Procedure for Testing Satisfiability in the Alternating-Time Temporal Logic ATL+. Pages 277–291 of: *IJCAR'14*. Lecture Notes in Computer Science, vol. 8562. Springer.

Chagrov, A., and Zakharyaschev, M. 1997. *Modal Logic*. Clarendon Press.

Chandra, A.K., Kozen, D.C., and Stockmeyer, L.J. 1981. Alternation. *Journal of the Association for Computing Machinery*, **28**(1), 114–133.

Chatterjee, K., Henzinger, T.A., and Piterman, N. 2010. Strategy Logic. *Information and Computation*, **208**(6), 677–693.

Chellas, B. 1980. *Modal Logic*. Cambridge University Press.

Chen, C.C., and Lin, I.P. 1993. The Computational Complexity of Satisfiability of Temporal Horn Formulas in Propositional Linear-Time Temporal Logic. *Information Processing Letters*, **45**, 131–136.

Clarke, E., and Emerson, E.A. 1981. Design and Synthesis of Synchronisation Skeletons Using Branching Time Temporal Logic. Pages 52–71 of: *Workshop on Logics of Programs*. Springer.

Clarke, E., Grumberg, O., and Peled, D. 2000. *Model Checking*. MIT Press.

Clarke, E.M., and Draghicescu, I.A. 1988. Expressibility Results for Linear-Time and Branching-Time Logics. Pages 428–437 of: *REX Workshop*. Lecture Notes in Computer Science, vol. 354. Springer.

Clarke, E.M., and Schlingloff, B.-H. 2001. Model Checking. Pages 1635–1790 of: Robinson, A., and Voronkov, A. (eds), *Handbook of Automated Reasoning*. Elsevier.

Clarke, E.M., Emerson, E.A., and Sistla, A.P. 1983 (Jan.). Automatic Verification of Finite State Concurrent Systems Using Temporal Logic Specifications: A Practical Approach. Pages 117–126 of: *POPL'83*.

Clarke, E.M., Emerson, E.A., and Sistla, A.P. 1986. Automatic Verification of Finite-State Concurrent Systems Using Temporal Logic Specifications. *ACM Transactions on Programming Languages and Systems*, **8**(2), 244–263.

Cleaveland, R. 1989. Tableau-Based Model Checking in the Propositional Mu-Calculus. *Acta Informatica*, **27**(8), 725–747.

Cleaveland, R., and Steffen, B. 1991. A Linear-Time Model-Checking Algorithm for the Alternation-Free Modal mu-Calculus. Pages 48–58 of: *CAV'91*. Lecture Notes in Computer Science, vol. 575. Springer.

Comon-Lundh, H., Dauchet, M., Gilleron, R., Löding, C., Jacquemard, F., Lugiez, D., Tison, S., and Tommasi, M. *Tree Automata Techniques and Applications*. Online book available at: http://tata.gforge.inria.fr.

Cook, S.A. 1971. The Complexity of Theorem-Proving Procedures. Pages 151–158 of: *STOC'71*. ACM.

Copeland, J. 2002. The Genesis of Possible Worlds Semantics. *Journal of Philosophical Logic*, **31**(1), 99–137.

Cristau, J. 2009. Automata and Temporal Logic over Arbitrary Linear Time. Pages 133–144 of: *FSTTCS'09*. LIPIcs, vol. 4. Schloss Dagstuhl – Leibniz-Zentrum fuer Informatik.

D'Agostino, G., and Lenzi, G. 2010. On the μ-Calculus Over Transitive and Finite Transitive Frames. *Theoretical Computer Science*, **411**(50), 4273–4290.

D'Agostino, G., Montanari, A., and Policriti, A. 1995. A Set-Theoretical Translation Method for Polymodal Logics. *Journal of Automated Reasoning*, **15**, 317–337.

D'Agostino, M., Gabbay, D.M., Hähnle, R., and Posegga, J. (eds). 1999. *Handbook of Tableau Methods*. Kluwer Academic.

Dam, M. 1994. CTL* and ECTL* as Fragments of the Modal μ-Calculus. *Theoretical Computer Science*, **126**, 77–96.

David, A. 2013. TATL: Implementation of ATL Tableau-Based Decision Procedure. Pages 97–103 of: *TABLEAUX'13*. Lecture Notes in Computer Science, vol. 8123. Springer.

David, A. 2015. Deciding ATL* Satisfiability by Tableaux. Pages 214–228 of: *CADE'15*. Lecture Notes in Computer Science, vol. 9195. Springer.

Dawar, A. 2005. How Many First-Order Variables Are Needed on Finite Ordered Structures? Pages 489–520 of: Artëmov, S., Barringer, H., d'Avila Garcez, A., Lamb, L., and Woods, J. (eds), *We Will Show Them! Essays in Honour of Dov Gabbay, Volume One*. College Publications.

Dawar, A., Grädel, E., and Kreutzer, S. 2004. Inflationary Fixed Points in Modal Logics. *ACM Transactions on Computational Logic*, **5**(2), 282–315.

Dax, C., and Lange, M. 2004. Game Over: The Foci Approach to LTL Satisfiability and Model Checking. Pages 33–49 of: *GDV'04*. Electronic Notes in Theoretical Computer Science, vol. 119. Elsevier.

de Bakker, J.W., and de Roever, W.P. 1972. A Calculus for Recursive Program Schemes. In: Nivat, M. (ed), *Proc. IRIA Symp. on Automata, Formal Languages and Programming*. North-Holland.

de Nivelle, H. 1998. A Resolution Decision Procedure for the Guarded Fragment. Pages 191–204 of: *CADE'98*. Lecture Notes in Computer Science, vol. 1421. Springer.

de Nivelle, H., and de Rijke, M. 2003. Deciding the Guarded Fragments with Resolution. *Journal of Symbolic Computation*, **35**(1), 21–58.

de Nivelle, H., and Pratt-Hartmann, I. 2001. A Resolution-Based Decision Procedure for the Two-Variable Fragment with Equality. Pages 211–225 of: *IJCAR'01*. Lecture Notes in Computer Science, vol. 2083. Springer.

Demri, S. 2003. A Polynomial Space Construction of Tree-like Models for Logics with Local Chains of Modal Connectives. *Theoretical Computer Science*, **300**(1–3), 235–258.

Demri, S., and de Nivelle, H. 2005. Deciding Regular Grammar Logics with Converse through First-Order Logic. *Journal of Logic, Language, and Information*, **14**(3), 289–329.

Demri, S., and Gastin, P. 2012. Specification and Verification Using Temporal Logics. Pages 457–494 of: *Modern Applications of Automata Theory*. IISc Research Monographs, vol. 2. World Scientific.

Demri, S., and Goré, R. 1999. Tractable Transformations from Modal Provability Logics into First-Order Logic. Pages 16–30 of: *CADE'99*. Lecture Notes in Artificial Intelligence, vol. 1632. Springer.

Demri, S., and Lugiez, D. 2010. Complexity of Modal Logics with Presburger Constraints. *Journal of Applied Logic*, **8**(3), 233–252.

Demri, S., and Schnoebelen, Ph. 2002. The Complexity of Propositional Linear Temporal Logics in Simple Cases. *Information and Computation*, **174**(1), 84–103.

Diekert, V., and Gastin, P. 2008. First-Order Definable Languages. Pages 261–306 of: *Logic and Automata: History and Perspectives*. Texts in Logic and Games, vol. 2. Amsterdam University Press.

Dima, C., and Tiplea, F.L. 2011. Model-Checking ATL under Imperfect Information and Perfect Recall Semantics is Undecidable. *CoRR*, **abs/1102.4225**.

D'Souza, D., and Shankar, P. (eds). 2012. *Modern Applications of Automata Theory*. IISc Research Monographs Series, no. 2. World Scientific.

Eisner, C., and Fisman, D. 2006. *A Practical Introduction to PSL*. Springer.

Emerson, E.A. 1983. Alternative Semantics for Temporal Logics. *Theoretical Computer Science*, **26**(1–2), 121–130.

Emerson, E.A. 1990. Temporal and Modal Logics. *In:* Leeuwen (1990).

Emerson, E.A. 1995. Automated Temporal Reasoning about Reactive Systems. Pages 41–101 of: *Banff Higher Order Workshop*.

Emerson, E.A., and Clarke, E.M. 1980. Characterizing Correctness Properties of Parallel Programs Using Fixpoints. Pages 169–181 of: *ICALP'80*. Lecture Notes in Computer Science, vol. 85. Springer.

Emerson, E.A., and Halpern, J.Y. 1982. Decision Procedures and Expressiveness in the Temporal Logic of Branching Time. Pages 169–180 of: *STOC'82*. ACM.

Emerson, E.A., and Halpern, J.Y. 1983. 'Sometimes' and 'Not Never' Revisited: On Branching versus Linear Time. Pages 127–140 of: *POPL'83*.

Emerson, E.A., and Halpern, J.Y. 1985. Decision Procedures and Expressiveness in the Temporal Logic of Branching Time. *Journal of Computer and System Sciences*, **30**, 1–24.

Emerson, E.A., and Halpern, J.Y. 1986. 'Sometimes' and 'Not Never' Revisited: On Branching versus Linear Time Temporal Logic. *Journal of the Association for Computing Machinery*, **33**, 151–178.

Emerson, E.A., and Jutla, C.S. 1988. The Complexity of Tree Automata and Logics of Programs (Extended Abstract). Pages 328–337 of: *FOCS'88*. IEEE.

Emerson, E.A., and Jutla, C.S. 1991. Tree Automata, Mu-Calculus and Determinacy (Extended Abstract). Pages 368–377 of: *FOCS'91*. IEEE.

Emerson, E.A., and Jutla, C.S. 2000. The Complexity of Tree Automata and Logics of Programs. *SIAM Journal of Computing*, **29**(1), 132–158.

Emerson, E.A., and Lei, C.-L. 1986 (16–18 June). Efficient Model Checking in Fragments of the Propositional Mu-Calculus (Extended Abstract). Pages 267–278 of: *LICS'86*. IEEE.

Emerson, E.A., and Lei, C.-L. 1987. Modalities for Model Checking: Branching Time Logic Strikes Back. *Science of Computer Programming*, **8**(3), 275–306.

Emerson, E.A., and Sistla, A.P. 1984. Deciding Full Branching Time Logic. *Information and Control*, **61**, 175–201.

Emerson, E.A., Jutla, C.S., and Sistla, A. 2001. On Model-Checking for μ-Calculus and Its Fragments. *Theoretical Computer Science*, **258**(1–2), 491–522.

Etessami, K., Vardi, M.Y., and Wilke, Th. 1997. First-Order Logic with Two Variables and Unary Temporal logics. Pages 228–235 of: *LICS'97*. IEEE.

Fagin, R., Halpern, J.Y., Moses, Y., and Vardi, M.Y. 1995. *Reasoning about Knowledge*. MIT Press.

Fernandez, J.-C. 1990. An Implementation of an Efficient Algorithm for Bisimulation Equivalence. *Science of Computer Programming*, **13**(2–3), 219–236.

Fine, K. 1970. Propositional Quantifiers in Modal Logic. *Theoria*, **36**, 336–346.

Fine, K. 1975. Some Connections between Elementary and Modal Logic. Pages 15–31 of: *3rd Scandinavian Logic Symposium*. North-Holland.

Fischer, M., and Ladner, R. 1979. Propositional Dynamic Logic of Regular Programs. *Journal of Computer and System Sciences*, **18**, 194–211.

Fisher, M. 2011. *An Introduction to Practical Formal Methods Using Temporal Logic*. Wiley.

Fisher, M., Dixon, C., and M.Peim. 2001. Clausal Temporal Resolution. *ACM Transactions on Computational Logic*, **2**(1), 12–56.

Fitting, M. 1972. Tableau Methods of Proof for Modal Logics. *Notre Dame Journal of Formal Logic*, **18**(2), 237–247.

Fitting, M. 1977. A Tableau System for Propositional S5. *Notre Dame Journal of Formal Logic*, **18**(2), 292–294.

Fitting, M. 1983. *Proof Methods for Modal and Intuitionistic Logics*. D. Reidel.

Fitting, M. 2007. Modal Proof Theory. *In:* Blackburn et al. (2007).

Fogarty, S., Kupferman, O., Vardi, M.Y., and Wilke, Th. 2011. Unifying Büchi Complementation Constructions. Pages 248–263 of: *CSL'11*. LIPIcs, for Schloss Dagstuhl–Leibniz-Zentrum fuer Informatik.

Francez, N. 1986. *Fairness*. Springer-Verlag.

Friedmann, O. 2009. An Exponential Lower Bound for the Parity Game Strategy Improvement Algorithm as We Know It. Pages 145–156 of: *LICS'09*. IEEE.

Friedmann, O. 2010. The Stevens-Stirling-Algorithm for Solving Parity Games Locally Requires Exponential Time. *International Journal of Foundations of Computer Science*, **21**(3), 277–287.

Friedmann, O. 2011a. An Exponential Lower Bound for the Latest Deterministic Strategy Iteration Algorithms. *Logical Methods in Computer Science*, **7**(3).

Friedmann, O. 2011b. Recursive Algorithm for Parity Games Requires Exponential Time. *RAIRO – Theoretical Informatics and Applications*, **45**(4), 449–457.

Friedmann, O. 2013. A Superpolynomial Lower Bound for Strategy Iteration Based on Snare Memorization. *Discrete Applied Mathematics*, **161**(10–11), 1317–1337.

Friedmann, O., and Lange, M. 2009. Solving Parity Games in Practice. Pages 182–196 of: *ATVA'09*. Lecture Notes in Computer Science, vol. 5799. Springer.

Friedmann, O., and Lange, M. 2010. A Solver for Modal Fixpoint Logics. Pages 99–111 of: *M4M-6*. Lecture Notes in Theoretical Computer Science, **262**, 99–111.

Friedmann, O., and Lange, M. 2012. Two Local Strategy Improvement Schemes for Parity Game Solving. *International Journal of Foundations of Computer Science*, **23**(3), 669–685.

Friedmann, O., and Lange, M. 2013. Deciding the Unguarded Modal μ-Calculus. *Journal of Applied Non-classical Logics*, **23**(4), 353–371.

Friedmann, O., Latte, M., and Lange, M. 2013. Satisfiability Games for Branching-Time Logics. *Logical Methods in Computer Science*, **9**(4).

Gabbay, D.M. 1972. A General Filtration Method for Modal Logics. *Journal of Philosophical Logic*, **1**, 29–34.

Gabbay, D.M. 1976. *Investigations in Modal and Tense Logics with Applications*. D. Reidel.

Gabbay, D.M. 1981. Expressive Functional Completeness in Tense Logic. Pages 91–117 of: *Aspects of Philosophical Logic*. Reidel.

Gabbay, D.M. 1989. The Declarative Past and Imperative Future: Executable Temporal Logic for Interactive Systems. Pages 409–448 of: *Colloquium on Temporal Logic in Specification*. Lecture Notes in Computer Science, vol. 398. Springer.

Gabbay, D.M., and Guenthner, F. (eds). 1984. *Handbook of Philosophical Logic*. Vol. 2. Reidel.

Gabbay, D.M., Pnueli, A., Shelah, S., and Stavi, J. 1980. On the Temporal Analysis of Fairness. Pages 163–173 of: *POPL'80*.

Gabbay, D.M., Hodkinson, I., and Reynolds, M. 1994. *Temporal Logic: Mathematical Foundations and Computational Aspects*. Oxford University Press.

Gabbay, D.M., Kurucz, A., Wolter, F., and Zakharyaschev, M. 2003. *Many-Dimensional Modal Logics: Theory and Practice*. Cambridge University Press.

Gale, D., and Stewart, F. 1953. Infinite Games with Perfect Information: Contributions to the Theory of Games. *Annals of Mathematics Studies*, **28**, 245–266.

Ganzinger, H., and de Nivelle, H. 1999. A Superposition Decision Procedure for the Guarded Fragment with Equality. Pages 295–305 of: *LICS'99*.

Gasquet, O., and Herzig, A. 1994. Translation-Based Deduction Methods for Modal Logics. Pages 399–408 of: *IPMU'94*. Lecture Notes in Computer Science, vol. 945. Springer.

Gastin, P., and Oddoux, D. 2001. Fast LTL to Büchi Automata Translation. Pages 53–65 of: *CAV'01*. Lecture Notes in Computer Science, vol. 2102. Springer.

German, S., and Sistla, A.P. 1992. Reasoning about Systems with Many Processes. *Journal of the Association for Computing Machinery*, **39**(3), 675–735.

Glabbeek, R.J. van. 2001. The Linear Time – Branching Time Spectrum I; The Semantics of Concrete, Sequential Processes. Chap. 1, pages 3–99 of: *Handbook of Process Algebra*. Elsevier.

Goldblatt, R. 1992. *Logics of Time and Computation*. 2nd edn. CSLI Lecture Notes, vol. 7. Center for the Study of Language and Information.

Goldblatt, R. 2005. *Handbook of the History of Logic*. Vol. 7. Elsevier.

Goldreich, O. 2008. *Computational Complexity - A Conceptual Perspective*. Cambridge University Press.

Goranko, V. 2000. Computation Tree Logics and Temporal Logics with Reference Pointers. *Journal of Applied Non-classical Logics*, **10**(3–4), 221–242.

Goranko, V. 2001. Coalition Games and Alternating Temporal Logics. Pages 259–272 of: *TARK VIII*. Morgan Kaufmann.

Goranko, V., and Galton, A. 2015. *Temporal Logics*. Entry in the Stanford Encyclopaedia of Philosophy, http://plato.stanford.edu/entries/logic-temporal/.

Goranko, V., and Jamroga, W. 2004. Comparing Semantics of Logics for Multi-agent Systems. *Synthese*, **139**(2), 241–280.

Goranko, V., and Otto, M. 2007. Model Theory of Modal Logic. *In:* Blackburn et al. (2007).

Goranko, V., and Shkatov, D. 2009a. Tableau-Based Decision Procedure for Full Coalitional Multiagent Temporal-Epistemic Logic of Linear Time. Pages 969–976 of: *AAMAS 2009*. IFAAMAS.

Goranko, V., and Shkatov, D. 2009b. Tableau-Based Decision Procedure for the Full Coalitional Multiagent Logic of Branching Time. In: *MALLOW'09*. CEUR Workshop Proceedings, vol. 494.

Goranko, V., and Shkatov, D. 2009c. Tableau-Based Decision Procedures for Logics of Strategic Ability in Multiagent Systems. *ACM Transactions on Computational Logic*, **11**(1).

Goranko, V., and van Drimmelen, G. 2006. Complete Axiomatization and Decidability of the Alternating-Time Temporal Logic. *Theoretical Computer Science*, **353**, 93–117.

Goranko, V., and Vester, S. 2014. Optimal Decision Procedures for Satisfiability in Fragments of Alternating-Time Temporal Logics. Pages 234–253 of: *Advances in Modal Logic*, vol. 10. College Publications.

Goranko, V., Kyrilov, A., and Shkatov, D. 2010. Tableau Tool for Testing Satisfiability in LTL: Implementation and Experimental Analysis. *Electronic Notes in Theoretical Computer Science*, **262**, 113–125.

Goré, R. 1991. Semi-analytic Tableaux for Propositional Modal Logics with Applications to Nonmonotonicity. *Logique et Analyse*, **133–134**, 73–104.

Goré, R. 1999. Tableaux Methods for Modal and Temporal Logics. Pages 297–396 of: *Handbook of Tableaux Methods*. Kluwer.

Goré, R., and Widmann, F. 2009. An Optimal On-the-Fly Tableau-Based Decision Procedure for PDL-Satisfiability. Pages 437–452 of: *CADE'09*. Lecture Notes in Computer Science, vol. 5663. Springer.

Goré, R., and Widmann, F. 2010. Optimal and Cut-Free Tableaux for Propositional Dynamic Logic with Converse. Pages 225–239 of: *IJCAR'10*. Lecture Notes in Computer Science, vol. 6173. Springer.

Gough, G. 1984. *Decision Procedures for Temporal Logic*. M.Phil. thesis, University of Manchester.

Grädel, E. 1999. On the Restraining Power of Guards. *The Journal of Symbolic Logic*, **64**(4), 1719–1742.

Grädel, E. 2002. Model Checking Games. Pages 15–34 of: *WOLLIC'02*. Electronic Notes in Theoretical Computer Science, vol. 67. Elsevier.

Grädel, E., Kolaitis, Ph., and Vardi, M.Y. 1997. On the Decision Problem for Two-Variable First-Order Logic. *Bulletin of Symbolic Logic*, **3**(1), 53–69.

Grädel, E., Thomas, W., and Wilke, Th. (eds). 2002. *Automata, Logics, and Infinite Games: A Guide to Current Research [outcome of a Dagstuhl seminar, February 2001]*. Lecture Notes in Computer Science, vol. 2500. Springer.

Grumberg, O., and Kurshan, R. 2001. Which Branching-Time Properties Are Effectively Linear. *Journal of Logic and Computation*, **11**(2), 201–228.

Grumberg, O., and Veith, H. (eds). 2008. *25 Years of Model Checking*. Lecture Notes in Computer Science, vol. 5000. Springer.

Gurevich, Y., and Harrington, L. 1982. Trees, Automata and Games. Pages 60–65 of: *STOC'82*. ACM.

Gutierrez, J., Klaedtke, F., and Lange, M. 2014. The μ-Calculus Alternation Hierarchy Collapses over Structures with Restricted Connectivity. *Theoretical Computer Science*, **560**(3), 292–306.

Hafer, T., and Thomas, W. 1987. Computation Tree Logic CTL* and Path Quantifiers in the Monadic Theory of the Binary Tree. Pages 270–279 of: *ICALP'87*. Lecture Notes in Computer Science, vol. 267. Springer.

Halpern, J.Y. 1995. The Effect of Bounding the Number of Primitive Propositions and the Depth of Nesting on the Complexity of Modal Logic. *Artificial Intelligence*, **75**(2), 361–372.

Halpern, J.Y., and Reif, H. 1983. The Propositional Dynamic Logic of Deterministic, Well-Structured Programs. *Theoretical Computer Science*, **27**, 127–165.

Halpern, J.Y., and Reif, J. 1981. The Propositional Dynamic Logic of Deterministic, Well-Structured Programs. Pages 322–344 of: *FOCS'81*.

Harel, D. 1983. Recurring Dominoes: Making the Highly Undecidable Highly Understandable. Pages 177–194 of: *Fundamentals of Computing Theory*. Lecture Notes in Computer Science, vol. 158. Springer.

Harel, D. 1985. Recurring Dominoes: Making the Highly Undecidable Highly Understandable. *Annals of Discrete Mathematics*, **24**, 51–72.

Harel, D., Kozen, D.C., and Tiuryn, J. 2000. *Dynamic Logic*. MIT Press.

Hartmanis, J., and Stearns, R. 1965. On the Computational Complexity of Algorithms. *Transactions of the American Mathematical Society*, **117**, 285–306.

Heljanko, K., Keinänen, M., Lange, M., and Niemelä, I. 2012. Solving Parity Games by a Reduction to SAT. *Journal of Computer and System Sciences*, **78**, 430–440.

Hemaspaandra, E. 1994. Complexity Transfer for Modal Logic (Extended Abstract). Pages 164–173 of: *LICS'94*. IEEE.

Hemaspaandra, E. 2001. The Complexity of Poor Man's Logic. *Journal of Logic and Computation*, **11**(4), 609–622.

Hennessy, M., and Milner, R. 1980. On Observing Nondeterminism and Concurrency. Pages 299–309 of: *ICALP'80*. Lecture Notes in Computer Science, vol. 85. Springer.

Hennessy, M., and Milner, R. 1985. Algebraic Laws for Nondeterminism and Concurrency. *Journal of the Association for Computing Machinery*, **32**(1), 137–161.

Henriksen, J., and Thiagarajan, P. 1999. Dynamic Linear Time Temporal Logic. *Annals of Pure and Applied Logic*, **96**(1–3), 187–207.

Henzinger, Th. A., and Prabhu, V.S. 2006. Timed Alternating-Time Temporal Logic. Pages 1–17 of: *FORMATS'06*.

Hintikka, J. 1962. *Knowledge and Belief*. Cornell University Press.

Hoare, C.A.R. 1985. *Communicating Sequential Processes*. Prentice Hall.

Hodges, W. 2013. *Logic and Games*. Entry in the Stanford Encyclopaedia of Philosophy, http://plato.stanford.edu/entries/logic-games/.

Hodkinson, I. 1999 (December). *Notes on Games in Temporal Logics*. Lectures notes for LUATCS Summer School, Johannesburg. Retrieved from http://www.doc.ic.ac.uk/ imh/papers/sa.ps.gz.

Hodkinson, I., and Reynolds, M. 2005. Separation – Past, Present, and Future. Pages 117–142 of: Artemov, S., Barringer, H., d'Avila Garcez, A., Lamb, L., and Woods, J. (eds), *We Will Show Them! (Essays in Honour of Dov Gabbay on his 60th Birthday)*, vol. 2. College Publications.

Hoek, W. van der, Lomuscio, A., and Wooldridge, M. 2006. On the Complexity of Practical ATL Model Checking. Pages 201–208 of: *AAMAS'06*.

Holzmann, G. 1997. The Model Checker SPIN. *IEEE Transactions on Software Engineering*, **23**(5), 279–295.

Hughes, G., and Cresswell, M. 1984. *A Companion to Modal Logic*. Methuen.

Hughes, G., and Cresswell, M. 1996. *A New Introduction to Modal Logic*. Routledge.

Huth, M., and Ryan, M. 2000. *Logic in Computer Science: Modelling and Reasoning about Systems*. Cambridge University Press.

Iman, S., and Joshi, S. 2004. *The e-Hardware Verification Language*. Kluwer.

Immerman, N. 1988. Nondeterministic Space Is Closed under Complementation. *SIAM Journal of Computing*, **17**, 935–938.

Jamroga, W., and Bulling, N. 2011. Comparing Variants of Strategic Ability. Pages 252–257 of: *IJCAI-11*.

Jamroga, W., and Dix, J. 2008. Model Checking Abilities of Agents: A Closer Look. *Theory of Computing Systems*, **42**(3), 366–410.

Janin, D., and Walukiewicz, I. 1996. On the Expressive Completeness of the Propositional mu-Calculus with Respect to Monadic Second Order Logic. Pages 263–277 of: *CONCUR'96*. Lecture Notes in Computer Science, vol. 1119. Springer.

Johannsen, J., and Lange, M. 2003. CTL^+ is Complete for Double Exponential Time. Pages 767 – 775 of: *ICALP'03*. Lecture Notes in Computer Science, vol. 2719. Springer.

Johnson, D. 2012. A Brief History of NP-Completeness, 1954–2012. Pages 359–376 of: *Optimization Stories*. DMV. Special volume of Documenta Mathematica.

Jónsson, B., and Tarski, A. 1951. Boolean Algebras with Operators. Part I. *American Journal of Mathematics*, **73**, 891–939.

Jungteerapanich, N. 2009. A Tableau System for the Modal μ-Calculus. Pages 220–234 of: *TABLEAUX'09*. Lecture Notes in Computer Science, vol. 5607. Springer.

Jurdziński, M. 1998. Deciding the Winner in Parity Games is in UP ∩ co-UP. *Information Processing Letters*, **68**(3), 119–124.

Jurdziński, M. 2000. Small Progress Measures for Solving Parity Games. Pages 290–301 of: *STACS'00*. Lecture Notes in Computer Science, vol. 1770. Springer.

Jurdziński, M., Paterson, M., and Zwick, U. 2008. A Deterministic Subexponential Algorithm for Solving Parity Games. *SIAM Journal of Computing*, **38**(4), 1519–1532.

Kähler, D., and Wilke, Th. 2008. Complementation, Disambiguation, and Determinization of Büchi Automata Unified. Pages 724–735 of: *ICALP'08*. Lecture Notes in Computer Science, vol. 5125. Springer.

Kaivola, R. 1995a. Axiomatising Linear Time Mu-Calculus. Pages 423–437 of: *CONCUR '95*. Lecture Notes in Computer Science, vol. 962. Springer.

Kaivola, R. 1995b. On Modal μ-Calculus and Büchi Tree Automata. *Information Processing Letters*, **54**(1), 17–22.

Kamp, J. 1968. *Tense Logic and the Theory of Linear Order*. Ph.D. thesis, UCLA.

Kanellakis, P.C., and Smolka, S.A. 1983. CCS Expressions, Finite State Processes, and Three Problems of Equivalence. Pages 228–240 of: *PODC'83*. ACM.

Kanger, S. 1957. *Provability in Logic*. Stockholm Studies in Philosophy, University of Stockholm. Almqvist and Wiksell.

Karp, R. M. 1972. Reducibility among Combinatorial Problems. Pages 85–103 of: Miller, R. E., and Thatcher, J. W. (eds), *Complexity of Computer Computations*. Plenum Press.

Keller, R.M. 1976. Formal Verification of Parallel Programs. *Communications of the ACM*, **19**(7), 371–384.

Kesten, Y., Manna, Z., McGuire, H., and Pnueli, A. 1993. A Decision Algorithm for Full Propositional Temporal Logic. Pages 97–109 of: *CAV'93*, Lectures Notes in Computer Science, vol. 697. Springer.

Kindler, E. 1994. Safety and Liveness Properties: A Survey. *Bulletin of the European Association of Theoretical Computer Science*, **53**, 268–272.

Klaedtke, F. 2002. Complementation of Büchi Automata Using Alternation. Pages 61–77 of: Grädel, E., Thomas, W., and Wilke, Th. (eds), *Automata, Logics and Infinite Games*. Lecture Notes in Computer Science, vol. 2500. Springer.

Klarlund, N. 1991. Progress Measures for Complementation of ω-Automata with Applications to Temporal Logic. Pages 358–367 of: *FOCS'91*. IEEE.

Kozen, D.C. 1976 (June). *On Parallelism in Turing Machines*. Tech. rept. TR76-282. Department of Computer Science, Cornell University.

Kozen, D.C. 1983. Results on the Propositional μ-Calculus. *Theoretical Computer Science*, **27**, 333–354.

Kozen, D.C. 1988. A Finite Model Theorem for the Propositional μ-Calculus. *Studia Logica*, **47**(3), 233–241.

Kozen, D.C. 2006. *Theory of Computation*. Texts in Computer Science. Springer.

Kozen, D.C., and Parikh, R. 1983. A Decision Procedure for the Propositional μ-Calculus. Pages 313–325 of: *Workshop on Logics of Programs*. Lecture Notes in Computer Science, vol. 164. Springer.

Kozen, D.C., and Tiuryn, J. 1990. Logics of Programs. *In:* Leeuwen (1990).

Kracht, M. 1995. *Tools and Techniques in Modal Logic*. Studies in Logic and the Foundations of Mathematics, vol. 142. Elsevier.

Kripke, S. 1963. Semantical Analysis of Modal Logic I. Normal Modal Propositional Calculi. *Zeitschrift für Mathematische Logik und Grundlagen der Mathematik*, **9**, 67–96.

Kröger, F. 1987. *Temporal Logic of Programs*. EATCS Monographs in Computer Science, vol. 8. Springer.

Kröger, F., and Merz, S. 2008. *Temporal Logic and State Systems*. EATCS Texts in Theoretical Computer Science. Springer.

Kuhtz, L., and Finkbeiner, B. 2009. LTL Path Checking Is Efficiently Parallelizable. Pages 235–246 of: *ICALP'09*. Lecture Notes in Computer Science, vol. 5556. Springer.

Kupferman, O., and Grumberg, O. 1996. Buy One, Get One Free!!! *Journal of Logic and Computation*, **6**(4), 523–539.

Kupferman, O., and Pnueli, A. 1995. Once and for All. Pages 25–35 of: *LICS'95*. IEEE Computer Society Press.

Kupferman, O., and Vardi, M.Y. 2001. Weak Alternating Automata Are Not That Weak. *ACM Transactions on Computational Logic*, **2**(3), 408–429.

Kupferman, O., Vardi, M.Y., and Wolper, P. 2000. An Automata-Theoretic Approach to Branching-Time Model Checking. *Journal of the Association for Computing Machinery*, **47**(2), 312–360.

Kupferman, O., Piterman, N., and Vardi, M.Y. 2001 (August). Extended Temporal Logic Revisited. Pages 519–535 of: *CONCUR'01*. Lecture Notes in Computer Science, vol. 2154. Springer.

Kupferman, O., Safra, S., and Vardi, M.Y. 2006. Relating Word and Tree Automata. *Annals of Pure and Applied Logic*, **138**, 126–146.

Kupferman, O., Pnueli, A., and Vardi, M.Y. 2012. Once and for All. *Journal of Computer and System Sciences*, **78**(3), 981–996.

Kučera, A., and Strejček, J. 2005. The Stuttering Principle Revisited. *Acta Informatica*, **41**(7–8), 415–434.

Ladner, R. 1977. The Computational Complexity of Provability in Systems of Modal Propositional Logic. *SIAM Journal of Computing*, **6**(3), 467–480.

Lamport, L. 1977. Proving the Correctness of Multiprocess Programs. *IEEE Transactions in Software Engineering*, **3**(2), 125–143.

Lamport, L. 1980. "Sometime" Is Sometimes "Not Never" – on the Temporal Logic of Programs. Pages 174–185 of: *POPL'80*.

Lange, M. 2002a. *Games for Modal and Temporal Logics*. Ph.D. thesis, LFCS, Division of Informatics, The University of Edinburgh. Tech. Rep. ECS-LFCS-03-431.

Lange, M. 2002b. Local Model Checking Games for Fixed Point Logic with Chop. Pages 240–254 of: *CONCUR'02*. Lecture Notes in Computer Science, vol. 2421. Springer.

Lange, M. 2005. Solving Parity Games by a Reduction to SAT. In: *Proc. Int. Workshop on Games in Design and Verification, GDV'05*.

Lange, M. 2007. Linear Time Logics around PSL: Complexity, Expressiveness, and a Little Bit of Succinctness. Pages 90–104 of: *CONCUR'07*. Lecture Notes in Computer Science, vol. 4703. Springer.

Lange, M. 2008. A Purely Model-Theoretic Proof of the Exponential Succinctness Gap between CTL$^+$ and CTL. *Information Processing Letters*, **108**(5), 308–312.

Lange, M., and Lozes, E. 2012. Model Checking the Higher-Dimensional Modal μ-Calculus. Pages 39–46 of: *FICS'12*. Electronic Notes in Theoretical Computer Science, vol. 77. Elsevier.

Lange, M., and Stirling, C. 2000. Model Checking Games for CTL*. Pages 115–125 of: *ICTL'00*.

Lange, M., and Stirling, C. 2001. Focus Games for Satisfiability and Completeness of Temporal Logic. Pages 357–365 of: *LICS'01*. IEEE.

Lange, M., and Stirling, C. 2002. Model Checking Games for Branching Time Logics. *Journal of Logic and Computation*, **12**(4), 623–639.

Lange, M., Lozes, E., and Guzmán, M. Vargas. 2014. Model-Checking Process Equivalences. *Theoretical Computer Science*, **560**, 326–347.

Laroussinie, F. 1994. *Logique temporelle avec passé pour la spécification et la vérification des systèmes réactifs*. Ph.D. thesis, Institut National Polytechnique de Grenoble.

Laroussinie, F. 1995. About the Expressive Power of CTL Combinators. *Information Processing Letters*, **54**, 343–345.

Laroussinie, F. 2010. Temporal Logics for Games. *Bulletin of the European Association of Theoretical Computer Science*, **100**, 79–98.

Laroussinie, F., and Schnoebelen, Ph. 1995. A Hierarchy of Temporal Logics with Past. *Theoretical Computer Science*, **148**, 303–324.

Laroussinie, F., and Schnoebelen, Ph. 2000. Specification in CTL+Past for Verification in CTL. *Information and Computation*, **156**(1–2), 236–263.

Laroussinie, F., Markey, N., and Schnoebelen, P. 2001. Model Checking CTL$^+$ and FCTL Is Hard. Pages 318–331 of: *FOSSACS'01*. Lecture Notes in Computer Science, vol. 2030. Springer.

Laroussinie, F., Markey, N., and Schnoebelen, Ph. 2002. Temporal Logic with Forgettable Past. Pages 383–392 of: *LICS'02*. IEEE.

Laroussinie, F., Markey, N., and Oreiby, G. 2008. On the Expressiveness and Complexity of ATL. *Logical Methods in Computer Science*, **4**(2).

Leeuwen, J. van (ed). 1990. *Handbook of Theoretical Computer Science*. Vol. B: *Formal Models and Semantics*. MIT Press.

Lehmann, D., Pnueli, A., and Stavi, J. 1981. Impartiality, Justice and Fairness: The Ethics of Concurrent Termination. Pages 264–277 of: *ICALP'81*. Lecture Notes in Computer Science, Vol. 115. Springer.

Lemmon, E.J., Scott, D., and Segerberg, K. 1977. *An Introduction to Modal Logic: Lemmon's Notes*. American Philosophical Quarterly.

Lenzi, G. 1996. A Hierarchy Theorem for the μ-Calculus. Pages 87–97 of: *ICALP'96*. Lecture Notes in Computer Science, vol. 1099. Springer.

Lewis, H. 1980. Complexity Results for classes of Quantificational formulas. *Journal of Computer and System Sciences*, **21**, 317–353.

Lichtenstein, O., and Pnueli, A. 2000. Propositional Temporal Logics: Decidability and Completeness. *Logic Journal of the IGPL*, **8**(1), 55–85.

Lichtenstein, O., Pnueli, A., and Zuck, L. 1985. The Glory of the Past. Pages 196–218 of: *Brooklyn College Conference on Logics of Programs*. Lecture Notes in Computer Science, vol. 193. Springer.

Löding, Ch., and Thomas, W. 2000. Alternating Automata and Logics over Infinite Words. Pages 521–535 of: *IFIP TCS' 2000*. Lecture Notes in Computer Science, vol. 1878. Springer.

Lopes, A. Da Costa, Laroussinie, F., and Markey, N. 2010. ATL with Strategy Contexts: Expressiveness and Model Checking. Pages 120–132 of: *FSTTCS'10*.

Lubarsky, R.S. 1993. μ-Definable Sets of Integers. *The Journal of Symbolic Logic*, **58**(1), 291–313.

Ludwig, W. 1995. A Subexponential Randomized Algorithm for the Simple Stochastic Game Problem. *Information and Computation*, **117**(1), 151–155.

Mader, A. 1997a. *Verification of Modal Properties Using Boolean Equation Systems*. Ph.D. thesis, Munich, University of Technology.

Mader, A. 1997b. *Verification of Modal Properties Using Boolean Equation Systems*. Bertz.

Manna, Z., and Pnueli, A. 1979. The Modal Logic of Programs. Pages 385–409 of: *ICALP'79*. Lecture Notes in Computer Science, vol. 71. Springer.

Manna, Z., and Pnueli, A. 1981. Verification of Concurrent Programs: The Temporal Framework. Pages 215–273 of: Boyer, R., and Moore, J. (eds), *The Correctness Problem in Computer Science*. Academic Press.

Manna, Z., and Pnueli, A. 1990. A Hierarchy of Temporal Properties. Pages 377–408 of: *PODC'90*. ACM Press.

Manna, Z., and Pnueli, A. 1992. *The Temporal Logic of Reactive and Concurrent Systems: Specifications*. Springer.

Manna, Z., and Pnueli, A. 1995. *Temporal Verification of Reactive Systems: Safety*. Springer.

Markey, N. 2002. Past If for Free: On the Complexity of Verifying Linear Temporal Properties with Past. In: *EXPRESS'02*. Electronic Notes in Theoretical Computer Science, vol. 68. Elsevier.

Markey, N. 2004. Past Is for Free: On the Complexity of Verifying Linear Temporal Properties with Past. *Acta Informatica*, **40**(6–7), 431–458.

Markey, N., and Schnoebelen, Ph. 2003. Model Checking a Path. Pages 251–261 of: *CONCUR'03*. Lecture Notes in Computer Science, vol. 2761. Springer.

Marx, M., and Venema, Y. 1997. *Multi-dimensional Modal Logic*. Applied Logic. Kluwer.

Mateescu, R. 2002. Local Model-Checking of Modal Mu-Calculus on Acyclic Labeled Transition Systems. Pages 281–295 of: *TACAS'02*. Lecture Notes in Computer Science, vol. 2280. Springer.

McMillan, K. 1993. *Symbolic Model Checking*. Kluwer Academic.

McNaughton, R. 1993. Infinite Games Played on Finite Graphs. *Annals of Pure and Applied Logic*, **65**(2), 149–184.

Meyer, A.R. 1973. *Weak Second Order Theory of Successor Is Not Elementary-Recursive*. Tech. rept. MAC TM-38. MIT.

Meyer, A.R. 1975. Weak Monadic Second-Order Theory of Successor Is Not Elementary Recursive. Pages 132–154 of: *Logic Colloquium*. Lecture Notes in Mathematics, vol. 453. Springer.

Michel, M. 1984. Algèbre de machines et logique temporelle. Pages 287–298 of: *STACS'84*. Lecture Notes in Computer Science, vol. 166. Springer.

Michel, M., and Stefani, J.-B. 1988. Interval Logics and Sequential Transducers. Pages 244–257 of: *CAAP'88*. Lecture Notes in Computer Science, vol. 299. Springer.

Milner, R. 1980. *A Calculus of Communicating Systems*. Lecture Notes in Computer Science, vol. 92. Springer.

Mints, G. 1988. Gentzen-Type and Resolution Rules Part I: Propositional Logic. Pages 198–231 of: *International Conference on Computer Logic, Tallinn*. Lecture Notes in Computer Science, vol. 417. Springer.

Miyano, S., and Hayashi, T. 1984. Alternating Finite Automata on ω-Words. *Theoretical Computer Science*, **32**(3), 321–330.

Mogavero, F., Murano, A., and Vardi, M.Y. 2010a. Reasoning about Strategies. Pages 133–144 of: *FSTTCS'10*.

Mogavero, F., Murano, A., and Vardi, M.Y. 2010b. Relentful Strategic Reasoning in Alternating-Time Temporal Logic. Pages 371–386 of: *LPAR'10*.

Mogavero, F., Murano, A., Perelli, G., and Vardi, M.Y. 2012. What Makes ATL* Decidable? A Decidable Fragment of Strategy Logic. Pages 193–208 of: *CONCUR'12*.

Moller, F., and Rabinovich, A. 2003. Counting on CTL*: On the Expressive Power of Monadic Path Logic. *Information and Computation*, **184**(1), 147–159.

Moore, R. C. 1977. Reasoning about Knowledge and Action. Pages 223–227 of: *IJCAI-5*.

Morgan, Ch. 1976. Methods for Automated Theorem Proving in Non-classical Logics. *IEEE Transactions on Computers*, **25**(8), 852–862.

Mortimer, M. 1975. On Language with Two Variables. *Zeitschrift für Mathematische Logik und Grundlagen der Mathematik*, **21**, 135–140.

Moschovakis, Y.N. 2006. *Notes on Set Theory*. 2nd edn. Undergraduate Texts in Mathematics. Springer.

Mostowski, A.W. 1984. Regular Expressions for Infinite Trees and a Standard Form of Automata. Pages 157–168 of: *5th Symp. on Computation Theory*. Lecture Notes in Computer Science, vol. 208. Springer.

Mukund, M. 2012. Finite-State Automata on Infinite Inputs. Pages 45–78 of: D'Souza, D., and Shankar, P. (eds), *Modern Applications of Automata Theory*. IISc Research Monographs Series, vol. 2. World Scientific.

Muller, D.E. 1963. Infinite Sequences and Finite Machines. Pages 3–16 of: *4th IEEE Symposium on Switching Circuit Theory and Logical Design*. IEEE.

Muller, D.E., and Schupp, P.E. 1987. Alternating Automata on Infinite Trees. *Theoretical Computer Science*, **54**, 267–276.

Muller, D.E., and Schupp, P.E. 1995. Simulating Alternating Tree Automata by Non-deterministic Automata: New Results and New Proofs of the Theorems of Rabin, McNaughton and Safra. *Theoretical Computer Science*, **141**(1–2), 69–107.

Muller, D.E., Saoudi, A., and Schupp, P.E. 1986. Alternating Automata, the Weak Monadic Theory of the Tree and Its Complexity. Pages 275–283 of: *ICALP'86*. Lecture Notes in Computer Science, vol. 226. Springer.

Muller, D.E., Saoudi, A., and Schupp, P.E. 1988. Weak Alternating Automata Give a Simple Explanation of Why Most Temporal and Dynamic Logics Are Decidable in Exponential Time. Pages 422–427 of: *LICS'88*. IEEE.

Müller-Olm, M. 1999. A Modal Fixpoint Logic with Chop. Pages 510–520 of: *STACS'99*. Lecture Notes in Computer Science, vol. 1563. Springer.

Nakamura, A., and Ono, H. 1980. On the Size of Refutation Kripke Models for Some Linear Modal and Tense Logics. *Studia Logica*, **39**(4), 325–333.

Nivelle, H. de, Schmidt, R., and Hustadt, U. 2000. Resolution-Based Methods for Modal Logics. *Logic Journal of the IGPL*, **8**(3), 265–292.

Niwiński, D. 1986. On Fixed-Point Clones. Pages 464–473 of: *ICALP'86*. Lecture Notes in Computer Science, vol. 226. Springer.

Niwiński, D. 1997. Fixed Point Characterization of Infinite Behavior of Finite-State Systems. *Theoretical Computer Science*, **189**(1–2), 1–69.

Niwiński, D. 2002. μ-Calculus via Games. Pages 27–43 of: *CSL'02*. Lecture Notes in Computer Science, vol. 2471. Springer.

Niwiński, D., and Walukiewicz, I. 1996. Games for the mu-Calculus. *Theoretical Computer Science*, **163**(1–2), 99–116.

Nonnengart, A. 1996. Resolution-Based Calculi for Modal and Temporal Logics. Pages 599–612 of: *CADE'96*. Lecture Notes in Artificial Intelligence, vol. 1104. Springer.

Ohlbach, H.J. 1993. Translation Methods for Non-classical Logics: An Overview. *Bulletin of the Interest Group in Propositional and Predicate Logics*, **1**(1), 69–90.

Ohlbach, H.J., Nonnengart, A., de Rijke, M., and Gabbay, D.M. 2001. Encoding Two-Valued Non-classical Logics in Classical Logic. Pages 1403–1486 of: *Handbook of Automated Reasoning*. MIT Press.

Øhrstrøm, P., and Hasle, P. F. V. 1995. *Temporal Logic: From Ancient Ideas to Artificial Intelligence*. Springer.

Orłowska, E. 1988. Relational Interpretation of Modal Logics. Pages 443–471 of: *Algebraic Logic. Colloquia Mathematica Societatis Janos Bolyai 54*. North-Holland.

Otto, M. 1999. Bisimulation-Invariant PTIME and Higher-Dimensional μ-Calculus. *Theoretical Computer Science*, **224**(1–2), 237–265.

Paige, R., and Tarjan, R.E. 1987. Three Partition Refinement Algorithms. *SIAM Journal of Computing*, **16**(6), 973–989.

Papadimitriou, C.H. 1994. *Computational Complexity*. Addison-Wesley.

Park, D. 1970. Fixpoint Induction and Proof of Program Semantics. Pages 59–78 of: *Machine Intelligence*, vol. 5. Edinburgh University Press.

Park, D. 1981. Concurrency and Automata on Infinite Sequences. Pages 167–183 of: *5th GI Conference on Theoretical Computer Science, Karlsruhe, Germany*. Lecture Notes in Computer Science, vol. 104. Springer.

Pauly, M. 2001a. *Logic for Social Software*. Ph.D. thesis, University of Amsterdam. ILLC Dissertation Series 2001-10.

Pauly, M. 2001b. A Logical Framework for Coalitional Effectivity in Dynamic Procedures. *Bulletin of Economic Research*, **53**(4), 305–324.

Pauly, M. 2002. A Modal Logic for Coalitional Power in Games. *Journal of Logic and Computation*, **12**(1), 149–166.

Pécuchet, J.-P. 1986. On the Complementation of Büchi Automata. *Theoretical Computer Science*, **47**(1), 95–98.

Peled, D., and Wilke, Th. 1997. Stutter-Invariant Temporal Properties Are Expressible without the Next-Time Operator. *Information Processing Letters*, **63**, 243–246.

Perrin, D., and Pin, J.-E. 2004. *Infinite Words: Automata, Semigroups, Logic and Games*. Elsevier.

Petersson, V., and Vorobyov, S. 2001. A Randomized Subexponential Algorithm for Parity Games. *Nordic Journal of Computing*, **8**(3), 324–345.

Pinchinat, S. 1992. Ordinal Processes in Comparative Concurrency Semantics. Pages 293–305 of: *CSL'91*. Lecture Notes in Computer Science, vol. 626. Springer.

Piterman, N. 2000. *Extending Temporal Logic with ω-Automata*. M.Phil. thesis, The Weizmann Institute of Science.

Piterman, N. 2006. From Nondeterministic Büchi and Streett Automata to Deterministic Parity Automata. Pages 255–264 of: *LICS'06*. IEEE.

Plotkin, G. 1981. *A Structural Approach to Operational Semantics*. Tech. report DAIMI FN-19. Aarhus Univ.

Pnueli, A. 1977. The Temporal Logic of Programs. Pages 46–57 of: *FOCS'77*. IEEE.

Pnueli, A. 1979. The Temporal Semantics of Concurrent Programs. Pages 1–20 of: *International Symposium on Semantics of Concurrent Computation 1979*. Lecture Notes in Computer Science, vol. 70. Springer.

Poizat, B. 1982. Deux ou trois choses que je sais de L_n. *The Journal of Symbolic Logic*, **47**, 641–658.

Popkorn, S. 1992. *First Steps in Modal Logic*. Cambridge University Press.

Pratt, V. 1979. A Practical Decision Method for Propositional Dynamic Logic. Pages 326–337 of: *10th Annual ACM Symposium on the Theory of Computing*. ACM.

Pratt, V. 1980. A Near Optimal Method for Reasoning about Actions. *Journal of Computer and System Sciences*, **20**, 231–254.

Pratt, V. R. 1981. A Decidable mu-Calculus. Pages 421–427 of: *FOCS'81*. IEEE.

Prior, A.N. 1957. *Time and Modality*. Clarendon Press.

Prior, A.N. 1967. *Past, Present and Future*. Oxford University Press.

Prior, A.N. 1968. *Papers on Time and Tense*. University of Oxford Press.

Prior, A.N. 1977. *Worlds, Times and Selves*. Edited by K. Fine. University of Massachusetts Press.

Puri, A. 1995. *Theory of Hybrid Systems and Discrete Event Systems*. Ph.D. thesis, University of California, Berkeley.

Queille, J.-P., and Sifakis, J. 1982a. Specification and Verification of Concurrent Systems in CESAR. Pages 337–351 of: *FOCS'82*. IEEE.

Queille, J.-P., and Sifakis, J. 1982b. A Temporal Logic to Deal with Fairness in Transition Systems. Pages 217–225 of: *FOCS'82*. IEEE.

Rabin, M. 1969. Decidability of Second-Order Theories and Automata on Infinite Trees. *Transactions of the American Mathematical Society*, **41**, 1–35.

Rabin, M. 1970. Weakly Definable Relations and Special Automata. Pages 1–23 of: Symposium on Mathematical Logic and Foundations of Set Theory. North-Holland.

Rabinovich, A. 2014. A Proof of Kamp's Theorem. *Logical Methods in Computer Science*, **10**(1).

Rescher, N., and Urquhart, A. 1971. *Temporal Logic*. Springer.

Reynolds, M. 2000. More Past Glories. Pages 229–240 of: *LICS'00*. IEEE.

Reynolds, M. 2001. An Axiomatization of Full Computation Tree Logic. *Journal of Symbolic Logic*, **66**(3), 1011–1057.

Reynolds, M. 2007. A Tableau for Bundled CTL*. *Journal of Logic and Computation*, **17**(1), 117–132.

Reynolds, M. 2009. A Tableau for CTL*. Pages 403–418 of: *FM'09*. Lecture Notes in Computer Science, vol. 5850, Springer.

Reynolds, M. 2011. A Tableau-Based Decision Procedure for CTL*. *Formal Aspects of Computing*, **23**(6), 739–779.

Reynolds, M. 2013. A Faster Tableau for CTL*. Pages 50–63 of: *GandALF'2013*.

Rich, D.I. 2003. The Evolution of SystemVerilog. *IEEE Design and Test of Computers*, **20**(4), 82–84.

Rohde, S. 1997. *Alternating Automata and the Temporal Logic of Ordinals*. Ph.D. thesis, University of Illinois.

Rosenstein, J.G. 1982. *Linear Ordering*. Academic Press.

Safra, S. 1988. On the Complexity of ω-Automata. Pages 319–327 of: *FOCS'88*. IEEE.

Safra, S. 1989. *Complexity of Automata on Infinite Objects*. Ph.D. thesis, Weizmann Institute of Science.

Sangiorgi, D. 2009. On the Origins of Bisimulation and Coinduction. *ACM Transactions on Programming Languages and Systems (TOPLAS)*, **31**(4).

Sangiorgi, D., and Rutten, J. (eds). 2012. *Advanced Topics in Bisimulation and Coinduction*. Cambridge Tracts in Theoretical Computer Science, vol. 52. Cambridge University Press.

Sattler, U., and Vardi, M.Y. 2001. The Hybrid μ-Calculus. Pages 76–91 of: *IJCAR'01*. Lecture Notes in Computer Science, vol. 2083. Springer.

Savitch, W.J. 1970. Relationships between Nondeterministic and Deterministic Tape Complexities. *Journal of Computer and System Sciences*, **4**(2), 177–192.

Schewe, S. 2007. Solving Parity Games in Big Steps. Pages 449–460 of: *FSTTCS'07*. Lecture Notes in Computer Science, vol. 4855. Springer.

Schewe, S. 2008a. ATL* Satisfiability is 2EXPTIME-Complete. Pages 373–385 of: *ICALP'08*. Lecture Notes in Computer Science, vol. 5126. Springer.

Schewe, S. 2008b. An Optimal Strategy Improvement Algorithm for Solving Parity and Payoff Games. Pages 369–384 of: *CSL'08*. Lecture Notes in Computer Science, vol. 5213. Springer.

Schewe, S. 2009. Tighter Bounds for the Determinisation of Büchi Automata. Pages 167–181 of: *FOSSACS'09*. Lecture Notes in Computer Science, vol. 5504. Springer.

Schewe, S., and Finkbeiner, B. 2006. Satisfiability and Finite Model Property for the Alternating-Time mu-Calculus. Pages 591–605 of: *CSL'06*. Lecture Notes in Computer Science, vol. 4207. Springer.

Schneider, K. 2004. *Verification of Reactive Systems: Formal Methods and Algorithms*. Springer.

Schnoebelen, Ph. 2003. The Complexity of Temporal Logic Model Checking. Pages 393–436 of: *AiML'02*. Advances in Modal Logic, vol. 4. King's College.

Schobbens, P.-Y. 2004. Alternating-Time Logic with Imperfect Recall. *Electronic Notes in Theoretical Computer Science*, **85**(2), 82–93.

Schwendimann, S. 1998a. *Aspects of Computational Logic*. Ph.D. thesis, Universität Bern, Switzerland.

Schwendimann, S. 1998b. A New One-Pass Tableau Calculus for PLTL. Pages 277–291 of: *TABLEAUX'98*. Lecture Notes in Artificial Intelligence, vol. 1397. Springer.

Scott, D. 1962. A Decision Method for Validity of Sentences in Two Variables. *The Journal of Symbolic Logic*, **27**, 377.

Segerberg, K. 1971. *An Essay in Classical Modal Logic*. Filosofiska Studier 13. University of Uppsala.

Seidl, H. 1996. Fast and Simple Nested Fixpoint. *Information Processing Letters*, **59**(6), 303–308.

Seidl, H., and Neumann, A. 1999. On Guarding Nested Fixpoints. Pages 484–498 of: *CSL'99*. Lecture Notes in Computer Science, vol. 1683. Springer.

Sifakis, J. 1980. Deadlocks and Livelocks in Transition Systems. Pages 587–600 of: *MFCS'80*. Lecture Notes in Computer Science, vol. 88. Springer.

Sistla, A.P. 1983. *Theoretical Issues in the Design of Distributed and Concurrent Systems*. Ph.D. thesis, Harvard University.

Sistla, A.P., and Clarke, E.M. 1982. The Complexity of Propositional Linear Temporal Logic. Pages 159–168 of: *STOCS'82*. ACM.

Sistla, A.P., and Clarke, E.M. 1985. The Complexity of Propositional Linear Temporal Logics. *Journal of the ACM*, **32**(3), 733–749.

Sistla, A.P., Vardi, M.Y., and Wolper, P. 1987. The Complementation Problem for Büchi Automata with Applications to Temporal Logic. *Theoretical Computer Science*, **49**, 217–237.

Slutzki, G. 1987. Alternating Tree Automata. *Theoretical Computer Science*, **41**, 305–318.

Smullyan, R.M. 1968. *First-Order Logic*. Springer.

Spaan, E. 1993a. *Complexity of Modal Logics*. Ph.D. thesis, ILLC, Amsterdam University.

Spaan, E. 1993b. The Complexity of Propositional Tense Logics. Pages 287–309 of: de Rijke, M. (ed), *Diamonds and Defaults*. Series Studies in Pure and Applied Intensional Logic, vol. 229. Kluwer Academic.

Stevens, P., and Stirling, C. 1998. Practical Model-Checking Using Games. Pages 85–101 of: *TACAS*. Lecture Notes in Computer Science, vol. 1384. Springer.

Stirling, C. 1987. Comparing Linear and Branching Time Temporal Logics. Pages 1–20 of: Banieqbal, B., Barringer, H., and Pnueli, A. (eds), *Temporal Logic in Specification*. Lecture Notes in Computer Science, vol. 398. Springer.

Stirling, C. 1992. Modal and Temporal Logics. Pages 477–563 of: *Handbook of Logic in Computer Science*, vol. 2 (Background: Computational Structures). Clarendon Press.

Stirling, C. 1995. Local Model Checking Games. Pages 1–11 of: *CONCUR'95*. Lecture Notes in Computer Science, vol. 962. Springer.

Stirling, C. 1996. Games and Modal Mu-Calculus. Pages 298–312 of: *TACAS'96*. Lecture Notes in Computer Science, vol. 1055. Springer.

Stirling, C. 1999. Bisimulation, Modal Logic and Model Checking Games. *Logic Journal of the IGPL*, **7**(1), 103–124.

Stirling, C. 2001. *Modal and Temporal Properties of Processes*. Springer.

Stirling, C., and Walker, D. 1989. Local Model Checking in the Modal Mu-Calculus. Pages 369–383 of: *TAPSOFT*, vol. 1. Lecture Notes in Computer Science, vol. 351. Springer.

Straubing, H. 1994. *Finite Automata, Formal Logic, and Circuit Complexity*. Progress in Theoretical Computer Science. Birkhäuser.

Streett, R.S. 1982. Propositional Dynamic Logic of Looping and Converse Is Elementarily Decidable. *Information and Control*, **54**(1/2), 121–141.

Streett, R.S., and Emerson, E.A. 1984. The Propositional μ-Calculus Is Elementary. Pages 465–472 of: *ICALP'84*. Lecture Notes in Computer Science, vol. 172. Springer.

Streett, R.S., and Emerson, E.A. 1989. An Automata Theoretic Decision Procedure for the Propositional Mu-Calculus. *Information and Computation*, **81**(3), 249–264.

Sundholm, G. 2001. Systems of Deduction. Pages 1–52 of: Gabbay, D.M., and Guenthner, F. (eds), *Handbook of Philosophical Logic*, vol. 2. Springer–Science & Business Media, B.V.

Szelepcsényi, R. 1988. The Method of Forced Enumeration for Nondeterministic Automata. *Acta Informatica*, **26**(3), 279–284.

Tarjan, R. E. 1972. Depth-First Search and Linear Graph Algorithms. *SIAM Journal of Computing*, **1**, 146–160.

Thomas, W. 1990. Automata on Infinite Objects. Pages 133–191 of: van Leeuwen, J. (ed), *Handbook of Theoretical Computer Science, Volume B, Formal Models and Semantics*. Elsevier.

Thomas, W. 1999. Complementation of Büchi Automata Revisited. Pages 109–122 of: J. Karhumäki et al. (ed), *Jewels Are Forever, Contributions on Theoretical Computer Science in Honor of Arto Salomaa*. Springer.

Thomason, R.H. 1984. Combinations of Tense and Modality. *In:* Gabbay and Guenthner (1984).

Troquard, N., and Walther, D. 2012. On Satisfiability of ATL with Strategy Contexts. Pages 398–410 of: *JELIA'12*. Lecture Notes in Artificial Intelligence, vol. 7519. Springer.

van Benthem, J. 1976. *Modal Correspondence Theory*. Ph.D. thesis, Mathematical Institute, Amsterdam University.

van Benthem, J. 1984. Correspondence Theory. *In:* Gabbay and Guenthner (1984).

van Benthem, J. 1985. *Modal Logic and Classical Logic*. Bibliopolis.

van Benthem, J. 1993. *The Logic of Time*. 2nd edn. Kluwer Academic.

van Benthem, J. 1995. Temporal Logic. Pages 241–351 of: Gabbay, D.M., Hogger, C.J., and Robinson, J.A. (eds), *Handbook of Logic in Artificial Intelligence and Logic Programming: Epistemic and Temporal Reasoning*, vol. 4. Oxford University Press.

van Benthem, J. 2014. *Logic in Games*. MIT Press.

van Benthem, J., and Bergstra, J.A. 1995. Logic of Transition Systems. *Journal of Logic, Language and Information*, **3**(4), 247–283.

van Benthem, J., van Eijck, D., and Stebletsova, V. 1993. *Modal Logic, Transition Systems and Processes*. Tech. rept. CS-R9321. Centrum voor Wiskunde en Informatica, Amsterdam.

van Dalen, D. 2004. *Logic and Structure*. Springer.

van Drimmelen, G. 2003. Satisfiability in Alternating-Time Temporal Logic. Pages 208–217 of: *LICS'03*.

van Emde Boas, P. 1997. The Convenience of Tilings. Pages 331–363 of: *Complexity, Logic, and Recursion Theory*. Lecture Notes in Pure and Applied Mathematics, vol. 187. Marcel Dekker.

Vardi, M.Y. 1988. A Temporal Fixpoint Calculus. Pages 250–259 of: *POPL'88*. ACM.

Vardi, M.Y. 1991. Verification of Concurrent Programs: The Automata-Theoretic Framework. *Annals of Pure and Applied Logic*, **51**(1–2), 79–98.

Vardi, M.Y. 1996. An Automata-Theoretic Approach to Linear Temporal Logic. Pages 238–266 of: Moller, F., and Birtwistle, G. (eds), *Logics of Concurrency: Structure versus Automata*. Lecture Notes in Computer Science, vol. 1043. Springer.

Vardi, M.Y. 1997. Alternating Automata: Unifying Truth and Validity Checking for Temporal Logics. Pages 191–206 of: *CADE'97*. Lecture Notes in Computer Science, vol. 1249. Springer.

Vardi, M.Y. 2001. Branching vs. Linear Time: Final Showdown. Pages 1–22 of: *TACAS'01*. Lecture Notes in Computer Science, vol. 2031. Springer.

Vardi, M.Y. 2007. Automata-Theoretic Techniques for Temporal Reasoning. Pages 971–990 of: Blackburn, P., Benthem, J. van, and Wolter, F. (eds), *Handbook of Modal Logic*. Elsevier.

Vardi, M.Y. 2009. From Philosophical to Industrial Logics. Pages 89–115 of: *ICLA'09*. Lecture Notes in Computer Science, vol. 5378. Springer.

Vardi, M.Y., and Stockmeyer, L.J. 1985. Improved Upper and Lower Bounds for Modal Logics of Programs. Pages 240–251 of: *STOC'85*. ACM.

Vardi, M.Y., and Wilke, Th. 2007. Automata: From Logics to Algorithms. Pages 629–736 of: *Logic and Automata: History and Perspectives*. Texts in Logic and Games, no. 2. Amsterdam University Press.

Vardi, M.Y., and Wolper, P. 1983. Yet Another Process Logic (Preliminary Version). Pages 501–512 of: *Logic of Programs*. Lecture Notes in Computer Science, vol. 164. Springer.

Vardi, M.Y., and Wolper, P. 1986a. Automata-Theoretic Approach to Automatic Program Verification. Pages 322–331 of: *LICS'86*. IEEE.

Vardi, M.Y., and Wolper, P. 1986b. Automata-Theoretic Techniques for Modal Logics of Programs. *Journal of Computer and System Sciences*, **32**, 183–221.

Vardi, M.Y., and Wolper, P. 1994. Reasoning about Infinite Computations. *Information and Computation*, **115**, 1–37.

Viswanathan, M., and Viswanathan, R. 2004. A Higher Order Modal Fixed Point Logic. Pages 512–528 of: *CONCUR'04*. Lecture Notes in Computer Science, vol. 3170. Springer.

Vöge, J., and Jurdziński, M. 2000. A Discrete Strategy Improvement Algorithm for Solving Parity Games. Pages 202–215 of: *CAV'00*. Lecture Notes in Computer Science, vol. 1855. Springer.

Walther, D., Lutz, C., Wolter, F., and Wooldridge, M. 2006. ATL Satisfiability Is Indeed ExpTime-Complete. *Journal of Logic and Computation*, **16**(6), 765–787.

Walther, D., van der Hoek, W., and Wooldridge, W. 2007. Alternating-Time Temporal Logic with Explicit Strategies. Pages 269–278 of: *TARK '07*. ACM.

Walukiewicz, I. 1996. Monadic Second Order Logic on Tree-Like Structures. Pages 401–413 of: *STACS'96*. Lecture Notes in Computer Science, vol. 1046. Springer.

Walukiewicz, I. 2000. Completeness of Kozen's Axiomatisation of the Propositional μ-Calculus. *Information and Computation*, **157**(1–2), 142–182.

Widmann, F. 2010. *Tableaux-Based Decision Procedures for Fixed Point Logics*. Ph.D. thesis, Australian National University.

Wilke, Th. 1999. CTL+ Is Exponentially More Succinct than CTL. Pages 110–121 of: *FSTTCS'99*. Lecture Notes in Computer Science, vol. 1999. Springer.

Wolper, P. 1981. Temporal Logic Can Be More Expressive. Pages 340–348 of: *FOCS'81*.

Wolper, P. 1983. Temporal Logic Can Be More Expressive. *Information and Control*, **56**, 72–99.

Wolper, P. 1985. The Tableau Method for Temporal Logic: An Overview. *Logique et Analyse*, **110–111**, 119–136.

Wolper, P. 1989. On the Relation of Programs and Computations to Models of Temporal Logic. Pages 75–123 of: Banieqbal, B., Barringer, H., and Pnueli, A. (eds), *Temporal Logic in Specification*. Springer.

Wolper, P. 2000. Constructing Automata from Temporal Logic Formulas: A Tutorial. Pages 261–277 of: *European Educational Forum: School on Formal Methods and Performance Analysis*. Lecture Notes in Computer Science, vol. 2090. Springer.

Zanardo, A. 1996. Branching Time Logic with Quantification over Branches: The Point of View of Modal Logic. *The Journal of Symbolic Logic*, **61**, 1–39.

Zeman, J. 1973. *The Lewis-Modal Systems*. Clarendon Press.

Zielonka, W. 1998. Infinite Games on Finitely Coloured Graphs with Applications to Automata on Infinite Trees. *Theoretical Computer Science*, **200**(1–2), 135–183.

Index